Hereford Cathedral School

Sarah Seymour, fourth Duchess of Somerset, 1631-92. Her bequests to Brasenose College, Oxford, and St John's College, Cambridge, enabled hundreds of Old Herefordians to study at these colleges over three centuries. The Duchess is shown holding a floral wreath, with her arm resting on what may be a funerary urn, so the original portrait, of which this is a copy, may have been painted shortly after the fourth duke's death in April 1675.

Hereford Cathedral School

A History Over 800 Years

FLOREAT SCHOLA HEREFORDENSIS

by

Howard Tomlinson

Logaston Press

LOGASTON PRESS
Little Logaston Woonton Almeley
Herefordshire HR3 6QH
logastonpress.co.uk

Published with the generous support of a grant
from the Geoffrey Walter Smith Fund of
the Woolhope Naturalists' Field Club

First published by Logaston Press 2018

ISBN 978 1 910839 23 2

Typeset by Logaston Press
and printed and bound in Poland by
www.lfbookservices.co.uk

In Loving Memory of

EDWARD ALEXANDER TOMLINSON (1981-2006)

Old Herefordian (HCS: 1995-2000) and
President of the Oxford Union Society, Hilary Term 2004

FOREWORD

by The Very Revd Michael Tavinor, Dean of Hereford
and President of Governors, Hereford Cathedral School

Hereford Cathedral may not be able to compare in its architecture with the massive splendours of York, Durham or Lincoln but its history and traditions rank it with the most venerable institutions in our country. Like mother, like offspring. Hereford Cathedral School may not have extensive buildings like Eton or be set in grand parkland like Stowe, but its past and customs – so closely linked with the cathedral – place it among the very oldest schools of the country, and give it an enviable and honoured place among its peers. There is more. Both cathedral and school are thorougly in tune with their surroundings. The soft sandstone of the cathedral seems to grow out of the surounding hills, with their soft, red soil. Likewise Hereford Cathedral School has always happily maintained a synergy with its surrounding rural landscape and agricultural community.

Cathedral and school have always celebrated the ethos of family. Canon Phillott in his diocesan history of 1888 puts it well, in speaking of the qualities of Hereford:

> These are of a more personal and domestic kind, not so heroic and impressive as elsewhere, perhaps … but containing elements more amenable to kindly personal influence, and more favourable to individual direction of character …

This understated confidence is something which has always joined diocese, cathedral and school.

No-one has understood better this subtle blend than Dr Howard Tomlinson. He is thoroughly well placed to write a history of this scope – an historian with 18 years' experience as Headmaster of Hereford Cathedral School and one long involved in cathedral life, not least as a lay canon. His fine scholarship and affection for the school and its close relationship with the cathedral come over loud and clear. In this wide-ranging volume, the reader will find glimpses into the school's early history, never before documented. In it, the reader will chart the long succession of triumphs and setbacks that have marked the school's progress over the centuries. Above all, readers will delight in the human stories, which bring to life the institution with humour and a lightness of touch. All who have an affection for the school will be indebted to Dr Tomlinson for this timely, comprehensive and well-researched volume.

Times have changed. The Dean is no longer chair of governors and cathedral and school are independent entities, yet the bonds of history and affection remain stronger than ever, and it is as President of the Cathedral School that the Dean maintains special links – presiding over school events, not least the annual service for the installation of Dean's scholars. It is as Dean and President that he is delighted to commend this book. It will long provide a definitive history of this great institution.

Michael Tavinor
All Saints Day, 2017

Preface and Acknowledgements

Over one hundred years ago, less than a month before the opening of the first hostilities of the Great War, two local Old Herefordian publishers, W.M. Wilson and W.J. Phillips, brought out A *Short History of Hereford School* by W.T. Carless, at the price of 7s 6d. The author, Hereford's Town Clerk for a brief period in 1911 (as was his OH father for a much longer reign) was also an Old Herefordian, and as Registrar of the Hereford County Court was one of a number of OH lawyers who dispensed justice in Herefordshire during the late Victorian and Edwardian eras. His history of HCS, the first ever undertaken, had only been commissioned by the OH Club the previous year. It was well received in the local press as 'a labour of love', and despite Carless' disclaimer that it was far from complete, it was held to have laid 'a very substantial foundation to any future editions of wider scope'.[1] Carless himself was unable to undertake that task, as had been his intention, for he had taken command of the Herefordshire Regiment in the Dardanelles campaign and was presumed killed in action on 12 August 1915, three days after landing at Suvla Bay. Nor was the task of revising the school's history fully taken up by J.C. Eales-White, whose *Records of Hereford Cathedral School* was produced for the '550th' celebrations of 1931. The history was again published by Wilson and Phillips, in a similar format to the 1914 volume but this time for 12s 6d, and was intended as 'a brief summary of the activities of the school' since Carless' book. To this, Eales-White added some biographical entries on Old Herefordians who had (in his own words) 'set out to leave the world better than they [had] found it'.[2] Less than ten years later, J.C. Wordsworth, the senior Classics master of the time, produced an 18-page booklet entitled *A Shorter History of The Cathedral School, Hereford*. This brief, well-written, chronological guide, with clear sub-headings, proved useful as an examination text for the boys but did not add materially to the earlier histories. It also suffered in appearance by comparison with its predecessors from being a war-time publication.[3] Forty years on, in the

1. *HT,* 18 July 1914, p.4. For the OH Club resolution of 26 July 1913 which commissions the History: *TH*, NS LXXIV (Dec. 1913), p.32.

2. Eales-White, foreword. For his school and army career, and his scientific interests – he wrote a number of (to my mind tedious) articles on 'bees and ants' for *The Herefordian*, under the nom de plume 'Selae' – see *ibid.*, pp.69-70; and *TH*, NS CLXXV (Jan. 1949), pp.34-35, for his obituary.

3. It was printed, with soft covers in limp binding, by the *Western Mail and Echo* press in Cardiff. For Wordsworth and the use made of the pamphlet for examination purposes, see below, pp.380, 399; and HCSA, GMB 1921-45, C.F. Scott's report, 23 July 1941.

early 1980s, Alan Morris brought together some interesting school memoirs, which were intended for publication but never published.[4] And more recently, Nicholas Orme and Egerton Parker contributed chapters on the Cathedral School for the millennium history of Hereford Cathedral.[5] Until now, however, no-one has attempted to write a more complete work on the history of HCS.

In doing so, I should first acknowledge my indebtedness to Carless, Eales-White, Wordsworth and the school's more modern authors. As will become apparent from the footnotes, their writings have proved to be important secondary sources for this book. For this history, however, I have adopted not only a different approach but a longer time-frame from my one predecessor who tried to cover the school's whole history. Of necessity, given that we are a century on from 1914, this work covers a longer time-span than Carless' *Short History*. There is also good reason, as Orme has shown and as I have argued in the Prologue, to take the foundation of Hereford's grammar school – the direct forerunner of HCS – back to the late twelfth century. As my title indicates, this makes the school more than 800 years old.

The sources preclude giving each century over that long period equal treatment. The medieval chapter, inevitably, is briefer than the others, as is the history of the past 30 years, for very different but equally obvious reasons. The centuries in between, from the post-Reformation settlement of the mid-sixteenth century to the late twentieth, provide the period for the most detailed narrative. And these four centuries are the most crucial for the school's modern history. It is not until the late sixteenth century that the school became a proper cathedral school rather than one controlled by the Chancellor; in the seventeenth century, HCS gained its crucial endowments; the eighteenth, while being far from a period of torpor, saw it fully established; in the late nineteenth, it emerged as a Victorian public school; in the twentieth, it was recognised as an 'efficient' school supported by government grants, and eventually in the 1970s as a co-educational establishment; and in the early twenty-first, it reverted to the status of a fully independent school. But even here, for the four centuries from the cathedral statutes of 1583 that remodels the Chancellor's old school to my arrival as Headmaster in 1987, I make no attempt to balance the narrative: the story expands as the quantity of evidence increases, so that over one-third of this history has been devoted to the twentieth century.

The general nature of this book needs further explanation. I have endeavoured to avoid a myopic vision by writing a history of greater breadth than is to be found in some official school chronicles. Too often, these possess a largely parochial appeal and owe more to the demands of public relations than to historical truth.[6] So although *A History Over 800 Years* covers the subject matter of most school histories by dealing with the Cathedral School's teachers; its pupils and their learning and play; its governance

4. As advertised in *TH*, CCXXVI (1980), p.39. I inherited a number of these reminiscences and articles in manuscript, many written by OHs and others no longer with us, which have been invaluable, not least the piece by the late Herbert Powell OH on the school's buildings.

5. Aylmer and Tiller, chapters 32 and 33, pp.565-78, 579-98.

6. Although emphatically this is not the case for such histories as those commissioned for Wellington College and Harrow School, written (respectively) by David Newsome and Christopher Tyerman.

and finances; its physical setting; and the highs and lows of its fortune, it is more than a narrow institutional history. For I have attempted to place the school's development within the context of its wider community. More than most schools – given its location over the centuries as a school both within the environs of a cathedral and at the centre of an ancient city – the history of HCS is intimately bound up with that of its neighbourhood. But beyond the narrow confines of the Close and Hereford itself, wherever appropriate, I have also tried to relate the Cathedral School's history to advances (or otherwise) at schools, locally and nationally; to the ancient universities HCS served, not least the colleges (Brasenose, Oxford, and St John's, Cambridge) which through the Somerset endowments it had the closest relationship; and to national educational developments, such as the Endowed Schools Commission of the 1860s. And in a sense, the history of HCS as an institution is also a microcosm of the history of England. For instance, the diocese's slow response to the Protestant Reformation; the parliamentary sieges of the city during the English civil war, when schoolboys manned the barricades in the royalist cause; the effects of regime change at the cathedral during the Interregnum and again at the Restoration of 1660 and (to a more limited extent) the Revolution of 1688, all had an effect on the school's governance. Equally, in an age of mass democracy, the people's wars of the twentieth century, when daily announcements of old boy casualties, the complete disruption of school routine, and (in the Second World War) the arrival in Hereford of evacuees from Birmingham and (in time) troops from America, brought home the realities of war to the smallest boy. Such cataclysmic events in our national story should not be ignored by a school historian, even one dealing with a small community remotely situated on England's western fringes.

In sum, I have tried to avoid the tunnel vision of too many historians of this notoriously difficult genre. As that distinguished historian Lord Blake wrote in his foreword about the history of another cathedral school:

> The trouble with institutional histories, whether of schools, businesses, livery companies or colleges is a tendency to be parochial. They are too often merely linear – catalogues of numbers, endowments, buildings, personalities and curriculum changes, without broadening out into the social economic, intellectual and other contemporary factors which were shaping the development of the body concerned. For a school no more exists in a vacuum than a person does. Circumstances are always altering and a school's history is largely the story of how it adapts – or fails to adapt – to those alterations. The historian has to steer somewhere between the parish pump and the broad delta.[7]

And if, occasionally, I have strayed too far from the 'parish pump' by concentrating too much on the 'broad delta', it has been done with the best of intentions.

In one important respect, however, this is a traditional school history. For the modern period (from 1697), I have followed the format of many other school histories by arranging the chronological narrative around the tenures of the school's Headmasters. And in this regard, I do so with good reason and without apology – and not simply because I once

---

7. Harries, Cattermole and Mackintosh, Lord Blake's foreword.

counted as one of their number. For there is something in Churchill's famous remark that 'Headmasters have powers at their disposal with which Prime Ministers have never yet been invested'. How far this is so today – even in an era of 'superheads' – at a time of delegated magisterial powers, government directives, legal restrictions and governor and parental involvement, is open to question.[8] But for times past, there is more than a grain of truth in Churchill's lament. Nicholas Orme, the foremost authority on English medieval schools, has argued that 'the schoolmaster ruled the school, except when … governing powers, local worthies or parents tried to influence what he did'.[9] This remained the case for HCS for much of its history. For centuries, the school was run by one master (the *Archididascalus*), who may or may not have appointed an Usher (the *Hypodidascalus*) as was required by the cathedral statutes. And as the earliest extant school rules of 1818 make clear, his powers were extensive. Sometimes, as in the 1665 orders (promulgated as a result of a dispute with the city fathers), the Dean and Chapter as the school's sole governors – as they were for over 300 years from the Elizabethan statutes to 1910 – would give general rules for its governance; at other times (as in 1795-96), they would try to restrict the play of the cathedral schoolboys in the churchyard in an attempt to preserve the cathedral windows. Occasionally, a powerful Dean like John Merewether (1832-50) might even re-order the school's classical curriculum or interfere with the disciplining of the boys, including those who were not members of his foundation. But for the most part, the major concerns of the residentiary canons as governors related to safeguarding the school's religious instruction, preserving its endowments, and electing – sometimes belatedly – the choristers and Langford (or later Dean's) scholars.

As for Professor Orme's local worthies and parents, only rarely until recent times do we hear of their direct involvement in the school's activities, by way of periodic visitations (for a period from the late seventeenth century) from the diocesan Bishop, the granting of a half-holidays and fielding complaints about a Headmaster's course of action. But over the centuries, with the exception of the extra half-holidays ('halves'), such interference was rare, and the Headmaster's absolute authority over his school remained relatively unfettered for much of this history. In very different ways, the late defining of his responsibilities and the late reform of what we would now consider irregular practice is significant. It was only in 1893 that the Headmaster's specific duties, as opposed to the vague requirements of the cathedral statutes, were prescribed in an official scheme of governance; until the Second World War, Headmasters pocketed the profits – and sustained the losses – of the boarding house they administered; four Headmasters (continuously from 1898 to 1945) were successive proprietors of their own preparatory school, which they ran as a private business; as late as the 1960s, the terms of contract of an assistant master required him 'to be at the Headmaster's discretion during the whole of the time that the school … [was] in session'; and the Headmaster's power to beat boys was not formally abolished by the governors until 1987. So there is good justification for an historian of HCS to shape his narrative around the Headmasters.

8. Although only a few years ago, a union leader complained that Heads 'have more power than Roman emperors', as reported in *The Times*, 9 April 2012, p.2.

9. Orme (2006), p.141.

For much of this story, moreover, the school's prosperity – intellectually as well as materially – depended mainly on the Headmaster. To take just one period: the early nineteenth century, when for the first time we have reliable evidence of pupil numbers. Under Dr Taylor (1807-26), HCS increased to over 100 boys; under his successors in the 1830s and '40s, the roll fell on occasions to single figures, the foundationers apart. Then, more quickly than now, a school's favourable reputation could vanish with a change of Headmaster. The boarders would leave and, as a scholar of classical education has observed, 'there would remain only a few local boys construing at one end of the schoolroom',[10] as was the case in the second quarter of the nineteenth century. How far these decades were exceptional is difficult to determine. Of one thing, however, we can be more confident. We know that not all our Headmasters were equally successful: sometimes external circumstances, like an economic downturn, the spread of an epidemic or the opening of a rival school would work against them; at other times, they may have been too unworldly to have been effective teachers of boys. Nevertheless, for the past three centuries, at least, it has been Hereford Cathedral School's good fortune to have had few rogues and many scholars, as well as a long succession of Christian gentlemen, all of whom were clerics until 1919, in the magisterial gallery. Even when they held livings elsewhere, as they did until 1839, the evidence suggests that in the main these Headmasters were committed to the school; and that they both preserved (and sometimes enhanced) its standing, and effectively directed the lives of the members of the community under their charge.

I wrote the first words of this book, an account of HCS in the 1860s, based on the fascinating memoirs of W.E. Vernon Yonge OH, in May 2007. During the ten years since, I have incurred obligations to many people. First, I must thank Michael Tavinor, Dean of Hereford and President of the school's governors, for writing the foreword and for his encouragement throughout this project. The medieval cathedral Chancellors were important, although frustratingly shadowy, cathedral dignitaries in the school's governance for its first 400 years. However, two of the most recent incumbents of this office, John Tiller and Chris Pullen, the present Chancellor, have been far from remote figures in the genesis of this work. I am indebted to them both. Paul Illes and Andrew Piper, the two Hereford Precentors in my time, have also been supportive of this project, as have Geraint Bowen and Roy Massey, the present cathedral organist and his immediate predecessor.

As will be appreciated from the footnotes, I have relied on the expertise of archivists and librarians at The National Archives, the British Library, Brasenose College, Oxford, St John's College, Cambridge, as well as the professionalism of historians at many colleges and schools. I would, however, like to pay particular tribute to past and present staff and volunteers at Hereford Cathedral library, where I have spent many happy days poring over documents at the desk overlooking the cathedral's west front, not far from the old cloistered schoolroom and the Great Room, both long demolished, where cathedral schoolboys were taught for well over two centuries. Joan Williams first suggested that I should write this history; Rosalind Caird, whose knowledge of the cathedral's manuscript collections is unsurpassed, put numerous documents my way and saved me from many errors; and Rosemary Firman, the cathedral's present librarian, has been unfailingly helpful. Among

10. Clarke (1945), p.19.

other Hereford librarians and archivists, I would particularly like to acknowledge the help given me by Marianne Percival at the city library and Rhys Griffith at the Herefordshire Archive and Records Centre.

This is not a commissioned history but it could not have been written without my first having been given access to the school's archives, as well as to private collections of documents relevant to the school's history. In this regard, I am particularly grateful to Paul Smith, my immediate successor and the present Headmaster, for locating Barry Sutton's papers; to Norman Moon, a former bursar, for finding the early governors' minute books, which I feared might have disappeared for ever; and to three daughters of past headmasters (or acting headmasters): Naomi Bell, Trish Brittain (née Hopewell) and the late Jillie Steele (née Peebles), who generously gave me access to their fathers' papers.

Past and current Headmasters and teachers have provided invaluable reminiscences of their time at the school. Of former Headmasters, I am especially sorry that David Richards (1968-75) and Barry Sutton (1975-87), who died within four months of each other in 2016-17, were unable to see this book in print. However, they had given me detailed recollections of their respective headmasterships and read early drafts of the sections on their tenures. I remain indebted to them both for their generosity and friendship over the years. Stephen Sides, Tim Lowe and Tim Wheeler, whose headmasterships at Hereford Cathedral Junior School cover some twenty-five years, have also written to me about their time at HCJS. Both Paul Smith and Rob Haydn Jones, the recently retired chairman of governors, have willingly answered my queries on the school's development over the past twelve years. Of my former colleagues, Alan Morris has written colourful pen-portraits of three Headmasters under whom he served; Egerton Parker and Richard Rhodes have provided me with material help and encouragement; Elizabeth Locke (née Whittaker), who was among the second girls' cohort to be admitted to the school, wrote a beautiful piece on the advent of co-education, 1972-74, from which I have quoted extensively; and Jon Priday OH and Marnie Wooderson, who are still teaching at HCS, gave me their recollections of developments at HCS over more than 30 years. Among other former colleagues, John Williams pointed me in the right direction with regard to both John Woolley's headmastership at Rossall and Dr Crees' benefaction to St John's College, Cambridge.

The Old Herefordians' Club, whose members kindly elected me their President despite my being only an honorary OH, generously funded part of my research expenses. The club's membership secretary, Helen Pearson, its recent magazine editor, Clare Adamson, and the school's development director, Claire Morgan-Jones, have all supported me through the writing of this history. Hundreds of Old Herefordians, the earliest of whom started at HCS before the Second World War, have written to me (not always favourably) about their times at the school. I have been able to use only a fraction of their contributions but all have added to my understanding of the Cathedral School's history in the mid to late twentieth century. Where I have used an individual's contribution, I have made reference in the footnotes, but here I would like to acknowledge the help of three OHs specifically: Paul Dodd for the loan of his thesis which aided my understanding of the Endowed Schools' Commission of the 1860s; Martin Everett for the gift of his meticulous study of OHs who fought in World War One and his help with the OH appendix; and Matthew Hall for the composition of his fine companion piece which introduces Chapter 8. Richard Birt is an Old Westminster rather than an Old Herefordian, but he is also an Oxford scholar from whom I have learned a great deal about Thomas Traherne, HCS's most celebrated poet. Henry Connor has done the same for some notable Old Herefordian medical men.

There are also those who have helped me with process of putting words and images on paper. Geoffrey Allibone, Charles Gordon Clarke and David Wyllie gave me the benefit of their expertise in classical languages and medieval Latin. The following read drafts of chapters for me and improved them considerably by their suggestions: Dudley Ankerson OH, Caroline Barron, the late Glen Butcher OH, Rosalind Caird, John Eisel OH, Joseph Goldsmith OH, the late Geoffrey Hughes OH, Paul Iles, Anthony Fletcher, David James OH, David Jones OH, David Lepine, the late Colin Oldroyd, Nicholas Orme, John Tiller, Nicholas Tyacke, Michael Walling OH, John Powell Ward OH, Anthony Weston OH, Jeremy Wilding OH and Peter Williams OH. I am further indebted to Joseph Goldsmith for his immaculate proof-reading; to Gordon Taylor for his skill and patience in producing the images; to Debbie Mumford for formatting and Tim Symons for copy-editing my type-script; and to my publisher, Andy and Karen Johnson, for taking on this venture towards the end of their prolific publishing careers at Logaston, saving me from many errors, compiling the index and seeing the book through the press. Most importantly of all, my wife, Heather, who has lived with this project for far too long, has vastly improved at least two drafts of the text through her meticulous attention to detail.

This history has indeed been an unconscionable time in the making. As a consequence, in addition to my two immediate predecessors already mentioned, it has appeared too late for a number of Old Herefordians to read. One of them, James A.W. Smith OH (1921-26) and former Somerset exhibitioner in Classics, wrote to me (aged 97) towards the end of my time as Headmaster, saying that he hoped to survive long enough to read the school's history that I had announced I would endeavour to write in my retirement. Although Mr Smith lived to 101, I fear that I failed him, as well as other OHs like Geoffrey Hughes and Colin Manning, who both sent me invaluable reminiscences of their schooldays. In this context, I would also like to acknowledge the contribution of our son, Edward Tomlinson OH, who gave me early encouragement when I first started this project, and to whose memory this book is dedicated.

I compose these last sentences, as I have written most of this book, from my Park Street study, looking out towards Bartonsham Meadow and Dinedor Hill. The house itself, built in the 1860s as one of the Hereford Freehold Land Society developments, was not so long ago occupied successively by two families whose children attended the Cathedral School. Two of the boys were choristers. But the landscape also has associations with both the cathedral and its school. The 'Scotch rowditch', from which line the Scottish army laid siege to the cathedral and city in 1645, lies at the bottom of the garden; Bartonsham Meadow, perhaps part of the cathedral demesne in medieval times, was explored as a site for the school's playing-fields before Wyeside was acquired; Dinedor Hill, where 'deep orchards' once nestled,[11] was the scene of many a paper-chase in Victorian and Edwardian times. As

11. At least according to the great Victorian lyricist, F.E. Weatherly OH, in his verse composition for the first issue of *The Herefordian*, as reprinted in the review in the *Hereford Times*, 23 Feb. 1878, p.5.

I gaze out on hill and meadow, I try to imagine how it might have been; and think how appropriate it is that my concluding words should be written within sight of fields once roamed by cathedral schoolboys, and within sound in a westerly breeze of the cathedral's bells. Like Carless' work, this book has been a labour of love – a story written by an historian who holds one of the city's oldest foundations in great affection – but not, I trust, a history of entirely uncritical piety.

Contents

Colour Plates

(Between pages 434 and 435)

Figures

Principal Abbreviations

BL Add. MS	British Library, Additional Manuscript
BNCA	Brasenose College, Oxford, Archives
Bodl.	Bodleian Library, Oxford
Brasenose Reg.	[C.B. Heberden], *Brasenose College Register* 1509-1909, 2 vols. in 1 (Oxford Historical Society lv, 1910)
BNEJ	*Building News and Engineering Journal*
CCCA	Corpus Christi College, Oxford, Archives
CRO	Cornwall Record Office
CSA	Crypt School Archives, Gloucester
CSPD	*Calendar of State Papers, Domestic Series, preserved in the Public Record Office, 1547-1704* (92 vols., London 1856-1972)
GBA	Governing Bodies Association
GMB	Governers' Minutes Book
HARC	Herefordshire Archive and Records Centre
HCA	Hereford Cathedral Archives
HCJSA	Hereford Cathedral Junior School Archives
HCL	Hereford Cathedral Library
HCN	*Hereford Cathedral News*
HCSA	Hereford Cathedral School Archives
HDM	*Hereford Diocesan Messenger*
HJ	*Hereford Journal*
HMC	Headmasters' Conference
HRL	Hereford Reference Library
HT	*Hereford Times*
KCA	King's College, Cambridge, Archives
LPL	Lambeth Palace Library
ODNB	*Oxford Dictionary of National Biography*, 60 vols. (Oxford, 2004)
OH	Old Herefordian (former pupil)
PRO	Pembrokeshire Record Office
PP	*Parliamentary Papers*
SA	Shropshire Archives
SJCA	St John's College, Cambridge, Archives
TH	*The Herefordian*

TNA	The National Archives
TRHS	*Transactions of the Royal Historical Society*
TWNFC	*Transactions of the Woolhope Naturalists' Field Club, Herefordshire*
VCH	*Victoria County History*
WAAS	Worcestershire Archive and Archaeology Service
WSA	Westminster School Archives

Conventions

Before 1752, dates are given in the new style, with the year stating on 1 January, rather than 25 March.

Spelling and punctuation in quotations have been modernised and standardised.

As the Prologue indicates, HCS has been known by a number of names through the centuries. In the text however (unless in direct quotation), I tend to refer to Hereford Cathedral School (or its diminutive the Cathedral School) rather than the Free School, the College School, Hereford Cathedral Grammar School, or any of its other former designations.

The Dean and Chapter, the Cathedral School & the College of Vicars Choral: A Constitutional Guide

As the Dean mentions in his Foreword, the cathedral and its school are now distinct entities. The present legal separation between the two bodies is not altogether different from the position in medieval times, when for the first 400 years of the school's existence from the late twelfth century, the school was personally controlled by the cathedral Chancellor and it was as much a city as a cathedral school. During this period, about which we know comparatively little, the cathedral had its own separate song school for the choristers, some of whom would have advanced to the senior grammar school.

The decisive shift occurred with the Elizabethan statutes of 1583, when the cathedral's medieval statutes were reformed and the grammar school established within the cathedral's precincts. The Dean and Chapter as a corporate body became its patrons, appointing the Headmaster for the first time in September of that year. The choristers were also absorbed from this date into the grammar school. From then onwards, our school properly became Hereford Cathedral School, although it was not always so named. From 1583, the Dean and Chapter were the school's sole governors for over 300 years.

The next major constitutional change occurred in June 1893, when a new scheme devised by the Charity Commissioners under the Endowed Schools Act of 1869, was approved by Her Majesty in Council. This gave HCS a definite foundation, with much of its assets being vested in independent trustees. The school site and buildings (then restricted to those shown on the cover photograph), however, continued to be vested in the Dean and Chapter who for a short time continued to constitute the governing body.

The constitutional story of the twentieth century is one of the cathedral's gradual withdrawal from control of the school. The first two lay governors were appointed in 1910. By 1919, the three Dean and Chapter representatives were outnumbered by the four other governors in a reconstituted scheme of governance. However, the Dean continued to chair the Board for most of the century, and two of his colleagues (usually the Precentor and Chancellor) continued to act as governors until the early years of this century. Today, while no members of the Dean and Chapter sit as active governors, as explained in the Epilogue, the Dean as President of the Board, and he and his Chapter colleagues as members of the Limited Company (established by the school in 1987), still have important formal roles to play in the governance of HCS, quite apart from their considerable influence in other ways. As for the vicars choral, junior clergy who sang services (among other duties) in the cathedral choir, their involvement in the school has long gone. The vicars were incorporated as a College in 1395 and remained an independent corporation until 1936, when the College was dissolved and its assets taken over by the Dean and Chapter. Their informal links with the school, however, were close until the late nineteenth century: through their provision of two choristers for the cathedral choir; from the vicars choral often being old boys of the school; from their role as masters within the school; and from the periodic emergency use by the school of their buildings – as from 1760 to 1778 and again from 1851 to 1875, part of their cloister garden continuning to be used by HCS boys as a playground until 1889.

As the Armies did against each other fight,
Even so doe our moderne Historians write:
Each for his side. The Stationer says, Buy both:
Compare them, and you may pick out the Truth.
(Clement Barksdale, Headmaster of HCS, 1637-46?)
Nymphal Liberthris or the Cotswold Muse (1651),
part 2, p.43, XLI: 'Upon the Histories of the late Wars')

This City is an Engin Great
That makes my pleasure more compleat,
The Sword, the Mace, the Magistrate
To honor Thee attends in State;
The whole Assembly sings
The Minster rings.
(Thomas Traherne OH, *On Christmas-Day*, Margoliouth, ii. 110)

O patience, heav'nly maid ...
Assist my flight! No common aid I ask,
To sing the tutor's multifarious task.
(Gibbons Bagnall, Headmaster of HCS, 1762-78, 1782-84,
From *Education an Essay* (1765))

Let others sing of famous schools by Thames or on the hill,
The Wye that runs by Hereford to us is dearer still.
Where'er we journey, near or far, whatever voices call,
The school that made us what we are, is dearest school of all.
Then *Floreat, semper floreat*, the dearest school of all.
(Fred E. Weatherly OH, '*Floreat!*', frontispiece to J.C. Eales-White,
Records of Hereford Cathedral School (1931))

We can't talk to the past
We're too concerned with what comes next;
What's gone
Talks to us, talks incessantly.
(R.D. Lancaster, Assistant Master HCS, 1947-88, 'Love to Jump',
The Herefordian, CCXXIV (Nov. 1978), p.4)

Prologue

Name, Place and Date

The grammar school that has been attached to the cathedral church of Hereford since medieval times has not always been known as Hereford Cathedral School. Variants over its long history include Hereford's grammar school, Free School or collegiate school, as well as its Cathedral School. Such names, as with grammar school (or as in the cathedral's early statutes '*de gymnasio, sive ludo literario*'), could accurately define function: the teaching of Latin grammar. However, other designations, like 'Free School' (or 'free grammar school', a name which was used as late as 1763) could cause confusion. For as the Chapter Clerk argued in 1890, the description of HCS as a 'Free School', whilst accurate in terms of its being available to any Hereford citizen irrespective of the Headmaster's wishes – thereby making it a public school as opposed a private or proprietary one – was inaccurate in terms of non-payment of fees. Such a term had sowed the seeds of conflict with the city fathers, who occasionally over the previous centuries claimed the right of free education at the school for their sons. And the name 'collegiate school', while it was perfectly appropriate during HCS's (as it turned out temporary) stay within the College of Vicars Choral in the 1760s and '70s, and from 1851 to 1875, continued to be used outside these periods. So Headmaster Squire (1784-1803) referred in his advertisements in the *Hereford Journal* to the 'Collegiate' or 'College' School, a much grander sounding title than the 'Grammar School at Hereford' used by his predecessor. The term College School and 'Old Collegians' lingered on (with greater justification in the third quarter of the century) under Squire's successors, and it was not until the mid-1870s that Hereford Cathedral School found universal acceptance in press notices and reports of sporting fixtures.[1]

But even then, although unlike its Gloucester and Worcester counterparts HCS did not alter its name in the late nineteenth century,[2] the Hereford Cathedral Grammar School

1. Squire's use of 'Collegiate School' may be found in his numerous notices in the *Hereford Journal* from 14 Oct. 1784. The earliest use of 'Cathedral School' I have found in the same journal relates to its masters (Picart and Garbett) presenting their report for the Chapter Audit, 19 Nov. 1806; and the last use of College School: *HT*, 14 Nov. 1874, report of a football match against Hereford City.

2. Both Gloucester and Worcester became 'King's Schools', which were appropriate designations for Reformation foundations. For an earlier reference to Gloucester and Worcester Cathedral Schools: *HT*, 28 Sept. 1872, p.2, list of cricket fixtures.

continued as its legal title, as in the 1893 scheme of governance which established the school as a separate corporation. This designation continued to be used in official documents for much of the twentieth century. Indeed, it was not until 1958 that the governors sanctioned the use of Hereford Cathedral School, which had by then come into customary usage, 'for all purposes', characteristically adding that the existing stocks of stationery, which included the name 'Grammar School', should first be used up.[3]

Although the school has always been situated within the vicinity of the great ecclesiastical building that has dominated Hereford for so many ages, its place of teaching, like its name, has not had a settled existence. Following its no doubt peripatetic existence around the Cathedral Close in medieval times, the earliest schoolroom that can be identified was that established over the west walk of the Bishop's Cloister in 1590. This lasted until its temporary move to the College in 1760. The schoolroom was then transferred in 1778 to the Great (or Music) Room, that grand – at least for a time – Georgian edifice (long demolished) adjacent to the cathedral's west front. After 57 years of increasingly uncomfortable existence there, teaching moved to the east of the cathedral in school yard, adjacent to the Headmaster's house, before reverting again in 1851 to the College's rooms for a generation. In 1875, the school acquired its first purpose-built schoolrooms on the corner of Castle and Quay Streets, a site it has continued to retain until the present day. The twentieth century has seen a gradual progression down these streets and around the Close: from its renting of Number 1 in 1911, which gave it access to East Street, followed by Old Deanery in 1945; to its acquisition from the 1970s of houses straddling both sides of Castle Street and Quay Street; to its procuring of the old Post Office Exchange Building in Church Street in 1996. The present locations, as shown on the plan on the rear endpaper, reveal a picture of a school that has grown haphazardly, in and around the cathedral precinct and adjacent areas, as needs have arisen and circumstances dictated.

The school's age as given in the book's title requires more detailed explanation, for the '800 Years' will be confusing for the many who remember the '600th' celebrations on that special summer's day in June 1981, as well as the very few centenarian (or near-centenarian) Old Herefordians – if there are any still alive – who can recall the '550th' commemoration in 1931. For all these, and for other generations of former pupils who have been brought up with the belief that the school's foundation dates from the early 1380s (whether 1381 or 1384), this prologue is also intended to disabuse them of their misapprehension.

As recently as 1989, a similar error was made. In that year, Hereford suitably celebrated the 800th year of the grant by Richard I of its first charter, which gave the citizens of 'Hereford in Wales' the rights of fortifying their town and holding it 'with all its liberties and free customs' independently of the sheriff's control. Among the memorabilia brought out to mark this significant milestone in the city's history was a commemorative booklet *Hereford 800: A Celebration* which gave a picture of its development over the centuries. Education was one of the chosen topics for consideration. The article on this theme started promisingly enough by pointing out that 'the church and the cathedral were probably providing education

3. HCSA, GMB 1945-82, p.122, meeting 8 Oct. 1958. 'All purposes' did not include schemes of governance; and as late as 1987, I inherited a Lloyds (Headmaster's) bank account in the name of Hereford Cathedral Grammar School.

in Hereford from an early date' and that 'the most ancient [educational] foundation documented is that of the Cathedral School'. Thereafter, the opening statement that the school was founded in 1381 by Bishop Gilbert 'to give free education to the sons of poor citizens of Hereford' could hardly have been more wrong: the school was not founded in 1381; Bishop Gilbert was not its founding father; and the education it provided was never wholly free.[4]

Given the weight of local antiquarian opinion over the previous 200 or so years, such mistakes are understandable. Many of the nineteenth-century county and city histories state unequivocally that the school was originally founded by Bishop Gilbert. John Duncumb's assertion, for example, that the school was 'founded under the auspices of Bishop Gilbert ... for the purpose of affording gratuitous instruction to the sons of poor citizens' was copied almost exactly by Richard Johnson, Hereford's Town Clerk from 1832 to 1868, in his book of ancient city customs. And the authors of early guidebooks and directories followed suit. Even a scholar like Canon Phillott wrote in his diocesan history that Gilbert 'deserves to be remembered as the founder' and W.T. Carless, the school's first chronicler, thought that he 'obtains more or less the credit of being its founder'.[5]

The school itself, however, must take responsibility for the incorrect dating of its origins. The mistake seems to have stemmed from the earliest issue in January 1878 of *The Herefordian*, the school magazine, on the front cover of which was engraved the motto: *Schola Cathedralis Herefordensis 1381*. It was a schoolboy error for it had long been recognised by local antiquarians – from at least as early as Duncumb's *Collections* in 1804 – that the then earliest known document specifically mentioning the Cathedral School was dated in the year 1384. Indeed, this had come to the school's notice by September 1878 when the second edition of the magazine was published.[6] However, the young Headmaster of the time showed a greater anxiety to promote the school than properly to investigate its origins. So despite the evidence to the contrary, its quincentenary was officially celebrated on 30 June and 1 July 1881. Thereafter, there was no going back on 1381, the '550th' celebrations taking place on 20-21 June 1931 and the '600th' on 27 June 1981, even though 1884, 1934 and 1984 would have been the more historically appropriate, if still inaccurate, years for commemorative junketing to honour the school's foundation.[7]

For it was on 26 December 1384, the feast day of the first Christian martyr, that the aforementioned John Gilbert – a member of the learned Dominican Order, a councillor to Richard II and (following his Bangor episcopate and prior to his translation to St David's) Bishop of Hereford from 1375 to 1389 – issued the writ from his Whitbourne Manor appointing Richard Cornwaille Master of the school. As this is the most important of the few records relating to the school in the medieval period, it is worth quoting extensively:

---

4. *Hereford 800: A Celebration* (Worcester, 1989), p.49.

5. Duncumb, i., p.590; Johnson, p.186; Rees, p.64; J. Jones, p.79; Phillott, (1888), p.110; Carless, p.6. J.C. Wordsworth, in his *Shorter History* (pp.1, 16), was nearer the mark when he observed that 'a cathedral school had been in existence for a long time before 1384', and that it was 'maintained by the cathedral authorities for years, perhaps for centuries, before Bishop Gilbert ...'

6. T.T. Davies, 'A Brief Historical Account of Hereford Cathedral School', *TH*, 2 (Sept. 1878), pp.45-49. Also see *ibid.*, 4 (Sept. 1879), p.168, for an anonymous article citing 1385 rather than 1384.

7. For the celebrations in 1881, 1931 and 1981 see below, pp.250, 390-91, 566-67.

> Seeing that by old custom the appointment and control of the Master of the grammar school in the city of Hereford belongs to the office of the Chancellor of the cathedral, and that we have repeatedly required and urged the Chancellor and his proctor to provide an adequate Master for our school, and that they have expressly refused to comply with our request to the prejudice of holy church and grave injury to the scholars who desire instruction. Wherefore we, having regard to the aptness of your person, finding you through examination to be capable and well-suited by your character and learning, and in view of the failure of either the Chancellor or his proctor to act, by virtue of our own episcopal authority and by means of this commission, valid for just one year, appoint you to have the rule and discipline, by birch and rod as is customary, of the grammar school.[8]

The most complete document relating to the school in the Middle Ages, however, neither signifies that Bishop Gilbert was the school's founder nor constitutes a founding charter. There is no evidence here of the creation of an endowment or new office for the school. As the editor of Bishop Gilbert's register indicated in 1913:

> Bishop Gilbert has been erroneously credited with the foundation of the Cathedral School, probably from a misunderstanding of an entry in the register. The truth was that in the exercise of his office and as a matter of discipline he restored to its proper work an institution of great antiquity which for a short time had fallen into neglect.[9]

A few years later, A.F. Leach, a renowned (but controversial) scholar of medieval schools, put it more acerbically. 'With the usual insouciance of the local medieval historian', he wrote, 'this [Bishop Gilbert's writ] has actually been quoted as the foundation of Herford Cathedral Grammar School, whereas it witnesses to its being even then ancient'.[10]

As Leach implied, it is clear from this register entry that the school's governance had long belonged by custom to the Chancellor; that Bishop Gilbert was acting outside his jurisdiction only after repeated attempts to persuade the cathedral authorities to make an appointment; and that he was respecting the Chancellor's rights in the matter by ensuring that the commission lasted for a finite period (one year). The Bishop had issued his writ on this occasion to deal with a temporary emergency. As with other secular cathedrals in the medieval period, this is another instance of evidence concerning their grammar school being written down as a result of a crisis.[11]

Bishop Gilbert's appointment of Richard Cornwaille as master of the school arose out of a dispute between the pope and the English crown over the right of patronage to the cathedral's office of Chancellor, one consequence of which was that there were untutored

8. Carless, pp.5-6. I am indebted to David Wyllie for his help in translating this document and for his translation of De Freine's poem (note 16). Also see, Parry (ed.), p.48. According to Parry, despite Gilbert's successive appointments in the 1380s as Chancellor of Ireland, Treasurer of England and a member of the subsequent ruling commission, the administration of his diocese did not unduly suffer by his absence.

9. *Ibid.*, p.v, Introduction.

10. Leach (1916), p.164. Although Leach himself mistakenly claimed that the writ dated from 1385.

11. Kathleen Edwards (pp.195-96), for example, has made the same point about troubles at Salisbury's grammar school in 1350-52 and 1468.

scholars in his school waiting for instruction. It is not known for how long this unsatisfactory state of affairs had obtained but it is possible that it had existed for much of Gilbert's early episcopate in Hereford and perhaps continued for the best part of a decade. The story of the Hereford chancellorship at this time is a complicated (and unusual) one but it seems that after the translation of Bishop William Courtenay (Gilbert's predecessor, 1369-75) to London in 1375 and following the demise of Thomas Hacluit (Chancellor, 1349-75), the Chancellor's duties were largely unperformed. It was not that there was a lack of candidates to fill his stall. Nicholas Hereford, later a follower of John Wycliffe, gained temporary possession and received papal confirmation of the dignity. His title, however, was subsequently questioned by the Bishop on the grounds that the patronage of the chancellorship belonged to the King during the vacancy of the see after Courtenay's translation. The King, indeed, seized the endowment of the chancery in 1375 and apparently held it until 1387, during which time the cathedral lacked a resident active Chancellor: Nicholas Hereford does not seem to have been installed and two absentee cardinals – one French (Bertrand Lagier to 1381) and the other Italian (Andreas Bontempi from 18 August 1381) – received nominations to the bare title only.[12] For us the important consequence of the lapse in the effective functioning of the chancellorship was, as we have seen, an appreciable gap in the school's governance and a consequent lack of continuity in its instruction.

If Bishop Gilbert's 1384 writ does not signify the school's foundation date, when was Hereford's medieval grammar school founded? As we will see, this is an impossible question to answer, for unlike medieval schools such as Winchester College, which can trace their foundations to a particular date through the legacies of their founding patrons, the origins of all secular cathedral schools are obscure.[13] Nevertheless, as has already been suggested, there is good cause to believe that a grammar school has been attached to Hereford Cathedral for at least 800 years, and perhaps even predated Richard I's famous charter granted to the city of Hereford in 1189.

Although we know that its existence has not been continuous, over these 800 years the school overcame the absences of medieval Chancellors; was strengthened by both the new cathedral statutes of 1583 and 1636 and the generosity of its early seventeenth-century patrons; weathered the storms of the civil war in the 1640s; survived the abolition of Deans and Chapters and continued (under different governors) as an educational establishment during the Interregnum; prospered during the Restoration period, when further rules were set (in 1665) for its existence, and became the almost accidental beneficiary (in the 1680s) of the Duchess of Somerset's largesse; endured the scandal of a headmaster who ran into financial difficulties in the late eighteenth century and had to be removed from office; avoided closure when numbers fell to single figures in the late 1840s; fought off threats

12. I am indebted to Nicholas Orme for his observations about the Hereford chancellorship during Gilbert's episcopacy. The story may be pieced together from Parry, pp.105-08 (Inquisition on the vacancy, 15 June 1387, grant to John Nottingham, Chancellor, of the profits of office during the vacancy to repair his residence, 24 Oct. 1387; and John Derlton's report to the Bishop on the vacancy, 24 Nov. 1387); Capes, p.xli; Aylmer and Tiller, pp.575, 640; Le Neve (2009), p.12. For the preferment of non-resident cardinals to English secular cathedral dignities by Clement VII and Urban VI: Edwards, pp.83-85.

13. Winchester College was founded by William Wykeham, its foundation charter being issued in 1382. Orme (2006), p.225. For schools attached to secular (non-monastic) cathedrals, see below, pp.7-8.

of mergers with the County College and then the Boys' High School fifty and more years later; was restored during the latter part of the Great War and the depression years of the 1920s and '30s; muddled through years of austerity during the Second World War and the immediate post-war years; was modernised in the 1950s and '60s; adopted co-education in the following decade, which helped offset the phasing out of direct grant and assisted places in 1976 and 1998; and has flourished as a fully independent school since 2004.

How Hereford Cathedral School survived such traumas and adapted to these changes forms a central theme of this book. And although for much of this narrative, the sources on which the book is based are the product of adult minds, from the first edition (in 1878) of *The Herefordian*, which was founded and edited by the boys themselves, this history is also periodically narrated through the voices of its former pupils. It is a rich and complex story of survival and growth of one Hereford's oldest living institutions; a story which as the school is reinvigorated each year with a fresh infusion of people, young and older, is still without end.

Chapter 1

The Chancellor's School

Bishop Gilbert's writ of 26 December 1384 shows that the Chancellor, through his right of nomination of the grammar master, was indispensable to the running of a secular cathedral grammar school in the medieval period. It also illustrates the weakness inherent in an institution dependent for its effective functioning on one man rather than a corporate body. So during its earliest history, Hereford's grammar school, as with those of other secular foundations (those staffed by canons rather than monks), had (as Nicholas Orme has observed) 'an equivocal status ... [being] neither fully part of the cathedral body, nor altogether detached from it'.[1] At Hereford, the arrangement of the grammar school being under the auspices of the Chancellor, and separate from the song school which was supervised by the Precentor or his deputy, continued through the Reformation period until the later sixteenth century.

The Chancellor's office gradually emerged as a separate dignity in the late twelfth century. During this period, the old cathedral teaching masters had begun to take on work as writers of letters and keepers of records as the demands of ecclesiastical administration

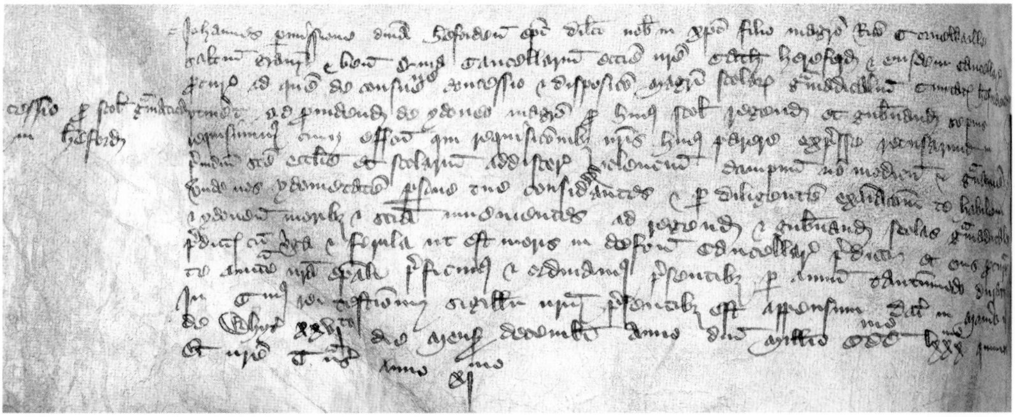

Fig. 1.1 Bishop Gilbert's original writ, 26 December 1384, appointing during a vacancy in the Chancellor's office, Richard Cornwaille as Master of the School.

1. Orme (1996), p.50.

grew. Consequently, they adopted the title of Chancellor to reflect their new responsibilities and appointed deputies of lower social standing to undertake their grammar duties. Their links with education were retained through their delivery of higher lectures on theology and canon law to local clergy – a duty at Hereford given over to the penitentiary by 1356 – and (importantly for our purposes) through the oversight of the school's operation.[2]

Twelfth-Century Origins

The evidence for a twelfth-century grammar school foundation at Hereford is indirectly suggested by the known existence of free-standing grammar schools at other secular cathedrals and more directly indicated by the early reference to a grammar master attached to Hereford Cathedral. The comparative examples are especially telling. Even in cathedral cities, no school is able to demonstrate by way of regular and frequent documentation a continuous history from early medieval times. Grammar schools, however, are known to have existed at most of the nine secular cathedral foundations before *c.*1200: at Salisbury and York by about 1100; at St Paul's and Wells by *c.*1102 and 1140 respectively; and at Exeter (although that city's school was *sui generis*), Lichfield and Lincoln by the end of the twelfth century.[3]

There is good reason to think that the developments at Hereford were similar to those at other secular cathedrals. Like Master Durand the *Scholasticus* at St Paul's in 1102, the Hugh *Grammaticus* whose son was one of the witnesses to a land conveyance at Brampton by the Bishop of Hereford in 1132 may have been a grammar school master. And while the emergence of the Chancellor's office was later at Hereford than at some of its sister foundations, it is likely that the pattern of the Chancellor having a grammar master as his deputy had already been established well before the time of appointment in *c.*1195 of Henry de Vere, the earliest known Chancellor to have formally held the dignity.[4] Most secular cathedrals appear to have fulfilled the spirit (although not the letter) of the Third Lateran Council edict of 1179, ordering every cathedral to provide a schoolmaster 'to teach the clerks of the same church and poor scholars freely', before its issue, even if the masters continued to levy fees on their charges because they never succeeded in securing the required benefice. This necessitated the promulgation of a similar edict in 1215 with the additional stipulation that a theologian should be selected for each metropolitan area 'to teach the priests and others in the sacred page and inform them especially in those matters which are recognised as pertaining to the soul'.[5]

Again, however, by 1215 – and before the establishment of the ancient universities – several English secular cathedrals had already organised scholarly gatherings for

2. See Edwards, pp.176-85, for the development of the dignity of Chancellors at secular cathedrals; Orme (2006), pp.81-83, 163-68, for the changed Chancellor's role and the emergence by *c.*1200 of the schoolmaster's office; and specifically, Orme (1976), pp.66, 82, for its separation from the chancellorship at Salisbury and Wells.

3. Orme (2006), pp.346ff, list of schools, 1066-1530. For Exeter, where (uniquely for secular foundations) the master was appointed by the Archdeacon and the school was more remote from the cathedral: Orme (1976), pp.46-47.

4. Capes, pp.7-8; Charles and Emanuel, i., p.3, no. 1095; Capes, pp.7-8; Le Neve (2002), pp.xxiv, 21.

5. *Ibid.*, p.203; Orme (2006), p.202; Leach (1911), pp.122-23, 142-44.

the edification of local clergy, even if the Chancellor had yet to assume responsibility for theological training in many of them. In Exeter, Lincoln and St Paul's, for example, leading scholars were appointed to canonries from the mid-twelfth century onwards.[6] And for a period before 1200, Hereford had gained renown in higher learning, in part through the influence of a succession of highly educated bishops. In the late twelfth century, Bishop Robert Foliot (1174-86) and especially his successor, William de Vere (1186-98), were particularly important in enticing a number of luminaries to the city. These included Nicholas, styled *Divinus*, a theologian who may have acted as master of the schools, if not Chancellor; the polymath and future Bishop of Lincoln, Robert Grosseteste, who was a member of the Bishop's household in the 1190s; and Walter Map, author and wit who wrote *De Nugis Curialium*, a collection of anecdotes and legends. Map was appointed a canon of Hereford, as was Gerald of Wales, who wrote a life of St Ethelbert, and Simon de Freine, who composed an Anglo-Norman poem on the life of St George.[7] It is de Freine's poem of the mid-1190s – this time in Latin – to Gerald of Wales which gives an indication of the flowering of scholarship in the Welsh Marches at the end of the twelfth century. The poem urges Gerald to visit Hereford, where he will find a greater study of the seven liberal arts and other subjects than anywhere else in England as this extract shows, in translation:

> Flower, glory of the cloth, come to our town;
> Where learned men are, you would hold the crown.
> Hereford truly suits you very well;
> Both trivium and quadrivium here do dwell.
> Especially within these thriving walls
> To these seven arts the highest honour falls.[8]

There is no reference in this poem to any kind of organised institution but a decade or so later Gerald himself wrote a letter alluding to the teaching of Master Albinus – then a Hereford canon and later (from *c.*1217) its Chancellor – 'at a school'. It is likely that this alludes to a school of theology rather than a grammar school, where by this time (*c.*1208) teaching would have been passed on to a deputy schoolmaster as we have seen. Nevertheless, the teaching of advanced subjects to local clerks at Hereford Cathedral by the turn of the twelfth century could hardly have occurred without there being preparatory facilities for the teaching of grammar to schoolboys nearby.[9]

The earliest surviving written statutes for the cathedral provide the final evidence that a grammar school, as well as a song school, existed in Hereford from an early date.

---

6. Orme (2006), p.80.

7. I am indebted to Rosemary Firman for a number of these observations. Also see: Le Neve (2002), pp.xxiv, 21 (for Nicholas Divinus); Aylmer and Tiller, pp.565-67; and (for a general survey of Hereford as a centre of medieval learning), Johnson and Shoesmith, pp.81-84, 89, 91.

8. Hunt, pp.36-37. The advanced subjects studied were Grammar, Logic, Rhetoric, Mathematics, Geometry, Music and Astronomy but de Freine also mentions Jurisprudence, as well as the work of astrologers and 'the geomancer', who practised the art of divination by means of lines and figures or geographical features. For a discussion of the study of mathematics and astronomy at Hereford in this period: Burnett, pp.50-59.

9. Aylmer and Tiller, pp.30, 40, 42-43, 565-67 and references there cited; Mynors and Thomson, p.xvii.

Although these statutes date from the mid-thirteenth century, they refer to practices which had long been established. From this evidence, it can be deduced that there were two further schools attached to Hereford cathedral: one of grammar; the other of song. A regent master of arts – a university MA and one who was still 'regent' or engaged in teaching – was to be appointed by the Chancellor to attend the choir in 'choir habit', organise those who were to read and 'hear the lessons in his master's place'. No mention was made of his duties in the school, nor were references made to his pupils, but as the Chancellor's deputy and given his required graduate status, it is apparent that he would also have undertaken the role of grammar master. The grammar school boys were distinct from the choir boys who were the cathedral's direct concern. They were supervised by the Succentor, the Precentor's deputy, and the other person in the cathedral hierarchy involved with education. The Succentor was to provide from 'his school' five boys, over whom he had extensive disciplinary powers, to sing in the cathedral choir.[10] Rules were laid down for their dress, ordering in procession, and proper behaviour and devotion in services. So as these statutes make apparent, there was a clear distinction between the choir boys, complete with their 'broad and comely' tonsures, and, by implication, the grammar school pupils. These two sets of boys were to learn in separate schools under different jurisdictions until after the Reformation.[11]

Hereford's possession of a grammar school before 1200, in addition to cathedral schools for song and theology, is not surprising given the city's status and increasing prosperity by that time. Hereford had long been established as a religious centre of significance, its bishopric being traceable from the late seventh century. Its cathedral building, too, was of Anglo-Saxon origin, the new Romanesque Norman cathedral completed in the 1140s being at least the third building on or around that site. A parochial system had probably been established by that decade. By 1200 the city itself, with its command of approaches to central Wales, was not only a useful resting place for peripatetic scholars like Gerald of Wales on their journeys across the Welsh Marches but also an important royal fortress of strategic significance. King John was one of the monarchs who made occasional visits, strengthening his castle and hunting in the royal forest of Haywood, during his reign (1199-1216). By this time, the city had gained independence from royal control, Richard I having sold its citizens a charter in 1189 for an annual £40 fee, enabling them to enclose the town with earthworks, which were replaced with gates and stone walls over the course of the next century. There are strong indications, too, of Hereford's economic advance during these years, despite the laying waste of the city and its suburbs east of the Wye bridge in 1139. Following the Norman Conquest, a market had developed to the

10. It is evident that at this time the Succentor was running a separate public institution, probably teaching boys to read Latin and sing plainsong. Such schools seem to have faded out by *c.*1300 because the provision of elementary education through small private schools became so common that it was not in the interest of the cathedral or its officers to run one. I am again indebted to Nicholas Orme for this observation.

11. The statutes' origins are discussed by Bannister pp.55ff and Leach (1916), p.164. Aylmer and Tiller, pp.567-68, 633-36, give further details on both their educational provisions and the cathedral's thirteenth-century constitution. For the educational responsibilities of the Precentor, Chancellor and their deputies as outlined in the actual statutes: Bradshaw and Wordsworth, ii., pp.63, 71, 76, 81, 82-84. The cathedral library holds a typescript copy, dated Nov. 1962, of E.F.H. Dunnicliff's translation.

north around the intersections of a new east-west route through High Town, which eventually stretched from St Peter's Church (*ante* 1085) to All Saints in the west. Trade began to flourish. After 1121, there was the attraction of the Bishop's three-day fair, extended to seven days in 1161. There is evidence, too, of the growth of diversified occupations connected with building, wine and textiles. Hereford was becoming a centre of the cloth trade and attracting a wealthy Jewish community. Immigration from rural villages and neighbouring towns was increasing; pilgrims were attracted (although less actively than elsewhere) by St Ethelbert's shrine in the cathedral; and there were fewer open spaces within the city's confines. Hereford was by no means the largest or richest town in the west of England but by *c.*1200 it dominated its immediate hinterland and was entering upon the highest point of its medieval development. In sum, Hereford, like other secular cathedral cities, enjoyed favourable conditions – not least a literate clergy and an increasingly prosperous trading class with sons to advance – for the growth of a flourishing grammar school before the end of the twelfth century.[12]

Masters and Their Work

The medieval grammar masters and their pupils are also well shrouded in the historical mists of time. Given that no personal correspondence survives of any Hereford Chancellor, who as we have seen took responsibility for the grammar master, we have to rely on material from a miscellaneous range of sources.[13] From such evidence, the names of five Hereford masters – only two of whom were certainly masters of the school – may be discerned. This tally is considerably fewer than the known grammar masters at other secular cathedrals.[14] We are even worse off for Hereford pupils, for whom the evidence is almost non-existent. As the earliest of the cathedral's Chapter Act books to have survived is dated from July 1512, this is so even for the choristers. Although we know the names of 18 choristers from the mid-sixteenth century, all of whom would have attended the cathedral song school, there is no telling how many would then have furthered their education at the grammar school.[15] As for masters, we know from York, Lincoln and various towns that the majority

12. For Hereford's development in the Middle Ages: Lobel, vol. I (Hereford); Tonkin, *passim*; Whitehead, (2007), chapters 2 and 3; and Johnson and Shoesmith, pp.101-111. For other English western cathedral cities in this period: Orme (1976), pp.35, 42, 57, 67, 78. There is little reliable evidence of the size of Hereford's population in the medieval period. The returns of the 1334 lay subsidy rank Hereford 14th among the major English provincial towns. The 1377 poll tax (intended to be levied on all people over 14), shows 1,903 persons paying the tax. From this, Lobel ('Hereford', p.8, note 27) estimates a population of at least 2,845. Orme suggests that this figure is an underestimate, given that the tax was widely evaded and no-one had the time to enforce the poor or recalcitrant to pay. Hereford's population was likely to have been far higher, perhaps 3,000 to 4,000 people, prior to the bubonic plagues which struck the city in 1348-49 and 1361.

13. For the chance survival of a Chancellor's correspondence at another secular cathedral: Cheney, p.634.

14. Seventeen are known from Exeter (1329-1555), 14 from Salisbury (*c.*1254-1474), 22 from Wells (*c.*1274-1561) and 12 from York (*c.*1266-1535). Orme, (1976), pp.56-57, 76, 89; Moran, pp.39-40.

15. The 18 choristers as listed in the first extant Chapter Act book. HCA, 7031/1, between fos. 80r and 172r, from 20 Dec. 1537 (William Lyde) to 30 Sept. 1563 (John Davis). At least four of these boys – Edward Hill, Henry Pye, Clement Lewys and William Walker – later became sub-deacons. It is likely that they would have attended the grammar school, as with some of their predecessors (including John? George and Roger Note) whom the Chapter warned in October 1531 and again in December 1533 not to neglect their studies (*ibid.*, fos. 67v, 72v).

of their tenures, at least in the fourteenth century, were likely to have been no more than five years. So a return of the names of five masters from the 100 or so who may have held the appointment over the 350 years from 1200, to say nothing of the thousands of nameless boys who would have attended the school over this time, is modest fare indeed. Nevertheless such limited sources, together with scraps of evidence from other secular cathedrals and elsewhere, still enable us to build up a picture of the workings of Hereford's oldest school during the later Middle Ages.

Of the five known Hereford grammar masters, only with Richard Cornwaille and John Dornell, appointed in 1384 and 1535 respectively, is there conclusive evidence in the form of an official writ or confirmation of title that they held the post of cathedral schoolmaster. However, it is fair to claim another three men: all three were described in contemporary records as teachers of grammar in Hereford, and each of them could only have worked at the Cathedral School, the sole public grammar school then existing in the city.[16]

John Lelamour, the earliest of the five, described himself in 1373, at the end of his translation of a Latin herbal treatise, as schoolmaster of 'Herford East', to distinguish it from 'Herford West' – the spelling later being standardised as 'Haverfordwest', the Pembrokeshire town. The translation, which contains orthography and words in common usage in Herefordshire in the late fourteenth century, suggests that Lelamour was a local man.

Of 'Master Richard Cornwaille', as the good Bishop described him, we know equally little. It was fanciful of the school's first historian to have suggested that he may have been a relative of (or indeed the same person as) the famous Oxford grammarian John Cornwall, who completed an influential Latin prose treatise, *Speculum Grammatice* ('A Mirror of Grammar'), in 1346 and died in 1349.[17] Not much may be assumed from Richard's surname except perhaps that in contrast with Lelamour he is unlikely to have been a local man. Nor does the description 'master' guarantee that he was a regent master of arts as was prescribed by the cathedral statutes. Although the degree of Master of Grammar had been introduced at Oxford by the late fourteenth century, grammar masters with degrees were in such short supply after the Black Death that some cathedrals, including Lincoln and Salisbury among the secular foundations, allowed men with lesser qualifications to teach in their schools.[18] The term 'master' was also increasingly being applied as a courtesy title for non-graduates, including vicars choral as well as schoolmasters. Whatever the exact meaning of his name and title, Richard Cornwaille would have left Hereford well before 1396, the year in which we hear about one Thomas More 'that was schoolmaster of Hereford' becoming embroiled in a protracted legal quarrel in a neighbouring city. The dispute in Gloucester between two local Augustinian priories, Llanthony and St Oswald's, arose because the latter had reopened (in *c.*1380) a school where More now taught, threatening the school owned by Llanthony. This controversy over the control of the city's grammar school, which dragged on for several years, need not concern us here except to say that it showed More to have

16. The following paragraphs on the masters are largely based on the researches of Nicholas Orme, as published in Aylmer and Tiller, pp.574-77.

17. Carless, *Short History*, p.7. On John Cornwall: Emden, i., p.490 and Orme (2006), pp.105-06, 110-111.

18. Orme (1989), pp.52-53.

been a tenacious and disputatious schoolmaster who may also have caused difficulties for his superiors at Hereford.[19]

We are left with the names of two other pre-Reformation masters both of whom have a more direct connection with Hereford Cathedral. We know about 'Master Richard Burgehyll' because following his death on 8 November 1492, he was commemorated (in Latin) in a monumental cathedral brass as having been 'formally teacher of grammar in this city' ('*quondam instructor gramatice istius civitatis*'). (Plate 1b). As with Cornwaille, his description as master may or may not have meant graduate status but his cathedral burial indicates that he had been master of the Cathedral School. He must also have been a prominent local personage (presumably from Burghill) for his brass plate, now in the south-east transept but originally placed near the third or fourth nave pillar, was inlaid with his (lost) effigy on a large floor marble. Like the effigy of the only other fifteenth-century schoolmaster known to have survived, that of Robert Londe (d.1462) of Newgate School Bristol, Burgehyll was not portrayed as a schoolmaster holding a birch, his symbol of office. But unlike Londe's depiction as a priest in mass vestments holding a host and chalice, Burgehyll was drawn as a prosperous man of Herefordshire: the long-haired figure, dressed in a fur-lined gown and under-tunic with braiding at the neck and cuffs and a large bag or purse hanging down from his waist, was clearly a man of substance. (Plate 1a). The day when a schoolmaster's position in society was sufficient to warrant him being commemorated in magisterial dress had not yet arrived.[20]

By 1535, when John Dornell's appointment was confirmed, a schoolmaster's status had been bolstered by greater security of tenure and additional remuneration consequent upon the foundation of newly endowed grammar schools. There are indications in the first half of the sixteenth century, too, of increasing numbers of intending or actual schoolmasters taking degrees in arts or grammar at Oxford and Cambridge which would have enhanced their social standing as well as their career prospects. John Dornell himself held a bachelor degree in civil (Roman) law – he was described as such when witnessing the Chapter's appeal in May 1535 against Archbishop Cranmer's threatened visitation – and had been admitted to the degree of BCL at Oxford on 8 April 1530 after studying at the university for five

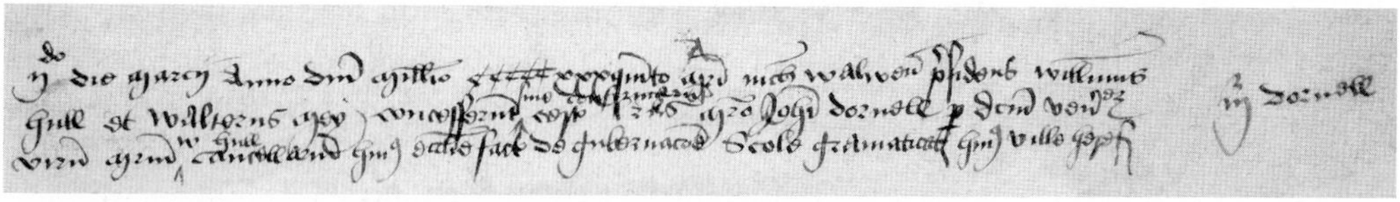

Fig. 1.2 The Chapter Act, passed in the presence of Nicholas Walwen (presiding), William Hull and Walter Mey, confirming John Dornell's appointment as Headmaster of the grammar school 'huius ville Herefordie'. *Hull, as Chancellor, clearly played a decisive role in Dornell's elevation, the appointment being made* 'per dictum venerabilem virium Magister W. Hull'.

19. Orme speculates that More may even have lost his job at Hereford – hence his move from an established grammar school to the newer one at St Oswald's (Aylmer and Tiller, pp.575-76). For More at Gloucester: Orme (1976), pp.61-63.

20. Winnington-Ingram, pp.15-16; Heseltine and Stuchfield, p.30. In 1717, Rawlinson (p.117) recorded the brass as being originally sited near the third nave pillar; Duncumb, some 90 years later (*Collections*, i., p.545, published in 1804 after the fall of the west end), as near the fourth pillar.

years. Dornell was also a good Latinist, who during his university studies had made friendships with Robert Joseph, the humanist monk of Evesham Abbey, and Edmund Field, the public schoolmaster there. Five years later he was considered by William Hull, the cathedral Chancellor, to be sufficiently worthy to take charge of Hereford's grammar school, his appointment being endorsed by the Chapter on 2 March 1535. Whether Dornell was still in office when he leased a tenement from the Chapter in Broad Cabbage Lane (now Church Street) in January 1552 is unknown.[21]

Lelamour, Cornwaille, More, Burgehyll and Dornell are the only known figures that were likely to have occupied the master's seat in Hereford's grammar school over 160 years in the later Middle Ages. Collectively, we can learn a little more. Three were designated 'master', although only one definitely held a degree. Most probably held the post in their twenties and for brief periods. None seems to have been ordained to the priesthood at the time they taught, although some may subsequently have been ordained and like 'John Schoolmaster', who became vicar of Blakemere in November 1546,[22] may have later held a Church benefice. Some, like More, may have become professional schoolmasters. All were obscure provincials even if they were not all local to Herefordshire. These certainties, such as they are, are far outweighed by the questions. What were their social origins and marital status? Who were their pupils and friends and who comprised their households? What did they read and write? How much did they earn from their fees? Did many return after university to teach at their old school?[23] We simply do not know. One thing, however, would have united them: a competence – and perhaps a brilliance for those appointed by scholarly Chancellors like John Castell and Richard Rotheram[24] – in Latin and some ability to instruct. We should now turn to their work, starting with where they might have plied their trade.

Although under the Chancellor's control, the medieval grammar school was as much a city as a cathedral school. It is significant that when Dornell's appointment as schoolmaster was confirmed, he was described in the Chapter Acts as having the rule of the town grammar school ('*de gubernacione scole grammaticalis huius ville Herefordie*') as opposed to the cathedral school. Choristers and grammar school boys kept separate existences, as already explained, although some former choir boys would have eventually progressed to Oxford via the grammar school.[25] Nevertheless, during their choir days, the five choristers (increased to seven in the early sixteenth century) not only lived within the Close – in July 1526, William Hull, prebendary of Putson Major and Chancellor, was required to

21. HCA, 7031/1, fos. 75v, 77r, 109r, Acts 2 March, 13 May 1535, 30 Jan. 1552; Aylmer and Tiller, pp.576-77; Orme (1989), pp.38-41. Catherine Dornell, described as a widow (and possibly John's widow), was given the lease of Old College by the College of Vicars Choral in September 1578, provided 'she shall well and sufficiently and town-like build a forefront upon the old building …' HCA, 7003/1/1, pp.13-14, lease, 5 Sept. 1578.

22. HCA, 7031/1, fo. 94v, 15 Nov. 1546. It should be remembered, however, that 'Schoolmaster' could have been an inherited surname.

23. In a similar way, perhaps, to Hereford's residentiary canons in the fifteenth century. David Lepine (p.182) has calculated that half of these men were local with origins in the diocese or nearby. Like their later counterparts, some of them would have attended the grammar school.

24. Respective Hereford Chancellors, 1425-28 and 1435-48. For their scholarship: Lepine, pp.187-91.

25. As with those boys who benefited from the 1529 will of Edmund Frowcester, Dean of Hereford, 1513-29, who asked for two of the 'most aptest' Hereford choristers to be supported at Oxford from his estate. *Ibid.*, p.185.

board his choristers in his canonical quarters rather than in Putson 'on account of the long and dangerous crossing of the Wye' – but were also taught there, in late 1530 in a house formerly belonging to one Thomas Coke.[26] If they strayed, as one chorister did in late 1517, when caught out with a vicar choral, who was frequenting *loca suspecta* and playing dice in the city, they were dealt with.[27] Most grammar school boys, however, were likely to have lived and all of them been educated outside the Close's strict confines. This was the case at other cathedral cities: the schools at Exeter, Salisbury and Gloucester, for example, were all sited away from the cathedral on the fringes of their city's commercial centre. In all likelihood, the situation was similar at Hereford. By around the late thirteenth century, a street in the city was called *Scolestrete*, and there is a reference in a document of 1365 to the grant to John Payne, a baker, of a house in *Oldescolestrete*, probably the narrow lane at the north-east of the Close leading to the present-day Harley Court. Given that the Chapter would have guarded its monopoly over the provision of grammar masters as jealously in Hereford as secular chapters did elsewhere, it is probable that *Scolestrete* and *Oldescolestrete* marked an early site of the old cathedral grammar school.[28]

This is not to imply that the living room in the present Headmaster's house in 5, Harley Court was the medieval schoolroom. Indeed, it is likely that it was part of a canonical residence dating from the early fifteenth century. Its four-bay hall, complete with its magnificent tie-beamed oak roof, massive floor-boards and raised dais, would have provided the space needed for the extensive hospitality resident canons were expected to provide.[29] Nevertheless, one can imagine that Hereford's late medieval schoolroom was not unlike the original Harley Court hall, with its 36 foot length, east-west axis in line with the cathedral, high window lights to prevent the boys being distracted from their work, and a raised dais where the grammar master, dominating his pupils crouched on forms beneath him, would have been seated.[30] His chambers, where pupils no doubt lodged to boost his fees – as they were found to have done in 1548 in private houses at Ledbury, much to the benefit of its local economy as well as its grammar school[31] – would have been attached. The Hereford schoolroom, in contrast to those at richly endowed schools in the late medieval period, was likely to have been a modest domestic building, at least until the late-sixteenth century.[32]

26. *Ibid.*, fos. 37v, 65r, 77r, Acts 6 July 1526, June 1530, 2 March 1535.

27. *Ibid.*, fo. 12r, undated but between Sept. and 23 Nov. 1517. The vicars choral were occasionally arraigned for failure to attend the offices, spending the night outside the College, 'incontinence' with women or other offences. See, for example, *ibid.*, fos. 12r, 13v, 18r-v, 30r, 41r, re charges against Roger Palmer, Hugh Fishpole, David Mey, Richard Baker, Roger Brayne and William Chell, between 1517 and 1527.

28. Orme (2006), p.136; Aylmer and Tiller, p.569; Carless, pp.3-4; Lobel, map 3 (Hereford). The name was still in use in the seventeenth century, as indicated in the College of Vicars 39 lease of a garden in *Old Schoole Streete* (St Peter's parish) for 6s. 8d annually and a couple of fat hens at Epiphany: HCA, 7003/1/1, p.200, 26 July 1631.

29. I am grateful to David Lepine for this suggestion. A lease of the house was granted to Master John Gatesby in 1406. Johnson and Shoesmith, p.125.

30. For W.W. Robinson's 1884 drawing of the original four-bay roof and the presumption of a dais: Watkins, pp.170-71, and below, p.21; for the hall's measurement, description, possible dating and an alternative proposition for its use (as a centre for the administration of the Duke of York's estates): D. Jones, (2008), pp.73, 88-90 and (2009), p.78; and for descriptions of medieval schoolrooms: Orme (2006), pp.135-41.

31. Leach (1896), p.93.

32. See below, pp.33-34, for the conversion of the cathedral library into a schoolroom.

Evidence about what was taught at Hereford's medieval grammar school also remains tantalisingly thin: two known manuscripts and one known early printed book containing school material with Hereford, although not necessarily Cathedral School, associations. The first of these is a lost fifteenth-century manuscript containing 95 folios (Jesus College, Oxford, MS 14) that once belonged to Roger Hygyns, who described himself as 'some-time clerk of Saint Nicholas parish in Hereford'. An 1852 catalogue shows that it contained five texts: a grammatical treatise by question and response in English which taught the eight parts of Latin speech ('How do you recognise the common gender?' etc.); questions on grammar, with answers, from an unnamed questioner, ending: 'Praises to Christ be raised – the work its course has run. / Thy name O Christ be praised – this volume now is done'; grammar rules put into hexameter verse, beginning: 'Sorbeo gives [as Perfect and Supine tenses for to swallow] both -ei, -itum, and sorpsi plus sorptum, / A point on which Prisianus's magnum opus is dumb';[33] a Latin-English vocabulary grouped by subject, the largest section of the volume at 34 leaves; and further grammar on irregularities.[34]

The other manuscript of the same period, written 'in a neat anglicana hand' and now deposited in the cathedral library, is a more advanced Latin work. It contains a list of the books of the Bible with mnemonic verses, notes on grammar and rhetoric, and extracts from a treatise on letter composition (*Dictamen*). The third fragment, one sheet of the Latin-English dictionary *Hortus vocabulorum* ('The Garden of Words'), one of its columns appropriately ending with the word *scholastic*, is also to be found in the cathedral library. It was printed in Rouen in 1517 by Eustace Hardy for Jean Gaschet, a French bookseller and bookbinder then dwelling in Hereford between periods in York.[35] To link all three or any of these items with the Cathedral School stretches the evidence: Roger Hygyns, the St Nicholas clerk, may or may not have been a pupil; the second manuscript is associated by nothing more than its place of deposit; the third came into the possession of Lady Hawkins School, Kington, which was not founded until 1632, although the French bookseller could well have sold other books, if not this particular dictionary, to the city's grammar master and his pupils. Nevertheless these fragmentary sources, despite their limitations, still give an indication of both the medieval school curriculum and the developing nature of education in the later Middle Ages.

The Hereford survivals are an indicator of what medieval grammar schools were in part about: the teaching of pupils to speak, read and write Latin. The Jesus College manuscript is typical of the grammar-school curriculum in which boys learned and memorised Latin parts of speech, tenses and vocabulary. The first part shows the importance of interrogatory teaching and is based on the *Accidence*, a tract by the Oxford schoolmaster, John Leland (d.1428), described by his contemporaries as the 'flower of grammarians'; some of the other

---

33. Prisian had taught at Constantinople in about 500. His *magnum opus* was an eighteen-volume prose work, *Institutiones Grammaticae*.

34. Coxe, ii., pp.6-7. I am further grateful to Owen McKnight, Librarian of Jesus College, for a copy of the catalogue entry on the manuscript which was described as 'missing March 1886'; and again indebted to David Wyllie for the translation.

35. Mynors and Thomson, p. 126; HCA, 3169 and Kington J.13B; Aylmer and Tiller, pp.577-78; HCL, Penelope E. Morgan, 'Catalogue of the Lady Hawkins School Library' (typescript, 1979), p.26; and P. Morgan (1981), p.223.

parts are similar to those practised in other schools. In the second (Hereford) manuscript, the more demanding grammar section, based on a popular treatise of 1427 written by either Reginald or Simon Alcock (a canon of Hereford, 1436-59) reveals that a medieval grammar school education also involved instruction in business skills such as the art of composing letters (as in this case) and the drawing up of legal documents and financial accounts, as well as the routine learning of Latin. And from the folio beginning *circuicio est color rethoricorum*, we can appreciate the importance of rhetoric to the educated medieval mind. Even though rhetoric does not appear in the school curriculum, at the higher level of study inter-school Latin disputations were sometimes held, as well as the more mundane requirement for boys to speak Latin within schools, the Wells choristers being enjoined at meal times from 1460, for example, to 'ask for anything they want in Latin not in English'. The manuscript further includes Bible verses and a pious distich on its cover, and this is a reminder that the masters were deputies of the cathedral Chancellor and that education in this period and long after was inextricably bound up with religious teaching. As Bishop Edmund Story of Chichester observed at the end of the fifteenth century, 'the teaching of grammarians', could 'profit for life eternal if it be taken up for the best purposes'.[36] Following prayers like the Paternoster, Ave Maria, Creed, Confession, graces and 'hours of Our Lady' which would all have been learned at a younger age, perhaps even before the study of Latin, grammar boys would have been taught to read the *Hymnal*, the Latin hymns of the daily services and mass, as well as composing Latin exercises relating to Christian virtue. That the manuscript was written on a single quire of 12 leaves, which would have cost about 6d in the early fifteenth century, also shows the increasing importance of paper in education from *c.*1400 when it became a less expensive material for writing purposes. Finally, by the early sixteenth century, printing had enabled the production and rapid circulation of Latin-English dictionaries, the *Hortus Vocabularum* being drawn from a number of medieval collections. It was first printed in 1500 and ran into several re-issues, which included the Hereford Rouen dictionary, over the next 30 years. The coming of the printed word, together with the diffusion of humanist texts, was eventually to revolutionise grammar teaching, not least following the Crown's imposition of uniform grammars in the 1540s.[37]

A central schoolroom activity was the composition and analysis of Latin sentences, known as latins or vulgaria, devised to explain grammatical rules and constructions. Although there is only the one Hereford exemplar (from the Jesus College manuscript), 17 major collections of these compositions exist from the fifteenth and early sixteenth centuries which do more to illuminate the work of grammar masters and their pupils than any other source. Masters used published texts or extemporised by composing exercises (in Latin and/or English) both to edify their pupils and gain their interest by drawing examples from everyday life. Numerous sentences are to be found referring to Christian virtues, the Christian calendar, devotion to the Virgin, pilgrimages and other church ceremonies, national events and matters like food and sex. For our purposes, it is what we can learn about school life that is especially relevant. Vulgaria on such themes show that the school day began early from six o'clock, the morning lasting until breakfast at the time of the

36. As quoted by Leach (1907), p.402, with regard to an endowment at Chichester Prebendal School.

37. Orme (2006), pp.58-59, 107-08, 111, 118-25, 148-49; and Orme (2013), pp.9, 25-26, 31.

services of prime or high mass (seven or nine), with a subsequent break for an hour or two for dinner from about eleven followed by a four-hour afternoon session until five. During this long day, the master was constantly busy in 'apposing', calling out individual pupils to test their knowledge and capabilities in composition. If mistakes were made punishments were likely. Discipline, as shown by Richard Cornwaille's commission to rule *cum virga et ferula* – the birch (applied to bare buttocks) and the rod with a hole in it (struck on the hand) – could be severe. There are sentences, too, on such valuable school items as equipment, supplied by the pupils themselves, which included a pen made with a penknife from a quill, an inkhorn and ink, tablets or paper and schoolbooks; as well as those composed about boarders, who if they lived with the schoolmaster (and no doubt with a Hereford canon) was expected to speak Latin in the house except on festival days when English was permitted as a treat.[38]

Such was the school regime as portrayed in these latins. In the absence of any Hereford vulgaria, apart from the one in the Jesus College catalogue entry, we are left with many unanswered questions. One cannot help wondering, for example, which Hereford masters would have been as revered and which as hated as the ones at Oxford; or whether football was played outside the grammar schoolroom, perhaps even in the nearby cathedral cemetery which had been enclosed in 1389, as the pupils at Beccles and Canterbury were held to have done; or whether Hereford's school would have moved out of the city with the cathedral residentiaries during the plague in the city in February 1551, as seems to have happened with Magdalen College School, Oxford, in similar circumstances earlier in the century. Overall, we have no reason to believe that a grammar boy's experience in Hereford would have been all that different from those lived by boys in schools at Barlinch (Somerset), Beccles, Bristol, Canterbury, Exeter, Lincoln, London, Oxford or Winchester from where such sentences were composed. The vulgars that were devised by or for Hereford pupils in the fifteenth and early sixteenth centuries would have had a different local emphasis but their concerns would have been similar. And of this we can be certain: the relief that would have been felt at the end of a hot and tiring day. As one Lincoln sentence put it: 'Be the summer day never so long, at last comes evensong'.[39]

Schools and the Reformation

The impact of the Protestant Reformation on the schools of England was the subject of fierce academic debate a hundred and more years ago. Arthur Francis Leach (1851-1915), the first real historian of early English schools, who as an assistant Charity Commissioner was also to undertake invaluable work for Hereford Cathedral School, was the chief protagonist in this controversy. As early as 1896, he had asserted in his book, *English Schools at the Reformation, 1546-48*, that the received wisdom of his day that Edward VI's government had established 51 new foundations was incorrect. He also claimed from his study of

38. *Ibid.*, pp.3-5, for the surviving collections of vulgaria; and pp.28-35, for the examples they give of school life. For the school hours at Canterbury in 1547 (from 6am to 5pm, with three breaks totalling four hours) and those at Salisbury and Wells in 1559: Frere and Kennedy, ii., pp.143; iii., pp.33, 36.

39. *Quam longa fuerit dies estiualis, tandem venit nox et vespere.* Orme (1989), p.85. For the 1389 enclosure: Aylmer and Tiller, p.304; and the 1551 plague in the city: HCA, 7031/1, fo. 106r, Act, 15 Feb. 1551.

chantry records that up to 200 grammar schools 'were for the most part abolished or crippled under him [Edward VI]' and that many other schools 'were swept away either under Henry or his son, or if not swept away, plundered and damaged'. A generation later, in the year of his death, he published his *Schools of Medieval England*, his *magnum opus* in which he investigated schools connected with cathedrals, collegiate churches, monasteries, hospitals and independent institutions in pre-Reformation England. Overall, Leach's views did not find favour with his own contemporaries, one distinguished medievalist of the time, for example, suggesting that he gave 'the rashest judgement about the most disputable matters'. Subsequent research over the past century has proved his detractors right: in general terms, Leach overstated the educational impact of the dissolution of the chantries and undervalued the devastation caused by the dissolution of the monasteries. Nevertheless, we should not completely dismiss his researches. Some of his individual school histories have stood the test of time and his general thesis, despite its obvious limitations, was both an important modification of the then prevailing view that the Protestant Reformation had revolutionised educational provision in England and a necessary reminder of the continuity of much of English education from medieval times if not from the time of the country's conversion to Christianity.[40]

Nevertheless, modern scholarship has shown that the Reformation still had a significant impact on schools nationally, as well as locally in Herefordshire. The suppression of about 840 monasteries, friaries and nunneries between 1536 and 1540 resulted in an estimated loss of at least 5,000 supported educational places in England, which were not wholly replaced by the creation of 12 permanent grammar schools in the new cathedral cities and the handful of other new foundations established by Henry VIII and Edward VI. During the 1540s, further educational provision was lost by the closure of the few hundred collegiate and chantry schools. These included five Herefordshire elementary chantry schools: those at St Owen's (Hereford), Kington, Much Cowarne, Staunton-on-Wye and Weobley, although the county's ten chantry grammar schools (mostly in north Herefordshire) survived albeit with reduced endowments. The one new educational foundation for the county during these years was in 1553 when a royal grammar school was established in Leominster – a town which in 1548 had a population of over 1,700, making it (according to the chantry certificates) 'the greatest market town' in Herefordshire – endowed, in part, by chantry property worth £20 *per annum*. But the losses were also partly offset by such measures as the introduction of two authorised and uniform books of grammar in 1540 and 1542, which continued to be used for more than three centuries, a uniform primer for school prayers in 1545 and (in 1548) an English catechism.[41]

The non-monastic schools of the nine secular English cathedrals, of which Hereford was one, remained intact during the years of the Reformation but were not wholly untouched by its provisions. In the summer of 1547 during Edward VI's first protectorate, royal injunctions were promulgated to the dignitaries of all cathedral and collegiate churches 'for

---

40. The best modern critique of Leach's historical work is provided by Orme (2006), pp.5-8, 49-50, 214, 221, 223, 236, 281, 291, 312, 334. Also see Foster Watson's biography of Leach, revised by Roger T Stearn: *ODNB*, vol. 32, pp.942-43.

41. Orme (2006), pp.299-335; Orme (1996), pp.59-61; Leach (1911), p.94.

the advancement of God's honour, increase of virtue and for good order'. Its educational provisions mirrored the practices of the new Henrician cathedral schools, which in turn had been modelled on the lines of later collegiate churches like St George's, Windsor, rather than the idiosyncratic medieval statutes of Hereford and other secular cathedrals. This had resulted in a far more coherent structure for the new foundations: masters were appointed by Deans and Chapters corporately rather than individually by the Chancellor; they had dwellings and dining rights similar to the lesser clergy and shared in the communal life of their churches; and they were paid a fixed stipend which enabled them to provide free teaching.[42] Similarly, the Edwardian injunctions ordered that a free grammar school was to be 'ordained and kept and maintained perpetually' from the cathedral's 'common lands and revenues', the master being given an annual salary of 20 marks [£13 6s 8d] and a rent-free house and the Usher £6 13s 4d with a free chamber. The requirement applied to Hereford and five other secular cathedrals whose schools still depended on the payment of fees, Chichester, Lichfield and St Paul's having already founded Free Schools. In addition, Deans and Chapters were to find grammar school places for 'choristers as have served in the church five years or more or hath their voices changed', giving them an annual maintenance allowance of £3 6s 8d each for five years to enable them to complete their education.[43] This implied that song schools for choristers continued, although it is evident (as the 1547 injunctions for Winchester College indicate) that antiphons to the Virgin Mary 'or any suchlike untrue or superstitious anthem' would have been dropped from the choristers' repertoire. Choristers' appearance would also have changed, as at Canterbury and Winchester where their heads were to be 'no more shaven, but only their hair to be rounded and clipped short'.[44]

It is apparent that the educational provisions of the 1547 injunctions were not implemented at Hereford during this period. We know that the Hereford Dean and Chapter only reluctantly embraced other aspects of the Protestant Reformation. Shrines were not removed until the summer of 1550, more than ten years after Thomas Cromwell's injunctions against them and over three years after Bishop Bonner's order that they should be removed; chantry masses for the dead appear to have continued for some time following the enactments at the end of Henry VIII's reign condemning them; other traditional observances were slowly abandoned in the face of the demands of the 1549 and 1552 prayer books; and the re-ordering of altars in the early 1550s seems to have been resisted. Following these reformist measures, the conservative Catholic injunctions, issued for Hereford by Bishop Pate of Worcester as Cardinal Pole's commissioner in the metropolitan visitation of 1556, may well have come as a relief to the cathedral authorities.[45] That the school is not mentioned is sufficient evidence to suggest that it remained firmly under the Chancellor's control. The presumption must be that he continued to appoint the grammar

42. The evolution of the new school foundations is discussed by Orme (2006), pp.302-07.

43. *Ibid.*, p.317; Frere and Kennedy, ii., pp.138-39.

44. *Ibid.*, pp.145, 148-49.

45. Among its provisions, the Dean and Chapter were to 'receive no bastards nor priest' children to be choristers'. For these injunctions: Frere and Kennedy, ii., pp.392-96. The cathedral's response to the Reformation is traced by Stanford Lehmberg in Aylmer and Tiller, pp.88-91.

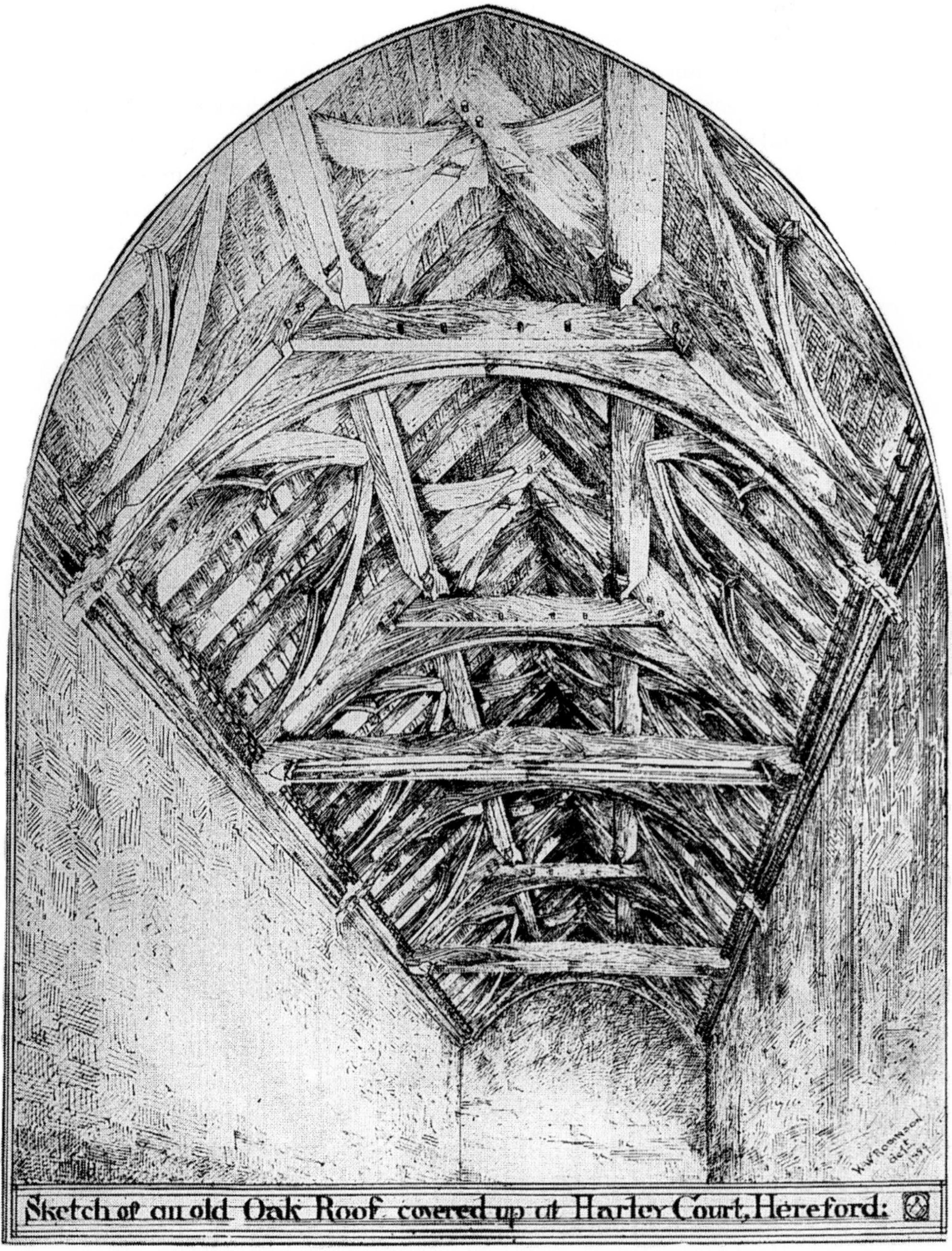

Sketch of an old Oak Roof covered up at Harley Court, Hereford:

Fig. 1.3 The roof of Number 5, Harley Court (the present Headmaster's house), as it appeared in 1884. A similar domestic building would have housed the late medieval school.

master and that both the old school building and the schoolmaster's medieval teaching methods continued well into the later sixteenth century.[46]

In conclusion, we do not need to subscribe to Leach's hypothesis that the cathedrals at Hereford and Worcester could well date their schools from the time of Bishop Putta in the late seventh century, to show that the early history of Hereford's cathedral and city grammar school from the late twelfth to the mid-sixteenth centuries is essentially one of continuity. And like many old endowed schools, Hereford Cathedral School owes a particular debt of gratitude to A.F. Leach. For Leach's research on the history of HCS, admittedly undertaken somewhat hurriedly and not without mistakes during the summer of 1889, was the first to reveal the full nature of the school's endowments. It was Leach, too, who was to do more than anyone else to help disentangle them.[47] It is to these late sixteenth and seventeenth century endowments – endowments which in time were to prove sufficient to secure its future – that we should now turn.

46. See below, pp.26, 27, 32. Contrary to the assertions of Carless (p.10), following Duncumb and other local antiquarians, I have found no evidence to suggest that a schoolroom was incorporated within the west walk of the Bishop's Cloister after a fire to the range during Edward VI's reign.

47. For Leach's 37-page report, dated 25 July 1889: TNA, ED 27/1606; and for his involvement with HCS: below, pp.291-93.

Chapter 2

The Endowed Grammar School, 1558-1697

Hereford was not the only prominent town at the end of the Middle Ages without an endowed grammar school. Bristol and Gloucester, for example, may be cited as other considerable centres where the grammar masters depended on charging fees. Other cathedral cities also lacked a free grammar school. Canterbury, Exeter, Norwich, Salisbury and York were (together with Hereford) among 16 out of 21 English cathedral cities before the 1530s not to have an endowed grammar foundation. So Hereford was by no means alone in its lack of scholastic endowment.

Nonetheless, Hereford was the poor relation compared with most other cathedral schools. Among the nine secular cathedrals, Lichfield, Chichester and St Paul's had been newly endowed by the early sixteenth century. Dean Colet's refoundation of St Paul's from 1508-12 was especially notable: for taking charge of the 153 boys, all of whom were to be educated free of charge, a 'high-master' was awarded an annual stipend of £35, together with an assistant at half that amount, sums which no other cathedral could match for its school.[1] But the remaining five unendowed secular cathedral schools all seem to have been wealthier than Hereford. Both York and Exeter, for example, were well provided for, and Lincoln's grammar school was likely to have prospered following the resolution of the dispute with its Dean and Chapter in 1407.[2] And while there is no evidence to indicate the wealth of Hereford's own grammar school, it is most unlikely that the cathedral Chancellor (responsible as we have seen for the school) would have been able to provide for it in a similar way. This is clearly suggested by the information gathered by Henry VIII's commissioners in 1536, at the time of the *Valor Ecclesiasticus*, when the Chancellor's dignity was assessed at £14 3s 4d – a substantially lower income than his counterparts received at sister foundations. That Hereford was among the poorest of the old foundations is further illustrated by the worth of its common fund, which was valued in 1536 at £423 17s 2¼d net, the lowest revenue at that time for any secular cathedral apart from Chichester.[3] A generation later the cathedral's plight may have been even worse.

1. J. Simon, pp.73-74; Orme (2006), pp.238, 245, 249.

2. Moran, pp.7-8; Orme (1976), pp.47-49; *VCH*: *Lincolnshire*, ii., p.425.

3. And Chichester's grammar school had already been re-endowed by this date – unusually through the attachment

So by the mid-sixteenth century, Hereford's grammar school was still unendowed and its schoolmaster still had to rely on fees, which may not have changed substantially from the 8d per quarter that was commonly levied a century earlier on each boy learning basic grammar at other schools.[4] These medieval practices remained unchanged at Hereford for a good part of Elizabeth I's reign (1558-1603) during a period when endowed foundations were becoming the rule rather than the exception. But new practices could not be for ever resisted even by a poor cathedral situated in a remote part of the western Marches.

The story of the school's endowment in this period in part relates to the cathedral's reluctant acceptance of the new statutes of 1583 and 1636. These constitutions, which as we will see were imposed by royal authority following resistance to episcopal visitations, systematically covered every aspect of cathedral life, including the running of the grammar school which was finally brought under the Dean and Chapter's direct jurisdiction and patronage. In 1583 the school also gained responsibility for the non-musical education of the choristers.[5] From this time, therefore, it can properly be named Hereford Cathedral School in the modern sense, and for the next three hundred years the sources for its history are mainly to be found in the cathedral archives.

As important to the school's long-term future, in an era when grammar schools and other institutions were increasingly being favoured by charitable giving from pious Protestants – not least in the five western counties south from Lancashire[6] – were the wills of three seventeenth-century benefactors: Dean Charles Langford (1607), Roger Philpotts (1615) and Sarah Alston, fourth Duchess of Somerset (1692). These three patrons left legacies which benefited the school partly as a result of their ties in terms of office or land with the city and region but overwhelmingly because of their concern to help 'banish ignorance and its handmaid poverty' through the means of a godly education. They thereby mirror the aspirations of many Protestant benefactors of the period.[7] These bequests, based as they were on landed rental income, are of considerable financial importance for the school. But they are also significant because they were complementary: the legacies of Philpotts and Somerset were intended for Cathedral School students going up to Oxford and Cambridge and so complemented the favour shown by Dean Langford to poor young scholars on their entry to the school. The Duchess' bequests (given to the colleges) further

of a canonry in 1498. (See A.F. Leach's chapter in *VCH*: Sussex, ii. 402). The relative incomes of the secular cathedrals and their dignitaries are given in the tables compiled by Lehmberg, p.27. For Hereford specifically also see Le Neve (2009), pp.xxii-xxiv.

4. No scale of fees is extant for Hereford in the early period but 8d per quarter was the amount charged by the masters in Hull (1454) and Newland (1446). In 1477 Ipswich, on the other hand, 10d a quarter was required for grammarians (8d if they were burgesses' sons). J. Simon, pp.22n, 28n, 30n.

5. Although this was not spelt out in the statutes, it is evident, as the vicars' replies to the 1588 college visitation indicate (HCA, 3395, responses of Luke Prosser and George Allin to the 13th article), that the choristers had joined the grammar boys for their main teaching.

6. In Herefordshire itself (the Cathedral School apart), grammar school endowments included those by Dame Margaret Hawkins (Kington, 1621), John Perryn (Bromyard, 1657), and William Crowther (Weobley, 1658). Jordan, pp.238, 246, 249.

7. *Ibid.*, p.267; Archer, pp.234-45.

strengthened the school's ties with Brasenose College, Oxford, and established links with St John's, Cambridge. Collectively, the re-ordered statutes and these new endowments were to re-invigorate the school.

By 1700, Hereford's grammar school had been transformed into a cathedral school, answerable to the Dean and Chapter as a whole rather than its Chancellor, with a schoolroom within the Close; its master had acquired a grace and favour house, as well as an assistant ('the Usher' or *Hypodidascalus* to the *Archididascalus*), both of whom were paid a fixed stipend from 1583; and some of its pupils, notably the choristers and such boys (in Dean Langford's words) 'poor and towardly for learning',[8] were able to claim free schooling as well as support for their university education. Even through the insecurities caused by the Scottish army's five weeks siege during the civil war, Hereford's subsequent fall as a royalist garrison in December 1645, and following the King's execution on 30 January 1649, the abolition of Deans and Chapters in the early months of the Interregnum, there is good evidence to suggest that the school continued to function albeit under a different guise.

And during this period the school's membership is not as anonymous to subsequent generations as in medieval times. An increased number of masters, over 30 in all, can be identified. The names of 120 or so of their pupils, a few of whom were to gain distinction in the church, at court and in the law, are also known,[9] even if the nature of their instruction and their preoccupations outside the schoolroom are still largely a matter of conjecture. The Cathedral School during these 140 years gradually becomes more recognisable as a successful living institution.

1558-1642

Hereford's insularity and conservative nature was fully apparent at the opening of the new reign, following Elizabeth I's accession in November 1558. The Protestant reformer, John Scory, the first Elizabethan Bishop of Hereford, who had been Cranmer's chaplain, as well as Bishop of Rochester and Chichester successively under Edward VI, found all but one of the residentiary canons (the indiscreet Walter Jones, the new Precentor) to be 'dissemblers and rank papists' on his accession to the see. The vicars were held to be similarly disposed, as were the deacons and sextons who were described as 'mortal enemies' of Protestantism. The tradesmen and city fathers, too, were suspect. Referring to the vigil of the Assumption of Mary (15 August) in 1560, the new Bishop could report:

> Upon Thursday last, there was not one butcher in Hereford that durst open his shop to sell a piece of flesh, and the next day there was not one in the whole city, gospeller nor other, that durst be known to work in his occupation or open his shop to sell anything, so duly and precisely was that abrogate fast and holiday kept.

---

8. 'Towardly', meaning having an aptness (for learning), was a word frequently applied about studious young persons in this period. For examples of usages from 1587 to 1660: Cressy, pp.72, 91, 100, 124.

9. The names of around 70 choristers are known for the seventeenth century, together with 15 from the Tudor period before they were members of the grammar school, and about 50 Langfordian scholars. I am grateful to Rosalind Caird for a copy of her list of choristers, held in the cathedral library. No school register of pupils exists before the early nineteenth century.

And among the members of the city's council, Scory continued, there was not one man 'that is counted favourable to this religion'.[10]

The strength of the old religion among the cathedral clergy is also evident from the resistance of some of them to the Elizabethan religious settlement. The newly appointed Marian Dean, Edmund Daniel, later described by recusancy commissioners as 'one that pretends a sobriety but yet stubborn',[11] refused the oath of allegiance to the new monarch and was deprived of his office. The same fate befell the Precentor, the Archdeacon and several other canons.[12] Edward Baskerville, the cathedral Chancellor 1555-67, maintained his office despite his Catholic sympathies. The presumption must be that he continued to appoint the grammar master and that the school maintained its old ways.

Indeed, it is evident that the new regime had little immediate impact on the school. It was not even mentioned in the new Queen's visitation articles for Hereford Cathedral in 1559, unlike the injunctions issued in the same year for Salisbury and Exeter where specific provision was made for the maintenance of former choristers at their respective grammar school.[13] Even if the Hereford articles had required that the cathedral provide for its singing boys in this way, it is likely that the requirement would have been ignored. As it was, despite the admission of a sympathetic new Dean in the person of John Ellis, five years after the promulgation of the 1559 articles, the communion was still not being administered monthly as had been laid down. The canons, moreover, refused to preach, read homilies 'or do anything to commend, beautify or set forward this religion but mutter against it [and] receive and maintain the enemies of religion, so that this church which should be the light of all the diocese is very darkness and an example of contempt of true religion whom the city and country about do follow'.[14] And even had the will to reform the school been apparent, the means to find an endowment was entirely lacking. As the Dean and Chapter wrote to Archbishop Matthew Parker in March 1561:

> And we most humbly pray also that [you] ... will have in your grace's consideration the poverty of this church and of the ministers thereof, the exility [meagreness] of the revenues greatly diminished and decayed, and the charge of hospitality whereunto we are bound, and especially the great charges which we very lately sustained in the Queen's Majesty's and other late visitations ...[15]

10. As quoted by Bannister, pp.85-86. Scory was later required to make a further report (following the Privy Council order of 17 October 1564), and dismissed the Chapter in similar terms, claiming that the cathedral did not obey the Queen's 1559 injunctions and that 21 council members were hostile to Protestantism and 10 indifferent towards it. Bateson, pp.13-14, 20-21.

11. *CSPD, 1601-03, Addenda 1547-65,* p.522.

12. For the deprivations of these residentiaries and the appointments of Walter Jones, John Ellis and Robert Crowley as Precentor, Dean and Archdeacon respectively, see HCA, 7031/1, fos 155r, 155v, 156v, 24 Dec. 1559, 18 Feb., 28 April 1560.

13. The educational clauses for these two cathedrals may be compared with those issued for Hereford in Frere and Kennedy, iii., pp.32-3, 40, 43, 47-48.

14. At least according to Bishop Scory. Bateson, p.21.

15. HCA, 7031/1, fos 158v-159r, 22 March 1561.

While taking into account an element of special pleading here – intent as they were to ward off an attempted visitation from their Bishop, the Chapter no doubt exaggerated its poverty – the canons' cry contains more than a semblance of truth.

There are other reasons to believe that the school's medieval constitution remained unchanged during the first half of Elizabeth's reign. No further mention of a schoolmaster's appointment is given in the Chapter Acts until the 1580s. Even in the detailed instructions governing the conduct of the residentiaries and prebendaries, issued in 1577 following John Watkins' appointment as Dean, the school is ignored. This disregard may be compared with the demands made of the master of the library, which the Dean and Chapter were required to visit once each year to ensure that it was 'clean and decently kept'.[16] It is clear that the grammar school, unlike the song school, was not yet an integral part of the cathedral's governance. And when the cathedral submitted to a further royal visitation in 1582 – the Dean and Chapter having successfully resisted both Archbishop Parker's cathedrals visitation of 1560 and Bishop Scory's repeated attempts to hold the canons to account – the Chapter was required for the first time to respond to an official enquiry about the school. It did so, at least in part, through the good offices of James Yaden, the Chapter Clerk. His written answer to the commissioners' fiftieth question (out of 52 articles) is instructive. When asked if there was a free grammar school 'supported or kept in the cathedral church, and if there be none by what means it may best be erected', he replied:

> There is none ... it would well be erected if it might please Her Majesty to bestow thereof some part of the possessions of late supressed chantries, the Lord Bishop ... being also a contributor and the Chapter likewise.[17]

This was the pathway to reform which was to result in the enshrining of a new school foundation, albeit one without the benefit of endowment from former chantry lands, in the cathedral statutes of the following year.

The reformation of Hereford's medieval statutes was the work of six commissioners, led by John Whitgift as Bishop of Worcester in the year before his elevation to Canterbury, three of whom assembled in the cathedral's chapter house on 5 September 1582 to begin the visitation.[18] From the articles of enquiry new statutes were drafted over the ensuing months, sent to the Privy Council the following February, promulgated on 26 March and published under the Queen's authority on 11 April 1583. They covered all aspects of the cathedral's life and governance. In Whitgift's own words, the commissioners 'had consideration as well to the present state of the church as also to the ancient state and orders in the same, reforming the abuses in them both and adding that which was therein wanting'.[19] Only one provision concerns us here and such is its importance to the school's history that the first part of this statute needs to be quoted in full:

---

16. *Ibid.*, fos 72v-74v.

17. HCA, 4642/1, *c.*Sept. 1582. As a layman and parishioner of All Saints, Yaden was unable (or unwilling) to answer many of the articles of enquiry concerning the cathedral's religious practices.

18. See HCA, 1553 for details re the issuing of the letters patent on 1 July, the citation to Dean Watkins on 5 August and the presentation of the articles of enquiry on 6 September.

19. Strype, i., p.214.

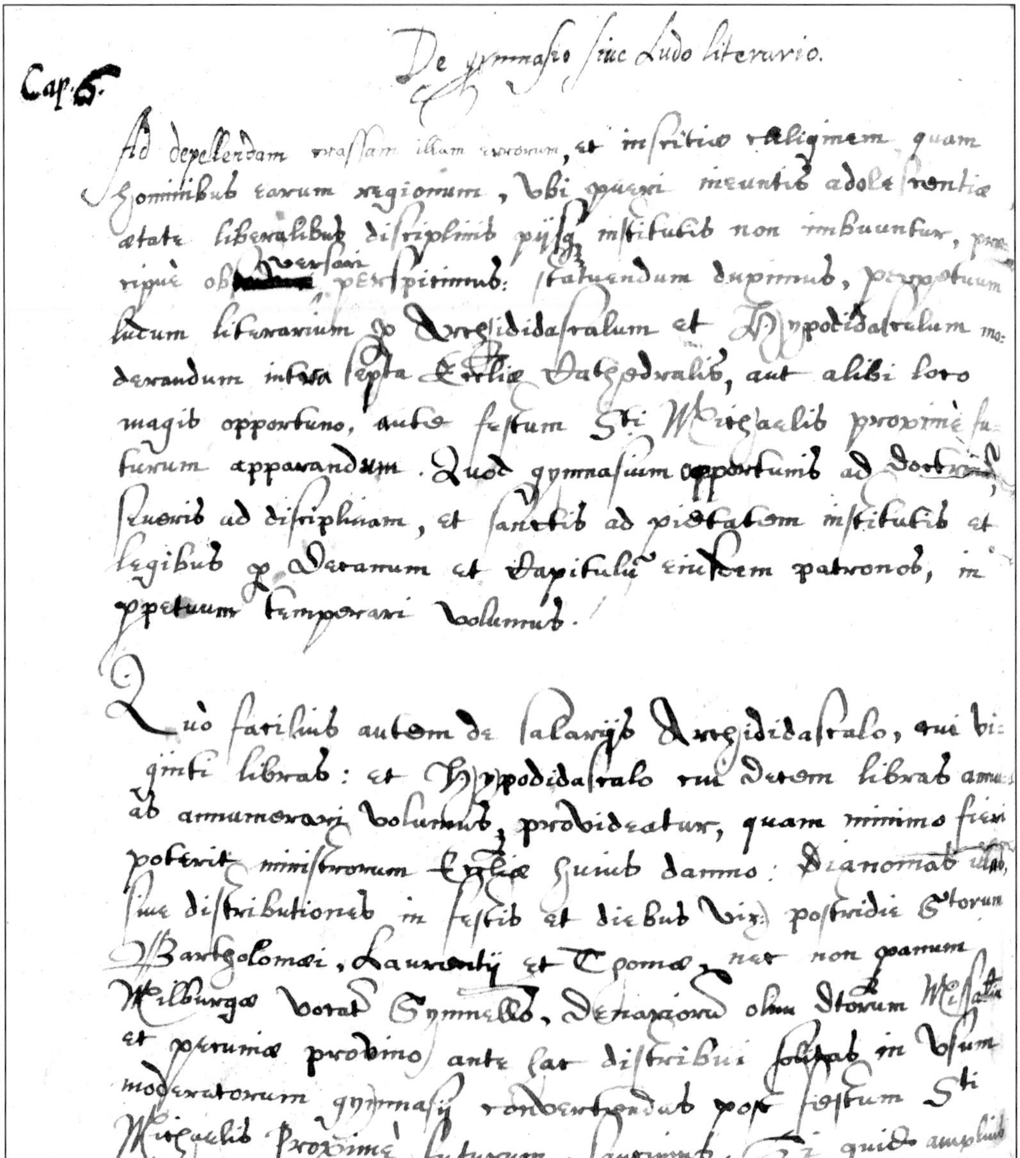

Cap. 6.

De Gymnasio sive Ludo literario.

Ad depellendam crassam illam errorum, et inscitiae caliginem quam hominibus earum regionum, ubi pueri ineuntis adolescentiae aetate liberalibus disciplinis piisque institutis non imbuuntur, praecipue obversari perspicimus: statuendum duximus, perpetuum ludum literarium per Archididascalum et Hypodidascalum moderandum intra septa Ecclesiae Cathedralis, aut alibi loco magis opportuno, ante festum Sti Michaelis proxime futurum apparandum. Quod gymnasium opportunis ad doctrinam, severis ad disciplinam, et sanctis ad pietatem institutis et legibus per Decanum et Capituli eiusdem patronos, in perpetuum temperari volumus.

Quo facilius autem de salariis Archididascalo, cui viginti libras: et Hypodidascalo cui decem libras annuas annumerari volumus, providebitur, quam minimo fieri poterit ministrorum Ecclesiae sumptu damno: Diaconatus sive distributiones in festis et diebus viz. postridie Sanctorum Bartholomaei, Laurentii et Thomae, nec non quarum Milburgae vocat Symnells, decreverunt olim Ssorum ... et proximae proximo ante hac distribui solitas in usum moderatorum gymnasii convertendas post festum Sti Michaelis proxime futurum, sancimus. Si quid amplius

Fig. 2.1 The important clause in the 1583 statutes vesting the school's governance in the Dean and Chapter.

> For dispelling that thick darkness of errors and ignorance which we see arise to the injury of most of the people of those places where children are not educated as they grow up in liberal studies and religious principles, we have ordered it to be settled that a permanent grammar school be provided before the next coming feast of St Michael within the precincts of the cathedral church, or at a more suitable place elsewhere, governed by a Headmaster and an Usher. Wherefore we wish that the school, meet for learning, strict for discipline and devout for piety be maintained in perpetuity by ordinances and laws through the Dean and Chapter as patrons.[20]

To help provide for the Headmaster's and Usher's salaries – respectively of £20 and £10 annually – funds earmarked for distribution to the poor on certain feast days, income from 'Milburga's bread called simnels', mass pence ('once so-called') and 'the money previously accustomed to be distributed for wine' were to be allocated to the school's use.[21] In sum, this statute was of revolutionary importance for the school's future: it wrested control of its affairs from the Chancellor alone to the Dean and Chapter; it looked to the provision of a permanent site within the Close; it authorised the appointment of an assistant to the Headmaster; and it hypothecated specific church revenues as an endowment for the masters' salaries, set at a rate commensurate with other educational foundations of the time, even if a house had not yet been provided.

But it could all have been so much more. When Whitgift submitted the draft statutes, following perusal by the residentiaries, he enclosed two petitions to Lord Treasurer Burghley. They were written in the name of the Dean and Chapter, although no doubt drafted upon Whitgift's instigation, for the Queen's consideration. Both concerned the settlement of additional revenues for further endowments: one for the divinity lecturer; the other for the school. The school petition – as opposed to that for the lecturer, which was granted in full – was met only in part. It is, nevertheless, worth hearing, if only to illustrate what might have been:

> That it would please her Majesty for the better support and furnishing of the new free grammar school to be erected in the said cathedral church; whereas there is now no Free School in all the city of Hereford, to grant back unto the said Dean and Chapter and their successors for ever, four pounds yearly by them paid out of the Rectory of Lugwardine aforesaid unto her Majesty as due unto her for obits [commemorations of the deceased], and five pounds for the like paid out of their appropriate Rectory of Shinfield ... And also whereas her Majesty of her princely liberality yieldeth yearly out of certain dissolved chantries unto a petit ['petty' or elementary] schoolmaster of Ledbury £3 12s 2d, and at Bosbury £8 4s 2d, and at Colwall £6 6s 8d and at

20. HCA, 7044/6. R.J.W. Bryer's English translation has been revised in the light of Jebb and Phillott's translation of the same Latin sentences in the 1636 statutes. (See below, note 61). A contemporary copy of the 1583 statutes is to be found in HCA, 7044/4, and Bannister (pp.88-92) summarises the main clauses.

21. The feast days were those of St Lawrence (10 August), St Bartholomew (24 August) and St Thomas (of Hereford) (2 October). Between 1174 and 1180, David de Aqua had granted tithes to the cathedral 'so that simnel cakes could be made annually on the feast of the Blessed Milburga' (23 February) for distribution to the canons, vicars and Hereford priests (Aylmer and Tiller, p.441); and one Hugh of St Martin had also apparently left land for buying wine for the chaplain (at least according to Carless, p.17.) The simnel cake deed is to be found in HCA, 1383; the Hugh of St Martin's endowment has not been traced.

Kinnersley £5 or £6 ... and doing small or no good at all by reason they are uplandish towns and ... of the smallness of their pensions; it would please her Highness to grant the said stipends in perpetuity to the foresaid cathedral church to the use of the said free grammar school to be erected in Hereford, being the shire town and serving as commodiously for the training up of the youths of south Wales which shall repair thither, as the school of Shrewsbury doth for the use of north Wales. So that the sums and distributions only for this purpose taken from the poor ministers of the said church to their great hindrance may in part, or at least be employed as before they have been; or else upon the said better allowances, the number of teachers may be increased, men of greater sufficiency placed in the rooms of teaching, and the teachers' houses and schoolhouses the better by them from time to time repaired and maintained.[22]

Here was a bold proposal: the diversion of annual fees worth well over £30 for the establishment of a boarding school to enable the boys of the southern Marches and south Wales to obtain an education in Hereford to rival that in Shrewsbury in the north, in exchange for the restoration to the Chapter of the proposed diversions (or some of them) from the existing common fund. It was not so far-fetched. There was at least one precedent elsewhere. In 1569 in another cathedral county, stipends worth over £26 had been alienated from endowed chantries in Bradford-on-Avon and Trowbridge, on the grounds that they were 'but upland towns and not a resort of gentlemen and merchants', to finance a second grammar school at Salisbury.[23] And there was no reason why the Hereford Dean and Chapter should not aspire to making their cathedral school another Shrewsbury. The Shropshire school was originally in part endowed in 1552 from the lands and tithes of two collegiate churches in the town. Under its influential master Thomas Ashton, it had expanded rapidly during the following decade, partly by attracting the sons of the gentry to the school from neighbouring counties (including Herefordshire), which resulted in the granting of a substantial additional endowment from the crown in 1571.[24] Hereford, moreover, was just as important a judicial, administrative and commercial centre for the southern Marches and south Wales as Shrewsbury was for the northern borderlands. By the 1580s, too, the city had recovered from its economic slump of the mid-sixteenth century, was growing in population and entering its late Elizabethan prosperity, symbolised by the building of the magnificent three-storeyed market hall in 1576 – which was still described in 1642 as 'the stateliest market-place in the Kingdom' – and its 1597 charter of incorporation.[25]

---

22. Strype, *Whitgift*, i., pp.215-16, Dean and Chapter petition, enclosed in a letter from Whitgift to Burghley, 11 Feb. 1583 (misdated by Strype). The Chapter had also requested the confirmation of its possession of the Lugwardine Rectory and its four chapels for the permanent endowment of a divinity lecturer.

23. Orme (1976), p.75; J. Simon, pp.312-13.

24. *Ibid*, pp.231-32, 315-16.

25. *CSPD, 1641-43*, p.399, Nehemiah Wharton to George Willingham, 7 Oct. 1642. The impressive market-hall consisted of eight bays, rested on 27 oak pillars, measured 85 feet by 35 feet and housed the market, the city's courts and rooms for 14 guilds. Drinkwater, pp.1-2, 7. John Eisel has argued convincingly that the hall was built in 1576 rather than at a later date. Eisel (2005), pp.26-27, 29. For Hereford's decline following the destruction of the fulling mills in 1527 and subsequent recovery in the late sixteenth and early seventeenth centuries: Dyer, *passim*.

There were good reasons then for the Dean and Chapter to hope that their petition for the new school might be granted. But it was not to be, which was just as well for the future generations of young country children who would have been deprived of any education in these elementary 'upland' schools by the cathedral's dubious proposal.[26] So the county's petty schools were saved and of the petitioners' requests only £2 from the annual rents of the Lugwardine Rectory and chapels was diverted for the school's use.[27] In retrospect, we can look back on the government's decision to reject the Dean and Chapter's request as a lost opportunity to provide a more substantially endowed cathedral grammar school. It was also one which would put further strain on the cathedral's own slender resources. As Whitgift recognised at the time, 'not that church only [Hereford] but divers others are greatly impoverished, partly by unreasonable leases and partly by other ways and means so that they are not able to perform that which is looked for'.[28] Nevertheless, we should still acknowledge the work of the Hereford commissioners – and especially the contribution of John Whitgift, one of the great educational patrons of the late Elizabethan age[29] – in establishing an endowed cathedral school.

Whitgift, perhaps fearing backsliding from the Hereford Chapter, acted promptly to ensure that the new school was ready to start by Michaelmas 1583 as the statutes required. Three months after their promulgation and shortly before Whitgift's translation from Worcester to Canterbury, the commissioners wrote a letter – tellingly from Hartlebury, the Bishop of Worcester's palace – to the Dean and Chapter in the following terms:

> Among other statutes, which we by virtue of our commission have made for the good government of the church [of Hereford], there is one that especially concerneth the erection of a free grammar school, to be moderated and taught by a schoolmaster and an Usher. And because we have a special care that the first man to be placed in the room of the schoolmaster there, should be such a one as may be an example for the like choice hereaft[er] when occasion shall require, we have thought good to commend unto you this bearer, Mr May, whom by good experience we know to be of very honest conversation, zealous in religion, skilful in the tongues, painful in teaching and in all respects very meet for that place. And therefore we heartily pray you as well to admit the said Mr May to be schoolmaster there, as also to make choice of some other honest, godly and painful man to be Usher, whom you shall think good. And also not doubting but that you remember to make ready the house for their lodgings that at Michaelmas next, being the time appointed for the school to begin,

26. These four schools still survived in the early nineteenth century. Carlisle, i., pp.481, 484-87, 501, 502.

27. As indicated by the entries in the surviving post-1583 clavigers' accounts (e.g. HCA, R591 for 1586-87), which list 40s being paid yearly (from the master of the library who evidently received the whole of the Lugwardine rents) towards the masters' salaries.

28. Strype, iii., pp.65-66, Whitgift to Burghley, 11 June 1583. Whitgift asked Burghley to defend the cathedral's interest with the Queen because of the Dean and Chapter's fears that there was 'some intendment to get from them Lugwardine parsonage, with the chapels annexed, under pretence that the same is concealed from her Majesty'. *Ibid.*, p.65.

29. Whitgift purchased a site in Croydon for his school on 6 October 1596; by 1599, the building had been completed at a cost of over £2,718; and on 25 June 1600, the foundation deed endowed the school and hospital with lands which were to produce an annual income of over £185. Sheils, *ODNB*, vol. 58, p.726

> they may enter upon the same accordingly, we commit you and all your doings to the direction of God's Holy Spirit.[30]

The admission of one William May MA as *Archididascalus* (the Usher is not mentioned) is then recorded in the Chapter Acts for 30 September 1583. It was the Chapter's first formal appointment of a grammar school Headmaster in its history.[31] Despite Whitgift's strong recommendation, May's tenure was not a success and he could hardly have been the example for future appointments. Within little more than a year, the Chapter was writing to the Archbishop about 'the great mistake had with our Schoolmaster and Usher' and petitioning him for their removal on these grounds:

> For that they do not teach by any method set down by public authority but only by imitation, whereby the scholars for this year now past have very little profited under them. Insomuch that divers of the church, with others more of the city and country, have been forced to take away their youth[s], to take elsewhere for their better education and likelihood of profit in learning, to their great charges and trouble.[32]

It had been an inauspicious start to the new regime.

Whatever happened to May and his colleague is not known but it is clear from existing records that they were not in office for an extended period. In early 1587, Whitgift, having heard that the schoolmaster's position was 'very shortly to be void', again pressed the cathedral to appoint another of his nominees, a Mr Rastall MA of Balliol College, Oxford. Rastall had been 'specially recommended unto me for many good respects by divers of the Heads and others of that university, as their letters of commendation here enclosed doth appear'. He was regarded as a good person 'for education of the youth', and the Dean and Chapter were urged by their Archbishop to 'consider of his meekness and sufficiency'.[33] Whether they took fright at another Whitgift nominee is not recorded, but a new Usher, George Quarrall, was certainly appointed in July 1587.[34] Less than four years later, one Thomas Cooke was termed 'schoolmaster' in the Vicars' Act book.[35] The rapid turnover of masters at this period is not surprising. The 1583 statutes had stated that the schoolmasters' tenures were not to be granted for life or a period of years, thereby implying that the offices were held only during their 'good behaviour'. May, for one, had not fulfilled this requirement.

Rooms appropriate to a cathedral grammar school were less easy to acquire than personnel. The lodgings that the commissioners ordered the Dean and Chapter to prepare for the masters were probably found within the College of Vicars Choral. Although there

30. HCA, 1532, letter from John Whitgift, Thomas Wilson and Richard Cosin, 22 July 1583.

31. HCA, 7031/2, fo 109v. As we have seen, John Dornell's 1535 appointment was mentioned in the Chapter Acts (HCA, 7031/1, fo 77r, 2 March 1535) but this Act simply confirmed the appointment, which had been made '*per dictum venerabilem virium*' William Hull, the then Chancellor.

32. HCA, 7031/2, fo 178r, Dean and Chapter to Archbishop Whitgift, 18 Nov. 1584.

33. Thomas Rastall had matriculated from Brasenose, at the age of 14, on 20 July 1578, but subsequently migrated to Balliol, taking his BA, 26 Jan. 1581, and his MA, 17 Jan. 1584. Foster (1891-2), iii., p.1234.

34. HCA, 4562, Whitgift to the Dean and Chapter, 11 Feb. 1587; HCA 7031/2, fo 129r, 15 July 1587.

35. HCA, 7003/1/1, p.79, 10 March 1591. Also note HCA, R592, R593, re payments to Cooke, 1592-93. Cooke's name was mistranscribed (at a later date) in the College Acts as 'Cooxy'.

is no evidence of May having lived in their quadrangle, subsequent Headmasters were housed there in the late sixteenth century. Thomas Cooke paid an annual rent of 10s for his chamber and [James?] Povey was allowed 'to be commensal at their table'.[36] They therefore joined the company of distinguished musicians who lived there. One such was 'the cathedral's most distinguished musical son' – the former Hereford chorister, and later its organist and master of choristers, John Bull – who was even given rooms in the cloisters when a gentleman of the chapel royal.[37] One of Bull's successors, John Farrant, having escaped from Salisbury where he tried to murder the Dean, was granted the lower chamber behind the hall next to the vicars' saffron garden as a room to instruct the choristers in May 1592, 'the choristers' chamber without College gate' being then handed over to the diocesan registrar. Within months, Farrant had been sconced 2s 11d for his abuse of a vicar choral and admonished for his 'filthy railing and contumelious speeches' against the Custos at supper in the hall.[38] It was, at times, a rumbustious fellowship.

It was not long, however, before the Headmasters had acquired a more appropriate and substantial residence. The first indication of this is a Chapter Act of 25 June 1608, when 'the dwelling house near the College in the east part of the graveyard in which Master Philip Kynvyn, lately prebendary of this church, lived' was converted for the Headmaster's use.[39] There is further evidence to suggest that this house may have been the one designated for the Headmaster, even if at this stage it did not become his permanent residence. During 1612-13, the Chapter paid £10 to a Mr Burghill 'for his lease of the house now appointed for the schoolmaster', and in 1619 John White Osgood was given permission to rent out for a year 'the house or lodgings called the schoolmaster's house lying in the graveyard'. By 1635, Bishop Matthew Wren could report that the schoolmaster's dwelling had been taken from him more than eight years previously, and that the Master had also been deprived of his small rental income in lieu. Wren then instructed the Dean and Chapter to ensure that the house was restored to its rightful owner. This would have been the house recognised in the 1636 statutes as the one 'formerly appointed for this office near to the Canon's Bakehouse', now known (after many alterations over the centuries) as School House.[40] The Headmaster, then, had been allocated a specific house on the east side of the cathedral by the early seventeenth century, but where did he teach?

The statutes had provided for a school within the Close 'or a more suitable place elsewhere', and it is evident that the old schoolroom – wherever that may have been – was used for teaching until 1590. On 16 February that year, the Chapter Acts record that following

---

36. HCA, 7003/1/1, pp.79, 97, Vicars' Acts, 10 March 1591, 15 Nov. 1595.

37. HCA, 7003/1/1, p.78, 18 Jan. 1591, when Bull was given (on Whitgift's order) 'the great upper chamber behind the college, appointed heretofore for the reader of the divinity lecture'. For Bull at Hereford: Aylmer and Tiller, pp.395-96.

38. *Ibid.*, p. 449; HCA, 7003/1/1, p.82, 13 May 1592; p.84, 14 Feb. 1593. Crump, the registrar in 1592, may be the same William Crump who rented a room in 1618-19 for 10s over the cathedral north porch, 'where he keepeth the records belonging to his office'. HCA, R601 (1618-19 fabric account), fo 10r.

39. HCA, 7031/3, p.56, 25 June 1608. Kynvyn was collated prebendary of Colwall in April 1580 and died *c.*1604. Le Neve (2014), p.40.

40. HCA, R600, clavigers' account entry, 1612-13; HCA, 7031/3, p.135, Chapter Act, 30 Sept. 1619; WAAS, 40/11240, p.216, Wren's presentments, 25 Oct. 1635. See below, pp.38-39, for the 1636 statute.

the library's move to the Lady Chapel, the old library room was to be given to the free grammar school, an external door being made 'outside the cemetery of the cathedral ... to the grammar school step'. The school thereby acquired the upper room over the west walk of the Bishop's Cloister, which had housed the cathedral library since the 1470s.[41] Over the summer of 1590, payments were made for making the room fit for school use, as well as establishing the library in its new location. If Miles Smith was supervising these works as residentiary canon, as seems likely, it was highly appropriate that a distinguished scholar who had himself attended the school in the 1560s was directing operations.[42]

There are no detailed accounts of the upper room's structure or refurbishment so whether it contained a fireplace or how its seating was arranged is unknown. We only know that it was accessed via a spiral staircase and that the old library may have occupied three bays.[43] If so, this would have allowed more than sufficient space for educating tens of pupils at any one time given the rudimentary architectural requirements for a school of this period. The room would have been inferior to the great purpose-built schoolrooms of the Elizabethan period at Guildford in 1557 (65 x 21 feet) or the Harrow plan of 1590 (56 x 20) but not so far off the country schoolrooms of the 1580s at Ashbourne (46 x 22) or Illminster (36 x 16). Nor was it unusual in the post-Reformation period for old buildings to be used for educational purposes. This was especially the case with the former monasteries, where there was an excess of building stock. Among the new cathedral foundations, Canterbury, Chester and Gloucester all used monastic buildings for their schools; and Norwich adapted the charnel-house for educational purposes. By comparison, Hereford's cloistered upper-storeyed room seems preferable. And among secular cathedrals, there was at least one precedent – at Wells in 1459 – for a schoolroom to have been built over a western range of cloisters. Indeed, some educationalists of the period thought that it was wise for the young to be instructed in a remote room where they were less likely to be distracted. Richard Mulcaster had even suggested in *Positions* (1581) that it was better for a grammar school to be sited on the first floor to protect scholars from 'too great noise if the place be ... enclosed with other building'.[44] And although the Hereford conversion cost no more than a few pounds, compared with the hundreds spent on the grandest of the Elizabethan schools,[45] its new schoolroom was an improvement on the domestic building that it replaced. Quite apart from its size and lofty eminence, not the least of its attractions would have been its beauty as a piece of architecture. Despite its 'very high antiquity', as one antiquarian was later to describe it,[46] this venerable schoolroom was to serve generations of cathedral school pupils for 170 years.

---

41. HCA, 7031/2, fo 140r, 2 Acts, 16 Feb. 1590; Aylmer and Tiller, pp.514-15.

42. HCA, R588 fo 20r, 29 June 1590, payment of 39s to Dr Lewis for money expended by Miles Smith on both school and library 'as by 3 several bills it doth appear'. Later, Dean Watkins was in charge of the library works. *Ibid.*, no date, re his expenditure of 52s 2d for boards, timber, labour and unnamed items in the Lady Chapel. For Miles Smith, see below pp.71-72 and Plate 2.

43. Mynors and Thomson, p.xxi; Lepine (2002) p.185, suggests the three bays.

44. The comparative material has been drawn from Seaborne, pp.8-9, 15-21, 23, 26; and (for Wells) Orme (1976), p.80 and Orme (2006), p.236.

45. Seaborne (p.31, note 23) estimates that the costs of a new school then ranged from £100 to £300.

46. Price, p.137.

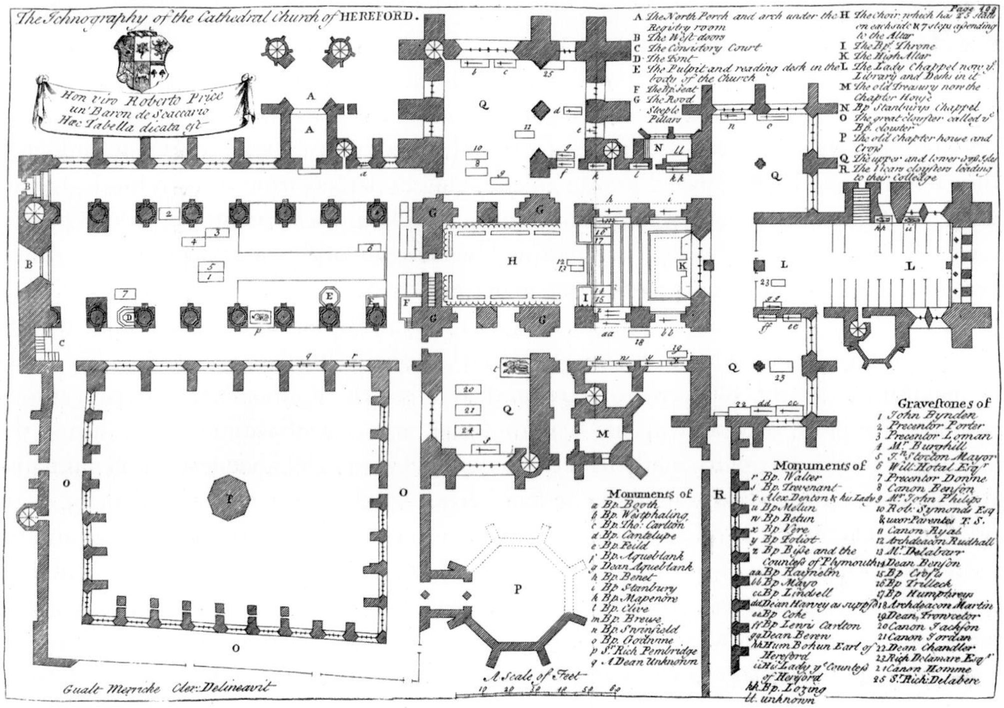

Fig. 2.2 Browne Willis' 1727 plan showing the spiral staircase (in the west cloister of the Lady Arbour) to the old schoolroom.

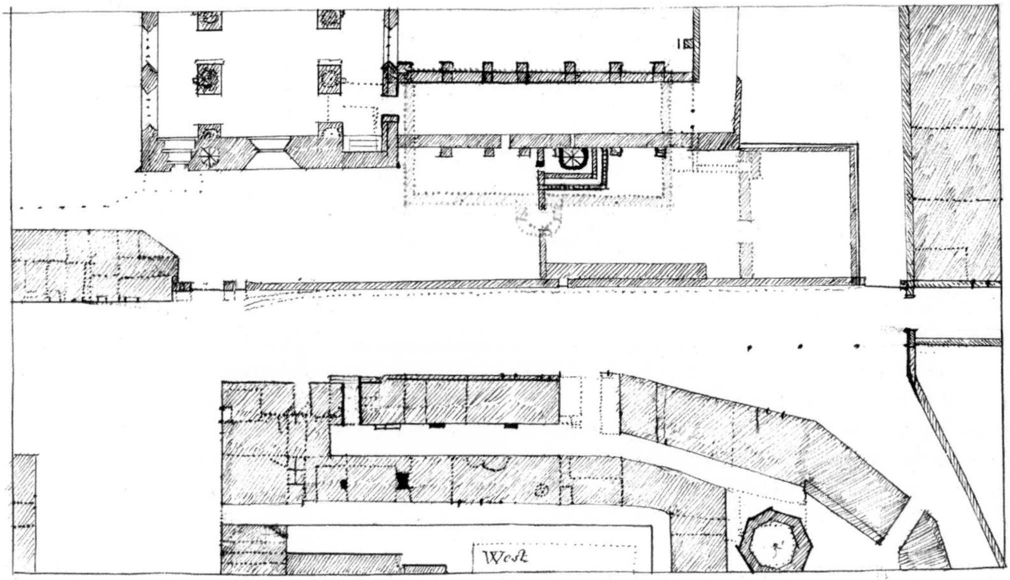

Fig. 2.3 A plan of the old schoolroom, with an outline plan for the Great Room, c.1760.

So by the end of Elizabeth's reign, the school had been refounded under the tutelage of a Headmaster and Usher and possessed for its sole use a fine schoolroom adjacent to the cathedral, where choristers as well as other local boys could study. It was now both a cathedral school, statutorily governed by the Dean and Chapter, and a 'free' grammar school for the city of Hereford. But despite its enhanced status, it was minimally endowed. The cathedral had been required to find an endowment, largely from its own funds, for the payment of the masters' fees. It had also endowed an Oxford scholarship for former pupils, as we will see,[47] but it still lacked rich patrons. In the years of the new Jacobean age, things were to change through the means of two generous legacies.

Charles Langford, Dean of Hereford from 1593 until 1607, gave the school its first substantial private endowment. By his will of 10 October, signed 18 days before his death, he bequeathed nearly 300 acres of farmland at Disserth, Radnorshire, for educational purposes. Langford had built up his Radnor estate, at a cost of around £500, during the last 20 years of his life, particularly in the years following his 1593 bequest (of £8 annually) to Brasenose College, Oxford, where he had been a scholar.[48] His will provided for quarterly payments of £2 13s 4d each to eight scholars: four from Ludlow 'in regard he and his ancestors ... being men of special rank within the town';[49] and four from 'the Free School of Hereford'. Each scholar was 'to be chosen out of such poor and towardly for learning', born within their respective towns and at least nine years old on their nomination – holding the scholarship until they were sixteen and no longer. Only the Hereford boys, however, were:

> Upon every Sabbath day and other festival days...[to] come to the divine service morning and evening into the choir of the said cathedral church, in gowns and surplices as the chorister ... use[d] to do, and to keep that order which the statutes and orders of the church shall require.[50]

The educational provisions of Langford's will were admirable and many boys were to benefit from his largesse for more than three centuries. Initially, however, there were problems with regard to its administration. A disputed title to a part of the estate was not resolved until 1613.[51] And then, ten years later, there was the claim from the parents of the Ludlow scholars that their boys had not received their due, the case being eventually heard before the Council in Wales, which ordered the cathedral Treasurer both to pay the arrears

---

47. Below, p.37 note 54.

48. Foster (1891-2), iii., p.876. The gradual (and often difficult) accumulation of Langford's lands in Disserth may be traced in Charles and Samuel, iii., pp.1318-19, 1321-26, 1328-33. The lands had cost Langford over £300 by September 1603, exclusive of at least two further purchases in October 1603 and July 1603 amounting to £185. HCA, 3110, 3111, 3119, 3120. The 1593 Brasenose bequest of £8, together with £4 from George Philpotts, was to be divided between two exhibitioners nominated and paid for by the Hereford Dean and Chapter. *Brasenose Quartercentenary Monographs* (1909), iv (General Benefactions, by A.J. Butler), p.21. I am indebted to Georgie Edwards, deputy archivist at BNC, for this reference.

49. HCA, 3134, undated petition from four Ludlow boys to the Council of Wales requesting payment.

50. HCA, 3123, copy of Langford's will, 10 Oct. 1607. The lands were vested in trust to four residentiaries: Giles Tomson, Thomas Singleton, Roger Bradshaw and Francis Kerry (the then cathedral Treasurer).

51. HCA, 5157, 3131, 3128, 3130, letters from Singleton to Kerry 12 Sept. 1611, 17 June 1613; expenses re the suit *c.*1612 (amounting to £11 1s 6d) and witness support for Singleton and Kerry, 26 March 1613.

and make new payments to the boys until they had reached their 16th birthdays, in accordance with Langford's will.[52] But in the long run, the main pity was that the Disserth estate was (in the words of a later parliamentary report) 'situated in a cold and bleak country, among hills and very bad roads', and that despite its acreage the returns were to remain poor.[53]

The 1615 bequest of Roger Philpotts was more valuable to the school in the long-term. It added to the existing provision for former pupils, whom the cathedral had favoured since the late sixteenth century by the grant of £1 or £2 annually in support of their studies at Oxford.[54] Philpotts' legacy was both similar in form to and complemented Langford's bequest. Like Dean Langford, he was a Brasenose man,[55] but unlike the Dean he was a Herefordian who probably attended the Cathedral School, eventually becoming mayor of the city in 1614. By Philpotts' will of 24 March 1615, Archdeacon Silvanus Griffiths, the cathedral residentiaries Francis Kerry and John Best, and Richard Vaughan, his son-in-law, were all made trustees of his estate. Following the death of his wife, he bequeathed his house 'at the east corner of the north end of Cabbage Lane' [Church Street] – then 'and still in some degree' (so it was reported in 1818), Hereford's vegetable market – for the school's benefit. The proceeds from this house, then let at £10 annually to one Thomas Quarrell, were to be used for the maintenance of two of the four Langford scholars at Brasenose College.[56] His widow may have outlived her husband by 15 and more years and it is not until 1639 that there is evidence that a payment was made from the Philpotts foundation by the Dean and his Chapter colleagues, who by this time were administering the fund.[57] As we will see, this foundation, which eventually accumulated large surpluses, was to sustain generations of Old Herefordians, some of whom had also held the Langford scholarship, during their studies at Oxford.[58]

52. Lloyd, p.49, re the parental petition of 1623 to the Ludlow bailiffs; and HCA, 3134-3140, for a copy of the actual petition to the President of the Council and details of the 1625 court proceedings.

53. Disserth lands were let at an annual rent of £24 (with £10 fine in 1673) for much of the seventeenth century; by 1780, the rent was only £38, which had been increased to £52 10s by 1830. HCA, 3132, 3142, indentures 28 Jan 1614, 26 June 1673; HCA, 7007/1; *Report of the Commissioners Concerning Charities*, xiii (1815-39), part 2, p.10.

54. HCA, R591, payment of 20s, 17 June 1587, to one Best for his son's Oxford exhibition; R595 (1608-09), R 600 (1612-13), re payments of £4 annually for 'our' two Oxford scholars (reflecting the 1593 BNC bequest). The 1624-25 payment 'to our scholar in Oxford the whole year, £4' (R601a) suggests an increase in living costs. The annual £4 payment continued through the mid-seventeenth century. It was paid to the Oxford student until he became a Master of Arts. See below, p.18; and LPL, COMM XIIa/10 fo 207, report on Thomas Reading of All Souls, 29 July 1649.

55. He matriculated, aged 18, on 9 March 1582; gained his BA on 19 Jan. 1586 (MA, 11 July 1589); and was made a college fellow, 14 Dec. 1588. George Philpotts is listed as a college benefactor in 1593 (the same year as Charles Langford); and Francis Philpotts, probably Roger's son, matriculated at the same college on 13 July 1613. *Brasenose Reg.*, i. 64, 123; Crook, p.437.

56. Carlisle, i., p.498. Report *of the Commissioners Concerning Charities*, xiii (1815-39), part 2, p.10. Philpotts' Hereford house is now part of Number 28, High Town.

57. HCA, R606, clavigers' account 1639-40, re the £8 paid to two Oxford scholars 'in performance of Mr Philpotts' gift'. There is no mention of the payment in the previous extant account (for 1630-31, HCA, R605) so it is likely that his widow died between 1631 and 1639.

58. See below, pp.74, 122, 185; and for the eventual use of the fund for internal scholarships, below, p.296.

Choristers had an occasional claim on one other early seventeenth-century legacy. This resulted from the will of 24 July 1619 of Richard Lane, alias Tomson.[59] It was similar in form to Philpotts' bequest, with the same three residentiaries having oversight of its execution. Land with an annual rental value of £20 was to be purchased – two farms, one in Norton Canon, covering some 177 acres were eventually secured – and vested in the Dean and Chapter. Most of the money was to be used in distributing bread doles to the poor – together with the £2 given annually to a deacon for 'for ever to prick [copy] fairly into books songs and church service[s]' – but every third Maundy Thursday the residue of the estate's profits could be used to bind a poor chorister in an apprenticeship 'to some honest trade'. Given that the surplus was unlikely to have been more than a pound or two, only modest trades would have been open in this period to Tomson's chorister children.[60]

The final school endowment prior to the civil war was enshrined in the new cathedral statues signed by Archbishop Laud and issued under royal authority on 31 May 1636.[61] These Caroline statutes, which were promulgated following another bout of wrangling between the Dean and Chapter and their diocesan Bishop and metropolitan Archbishop over visitations,[62] further increased the Headmaster's reward as this passage illustrates:

Fig. 2.4 The site of Roger Philpotts' house, the rents from which financed scholarships for over 300 years. For much of the twentieth century the property was let to Boots. It was sold by the school in 1966.

59. HCA, 3957. The will is outlined in Aylmer and Tiller, pp.645-46. Richard Tomson gained some of his wealth from his brother Giles Tomson (1553-1612), who gained the plum deanery of Windsor in February 1603 and became Bishop of Gloucester in 1611.

60. For example, in 44 extant Bristol apprenticeship agreements recording premiums from 1615 to 1630, £70 was the highest sum paid (to a mercer) and between £1 and £4 the lowest sums (paid to a shoe-maker, button-maker, tiler, rope-maker and mariner). Jewell, pp.108-09.

61. The statutes have been translated (although misdated) by J. Jebb and H.W. Phillott. They were published as *The Statutes of the Cathedral Church of Hereford, promulgated AD 1637* [*sic*] (Oxford, 1882); pp.30-33 relating to the school clauses.

62. The Chapter eventually succumbed to Charles I's commands and Archbishop Laud's will. For this: Bannister, pp.94, 178-80, especially Laud's letter to the Dean and Chapter of 22 Sept. 1634.

> And that the Headmaster may be more careful to teach the boys, he shall have assigned to him the house formerly appointed for this office, near to the Canon's Bakehouse on the west, with the garden adjoining, at the yearly rent of six shillings and eight pence, so long as he shall continue Headmaster.

This addition to the Headmaster's remuneration was of the utmost importance to the school's future: it gave him and his successors the security of a permanent residence in perpetuity in return for a nominal rent.[63] This would better enable them to undertake their duties; encourage more boarders; and attract masters of a higher quality, particularly as the Headmaster's and Usher's salaries remained fixed at the sums set in 1583 (£20 and £10 respectively) despite the subsequent climb in the costs of foodstuffs and other goods.[64] But there was a price to be paid for this enhanced status. A clause which did not appear in the 1583 statutes suggests that over the ensuing 50 years masters had failed in their duties and their superiors had been negligent in their governance:

> Let the Dean and Chapter take great care that both the masters execute their office uprightly and piously, that they teach such authors as are fit for their scholars, and that they instruct them faithfully in the catechism set forth in the liturgy of the Church of England, and that they form them strictly to good conduct as well by their daily discipline as by their own example. But if they shall be slothful or negligent, and do not perform their duty in every respect with fidelity and without reproach, let them be cited into the Chapter by public monition and be reproved once or twice, and then, if after two monitions they do not thoroughly amend themselves, let them be removed for ever.

In 1637 Clement Barksdale, an Oxford MA and ordained clergyman, was assigned to undertake these responsibilities, the first Headmaster known to have been appointed under the new statutes. Four years later he was made a vicar choral and rector of St Nicholas, possibly in addition to his responsibilities at the school. A firm royalist, he remained in Hereford until parliamentary forces occupied the city in 1646. Other than his appointment in 1641 of William Harvey, who also hailed from Winchcombe and like Barksdale had studied at Gloucester Hall, Oxford, as his Usher,[65] little is known about his doings at the school. We do know from his later writings, however, that he was both a doughty defender of the church and a noted scholar. An early work, *Monumenta Literaria*, was first published in 1640 when he was Headmaster of the school, and this was followed by around 30 other

63. It is possible that the Headmaster's house given by the 1636 statutes was the same one as had been occupied earlier in the century, although it then was leased in 1612-13 (at a £10 rent paid to Mr Burghill) and for one year in 1619. See p.33 above. The 6s 8d payment to the chapter was maintained as a separate item in the school accounts until 1970-71 when it was changed to 33p as a result of decimalisation.

64. Not least during the inflation decades of the 1590s, 1610s and 1630s. For the near doubling of food prices between 1580 and 1640: Outhwaite, p.10.

65. 'Mr Harvey' was paid his £2 10s quarterly fee as the new Usher (a 'Mr Allen' having received the same amount in November 1640) on 7 August 1641, the same day that Barksdale was paid £5. HCA, R607, clavigers' entry book 1640-41. Harvey was clearly the William Harvey (listed by Foster (1891-2) ii. 668) who matriculated at Gloucester Hall, 12 December 1634.

books, including translations, collections of biographies and sayings, as well as a volume of poetry and several more of his own sermons. Modern examination of some of these works gives the lie to Anthony Wood's waspish comment that they were mostly 'mere scribbles'. Barksdale laboured in his life's work to fashion Anglicanism as a 'tolerant, ecumenical, rational and learned' creed. All this was in the future. Nevertheless, in 1637 Jonathan Brown, the new Dean, no doubt saw Barksdale – even at 28 – as the man to put the school on the right path and perhaps raise it to new heights. He had little more than four years to do so before the city was engulfed by the civil war.[66]

1642-1660

Herefordshire's royalism was evident well before the official beginning of the civil war, signified by the raising of Charles I's shaky standard – it blew down on the first night – on a mound above Nottingham Castle on 22 August 1642. And although the loyalty of most of the county's ruling elite was paralleled in other regions – loyalist petitions were mobilising opinion in neighbouring Worcestershire and counties as far afield as Cornwall, Kent and Yorkshire in that spring and early summer – Herefordshire's stance was unique, as one scholar observes, 'in the strength and clarity with which its royalism was expressed and recorded'.[67] One early manifestation of this is the pro-episcopacy petition presented to local justices at the January 1642 Quarter Sessions, in response to the parliamentary arrest and detention of Bishop Coke of Hereford and 11 other prelates for affirming their right to sit in the House of Lords. The petition – having been signed, so it was claimed, by 68 gentry, 8 doctors, 150 clergymen and other ministers and 3,600 local inhabitants – was eventually printed in May, although there is no record in the Commons or Lords Journals of its ever having been presented to either of the two Houses of Parliament. As well as its staunch defence of bishops, the petitioners demanded 'that cathedrals, the monuments of our forefathers' charity, the reward of present literature and furtherance of piety be also retained'.[68]

Cathedral communities were both instinctively loyal and among the staunchest supporters of the King's position as 'defender of the faith'. And in the late 1630s, Hereford Cathedral in particular embraced with enthusiasm Laudian ornamentation and ceremony, as imposed by the Archbishop of Canterbury, William Laud. Bishop Matthew Wren, on the eve of his translation to Norwich in October 1635, gave the most elaborate instructions for reverent worship to be found in any refurbished cathedral choir to the Hereford Dean and Chapter. Some of these injunctions were incorporated into the new cathedral statutes of 1636.[69] So it is realistic to suggest that the cathedral clergy, together with Barksdale as *Archididascalus*, would have been among the 'ministers of good report' who defended the bishops and subscribed to the May 1642 petition. We know that one Hereford priest in particular, the well-established canon but new residentiary Dr Henry Rogers, used the

66. On Barksdale in general, and particularly his later success as a schoolmaster at Hawling and his influential translations of Grotius' works: Anthony Wood, iv. 221-25; Coffey, *ODNB*, vol. 3, p.907.

67. Eales, p.127.

68. J. and T.W. Webb (1879), ii., pp.337-38.

69. As outlined by Fincham and Tyacke, pp.235-36, from WAAS, 40/11240, pp.201-16, Wren's presentments, 25 Oct. 1635. In early 1642, the cathedral removed many of its Laudian trappings. Eales, p.131.

cathedral pulpit to further the King's cause. In a sermon on 27 April 1642, for example, he railed against the levelling tendencies of the King's opponents, who 'would have no man above another but all men alike and to throw down all government, learning and religion'.[70] As far as the school was concerned – and the two masters, seven choristers and Langford scholars were all likely to have heard his thundering – he would have been preaching to the converted.

Hereford's importance during the civil war as an essential strategic link in the 'cavalier corridor' between the west of England and south Wales meant that it was soon caught up in the conflict. On 14 July 1642, over one month before the raising of the King's standard, 150 volunteers and a hundred or two other troops mustered outside the city walls. There, 'A Declaration of Resolution of the County of Hereford' in favour of the Protestant religion, the monarch's 'just power', the laws of the land and the subject's liberty was read, the 'faithful subjects' resolving to defend the King with their 'lives and fortunes'. In the words of Professor Fletcher, this pledge 'exhibited a lofty strain of royalist sentiment that had not at that stage been heard from any other county'.[71] So for the first few weeks of the war, the city was firmly under royalist command. However, control of Hereford was to be determined more by the fluctuating movements of field armies than by its royalist sentiment, and within weeks parliamentary forces had secured the city.

Hereford's occupation by the Earl of Stamford and his troops from 1 October to 14 December 1642 and by General Sir William Waller and his men for less than a month from 25 April 1643; its siege from 30 July 1645 until its relief by the approach of Charles I's forces on 2 September in the King's last significant victory of the war; and its final capture by Colonel John Birch's subterfuge on the snowy night of 18 December that year – all this need not long detain us here.[72] There are few records to determine how far the school was caught up in these momentous events but it is impossible to imagine that it would have been unaffected by the war. Given the flight from the city like the one reported in late September 1642, when with a large parliamentary army at Worcester, 'many of the people with their children' escaped from Hereford, it is probable that the school population reduced in size as happened at Shrewsbury during the war years.[73] Given, too, the dangers of travel even over a few miles on the county's wretched roads, boarding numbers might have been especially vulnerable.[74] Money would also have been even tighter following Stamford's appropriation of cathedral revenues in late 1642, and there would have been little spare to spend on the school.[75] And throughout the war, the febrile atmosphere within Hereford would have disrupted learning. For a royalist garrison town subject to periodic attack, these were years of acute anxiety for the native population.

70. *Ibid.*, p.140. Lady Brilliana Harley took strong exception to Rogers' royalist sermons and thought that 'it were a most just work to punish him'. Lewis, p.174, letter to her son 'Ned', 27 June 1642.

71. Eales, p.128; Ross, pp.37-38; J. and T.W. Webb (1879), ii., pp.343-44; Fletcher (1981), p.305.

72. Ross (pp.27-124) gives the best modern account of how the city fared during the war.

73. *CSPD, 1641-43*, p.399, Nehemiah Warton to George Willingham, 7 Oct. 1642; Vincent, (1950), p.42.

74. For an evocative description of the state of the Herefordshire byways in this period: J. and T.W. Webb (1879), i., pp.7-9.

75. Ross, p.54.

As prominent defenders of the *ancien régime*, the cathedral community was particularly at risk during the occupations. And the school's seven choristers, together with the singing-men, were sometimes on the front line. Despite being mocked, their courage and constancy are evident from Sergeant Nehemiah Wharton's account of the cathedral service that occurred on Sunday 1 October 1642, when the parliamentary forces first occupied the city:

> Sabbath day, about the time of morning prayer, we went to the minster when the pipes played and the puppets sang so sweetly that some of our soldiers could not forbear dancing in the holy quire, whereat the Baalists were sore displeased. [When] the anthem ended they fell to prayer, and prayed devoutly for the King [and] the bishops ..., and one of our soldiers with a loud voice said, 'What! Never a bit for the parliament?' which offended them much more.[76]

Other boys showed even greater bravery during the defence of their city and outside its fortification, as on 17 August 1645 when: 'a noble sally was made at St Owen's church with great execution and divers prisoners taken with the loss of only one man, at which time little boys strived which should carry first torches and faggots to fire their works, which was performed to some purpose'. Later that month St Owen's was counter-mined, and Sir Barnabas Scudamore, the royalist commander, 'employed our boys by day and night to steal out and fire their works, securing their retreat under the protection of our musketeers on the wall'.[77] It would be good to know whether cathedral schoolboys were among their number.

The boys were vulnerable during the civil war but so too were their governors. Although one of the terms of the city's surrender to Waller in April 1643 stated that 'the Bishop and Dean and Chapter and the collegiates' were to be 'freed in their persons from violence and in their goods from plunder', the 'persons of consequence' taken prisoner included Bishop Coke, as well as Lady Brilliana's *bête noire* Henry Rogers and his two colleagues, Thomas Godwyn and William Evans. By this time Dean Brown had already been sequestrated of his Rectory of St Faith's in London.[78] His successor suffered even greater trials. Following Hereford's final capture on 18 December 1645, Dean Croft stoutly defended his cathedral from the parliamentary soldiers, who (according to Colonel Birch) were 'so enraged' from being shot at by the townsmen in the streets 'that we could not stop them from plundering'. As Birch's later memoir puts it: 'The doctor [Croft] is said to have preached so vigorously against sacrilege that the soldiers were preparing to level their firearms against him but were restrained by their commander [Birch himself]'.[79] Within months, the brave Dean had been deprived of the deanery as well as his other preferments and had retired to a country retreat.[80]

---

76. *CSPD, 1641-43*, p.399, Wharton to Willingham, 7 Oct. 1642.

77. Scudamore to Lord Digby, as printed in a royalist Oxford pamphlet of 1645 and cited by J. and T.W. Webb (1879), ii., p.387.

78. *Ibid,* i., pp.257-58, 262; ii., p.23.

79. HCL, X.13.2/16, Birch to the parliamentary commissioners, 18 Dec. 1645; J. and T.W. Webb (1873), p.198. The 'Croft' pulpit, from which the soldiers were alleged to have been berated, was probably made in *c.*1617 and is now placed in the south-east transept. Aylmer and Tiller, p.103.

80. Where he married (by 1651), Anne, the daughter of Jonathan Brown, his predecessor. There is also a happy

Despite the turbulence of these years, Hereford cathedral itself, directly as a consequence of the city being under royalist control for all but three of the 40 war months, survived (the odd musket-shot mark apart) unscathed. It was more fortunate than some of its sister foundations like Lichfield and Carlisle which suffered direct bombardment; or indeed St Giles' chapel, St Martin's and St Owen's, all of which were situated outside Hereford's walls and reduced to near ruin.[81] The cathedral community, like its church building, also held together during the civil war. There is good evidence for this in the chance survival of the one cathedral financial account for the war years: that between Michaelmas 1644 and 1645. In the absence of the Chapter Acts and other cathedral records, despoiled after the city's capture, it is worth examining in some detail.[82]

The clavigers' entries for 1644-45 differ little from those in the pre-war accounts.[83] Receipts included the £2 forwarded by the master of the library, from Philip Traherne's rent (of £8 6s 8d) for the Lugwardine rectory and chapels, towards the schoolmasters' salaries; £24 from Richard Rea for his rent of the Disserth lands for the eight Langfordian scholars; and £8 from Robert Weaver 'for that part of his house to discharge Mr Philpotts' gift'. And among the payments, George Lea collected £1 on the King's behalf for the obits (from Sellack, Kings Caple and Pencoyd) 'called mass pence and now converted to the maintenance of the schoolmaster and Usher'; the schoolmaster and Usher themselves received £20 and £10 respectively for their salaries; the eight Langfordians, £21 6s 8d; the scholars 10s following the audit; and Jones and Powell ('Mr Philpotts' scholars' in Oxford) £8 between them.[84] Cathedral music, too, continued to aid worship: the organist's salary was augmented by £2 13s 4d; the deacons were paid £15 12s for their services in the choir; John Watkins, 'blower of the bellows', received his annual £1 fee; and the choristers were apparelled and recompensed as usual, the following payments being recorded: £2 to a Mr Norman for cloth for their garments and 7s to the tailor for making them; 16s 8d for their 'shoes and stockings at Christmas' [1644]; £1 15s 4d 'for their whole year's wages, one being wanting for the last 2 quarters'; and £1 each to Lord, Caldicot, Adams, Smith and Black – the five Dean and Chapter choristers (the vicars choral supported the other two) – 'for their gowns'.[85] In the whole account, the few indicators of war were the 20s paid to

---

ending to Croft's deprivations. He was reinstated as Dean at the Restoration and two years later, on 9 February 1662, consecrated Bishop of Hereford. Marshall (2004), *ODNB*, vol. 14, p.240.

81. Aylmer and Tiller, p.102; J. and T.W. Webb, ii., pp.217, 219; LPL, COMM XIIa/10, fo 178. There seems to be no contemporary evidence that the Chapter House roof was stripped of its lead for bullets or that cathedral brasses were melted down for the same purpose, as claimed by later historians. Ross, p.108. As far as the Chapter House is concerned, it is more likely that its lead was used to repair the castle tower keep following the city's final surrender. Whitehead, pp.49, 51.

82. Silas Taylor, one of the Herefordshire sequestrators, may have been responsible for the loss of some manuscripts. Aylmer and Tiller, pp.521-22.

83. HCA, 2384, Francis Kerry's and Henry Rogers' clavigers account for that year. It may be compared with HCA, R608 (for 1640-41), the last extant account before the outbreak of the civil war. Two clavigers (literally 'key-holders') were appointed annually from the residentiary canons to administer general cathedral expenditure, excluding fabric money which was separately accounted for.

84. Possibly the Thomas Jones and James Powell, who matriculated at Balliol and Brasenose respectively on 16 March 1638 and 22 Nov. 1639, both of whom came from Hereford. Foster (1891-2), ii., p.830; iii., p.1191.

85. The young Adams himself, so his father (Anthony Adams) was later to claim, had the distinction of singing

the ringers for four celebratory peals; the 13s given to the king's lifeguard, in addition to 6s to soldiers by the advice of two residentiary canons; and (in the fabric account) the 2s 4d paid 'for Mr Addis his man killed in the siege'. Indeed, it is the fabric account that reveals the best evidence that life still went on. The 3s 4d received 'for burying Mr Barksdale's child' was one of 12 child burials recorded for 1644-45, out of 28 in the cathedral that year, a powerful reminder that (in Professor Aylmer's words) 'much of the normal pattern of private and family life – work and leisure, joy and sorrow – continued unaffected in the 1640s and '50s' despite the upheavals of the period.[86]

But the oversight of the cathedral and its school was to be affected for a generation. We can be sure, following the city's capture on that wintry day of 18 December 1645, that the cathedral's Christmas celebrations a week later would have been muted compared to those of the previous year; and that the prospects for a school of royalist sympathies under occupation would have been uncertain during the early weeks of 1646. We know nothing about how the school functioned during this time, and precious little about its operations over the next 14 years except that it came under new rule. Clement Barksdale, the school's erstwhile and perhaps continuing Headmaster, who had buried his daughter in the south transept the previous year, was ousted from his preferments and left the city for a chaplaincy at Sudely Castle, where he 'exercised his ministry and submitted to the men in power'. Later he was to reflect on his last days in Hereford and the loss of his chamber. His bitterness is apparent in this satirical verse addressed to Colonel Birch who had turned the College of the Vicars Choral into an alms-house for the poor:

> Sir, we are not so bold to fight with God
> But meekly do submit unto his rod;
> Yet we may ask, why thus you do give leave
> The nasty beggars should our chambers have.
> Do strangers spoil's for incivility?
> All strangers drunk of our humanity?
> Do th' poor possesseth all, 'cause we did not give
> due alms? Poor people we did still relieve.
> D' ye mean, because you think that we want grace,
> To turn us out into the beggars' place,
> As they're in ours? What ere 'tis, we go hence:
> Religion hath taught us patience.[87]

His seniors were no less unfortunate. Dean Croft, as we have seen, retired to a private estate. Other Chapter members also suffered sequestration. From 25 March 1646, the

---

'the last anthem in the choir before King Charles the first'. (HCA, 7031/3, p.224, note of the £7 claim from the Tomson bequest 'in Dr Benson's hands', 22 Sept. 1663). This may have been at the morning service on 7 September 1645, when the King was present at 'a solemn thanksgiving' for the city's deliverance. (*CSPD, 1645-47*, Lord Digby to Prince of Wales, 7 Sept. 1645). The King's movements after the relief of the Hereford garrison in early September 1645 are documented in Long, pp.232, 238, 240; and by Ross, pp.111-113.

86. Aylmer (1972), p.384.

87. Anthony Wood, iv., p.221; Barksdale p.56 no. vi, 'Upon Beggars lodg'd in the College' (spelling and capitalisation modernised); and *ibid.*, p.12 no. xxiv, 'Upon the Decease of my Infant Lady', for his daughter.

Deanery and the prebendal houses in the Close in 'Broad Cabbage Lane' (modern Church Street) and Broad Street were rented out to the members of the all-powerful county committee, who now administered the Chapter properties and revenues 'to the use of the state'.[88] The Dean, residentiaries and evicted clergy were replaced by six Presbyterian ministers, three of whom were to officiate in the cathedral 'to preach in turn ... there on the Lord's days ... both morning and afternoon', as well as twice during the week. They were awarded an annual salary of £150 each, together with rent-free accommodation, although only one minister is known to have been given a canon's house as the ordinance required.[89] With the notable exception of Richard Delamaine the younger, most of these ministers seem to have lived up to their description as 'able, godly and learned divines'.[90] Their services, however, would have been based on the puritan *Directory for Public Worship* rather than the *Book of Common Prayer*, with the emphasis on the written and spoken word. Music was confined to psalm singing, whereby the voice was to be 'tuneably and gravely ordered', and the psalms sung 'with understanding and with grace in the heart, making melody unto the Lord'. In Hereford, the cathedral's organ was dismantled by March 1647, and the lead for the psalms was given (in 1647) by the Langford scholar, Robert Weaver. Other liturgical changes were imposed, as on 8 June 1647 when 'the feasts of the nativity of Christ, Easter and Whitsuntide and other festivals commonly called holy days', which (it was alleged) had 'been heretofore superstitiously used and observed', were abolished. To compensate, scholars, together with apprentices and other servants, were given leave to have 'reasonable recreation and relaxation from their constant and ordinary labours' on the second Tuesday of each month.[91] Feast days had been done away with, the vicars choral dispersed, the choristers proscribed – probably for the first time in almost a millennium – and a near musical silence imposed on the cathedral well before the official abolition of Deans and Chapters in April 1649.

This does not imply that the Cathedral School followed the musicians into temporary oblivion. Indeed, there is sufficient evidence to indicate that following Hereford's capture, the school, unlike Shrewsbury in 1644,[92] continued with little interruption.

88. BL Add. MS, 16,178, fos 4r, 6v, 34r (13 March-20 April 1646), re rents to be paid by Henry Jones (£5 for Dr Skinner's house in Broad Cabbage Lane), Thomas Rawlins (£4 for Dr Benson's in Broad Street), John Flackett (£4 for Mr Bassett's in the 'churchyard') and Dr Nathaniel Wright (£6 for the Deanery, complete with orchards).

89. Firth and Rait, i., pp.840-41. Timothy Woodroffe, who took over Dr Rogers's house (BL Add. MS, 16,178, fo 116v, 10 Nov. 1646), was the exception in terms of accommodation.

90. To the names of the six preachers mentioned in Aylmer and Tiller, p.106 (George Primrose, William Lowe, Samuel Smith, William Voyle, Richard Harrison and Edward Delamaine) – at least four of whom were graduates (including Voyle, who matriculated at Brasenose in December 1609 and probably attended the Cathedral School) – should be added John Somers, who officiated in the cathedral for several weeks in early 1646, and William Newport and Timothy Woodroffe who joined the city ministerial team in late 1646. In early/mid-1647, Smith and Woodroffe were described as cathedral ministers and Voyle, Lowe and Primrose as ministers at (respectively) St Peter's, All Saints and St Nicholas. BL Add. MS, 16,178, fos 110r, 113r, 121v, 138v, 151v, payment warrants, 19 Oct. 1646-6 March 1647; TNA, SP 28/228, part 5, warrant, 28 June 1647. For the younger Richard Delamaine: below, note 94.

91. Firth and Rait, i., pp.607, 954, 4 Jan. 1645, 8 June 1647; BL Add. MS, 16,178, fo 150r, 5 March 1647, 5s payment for dismantling the organ case; TNA, SP 28/228 part 5, warrant for 30s to Weaver, 22 Dec. 1647, and SP 28/229, part 1, warrant for payment to Weaver as a Langford scholar, 17 Dec. 1647.

92. Vincent (1950), p.42.

The post-regicide boast that 'the Commons assembled in parliament have ever been zealous to continue and establish all works and foundations tending to the advancement of learning' is confirmed at a local level by what happened to Hereford's school.[93] In the early months of the city's parliamentary occupation, for which a unique account survives, the county committee made its first salary payments on 20 May 1646 to Mr Seaborne and Mr Allen 'schoolmaster and Usher of the Free School of Hereford' less than two months after they were due. These were continued at regular intervals over the following weeks.[94] Langford scholars were also paid their allowances, if not quite in full at least as much as was realised by the Disserth rents. And although it took a little longer and an approach from Dr Kerry, the old cathedral Treasurer, the Dean and Chapter's annual £4 payment to an Oxford student, bestowed 'in favour of learning for the help of such poor scholars as should be commended to them by the head schoolmaster of the said [free] school', was resumed.[95] The wherewithal for the continuation of the school, too, was provided. For those senior boys who may have had access to local treasures, the college and cathedral libraries, having been 'lately spoiled and many of the books thereof purloined', were brought together and the ministers charged to make two catalogues 'fairly written' of the remaining collections. A few weeks later, within the college itself, orders were given for a census to be taken of its occupants, who were further charged with keeping the rooms 'clean and sweet' and preserving the utensils and 'all things belonging to the Free School of the said college'. That this was a reference to property formerly used by the masters and the college choristers who lived there, rather than by the school as a whole, is suggested by later repairs to the school door-lock and for the provision of a lock and key 'for the cloister door below the school', which clearly indicates that the school had not moved from its 1590 schoolroom.[96] And at the traditional time of year, in mid-December [1646], the generous sum of 20s was given 'to the scholars of the Free School at their declamations', speeches made by pupils in the learned tongues such as those that were undertaken by Samuel

93. Firth and Rait, ii., p.256 from 'An Act for the continuance and maintenance of the school and alms-houses of Westminster, 26 September 1649'. Parliamentary support for grammar schools in this period is covered by Vincent (1950), pp.94-108; and Vincent (1969) pp.9-16.

94. BL Add. MS, 16,178, fos 45v, 108r, 129v, 167r, warrants, 20 May 1646- 6 April 1647; TNA, SP 28/228, part 5, warrants, Sept., 14 Dec. 1647. William Seaborne matriculated at Oriel College, Oxford, on 8 May 1635 aged 17. Foster (1891-2), iv. 1328. He was the 'Mr S' who quarrelled with Richard Delamaine over the authority of scripture. (*Impostor Magnus or the Legerdemain of Richard Delamain* ... (London, 1654), p.6. Thomas Higgs, who had replaced William Allen as Usher by September 1647, matriculated at New College, Oxford, on 14 Feb. 1640 aged 16. Foster (1891-2), ii. 708; and above, note 64, for Allen.

95. BL Add. MS, 16,178, fos.113v, 138v, warrants, 26 Oct. 1646, 28 Jan. 1647. For the Langford payments also see below, note 94. TNA, SP/228, part 5, warrants, 2 June, 8 July 1647 (the latter for a 40s payment to Thomas Reading, late Langford scholar).

96. BL Add. MS, 16,178, fos 113r, 124r, orders, 20 Oct., 2 Dec. 1646; TNA, SP 28/228, part 5, warrant for payment of sextons, Sept. 1647. By January 1649, John Probin and Hosea Best had fitted 51 feet of new glass in the schoolroom windows and re-leaded the old glass; and by May that year, John Ansell was paid 30s 'for writing and fitting ten catalogues of books to be placed in tables for the use of the library', as well as 15s 6d for 12 new chains, 36 clasps and for chaining 32 books. TNA, SP 29/229, part 1, warrants, 19 Jan., 10 May 1649.

Pepys at St Paul's at much the same time.[97] Within a few months of the royalists' demise in Hereford, normal school life had certainly returned.

On the ground, therefore, puritan control of cathedrals occurred several years before the parliamentary enactment of 30 April 1649 abolishing Deans and Chapters, canons, prebendaries – as well as 'other officers and titles of or belonging to any cathedral or collegiate church or chapel' – within England and Wales. But there were notable exceptions to this blanket uprooting of royalist foundations. The 'Act' did not apply to Christ Church, Oxford, Westminster, Winchester and Eton; and as with the earlier ordinance for the abolition of bishops, all revenues that had been allowed (before 1 December 1641) for the maintenance of grammar schools and their scholars, the repair of schoolhouses and almshouses, in addition to those for other charitable uses, were exempted from its provisions.[98] The details of the dispersal of Hereford's capitular wealth need not concern us here. One important financial development concerning the school, however, came about as a result of the 1649 enactment. Following the survey of Dean and Chapter lands and properties undertaken during the summer and autumn of 1649, the 209-acre Manor of Preston-upon-Wye was sold in June 1650 for £828 11s 3d to Owen Roe of London, the purchaser guaranteeing the payment of the schoolmasters' salaries in perpetuity.[99] It was a neater solution than the old cathedral system of basing the payments on the income of several rectories and other sources, but unlike other schools there is no indication during the Interregnum that the salaries of the Hereford Headmaster and Usher were augmented beyond the by then modest sums (£20 and £10 annually) set by the Elizabethan statutes.[100]

How far Hereford's schoolmasters went along with the post-regicide regimes during the 1650s is unknown. There are no extant records to determine, for example, whether any master was suspended from office like William Lowe and George Primrose, the Presbyterian ministers, had been for refusing to take the Engagement, the Commonwealth's loyalty oath.[101] Nor is it known whether a Hereford master was caught out by the Lord Protector's order of 28 August 1654 'for ejecting scandalous, ignorant and insufficient ministers and schoolmasters', the insufficiencies being spelt out for the first time. In addition to absence from school and neglect of teaching duties, these included blasphemous, atheistical or popish opinions; open disaffection to the government; swearing, perjury, adultery and fornication;

97. BL Add. MS, 16,178, fo 130r, Rawlins' payment warrant, 19 Dec. 1646. Pepys, who was a pupil at St Paul's from *c.*1645 to 1650, recorded in his diary a visit to his *alma mater* for 'Apposition Day' on 4 February 1663, when he considered that the speeches were 'not so good as ours were in our time'. Latham and Matthews, iv., p.33. Also see below, pp.51, 62, for Dean and Chapter payments to scholars for Latin speeches.

98. Firth and Rait, ii., pp.81-104, 'An Act for abolishing of Deans, Deans and Chapters, Canons, Prebendaries and Other Officers ...', 30 April 1649; and i., p.88, for the exemption clause in the ordinance abolishing bishops, 9 Oct. 1646. Details of the sale of Hereford's ecclesiastical lands and properties and an estimate of the value of prebends for the Interregnum period are outlined in Aylmer and Tiller, pp.102, 104-06.

99. HCA, 7007/1, fos 377-83, copy indenture, 20 June 1650. The survey of the tithes belonging to the Rectory of Preston with Blakemere (among other Dean and Chapter estates) was completed on 26 July 1649. LPL, MS COMM. XIIa/10, fo 204.

100. See, for example, LPL, MS COMM IX/1, p.87, for the increase in annual allowances to John Greenhalye (from £10 to £36) and John Pack (from £10 to £19), schoolmaster and Usher at Chester Free School.

101. Or so it was presumed by Edmund Calamy. Matthews, p.329. Both Lowe and Primrose were reinstated by order of the Council on 30 March 1654.

drunkenness and common haunting of taverns; frequent quarrelling, fighting and playing at cards or dice; prophaning the Sabbath day; the public use of the Book of Common Prayer; and support for 'any Whitsun ales, wakes, morris-dancers, maypoles, stage-plays or such like licentious practices by which men are encouraged in a loose and prophane conversation'. The judgement of the licentious was to be undertaken by five specially appointed commissioners and five ministers, including those who served the cathedral.[102] But perhaps the Hereford masters of the Interregnum were unaffected by Cromwell's puritanical injunction. Like Barksdale at Hawling, his Cotswolds school, and many of the county's parish clergy, they may well have conformed to the existing regime and kept their heads down.

After all, they had a living to make and there were still boys wanting to learn. We know the names of a few of them: the Langford scholars for the late 1640s. Thomas Reading, James Boyle, Owen Phillips, William Langford; and Simon Beavan, Herbert Vicars, John Garnons and Thomas Beazer, their predecessors, all signed a receipt for their scholarships – in bold hands – on 27 October 1646, the first boys' signatures from the school to have survived. A year later, Reading and Philipps had been replaced by Thomas Lawrence and Robert Weaver.[103] Of these ten, three (Reading, Langford and Weaver) went to Brasenose. Sixteen other Herefordshire boys, a majority of whom had probably attended the Cathedral School, were also admitted to Brasenose between 1647 and 1660, including the celebrated Thomas Traherne, who matriculated on 2 April 1653, following his admission to the college a month earlier at the age of 15.[104] At Oxford, Traherne was to receive (in his own words) 'the taste and tincture of another education ... glorious secrets and glorious persons past imagination' of which he had never dreamed. Yet it was Hereford that had set him on his way. And for his Hereford masters, boys like Traherne would have been rewarding to teach, even if 'there was never a tutor that did professly teach felicity'; and the obligation to listen to long and frequent puritan sermonising, in a cathedral pulpit complete with hour glass and velvet and purple serge-silk cloth and cushion, may not always have been appropriate for him, his contemporaries, or, indeed, their masters.[105]

But when the tide eventually turned, many from the school and its wider community must have rejoiced with the Herefordshire gentry, who in May 1660 opened their address to Charles II with these words: 'Upon restoration to your throne and people, we do find in ourselves a certain joy which is unspeakable both for kind and degree'.[106] Among the 106 or

---

102. Firth and Rait, ii., pp.968ff, 28 Aug. 1654; Vincent (1950), pp.97-98.

103. TNA, SP 28/228, part 5, receipt for payment of £19 4s (at the rate of 6s per quarter), 27 Oct. 1646; TNA, SP 28/229, part 1, payment order, 17 Dec. and receipt, 18 Dec. 1647.

104. *Brasenose Reg.*, i., pp.183-206. Although I have found no conclusive evidence, Traherne may have been a Langford scholar even though he would have held the award for less than the seven years stipulated by the Dean's will. It was not unknown at this time for other boys to have done the same, as with Robert Weaver, who was made a Langfordian between October 1646 and December 1647 (compare the respective payment warrants: TNA, SP 28/228 part 5, 27 Oct. 1646; and TNA, SP 28/229 part 1, 17 Dec. 1647), and was admitted at Brasenose (aged 16) on 28 July 1651 having held the scholarship for around four years.

105. Margoliouth, i., p.132, (*Centuries*, 3.36, 37); BL Add. MS, 16,178, fo 174v, warrant for payment of £4 12s 6d to Woodroffe for pulpit adornments, 17 April 1647; TNA, SP 28/228, part 5, 4s warrant to same for four hour-glasses, 18 June 1647.

106. TNA, State Papers Charles II, vol. 1, no. 62.

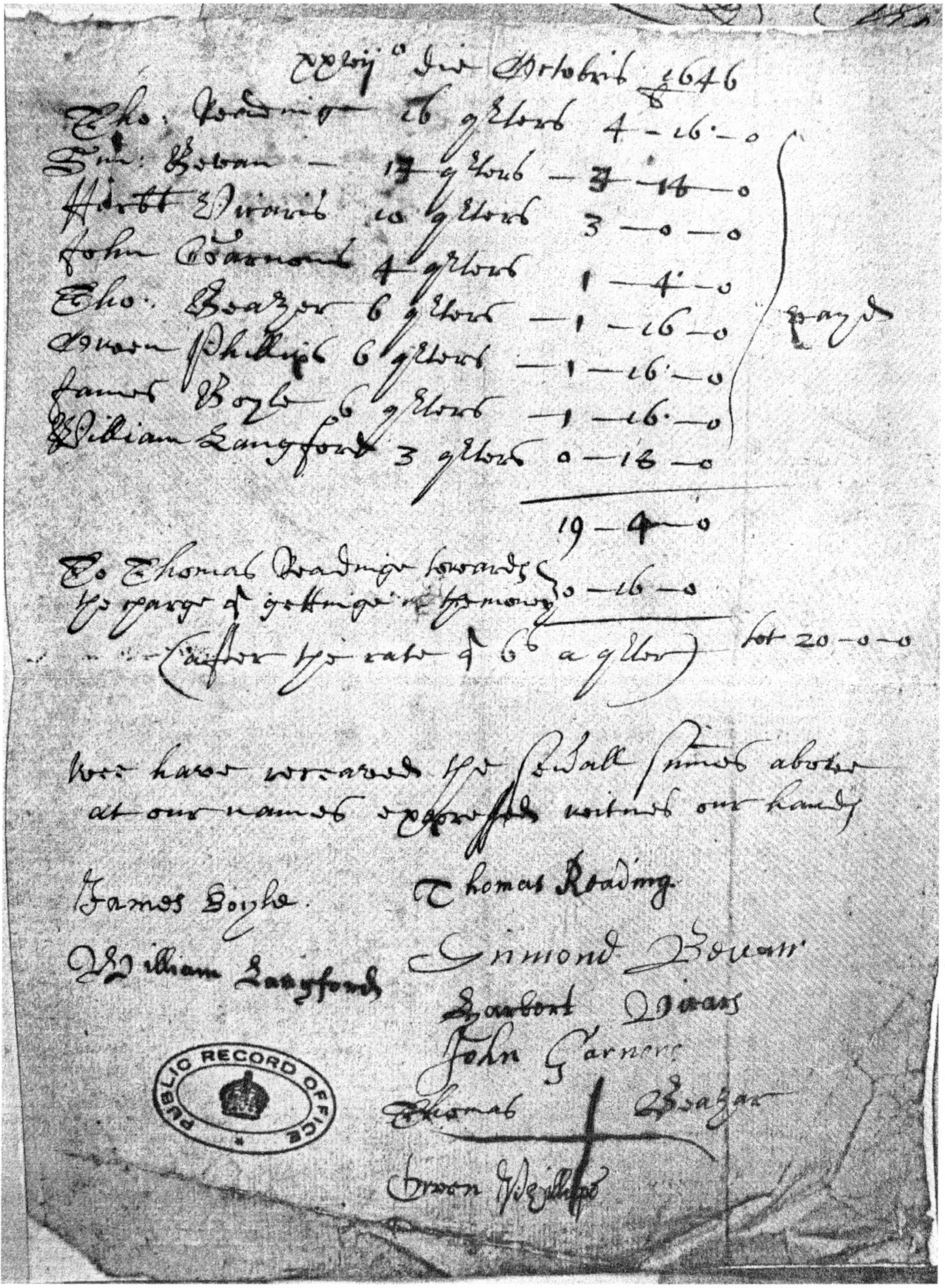
xxvij° die Octobris 1646

Tho. Readinge 16 [illegible] 4-16-0
Sim: Bowen 17 [illegible] [illegible]
Herbt Divers 10 [illegible] 3-0-0
John Garner 4 [illegible] 1-4-0
Tho. Beazer 6 [illegible] 1-16-0
Owen Phillips 6 [illegible] 1-16-0
James Boyle 6 [illegible] 1-16-0
William Langford 3 [illegible] 0-18-0
paid
19-4-0

To Thomas Readinge towards the charge of gettinge in the money 0-16-0
(after the rate of 6d a [illegible]) tot 20-0-0

Wee have received the severall sumes above at our names expressed witnes our hands

James Boyle
William Langford
Thomas Reading
Simond Bowen
Harbert Divers
John Garner
Thomas Beazer
Owen Phillips

Fig. 2.5 The first surviving boy signatures: eight Langfordians sign a receipt for their scholarships, 27 October 1646.

so signatures to this loyal petition was one boldly written by 'W Gregory'. Son of the vicar of Fownhope and rector of Sutton St Nicholas, and an Old Herefordian (almost certainly) who had risen to become deputy steward of Hereford, he was to be instrumental in the late seventeenth century in gaining the school its most influential endowment.[107]

1660-1697

William Gregory's signature on Herefordshire's loyal address indicates that he was already among the county's ruling elite by 1660. The King's restoration was also to enhance his position within the church as both office and land-holder. A month after the first meeting of the restored cathedral Chapter on 8 August, he had been appointed *conciliarius*, the lawyer who proffered legal advice and prosecuted suits on the cathedral's behalf, a position he held until January 1665; and on 20 October 1660, he secured the title to lands 'supposed to belong to the Dean and Chapter' at Woolhope which he had purchased in 1653.[108] Over 20 years later, Gregory had risen to high political and legal office, having been made Speaker during the First Exclusion Parliament in 1679, when the *Habeas Corpus* amendment act was passed, and being knighted and appointed a baron of the Exchequer immediately following the parliament's dissolution. He was now in a position to do great service to his *alma mater*. (Plate 4). But before we turn to Sir William's role in extending its influence – if not strictly its endowments, the Duchess of Somerset's lands being granted to St John's College, Cambridge, and Brasenose College, Oxford, rather than the school – we need to examine how the school fared in the years following the return of Charles II from his years in exile.[109]

The pace of the royalist recovery of the county in civil affairs, as indicated by the composition of the 1660 commission of the peace, the election of members of parliament in early 1661 and the purging of Hereford's municipal corporation under the 1661 Act,[110] was matched by the speed of the cathedral's restoration. The city's surviving puritan preachers were summarily ejected from their posts, and the first formal meeting of the general Chapter for almost 15 years occurred on 8 August 1660. Dean Croft, then the only living cathedral residentiary, together with three surviving prebendaries, thus began the task of filling the depleted ranks of the cathedral staff.[111] Among the earliest appointments were those of John Badham, the organist and one of the three new vicars choral. Given that the last cathedral service was sung before any of the new choristers had been born, he would have had his work cut out to train up the boys to the requisite standard. As an inducement, they were

107. See below, pp.56-57.

108. HCA, 7031/3, pp.188, 237, Acts 8 Sept. 1660, 17 Jan. 1665; HCA, 7007/1, pp.373-75, deed of exchange between Gregory and Dean Croft (Gregory releasing his title to Woolhope Court), 20 Oct. 1660.

109. For Gregory and the Duchess of Somerset, see below, p.57.

110. Aylmer (1972), p.383. Members of local royalist families (Brabazon, Coningsby, Cornewall, Lingen, Scudamore, Skipp, Tomkyns, Vaughan and Whitney), absent from the county's administration since 1645, now shared power with former republicans.

111. HCA, 7031/3, p.183, Acts, 8 Aug. 1660. Re the city preachers, Calamy (Matthews, pp.250, 329, 399, 448, 504) suggested that Richard Harrison, William Lowe, George Primrose, Samuel Smith and William Voyle were all active in Hereford until the Restoration but the exact date of their dismissal is unknown. Cathedral appointments are detailed by the author in Aylmer and Tiller, pp.109-112.

given half-a-crown for their encouragement 'when they began to sing alone in the choir'.[112] For Broad, Davis, Williamson and Rogers, the four Langford scholars, the re-establishment of processions and the regular celebration of Holy Communion at major festivals and on the first Sunday of each month would also have been a new experience in this period of liturgical uncertainty before the new prayer book was enacted in May 1662.[113] But for the school in general, there was no immediate break in continuity. Lessons would have been taught in 1660 – as (no doubt) in 1659 – by Mr Morris and his youthful Usher Mr Broad, in the cloister schoolroom, the windows of which were soon to be re-glazed like they had been from time to time over the previous decades. And the scholars were again paid 'at the breaking up at Christmas when they make their oration'.[114]

In following years, however, there are signs of change, three Headmasters – Barrow, Lane and Thomas Smyth – coming after Morris in quick succession.[115] Smyth left after a year to be replaced in 1663 by William Wakeman, whose tenure lasted throughout the late 1660s and whose impact on the school was of more consequence. That he was admonished in September 1670 by the Dean and Chapter for neglecting to receive communion each month, 'contrary to the ecclesiastical canons and rights of the church,' would have affected his own well-being but it was of less consequence for the school's history than the 1665 orders for its governance.[116]

These were drawn up by the cathedral for 'the government of the grammar school in the city of Hereford which is in the disposition, survey, governance and protection of the Dean and Chapter' and agreed to by both Wakeman and his Usher, William Langford.[117] The orders were promulgated as a response to the 'disputes and questions' that had arisen concerning the charging of fees to freemen of the city, a presentment having been taken to a court of frankpledge against 'the schoolmasters of the Free School', who (it was alleged) contrary to 'ancient custom' had exacted greater fees for the education of freemen's children

112. HCA, 7031/ 3, p.192, 27 Sept. 1660 (Badham's admission); HCA, R609, undated payment (for 1660) of 2s 6d. The names of these choristers are unknown, the earliest chorister appointment in the Restoration Chapter Acts being that of Rowland Pearce in place of William Pearce 'defunct'. HCA, 7031/3, p.196, 24 Jan. 1661.

113. HCA, R610, payment of £5 6s 8d to the four named Langfordians, for the half-year ending 24 June 1662. Henry Davis matriculated (at Brasenose), on 16 December 1664, aged 17. *Brasenose Reg.*, i., p.212.

114. HCA, R609 (for the scholars); payment of £1 16s 6d to William Hayfold for Charles Taylor; and various payments to 'Morrice' and Broad (together with his father in 1660). The masters are not readily identifiable, but possible candidates include the John Morris, who was admitted at Brasenose (aged 18) and matriculated on 10 March 1637; the Richard Morris, who matriculated at Christ Church, 17 Dec. 1640; and (more definitely) Thomas 'Broade', who was admitted at Brasenose (aged 17) on 17 July 1656. *Brasenose Reg.*, i., pp.173, 198; Foster (1891-2), i., p.184, iii., pp.1035, 1036.

115. HCA, R609, R610 *passim*, clavigers' accounts from 1660; HCA, 7031/3, pp.198, 201, Acts 10 July 1661, 23 June 1662; CCCA, MS 390/1, fo 209, Harvey's list, 4 April 1674. It is tempting to suggest that Smyth was the distinguished orientalist and antiquary Thomas Smith (1638-1710), who became master of Magdalen College School in 1663, but there is no extant evidence to connect him with Hereford. For this Smith: *ODNB*, vol. 51, pp.335-37.

116. HCA, R610, 1663-64 account; HCA, 7031/3, p.281, Act 29 Sept. 1670. Wakeman was probably the William Wakeman of Gloucestershire who was admitted sizar at Trinity College, Cambridge, on 14 November 1656. Venn, part I, iv., p.313.

117. For Langford, see below, p.64. The 1665 manuscript (with the masters' signatures) is to be found in HCA, 1530, and is printed by both Carlisle (i., pp.491-92) and Carless (pp.30-31).

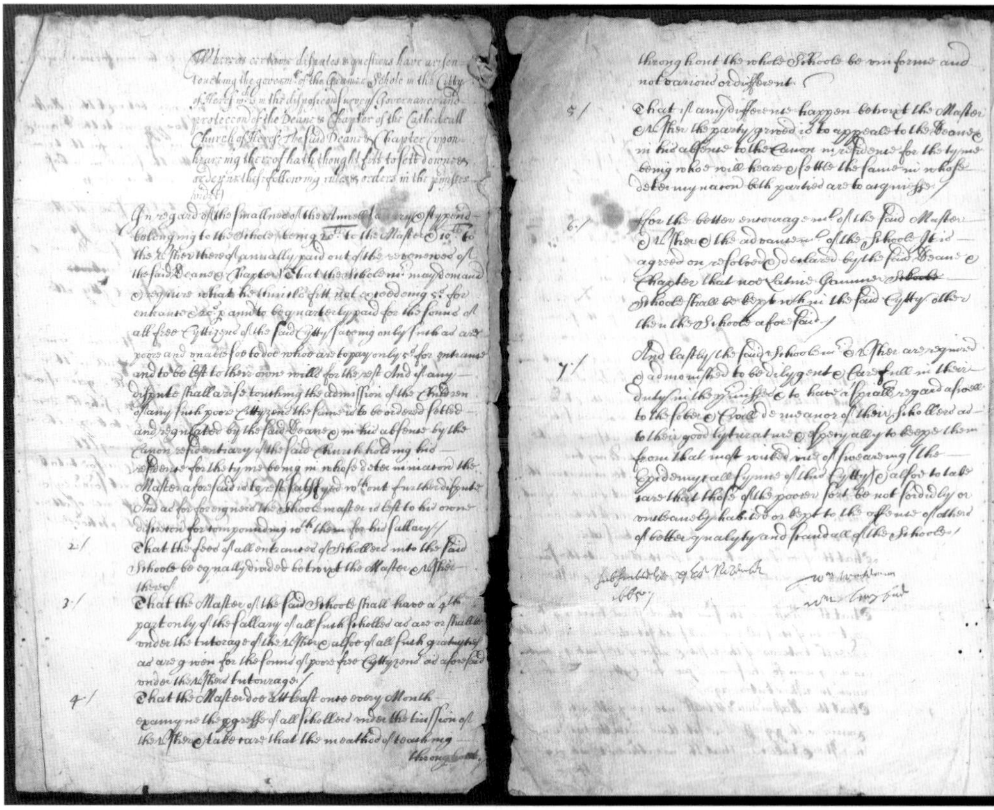

Fig. 2.6 The 1665 orders, issued by the Dean and Chapter for the school's governance and signed by the Headmaster and Usher.

'than ever formerly hath been given or ever due'.[118] There may also have been rivalry between the two masters over the distribution of fees, as well as other anxieties regarding the quality of the teaching and the pupils' behaviour. Beyond the freemen, it is uncertain how widespread these general concerns were, but the cathedral authorities evidently thought it necessary to set down rules governing the school's conduct, the Dean or in his absence the residentiary canon reserving their rights to arbitrate on future disputes.

The two masters' annual salaries (£20 and £10) were recognised as inadequate and compensated for by allowing the Headmaster to levy 'what he thinks fit' as a fee, which was not to exceed 5s for entrance and 20s annually (paid quarterly) for the sons of Hereford freemen, excepting 'such as are poor and unable so to do' who were to pay the entrance charge 'and to be left to their own will for the rest'. As for 'foreigners', the Headmaster was given discretion 'for compounding with them for his salary'.[119] All entrance fees were to be

118. HARC, Transcripts of Sack Books 24-27, p.269.

119. 'Foreigners' were boys who were born or resided without the city's boundaries, as with other school statutes of the period such as those devised by Peter Blundell, who in his will (9 June 1599) directed that the school was to be filled up with 'children of foreigners' after preference had been given to those born or brought up in the town or parish of Tiverton. Vincent (1969), p.44. Many 'foreigners' would also have supplemented the Headmaster's salary by the payment of a boarding as well as a tuition fee. For lists of 'foreigners' at Lady Hawkins' School, Kington,

equally divided between the two masters but the Headmaster was to claim only a quarter of the fees paid for those boys under the Usher's tutelage, implying perhaps that his assistant had been short-changed in this respect in the past. In return, the Headmaster was required at least once a month to examine the progress of the Usher's scholars 'and take care that the method of teaching throughout the whole school be uniform and not various or different', an indication that previously there had been little consistency in the approaches to learning between the two teachers. But for their 'better encouragement' the Dean and Chapter resolved that no other 'Latin grammar school' should be maintained in Hereford, the cathedral thereby confirming their ancient right of monopoly over grammar education within the city. Finally, there was this revealing clause relating to the masters' responsibilities both to encourage good reading and instil sound morals and manners among their charges:

> And lastly, the said schoolmaster and Usher are required and admonished to be diligent and careful in their duty in the premises, and to have special regard, as well to the sober and civil demeanour of their scholars as to their good literature, and especially to keep them from that most wicked vice of swearing, the epidemical sin of this city. And also to take care that those of the poorer sort be not sordidly or uncleanly habited or kept to the offence of others of better quality and to the scandal of the school.

Such were the earliest extant rules (the cathedral statutes apart) for the school's good governance. They were not novel in the sense that newer grammar school foundations often anticipated some of these orders in their founding statutes. The one relating to the conduct of Hereford pupils, for instance, is mirrored in those for Newport (Shropshire) in 1656 and Wigan in 1664.[120] Nor did these rules permanently resolve conflicts over fees with the city's freemen. This is clearly indicated by a dispute in April 1686, when Robert Phillips, the new Headmaster, was presented at a court of frankpledge 'for taking and exacting of the freemen and inhabitants of the city the sum of five shillings a quarter for teaching many of the said freemen's and inhabitants' children', the mayor and council being requested to consult with the Dean and Chapter to maintain 'the ancient freedom' of free education.[121] The 1665 orders may not have resolved all grievances but they at least provided a framework for the future conduct of masters and their boys.

How far these orders were observed under William Wakeman is unknown. Nevertheless, his headmastership, now bolstered by official recognition of the profitable taking of fees, lasted over seven years, considerably longer than the tenures of his immediate predecessors. 1671, however, marked the appointment of Joseph Harvey, whose headmastership was to be of greater significance. Harvey had already acquired the status of commoner of the College of Vicars Choral, paying 8d for each meal (exclusive of the cost of beer and bread at other times),

from 1632: HCA, D853/2, *passim*.

120. Foster Watson (pp.132-36) gives details of these orders against swearing and 'gaming for anything of price', as well as other statutes governing pupils' manners and morals from 1528 to the mid-seventeenth century.

121. HARC, BG11/3/7, Phillips' presentment, among Hereford Law Day records, 1684-96 (incorrectly transcribed by Carless, pp.31-32). I am indebted to Stephen Rexworthy for locating this document. There is no evidence that the Dean and Chapter changed their minds over the payment of fees. For various interpretations of the meaning of 'Free School' at this time: Vincent (1969), pp.40ff.

13s 4d for his linen and £1 annually for his chamber[122] before he was admitted *Archididascalus* of the free grammar school on 6 December 1671. In Harvey's case, there exists the first known patent for the appointment of a Hereford Cathedral schoolmaster. His tenure was dependent on the faithful exercise of his duties, Dean Hodges giving him the office 'on account of … [his] knowledge of learning … probity of life … honesty of manners', his experience in educating boys, and his 'other gifts of virtue to which in our presence we confidently receive most worthy testimonies'.[123] Harvey's testimonies do not survive and whether these laudatory phrases are anything more than formulaic platitudes is anybody's guess. However, we do know something about his background from university records: he was a Shropshire boy who matriculated from Christ Church, Oxford, on 30 March 1666, taking his BA in 1669 and his MA in 1672.[124] At the time of his appointment, therefore, he would have been around 22, young but given that it was then not unusual for a university student to matriculate at an even younger age than Harvey (he was 16), not excessively so. Moreover, from the 13 extant letters he wrote over a four-year period in the mid-1670s, the first surviving correspondence for any of our Headmasters, he seems to have been a fit man for the position.[125]

These letters, all from Hereford, were written to Christopher Wase, who at the time held the grand titles of Architypographus and Superior Bedell of Civil Law at Oxford. Wase was conducting a survey of the country's Free Schools, promoted to counter opinion – peddled by Joseph Howell, an old boy of the school, among others[126] – that these schools were producing too many scholars for the learned professions to absorb; that 'the multiplying [of] these foundations' was 'dangerous to the government'; and, especially, that the 'late civil commotions' could be attributed to the education given to endowed scholars.[127] From the outset, Joseph Harvey was supportive of Wase's 'excellent work', and as Wase's key intermediary in Herefordshire, did his utmost to provide the evidence required, periodically cajoling Griffith Reynolds, the Bishop's deputy registrar, to prompt local schoolmasters for details about their schools. In this, he was not altogether successful. Although the evidence he passed on helped to give Wase a more complete picture of education in the diocese than in most others, the busyness of the registrar, the incomplete state of school records, the truculence or fearfulness of the schoolmasters themselves and the unwillingness of some governors (including, it appears, the Dean and Chapter) to give information about their foundation to a third party, resulted in an incomplete survey even for the Hereford archdeaconry.[128] Its details have more

122. HCA, 7003/1/3, p.47, 22 Aug. 1671.

123. HCA, 7031/3, p.288, Harvey admission, 6 Dec. 1671; HCA, 1531, Hodges grant (under the Chapter's common seal) [in Latin], 6 Dec. 1671. I am indebted to Charles Gordon Clark for his translation of this document.

124. Foster (1891-2), ii., p.667.

125. CCCA, MSS 390/1, fos 176-95; 391/1, fos 112-15, letters from Joseph Harvey to Christopher Wase, 26 Sept. 1673-25 June 1677.

126. As in Jacobs, pp.523-27, Howell to Edward Sackville, Earl of Dorset, *c.*1651.

127. For the Wase enquiry in general, see Vincent (1969), chapter 2; and for his views: Wase, pp.1-2, 10-11, 51-52.

128. CCCA, Oxford, MSS 390/3, fo 181, diocesan returns for individual schools; 393/1, fo 94, list of national returns by county. Of the 18 schools in the Hereford archdeaconry, eight (including the two under Dean and Chapter control) were marked with a cross, whereas only three out of the 12 schools in the Shropshire archdeaconry had failed to respond. At a national level, Shropshire was first and Herefordshire fourth in terms of the number of schools responding. There was no response from any school in Norfolk, Cumberland, Westmorland

relevance for a history of the county's Free Schools than one for the Cathedral School. Harvey did succeed, however, in gathering together 'the names of all those who have been schoolmaster [at Hereford] in the remembrance of those who have longest lived here' – an observation which reveals the limitations of the school's record-keeping, although the list itself usefully supplements records of schoolmasters in the cathedral's own archive. Nevertheless, despite the shortcomings of the correspondence in terms of our own history, Harvey's letters give us some insight into the nature of the man: his meticulousness as a correspondent; his capacity for friendship; his antiquarian instincts, as shown by his forwarding a catalogue of over 140 manuscripts from the cathedral library; and his concern for his former students, his final letter of June 1677 asking Wase to matriculate 'a scholar of mine now come to settle in the university'. At this time, Harvey was still hoping that Bishop Croft would 'meet with schoolmasters behind with their answers' during his diocesan visitation that summer, even though Harvey feared that they would 'come too late for your purpose'.

The first successful diocesan visitation of the cathedral, accomplished by Bishop Croft, also occurred in that year of 1677 when Harvey was still in charge of the school.[129] Of the 60 articles covering all aspects of the cathedral's governance two concern the choristers and two the school itself. The following questions were asked. Were the choir's surplices 'decent and clean', and were the choristers kept in good order 'without babbling or running about from place to place more than absolutely necessary'? Did they regularly attend the grammar school or for 'such as have not natural capacities fit for that', the writing school? Were they taught a musical instrument 'such as may be useful for church service'? Were they employed in some 'honest way' to support their future livelihoods or did they spend their time 'in idle wandering ... or in such service and attendance as will not improve them'? Above all, were they both catechised and educated in 'pious and divine matters' which would lead 'to a holy Christian conversation all their lives'? Two questions relating to the grammar school were on similar lines. Was it governed by able masters who were diligent in instructing their scholars in both church catechism and 'humane learning'? And were the boys 'well trained up in piety, sobriety, modesty, obedience and all good discipline'? Bishop Croft's final educational query related to the school's oversight. Did the Dean and Chapter visit the school at least twice a year to examine the scholars 'to find out whether ... things ... [were] effectually performed as they ought [to have been]'?[130]

Such were the questions Croft posed for the schoolmasters and their governors. No answers survive from his enquiries but if they were anything like the anodyne replies given to Bishop Wren in 1635 they would not have been particularly illuminating.[131] Nevertheless, given that Herbert Croft held Joseph Harvey in high regard (as we have seen) and that none of his surviving post-visitation injunctions (for the cathedral's improvement) relate to the

and Northumberland, and only one return from a Suffolk school.

129. For the cathedral's resistance to episcopal visitations in the medieval period: Lepine (2009), pp.xviii-xix; and for the incomplete diocesan visitations by Bishops Lindsell, Wren and Croft, respectively in 1634, 1635 and 1662: Bannister, pp.101-02, 178-80; HCA, 1560-1562, 1565 for Lindsell's 31, Wren's 53 and Croft's 46 visitation articles; Aylmer and Tiller, pp.116-17.

130. HARC, AL 19/18, fos 254r, 255r, 257r, articles 9, 18, 47, 48.

131. As with the two extant answers given by Drs Skyrme and Kerry to Wren's articles of 22 September 1635, found in HCA, 1558, no. 29; 1559, no. 28. See below, p.62, for Skyrme's observation.

school, the bishop may have concluded that the boys were receiving a sound Christian education. At this time at any rate, the school, like the cathedral itself, where for nearly 20 years from 1672 Dean George Benson formed a close and effective partnership with his friend Bishop Croft, seems to have been in safe hands.[132]

Joseph Harvey's career in the Hereford diocese continued to prosper. He was collated prebend of Withington in May 1678 and presented to the vicarage of Upton Bishop in December 1679. Little more than two years later, he was also installed as cathedral Chancellor, the first known Headmaster to have attained this office.[133] Even though he was not made a residentiary canon and he had a youthful deputy in Charles Manfield,[134] it is to be doubted whether even Harvey was able to exercise his pedagogical duties effectively in addition to these responsibilities, and his resignation as *Archididascalus* in December 1685 must have come as a relief to both himself and the school. The election of Robert Phillips MA in his stead suggests that the school – unsurprisingly – was in some disarray at the end of Harvey's tenure.[135] Accompanying Phillips' appointment, the Dean and Chapter required that these two orders should be observed and displayed 'in the Free School':

> That the Master and Usher shall, with what convenient speed they can, introduce the discipline of Westminster School.
>
> That there shall be no play days given by the Master or Usher upon any particular man's request, but upon Tuesday or Thursday in the afternoon, except it be by the appointment of the Bishop or Dean or Chapter.

Phillips was clearly appointed to tighten up on discipline, and to do so in the style of the great Dr Busby, the Headmaster of Westminster from 1638 to 1695, who was renowned for the strictness of his regime, even (so it is alleged) keeping his hat on to ensure that his authority was not undermined in front of the boys when Charles II visited the school. It is conceivable that Phillips himself had attended Westminster under Dr Busby, one Robert Phillips having been a King's scholar at Westminster in 1668 before going on to Trinity College, Cambridge, in 1671.[136] Whatever the truth, the fact that Phillips survived at Hereford for more than a decade perhaps indicates that he was successful in curbing the wilder excesses of its schoolboys. More significantly, at least in the longer term, the school during the 1680s became a beneficiary of the Duchess of Somerset's largesse.

Although Brasenose, Oxford, and St John's, Cambridge – rather than Hereford Cathedral School – were the direct beneficiaries of her munificence, such is the importance

---

132. Croft's 33 injunctions resulting from his 1677 visitation, together with George Benson and Herbert Croft's strong alliance, are covered in the author's chapter in Aylmer and Tiller, pp.116-22.

133. HCA, 7031/3, pp.353, 378, 397-98; Acts, 17 May 1678, 4 Dec. 1679, 27 Feb. 1682.

134. *Ibid.*, p.387, 3 Dec. 1680, election of Manfield as Usher following William Langford's death. Manfield (a former Langford scholar), having matriculated at Christ Church on 19 July 1673 aged 16, was around 23 at the time of his appointment to his old school. He was installed as vicar of Kenchester in 1681 and rector of Ullingswick in 1688. Foster (1891-2), iii., p.965; and Marshall (2009), p.75, for William Gregory's patronage.

135. HCA, 7031/3, p.442, 11 Dec. 1685.

136. Barker, p.51; Venn, part I iii., p.356. I am indebted to Elizabeth Wells, archivist at Westminster School, for the reference to Phillips and for her observations on Dr Busby.

of her legacies over 300 years to both the school and its former pupils that it is necessary to examine her bequests to these colleges.[137] The first grants were made before the Duchess' death in October 1692, thereby fulfilling the precepts of seventeenth-century Protestant moralists who saw charitable life-time giving as a nobler sacrifice than mere death-bed legacies through the giver's will.[138] From the bequest to Brasenose, her first husband's college, of 17 February 1680, scholars born in Herefordshire benefited only if there were no suitable candidates from Manchester Grammar School. Some two years later, on 12 July 1682, she made a similar grant to St John's, her father's college, but this time the endowment of five scholarships were for scholars 'out of the Free School of Hereford'. Additional endowments were made to the same colleges by the terms of her will of 17 May 1686, with a codicil dated 10 February 1691, for the provision of scholars in strict order from the 'Free Schools' of Manchester, Hereford and Marlborough (in this rotation for Brasenose, the order being reversed for St John's, HCS being the middle school in both turns), the 12 scholarships being reserved for 'such as ... intend to take upon them the ministry ... and dispose themselves to the study of divinity'.

Fig. 2.7 Part of the Latin epitaph on the tombstone of Sir William Gregory, the most influential Old Herefordian of the seventeenth century.

The question remains as to why the Cathedral School was favoured in this way. The answer is almost certainly to be found in the person of William Gregory, who in addition to his legal offices became the Duchess of Somerset's agent for her Herefordshire lands. Quite when is unknown but his service for the Duchess – and for his father Robert Gregory, vicar of Fownhope 1619-43, posthumously – was shown when he facilitated the transfer of Fownhope Manor, together with 400 acres of woods and land from the Somerset estate, to its then vicar, Walter Rogers and his successors for their 'better support and maintenance ... and ... [their] encouragement ... to be resident ... so they may the better ... attend the care of the souls within the said parish'.[139] When Gregory himself died more than a decade later on 28 May 1696, he was buried in the church of St

137. Copies of these grants are to be found in HCA, 7044/17, pp.96-105, 108-117. The Duchess' will and codicil is extant (TNA, PROB 11/474); and for an outline of her life, see the author's article, *ODNB* Online.

138. For the arguments of some seventeenth-century divines on these lines: Archer, p.238.

139. HCA, 7007/1, pp.389-94, indenture between Sir William Gregory and Walter Rogers, 20 Jan. 1686.

Andrew and St Mary, How Caple, adjacent to his country seat. He was commemorated with an elaborate Latin epitaph on his tombstone there, part of which in English reads:

> Sacred to the memory of Sir William Gregory. The Parliament of the whole of England heard him as Speaker from the chair; the learned branches of the judiciary honoured him as now baron of the exchequer and then in the royal court of justices. When he was ... in the yearly circuit of the law-courts, justice uncorrupted always sat as his companion, and when he was likewise dealing with his own people. The whole neighbourhood did not find anywhere a more far-sighted friend, nor the Church a more generous patron.

The inscription might well have added that he also ensured that his old school received, through the Duchess' generosity, its greatest legacy.

Sir William's restorations within How Caple church included the magnificent chancel screen, reputedly carved by Grinling Gibbons, crowned by the William and Mary coat of arms, showing his acceptance of the 1688 Revolution. Not everyone in the county was so prepared to abandon their loyalty to the Catholic James II, who had fled the throne that December. Eleven ordained clergy, including at least two cathedral canons, refused to swear an oath of allegiance to the new monarchs and lost their livings.[140] But even for those like Bishop Croft and Dean Benson who reluctantly accepted the new regime, the changes wrought by the 1688 Revolution would have made them weary of this world as they prepared to meet the next. As Bishop Croft wrote in his will, signed on 4 January 1689 during the darkest days of the country's second revolution:

> Jacob said: 'Few and evil have the days of the years of my life been'. But I say many and evil have the days of the years of my life been. For we Christians, whom our blessed saviour, Jesus, hath both by himself and his holy apostles so fully assured that we shall enjoy his gracious and glorious presence after our death, should think every day a year 'till we arrive to that blessed enjoyment; and especially in these evil days wherein we have lived to see such sad revolution and dismal catastrophes. And now when we looked for peace there is no good; and for the time of healing and behold trouble ... How can we then but wish and pray for our hastening out of this comfortless life, and gathering to Christ who is the life, the joy, the bliss of our souls.[141]

And yet the school, like the cathedral itself, faced little disruption, although towards the end of 1689 the Usher, Thomas Gwillym, a vicar choral, resigned his post on his election as one of the College's four minor canons. But Robert Phillips, the Headmaster, remained in post through much of the 1690s – no doubt continuing to administer 'the discipline of Westminster' – until he too resigned in November 1697 on his admission as vicar of Fownhope.[142] It was this resignation, rather than the 1688 Revolution, which led to the

140. Aylmer and Tiller, pp.120-21. The cathedral Chancellor and former Headmaster, Joseph Harvey, eventually quitted all his preferments in 1716, having refused to abjure his oath to James II. Le Neve (2014), pp.23, 38.

141. TNA, PROB 11/405, fos 187ff; HCA, 7005/1, pp.210-11 (extract).

142. HCA, 7031/3, pp.477, 517, Acts 7 Nov. 1689, 11 Nov. 1697.

biggest hiatus in the school's history during the later seventeenth century. It is a story which will be recounted in the next chapter.

'Towardly' Pupils and Their Learning

Unlike the new sixteenth- and seventeenth-century grammar schools, where foundation statutes often give detailed instructions as to a master's qualifications, a scholar's demeanour and the nature of the godly and classical teaching that a pupil would receive, there is no one document prescribing what was expected from the masters and boys of the Cathedral School.[143] However, the cathedral statutes and various acts and other orders are sufficient to indicate what expectations the Dean and Chapter had for a boy's learning at Hereford during this period. As we have seen, in 1583 the children were to be versed in 'liberal studies and religious principles', the school being 'meet for learning, strict for discipline and devout for piety'. Similarly, the Laudian statutes of 1636 prescribed that the masters should teach 'such authors as are fit for their scholars', and that they should be instructed 'faithfully in the catechism set forth in the liturgy' (to prevent the use of unauthorised Puritan catechisms) and 'form them strictly to good conduct'. 'Good literature' and 'sober and civil demeanour' were also an element of the 1665 orders; and mastery of the church catechism, 'humane learning' and virtuous living, the essence of Croft's 1677 visitation articles for the grammar school.[144] From this, we can gather that there were three essential elements to a cathedral-school education in this period.

Firstly, it was above all else a godly education, a key part of which was the catechism, the short text of Christian doctrine which was capable of being committed to memory. In all probability, it would have been based on one of Dean Nowell's catechisms of 1570 which became the main instrument of the church's religious instruction in the seventeenth century, as required by the 1604 canons when schoolmasters were bidden to teach his longer or shorter catechisms (in English or Latin) 'as the children are able to hear'. Catechising often took place on a Saturday afternoon, as with the grammar schools at Guildford, Chigwell and (nearer home) Newport, Shropshire. Bible teaching, too, was essential, the same article in the 1604 canons (number 79) laying down that upon days other than holy days and festivals the children were to be taught 'such sentences of holy scripture as shall be most expedient to induce then to all godliness'. Regular school prayers were also practised, perhaps twice each day as at Colwall in 1612, and regular church attendance observed on holy and festival days (again as required in 1604), after which pupils were to be examined on the sermons they had heard. Langfordians, like the choristers, were to process in gowns and surplices twice every Sunday, as well as on other festivals. As Foster Watson has observed, 'the whole school round of religious observances, catechisms, primers and Bible-reading show the permeation of the school work with religious instruction'.[145]

Secondly, the statutes and orders indicate that the cultivation of good morals and manners through strict discipline was related to a godly education. The masters were to

143. Foster Watson (pp.38-49, 79-92, 126-36, 316-18) lists extracts from the statutes of some new foundations, relating to religious observance, catechisms, manners and morals and spoken Latin.

144. See above, pp.29, 39, 53 and 55.

145. Foster Watson, pp.34-36, 43, 48, 57, 60.

be exemplars in this respect. As the 1636 statutes put it, they were to form their pupils 'to good conduct as well by their daily discipline as by their own example'. And good conduct, in the terms of the 1665 orders meant 'sober and civil demeanour', including refraining from swearing – 'the epidemical sin of this city' – and clean habits from 'the poorer sort'. The virtues of 'piety, sobriety, modesty and all good discipline' were again emphasised by Bishop Croft in his 1677 visitation. Such rules of conduct for a moral education were advocated by enlightened writers from Erasmus in 1526 to Comenius a century later and similarly enshrined in grammar school statutes over the same period. Even as late as 1693, John Locke in his *Thoughts on Education* stated that virtue, wisdom, manners and learning were the true aims of education – and in that order of importance.[146]

Thirdly, the nature of that learning within a grammar school of this period was almost exclusively literary. At Hereford, there is no evidence that Arithmetic was taught unless it was to the choristers preparing for apprenticeships, Tomson's bequest having provided every third year for the binding of a poor chorister and the 1677 visitation articles making clear that they were to be prepared for their future livelihoods if they could not cope with the rigours of the grammar school. The same visitation, too, shows that the choristers, if they were not fit for grammar, were to be prepared for employment at a writing school. We know that there was a writing school in Hereford several decades earlier at the beginning

Fig. 2.8 John Davies of Hereford, poet and writing-master, celebrated (by Thomas Fuller) as 'the greatest master of the pen that England in her age beheld'.

146. See Foster Watson (pp.98-136) on the teaching of morals and education.

of the seventeenth century, for Richard Gething (1585?-1652?) studied at one under the noted poet and writing-master, John Davies (1564/5-1618), who signified on his title pages that he was the John Davies of Hereford to distinguish himself from his more prominent contemporary namesake, Sir John Davies, the poet. Both the Hereford Davies and Gething may well have been old boys.[147] How far the Usher taught such subjects as penmanship within the Cathedral School is unknown. At the other end of the scale, the highest scholars may have been taught Greek and Hebrew – the 'holy' languages – perhaps even occasionally by the Dean or a canon such as Miles Smith.[148] But these were peripheral subjects for in essence HCS, like other grammar schools of this period, was a Latin school.

Here again there is no extant evidence for our school as to what constituted 'fit' authors or 'good literature', as specified by the 1636 statutes and 1665 orders. Nor do we know what texts might have been used for the seemingly endless round of classical compositions, albeit in the differing forms of letter-writing, theme verses and orations. Charles Hoole, the contemporary educational writer and teacher, considered that over 300 books would have been within the capacities of the mid-seventeenth-century grammar schoolboy. He also advocated an elaborate means of storage for every book, including a library for 'every school of note', although only around one in five grammar schools could lay claim to one according to Wase's survey in the 1670s.[149] The Cathedral School would undoubtedly have been among their number. There survives an eighteenth-century copy of a library list, entitled 'a catalogue of the books in the library belonging to the Free School in Hereford'. Although it includes books such as Richard Bentley's *Horace,* first published in 1712, judging by some of the other books and the school's given title, the list may have originated in the late seventeenth century. It is a catalogue of over 50 specialist works, clearly intended for the consultation by the masters and senior pupils. It comprises alternative grammars, advanced classical texts, historical works, anthologies, commentaries and lexicons, including a Hebrew dictionary and John Minsheu's *Guide into Tongues* (1617), the first book published by subscription, which contained equivalents in eleven languages. The books were mostly in Latin but also included Chaucer's works, and heading the list – appropriately (for a cathedral school) – the works of Charles I 'with his life and martyrdom'.[150] This catalogue was likely to have been incomplete. Nonetheless, the Cathedral School library holdings would have paled into insignificance compared with the seventeenth-century collections of some of the larger schools. Even Lady Hawkins, Kington (founded 1632), could eventually boast 156 printed works from the sixteenth and seventeenth centuries, of which around 100 were *in situ* by September 1673.[151]

147. Although there is no direct evidence of this for either of them, it is a fair presumption.

148. As a Hereford residentiary (1587-1624), Miles Smith, like his fellow translator of the King James' Bible Lancelot Andrews, who as Dean of Westminster in the early seventeenth century 'in the evenings would send for the elder boys to the Deanery, and teach them Greek and Hebrew from eight to eleven o'clock' (Foster Watson, p.497), would have been eminently qualified for this task.

149. *Ibid.*, p.5 and *passim*; Green, pp.47, 50.

150. HCA, 6284. The catalogue does not truly reflect the number of books that would have been in circulation at the school. Cheap editions of grammars, Latin texts, as well as a Bible, prayer book or psalter and an elementary catechism, would have been owned outright or lent to the boys. Green, p.49.

151. P.E. Morgan, pp.46-62; CCCA, Wase MS 390/1, fo 210, report on Kington's 'small library', 26 Sept. 1673.

One item in the Hereford catalogue is a book of orations from Greek and Latin histories. We also know from other sources that boys at the school regularly made Latin speeches. Cathedral and other seventeenth-century accounts record payments to 'scholars that declaimed' when they broke up each Christmas: 4s, 6s or 7s in the 1620s; 10s – the same amount given in 1629-30 to scholars who 'played' at the Dean's house, although whether it was for Latin play-acting or music is uncertain – immediately before the civil war; 10s again at the Restoration, except for 1665 when 8s was given; and the unheard of sum of 20s in December 1646, the year following the fall of the royalist garrison.[152] The mid-1660s payments indicate that the boys were examined by Dr Thomas Good, the residentiary canon (and holder of the valuable Bishop's prebend) from 1660 to 1678, who was an active tutor of Balliol College, Oxford, before the civil war and became its Master in 1672. We can safely assume, therefore, that the boys would have been under scholarly scrutiny during these linguistic trials. However, it is unclear whether the speeches were strictly declamations (themes on disputable topics sometimes delivered extempore), as the payments in the 1620s and 1646 indicate, or whether they were prepared orations on set subjects, which could range from scriptural or moral themes to topics arising from general observation to those relating to praise for a school's benefactor. Nonetheless, the regularity of these public occasions at the end of each Christmas term, when Latin exercises would be delivered, underlines the importance of the teaching of Rhetoric to the highest pupils in a seventeenth-century grammar school.[153] And for the university student – not least the Somerset scholar, who was bidden by the Duchess (under 2d penalty for every default) 'to speak the Latin tongue both in their public and private conferences with one another' as well as give a Latin oration in her memory – the ability to show fluency in Latin speech was even more critical.[154]

But is it possible to gauge how well pupils were taught? Again, the evidence is frustratingly thin. The few surviving answers to Bishop Wren's incomplete 1635 visitation and to Archbishop Laud's 1636 articles give some little indication as to the quality of a boy's learning at this time. The scholars were 'duly taught and well governed by the schoolmaster and Usher' claimed one in 1635; in the following year, we are told that the master of choristers, appointed to catechise his charges, said that he had done so, and that the grammar masters themselves 'well perform their duties, as I hear, and are duly paid'.[155] Such witnesses

---

See, CCCA, Wase 390/3, fos 216-17 for an unidentified school library, *c.*1676; and Green, pp.51-52, for the seventeent-century libraries at Westminster and St Paul's, as well as those at other grammar schools. The 1695 catalogue of Roger Williams, a Hereford bookseller, also survives. It contains 171 items, including dictionaries, lexicons, grammars and other texts which would have been used by the school. Among them were two works by an old boy, James Howell: *Six Cordealls* (1661) and his new English grammar (1662). F.C. Morgan, pp.22-36.

152. HCA, R 601a-R606, R608, R610, clavigers' accounts, miscellaneous payments, 1624-30, 1639-41, 1663-65. The 1646 payments are recorded in BL Add. MS., 16,178, fo 130r, 19 Dec. 1646; and TNA, SP 28/228, part 5, invoice of the same date. Also see the disbursements (of 10s) made by the vicars choral in 1673-74 for the scholars 'at the play' and 'when they acted at the Free School'. HCA, 7003/2/1/1, steward's accounts, 1671-1747. I am grateful to Rosalind Caird for this reference.

153. For declamations and the teaching of Rhetoric: Foster Watson, pp.434-35 and 440ff.

154. *Ibid.*, pp.308-09 on Latin-speaking at the universities; and HCA, 7044/17, pp.103, 113-15, re the spoken Latin requirements for Somerset scholars at both Brasenose and St John's, Cambridge.

155. HCA, 1558, Dr William Skyrme's 29th answer to the articles of 22 Sept. 1635; HCA, 1564, Dr William

do not help us a great deal: as prebendaries, they were hardly either informed or impartial observers; and their answers, often based on hearsay, tell us little more than the question asked. We can, however, learn more about how well the school functioned from the background and careers of the masters themselves.

Of the 16 known Headmasters from 1583 to 1699 whose details can be uncovered, most were appointed in their late twenties, and (as may be expected from the statutes), all were Bachelors or Masters of Arts, the majority holding the higher degree and most graduating from Oxford.[156] Youthful vigour and the holding of a degree did not, of course, necessarily mean that the master was an inspiring or even competent practitioner in the schoolroom. We have seen, for example, that William May MA, despite his being held by Whitgift to be 'skilful in the tongues' and 'painful in teaching', was within months of his appointment in 1583 being criticised by parents and others for his outdated teaching methods. Nevertheless, a number of Hereford Headmasters of the period were distinguished for their scholarship and (for one or two of them) their teaching. Richard Dugard, given leave to study in Cambridge for a year in June 1613, became a noted tutor of Sidney Sussex College and a close friend of Milton.[157] Clement Barksdale, as we have seen, was a doughty polemicist, whose *Cotswold Muse* of 1651, 'presenting some extempore verses to the imitation of young scholars', no doubt succeeded in capturing the imagination of his pupils as these amusing verses demonstrate:

> Is not wondrous hot! O dear
> Father Apollo, shoot thy rays
> more gently: knowest thou not that here
> thy loved muses make their lays?
> Besides, O hear!
> Our plants are young
> and cannot bear
> thy scorching sun.
>
> As tender parents, with their children, may
> go to 'hide and seek' and other childish play,
> so I that should have clos'd this youthly vein
> long since, for your sakes open it again.

Skinner's 9th and 17th answers to Laud's 1636 Articles. Dr Kerry, the cathedral Treasurer who should have been better informed, also reported favourably on the grammar school in his response to Wren's 1635 articles. HCA, 1559, answer no. 28 (partly indecipherable).

156. See appendix below, p.597, for the names of the identifiable Headmasters during this period. The known exceptions in terms of age were Richard Dugard and Joseph Harvey (both of whom were in their early 20s on appointment) and Richard Traherne who was around 31 at the time of his unanimous election on 28 June 1699. Of the 16 known Headmasters, only four (William May, Richard Dugard, William Wakeman and Robert Phillips) took their first degree at Cambridge. None of the 13 Ushers can be identified as Cambridge men.

157. J. and J.A. Venn, part I ii., p.72; HCA, 7031/3, pp.91-92, 25 June 1613 (for the leave). Dugard was allowed to return once every quarter to the school 'at his pleasure'. The one letter (in Latin) from Richard Dugard in the cathedral archives (HCA, 4650, letter, 25 Jan. 1627) deals mainly with university gossip, but also thanks the unnamed recipient for his support in helping him secure his university position.

This print's so fair and bright, in th' others stead,
the letter now invites and cries, 'Come, read'.
My little boys are so tane [taken] with 't that they
printers will be and stationers, they say.
I bid them, be good scholars: to write well
is better than to print or sell.[158]

And in the late seventeenth century, Joseph Harvey's erudition was further recognised by his appointment as cathedral Chancellor. His period in office (as *Archididascalus*) lasted 14 years, and the rule of his successor Robert Phillips, the Westminster disciplinarian, 12 years. These were by far the longest tenures of the period, which suggests that they were, at the least, respected masters.

The 13 Ushers of this period for whom we have names have different profiles. The job was less profitable, carrying half the Headmaster's salary and smaller fees, and the tasks more menial. As with Barksdale and William Harvey, both of whom came from Winchcombe in Gloucestershire and matriculated from Gloucester Hall, it is likely that the Headmaster selected his own Usher, the appointment then being confirmed by the Dean and Chapter. The Headmaster, who was required regularly to examine the Usher's pupils (at least from 1665), would then allocate lesser duties to his junior. The exact nature of the Usher's role at Hereford was not specified but the practice in other grammar schools indicates that it would have involved elementary instruction in basic grammar and possibly hand-writing.[159] As a consequence, the Hereford Ushers of the period were less well qualified than their masters. Although the majority of the 13 attended university not all had completed their degree by the time of their appointment. Thomas Broad, for example, the Usher at the Restoration, was not awarded his degree until 1669, although he had matriculated from Brasenose in July 1656. William Langford, one of his successors and a former Langfordian, had matriculated from Brasenose several years earlier in June 1649 but may never have taken a degree. He died in post in 1680 after some 15 years service at the school. Similarly, Benjamin Prosser, a former Philpotts scholar and Usher for a year or two in the mid-1680s, does not appear to have graduated.[160] Three other Ushers of the late seventeenth century, Charles Manfield (another Langfordian scholar), Thomas Gwillym (a vicar choral at the time of his appointment) and Richard Traherne, were all degree men but of these only Traherne stayed as Usher for any length of time, the other two soon progressing to richer pickings within the church.

Overall, the impression given from an examination of the careers of these Hereford masters, almost all of whom were ordained by the time or soon after their appointment, was that teaching was either a prelude to a clerical career or at best – from the late seventeenth century – an extended employment held in combination with a church living elsewhere. Despite the improved status of teachers from the time of Elizabeth's accession, by 1700,

158. Barksdale, part 1, p.21, 'Upon the school extreme hot in the summer'; p.22, 'To his scholars'; and part 2, p.47, 'Upon the new printing'.

159. Foster Watson, pp.151, 176, 189.

160. *Brasenose Reg.*, i., pp.186, 198. HCA, 7031/3, p.221, 15 Sept. 1663 (for Prosser's election as a Philpott scholar at Brasenose, although he does not appear in the college register.)

in Hereford at least, the age of school-mastering as a single vocation had not yet arrived. And for most of this period, as the grammarian John Brinsley observed in 1612, 'the often change of schoolmasters' could also hinder a pupil's education.[161] But who learned at the Elizabethan and Stuart Cathedral School and how 'towardly' anyway were they for learning?

Of the several thousand boys likely to have gone through the school during these 140 years, for only a few do we have details of their backgrounds. Nevertheless, from these it is possible to determine something of the character of the pupil body.[162] Of prominent individuals, Miles Smith (d.1624) was the son of a Hereford fletcher, a maker of bows and arrows, which trade, despite the development of ordnance in warfare, still flourished in the sixteenth century. John Guillim (1550-1621), a near contemporary who became famed for his *Display of Heraldrie* (1611), was the son of a Gloucestershire gentry family. Richard Gardiner (1590/91-1670), clergyman, benefactor and Oxford's deputy orator, was born in the city in modest circumstances. James Howell (1594?-1666), the first historiographer royal, whose *Familiar Letters* of the 1640s referred to his education at 'a choice methodical school ... under a learned though lashing master' and his carrying 'a calf-leather satchel to school in Hereford',[163] came from a Welsh clerical family. Fitzwilliam Coningsby of Hampton Court (*c*.1595-1666), 'sometime commensal' of the College and 'a scholar in the Free School', had donated books and furnishings to the vicars choral library. He was an MP for the county in 1640-41, a governor of the city during the civil war and a member of one of Herefordshire's dominant families.[164] William Gregory (1625-96) was the son of the rector of Sutton St Nicholas and vicar of Fownhope, the place where Richard Harley and Robert Phillips were also preferred (after resigning their headmasterships at either end of the seventeenth century); and Thomas Traherne (*c*.1637-74), the son of a Hereford shoemaker.

And then there were the choristers whose worldly achievements were of lesser significance. For this period there is no record of the names of any seven choristers serving together simultaneously until the late seventeenth century;[165] and only rarely are the names of all five Dean and Chapter choristers recorded, the clavigers' account of 1644-45, when £5 (in total) was paid to John Lord, Caldicot, Adams, Smith and Black 'for [in lieu of] their gowns',[166] being one exception. Individual names, however, are to be found in the Chapter

161. From Brinsley's *Ludus Literarius* (with regard to the difficulties of teaching writing), as quoted by Foster Watson, p.196.

162. Of the following seven luminaries, all but one (Fitzwilliam Coningsby) are listed in the *ODNB*. In alphabetical order: vols 21, pp.425; 23, pp.687-88; 24, pp.193-94; 28, pp.500-05; 51, pp.259-61; 55, pp.205-08.

163. Jacobs, pp.19, 71, Howell's letters to his father, 1 March 1618; and to Dr Francis Mansell, 25 June 1621.

164. HCA, 7003/1/4, p.317, copy letter from Morgan Cove to Lady Frances Coningsby, 13 Dec. 1766, re Fitzwilliam Coningsby's gifts. Rawlinson, p.58; Duncumb, i., p.589. Coningsby's name, with those of other benefactors, was listed on a vellum parchment (now lost). He graduated from Oxford in 1613, and would have been a pupil at HCS in the early years of the seventeenth century. For an outline of his life: Keeler, pp.139-40.

165. Lists of the seven serving choristers – as recorded by the boys themselves in the Hereford set of John Barnard's part-books, sold by the Chapter for £100 to Christ Church, Oxford, in 1917 – exist for 1687, 1690, 1700, 1720 and 1731. The choristers for these dates are listed in HCA, 5983, chorister magazine, Sept. 1921; and Carless, pp.79-80. For the part books: Aylmer and Tiller, p.401 (especially note 15).

166. HCA, 2384.

Acts at the time of a chorister's appointment but only very occasionally are their families mentioned, as in June 1670 with the election of Richard Rogers, whose father was recorded as being a barber in the city.[167] While at school, as the visitations to the college in 1667 and the cathedral a decade later indicate, the choristers were expected to have the capacity to learn a musical instrument 'useful for church service', as well as sing, but it was recognised that they might not be able to cope with the rigours of Latin grammar.[168] So the academic expectations of choristers were as modest as their backgrounds appear to have been. And after they had left the choir, and probably the school, for they rarely proceeded to one of the universities, they were often found the wherewithal for an apprenticeship, primarily from Tomson's gift.[169] Periodically, other posts came their way as with Richard Floyd, who having been admitted a deacon after his voice broke in May 1688, was appointed sexton seven years later.[170] And for the fortunate, there was the prospect of an incumbency, at least until the closing years of the seventeenth century, as is evident from this Chapter petition to the Archbishop of Canterbury:

> A custom had formerly obtained at Hereford that when choristers had grown to maturity of years, they without any academical education, learning or degrees, were brought into sacred orders (whereof they were very unworthy) and so were presented to benefices in the Dean and Chapter's gift ... whereby they were not only vicars choral but parochial vicars or parsons.

As a result, 'ignorance and disorders ... attended so sorry a ministry and thus the clergy and college were brought into no small contempt'. Within the previous 20 or 30 years, however, the Dean and Chapter had admitted none as vicars 'save such as were bred up in the universities' and taught 'to sing skilfully in the colleges and chapels there'. By 1709, when the petition was presented, all but one of the vicars choral held degrees and – Mr Astrey apart – were proficient singers.[171] So well before 1700, it seemed that even this avenue of preferment had been denied the former singing-boys.

The Langfordians were different, academically certainly and perhaps socially as well. Although Dean Langford's legacy had been directed towards poor local boys, it is doubtful whether many of his scholars fulfilled the terms of his bequest in this regard. Few of the city's labouring poor could have survived for long without their children's labour. And even at Hereford's 'free' school, the 1665 orders show that although the Headmaster had

167. HCA, 7031/3, p.278, 30 June 1670.

168. HCA, 4621, vicars' answers to the visitation, 25 July 1667; and above, p.55, for the 1677 visitation.

169. There is considerable evidence of former choristers receiving payments for apprenticeships: HCA, R602, 10s to 'Howells when he went to London as an apprentice' (1625-26); HCA, 7031/3, pp.258, 278, 303, 348, 395, 397, payments to William Hayfield, Richard Rogers, John Fisher, William Bedford, Charles Gunter, Francis Seaborne and William Badham, 25 June 1667-2 Dec. 1681. Hayfield had been awarded £10, twice as much as later payments, the annual rents from Tomson's legacy having fallen from £16 to £8 by 1673. *Ibid.*, p.302, 26 March 1673.

170. *Ibid.*, p.467, 14 May 1688; p.508, 2 April 1695.

171. HCA, 7003/1/3, pp.230-231, copy of a Dean and Chapter letter to Thomas Tenison, Archbishop of Canterbury, re the election of John Moore as Custos, 1709. An earlier copy survives in HCA, 7003/1/2, first item.

discretion as to the amount, the poor were still required to pay an entrance fee. Moreover, the cost of books, writing paper (the Chapter paid 4d for a quire in 1608-09 and again in 1630-31 but 9s 6d 'for 4 small paper books' in 1662-63), ink, writing implements and wax candles for the winter months – all contained within a satchel – would have put an education, even for a prospective Langfordian, out of reach for the genuinely poor.[172] From what little we know of these scholars, by the mid and late seventeenth century a number were the sons of respectable widows who had fallen upon hard times. Thomas Reading's mother, Elizabeth, who was able to sign her name for her son's Oxford scholarship, was a clerical widow of a former Headmaster.[173] Similarly, the mother of Charles Manfield was the widow of a vicar choral when her boy was placed on the Langfordian list in June 1667; the sons of Widow Owens, Widow Hill of All Saints and Widow Bannister were all considered for the scholarship over the following years; and William Langford, whose mother Elizabeth was probably the widow of the Usher, became a Langfordian in 1681 but he, like his father before him, would have had a stronger claim as founder's kin.[174] And then there were the sons of local tradesmen: John Hancox, was the son of Thomas Hancox, bookseller and stationer; Stephen Phillips, the son of a father of like name who was a 'corviser' or shoemaker; Thomas Rodd, was the son of Humphrey Rodd, a glover; and William Seward, the son of a deceased apothecary also called William, who was no doubt related to the then Chapter Clerk, Abraham Seward.[175] Abraham Fisher, who became a Langfordian in 1684, also had cathedral connections. He was the son of Humphrey (vicar choral and successively of Holmer and Pipe, 1665-1702) who transcribed the college Act books and was largely responsible for the improvement of its library and hall.[176] So as in many of these cases, the gaining of the scholarship depended in part on the good offices of your patron, which again would have put them out of reach of the poverty stricken.

A good recommendation apart, it is unclear whether entrance requirements from prospective Langfordians went beyond the Dean's stipulations in his will. However, we do know, at least from an examination of their future Oxford careers, that some of these scholars were 'towardly for learning'. As the Dean would have anticipated, his scholarships gave greater opportunities for Hereford boys, after a sound education at school, to gain a degree and return to strengthen the church's ministry in the diocese.[177] Roger Philpotts,

172. For the writing implements in use in this period: Foster Watson, pp.190, 194; and for the cost of paper, the entries in these Hereford clavigers' accounts: HCA, R595 (1608-09), R605 (1630-31), R610 (1662-63).

173. TNA, SP 28/228, part 5, receipt 27 Oct. 1646; warrants 24 June, 25 Dec. 1647; SP 28/229, part 1, warrant 17 Jan. 1648; CCCA, MS 390/1, fo 209, Harvey's list, 4 April 1674.

174. HCA, 7031/3, pp.258, 280, 284, 304, 319, 397; Chapter Acts, 28 June 1667, 29 Sept. 1670, 6 April 1671, 25 June 1673, 25 Feb. 1675, 8 July 1681.

175. *Ibid.*, pp.365, 402, 423, 475; Acts, 30 Nov. 1678, 26 June 1682, 25 June 1684, 9 Aug. 1689. For Abraham Seward, see Aylmer and Tiller, pp.116, 549.

176. *Ibid.*, pp. 452, 549; HCA, 7031/3, p.434, Chapter Act, 4 Dec. 1684.

177. Indeed, in the Hereford diocese, it has been estimated (Marshall (2009), p.85) that in the seventeenth century around one in four of the parishes with Oxford graduates had Brasenose men. Moreover, during the period 1558-1688, at least 17 Herefordshire schoolboys with Brasenose connections eventually became Hereford Cathedral prebendaries. These included three Deans (Charles Langford, Silvanus Griffiths and John Tyler) and five residentiary canons (Miles Smith, John Best, William Skinner, Stephen Phillips sr and William Watts sr), many of whom would have been old boys as well as the school's governors. In addition, Thomas Singleton (residentiary, 1605-14)

another Brasenose *alumnus*, then strengthened the school's link with a college which has been described as being (in the early seventeenth century) 'theologically Calvinist, institutionally Episcopalian and presentationally evangelical'.[178] A firm relationship had already been established between the school, cathedral foundation and college during Elizabeth I's reign (1558-1602), when 62 Herefordshire boys are listed in the Brasenose registers as having connections with the college. In the seventeenth century these numbers increased: 70 in James I's reign (1603-25); 51 under Charles I (1625-59); 14 during the Interregnum (1649-60); and 99 from 1660-1702, during which period the first of the school's Somerset scholars was elected.[179] Not all the 300 or so Herefordshire boys identified over this period as having had a Brasenose connection were *alumni* of the school. A number of the sons of leading county families would have been educated at national boarding schools, if not privately, and some local boys would have found their way to university from one of the county's other grammar schools despite their limited endowments.[180] Nevertheless, many Herefordshire Brasenose men are likely to have been old boys. Of these, only a minority were former Langfordians; and not all the Langford scholars would have gone on to Oxford let alone taken a degree there.[181] But the expectation was that Langfordians should complete their education at Oxford, as is evident from the Chapter Act of 26 June 1682, when John Hancox's school scholarship was described as being vacated as he had been 'admitted a Langfordian at the University of Oxford according to Mr Philpotts' will'.[182] Thanks to the munificence of the school's benefactors in this period, many other boys 'towardly for learning' also took advantage of their good fortune.

It took an exceptional and unworldly boy to be 'towardly' all the time. And most schoolboys are not like that even when faced with the threat of physical punishment. We get occasional glimpses later in the period of poor behaviour from individual choristers and Langfordians. The chorister William Roberts, for example, was given a last chance to mend his ways. However, if in future he was found 'drinking, swearing, cursing, fighting or neglecting his duty in the church', the hebdomadary (the duty member of Chapter) was 'to out him'. Around the same time in June 1683, John Silvester was turned out of his Dean's

---

was Principal of Brasenose and the college's first university Vice-Chancellor (1598-99, 1611-14). Outside the established church, the Herefordshire/BNC connection produced one cathedral Presbyterian minister (William Voyle) and the founder of the Welsh Baptists (John Miles).

178. Crook, p.43.

179. Thomas Smith, elected on 21 September 1691, was the 13th boy (but 12th in terms of election) on the college's list of Somerset (Thornhill) scholars from 1680 and the first who can be identified with the Cathedral School, he being admitted as a Langfordian on 30 June 1683. (*Brasenose Reg*., ii., p.124; HCA, 7031/3, p.411.) The numbers of Herefordshire boys at BNC have been calculated from the college register, pp.28-278.

180. From the evidence presented to Wase in the 1670s, the stronger 'Free Schools' in Herefordshire appear to have been at Colwall, Kington, Ledbury, Leominster and (from 1663) Weobley. CCCA, MS 390/1, fos 197-208, school returns *c*.1673-74.

181. From the only complete list we have of serving Langford scholars, as listed in the receipt of 27 October 1646 (TNA, SP 28/228, part 5), five of the eight boys who signed for their scholarship are known to have been admitted to Oxford colleges (two, Reading and Langford, at Brasenose), and only two (Reading and, possibly, Phillips) are likely to have taken their degree.

182. HCA, 7031/3, p.402.

scholarship for 'absenting himself from school and choir since Easter last and for breaking the new brick wall, abusing the verger and for several other miscarriages'. Silvester was replaced by Charles Tucker but he, too, was upbraided by the Chapter for 'not going legally from school' and his Oxford allowance was eventually withdrawn.[183] Some years afterwards, it was enacted that no Langfordian should 'have the exhibition that goes to Oxford before the Dean and Chapter be acquainted with his or their going', so his may not have been an isolated case.[184]

There is no evidence implicating cathedral schoolboys during this period with involvement in the type of ill-discipline common in other schools of the time. There are no indications of boys having carved their names on the walls of the schoolroom or on their desks, even supposing that the grammar boys like the choristers (by 1617-18) wrote on desks rather than their knees.[185] There are no records of boys having left their lofted eyrie, as they surely must have done, on their 'necessary occasions, real or pretended'.[186] There are no specific instances of boys having deliberately broken windows – window-smashing was a regular occurrence at many schools of the time, not least at the end of term or on a master's departure – although given the number of payments to glaziers for schoolroom repairs recorded in the cathedral fabric accounts it is tempting to suggest that this regularly happened.[187] Whether these reparations were the result of barring-out – a mode of schoolboy rebellion, especially prevalent in the midlands and north of the country, when masters were shut out from the schoolroom until the boys' demands were conceded – is, of course, another question.[188] One specific example of riotous behaviour among Hereford schoolboys to have been recorded again concerns the choristers. It occurred during the late summer of 1676 and involved persecution of the Quakers. After a warning given by Henry Caldicott, that year's Hereford mayor, against their unlawful assembly, and a series of assaults on their meeting-house, the following incident appears to have taken place within the city:

183. *Ibid.*, pp.409, 413, 418, 477, Chapter Acts, 2 Dec. 1682, 30 June 1683, 7 Nov. 1689. Tucker was noted as 'now gone' on 25 June 1685 (*ibid.*, p.249), and matriculated from Brasenose on 22 April 1687, aged 17. *Ibid.*, p.249; *Brasenose Reg.*, i., p.254. He may, therefore, have absconded from HCS and gone to Gloucester to complete his school education as he is noted in the BNC register as hailing from 'Gloucs. or Herefs.'.

184. *Ibid.*, p.515, 25 June 1697.

185. HCA, R601, fo 8v, 2s 8d payment to Thomas Smith for two locks for the choristers' desks. For boys' carvings in the late nineteenth century on the then playground wall (now the wall of the organist's garden), see Fig. 6.5 (p.257, below).

186. Parkinson, p.15. For repairs to the school 'privihouse' or 'boghouse' in 1742 and 1748: HCA, 5715/2/13, 19, fabric vouchers, 18 Jan. 1742, 1 Oct. 1748.

187. For example, see the following payments: HCA, R600 (1612-13), 10s to Morgan, the plumber; R604 (1629-30), 3s to 'Mr Reading' for glazing (and 10s to Matthew the mason for repairing the school door); R606 (1639-40) £10 17s (the largest single disbursement for the year) to Morgan, the plumber for unspecified work done in the school; TNA, 0 SP 28/229, part 1, warrant 19 Jan. 1649, for payment of £5 5s to John Probin and Hosea Best for various works including 51 feet of new glass for the school.

188. At Durham, the Chapter had prohibited the practice in 1595. For the tradition of barring-out: Thomas, pp.21-35; for an example at King Edward's School, Birmingham (on 26, 28 Nov. 1667) which ended in riot: Cressy, pp.93-94; and for a much later incident at HCS: below, pp.162-63.

> On the 17th [September], the outrageous mob, part of which were choristers or singing-boys of the cathedral, encouraged by their superiors, broke in pieces the remainder of the glass windows with the window frames and some of the walls of the house. After meeting they pursued the country friends, pelting them with stones, about a quarter of a mile.

But as is hinted at here, the choristers' behaviour does not seem to have been regarded by the cathedral authorities as a serious breach of discipline. Indeed, a day or two later Walter Rogers, one of the residentiary canons, is alleged to have said that 'they who did it were very good boys and had done their work better than he [had] thought ...'[189]

Despite such acts, the school's position as it entered the new century was far stronger than it had been at the beginning of the Elizabethan age. Over these 140 years, it had evolved from the Chancellor's school to a cathedral grammar school; gained valuable endowments; secured the education of the choristers; acquired a permanent schoolroom within the Close; and had put the masters' remuneration on a sounder footing. As a testimony to its efficiency, moreover, it had also produced some 'towardly' pupils who were to make their mark in the world.

But, as we have seen, we know the names of only a small proportion of these pupils: hundreds more who passed through the school's doors have been lost to posterity. It is likely, however, that as at other grammar schools, they came from a wide range of social backgrounds, judging by surviving records of entrance fees charged by masters elsewhere. At Shrewsbury School in the 1570s, for example, the sons of a lord were charged 10s; sons of knights and gentlemen (eldest sons were charged more) 6s 8d, 3s 4d or 2s 6d; 'those of lower degree' either 2s, for those born out of the county, or 1s; and sons of local inhabitants, depending on whether they were burgesses or not, 8d or 4d. At Kington 60 years later, local boys were to be educated free but there was a 5s entrance fee for the son of a knight or gentleman, 2s 6d for a yeoman's son and 1s for 'the poorer sort', as well as an additional charge of 5s quarterly in advance.[190] Although there are no extant accounts of the fees levied at Hereford, the 1665 orders indicate that a similar sliding-scale operated, differential fees being paid by the sons of freemen, 'foreigners' and the poor, the Headmaster having considerable discretion as to the exact amount. The social range encompassed by the pupil population was further emphasised when the 'poorer sort' were not to offend 'others of better quality' by their unkempt habits. Despite a handful of Langfordians during the late seventeenth century matriculating at Brasenose as 'poor boys',[191] the 'poorer sort', as has been shown, were probably not as destitute as Dean Langford would have liked and few, if any, of those of 'better quality' would have been sons of peers. But Fitzwilliam Coningsby cannot have been the only member of the local gentry to have been educated at the school

189. Besse, i., p.259. I am indebted to Michael Tavinor for this reference. The persecution of local Quakers in 1676 may be compared with their situation a 100 years later, when at their annual meeting in Hereford it was reported that 'they were treated by the inhabitants of all ranks with the politeness and attention due to so useful, inoffensive and worth a sect'. *HJ,* 28 Sept. 1780.

190. O'Day, p.32; P.E. Morgan, p.46.

191. For example: William Caldicot (1667), Francis Owens (1673) and John Hancox (1682). *Brasenose Reg.*, i., pp.217, 229, 146.

in the late sixteenth and seventeenth centuries, even though they would have been outnumbered by sons of clergy, freemen and the 'middling' classes. Few of these pupils would have been scholars in the modern sense but most would have gained a grounding in Latin, together with a knowledge of 'true religion' and 'civility', which would have served them in good stead in life as well as the learned professions.

And during their time at school they would not only have had to suffer the rigours of a largely classical curriculum over at least an eight hour day six days a week but also survive the conditions of a cloistered medieval schoolroom, an upper chamber which as Barkesdale himself acknowledged could be 'extreme hot in the summer', and presumably desperately cold and gloomy in the winter months. Not that it was all academic grind as the 1685 Chapter Act indicates. Indeed, the restriction of 'play days' to Tuesday or Thursday afternoons, with the further proviso that no additional days should be sanctioned without proper ecclesiastical authorisation, indicates that the masters had previously been too lenient in bowing to requests for holidays from influential outsiders. Masters as well as pupils needed breaks from the academic drudgery. And no doubt Joseph Harvey (whose successor was required to abide by the 1685 provisions) had been as pleased to submit to a grandee's request for time off for his pupils as Sir Hugh Evans was in *The Merry Wives of Windsor* when Master Slender obtained leave for the boys to play.[192] While Harvey attended his other clerical duties, perhaps some of his boys, like their contemporaries elsewhere, were indulging in activities such as shooting with long bows, chess, wrestling, leaping, driving a top or tossing a handball.[193]

Nevertheless, despite the play days, occasional church holy days and longer vacations – perhaps six weeks annually taken around the Christmas, Easter and Whitsun festivals – the school system of these times appears to modern eyes to be a repressive, limited and largely untempered regime. It is telling, as Keith Thomas has pointed out, that the attitude of old boys at the feasts and reunions which sprang up for the larger schools in the late seventeenth century seems to have been one of self-congratulation at having survived such an ordeal.[194] Yet notwithstanding the privations, the grammar schools of the late Tudor and Stuart period produced, in the words of another authority, 'a fine breed of men and eminent scholars'.[195] One such was our own Miles Smith, Bishop of Gloucester , who wrote the preface and was one of the key translators of the King James' Bible, and of whom this was written in the decade after his death:

> For his sufficiency in learning, as therein I suppose he was inferior to none, either for knowledge in divinity or skill in the eastern tongues, so joining to the height of his knowledge the humility of his mind, for my part I must confess that I never knew nor heard of his match.

192. Act IV, scene 1. For the granting of play days in this period: Thomas, pp.17-20.

193. Vincent, (1969), p.59.

194. Thomas, pp.14-15.

195. Vincent (1969), p.90.

From his youth, his biographer continued, 'he constantly applied himself ... to the reading of ancient classical authors of the best note in their own languages ... and lusted after no worldly thing so much as books'.[196] (Plate 2).

Few schoolboys could have matched Miles Smith's erudition, but whether they had been tutored by kindly masters or, like James Howell, had suffered under 'a learned though lashing master', the Cathedral School had helped form them as at least one old boy of the period later acknowledged in print. This heartfelt dedication to his *alma mater* in *Specimen Oratorium* (1653), written originally in elegant Latin, was penned by Dr Richard Gardiner, the Oxford public orator, around 50 years after he had attended the Cathedral School in the early years of the seventeenth century:

> In token of his gratitude, Richard Gardiner, author and augmenter of the present collection [of sermons], dedicates this meagre testimony of his highest good will to Hereford's Free School, where, in his tender years, under Christ's auspices, he spent his time, to good effect, on the fostering of liberal studies and his early schooling.

It was Gardiner, too, who gave the ingenious rebus that was painted on the screen of College Hall, to the vicars choral in gratitude for the happy hours he had spent there as their resident dining companion.[197] (Plate 3). Nor did he neglect his home city. He endowed £100 for the relief of six 'poor and indigent' Hereford housekeepers and for the binding of a poor child 'apprentice to some handicraft trade'; together with a similar sum, to be lent out as interest free loans in £20 lots, to further the trades of 'five honest and sober citizens of Hereford, not being ale-sellers or vintners or bearing any office or benefit'. Like other benefactors of this philanthropic age, Richard Gardiner remembered the place of his birth and early schooling with affection and gratitude.[198]

---

196. J.S., biographical preface, in Miles Smith, *Sermons of the ... Bishop of Gloucester* (1632).

197. HCA, 7003/1/1, p.223, for Gardiner's rental of a chamber at the College, 2 Sept. 1642.

198. And, it should be added, his old university. The Hereford gifts (the first of which resulted in a £6 annual rental from the purchase of the 20 acre Wear meadow) were administered by the city corporation and are detailed in the *Report of the Commissioners Concerning Charities*, xiii (1815-39), part 2, pp.33-34. For Gardiner's donations and benefactions to Christ Church, Oxford: *ODNB*, vol. 21, p.425.

Chapter 3

The 'Settled' Century?: The School, 1697-1803

The late sixteenth and seventeenth centuries had seen HCS firmly established as an endowed cathedral school. By contrast, the school during the eighteenth century was both unchanged in its governance and lacking in significant new endowments. This did not mean, however, that it was a period without development. Still less does it indicate that it was one of 'slumber' for either the city or its cathedral, as Arthur Bannister, cathedral residentiary and school governor, 1909-36, implied when writing the cathedral's history in the early 1920s.[1] To Canon Bannister, the cathedral may have seemed 'settled' compared with what came before, but its school in the years from the disputed election and headmastership of Richard Traherne (1697-1731) to Robert Squire's tenure (1784-1803), did not endure a period of stagnation. Indeed, there is sufficient evidence to suggest that the Cathedral School made important advances over these years. Like the church in the Hereford diocese (and, in truth, the cathedral itself), the eighteenth-century Cathedral School was 'neither asleep nor decadent'.[2]

It is true, however, that by 1700 the great period of grammar school endowment had passed. In terms of educational philanthropy, and quite apart from the numerous private academies established in the eighteenth century, the real weight of charitable giving in this period went towards the establishment of elementary charity schools. These were designed for the teaching of English, reading, writing, and some accounts, as opposed to the endowment of classical grammar schools for the poor. Under the auspices of the Society for the Promotion of Christian Knowledge from 1699, thousands of these charity schools were founded during this century, often by local public subscription encouraged by charity sermons. One such was established in Hereford in 1710. Within a decade, it was educating 60 boys and 40 girls, the distinctive blue coats that they wore around the city being a constant reminder to the local population of their support for the Blue Coat School, and not least the Dean and Chapter and corporation, which bodies subscribed £15 and £20 respectively each year towards the school's maintenance.[3] By way of contrast, only 128

1. Bannister, p.101, in a chapter entitled 'The Settled Centuries'.

2. Marshall (2009), p.209. Also see the author's chapter in Aylmer and Tiller, pp.122ff, for the eighteenth-century cathedral.

3. Marshall (2009), pp.116, 119; HCA, 7100/1, clavigers' accounts, payments from 1712-13; HARC, BG 11/1

grammar schools, 19 fewer than in the 54 years of the later Stuart period (1660-1714), were founded during the whole of the eighteenth century. Lucton School, founded by John Pierrepont in 1708 and endowed with tithes from five Herefordshire parishes, was one of these eighteenth-century grammar school foundations.[4]

On the other hand, no significant new endowments were received by the Cathedral School during this century.[5] However, the income from the Langford and Philpotts estates, like the Somerset foundations at the school's colleges, markedly increased through better management in the 1790s. The Langford estate at Disserth, which brought in an annual revenue of £24 for most of the century, was realising £54 18s by 1798. As a consequence, the annual payment to each Hereford Langfordian almost doubled over the century: from £2 13s 4d at its start to £4 3s 4d before its end. Similarly, the accumulated revenue from Philpotts' house in High Town had increased to £290 by 1802-03, although Oxford Langfordians do not seem to have been beneficiaries of this increase.[6]

The school's governance remained unchanged throughout this century. The Dean and Chapter's overwhelming concern during these years was that the cathedral's statutes should be properly fulfilled. As we will see with Richard Traherne's eventual unanimous election to the headmastership in 1698, this could mean that an appointment was subject to the conflicting pressures of factions within the Chapter, thereby delaying the decision (in Traherne's case) by over 18 months while the appeal process to the diocesan and metropolitan was played out. This could hardly have been in the school's best interests. But the Hereford residentiary canons exercised due diligence over the election, as well as such matters as the clothing of its five choristers (the clavigers' accounts giving a detailed annual account of the sums spent on apparel), the appointment of Langfordian scholars, the proper administration of Philpotts' bequest to Langfordians at Brasenose and the £4 annual payment to their Oxford scholar.[7] And from time to time, as can be seen from the thousands of extant tradesmen's bills, they paid for the repair of the schoolhouse, and in 1700 even provided for the building of a 'necessary house' or 'house of office' from old brick and 'other rubbish stone' for the boys' comfort.[8] Apart from these time-honoured duties and very occasional admonitions to boys for their misbehaviour, there is little evidence to suggest that the cathedral

---

A/2, fo 11v, no date but after 19 Nov. 1709.

4. Marshall (2009), p.116; Vincent (1969), p.16; Carlisle, i., p.503.

5. In terms of new endowments, the 1698 bequest of Robert Jones ('late of Cheltenham' but the legacy appears to have been based on a house in Widemarsh Street), who provided for a £1 gift to be made to the Headmaster annually (10s for teaching and 10s for books) to educate a boy from All Saints parish, should be noted. These payments were later transferred to the Blue Coat School. HCA, 7031/4, p.125, Chapter Act re new trustees, 9 May 1727; *Report of the Commissioners Concerning Charities*, xiii (1815-39), part 2, pp.330-31.

6. Figures from HCA, 7104/2-4, accounts of the Langford (and Tomson) estates, from 1719/20, and the Philpotts estate from 1778-79; HCA, 7105/2, pp.179-18, 199-200, consolidated accounts for both estates.

7. The £4 payment continued throughout the century. For example: HCA, 7031/4, pp.369, 424, 450; 7031/5, pp. 48, 96, 225r, 291v, Chapter Acts, 8 Nov. 1769-8 Nov. 1792. The regulation of awards to Langfordians at Oxford (following the Headmaster's recommendation) was enshrined in the Chapter's standing orders of 1713. HCA, 7031/4 (back), nos 4 to 6.

8. The boghouse was built on adjacent land belonging to the vicar of St John the Baptist (Thomas Gwillim, formerly Usher of the school). HCA, 7031/3, p.532, Chapter Act 14 Nov. 1700. Thirty years later, a new one was built. See below, p.82.

authorities took an active interest in the school's fortunes despite the injunction in Croft's 1677 visitation articles that the Dean and Chapter should formally examine the scholars twice each year. Even the 10s payment to scholars 'at their breaking up' drops out as an item in the accounts at the beginning of the century.[9] Presumably, given the lack of contrary evidence, and with the notable exception of Abraham Rudd who lost office in 1782 when he became insolvent, the Dean and Chapter, like the eighteenth-century bishops at their visitations, were generally satisfied that the masters continued to teach and act in accord with their responsibilities under the 1636 Laudian statutes.

Of the six eighteenth-century Headmasters, the first three were home grown and knew the school well on appointment, being both old boys (in all probability) and former Ushers. Indeed, one of them, John Stephens, had received the full gamut of the cathedral's educational patronage. Whether this inbreeding brought about any stagnancy in the school's management in the first half of the century, as it might well have done when more often than not both Headmaster and Usher were old boys, is impossible to tell. In the second half, however, the three 'foreign' Headmasters (at least in origins) made up for any insularity in their earlier Georgian predecessors by introducing some important changes to the school's operation. But there were also similarities between the century's Headmasters: all six were ordained and five held an MA or higher degree on their appointment (Traherne being the exception); all were given Chapter livings to supplement their statutory salary; and five out of our six incumbents (again bar Traherne) were prebendaries, the Hereford bishops from James Beauclerk's long episcopate (1746-87) onwards using the office to help support the cathedral foundation as well as to recognise outstanding clergy.[10] However, there is nothing to suggest that the school, as opposed to the Headmasters' parishes which would have been administered by a curate at least during term-time, suffered by this arrangement.[11] The Cathedral School Headmasters of the period seem to have resided mainly in their Close house – there is no evidence of any absenteeism – and to have regarded teaching as their main profession.[12]

What of their teaching and pupils? Their curriculum, at least for the early part of the century, probably remained an unchanged diet of Classics and Religious Instruction. Before its end, Squire had ensured that it had broadened considerably so that an observer could report that 'besides the Classics and a regular preparation for the university, the Mathematics, Drawing, French, Accompts etc. are taught by proper masters in the same school which has for a long time past been conducted upon the true principles of a public institution'.[13] And for the first time, we can also be certain that by the 1790s the boys were playing vigorous – and unsupervised – games within the cathedral precincts. No register

9. The last clavigers' account I have found with this entry is that of 1700-01. HCA, 7100/1.

10. Le Neve (2014), pp.90, 119 (Willim); 80, 99 (Stephens); 33, 91, 120, 141 (Bagnall); 59 (Rudd); 34, 91 (Squire). Bagnall was the one eighteenth-century Headmaster to be installed as a prebendary before his magisterial election.

11. And even the ill effects of non-residence in parishes have been exaggerated, as Marshall (2009, p.87) has demonstrated from the Hereford diocesan visitation returns of 1716, 1719 and 1722.

12. For the growth of school-mastering as a profession in the first part of this period: Holmes, pp.43-80.

13. Price, p.137.

of pupil names for this period survives so we have little idea as to who these boys were. As in the previous century, we know most about the foundationers, many of whom were tradesmen's sons, which ensured that the school continued to educate boys from diverse backgrounds. Former choristers continued to be apprenticed and benefit from Tomson's bequest, although a greater number now went on to university and then returned to the cathedral choir as vicars choral. Langfordians and other boys still progressed to Oxford, but at an older age and increasingly to Cambridge as well through the Somerset legacy. They, too, sometimes returned to benefices within Herefordshire, the still significant (although declining) number of Brasenose men in the county's parishes testifying to the school's continued importance in supplying clergy for the diocese.[14] Few of these clergy became bishops or cathedral canons. Even fewer Old Herefordians of this century became distinguished in other fields. But the advent from the 1780s of OH dinners at local hostelries – and briefly, for a time, in London – is testimony to the growing corporate strength of the school's old boys.

In terms of the school's foundation, then, the eighteenth century brought no change. The longer tenures of its Headmasters – of the six during this period only Rudd failed to complete at least ten years in office, in marked contrast to many of their predecessors – also provided greater continuity, as often did the Ushers at the times when a new Headmaster was appointed. This does not mean, however, that there were no major structural developments. Indeed, the school's very name changed as the century progressed, being described initially as a Free School, then as a free-grammar or simply a grammar school, and eventually from 1785 as a college school, but not yet widely as a cathedral school. Before 1800, too, two extended holidays either side of four to five month terms, had been established. And while Classics remained a schoolboy's staple academic diet, the curriculum was broadened as has already been indicated.

The school's physical development in the late eighteenth century was as significant. Its eventual acquisition of the music or Great Room in 1778, built early the previous decade for Hereford's triennial music meeting and other charitable causes, was a significant advance on its cloistered medieval schoolroom. Similarly, the Headmaster's house was rebuilt in 1778-79, in part – and to his later financial embarrassment – at Rudd's own expense, and further refurbished by Squire, so that by the end of the period it was described as having 'several good apartments' and being 'well adapted for the accommodation of pupils'.[15] These alterations would have given rise to an increase in numbers, especially gentlemen boarders upon whom the Headmaster's income in part depended. The expansion here was a reflection of a wider catchment brought about by improved travel to the city through the stage-coach's arrival in the second half of the century. By the early 1800s, two companies were operating ten stage-coaches running return journeys several times each week from the new City Arms, the Green Dragon and the Greyhound hotels to London, Bath, Bristol, Holyhead, Milford

14. By 1759, the proportion of Brasenose graduates in Herefordshire parishes with Oxford educated clergy had dropped from one in four to 15.4 *per cent*, but among these men it still remained the most popular college. Marshall (2009), p.85.

15. Rees, p.105.

Haven and points between.[16] The coaches even served the Hereford ladies' boarding schools which 'drew pupils from a considerable distance' and were 'in high repute' at this time.[17]

Such advances should also be put in the context of the city's development in the late eighteenth century. Early in the century Hereford was often described by observant travellers as being old, mean-built and dirty.[18] And even by 1774, the clauses of the Paving, Cleansing and Lighting Act, passed three years after Dean Wetherell (in his capacity as the university Vice-Chancellor) had helped draft the Oxford Improvement Act, reveal that the city's streets were in a poor condition, ill-lit and 'dangerous for carriages and persons passing on horseback and on trot', and that many of its buildings were 'ruinous'. This Act provided the legal framework for such measures as the paving, lighting and widening of the streets; the prohibition of street fireworks, bonfires and abattoirs; the restriction of boghouse clearances to the early hours; and the enclosure of Widemarsh and Monk Moor.[19] Such were the improvements, that John Price a generation later reckoned that the city possessed nine broad and well-paved streets.[20] Its stock of public buildings, their construction a testimony to the public spirit and social conscience of their private benefactors, also increased in the latter half of the century. In addition to the Great Room, an infirmary on the bank of the Wye was opened in 1783; a modern county gaol was built, 1793-96, to John Nash's severe neo-classical style; and a new lunatic asylum was erected the following year. James Wyatt was responsible for the design of the cathedral's west front, following its collapse on Easter Monday 1786, the building being completed in time for the opening service of the three choirs in September 1795. As with the school itself, Hereford's physical changes in the last decades of the century were marked during this period, not least the alterations to the market hall and the gradual dismantling of the city gates and walls.[21]

So by the beginning of the nineteenth century, Hereford was coming to terms with the modern age. Its population, too, had grown from an estimate of 5,592 in 1757 (including 1,776 people without the walls) to 6,828 by the time of the 1801 census, a marked increase for a small city.[22] By the time of the census, too, its main school – it is

16. *Ibid.*, pp.155-56.

17. *Ibid.*, pp.65, 153. Rees lists such schools in St Owen's Street (Miss Cook), Widemarsh Street (Miss Griffiths) and Harley Court (Mrs Lincoln), together with reading and writing schools and various music, dancing, drawing and French masters.

18. For instance: Defoe, ii., p.50; Cox, *Magna Britannia*, p.928; and Macky, ii., p.137. The views of these more authoritative observers may be compared with the opinion of Celia Fiennes, who in her visit to 'Herriford' around 1696 thought that it was 'a pretty little town of timber buildings' and that its streets were 'well pitched and handsome as to breadth and length'. Morris, p.65.

19. 14 Geo. 3. c. 38 for the 1774 Act; and *VCH, Oxon.* iv., pp.188-89, 232-33 and Darwall-Smith, p.291, for Wetherell and the Oxford Improvement Act.

20. Price, pp.59-60. The streets were: St Owen's, Bye Street, High Town, Widemarsh Street, and Eign, Broad, Castle, King and Wyebridge Streets.

21. For these developments: Lobel, i., p.11; Aylmer and Tiller, p.142; Johnson and Shoesmith, chapter 12. Some idea of the city's alterations in this period may also be gained from its Common Council minute books: HARC, BG 11/1 A3 (1755-78) and BG 11/1 A4 (1776-99).

22. J. Taylor's map, published 21 March 1757; 1801 census. The expansion is even more marked within the city walls: from 3,826 in 1757 to 6,224 (for the five central parishes, excluding 604 people living outside the walls in St Martin's parish) in 1801, a population increase of nearly two-thirds.

'the cathedral or college grammar school [which] claims first notice' as one guide rightly observed[23] – like the new brick-clad fronts pinned onto the old timber-framed houses of its Castle Street neighbours, was adapting to the Georgian era. Its steady governance, endowments and university connections, as well as the competence and longevity of most of its Headmasters, had ensured that it neither suffered the same fate as some rural grammar schools, nor justified Lord Chief Justice Kenyon's famous 1795 description of grammar schools as 'empty walls without scholars and everything neglected but the receipt of salaries and emoluments'.[24]

The Three Headmasters, 1697-1762

The school's stability, in terms of the length of Headmasters' tenures, during the last 30 years of the seventeenth century continued into the eighteenth. Indeed, only three men held this office during these 64 years, the first, Richard Traherne, holding the post for over 30 years, the longest known headmastership in the Cathedral School's history.

Richard Traherne (son of John) was a native of the city and probably an old boy. If so, he was educated under Joseph Harvey in the late 1670s and early 1680s, progressing at the age of 17 in 1685 to Christ Church, Oxford, and taking his BA degree four years later in the early months of the Glorious Revolution. He then returned to Hereford. Like Charles Manfield before him, he turned to school-mastering, becoming Phillips' Usher in late 1689. Although continuing with his teaching career, he also held the livings of Dinedor from 1692 and Little Birch from 1706.[25] It was on Phillips' resignation in November 1697 that Traherne assumed his master's mantle – illegally, as it turned out – and there followed a turbulent 18 months for both the school and the new assumed Headmaster.

The story may be briefly told. John Tyler had succeeded Benson as Dean in October 1692. Five years later, at the time of Phillips' resignation, he had refused to endorse the action of four residentiaries – the fifth member of the Chapter, William Watts, 'although sent to' was conveniently absent from the cathedral – who independently and (as it turned out) unlawfully, elected the Usher, Richard Traherne, as Phillips' successor. We do not know why Tyler acted as he did. As a man of Herefordshire – he had attended Lady Hawkins' school at Kington – and near contemporary of Thomas Traherne, perhaps he had a personal grudge against the family; perhaps the Dean thought that it was unwise to promote a lowly Usher without an MA to the headmastership; perhaps Traherne's political or religious views were inimical to those of the moderate Whig Dean; or perhaps Tyler had another candidate in mind; or perhaps it was a combination of these things. Whatever his reasoning, the wrangle between the Dean and his Chapter meant that for 18 months from November 1697 the school was without a lawful Headmaster. The Dean successfully

23. Rees, p.64.

24. Quoted by Tompson, p.100. The case concerned the Archbishop of York's right to examine a candidate for a schoolmaster's licence. For the state of some grammar schools in the late eighteenth century, also see Vincent (1969), pp.20-21 and O'Day, pp.200ff. It is significant that almost half of the 21 'Free Schools' in the Hereford diocese listed by Christopher Wase *c.*1675 had disappeared by the time of Nicholas Carlisle's 1818 survey: CCCA, Wase Mss 390/3, fo 192; Carlisle, i., pp.480-507; ii., pp.340-99.

25. Foster (1891-2), iv., p.1502. HCA, 7031/3, p.477, Act appointing Traherne as 'under schoolmaster', in Thomas Gwillym's place, 7 Nov. 1689. For Manfield: see above, p.56 note 134.

appealed to Bishop Ironside of Hereford. Dr Ottley, one of the residentiaries, then made his pitch on the Chapter's behalf to the Archbishop of Canterbury. This, in turn, prompted a learned counter-appeal from Dean Tyler to Lambeth as to why Traherne's election was invalid. Eventually, on 28 June 1699, after much ink had been spilt 'and for the amicable composure of this difference', the Dean and his Chapter proceeded to a new election 'upon the voluntary resignation of the said Mr Richard Traherne and the cancelling of his patent', which resulted in the proper election of Traherne as Headmaster and Thomas Jones as Usher 'of the Free School'.[26] How the school managed during this time of uncertainty is unknown, but we can safely assume that in the last years of the seventeenth century, even if Traherne was in actual 'possession of the school',[27] it would have lacked firm direction as a consequence of the conflict between the Dean and his canons over the suitability of Richard Traherne for the post to which he was eventually unanimously and legally appointed.

There is little to suggest that Traherne's unfortunate start to his tenure presaged a stormy career as Headmaster. Indeed, quite the opposite seems to have applied. John Tyler, who continued as Dean until his death, aged 91, in July 1724,[28] made no further attempt to unseat Traherne which indicates that the dispute was as much to do with correct protocol as with the choice of candidate. So for the first quarter of the eighteenth century the Cathedral School was governed by the same Dean. The same team of Traherne as Headmaster and John Andrews (his fellow Christ Church student) as Usher also taught there together for over 20 years from 1708 to 1730.[29] In such circumstances, it is likely that the conduct of the school continued much as before. Certainly, the surviving records, such as they are, indicate that the masters and their governors were faced with the same age-old issues. Under Traherne's rule, Langfordians continued to benefit from Philpotts exhibitions to Brasenose, although the Chapter's standing orders of 1713 tightened up their award.[30] Nor is it surprising to learn that some boys continued to misbehave, as indicated (for example) by the new 1710 visitation article which advocated an officer's appointment to regulate the boys' play.[31] Periodic restorations, too, continued to be made to the school's fabric. The re-glazing of windows and repair of doors perhaps were a direct consequence of over-exuberant youth; other repairs like the building of a new fence between the schoolhouse

26. HCA, 7031/3, pp.517, 526, Acts, 11 Nov. 1697, 28 June 1699. Dean Tyler's submissions are to be found in HCA, 1533.

27. As Ottley seems to have indicated in his appeal. *Ibid.*, document K, point 7.

28. Bodl., MS Willis 81, fo 28r. Tyler died on either the 6th or 8th July (Le Neve (2014), p.13) at the old Elizabethan Deanery, having completed almost 32 years as Dean, the second longest tenure (after Nathan Wetherell, 1771-1807) in modern times.

29. Foster (1891-2), i., p.24. HCA, 7031/3, p.579, Act electing Andrews, 25 June 1708; HCA, 7031/4, p.140, Act electing Willim as Usher (following Andrews' death), 1 April 1730. Traherne died (also in office) the following year. *Ibid.*, p.145, Act electing Willim as Headmaster, 24 March 1731.

30. A putative scholar needed the Headmaster's validation, the award being withdrawn if the student was absent from Oxford for more than one term (unless the circumstances were exceptional). Following the granting of a BA, the exhibition could be continued for a maximum of eight terms, on the production of a favourable testimonial, provided that the candidate had not accepted a curacy, schoolmaster's position or a fellowship. *Ibid.*, 1713 orders (at back of the Act book).

31. See below, p.113.

garden and the Canon's Bakehouse in 1709-10, were no doubt a result of the need to define physical boundaries.[32]

We know nothing either about the manner of Traherne's teaching or the effectiveness of his administration, but four of his letters to Browne Willis, the antiquary, who had an estate nearby at Burlton Manor, Burghill, survive and provide an insight into Traherne's character and interests.[33] They mainly relate to material that Traherne was gathering on Hereford for Willis' survey of ten cathedrals, which was eventually published in 1727. So Traherne reported on the cathedral's 'scandalous' sale of a grove of oak trees in 1719; the value of the Bishop's prebend (who occupied a house in Broad Street adjacent to Traherne's); the 'unparalleled impudence' of Dr John Hoadley's admission as a Chapter member, 'contrary to the principles of all good Christians which oblige them to keep heterodox miscreants out of the Church'; and the names and careers of other canons. It is not much to go on, but from this series we can gather something of Traherne's fiery temperament, his antiquarian interests, his Tory sympathies and low opinion of some Chapter members – Richard Smalbroke, canon residentiary and Bishop's prebend, 1710-24, comes in for particular criticism – and, as a high churchman, his stout defence of the rights and orthodoxies of the established Church.[34] One undated letter of early 1723 contains this apology for Traherne's delay in sending Willis details of tomb inscriptions and is of more direct relevance:

> When you consider the little leisure I've had since the receipt of yours, it being brought to me the day that school began after our Christmas vacation, the extraordinary badness of our roads and the ill state of my health ... I persuade myself that you will not think your request slighted.

Such are also the pleadings of a hard-pressed and hard-working schoolmaster.

He was also a wealthy one. Although he died intestate, Edward Traherne, his clerical son and Brasenose fellow, compiled 'a true and perfect inventory' of his late father's estate in a suit against his brother-in-law Samuel Bird (a vicar choral) and his two sisters.[35] According to these sworn and witnessed documents – and there is no reason to doubt their veracity, despite their being drawn up more than six years after Richard Traherne's death – debts of over £230 (which included a small sum that he owed his Usher 'Mr Willim') were totally eclipsed by assets valued at almost £1,900, excluding plate, linen and miscellaneous household goods. The estate consisted of over £344 in various goods and chattels, including £87 in cash and 'books of all sorts' (unfortunately not listed) worth £14 12s 11d. The vast

32. HCA, 5715/2/1, John Dance's and William Griffith's bills (paid, 6 March, 12 April, 1727) for glazing, lead and 'hanging windows' at the 'Free School'; HCA, 5715/2/2, bill of Richard Beavan for stays (19 Oct. 1727), and one for work done by John Lane, 15 Feb. 1728, for 'fastening the Free School door'; HCA, 7020/2/1, fabric account 1709-10.

33. Bodl., MS Willis 72, fos 126-131v, letters of 1, 22 Dec. 1722, 25 Feb. 1723, and an undated letter of early 1723.

34. The author describes the factions within the Chapter in this period and the dispute over Hoadley's election in Aylmer and Tiller, pp.122-24.

35. There were two documents: HCA, 5344/1 (re Traherne's debts); and 5344/2 (relating to his 'goods, chattels and credits'). Both were dated 22 June 1737 and witnessed by Thomas Barnes. Richard Traherne died in office sometime before Thomas Willim's election as Headmaster on 24 March 1731. HCA, 7031/4, p.145.

bulk of the estate, however, comprised 'credits' in the form of dues owed by his Dinedor parishioners, various rents, debts upon bonds and mortgages and several loans. What is instructive for this history is the money owed him for running the school: £7 10s for several months of his Headmaster's salary; £2 'from Howlands for schooling' and 5s more from 'Morse' for the same – names which were listed separately perhaps because they were private pupils; £5 17s in unpaid fees from nine day pupils, including the two Jones and two Jauncey brothers; and the astonishing sum of £43 1s 7d – £19 7s of which was due from one 'Sandford' – from five others boys 'for boarding and disbursements'.[36] There is, of course, no way to ascertain the school's total size from these meagre lists for we have no idea of the numbers paying fees and no indication of how many fees were paid on time, but clearly bad debts were a worry even for an eighteenth century schoolmaster.

How Traherne's estate was eventually settled is also unknown, but it is nice to think that Thomas Willim, his Usher from April 1730, would have eventually received the £1 2s 6d he was owed by his former master. In any case, Willim inherited his crown, becoming Headmaster in March 1731 and succeeding too to the living of Little Birch in August that year. Four years later, he was also collated rector of Eaton Bishop in plurality with his headmastership.[37] In all, Willim served the school for over 19 years, working with Henry Vere (1731-38), William Davies (1740-42) and John Stephens (1742-49) as his Ushers,[38] before resigning 'the office of Headmaster of the public school founded in the said cathedral, together with all rights, profits and emoluments belonging' on 30 September 1749.[39] By this time, Willim had already been installed as a prebendary (of Piona Parva in May 1733) and his resignation in 1749 was a result of his election as praelector, an important preaching role within the cathedral.[40] Although there is no surviving evidence as to his qualities as a schoolmaster, it is clear that he was a highly respected churchman within the diocese.

The same may be said about Willim's successor, John Stephens, who was Headmaster from 1749 to 1762. Stephens was even more steeped in the ways of the cathedral than his predecessor. Willim, as the son of a gentleman of St Nicholas' parish, was probably an old boy but we have sure evidence that Stephens was a member of the cathedral foundation from the age of eight, being successively a chorister (from June 1725), Langfordian scholar (1727-32) and Philpotts scholar at Brasenose (matriculating at the age of 16 in May 1733) before becoming Willim's Usher.[41] He is, thereby, the only known Headmaster to have

36. William and Benjamin Jauncey were Langfordians, and one of the other brothers may have been Joseph Jones, also a Langfordian scholar. HCA, 7031/4, pp.127, 132, 158, Chapter Acts, 11 Nov. 1727, 13 Nov. 1728, 8 Nov. 1733. The other boys have not been traced.

37. HARC, HD 6/56/4, fos. 89r, 102r.

38. HCA, 7031/4, pp.145, 186, 193; 7032/1, p.111, Vere's resignation. There is no indication in the Chapter Acts that any Usher was appointed from 1738 to 1740 (between Vere and Davies).

39. As it said in his resignation letter, as copied into the Chapter Clerk's precedent book: HCA, 7032/1, p.93. This is the first reference to HCS being described as a 'public school' (as opposed to a 'Free School') that I have come across.

40. Le Neve (2014), pp.90, 119. Piona Parva prebend was endowed with land in the parish of Canon Pyon.

41. HCA, 7031/4, pp.116, 127, 154, 193, 239, Acts 25 June 1725-30 Sept. 1749. Stephens was baptised on 11 November 1716 and I have assumed that he was eight years old on becoming a chorister. Francis Bell, an earlier

been the beneficiary of every part of the foundation's educational largesse. Unusually, he was also awarded an Oxford law degree (the BCL in 1743) in addition to his BA and MA, and shortly after his elevation as Headmaster, had married the daughter of a vicar choral.[42] Again, he remains an obscure figure as a teacher but he was well rewarded with the Chapter livings of both Ocle Pychard and Kempley, which he was allowed to hold in plurality from September 1760, following his recognition as prebendary of Moreton Parva (1754-56) and then Preston (1756-62).[43] And, as we will see, before his resignation as Headmaster in June 1762, he had successfully moved the school to new quarters.

During the 30 years covering the headmasterships of Thomas Willim and John Stephens, there are indications of improvements to the school's fabric. Willim was the initiator of a substantial re-modelling of the Headmaster's house in the early 1730s when he persuaded the Chapter to lay out half the cost of 'repairing and improving the dwelling house belonging to him as schoolmaster'. In return, he promised to keep the same 'in good repair', the inference being that it had been run down by Traherne. These are obviously references to the present School House as the building was described as being 'near to the College', but what exactly was done there is unclear. Nevertheless, the £50 spent on the project was a considerable sum – Willim himself laying out £25 from his own pocket to match the Chapter's contribution – and equivalent to over 40 *per cent* of the total cost of the cathedral's repair bill for 1732-33. These alterations would have significantly increased the house's boarding capacity, as well as Willim's income. A year later, he also rented land from the keeper of the Canon's Bakehouse (at a rate of 10s annually), which no doubt increased the size of his own garden and gave the boys further room to play.[44]

The school on the west side of the Close was improved as well. In June 1731, 30 years after the building of the old one, it was agreed that the charge 'of sinking and making the vault [for] building the house office for the use of the church school' should be paid for from cathedral funds. Subsequently, as the tradesmen's bills in the 1740s and '50s for repairs to the 'privihouse' or 'boghouse' indicate, the cathedral also paid for its upkeep.[45] The old schoolroom, too, was made more comfortable, forms being repaired in 1736 and a chimney added in 1751, which were the first signs in the extant records that the boys had both seats on which to learn and some warmth from a fire in winter, together (in the latter

---

Langfordian who also went to Brasenose, took over from Stephens as Usher. *Ibid.*, pp.50, 63, 239, Acts 25 June 1718, 25 June 1720, 30 Sept. 1749.

42. *Brasenose Reg.*, i., p.324; HCA, 7003/4/3, William Cooke's biographical memoir no. 31 (Richard Waring). Stephens married Margaret Waring, Richard's eldest daughter, at Preston Wynne on 1 December 1749.

43. HCA, 7031/4, p.384, Act 18 Sept. 1760; Le Neve (2014), pp.80, 99. Moreton Parva was endowed with land in the parish of Moreton-on Lugg, and Preston with land in the hamlet of Preston within Withington parish.

44. HCA, 7031/4, pp.150, 153, 158, Acts 27 June, 10 Nov. 1732, 8 Nov. 1733. The total disbursements in the 1732-33 fabric accounts (HCA, 7020/2/1) come to £123 6s 5½d, excluding the £25 chapter contribution to the refurbishment. The detailed fabric vouchers for 1731-33 are missing and there are no extant plans of these alterations.

45. HCA, 7031/4, p.146, Act 25 June 1731; HCA, 5715/2/13, Thomas Prichard's bill, allowed 13 May 1742; HCA, 5715/2/19 and 23, Richard Reece's bills for tiling 28 July 1748 and 17 July 1752. One James Traherne also put in a bill 'for sinking the little house at the school', which may well have been another such facility. HCA, 5715/2/20, 28 Sept. 1748.

year) with a window over the master's seat.[46] The annual 25s rent paid to the vicar of St John's from 1740 for the use of the garden which adjoined the school, and the building of a substantial boundary wall in August 1741, using stone from the 'old chapel', to separate it from the timber-yard, also increased the school's play area and made it more secure.[47] And then there were the seemingly endless repairs to the roof, windows, flooring, door and steps of the medieval schoolroom, to say nothing of the work done in the mid-1750s to shore up the crumbling stonework and mend the leaking tiles of the Bishop's Cloister where the school was situated.[48]

By the mid-eighteenth century, it was becoming increasingly clear that the old schoolroom was no longer fit for purpose. It was John Stephens who, after not far short of two centuries in their old abode, led the school to a new temporary home in the College of the Vicars Choral. An Act of theirs gives the sole surviving reference to this upheaval:

> Whereas ... the Lord Bishop of Hereford [Beauclerk] has generously taken great pains to raise contributions in order to build a room large enough to serve the purposes of the music meetings in the city of Hereford; and whereas the present school belonging to the Dean and Chapter of Hereford must be pulled down in order to make room for the said new building, and a place will be wanting where to teach the scholars of the said school; we the Custos and Vicars in Chapter assembled, being willing to contribute our endeavours towards promoting so good a design, do, as far as lies in our power, give our consent that the Reverend Mr Cove may lend his rooms and Mr Clack the singing school, which he rents off the College, for the use and accommodation of the said scholars during the time of rebuilding the said school.[49]

Morgan Cove's rooms were available because in 1760 he had been presented to the living of Pipe, where he died in 1768. The song school during Richard Clack's tenure as organist (1754-79) was in the north-west corner of the College and Cove's rooms were probably adjacent to it. Altogether, the space given over to the school was unlikely to have been more than three or four rooms and was bound to have been cramped.[50] The school's stay in their different cloister lasted for a generation. Stephens himself, however, having resigned the headmastership on 25 June 1762, was destined to complete his teaching career in the College rather than the new building. This also applied to his successor, Gibbons Bagnall,

46. HCA, 5715/2/7, Thomas Hope, the carpenter's bill, for £1 0s 2d; HCA, 5715/2/22, various bills especially William Reece's for the window, 23 Jan. 1751, and Richard Reece's bill for work on 13 Jan. 1751 for 'taking down the stone wall and building the chimble at the scolle'.

47. HCA, 7031/4, p.187, Act 9 Sept. 1740; 7101, fabric account 1740-41, garden rental payment to Woodcock; 5715/2/12, Thomas Prichard's bill (allowed 11 Nov. 1741) for £20 10s 9d for the new wall.

48. The fabric vouchers (HCA, 5715/2/file 7 onwards) contain many references to school repairs in this period. For the Bishop's Cloister restoration: HCA, 5715/2/26, payments of £8 0s 3d to Richard Hawkins for Capler stone and repaving the arches, 8 Nov. 1754-9 March 1755 (paid 26 April 1755) and £8 8s 4d to William Powell for tiling etc. (paid 10 Oct. 1755). In early 1763, the cloister was still 'in danger of falling'. Two buttresses were then built to help secure it. HCA, 7031/4, p.419, Act 24 March 1763; HCA, 5715/2/34, payments to Richard Hawkins, mason, 16 July, 9 Nov. 1763; Aylmer and Tiller, p.255.

49. HCA, 7003/1/4, p.161, 19 July 1760.

50. HCA, 7003/1/4, Cooke's biographies nos 50, 66; Aylmer and Tiller, p.458, note 101.

throughout the 18 years of his first tenure.[51] But before we consider his headmastership, we need to turn to the 'Great Room' that was being built on the western range of the Bishop's Cloister, a room which the school was eventually to inherit as its own schoolroom.

The Great Room

As the vicars choral had made clear, the building of the new schoolroom was intimately bound up with the need for a larger space for the holding of concerts for the triennial music meeting. College Hall had been enlarged and boarded by William Baker, an undertaker, for the evening concerts in Hereford in 1753. This followed the vicars' agreement three years earlier that the hall was 'too small to contain enough to defray the expenses of the triennial music meeting' and the consequent gathering of subscriptions from 'the gentlemen and clergymen of this country [county]'.[52] By 1759, however, even the new hall was insufficient, Handel's *Messiah* being performed (a few months after his death) for the first time that year in the choir of the cathedral, previously exclusively preserved for services and anthems, the concert notices explaining that it was the only sizeable building in Hereford that was not 'ruinous'.[53] Given the lack of a suitable alternative room to accommodate the increasingly large audiences, it was imperative that a new building should be acquired for the evening concerts for the 1762 meeting. The question was where.

The favoured solution had been for a joint enterprise between the clergy and the city. This would have involved the rebuilding of the old 'tolsey' (market toll-house), which was in a parlous state, on a more central site. The city fathers indeed had approved a scheme in the summer of 1759 for a new guildhall 'so as to have a room proper for the reception of the company at the meetings of the choirs of Hereford, Gloucester and Worcester, as well as for the general convenience and use of the said city'. An appeal went out for contributions, the estimated additional expenditure 'greatly' exceeding the sum that the corporation proposed to spend on the new building. But the county's great and good were insufficiently generous and the plan foundered, a delegation from the corporation thanking Bishop Beauclerk in person for his 'steady and earnest endeavours to promote an undertaking so well intended'.[54] The Bishop was presumably (there are no extant records) also instrumental in persuading the Dean and Chapter to release the western range of the old Bishop's Cloister, where the school was situated, as the new site for the music room: hence the necessity for the school to move to other quarters in the College of Vicars Choral.

We have no knowledge of the building of what became known as the 'Great Room' except that it was accomplished 'by means of the liberal contributions of many of the nobility, gentry and clergy' (the corporation agreeing in August 1760 to donate £50), and it was completed under Bishop Beauclerk's management in time for the Hereford meeting

51. HCA, 7031/4, p.410, Chapter Act, 25 June 1762, recording Stephens' resignation and Bagnall's appointment.

52. HCA, 7003/4 p.114, Cicars' Act, 31 March 1750.

53. Boden and Hedley, pp.45-46; Lysons, pp.36, 123; Carless, *Short History*, p.35.

54. HARC, BG 11/1 A3, pp.60, 62, 64, 69, 72, minutes 4 May, 28 June, 20 July, 24 Aug., 18 Sept. 1759. The city's plan to erect a new building 'to answer the purposes of the corporation only' was itself shelved a few months later, when it was ordered that repairs should be made to the old 'tolsey'. The repairs proved largely ineffective and before the end of the decade the corporation was meeting at Mr Newton's White Lion Inn, Byestreet, and the old 'tolsey' was taken down. *Ibid.*, pp.87, 250, 22 April 1760, 28 June 1768.

in September 1762 when Handel's last oratorio, *Jephthah*, was performed on the first evening.[55] It did not come into use as a schoolroom at that time, although in February 1763 the Chapter allowed old timber to be used for 'setting up desks in the new schoolroom' provided that no more were made than were 'absolutely necessary according to the number of the scholars'. Twenty elm forms for the 'Latin school' were also being crafted at the same time.[56] Even the making of suitable desks and benches, however, does not signify that the new building was immediately available for the school. Indeed, there is good evidence to suggest that the school's occupation of the Great Room was delayed until 1778.

Protracted negotiations between the Dean and Chapter and Bishop Beauclerk over its usage took place in 1763-64. The situation was complicated by the cathedral's need for another timber-yard, the new porticoed music room and its 'commodious and ornamental approach' necessary for 'coaches, carriages and servants in such sort, manner and form' as was customary 'at all well-regulated places of public resort' having effectively destroyed the yard outside the western range of the old cloister. The cathedral got round this by creating a new yard in the Chapter House garden, but a suitable way had then to be made for the carriage of timber and other materials through the back court of the Bishop's Palace. There was also the further issue of making good any damage that might be caused by public use, Bishop Beauclerk promising to recompense the cathedral in such cases, although not when damage occurred through the carriage of timber or 'by means ... of the said free grammar school being held or kept within the same'.[57] As late as August 1764, Dean Webber could openly declare that the Bishop had only 'in private conversation ... relating to the Great Room' accepted the cathedral's 'right thereto'. As it was not 'wanted immediately for a schoolroom', the Chapter were 'content to make no further application at present to be put in possession but to wait somewhat longer for it'.[58]

By the mid-1770s, another Dean – Nathan Wetherell having been installed in November 1771 following Webber's death – and his Chapter colleagues were still waiting for their new schoolroom. Around this time, it is evident that an increase in pupil numbers (it is not known by how many) was putting added pressure on the school's existing rooms which may by then have been moved to the Headmaster's own house.[59] But wherever they were

---

55. *Ibid.*, p.94, minute 1 Aug. 1760; HCA, 5703/1, draft indenture, Nov. 1763; Lysons, p.39.

56. HCA, 7031/4, p.418, Act 10 Feb. 1763; HCA, 5715/2/34, Philip Evans' bill for £3 12s 8d, work beginning 15 Jan. and payment 6 May 1763. It is impossible to judge the school's size from these bills: it is not known how many desks were made nor how many boys sat on each form.

57. HCA, 5703/1-8, draft indenture, Nov. 1763, together with plans and correspondence relating to the new building; HCA, 7031/4, pp.417, 422, Acts 4 Dec. 1762, 25 June 1763. The situation was further complicated by the fact that the cathedral rented the land (from the vicar of St John the Baptist at 25s *per annum*) on which the old timber-yard had stood. Agreement was reached with the bishop over the carriage-way in September 1763 but this did not prevent a protracted dispute between the cathedral and palace in 1768 regarding its use: *ibid.*, Acts 27 Jan., 24 March, 19 April 1768; 5703/9-15, drafts, 27 Jan. to 19 April 1768, especially the Chapter Clerk's note of 15 April which illustrates Bishop Beauclerk's aristocratic *hauteur* as well as his short temper.

58. HCA, 7031/4, p.432, Act 31 Aug. 1764.

59. Although their location is uncertain, it may be that the school had moved out of the College after Morgan Cove's death in 1768, especially as the vicars choral had given over their rooms only 'during the time of rebuilding the said school'. (See above, p.83). There is, moreover, no further reference in the vicars' Act Book either to the school's occupation of the College or its alteration of the rooms in the mid-1770s.

situated, in late 1775 the Chapter ordered that the partition between the then schoolrooms and the adjoining passage should be taken down and a further enlargement made 'by carrying forward the upper room if the present school be found too small'.[60] These modifications, however, soon proved insufficient for the school's growing needs for three years later, following the resignations of Gibbons Bagnall and Richard Underwood (as, Headmaster and Usher respectively), the new masters were given formal permission to move into the Great Room.[61]

But it was to be a shared occupation, the original agreement having been for its use as a music room for the Hereford meetings and also a place 'for any other charitable or useful occasions ... meriting encouragement over and above the purposes of the said free grammar school'.[62] This must have posed problems for both masters and boys. In 1779, indeed, a new Headmaster's house was built, as we will see, together with an alternative schoolroom for occupation when the music room was being used for the three concerts during the triennial gatherings.[63] There were compensations at these times, however, the room being regularly cleaned and repaired and its surroundings beautified to suitably accommodate the county set at the evening music-making.[64] With the Bishop, Dean and residentiary canons all being able to sanction the room's use, the school may have been more disrupted when its schoolroom was given over to other causes. This was certainly the case with the grand balls – conducted (at 5s per ticket), it was said in 1772, 'with the utmost elegance and politeness'[65] – held there for three nights every August during the Hereford races. By August 1794, the very month that the county was raising a volunteer force for the kingdom's defence, the cathedral authorities had had enough as the Chapter's respectful but firm reply to that year's race steward reveals:

> The Dean and Chapter present their compliments to you and are sorry they cannot comply with your request to have the use of the schoolroom for public entertainment during the races. In a time of dissipation, some place of restraint for keeping the young gentlemen within bounds, secure from danger, is particularly necessary. If the scholars were left at large and any misfortune or misconduct should occur, an

60. HCA, 7031/5, pp.131, 135, Acts 19 Oct., 9 Nov. 1775, which follow the Chapter's request a year earlier for an estimate of the cost of altering 'the rooms now used for school'. *Ibid.*, p.122, 10 Nov. 1774. The tradesmen's bills from James Holland (for 21 feet of elm), William Hargest (5 days labour, 3 bags of lime and 2 bushels of hair), Phillip Williams (bars for the windows) and Philip Evans (wooden girder and prop) are extant for work done at the schoolroom in early November 1775. HCA, 5715/2/44.

61. *Ibid.*, pp.162, 163, 166, Acts 25 June, 23 July, 12 Nov. 1778. The two new masters were Abraham Rudd and Henry William Barry. See below, pp.95-96.

62. HCA, 5703/1, draft indenture between Bishop Beauclerk and the Dean and Chapter, Nov. 1763.

63. See below, pp.96-97, for the new buildings.

64. For Chapter Acts ordering works on the room in Hereford years: HCA, 7031/4, p.462, 13 Nov. 1766 and HCA, 7031/5, p.33, 31 Aug. 1769 (appointment of James Holland as cleaner); *ibid.*, p.118, 25 June 1774 (cleaning, whitewashing and painting); p.151, 25 June 1777 (new lamps in the churchyard); fo 242r, 31 Aug. 1786 (orchestra gallery); HCA, 7031/6, p.5, 4 Aug. 1801 (deal benches). Numerous miscellaneous tradesmen's bills detail the refurbishing of the music room and its surrounds, particularly in the months before the triennial meetings, as in HCA, 5715/3/ 39, 42, 45, 48, 51, 54, 57 and 60 for the Hereford years, 1768-92.

65. *HJ*, 27 Aug. 1772.

> event naturally to be expected, they would think themselves blameable for any bad consequence that may follow. They charge me [the Chapter Clerk] to express in their strongest terms their personal esteem and regard for you.

The Chapter then ordered that in future the room should be granted for use by the canon in residence only for the triennial music meeting. Interestingly, Gibbons Bagnall, the former Headmaster, was the one residentiary who disagreed with his colleagues' resolve to send the letter. But he was out-voted so the race-goers had to make do with a ball at Preece's coffee-house.[66]

As for the building itself, one of the few contemporary illustrations was a partial view drawn by James Wathen on 18 April 1786, the day following the collapse of the cathedral's west front when the music room was also 'considerably injured'. This drawing shows only the top storey of the north-west corner of the building, with its hipped roof protruding above the elm trees. Two sash windows can be seen on the west side, and a dormer attic together with a blank window on the northern front. An alarming crack, from the roof slates down through the blank window, is depicted as a jagged line on the middle of this façade. Before the end of June, the wall had been propped-up and by early August it had been rebuilt. The windows, too, were re-hung, the orchestral gallery on the south side re-made and the room repainted in time for the evening concerts at the Hereford triennial meeting in September, although the two morning performances had to be transferred from the cathedral to St Peter's church.[67] The *Hereford Journal* reported that the 'meeting though not numerous was very genteel' and the music 'finely executed by the different performers, whose excellence ... stands high if not unequalled in the opinions of some of the most competent judges'.[68] But how did this Great Room, designed by Bishop Beauclerk as a prestige building for the county as much as a place of learning for the cathedral's grammar boys, work as a schoolroom?

There are no surviving pictures of the interior but its dimensions are known, as are some details of the layout and fittings.[69] Its size – 80 feet long, 40 feet wide and 40 feet high – compared favourably to those schools with earlier purpose-built schoolrooms, including the new room (now 'School') at Winchester, built 1683-87 at a cost of £2,600 possibly to Wren's design. More locally, the music room was double the size of Lucton's schoolroom erected more than 50 years earlier. Lucton's room, moreover, was without a fireplace, which according to one contemporary source was a 'great discouragement' to regular attendance,

---

66. HCA, 7031/5, fo 303v, letter to Richard Cope Hopton, 12 Aug. 1794; *HJ*, 6, 20 Aug. (reports on the meetings – which included Hugh Morgan, the cathedral residentiary, and Thomas Russell, the praelector – for raising a corps of yeomanry); and 27 Aug. 1794 for Preece's coffee-house.

67. HCL, B 3 18, Wathen's engraving (published 12 April 1788 by F. Jukes); *HJ*, 20 April 1786; HCA, 5715/2/54, bills from: Philip Evans, including an item for 'propping the end of the music room' (paid 9 July); William Hargest, £18 for rebuilding the north wall (paid 3 Aug); and William Parker, various items including the windows and 'work done at the orchestra', £28 10s paid 10 Oct. 1786.

68. *HJ*, 28 Sept. 1786.

69. The following details on the Hereford Great Room are based on: J. and H.S. Storer's 1815 cathedral plan; Carlisle, i., p.493; Caird, pp.28-31; and numerous miscellaneous tradesmen's bills (HCA, 5715/2/37-61, 1766-96.) For the 1798 numbers: *HJ*, 3 Oct. 1798.

Fig. 3.1 James Wathen's drawing of 18 April 1786, of the collapse of the west end of the cathedral, showing the damage done to the Great Room.

compared with the two on the east side of Hereford's room.[70] The Great Room was not only spacious enough to accommodate 476 people at a Three Choirs concert in 1798 but also well-lit. Originally, there were nine sash windows on the imposing western public façade, five with 20 lights on the upper level and four at ground level (later blocked up: Plate 6), and at least one grand one, repaired with '6 squares of crown glass' before the Hereford music meeting in 1780, facing the bishop's palace. Judging by the number of expensive window repairs (at 1s 9d per square by 1791) regularly made by the cathedral glaziers, these lights may have proved too great a temptation to the boys, and the openness of the western side to the city's daily traffic may have been a distraction. However, the profusion of natural light through the windows, together with the 36 candles in the four chandeliers and other lamps, at least gave them more light to do their work as the sun rose during the day, there being no windows on the eastern façade until 1804. The Great Room offered other advantages. The south end orchestral gallery provided the Headmaster with an excellent view of his charges, as we will see, although whether the permanent north gallery (with 28 pillars), made in 1789, was used in the same way is unknown. Other spaces utilised by the school were identified in tradesmen's bills: a 'lower room' and 'lower gallery' and a 'privy house' where '7 old sash squares' were fitted for 1s 2d before the triennial meeting in 1780; and a library for which a key was made in December 1782. These may all have been on the south side of the building where there was a staircase to the gallery and a lobby connecting the Great Room to the rest of the cloister, so the boys could still take advantage of an outside play area in wet weather. The most imposing feature of the schoolroom, however, would have been the porticoed entrance on its fenestrated west façade, enhanced by the addition of white painted 'china rails and obelisks', perhaps providing lights to the pedimented doorway. It was all too grand, of course, for schoolboys, and the brick would have contrasted strangely with the cathedral's stonework. Nevertheless, before its reconstruction in 1804, the Great Room was regarded as a significant Georgian building.[71]

The Three Headmasters, 1762-1803

Gibbons Bagnall, Abraham Rudd and Robert Squire, the three clerics who occupied the position of Headmaster over these 40 years, were all men of vision. Rudd and Squire were clerical entrepreneurs of a new age: Rudd re-built the Headmaster's house and advertised widely to try to fill it but over-extended himself and lasted only four years; Squire was more successful through his tenure of almost 20 years, extending the school's provision and promoting it as never before. Both advanced the school as a business, even though it meant insolvency for one of them. But Gibbons Bagnall, the first of these men, was a different kind of visionary: he was a poet and enlightened Headmaster, whose pupils later gathered together as old boys to dine in his honour.[72] It is to him that we first turn.

70. Seaborne, pp.72 (Winchester), 85 (eighteenth-century usage of old schoolrooms), 90-91 (Lucton). See above, p.34, for the dimensions of some late-sixteenth-century schoolrooms.

71. For example: Price (p.136) viewed it as 'a very spacious and superb brick building'. For the 1804 re-modelling and later opinions on the room, see below pp.127-128.

72. In my chapter of the cathedral history, written 20 years ago, I considered that Bagnall was probably not 'a great visionary' (Aylmer and Tiller, p.139). I am pleased now to be able to correct that mistaken view.

Bagnall, Headmaster for 18 years in all (1762-78 and 1782-84), rose higher in the cathedral hierarchy than any other master of the period. He was the only Headmaster of the century to have been made a prebendary (in 1760) before he took charge of the school; he was the only one to have been appointed Headmaster twice (assuming office again at the age of 63), one of two (with Thomas Willim) to have been elected praelector (in 1782) but the only one to have become (in 1783) a residentiary canon.[73] As importantly, Bagnall was the only eighteenth-century Headmaster who was a published poet.

Fig. 3.2 Gibbon Bagnall's bookplate. Following his death in December 1800, among his effects was a library of around 700 books.

Bagnall's preface to his translation of Fenélon's *Telemachus*, which he worked on and published in 1756 as vicar of Holme Lacy, not only reveals his admiration for his subject's learning and relevance for all ages – Telemachus (Odysseus' son in Greek mythology), Bagnall tells us, 'has ransacked all the treasures of both sacred and profane history ... and will be respected by all so long as any taste shall remain for virtue and politeness' – but also gives an insight into the translator's own character as this passage indicates:

> I confess myself extremely diffident of success ... Whatever may be the fate of this translation when published, it has amused me in some solitary and very melancholy hours. To its author, therefore, it hath already been of singular service ... at the worst, I would recommend it as a good narcotic which may administer comfort to all those who are in want of sleep. And I see no manner of reason why they, and I, may not nod together, when the great Homer has done the same before us.[74]

Bagnall's qualities of self-deprecation, humanity and humour, as illustrated here, would have gone down well with the boys whom he taught. Similarly, his enlightened philosophy of education, as portrayed in his *Education an Essay*, the verse treatise he published nine years later while serving as the Cathedral School's Headmaster, may also have been appreciated, at least in retrospect, by his charges.[75]

---

73. HCA, 7031/4, pp.379-80, 410; 7031/5, p.163, fo 211r; Le Neve (2014), pp.91, 119, 120, 141.

74. Bagnall's pessimism about the fate of his translation was not borne out. Although a contemporary (in *A New Catalogue of Living English Authors* ... 1799) claimed that it lacked 'the cadenced prose' of Fenélon's original, at least two further editions were published in his own life time: in Hereford in 1790 and Dublin in 1792. His reason for using the phrase 'solitary and very melancholy hours' is unknown.

75. Gibbons Bagnall, *Education an Essay*, (London, 1765).

Despite its being in verse and only 18 stanzas long, the first extant educational treatise of any Hereford Headmaster – and the only known published one for 150 years[76] – repays further scrutiny. First, Bagnall recognised both the importance and the demands of the schoolmaster's vocation, 'the tutor's multifarious task' as he termed it. After 'some fair Madam Slipslop' has taught 'the future scholar how to read', he is admitted 'for pelf' by 'some smatt'rer soul' to his 'paltry school' – preferably (according to Bagnall) at a 'public school' where 'education holds the foremost place' rather than a private institution – and 'to odious Latin, Cato and Corderius'.[77] It is there that the schoolmaster could experience both the frustrations and the rewards of teaching:

Behold him now for eight long tedious years!
When ripe for *alma mater* he appears.
No single passage can he justly speak
yet studies Virgil and has heard of Greek.
Without one spark of taste or general fire,
which Cam or Isis will (we hope) inspire.
Not so the gen'rous youth, whose cultur'd mind
betimes to Attic elegance inclin'd.
Like flexile osiers[78] hath been taught to bend,
and well concerted discipline attend.
No stranger he to Ciceronian sense,
or secret pow'rs of eloquence.
He sees its force in each harmonious line,
his bosom glows with sympathy divine.

Bagnall next considered the variety of teaching methods masters adopted in the mid-eighteenth century, and came out firmly in favour of a benign approach to discipline:

Of masters next, though qualified to teach
no tongue the vast variety can reach.
Some think that boys should endless vigils keep;
some lash (as they their tops) 'till fast asleep.
Ingenious nature thus recoil at once,
and dawning merit dwindles into dunce.
They shrink, of sour severity afraid:
stern Busby spoil'd more scholars than he made.[79]
Alas! We gain not learning in a trice.
Keep rods for wilful wickedness and vice.
'Tis emulation and desire of fame
that leads to honour and secures from blame.

---

76. See below, p.98, for the possibility that Abraham Rudd, Bagnall's successor, published a book on education in 1780; and below, pp.376-77, for J.H.E. Crees' *Didascalus Patiens: A Satire, A Medley, A Romance*, (London, 1915).

77. 'Madam Slipslop' was a character in Henry Fielding's novel, *The History of the Adventures of Joseph Andrews* …, first published in 1742; 'pelf' means money and 'smatterer', a mere 'dabbler'. Bagnall noted that Cato and Corderius were 'two of the first books' which boys were 'generally put to read'.

78. A species of willow used in basket-work.

79. For Busby, see above, p.56.

However, it is Bagnall's views on the curriculum that really marked him out as an enlightened Headmaster of his time. Over half the poem is devoted to a disquisition on the importance of the scholar gaining a wide range of knowledge. Latin and Greek were to be the vehicles for this, which involved attendance to 'orthographic rules' for 'what in nature more reflects disgrace than spelling bad and accents out of place'? So grammar had to be mastered but this did not indicate that Bagnall thought that learning needed to be narrowly focused on the classical languages. The greats of the classical world should be used to captivate the young, for the 'historic page … suits that study with our tend'rest age' and 'to make it please should geography unite and clear chronology must give us light'. Nor should 'the mother-tongue' be neglected for 'we too have speakers that display with ease the fire of Rome and elegance of Greece'. Among the English poets, he paid tribute to Milton, 'with idioms borrowed from the sacred page', together with John Philips, the poet of Herefordshire cider and 'the pride of Ariconian plains',[80] and Waller, Dryden and Pope who all 'divinely sing'; and emphasised the importance of learning to soar with Shakespeare 'to seraphic height'. And among the prose writers, he favoured 'nervous Swift's honest rage', 'polish'd Addison' and 'smooth … Atterbury's quill'. But above all, truth and moral teaching should come 'to him from whom all benefits descend' and the 'Christian and scholar should go hand in hand'. Otherwise, irrespective of the development of 'a philosophic mind, improv'd by study and by arts refin'd', it was but 'pedantry and false parade'. 'Religion, polar star, must point the way', by which, of course, he meant the articles and liturgy of the Church of England – the spiritual element of the country's 'excellent constitution' (as he described it in his *Telemachus* preface) – to which he had several times subscribed as priest, prebendary and schoolmaster.[81]

How successful Bagnall was in convincing 'the weak, the timid and the slow' that it was 'a Godlike attribute to know' is impossible to gauge. But on becoming Headmaster at around 43 in 1762, he was not only well suited to the position in terms of his intellect and temperament but also sufficiently mature and experienced to do it well. The formulaic references, in both his Chapter patent of appointment and Bishop's teaching licence, to Bagnall's 'integrity, piety and good learning' and his 'learning, industry and good morals' seem justified.[82] Moreover, he established long partnerships with his first two Ushers, both of whom were old boys of the school. He inherited Francis Bell, a Langfordian and Brasenose Philpotts scholar, who was Usher for 20 years from his appointment under John Stephens in 1749 to his death in office at 65 in 1769.[83] The career of Richard Underwood, his successor, was more remarkable for in addition to his position as Bagnall's Under-Master (1769-78), and following his time as a Hereford chorister and Christ Church undergraduate, he became successively a vicar choral (from 1766 with 'a mellow tenor voice'),

80. In his *Cyder* (1708), Philips described legends like the disappearance of Ariconium, near Weston-under-Penyard, which he imagined 'sinking into the earth to yield huge bones to frighten the ploughman'. Weaver, p.314.

81. For three of Bagnall's subscriptions (with his signature): HARC, HD 6/56/5, fos 4v-5r, 23 Oct. 1744; HARC, HD 6/57/2, fos 79v, 6 June 1782; 179r, 9 Oct. 1790.

82. HCA, 7005/2, p.268, patent, 20 June 1762; HCA, 1534, licence, 1 July 1762.

83. HCA, 7031/3, p.610, 24 June 1712; HCA, 7031/4, pp.63, 239, 25 June 1720 and 30 Sept. 1749; HCA, 7031/5, p.31, 14 July 1769.

Fig. 3.3 Richard Underwood OH, under-master and vicar choral with a 'mellow tenor' voice, and an influential cleric in the diocese.

curate of Canon Pyon (1769), chaplain of the county gaol, vicar of Weston Beggard (1775) and rector of St Nicholas. These preferments, according to the biographer of the lives of the vicars choral, 'induced him to resign his office in the grammar school', together no doubt with the security provided by a favourable marriage in 1771 to an heiress 'with a £2,000 fortune'. Thereafter, he continued to rise within the county, as magistrate and grand master of the Freemasons, as well as the diocese as Bishop Beauclerk's domestic chaplain, prebend of Hampton (1780) and Wellington (1780-1801), vicar of St John the Baptist and Custos of the vicars choral from 1794 until his death in May 1819.[84] No other Usher of the century gained such favour, but at least Underwood's stay of nine years, together with Bell's long tenure, provided some continuity in the school's leadership over two decades.

Whether Bagnall succeeded in widening the curriculum, as he had advocated in his verse treatise, is also difficult to know: unlike his successors he did not advertise the school's educational wares in the weekly *Hereford Journal*, first published on 9 August 1770 during the time of his headmastership.[85] From the evidence of the school's earliest surviving library catalogue, which was overwhelmingly classical and linguistic, it certainly needed broadening.[86] Bagnall would have had an opportunity to provide the wherewithal to do this as the following ingenious order from the Dean and Chapter indicates:

> The master of the school be directed not to grant any play days to his scholars for the future unless the person applying shall pay into his hands the sum of half a guinea to be laid out in books for the use of the school; excepting at the request of the Lord Bishop, or one play day to each canon during his residence, or to each prebendary or dignitary at the time of his installation. The books [are] to be purchased with the advice of the Chapter.[87]

---

84. Richard Underwood's career is outlined in William Cooke's unpublished 'Biographical Memoirs of the Custos and Vicars … from 1660 to 1823', vol ii, no. 62 (HCA, 7003/4/4). For his school career: HCA, 7031/4, p.424, Act 27 July 1763; HCA, 7031/5, pp.31, 162, Acts, 14 July 1769, 25 June 1778. For his prebendal appointments: Le Neve (2014), pp.59, 109; and his marriage: *HJ*, 4 April 1771.

85. As *The British Chronicle or Pugh's Historical Journal*, issued free for the first number and then at 2½d per copy. Pugh apologised in his first editorial for there not having been such a journal 'in these parts' before, 'where there is scarce a county in England that does not support a newspaper'.

86. HCA, 6284. See above, p.61.

87. HCA, 7031/5, p.122, 10 Nov. 1774.

Given that there were six annual periods of canonical residence, as well as occasional installations and (no doubt) intermittent episcopal gifts, the library would have been built up from the mid-1770s by donations worth several guineas each year, although there is no suggestion as to the kind of books that would have been deemed worth of purchase.

The only external validation of the school under Bagnall's tutelage that we have is contained in the surviving written answers from three members of the foundation (two residentiaries and one vicar choral) out of the 47 dignitaries summoned by Bishop Beauclerk to his cathedral visitation in 1765.[88] Although the three questions relating to the choristers' appearance, behaviour and training and the two directly concerning the school are exactly the same as those posed by Bishops Croft and Bisse, respectively in 1677 and 1716,[89] the extant responses put Bagnall and Bell, his Usher, in a good light: Canons Whishaw and Russell, as well as Morgan Cove, all asserting that the masters were able and diligent and took proper care in educating their scholars. As to whether the residentiaries visited the school twice each year, as required by Bishop Croft in 1677, it is clear that the Chapter's examination of the scholars had lapsed, if indeed it had ever happened on so regular a basis. As the clerk who summarised the responses put it, 'the school [was] not visited'. Bagnall's and Bell's own thoughts on this, or, indeed, on other aspects of the school and cathedral, have not survived. Nevertheless, despite the meagre evidence and the Chapter's own failings in supervision, it is fair to conclude that both masters were well respected by their peers in 1765.

That Gibbons Bagnall was also esteemed by his colleagues is apparent from his second spell as Headmaster over the 18 months from December 1782. He was appointed in an emergency as a safe pair of hands four-and a-half years following his first retirement from the school and days after the resignation of Abraham Rudd, his successor, in dubious circumstances.[90] By this time Bagnall was also the cathedral's praelector, an office he resigned on his final election as a full residentiary in June 1783.[91] It was a heavy burden that Bagnall carried in the cathedral over the following year for he spent four months in residence as hebdomadary (June, July, October and November 1783), he was elected master of the fabric that November and he attended every Chapter meeting bar one during this time. In addition, on 25 June 1783, he had been presented to the vicarage of Sellack, with King's Caple.[92] Given these responsibilities, the immediate appointment of Robert Squire as his successor, following his second resignation on 25 June 1784, must have come as a relief.

It is by no means the end of the Bagnall story for his work on the Chapter was not yet complete. Indeed, he continued as a wise, well-respected and conscientious (although

88. HCA, 1575, list of those summoned; HCA, 1543, 5559 and 6247, answers from Whishaw, Russell and Cove. Robert Breton's responses are also extant (HCA, 5125) but he did not answer the school articles (nos 49 and 50). HCA, 1573 summarises some of the dignitaries' criticisms, including the one about the Chapter's failure to visit the school. The 1765 visitation in general is covered in the author's chapter in Aylmer and Tiller, pp.132-34.

89. See HCA, 1579 for Bisse's articles of 1716, and above, p.55, for Croft's of 1677.

90. HCA, 7031/5, fos 211r, 214v, 215v, Acts, 25 June 1782, 14 Nov., 6 Dec. 1782. Although Gibbons' second appointment dated from the latter date, it is clear from the notice in the *Hereford Journal* of 21 November 1782 that he was in harness again less than a week after Rudd's resignation.

91. *Ibid.*, fos 217v-18r, 218v, 219r, Acts 12 April, 2 June 1783.

92. *Ibid.*, fos 219v-228v, Acts 4 June 1783 to 25 June 1784.

increasingly gout-ridden) residentiary canon for another 16 years during the cathedral's greatest period of rebuilding in its modern history, following the west front's collapse on that fateful Easter Monday in April 1786.[93] However, his active involvement as Headmaster over 18 years had finally drawn to a close. This notice, published in the *Hereford Journal* shortly after his second retirement from the school, gives some indication of the regard with which he was also held by his former pupils:

> Several gentlemen educated under the Reverend Mr Bagnall, being desirous of showing their respect for him and also of renewing their early connections, have appointed a meeting at the New Inn in this city upon Tuesday the 21st September ... Dinner at three o'clock and tickets at 10s 6d each to be had at the bar of the New Inn.

Thus Gibbons Bagnall was honoured by Edmund Pateshall, Hugh Morgan and their fellows.[94]

Abraham Rudd's headmastership from 23 July 1778 to 14 November 1782 bridges Bagnall's two tenures. He was the son of a fellow of St John's, Oxford, but completed his own education in the 1770s at University College. There, Rudd came under the influence of his 'learned and ingenious friend' Dr George Croft, a college fellow and Bampton lecturer, who Rudd later claimed had taken 'great care' in supervising his education.[95] As important for Rudd's future career was the figure of Nathan Wetherell, who not only transformed the fortunes of that college during his long tenure as its master (1764-1807) but was also instrumental in reforming the university and city of Oxford during his influential tenure as vice-Chancellor (1768-72). It was during this period as the university's chief officer that Wetherell, through his political connections and the favour of the then Prime Minister, Lord North, gained the Hereford deanery in 1771, a post he was to hold for 36 years – like his college mastership, he retained this position for a longer period than any of his predecessors.[96] It was, therefore, natural that when Bagnall resigned for the first time in July 1778, a strong Dean should want a man from his own college as Headmaster of his Cathedral School. Thus began Rudd's extraordinary four-year headship.

It is 'extraordinary' not simply because he was the only Headmaster in modern times for whom the Dean and Chapter may have had to invoke the 'good behaviour' clause of his contract but also because of the changes undertaken during his tenure. In his mid-twenties in 1778, after seven years at Oxford, he (with Willim) was the youngest Headmaster of the century on taking up office. Together with the appointment of Henry William Barry 'late'

---

93. Gibbons Bagnall had the misfortune to be the canon in residence on the evening of 17 April 1786 when the west front fell. William Cooke gives an account of how the news was brought to another prebendary (and an old boy of the school) Dr Thomas Luntley at his house (Old College) in Castle Street. HCA, 7003/3/4, no. 62. For the fall and rebuilding: Aylmer and Tiller, pp.139-42, 258-62. Bagnall died in his 82nd year in December 1800. Among his household effects was a library of 700 or so books. *HJ*, notices 31 Dec. 1800, 7 Jan. 1801.

94. *HJ*, 26 August 1784. The notice was signed by the two men, who acted as stewards for the dinner. The 1784 old boys' dinner was the first in a long series of annual gatherings. See below, p.115.

95. Rudd, dedication.

96. See Darwall-Smith, chapter 13 *passim*, on Wetherell's reforms at the college during his early tenure; and pp.291-92, on his work as vice-Chancellor and his appointment to Hereford. Wetherell returned Lord North's favour by engineering the Prime Minister's election as Oxford's Chancellor in 1782. *Ibid.*, pp.292-93.

of Pembroke, Oxford, as the new Usher, it would have seemed to both the canon residentiaries and the boys that a new era had dawned, an impression that would have been reinforced by the alterations to the school's buildings which were accomplished within months of their arrival.[97]

For as we have seen, it was Rudd and his colleague who benefited from the school's move to the Great Room. Precisely when this was accomplished is unclear but it must have been towards the end of 1778. That summer, we know that the cathedral carpenters were busy making and fitting school benches, as well as constructing a large master's desk, strengthening the gallery on which it was to stand and 'getting the desk up in the gallery and fixing it'.[98] And then on 12 November that year came the momentous Chapter decision permitting the schoolmasters 'to use the Great Room and teach school therein'. At the same time, this equally significant enactment was passed which was to have far-reaching consequences for both the school and for Rudd personally:

> Whereas the present schoolmaster's house is incapable of reparation and it is thought necessary to erect a new one in the stead thereof, we whose names are subscribed do engage to give the sum of one hundred guineas towards the erecting [of] such [a] new house: N. Wetherell, Dean; Henry Whishaw ... Thomas Russell ... John Evans ... James Birt ... John Woodcock [residentiary canons].

The site was to include the cathedral glazier's lead-house which was to be demolished and added to the schoolmaster's house on its southern side 'and in future become an appurtenant thereto'.[99] Dean Wetherell and the five residentiary canons had thereby committed themselves to finance (in part) the rebuilding of the Headmaster's house as well as increase its acreage. The young Headmaster must have felt that his decision to accept his new office had been fully vindicated.

Over the following year, something resembling today's School House became a reality. We are able to trace its construction from a remarkably complete set of tradesmen's bills which document the spending of the residentiaries' £105 from 28 December 1778 to 9 November 1779. Of this amount, £33 1s was paid to Philip Evans for desks, benches and other carpentry work; over £28 to William Hargest for laying the 8,400 bricks provided by J. Whitmore and Charles Cooke (costing £9 10s); and 5s 6d to William Phillips for 'opening the well ... moving the pump and covering the well' and the cost (1s 6d) of 'a bucket leather'. The rest of the money paid for other materials – excluding the 25 tons of wood the Chapter allowed to be used from the timber-yard – such as boards, lime,

97. Rudd's patent of appointment has not survived but it cannot have differed in essentials from the one for Bagnall, who was bidden 'to hold and enjoy' the office provided he 'behave[d] ... well, diligently and religiously'. HCA, 7005/2, p.268, 20 June 1762. For Rudd's university career and his and Barry's appointments: Foster (1887-8), iii., p.1233 and HCA, 7031/5, pp.163, 164, Acts 23 July 1778. Barry does not appear to have taken a degree and did not last long at the school. John Lodge, also (like Rudd) from University College, replaced him in early 1780, although he does not appear to have gained his BA until 1782. *Ibid.*, p.179, Act 1 Feb. 1780; Foster (1887-8), iii., p.868.

98. HCA, 5715/2/46, Philip Evans' bills, 5 and 7 Sept. 1778.

99. HCA, 7031/5, p.166, Acts 12 November 1778. Prior to this, the lead-house had always been excluded from leases, as in those of 25 June 1756 and 25 June 1765: HCA, 7005/2, pp.112-15, 339-43, leases no. 27 and 79.

iron-work (including a chimney, grate, stove and window bars), as well as haulage. From these accounts, we can also chart the progress of the work from the first making of the desks in November 1778, through the receipt and laying of the bricks early the following summer, to the installing of the pump in July and the 'turning bannisters for a staircase' on 28 August 1779. And in conjunction with the Chapter order of 1 March 1779, when it was again ordered that the lead-house should be demolished as it had been 'found impracticable to raise an attic storey on the schoolmasters' house', these bills further reveal that the old lead-room was taken down before that month was out. Rudd's dream of erecting another teaching space within the eaves of his new house had been shattered, but at least he could claim the lead-house site to build an additional schoolroom for use whenever the Great Room was needed for other causes.[100]

We know nothing about this room except that it existed, a later Headmaster revealing that in 1779 'a large room was added by voluntary subscription for the purposes of a school when the music room should be applied to county business'.[101] How much money Rudd managed to raise is unknown but the appeal may have fallen well short of his actual expenditure. This was one possible cause of his later financial difficulties. In all probability, Rudd's petition to the city fathers was for money for this new building, but as this minute reveals they were unwilling to meet the sum that was expected from them:

> The mayor and corporation, highly sensible of Mr Rudd's merit and of the expediency of the plan proposed for enlarging the house belonging to the master of the grammar school, have unanimously agreed to subscribe the sum of thirty guineas towards the completion of the work, and they [there] would with cheerfulness have been more ample contributions if their ability to give was not limited by other calls of a public nature.[102]

As for the appearance of the house, there is little to go by except James Wathen's south-east view of the cathedral, sketched on 21 May 1799. This was drawn from the Headmaster's garden and shows the bricked corner of a two-storey building, with a double gabled roof-line, smoking chimney, upper casemented window and garden entrance. (Plate 7). It looks a comfortable enough dwelling, and had indeed been described as 'a very good house' some three years earlier.[103] Wetherell and his colleagues had done their duty by their Headmaster but the final cost of the construction and furnishing of his residence, as well as the additional schoolroom, must have been well in excess of their hundred guinea donation.

At the end of Rudd's first term, before a brick had been laid, this advertisement was published in the *Hereford Journal*:

---

100. HCA, 5715/1/47, miscellaneous bills to 11 contractors, each of whom employed several additional workmen (many of whose names are recorded in these bills), 1778-79; HCA, 7031/5, pp.167, 169, Chapter Acts (on the use of timber and the lead-house) 17 Nov. 1778, 1 March 1779.

101. Carlisle, i., p.493. Charles Taylor (senior) was the Headmaster at the time of Carlisle's survey.

102. HARC, BG 11/1 A4, council minute of the 'answer [to] be given to a memorial presented by the Revd Mr Abraham Rudd', 4 May 1779.

103. Price, p.136. For Squire's additions to the house in the mid-1780s: below, p.103.

> The grammar school at Hereford will be opened after the Christmas holidays on Monday 11 January 1779. Particulars with regard to the plan of education and the expenses attending it may be had by applying to the following persons: Messrs Williams and Price, mercers in Brecon; Mrs Williams, stationer, Carmarthen; Mr Wilmot, bookseller, Pembroke; Mr William Bowen, Haverfordwest; Mr Benjamin Thomas, mercer, Cowbridge, Glamorgan; Mr Williams, bookseller in Monmouth; Mr Turner, bookseller in Ludlow; Mr Andrews, bookseller in Worcester; and Mr Pytt, printer in Gloucester.

The notice, which was repeated on successive Thursdays over the change of year and three times more in subsequent months,[104] was of historic significance being the first such advertisement in the school's history. As importantly, apart from illustrating the *Hereford Journal's* wide circulation within the far-reaches of Wales, Shropshire and the three counties, it reveals the extent of Rudd's ambition for the school and the necessity of his gaining boarding pupils to fill his new house. And perhaps also for the first time, it indicates that the school's curriculum and fees had been printed and widely circulated. In Ambrose Rudd, the Chapter had found an ambitious young Headmaster who was intent on promoting both himself and the school under his care.

No copies of Rudd's 'plan of education' have survived; nor has his 'Cursory Remarks on Education', advertised in September 1780 as a forthcoming publication for the price of one shilling, if indeed it were ever published.[105] The nearest we can come to an understanding of Rudd's philosophy is in his book of collected sermons, published when he was reader at Ludlow parish church, more than three years after his resignation as Headmaster. And even here, he gives little insight as to his educational views beyond his sermon – with *Proverbs* 22, verse 6: 'Train up a child in the way he should go: and when he is old, he will not depart from it', as his text – on 'the great importance of an early and virtuous education'.[106] This was conventional stuff for the time. As he wrote in his introduction to the volume:

> If I have been able to execute my own ideas, the sincere Christian will find nothing to shock his creed, nor the good citizen anything that will violate his regard for the venerable constitution of his country in church or state.

As befitted as student from Wetherell's college, here was a high church Tory presenting his orthodox conservative views to a largely sympathetic wider public.

Financial necessity, at least in part, must have driven Rudd to publish his book of sermons. There is no evidence as to how profitable a venture it was – although well before its publication Rudd had laid claim to having both 'numerous subscribers' and 'honourable patronage' which twice delayed its publication[107] – but at the time he was certainly in

---

104. *HJ*, 24, 31 Dec. 1778; 7 Jan., 20 May, 23, 30 Dec. 1779. By that December, a Mr R. Thomas had replaced Turner as the Ludlow distributor.

105. *HJ*, 14 Sept. 1780. This is the only advertisement I have found for the book.

106. Rudd, pp.113-25. Most sermons are undated, and only 'The benefit of General Infirmaries Illustrated' (pp.127-43), delivered on 3 July 1781, can be definitely dated to Rudd's time in Hereford.

107. *HJ*, 15 April 1784, 3 Feb. 1785. For the latter notice, Rudd listed his agents in Hereford, Leominster, Ross and Ludlow, one of whom (Thomas of Ludlow) corresponded with the distributor of his 'plan of education'.

financial distress. In order to try to understand how this state of affairs had come about, we need to turn to his final months as Headmaster.

Quite apart from his mounting money worries, it was an unhappy period for Rudd because of a personal loss: his wife died at the age of 28 on 23 August 1781. Anne Rudd was interred in a vault opposite the high altar in the cathedral's north aisle, her husband composing the words on her elegant marble monument. As the inscription relates, this was done both to acknowledge her virtues (which included 'a mind enriched' by her 'acquaintance with useful science') and 'to alleviate those pangs of separation which they only can adequately conceive whose similarity of suffering may have taught sympathy of sensation'.[108] Although Rudd's painful bereavement may have been linked to his resignation as a prebendary days after his wife's death,[109] the tragedy cannot explain his resignation as Headmaster more than a year later. This occurred as a result of financial failure: in all probability, Rudd over-extended himself through the building of the new house and schoolroom, and despite his best efforts to promote the school, boarders may not have materialised in sufficient numbers to offset his debts.

The evidence for Rudd's insolvency rests on two newspaper notices posted in the weeks after his resignation. The first appeared in the *London Gazette* of 17 December 1782, as follows:

> The Reverend Mr Abraham Rudd, late of University College, Oxford, and now of the city of Hereford, having assigned his estate and effects to trustees for the benefit of his creditors, all persons who have any demands upon him are desired forthwith to send an account thereof to Messrs Brograve and Lyon, Gray's Inn, London, or to Mr Bourne, attorney in Hereford.[110]

Less than six months later, this second announcement was printed in the *Hereford Journal*:

> Such of the creditors of the Reverend Abraham Rudd, late of the city of Hereford, who have sent in an account of their demands, may receive a dividend of eight shillings in the pound upon their respective debts by applying to Mr Bourne, attorney at law in Hereford.[111]

It is a moot point as to whether these proceedings meant that Rudd had been declared bankrupt or whether they indicated some lesser financial illegality, but it is clear that having resigned his headmastership he obeyed the letter of the law and escaped gaol.[112] Either

108. As recorded by Price, p.96. Rudd paid £2 for his wife's vault. HCA, 7101/2, p.157.

109. Le Neve (2014), p.59.

110. The notice was repeated in the *Hereford Journal*, 26 Dec. 1782; 2, 9 Jan. 1783.

111. *Ibid.*, 12 June 1783.

112. The assignment of Rudd's estate to trustees, rather than a commission of bankruptcy, may indicate that Rudd escaped formal bankruptcy proceedings. I am indebted to Joseph Goldsmith for this observation. That Rudd was not among those in the alphabetical list of the country's bankrupts (between 1 Jan. 1774 and 13 June 1786, as published that year) supports this view.

way, he was not the only clergyman of the period to have fallen foul of the law in this regard.[113] And he was also able to hold on to his vicarage, to which he had been presented in September 1781, and was soon to be instituted by the bailiffs and corporation of Ludlow to the readership of St Laurence parish church, showing the extent to which eighteenth-century Anglican divines enjoyed security of tenure in terms of their livings if not always their offices.[114] So together with the proceeds from his book, published under the name 'A. Blackstone' rather than 'Abraham Rudd', he would have had enough to get by, and certainly more than many impecunious clerics of the period. And although through his ambition – and even neglect – he had left the school in the lurch, maybe Rudd's undoubted talents were never suited to school-mastering and he eventually found his true vocation as a preacher and lecturer. It is significant that in the dedication to his collected sermons, he made this passing reference to his erstwhile tutor and fellow of University College, who became master of the grammar schools at Beverley and then Brewood. 'Why does the caprice of fortune suffer so much genius and industry to be buried in the dust of a provincial school?' – a lament that perhaps applied as much to Rudd himself as to his mentor, George Croft.[115]

Robert D'Lambert Squire, Headmaster for over nineteen years (1784-1803), followed Bagnall's short interim tenure. Of humble origins, he hailed from Heversham in Westmorland and was probably educated at the grammar school there. He then entered (as a batteler) The Queen's College, Oxford, later claiming he was 'in constant residence' there 'for upwards of eight years'. Oxford was followed (in his own vainglorious words) with 'success … in other seminaries' – where we know not – before his Hereford appointment, at the age of 29, on 25 June 1784, almost ten years to the day after his university matriculation.[116]

Although two years younger, Squire was of Rudd's generation and possessed similar drive. Equally a man of business, and building on Rudd's work, he was a better self-publicist and much more successful in his promotion of the school. As befitted his name, he was a man of some style as is evident from the school's *Hereford Journal* advertisements, which had again lapsed under Bagnall between 1782 and 1784. Within his first months as Headmaster, Squire had placed this notice in the newspaper:

> The Revd R.D. Squire MA, Headmaster of the Collegiate School, Hereford, begs leave to inform the public that his house in the churchyard will be genteely fitted up

113. William Couture is one such example. He matriculated from University College in 1771, the same year as Rudd, was frequently indebted and died (in 1820) insolvent in his college living. Darwall-Smith, pp.297-98.

114. HCA, 7031/5, fo 202v, Chapter Act presenting Rudd to the college living of Diddlebury, Shropshire, 6 Sept. 1781; HARC, CA119/1, fo 61r, his subscriptions, 7 Sept. 1781; *HJ*, 3 Feb. 1785, re his readership; and SRO, LB7/149, re complaints about Rudd's conduct of the 6 o'clock prayers at Ludlow, and his high-handed reply to the churchwardens, 22 April 1786.

115. Rudd died suddenly in his early forties on 11 December 1794, John Price paying tribute a year or so later to his 'unfortunate memory'. *HJ*, 17 Dec. 1794; Foster (1887-8), iii., p.1233; Price, p.96.

116. Foster (1887-8), iv., p.1339; *HJ*, 30 Dec. 1784; HCA, 7031/5, fo 229r, Chapter Act, 25 June 1784. As a batteler, Squire would have paid for his tuition and accommodation (his batells) but received his basic food (or commons) free. I am indebted to Michael Riordan for this observation. For battelers at Brasenose in this period: Crook pp.97, 104-05.

> for the reception of boarders immediately after the Christmas recess (January 1785), where every polite attention will be paid to moral and literary improvements. Letters (post-paid) will be immediately attended to.

At a stroke, Squire had changed the school's name from 'grammar' to the grander sounding 'collegiate' school – a name which continued in public announcements until well into the following century – and had made his pitch to attract gentlemen boarders to the school.[117]

Nor did the new collegiate title carry with it the associations implied by the old grammar school name. This was of increasing importance commercially at a time when other schools were abandoning their narrow classical focus. To take just one local example: before the end of the century Lucton School boasted that it 'taught the English, French, Latin and Greek languages; all the useful parts of Mathematics, both in theory and practice; merchants' accounts by the common and Italian methods; [and] penmanship in all the hands now in use'. The classical subjects were taught by old Robert Simpkinson, the Headmaster who had been in post for almost 40 years, whilst J. Pott, formerly a master at an academy in Rotherhithe, had been hired to look after boarding together with the rest of the curriculum.[118] Squire could not go as far as this. Quite apart from the cathedral's need for its statutes to be observed – and as we will see, the Chapter were worried on this score at the beginning of the next headmastership – a predominantly classical curriculum was still of particular importance for attracting the sons of local gentry, as well as clergymen and others who wanted their boys to progress to the universities prior to a career in the church. That the new Headmaster was prepared to maintain the school's traditional strengths is perhaps suggested by the two masters each being given separate keys to the cathedral library early in Squire's reign.[119] Nevertheless, the following notice published a little more than a month later – the first indication of the school's work in the later eighteenth century – illustrates both Squire's teaching method and his intent to remodel the curriculum for his boarding community:

> The young gentlemen more immediately under Mr Squire's care as boarders, will have many opportunities of being made critically acquainted with the various departments of the *belles lettres*; and as they advance forward in their different classes, the elements of Logic, Ethics, Mathematics and Hebrew will be periodically laid before them in a series of private lectures. To obviate vague and irregular private studies, so extremely fallacious and unfriendly to solid acquirements, a syllabus will be put into the hands of each boarder at his entrance, specifying at what certain periods he will be called upon to give an account of particular books and sciences, according to the rank he

117. *HJ*, 4 Nov. 1784, following a briefer notice of 14 October. John Lodge, the Under-Master, also advertised for 'four young gentlemen' to board in his churchyard house 'in a retired and healthy part of the town'. *Ibid.*, 25 Nov., 2 Dec. 1784. The only subsequent public use of the name 'Hereford grammar school' in this period that I have come across was by an old boy when advertising the annual dinner. *Ibid.*, 27 Sept. 1787.

118. *Ibid.*, 13 Jan. 1796. By the following year Pott claimed that only three boarding places remained unfilled. *Ibid.*, 14 Jan. 1797. Simpkinson had been appointed as Lucton's third Headmaster in 1759 and remained in post until 1801. For the proliferation of academies in general (but not Rotherhithe): Hans, pp.63-116.

119. HCA, 7031/5, fo 231r, Chapter Act, 11 Nov. 1784.

holds in the above seminary ... French, Drawing, Writing, Arithmetic and the use of globes will be taught by approved masters, and in future in the College School or the rooms adjoining.[120]

Squire's annual terms for such services were 18 guineas for board and three for tuition, apart presumably for fees for the extras provided by the 'approved masters'.[121]

Squire was also anxious to advance the study of English and announced in June 1785 that he would ensure that one class was 'regularly set apart ... for the study of the English language, viz: Grammar, History, Geography and the varied modes of English composition'.[122] Nothing more is known about this arrangement but there is good evidence to suggest that English as well as Latin composition became an important element in the curriculum, not least for those boys near the top of the school. For in late 1789, the stewards organising that year's old boys' dinner not only awarded 'a premium' (its value was unstated) to one Williams for his Latin verse on civil discord, but also gave a prize to Thomas Underwood, son of the former Usher, for his English poem on canals. Both subjects were of particular relevance at that time: a revolution had broken out in France in June 1789, and an application had been made that summer for a parliamentary bill to be brought forward 'for making a navigable cut or canal' from Ledbury to the River Severn.[123] Although not mentioned again during this period, such awards may have become a regular feature of these dinners. And we know that English composition continued at the school. Thomas Watkins' poem 'Ode to Health' was printed in the *Hereford Journal* in January 1792, the first known publication by a Hereford boy while still at school, and this was followed some eight years later by P. Moore's English verses (with Greek text) 'On the Blindness of Homer'.[124]

Squire's promotion of the school went beyond curriculum notices. For the first time, he published details of its valuable leaving scholarships. In the same advertisement as the one about the English class, he announced that following the receipt of letters from the Principal of Brasenose and the Master of St John's, Cambridge – 'in which young gentlemen of the school are particularly interested' – 'Hereford School' in turn with the grammar schools at Manchester and Marlborough had claim on the 17 Brasenose scholarships (worth £17 annually), as well as the 15 at St John's (from £19 to £26) 'in preference to any other school or seminary'. Such notices were repeated at regular intervals, details being given of any increase in their value, as in 1786-87 when 'the increase in the [Somerset] estates had enabled the trustees to add two to the former number'. Squire then brought to the public's attention (by a pointed finger in the advertisement) the 1691 codicil to the Duchess' will about her scholars having preference 'in case of vacancy, to the valuable

120. *HJ*, 30 Dec. 1784, 6 Jan. 1785. An undated (and slightly emended) copy of this notice later appeared in the school magazine: *TH*, NS CIV (April 1924), pp.13-14.

121. *HJ*, 13 Jan. 1785. Tuition fees were one guinea more than those Willim had charged David Renaud for his son's Hereford 'schooling' in 1741. HARC, A 98/1, fo 89.

122. *HJ*, 30 June 1785.

123. *Ibid.*, 9 Sept., 28 Oct., 4 Nov. 1789. Two years later, an Act was passed 'for making and maintaining a navigable canal from the city of Hereford to the city of Gloucester' (via Newent). 31 Geo. III, c. 89.

124. *Ibid.*, 11 Jan. 1792; 9 July 1800. Both verses were signed as being from 'The College School, Hereford', and dated Dec. 1791 and 10 June 1800 respectively.

living of Wotton-Rivers in Wiltshire' – an announcement obviously directed at the sons of clergyman, as well perhaps as younger sons of local gentry. At the same time, he declared that he had recently made 'some very considerable additional buildings to his house for the accommodation of young gentlemen'.[125]

Given the lack of an extant register before the nineteenth century, the effectiveness of Squire's promotion of the school in terms of pupil numbers cannot be accurately measured. Nevertheless, it is significant that after his first two or three years as Headmaster, his advertisements become less detailed, if not less regular, simply announcing when the school would reassemble, with the occasional brief reference to the Somerset endowment. Even though boarding numbers appear to have been modest even by the end of the century – Squire's pew rent payments from 1795 to 1803 averaged out at 12 persons each year[126] – Old Herefordians, at any rate, believed that the school had prospered under Squire's charge, as this report on a convivial gathering at the old boys' anniversary dinner of 1800 indicates:

> The uninterrupted prosperity of this seminary for a series of years has been uniformly acknowledged, and the high respectability of the present establishment precludes the dread of any diminution of its former celebrity.[127]

So Robert Squire was also esteemed by the school's old boys, if not always by his early Ushers, or Under-Masters as they came to be called, in the 1780s.[128] But there is no gainsaying his successful tenure as Headmaster or his progression as a clergyman: as vicar of Kempley in 1787; the Earl of Oxford's chaplain in 1790; and prebendary of Piona Parva (Canons Pyon) in 1795, and after Bagnall's death, of Bartonsham in 1800.[129] He was also a man of some prosperity, altering his Headmaster's house, rebuilding the Kempley vicarage, 'the old one being totally dilapidated and the site in a bog', and leasing Chapter property in and around Castle Street.[130] He would have gained a part of this wealth through running the school, but he had also taken a risk when accepting the headmastership, after a period of uncertainty, and changing its course of direction. Nevertheless, as the old boys declared

---

125. *Ibid.*, 30 June 1785; 28 Dec. 1786. The latter notice (on the Somerset foundation) was repeated on 4, 11, 18, 25 January 1787, the most for any Squire advertisement. We know nothing about his additions to the Headmaster's house, but see above, p.76, for Rees' description of the house in the early nineteenth century.

126. Following the temporary use of the north choir gallery for the school, the north transept was furnished with pews in 1795 for the parish of St John the Baptist, 'for any inhabitants who shall agree to make an annual payment ... to the fabric fund'. Squire rented pews no. 47 and 48 (with eleven kneelings) at 4s for each seat, together with an extra three seats in 1799-1800 and four the following year. His annual payments ranged from £3 (1795-97, 1800-01) to £2 4s (1797-99, 1801-03). HCA, 7031/5, fos 302v, 311r, Chapter Acts, 25 June 1794, 25 June 1795; HCA, 7101/2, pp.339-46, pew rents.

127. *HJ*, 15 Oct. 1800.

128. He ran through four of them from 1784 to 1790: John Lodge (whom he inherited), Thomas Fowle, Abraham Swann and Samuel Waring (who died in post). The fifth, John Dyer, stayed with him throughout his last 14 years as Headmaster. HCA, 7031/5, p.179, fo 250r, 254r, 265r, 278r, Chapter Acts, 1 Feb. 1780, 8 Nov. 1787, 28 Jan. 1788, 24 March 1789, 11 Nov. 1790; HCA, 7031/6, p. 21, Act 20 Sept. 1803.

129. *HJ*, 15 Nov. 1787, 29 Dec. 1800; Le Neve (2014), pp.34, 91.

130. HCA, 7031/5, fo 325v, Chapter Act, 25 June 1796; HCA, 7101/2, pp.246-319, Squire's leases, 1795/6-1808/09, for which he paid 14s 1d until 1806-07; then 8s 6d for the remaining two years.

at the beginning of the new century, Squire had by then enhanced the school's reputation. They were wrong, however, to imply that the 'high respectability' that Squire had gained for the school by 1800 guaranteed its future success: small schools especially still depended heavily not only on the Headmaster's standing but also on local circumstances. When a few days after his Under-Master's resignation, Squire gave the Chapter notice of his own intention to depart at the 1803 Michaelmas audit. One reason for his decision may well have been a scarlet fever outbreak which resulted in a pupil's death and sent numbers tumbling from 80 or 90 boys to around 30.[131] And as we will see in the next chapter, under an unpopular Headmaster it was not easy for a school to recover from this plight.

Boys and Old Boys

Virtually nothing is known about most of the hundreds of boys who went through the eighteenth-century school – many, perhaps, staying for not more than two or three years – apart from the names of 230 or so choristers and Langfordians, together sometimes with their ages and fathers' occupations.[132] These foundationers never comprised more than 11 pupils, seven choristers and four Langfordians (named Dean's scholars from the early 1770s), at any one time. Numbers would have fluctuated throughout the century,[133] but if we assume that they increased in the final two decades as seems likely as a result of the school's use of the Great Room, the increase of its boarding facilities and Squire's prominent advertising, the proportion of foundationers to others would have decreased as the century progressed. By around 1800, even if the roll of 80 or 90 boys, as remembered by that 'very old boy' T.T. Davies over 70 years later, is taken as the school's high-water mark for this period, the foundation boys would have represented one in eight (at best) of the pupil body. For Old Herefordians there is a little more to be learned, particularly if an old boy entered Oxford or Cambridge, came into prominence locally or gained national recognition.[134] But Davies' brief comments apart, there are no old boy recollections on which we can draw. So this account of eighteenth-century boys and old boys – their backgrounds, study, capers and careers – can be nothing more than an impressionistic survey of the few who have left a mark on the school's history. As with earlier centuries, for the vast majority there is nothing but silence.

A chorister's musical education, which was not the school's responsibility, seems to have been haphazardly conducted in the mid-eighteenth century, judging by the admonitions given to Richard Clack and William Perry, successive Hereford organists, about their failure

131. The evidence is based solely on T.T. Davies' testimony over 70 years after he had left the school. *TH*, No. 2 (Sept. 1878), p.48. For Dyer's and Squire's resignations: HCA, 7031/6 pp.21, 22, Chapter Acts, 20 Sept., 4 Oct. 1803. Squire's wife, Mary, had died (aged 48) on 2 April 1802. Duncomb i., p.585.

132. 142 choristers and 86 Langfordians have been identified for the period 1698-1802 from the Chapter Act books. HCA, 7031/3-6, *passim*. For names of Hereford choristers, as written between 1686 and 1731 on the covers of Barnard's part-books: below, chapter 2, note 165.

133. Sometimes wildly as in 1803 with the advent of scarlet fever, and perhaps also following the smallpox outbreaks in Hereford in June 1736 and September 1742. HCA, 7031/4, p.168, Chapter Act (re residences) 25 June 1736; HARC, A 98/1, fo 90, re David Renaud, who contracted the disease while a day pupil at the school.

134. Despite my description here, it is not until the late nineteenth century that the name 'Old Herefordian' is commonly used to describe a former pupil.

to teach the choristers. Musical training did not feature highly among their priorities.[135] A chorister's general education, however, would have posed problems even for the most conscientious Hereford schoolmaster of the period. Quite apart from the occasional practices and regular choir services – sometimes irregularly attended as Dean Webber discovered when he found out that the boys were left to chant psalms and hymns by themselves[136] – interrupting study either side of morning worship, there were the problems associated with teaching younger choristers. Where we know their ages on admission to the choir, most were aged nine or ten but some were younger. To take three examples from the late 1780s and early 1790s: Thomas Gwillim and James Payne were eight and William Cooke seven. A few years earlier, Thomas Hill may have been even younger for he was elected a chorister 'notwithstanding his age' 'on account of his proficiency in music and being immediately useful in the choir now'.[137] It seems from the visitation articles and replies that these younger boys were first placed in an elementary 'writing school'.[138] And many of them would have had long enough careers as trebles, and perhaps on the back row, to enable them to graduate from there to the Cathedral School proper if they were sufficiently able to do so. Six or seven years' service in the choir was not unusual and there are examples throughout the century of boys remaining in the choir for even longer. Francis Hill (1700-08), Samuel Hayward (1701-09), James Rawlinson (1730-38), James Garbett (1782-90), Christopher Jones (1794-1802) and James Payne (1795-1803) all served around eight years; Richard Lloyd (1708-18), Philip Lewis (1770-79), Matthew Hill (1781-90) and William Cooke (1793-1802) nine; and Francis Lewis (1725-36) – whom we will meet again – well over ten years, a record unlikely ever to have been surpassed.[139]

Not all choristers stayed the course. Henry Jones and John Eckley both died in harness.[140] Others misbehaved and were summarily dismissed. Assuming that the squib allegedly thrown by Thomas Bayley from the organ loft into the choir at Evensong on bonfire night 1699 had nothing to do with a chorister, the most notorious chorister felony of the period was committed by Thomas Bell who assaulted William Fisher, the verger, in College Cloisters in late 1709, 5s being docked from Bell's annual income of £1 to pay a surgeon 'for the cure of his [Fisher's] wounds'. The reason for the dismissal of other choristers like Thomas Gladden are not given. However, Charles Skyrme, described by one of his own as being as 'great a

135. HCA, 7031/4, p.450; 7031/5, fo 238r; Chapter Acts, 24 March 1766, 23 Dec. 1785, ordering Clack to teach the choristers three times weekly, and Perry to do so on Tuesdays and Thursdays on pain of 2s 6d fines for neglect. For the negligence of Clack and Perry in particular: Aylmer and Tiller, pp.411-12; and for observations about the limitations of organists in provincial Georgian cathedrals in general: Mould, p.148.

136. HCA, 7003/1/4, p.154, Webber (from Oxford) to the vicars choral, 22 April 1758.

137. HCA, 7031/5, fos 263v, 293v, 315v, elections of Gwillim, Cooke and Payne, 15 Nov. 1788, 23 March 1793, 12 Nov. 1795; p.132, Hill's election, 9 Nov. 1775.

138. See, for example, Thomas Russell's answer to question 19 of Bishop Beauclerk's 1765 visitation. HCA, 5599.

139. For the exact dates of admission and replacement of these choristers, see the relevant entries in the Chapter Acts, HCA, 7031/3-6, *passim*. Lewis matriculated at 17 from Wadham College, Oxford, on 8 June 1736, so he would have been around six at his entry to the Hereford choir nearly 11 years earlier. For his election and eventual replacement (by William Symonds): HCA, 7031/4, pp.172, 116, 172, Chapter Acts, 25 June 1725, 24 March 1737.

140. HCA, 7031/4 p.206, Chapter Act 8 Nov. 1744; 7031/5, p.176, 11 Nov. 1779.

rogue as ever gallows did hold', lasted three years in the choir in the early 1730s despite his lack of discipline.[141] Indeed, some of these boys would have been rough diamonds, being sons of local shoemakers, carpenters, saddlers, joiners, hairdressers and victuallers, and even (in the 1790s) of an excise-man and a sergeant in the yeomen cavalry.[142]

But for the majority who had served the cathedral loyally, there were rewards. Many choristers on leaving the school and choir could look forward to a payment from Tomson's charity (distributed every third year) of £5 towards an apprenticeship, the amount being doubled to £10 in the 1790s from the want of claimants and an increase in landed rents.[143] And increasingly, former choristers progressed from the school to the universities, especially to Christ Church, Oxford. Of the 20 or so Hereford choristers who gained Oxford degrees in this period, a number returned to serve as priests in the diocese. One, John Greenly, was wounded at Trafalgar and then became vicar of Salisbury Close and an ineffective schoolmaster, and about half of them were appointed vicars choral at Hereford. William Cooke, the vicars' biographer, commends most of them.[144] We have already heard about Richard Underwood, Bagnall's Under-Master, and we will hear more about James Garbett and Samuel Picart, Under-Master and Headmaster respectively in the early-nineteenth century. Of the rest, Richard Lloyd showed a 'professional formality of penmanship' as chief clerk and buttery steward; Benjamin Winston had 'a strong bass voice', transcribed glee books, the Caroline statutes and other College records, and was held in high regard by the choristers 'whom he encouraged to good conduct by advice and suitable rewards'; Francis Woodcock, an excellent counter-tenor, was 'full of intellectual resources', had 'great conversational powers and 'accumulated a capital library'; James Bullock became a prebendary (of Ewithington, 1786-1815) and survived several Chapter admonitions before his resignation from the College in 1796; Robert Pearce, whose treble voice had been much admired, had 'an aptitude for business, vocal talent and agreeable manners'; Matthew Hill, who was regarded by John Lodge, the Under-Master, as being an extraordinarily talented pupil, assisted Dr Robert Holmes, a Hereford prebendary, in his collation of manuscripts of the Septuagint,[145] and 'in talents natural and acquired was seldom surpassed'; and Christopher Jones, who learned to play the harpsichord while at school and later developed a high tenor voice, eventually followed Pearce as Custos (in 1850). All of these old boy vicars had musical and intellectual gifts and became important members of the College and respected parish priests. There was

141. HARC, HD 7/32, part 3 and Marshall, p.68 (for Bayley); HCA, 7031/3, pp.584, 591, Chapter Acts, 24 March, 10 Nov. 1709, for Gladden and Bell; Carless, p.80 and HCA, 7031/5, pp.149, 164 (Chapter Acts, 24 March 1732 and 25 June 1735), for Skyrme.

142. Occasionally at a chorister's election, a father's occupation is recorded in the Act books as in: HCA, 7031/4 pp.165 (for Richard Lloyd), 254 (Thomas Davies); 7031/5, fos 293v (William Cooke), 302r (Christopher Jones), 315v (James Payne), 324r (William Garland), 338v (Samuel Grainger), 344r (William Watkins).

143. The first £10 recipient seems to have been Joseph Smallman: In July 1793, John Rawlings, a joiner, was paid the sum for taking on Smallman on as an apprentice. HCA, 7031/5 fo 297v, Chapter Act, 29 July 1793; and fo 311r, 25 June 1795, for the accumulated surplus in Tomson's charity. Names of chorister apprentices (and occasionally their residentiary canon), 1758-71, are recorded in Tomson's accounts: HCA, 7105/2, pp.193-95.

144. The following account is based on William Cooke's two volume manuscript: 'Biographical Memoirs of the Custos and Vicars admitted into the College at Hereford from 1660 70 1823'. HCA, 7003/4/3-4. For Greenly's chorister election and career: HCA, 7031/5, fo 234r, 24 March 1785; Foster (1891-2), ii., p.559; Mould, p.162.

145. The Greek version of the Old Testament.

but one rogue among them: Francis Lewis, who neglected his duty, misappropriated funds as steward and was formally expelled – the only corrupt officer in Cooke's account of nearly one hundred vicars from 1660 to 1823. Later Lewis gave assistance to Samuel Johnson as a translator and (according to Boswell) 'hung loose upon society'.[146]

Several vicars had also been Langfordian scholars, including Thomas Barnes, John Stone, Thomas Luntley and Thomas Watkins in this period. The first three became prebendaries.[147] Watkins (the author of the published ode) was Squire's chief classical assistant for two years before Oxford, became a private tutor to make up for his lack of preferment as a junior vicar and eventually found advancement outside the diocese as Precentor of Winchester cathedral, chaplain to the college and vicar of two southern livings.[148] But Watkins was the exception: it was more usual for ordained Langfordians to be advanced within the Hereford diocese. It is to these scholars that we now turn.

Exceptionally, choristers might become Langford scholars (and visa-versa). John Stephens (in 1725 and 1727), John Palmer (in 1768), Thomas Ridler (in 1774 and 1776), and David Renaud (in 1781 and 1782) moved from one office to the other but neither was held at the same time. And while the backgrounds of choristers and Langfordians were similar – as we will see, Dean's scholars were also sons of widows, clergymen and artificers – there were differences between these two types of foundationer. Langfordians were older: a boy was often ten or eleven at the time of his election.[149] Their tenures, thereby, were generally shorter than the seven years that Langford intended. Above all, they were either attending the grammar school already or sufficiently advanced in their studies to start there rather than at the writing school. This should not imply that Langfordians were always highly motivated. Although subject to dismissal for less spectacular acts than some choristers, there are enough instances throughout the century of Dean's scholars being removed from the foundation for absconding, persistent absence or other unspecified misdemeanours to suggest that their elections may not have been a particularly rigorous process.[150] Whether the increase of the Langfordians' annual allowance in the 1790s by £1 3s 4d occasioned by the increasing profitability of the Disserth estate, as already mentioned, made any difference to their attitude is hard to tell.[151]

146. For Lewis' neglect of his duties as steward, choir absences and eventual expulsion: HCA, 7003/1/4, p.105, vicars' Acts 10 Nov. 1747; HCA, 7031/4, pp.230, 247, 250, 253, Chapter Acts, 24 March 1748-24 March 1751.

147. Respectively of Pratum Minus (parish of Withington), (1736-47); Eign (1776-78) and Moreton Magna (1778-83); and Withington Parva (1776-1800). Le Neve (2014), pp.97 (Barnes), 46, 77 (Stone), and 112 (Luntley).

148. As a private tutor, Watkins had advertised for eight 'young gentlemen' for instruction in the Greek and Roman classics and other branches of 'polite and useful' English literature. He considered that a small class was 'sufficient for the excitement of emulation, without hazarding their morals by those vices which are too prevalent in larger seminaries'. *HJ*, 25 June 1800.

149. Some were even older: George de Foreville, for instance, was 14. HCA, 7031/4, pp.81, 114, Chapter Acts, 14 April 1722, 20 Nov. 1724.

150. Apart from the three mentioned in the following paragraph, see HCA, 7031/3, p.55; 7031/4 pp.99, 186, 223, 240, 342; 7031/5, p.113, for the suspensions or expulsions of Thomas Matthews, Benjamin Lloyd, Thomas Rudd, Richard Jenkins, John Fisher, John Palmer, among others, 24 March 1703, 15 Nov. 1723, 26 June 1740, 26 Aug., 9 Nov. 1749, 25 June 1757, 24 March 1774.

151. HCA, 7031/5, fos 292r, 335v, Chapter Acts 8 Nov. 1792, 11 Nov. 1796, the latter reference clarifying that

The impression that the Langfordians were not always elected because they were 'towardly for learning' is further suggested by the chance survival from the 1750s of 11 parental petitions to the Dean and Chapter for their sons to be considered for scholarships.[152] Almost all the petitioners stated their occupations to ensure that their boys fell within the terms of Langford's bequest. So we find one widow with five small children, and Hereford working men of seven different trades: two glovers, a baker, a joiner, a tiler, a writing-master, a shoemaker and a saddler. Similarly, the boys' ages are given, together with evidence of their baptism, and for Widow Beard signed certificates from her eldest son's midwife and godfathers as well. By contrast, there are no corroborative letters relating to academic progress and potential, although William Hollings stated that his son (also named William) wrote and read 'very well' and was 'very capable and desirous of learning' and 'of the age of nine years and a scholar in the grammar school under your reverences'. Similarly, Thomas Rodd was 'under the care of the Under-Master of your church school' and 'by his age, place of birth and towardly disposition for learning' was held to be qualified for consideration. Some of the others, like the ten-year-old Robert Beard (together with John, his brother, who was a year younger), James Holland and Thomas Luntley ('upwards of 12 years'), also attended the school. There are no surviving letters, as we might expect, from the Headmaster or his Usher as to how they were progressing. Nevertheless, nine of the 11 were granted the scholarship, the sons of the writing-master and the saddler being the unsuccessful candidates. Only Luntley and Hollings, however, eventually proceeded from the school to Oxford, and only Hollings to Brasenose.[153] Of the other Langfordians, we know that three dropped out before finishing their schooling, a letter of 20 September 1757 (possibly from John Stephens) testifying that Robert Beard had been 'absent for these two years past and [had] now gone to sea'; George Powis had been 'absent since Whitsuntide last'; and Benjamin Spencer had 'not been at school since elected and of late seldom attended church'. It was a poor return from the nine Hereford boys who had been granted the cathedral's favour and a far cry from Philpotts' intention that half the Langfordians at any one time should proceed to Brasenose to continue their education.

In contrast, too, with the previous century, undergraduate admission at the universities generally were in decline during much of this period but at both Oxford and Cambridge Old Herefordians continued to receive preference. At Oxford, although (as already described) Christ Church had come into favour among former choristers as the century progressed, Brasenose was still the school's choice for many boys. Almost half of

---

the overall increase of £9 6s 8d was meant for the four Ludlow boys as well as the four Hereford Langfordians.

152. HCA, 4977. The parental petitions date from between the years 1753 and 1757. Petitions for the Philpotts exhibition on behalf of three earlier Langfordians – Daniel Price (son of a maltster), Michael Hollings (son of a baker and elder brother of William) and Philip Watkins (son of a tanner) – also survive in this series (Hollings and Price were successful); together with Daniel Price's letter of 16 January 1761, asking for his Oxford award to be continued as there was 'no-one qualified to succeed him' and it would 'enable him to take the degree of Master of Arts'. Price took his MA in 1763 after seven years at Brasenose so presumably his request was granted.

153. Luntley became a college fellow, a DCL of the university and prebendary of Withington Parva; and Hollings, following his lack of preferment after ordination, ended his days a miser and recluse. HCA, 7003/4/4, Cooke's biographies no. 2; Le Neve (2014), p.112; *Brasenose Reg.*, i., p.361; Carless, pp.34, 75-77.

Fig. 3.4 The Revd William Hollings OH, a Langfordian who ended his days a miser and a recluse. According to his obituarist in the Gentleman's Magazine *(April, 1820), a fishing basket on his back served the double purpose 'of containing his plunder and concealing the hole in his coat'.*

the 110 Herefordshire students admitted at Brasenose, 1698-1802, have been identified as old boys, most entering the college on the Philpotts and Somerset foundations.[154] And for those with sufficient tenacity and resources to stay the four or seven years to complete the desultory courses for their BA or MA degrees – an outmoded examination system as John Napleton, another Somerset scholar (from Marlborough Grammar School) and later reforming Hereford residentiary, had pointed out in his anonymous 1773 treatise[155] – there was the expectation of further advancement. For the young men entering into Holy Orders – and the church remained the likeliest career for the majority of old boy graduates – the brightest could hope for a college fellowship. Herbert and John Pritchard (1702 and 1717), Edward Traherne (1722) and Herbert Mayo (1739) became vice-principals of Brasenose; James Bowdler (1725), William Mayo (1742), Samuel Bethell (1774), a founder member of The Club, a university dining society established in 1790 to promote liberal principles,[156] and John Huish (1790), fellows of the college. Others returned to the diocese where they had been educated: William Seward (1695), Charles Griffiths (1703), John Lloyd (1710), Charles Tucker (1740), Theophilus Lane and Daniel Price (1756), for example, were all Brasenose men who gained local preferment. Lane excepted, all were Langfordians, as were Francis Bell (1720), John Stephens (1733) and Samuel Picart (1792), who were appointed masters at their old school. At least one Brasenose old boy gained national prominence: John Mayo (1778) became a distinguished London medical practitioner and physician-in-ordinary to Caroline, princess of Wales, his son's publication of *Remarks on Insanity* in 1817 being based on his father's practice. William Lambe, one of Mayo's school contemporaries (although four years junior) and also a Somerset scholar, was to follow in his footsteps from St John's College, Cambridge.

For in the eighteenth century, St John's was beginning to attract old boys, the increased value of its Somerset awards, worth annually some £2 to £9 more than those at Brasenose by 1785 (as we have seen), no doubt being an additional enticement. Old Herefordians are particularly evident for the first half of the century in the college's admission registers, which often list the schoolmasters under whom the boys had studied.[157] Between the registrations of Robert Hathway, our first Cambridge Somerset scholar, on 9 January 1683, and Peter Moore, the author of the ode on Homer's blindness, in 1802, around 50 old boys were admitted to the college, mostly as Somerset scholars. From this list, it is possible to draw a picture of the boys on their entry and reconstruct something of their lives. We know of two recommendations from Richard Traherne for William Powell and Thomas Ford from 1722-23, certifying that the bearers had been educated in the 'Free School of Hereford' and qualified for a Somerset scholarship provided that their 'learning' was approved.[158]

---

154. *Brasenose Reg.*, i., pp.270-411, from which the later details of OH careers are taken (with the year of admission in brackets). For the decline in admissions at Oxford and Cambridge until the closing decades of the eighteenth century: Sutherland and Mitchell, pp.309-13; Searby, pp.12, 61.

155. Sutherland and Mitchell, pp.568-69; Crook, p.159 (incorrectly citing Manchester Grammar School); Aylmer and Tiller, pp.150-53; HCA, 6434, W.J. Rees' manuscript memoir of Napleton's life, *passim*.

156. Crook, p.191.

157. The following details (again with admission dates in brackets) are based on SJCA, C4 1-4, admission registers from 1630; Mayor, *passim*; and a manuscript list of Somerset scholars held by the college.

158. SJCA, D 94/354 and 355, certificates, 15 Dec. 1722; 22 June 1723.

Boys tended to be at least 17 on their admission, a year or two older than in the previous century. Their places of birth are scattered. Many hailed from Herefordshire but by no means all. A number were born (and probably lived) in Wales: John Morgan (1719) was from Carmarthen; William Powell, Cardiganshire; Walter Cuny, Pembroke; and Morgan Price, Llandaff – and some further afield. These boys, and others who lived in the remoter reaches of the diocese (or even nearer Hereford), would have stayed during term either with the Headmaster or like David Renaud, whose father was rector of Whitchurch and who paid a Mrs Jones £14 for his son's board in May 1741,[159] with a Hereford landlady.

The social backgrounds of the St John's boys are also more varied than the Langfordians at Brasenose. Where occupations are given, the seven sons (all under Traherne or his predecessors) of 'gentlemen' not quite matching the ten sons of the cloth. There are six Old Herefordians with fathers in other professions. Timothy Geers (1712), the two John Cams (1749 and 1791) and Robert Sayer (1737) all have medical backgrounds; and the fathers of two others, John Morgan (1719) and John Ross (1737), are listed respectively as 'registrar of Wales' and 'attorney at law'. Finally, there are the boys of whom the Duchess would have most approved: the sons of an inn-keeper, baker, grazier, brazier and a free-holder. Many such undergraduates, together with some clerical sons, would have worked as sizars – poor students who served at table, lit fires and performed other menial tasks to pay their way through the college.[160]

As the Duchess would have expected, many of these Cambridge Somerset scholars, like their Oxford counterparts, became ordained. A few returned to livings within the Hereford diocese, including Joseph Guest (1741) and Thomas Russell (1773), who both became prebendaries and residentiary canons. Of those prominent elsewhere or in other fields, Thomas Pennoyre (1715) of The Moor, Clifford, was High Sheriff of the county for 1755; John Morgan (1719), a senior college fellow and Precentor of St David's; John Cam (1749), a Hereford physician and receiver-general of Herefordshire; William Barrol (1752), the son of the grazier and rector of Sassafras in Maryland, lost his benefice in 1777 on his refusing to renounce his allegiance to George III but left descendants who gained distinction within the American church, army and bar; and William Lambe (1782), fourth wrangler in 1786 (having been listed fourth among the first-class degrees in Mathematics at Cambridge that year) and then a foundress fellow, held important offices at the Royal College of Physicians and was the doctor who ordered Keats abroad on what proved to be the poet's last journey. But the most notable Old Herefordian Somerset scholar of the period – and apart from the co-founder and leader of Welsh Methodism, Daniel Rowland (Plate 5), perhaps the most distinguished old boy of the century – was John Ross (1737), a college fellow who was consecrated Bishop of Exeter in 1778, elected a member of the Royal Society, welcomed John Wesley to his palace and was held to be 'as modest as he was learned'. His career contrasts strangely with one of his Old Herefordian students: Walter Edwards (1754), a poor sizar, who was expelled from

159. HARC, A 98/1, fo 89, entry in Renaud's notebook, 25 May 1741.

160. Eight are listed as sizars: Morgan Price (1744); Thomas Manlove (1747); William Barrol (1752); Walter Edwards (1754); George Luggon (1757); Richard Palmer (1760); Thomas Honniatt (1799); and John Dyer (1786). For a further indication of their menial duties (and status within the college): Lineham, pp.120-21.

St John's in April 1757, 'he having melted down a silver spoon ... and sold part of it to a silver-smith in the town'.[161]

But what of the patterns of work and play while boys were still at school? The answer is that we know little about the hours worked or the method of teaching, and not much more about the curriculum except that it became more diversified. As we have seen, Bagnall was philosophically disposed to introducing a wider range of English studies, and by the time Squire was advertising the school's wares in the mid-1780s, the boarders were gaining the benefit of his lectures in a range of disciplines and 'approved masters' were being brought in to deliver subjects outside his own range of expertise. Nevertheless, despite these advances, Classics would still have been at the heart of the school's learning. Even by the end of the century, there would have been no getting away from the dull routine of classical instruction, despite Squire having changed the school's name from a 'grammar' to a 'college' school. As a Madley private tutor informed the public in 1794 in a notice for young gentlemen designed for the universities, professions or 'superior lines of trade':

> The great advantages of classical learning are universally known. It is most justly considered as the groundwork of general information and the best preparatory discipline for future improvement in every department of science ... Accurate grammatical investigations, examinations, constant application of grammar rules, repetitions, translations and regular exercises in composition are the only means by which it is practicable to acquire any degree of excellence in school learning.[162]

By the early 1790s, too, such instruction in Hereford was being delivered by Thomas Watkins, who acted as Squire's classical assistant for two years before entering Oxford. The same office may also have been performed towards the end of the decade by young Moore, the school's other published boy poet of the period, and perhaps also by John Parsons, eldest son of the Reverend William Parsons of Stretton Grandison, who following his election to the Brasenose Somerset scholarship is described as 'senior boy of the College School in this city'.[163]

Although we have little idea of the nature and length of the school day, we know about the pattern of the school year towards the end of the period from the regular advertisements posted by Rudd and Squire in the *Hereford Journal*. From these, it is apparent that there was an extended holiday of four weeks over Christmas and a break of three or so weeks in late May and early June around Whitsuntide, its length probably being reduced by Squire who instituted a 'midsummer vacation' in July.[164] So four to five month terms, punctuated by two extended holidays, became the normal pattern of the school year well before the

161. C.F. Scott's biographies of a number of Old Herefordians are to be found in his edition of Mayor, vol iii., p.298 (Pennoyre) to p.697 (Sayer). For Lambe, Ross and Rowland: *ODNB*, vols 32., pp.302-03; 47., pp.825-26; 48., pp.2-3.

162. *HJ*, 8 January 1794, notice by Revd Henry Davis BA about his private school at Madley.

163. *Ibid.*, 24 Dec. 1800, the notice also announcing that Parsons was the school's second Somerset election at the college that year, following that of Francis Woodcock (son of a Hereford prebendary). For their elections: *Brasenose Reg.*, i., p.407; and for Watkins, above, pp.102, 107.

164. See, for example, these notices: *HJ*, 18 May 1780; 21 Dec. 1780; 12 July 1787.

end of the century. But it is also clear from the Dean and Chapter's directive to Bagnall of November 1774, that the Headmaster had discretion to grant 'play days' during term, following requests from the bishop, prebendaries at their installation, canons in residence and visiting dignitaries.[165] Several were no doubt granted each year.

And for the first time there is an indication of what boys got up to either on their 'play days' or during their free time in normal school. Play areas would have been necessarily restricted within the eighteenth-century Cathedral Close. There were, however, gardens near the school, including the Headmaster's garden, which might have been used for quieter recreational activities.[166] But for the most part the cathedral, its buildings and the churchyard itself would have been the children's playground, despite the 1710 prohibition against boys playing 'in the cathedral ... cloisters, churchyard or other places belonging to the ... church upon Sundays, holy days and at other times'.[167] The walls of buildings, especially those that were buttressed, would have made excellent fives courts, as suggested by the Chapter's order to their carpenter to fix posts 'to prevent the boys and others playing at ball against the church or school at the west end thereof'.[168] And the churchyard itself would have made an interesting place to play rudimentary sports, irrespective of the obstructions caused by carriages, waggons, sedan chairs and beasts, and even (by 1790) the dangers posed to health from 'the many putrid limbs continually thrown out and exposed to public view' by an over-crowded burial ground.[169] A Chapter Act of 10 November 1796, limiting the playing of games to outside the railed walks which Dr Woodcock had first established 'in the manner the Mall is in St James' Park' a generation earlier, gives us the first indication of what these games might have been:

> Ordered that no boys except Mr Squire's be suffered to play in the churchyard, and that they be restrained from playing at all in the walks or within the rails at cricket, bandy [a primitive form of hockey] or any other diversion that may endanger the passengers or the windows of the cathedral.[170]

The boys soon over-reached themselves, however, for by the following midsummer, Squire was required 'in order to preserve the cathedral windows as much as possible', to prevent

165. See above, p.93. At Salisbury the duty canon could award two full holidays to the school during his residence by ancient custom. Mould, p.162.

166. HCA, 7031/4, p.187, Chapter Act, 13 Nov. 1740, ordering the master of the fabric to rent the garden 'lying by the school' (for a timber-yard); Act, 12 Nov. 1767, pales between the schoolmaster's garden and the way to the Canon's Bakehouse to be repaired; HCA, 7031/5, fo 236r, Act, 30 Sept. 1785, giving permission for Squire to use the Chapter garden. Also, see above, p.82, for Willim's addition to the Headmaster's garden in 1733.

167. HCA, 1569, Bishop Humphreys' visitation article, no. 23.

168. HCA, 7031/4, Chapter Order, 6 May 1767, for Philip Evans to fix posts as directed by Dr Russell.

169. For such nuisances over this period, see the following Chapter Acts: *Ibid.*, p.123, 10 Nov. 1726 (coaches); p.354, 20 April 1758 (carriages); p.440, 25 June 1765 ('horses, asses or other beasts'); HCA, 7031/5, p.159, 8 Jan. 1778 (gate locks to keep out 'sedan chairmen'); fo 277r, 11 Sept. 1790 ('putrid limbs'); HCA, 7031/6, p.14, 11 Nov. 1802 (waggons and carts).

170. HCA, 7031/5, fo 335r, 10 Nov. 1796 (incorporated in the 1800 standing regulations, fo 352r); *ibid.*, pp.78, 134, for the Chapter Acts of 20 Feb. 1772 and 9 Nov. 1775 re the railed paths; and HCL, B.3.17 for Wathen's view of the railed walk leading to the Booth porch, 18 April 1786.

Fig. 3.5 James Wathen's drawing of the fall of the west end of the cathedral, from the north-west, showing the railed walks and gravestones in the Close, which the boys used as their playground until 1851.

his boys from 'playing at ball' in the churchyard at all. How easy it would have been, in any case, for the boys to play bandy and cricket among the gravestones outside these gravelled paths is a matter of conjecture, but at least they had the exclusive use of the area for their quieter pastimes, as the Chapter reiterated the following year, when the Close constable was ordered to inspect the churchyard at least twice a day 'and turn out all the boys except the College schoolboys'.[171]

No doubt other recreations like boating and fishing were pursued on the Wye, and perhaps even real tennis would have been played on the court nearby.[172] Of boys' involvement in these, or less innocent sports like cock-fighting, we know nothing. Some senior boys, however, may have kept horses. The Chapter directed in March 1772 that no part of the Canon's Bakehouse was to be used by the schoolmaster or inhabitants of his house as a stable 'as many inconveniences may arise thereby',[173] so at that time riding may have been

171. HCA, 1535, Chapter Clerk to Squire, 28 July 1787; HCA, 7031/5, fo 337v, 16 May 1797. Even the military were forbidden to muster in the churchyard. *Ibid.*, fo 338v, 26 June 1797.

172. HCA, 5714, accounts of Henry Jones (parish collector of the common rents), 1674-1713, listing annual receipts of 3s 'for the tennis court' within St John parish.

173. HCA, 7031/4, p.80, Chapter Act, 24 March 1772.

an option for the few boys rich enough to be able to afford it. For the rest, open-air recreation would have consisted of long walks in the Herefordshire countryside. Of two other activities we can be more certain: in November 1790, Kemble's 'elegant theatre', established in the Half Moon, Broad Street, 12 years earlier, put on two 'fashionable' three-act plays, together with a 'new harlequin entertainment', at the request 'of the young gentlemen of the College School', who no doubt attended the performance; and in April 1799, Squire and a different cohort of 'young gentlemen' contributed £5 towards the mayor's appeal on behalf of one Thomas Creed, whose wife and apprentice had died in a devastating fire which had destroyed his business, the first known instance of a charitable collection by the school.[174]

Whatever a boy's experience at the time, by the late eighteenth century a number of alumni took sufficient pride in their school to relive old times. As already described, the first formal gathering of this school's old boys occurred in Hereford on 21 September 1784 as a tribute to their Headmaster, Gibbins Bagnall, at the end of his second magisterial tenure. Two years later, its clientèle was widened and 'gentlemen educated under other masters' were invited to dine. Thus began the first series of annual old boy dinners which lasted almost without interruption for 48 years, albeit a century later than those of the great schools and a decade after Mr Rodd's former scholars from the charity school had gathered together at Woodcock's coffee house.[175] Apart from honouring (and perhaps dishonouring) their masters, one purpose of these dinners (as in 1789) was to reward boys at the top of the school for their compositions.[176] Given that many of the guests would have been clergymen and others of a strong Tory hue, another would have been to discuss matters of church and state. Perhaps this was especially so at the London dinners held in the early 1790s at a time when the French Revolution was beginning to become more violent. But like today, the main reason for the gatherings would have been for old boys to share together in convivial surroundings 'endearing recollection of youthful pleasures'. Or in the words of the 1791 anniversary report: 'The remembrance of youthful exploits gave a high zest to present enjoyment'; the party breaking up 'at a very seasonable hour, a little pleased with their encouragement and with each other'. The following year this tribute was paid to the alumni who had organised the meeting: 'The whole entertainment was conducted upon such a scale as to reflect the highest honour upon the taste and liberality of the two gentlemen who discharged the office of stewards'.[177] It is these gentlemen that we finally observe.

Like the triennial music meeting, where six stewards were generally employed rather than the two at the Hereford old boy dinners, each lay steward was balanced by a clergyman.

---

174. *HJ*, 31 Dec. 1778 (for Kemble); 17, 24 Nov. 1790; 16, 24 April 1799.

175. These 48 early dinners were held at the New Inn (1784-89, 1807-08), the Bowling Green (1790-99, 1809), the Green Dragon (1800-06, 1832), the City Arms (1810-12) and the Greyhound Inn (1813-30). Similar annual dinners were held in London, 1791-94. I am indebted to John Eisel for this information and details about the stewards. See Thomas, p.15 note 61, for the late-seventeenth century feasts and reunions at St Paul's, Eton, Westminster, Merchant Taylors' and other schools; and *HJ*, 18 Aug. 1772, 26 Aug. 1784, 31 Aug. 1786, for Rodd's gatherings (which had started in 1771) and the 1784 and 1786 dinners.

176. See above, p.102.

177. For these reports: *Ibid.*, 16 Nov. 1791; 10 Oct. 1792; 15 Oct. 1800.

Their names are given in the *Hereford Journal* notices, posted each year a few weeks before the autumn dinner. Little more can be said about the laymen except that they were all likely to have been prominent city and county figures. In 1807, for example, Sir John Geers Cotterell of Garnons, a substantial local landowner and one of the two county MPs for Herefordshire, was one of the stewards. Three years later, Thomas Bird, a Hereford solicitor and businessman who became clerk of the peace, had taken over the office. Earlier, in the 1790s, the London Old Herefordians had assembled first (in 1791) at Mr Greenly's 'Crown and Rolls' in Chancery Lane and then for three successive years at Grays Inn coffee-house, Holborn, which suggests that the hosts, all of whom were laymen, and perhaps many of the company, were lawyers.[178]

More is known about the clergymen stewards at the Hereford meetings: as might have been expected, they were all prominent alumni within the cathedral, college and diocese. Six of the 20 clerics organising the dinner from 1784 to 1803, became (or were already) residentiary canons: Hugh Morgan (1784), Thomas Russell (1786), Charles Morgan (1787), James Jones (1789), Thomas Underwood (1799) and Morgan Cove (1800). Thomas Clarke (1791) and James Bullock (1794) were prebendaries although not members of the Chapter. Of the five who were vicars choral, two, Benjamin Winston (1785) and Robert Pearce (1801), became College Custos. In 1802, Thomas Kidley, was the clerical steward. With his mellow bass voice, wide knowledge of literature and lively conversation, he would have made a brilliant host. And perhaps he also wore his favoured but unsightly bush-wig for the occasion, an increasingly unfashionable adornment which his biographer considered 'a very unbecoming appendage to his tall and slender frame'. Two years later, it was the turn of another vicar choral. Samuel Picart, the first appointed Headmaster of the nineteenth century, could match Kidley neither as a singer nor as a conversationalist but being over 30 years his junior, he was a man of a new age.[179]

---

178. *Ibid.*, 2 Feb. 1791; 8 Feb. 1792; 27 Feb. 1793; 12 Feb. 1794.

179. See HCA, 7003/4/4, nos 61, 81 for Cooke's pen-portraits. Kidley was born on 28 Sept. 1742 and Picart in 1774.

CHAPTER 4

RISE AND DECLINE, 1803-1851

Between the period of the Napoleonic wars, when redcoats roamed the local streets, and the Great Exhibition in Hyde Park of 1851, Hereford's population steadily increased from the 6,828 souls recorded in the first census of 1801 to the 11,151 registered five decades later. Most of these new-comers were accommodated within the old city boundaries, either through new infilling or in existing slum dwellings, rather than in the suburbs, which did not markedly expand until the later Victorian period. Nevertheless, by 1851 the compiler of Lascelles' *Directory* could point to Hereford's 'clean and healthy appearance', its streets being 'well paved and lighted with gas' and its roads 'macadamised'. 'The streets in general', the author continued, 'are of moderate width, containing excellent shops and private dwellings [and] there are reading rooms and numerous public institutions in addition to the delightful walks in the neighbourhood which add greatly to the comfort of the inhabitants'.[1]

As befitted Hereford's dominant position as the county's great service centre that it had established in the Georgian era, trades and professional businesses proliferated. By the mid-nineteenth century, in addition to the 155 residents listed as clergy and gentry, more than one hundred trades and professions from accountants to wool-staplers were categorised in the 1851 Gazetteer, employing over 1,000 people (around ten *per cent* of the city's population). Fifteen or so can be classified as professional. Twenty-eight solicitors headed the list, followed by the insurance agents (27), chemists and 'druggists' (13), other types of agent (11), medical men, of whom 11 were surgeons (including 2 veterinary) and 7 physicians, accountants and land surveyors (7 in each category), auctioneers and appraisers (6), bankers (5) and architects and surveyors (2). Education was represented by 5 self-styled 'professors' and jobbing teachers, and those who staffed the 13 boarding (7 for ladies and 6 for gentlemen) and 9 day schools.[2]

Of these, by far the most important was the Collegiate or Cathedral School as it increasingly came to be called, at least until it moved back into the College in the mid-century.

1. Gretton, p.10 ('importations of redcoats [into Hereford] kept us alive and merry'); Johnson and Shoesmith, pp.196, 221; Lascelles, p.5.

2. *Ibid.*, pp.19, 37-69. The number of professionals pales into insignificance compared with the 72 boot and shoemakers; the 68 hoteliers, inn and tavern-keepers; the 58 shopkeepers and 44 tailors. The day schools include the three St Peter's schools for girls, boys and infants in Union Street.

Hereford's richer clergy and burgeoning professional class, together with a proportion of the wealthier local tradesmen, could all have afforded the school's annual tuition fee (10 guineas by 1851), and the 30 or so extra guineas for boarding would have been well within the compass of the gentry and middle classes in Herefordshire and neighbouring counties. Indeed, many paid up, particularly during the headmastership of 'the great' Dr Taylor (1807-26), during which time numbers peaked at over one hundred pupils. One anonymous old boy in the mid-1850s fondly recalled 'the dynasty of the good old Doctor' as a period when 'the scions of the aristocracy' were 'nurtured in common' with the foundations boys 'to the equal advantage of both classes; and many of them afterwards [he continued] fought their way together at college and in the world, to the highest distinction in intellectual attainments'. He also remembered that it was during the 'palmy days' of Dr Taylor's headmastership that the '*floreat schola Herefordensis*' toast was drunk at the school's pre-vacation banquet, the first indication we have of the use of these words of felicitation.[3]

In contrast, the tenures of the other five Headmasters of the period – Samuel Picart (1803-07), Charles Taylor junior (1826-39), William Ley (1839-42), John Woolley (1842-44) and Thomas Layng (1844-51) – were less lustrous, and the school's reputation declined. Numbers fluctuated, sometimes wildly, reaching the nadir of eight fee-payers as Dr Layng's tenure closed. All these clerical gentlemen were good scholars; all but two were young and inexperienced on taking up their posts; until 1839, when the post was advertised for the first time, all held local livings with their headmasterships; the Taylors apart, none stayed long enough to make much of a mark on the school; and with the significant exception of Dr Taylor, none ran a sufficiently attractive school to compete with neighbouring rivals. On the one hand, local commercial schools proved a preferable alternative for the tradesman; on the other, many gentry and wealthier professional families looked to major schools for the education of their sons. Even with the sons of the Cathedral Close, there was no guarantee that they would complete their education at HCS. Frederick Gretton, the Dean's son, provides one example of a boy who started his classical tuition at the school before moving in 1814 to Shrewsbury. The Hereford boys (he remembered a near life-time later) were 'a very mixed and untoward lot', whereas Shrewsbury was in the process of being transformed under the ministrations of that remarkable Headmaster, Dr Samuel Butler (1798-1836). In addition to the regeneration of older foundations, towards the end of the period the Cathedral School had to face the challenge of a succession of new public schools which were founded in the first part of Victoria's reign. Cheltenham College, which opened in 1841, was the earliest of these, the first boy to be enrolled there being one Henry James, a Herefordian who became Gladstone's attorney-general and was ennobled as Baron James of Hereford.[4] Three years later, HCS lost a few boys to another new proprietary college at Rossall in Fleetwood (Lancashire) when Dr Woolley left to become its first Headmaster.

It was not that the Cathedral School stagnated during this near half-century. The nature and location of its schoolroom, for example, changed. Despite the 1804 alteration to its

3. *HJ*, 18 Nov. 1857, letter from 'An Old Boy'. The old boy observed that he could still 'most heartily repeat' the '*floreat*' toast ('the concluding toast of our scholastic table'), but lamented that he could no longer join in the old refrain: '*gaudiamus igitur, juvenes dum summus*' ('Let us, therefore, rejoice while we are young').

4. Fisher, pp.262-324; Askwith, p.14.

fenestration, the Great Room, after having been abandoned for Smirke's 'Grecian' shire-hall by the triennial music meeting from 1819, gradually fell into disrepair and was eventually demolished in 1835. A time of uncertainty followed before a new schoolroom was built on the back of the Canon's Bakehouse. Two years later, the Headmaster's house was improved – the school being closed for a while before Ley and his new bride were ensconced there – and additional boarding accommodation provided for 40 boys, a number which was never realised during this period, although the Headmaster's private pupils may have in part made up the shortfall. And in 1842, John Woolley acquired the College chapel, which had been rebuilt seven years earlier, for the school's worship. These school buildings were not grand but by the 1840s its teaching, boarding accommodation and chapel were situated on adjacent parts of the Close.

There were other important developments. At the beginning of Picart's reign, the Dean and Chapter, mindful perhaps of the recent national charge that endowed schools were systematically neglecting the teaching of Christian education,[5] required the Headmaster to make an annual report on Religious Instruction within the Cathedral School. By Layng's time, this had metamorphosed into a general report on the doings of the foundationers, the decline of boarding and Oxford entries.

As for the rest of the curriculum, all the evidence points to the continued supremacy of the Classics. And from the chance survival of Dr Taylor's register, a remarkable record of the school's academic doings from 1818 to 1825, we have a detailed account of the texts studied and the lines supposedly learned, month by month, by the boys in each class. This was in accord with his adoption in 1818 of the mutual (or 'Madras') system of boy tuition,[6] which was made famous by Dr Bell – popularly known as the 'school Bell' – who for a short time was a Hereford residentiary canon. Although popular for the mass education of children in elementary schools, Hereford was one of the few classical schools to have used this method of instruction. Dr Taylor even published a grammar for use by his Hereford boys. The new system was not always well received by traditionalists like James Bullock, an old boy who wrote a vituperative pamphlet against its use, and it did not last. Its end at Hereford was probably sealed by the dramatic decline in numbers during the headmastership of Taylor's son, the method probably foundering by the early 1830s when Dean Merewether insisted on the re-adoption of the Eton Grammar. By Woolley's time, the classes had been renumbered in the traditional manner, with the IVth or Vth again designating the top form. Like Dr Russell at Charterhouse, Dr Taylor's bold experiment was successful in coping with the classical education of a large number of pupils but failed when the school was declining and the system was administered by less capable hands.

Religious and classical instruction aside, other subjects like Ancient History and Geography were taught even under Dr Taylor's regime. Arithmetic (and some Accounts) was the purview of the supernumerary writing-master – hired like other assistants (the Usher apart) at the Headmaster's expense – at least until 1840 when a graduate 'mathematical

5. The charge had been made a year of two earlier by Dr Rennell, the master of the Temple, as well as by the Bishop of Meath from the pulpit of St Paul's, and was answered in 1802 in a pamphlet written by William Vincent, the Headmaster of Westminster. Adamson, pp.45-46.

6. See below, p.137.

master' was appointed. The most important of these men until his retirement in 1825 was Benjamin Powle, whose influence was such that his commendation of a pupil, the meritorious Thomas Pitt, was recorded in Dr Taylor's register. His other pupils included Richard Gwatkin, who was senior wrangler in 1814, and Edward William Lane, the great orientalist, whose proficiency as a boy was such that as a prospective Cambridge undergraduate he solved all the questions posed in a mathematical tripos paper.[7] So for the very gifted, mathematical teaching appears to have been of a high order in the early decades of the century, although a generation later, Woolley felt unable to award a mathematical prize in the December 1842 examinations.[8] In sum, Classics (overwhelmingly), Divinity, some Mathematics and a little of the modern humanities formed the staple subjects of the curriculum. No Science was taught; nor was teaching in Modern Languages widely available, French being no more than an optional extra, and simply viewed like Dancing, Drawing, Fencing and Music as a desirable gentleman's accomplishment for his leisure hours.

And there was much leisure, despite the demands of two 20-week terms, 35 tuition hours over a six-day week and a long day starting around seven and finishing at five – albeit one punctuated by three breaks.[9] Some of the free-time was unofficial. As is evident from Dr Taylor's register, which not only details instances of boarders running away from school but also records a high rate of absenteeism, very few boys attended every session. But there were also official holidays during term-time. A few of these were authorised by dignitaries or old boys who had gained academic success but, more regularly, half-holidays were given on two days each week. In Dr Taylor's time, these were on Thursdays and Saturdays when boys were released at noon. An insight into what they did during these afternoons is provided by two late-nineteenth-century reminiscences.[10] T.T. Davies whose memory went back to Picart, suggested that bandy and cricket – although not football which 'was [then] considered a low game, only indulged in by boys of an inferior grade' – continued to be played in the churchyard, and before the erection of Nelson's column in 1809, on Castle Green. And F.W. Bennett left these details about the school's bounds and its pupils' extracurricular activities in the 1840s:

> Bounds comprised the cathedral yard as far as the path leading from the north porch, Castle Street and the Castle Green, extended in summer to the 'Bassom' [Bartonsham] meadow where we bathed, but the elder boys could always get leave to go into the town. Playground we had none, but the boarders utilised that part of the cathedral yard between the school buildings and the cloisters leading from the College to the cathedral, and the day boys the part opposite to the Deanery. Our fights generally came off at the bathing place but sometimes in the before-mentioned cloisters where I had my last 'turn up' (with the late Beresford Harris) a few days before I left school.

7. The answer to one of them coming to him in the middle of the night. The story is told in *TH*, no. 3 (Jan. 1879), p.121.

8. HCSA, Dr Taylor's register (back pages), Woolley's prize-list, Christmas 1842.

9. At least during Charles Taylor junior's time, when boys attended at 7.30 (rather than 7.15 under his father), 9.30, Noon and 3pm. HCA, 7031/18, p.442, Chapter order 9 Aug. 1834, refusing Taylor's request that the ringing of the school bell should be changed from 7am and 1 o'clock to the above times.

10. *TH*, no. 2 (Sept. 1878), p.49; and XVI (Nov. 1891), p.21.

> We had no monitor or anyone to look after us out of school so fights were frequent, although a black eye or swollen lip always entailed a heavy 'impot' [imposition].

But there were no regularly organised team games, and as Bennett observed, no playground to play them in, the pupils still having to make do and the citizens having to bear (in Canon Musgrave's words) 'the unseemly sight of … [boys] playing over the tombs in the Close … or … running about the streets'.[11] Towards the end of the period, however, occasional cricket matches were organised by the boys themselves, the earliest reported one being the match played in a Bartonsham field in early October 1840 'between eleven young gentlemen of the College School … against eleven of the Widemarsh Commoners', the Commoners winning by 109 runs 'after three days fine play on both sides'. Two later contests (in 1848) were between the school and the 'Break-of-Day' club, both of which resulted in victories for the cathedral boys. By 1850, the boys had formed their own club, which resulted in a 'spirited' but low-scoring internal match between a team of ten and one of five pupils – the majority side winning despite the lowly contributions of the Headmaster's three sons – and a draw in the 11 a-side game against Mr Hayter's school.[12] As for 'boating', the only evidence that it might have been taken seriously is provided by John Oakes Taylor and Edward Garbett, two old boys who both rowed for Brasenose in 'Torpids' in 1839, which does not necessarily mean that they had taken up rowing at school.[13] But such sports as football (of either variety) and athletics, were in their modern form, late Victorian inventions.

So for an observer of the school in 1850, it would not have appeared inevitable that a boy's freedom to indulge in individual pastimes on his half-holidays would soon be replaced by organised team games. As is revealed in the account which ends this chapter of the extraordinary misadventures of a chorister, Robert Carpenter, in the spring of 1820, walking, fishing and music-making made up the kind of activities that boys enjoyed during their extensive leisure hours. To these might be added games in the Close which neither disturbed cathedral services nor endangered its windows; pursuits like bathing, boating and fighting; and, in Carpenter's case, riding, drinking and (possibly) arson. For the latter alleged offence, he was imprisoned and then brought before a grand jury at that year's midsummer assizes where the case was dismissed.

It was and remains highly unusual for any schoolboy to be imprisoned and tried in a court of law but as is shown by Taylor's 1818 school rules – the first that have survived – punishments for even minor misdemeanours could be severe. Before enforcing the final sanction of expulsion, these punishments were available under Dr Taylor's regime: transcriptions of sermons, appropriately for writing on walls and carving names on desks;

---

11. As reported in the *HJ*, 7 May 1851. It seems that Charles Taylor junior's request to the Chapter in late 1827 for a new playground (HCA, 7031/18, p.258) was ignored.

12. Anthony, pp.27, 52; *HJ*, 7 Oct. 1840, 18 Sept. 1850; *HT*, 17 Oct. 1840, 14, 28 Sept. 1850. In the internal match F. Layng, T.B. Layng and C. Layng scored nine runs between them. For G.G. Hayter and his school: below, pp.163, 184.

13. *Brasenose Reg.*, i., pp.508, 509. Unlike cricket, an undergraduate – then and today – could become proficient at rowing without prior experience. Given that the two OHs rowed in 'torpids' (at the time bumping races for College second boats) may indicate that they had not rowed much at school.

forfeitures and fines; parading around as a named 'sloven' and public humiliations like the dreaded 'mark';[14] and corporal punishments such as cuts on the hand and floggings. Much of his regime was administered by monitors, whose powers were wide-ranging when the boys were in school. As well as keeping regular discipline, as Woolley required them to do in the College chapel, they were allowed to flog until the Dean and Chapter put an end to the practice in December 1834 in no uncertain terms.[15] And the most senior boy had additional duties, including (as related in the 1818 rules) undertaking the office of treasurer of the school's general fund.[16] How effective all this was in maintaining good order, let alone in promoting behaviour worthy of a Christian gentleman, is impossible to determine but apart from one barring-out incident in late 1844, HCS seems to have escaped the boy rebellions suffered by the major boarding schools.[17]

The Cathedral School also continued to provide a regular supply of boys to the ancient universities, the professions and trades. Oxford remained the preferred destination, although for those gaining entry to the school's colleges not by much, around 26 old boys proceeding to Brasenose and 20 to St John's, Cambridge, during this period.[18] The number of Langfordians going on to Brasenose, however, declined markedly as is evident from the few distributions made to them from Philpotts' charity: only £245 being paid out between 1790 and 1833. As a consequence, its accumulating funds were used for other purposes, nearly £2,000 worth of loans being transferred from Philpotts to the cathedral fabric fund (at four *per cent* interest) by 1829. Almost 20 years later, the charity's investments were being used to help pay off the fabric debt.[19] So Langfordians increasingly forsook the expense of an Oxford education for the more certain returns of trade, the Chapter using Tomson's charity for 'placing out' these boys 'towards their advancement in life'. It was the same with former choristers. Only exceptionally do they proceed to university, the vast majority being granted £10 at their leaving towards an apprenticeship, unless (as with

---

14. 'La marque' was a stigma passed on from one pupil to another in this period, the original holder having detected and denounced another boy in a lapse of the school rules. At HCS, Taylor used the mark to punish bad language, those boys carrying the mark either at 9.30am or 3pm being fined by a monitor. See below, p.134. For its use elsewhere (particularly in French and private schools) at this time: Chandos, pp.53-54.

15. See HCA, 7031/18, p.481, for the letter to Taylor, 9 Dec. 1834, requiring that 'the infliction of corporal punishment' should 'not on any account [be] delegated'.

16. A list of senior scholars from 1807, mistakenly headed 'captains', was published in *TH*, no. 4 (Sept. 1879), pp.193-94. This was evidently compiled from both Dr Taylor's register and his Usher, William Cooke's register dated 1812-24. *Ibid*, no. 3 (Jan. 1879), p.145. Sadly, this latter source is now lost.

17. In 1818, for example, rebellion broke out in all but one of the major public schools. For accounts of these and other school rebellions during the early nineteenth century: Chandos, pp.167-95.

18. *Brasenose Reg.*, i., pp.414, 426, 438, 440, 450, 455, 459, 462, 466, 469, 475, 484, 487, 488, 495, 501, 508, 509, 514, 521, 528, 531,537, 548; SJCA, C4/5 and 6, entry books 1802-35, 1835-84 *passim*. For correspondence relating to one of them, James Esdaile, who was elected onto the Somerset foundation at BNC at Christmas 1809, and his father's concerns about the administration of the scholarship: HCA, 1536.

19. HCA, 7105/5, 1829 account; HCA, 7105/6, 1847 account, showing transfer of consoles valued at £1,233 12s 8d; *Reports of the Commissioners ... Concerning Charities and Education, XIII (Hereford, 1815-39)*, pp.300-301. As early as 1814, the Brasenose Principal made enquiries as to why Langfordians no longer applied to his college. See BNCA, A3.19 p.350, for James Bullock's reply to Thomas Yate, 8 Dec. 1814, about the 'want of proper applicants'.

Byers in 1847) the master was a Roman Catholic.[20] Of these and other old boys of the first half of the nineteenth century, a few made their mark nationally, among them the Garbetts in the church; Judges John Maurice Herbert and William Henry Cooke in the law; and Edward William Lane and David Cox, junior, in the scholastic and artistic worlds. Most old boys, however, were content to remain in the region where they went to school, some later becoming prominent in Hereford's corporate and civic life. Robert Carpenter, as we will see, was one of these but there were many others. And some returned from the ancient universities to become ordained clergymen, as they had done for centuries, serving the people of the Hereford diocese as parish priests and often the cathedral foundation as vicars choral. Edward Higgins was just one prominent old boy cleric who came back to his native county after his Oxford years at Brasenose, rebuilding Bosbury House and landscaping its grounds, indulging his antiquarian passions and policing his local community as a magistrate.[21] In all these ways, the Cathedral School fulfilled its historic mission, even if, with its fluctuating numbers, it struggled to do so in the second quarter of the century.

Alfred Salway, the Ludlow MP's son and the solitary boarder in *c.*1836, may have been called 'school' by his friends and the townsfolk, but that sobriquet could equally have been applied to the nameless solitary boarder in 1844 or the one day pupil in 1851.[22] The nickname would not have reflected reality, of course. Salway and the two other boys may have been the sole fee-payers but there were 12 additional foundationers, making a school of at least 13 pupils in these years. It matters not whether the story is apocryphal; what matters is that it indicates the extent of the Cathedral School's decline in the 1830s and 1840s compared with the heady days of Dr Taylor's regime a generation earlier. This decline coincided with John Merewether's divisive period as Dean (1832-50).

Towards the beginning of his tenure, the new reforming Tory Dean expressed these sentiments in an open letter to Charles Taylor, the Headmaster: 'You have my best wishes for the rapid increase and prosperity of the school, in which I feel a great interest, and to which while I am resident at Hereford, I hope to give some of my time'.[23] The Dean's hopes for the school proved illusory. It was not that he was inactive or that his heart was in the wrong place. He immediately required Taylor to revert to the Eton Grammar, which despite its antiquity and limitations was then used by all the major schools; he endowed new prizes; he examined the boys; he sent four sons to the school; and he opened the headmastership to competition and required that an incumbency should no longer be attached to it. These were considerable advancements. But the forces against him were too strong to enable the Cathedral School to regain the position it had enjoyed earlier in the century: the turnover

20. The following nine choristers have been identified from the Act books and Foster's *Alumni Oxonienses*, as having matriculated at Oxford in this period: Edward Howells, William Watkins, Thomas Hill, Henry Pearce, John Prosser, Albert Jones, John Griffiths, Ezekiel Mills and Christopher Jones. The apprentice fees paid out to foundationers from Tomson's charity are listed in its nineteenth-century accounts: HCA, 7104/4-5, *passim*. For the chapter's refusal to pay Byers: HCA, 7031/20, p.95, 25 March 1847.

21. The above names (Judge Herbert and Robert Carpenter apart) are listed in Weaver, pp.104, 112, 167, 211, 245.

22. Salway matriculated from BNC (aged 21) in June 1838 but only lasted at Oxford for one year. He later became a commissary-general in the army. *Brasenose Reg.*, i., p.514. For the solitary numbers in *c.*1836, 1844 and 1851: Carless, p.42, and below, p.165 (including note 164).

23. Merewether's letter was published in the *Hereford Journal*, 27 Feb. 1833.

Fig. 4.1 John Merewether, an imperious Dean who was unable to stem the school's decline.

of Headmasters was too rapid; the school's infrastructure too insecure; and the competition too intense, especially in the period of economic depression during the late 1830s and early 1840s and before the coming of the railways to Hereford in the early 1850s widened the school's boarding catchment and increased the city's prosperity. Dean Merewether, moreover, was too preoccupied with the state of the cathedral to devote sufficient time to the school. And he was not always helpful to his Headmaster. Two illustrations will suffice. Despite Taylor's urgent appeals, he delayed the rebuilding of the schoolroom in the mid-1830s; and a decade later in Dr Layng's time, the Headmaster's authority was compromised by the Dean's forceful espousal of a residentiary's right to punish the misconduct of any boy by awarding impositions. It was something that Thomas Arnold, for one, would never have stood for, and Layng was no Arnold.[24] So at Merewether's death in the spring of 1850, the school was in a parlous state. It was left to Dean Dawes, his successor, a churchman of very different character – and, importantly, an innovative educationalist – to rescue the Cathedral School (in Dawes' own words in April 1851) 'from its present humiliating position'.[25]

The Vicars Choral Masters, 1803-1807

Samuel Picart and James Garbett were in harness together as Headmaster and Under-Master for three-and-a-half years from November 1803. Born within a few months of each other in 1774, they both worked together as Hereford choristers, Oxford students and vicars choral. As masters of the Cathedral School and at the same time fellow members of the College, they were the last such pairing in the school's history. There the resemblance ends for their backgrounds, voices and temperaments differed markedly. Picart was the son of a curate from Ross-on-Wye; Garbett, the son of a carpenter and joiner with extensive business interests.[26] As fellow cathedral choristers in the 1780s, Garbett was the better singer – although whether he had the voice of an angel is unrecorded – serving eight years as a treble, one of the longer tenures of the century. Picart, on the other hand, lasted only two, his biographer noting that 'his voice ... proved so utterly useless that although he remained a pupil in the school, the organist (Mr Coyle) requested that the Dean and Chapter would remove him from the choir'. This was also said of him as a vicar choral:

> Had his vocal powers been equal to his knowledge of choral duty, no-one would have excelled him, but he laboured under some organic defect which rendered his voice inflexible, and from the same cause he was often inarticulate both in reading and conversation.

---

24. For the incident, which concerned a former Dean's scholar, F.W. Bennett: HCA, 7031/20, pp.42-43, 25 Aug. 1842, when Merewether dressed down Layng in Chapter. At Rugby, Arnold had insisted from the first that he must be 'completely independent' of his trustees in the actual working of the school. Stanley, i, p.102.

25. Dawes used the phrase in his letter to the vicars choral of 17 April 1851 (HCA, 7003/1/6, p.118). For Merewether's controversial period as Dean: Aylmer and Tiller, pp.156-161.

26. HCA, 7003/4/4, Cooke's memoir, nos 80 and 81. Picart was orphaned when he was ten and was then befriended by Hugh Morgan, the vicar of Ross and a cathedral residentiary, who (presumably) placed him in the cathedral choir. For Philip Garbett's business interests: *HJ*, 6 Jan. 1785, advertisement announcing his taking over 'a large and commodious malthouse'.

It was hardly a recommendation for a career as a schoolmaster.[27]

But both came to HCS with some experience of the profession. Immediately after Picart had taken his BA in 1796 – the same year as Garbett but (as a former Langfordian) from Brasenose rather than Garbett's Christ Church – he became a classical assistant at Warwick grammar school. A few years later, we find him advertising 'to engage in the education of six young gentlemen' from his rooms in the College. One of his students was Christopher Jones, a former chorister and future vicar choral and Custos, who was placed with Picart for classical tuition between his leaving the school and his going up to Oxford. Garbett, too, tutored privately as a vicar choral, announcing in July 1802 that he was able to school eight young men in the Greek and Latin Classics, four of whom were to live as boarders with his own family where 'every attention', it was alleged, would be paid 'to their health, comfort and morals'.[28] But as schoolmasters of the Classics, their attitudes could hardly have been more different. In the words of T.T. Davies over 70 years later, Picart was 'a good scholar but irritable and very severe in correcting the boys', whereas Garbett was 'of a mild temperament, kind and affable'. Garbett was later described as 'one whose character for truth and honour never was and never will be doubted'.[29]

Fig. 4.2 James Garbett OH: Under-Master for less than four years; vicar choral for over 40; and founder of a notable clerical dynasty.

Picart and Garbett had complementary gifts but the school did not flourish under their tutelage. According to Davies, numbers declined by 50 or so boys, partly because of a scarlet fever outbreak which resulted in the death of a pupil. By the time of their departure in midsummer 1807, only 24 boys were listed as 'left by Mr Picart' on his successor's school register.[30] The decline in numbers would obviously have meant a considerable reduction in their fees.[31]

27. HCA, 7031/5, fos 214v, 378v, Acts 14 Nov. 1782, 11 Nov. 1790 and fos 250r, 269v, 10 Nov. 1787, 12 Nov. 1789 for Garbett's and Picart's chorister tenures; and HCA, 7003/4/4, for Cooke's observations about Picart's voice.

28. *HJ*, 7 Jan. 1801, 14 July 1802. Garbett took over the business from Thomas Watkins, also a vicar choral old boy. For Watkins, see above, pp.102, 107, 112; and for Watkins and Jones: HCA, 7003/4/4, nos 82 and 85.

29. By Canon John Clutton in a dispute with Dean Merewether. HCA, 7031/19, p.336, 18 April 1838.

30. *TH*, no. 2 (Sept. 1878), p.48 (T.T. Davies); HCA, 7031/6, p.44, Act 25 June 1807 for Picart's and Garbett's resignations; and below, p.131, for the 1807 numbers as listed in the first extant school register.

31. HCA, 7031/6, p.23, Act 10 Nov. 1803, for Picart's and Garbett's appointments and sharing of the fees (three-fifths to the Headmaster and the remaining two-fifths to the Under-Master). The Chapter also ordered that the

Nevertheless, improvements to both the curriculum and the schoolroom were made during these few years as a result of Chapter initiatives. This order from the beginning of Picart's reign indicates that the Dean and his colleagues were determined to ensure that religious instruction was improved and the cathedral's statutes followed:

> In consideration of the general importance of religious education in seminaries of learning and of the special provision of the statute *de gymnasio sive ludo literario*, the Dean and Chapter ordain these standing regulations concerning the Cathedral School:
>
> 1. That the masters do on some day every week instruct and examine every scholar in the doctrines and precepts of the Christian religion as established and taught in the Church of England and Ireland, making the church catechism, with some approved comment, the basis of such instruction and examination.
> 2. That they do, at every audit chapter, give in a written report of the plan which they have adopted for this purpose, and of the progress which they have made in the year preceding.[32]

The masters' subsequent annual reports, the first such accounts ever entered in the Act books, reveal the nature of the books used: Lewis' explanation of the catechism, 'in which the obscure parts of it are explained and the texts of scripture adduced by which its doctrines are confirmed', and Sellous' abridgement of scripture history for the lower forms; the Greek Testament, Sayer's principles of Christianity, and two abridged editions of works on Christian theology by former bishops of Lincoln and London. From these reports, we also learn something about how and when the material was taught. All the texts were to be 'reduced by the boys into question and answer and learned to be repeated' on at least one day each week, with an additional lesson for the senior boys on Monday mornings, the boys being divided into five classes (in 1806) for this instruction. It is also evident that the Dean and Chapter approved Picart and Garbett's scheme, the masters being thanked one year for their 'exemplary attention'.[33]

The schoolroom improvements again occurred as a result of the requirements of the triennial music meeting. The first intimation of the remodelling of the Great Room came with the Chapter order of 25 June 1804 that its windows should be moved from the west to the east side according to a plan drawn by a Mr James. Over the following weeks, as the tradesmen's bills reveal, the western windows on the public façade were blocked up with over 5,000 bricks, and three new tripartite arched gothic windows were created on the eastern side overlooking the Lady Arbour. In addition, the roof was repaired with some 5,150 'ladies' slate' and the west portico taken down, the door leading to the lobby on the south side now providing the only access to the building. The Great Room itself was

---

foundationers were not to pay entrance fees and the four Hereford Langfordians were each to be given eight guineas annually 'as an equivalent for their education'.

32. HCA, 7031/6, pp.22-23, 10 Nov. 1803. The Latin phrase relates to Chapter VI of the 1636 Laudian statutes, 'Concerning the Grammar School'.

33. *Ibid.*, pp.28, 35, 40, reports 8 Nov. 1804, 14 Nov. 1805, 13 Nov. 1806. For details of Lewis' catechism and the Bishop of Lincoln's abridgement, see below, p.144, note 86.

replastered and repainted in alabaster, spruce ochre, turkey umber and blue over the period 28 July to 22 September. To ensure that the paint had dried in time for the performance of Handel's *Samson* at the first concert of the triennial meeting on the Wednesday evening, one James Pitchford was employed (at 4s per night) 'for sitting up four nights in the music room to keep and watch the fires'.[34]

Despite his absence from Chapter on 25 June 1804, the impetus for the remodelling of the Georgian music room may well have come from Dean Wetherell. He liked the 'Gothick' style and employed it in all the building projects he was associated with as Master of University College, as well as at Hereford with James Wyatt's design of the cathedral's new west front, completed in 1795.[35] Although the incongruous style of the building as a whole was eventually deplored, as we will see, its hidden east front, at least, found immediate favour, one authority in the year of its transformation commenting upon its 'three handsome windows under pointed arches'.[36] And for the school itself under Picart and during the early years of his successor, before the Great Room had deteriorated, the 1804 schoolroom provided welcome morning light in a refurbished building, even if the Chapter had required in its original order that the new façade should be railed 'to prevent the playing of ball against the schoolroom'.

Samuel Picart and James Garbett resigned together at the midsummer Chapter of 1807.[37] In their early thirties when they relinquished their positions, they both had sufficient time to advance within the church. Having been appointed a prebendary by Bishop Cornewall in 1805, Picart became his domestic chaplain, and then on Cornewall's translation to Worcester, he found preferment outside the Hereford diocese, eventually becoming rector of Hartlebury in 1817, a living with tithes and glebe land worth £2,500 *per annum*. There he was known for his benevolent rule and generous hospitality. His music library, it was said, 'could scarcely be found elsewhere in any private collection', and at his death in 1835 he left five volumes of Handel's songs to the College of Vicars Choral where his old friend James Garbett was now Custos. Garbett himself had trodden a less remunerative but well-worn path within the Hereford diocese: as a prebendary (from 1813 until his death in 1857) and holder of six livings before his presentation – despite Dean Merewether's protest – to Upton Bishop in 1839, a favourable lease of its great tithes being given him 'in consideration of his long and valuable services in this cathedral'. He then relinquished his living as vicar of St John the Baptist, as well as his position as vicar choral after over 40 years as a member of the College.[38] As significantly in the long run to the wider established church,

34. HCA, 7031/6, p.25, Act 25 June 1804; HCA, 5715/3/85, fabric vouchers nos 166, 170, 172, 177, 182, 185-89, 192; Caird, p.30; Lysons, p.82 (for *Samson*).

35. Darwall-Smith, p.299; Aylmer and Tiller, pp.140-42, 261-65.

36. Duncumb, i, p.586.

37. HCA, 7031/6, p.44, Act 25 June 1807. Picart's resignation and his successor's appointment had already been announced in the *Hereford Journal* of 15 April 1807. For Picart's and Garbett's later careers: HCA, 7003/4/4, Cooke's memoir, nos 80 and 81; and for their appointments as prebendaries: Le Neve (2014), pp.62, 80.

38. HCA, 7031/19, pp.453, 454, for the tithes lease and Garbett's presentation to Upton Bishop, 7, 14 Nov. 1839; p.473, 24 March 1840, for the handing over of St John the Baptist to John Hanbury; and HCA, 7003/4/4, Cooke's memoir no. 80, for his other benefices and tenure as Custos.

Garbett founded a notable clerical dynasty.[39] Picart's and Garbett's short tenures as masters of the Cathedral School were unrenowned but their services to the Anglican Church and its people were inestimable.

'The Great Dr Taylor', 1807-1826

Over 30 years after Charles Taylor had left office, one of his former pupils lamented the school's subsequent decline. 'This institution as a classical establishment', he suggested, 'has never recovered [from] the blow it received by the resignation of the late lamented Rev. Dr Taylor, whose amicable and bland method of imparting instruction still dwells in the memory of his former pupils'.[40] And almost 90 years after Taylor had left the school, his tenure was being celebrated at a dinner to mark a later Headmaster's retirement. The toast to George V having been drunk 'with feelings of intense loyalty' in April 1913, Colonel M.J.G. Scobie, who presided at the occasion, referred to Taylor's headmastership as 'the first landmark' in the school's modern history. 'Some of the old boys who were at school even in his [Colonel Scobie's] time', it was reported, 'had heard the traditions of the great Dr Taylor'.[41] What these traditions were is not related but for them to have been talked about years afterwards is an indication of his lasting influence. Two contemporary references to the school's burgeoning reputation provide further evidence of his successful tenure. In December 1819, at the height of its growth to over a hundred pupils, it was described by a former employee about to set up his own establishment, as a school of 'much celebrity'.[42] A year or two later, Maria Hackett, 'the choirboys' friend' praised Hereford's 'flourishing school' – in contrast to the educational provision of some other foundations – with its 'ancient academical discipline' and the masters' readiness to receive an extra chorister 'for gratuitous instruction', excepting writing and arithmetic.[43]

Unlike his immediate predecessors, Charles Taylor had not been a member of the foundation as a boy. The son of an Oxford college servant, he was a Magdalen chorister

---

39. Four of his six sons won Somerset scholarships from the Cathedral School to Brasenose in 1819, 1828, 1834 and 1837 respectively, and were subsequently ordained. Two of these four, James Garbett (1802-79) and Edward Garbett (1817-87), were prominent evangelical apologists; and a third, Charles Garbett (1813-95), the father (by his second wife) of Cyril Forster Garbett (1875-1955), sometime Bishop of Southwark, Winchester and Archbishop of York. James junior, as Archdeacon of Chichester, conducted James senior's second marriage service in 1852, 'perhaps a solitary instance' (commented Cooke) 'where a venerable archdeacon has officiated at his father's nuptials'.

40. *HJ*, 18 Nov. 1857, letter from 'An Old Boy'.

41. *HT*, 5 April 1913 p.5, report on the dinner to mark Murray Ragg's retirement. Mackay John Graham Scobie (1852-1930) had attended HCS from 1869 to 1875. For his career and offices as a prominent Hereford citizen: Eales-White, pp.106-07.

42. In a notice by T. Collier, a former chorister whom Taylor later employed as an assistant master: *HJ*, 15 Dec. 1819. For pupil numbers during Taylor's tenure, see below, pp.131, 146 (especially note 96).

43. Hackett, pp.34-35. The passage was written after the death (on 5 Sept. 1821) of George Cope, who left a £200 legacy for an additional chorister to attend the junior canon (at that time Hugh Hanmer Morgan), at an annual gratuity of five guineas. This made up the chorister establishment to eight for the first time. Charles Woodward was the first established eighth chorister, his election on 8 November 1821 being 'considered as taking place' from the following Christmas (HCA, 7031/18, p.184). For Maria Hackett's life, criticisms of the academic provision for choristers and the compilation of her *Brief Account*: Mould, pp.154, 158, 161-62, 164, 167-76, 316-17 note 1.

for six years, he then entered Balliol College, where his father had been cook and then manciple, at 16 in 1796, taking his BA degree in 1800.[44] The following year, he was appointed Headmaster of Ludlow Grammar School at an annual salary of £60. After his ordination, he also became curate at Diddlebury.[45] Although not yet 22 on taking up his magisterial office at Christmas 1801, the school's governors were sufficiently confident of his abilities to build an addition to the school house at a cost of several hundred pounds.[46] Little more is known about Taylor's work there, but such was his following that his appointment to Hereford in March 1807, together with his Under-Master's simultaneous move to another school, caused the Ludlow governors considerable difficulties. As the Town Clerk observed: 'I am told that Mr Taylor will take with him to Hereford several of his Ludlow scholars and the Under-Master who is appointed to Bitterly School will do the same, which will very much and probably for some time lessen the advantages [of Ludlow for their successors]'.[47]

Taylor's talents and six years' experience of running the medieval foundation which shared Dean Langford's bequest were complemented by those of William Cooke, who following Garbett's resignation became Under-Master on the same day as Taylor's appointment. Like his predecessor, Cooke was born in Hereford into an artisan family. The son of a saddler, he again served a long time – over nine years – as a cathedral chorister before going on to Oxford, matriculating from New College on 18 November 1802, aged 17, and gaining his BA degree in 1806. Like Garbett, too, he became a vicar choral, his election in July 1808 being conditional upon his obtaining Holy Orders at the following ordination, and gave 'constant attention' (it was later claimed) to the College's interests for nearly 30 years, eventually becoming its chronicler. As a teacher, Cooke was also fondly remembered. 'His firm yet cheerful method of stimulating the studies of his pupils', his obituarist wrote, 'induced a feeling of ready obedience and filial regard which ripened into pleasing friendship, and which in after years tutor and pupil used to recur to with mutual delight'. Cooke stayed with Taylor for all but two of his 19 years in charge. The stability of their partnership explains in no small measure the school's success during these years.[48]

---

44. Foster (1887-8), iv., p.1392; Lloyd, pp.86, 87. As a manciple, Taylor's father would have bought provisions for the college. Dr Taylor's university subscription and Balliol certificates are to be found in HCA, 1536.

45. SA, LB2/1/7, p.139, Ludlow corporation minute, 28 Oct. 1801. Taylor's schoolmaster's licence (HARC, HD 6/56/5, fo. 46v) is dated 13 July 1802. After his ordination, Taylor also became curate at Diddlebury, as is evident from the anxious letter the vicar later wrote concerning Taylor's successor, a letter which nicely illustrates how curates were appointed in this period. SA, LB7/21, J.L. Baugh to James Baxter (Ludlow Town Clerk), 27 May 1807.

46. SA, LB2/1/7, p.150, minute 13 Oct. 1802; LB7/1389, committee minutes, 22 Dec. 1801, 28 Feb. 1802.

47. SA, LB7/20, Baxter's draft letter (to Baugh), no date; also see LB7/18, his draft letter to Haggitt, 19 May 1807, expressing concerns about 'both the present masters quitting the school' to Taylor's potential successor. Taylor's election as Headmaster of the Cathedral School was recognised by the Chapter Act of 25 June 1807 (HCA, 7031/6, p.44), although he had been appointed on 24 March as shown by his resignation letter to the Ludlow Corporation of the following day. SA, LB7/15.

48. HCA, 7031/5 fo 293v, 23 March 1793, and 7031/6, p.14, 11 Nov. 1802, for Cooke's chorister election and his place being declared void as he was 'going the university'; *ibid.*, pp.44, 61, for his elections as Under-Master and vicar choral, 25 June 1807, 23 July 1808, and HCA, 7031/8 p.218, for his resignation from the school, 25 June 1824. Also see HCA, 7003/4/3-4 for his invaluable vicar choral memoirs, no. 86 being Cooke's own *HJ* obituary of 25 Oct. 1854; and Foster (1887-8), i., p.290, for his university career.

One of the immediate benefits of Taylor's election at Hereford was that he brought with him ten scholars from Ludlow grammar, which increased the Cathedral School roll by almost one-third to 34 pupils. Within six months 12 more boys, almost all of whom were local, had been added. And the roll continued to expand: from 72 by January 1809 to 80 by that July, numbers dipping to 78 by the following January. Lists are incomplete from then onwards until January 1818, when for the first time we can be certain that numbers had reached three figures, but the periodic details of new-boy entries in Taylor's register are a further indication of the school's continued popularity in these intervening years.[49] We also know that Taylor recruited from a wide catchment and attracted boys from a broad social class. Over the decade from 1809, one in three boys came from the city and most of the others from elsewhere in the county, the Marches borderlands and Gloucestershire. But some hailed from further afield. It is unsurprising to find boys who lived in west Wales, or occasionally Bath, Birmingham and London, being schooled in Hereford, but more so to learn that 14 of those registered at the Cathedral School in this period came from the West Indies. These were mostly children of planters and merchants from Jamaica, Tobago, St Lucia and elsewhere but included the sons of a governor and a chief justice of Jamaica, as well as a general stationed in the 'East Indies'.[50]

The backgrounds of other boys who entered the school during these years are also known. Again, to find that the fathers of one in five boys were ordained causes no surprise. Aside from Taylor's own sons, these boys included the Garbett brothers; Frederick Gretton and Thomas Clutton, the sons of the Dean and one of the residentiaries; and, in William Cooke and Edward Lane, who both entered the school on 28 July 1817, two of the most distinguished old boys of the century.[51] But the sons of the cloth mixed with a similar number of those whose fathers were styled 'Esq' or 'Gent', who could boast such addresses as Purslow Hall, Shropshire; Leckhampton Court, Gloucestershire; Alton Court and The Lawns, Monmouthshire; and Whitney Court and Harewood House, Herefordshire.[52] They also rubbed shoulders with sons of military and naval officers and yeomen farmers. Much more numerous, however, were the children of prosperous tradesmen such as glovers, butchers, grocers, maltsters, 'druggists', inn-keepers, a coach-proprietor (John Bosley) and timber and iron merchants, as well as the rising professional classes. Among these professional fathers, lawyers, especially, and medical men predominated. But (among others) the

---

49. So 15 boys were admitted during the first half of 1810 and 22 and 12 respectively for the second halves of 1812 and 1813. Thereafter, for the seven years from 1814 to 1820, the average annual entry was 23. For further figures, see below, p.146 (especially note 96).

50. The sons of the governor, chief justice and general were respectively: S. and A. [possibly Augustine] Wentworth (entered on 26 July 1809); Thomas and Robert Jackson (22 July 1816); and Charles and William Taylor (January 1819). The general, who may have been an old boy, was Major-General Aldwell William Taylor (1759-1817), the son of William Taylor of Yatton. HCSA, P.A. Wilde Parsons to Barry Sutton, 1 Dec. 1975.

51. The Unde-Master's son, William Henry Cooke (1811-94), became a judge and prominent local antiquary; and Edward William Lane (1801-76), the son of Dr Theophilus Lane, prebendary of Withington Parva, the foremost Orientalist of his time. See below, note 59, for Cooke; and *ODNB*, vol. 32, pp.418-20, for Lane.

52. As with the entries for 23 Jan. 1809 (T. Powell of Whitney Court), 22 Jan. 1810 (Angelo Browning of Purslow Hall), 24 July 1815 (William and John Curre of Alton Court), 27 July 1818 (John Trye of Leckhampton Court), July 1819 (William Trumper of The Lawns) and 24 July 1820 (Chandos Hoskyns, son of Hungerford Hoskyns, 7th Baronet of Harewood).

local dancing and drawing-masters (one Peene and David Cox), the occasional banker, the clerk to the (paving?) commissioners (John Bell) and the surgeon to the Hereford militia (Mr Dunne) also felt that the Cathedral School was good enough for their boys.[53] Overall, the pupil body Taylor presided over was a wide and diverse mix of the gentry, professional and artisan classes. Some parents, indeed, considered the social spectrum too broad. Not the least of these was Dean Gretton. His son's experiences during his short stay at the Cathedral School from 1812 to 1814 were clearly too much for his parents, as Frederick Gretton described more than 70 years later:

> There a little Latin grammar was caned into me by an ill-grained Usher, and a rise up to extracts from Ovid taken out of the Second Master. But from the boys – a very mixed and untoward lot – as my private tutors, I learnt bad words and bad tricks, which naturally oozed out at home, so out of the present evil came the lasting good: it was at once determined that I must be sent from home ... [and] transplanted from Hereford School to Shrewsbury.[54]

And he was not the only boy in Taylor's time to desert the Hereford ship for a large public school.[55] Nevertheless, the school during Taylor's reign, for the most part, became increasingly well regarded. And as numbers grew, so its superintendence improved as is evident from the detailed rules that the Headmaster devised to govern his boys' behaviour, progress and moral welfare.

The 31 'general rules to be observed by the boys of Hereford Cathedral School' were promulgated by Charles Taylor and printed by E.G. Wright, a local printer who had been responsible for producing an early guide to the city. This detailed code is undated but was probably put together, no doubt from earlier versions, in 1818 at the time of the introduction of the mutual or Madras system at the school. It is the earliest surviving set of rules for any Hereford Headmaster, and repays scrutiny as it throws considerable light on the school's operation during the Taylor era.[56]

The school day strikes a modern reader as being excessively long, with the school doors being opened at seven in the morning and closed after five in the afternoon. During these hours, the boys were required to work more than seven hours, with one half-hour and two one-hour breaks, four days per week. On Thursdays and Saturdays, school started at 9.30 and the morning session was reduced to a two-and-a-half hours, the boys then being 'released for the rest of the day'. In addition, 'an accidental half-holiday' could be given on a

53. Entries are listed in the register for 19 out of the 24 (half-yearly) terms, 1809-20. During this period, out of the 237 boys admitted, 13 were officers' sons; 20 came from farming families; 53 boys were sons of tradesmen (with the 50 clerics, the largest grouping); and 40 came from professional (non-clerical) backgrounds.

54. Gretton, pp.21-22.

55. The names of those leaving HCS for other schools are generally not given in Taylor's register. A list of December 1809, however, shows that three out of the 15 leavers went to more prestigious schools: Andrew Knight (of Downton Castle) and Salway to Eton, and P. Puget 'to Charter House'. Thomas Andrew Knight, the only son of the famous horticulturist, died aged 32, in a shooting accident at Downton, on 29 Nov. 1827. *TWNFC* (1869), p.59.

56. The rules are pasted to the front cover of Taylor's register, and were printed in Carless, pp.70-74, from *The Herefordian* of March 1900.

GENERAL RULES

TO BE OBSERVED BY THE BOYS

OF HEREFORD CATHEDRAL SCHOOL.

1. THE School Doors are opened at Seven o'Clock in the Morning, and every Boy must be in his place from a quarter after 7 till 9.—From half-past 9 till 11.—From 12 till 2.—From 3 till 5 o'Clock.

2. Thursdays and Saturdays are regular half-holidays, when the Boys stay in School from half-past 9 till 12, and are released for the rest of the day.

3. No accidental half-holiday is given but on a Tuesday, and then only upon the application of the Bishop, the Dean, or Canon in Residence, the Members of Parliament, the Judges on the Circuit, the High Sheriff, or an Old Scholar, who having obtained honours in the University, is entitled to ask for one holiday after such distinction.

4. Two of the most exemplary Boys out of each class shall be selected for a Teacher and Assistant. Their duty is to hear the class and perfect them in their lessons before they go up to the Master; to keep silence and good order; to see that each Boy has his requisites; to keep the roll; report all absentees and defaulters; and to keep their class in the highest possible state of good discipline.

5. Every Boy as soon as he comes into School shall go quietly to his box, and take out whatever he may want during the School hours.

6. Every Boy shall be furnished with a pen-case, containing at all times not less than three pens, a slate pencil, and a lead pencil, and also with a ruler and a penknife.

7. A Boy not having these requisites together with a slate lying by him during School hours, shall be reported by the Assistant Teacher to the Master, and receive a cut on the hand.

8. The Boys in the junior classes are not to have penknives, unless ordered to procure them.

9. A Boy absent from roll-call forfeits one penny, or receives three cuts on the hand: if tardy, he forfeits one half-penny, or receives two cuts on the hand.

10. A Boy leaving his book out of its place forfeits one half-penny.

11. The Boy who has the upper or lower School mark at half-past Nine or Three o'Clock forfeits one half-penny; the mark to be passed for using any improper language, and to be shown to the Monitor at the above hours.

12. No Boy to return to his box before the School is over, except at the express permission of the Master.

13. When the hour of accounts is finished, each Boy shall deliver his account-book to the junior of his class, who shall deposit it in the proper place, and report any defaulter to the Writing-master.

14. All the Boys when a Master comes into School shall rise, and stand until he has taken his seat, or desires them to sit down. If a stranger come in, each class shall rise as he passes them, and then sit down and proceed with their work as if no one more than usual were present.

15. Those Boys who learn French, Dancing, or Drawing, shall not leave the School before their respective Masters call for them.

16. A Boy dirting the yard or parts adjacent, shall forfeit three-pence to the person cleaning the School, and three-pence to the prize box.

17. A Boy knowing another to be guilty of the above offence and not reporting him immediately shall incur the same penalty.

18. If the Boy cannot be discovered three-pence shall be paid out of the general fund to the person cleaning the School.

19. Any Boy writing on the walls, cutting the desks, doors, or rails in the Church-yard, shall transcribe a Sermon.

20. As Boys are required to come into School without noise, so will they be to depart from it in the same manner, and therefore, when the word has been given to leave off, every Boy shall go to his box, put up his books, and wait in silence until notice is given, and then leave the School two and two in the order of the classes.

21. Whatever benches or windows may be broken or other damage done shall be repaired by those who do it, if they can be discovered, or otherwise from the general fund to be raised by subscription among the Boys.

22. The senior Boy shall be Treasurer of the above fund and keep an account to be audited quarterly by the Master.

23. All games are prohibited in the Church-yard which may endanger the church windows, or disturb the service of the church.

24. All lying, swearing, or prophaning the name of God, shall invariably be punished with a flogging.

25. All cruelty to animals shall be severely punished.

26. Genteel and polite behaviour, cleanliness in person, and neatness in dress, next to GOOD MORALS, shall be principal objects of attention.

27. A Boy shall not pass a Master out of School without touching his hat.

28. Dirty hands or face, or holes in the clothes, shall be punished with a cut on the hand for each, and if this will not correct the *Sloven*, this name shall be affixed to his back in large letters.

29. All buying, selling, or lending among the Boys is strictly prohibited.

30. If a Boy *find* any thing he must bring it to the Master.

31. If a Boy retain any thing in his possession belonging to another, he shall receive for the first offence three cuts on the hand, for the second six, and for every succeeding offence a flogging or expulsion.

Prize Exercises.

IN THE UPPER SCHOOL.—Five weeks before the Holidays, the subjects for a Copy of Latin and English Verse, and for a Latin and English Essay, shall be affixed to the usual place.——The Latin Verses shall be shown up at the end of the first week.——The Latin Theme at the end of the second.——The English Verses at the end of the third.——The English Theme at the end of the fourth week from the time the Subjects are given out.—Every Boy in the Upper School will be required to write upon them, and those who neglect it will be deprived of the benefits arising from any Scholarship or Exhibition belonging to the School.

IN THE MIDDLE SCHOOL.—The Prize Exercises are—A Copy of Latin Verses—A Translation from English into Latin—An English Theme—A Copy of English Verses.—The Subjects to be given three weeks before the Holidays, and the Compositions to be completed in a fortnight.

IN THE LOWER SCHOOL.—A Translation from Latin into English—A Translation from English into Latin—A Conjugation of a Verb well written—A Composition in English.—The above Exercises to be shown up the week before the Holidays. One day allowed for the completion of each.—Whatever Exercise falls on the 15th of each Month to be considered as a Prize Exercise.—The Best Writing in each class exhibited on the last Saturday in each Month to be entitled to a Bene.—The reward for the other Prizes to be a Card, value four Optimes, except for the Prize on the 15th of the Month, the reward for which is an Optime—value of an Optime two Benes. The Boy who has the greater number of Benes at the end of the half year is entitled to a Book value 10*s.* 6*d.* to be p[illegible] out of the Forfeit Box.

PRIVATE TUTOR attends on Thursday and Saturday, from 12 to 1, every other day an hour in the Evening.——FRENCH MASTER, on Tuesday, from 8 to 9; on Thursday and Saturday, from 11 to 12.——DANCING MASTER, on Wednesday, from 8 to 9, and 12½ to 2.——DRAWING MASTER on Monday and Thursday, from 1 to 2.——FENCING MASTER, on Thursday and Saturday, from 2 to 3.——MUSIC MASTER, on Thursday and Saturday, from 4 to 5.

Each Boy shall produce a Copy of these Rules to the Master the Saturday before the Monthly Examination.

E. G. WRIGHT, PRINTER, HEREFORD.

Fig. 4.3 Dr Taylor's school rules and prize exercises, c.*1818.*

Tuesday but only by ecclesiastical authority (as the Dean and Chapter had stated in 1774), one of the Members of Parliament, a judge on the circuit, the High Sheriff or (once only) by an old scholar who had 'obtained honours in the university'. Nevertheless, aside from these special dispensations, the normal routine would have meant a 35-hour working week over two half-yearly terms of nigh-on five months each.

Punishments were severe if boys fell below the high standards expected, 'the principal objects of attention' being described in one of the rules as 'genteel and polite behaviour, cleanliness in person and neatness of dress, next to good morals'. Genteel and polite behaviour was to be demonstrated by all boys rising when a master came into the school. If a stranger entered, each class was to stand up as he passed the boys who were then 'to sit down and proceed with their work as if no-one more than usual was present'. Every boy was to enter the school quietly, and after leaving his books in 'his box' depart from it without noise 'two and two in the order of the classes'. Out of school, due decorum was to be preserved, each boy being expected to touch his hat when he passed a master. Uncleanliness and unkempt appearance were to be severely dealt with as this rule reveals: 'Dirty hands or face or holes in the clothes shall be punished with a cut on the hand for each,[57] and if this will not correct the sloven this name shall be affixed to his back in large letters'. But cleanliness was only next to godliness. 'All lying, swearing or prophaning the name of God' were 'invariably [to] be punished with a flogging'; and all games which were likely to endanger the church windows or disturb the cathedral services were prohibited, the rule thereby reinforcing the 1796-97 Chapter orders. Other punishments were also designed to promote moral behaviour. Cruelty to animals was to be 'severely punished' (how was not specified); any boy retaining another's possession was to receive 'three cuts on the hand' for a first offence, six for a second 'and for every succeeding offence a flogging or expulsion'; and the possessor of the upper or lower school 'mark' at either half past nine in the morning or three in the afternoon was to forfeit a half-penny, 'the mark to be passed for using any improper language and to be shown to the monitor at the above hours'.[58]

Fines or physical punishments were also set down to encourage good learning habits, punctuality and tidiness and discourage vandalism. Every boy was to possess a slate, together with a 'pen-case' containing at least three pens, a slate and lead pencil, a ruler and (the junior classes apart) a penknife. A boy would receive 'a cut on the hand' if found without any of these 'requisites'. Boys absent from roll-call or 'tardy' had the choice of a 'forfeit' or a 'cut': for absence a penny fine or three cuts; for lateness, a half-penny or two cuts. A boy could also be fined a half-penny for leaving a book out of place. Forfeits were similarly devised for 'dirting the yard or parts adjacent': three-pence to the school cleaner and three-pence for the prize box. Repairs to benches or windows broken by boys were to be paid for out of a general fund, administered by the senior boy, the bill being raised by a school subscription. For 'writing on the walls [or] cutting the desks, doors or rails in the churchyard,' the unusual punishment of transcribing a sermon was required. Two boys who

57. A cut may have been administered by the Headmaster 'switching [swishing?] of the back of the hands with a birch', as was practised at Westminster School where it was called a 'handing': Chandos, p.67

58. As at other schools of the period, the mark 'was never quiescent [and] … had to be passed on by the holder … by detecting and denouncing some other unfortunate comrade in a lapse'. *Ibid*, p.53.

offended in this way for 'writing on wall' in late 1825 were Charles Bowen and William Cooke (son of the Under-Master), who as foundationers should have been well practised in hearing – if not listening to – sermons.[59]

No punishment books from the period survive so we do not know how rigorously these rules were enforced but there are occasional entries in Taylor's register of the sums raised through 'forfeitures': £3 10s for the half-year to July 1819 and £3 4s from August to December 1820. For the same months a year later 19s was levied and for the first half of 1825 £1 3s 6d, although it is uncertain whether these reduced sums were due to improved behaviour or a more relaxed attitude among the authorities. There is also evidence in Taylor's register of boy absences and 'tardy' behaviour. From these lists covering the period August 1819 to November 1824, the number of boys being marked down as either absent or late were far greater than would be tolerated today, not least for 1819 when it is not so unusual to find individuals being recorded as absent or 'tardy' ten or more times in any one month.[60]

Occasionally, from the Headmaster's comments, we know the reasons for the absences. So C. Hatton was expelled on 9 May 1820 'for disobedience'; Higgins had 'idled at home the whole quarter' from October 1822; Charles Freeman was 'sent home for filth' at the end of that year; and Johnstone was advised to stay at home for at least a year in early 1825 because he was 'liable to such dreadful attacks'. But Taylor also comments when boys abscond. This observation was recorded against William Jay's name in early 1820: 'Ran home without leave before the examination. Was over for him and his brother [James] when they return'. Taylor showed leniency in this case, as he did in others. On 7 May 1818, John Hooper, having run away home four days earlier, was received back at school 'upon his submission to proper punishment and it being understood that he would be expelled for a second offence'; and on 27 March 1819, four boys – Edward De Visme, John and William Curre and William Biscoe, the latter two having escaped through their dormitory window to go to the theatre – were all readmitted after absconding, following their signing of a submissive declaration before the whole school acknowledging their bad example, 'the impression of which', they vowed, would be 'the study of my future life to obliterate'. These were all routine enough misdemeanours but Taylor's note against the name of Robert Carpenter, a senior chorister, was of a quite different order. It read: 'May 16. Was sent to prison charged with firing the College'. We will come across Carpenter again.[61]

59. Charles Bowen had been elected chorister (aged 8) on 26 January 1819, and William Cooke a Langfordian (aged 10) on 18 September 1821. HCA, 7031/18, pp.126, 178. Cooke, at least from Taylor's occasional remark in his register, had a chequered school career, being demoted from the top to the bottom of class 3 – then described as the 'worst class in the school for practising deceit' – in mid-1825. Such misdemeanours did not prevent him from either gaining a Somerset scholarship at Brasenose in 1830 or becoming a QC in 1863, Recorder of Oxford in 1866 and a county court judge in 1874, as well as a noted antiquary. See *Brasenose Reg*, i., p.488 and Weaver, p.104, for Cooke's career, although Weaver mistakes this Cooke for his father with regard to the biographies of the vicars choral.

60. The record being held by Edward De Visme for 44 absences that November and Cox for being 'tardy' 14 times in October. The 95 recorded absences against John Hanson's name for the three months from August to October 1819 did not prevent his being awarded a Somerset scholarship at Brasenose in early 1820. He later (in 1835) became vicar of Burghill. *Brasenose Reg*, i., p.459.

61. For a detailed account of this incident, see the section below, p.165ff.

Aside from behaviour, several rules throw light on teaching instructors who were not part of the school's official establishment. The writing-master was still of considerable importance, each boy when 'the hour of accounts' was finished being exhorted to deliver his account book to the junior of his class so that it could be put in its proper place, any defaulter being reported to the writing-master himself. His name at the time these rules were devised was Benjamin Powle. In 1791 he had styled himself as a 'writing-master and accomptant' and advertised that he was able to teach 'the elements of geometry, conic sections, algebra, fluxions [calculus] and all higher departments of mathematical instruction'. Whether he was free to impart the full range of his expertise in a predominantly classical school is unknown, but at the end of his 50-year tenure at least 80 of his former pupils and well-wishers were appreciative enough to raise around £150 for his testimonial.[62] We also know that Taylor advertised for an assistant who was to be qualified 'to teach the Eton grammar to the lower forms and … assist the writing masters'.[63] In addition to these masters, the rules indicate that Taylor also hired part-time assistants to give instruction in French, Dancing and Drawing, the boys opting for these supplementary subjects being commanded not to leave school 'before their respective masters call for them'.[64] The names of three such part-time assistants employed by Taylor are known: Le Conte de Crenolle, one of the old French *noblesse*, who after ten years at the school returned to France on the Bourbons' restoration in 1815; a Mr Frere, who promoted himself in 1824 as 'French instructor at the College School' (terms one guinea per quarter) and author of the lyric poem 'Ode sur la Guerre'; and the artist David Cox, who served as drawing-master at a modest annual stipend for more than a decade from *c.*1815.[65]

Finally, one rule gives an insight into teaching methods and the role of senior boy teachers. Such is its importance it is worth quoting in full:

> Two of the most exemplary boys out of each class shall be selected for a teacher and assistant. Their duty is to hear the class and perfect them in their lessons before they go up to the master; to keep silence and good order; to see that each boy has his requisites; to keep the roll; report all absentees and defaulters; and to keep their class in the highest possible state of good discipline.

---

62. The list was headed by Revd Richard Gwatkin of Cambridge (Senior Wrangler in 1814) who gave £15, followed by the two Headmasters (Taylor and Picart) and George Wyllim of Eaton Bishop with donations of five guineas each. *HJ*, 13 July 1791, 21 Dec. 1825, 18 Jan. 1826. Powle's death, aged 75, was recorded in the same journal on 8 August 1832.

63. *Ibid.*, 31 Aug., 7 Sept. 1808. He may also have occupied the role of private tutor, who was listed in the rules as being in attendance at the school for the first hour on the half-holidays and for an hour in the evening every other day.

64. The French master taught for three hours per week on Tuesdays from 8-9am, and on Thursdays and Saturdays from 11-12am; the dancing master for two-and-a-half hours each Wednesday; and the drawing-master for two hours each week on a Monday and Thursday from 1-2pm. Fencing and Music masters were also employed for one hour each Thursday and Saturday afternoons, the only organised activity (private tutoring apart) during the boys' half-holidays.

65. Carless, p.56; *HJ*, 11 Feb. 1824; Redgrave, p.20. David Cox junior, who himself became a watercolour artist, entered HCS on 22 July 1816 (when his father is described in Taylor's register as drawing-master) and left, as fourth student in the top class, in the summer of 1825.

The origins of this system of instruction lay in the educational theories of Dr Andrew Bell, who, despite his contravention of the cathedral statutes by not having a degree from an English university,[66] held the Bishop's prebend and became a Hereford residentiary for a few months in 1818-19 before swapping Hereford for a Westminster stall. Bell's method, first practised in Madras as early as 1789, was based on the use of monitors, after suitable training from a master, to pass on to their fellows the instruction that they themselves had received. It made possible the introduction of an elementary system on a national scale for the first time and was also taken up at Charterhouse as well as a number of private schools. We know exactly when it was first used at Hereford for Taylor writes in his register on 27 April 1818 that 'Dr Bell's system was tried and after a month's experience of its beneficial effects was adopted'. This was three years after the publication of Bell's *Elements of Tuition* (for the teaching of classical languages) and two after Jeremy Bentham's *Chrestomathia* where he had praised 'the matchless excellence … of its illustrious inventor' and advocated its application 'to the higher, not to say the highest, branches of intellectual instruction'.[67] More significantly, perhaps, although there is no evidence of the Chapter's direct interference, the school started using the mutual system just over a month after Bell's admission as a residentiary canon. But irrespective of whether the Headmaster had been pressured into using a different method of instruction, the new scheme no doubt also appealed to Taylor as the best and cheapest way for a school with an increasing roll but a small establishment of two masters and a few supernumeraries to be efficiently taught. But how effective was Bell's system as a means of instruction?

Apart from the negligible costs involved in training monitors at a time of a national dearth of teachers, the scheme's virtues, as trumpeted by its promoters, were that the pupils received more individual attention in a mutual school, they were better focused and more easily controlled and 'every boy was forced to use and exercise his own faculties'.[68] One supporter of the use of the Madras system for classical instruction pointed out the limitations of the old system of teaching the ancient languages. In a long letter to the *Hereford Journal*, he referred to 'that morosity and tyranny of masters which instead of leading their pupils gradually and kindly up the rugged ascent, goad and impel them with [the] relentless cruelty' of physical chastisement, occasioned by each boy repeating his individual task before the teacher:[69]

> See while the master is hearing and tormenting these, how 5 or 6 more are standing trembling before him! But suppose a boy should repeat his declension correctly, the master immediately returns his book and another boy commences. But no examination

66. Le Neve (2014), pp.50, 142. Bishop Huntingford made an exception in Bell's case despite the statutes (Bell held degrees from St Andrews as well as a Lambeth LL.D) and the formal protest of Canons Clutton and Cope, who while recognising Bell's 'services to national education' were intent 'to preserve inviolate the integrity of the statutes'. HCA, 7031/18, pp.102-06, 110-11, for Bell's installation as prebend, admission as residentiary and the canons' protest, 28 Feb. to 4 May 1818.

67. *Chrestomathia*, appendix 1, as cited by Adamson, p.103.

68. *Ibid.*, pp.25 and 102-03 for the endorsements of Sir Thomas Bernard and Bell's rival Joseph Lancaster, as well as Bentham.

69. *HJ*, 8 Aug. 1821, letter from 'B. Senior', written from Durham and dated 24 July 1821.

> takes place in the boy's general understanding of what he says; there is no explanation of the connection, reason, analogy or meaning of the declensions ... Each lesson is an arduous and an independent undertaking. The boy has the same toils to encounter; the master is wearied with the same daily and hourly repetition.

Whereas the nature and abilities of the 'never-tired, never-wearied, ever-anxious little teachers' corresponded 'with the instruction to be imparted'. 'I fearlessly declare', our correspondent observed, 'that young lads of tolerable genius and good dispositions, under a master of intelligence, will teach the elementary parts of the dead languages with greater exactness, greater impression, greater pleasure than any adult'. And this also applied, he suggested, to the higher classes:

> Not only are the classes improved by having boys to teach them but the monitors are, by the act of teaching, compelled to exert their own powers, to act for themselves, to exercise their memory, to employ their own thoughts, to lay up in their minds the master's instruction, and to search for every species of information which may be necessary to the full understanding of their lessons; as well as to acquire habits of close attention, of precision in pronunciation, grammar, translation: in short to judge of elegance of style and excellence of language.

However, he continued, 'suppose some pretty allusion, some historic fact, some national custom should slip his memory', the master would discover it; if not, his dictionary or commentary would be at hand. Besides, the 'law of classification' would:

> by uniting so many boys together, and using the excitements of emulation and honorary distinction, renders their [the boy teachers'] tasks far easier and the repetition far less. But the shortness of the lesson [under Bell's system], the briskness of its circulation, the vigilance which is necessarily attached to the office of monitor, make it impossible for any inattention or indolence to escape instant detection.

For watching overall was the ever vigilant master, who through his 'constant superintendence ... can discern and correct whatever may be verging to disorder or irregularity'. Such was the ideal.

In practice, however – and irrespective of the masters' virtues – one can question how far 'the little monitors at the head of their classes' would have devoted 'their whole mind to the task' as was inferred. Indeed, evidence from Taylor's register suggests that some of them were not able to live up to their Headmaster's trust, for he not infrequently had to replace the boys whom he had put in charge (one as teacher, the other as his assistant) of each class. From his first appointment of 14 boys as teachers and assistants for the eight classes in April 1818, he had trouble with the junior monitors. So Richard Higgins and Charles Hatton, teacher and assistant of class 8, were soon demoted but then restored 'on the promise of paying more attention', presumably because their successors, Thomas Clarke and John Hopton, proved even more irresponsible; finally they swapped offices, with Hatton being promoted before May 1818 was out. Thereafter, Taylor's register shows over 30 boys in these positions leaving their class mid-term over the seven years from

1819. Some of these were demoted a class 'for inattention', 'negligence' or an unspecified offence;[70] others were either promoted to a higher class or gave up their post as a result of leaving the school. On one occasion the Headmaster noted that all the boys in class six under the tuition of H. Taylor and William Bird, having been promoted after the March 1821 examination, were then sent home the following quarter 'for telling lies'. How far the monitors were to blame is not disclosed. Nevertheless, the disruptions caused by the comings and goings of the boy teachers can hardly have provided the necessary continuity for good learning. Nor, given that some of these tutors were only 11 or 12 years of age (or even younger), should we be surprised to discover that a number of them failed to execute their duties responsibly.[71]

One old boy, in particular, vehemently questioned the efficacy of the mutual system for a classical school like Hereford. The controversy was played out anonymously in the *Hereford Journal* over the summer of 1821 and became something of a *cause célèbre*.[72] Most of the correspondents were hostile to the scheme. The paper war was started by 'A Father', anxious for 'the improvement of my children', who queried whether the Madras system was 'applicable to the higher Classics' and 'preferable to the old system'. This resulted in a ferocious barrage, in support of 'A Father', the following week from 'A Brother'. The author, almost certainly, was the Revd James Bullock, Old Herefordian, Somerset Brasenose scholar and fellow of Worcester College, Oxford, who was to become the major protagonist in the debate.[73] Bullock questioned the wisdom of the whole system 'as a method of classical instruction'. In his view, the 'constant superintendence' of a master, rather than 'one boy of eight or ten ... as the teacher of a class whose ages and abilities are nearly equal with his own', was vital for laying the foundations for learning 'dead languages'; for the higher classes, on the other hand, 'a durability and polish' was required to teach boys 'to translate ... with accuracy ... [and] elegance' which could only be supplied by a master; in immaturity, 'fear of the birch rather than the desire of excelling' was 'the great spur to exertion'; and until 'emulation, industry and attention, instead of thoughtlessness, indolence and apathy became the *primum mobile* of boyhood', it was unwise of 'classical seminaries [to] adopt such a system'. Bullock concluded:

> A system which renders the master slothful and the pupil ignorant and which ... never has nor ever will ... be introduced into Eton, Westminster, Winchester, Rugby or any public classical school (the Charterhouse excepted) in the kingdom ... A system in short which while ministering to the indolence of a master and the vanity of a parent,

70. Some demoted boys, of course, made good. J. Trye, for example, was twice 'degraded' from class 6 in 1819-20 but by the end of 1822 was listed as the sixth boy in the top class, gaining a string of 'optime' marks in the monthly Greek and Latin examinations.

71. We know the ages of three chorister monitors: Edward Howells, Henry Hughes and John Griffiths were seven, nine and eight respectively at the time of their chorister elections. (HCA, 7031/18, pp.126, 156, 174, 26 Jan. 1819, 23 Aug. 1820, 25 June 1821.) Therefore, they cannot have been more than 9, 12 and 11 respectively when they were they were put in charge of their classes in 1820, 1823 and 1824.

72. *HJ*, letters 11, 18, 25 July; 1, 8, 15 Aug. 1821.

73. Bullock matriculated at Oxford, aged 19, on 29 March 1814, gaining his BA in 1817 and his MA in 1820. *Brasenose Reg*, i., p.438.

who perhaps is flattered at hearing little Master Jackey, an urchin newly breeched, ycleped [called] a 'teacher', sacrifices the best, the dearest and most important interest of the pupil.

The Headmaster's actions following this broadside were, to say the least, unfortunate. Posing in print as 'A Friend to a Liberal Education', he praised the 'excellency and beauty of the [Madras] system'; denounced his adversary as being totally ignorant of the subject; and advised him both to ponder on Moses' practice in choosing 'able men' as judges of the people and to read an essay by Lord Kenyon's chaplain which showed 'the practicability of ... [its] application ... to the higher branches of education'. This, Taylor asserted, would lead Bullock 'to regret his indiscriminate abuse of the masters who instead of lying idly on their oars have taken the pains to examine and have [had] the courage enough to adopt it'. The Headmaster's angry response, in his turn, allowed him to be condemned for losing his temper and using 'sophistical exceptions and the empty parade of biblical quotation' instead of 'solid reasoning' to answer his detractors, and to be stigmatised as a literary radical and a friend of 'a party'. Even worse than Taylor's ill-judged *apologia* was his decision two days later to remove Bullock's younger brothers from the school on the grounds that 'there can be no hope of boys being improved by any labour and care we can bestow upon them, who are taught at home to consider their masters as idle and slothful and the system of instruction adopted as one calculated only to ensure the disgrace of the scholars'. This resulted in Bullock publishing a vituperative pamphlet condemning the masters' action as 'an act of flagrant injustice'.[74] Thereafter, the Dean and Chapter were inevitably dragged in to the controversy; the boys were reinstated and then dismissed again; and further notices from both sides were published in the local press, including one from Taylor and Cooke inviting 'any person interested in the school ... [to] attend the public examinations' and judge for himself 'both of the mode of instruction and of the acquirements of the boys'. At the same time, the Chapter publically expressed its support for the masters in their conduct of the school, declaring that they had 'done their duty with propriety and success' and that any 'charges of indolence and neglect' were 'entirely without foundation'.[75]

Like most others, this crisis eventually blew over. It had generated more heat than light but demonstrated the unpopularity of the Madras system and not only among the Bullock family. James Bullock himself had hinted that one third of pupils (and presumably their parents) had questioned 'the practicability of a modern system of education', and that William Cooke, the Under-Master, initially considered it 'a tender subject' and a 'matter

---

74. *A Fair, Candid and Impartial State of the Case Between the Masters of the College School and the Rev. James Bullock* (HCL, 96/845), in which is published the masters' letter of dismissal of 27 July 1821 and Widow Jane Bullock's judicious reply, together with her son's intransigent one. Bullock claimed that the pamphlet had 'extensive circulation', which seems to be corroborated by the publication of a second edition within days of the publication of the first. *HJ*, 8, 22 Aug. 1821.

75. *Ibid.*, notices 3, 10, 17 Oct. 1821; HCA, 7031/ 18, pp.178-79, copy of Jane Bullock's appeal, 6 Sept. and the Chapter's reply, 18 Sept. 1821. Taylor's register shows that the two younger brothers entered the school in May 1821. The younger boy (with his fellows in class 6) had been 'sent home for telling lies' during the May quarter 1821 and this may have been the spur for James Bullock's public attack on the school.

of experiment'.[76] This is not surprising given both the long history of traditional methods of instruction in the ancient languages and that the efficacy of the new system was largely unproven, few schools having adopted Bell's method for higher classical teaching. One contemporary correspondent to the *Hereford Journal*, who was favourable in principle to the scheme, considered that its drawback was that 'no well-arranged, simplified introduction from the common grammar' had been published to aid its implementation.[77] It was this deficiency that Charles Taylor, who had been using the long established but limited Eton grammars, sought to remedy. His Latin grammar, 'with progressive lessons attached to each rule', was published in 1823 priced 3s 6d 'for the use of the Cathedral School, Hereford'. According to Taylor's preface:

> [the] arrangement and compression of the Latin syntax was undertaken in consequence of an intercourse with Dr A. Bell, the well-known author of the Madras system of education, which induced me to consider more minutely than I had before done ... the syntax originally drawn up by Lily and afterwards compressed at Eton.

His intent was 'to conduct the learner in his progress step by step while adhering strictly to the soundest principles of the old grammarians'.[78]

Although the grammar was warmly received by the *Oxford Herald*,[79] it is doubtful whether it persuaded many of the bigger classical schools to convert to the Madras system. But Taylor's register for the seven years from 1819 provides proof that it continued at Hereford during the remainder of his tenure. For as Bell required, the register lists the progress of every boy in their separate classes. It charts their performance, month by month, in the Greek (for class 5 and above) and Latin examinations, as well as their overall ranking in the class. A 'black list' (presumably for poor work) and lists for 'absence', 'tardy' and 'prizes' complete the monthly register.[80]

The subjects for half-yearly prize exercises are also recorded, the nature of these competitions having been precisely stated in the 1818 rules. So in the upper school, the general subjects for a copy of Latin and English verses and for a Latin and English essay were to be 'affixed to the usual place' five weeks before the beginning of the holidays, those boys who neglected to write on them being 'deprived of the benefits arising from any scholarship or exhibition belonging to the school'. In the middle school, the prize exercises again consisted of a copy of Latin and English verses and an English theme, together with a translation

---

76. Bullock, pp.9, 16. Bullock, of course, is not the most impartial source for these assertions.

77. *HJ*, 15 Aug. 1821, anonymous letter, written 7 Aug. The correspondent remarked that the one prepared for Newark Grammar School was 'shamefully expensive' and 'too imperfectly executed', and that Dr Russell's at Charterhouse needed to be 'devoid of peculiarities'.

78. C. Taylor, pp.i, ii. For Eton's adaption of Lily's Latin Grammar in 1758, and Hereford's use of the Eton Latin and Greek grammars in 1818: Foster Watson, p.259, and Carlisle, i., p.493.

79. *HJ*, 23 July 1823, reprints the review of the *Oxford Herald* which had strongly recommended 'this very useful publication'.

80. Bell's elaborate recommendations on the record-keeping necessary for the efficient working of his system, including a 'paidometer' which tracked each pupil's progress throughout his school career, are detailed in his *Instructions for Conducting Schools*, pp.52-57. Taylor's Hereford register, therefore, was almost certainly based on a series of other records which are now lost.

from English into Latin, the subjects being announced three weeks before the holidays and the compositions to be completed in a fortnight. In the lower school, although the exercises were easier, the incentives were more complicated. Translations were to be made from Latin into English and English into Latin, as well as a 'well written' conjugation of a verb and an English composition, the subjects being shown a week before the holidays, one day being allowed for the completion of each. In addition, whatever work was being done on the fifteenth of each month was to count as a prize exercise and the boy with the best writing from each class on the last Saturday in each month was entitled to 'a Bene'. The rewards for the other prizes were a card valued at 'four Optimes', except for the one on the fifteenth when an Optime, equal to 'two Benes', was awarded. The boy with the greatest number of Benes at the end of the half-year was entitled to a book worth 10s 6d to be paid for from the forfeit box.

Subjects for the mid-summer and Christmas senior prize compositions in English and Latin verse and themes and Greek verse, are recorded in the register. These range from a wide variety of classical texts to such English moral, topical and general themes as: 'decency of conduct', 'calumny', 'rebellion' (for Christmas 1819, at a time of radical agitation and a few months after the Peterloo 'massacre'), 'the accession of George IV' (for June 1820), 'emigration', 'the advantages of history', 'sacrilege', 'chronology' and 'patriotism'. Latin subjects included 'wisdom the best of possessions' and 'love of one's country', as well as the importance of maintaining 'due proportion in all things', letting 'sleeping dogs lie' and 'listening a lot and saying little'. An ancient history question on the battles of Cannae and Capua (216 and 211 BC, respectively) was set as the Latin theme for 1821;[81] 'fishing' was the subject for the Latin verse for 1826; and the 120 or so lines from Act II scene III of Shakespeare's *Henry VIII*, the one for the 1825 Greek verses.[82] Prizes are also occasionally listed, such as those won by the scholars' efforts at midsummer 1819, funded by the £3 10s collected in fines. These comprised an edition of Herodotus, Lambert Bos' *The Antiquities of Greece*, Picquot's *Elements of Universal Geography Ancient and Modern* and Isaac Taylor's *Self-Cultivation*, an improving text for 'a youth leaving school'. This latter volume was illustrated by a print showing a young man earnestly reading at a table with his back turned on boyhood pleasures.[83]

Taylor's register also contains a record of the 'quantity read by each class' every half-year. The amount of classical literature covered is astonishing to the modern reader. For example, in the four months from August 1819 during the early days of the operation of the Madras system, the three senior boys in class 1 read the following classical authors: Livy (book 1 to the twentieth chapter of book 2), Horace (his odes), Demosthenes (six orations), Thucydides (book 2), and Homer (five books). In the second class of nine boys, the fourth

81. The English translation of which reads: 'Marcellus seems indeed to have declared that the battle of Capua was Hannibal's own "Cannae"'. In dating Capua, I have assumed that the question referred to the second rather than the first battle which took place a year earlier.

82. Which finds Anne Boleyn in an antechamber of the Queen's apartments. For a discussion of the resurgence of Greek studies at Shrewsbury School under Samuel Butler in the early nineteenth century: Clarke (1959), pp.76-78.

83. I. Taylor, frontispiece. Taylor described self-cultivation (*ibid.*, p.8) as the mind cultivating 'all its powers', which would 'repay all the toils it occasions, by steady usefulness and respectable rank in society'.

and fifth books of Virgil were read, together with 18 pages of Sallust and 18 of the 'Greek primitives', and selections from the minor Greek poets Anacreon, Bion, Moschus, Musaeus and Tyrtaeus.[84] In addition, all these boys studied the Greek testament (St Paul's epistle to the Romans) and wrote themes, verses and translations. Class 3 got away with seven of Virgil's eclogues, 68 chapters of Caesar, ten of Burnet, 31 Aesop fables (in the original) and the first three chapters of St John's Gospel also in Greek; class 4 with 30 chapters of Caesar, 12 pages of Ovid and 27 of the Greek grammar 'with exercises'; and class 5 with 11 chapters (presumably from Thucydides' *History of the Peloponnesian War*) on Alcibiades, four about Thrasybulus and three on Conon, as well as 20 pages of grammar and exercises. The syllabus for the bottom two classes related almost exclusively to grammar schemes: 61 'vocabularies', the same number of 'lessons' and 13 'rules with exceptions and exercises' for class 6; and 54 'first pages in the Latin Grammar with exercises' for class 7. The following term we have some idea of the homework expected from the juniors who were to transcribe 'a noun or verb … every night'. Subsequent lists outline the nature of their regime: epitomes, translations, grammar lines, verb conjugations, noun declensions, occasional sense and nonsense verses, alphabets, 'dictates', syntax rules, cautions, tables and the rest. Nor were these academic requirements exceptional. Indeed, the volume of classical work covered comes across even more clearly for the school as a whole from the abstracts detailing the hundreds of lines construed, repeated and translated every month, as meticulously listed in Taylor's register from August 1819 to March 1825.[85]

From these lists we can also glean something about non-linguistic instruction under Madras. A chart of Ancient History was made by the top class in February 1820. An unspecified history of Rome was listed for classes 7 and 8 in early 1821, and a history of England is regularly prescribed in 1820 and subsequently for the junior classes. Geography is a staple diet for the middle school, the number of lines being read amounting to well over one thousand per class in most terms. Unsurprisingly, Religious Instruction is shown to occupy a central part of the curriculum. Books from the Greek Testament, as we have seen, were taught to the top classes, and the church catechism – and sometimes sermons – were drilled into the others.

Taylor's and Cooke's first annual report to the Dean and Chapter on this subject amplify both their teaching methods and the texts they used in 1807:

> Saturday is the day particularly set apart for religious instruction. Before breakfast, all the boys repeat their church catechism which is explained *viva voce*; after breakfast, those in the lower school learn different parts of Lewis' catechism and in the upper school read the Greek Testament. For Sunday's exercise the junior classes write out and learn the collect with a portion of Lewis' catechism, the senior answer on paper

84. The exact works were generally not listed but Demosthenes' orations were selected from William Allen's edition of 1755 (all 12 speeches were read from this book the following term) and the poems (for the first four Greek poets) probably came from one of Francis Fawkes' five editions published between 1760 and 1813. For these editions: Clarke, (1945), pp.36, 229, 235.

85. To take just one example: the top class (who, of course, worked faster than the others) over the four months from August to November 1819 construed 5,002 lines of Sophocles, 3,163 of Juvenal and 2,490 of Livy; repeated 329 lines of Homer and 208 of Virgil; read 341 verses of the Greek Testament; translated 510 lines into or from Latin; and wrote 13 Latin verse copies and three themes.

> the questions at the end of Sayer's evidences, and after they have gone through them translate Clapham's abridgement into Latin. A portion of the prayers of the church is likewise read every day in school.[86]

Thereafter, they made periodic additions to their syllabus. In 1808, one of the psalms was occasionally translated into Latin verse. In 1813, the instruction received by the boys in the lower school was largely the same, although they had to transcribe the catechism, with the appropriate collect and text as a Monday morning exercise; whilst the upper school boys that year read through St Paul's 'and the Catholic epistles' with commentaries, repeated the church catechism monthly and had either reported on the cathedral sermons, translated Clapham as before or written an English essay on a scriptural text. Four years later, the translation of Burnet's *De Fide Officies Christianorum* was added as a Sunday evening task for the top class in the lower school and a selection from the notes of the SPCK family Bible for the senior boys. The broken catechism from SPCK, as well as the *Epitome Sacrae Historiae*, was used for the juniors in 1819, and in 1823 the seniors paid closer attention to the gospels and Acts of the Apostles in the Greek Testament.[87]

The additional religious texts that the masters required their pupils to learn comprised just one aspect of a curriculum that was becoming increasingly burdensome. From Taylor's abstracts, we know exactly how many lines the boys read, learned, construed, repeated, memorised and wrote in all subjects every month under the Madras system. A recitation of the totals for each class for the term from August to November 1819 will suffice to illustrate the point: class 1, 12,059 lines; class 2, 7,290; class 3, 6,610; class 4, 4,441; class 5, 3,918; class 6, 3,789; class 7, 2,581; class 8 (for August and September only), 1,699. For the modern reader, it comes as a relief to read the note at the end of these figures that 'the music meeting in September was the occasion of less being done in all the classes'.[88] Nevertheless, the reading and learning of these lines must have imposed extraordinary burdens of mechanistic rote-learning upon young people, even if, given that the lists were in part composed by the boys themselves, the totals should not necessarily be regarded as an accurate reflection of their labours. It was the factory system being applied to education, the mechanical and factory-like character of the teaching being seen by its promoters as one of the great virtues of mutual schools.[89]

Many, no doubt, fell by the wayside. But for those who could withstand both the pressures and the monotony of learning and worked their way through the school to the upper

---

86. HCA, 7031/6, p.47, the masters' report (from 'Hereford College School'), 12 Nov. 1807. John Lewis' *Church Catechism* had gone into 35 editions by 1784; and the second edition of Samuel Clapham's abridgement of the Bishop of Lincoln's *Elements of Christian Theology* had been published in 1804.

87. HCA, 7031/6, pp.65, 142, reports 10 Nov. 1808, 11 Nov. 1813; HCA, 7031/18, pp.95-96, 147-48, 213, reports 13 Nov. 1817, 11 Nov. 1819, 13 Nov. 1823. Taylor was the local secretary of the Society for the Propagation of Christian Knowledge.

88. The equivalent figures for seven classes from August to November 1824, the last complete termly abstract in Taylor's register, were: 16,005; 9,585; 7,885; 8,255; 2,999; 4,239; and an astonishing 27,336 (including over 15,000 lines of Latin grammar) for the lowest class.

89. Samuel Coleridge, for instance, referred to the method as 'an especial gift of Providence to the human race … this incomparable machine, this vast moral steam-engine'. As quoted by White, p.27.

classes, there were sufficient rewards. Despite Bullock's fears that 'the system [would] ... neither ... [make] a boy a sound scholar in the first nor a brilliant one in the last form', we know of 12 boys from the school who entered the two ancient universities between 1820 and 1825, as well as the names of a few 'who left for the law' and medical professions.[90] Nor did Bullock's warning that even if a boy should go on to university after having been tutored under the Madras system, it would 'all but ... [ensure] his being plucked [rejected]', stand the test of time, at least as far as the Brasenose Old Herefordians were concerned.[91] For such men as these, the Madras system worked to their considerable benefit.

Taylor's faith that the mutual system could be successfully applied to a classical school had, to this extent at least, been vindicated. He also continued to maintain both the Dean and Chapter's confidence and the patronage of Bishop Hungerford (Bishop of Hereford, 1815-32), himself a considerable classical scholar and one of Lord Liverpool's 'Greek play bishops', to whom the Headmaster had dedicated his Latin grammar.[92] Taylor's elevation to Long Staunton in 1815 – a Shropshire parish made void, ironically, by the death of James Bullock's father – and then Madley in 1821, a Chapter living Dean Merewether was later to occupy; his installation as Prebend of Moreton Magna in 1820; and his appointment as diocesan Chancellor and vicar-general in 1825 is testimony to the respect with which he was held by his patrons.[93] He also exercised authority as a magistrate, his severity on the bench giving rise to this *jeu d'esprit* written shortly after his preferment as a prebendary:

What bid the rod o'er truant wave
The very morn his lordship gave
Preferment in the Church?
If it be so, then *entre nous*,
'Twere fitter he had given you
Not Moreton, Sir, but Birch.[94]

As a strict disciplinarian, Taylor would also have driven his boys hard as Headmaster. Even so, it is unlikely that he would have matched the record of his contemporary John

90. Taylor recorded in his register that John Hanson, Edward Higgins, John Hill, Charles Taylor (the Headmaster's son), Josiah James and William Duncomb went on to Brasenose (James later moving to St John's, Cambridge); Tomkins and Evans to Jesus, Oxford; Strong to Wadham; Wynne to St John's, Oxford; and Pitt and Woodward to St John's, Cambridge. In addition, he noted that McGuire had entered 'Dublin College'; Trye, Hone and (another) Strong had 'left for the Law' and H. Taylor 'for surgery'. Earlier, H. Garbett had 'gone to Mr Tully at the Infirmary' (September 1819); and Braithwaite and C. Garbett had been 'apprenticed to Mr Griffiths, surgeon', May 1820.

91. All six took their degrees (James from St John's, Cambridge); two (Higgins and Hill) became Hulme exhibitioners; and four returned to livings within the Hereford diocese. *Brasenose Reg.*, i., pp.459, 462, 466, 469, 475.

92. See Clarke (1945), pp.83-84, 231, for Hungerford's publications in the 1780s (to critical reviews) of original Greek verse; and Brock and Curthoys, p.15, for Liverpool's patronage. The senior boys at HCS regularly used one of Hungerford's works, perhaps his *Short Introduction to the Writing of Greek*.

93. HCA, 7031/6, p.186, presentation, 24 March 1815; HCA, 7031/18, pp.155, 185, 223, grants 8 Aug. 1820, 8 Nov. 1821, 24 March 1824. Taylor was elected to Madley, following Dean Carr's proposal, by three Chapter votes to two.

94. As recited by Bullock, p.19. It is also unclear whether Taylor was acting in this context as a magistrate or Headmaster. If the allegation was true, and the punishment was delivered on the morning Taylor's installation, it occurred on 8 August 1820.

Fig. 4.4 A cartoon drawn by J.T.O. Fowler, who was a boy at HCS in the 1840s. The Latin is from Virgil's Aeneid, *and may be rendered as: 'One day, we'll look back on this and smile'. Fowler described the sketch (together with the Woollam drawing, figure 5.3) as 'old reminiscences of the Cathedral School at Hereford'. The scene may well have been apocryphal, but it illustrates the prevalence of birching as an instrument of punishment in schools at this time.*

Keate, Headmaster of Eton 1809-34, who is estimated to have flogged about ten boys a day – Sundays excepted – during his long tenure.[95] Nevertheless, this was the custom of the times, and (as already related) even his adversary James Bullock reckoned that 'fear of the birch' was the greatest incentive for learning. And, overall, Taylor ran a successful school. As we have also seen, before the end of 1807, numbers had almost doubled from the 24 boys left by Picart; less than two years later, they had reached 80; and for each term of the three years, 1818-20, over one hundred. Thereafter, numbers fell away, but Taylor was still able to hand over to his son a viable school of 58 boys, of whom around 15 were boarders, by the time he left office.[96] It was, however, to the school's detriment that nepotism governed

95. For flogging in the big public boarding schools in this period, and for Keate in particular: Chandos, pp.202, 221-22, 225-27, 232 note. One of Keate's victims (on at least one occasion) was William Gladstone. *ODNB,* vol. 22, p.384.

96. Approximate numbers during Taylor's tenure, as recorded intermittently and calculated from his register, are as follows: Dec. 1807: 46; Jan. 1808: 72; July 1809: 80; Jan. 1810: 78; Jan. 1818: 107; July 1818: 115; Jan. 1819:

the succession, which resulted in Charles Taylor junior inheriting his father's crown. The responsibility for this lay firmly at the father's door.

Charles Taylor, Junior, 1826-1839

Taylor had petitioned the Chapter in June 1826 to be allowed to resign the headmastership in favour of his eldest son at the following audit. The Dean and residentiaries eventually agreed provided that the young man should by then be in deacon's orders. Accordingly, on 9 November 1826, Taylor's resignation was accepted and the headmastership declared void. The next day, his son appeared in Chapter and after taking the usual oaths was appointed Headmaster.[97] The appointment had the benefit of convenience and provided continuity but did not prove to be in the school's best interests.

The second Charles Taylor was an able enough scholar. A former pupil, he had steadily worked his way to the top of the school, gaining commendable marks under his father's tutelage. He proceeded to Brasenose on 10 October 1822, held the Somerset scholarship for three years and was awarded his BA degree in 1826, his MA not being granted until 1831. His appointment, therefore, was in contravention of the cathedral statute requiring the Headmaster to hold a higher degree. More significantly, at the age of 23, he lacked his father's experience of having run another school before Hereford. Nor could he rely on someone as steadfast as William Cooke as his Under-Master, Cooke having resigned in 1824. His successor, Albert Jones, a chorister for nine years and vicar choral, had lasted but a year, to be replaced by Henry Law Bamford, the assistant who was promoted to the second mastership without having a degree. Bamford remained at the school for eight-and-a-half more years, during which time he acted as the secretary for the Old Herefordian dinners, but resigned in February 1834 'finding it necessary to reside on his curacy at Bellingham'.[98] Thereafter, Taylor managed without an Under-Master, a reflection of the drop in numbers and one sign of the extent to which the school had declined since the heady days of his father.

Although the sources are thin for the son's reign – unlike his father, his register has not survived, and we have to rely heavily on the hints provided in the Chapter Acts and newspaper notices – there is sufficient evidence to suggest that this was far from being a glorious period in the school's history. In the absence of a register, it is not known how long the new Headmaster continued with the Madras method of teaching, although having himself been brought up in the school under the mutual system, as well as for reasons of filial piety, it is unlikely that he would have abandoned his father's practice. The publication of a third edition of Dr Taylor's *Latin Grammar* (for 2s 6d) in 1827 also suggests that the school's classical curriculum continued to be taught under the new methods, at least

113; Dec. 1819: 108; May 1820: 107; Dec. 1820: 102; June 1821: 99; Dec. 1821: 89; Dec. 1823: 75; June 1824: 79; Dec. 1824: 70; June 1825: 69; Dec. 1825: 70; June 1826: 58.

97. HCA, 7031/8, pp.236-37, 238, 242,243, Chapter Acts, 26 June, 11 July, 9, 10 Nov. 1826.

98. *Ibid.*, pp.218, 228, 420, Chapter Acts, 25 June 1824, 9 Aug. 1825, 4 Feb. 1834; and *HJ*, 15 Oct. 1828 for his secretaryship. For the vicars' glowing testimonial for Albert Jones' preferment to Marden: HCA, 7003/1/6, pp.87-89, 6 Feb. 1847.

Fig. 4.5 Charles Taylor junior, a less successful Headmaster than his father.

until the arrival of a vigorous young Dean in the person of John Merewether.[99] Within months of Merewether's installation in June 1832, he had informed Taylor that he doubted the wisdom of 'the use of a Grammar peculiar to one school only', and with the Chapter's unanimous agreement advocated 'that the Grammar most in use in the country in general should be the established Grammar of the Hereford School'. This necessitated a return to the Eton Grammar, despite Merewether's claim that he recognised the superiority of Dr Taylor's version 'both as to arrangements and accuracy'. Under this forceful direction, and with his father's willingness 'to waive all personal considerations', the younger Taylor would have had no other option than to succumb to the forces ranged against him whatever his private reservations might have been.[100]

In his letter advocating the change, Dean Merewether endowed two new prizes: one to the lower school boy who had 'made the greatest proficiency in grammatical knowledge'; the other to an upper school pupil who wrote 'the best essay in the prophetical allusions to the Messiah contained in the five books of Moses', the prize being rehearsed at the general examination and its delivery to take at least 20 minutes. We have no idea as to who might have won these prizes, but the *Hereford Journal* carried reports of the prize ceremonies conducted before the midsummer and Christmas holidays in 1832-33 and again in 1835-36.[101] From these, it is evident that the traditions of Dr Taylor were continued in the awarding of prizes for Latin (and sometimes Greek) verse and theme and for English compositions on such topics as the advantages of history, national honours and the importance of discretion. These reports also give us the first indication we have of the nature of formal speech recitations on these occasions. So on 21 June 1832, 'before the canon in residence and other friends of the establishment', the speeches of Latinus, Turnus and Drances were recited, together with one from Addison's Tragedy of Cato. The prize for the best speaker, presented to James Lane Taylor at that ceremony, was 'a very handsome edition of the Spectator'.[102] At a later ceremony in December 1835, the Chapter praised the prize-winners 'on the advancement they had made in their general studies, on the accuracy and classical style in which they construed difficult passages of Thucydides, Sophocles and other authors, and on the gratifying and creditable manner in which they passed their examination in the Greek Testament and Theology'.[103] One of them, Edward Garbett, recited his 134-line prize poem 'Lucretia' ('So well she lived – so nobly dared to die'), which was later

99. *HJ*, 15 August 1827, advert for the Grammar's publication (without its new exercises), 'for the use of Hereford Cathedral School'.

100. Merewether further suggested that his letter to the Headmaster urging the change should be made public, and it was published in the *HJ*, 27 Feb. 1833. The matter was formally resolved in Chapter on 19 February (the date of the Dean's letter to Taylor): HCA, 7031/8, p.394.

101. *HJ*, 27 June, 26 Dec. 1832; 26 June, 25 Dec. 1833; 23 Dec. 1835; 28 Dec. 1836.

102. The classical speeches were from Book 11 of Virgil's *Aeneid*. Joseph Addison (1672-1719) was an essayist, poet, playwright and statesman, whose Cato was based on the final days of Cato the younger (95-46 BC); and the *Spectator* edition may have been from Addison's revival of the periodical, which ran to 18 issues in 1714, rather than the (then) radical political magazine first issued on 5 December 1828. James Taylor, first listed in Dr Taylor's register as a pupil in Class 8 for late 1824, was probably the Headmaster's half-brother. James Taylor's younger brother, John Oakes Taylor, was awarded the prize for English verse in December 1833.

103. The following year, Dean Merewether complimented the top class on their proficiency in Aristotle, Pindar, Thucydides, Logic, Cicero and Livy.

published in its entirety. It was not the last publication of the boy who was to become a prominent evangelical apologist.[104]

The problem as far as the school was concerned, however, was not so much the number of prize-winners – although there were far fewer of them in this period proceeding to the ancient universities even on the Somerset foundation[105] – as the total roll. Despite the absence of a register, there is clear evidence that numbers had steeply declined by the mid-1830s. Bamford, as we have seen, was not replaced as Under-Master following his resignation in February 1834; one of Bishop Grey's injunctions, after his visitation of June 1835 required that the Chapter should 'minutely enquire in to the falling off of the Cathedral School', as well as provide a new schoolroom and 'a diligent Usher'; and in January 1836, Dean Merewether and the hebdomadary could report that there were 'only twenty-one boys in the school in all'.[106] The question remains as to why there was such a decline in the school's population in less than a decade.

One reason may well have been that its overwhelmingly classical curriculum was seen as being increasingly outmoded in an industrial age. While assistants were hired for mathematical instruction, Accounts, French and musical tuition, as shown by the 1818 rules, the formal establishment still only consisted of the two classical masters as provided by the cathedral statutes. Of the assistants, the most important was the writing-master, styled 'the writing and mathematical master' by this time in acknowledgment of the increasing importance of his arithmetical duties. As we have seen, Benjamin Powle served the Cathedral School loyally in this regard for nearly 50 years. One of his successors was John Goundry, who left in 1825 to take up the mastership of Easington School, a parish school in Durham established on the lines of Dr Bell's system. Thereafter, it was Taylor's misfortune that William Bunning should resign this position at midsummer 1829 'to devote his attention exclusively' to his own school in Bridge Street. Here young gentlemen were 'carefully instructed in writing the proper hands for business, commercial arithmetic with vulgar and decimal fractions, Book-keeping by single and double entry, grammatical composition, Geography with mapping etc., mensuration and the higher branches of mathematics'. By the end of the year, the school was advertised as a 'classical, mathematical and commercial academy' and had moved (briefly) to new premises in Widemarsh Street.[107] And there were other competitors nearby: Collier was still providing a 'classical and commercial education' in St Owen's Street; W. Howell had established a similar academy in Castle Street by 1830, as had a Mr Fowler in Berrington Street. This latter establishment (it was claimed)

---

104. Nearly 50 of his works are listed (*Brasenose Reg.*, i., p.509) as being published, 1850-79. Lucretia is the legendary heroine of ancient Rome whose suicide (*c.*509 BC) was the catalyst for the overthrow of the monarchy and foundation of the Roman republic.

105. Of the Brasenose Somerset scholars, only the three Garbetts (George in 1828, Charles in 1834 and Edward in 1837), W.H. Cooke and John Oakes Taylor (in 1830 and 1836 respectively) can be definitely identified as old boys. At St John's, Cambridge, no Hereford Somerset scholars were elected during this period, John Maurice Herbert gaining his award on 6 November 1826 before Taylor junior's appointment as Headmaster. *Brasenose Reg.*, i., pp.484, 488, 501, 508,509; *HJ*, 15 Nov. 1826; SJCA, typescript of Somerset scholars.

106. HCA, 7031/19, p.26, injunction 12; p.53, report 15 Jan. 1836. For Bamford, see above, p.147.

107. *HJ*, 9 March 1825 (Goundry), 11 March, 1 July, 30 Dec. 1829, 7 July 1830 (on Bunning's return to Bridge Street); Carless, p.42.

combined 'all the advantages of a grammar school with those of an academy', including the teaching of the classical languages, History, Mathematics and book-keeping to the higher classes.[108] Such academies did not have the cachet or patronage of the Cathedral School but they provided a vocational training which must have been an attractive proposition for some parents. Their fees, too, compared favourably. In 1829, for example, Bunning charged an annual fee of 25 guineas for boarders and 4 guineas for day pupils (with no entrance fees), compared with the 40 guineas Taylor required for his boarders in the same year. Three years later, Taylor's charges came out at £31 10s for board, 6 guineas for classical tuition, 2 guineas for washing and one guinea for 'hair cutter and shoe black'.[109]

And at times some parents must have wondered whether the state of the Cathedral School justified such fees, whatever the quality of the teaching. The school-house, where Taylor lived with his boarders, was in disrepair for the early part of his headmastership. When he approached the Chapter with his concerns in 1828, the matter was postponed, 'the Chapter not recognising their liability'. In May 1832, some repairs were allowed but it was not until late 1833 that a major reconstruction was undertaken by Leonard Johnson, a local builder who was restoring the College of Vicars Choral after the 1828 fire, at a cost of nearly £130. Earlier that year, the dilapidated long room, which Headmasters had used for teaching during the Hereford music meeting since Rudd's time, had been taken down. This was not quite the end of the renovations for in June 1837 one of the rooms that had been 'much damaged by the boys' during its temporary use as a schoolroom was repaired. The Chapter, however, regarded Taylor's request for a new garden pump as being 'not requisite'.[110]

The schoolroom's condition, however, was much more important to the lives of most boys than that of the school-house. And through much of Taylor's tenure the school suffered from inadequate teaching accommodation. Despite its gothic facelift in 1804, the Great Room, which (as we have seen) had been used as a schoolroom since 1778, was by this time unloved. Its last major renewal had been in the late summer of 1816, when it was patched up for the final Three Choirs concert to be held in the building.[111] Thereafter, following the use of Robert Smirke's new Shire Hall for the music meetings from 1819, the old room, lacking its triennial makeover, had gradually fallen into disrepair. By 1832, its walls were being used by members of the public for posting bills.[112] Architectural tastes, too, had changed so that the lauded building of the early 1760s was seen to be an eyesore by the end of the Georgian period. Writing in about 1830, John Britton's dismissal of the once Great Room that had housed 19 Three Choirs meetings as nothing more than a 'brick building of

108. *HJ*, 20 Jan., 7, July 1830; 13 July 1831; 11 Jan. 1832.

109. *Ibid*, 21 Jan., 1 July 1829; 11 Jan. 1832.

110. HCA, 7031/8, pp.265, 267, 341, 395, 396, 399, 401, 402, 404, 409, Chapter Acts, 13 Nov., 2 Dec. 1828; 3 May 1832; 4 March, 10 April, 13 May, 3, 7 June, 17 Sept. 1833. HCA, 7031/19, p.117, Chapter Act, 26 June 1837. For the vicars choral approval of Johnson's plan for repairing the College, see HCA, 7003/1/5, p.238, 9 Aug. 1828.

111. See HCA, 5715/2/64-65, for the cleaning bills from 19 August, as well as the vouchers of the blacksmith (James Bruton), carpenter (Garstone), mason (William Preece) and painter (Price).

112. HCA, 7031/18, p.301, Chapter order, 8 Nov. 1832, prohibiting the practice.

most unsightly and unmeaning character' and a 'warehouse-looking pile',[113] was a view that was shared by many at that time.

It was certainly held by Dean Merewether who had a 'horror of bricks' and, as befitted an *alumnus* of Queen's, Oxford, a love of architectural uniformity. But his proposal to dismantle the schoolroom was not accepted by all his colleagues, Canon Clutton among others arguing that after suitable conversion it should become the parish church of St John.[114] Eventually, however, the following chapter order of mid-July 1834 was agreed:

> Resolved that in consequence of the dilapidated and unsafe condition of the schoolrooms and other buildings near the west end of the cathedral, the same be taken down, the materials sold and cleared away, and that the purchase money be invested in a separate fund and the interest allowed to accumulate for the purpose of building a new schoolroom elsewhere. And that the Dean may be authorised to confer with Leonard Johnson, builder, or any other person he think proper, and enter into the necessary arrangements for carrying the above resolution into effect.

The implementation of the resolution was twice postponed, initially because of the music meeting, and it was not until the following spring that it was acted upon, the building being demolished without Bishop Grey's permission which in itself caused a rumpus.[115] The schoolroom was then temporarily removed to unsuitable quarters – a poky room 16 feet by 11 – in the Headmaster's house, the unfitness of which is nicely illustrated in this letter from a worried chorister mother to the Dean:

> I am sorry to observe that my boy has suffered ... in his constitution by being close pent-up in a room, or closet rather, among so many boys, where in the months of October and November they could not breathe without the window and door open and the fire being put out. Six weeks previous to the vacation, my boy came home dangerously ill. I consulted two medical gentlemen ... about him who both gave it as their decided opinion that his life would be in sacrifice if he were permitted to go again to school. I am obliged to give him private instruction, at a great expense, in order that he may be able to go up with his class at the examination.

This resulted, at Merewether's insistence and despite Taylor dragging his feet, in the school moving yet again to a larger room at the southern end of the house, where it stayed for more than a year.[116]

Meanwhile, despite the Headmaster's urgent appeals, the Chapter repeatedly delayed making a decision about rebuilding the schoolroom, one reason being in order to see whether (in Dean Merewether's words) 'the College rooms might not supply the need

---

113. Britton, pp.38, 53.

114. HCA, 7031/19, pp.152, 155, 190, 340, letters to Bishop Grey, 31 May, 1 June 1837, 18 April 1838.

115. HCA, 7031/18, pp.436, 439, 450, Chapter Acts, 15, 29 July, 1 Oct. 1834; 7031/19, pp.13, 15, 18, Chapter Acts, 17 Jan., 3 March, 21 April 1835; *ibid.*, pp.190-91, Matthews to Grey, 1 June 1837.

116. *Ibid.*, pp.51-52, letter to the Dean (read out in Chapter 1 Feb. 1836), from Mrs Vaughan, the mother of James Henry Vaughan (elected a probationer, 'nearly seven years', on 10 August 1831 and a full chorister on 16 January 1832: HCA, 7031/18, pp.315, 333); HCA, 7031/19, pp.53, 56, Chapter Acts, 15 Feb., 7 March 1836.

and save the outlay'.[117] Eventually, a new site was the preferred option, the west end of the Canon's Bakehouse being chosen 'on account of its propinquity to the Master's house and every other circumstance the most eligible for the purpose'. Leonard Johnson was again chosen as the contractor, and on 26 June 1836 the Chapter agreed the following resolution: 'that the Canon's Bakehouse be converted into a room according to the specification and estimate now laid before the Chapter and approved, which shall be used as the schoolroom for the Cathedral School during the pleasure of the Dean and Chapter'. Details of the cost are not given but presumably it would have been largely covered by the £210 that Johnson had paid a year earlier for the materials from the old schoolroom, apart from £31 Johnson spent on a porch, shed (for faggots, coal and the cathedral scaffolding) and drains, including a culvert 'from the boys' privy to the common sewer in the lane'. Nor has a plan of the building survived, although we know that it was a room of 35 feet by 21 which was considered 'sufficient not only for the present boys but also for the accommodation of a large addition to the number, more than it is probable may be added'. Given the size and the money available, when it was opened for the beginning of term on 7 August 1837, it could only have been a pale imitation of the Great Room. But at least the school had secured a site adjacent to the school-house for its teaching, even if the Chapter had reserved its right to 'make use of the said room for any other purpose at any time as they may think proper and to suspend the use of it as a schoolroom if occasion should seem to them so to require'.[118]

So the school had finally gained a permanent schoolroom in a convenient location. However, the previous three years of teaching in a condemned building and then in two temporary rooms, before the final move to a purpose-built schoolroom, would have tested the resolve and patience of any Headmaster, not least one whose hold on the school was insecure. For even before the school's peripatetic existence in the mid-1830s, there were signs of parental and pupil dissatisfaction. Unusually, some grievances which had reached the ears of the school's governors are recorded in the Chapter Acts. The details of each case remain shadowy but we know that in early 1830 one Captain Bennett made a formal complaint against the Headmaster. A few years afterwards, we find that three boys had gone on strike and had refused 'to learn their grammar lessons'.[119] Later in 1834, following representation from a Mr Hughes, the senior chorister's father, the Chapter recommended that Taylor should reinstate the excluded boy, following his contrition and completion of the required translation. They then rebuked the Headmaster in these terms:

117. *Ibid.*, p.104, Merewether to Grey, 1 March 1837. The decision had been postponed five times from June 1835. Canon Matthews later asserted, in contradiction of Merewether's claim that he had pressed for the schoolroom's rebuilding, that that the Dean was primarily responsible for this delay. *Ibid.*, pp.21, 30, 31, 34, 44, Chapter Acts, 25 June, 18 Aug., 2 Sept., 1 Oct., 24 Nov. 1835; p.104, Merewether to Grey, 1 March 1837; p.190, Matthews to Grey, 1 June 1837.

118. *Ibid.*, pp. 62, 63, 66, 109, 110, Chapter Acts 6, 26 April, 25 June 1836, 21, 25 April 1837; *HJ,* 2 Aug. 1837; HCA, 5715/2/75, 76, various tradesmen's vouchers, including Joseph Jeynes carpenter's bill (*c.*23 Sept. 1837) for four ten-feet-long oak desks 'made particularly strong with iron edges' (53s each), four forms (10s each) and 'a master desk of oak' with lock and chair (£1 17s 6d); and Richard Spencer's painting bill for £2 0s 5d (including rails for hats and 'blacking 51 iron pins' [for cloaks?]).

119. HCA, 7031/18, pp.280-81, 442-43, Chapter Acts 2 March 1830, 9 Aug. 1834.

> The Dean and Chapter have to express their regret that the exercise happened to be set at the time of the audit, and they desire the Headmaster in future to avoid the suspension of either of the cathedral boys from the privilege of attendance at school in which he would not be justified. They recommend that the boys be not sent out of his house for their instruction in writing, and that the infliction of corporal punishment be not on any account delegated to any of their school fellows.

A letter to the parent of the same date expressed confidence that Taylor was 'sufficiently experienced in tuition to regulate the internal management of the school', deprecated Hughes' interference with the school's regulations and stressed 'the importance of [his] co-operation with the Master in promoting regularity of attendance'.[120] In all three cases, the Dean and Chapter had supported their Headmaster, but one is left pondering how many other parents were dissatisfied with the running of the school and how many boys took the liberty of defying him by their frequent absences like the foundationers did in 1837.[121] Given such circumstances, it is little wonder either that numbers were going south or that Bishop Grey had expressed concerns about the school after his cathedral visitation in 1835.

Taylor struggled on as the lone established master for four more years. He saw the school settled into its new home but following his preferment as vicar of Lydney, he gave his governors three months' notice of his intention to resign the headmastership from 24 March 1839.[122] His tenure had not been an unalloyed success. He had been appointed too young and with no school-mastering experience; he had gradually lost the confidence of influential parents; and unlike some of his predecessors, he did not have the vision, entrepreneurial skills or drive – and perhaps personality – to compete effectively with his commercial rivals. It was not, of course, all his fault. The squabbling in Chapter over the schoolroom in the mid-1830s, in particular, did not help Taylor's cause. As one of the canons wrote at the time: 'Letter after letter did he [the Dean] receive from the master of the school [about the rebuilding] and month after month did he postpone its consideration'.[123] Nevertheless, one cannot avoid the conclusion that Taylor was a better churchman than Headmaster, even when his competence as a scholar and teacher are acknowledged. Judging by his preferments and prebendal appointments – like his predecessors he was made a prebendary while still in magisterial office[124] – he was in good standing within the diocese, and some idea of his conscientiousness (at least) as a priest may be gathered from the surviving list of the 52 sermons he gave in seven parishes in the

120. *Ibid.*, pp.481-82, Chapter Clerk's letters to Taylor and Hughes, 9 Dec. 1834. For Charles Hughes' chequered career as a chorister and eventual retirement: HCA, 7031/19, pp.15, 30, 31, 122, 223, Chapter Acts, 3 March, 18 Aug., 2 Sept. 1835, 22 July 1837, 2 Jan. 1838.

121. *Ibid.*, p.223, Taylor's complaint in Chapter, 2 Jan. 1838.

122. *Ibid.*, p.399, 18 Dec. 1838.

123. *Ibid.*, p.190, Matthews to Grey, 1 June 1837.

124. He followed Picart as prebendary of Moreton Parva (1835-36), and after his father's tragic death became prebendary of Moreton Magna (1836-81): Le Neve (2014), pp.77, 80. For the 'dreadful accident' involving Dr Taylor's phaeton in Bridge Street: *HJ*, 15 June 1836.

year from November 1835.[125] However, as to the school – and unlike his father – he could not arrest its decline.

Three Short Interludes, 1839-1851

These 12 years cover the Headmasterships of William Henry Ley (1839-42), John Woolley (1842-44) and Thomas Francis Layng (1844-51). All three were good clergymen scholars. Woolley and Layng held doctorates; Ley and Woolley came to Hereford straight from Oxford, following their marriages, both having held fellowships at their respective colleges; both were in their mid-twenties and neither had any experience of school-mastering. Layng, on the other hand, was appointed in his mid-thirties after teaching at and running several schools. Overall, despite their academic credentials and their appointments being made without the encumbrance of parochial duties, none of the three tenures was distinguished. Neither Ley nor Woolley stayed long enough to make much of an impact on the school's development, nor did Layng's seven years see a rise in the school's fortunes. For several of these years the school was without an Under-Master; for a short while in 1839, it was closed; and for a period in 1844, there was only one boarder, and for a time in 1851, only one non-foundationer day boy. Overall, although improvements were made to School House in 1839 so that it could accommodate about 40 boarders, boarding numbers fluctuated wildly and there is no evidence for this period that it was ever more than half-full. Nor were there always 12 foundationers (eight choristers and four Langfordian scholars) to be added to the day number, the Chapter often being tardy in their replacement. And while the school obtained the College chapel for their services from 1842, for much of this period the foundationers were excluded from the cathedral while the building was being repaired. For both school and cathedral the 1840s proved to be a time of trial.

Two weeks after the *Hereford Times* had announced the presentation of the Lydney living to Charles Taylor, the newspaper published an article on 'Hereford Collegiate School', the old name for the school which was by then rarely used except by old boys.[126] Its author wrote that Taylor's preferment had given the Dean and Chapter an opportunity 'to adopt some means which shall not only restore the establishment to its former flourishing state' but would 'also place it in the first rank of the public schools of this kingdom'. He then indicated that its valuable leaving scholarships to the universities could be the means 'for the formation of a public school which might be wrought to good purpose by skilful hands', and that 'eminent men' could be found to 'enter the lists of candidates for the headmastership, gentlemen who would derive a handsome income from the school and confer honour and benefit on the city and county'. More contentious was the suggestion that its governors should 'give their suffrages to a gentleman of established scholarship and scientific acquirements ... whose intellectual lights have extended far beyond the confines of this county'; and (in an oblique reference to Taylor's elevation the previous

125. HCA, 7031/19, p.77, Taylor's schedule of the place, time and number of sermons preached at Madley, Pipe, Tiberton, Moreton-upon-Lugg (where he was rector), Eaton Bishop, Hentland and Dewchurch and Little Dewchurch on 33 days, 1 Nov. 1835-6 Nov. 1836, 'which prevented my personal attendance at the cathedral'.

126. *HT*, 10, 24 Nov. 1838. The article may well have been written by its reforming editor, Charles Anthony, who had bought the paper some six years earlier.

decade) that the appointment was 'not a party question, nor one in which the ties of friendship or kindred should have sway'. The following week, a correspondent reassured the editor that the Dean had fully concurred with Taylor's preferment at Lydney 'having in view probably a complete reform of the school', and that his strong favour of open competition accorded with 'his liberal views and acknowledged anxiety for the best interests of this city and neighbourhood'.[127]

Dean Merewether did not disappoint his liberal followers. At the December meeting which received Taylor's resignation, prior to a statement that legal advice would be sought about an anonymous letter, allegedly 'of a libellous nature', which had also appeared in the *Hereford Times*,[128] the Chapter stated that the Headmaster's appointment would be open to public competition with the proviso that all the candidates should be in Holy Orders. The post was then advertised for the first time in the school's history, and in late March William Henry Ley was elected Headmaster from a short-list of six eligible clergymen.[129] Having matriculated at Oxford in 1831 at the then early age of 16, and as a scholar of two colleges and a fellow of Trinity 1836-39, Ley was academically well qualified for his teaching responsibilities. And it was certainly well received by the *Hereford Journal* which announced the Headmaster's appointment to 'our grammar school', from a list of 14 or 15 competitors, in these triumphant terms:

> The high distinction with which Mr Ley graduated at Oxford, having attained the foremost rank in *literis humanioribus* – as well as the various and ample testimonials exhibited in his behalf from many of the chief authorities and ornaments of that university – render the appointment … a just subject of congratulation to the city and county of Hereford, as bringing the means of first-rate education within easy reach, under the direction of a pre-eminent scholar already well known for his successful preparation of candidates for the highest academical honours, and for the possession of qualifications rarely combined for the instruction and guardianship of youth.[130]

It must have seemed to Dean Merewether and his colleagues that the £5 2s they paid for advertising the post in four newspapers was money well spent.[131]

Yet the task of revitalising the school needed more than intellectual prowess. The state of the Headmaster's house was such that the opening of the school was delayed while

127. *Ibid.*, 1 Dec. 1838, letter from 'A Looker On', who also explained that the Dean had opposed Thomas Underwood's preferment to Diddlebury on the ground that he was not a member of the cathedral foundation.

128. Perhaps the letter from 'A Conservative' of 1 Dec. 1838 which questioned whether the governors' authority was sufficient 'for the subversion of the grand principles of the foundation, namely gratuitous instruction laid down by the founder …' There is no indication in the Chapter Acts that any further action was taken.

129. Of the six candidates, William Fletcher, Henry Cape and Ley himself had been fellows of their respective colleges; George Thompson and Cape, had previously been Headmasters – of Wisbech and Doncaster grammar schools respectively; and Samuel Stead was a student at Brasenose before his preferment as vicar of Burton-upon-Trent. Only John Skally had a local connection (as curate of Cleobury Mortimer). Foster (1887-8), ii., p.471, iii., p.850, iv., pp.1346, 1410; Venn, part II, i., p.507, v., p.524.

130. *HJ*, 27 March 1839.

131. HCA, 7105/5, p.397, 1839 clavigers' account. The headmastership was advertised in the two local papers, the *Oxford Herald* and a Cambridge journal (possibly the *Cambridge Chronicle*).

improvements, publically stated as being 'designed for the better accommodation of boarders', were undertaken.[132] Beyond the need for a water-closet 'for the use of the family' and a new 'privy' for the servants, it is not clear what restoration work was required but what is certain is that the Dean and Chapter refused to pledge more than £500. This sum was 'to be in full of all claims upon them for taking down and rebuilding, repairs or otherwise'. The Headmaster himself was to take on 'all responsibility beyond that amount', contract with the builders for the works and then maintain the premises in good repair at his own expense.[133] Well might Ley have pressed his governors on 9 May to approve the rebuilding plan, 'time being of the greatest importance to the interests of the school'. Even so, the decision to go ahead was not taken until the end of that month. Meanwhile, John Williams, a chorister, was being schooled by the verger, 'during the time the Cathedral School was closed'. Other boys, no doubt, found tuition elsewhere. And having married Mary Pritchard at St Augustine's, Bristol, on 15 June, the new Headmaster waited for his Hereford house to be made ready, both for his new bride and the boarding boys, and the school itself to be prepared for the delayed start of his first term. It was finally announced that the Cathedral School would re-open on Monday 30 September 1839.[134] It had been a long six months since Taylor's departure but the boarders at least now inhabited a new two-storey building adjacent to the Headmaster's house, containing two studies for the boys and a long dining-room as well as dormitory accommodation.[135]

Whether the delayed start to Ley's tenure markedly affected the pupil roll, and how far the new school house attracted boys from outside the county is unknown: no register survives from his period in office. Nor can much be discerned from other sources as to how the school operated during the two years of the Ley regime, although life for the foundationers would have changed significantly during the Forties. For during this decade, the Cottinghams made extensive repairs to the cathedral tower, Lady Chapel and choir during which works the daily choral service was transferred to the chapel of the College of Vicars Choral and later for most of the decade to All Saints church.[136] As to the boys generally, their appearance was smartened up when Ley required them to wear caps and gowns.[137] There is little indication, however, that any significant alterations were made to the nature of their academic studies. Ley's book of *Scripture Studies,* published 50 years later, shows that he was a biblical scholar of some distinction but there is no evidence from his one surviving submission on the boys' religious instruction that he did more in his headmastering days

132. *HJ*, 29 May, 28 Aug. 1839.

133. HCA, 7031/19, pp.439-43, 446, Chapter Acts, 17, 25 April, 31 May, 25 June 1839. The contract has not survived but the approved plan was prepared by Messrs Pearson and Johnson who presumably executed the work.

134. *Ibid.*, p.450, Chapter Act, 25 Oct. 1839, authorising the verger's payment of £1 11s 6d; HCA, 7105/5, p.400, 1839 clavigers' account, payment to John Davis; *HJ*, 26 June, 28 Aug., 4 Sept. 1839. Ley probably spent most of the summer of 1839 at Trinity College, Oxford, where letters of application for new entries were to be forwarded. School prospectuses were available from a Mr Jones, bookseller, Broad Street.

135. As described 50 years later by F.W. Bennett: *TH*, XVI (Nov. 1891), p.21.

136. HCA, 7031/9, pp.512, 513, 584, Chapter Acts, 14, 17 Aug. 1841, 15 Jan. 1844; HCA, 7003/1/6, pp.60-61, Merewether to vicars, 15 Jan. 1844. For L.N. and N.J. Cottingham's restorations in the 1840s: Aylmer and Tiller, pp.269-74.

137. HCA, 7031/9, p.505, Chapter Act, 29 June 1841.

than add 'some short book on the Articles' to the old syllabus.[138] Nevertheless, the high standards of tuition would have continued under the scholarly Headmaster as we can gather from reports on two prize ceremonies. In December 1840, in the presence of Bishop Musgrave, Dean Merewether and other dignitaries, the two senior classes were examined in several biblical passages, Sophocles' *Antigone*, a work of Thucydides and Horace's *Epistles* and 'acquitted themselves much to the satisfaction of all present'. Six boys were awarded prizes that year, the one for Latin verse composition being appropriately awarded to John Merewether, the Dean's eldest son, whose 120 line poem on 'Attila' ('Such men as these are God's own instruments / To work great actions, tho' with bad intents') was dutifully published in the original in the *Hereford Journal*. A year later, following the governors' £5 gift for two further prizes, the young Merewether did one better, by winning the competitions for both Latin verse (on 'Vaga Flumen') and Greek iambics (a scene from *Macbeth*).[139]

Significantly that year, in addition to the other classical awards and those for each of the six forms, two prizes were given for progress in Mathematics. This followed the appointment by June 1840 of a graduate 'mathematical master'. Robert Potter was a no-nonsense Lancastrian and a Cambridge graduate with some experience of teaching Mathematics at Bristol College when he arrived in Hereford in 1840 to become ordained. One old boy later remembered him as 'a good scholar' with 'an awful temper'. He would not have remained at the school beyond the mid-1840s when his clerical duties took him from the curacy at Clehonger and Eaton Bishop to Broadwell, but Ley's appointment of a mathematician as his Under-Master indicates that the subject was being taken more seriously as an academic discipline.[140]

By this time, Ley himself had gone on to pastures new. In November 1841, he was presented to the living of Sellack and King's Capel, resigning the headmastership early the following year.[141] The reasons for his preferment and consequent resignation are unclear but perhaps Ley's intellectual and pastoral gifts were better suited to rural ministry than schoolmastering, as he stayed in the same incumbency for over 45 years until his death in March 1887.[142] Whatever the reason, Ley's departure made way for the appointment of the most distinguished Headmaster of the period.

John Woolley, like Ley, had matriculated at Oxford aged 16 in June 1832, a few months after his predecessor. Like Ley, he gained a first in Greats, which led to an open

138. *Ibid.*, p.527, Ley's report 11 Nov. 1841. His *Scripture Studies* (London, 1872), consists of 92 biblical studies ranging from a homily on Adam ('I picture him before the Fall as the most perfect gentleman that ever was') to learned disquisitions on the Psalms, the Gospels, the 'Restoration of the Jews' and other sacred themes.

139. *HJ*, 18 Dec. 1840; HCA, 7031/19, p.498, Chapter Act, 28 April 1841; *TH*, XV (June 1891), p.15, list based on Hook's copy of the prize exercises 'recited at the public examination', 15 Dec. 1841, when classical prizes were also won by I.T. Prichard and W. de Boinville.

140. *HJ*, 24 June 1840; Venn part II, v., p.167; *TH*, XVI (Nov. 1891), p.20, reminiscences of F.W. Bennett. For Potter's successors as Under-Master in the 1840s, see below, pp.162-63.

141. HCA, 7031/18, pp.526, 530, Chapter Acts, 11 Nov. 1831, 28 Jan. 1842.

142. It is possible that Ley's health broke down. F.W. Bennett, who arrived at HCS as a Langfordian scholar in 1840, stated that the then Headmaster Dr Woolley was 'a great invalid'. (*TH*, XVI [Nov. 1891], p.20). Given Woolley's later career, it seems an inappropriate description. In any case, Woolley was not appointed until 1842 so Bennett could have meant Ley. After 50 years his memory may well have been playing tricks on him.

scholarship and then a college fellowship (at University College, 1837-43). Like Ley, too, while he may have undertaken some private coaching, he had no experience of school-mastering before he came to Hereford. But Woolley had the good fortune of being at University College at the same time as Arthur Stanley, who had won his fellowship in 1838, two years before Woolley became a fellow. In a small fellowship of around a dozen dons, he would have known Stanley well. And even though Stanley compiled his famous biography of the great Thomas Arnold as a memorial to his Rugby Headmaster after Woolley's departure from Oxford, it is reasonable to suppose that Woolley would have absorbed some of Arnold's ideas on headmastering from his greatest disciple. Be that as it may, Woolley's academic record was sufficiently distinguished for him to be 'unanimously appointed' by the Hereford governors on 24 March 1842, shortly before his marriage to Margaret Turner that July.[143]

Fig. 4.6 Dr John Woolley, Headmaster of HCS for only two years but a notable Victorian educationalist.

Woolley wasted no time in attempting to evoke the spirit of Thomas Arnold at the school. Within weeks of embarking upon his headship, he enquired whether he could use the College chapel, which had been adapted for cathedral worship, to read the daily service 'at an early hour' to his boys. Woolley's letter to the Custos and vicars choral is revealing:

> I make this request believing that you feel with me the very great importance of the daily service in the education of young minds, and hoping that as our hopes of securing that great advantage depend ... entirely upon you, you will be inclined kindly to give us your assistance. I am fully sensible of the magnitude of the favour which I am asking, and if you grant it shall always esteem myself – as well as my pupils and their parents – deeply obliged to your society, and shall study in every way to prove my gratitude is sincere. I am also aware that considerable difficulties and objections at first sight oppose themselves to my success – the most considerable, with which I myself seriously sympathise, arising from the danger of noise or disturbance being excited by the boys in going and returning, and from the damage which might happen to the seats in the chapel itself. I trust, however, that I should be able to obviate these,

143. Foster, (1887-8), iv., p.1608; *ODNB*, vol. 60, p.274; Darwall-Smith, pp.356-59 (on Stanley). I am indebted to Robin Darwall-Smith for details about Woolley's University College career. Following his marriage, Woolley had to resign his college post but he was allowed to retain his fellowship for a further year, its stipend no doubt cushioning the financial blow of moving from Oxford to Hereford.

the former by mustering the boys in the schoolroom and attending them myself both to and from [the] service, whilst at all other times the College would, of course, remain, as it now is, strictly out of bounds even to the senior boys. The second danger I shall feel confident of preventing, partly by my own vigilance, partly by the care of my monitors, and in some degree I trust by the good feeling of the boys themselves.

The request was granted, subject to Chapter approval, although how the boys responded to listening to their Headmaster's reading is unrecorded. Despite the chapel's small size, dampness and 'inutility of the organ', Woolley clearly thought the experiment worthwhile for shortly afterwards the vicars agreed that it could also be used for Sunday morning services 'at eleven o'clock', a magisterial lecture taking the place of the sermon.[144]

Woolley's first report to the Chapter, the fullest of all the Headmasters' reports since their inception in 1803 – gives a further indication of the nature of his theological instruction.[145] Work for the various forms was appropriately differentiated. The lower classes used elementary commentaries on the church catechism, the upper remove also having to learn a psalm 'accommodated as much as may be to the services of the Sunday following', all the lessons being repeated in the mornings after chapel. Twice a week boys in the second and third classes studied sections from Watts' *Catechism*, in addition to 'construing lessons in the Gospels' from which 'explanations ... [were] given of the historical or doctrinal difficulties which may occur'. And boys in the fourth, 'at present my highest class', were required every Monday to submit an abstract and answer any questions put to them on the ten chapters of the historical books of the Old Testament. Judges was the relevant book in November 1842, the principal object being to ensure that the boys had read and remembered the text with Woolley making 'general allusions to ... prophetical or typical peculiarities'. In addition every Sunday evening, boarders in the higher classes read and made notes on a chapter of the New Testament, the Headmaster examining them the following morning. Overall, Woolley felt that there was a need for further tuition in both the Creed and the Articles – a knowledge of which was 'now generally required at the Oxford matriculation' – a need which he met for the boarders in 1843 through his Sunday morning lectures. He further planned to rearrange his timetable to find another hour for critical reading of the New Testament with his top class. Despite this full programme of religious instruction, it is apparent from the surviving list of subjects set for the examination of the senior classes in June and December 1843 that Classics still formed the major part of the curriculum. The book of Kings, Daniel, St Matthew's Gospel and the Greek Testament appear on the examination syllabus, as do topics in Greek History, Adams' *Roman Antiquities* and 'ancient and modern' Geography, but classical authors – Homer, Sophocles, Herodotus, Euripides, Ovid, Virgil and Livy – dominate the list of set works. Nevertheless, Woolley's rigorous

144. HCA, 7003/1/6, pp.45-46, copy of Woolley's letter to the Custos and vicars, 23 Sept. 1842; p.51, vicars' Act 4 March 1843; pp.60-61, Merewether to vicars, 15 Jan. 1844 (on the chapel's condition). None of Woolley's Hereford lectures survive, although in his 1842 report (HCA, 7031/19, p.555, 11 Nov. 1842) he had stated that he would 'deliver an explanation of the creed accommodated to the age of the hearers, of which I should require them to exhibit an abstract on [the following] Tuesday morning'. His later Rossall sermons, published in 1847, reveal a decidedly Arnoldian bent.

145. HCA, 7031/19, pp.553-55, 11 Nov. 1842.

half-yearly examinations, each spread over five days, would no doubt have received Arnold's plaudits, even if the results would not have matched those of the Rugby scholars.[146]

With a school of 340, attracting pupils from all over England, Rugby dwarfed Hereford's 30 or so boys. Despite advertising locally that the Cathedral School was an 'ancient foundation' situated 'in the most retired part of the Close and separate from all communication with the town'; that it possessed valuable scholarships at Oxford and Cambridge; and that its studies were 'conducted upon the principle of the great public schools: the union of religious and moral with intellectual discipline' – all at a rate of 10 guineas annually for tuition and 44 for board and washing – there is no evidence that the roll increased during Woolley's time.[147] Indeed, he had little time to build up numbers for he resigned in March 1844 after less than two years in post. Some weeks later, he had been appointed the first Headmaster of the new 'Northern Church of England School' at Rossall Hall, at a minimum annual salary of £600, riches compared with Hereford's meagre stipend.[148] There he was loved by the senior scholars, at least two of whom had exchanged Hereford for the Fylde coast,[149] his captain of school later writing of him as 'a man of the highest culture and sweetest temper, whose only fault was putting too much trust in the goodness of human nature'. He stayed at Rossall for five years, establishing the school on Arnoldian lines, before falling foul of his governors. He then moved to the grammar school at Norwich, where Arthur Stanley's father was bishop, before becoming principal of the newly formed University of Sydney in 1852 and later one of the original trustees of Sydney Grammar School.[150] Woolley's tenure at Hereford was too short to be of lasting significance but at least it proved to be a training ground for his career as a notable Victorian educationalist.

Woolley's departure to the bleak north-west in mid-1844 did not quite sever his ties with Hereford. For during that summer, a serious dispute arose over the state of School House, his successor taking counsel's advice as to the extent of his own liability and the Dean and Chapter feeling obliged to write to Woolley to insist that he make good the repairs 'committed or permitted during his occupation'. His reply, which has not survived, cannot have been a positive one for the cathedral eventually paid for the restoration of the 'greatly dilapidated' school premises, whilst ensuring that the new Headmaster entered into an agreement to hand over the house 'in good and tenantable repair' at the end of his

146. See HCSA, Dr Taylor's register (end) for these examination details, prize-men and pupil lists, 1842-44. Of the boys examined during Woolley's tenure, W.H. Thackwell, L.H. Rumsey, E.B. Smith (via Rossall) and C.J. Jones all became Brasenose Somerset scholars, and W.H.E. Merewether (the Dean's second son) followed his brother, John, to Oriel College in November 1845. *Brasenose Reg.*, i., pp.531, 537, 545, 548; Foster (1887-8), iii., p.945.

147. Bamford (1960), p.156; HCSA, Dr Taylor's register, pupil lists for Christmas 1842 and Easter 1843; *HJ*, 25 Jan. 1843.

148. HCA, 7031/20, pp.9, 12, Chapter Acts, 8, 25 March 1844, which both give notice of Woolley's resignation. His appointment to Rossall could not have occurred until after 7 May 1844 when its governors advertised for a Headmaster. Bennett, p.23

149. E.B. Smith and C.A. Woolley. For Smith, see above, note 146; and for Charles Woolley, the Headmaster's younger brother: Bennett, p.56.

150. Rowbotham, p.49 (quoting T.W. Sharpe); Bennett, pp.31-57; *ODNB*, vol. 60, p.274. Woolley died, aged 49, returning to Australia on board the *London* in January 1866 when it foundered in the Bay of Biscay. He was last seen manning the pumps in a forlorn attempt to save the vessel. The father of J.A. Bevan (below, pp.263, note 98) perished with Woolley on the same steamship.

own occupancy.[151] The renovation, which was undertaken in early 1845, involved extensive re-plastering and painting, as well as the mending of 30 broken windows, at costs in excess of £50. The whole episode makes one wonder how far Woolley was able to control his boys at Hereford, his failure to maintain good discipline being also a charge levelled against him at Rossall. Meanwhile, his successor justly considered that he had been 'much prejudiced' by the school's condition and 'that he would be permanently injured if prompt means were not adopted to put the premises in a state fit for the reception of his scholars'.[152]

That successor was an experienced schoolmaster. On Woolley's resignation, the post was again advertised, the particulars stating that no clerical duties were attached to the appointment as it was 'thought desirable that … [the Headmaster] should not engage in regular duty lest it should interfere with his personal attention to the school'.[153] Within weeks Thomas Francis Layng had been appointed Headmaster. This time, Merewether and his colleagues elected an older man, aged 35; a Cambridge graduate, the first for the century; and a clergyman who had (in the words of the *Hereford Journal*) 'for many years been successfully engaged in the duties of instruction' as Second Master at Oundle and Headmaster of both Chipping Campden Grammar School and the junior department of Bristol College.[154] Layng stayed for nearly seven years and following the short tenures of his immediate predecessors provided some stability for the school in the late 1840s. At least one old boy, Francis William Bennett, remembered him with affection. He had been a Langfordian scholar and a spirited boy at school, who had once refused to undertake Merewether's imposition on the grounds that Layng himself had denied the Dean's authority to punish boys. Bennett later wrote: 'Dr Lang [*sic*] … was one of the best masters I was ever under. He was very strict but very fair, not much given to punish but when he did there was no mistake about it, and I can well remember a visit to his study and the effects thereof!'[155]

From this testimony, Layng was an able teacher. He was less fortunate, however, with his assistant masters. The second mastership was vacant on his appointment, Potter having presumably left at the same time as Woolley, but local notice was given that it would soon be filled by an Oxford graduate, no doubt to complement the Headmaster's university. Layng's choice proved disastrous. Nearly 50 years later, Bennett remembered a 'Revd H' as 'a perfect brute, who made himself so hated by the boys that we barred him out, for which nearly all the school was punished by Dean Merewether, who at the same time advised Mr

151. HCA, 7031/20, pp.21, 23, 31, Acts re the 'dilapidations', 12 Aug., 5 Oct. 1844 and 16 Jan. 1845, when 'sundry letters' from Ley, Woolley and Layng were read in Chapter.

152. HCA, 7031/20, pp.29-30, Layng's report and Chapter order for repairs, 7 Jan. 1845. Tradesmen's vouchers for these repairs are to be found in HCA, 5715/2/78, bills of William Newman (carpenter), James Preece (mason) and Alfred Tristram (painter), various dates in 1845. For Woolley's disciplinary problems at Rossall: Bennett, pp.33-35, 47-48.

153. HCA, 7032/1, p.340.

154. HCA, 7031/20, p.12, Chapter sealing of Layng's appointment, 25 March 1844; *HJ*, 24 April 1844. Venn (part II, iv., p.119) also suggests that Layng had been Headmaster of Bristol Cathedral School, 1842-43. The Chapter had advertised the post in the London *Times* and (as for Woolley) in the *Oxford Herald*. HCA, 7105, pp.613, 697, payments of 17s 3d (1844) and £2 13s 8d (1846).

155. As published in *TH*, XVI (Nov. 1891), p.20. Bennett was elected a Langfordian scholar in 1840 but resigned the scholarship two years later. HCA, 7031/19, pp.485, 551, Chapter Acts, 12 Nov. 1840, 8 Nov. 1842. For the contretemps with the Dean, see above, p.125.

H to resign, which to our great joy he did'. There is, of course, no reference to this incident of 'barring-out' – a late example of this particular form of schoolboy rebellion[156] – in the official records but it is likely to have occurred as the Chapter's order of 7 January 1845 reveals:

> The Dean and Chapter, having ... fully considered the present circumstances of the school, and without any expression of censure, deemed it better for all parties that as there was not any probability that Mr Layng and Mr Hall would act together with the consent and harmony necessary for the prosperity of the school, that Mr Hall, the Under-Master, should be recommended to retire.

He had left by the following month, the Chapter turning down Hall's request for an additional payment for the expenses he had incurred in a job that he had held 'for so short a time'.[157] Layng made do without an official assistant for that term, the Chapter having deferred the appointment of Hall's successor until June 1845 when George Goodenough Hayter, an old boy who went on to Oriel College, Oxford, was unanimously elected Under-Master. Judging by the way the Chapter expressed regret at the receipt of his letter of resignation 18 months later, it would seem that Hayter made a success of his appointment. He left to run his own school in Castle Street, where he had taken young boarders and given private tuition in composition to older cathedral boys from January 1847. Hayter's resignation was thereby a double blow to Layng: he had lost a good Under-Master, a post that was in abeyance for the rest of his tenure; and his former colleague had opened a rival school within a stone's throw of his own establishment.[158]

The Cathedral School's welfare following Hayter's departure may be gauged from Layng's three surviving Headmaster's reports, 1847-49, which for the first time go beyond his predecessors' schemes of religious instruction.[159] Indeed, his reports are not primarily academic, although in 1847 he remarked that two leavers had gone on to Brasenose and Wadham and a remaining boarder had already been admitted a fellow of Jesus College, Oxford; and the following year, he observed that the Fifth Form was reading Sophocles' *Oedipus Tyrannus* and that 'considerable attention' had been paid to the works of Homer, Horace and Virgil.[160] Principally, however, Layng kept the Chapter informed about the

156. Although there are further examples from the mid to late-nineteenth century of the forced exclusion of a master from the schoolroom at other grammar schools, as given by Thomas, pp.28-29.

157. HCA, 7031/20, pp.30, 34, Chapter Acts, 7 Jan., 24 Feb. 1845. 'Mr Hall' may have been either John Hall or William Swanbrook (or Twambrooke) Hall, sons of William Hall of Warrington, both of whom had studied at Brasenose. Foster (1887-8), ii., pp.588, 590; *Brasenose Reg.*, i., pp.504, 525.

158. HCA, 7031/20, pp.37, 38, 41, 86, Chapter Acts, 28 April, 11, 25 June 1845; 11 Jan. 1847. Hayter regularly advertised in the *Hereford Journal*, as on 2 Dec. 1846, 9 June 1847, 12 July 1848, 3 Jan. 1849 and 16 July 1851, by which time he had employed John Goss, a vicar choral, as his assistant.

159. HCA, 7031/20, pp. 109-10, 148-49, 185-86, reports considered by the Chapter on 11 Nov. 1847, 7 Nov. 1848, 8 Nov. 1849. Layng's fuller reports stem from the Chapter's return of his 1845 effort, which he was asked to make 'more detailed and specific'. (*Ibid.*, p.51, 13 Nov. 1845.) Only three of Layng's seven annual reports were copied into the Dean and Chapter Act book.

160. The BNC leaver was George Waudby who matriculated on 4 February. *Brasenose Reg.*, i., p.546; *HJ*, 17 March 1847. The Wadham and Jesus College students have not been identified.

foundationers' behaviour and attendance, general disciplinary matters and pupil numbers. So the choristers had made 'considerable improvement' 'with respect to their regularity' in 1847, and the whole school was 'in a better state of discipline' and more orderly when assembling in the Close. In November 1848, Layng again claimed that he had less reason to complain 'as to the regularity and punctuality of the choristers', despite the absences of Morgan and Thomas Carpenter (the latter 'with your sanction I was informed by his father'). Joseph James and Joseph Cole had been punished during that term 'for using language of an immoral kind', but he could speak 'with full satisfaction' about 'the general discipline and good order of the boys altogether'. A year later, Layng could observe that the choristers' general conduct had been 'satisfactory' but that Guy's and Pearce's attendance was irregular 'from ill-health'; Robinson likewise was often absent, although he had not always 'been able to avail himself of the same excuse' and he did not 'value the privilege of attending the school'; and Morgan was 'regular and punctual but idle'. Jones, on the other hand, was commended for his good behaviour and erudition, and had 'lately commenced reading Livy and Herodotus with the Fifth Form'.[161] However, Layng's greatest concern related to pupil numbers, especially the boarders from whom the principal part of his income derived. He had started the half-year in August 1847 with a school of 27 boys, three short of the proper number had there been a full complement of foundationers. Of his six boarders, two had left that Michaelmas. His lament continued:

> One great disadvantage [during my tenure] ... has been the age and condition of my boarders. They have in several cases come when they ought almost to have been leaving and possessing little information for their years. The necessary consequence has been that the removals have been too rapid not only to gain an increase but have caused a decrease in the number. This must still be the case with the four now in my house, being all of such an age that I expect they will shortly withdraw.

He was proved right that Christmas but admissions in 1848 brought boarding numbers back to nine, which together with his three sons and four other day boys resulted in a school roll of 16 non-foundationers.[162] The situation was dire.

Nor did it improve, as can be seen from the particulars that the Chapter Clerk sent out to candidates aspiring to succeed Layng following his presentation to Marden in November 1850 and his subsequent resignation from the school.[163] The prospectus outlined the annual fees (tuition 10 guineas, board 'with single bed' 30, washing 4 and entrance 1); the optional

161. With the exception of Percy Pearce, who was a Langfordian scholar, J.A. Morgan, Thomas Carpenter, Joseph James, Joseph James Cole, Alfred Jones, Edwin Guy and Christopher William Robinson were all choristers who were elected between 14 February 1843 and 10 November 1848. HCA, 5983; HCA, 7031/19, pp.560, 575; 7031/20, pp.33, 95, 108, 148, 185-6.

162. Which meant a total school of 30 boys provided there was a full complement of eight choristers, two probationers and four Langfordians. This was often not the case as Layng had pointed out in his 1847 report. For the year's delay in the Chapter appointing a successor to William Meyler Milton as a Dean's scholar (Langfordian), for example, see HCA, 7031/20, pp.141, 143, 147, 157, 173, 175, Acts 26 June, 14 Oct., 10, 27 Nov. 1848, 16 May and 25 June 1849, when Richard Tench was elected.

163. HCA, 7031/20, pp.207, 222, 223 re the Marden presentation, 14 Nov. 1850; Layng's resignation letter of 20 March; and the forwarding of his £35 15s 3d dilapidations bill, 26 April 1851.

subjects (German, French, Italian and Dancing at one guinea per quarter and Drawing at one-and-a-half); the general age of admission (between 7 and 15, no boy being received 'unless qualified to begin Latin Accidence immediately on entering the school'); the notice period (three months or a quarter's board 'before removal'); the vacations (six weeks at both summer and Christmas, the holidays starting on 21 June and 21 December respectively); the university scholarships attached to the school; and the requirement for each boarder 'to bring six towels and a silver fork and dessert spoon'. The details of the Headmaster's package were also given: £20 annual salary, plus an additional £10 during the Under-Master's vacancy; 8 guineas annually for the four Langfordians' tuition; and three-fifths of the annual day tuition fees of 10 guineas for the seniors and eight for the juniors, the Under-Master (when in post) receiving the remainder. In addition, it was stated that the Headmaster paid £5 4s 6d each year for the rent of the school premises belonging to the cathedral fabric estate, and (optimistically) that the School House would accommodate about 40 boarders. The sting, however, was in the final sentence: 'There was recently fifteen boarders but this number is now reduced to seven, it being known that ... Dr Layng was about to retire. At present, there is only one day scholar'. It was the same number of non-foundationers that Layng had inherited from Woolley, although in 1844 day and boarding numbers were reversed.[164] As we will see, it took all the skills of the new Dean – that pioneering educationalist, Dean Dawes – to place the school on a different footing so that the right candidate could be attracted to turn things around.

A Disaffected Chorister

This almost unbelievable, yet true story concerns the notorious escapades within the College of Vicars Choral of one Robert Carpenter, then a senior chorister, during the summer of 1820.[165]

Robert Carpenter was elected a chorister, aged eight, on 10 December 1811. He served the cathedral in this capacity for over eight years, his formal resignation being recorded in the Chapter Acts on 23 August 1820.[166] As far as we can tell from Taylor's register, he made good academic progress, as befitted the son of a Hereford schoolmaster, working his way up to and more than holding his own in the second class by 1819. In the early months of 1820, however, a change can be detected in his behaviour. Although his academic work does not seem to have unduly suffered – he was still ranked about the middle of his class – for the three months from February to April, he had chalked up 39 absences, the second worst record in the school after Robert Jackson, the Jamaican Chief Justice's naughty younger son.

164. Two copies of the 1851 particulars survive in: HCA, 1536 and (in part) HCA, 7032/6, p.87. For the 1844 prospective Headmaster's notice that there had been 'lately' about 15 boarders but 'only one at present' (together with the eight 'day-scholars'): HCA, 7032/1, pp.339-40. Thirty years later, in palmier days, William Peete Musgrave (canon residentiary, 1844-92) remembered (inaccurately) the time when there was only one boy at the school. *TH*, No. 6 (Sept.1880), p.49, his speech possibly referring to the one boarder on his arrival in 1844 rather than the one day boy in 1851.

165. The following account is based on a copy of the prosecution's brief, together with statements prepared for Carpenter's hearing at the Herefordshire summer assizes in 1820, to be found in HCA, 3835/1-3. I am indebted to Rosalind Caird for bringing these extraordinary documents to my attention.

166. HCA, 7031/6 p.119, Act, 10 Dec. 1811; 7031/18 p.156, Act, 23 Aug. 1820.

His absences for early May are not recorded but we do know that he had neglected his chorister duties and bunked off school on Friday 12 May 1820. Carpenter had been befriended by Henry Pearce, a former chorister and by this date a young and unruly vicar choral.[167] Pearce, according to his later testimony, was subject to 'sudden illness' and had allowed Carpenter to stay in his College apartment, 'holding him to be a lad of good character and principles'. On the day in question, he had lent Carpenter his horse to undertake some business of Pearce's in Norton Canon, a round journey of about 20 miles. Having executed the errand, rather than riding straight back to Hereford, Carpenter had decided to go on to Hay and dine at the Swan Inn where he was acquainted with the landlord. What he ate there is not known but he had enjoyed glasses of negus – wine and hot water sweetened with lemon and spices – with his meal and peppermint afterwards. On his way back from Hay, he had stopped off at the Portway Inn, had his horse rubbed down and drank some rum and milk. He had then returned to Hereford via Norton Canon, drinking another glass – this time of cider – at Mr Tunstall's. Arriving in Hereford at about 8.30 that evening, he immediately went to the Sun Tavern to stable the horse and dry off, it having been wet on the road. There he had met up with Joseph Tyler, the College groom, and James Bruton the blacksmith, and treated them to several drinks, Carpenter himself downing two or three glasses of brandy and water. He came back to the College about ten o'clock and was alone in Pearce's chambers for a few minutes. Carpenter then proceeded to the College Buttery, falling off a table while he was there, and after the servants had gone to bed, no doubt in an attempt to sober up, staggered about the gardens with Benjamin Matthews, the watchman. He accompanied him on his rounds of the College, twice asking if he smelt fire. Refusing to remain in Pearce's rooms, Carpenter returned to the cloisters and was promptly sick.

Pearce himself, whose misjudgement of Carpenter had set the events of that day in motion, came back to the College at about 11.25 that night. Pearce and Matthews then left Carpenter at the gate while they investigated a suspicious looking character in the churchyard (it turned out to be a fellow watchman), and taking no notice of a flickering light in one of the College windows, thinking it was but a reflection from the stars, they returned with Carpenter to the vicar's rooms. There Pearce discovered that the light was indeed that of a lit candle which had been placed against lathes within an upper lumber room. The flame had scorched part of a lath and plaster partition. Carpenter now became a suspect. Custos Garbett was called – the very man who had been Under-Master of the Cathedral School less than 15 years earlier – and Carpenter was accused of being intoxicated and of having placed the candle in the wainscot. The chorister (according to Pearce's account) 'cried a good deal but asserted his innocence' of the crime. Carpenter refused to go home, claiming his father would not wish to be disturbed at such a late hour – by then it was past midnight – so he was allowed to remain in his rooms for the rest of the night, Pearce having agreed to be responsible for his conduct. The next morning, he was examined by a city magistrate and imprisoned on suspicion of having set fire to the College. Such were

167. According to Cooke's biography, Pearce defied 'all rule, all authority and all power'. HCA, 7003/4/4, no. 93. His attempt to introduce his wife as a permanent College resident in 1833 (and later a female servant) was one such act of defiance. See HCA, 7003/1/5, pp.273ff, for this protracted dispute.

the events which led to Carpenter's hearing before a grand jury at the Herefordshire assizes later that summer.

The fire on the evening of 12 May was the last of five arson attempts that the vicars had suffered in two months during the course of that spring.[168] The first of these was successful, for on the evening of 15 March, the vicars' six stables were completely destroyed, only the horses being saved – hence their temporary stabling at the Sun Tavern. On the following Easter Sunday (2 April), a fire broke out in the College itself. Aaron Hayter, the cathedral organist, had left the church earlier than usual that morning, 'it being a sacrament day' and having completed his duties at the organ. He looked upwards as he was entering the College to watch a hawk flying over the quadrangle, and saw smoke coming from the roof of the south-eastern range of the building. He raised the alarm and the fire was quickly put out without much damage being done. A further fire was discovered in an unoccupied room on the west side of the College on the evening of 10 April, and again extinguished before it took hold. Three weeks later, on the night of 2 May, an upper room on the north range occupied by John Hill, a cathedral schoolboy to whom we will return, was badly damaged by a fire set alight in three distinct places, although Hill himself was unhurt. Finally, ten days later, there was the burning in the lumber room already described.

Suspicious circumstances surrounded each of these incidents: a mysterious note was addressed to the College butler after the stable fire; an oil flask which had contained turpentine was found after the second one; and candles and other combustible materials were discovered following the others. It was quite clear, too, that it was an inside job. The arsonist knew his way around the College, the fires having been started in hidden away places, adjacent to rooms seldom frequented and where water access was difficult. The vital question was this. Who was both (as the local journal put it) 'well acquainted with the College and possessed of daring and wicked cunning equal to the horrible crime he attempted to perpetrate'?

It took some time for the authorities to suspect that Carpenter was the culprit. Indeed, after the Easter Sunday incident and until he could provide a cast-iron alibi for his whereabouts on 2 May, Aaron Hayter, the organist, was considered to be the more likely arsonist, and was actually imprisoned for a while following an investigation by a Mr Lavender, a Bow Street officer engaged by the city corporation to investigate the crimes. Carpenter himself had been first formally examined by a city magistrate on 3 May, but as stated in the later prosecution brief, the case against him was 'too vague and undefined a character to warrant at that time proceeding against him'. But after his drunken return from Hay ten days later and the taking of several more statements on oath, 'the whole body of evidence pressed so strongly upon Robert Carpenter … that he was fully committed [to prison] to take his trial for the offence'.

The hearing duly took place that August at the same county midsummer assizes which tried 35 other prisoners charged with horse and sheep stealing, household burglary, possession of forged bank notes, abetting a rape and other criminal offences.[169] Carpenter himself

168. Details of these fires are given in the depositions (as in note 164), the vicars' Acts (HCA, 7003/1/5, pp.181-86), and *HJ*, 22 March; 5, 12 April; 3, 17 May 1820.

169. *Ibid*, 2, 9 August 1820.

appeared before a grand jury of 20 of the county's great and good, some of whom were friends of the school. He was indicted on eight counts for 'feloniously, wilfully and maliciously' setting fire to the vicars' houses on 12 May 1820 'against the peace of our said Lord the King, his Crown and dignity'. Unsurprisingly, given its circumstantial nature, and despite the College butler, groom, boy and watchman, as well as Pearce and Custos Garbett, all being sworn as witnesses, the evidence was insufficient for Carpenter to be tried before a 'petty jury' and the case was dismissed.[170] As Taylor accurately recorded in his register: 'No bill was found against this boy'. But it is surely not without significance that from the time of Carpenter's apprehension, (again in the prosecutor's words) 'no fresh attempt has been made [to fire the College], no alarm whatever has been excited, the confidence of the members and servants of the College has been completely restored and they have returned to rest without the appalling apprehension of being burnt in their beds'. Eight years later, the vicars had to endure a more disastrous fire in their College, which saw the death of John Constable, their butler, but foul play was not suspected and Carpenter had long since departed the school.[171]

Thus Carpenter escaped a trial before 12 good men and true. However, his story during the summer of 1820, as reconstructed from the depositions taken for his hearing, is much more than an account of one disaffected chorister's wayward behaviour. For these documents reveal much about the daily routine of the three cathedral schoolboys who were questioned. Indeed, their surviving statements give a unique glimpse into their lives during a couple of days in May 1820 at the height of Charles Taylor's headmastership.

Carpenter apart, the two boys interviewed before John Matthews JP after the fire of 2 May were John Hill, whose chamber was set ablaze, and Robert Woodward. Hill, the son of a vicar choral, stayed in his father's College room on Monday 1 May, his mother having insisted that he should return to the vicarage at Sutton St Nicholas after the Easter fire 'for fear of accident'. We know from Taylor's register that the bookish Hill was among the best scholars in the school, tutoring class 2, gaining high marks in the Greek and Latin monthly exercises in 1819-20, and having a good attendance record.[172] He kept his books in a box, together with his tinder box for lighting fires and candles, so (his deposition of 3 May goes) 'that he might know when to lay his hand upon it in the dark, being in the habit of reading early in the morning'. Robert Carpenter, his 16-year-old contemporary, although they were not close friends, often borrowed a book from Hill's room, where Carpenter's exercise book was discovered. Eleanor Jones, the College cook, found Hill reading when she dusted his room on 2 May just before he left to go to school at noon that day. After the mid-day session, he had walked on Castle Green, dined at his cousin's in King Street until half past three and then walked the four miles to his father's house at Sutton, returning before nine to eat again with his cousin and getting back to College by ten.

170. For Carpenter's indictment ('ignor' for ignoramus being written over his name, signifying that the case was dismissed), which includes the names of the sworn witnesses: TNA, ASSI 5/140/9. Two of the four local baronets picked for those assizes had acted as stewards for Old Herefordian dinners: Sir John Geers Cotterell in 1807 and Sir Hungerford Hoskyns in 1817. Hoskyns was a school parent, and both may have been old boys.

171. For a contemporary account of the 1828 fire: HCA, 7003/1/5, p.237, vicars choral Acts, 9 August 1828.

172. Hill matriculated at Oxford on 3 July 1821. He was a Somerset scholar and then a Hulme exhibitioner at Brasenose, gaining his BA in 1825 and MA in 1828. *Brasenose Reg.*, i., p.462.

Carpenter, who was also interviewed before the JP on the same day, claimed that he had attended school between 7 and 9 before breakfasting at his father's. He had returned to school at half past nine, staying there until 11 and going back again, after the cathedral service, for an hour from mid-day. He had then dined at his father's until around quarter past two and visited the cathedral for half an hour until about three, staying in the organ loft rather than going 'in his surplice in his proper place'. After the service, he had walked to the bridge with Woodward (whom we will soon meet), played the harpsichord in Pearce's room, gone with three other choristers (Bowen, Howells and Morgan) to fish in the river from Easton's yard,[173] and returned to the Close via Castle Green. Shortly after 4, he had taken tea at his father's, walked to Widemarsh Common at 6 with John Mills, a young chorister, and had returned with him around 7.30 to Mills' father's house where Hayter lodged. They then had a jolly musical evening together until near 10 when Carpenter went home – for the fourth time that day – before returning to his chamber in the College.

Robert Woodward, another chorister,[174] gave his deposition on 5 May, when he recalled his movements during the previous Tuesday afternoon. He corroborated Carpenter's account, but only in part: that Carpenter had come into the organ loft while he (Woodward) accompanied the service. After church, in contradiction of Carpenter, he said that they had not parted at the bridge but had returned together to the College so that Woodward could borrow a copy of Gay's *Fables*.[175] There they had visited Pearce's room where Carpenter had played the harpsichord. Pearce's return had prompted them to leave: Carpenter to the Buttery and Woodward to go home.

Such are the glimpses into the lives of these schoolboys on 2 May 1820. The overwhelming impression that the depositions make upon a modern reader nearly two hundred years later concerns the freedom enjoyed by these senior boys to roam widely and unsupervised within and without the city. None of the three attended school that afternoon, even though a Tuesday was not an official half-holiday, and Hill may also have missed the early morning session. Walking and wandering, fishing and music-making were the orders of that particular afternoon and evening. Carpenter's excursion ten days later may have been exceptional, although he admitted that he had previously hired a horse from the Black Lion and perhaps elsewhere. Choristers especially had sufficient funds at their disposal to finance such expeditions. In addition to his occasional fees and regular payments – three five shilling quarterly allowances and the December bonus of £1 12s 8d – Carpenter had received the then enormous sum of 31 shillings in Christmas boxes in December 1819. He claimed

173. Easton's yard at Castle Quay was owned at the time by John Easton, who operated a river transportation business from Hereford to Bristol. For its sale to William Bunning (the school's former mathematical and drawing-master) in 1835: *HJ*, 4 March, 17 June 1835; and for its boat-building activities, 1822-32, and Hereford's river trade in general at this time: Johnson and Shoesmith, pp.207-10. Re the three choristers, Charles Bowen (aged 8) and Edward Howells (7) were elected choristers on 26 January 1819 and Thomas Morgan (8) on 24 March 1820. HCA, 7031/18, pp.126, 150.

174. Taylor later notes in his register that he entered St John's, Cambridge, on 10 October 1823. He gained his BA in 1827 and was ordained in Hereford, 1827-28, before leaving the diocese for Northamptonshire. Venn, part II, 6., p.575. He was probably the elder brother of Charles Woodward, the eighth chorister.

175. Perhaps the new 1820 edition, 'with upwards of one hundred embellishments', which was printed at Chiswick that year by C. Whittingham.

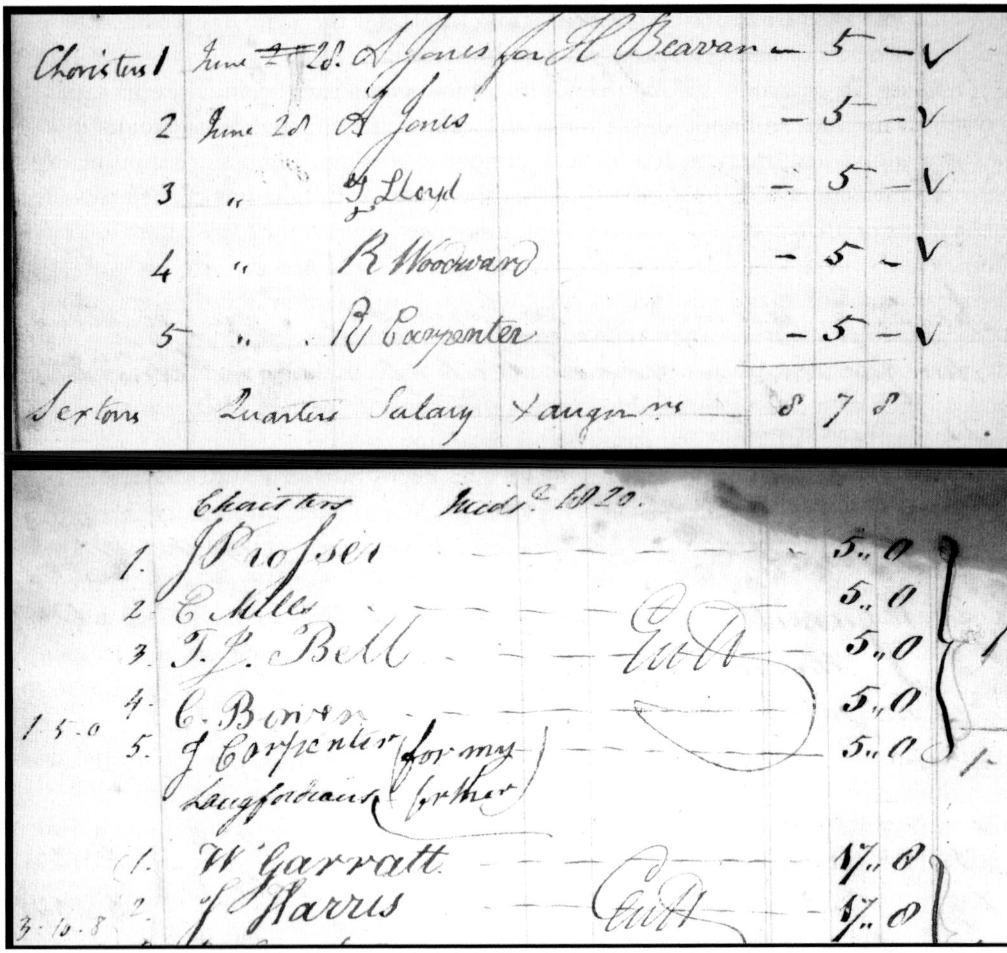

Fig. 4.7 Robert Carpenter's signature for his quarterly chorister's fee of 5s, Midsummer 1814. Six years later, during the court case, the fee is signed for by his brother.

that he had given his mother £1 of this sum. If so, the 10 or 11 shillings remaining, even if it had been insufficient to cover the cost of hiring a horse (had he been required to do so), was more than enough to pay for the drinks and meal he had bought on 12 May: the Sun Tavern liquor having cost him four shillings, the Portway drink of rum and milk 6d, and his dinner 18d. Such abuse of these collections no doubt later persuaded the Chapter to abolish the custom of choristers soliciting Christmas boxes.[176]

We do not know why Carpenter acted as he did during these extraordinary weeks. Getting drunk was not unusual for a schoolboy in this period, and the availability of beer

176. HCA, 7031/8, p.213, 13 Nov. 1823. Despite this order, the custom continued as is evident from a Chapter Act of 23 March 1829 (*ibid*, p.269) – following a complaint made against choristers 'going round from house to house soliciting Christmas boxes' – which threatened a chorister with expulsion from the choir if he persisted with the practice. The quarterly chorister (and Langfordian) payments, 1813-23, are recorded in HCA, 7100/4, Robert Carpenter's final 5s allowance for midsummer 1820 being signed for by his brother.

and cider in College may have meant that choristers were sometimes the worse for wear.[177] Nor, as has already been recounted, was chorister misbehaviour unusual.[178] Nevertheless – and making the unproven and unprovable assumption that Carpenter was the arsonist – for a pupil to have set buildings on fire is without precedent in the school's recorded history. For every disaffected chorister like Robert Carpenter, however, there were the vast majority who were rewarded for their loyal service with a grant from Tomson's charity (usually of £10 by this period) towards the cost of their apprenticeships. And occasionally, if they were clever enough, they gained special exhibitions to see them through Oxford, like the £10 given to John Griffiths annually for four years towards his support at Christ Church 'in consequence of … [his] meritorious conduct while chorister of our cathedral'.[179] By way of contrast, Carpenter, who seems at times to have acted as if he hoped that the fires that he had in all probability started would be discovered, had outrageously betrayed the trust bestowed upon him. But it is comforting to learn that he was later to make amends and repay his debts both to society and to the cathedral. To society, by taking on his father's mantle and becoming a local schoolmaster; and to the cathedral, by his contributions as a supernumerary bass at All Saints (at 2s per service) from 1844 to 1850 during the cathedral repairs, and then through his son, Thomas Carpenter, who followed his father as both chorister (1841-51) and a bass lay clerk for 13 years from 1855.[180]

By the time Thomas Carpenter had left Hereford in October 1868 for Cork, where he died in the workhouse, the freedom that he and his father had enjoyed at school was beginning to be curtailed. For some, like the studious John Hill, the College's other schoolboy resident in May 1820, the educational value of that leisure time was properly used for

177. See, for example, the following vicars' Acts: HCA, 7007/1/4 p.212, 9 Oct. 1772, forbidding the two College choristers from drawing beer; and HCA, 7003/1/5, p.202, 29 Nov. 1823, order for the purchase of two hogsheads of cider 'in consequence of the present low price … [and] the late preference given in the Common Room to this beverage …'

178. Although if William Pritchard, a chorister whose voice was on the wane and who was jealous of one of his fellows, did indeed hide a monkey under his surplice during a service with the intention of releasing it during his rival's solo, it was an unusual form of high jinks, even though the monkey allegedly escaped (to the congregation's consternation) before Pritchard could put his plan into action. For this story, which may have occurred in the latter part of this period, see Carless, p.40. I have been unable to verify it but Percy Hull, cathedral organist 1918-49, heard the tale from the horse's mouth many years later when Pritchard was running the tailoring business in High Town founded by his uncle (marginal annotation from Hull's copy of Carless) and believed it to be true.

179. See HCA, 7104/4 *passim*, for the regular Tomson grants to former choristers from *c.*1790 to 1837. Griffiths' award from the vicars choral (HCA, 7003/1/5, p.259, 15 May 1832) was supplemented by periodic grants (amounting to £35) from Tomson's charity over the period 1832 to 1835. Griffiths was later to become senior chaplain at Madras Cathedral, 1866-73. Foster (1887-8), ii., p.569.

180. Robert Carpenter is listed as a schoolmaster, aged 48, living in St Owen's parish, in the 1851 census, together with his son Thomas (aged 17), who is described as a 'writer'. Ten years later, Thomas was named in the census as a 'professor of music' in St Martin's parish. Their respective cathedral appointments are recorded in the Act books: HCA, 7031/19, pp.560, 585, 14 Feb. 1843, 15 Jan. 1844; HCA, 7031/20, p.344, 25 June 1855. Thomas was given notice as a lay vicar on 14 Nov. 1867 and left Hereford for Cork on 12 Oct. 1868 (HCA, 7031/21, pp.298-99; 30. B. 32). Robert was listed in 1851 (Lascelles, p.19) as master of St Peter's National School for Boys; and his father in 1806 (Rees, p.63), as master of a school in Packer's Lane. Thomas Carpenter later established a commercial school in Castle Street and then Widemarsh Street. See *HJ*, 7 July 1852, 5 Jan. 1853, for his advertisements aimed at 'the agriculturalist and the tradesman'.

Fig. 4.8 Thomas Carpenter (seated, front right), with his five fellow lay vicars, in the 1860s.

self-cultivation and improvement; but for many, like Robert Carpenter, the devil made work for idle hands. As an Old Rugbeian observed later in the century:

> Much … old mischief arose from [boys] having nothing else to do … They prefer to run, leap, climb, catch, kill and carry off something. And if these adventurous desires have given place to universal cricket, House matches and the domination of the umpire, we must not too much murmur at that which has brought about the change.[181]

That change did not happen overnight. As early as 1835, a writer in the *Quarterly Journal of Education* had advocated that masters should more closely govern their boys' out-of-school hours,[182] but it was to take more than a generation for this public school revolution to occur. As we will see in the following chapters, it was not fully realised at Hereford until the 1870s and '80s – principally through compulsory drill and organised team games.

181. As quoted in Bamford (1960), p.188.

182. Mack (1938), p.218.

Chapter 5

An Age of Restoration and Improvement, 1851-1875

At one of the school's earliest speech days, held in College Hall on 17 June 1863, a few days before the grand re-opening of the cathedral itself, the *Hereford Times* reported that Prebendary Frederick Custance, the rector of Colwall, had been applauded for these words in his vote of thanks: 'This was called "the age of restoration" ... and he hoped it was the age for restoring cathedral schools to that position which they once held in public opinion'.[1]

The mid-Victorian period was indeed a time of restoration and improvement for the school, as we shall see, but also for its cathedral and the city. Hereford Cathedral, following on from Cottingham's repair work in the 1840s, was restored by George Gilbert Scott in the late 1850s and early 1860s.[2] When the cathedral re-opened in June 1863, Scott's works attracted considerable public interest, which raised over £1,500 for the cathedral in admission donations in less than five years.[3]

The school, too, witnessed a revival in its fortunes under the guidance of three gifted young Headmasters – the Reverends Thomas Power (1851-57), John Woollam (1857-69) and Eric Rudd (1869-75). During their stewardship, pupil and staff numbers increased, and the curriculum was remodelled. The school site, too, was developed by way of the lease of a corner wing of the adjacent College of Vicars Choral and the extension of the playground at the back of that side of the College. As a consequence, cathedral schoolboys became known to the wider public – in this period and in the years beyond – as 'collegians', and their school

1. *HT*, 20 June 1863, p.3. For Custance, see HCA, 7983/8, Choristers' Magazine (Jan. 1923), p.10.

2. See Aylmer and Tiller, pp.269-79, for L.J. Cottingham's saving of the cathedral; his son's, N.J. Cottingham's, incomplete and inferior work; and Scott's restoration of the transepts, choir aisles and Lady Chapel, his external alterations and the designs of the Skidmore screen and Dawes' monument. Also HCA, 7031/20, pp.298-99, 306-07, for the ordering of Scott's initial survey and his report, 7 Nov. 1854; pp.405-08, for his estimates, Nov. 1857; and pp.419, 421, 426-27, for the tenders and additional external works, 6 Feb. to 29 May 1858.

3. Visitors were encouraged to donate at least sixpence. The salaries of the verger and two sextons, together with an additional fee (ten *per cent* of the proceeds shared equally between the three officers) and cleaning costs, need to be deducted from this sum, which was then paid into the fabric fund. HCA, 7032/6, p.392.

as the College School as well as the Cathedral Grammar School. The extension over the College wall was by no means a permanent solution to the problems posed by the restricted site between Quay Street and the Lady Chapel, but it gave the school a breathing space in which to consolidate its gains before a more permanent solution could be found. Richard Dawes, the energetic and radical Whig Dean of Hereford (1850-67), was the common factor behind both the cathedral and school revivals. (Plates 8 and 9). Nominated by the Liberal Prime Minister, Lord John Russell, Dawes had come to Hereford with a reputation for meticulous financial management and educational reform, first as bursar of the newly founded Downing College, Cambridge, and then as Rector of King's Somborne, where he had established a model elementary school and come to the notice of the committee of council on education. When Dean, he was even invited by the Prince Consort to submit a scheme of education for the proposed Wellington College, although he was not consulted – as he should have been – by the Newcastle Commission on elementary education.[4] And following his arrival in Hereford, a colleague had referred to him as a gentleman 'of active and business habits ... sincere in his efforts for improvements'. 'Being from the north', he added, 'there was no doubt that he would carry them out with effect and judgement'.[5]

But like Bishop Percival at the end of the century, it was not easy for a reform-minded Liberal to lead a conservative church. This is exemplified in the Chapter Acts of the period which are full of protests entered in the Dean's name after he had found himself outvoted by his Chapter in matters as diverse as presentations, the supplementing of clerical stipends, accounting procedures, lease renewals and the occupancy of residentiary houses. On such issues, the Dean was invariably in a minority of one.[6]

However, there is no doubting the force of Dean Dawes' personality in bringing about change in his cathedral, as for example in his personal initiatives to recruit lay clerks (despite the organist's strong opposition) to remedy 'the inefficient manner in which the choral service is performed', and to appoint Francis Tebbs Havergal as deputy librarian with a brief to reform the library.[7] The Dean also restored and enlarged the Deanery, unoccupied in 1850, which became 'the scene during his entire decanal residence of frank, refined and generous hospitality', and built a new wing of 12 residences at St Katherine's Hospital, Ledbury.[8] All this was quite apart from Dawes' support for – and, not least, his astute financial management of – his architect's plans to complete the cathedral's restoration, symbolised posthumously by Scott's 1867 design of Dawes' marble monument in the north-east transept in recognition of the Dean's 'kindly and friendly assistance'; and (as we will see) his drive to improve the school. Dean Dawes, with his Chapter colleagues, was also responsible

4. Newsome (1959), pp.28-29. Dawes had proposed an essentially practical time-table for the new college which was very different from the one eventually established under Wellington's first Master, Edward White Benson. For the Newcastle Commission, see below, p.178.

5. *HJ*, 7 May 1851, Canon William Peete Musgrave's reported speech before the mayor and council.

6. HCA, 7031/20, pp.204-05, 14 Nov. 1850; pp.244-45, 24 March 1852; p.262, 11 Nov. 1852; pp.304, 308, 9 Nov. 1854; p.348, 8 Nov. 1855; pp.424-25, 24 March 1858; pp.477-78, 10 Nov. 1859.

7. Aylmer and Tiller, pp.422-23, 525-27. Letters entered in the Act book to Dean Dawes from G. Townshend Smith (the organist) and Havergal clearly indicate that it was the Dean who was the prime mover behind both reforms. HCA, 7031/20, pp.209ff, read 11 Nov. 1850; pp.301-03, letter 6 Nov. 1854.

8. *HT*, obituary notice, 16 March 1867.

in his first months in office for laying out the Close, which improvements the city fathers considered were 'as great a credit to the city as they are satisfactory to the inhabitants', and further busied himself with educational matters – notably at the Blue Coat School – and campaigned for other improvements within and beyond the precincts.[9]

For this was also an age of improvement and a period of some prosperity for the city itself, to which the church contributed its part. Following the damning report of T.W. Rammel (the health inspector) on the unsanitary state of the city, the great Hereford Improvement Act was belatedly passed in June 1854, which gave the council powers to provide directly for the public health of Herefordians. This resulted in the construction in 1856 of the cattle market in Newmarket Street, taking cattle trading off the streets; the provision of the city's first sewers and drainage works (which did not altogether prevent the horrid stench emanating from the Wye in the summer months, by reason of the city's sewage being emptied into the river at Eign); and the building of the Broomy Hill water-works, powered by the pump-house beam engine dismantled from the 1851 Great Exhibition. Nearby, following the closure of the All Saints burial ground and the formation of the council's cemetery committee in 1856, Bishop Hampden offered eight acres of land between Breinton Road and White Horse Lane as a united parish burial ground. This offer was accepted, albeit reluctantly given the Bishop's insistence on preserving parish burial rights, and the new cemetery was consecrated on 28 May 1863. In addition to these municipal schemes, a grand porticoed corn exchange had been opened on Broad Street in January 1858, at a cost of £3,500, and within the first year of the new decade, the mayor had opened the vast glass-roofed butter and poultry market.[10] One observer, writing to the *Hereford Times* shortly after that ceremony had been performed, suggested that no town in the kingdom had 'made such gigantic advances in the path of progress as "the ancient city" has done since the year 1854'.[11] It was a fair claim, even though C.H. Edwards' fine 120-foot high clock tower and drinking fountain, a sketch of which had been proudly displayed as the centrepiece of that paper's 1861 New Year almanac, was not to be built.

Such improvements coincided with, and were in part prompted by, the belated coming of the railways to the city. In 1852, in the eyes of the leading historian of British railways, Hereford was one of the three foremost towns in the country not to be connected with the English rail network.[12] A decade later, it had two stations – Barton and Barr's Court (opened in 1854 and 1855, respectively) – and railwaylines operating in four directions: north to Shrewsbury, west to Newport, south and east to Ross and Gloucester, and east to

9. HCA, 7031/20, pp.238-39, for the vote of thanks passed by the commissioners of paving and lighting, 3 Dec. 1851; *ibid*, pp.204-05, for Dawes' proposal for a model parish school at Madley, 14 Nov. 1850; Aylmer and Tiller, p.165, for other reforms; *HT*, 10 Jan. 1852 p.5, re his chairing Thomas Carpenter's lecture on 'The Modern System of Education Illustrated', at the Blue Coat School; *HT*, 9 Dec.1854 p.10, for the exhibition of prize drawings promoted through the Dean's 'kind exertions'; *HT*, 16 March 1867, obituary notice.

10. For these improvements: Roberts, pp.13, 16, 106ff; Currie, pp.389-401; Allfield, pp.347-70. The expense of enclosing three acres for the parishes of All Saints, St Nicholas and St John's and building a common chapel was estimated at £600 in 1860. HCA, 7031/20, p.510, Goss' letter, 25 Aug. 1860.

11. *HT*, 23 Feb. 1861, p.12, letter from 'a citizen'.

12. Jack Simmons, *The Railways of Britain* (1961), p.18; quoted by Best, p.70. The other towns were Yeovil and Weymouth.

Worcester. A fifth line, to Hay and Brecon, opened in 1863 and operated from the city's third station at Moorfields.[13] Well might the *Hereford Times* have recorded the coming of the second of these lines (from Newport) on 6 December 1853, which united 'our fair and fertile county with the great world of manufacturing industry for which she has been for so long and … so injuriously divided', in unrestrained prose:

> The iron bands, [the correspondent continued] symbolical we believe of the lasting nature of the benefits which the union of Herefordshire with the railway world will confer, have at last been riveted amid a demonstration of public joy unsurpassed in the annals of the railways.[14]

Nearly 18 months later, the opening of the Hereford, Ross and Gloucester railway was hailed by the same journal in a similar manner. The same issue further sported a drawing of the new grand brick palace that was Barr's Court station, which had been designed in the fashionable style by Mr T.M. Penson of Chester.[15]

The coming of the railways to Hereford was instrumental in the extraordinary increase of the city's population during the 1850s and 1860s, from 12,128 in the 1851 census to 18,345 in 1871. The rise was especially marked – an increase of around 26 *per cent* – during the growth of the rail network in the 1850s.[16] The expansion of the railways also had a direct bearing on the school's expansion in the mid-Victorian period – particularly on the increase in day boy numbers – as John Woollam admitted in his evidence to the Endowed Schools' Commission in 1865. That same commission described Hereford as 'an important county town' of 15,587 people, which was 'prosperous and increasing'.[17]

Educational Reform

The transformation of Hereford, the rebuilding of the cathedral and the revival of its school in the 1850s and 1860s, coincided with the greatest period of sustained educational enquiry and legislation in English history. Although the immediate impact of these reforms on the Cathedral School was limited, cumulatively they were to have a profound effect on the working of the school in the later years of the nineteenth century.

The first enquiry of the period – the Royal Commission appointed on 10 November 1852, 'to inquire into the state and conditions of the cathedrals and collegiate churches

13. Roberts, pp.49-50; Currie, p.397; Wood (2003), p.47.

14. *HT*, 10 Dec. 1853, p.6.

15. *Ibid.*, 2 June 1855, p.12: the line thereby uniting Hereford 'by three links of iron to the vast railway system which has done so much and promises so much for the advancement of civilisation', and giving the city 'ready communication' with the metropolis, 'the greatest mart in the world … [and] the spur to intellectual, social and commercial activity'.

16. Grundy, pp.488-97. One indicator of this growth is provided by the Chapter's letter to the Ecclesiastical Commissioners of 18 January 1860, recommending an augmentation to the stipend of the vicar of All Saints, 'considering the extent of its [the parish's] present and increasing population, now between four and five thousand, and the smallness of its endowment'. HCA, 7031/20, p.487. In 1861, All Saints parish numbered 4,525 out of a total population of 14,443 in the six Hereford city parishes, some 1,500 more populous than St Peter's, the next biggest parish. HCA, 7032/6, p.70.

17. HCA, 1537, form B answer 3; *PP 1867-68, XXVIII (part 7),* p.4, Bompas' report.

in England and Wales' – was only tangentially to do with schools, as opposed to religious education, and did not result in parliamentary legislation. Nevertheless, it did require each Headmaster within these foundations to submit a detailed return to the commission about the state of his school. In the third and final report (presented on 25 May 1855) general observations were made on their condition, together with recommendations for improvement. It was found that:

> Although laudable efforts have been made, in some instances, to re-invigorate them, yet for the most part they are not in a flourishing condition, and do not occupy the place in the capitular institutions which their founders designed of them.

In particular, the headmasterships were insufficiently well endowed:

> to secure the services of competent instructors, or are at least not adequate to compensate them, and that these masters are compelled to make considerable sacrifices from their own stipends for the remuneration of assistant masters and to depend mainly for their subsistence on the fees they receive from town boys and boarders – a very precarious source of income; and that consequently the capitular schools are for the most part in an unprosperous state ...

As we will see, this exactly described the position at Hereford.

To alleviate the distress of these institutions, it was recommended that the endowments to the masters should be improved so that not less than £150 *per annum* could be assigned to the Headmaster, 'with a commodious house, rent free, for the reception of boarders', and £100 *per annum* and a house for the Second Master. Special provision should also be made for the foundationers, who 'should be entitled to a liberal education free of expense'. At least one exhibition should be awarded to the universities each year. Special attention was to be given to the well-being of the choristers, who should be placed 'under the spiritual care of one of the canons'; and who should receive 'a sound, religious, liberal and useful education, in addition to their musical training', as well as an apprenticeship fee on their leaving the choir. On admission, preference should be given to choristers 'as are likely to be afterwards fit to pursue their studies in the grammar school'. Finally, overall superintendence of each school should be committed to the Dean or a residentiary canon, who should examine the boys on admission and the scholars every six months, as well as make periodic reports on the state of the school to both the Chapter and the Bishop.[18] Although at Hereford it took many years before all these provisions were met, they provided a timely reminder to the Chapter – if not the learned Dean Dawes who needed no such prompting – about the importance of their scholastic foundation, as well as a yardstick by which the school could be judged.

Ironically, the reform of the statutes of the colleges of Oxford and Cambridge in the 1850s had a more immediate impact on the Cathedral School. The royal commissions of

18. *PP (1854-55) XV*, pp.56, 70-71. Not all cathedral schools were condemned by the commissioners – those at Durham and Worcester, for example, were singled out for praise, as was 'the comparative success which, under very difficult circumstances, this Cathedral School [at Carlisle] has attained'. *Ibid.*, pp.75, 76, 78.

enquiry into the ancient universities preceded that of the Cathedral Commission by more than two years, as did the 1852 reports which detailed extensive abuses within the universities. Of the many recommendations, those dealing with the abolition of 'closed' entrance scholarships in favour of open competition would have the most bearing on those endowed grammar schools that had the right to nominate pupils for awards at specific colleges. This time the commission reports did result in legislation in the form of the Oxford University Act of 1854 and the Cambridge Act of 1856. In both cases, however, the effect of the enactments were less radical than the reformers would have wished, partly as a result of the removal from the original Bill of the clauses relating to the universities' colleges. Increased statutory powers were therefore given to the executive commissioners, who were to ensure that the colleges recast their own statutes by a given date. And crucially, as far as schools like Hereford were concerned, the vested interests of particular schools were to be respected if the governors or the Charity Commissioners (established by the Charitable Trusts Act of 1853) so desired. The consequences for Hereford, in terms of the new schemes for the Somerset awards at Brasenose and St John's, Cambridge, were wholly favourable, despite the late nineteenth-century decline in the proportion of grammar school boys entering the universities as a whole.[19]

The university Acts opened the way for government intervention and change in the English schools system itself. The key enquiry for the grammar schools was that established by letters patent dated 28 December 1864, and became known as the Taunton Commission after its chairman Henry Labouchere, first Baron Taunton. It was the third great schools' commission in six years, and was authorised to enquire into education in schools not within the scope of either the Newcastle Commission, 1859-61 (the elementary schools) or the Clarendon Commission, 1861-64, which investigated the nine 'great' or 'public' schools.[20] This new commission was therefore to examine the state of education for 'those large classes of English society which are comprised between the humblest and the very highest', and was to consider 'what measures (if any) are required for the improvement of such education, having especial regard to all endowments applicable ... thereto'.

This huge task of enquiry into 'all schools which educated children excluded from the parliamentary grant' involved a massive investigation into nearly 800 schools 'endowed by a permanent charitable endowment' (the nine 'great' schools and the colleges of Cheltenham, Marlborough and Wellington – which had all given evidence to the Clarendon Commission – being excepted); as well as 2,200 private and proprietary schools. It was the greatest investigation of middle-class schooling ever undertaken. The bulk of the work was done by 12 assistant commissioners, one of whom was the barrister, H.M. Bompas, who was responsible for schools in the western region, including four Welsh counties, Monmouthshire and the Marches. There was a further report by another barrister, C.J. Elton, 'on the claims of cathedral schools to a larger share of the cathedral endowments'.

19. For a summary of the move to re-organise the universities, the work of the commissions and the subsequent legislation, see Simon (1960), pp.281-99, and 299 note for the decline in grammar school boys; and below, p.192, for the new Somerset schemes.

20. Charterhouse, Eton, Harrow, Rugby, Shrewsbury, Westminster and Winchester, together with two predominately day schools – St Paul's and the Merchant Taylors'.

The specific findings concerning Hereford Cathedral School will be dealt with later in this chapter. Here it is simply necessary to add that in general terms – although as we will see, HCS was the county's only endowed school to be exempted from severe criticism – the English endowed schools were in very poor order. The commission held that their failings were due to 'untrained teachers and bad methods of teaching, uninspected work by workmen without adequate motive, unrevised or ill-revised statutes, and the complete absence of all organisation of schools in relation to one another'. To remedy these defects, three grades of schools were recommended, schools of the first grade like Hereford serving the upper middle and professional classes, keeping their pupils until 18 and educating them for the universities. The fees of each grade of school, it was suggested, should be regulated (with the first grade boarding school charging fees between £60 and £120 *per annum*) enabling each type of school to keep to its intended grade, audience and curriculum. Further proposals concerned the transfer of endowments to finance scholarships, the setting up of effective governing bodies, the establishment of examinations, the inspection of endowed schools and the formation of controlling regional and national authorities.

The Taunton Commission's report, together with the evidence, was published in full in 20 volumes in 1868. A year later the Endowed Schools Act became law. Instead of creating a central educational authority, it provided for the appointment of three commissioners (with seven assistants) to reform the endowed schools, although on a more limited basis than that envisaged by the Taunton report or indeed the 1869 Bill. It was in this year that a grouping of headmasters came together as a direct result of the threats to the independence of schools (outside the nine Clarendon schools) that were contained in the original Endowed Schools Bill.[21] The Headmaster of HCS was not one of the 13 present at the first formal meeting on 21 December 1869, called by Edward Thring of Uppingham 'to discuss the existing state of things in schools ... [and] set on foot a society to meet annually in order that schoolmasters may communicate with each other and give and receive good feeling and general experience from year to year'. As Harper of Sherborne put it: 'now they were each doing their duty separately like scattered stars; if the light could be brought into one focus, the effect would be very different'.[22]

The election of Disraeli's Conservative government in 1874 ended more than two decades of Liberal-inspired educational reform and removed the threat of immediate government interference. In that year, the Endowed Schools' Commissioners were abolished as a separate department, their work being continued on similar lines by the Charity Commissioners until the end of the century. It was during this period that HCS was eventually to benefit from the work of civil servants within this department, and in particular from the support of that considerable historian of medieval foundations, A.F. Leach, who for much of his career worked as an assistant charity commissioner. But first we need to turn to the school's development during the mid-Victorian heyday of Liberal reform.

---

21. HCA, 1540, contains a draft copy of the 1869 Bill, which includes provisions in part II for the establishment of an educational council for the examination of teachers and schools. After fierce opposition, these provisions were subsequently dropped. For the hostile reaction of E.W. Benson, Master of Wellington College, to the Bill: Newsome (1959), pp.135-43.

22. *HMC Report 1869,* pp.3, 6.

New Buildings and the Move to the College

As 'a practical educator', Dean Dawes was the prime mover in the school's improvement in the early 1850s. The first step was to deal with an unsanitary School House. On 24 March 1851, within days of Layng's resignation, the Dean had proposed to his Chapter:

> That the Canon's Bakehouse and adjoining wooden building be taken down with a view to improving the school house and offices belonging to it which are now in a state requiring the attention of a sanitary commission.

It was agreed that these buildings, which included the old schoolroom – the size of a small barn – behind the Headmaster's house, should be removed 'under the superintendence of the Dean', and that an estimate should be made of how much Dr Layng owed for the School House 'dilapidations'.[23] These were later costed at £35 15s 3d.[24] However, the old Castle Street house belonging to the Master of the Canon's Bakehouse survived; and the bread dole which had been distributed to the county's poor for hundreds of years was not formally discontinued until January 1856, when the Master's house itself was repaired and let at an annual rent of 19 guineas to John Woollam, then Second Master.[25] By then, the boys had long enjoyed a proper playground which had been provided for them by the demolition of the old buildings.[26] During the period as a whole, many boys who played here left a permanent memorial by carving their names or initials on the wall of the College of Vicars Choral.[27] The Headmaster's house was also considerably refurbished, for on 9 May 1851, Dean Dawes had displayed in Chapter Thomas Nicholson's scheme 'for the improvement of the house of the Headmaster ... and for the appropriation of a portion of the College for a new schoolroom'. Having inspected the premises, the Chapter approved the plans and specifications, and before the end of that term contracts valued at more than £285 had been made with various artificers 'for the alterations and improvement of the Cathedral School'. It was stipulated that the work was to be completed before 20 July that year.[28]

---

23. HCA, 7031/20, pp.220-22, Layng's resignation, 20 March, and Dawes' proposal, 24 March 1851. The 'practical educator' quotation is Dawes' own self-assessment from his 1849 pamphlet, p.54. The old schoolroom measured 34 x 26 yards. HCA, 5067, ground plan.

24. HCA, 7031/20, p.223, 26 April 1851, estimate by Jeynes and Williams.

25. *Ibid.*, pp.353, 357-58, 359, Acts, 24 Nov. 1855, 5, 14 Jan. 1856; pp.366, 374, 25 June, 13 Nov. 1856 re further repairs. The dole itself was commuted into a payment (of money or bread) made direct to the parish clergy for the relief of poverty. Also see Aylmer and Tiller, pp.34, 54, 589, 644-45, for the history of the Canon's Bakehouse.

26. *HT* notices of 28 July and 20 Dec. 1851 indicate that the old schoolroom had been pulled down and a new playground built by the end of that year. Also see, HCA, 7105/6, clavigers' 1852 account, payment to J. Crabbe for building a wall in the Cathedral Close 'round the school garden'; and the Dean and Chapter's statement in one of the 1865 College visitation articles (HCA, 7003/1/6, p.244, no. 15, 7 Dec.1865) that as a result of the 1851 agreement with the vicars choral, they 'were induced to pull down a large schoolroom, erected by us only a few years before at a very considerable cost, and also pull down the large buildings known as the Canon's Bakehouse in order to afford a better playground for the boys'.

27. A few names and over 50 initials can still be deciphered on the garden wall of the present organist's house. The five legible dates were all carved in the 1870s and '80s.

28. HCA, 7031/20, pp.224-25, 9 May, 9 June 1851. The final cost for all the alterations, including the architect's

As Dean Dawes had indicated in early May, a key part of his plan was for the school to extend into a vacant part of the College Cloisters, which were considerably under-used at the time as a result of the reduction in the number of vicars choral by the 1840 Cathedrals Act.[29] Indeed, it was Dawes' firm belief that the property was so ill-managed that it should be vested in the Dean and Chapter,[30] a move that was successfully resisted for a further 80 years. For a priest who set so much store by the education of the young, it was natural that Dawes should look to the adjoining College to enlarge the site of a cramped school, even though the Dean's writ did not run within the walls of the neighbouring corporation of vicars. On 17 April 1851, with the knowledge but without the formal consent of his Chapter, the Dean enquired whether the Custos and vicars would release the north-east corner of the College, including 'the room formerly used as a chapel ... with the gardens between the buildings and Quay Lane [*sic*] ... for school purposes'. He suggested a rental of £5 *per annum* for the rooms, which would be adapted 'to school wants', the old wall between the College and the Canon's Bakehouse being pulled down. Dawes assured the Custos and his fellow vicars that access to the building would be on the school side of Quay Lane, and optimistically concluded his letter by denying that the school would be much of a nuisance to the vicars:

> In fact it need in no way disturb the privacy of the College. The only person disturbed by it will be the Custos ... but I am sure that for so useful a purpose...he will very readily make the sacrifice in order to give the School a chance of rising again from its present humiliating position.

Within two days the new Dean's proposal had been accepted on condition that the premises were kept in repair, the College privacy was respected and 'boundary stones [were] placed between the respective properties with the usual initials'. Thus the arrangements that had been made for the use of these rooms in times past were re-established.[31]

The boys' accommodation now consisted of dormitories in the Headmaster's house, together with a long room overlooking the Close, where the boarders had their meals and kept their books, and the new rooms in the north-eastern corner of the College. They were later described by an old boy who had attended the school in the 1860s but they can have changed little in the intervening years:

> Crossing a narrow alley, a part of the playground, you passed through a fairly spacious lobby, where we kept our play-boxes, hung up our nets etc., and which was also used for practising the noble art of self-defence with the gloves ... At one end of the lobby

fee, came to £316 10s 2d. HCA, 7105/6, 1851 clavigers' account.

29. In February 1850, the following rooms in the College Cloisters were being used: nos 9, 17, 2 & 3, 13, 16 and 12 by the vicars choral, who had been reduced to six by virtue of 3 & 4 Vic., cap 113. HCA, 7003/1/6, p.109, 23 Feb. 1850. For the 1840 Act: Barrett, p.24.

30. Aylmer and Tiller, p.457.

31. HCA, 7003/1/6, pp.118-19, Dawes to Custos and vicars, 17 April, and their reply of 19 April 1851. For the school's use of College rooms in the mid-eighteenth century and Woolley's 1842 request for use of the chapel, see above, pp.83, 159-60.

Fig. 5.1 The north-east corner of the College of Vicars Choral, which accommodated the school, 1851-75.

rose the stairs leading to the upper schoolroom. At the bottom of these stairs was the Fifth-form room, where was a piano and where the French classes were taken. At the very top of these stairs, on the left hand, was the apartment sacred … to their worships, the Sixth Form … Outside the Sixth-form room, to the right of the stairs, was a door leading to the dormitory … known as the 'College room'. It was considered a privilege and high promotion to be lodged there. The upper schoolroom itself faced the stair top. It was a very large room – six windows, three looking into the College quadrangle … and the other three in the school yard or playground. There were long rows of desks and forms tier upon tier. A stove [was] in the centre where, out of school, we were wont to roast potatoes, chestnuts etc. On one side of the big room were two desks for the second and third masters' use, and at the far end the Head's table … at right angles to … [which] was the Sixth Form desk. Thence you passed through a smaller lobby, where the day boys kept their books, and went down a sort of Jacob's ladder … into the lower schoolroom … once the private chapel of the vicars … This room done with, you passed into a large lobby, stone paved with gravestones … There were two huge open fireplaces and I think this must once have been the College kitchen … At the far end was the only miserable apology for a 'lavatory' which we had: just a tin basin and a towel of doubtful purity. But it came in very handy after … fights.[32]

32. *TH*, NS LXI (July 1909), pp.31-32. The author was W.E. Vernon Yonge, for whom see below, pp.215, 217ff.

Thomas Barratt Power, 1851-1857

Dean Dawes secured the College's agreement to the school's use of part of their cloisters just in time to entice the Reverend Thomas Barratt Power, who had responded to the advertisement placed in the *Cambridge Chronicle*, to accept his offer of the headmastership.[33] A fellow and assistant tutor of Emmanuel College, Cambridge, Power was quite a catch for a school on its uppers. The proposed £30 annual salary (which included the Usher's £10) was a paltry sum, and even though it was supplemented by profits from the boys' fees, it is little wonder that his acceptance of the position was contingent on the school accommodation being improved. Nevertheless, when his instrument of appointment was finally sealed in Chapter on 25 June 1851, a good start to the building programme had at least been made, as is apparent from this rather defensive notice posted by the new Headmaster in the following Saturday's *Hereford Times*:

> This school [HCS] will be re-opened on the first of August, with considerable improvements. The old schoolroom has been pulled down, and a portion of the College of Vicars Choral appointed for school purposes. This affords an opportunity for a large and extensive playground, which was very much needed. There will be a lower department of the school, in which a good practical education will be given.[34]

By the end of 1851, Power could boast in the local press that the school had been 're-opened under entirely different circumstances, and with carefully improved accommodation, including a new playground and schoolroom'. Prominent reference was made to the 23 Somerset awards, 'with rooms, a cap and gown and books exclusively for boys educated at Hereford School', together with the announcement that the Headmaster would soon 'be assisted by a first-class classical master'.[35] The Revd J.H. Glover MA, a fellow of Clare Hall, Cambridge, was appointed assistant master early in the following year, but was soon replaced by John Woollam, formerly of St John's, Oxford, ('1st class in Classics, 1850') who was to play a significant part in the school's history. Further assistant masters were added to the staff in 1853: The Revd John Goss (St Mary's Hall, Oxford), Mr Halsted ('late master of King's Somborne School') as English teacher, an assistant no doubt personally secured by the Dean; and the exotic figure of Monsieur Severin de Dziewicki, a Polish gentleman, as a part-time assistant in French. Richard Bustin was soon to be engaged, on a similar basis, as drawing-master, initially for the choristers, as was Burville the new choristers' master, who taught them (among other things, no doubt, 'how to handle the goose quill') separately

---

33. HCA, 7003/1/6, p.119, postscript to Dawes' letter to the Custos, 17 April 1857; HCA, 7105/6, clavigers' 1852 account, payment no. 42 re the 6s for the Cambridge advertisement.

34. *HT*, 28 June 1851, p.4, repeating the *HJ* announcement of 18 June.

35. *HT*, 20 Dec. 1851, p.5; *HJ*, 24 Dec. 1851. The Somerset awards exclusive to HCS at this time were as follows: 12 at Brasenose worth £36 8s *per annum* each, six at St John's at £39 and a further five at £13 *per annum*. In addition, the school had a share 'every third turn' in six additional Brasenose awards worth £52. Other contingent scholarships and the two Brasenose fellowships 'appropriated to natives of the county of Hereford' were also listed. By January 1854, the respective St John's awards had increased to £40 and 'more than £20'. *PP 1854, XXV*, p.745, Power's evidence to the Cathedral Commission, 31 Jan. 1854.

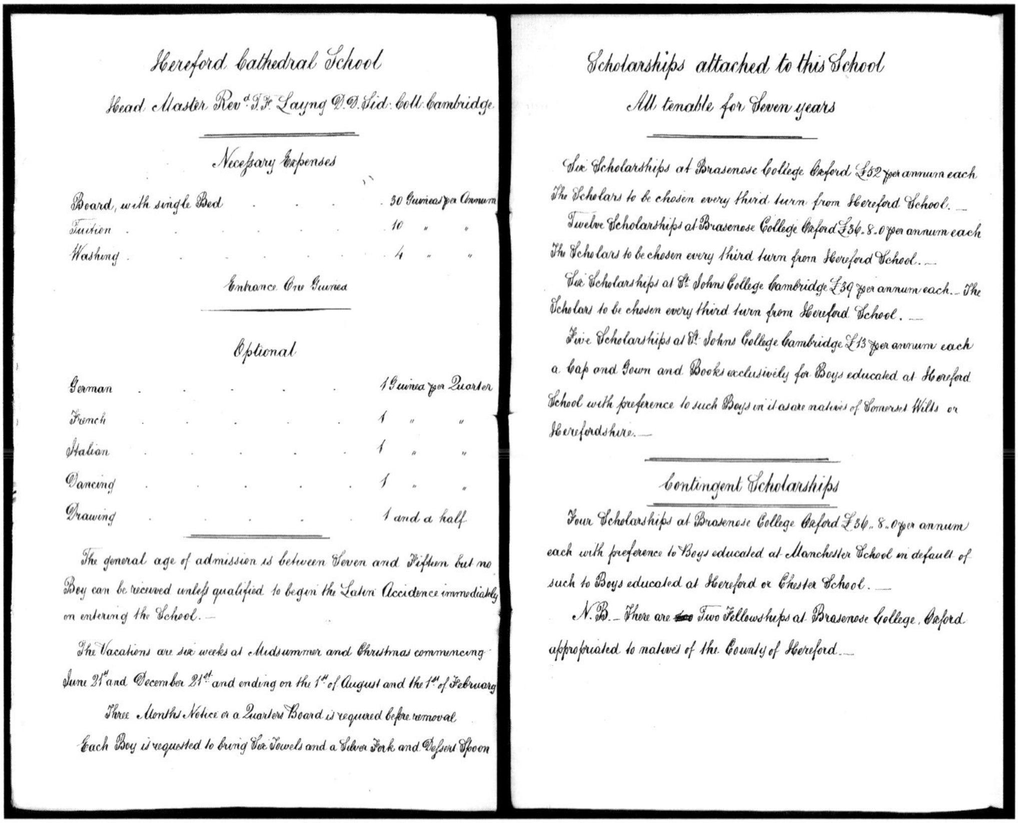
Hereford Cathedral School

Head Master Revd T. F. Layng D.D. Sid: Coll: Cambridge

Necessary Expenses

Board, with single Bed	50 Guineas per Annum
Tuition	10 " "
Washing	4 " "

Entrance One Guinea

Optional

German	1 Guinea per Quarter
French	1 " "
Italian	1 " "
Dancing	1 " "
Drawing	1 and a half

The general age of admission is between Seven and Fifteen but no Boy can be received unless qualified to begin the Latin Accidence immediately on entering the School.—

The Vacations are six weeks at Midsummer and Christmas commencing June 21st and December 21st and ending on the 1st of August and the 1st of February

Three Months Notice or a Quarters Board is required before removal

Each Boy is requested to bring Six Towels and a Silver Fork and Dessert Spoon

Scholarships attached to this School

All tenable for Seven years

Six Scholarships at Brasenose College Oxford £52 per annum each The Scholars to be chosen every third turn from Hereford School.—

Twelve Scholarships at Brasenose College Oxford £36.8.0 per annum each The Scholars to be chosen every third turn from Hereford School.—

Six Scholarships at St Johns College Cambridge £39 per annum each.— The Scholars to be chosen every third turn from Hereford School.—

Five Scholarships at St Johns College Cambridge £13 per annum each a Cap and Gown and Books exclusively for Boys educated at Hereford School with preference to such Boys as are natives of Somerset Wilts or Herefordshire.—

Contingent Scholarships

Four Scholarships at Brasenose College Oxford £36.8.0 per annum each with preference to Boys educated at Manchester School in default of such to Boys educated at Hereford or Chester School.—

N.B.— There are Two Fellowships at Brasenose College, Oxford appropriated to natives of the County of Hereford.—

Fig. 5.2 A school prospectus, 1856.

in the old College chapel.[36] Through the drive of its new Headmaster, and also partly as a result of the closing of 'Hayters', the private school in Castle Street (now Number 28), and the coming of the railways, the school roll was expanding, despite the increase in fees – the 8 guineas annual lower school charge being soon abandoned in favour of a 10 guinea flat rate fee for all day boys. By early 1856, if not before, the boarding fee was set at 50 guineas, with a 5 guinea discount for clergy sons.[37]

Within three years of Power assuming the headship, the school had expanded from a close-knit to an extended family, numbers having increased to 60 pupils (aged 10 to 18), ten of whom were choristers. 'On my appointment', Power explained to the cathedral commissioners in his evidence of 31 January 1854:

36. These appointments may be traced in successive notices: *HT*, 5 June 1852, p.4; 1 Jan. p.4; 29 Jan. p.5; 25 June 1853, p.5. For Dziewicki: Pitman, pp.77-81; for Bustin, see the references of payments (in 1853) to 'the government drawing school in Hereford' and to him personally (for example, in 1857) in the clavigers' accounts, HCA, 7105/6; and for Burville: *TH*, no. 3 (Jan. 1879), p.116. In November 1857, HCS won six medals (the only city school to do so) and four prizes in the annual drawing examination under the government scheme. *HJ*, 25 Nov. 1857 p.5.

37. *HT*, notices for 5, 12, 19 Jan. 1856.

> I found that in consequence of the low state of the school, it had been the custom for many years only to appoint a Headmaster and leave the other arrangements with him. This plan the Dean and Chapter have hitherto adopted in my case, and I have appointed assistant masters as the school required, receiving a stipend of £30 from the Dean and Chapter.[38]

The permanent staff of two clerical assistants, an English master and a master for the choristers, cost Power £420. This would have left him a tidy profit, given the fees demanded from the 50 or so non-chorister parents.[39] Power further admitted to the commissioners that his main problems concerned the education of the choristers, who:

> enter the school very young, and scarcely able to read or write (being generally from the charity schools of the city). I have therefore appointed a master for the choristers alone, and if before leaving they are sufficiently advanced, I take them into the classical school. They are generally apprenticed to some trade between the ages of 12 and 15, and seldom obtain much more than a fair knowledge of their own language, especially as they have a comparatively small portion of time allotted to school.

It was a problem that Power was never to solve, despite Burville's appointment and the Headmaster's suggestion in 1856 that the Dean and Chapter should find 'some new arrangement for the education of the choristers', Power offering to give up his £30 salary 'in furtherance of such an arrangement'.[40]

Nothing more was done at this time, but one important advance was made by the Dean and Chapter before the end of Power's tenure, following the Charity Commissioners' investigation of the Hereford city charities in the mid-1850s, and that was their reform of the Philpotts charity. From 1857, Philpotts' accumulated funds, which yielded an annual income of £185, were applied towards the award of three open exhibitions of £50 *per annum* at Brasenose College, one of which was to be awarded each year after a competitive examination.[41] In November 1857, the cathedral also increased its annual payment for the four Langfordian scholars' tuition, which was increased from 8 guineas to £20.[42]

Nevertheless, despite these initiatives, the apparent neglect of the foundation boys was an issue that came to the notice of the wider public through the correspondence columns of the *Hereford Journal*, an episode that was to blight Power's last days in office by calling into

38. *PP 1854 XXV*, pp.744-45, Power to the Secretary of the Cathedral Commission, 31 Jan. 1854.

39. Assuming 20 boarders – and allowing for half of them paying the clerical reduction – and 30 day boys, this would mean (at the 1856 fee levels above) a total fee income of *c.*£1,300, leaving more than £890 to Power after he had paid the salaries of his four assistants. From this sum, there would have been additional outlay for ancillary staff, boarders' food and internal repair bills to School House. Economies of scale probably made the school more profitable under Power than under his two immediate successors.

40. HCA, 7031/20, p.365, 25 June 1856.

41. *Ibid.*, pp.379-80, 390, Dean and Chapter to the Charity Commissioners, 22 Dec. 1856; and their reply of 13 June 1857. Although preference was still given to a Langfordian scholar, this was a significant reform in that prior to this time (and in accordance with Roger Philpotts' will), the exhibitions were *exclusive* to Langfordians. The Philpotts fund had accumulated because so few Langfordians were qualified to benefit from the charity.

42. HCA, 7031/20, p.412.

question not only the quality of chorister tuition but also the value of a classical education. This was quite apart from the personal attack on Power himself, who was branded as both inefficient and corrupt by perverting the cathedral's statutory requirements 'for purposes of private gain'. Another anonymous correspondent, possibly the cathedral's new young Precentor, Sir Frederick Ouseley, refuted the worst of these allegations but the school's reputation was in danger of being badly damaged by this unholy public row. When, in a letter of mid-November 1857, an 'old boy' questioned the school's management, demanded a public investigation and made more than a passing comparison to the notorious case of Robert Whiston, the Headmaster of Rochester Grammar School, who some years previously had sued his clerical governors, the Dean and Chapter must have felt that the matter was getting out of hand.[43]

Power stoutly defended himself from the blow 'Paterfamilias' had delivered him in the *Journal.* 'I cannot conclude', the Headmaster wrote to the Dean and Chapter, 'without referring to a most unjustifiable attack on myself and the state of the school which appeared in the *Hereford Journal* of last week'. He continued:

> I can assure you that I have always had expressions of great confidence towards me from the parents of the boys under my care, and that I utterly repudiate the charge made against the school. I certainly have had one or two bad cases arising either from early neglect ... or from extreme incapacity but this must be so in every school, and it is next to impossible in two or three years to do away with the effect of early neglect.

It was the cry of Headmasters throughout the ages; and whilst admitting that the choristers were 'in an unsatisfactory state', he denied that any leaving chorister was 'as grossly ignorant as represented in the libel of the *Journal*'. Nevertheless, Power was still smarting, and he feared for the school's future:

> I cannot help feeling much hurt at this attack, especially as I have taken such pains to provide efficient masters and the school is at this time in such a promising state. And tho' I do not fear its effect in the city, where the school is known, yet I cannot but think it may prove injurious in the county where there are not the same opportunities of obtaining a knowledge of the truth.

Power ended his statement defiantly. 'I am resolved to see myself righted in the matter', were the last words of his first and only formal report to his governors.[44]

Whether Power carried out his threat is unknown. Perhaps, after his initial anger had subsided, he felt that he had less need to seek formal redress, for at the same Chapter

43. *HJ*, 4 Nov. p.5 ('Paterfamilias'), 11 Nov. p.5 ('Lector'), 18 Nov. p.5 ('An Old Boy'), 2 Dec. p.4 ('Lector', 'Investigator', 'Observer'), 9 Dec. 1857, p.5 ('An Old Boy'). There is a remarkable similarity between the chorister references in 'Lector's' letter of 30 Nov. (published on 2 Dec.) and those of Ouseley in his letter to the Dean and Chapter earlier that year. HCA, 7003/1/6, pp.148-52, 21 July 1857. For the Rochester scandal: Arnold, *passim;* and Barrett, p.273.

44. HCA, 7031/20, pp.403-04, 12-14 Nov. 1857. Power's first sentence to the Dean and Chapter ('As I have been requested to send in a report of the School ...') indicates that he had not made such a report to his governors before then.

meeting he had been unanimously elected – and his presentation sealed – to the rich living of Upton Bishop.[45] Within hours, and without advertisement, John Woollam, the Under-Master, had been appointed Power's successor, as from Christmas 1857.[46] In the circumstances, it was a shrewd appointment.

Power's turbulent end as Headmaster, after over six years at the helm, should not cloud our judgement on his tenure. Although the sources for the 1850s school are fragmentary, they all indicate that Power – in partnership with Dean Dawes – started HCS on the road to recovery from its lamentable state in 1850. And not the least of his achievements was the loyalty he inspired among his pupils and the *esprit de corps* he built up within the school.[47] It is just to leave the final word to the Headmaster who departed in such trying circumstances but whose name lives on in the shape of the Power Memorial Prize for Mathematics:

> During the past quarter, the school has consisted of 21 boarders and 20 day boys, besides the Dean's [Langfordian] scholars and choristers. During the time I have held the headmastership, fourteen pupils have proceeded to the university, eleven of whom have obtained scholarships or exhibitions and all a fair average. Five others have obtained government appointments after examination. I am happy to say that a good tone prevails generally throughout the school and I very seldom have a serious case brought under my notice. With regard to the proficiency of the boys, the Dean who took some part in the June examination will be able partially to bear testimony.[48]

John Woollam, 1857-1869

In one sense, given the outcry over the foundation boys in the *Journal's* correspondence columns, Woollam could not have started his tenure as Headmaster at a less propitious time. In another sense, Woollam had nothing to lose. Unlike Power in 1851, he was inheriting a basically sound school, and as a respected Classics teacher, who had an intimate knowledge of the school's workings over five years, he knew the school's strengths and how they might be built on and its weaknesses in relation to chorister tuition. He also had the unwavering support of the Dean and Chapter, who could not afford public outrage over the education of the choristers to fester into a scandal of Rochester proportions. The favourable greeting of his appointment by the old boy who was openly critical in the *Journal* of the Dean and Chapter's governance was a good sign that public opinion was beginning to swing in the school's direction.[49]

45. A list of *c.*1850 indicates that Upton Bishop had an annual value of £708, the second richest Dean and Chapter benefice, after Lydney with St Briavels and Hewelsfield. However, by March 1874, its net income had reduced to £482 17s 9d. HCA, 7032/6, pp.334, 636.

46. HCA, 7031/20, pp.403, 414, 12-14 Nov. 1857.

47. *HT*, 25 July 1874 p.8, Rudd's comment on speech day, following Power's death.

48. *Ibid.*, p.403, Power's report, 12-14 Nov. 1857. Power's widow outlived him by over 33 years. By her will of 6 June 1898, she bequeathed £350 to be invested by the Dean and Chapter for 'The Power Memorial Prize', to be awarded to a boy who had shown 'considerable proficiency in Mathematics', preference being given to boys entering Cambridge. HCA, 7031/23, pp.418-19; HCA, 7106/5, fos. 357v-358r, account 1908-14, showing an annual dividend in excess of £9.

49. *HJ*, 18 Nov. 1857 p.5. The old boy commented 'so far so good' on Power's replacement by Woollam but recommended that the OH annual dinners should be revived to 'popularise his appointment'.

Fig. 5.3 John Woollam: as Second Master in the early 1850s (left), as drawn by J.T.O. Fowler OH 'after a party at the Bank for Savings', then situated on the corner of St John and East Streets; and (right) in a more formal pose as Headmaster.

Woollam worked fast to repair the damage over the Christmas holiday of 1857, and by 29 December he had submitted a long letter to the Dean and Chapter 'suggesting a modification of the present system of education so far as regards the education of the choristers and on sundry other matters relating to the school'.[50] The letter was not transcribed into the Act book and is now lost to history. However, it is evident from Woollam's first report of November 1858 that the choristers' curriculum had been revised and that the Headmaster had taken personal responsibility for their tuition. Thereby, as Ouseley had advocated, 'those intellectual advantages which the Cathedral Grammar School formerly afforded to them' were restored.[51] Thanks to Woollam's quick response, the storm over the foundation

50. HCA, 7031/20, p.417.

51. *Ibid.*, p.451 for the choristers' new curriculum, which comprised Bible reading, catechism and collects; English grammar and spelling; History and Geography; Latin grammar and Delectus; French exercises; and Arithmetic ('from simple rules to vulgar fractions') and 'a little Euclid for two senior boys'. *Ibid.*, p.514, Woollam to the Chapter Clerk, 5 Nov. 1860, re the chorister tuition fees. *Ibid.*, p.151, for Ouseley's comment in his letter to the Dean and Chapter of 21 July 1857. These reforms did not prevent senior choristers leaving the choir 'long before the loss of voice' in order to obtain the valuable apprentice fees from Tomson's charity. See *Ibid.*, p.479, for Townshend Smith's complaint on this score to the Dean and Chapter, 10 Nov. 1859.

boys subsided as quickly as it had arisen. It is little wonder that the Chapter Clerk was directed to convey the Dean and Chapter's 'great satisfaction' with his first report.

The increase in pupil numbers – from 62 in November 1857 to 78 by the following year and thereafter an average of over 90 until numbers declined in Woollam's final year[52] – also indicates a growing confidence in the school. This increase had partly been effected by the building of an extra dormitory for boarders within the roof of School House, 'in consequence of the numerous applications to enter scholars at midsummer [1859]'. This was erected over that summer at Woollam's own expense, the Chapter lending him £200 for the conversion to be repaid over two years. Woollam was well pleased with the result, which gave him 'a spacious, well ventilated dormitory, containing ample sleeping room for seventeen boys, and supplied with gas, water and other conveniences'. Here the boys slept in curtained-off double cubicles, with sufficient space down the middle of the room for pillow fights and a leap-frog game they called 'high cock-a-lorum'.[53] Despite such shenanigans, the provision of some decent accommodation, together with the appointment in 1858 of two able lieutenants, both of whom were to remain with Woollam for most of his headship, meant that the Cathedral School was set fair to prosper in the 1860s – academically not least.

Woollam himself was a fine scholar and teacher, whose 'knowledge was equal to his humility'. As his former Headmaster had boasted to the *Hereford Times*, in 1850 he had attained a first-class degree in Classics from Oxford, where he was also a prizeman. Former pupils – at least the brightest of them – remembered him with considerable warmth and gratitude. One, W.E. Vernon Yonge, held him in the highest regard and 50 years later dedicated reminiscences about his time at school to his memory. Another, F.E. Weatherly, referred in his autobiography to Woollam as 'a man of high culture and literary tastes', who had he gained his deserts 'should have been made a fellow of his college (St John's, Oxford) and eventually President, instead of being merely Archididaskelos [*sic*] ... of a small Cathedral School'.[54]

Woollam's considerable abilities as a teacher were supplemented by those of his two able ordained assistants – the mathematical master, Robert Dixon, and the assistant classical master, J. Capel Hanbury, Woollam's first appointments in 1858. Within a year or two, a third assistant master (T. Taylor who was later replaced by A.G. Jones) had been added to the staff. All were degree men. Mr Weymss was not, but as a former mayor and editor of the *Hereford Journal* he had useful political connections, and he was able to teach elementary Classics, as well as act as Woollam's secretary and start up a school journal. It was a small but stable team, the senior partners of which stayed together for ten years. As Woollam explained in his final report to the Dean and Chapter in November 1868: 'The labours of

52. There were 69 names on the school register in June 1869 at the time of Rudd's appointment. Other figures are taken from Woollam's November audit reports to the Dean and Chapter. See below, note 68.

53. HCA, 7031/20, p.485, Woollam's report, 7 Nov. 1859; *TH*, LXI (July 1909), p.32. By the time of the 1861 census, School House contained 44 boarders, aged 9 to 18, over half of them being 12 and under, besides Woollam himself and five ancillary staff (a housekeeper, cook, servant, and two housemaids).

54. For Woollam's natural modesty, see Lord Saye and Sele's tribute, *HT*, 23 July 1870, p.3. Both Yonge and Weatherly won Somerset scholarships to Oxford. See below, p.215ff; and Weatherly, pp.34-35. Weatherly found it difficult to cope with his Brasenose tutors after Woollam's patient teaching at Hereford. *Ibid.*, p.75.

these gentlemen in connection with the school were most assiduous and valuable and on our own account we greatly regret their departure'. Dixon had left 'to an important sphere of labour' as Headmaster of Nottingham High School and Hanbury to a time of residence abroad.[55] It was to be only a matter of months before Woollam himself was to depart after nearly 17 years' distinguished service to the school.

The opening up and competitive award of the Philpotts scholarship also helped Woollam to improve the school's academic standing. As a consequence in 1857, for only the third time in 20 years, pupils were awarded the Philpotts scholarship of £50 *per annum* to attend Brasenose. Thereafter, a Cathedral School leaver was regularly given one of the Philpotts awards to fulfil the requirement that there should be three such scholarships held by Old Herefordians at any one time at the founder's designated college.[56]

As important as the beneficial use of Roger Philpotts' bequest was the requirement that the award should be made annually at midsummer 'at a competitive examination open to the whole of the Cathedral School'. For the first time in the school's history, the examinations were to be conducted by external examiners. In 1859, the three candidates for the Philpottine scholarship were examined by the rector of Dinedor, the Reverend Rowland Muckleston, 'a gentleman of great experience in these matters and who was well known at Oxford'.[57] He was paid £10 for the privilege of being the school's first external examiner, a fee that was to be increased to ten guineas to his successors from 1862 and then to 15 guineas from 1870. In the mid-1860s, there were two examiners, both at the time fellows of St John's, Cambridge, who were later to become eminent in their respective fields: the geologist, Thomas George Bonney (1823-1923) – or 'the Revd Mr Bunney' as reported in the *Hereford Times* – 'who used to ... go bathing with us', as one boy later remembered; and the great classicist, Sir John Edwin Sandys (1844-1922). Each examined three times – Bonney from 1864 to 1866, and Sandys in 1867, 1868 and 1872.[58] Such was the stature of some of these early examiners.

To pass the examinations, as Dean Dawes explained to the company assembled in College Hall at the 1859 speech day, 'the boy must have good acquirement'. In that year, the candidates were examined in Latin roots, Theology (in three papers on the Old and New Testaments and the 39 Articles), original composition, translations from English into Greek and English into Latin prose and verse. Mathematics was later added as a discrete subject. Within a few years, the examiner was not simply testing those boys who had elected to try

---

55. Dixon, a scholar of St John's, Cambridge, was Woollam's first appointment in early 1858. He replaced Woollam as tenant of the old Canon's Bakehouse (at £1 rent) 'for the more efficient superintendence of the scholars'. John Capel Hanbury, who had just been ordained, replaced Goss as assistant master in the summer of 1858. For their appointments, see *HT*, notices, 23 Jan. p.5, 5 June p.9, 3 July 1858, p.5; and their departures, HCA, 7031/21, p.347, 7 Nov. 1868. Their places were 'by no means inadequately supplied' by C.E. Hargreen, a wrangler, and the Revd J. St Maur Russell. For E. Weymss' obituary, see *TH*, no. 3 (Jan. 1879), pp.160-61.

56. HCA, 7104/5 and 6, Philpotts charity accounts, 1838 onwards, for the awards and subsequent evidence about the examinations, examiners and prizes. Philpotts scholarships were not awarded in 1861, 1865-66, 1869 and 1871. For their reform, see above, note 41.

57. Dean Dawes' phrase as reported in the *HT,* 18 June 1859, p.8. Muckleston had been a fellow of Worcester College: Brock and Curthoys, p.151.

58. Two examiners were appointed each year from 1873 at a combined fee of £15. The comment about Bonney was made by W.E. Vernon Yonge: *HT*, 14 Oct. 1909.

for a Philpotts scholarship but the whole school. This was an elaborate formal examination, with question papers being printed by the Cambridge University Press, which received more than £40 for the commission over the years 1863 to 1870. In these circumstances, the remarks made by Dean Dawes and Examiner Bonney respectively on the speech days of 1863 and 1865 are perfectly understandable:[59]

> It must not be imagined that the examination was a matter of form, for it really was not so. While in many respects the examination was exceedingly interesting, it also tested the boys' capabilities and showed what progress had been made. It was now the custom for candidates for professional and public services to undergo examinations; and it could not be doubted that examinations, while often interesting on account of the talent they developed, were very useful.
>
> [Bonney] then referred to the middle-class examinations, the advantages of which to parents who did not intend sending their sons to the university he dwelt upon, contending that it was a good thing for a boy to submit himself to an examination ... as it enabled him to wrap up and put together what he knew correctly, neatly and concisely. Another of the advantages of their examinations was that as they were principally for the elementary branches of knowledge, they got the student well-grounded in the elements, without a good knowledge of which it would be impossible for him to get passed in the higher branches.

Such speeches were also a reminder that in the 1850s admission to the public service by patronage was being replaced by a service open to talent through the adoption of entry tests, a reform for which Dean Dawes himself was a powerful advocate.[60] For example, competitive examinations for the Indian Civil Service were introduced in 1853; two years later the home civil service followed suit, albeit in a more limited way. In 1857 and 1858, the regulations for admission to Woolwich and Sandhurst were also altered to enable entrance by examination, the age of entry having been raised to between 16 and 19. At a school level, boards for the 'locals' examinations – which individual pupils might elect to take – had been founded by Oxford in 1857 and Cambridge in 1858.

One further advantage that accrued to the Cathedral School as a result of the reform of the Philpotts charity was the award of speech day prizes – handsomely bound books, adorned with the school crest[61] – from its proceeds. In the seven years from 1864 to 1870, over £90 was paid to booksellers William Phillips, Joseph Head and W.H. Bartlett & Co. for these prize volumes. The prizes awarded on speech day mounted during the 1860s, which reflects Woollam's academic reordering of the school. In 1859, ten prizes were awarded – six classical prizes for the six classes, and three other subject prizes for Mathematics, Arithmetic and French, as well as the choristers' prize. By 1863, the form classical prizes had increased to seven through the addition of a 'modern division' in Class 3, and by the splitting of the junior forms into Class 6 A and B; and although there were still only two prizes for the four mathematical divisions, there were three for the six French classes. Further prizes were

59. As reported: *HT*, 20 June 1863, 24 June 1865.

60. Dawes (1854). Also see Roach (1971), pp.29-30, 63.

61. The phrase is from Yonge's concluding article: *HT*, 14 October 1909.

awarded for Divinity ('presented by R. Johnson, Esq., Town Clerk'), English and Latin verse, English essays, Chemistry and Music. The following year, as a result of the addition of extra classes both at the top and bottom of the school, two further classical prizes were awarded; and by 1865 Woollam had added a prize for German.[62] This increase of classes and prizes indicates an increasingly successful school under Woollam's tenure, an impression sustained by the evidence of the growing numbers of his pupils being awarded places at the ancient universities.

Woollam was again fortunate with his inheritance in that the reform of the statutes of the school's colleges coincided with the re-ordering of the Philpotts charity. The revision of the Brasenose statutes governing the Somerset awards was completed on 9 January 1858, and those at St John's, Cambridge, on 1 August 1860 and 16 April 1861.[63] The reforming ordinances abolished the birthplace qualifications; required that only candidates who had been educated at HCS, Manchester Grammar School or Marlborough Grammar for at least two years should qualify for an award; and tightened up the regulations for the examining of candidates, the awards being thrown open to general competition if there were no suitably qualified candidates from any of the three Somerset schools. Nevertheless, the reforms worked to the advantage of Woollam's best scholars in terms of the value of the Cambridge awards. At Brasenose, neither the value nor the number of Somerset scholarships was specified in the new statute, and it appears from Woollam's 1864 return to the Endowed Schools' Commission that they remained as they had been, with two open to the school at £52 *per annum* and four at £36 8s. *per annum* on the Somerset Thornhill Manor and Thornhill estates. At St John's, the number of Somerset exhibitions was to be determined by the proceeds of the estates in any one year, but the Hereford only exhibitions (on the March estate) were each valued at £40 *per annum* and tenable for four years, and the exhibitions for the Somerset schools in turn (on the Wootton Rivers estate) were put at £50 *per annum* for three years. In 1864, Woollam reckoned that eight of the £40 exhibitions and four to the value of £50 were available for Hereford's use at Cambridge, making a total of 18 closed scholarships and exhibitions at the two universities.[64]

These close awards, together with the Philpotts scholarships, were of huge value to a small school like Hereford. Bompas, the Endowed Schools' Assistant Commissioner for the region, calculated their total worth at nearly £920, which made HCS richer in terms of its university provision (although decidedly not in terms of its foundation entry awards) than some of the Clarendon schools.[65] Although the total value of the close awards

62. *HT*, HCS speech day reports, 18 June 1859, 20 June 1863, 11 June 1864, and 24 June 1865.

63. See HCA, 1536, for copies of both the Brasenose ordinance and the draft St John's statutes; and HCA, 7031/20, pp.446-47, 501, 514-16, re revision of the St John's statutes from 9 Nov. 1858, including the letters from Dr Bateson to Woollam, 20 Oct. 1860, and Woollam to the Chapter Clerk, 5 Nov. 1860. Woollam considered that the alterations 'would much conduce to the advantage of the school'.

64. 'Closed' because they were only available to candidates (like Old Herefordians in this case) who fitted specific conditions. For Woollam's 1864 calculation, see HCA, 1537, form A, answer 29. The Brasenose Somerset reforms are complicated. The original college proposal of 1855 for an increase in the value but reduction of the number of scholarships was contested by the trustees of Marlborough Grammar School and was not implemented. HCA, 1536, Halcomb (trustees' clerk) to the Dean and Chapter, 19 Dec. 1855, enclosing the BNC proposal.

65. For their names: see above, p.178, note 20.

at HCS were dwarfed by those at Merchant Taylors' and Westminster, for example, they were more valuable by over £300 and £600 respectively than those at Eton and Harrow.[66] They were, moreover, beginning to be well used by the school in this period. In May 1867, for example, there were six of Woollam's former pupils at Brasenose or St John's, all with closed scholarships or exhibitions.[67] The school did not take up its full allocation of Somerset awards during Woollam's tenure, and his successors were to be even more successful with their best pupils, but it was Woollam who set the pattern for later scholastic achievements.

Woollam's series of annual reports to the Dean and Chapter each November audit provides further evidence of the school's progress under his headship.[68] Although Woollam had complete control over his assistant masters, as *Archididascalus* he was obliged to ensure that the Dean and Chapter approved his curriculum, so his report contained considerable detail of the subjects and books – and particularly the religious and classical texts – studied by each class. Nothing at all was reported on the boys' activities outside the classroom, except a brief introductory acknowledgement that no 'circumstances of an unfavourable character' (including health scares) had occurred during the previous year. And at the end of each report, Woollam often invoked divine providence, as he did in 1862:

> And in conclusion, I would express a hope that they … who are receiving their training at our hands, may with the divine co-operation be enabled (in the words of our cathedral prayer) so to prepare themselves now, as hereafter, to serve God faithfully in Church and State.

Nevertheless, despite the formulaic nature of much of Woollam's writing, his reports do give good evidence of a prospering school, and not least in terms of pupil numbers.

These reports also show the gradual development of new classes and courses. By 1859, pupils had been arranged in six classes with five divisions for Mathematics and separate senior and junior French classes. Two years later, a 'modern' class was introduced in the middle school, 'which while omitting Greek pays especial attention to Latin, French, English and other more directly practical studies'. German was added in the following year. The more practical elements of the curriculum – aside from the heavy diet of scripture, languages and mathematics – included a 'tolerably numerous' weekly singing class, dancing, drill, drawing instruction 'under the government system', which led to an annual examination by the government inspector, Book-keeping and a course of lectures in Natural Philosophy 'under the able direction of Mr With'. In 1863, these involved Chemistry lectures for the first half-year and a course in Astronomy, 'rendered highly interesting by excellent illustration and delineation of telescopic scenes', for the second

---

66. *PP 1867-68 XXVIII,* part I, appendix V. The close awards at Merchant Taylors' were valued at £3,330 and at Westminster at £1,247. Bompas' figure for Hereford was worked out as follows: £249 12s. for the six scholarships at BNC; £520 for the 12 exhibitions at St John's; and £150 for the Philpotts scholarships.

67. *Ibid.,* p.165. Woollam had earlier made a list for the Endowed Schools' Commission of 14 of his former pupils who had attended university in the five years, 1859-64. HCA, 1537.

68. HCA, 7031/20, pp.449-51, 483-85; 7031/21 pp.33-35, 104-06, 157-59, 189-92, 222-24, 267-70, 303-05, 345-48, Woollam's reports, 1858-59, 1861-68. There is no report entered in the Act book for 1860.

half. Such courses seem to have been open to most boys. The choristers' curriculum, however, was inevitably restricted. The resumption of the second daily cathedral service, following its re-opening in 1863, 'made an additional claim on the school time of the choristers' in the second half of that year, although Woollam was careful to reassure his governors that their lessons had been re-adapted, which enabled them 'to keep pace very tolerably with their respective classes'.

Woollam's curriculum was subject to other pressures apart from Dean and Chapter approval. Although Woollam went beyond the subjects appointed by St John's for its closed exhibition examinations, the academic requirements of the school's Cambridge college, in particular, were beginning to have a bearing on what was taught at the top of the school. So in 1862, the upper class read Plato's *Apology,* Virgil's fourth *Georgic,* Horace's *Ars Poetica,* Aeschylus' *Prometheus Vinctus* and the *De Senectute,* on top of the prescribed college texts of Sophocles and Cicero. In Mathematics, St John's required mastery of Euclid, books I-VI and XI, as well as trigonometry, algebra 'and the whole of arithmetic'. In the junior classes, Woollam showed sufficient flexibility outside the fundamentals of grammar, composition, arithmetic and scripture to be guided by 'the taste of the boys themselves, their probable calling in life or the wishes of the parents'.

One other way in which we can measure the success of the school under Woollam is by the examiners' annual reports, some of which have survived as verbatim accounts in the Chapter Act books.[69] Overall, they tell a story of steady improvement in the academic standing of a school, which was recognised throughout the period as being well disciplined. As the Revd R.W. Taylor, a fellow of St John's, who examined in 1862 and 1863, observed in his first year: 'I have been much pleased with the gentlemanly bearing of the boys and the generally healthy tone of the school'. His successors would have agreed. In 1862, Taylor also complimented Woollam for the attention paid to Natural Science (with regard to With's Chemistry lectures), 'a feature in its courses in which your school sets a good example to other similar establishments'. Taylor was more critical, however, in other areas. He damned the mathematical learning with faint praise. Some boys had shown 'a fair amount of proficiency in the more elementary subjects of mathematical study', but the generality had in these subjects 'formed the least satisfactory part of the examination'. By 1863, when printed papers had been extended to the three senior classes, 'with very satisfactory results', the mathematical questions had again been answered poorly, and even the top boys in the first division had shown 'a reprehensible slovenliness of style'. In general, the upper classes, 'owing to unavoidable changes produced by the removal [leaving] of boys' were 'scarcely in such an efficient state as when I last addressed you'. This may also have been the result of an increase in their examinable subjects, which were in that year 'much more difficult'. By contrast throughout the lower classes, 'there were not wanting satisfactory signs of progress', although in at least one class, the *viva voce* examination was conducted in cramped conditions which distracted attention.

---

69. *Ibid.,* pp.93-95, 143, 146-67, 255-56, 287-89, examiners' reports, 1862-63, 1866-67. The reports for 1864-65 were not mentioned in the Act book, and those for 1868-69 were read out at Chapter (pp.331, 372) but not transcribed. The examiners' speech day addresses were also sometimes reported on in the local press. See, for example: *HT*, 18 June 1859, 20 June 1863, 11 June 1864, 24 June 1865, 22 June 1867 and 20 June 1868.

A few years later, the reports of Bonney and Sandys were much more positive. In 1866, there had been overall improvement at the top of the school, the senior boys having 'acquitted themselves with credit' in Latin, Greek, History and Divinity. 'I was much struck', Bonney continued, 'with the general care and accuracy with which their work had been prepared and the evidence which it affords of sound training'. The papers in Mathematics (trigonometry, algebra, Euclid and arithmetic) were also well done, 'and showed that the general teaching was efficient'. If Bonney was positive, the young Sandys, Cambridge's senior classic in 1866 and the school's examiner in 1867, was rhapsodic in terms of the classical side, the single flaw being the boys 'almost unaccountable misapprehension of the main facts of Greek and Roman History'. With this exception, the papers were 'eminently satisfactory both in matter and in manner'. And:

> The penmanship was, in the majority of cases, worthy of the school that had educated John Davies and Richard Gethinge; while the translations were executed with a correctness and spirit that show that the present pupils are not unworthy of the place where Miles Smith of Gloucester was trained to be one of the translators of the Bible.

After a further comment on the compositions ('elegant but diffuse and not quite equal to the translations'), Sandys ended his report on a subtly discordant note, which echoed that of his colleague a few years earlier: 'Hoping that the Cathedral School of Hereford will continue to be as useful and successful as hitherto, and will ere long be honoured with a "local habitation" worthy of its name'.[70]

A further indicator of the school's academic achievement and progress under Woollam relates to the destinations of its leavers. A number of his more able pupils gained admission to Oxford and Cambridge through the closed scholarships to Brasenose and St John's, as we have seen, but the school also served other colleges and universities, such as Balliol, Durham and King's, London, during the 1860s.[71] Overall, the numbers going on to university were not large – three on average, *per annum*, in the period 1859-64 – but neither was the upper part of the school, the top two classes being reduced from 13 to six boys in the year between the Taylor reports (1862-63). It is further evident that some of the best scholars left Hereford in their teens to attend larger public schools – as was the case with John Spencer Phillips, the outstanding scholar of the early-1860s, who went on to Shrewsbury.[72] In the same five-year period from 1859, as Woollam informed the Endowed Schools' Commission, 16 pupils moved on from Hereford to other schools, two more than had gone on to university straight from the Cathedral School.[73] And, in any case, the

70. Sandys, who also examined the school in 1868, again reminded his audience that the classrooms were 'inconceivably inconvenient, as any examiner can see and as all the teachers and boys must constantly know by experience'. *Ibid.*, p.7.

71. HCA, 7031/21, p.35, Woollam's (November 1861) references to Balliol and King's, London medical department; HCA, 1537, form G ('Distinctions') references to scholarships gained by pupils at Durham and King's, London (a 'Warnford scholarship', won by Miles Astman Wood, who later became a Ledbury physician).

72. Phillips, the son of the rector of Ludlow, attended HCS from 1859 to 1863. See below, note 181; and Money, p.64, for Phillips' splendid rejoinder (as captain of the Shrewsbury XI) to E. Oliver, his Westminster counterpart.

73. HCA, 1537, Woollam's pencil list for his answer to question B7 on the Endowed Schools' form, together with

majority of leavers were not bound for university. In the same return, Woollam listed 21 of his former pupils who had gone straight into business in those five years, and 24 more who had graduated to private tutors and foreign and military schools, no doubt to gain the extra tuition and experience necessary for direct entry to the army, navy or civil and foreign services. Nevertheless, although the majority of leavers in the 1860s were unable (for whatever reason) to take advantage of the generous number of Somerset awards that had been endowed for the school, Bonney's concluding observation following his 1866 examination, holds true for the school during the whole of Woollam's headmastership:

> On the whole ... I am very well pleased with the general state of the school, and think that its scholars have every opportunity of obtaining a sound and useful education, and of being prepared either for the universities or for other walks in life.

HCS and the Endowed Schools' Commission

The school received its biggest external validation during Woollam's headship from the Endowed Schools' Commission, in the person of its Assistant Commissioner, H.M. Bompas, the barrister who, fortuitously, also happened to have been a fellow of St John's College, Cambridge. It was an exhaustive enquiry, which involved both the Dean and Chapter and the Headmaster giving detailed answers to nearly 150 questions – on the constitution, endowment and government of the school; its character and buildings; the nature of its instruction and discipline; and the play and recreational opportunities that were provided. The final questions related to general educational issues, such as the subjects and examinations that the Headmaster considered were best suited for his pupils. Woollam was also required to complete a set of seven statistical returns on pupil numbers, parental professions, school fees – including a sample of three boarders' bills (which ranged from £53 2s to £74 10s, *per annum*), the curriculum ('names and precise quantity of authors read or text books used' for three classes in each subject) and a list of 'distinctions' gained by leavers over the previous ten years (1855-64).[74] It was a heavy additional work-load for the Headmaster during the period from late April to early June 1865, when the forms were returned. In addition to this giant paper exercise, Bompas paid a personal visit to Hereford in early December 1865, when College Hall was placed at his disposal so that he could formally examine the Cathedral School pupils, as well as those from five other Hereford schools.[75]

The draft report, approved by the Dean and Chapter in May 1867,[76] must also have met with their especial approbation following publication of the report in full, when they would have been able to read the strictures advanced against the county's other endowed schools,

---

his draft forms and notes for their completion. Also see, HCA, 7032/6, pp.88-90, for a copy of the cathedral's answers to the Commission.

74. Ibid., J. Roby to Woollam, 20 April 1865. The Dean and Chapter signed their form on 16 June. Woollam answered over 130 questions himself, as well as completing the statistical returns.

75. *HT*, p.7, 9 Dec. 1865. The schools were Barr's Court, the Gate House (Mr Boswell's), the Ladies' College and Miss Morris' and Mrs Melles' academies.

76. HCA, 7031/21, p.281, 29 May 1867.

few of whose endowments were being used to best advantage.[77] Lucton Free School, handsomely endowed to the tune of £1,346, was especially criticised, and not least because its long-standing Headmaster, the Revd C.C. Walkey (who refused Bompas permission to examine his pupils) put his boarders on the foundation so that they might qualify for one of the school's four university exhibitions.[78] One of Hereford's other potential rivals, Monmouth Grammar School, was even more heavily censured as a middle school for the sons of labourers and small tradesmen. 'The sons of professional men in the neighbourhood hardly ever attend', Bombas reported, 'an objection being felt by their parents to their associating with the lower class of boys in the school'.[79] As we shall see, this state of affairs was not to outlive Woollam's headmastership.[80]

HCS, however, was recognised by the Endowed Schools' Commission as having become under Woollam's management 'a good classical school', where the boys were found to be well taught and well disciplined. Bompas attributed the school's success to the attraction of the leaving scholarships, as well as the Headmaster's own capabilities.[81] However, he regarded the close awards as a double edged sword, their value to the school being offset, in his judgement, by them affording 'little incentive' for the boys to work, all entered candidates in Woollam's time having gained the scholarship or exhibition. Although this opinion was unfair to Woollam, who had given evidence that careful preparation was still required for the Somerset awards 'as the examination was one of some difficulty', Bompas regarded closed scholarship endowments as contrary to the spirit of the University Commission and recommended that they should be further regulated.[82] Fortunately for the Cathedral School his view did not prevail.

On the other hand, there were no recommendations to reform the nature of instruction at the school. Bompas had been told, presumably on his visit to Hereford, that the school would have been more useful to the choristers, who were mostly 'sons of the upper class of tradesmen', had its curriculum been more directed towards 'commercial education', but he firmly rejected this suggestion. He reported that a proprietary school had been founded in Hereford for the express purpose of affording a good, cheap commercial education. This was the Hereford Proprietary School, Barr's Court – which the boys called 'Lomax's', after its Headmaster – established in 1855.[83] Moreover, as Bompas reminded his readership, the choristers' timetable had already been adjusted so that that their two hour daily loss of school time was rendered 'as small an evil as may be'. He concluded that the choristers occupied 'a fair position in the school', and that periodically they had returned from

---

77. *PP 1867-68, XXVIII part XII,* pp.205-60. The Cathedral School was the only first-grade school out of the four (Bromyard, Hereford, Kington and Lucton) categorised as grammar schools.

78. For local outrage in the county against the Lucton charity, see the letters from 'A Commercial', published in the *HT*, 3 June, 5 August 1865.

79. *PP 1867-68, XXVIII part XII,* p.540.

80. See below, p.201.

81. For this and subsequent evidence, see *PP 1867-68, XVIII part XII,* pp.215-22.

82. *Ibid.*, p.71.

83. For its foundation (to supply 'a sound general education suitable to the wants of the present day and conducted according to the most improved plans of education'), see the notice in *HT*, 30 June 1855, p.5.

university as a vicar choral so 'the opportunity of obtaining a classical education appears … to … [have been] advantageous to them'.

So on the central question, there was no doubt that HCS would remain a first-grade classical school. This would have been to Woollam's considerable relief, for in his evidence had stressed the value of Classics as a general education:

> After the experience of 13 years, I feel convinced that in ordinary cases the regular classical routine, combined with the study of Arithmetic and Mathematics and French (a small portion of time being devoted to Geography and History), embraces the course best fitted for the education of those whose school-life may be made to extend over a period of several years. It is sometimes forgotten that each classical lesson of translation & composition is almost equally valuable as a lesson in English, imparting a knowledge of the definitions & shades of meaning of English words & facilitating their early use and application.[84]

The point had been even more forcibly made – and directly to the assembled parents – by Thomas Bonney, at the speech day in June 1864:

> … the examiner said he could not sit down without congratulating the ladies and gentlemen present on the efficient state of the school, and he thought them most fortunate in having a school at their own doors where their children could be thoroughly well grounded in Classics. Of late … it was said that boys of the present day could do as well without it as their fathers did, but he believed that the best training which could be given to anybody was to be made well acquainted with Latin, Greek and Mathematics. He was quite sure that those who had had experience in teaching would agree with him in saying that there was nothing so good as Mathematics and those two languages to prepare a boy for other pursuits. The great mistake was in thinking that a classical education was only fit for certain callings in life, but the words of a certain reformer should not be forgotten: 'There are many things which benefit the mind when forgotten, just as good soil benefits the field if it is ploughed up'.[85]

It is an image that would have struck home with his audience. Moreover, as a wrangler and classicist, who was to become a professor of geology within seven years, Bonney was a living proof of the efficacy of his own educational creed.

The Endowed Schools' report did not allude directly to Hereford's main constitutional weakness – the limited educational endowment within the cathedral foundation – although, as has been shown, this had been spelled out in general terms clearly enough by the Cathedral Commissioners in the early 1850s.[86] And the evidence submitted by Woollam in answer to the question: 'What difficulties, if any, do you find in the discharge of your duty?' clearly pointed out both the financial constraints the Headmaster operated under and their educational consequences:

84. HCA, 1537, Endowed Schools' form B, answer to question 79.

85. As reported in the *HT*, 11 June 1864, p.7.

86. See above, p.177.

> Although a larger sum is expended annually in stipends & expenses of masters than the school receipts would fully warrant, yet the fact that the endowment for masters is almost minimal ... fetters the Head Master in affording those tutorial advantages to his pupils which he would desire.

Woollam had also advised that the salaries and expenses of his six permanent assistants (three graduates, two of whom were in Holy Orders, and the resident foreign master) amounted to £650, and that the tuition fees of the past six years had averaged out at little over £700 *per annum.* The Headmaster's £50 surplus was supplemented by the £30 foundation fee and the £40 tuition fees for the four Dean's (Langfordian) scholars. Out of this annual income of £120 and the uncertain boarding profits, the Headmaster was expected to defray the costs of interior maintenance, cleaning of the school, and all other expenses, including the pupils' food. As Woollam informed the Commission, in his characteristically understated way: 'The endowment is in fact inadequate & presents strong claims on the interposition of the Ecclesiastical Commissioners'.[87] He was right, for the total average annual cost of the school to the Dean and Chapter at this time amounted to less than £250.[88] A year or two later, in a report to the Ecclesiastical Commissioners, the Dean and Chapter confirmed that the school's finances were in a precarious state:

> It will be observed ... that the efficiency of the school mainly depends upon the number of boarders in the Head Master's house which is necessarily subject to great fluctuation. The stipends to assistant masters and general school expenditure cannot be estimated at less than £750 *per annum* which would nearly absorb the statutable endowment and tuition fees. The tuitional services of [the] Head Master are thus given gratuitously and the means of providing an efficient staff of masters are at any time liable to fail.

The Dean and Chapter recommended that the Ecclesiastical Commissioners should help rectify this situation by providing an annual stipend of at least £250 for the Headmaster and £150 for the Second Master.[89] It was all a far cry from the stipends received by the Headmasters of richer foundations or even the £150 earned by George Townshend Smith, the cathedral organist.[90]

If Bompas had skated over the school's peculiar financial problems, his findings did not disguise its lack of decent buildings. The Headmaster's house was held to be inadequate; it provided room for up to 45 boarders 'but only by occupying so much of the ... house to leave insufficient accommodation for any master who was not, like the present one, a

87. HCA, 1537, Endowed Schools' form A, answer 63; B, answer 81.

88. I.e. the £30 stipend, £50 in external repairs, £5 rent of College, £60 for six choristers' fees (plus the £10 cost of their school books), £40 fees for the four Langfordians, plus £23 2s 8d in additional money and for their clothes, and £26 10s for the examination and prizes. *Ibid.*, pp.72-73; *PP1867-68 XXVIII,* p.217. I have not considered the cost of the apprentice fee, usually ranging from £10-£20, paid to the family after a chorister had left the choir (and school).

89. HCA, 7005/10, p.73, Dean and Chapter's 23 Jan. 1868 return.

90. The organist's duties then involved playing at the two daily services (three on saints' days) and rehearsing the choristers four days weekly, plus the weekly practice for the whole choir. *Ibid.* p.74.

single man'. The College classrooms were both small and insufficient so that two classes had to be taught in the Headmaster's dining-room. The largest College room (the upper schoolroom) was only just sufficient for assembly.[91] More importantly, the rooms were held on an uncertain tenure, and if the vicars were to resume possession 'the school could not be carried on'. Bompas outlined three possible schemes for improvement: the school securing, on a permanent basis, a larger portion of the College; the removal of the school 'to an entirely new spot a little outside the town'; and building on land adjoining the play-ground, on which the St John's vicarage then stood, 'and purchasing any other buildings or land that might be necessary'. Of these, Bompas favoured the third solution as the vicars would not accede to the further extension of the school into the College, which would not in any case have provided the most suitable accommodation, and the move to a new site would necessitate the choristers being taught separately. If, however, a good schoolroom, dining-room, dormitory, 'and if possible a separate infirmary', could be built, and the College classrooms retained, then 'the school would ... be provided with the necessary accommodation'.

Coda

The school's hold on the College rooms, however, was even more precarious than perhaps Bompas had realised on his visit to Hereford in December 1865, for in the autumn of that year the Custos and vicars had given the Dean and Chapter six months' notice to quit its occupation of the College premises.[92] By early November, however, the vicars had moderated their stance somewhat, provided that the Dean and Chapter were prepared to lease the schoolrooms 'for some certain and definite period' and a formal agreement was entered into 'setting out the terms of such occupation'.[93] These demands so angered the Dean and Chapter that it imposed, on 7 December 1865, the first visitation order on the College for nearly 150 years. In the end, the visitation was not actually carried out, but it was a threat which hung over the heads of the vicars choral for more than two years.[94]

An account of the acrimonious dispute which followed between cathedral and College over the next four or five years does not belong in a school history. As far as the school is concerned, however, it is evident from the Act books of the respective corporations that there were tensions within the Chapter itself over the school's use of the College's accommodation. Dean Dawes supported Woollam and pressed hard for the premises to be maintained as classrooms but occupied on a permanent basis; and his Precentor (Sir Frederick Ouseley), who chaired the committee established to try to resolve the dispute, favoured their use for boarder choristers as part of the establishment of a choral

91. Where (as Yonge later remembered), Woollam 'read prayers, called out impos, announced half-holidays – oh joy – and occasionally gave solemn orations, which we called "jaws" '. *TH*, NS LXI (July 1909), p.32.

92. HCA, 7003/1/6, p.238, 22 Sept. 1865. A copy of the notice is contained in the minute of Woollam's 1865 audit report, 7031/21, p.223.

93. HCA, 7003/1/6, p.239, 5 Nov. 1865.

94. See *ibid.* pp.242-46, 279-80, for the 46 visitation articles, and the effective ending of the visitation on 23 March 1868.

foundation within the College on the lines of St Michael's, Tenbury, which he had founded in 1856.[95] Neither side prevailed. Although a new scheme of governance was established for the College in 1870-71, it only exacerbated the problems posed by the school's occupation of the College. Woollam left the school nearly two years before this scheme received the Bishop's seal, with the issue of the school's use of the College rooms still unresolved.

By the autumn of 1868, Woollam had been connected with the Cathedral School, as Headmaster or Second Master, for 16 years, a period which coincided with the great state enquiries into the running of cathedrals and endowed grammar schools. Over this time, particularly during Woollam's headship – and with the wise counsel of Dean Dawes and able support of the Headmaster's assistants – the school had begun to flourish, sustaining a pupil population of near 100 pupils for much of the 1860s. A number of these pupils, too, had gained distinctions both at the ancient universities – none more so than George Yeld, who in 1866 won the Newdigate Prize for English verse at Oxford – and in competition for entry to the army, navy or civil service. One or two had even done well in the new Cambridge 'middle class' examinations.

Despite these successes, Woollam must have felt, after ten years as Headmaster, that he had done all he could for the school. His trusted senior lieutenants had recently left. The boarding numbers, on which HCS depended for its efficiency and the Headmaster for his profit, were beginning to dip in the face of competition from the new 'public' schools like Clifton and Malvern Colleges. Reformed grammar schools such as Monmouth, which had been placed by the Charity Commissioners under a new scheme of governance as early as June 1868,[96] were also emerging in localities which had (in Woollam's words) 'for a considerable time furnished us with a certain proportion of pupils'. Moreover, no way had yet been found to improve the inadequacies (and insecure tenure) of the school buildings, despite Bompas' report, the promptings of successive examiners and his own yearly reminders to the governors. And although by 1867 the means existed through the Ecclesiastical Commissioners to augment the educational foundations of cathedrals and collegiate churches, the time was not yet right for Hereford to exploit this particular source of revenue for the school's advantage.[97]

In these circumstances, it was not surprising that Woollam put himself forward for the first convenient vacancy of a Dean and Chapter living, the traditional way of escape for Headmasters who had served their cathedral well.[98] On 16 October 1868, he applied formally for preferment at Yarkhill, a living among the poorest in the Chapter's gift. Nevertheless, it was still worth between £200 and £250 *per annum* with a vicarage attached

95. *Ibid.*, p.249, 4 March 1866; pp.263-64, for Ouseley's (and the committee's) proposals. Three prebendaries made up the rest of the committee: Thomas Power (the former Headmaster), John Jebb and Henry Phillott.

96. The Haberdashers' Company, which administered the school, thereby forestalling any attempt at government reform. See, Allsobrook, pp.196-97.

97. HCS was not to take advantage of the relevant enactment (29 & 30 Vic., cap 111, section 18) for another generation. See below, p.292ff.

98. See Woollam's own answer to the Endowed Schools' Commission question about superannuation, HCA, 1537, form A, no. 64.

that was little more than ten years old.[99] He did so in words which showed his justified pride in the school's advancement during his period in office:

> The state and efficiency of the school, as attested by the annual reports of your examiners, the public opinion both of the city and county, and even of more distant localities, have been of an eminently satisfactory character. The number of pupils, both boarders and day scholars, availing themselves of the advantages of the school, has been large. Many have been directly prepared for the various duties of professional and practical life. Others have, each year, proceeded to the universities, in the enjoyment of the exhibitions and scholarships attached to the school, and of these a not inconsiderable number have subsequently entered Holy Orders and are pursuing the duties of their sacred calling with exemplary assiduity.

Having made his final report, Woollam's presentation to the vicarage of Yarkhill, together with the perpetual curacy of Moreton Jeffries, was signed and sealed in his presence at Chapter on 12 November 1868.[100] Woollam continued his duties at the school until the following midsummer. His last official duties should have taken place at the prize-giving ceremony in College Hall on 16 June 1869 but his father's burial on that day prevented his attendance. This necessitated the postponement of the presentation of a handsome electro-plated flower or fruit stand, manufactured by Woodward & Co. of Birmingham, together with the following address, penned in fine ornamental writing by Mr Henry Edwards of East Street, from his adoring pupils: 'The kindness we have always experienced at your hands, the anxiety you have constantly displayed in our welfare, and the care which you have invariably exercised in our instruction will ever be a source of gratitude to us, as well as no small influence on the future career of each one'. Woollam had to wait until the speech day of 1870 for his well-merited public acclamation.[101]

Eric John Sutherland Rudd, 1869-1875

As with Power's appointment in 1851, following Woollam's resignation, the headmastership was advertised – and this time more widely, notices being placed in the *Times, Standard, Guardian* (a Church of England newspaper), *Midland Counties Herald* and *Cambridge Journal,* as well as the *Hereford Times* and *Journal,* at a cost to the cathedral of £4 16s. It was money well spent and resulted in a country-wide response from 180 gentlemen who applied for particulars of the impending vacancy. Less than one third of them, however, made formal applications, the majority having no doubt been put off by the advertised stipend of £70 *per annum.* This lowly salary, less than one tenth of the sum offered a few years earlier to the first Headmaster of Malvern College, was clearly insufficiently compensated by the rent-free

99. HCA, 7031/21, p.344, Woollam to the Dean and Chapter, 16 Oct. 1868; HCA, 7031-20, p.337, 24 March 1855, re approval of the new vicarage. See HCA, 7032/6, p.636, for the value of each of the 26 chapter benefices in *c.*1850. Even with Moreton Jeffries, there were only six poorer livings (Weston Beggard, Long Stanton, St John Baptist, Norton Canon, Putley and Brockhampton).

100. HCA, 7031/21, p.343. His presentation to Moreton Jeffries was cancelled two months later 'in consequence of his not being able to hold the same with Yarkhill Vicarage' under the Pluralities Act. *Ibid.,* p.355, Act 14 Jan. 1869; HCA, 7005/10, p.201.

101. *HT,* 19 June 1869, p.7; 23 July 1870, p.3, for Lord Saye and Sele's tribute and Woollam's reply.

accommodation ('subject to the payment of parochial rates and taxes' and the cost of 'interior repairs'), the (unstated) possibility of profit from the fees (10 guineas for tuition and 50 guineas for boarding, less 5 guineas for clergy sons and brothers) and the more distant prospect of retirement to a Chapter living 'after having held the office for a certain number of years'. Nevertheless many of the 58 who submitted testimonials – the vast majority of whom were ordained – came from respectable schools, even if the prospective candidates from Dulwich, Haileybury, Magdalen College School and King Edward's, Birmingham, among other well-known schools, had not been tempted to apply. The interest shown in the position was in itself a tribute to the reputation HCS had gained under Woollam.[102]

At the Lady Day Chapter of 1869, the appointment was postponed until the following month 'to afford time for examination of the large number of testimonials sent in by the various applicants'. On 10 April, the testimonials of five reverend gentlemen: E.J.S. Rudd, G.J. Hall, A.C. Wilson, W.M. Hatch and E. Summers – the first three of whom we know had school-mastering experience at respectively Malvern, Shrewsbury and Lancing – were selected for further consideration. Eleven days later, the Hon. George Herbert, who following Dawes' death had been appointed Dean of Hereford during Lord Derby's administration some two years earlier, was requested to approach Mr Rudd, with a view to his being appointed Headmaster at the Midsummer Chapter, 'if the result of such communication should prove satisfactory'. The result of the Dean's 'communication' was indeed favourable – although precisely how Herbert conducted it is not recorded in the Chapter Acts – and on 2 June, Rudd attended his first Chapter meeting. He was then formally appointed Headmaster on 25 June 1869: 'to have, hold, enjoy the same place ... with all and singular the salaries, fees, profits and emoluments whatsoever to the said office by law, custom or otherwise belonging, as long as you shall behave yourself well, diligently and religiously therein ...'[103]

Today, the appointment of a young man of 28 as Headmaster of even a small secondary school would be regarded as a considerable risk. In the mid-Victorian period, however, it was not that unusual. For example, a decade earlier, Edward White Benson had been appointed as Wellington College's first 'Master' at 29, a year older than John Percival on his appointment as Headmaster of the new Clifton College in 1862. Nor was Rudd without experience of school-mastering, having been for two years (1863-64) Second Master of Sheffield College, prior to his appointment as one of Malvern College's first five assistant masters at its opening in January 1865. He was also a fellow of St John's, Cambridge. Indeed, it is Rudd's close connection with the Cathedral School's own college, where from Bedford School (under Mr Fanshawe, whom he revered) he had also been elected in 1859 to a Somerset scholarship, together with his strong university record – he had been 26th wrangler and gained a first in Classics in 1863 – that no doubt helped persuade Dean Herbert of Rudd's 'integrity, virtues and good learning'.[104] Herbert's confidence in his protégé was

102. HCA, 7105/7, 1869 payment no. 80 (for the advertisements). For the original particulars of 5 March 1869, together with the enquiry and applications list, see HCA, 7032/6, pp.332-41, 432.

103. HCA, 7031/21, p.357, 16 Feb.; p.362, 24 March; p. 363, 10 April; p.364, 21 April; p.366, 2 June; p.372, 25 June 1869. HCA, 7005/10, pp.231-32, Rudd's patent of appointment, 25 June 1869.

104. As cited in Rudd's patent, *ibid.*, p.232. That St John's was also Dean Herbert's own college was no doubt an additional recommendation.

Fig. 5.4 Eric Rudd: his short but significant tenure further raised the school's reputation.

not misplaced. Rudd's academic abilities were revealed from the start when he acted as the school's examiner for its midsummer examination in 1869, thus completing the remarkable succession of examiners during that decade. Although not in the same way as Woollam in 1857, by the time of Rudd's formal appointment, he was in the enviable position of taking over a school of which he had a personal knowledge.

Rudd's six annual reports to his governors, from his first for the November audit of 1869 to his last of 1874 – the only Headmaster of the period for whom the complete set is extant – reveal him to be a progressive teacher of high expectations and a far-sighted administrator who was well aware of the demands facing Headmasters of endowed schools at that time.[105] In his first months in office, the Endowed Schools Bill was going through Parliament, and although its provisions were to be considerably watered down,[106] it was by no means certain how the proposed new commissioners would view cathedral schools. And so in November 1870, Rudd informed his governors that as with all other endowed schools, the commissioners would now require Deans and Chapters to implement new schemes of governance, and that it was vital for HCS's future that it should be selected as the only first-grade school for the county. Although he was unclear how this might be best accomplished, he sent his governors reports of the county meetings at York and Exeter, where local committees had been appointed to act with the commissioners, and referred them to discussions in the church congress on 'the duty of the Church as to middle class education and the Endowed Schools Act'. By the following November, the point had been won, but this did not necessarily mean that that the Somerset scholarships were safe. Indeed, Rudd feared the worst and asked the Chapter to take 'immediate steps' to meet what he perceived would be an attack by the Endowed Commissioners 'upon the only valuable endowment which Hereford School possesses'. That attack, too, did not materialise.

New and Old Learning

Like Woollam, one of Rudd's priorities was to try to ensure a decent education for the choristers. Indeed, even before his arrival as Headmaster, their conditions had considerably improved as indicated by the following new scheme, sanctioned at the 1869 Midsummer Chapter, which established (or re-established) a complement of eight choristers and four probationers, appointed by the Chapter after trial by the Precentor, Succentor and organist; the abolition of any fee payment on appointment; free education at HCS, excluding French tuition but including the provision of books and free singing lessons from the organist; and a 48 week singing year. In addition, the choristers – except two of their number, who were each still paid at a rate of £10 *per annum* by the Custos and vicars as they had refused to accept these new financial arrangements – would receive a payment of between £8 and £10 *per annum*, depending on their seniority. Half of the sum was to be paid to the parents, and the other half deposited directly into a savings bank, to be paid out with an additional sum from Tomson's charity towards an apprenticeship 'or other advancement in life'. To

105. HCA, 7031/21, pp.379-83, 429-35, 473-76, reports, 1869-71; HCA, 7005/10, pp.450-52, report of 1872; HCA, 7031/22, pp.58-63, 114-19, reports, 1873-74. The reports are nothing if not thorough, and indicate that school lists and detailed curricula were often attached to them.

106. See above, p.179.

encourage boarding – an end Precentor Ouseley had long desired – the fees were substantially reduced to £25 *per annum* for probationers and £15 for full choristers (excluding extras), with a £5 annual supplement given to the school from Tomson's charity towards the cost of each chorister boarder.[107] There is some evidence that this new arrangement increased both chorister recruitment, which averaged more than three applicants for every place in these years, and the number of boarding choristers, for whom advertisements were placed in the *Yorkshire Post* and *Western Mail* as well as the *Guardian* and local newspapers.[108] However, the increased interest shown by parents in putting their sons forward as potential choristers did not ease Rudd's worries about the insufficiency of their education. Having initially observed in November 1869 that the choristers' teaching was carried on only 'under great difficulties and is far from satisfactory', the following year he was able to give his governors a more encouraging report:

> The chief difficulty attending their education is that all the class instruction which they can receive with the other boys must be given between 11am and 4pm; and of this time I can scarcely allow less than 2 hours for dinner. I have at present arranged for them to receive instruction in arithmetic by themselves during the hour before breakfast, 7.15 to 8.15am, which I have added to the school time for such boys as live within a mile of the school. This arrangement leaves the rest of their time available for other studies, and will work (I think) satisfactorily for the present, but much greater difficulties will arise when any of the choristers gain a higher position in the school, as the presence even of a single chorister in any class requires that the work of that class should be arranged with reference to him.

Given that Matins was a sung service, there was little more that could be done by way of reorganisation. The chorister issue subsequently disappeared from Rudd's annual reports, apart from his comment in 1873 that the new probationers were much better than their predecessors 'both in their conduct and their previous training'.

Rudd further improved the quality of teaching and learning for all the boys. Among his first initiatives were his proposals to divide the school year into three (rather than two) terms, 'as at most public schools', and to move the annual examination from June to July. This was accepted by the Chapter, apparently with little demur, and first implemented in 1870 to the approval of the majority of parents.[109] Even more radical was the instigation

107. HCA, 7031/21, pp.366-68, 2 June 1869. See HCA, 7032/6, p.58, for the printed circular for the new scheme, and above, pp.200-01, for Ouseley's advocacy of chorister boarding. The diversion of Tomson's charity funds to pay for chorister boarding and singing lessons was subsequently held by the Charity Commissioners to have been illegal. See TNA, ED 27/1605, no. 45, note by H.P. Morris, 31 Oct. 1889.

108. See *HT*, 7 Aug. 1869, p.7, for the initial response to the notices which was mainly from potential boarding choristers; and HCA, 7032/6, pp.58-59, 61-63, 215, for lists of chorister applications and appointments, 1869-70 and 1873-75. There are no similar figures extant for the previous decade. For the increase in applications for chorister boarding after the new scheme was announced, see *HT*, 7 August 1869, p.7; the Chapter payments to Rudd for boarder choristers (£5 each under the new scheme), HCA, 7104/5, 6 *passim,* payments 1870-74, which averaged over £17 *per annum* for these five years; and HCA, 7105/8, payment no. 31, for the advertisements.

109. See HCA, 7031/21, pp.385-86, 17 Dec. 1869; and *HT,* 16 April 1870, p.5, for the first announcement of the new summer term, which began on 20 April that year.

a few months later of an examination for all prospective Langfordian scholars, thereby taking the choice away from the Chapter – to their evident relief – and the introduction in late 1872 of an entrance examination in 'elementary English subjects' for all prospective pupils.[110] Whilst not making major curriculum changes – Rudd's Dean and Chapter reports were divided into the five heads of Divinity, Classics, Mathematics, English and French, which remained the staple subjects during his tenure[111] – he increased academic competition within the school. He introduced an annual prize examination in Divinity each December from 1869, as well as an examination in English based subjects (including History and Geography) after that Christmas 'in hopes that some at least [of the senior boys] may be induced to take up these subjects for themselves'. He then created new prizes, such as the two English prizes first awarded in 1870 'partly because there was an erroneous impression abroad that they did not teach English in classical schools', and those for Latin and English verse composition – the latter being given by Fred Weatherly, following his own poetic triumph on the occasion of the Marquis of Salisbury's installation as Chancellor of Oxford, and the winning entry being printed in the speech day programme. A chorister's prize was added in the same year (1872) 'to encourage … and … promote emulation' among their number, and in recognition that they 'laboured under some disadvantage'.[112]

Rudd was also willing to support less able boys by allowing a few of them to take German, together with extra Maths and English, instead of Greek, provided that they were over 14 and a specific parental request had been made.[113] However, as Rudd himself had admitted in 1871, this was far from establishing a modern side:

> I cannot but recognise the necessity of establishing a modern department, and of introducing into the school certain subjects which are now very generally adopted in the best schools. If I were to attempt to do so in the present state of the school, I should most probably impair the efficiency of the classical instruction and carry out but imperfectly the modern education. The very inadequate accommodation is of itself sufficient to deter me from making such an attempt, much as I think the change would be for the advantage of the school, and strongly as I feel that delay is for many reasons unwise.

It is probable that Rudd was thinking here primarily about the teaching of Natural Sciences, which during the 1860s had become among a number of intellectuals 'the one panacea for England's troubles', and which in the early 1870s was the subject of yet another

---

110. *Ibid.,* 23 July 1870, p.3 (Dean Herbert's speech); and the notices of 2 July 1870; 21 Jan. 1871, p.5; 14 Sept. 1872, p.5; 30 Nov. 1872, p.4.

111. For most senior boys, the curriculum remained overwhelmingly classical. In 1870, the weekly classical work for Form V boys involved two exercises from Bradley's lessons in continuous Latin prose, two exercises from Arnold's introduction to Greek prose composition, 12 to 14 lines of English poetry for translation into Latin elegiacs, and one or two passages of Greek or Latin authors for unseen translation (the Greek lexicon being generally allowed but not the Latin dictionary), with the occasional English essay in place of some of the exercises. HCA, 7031/21, p.431.

112. See the *HT*, 23 July 1870, p.3; 27 July 1872, p.7.

113. *Ibid.*, 16 July 1870, p.5 for the notice about the formation of a modern class and the division of the school into upper and lower departments.

royal commission.[114] Rugby, under the guidance of James Maurice Wilson, a mathematician turned science teacher, had shown the way by building a Natural Science school (to Gilbert Scott's design), and by making the subject compulsory in 1864 for all boys below the upper school.[115] Hereford, however, at a time when there were few serviceable classrooms let alone laboratories, could not possibly have sustained a modern curriculum – even if it had been modified to exclude science like the one that had been introduced at Malvern in 1867[116] – and Rudd's judgement not to press ahead with a modern side was sound. It was to be 30 years before conditions had changed sufficiently for Chemistry to be added as a regular curriculum subject.

The external examination reports give some indication of the school's academic standing in the early 1870s.[117] There were the inevitable caveats with regard to performance in individual subjects. For example: the poor standard of the classical prose and verse compositions in 1871 prompted Prebendary Gregory Smith to sponsor a prize for Latin verse; J.E. Sandys, examining for the third and last time in 1872, was surprised that the juniors were unable to cope with the questions on the Holy Land considering 'the increasing importance of Scripture Geography in this country with recent researches in Palestine'; in 1873, R.R. Webb, a Monmouth boy who had been elected senior wrangler the previous year, thought that the lower mathematical divisions showed little aptitude for 'solving elementary problems which required the assistance of a fundamental abstract principle'; and in 1874, H.M. Dymock pointed out the weaknesses in the boys' Latin prose ('English prose in a Latin dress'), their 'false quantities' in Greek verse and the fact that the Cyclops still 'seemed too much of a giant'. Nevertheless, over these years the examiners were broadly complimentary about the boys' academic performance. They praised their 'honest and hearty work' in 1870 and the 'unmistakeable evidence of real work' they produced in 1871; in 1872, they remarked on their 'thorough efficiency' in attaining satisfactory results and the 'honourable feeling and good tone existing in the school'; in 1873, they sensed the 'strong spirit of honourable emulation seconded by an indefatigable supervision' and in 1874, the school's elevated 'intellectual and moral air'. This is all very commendable: there is a sense here of the sound learning and energetic teaching – to say nothing of the honourable academic conduct and 'pure tone' – that seems to have been prevalent at HCS in the early 1870s, which resulted in many boys

114. The ('panacea') phrase is Mack's (1941), p.50. The commission was chaired by the seventh duke of Devonshire, and sought information from over 200 endowed schools. Of the 128 which replied, only 63 were found to teach Science, most cursorily. Roach (1991), p.33.

115. Hope Simpson, pp.46ff. Wilson was a polymath, who succeeded Percival as Headmaster of Clifton, and later became a Canon of Worcester. He left St John's, Cambridge, in 1859 (as senior wrangler) just before Rudd arrived, but Rudd would have known about him through his influential contribution on Science teaching in *Essays on a Liberal Education*, published in 1867 and edited by F.W. Farrar, himself a forceful advocate of a modern curriculum.

116. Blumenau, p.13. Faber's introduction of this modern department (where Chemistry was taught, at extra cost, as an optional extra) coincided with Rudd's last term at the school.

117. As published in the *HT*, 23 July 1870, p.3; 22 July 1871, p.8; 27 July 1872, p.7; 25 July 1874, p.8; 31 July 1875, p.13. I have not been able to trace Rudd's own report of 1869, when he was the examiner. The 1873 speech day was not reported on in the *HT*, but a copy of the examiners' report is transcribed in the Act book. HCA, 7031/22, pp.56-58, Oct. 1873.

being well-grounded in the educational basics of a first-grade classical school. Reading between the lines, however, these examiners also present a picture of an over-prescribed curriculum – Dymock, for example, referred in 1873 to the 'numerous and heavy' nature of the examination subjects – that was beyond the reach of many boys, who had no alternative but to resort to rote-learning. Such reports would have furthered the case of the liberal educational reformers of the period.[118]

Rudd, as we have seen, was well aware of the inadequacies of his own school's curriculum, as he was of the dangers of cramming, which he considered to be almost inevitable in a school like Hereford. As he admitted in his final report of November 1874, ideally he would have liked to have seen more competition for the school's university scholarships and exhibitions:

> instead of our being obliged sometimes almost to cram some of the candidates. But it is hardly possible for a school of 100 boys to be represented by 19 undergraduates at Oxford and Cambridge, much less that they should all reach the standard which I should expect from scholars & exhibitioners.

Still, despite the pedagogic limitations imposed by the school's public need to fill its quota of Somerset awards from a Sixth and Upper Fifth Form (the distinction between the two seems to have been nominal) which never exceeded ten pupils at this time, it should be recorded that Rudd's teaching of the senior boys was increasingly successful in terms of results. Over the six years of Rudd's tenure, 24 boys were elected to hold one of the school's Somerset awards. This does not mean that they were necessarily academically distinguished. Indeed in 1871, Rudd himself was surprised when a boy who was placed 17th in the school list was elected to a Somerset exhibition at St John's, albeit with the Master's warning that 'the College was far from satisfied and must raise the standard in future'. In subsequent years this seems to have happened, which Rudd considered (in 1873) to have 'done much good to those boys of moderate abilities who are anxious to go to the university'. By November 1874, Rudd was 'well satisfied' with the recent academic achievements of his senior boys. They had gained both the Somerset scholarships at Brasenose – Hereford boys thereby occupying all six such scholarships at the college for the first time; five Somerset exhibitions at St John's, even though only four were initially on offer; one open award in Mathematics at the same college, won by W.F. Burville, the music master's younger son; and a third place (achieved by W.P. Symonds from 207 candidates) in the Indian Civil Service examination.[119] And it was recognised that Rudd himself was responsible for many of these

118. Like E.E. Bowen, a Harrow schoolmaster, who wished both to humanise the classical curriculum and to provide alternative subjects for those not able to profit by studying the Classics. His arguments in his chapter on 'Teaching by Means of Grammar', which he considered 'repulsive and infructuous' in *Essays on a Liberal Education* (1867), proved so persuasive – at least to his paymasters, if not more generally – that the Harrow authorities allowed him to start a modern side there in 1869. Mack (1941), p.64; Tyerman, pp.289-90.

119. The speech day honours list of July 1874 also included the names of two boys who had matriculated in the first division at London University and another who had been placed in the first class of the Cambridge junior local examination, as well as other graduate successes. Rudd hoped that in the future there would be an even 'higher and more honourable list'. *HT*, 25 July 1874, p.8.

successes. In 1874, for example, Examiner Dymock detected the 'stamp of the Headmaster' in much of the school's good work, and not least through his teaching of the lower forms, which he held to be 'a very great stimulus indeed in a public school' and one which was seldom practised. These plaudits were repeated by Dymock in his third successive year as examiner, on Rudd's retirement as Headmaster in July 1875, when he considered that the boys had been placed 'on a good footing in all subjects' and that the Headmaster's mark – as a scholar, mathematician, first-rate teacher, disciplinarian and manager – was everywhere apparent in the school.

Numbers, Assistants and 'Machinery'

During Rudd's tenure there was a steady expansion of pupil numbers, proof (as Dean Herbert observed in July 1874, at his opening speech day address) 'not only of continued confidence but of increased confidence on the part of parents who reside in the city of Hereford and its neighbourhood in the system of education which is promoted here'.[120] Rudd was fortunate in being in post at the tail end of mid-Victorian prosperity in the county, one indication of which is the marked increase in a residentiary canon's income, which averaged in excess of £753 *per annum* for the period 1870-76, almost £100 greater than the septennial average for 1859-65.[121] This meant that an increasing number of prospective parents, most of whose livelihoods were based – indirectly or directly – on the land, would have been able to meet the fees, even when they were increased to 12 guineas *per annum* for basic tuition (for boys over 12), and to £75 for boarding.[122] Nevertheless, a school has to be worthy of the fees it charges, and there is no contradicting the growth of pupil numbers over Rudd's tenure, which after a levelling off in the two years following Woollam's retirement, increased annually in Rudd's last three years to reach the high water mark of 112 boys on the school roll in July 1875, the highest number for over 50 years.[123]

The increase justified Rudd's decision to establish a new junior boarding house, 'under the charge of a married master'. He hoped that this initiative would attract those

---

120. *HT*, 25 July 1874, p.8.

121. HCA, 7032/6, pp.54-56. I have not traced the figures for the late 1860s, but there was a marked down-turn in the 1880s. *Ibid.*, frontispiece, showing an average of nearly £594 for 1882-88, with an expectation of £450-80 for the following three years.

122. Rudd increased the tuition fee in 1870, maintaining the 10 guinea rate for boys under 12. French and 'Drilling' were extras – respectively at 2 guineas and half-a-guinea *per annum.* The boarding fees, which included tuition, the above extras and washing, were probably increased for the autumn term 1873. The fees for junior boarders (under 13) 'in Mr Brown's house' were £63 *per annum,* with a £5 boarding concession for all clergy sons. *Ibid.*, p.432. The fees in 1864, as listed in Woollam's report for the Endowed Schools' Commission, were 10 guineas for tuition (with the following optional charges: French and German an extra 2 guineas each, and Music 4 guineas); and £52 10s for boarders (£47 5s for brothers and clergy sons), including basic tuition.

123. *HT,* 31 July 1875, p.13, Dean Herbert's speech. The exact numbers at each November audit, 1869-74, were: 77, 72, 75, 90, 98 and 108, with boarding numbers increasing correspondingly over the same period from 24 to 35 (including the seven boys in the junior house). The rise of 15 pupils overall, 1871-72, necessitated an increase in the number of classes from five to seven – (in Rudd's words) 'the least number which I can consider at all satisfactory' – and the appointment of an additional master (W.H. Mills). The 1871 census lists 23 boarders (aged 9 to 18) in School House, plus the Headmaster, his sister Sarah Ann, and Ann Turner, the matron.

younger boys, who had hitherto been sent 'to one of the numerous preparatory schools in Hereford' before their entry to HCS.[124] Despite the difficulty in finding suitable accommodation, by early 1874, Rudd had persuaded James Brown, a personal friend 'who had been for many years the Head Master of 2 grammar schools in the eastern counties', to become master of the lower school and Housemaster of the new junior boarding house, which was opened that April at 9 St Owen's Street for boys under 13.[125] By the end of that year Rudd could report that there had already been 'a considerable increase' in the number of younger pupils, and that the lower school met separately for prayers from the upper school – there being, in any case, no one room which could hold all 108 boys. He hoped that 'as soon as practicable' the lower school would 'have its own masters under Mr Brown', as well as separate classrooms, an aspiration that was not to be fully realised until near the end of the century.

Rudd was relieved following James Brown's appointment to be 'comparatively free from anxiety with regard to the lower classes by reason of the confidence which I can repose in an experienced master'. His appointment may have given the prospect of stability for the junior boys but it did nothing to solve an inherent weakness in the teaching of the rest of the school: the rapid turn-over of assistant masters. In this respect, Rudd was much less fortunate than his predecessor.

As we will see, the foreign language masters were mercilessly bullied by the boys and seldom lasted longer than a year under Woollam. This pattern continued in Rudd's first two years, 1869 and 1870, when the start of the Franco-Prussian war deprived him of the teaching of the new 'foreign master', Mr Ehrethall, who was called to higher service in the Prussian army. M. Ménard, Rudd's former colleague at Malvern, filled the gap – Rudd and two assistants initially undertaking 'the construing lessons' in preparation for Ménard's weekly appearance – and then was engaged more fully, remaining a 'universally popular' teacher for almost 11 years (1870-81).[126] The short tenures of the other masters, none of whom – Burville, the music master apart – stayed with Rudd for the six years of his headmastership,[127] proved more serious. In November 1874, he bemoaned the frequent change of his assistants and the difficulty he had in finding experienced replacements, 'owing to the small salaries which I am able to offer and the want of other inducements such as the prospect of a boarding house'. He cited T.H. Belcher's leaving to take up a house at Malvern College – even though he had supplemented his income by singing as an assistant

124. Rudd had little confidence in the educational standards of these schools. 'It is not uncommon', he had written in November 1872, 'for a boy of 12 or 13 years to come to school knowing less than might be expected from an average boy of 10 years old.' It is at this point that he first suggested the formation of an entirely separate junior or preparatory school. HCA, 7005/10, p.452, 12 Nov. 1872. I have discovered about ten boys' preparatory schools within Hereford that placed notices in the *HT* during the period, some within a stone's throw of HCS, and perhaps a further six for 'young ladies'.

125. *HT*, 28 Feb.1874, p.8; 11 April 1874, p.4. The notices indicate that Brown was also ready to 'receive boys to be prepared' for HCS.

126. *TH*, No. 8 (Sept. 1881), pp.96-97. For the bullying of French masters in the 1860s, see below, pp.218-19.

127. Of the staff Rudd inherited, J. St Maur Russell had left by January 1870, C.S. Hargreen left in late 1871 and W.W. White in July 1871. Ménard apart, of Rudd's own appointments, only Knowles, the English master, and A.W. Hales stayed for more than three years.

vicar in the cathedral choir, and had free lodging and board in the cloisters[128] – as a case in point. He continued in this vein to his governors:

> Owing to the increased numbers & the addition which the Chapter has kindly made to the Headmaster's statutable stipend, my own salary and those of the other masters ... will contrast favourably with the earlier years of my mastership. But I am not going too far in saying that at most of the schools with which Hereford is called upon to compete, the assistant masters would be very loath to exchange their position even with mine.[129]

Rudd considered – and this was the important point – that the loss of such schoolmasters as Belcher had had a serious impact on the education of some pupils, and he was having to resort to teaching Divinity, Greek and Algebra to the middle forms to the neglect of the senior boys.

Rudd was even less able to do anything about the school's other structural weakness – the desperate need (as Rudd himself put it in 1872) for 'better provision' for the boys' teaching, lodging and recreation, referred to contemporaneously by Thring of Uppingham as the 'machinery' of any school.[130] As we have seen, the poor accommodation had been commented upon by Bompas for the Endowed Schools' Commission and had been a perennial complaint from Woollam and his examiners in the 1860s. As the school roll increased in the early 1870s, the situation only got worse and the Headmaster's pleas ever more plaintive. Despite the building of a new staircase, amongst other repairs in school house which cost the Dean and Chapter nearly £260,[131] within a few months of his taking office Rudd was informing his governors that 'the masters perform their work under great disadvantages and that much confusion arises from the imperfect accommodation'. Even more pressing was 'the want of a good playground set apart from the school & within easy reach of it'. Two years later, in 1871, he suggested that when a good site for the play area had been found:

128. T. Hayes Belcher was Housemaster of Number 1 at Malvern from 1874 to 1881, when he left to become Headmaster of Brighton College. Blumenau, pp.29, 179. He had been F.T. Havergal's curate at Lyde (HCA, 7003/1/6, pp.337-38, his letter to the Custos and vicars, *c.*June 1873), and was also a very useful cricketer. *HT*, 1 June 1872, p. 8, report on his 'extremely good' bowling for HCS v West Herefordshire, and above, p.230.

129. In 1873, Rudd was paying the following salaries to his assistants: Mills £160; Stebbing (with partial board) £150; Belcher £120; Hales (plus board and lodging) £70; Knowles (for two terms, with partial board) £64 14s; Warner (one term, with partial board) £45; Ménard (plus partial board) £80; the drill sergeant £20; plus a further £72 12s for 'occasional masters' and 'partial board of 4 masters'. Rudd spent £120 on rates, taxes, coals, gas, furniture, repairs and cleaning, leaving him a profit from the fees of £335 10s 6d. His official stipend (which now excluded the £50 or so annual tuition fees for the four Langfordian scholars) had been increased to £120 *per annum* from Lady Day 1873. HCA, 7031/22, pp.40, 41, Acts, 24 March, 4 June 1873.

130. Most conspicuously in his *Education and School*, published in 1867. The usage was not original. See, for example, Benson's comment to Canon Wickendon of April 1858, on Wellington College's 'fine and well-ordered and wealthy "plant" and machinery ...' Newsome, (1959), p.79.

131. HCA, 7031/21, p.371, 25 June 1869, acceptance of William Beavan's £220 estimate. The actual cost (including the fee of W.H. Knight, the architect) was £259 11s. HCA, 7105/7, 1870, payment no. 106; HCA, 7105/8, payments nos 107-09.

> Improved boarding accommodation might be provided, as has been the case in other places by private enterprise. A good boarding house or hostel, on a healthy site outside the town and near to a good playground, would attract to the school many boys whose parents are unwilling to have them board in the middle of a town, but would gladly pay higher terms for improved accommodation such as is met with at newly founded colleges, e.g. Clifton and Malvern.

And within a few months, he was even proposing an 'alliance between the cathedral and Barr's Court schools but with distinct buildings and playgrounds',[132] an idea that was still being publicly aired nearly two years later. However, it is unlikely that the Chapter would have seriously considered any proposal which threatened to take the choristers away from their education within the Close.

In November 1873, Rudd considered that the boys' illnesses of that term were attributable not only to the bad weather but also 'in a great measure ... due to the unfitness of the classrooms for that purpose', an observation that Dymock (the examiner) had already made that year. 'With our present number', Rudd continued, 'it is almost impossible to keep them properly ventilated and well warmed at the same time'. By the time of his 1874 report, Rudd – as an increasingly confident Headmaster, who had been fortified by the school's expanding roll and growing academic reputation – confronted his governors even more directly. Moreover, the recent transfer of the Endowed Schools Commissioners' powers to the Charity Commission had, he believed, given HCS an opportunity for the unlocking of funds that might not come again. There is a tone of desperation in his voice as he pressed the Chapter to seize the moment 'and come to a decision on these matters':

> I feel that I have done all I can without further aid, and that the result, however encouraging, falls very far short of what it might have been if we had had the advantages possessed by almost all other schools with which the school is brought into competition. Considering the great changes which have taken place during the last few years it would be absurd to expect any increase in the number of boarders until there are good school buildings, a proper playground & better boarding accommodation. I am continually told by my own friends & by persons in Hereford that their recommendations to send boys to this school are almost always useless because the first question is about playground & buildings, and to this they cannot give a satisfactory answer.

Rudd's forceful argument that this was the moment for Dean Herbert and his Chapter to commit funds to rebuild the school was reinforced by the actions of the Custos and vicars choral. The school's rent of the small rooms in their College, which Dean Dawes had pushed through nearly a quarter of a century earlier, could never have provided the required space for a school of 100 or more boys. In any case, the College's periodic spats with the cathedral – one noted illustration of which concerned the vicars' refusal to accept the new

132. HCA, 7031/22, p.7, 18 Jan.1872. At prize-giving in July 1871, the Mayor (T. Llanwarne), himself an old boy, suggested in public that the school should have 'as large a building on some more open site' which would enable it to 'compete not only with the colleges of Cheltenham and Malvern, but other public schools in the country'. *HT*, 22 July 1871, p.8.

chorister scheme of 1869[133] – could only be exacerbated by the school's continued use of part of the cloisters. As early as June 1869, Rudd's request for the building of a skylight in one of the College rooms, 'hitherto used by Mr Woollam as a dormitory', so that it could be converted into a classroom, was refused.[134] But this was only a minor skirmish compared with the increasingly hostile battles in the ensuing years between the Chapter and the vicars over the school's occupation of the College premises.

The campaign lasted well over two years from 23 March 1872, when the Custos and vicars first raised the issue, to the final Chapter decision of 4 January 1875 'that possession of such premises be given up to the College'.[135] The root of the problem stemmed from the new College statutes of 1871, which intended that the 'greater number' of the seven ordained assistant vicars, appointed to replace the lay clerks, should reside with the six vicars in the College. This inevitably brought the school's continued use of the College rooms, occupied at a nominal £5 annual rent since 1851, into sharp focus, especially when the Chapter refused to pay the £280 asked for as a contribution towards the restoration of the western cloister. Further negotiations stalled, which led to the vicars giving the Chapter a year's notice to quit the accommodation by September 1874. For more than a year the Chapter temporised, and it was in vain that they argued (as late as 13 November 1874) that the school's occupation of part of the College could only in equity be terminated by common agreement. Their final exhortation that: 'in the interests of the public, the Dean and Chapter deprecate the extrusion of the school as it might lead to the embarrassment of the Headmaster and to the partial dispersion ... of the scholars' had no effect on the collective vicars' mind. They then served a formal writ of ejectment on the Chapter on Christmas Eve 1874, and it was only after counsel's opinion had been taken that the cathedral's claim on the College rooms was finally abandoned early in the ensuing New Year. A tenancy agreement was then made with Rudd for him to rent the rooms temporarily but at the original rate.[136]

Two issues remained: the cost of the 'dilapidations' after 24 years of school occupation; and the school's continued use of College land for the extended playground. The repair bill was eventually agreed, after arbitration, at £35 'in full of all claims against the Dean and Chapter'; it took another generation, however, for the little matter of the play area to be settled (again by *force majeure*).[137]

---

133. HCA, 7003/1/6, p.287, Beddoe to Chapter Clerks, 23 June 1869. They eventually accepted the scheme, which involved their contributing one quarter of the choristers' costs, following their approval of the new College statutes in 1870-71. *Ibid.*, pp.300-10.

134. *Ibid.*, p.288, Rudd to Custos and vicars, 30 June; and the declining of the request on the 3 July 1869. Rudd's letter was written from East Street, where he was presumably temporarily residing, pending the completion of the repairs to School House.

135. This protracted dispute may be followed in the Chapter and College Act books: HCA, 7031/22, pp.13, 16, 73, 109ff, 126; HCA, 7003/1/6, pp.321-23, 329-30, 340-42, 355-56, 369-70, 371ff. The vicars choral were unanimous in their decision to resume possession of the rooms, although one of them, A.J. Capel, privately apologised to the Chapter. Custos Goss later alleged that his action influenced the cathedral in Capel's subsequent appointment to a minor canonry ahead of senior and better qualified candidates. *HT,* 3 April 1875, p.8.

136. HCA, 7003/1/6, pp.379, 382-83, Acts, 6 Feb., 12 April 1875.

137. *Ibid.,* pp.393, 395-96, 398, Acts, 7 Aug., 4 Dec. 1875, 24 March 1876; 7031/22, 7 March 1876. HCA, 7105/8, fo 195r, payment no. 120, for fees of the Chapter Clerks and counsel (Henry Matthews QC). See below, p.274, re the playground.

Legacy

Given this turn of events, there was no option but for Dean Herbert and his colleagues to take the necessary measures to reconstruct the school. The story of its rebuilding is properly told in the next chapter, for by the time of its completion – although not at the time of its commencement – Rudd had departed for a living in Walsall. He left his successor a strong legacy: a school that filled the old buildings to the brim, and one that was being renewed in the biggest building project undertaken up to that time in the school's history.

Rudd's last public occasion, speech day 1875, was a poignant affair. He responded to the school captain's presentation of a 'splendid time-piece, with mercurial pendulum', together with a testimonial that acknowledged the school's great increase in numbers and prosperity under his tenure, by urging his own pupils to rally around the new Headmaster in the same way that Power's and Woollam's old boys had supported him. Earlier in the proceedings, Dean Herbert had paid tribute to Rudd by recognising that he had not merely sustained but had raised the character of the school. There is no need to gainsay this judgement on Eric Rudd: his was a short but significant tenure which brought the Cathedral School within sight of the modern age.[138]

School Life in mid-Victorian Times

A number of old boy reminiscences, written 30 years or so after the events described for the early editions of the school magazine, provide an impression of boy-life at the Cathedral School during the 1850s.[139] For the following decade, we can draw on two more substantial memoirs. The first and most important was written by W.E. Vernon Yonge, who attended HCS from 1859 to 1868. The author was in his late fifties when he composed his articles, and they were published – in Woollam's memory, over a 21-week period – in the *Hereford Times* of 1909.[140] Yonge's reminiscences can be supplemented by those of his friend, Fred Weatherly, Yonge's *fidus Achates* and contemporary at school and at Oxford. The Hereford chapter in Weatherly's 1926 memoir, *Piano and Gown,* is different in style and substance from Yonge's 1909 pieces, being much less detailed and as an autobiography written for a different audience. It was also penned from the perspective of an aesthete rather than a 'blood', albeit one who could not only 'beat the big ones' at running games like 'prisoners'

138. For Rudd's resignation, see HCA, 7031/22, p.132, 24 March 1875; and pp.168-69, for his letter of 8 Nov. 1875 to the Chapter, from Aldridge Rectory, Walsall. The school captain was Raymond Gee, later Headmaster of Perth Grammar School, Australia. Tributes to Rudd are reported in *HT*, 31 July 1875, p.13. There is retrospective evidence (in *HT*, 16 Nov. 1889, p.8) to suggest that Rudd resigned because of his despair about the school's prospects, which does not correspond with Rudd's public admission on his last speech day that he was leaving because he had insufficient energy to carry out the 'much hard work [that] still needed to be done'.

139. *TH*, no. 3 (Jan. 1879), pp.115-19, 135-14; no. 4 (Sept. 1879), pp.172-79; no. 8 (Jan. 1882), pp.5-8; no. 9 (Sept. 1882), pp. 27-32; articles by 'The Beetle', Y.S.L. and J.W.C. (John Wilson Cooper).

140. *HT* from 10 April 1909, the articles being completed by Yonge on 14 October 1909. See HARC, M 90/1, pp.50ff, for newspaper cuttings of these articles, except parts 4 and 8. Yonge came from a distinguished clerical family, which was closely connected to both the school and the diocese. His distant forebear, George Gretton, had been Dean of Hereford from 1809 to 1820; his grandfather had been educated at the Cathedral School, as were at least two of his brothers; and, perhaps more relevantly for Yonge's schooling in 1859, his great uncle, Thomas Gretton, as Succentor of the cathedral, was then living in Hereford. His great-uncle was also incumbent of Pipe and Lyde, where Yonge's father had served his first curacy.

base' but who could also more than hold his own in a fight against a bigger opponent.[141] For these sources, it is necessary to heed Yonge's warning that 'memory is treacherous'. Nevertheless, his descriptions 'embracing school life generally and some Hereford bygone worthies and characters incidentally', together with his friend's later account, combine to give a unique picture of HCS life in the 1860s.

For Rudd's brief reign, however, there are no such descriptions. And aside from reports of occasional bouts of illness – an isolated case of scarlet fever in 1873 (when the adjacent St John's vicarage was used as an infirmary) and unspecified illnesses which badly interrupted academic progress in the following year[142] – there are no indications in his November audit reports of what the pupils were doing in their leisure hours. Clearly, it was not considered a part of a Headmaster's duty at that time to inform his governors about what we would today term extra-curricular activities. And so for the early 1870s, at a time before the advent of the school journal, we are left with the clues provided about cathedral boys in the columns of the local newspapers. These news reports, however, when combined with the earlier recollections, are sufficient to illustrate Cathedral School life during the period which has been described as 'an interesting transitional stage' in the history of public schools in the third quarter of the nineteenth century between the Victorian ideals of 'godliness and good learning' and 'godliness and manliness'.[143]

In the early 1850s, one Old Herefordian recollected that given the small number of boys, 'we consisted more of a family' than a school, the Head Boy 'Jack' Taylor acting as elder brother by helping with translations and equations, reading Shakespeare on winter evenings and playing 'back-up' in the pre-breakfast football 'scrimmages', as the boarders returned from the early morning saints' day services.[144] These recollections indicate that apart from an occasional cricket match – like the one against the town juniors, where 'Jack' fielded long-stop with 'great pluck' on rough ground 'to the fast and erratic bowling of A.G. Decico' – boarders against day-boy football games and rowing expeditions up river to Sugwas, there were few structured activities at this time beyond the schoolroom.[145] And what activities there were, were organised by the boys themselves. Indeed, the boys would have considered a master's involvement in their pastimes as a breach of privilege and not to be borne.[146]

141. Weatherly, pp.26-38. Weatherly's chapter on Hereford was written at an older age and may be less reliable than Yonge's reminiscences. See, for example, his mistaken references to 'Precentor Duncombe' (p.27) and 'Parson Green' of Allensmore (p.31). The fight took place before the whole school on Wye meadow.

142. A few days after his November governors' report, Rudd felt the need to scotch rumours of a more serious outbreak by stating the true facts (three mild cases of the fever by early December) in the local press. *Ibid.,* 22 Nov. 1873, p.5; 6 Dec. 1873, p.5.

143. See Newsome (1962), pp.219-20, and chapter IV generally for his discussion on the changing Victorian ideal.

144. W.T. Taylor was a boy at HCS, 1852-54, between the ages of 18 and 20. After St John's, Cambridge (1854-58), he was ordained, becoming curate (1861-68) and then vicar ('the people's parson') of Oldbury, Worcestershire, 1868-92. See *TH*, NS XVII (March 1892), pp.10-11, for his obituary.

145. Although there is evidence that a Debating Society was first formed in 1857 and then revived in October 1875. *Ibid.*, no. 2 (September 1878), p.81.

146. See below, p.226, for the situation in the 1860s. Even as late as 1878, the vote in favour of admitting masters to debates, led to the resignation of E.A. Chattock, the (boy) president of the Debating Society. *Ibid.*, no. 2 (Sept. 1878), p.82.

So for a good deal of the day the boys were still left to their own devices. This 'want of well organised amusement and exercise', as an old boy who styled himself 'the Beetle' later explained, could lead to 'listless loafing and much time and money' spent in buying tuck at Widow Spencer's in Church Street, Boulton's – a pastry cook in Broad Street – and Mrs Jones's, the fruiterer next to the Globe Inn, also in Broad Street. And on the two weekly half-holidays, as well as the occasional 'whole' – such as the one the Headmaster gave on the report of a victory in the Crimea, a band proclaiming the news around the town – there was even more time for the boys to explore.

Hereford in the 1850s was an exciting place for an adventurous boy to live. 'The Beetle' again gives us a vivid description of his outdoor activities during these years of the railway boom:

> Making the railways was a work of very great interest to us. Hundreds, I suppose I might say thousands, of navvies were living in the town, and their great physical strength and occasional outbursts of rioting made us regard them with a respectful wonder. I have spent many half-holidays on the Newport and Abergavenny and Shrewsbury railways watching the tipping or the bridge building. When the piers were first laid for the bridge across the Wye below Hunderton, I walked from one to the other on a balk of timber. I was not intended by nature for rope-dancing or any such feats, but I was out with a big boy who chose to go and of course I was bound to follow.

Occasionally on other days there could be an important cricket match to see, as in late August 1852, when the play of 22 of the county against an England XI was watched on the new racecourse ground by 'two little schoolboys in very big mortarboards'. And in a city then without suburbs, the countryside immediately beyond its walls was almost instantly accessible for walking, fishing, nutting and stick-cutting expeditions – and after the building of the Hereford, Hay and Brecon railway, egg collecting on Llangorse lake, 'the rage for egg collecting … [being] as regular as the season'. Such pursuits must have made for an idyllic existence, even if the school's accommodation in this decade was considered – at least in retrospect – to have been 'very poor', and the cathedral had 'a shabby, incomplete appearance', with the nave separated from the rest of the church during its restoration 'by a vast dingy canvas screen'.

Yonge writes affectionately about the school staff of the 1860s. As a boarder, and also as a new-boy who was placed in Woollam's own class (the 'Fifth class', which he superintended 'as well as his peculiar care, the Sixth Form or First class') – and eventually as 'school captain'[147] – Yonge got to know his Headmaster well. He viewed Woollam as a kindly man, 'perhaps too much so to unruly boys', a fine scholar, and a patient and sympathetic teacher who brought out the best in his pupils. By contrast, Robert Dixon, the Second Master and curate of St Nicholas church, who before the end of Yonge's school career had been appointed to 'the great position' at Nottingham High School (as we have seen) was by

147. In 1867-68, as listed in *TH*, no. 2 (Sept. 1878), p.75. The magazine lists the 23 boys who captained the school, 1856-78, from F.A. Best to W.G. Cazalet. All but three subsequently held Somerset awards, the vast majority at Brasenose.

virtue of his being teacher of Mathematics, Yonge's 'particular dread'. The Second Master's 'box on the ear' also 'meant something', although Yonge insisted that this particular form of muscular Christianity was sparingly used. Dixon was 'a tower of strength' when he played in the cricket XI – as a wicket-keeper batsman, who could hit a ball 'like a horse kicking' – and an 'eloquent preacher with a good manner and effective voice power'.[148] John Capel Hanbury was third master in Yonge's time. Although not a cricketer like Dixon, he was 'no mean performer' at fives, as well as being a good organist and a 'tender and sympathetic' pastoral figure. He also held the curacy of Pipe and Lyde (as Woollam had done before him) and was himself later succeeded as curate there by the 'wrangler' and Dixon's replacement, C.S. Hargreen, forging another link between that parish and the Cathedral School. Yonge was also indebted to other masters, like A.G. Jones, who was later ordained curate at St John's, and William Walmisley White, 'a deeply earnest, spiritually-minded man' who was 'reading up' for an Oxford degree – the former because he was an efficient, genial and understanding teacher and an excellent cricketer; the latter for the use of his Horace notes. 'Tom' Taylor, an imposing Yorkshireman and another young assistant master, was less congenial because of his 'very heavy hand' when boxing ears. Nevertheless, Yonge held most of his masters in high regard, and not least because they were ordained clergymen – as well as curates in the diocese – and so kept school life 'generally at a fairly high level in things that mattered'.

Yonge also sketched memorable portraits of the part-time assistants. These included 'old Mr Weymss', the city librarian, who acted as an extra Latin tutor to the youngest boys; R.B. Bustin, the Hereford photographer and the school 'drawing-master', who also taught geometry; Burville, the alto lay vicar and writing-master, who had a 'special charge' of the choristers and taught lower school arithmetic; and With, Headmaster of the Blue Coat School, who occasionally gave explosive chemical demonstrations.

The masters who tried to teach French to the cathedral boys of the 1860s were even more memorably described. French was taught in the Fifth Form room and was a compulsory subject, but in the days before *l'entente cordial* most native French teachers were looked upon as something of a joke by their pupils and did not last long at the school. Fifty years later, Yonge ruminated about their treatment at the hands of his unruly contemporaries:

> How is it, I wonder, that in the old days at any rate, French masters were looked upon generally in the light of 'fair game'? They seem to have been regarded chiefly by the boys of that day – and possibly so now – as a sort of providential arrangement for us to make sport of, and as convenient and handy subjects to sharpen such wits upon as we possessed ... Little wonder that they looked upon [us] as 'young barbarians at play', and treated us accordingly. May one hope they have forgiven us!

There was M. Blàzer, a blue-bespectacled Swiss gentleman, whose 'knowledge of English was as limited as his patience' and who also had a heavy hand for 'la boxe'. The boys nick-named him 'Blue Blazes' after a celebrated race-horse of the day. Then there was

148. See *HT*, 27 June 1869, p.7, for the testimonial and presents (a chemical cabinet and dining-room clock) given to Dixon on his leaving HCS. In the HMC committee report of 2 Dec. 1880, Revd R. Dixon LL.D was listed as Headmaster of Nottingham High School.

M. Schwellenbach, a German whom Yonge remembered as 'big and black'. He viewed M. Sand-Mayer, however, as 'a true Frenchman ... [and] a thorough gentleman', and M. Ruinart as 'the most efficient of the lot [and] very good natured', with a commanding presence and easy conversational manners.[149] M. Ruinart also had a good baritone voice, and his rendition of the song 'Mon âme, à Dieu, mon coeur à toi' – about the parting of a Breton sailor from his mother – brought the house down in Yonge's final College Hall concert.

And there were also the domestic and other servants like old Christopher, the organ blower, who worked the bellows and blackened the boys' boots. The affectionate care of the two matrons of Yonge's time, 'the motherly Miss Curtis' and Miss Stanley, was lovingly remembered – as was old Isgrove ('Ige'), the fat school butler with the glistening smile, whom Yonge mistook for one of the masters when awoken by him at 6.30 on his first morning. The Hereford militia sergeant, whom Woollam employed to drill the boys for an hour before lunch on a Saturday morning and to supervise them during cricket practice on Widemarsh Common on Wednesday and Saturday summer afternoons, was fondly recalled.[150] Even Croft, the glazier who had a lucrative business mending the classroom windows broken by the boys' over-exuberant play at cricket or fives, was remembered as a school character. Dressed in a fading 'chimney-pot hat', he became the object of the boys' badinage but gave as good as he got, 'hurling back repartee, with a fair local accent, in reply to our impertinences' from the top of his ladder.[151]

Yonge delighted in describing the wider life of the school. Apart from the choristers, whose cathedral duties 'took up much of their school hours', the pupils in Yonge's time only attended the cathedral on a Sunday when the boarders sat through both morning and evening services. The boys were not best placed for participating in the worship, being seated on a platform under the arches between the nave and the north aisle during Sir Gilbert Scott's restoration. Once the building work was completed, they were 'banished' to the south transept with the girls of Hereford Ladies' College and Miss Morris' Academy.[152]

---

149. Yonge had forgotten M. de Dziewicki, of the University of Warsaw, who was employed as a language teacher in Yonge's early years. See above (p.183) and the advertisements in the *HT*, 22 Jan. 1859, 11 August 1860 (for the Ladies College), and 13 July 1861.

150. There were two drill sergeants in Yonge's time: MacNicholl and then Evans. Yonge describes 'single stick', with hazel or ash sticks, 'by which we learned cut and guards', as being a pleasant interlude to the drill. The national volunteer movement in the public schools began at Eton, having also been adopted at Oxford. See *HT*, editorial, 25 Feb. 1860, about a meeting in London to establish drill in public schools; and Newsome, (1961), pp.224, 237, for the operation of drill squads at Oxford and Eton, and the impact of the 1859 war-scare on the volunteer movement.

151. H. Croft, the glazier, was paid £12 7s for painting School House in 1866. HCA, 7105/7, 1866 payment no. 67.

152. Scott signed an extensive contract for the rebuilding of the cathedral on 8 October 1858, and the restoration work was completed by June 1863. Aylmer and Tiller, pp.275-89. Hereford Ladies' College was established in Widemarsh Street (nos 35-36) in 1860, the first term starting on 18 August. Like many other mid-Victorian schools, it was founded as a joint stock company venture. Some of the assistant staff at HCS (Bustin, de Dziewicki, as well as Townshend Smith, the cathedral organist) also taught at the new college. For the elegant façade and details about the new school, see *HT*, 9, 23 June, 11 Aug., 22 Dec. 1860. Miss Mary Morris' academy at Vaga House (Quay Street) was one of a number of dame schools in Hereford listed in J. Littlebury's first Herefordshire directory of 1867. In the 1861 census, there are three teachers (including Mary Morris, aged 53), a cook, a housemaid and nine pupils (aged 7 to 21) registered as living at Vaga House. The school later moved to the Vinery, Aylestone Hill, and then to 4, St Ethelbert Street.

The boys' Sunday exile to the farther recesses of the cathedral still rankled with Yonge nearly fifty years later. Not surprisingly, Yonge recollected that these services were 'somewhat tiring'. He and some of his contemporaries enjoyed the music, but they really 'bucked up' when the congregation was invited to pray 'for the school attached to this cathedral church'. Yonge reflected that it was not so much the bidding prayer itself that was appreciated, but that its saying signalled the ending of the service and the drawing closer of Sunday 'dinner' – 'a thing to be remembered' about the school in those days and an occasion which deserved a special grace before and after the meal.

The little music there was in the school in the 1860s largely centred on the performing talents of the much derided choristers in the annual concerts. These were apparently started in 1865, and Yonge ascribed 'their modest beginnings and ultimate success' to Mr Burville's considerable efforts in rehearsing the glees and part songs, aided by those of Mr Duncombe, his fellow vicar choral. College Hall, elaborately decorated 'with long festoons of evergreens and flowers', was also used as the venue for speech day, held each year at the close of the summer 'half'. This ceremony included not only the giving of handsomely bound books stamped with the school crest as prizes, but also the recitation of extracts from classical and modern authors by the boys themselves as well as the official proceedings.

As a former captain of the XI for two seasons ('though a very unworthy one'), Yonge gives particular prominence to cricket in his account of school games. Yet in the 1860s, cricket, although the pre-eminent sport at HCS, was hardly the game it was to become a decade or two later. There were few school matches. Yonge recorded three school games, all of which were lost – one played away on the side of a hill against the then recently founded Malvern College; a match on a special whole day's holiday against Barr's Court School or 'Lomax's' for which HCS put out a 2nd XI, the better cricketers having refused to play, for whatever reason, against their local rivals; and an unofficial fixture – the boys not being allowed to accept the original term-time challenge – against Lucton School, played at Leominster on the first day of the summer holidays.[153] The vast majority of matches then were the home and away games against local club sides, which could be grand and bibulous affairs.[154] A highlight of the season was the Michaelmas day fixture at Allensmore, hosted by Frank Baker, a sporting clergyman 'who took a very kindly and substantial interest in the school'.[155] Home matches and practice games were played on Widemarsh Common, which to Yonge was a place of veneration, as is apparent from this extract:

---

153. The foundation stone of Malvern College had been laid in July 1863 (*HT*, 25 July 1863 report); the principal of the proprietary school at Barr's Court was Mr J.J. Lomax – hence the sobriquet, the cathedral boys being nicknamed 'mortar boards'; for Lucton School at this time, see above, p.197.

154. See, for example, the reports of the 1861 Whitsun fixture at Widemarsh against the Hereford club, watched by 'many of our hard-working clergy' and other spectators; and the match against Bishopstone the following May, when the archdeacon provided a lavish dinner 'at which the wine cup was not absent'. *HJ*, 22 May 1861, p.5; 24 May 1862, p.5.

155. Frank Baker was regarded by 'The Beetle' (*TH*, no. 8 [Jan. 1882], p.7) as 'the father of Herefordshire cricket: a man of great simplicity of life [and] extraordinary powers of endurance, whose quaint ways and eccentricities would fill a volume'. He died in 1867 and his obituary in the *Pall Mall Gazette* (as cited by J. Wilson Cooper, *TH*, no. 9 [Sept. 1882], pp.31-32) described him as 'a prodigy in his peculiar way and ... one of the finest made men in England', having as a youth fought Tom Spring 'in his glory' at the 'Castle', Holborn. Also see, Anthony, pp.12-13, 57, 74-76.

> We of the Cathedral School had to play cricket in my day under certain difficulties ... To start with we had a mile or more to get over before we reached our ground. But when we did get there it was a ground worth reaching ... Such turf! These were not the days of made and faked wickets ... No! The bowler had a chance then and it was his own fault if he did not make the most of it. For matches a good heavy roller was all that was required on Widemarsh at least. For our ordinary practice we simply took the best pitch we could get ... Probably there would be a 'baker's dozen' of games going on together any Wednesday and Saturday on dear old Widemarsh. These were our half-holidays, and the fleetest runners were started off to 'bag a pitch'. Not an easy matter when the Barr's Court School ... lived close to the Common.

Yonge goes on to describe the loose organisation of the school's cricket at the time:

> At Hereford School in my day almost every boy played cricket. There was no compulsion. We took to it as a duck to water. There were four elevens, made up indiscriminately from the best choices amongst boarders and day boys. Each eleven had their own colours – very primitive in those days. No blazers – simply ribbons for each eleven round the hat (straw), perhaps with a 'tie' of the same. Those were the 'use' in my earliest days ... but long before I left we had arrived at 'one colour' ... for the whole school ... In those times boys had not the enjoyment of all the ... cricket paraphernalia of today – much to the good of their governor's pockets, if not their personal comfort. For instance, a private bat was the exception ... There were so many club bats for each eleven. Flannels were only sported for matches – and precious hot and uncomfortable we were without them! But if we played more or less often in trousers and braces ... we played for all we were worth and enjoyed it nonetheless.

Although as we have seen, one or two masters played in the XI, and as Yonge later makes clear, the boys 'were allowed the occasional services of their [the county's] professional bowler on easy terms', HCS cricket in the 1860s – while being immensely popular – was casually structured and largely organised by the boys themselves. The services of a cricket professional like Morton Fessey (a Nottinghamshire fast bowler) were clearly paid for by the senior pupils, who would also instruct the younger boys on cricket's rudimentary arts in the school playground. And on half-holidays at Widemarsh Common, 'picked-up sides' between boarders and day boys, dormitories against school, North versus South and the 1st XI against the next 18 or 22 provided the staple diet for internal school cricket in this decade.

Other sporting pursuits like fives were not as well-established. Mr Hanbury, no doubt, was a good fives player, but the court was a plain wall, a primitive affair built against one of the playground's boundary walls. The game may have been popular, judging by the lost fives balls illegally retrieved on one occasion from the college roof, but it is likely that fives at this time was little more than a recreational activity played on a poor facility.[156]

This was even true of football before it had been codified as the rugby game. Yonge himself was never an enthusiast, although he admitted that the school had 'its good and

156. The boy who retrieved the balls was probably V.C. Yonge, Yonge's younger brother and 'a daring climber'. For the state of the fives court in 1874, see below, p.233.

manly footballers', one of whom – J.E. Deakin – was to represent Cambridge in 1872 in the first varsity (20 a-side) rugby match.[157] But apart from the annual boarder versus day-boy fixtures on the barrack parade ground (which had been opened, with the militia buildings, on the Bartonsham estate in 1857), and the special match organised by Sir Herbert Croft against the militia at the same venue, there were hardly any proper matches; and like the cricket practices on Widemarsh, the teams were again based on 'picked-up sides' but with unlimited numbers on each team. Most of the games were played on the school playground, which measured 36 by 18 yards, excluding the 23-yard near square at the back of the College, 'which bounded our yard on two sides'.[158] This proved to be an admirable stadium for such a sport. There was much gravel and many corners formed by the angles of the College buildings; there were 'grand openings' for scrimmages; the big doors to 'Quay Lane' and the iron gate opening into the Close formed the goals (with no limit to the number of goal-keepers); and 'the bridge', an over-head passage leading from the Headmaster's house to the College rooms, acted as a rudimentary cross-bar for well booted free-kicks. Yonge described the school's football as being something like the Harrow game, 'played in a rough and ready fashion'.[159] The ball could not be handled except by 'fair catch'. The catcher then called three yards, and could make the best of a free-kick by punt or drop. 'Dribbling', 'charging' (of man as well as ball) and 'scrimmages' were the other features of the game, Yonge vividly recollecting 'two seething and perspiring groups of humanity all mixed up together, with the ball – invisible – somewhere in the centre'. Yet goals were still apparently scored, sometimes by a cleverly judged kick over the bridge and against the Close wall goal but 'more often carried by a combined weight and rush'. Yonge admitted that this rough game inevitably resulted in torn clothes and damaged limbs, yet from the safe distance of 50 years he recognised its great value in the training of character, and not least in the preparing of Old Herefordians for 'colonial hardships':

> Still though not strictly scientific, and an object no doubt of derision to modern football[ers], yet it was a good, manly and wholesome game, and helped as much as anything to foster that hardiness and carelessness of personal discomfort and pain, which was one of our proud traditions ...

Although Dick Jordan's boatshed became for Cathedral boys of the 1860s like 'an informal club', even for non-oarsmen (of whom Yonge was one), there was no competitive rowing at the school. Boys needed special leave before they were allowed out on the river, which was not forthcoming unless they could swim – and there was no encouragement of swimming. The 'heroic exploits' of H.F. Baxter OH of Sibdon Castle, a university oar

157. For Deakin's 'gallant' play for the school, in a match in Yonge's last year against the Lugwardine Courtiers, see *HJ*, 23 Nov. 1867, p.5.

158. The playground measurements are from TNA, ED 27/1606, Leach's report, 25 July 1889.

159. For Harrow football: Tyerman, pp.213, 471-72. The 'Rules of Football as Played at Hereford Cathedral School, 1868' were printed in *TH*, NS LI (March 1906), pp.16-17. Although handling was allowed in order to stop and place the ball, it was mainly a kicking game. As it was to be played on a ground 100 yards long and of unlimited breadth, with a 12-yard wide goal, the rules were perhaps designed for early matches on Barrack Field (Harold Street).

before Yonge's time, were often mentioned but there was no recognised school crew in this period. Neither was the school allowed to compete in the recently established city regatta, although the few boys who rowed during Yonge's day could pull 'a very decent four' up to 'Sugwas boat' and back.[160]

If rowing at the school was in its infancy in this decade, the annual athletic sports evolved from small beginnings to an event that was recognisably modern by the time Yonge had left. In Yonge's earliest years, the sports day was simply called 'the races'. These consisted of six or so 'flat races' which gradually increased in length according to the ages of the participants. There were no distance races or jumping events or throwing competitions. Money prizes were based on the size of the individual entrance fee, the younger pupils paying a smaller fee. As the winner of each event also collected the combined fees for that age group, the winning of a race – as Yonge did in his 100 yards 'nursery stakes' – 'added appreciably to one's modest pocket money'. By the late 1860s, Hereford had followed the lead of the bigger public schools and things changed appreciably. A committee was formed to draw up the programme; the number of events was increased; and the boys had started canvassing the city and neighbourhood for subscriptions, receiving a 'very gratifying response' – not least from hopeful candidates during the 1866 general election.[161] Sports day itself, too, had been made much more of an occasion. It was held on the Barrack Ground (Harold Street) on a well-marked course. There was a committee tent, and the militia band accompanied the proceedings, which were watched by a good many spectators, the lady element being 'especially strong'. Each competitor ran in his own colours displayed as 'a scarf of ribbon over one shoulder and passing under the other'. Money prizes had been replaced by cups or 'pewters', which had 'made a brave display for a few days [before-hand] in Mr Besant's window in High Street' before being transferred to the committee tent for show on the day itself. But sports day was not yet a totally serious event. Yonge was tripped up by the Revd John Goss' black retriever on the final hurdle of one of his races, and little notice was taken of records – the exception being the 16-year-old A.W.L. Brodie's exhibition cricket ball throw of over 111 yards in 1866, a national schoolboy record that Yonge claimed stood for more than 40 years.[162]

---

160. Richard Rivers Felix ('Dick') Jordan, who died aged 62 on 27 December 1887, was in charge of the boathouse for 40 years. The early regattas of the period were held on 8 July 1856, 18 June 1859, 27 August 1860 and 27 August 1861 – the first one organised by the newly constituted Hereford rowing club. An HCS crew did not compete in this city regatta until the late-nineteenth century. See Eisel, pp.135-41; *TH*, NS V (Feb. 1888); and the unpublished typescript: 'The Hereford Rowing Club: Its History and Development', pp.1-4, 32, 37. And for Henry Fleming Baxter's undergraduate rowing feats: Crook, pp.268, 284.

161. During this election, when Sir Richard Baggallay was one of the two members for Hereford who was returned, a number of candidates were approached, including a naval captain staying at the Green Dragon, who gave one guinea. According to Yonge, Hereford at that time had a reputation 'perhaps not wholly undeserved, of being a constituency which was not altogether insensible to persuasion of a very practical nature'.

162. John Goss was a vicar choral from March 1853, and as a disputatious Custos of the College (1873-77), he entered into a fierce public denunciation of the Chapter in 1875, sparked by their appointment of A.J. Capel to a minor canonry. He was also vicar of St John the Baptist in the cathedral. The large window in the north-east transept is in his memory. Aylmer and Tiller, pp.320, 426; *HT* letters, 27 March p.8, 31 March p.8, 1 May p.8, 29 May p.5, 5 June 1875, p.8. Brodie – whose throw of over 102 yards in the 1867 athletic sports was also recorded (*HJ*, 28 Sept. 1867, p.5) – was the nephew of Frank Baker (note 155 above), another prodigious thrower of a

Yonge described other pursuits, pastimes and customs, which were an integral part of life for him and his contemporaries in the 1860s. 'Prisoner's base' and 'Blackthorn' – involving two sides charging at each other on the hop – were among the other playground games; and marbles, bought from Jones' stationery and toy shop in Broad Street, playing with catapults – 'the bane and holy terror of all the grooms and gardeners who occupied premises at the back of Castle Street and nicely within range' – and pea-shooting were all popular. Tree climbing provided a pleasant diversion, except when the boy concerned was caught by Bishop Hampden, as happened to Yonge's little brother when retrieving cricket and fives balls from the college roof.[163]

Fights could be even more intimidating. Yonge recorded that in his day the boys – following the Rugby School tradition as portrayed in *Tom Brown*[164] – did 'a good deal of this sort of thing', he himself admitting to two serious fights during his school career. These fights usually happened in the 'lobby', formerly the vicars' kitchen, which had a stone floor with a 'handy' wash basin nearby, but sometimes fights would occur on open ground – as on that Sunday in the school yard, when two Sixth-formers broke ranks as the boys were pairing up before the cathedral service, and went at each other hammer and tongs for several minutes before Woollam could restore order. Yonge remembered that both boys were disfigured but did not record the further outcome of that particular bloody duel. Group fighting against local boys was not uncommon. A senior boy, like C.A.S. Nicholl, with 'a neck like a bull and thighs and sinews to match' would tackle half a dozen 'town cads' in a row by himself.[165] Running fights, too, happened when local children pinched the school football which had been booted ('sometimes I fear on purpose') into 'Quay Lane', and then hurried off with their prize down Castle Street towards St Owens:

> We were only too ready and after it. Over the wall in a trice went the whole body of players, cheering and yelling like a lot of lunatics we chased our prey ... Nor can I remember an occasion when we were bested or failed to recover our quarry.

Yonge also recorded 'some old school customs' from the 1860s. Although 29 May had long since ceased to be observed in Anglican churches as a day of thanksgiving,[166] every pupil was expected to wear on the morning of that day a sprig of oak, in memory of the Restoration two centuries earlier. The Advent 'celebrations' on the three last Sundays of the winter 'half' were traditions peculiar to boarders. They became known as 'Rag Sunday',

---

cricket ball. According to Yonge, a Denstone College boy broke Brodie's record with a throw of 113 yards in the spring of 1909.

163. Dr Renn Dickson Hampden was Bishop of Hereford, 1848-68. Yonge's brother (note 156) was cautioned and then given a 'douceur'.

164. See Newsome (1961), pp.36-37, 212-15, for the influence of Thomas Hughes' novel (first published in 1857) on the development of 'manliness' in English public schools.

165. Nicholl's monumental cricketing feats were periodically reported in the local press about this time, as in *HT*, 27 Sept. 1856, p.4; *HJ*, 11 Aug. 1858, p.8; 1 Sept. 1858, p.8; 21 Sept. 1859, p.8; 22 Aug. 1860, p.3.

166. However, the 29 May service – together with those of 30 January and 5 November, commemorating Charles I's execution and the Gunpowder plot/William of Orange's landing – was not finally removed from the Book of Common Prayer until 1859.

when the boys carried a holed pocket handkerchief, which was duly flourished on the way to church; 'Cock Hat Sunday', when mortar boards or college caps were worn at an angle, 'the more exaggerated or more "cocked" ... the better'; and 'Kick and Stamp Sunday', when each boarder put on his heaviest boots and stamped as hard as he could, as he processed (in order of seniority) to the cathedral via the north porch or through the College Cloisters. On the last Sunday (as term neared its end) it was incumbent on the boys 'as a point of honour to administer a good hearty kick to the unoffending cathedral doors on leaving the sacred edifice'. One year when the door kicks came to the Dean's attention, the boys had to swear a solemn oath to the Headmaster that the offence would never be repeated.[167]

Yonge mentioned other occasions when events in the city during the 1860s impinged on his life as a cathedral schoolboy. He attended the Three Choirs Festival of 1860, although as we shall see, he did not benefit as much from Hereford's musical life as Fred Weatherly. Perhaps Yonge got more out of the May Fair, or (as he later called it) the yearly 'Saturnalia'. Even though it was out of bounds and the route to Widemarsh was 'mapped out afresh' for the fair's duration, the boys still went via Broad Street on their way to cricket practice, despite the difficulty of walking through the crowds, 'for that thoroughfare was scarcely broad enough for the booths and shows and sight-seers'. Yonge remembered seeing a 'savage' outside one of the booths who 'regaled himself with raw liver ... a disgusting exhibition'.

Yonge and some of his fellows also went out of bounds and skipped morning prep, to view one of the last public executions in Hereford. He did not have time to see the actual execution, but he recollected scaling the wall to see the gallows and 'the huge black erection on the top of the gaol gateway'. He also witnessed the gathering crowds, 'the ribald and unseemly jests', the 'last speech and confession being hawked about', the street preachers 'improving the occasion', and Mr Calcraft – the public hangman with his 'huge white beard' – adjusting the rope on the scaffold. Had the truants been caught, he mused in later life, they all would have been 'swished' ('and had richly deserved it') but they returned safely to school without being missed, although Yonge himself had a poor appetite for breakfast that morning and 'several ghastly dreams for nights after'.[168]

What does Yonge's invaluable memoir reveal about education at the Cathedral School in the 1860s?

As Yonge himself observed 50 years later, it was a limited education compared to that given in the early twentieth century, 'possibly not so much in scholastic and university distinctions', but compared with the 'higher tone and discipline and the gentlemanly demeanour and bearing of the boys' in more modern times. Yonge also recognised that in his day the curriculum was narrow and the teaching restricted:

167. The incident possibly took place in late 1867, during Yonge's final year at school, in which case Dean Herbert, who had recently been installed, was obviously intent on making his mark.

168. The details are essentially the same as those given by Weatherly (pp.243-45), although he adds that the year was 1866 (two years before public executions were abolished), that the man hanged was one Jem Hope of Allensmore and that the executioner was dressed in a black frock coat and silk hat. On a later visit to Hereford in 1913, Weatherly met the warder, who was also on the platform with the executioner that day, in Pritchard's (the school tailor's) shop.

> There was hardly any individual teaching or provision for a boy's natural leanings outside Classics and Mathematics. If you fancied anything else then, for the most part you had to puzzle it out for yourself. There was not even the slightest pretence or apology for a school library in my day. The consequence – and a baneful one it was to many a one besides the writer – was a resort to the circulating libraries whence much rubbish was eagerly devoured.

Moreover, the masters' duties were not extensive beyond the classroom. In a telling comment, Yonge observed that although the drill sergeant kept a friendly eye on the boys at Widemarsh, there was no 'espionage' or 'bossing', and in the playground duty masters were unknown. Had it been otherwise, he claimed that his contemporaries 'would not ... have put up with it for a moment'. Much of the out-of-class supervision, therefore, rested on the shoulders of the monitors, a system which according to Yonge had been copied from Rugby School, although he noted that 'at Hereford ... the monitors had not quite so much power or responsibility as the Rugby praepostors'.[169] The monitors were often young men – 'in stature if not wisdom' – in their late teens, resplendent in their tailcoats and 'incipient whiskers', who had stayed on at school to claim the valuable university entrance prizes, and as such were objects of genuine hero worship among the younger boys. They acted in pairs and a week at a time, their chief duties being keeping order during the boarders' daily preparation times – an hour in the early morning (7-8am) and a period in the late afternoons – ensuring that there was no bullying in the dormitories, and general supervising outside school. Woollam gave them strong support 'and anything like systematic disobedience to our delegated authority was sure to meet with condign punishment'. Even though these responsibilities were considerable, there were few privileges, apart from the fresh morning loaf and butter for the duty monitors, 'a welcome change from the ordinary thick bread and butter which in those days was the sole breakfast menu'. Nevertheless, Yonge reckoned that the monitors generally carried out their duties 'wisely and well'.

For Fred Weatherly, 'it was the music of the place for which my thanksgiving is deepest'. The standard of singing of the cathedral choir at the Sunday services and at Evensong, which he attended if he 'could squeeze in half an hour between football and tea', he never heard bettered 'in a wide experience of collegiate music'. And then there were the delights of the concerts – those of the philharmonic society and the three Hereford festivals he attended during his eight years at school – for which Weatherly saved up a good deal of his pocket money. There may not have been so much music taught in the school itself, but he remembered with fondness the singing classes of 'old Burville, who sang alto in the choir and tenor or bass when he was teaching us', from whom he learnt 'the good old glees and madrigals'. Outside class, the boys lustily roared out such songs as 'Trank-a-dillo', 'The soldier of the line' and 'Three jolly post boys'.

Weatherly was well grounded in classical literature. Like Yonge, he had experienced the great benefit of Woollam's learning – 'a man of high culture and literary tastes', from whom 'I first learnt to love my Virgil, Horace, Juvenal, Euripides and Homer' – but he also read extensively beyond the ancient texts, buying novels 'at a penny a volume' from

169. See Newsome (1961), pp.34, 41-42, on Thomas Arnold's re-modelling of the prefectorial system at Rugby.

Jakeman's bookshop. The works of Marryat, Harrison Ainsworth, G.P.R. James, James Grant, Dickens and Walter Scott, were 'devoured with ... enthusiasm', as was the poetry of Tennyson, Byron and Longfellow, together with 'the poetical books' of the Bible and Shakespeare. These works were his 'playtime reading', for apart from the ancient Classics, he had no-one like Miss Fanny Crisp, the schoolmistress at his former Bristol dame's school, to take him through 'the wonderland of books'. It was through Weatherly's own initiative, too, that 'theatricals' were started at Hereford, Woollam stipulating that only classical plays should be performed – so a burlesque of a Greek tragedy was followed by Hamlet and then Macbeth, when Weatherly played the leading thane. It was in this production that the paisley shawl borrowed from Miss Curtis ('our beloved matron') fell from Macbeth's shoulders onto a stage light and was badly burnt, the actors giving her a cameo brooch in recompense. Such cultural pursuits were largely of the boys' making, although it was the two official 'exceedingly doleful' elegies (in both Latin and English), composed on the death of Dean Dawes, the English version of which was published in the *Hereford Times*, that first gave Weatherly a taste for the versification for which he was to become world renowned in later life.[170]

Fig. 5.5 Fred Weatherly in his sixties. He was the most prolific songwriter of the late Victorian and Edwardian age.

Weatherly described other aspects of school and Hereford life. He was something of an artist at school and at the age of 12 won a Kensington School of Art prize, Bustin, the drawing-master having taught him enough 'to appreciate a good picture ... and make respectable copies'. Although he could not swim and was by no means a sportsman, he enjoyed rowing[171] and took pride in the

170. See Weatherly's *ODNB* entry (by John D. Pickles); and *HT*, 23 March 1867, ('What means the pealing of this solemn knell/ Thrilling the lonely student's cloistered cell? ...') for the elegy. More than 1,500 of Weatherly's songs were published, including *Nancy Lee* (1876), *The Holy City* (1892), *Danny Boy* (1912) and *Roses of Picardy* (1916).

171. Weatherly 'earned some considerable fame as being a main instrument in creating the cox-swainless fours' at Henley in 1868. See his obituary notice in *Brazen Nose*, vol. V (Nov. 1928), no. I, p.12; and the detailed account in Weatherly, pp.69-72.

exploits of the school and county XIs, 'of whom so many of our old boys were playing members'. He also remembered the cricket out-matches – 'to which in coach and four we went so gaily' – to Allensmore, as well as those against St Michael's Tenbury, played through the good offices of Sir Frederick Ouseley, that school's founder and the cathedral's Precentor. Weatherly corroborated Yonge's story of the boys' truanting to see the hanging at Hereford gaol, and authenticated his account of the illicit visits to the city fair, adding that they had also broken school rules by entering the fighting tents and fat ladies' booths. This was once accomplished by bribing the driver of a steam roundabout five shillings to keep it going for half an hour with the supervising junior master on board, 'and while poor Mr White was being whirled round till his face was the colour of his name, we saw the fighting in a neighbouring tent'. Above all, Weatherly provided further evidence of 'the long hard days of work, undreamt of in these easier times' for all pupils at the school. For the boarders it was two-and-a-half hours of preparation daily (7-8am and 7-8.30pm); and for everyone, six hours of schooling (9-12am and 2-5pm) Monday to Saturday, except for the half-holidays on Wednesday and Saturday afternoons. And this unremitting regime was conducted over two long 'halves', each of 20 weeks duration.[172]

Nevertheless, Weatherly, Yonge and their fellows had a degree of freedom in the 1860s, estimated by Woollam himself as some 28 hours per week for the boarders, that would have surprised even those boys who entered the school a generation or two later. Although cricket was almost universally popular, games were not compulsory. Neither was drill, for which parents paid 5 shillings per term as an optional extra.[173] The long daily breaks and the Wednesday and Saturday half-holidays, together with the special holidays not infrequently asked for by cathedral or other dignitaries,[174] gave ample time for other pursuits. These included walks in the country, provided permission had been granted by the duty master and the route had been specified, as well as 'some boating and bathing' and winter boxing ('with gloves') for the boarders. During the two hour mid-day break, most day boys also went home for lunch.[175]

Indeed, apart for the occasional local match, there were no competitive sports fixtures against other schools. Nor was there a gymnasium or a school playing field so the incomparable 'sward' of Widemarsh Common, the militia's Barrack Field and, above all, the school yard playground (with a small covered play area for boarders in wet weather) were the pupils' sporting grounds.[176] The Wye also provided a good reach for rowing, but that sport was in its infancy at HCS and its football was a throw-back to an earlier age. Although

172. In 1865 Woollam estimated that the full working time for boarders was 43 hours per week, and that the regular hours for the whole school (day and boarders) were 29 hours each week, the 14 hour differential being accounted for by prep time and Sunday lessons. HCA, 1537, schedule B, Woollam's draft answers to the Endowed Schools' Commission, nos 27 and 28.

173. For the boarders' week and drill, *ibid.,* nos 72, 77.

174. Both the Bishops (Hampden and Atlay) and Deans (Dawes and Herbert) in Yonge's time were apparently good for 'an extra half'. Weatherly relates elsewhere how Woollam granted the school an additional holiday, following the mistaken sighting of 'Prince Alfred' in the cathedral one Sunday morning. *TH*, no. 12 (Oct. 1883), pp.32-35; HARC, M 90/1, p.19, cutting 26 May 1900.

175. HCA, 1537, schedule B return, nos 5, 73, 77 and 78.

176. *Ibid.,* nos 71, 76.

the athletic sports were beginning to be organised on a more competitive basis, and school colours had begun to be worn at least in cricket, the 'cult of athleticism', which is such a marked feature of public school life by the end of the century, was not much practised in Hereford in the 1860s. A small, sensitive and bookish boy like Weatherly could flourish just as well as a sportsman like Yonge. It is significant, nonetheless, that Woollam could inform the Endowed Schools' Commission in 1865 that former pupils at Oxford and Cambridge were 'often members of the college eleven or eight' and that 'one within the last few years was a member of the university eight'.[177]

HCS in the 1860s, was a tough school but one that fostered a sense of independence, initiative and self-reliance among its pupils. Corporal punishment (caning as opposed to 'la boxe') was officially administered by the Headmaster – but only infrequently, for 'moral' offences or rowdy behaviour, and in private – and unofficially and rarely by a senior boy 'for some very serious offence against school morality and traditions'.[178] For the most part, however, the monitors do not appear to have abused their position, and there seems to have been little bullying or 'fagging', although fighting, as we have seen, was commonplace.[179] Above all, Christian values were underpinned by the ordained staff and accepted by the pupils themselves, many of whom were sons of clergymen. The school day opened and closed with prayer. In addition, the boarders attended morning and evening prayer daily in the Headmaster's house, and had two extra Sunday periods for reading the Bible and learning the catechism, as well as the two cathedral Sunday services.[180]

Yonge realised the limitations of aspects of his education as he looked back over 50 years, but he also recognised that the school regime of his day inculcated a 'brave and hardy manliness' among its charges. These included some fine sportsmen, whose 'names stood as high in the class list as they did between the wickets and on the river', as well as in later years from among his own contemporaries, a number of notable Old Herefordians – not least, Fred Weatherly himself.[181]

Yonge's and Weatherly's memoirs, then, give us a fascinating insight into a boy's life during the 1860s. As we have observed, however, there are no equivalent sources for Rudd's headmastership. For his few years, we are dependent on fragmentary local accounts of school activities – in particular, newspaper reports of the boys' prowess, or otherwise, at sport during the early 1870s, when games were taken more seriously and regular inter-school matches become more prevalent.

---

177. *Ibid.*, no. 77. The rowing 'Blue' was H.F. Baxter. See above, pp.222-23 and note 160.

178. HCA, 1537, schedule B return, nos 53-55. Officially, the assistant masters could only punish through impositions and detentions (nos 53, 56), although, as Yonge explained, this did not stop them 'boxing ears'. Yonge remembered only two 'strappings' by senior boys during the whole of his school career. *TH*, NS LXI (July 1909), p.31

179. *Ibid.*, nos 59-61. It is significant that neither Yonge nor Weatherly mentioned 'fagging'.

180. *Ibid.*, nos 46, 50, 51. A school register, 1858-66, indicates that on average one fifth of new entrants came from clerical families. See below, p.275, note 147, for the number of boys in a later period whose fathers were clergymen.

181. Weatherly and a number of sportsmen apart, Yonge mentioned John Spencer Phillips, later chairman of Lloyds Bank, 'genial' Joe Carless, Hereford Town Clerk (1868-1909), and John Taylor Lingen, son of the school doctor who in 1870 became 20th wrangler at Cambridge. (*HT*, 5 Feb. 1870, p.7) Weatherly (p.37) added the name of Watkins, who 'became the Registrar of one of the county courts in Monmouthshire'.

Cricket, as we have seen, was firmly established in the previous decade as the pre-eminent Cathedral School game, but there were further developments in the following decade. The school matches of the earlier period may best be described as social cricket against local sides – apart from the match between the 'Old Collegians' and 'The Present' which can be traced back as far as 1860[182] – with the boys' team invariably being bolstered by the addition of a master or two to even up the contest. Schools were occasionally 'challenged' by the boys themselves and school colours were worn for these contests, but no regular inter-school matches were played as we would understand them. A change occurred in the early 1870s. Although social cricket continued – as in the away match played at Staunton on Wye in June 1870 against Portway Cricket Club where it was recorded that the batting of C.F. Eagles and J.E. Deakin was 'decidedly not altered for the better' after their partaking of 'dinner' at the local hostelry – things were to change over the following years. The 1872 season was significant with the inaugural matches against Gloucester and Worcester Cathedral Schools (as they then were). Fixtures against 'the New College, Brecon' and Monmouth were added in 1873 and 1874 respectively.[183] In these years, the XI's complete results, as well as the school batting averages (headed in 1873 by E.L. Browne at 17.2) were published in the *Hereford Times* for the first time.[184] One important reason for the school's improvement in cricket and for the growth of a more competitive fixture list was the Revd T. Hayes Belcher's arrival as an assistant master and vicar choral in January 1872. Belcher was a formidable cricketer, who had gained an Oxford 'Blue' in 1870, and in the September return match of 1872 against Gloucester took 18 wickets (bowling round arm) and scored a 50. Belcher's match heralded the end of teachers playing in school games, although this was not the case with club fixtures, as with the school XI on 26 July 1873, which included the examiner H.M. Dymock (bowled Baskerville, 0) as well as three masters, in the game against Wyeside Wanderers.[185]

Football, the main winter game, was less well established than cricket, the laws of the summer game having been codified by the late eighteenth century. As the *Hereford Times* correspondent noted as late as November 1872, 'love of football is making rapid progress throughout the country and perhaps the only thing to give it equal popularity with cricket ... is a settled and general code of rules', despite 'two excellent codes' having been drawn up by the Rugby Union and the Football Association.[186] As we have seen, the school had long played a game akin to Harrow football, and it was only gradually in this decade that it adopted the Union rules. In the early 1870s, inter-school football fixtures were slowly established. A 15-a-side away game against Worcester Cathedral School on 29 November 1871 was lost by one goal, but 15 months later a 12 a-side contest against Gloucester

182. *HT*, 11 Aug. 1860, p.3. 'The Present' (which included Mr Dixon) lost by 17 runs in a two-innings match.

183. For the Portway game and the inter-school matches, see the *HT* match reports of 11 June 1870, p.2; 11 May 1872, p.8; 15 June 1872, p.8; 7 June 1873, p.3; 6 June 1874, p.3.

184. *Ibid.*, 4 Oct. 1873, p.3. In the following season, when only six matches were played, his brother, A.B. Browne, headed the boy batting averages with 16.4. *Ibid.*, 7 Nov. 1874, p.3.

185. *Ibid.*, 21 Sept. 1872, p.2; 2 Aug. 1873, p.3.

186. *Ibid.*, 2 Nov. 1872, p.8, report on the match between 'Old Hereford Collegians' against the rest of the Hereford Club. The Rugby Football and 'Association' codes were first differentiated in 1863.

Cathedral School at the Barrack Ground 'ended in a most decisive victory for Hereford, the latter winning by two goals ... and ten touch-downs to nothing'.[187] The Barrack Ground was the scene of other notable encounters against adults as on 10 March 1870, 'when the play was spirited and severe, the four goals [three by the school] occupying about two hours' in another 12-a-side match against the city club; 22 February 1872, when a game against the old boys resulted in a victory for the first time in their favour; and 27 February 1873, when the 'collegians' defended their line successfully for more than an hour in a return game (this time 11-a-side) against the Hereford club, before the opposing captain (Frederick Wilding, himself an old boy) kicked the only goal of the afternoon. The three masters who had played in that match were noticeable by their absences in school matches. Less than two years later in the game against the city club, it was reported in the *Hereford Times* that several boys had shown 'form worthy of any public school in England'.[188]

No school fixtures are recorded in this period for any other type of game but there were other sports to occupy a boy's time. As we have seen, athletic sports had been held annually on the Barrack Ground before Rudd's time. Indeed, by 1868 they had become an 'institution' which had 'within a very short time attained an amazing popularity', several years before the city had first established its own 'open amateur athletic meeting'.[189] So in this period, it was simply a matter for the boys' committee, which organised the event, to build upon the pattern set by its predecessors by adding additional events. These included (in 1871) a 'Siamese race ... introduced for amusement', and putting the 14lb weight, where a seven yard rather than the official seven feet run-up was allowed. A local reporter recorded one such meeting on a warm day in late October 1873: 'the young gladiators were arrayed in their handsome costumes of mauve, blue, serge, pink or whatever colour it was under which they had resolved to enter the lists to contend for athletic honours'; the 14 pieces of silver-ware, pencil cases, ornamental articles and other prizes made an imposing display in the tent; and the Herefordshire militia band ('by the kind permission of Captain Doughty') which played for the many visitors present, and not least the ladies 'accommodated with seats on the far side of the enclosure', throughout the afternoon. This 'gay and animated picture' provided the essential back-drop to the athletic events. The following year the weather was not so benign, the boys being made blue by the 'keen and bracing wind'. Despite the failure of entrants to show up for some jumping events, the races were popular enough with 33 boys running the handicapped mile, 26 the quarter-mile and 220 yards consolation races and 27 the strangers' quarter-mile handicap. The competitors do not seem to have been unduly disturbed by the antics of a pony 'career[ing] about the field in the wildest manner' during one of the events.[190]

Rowing in the 1860s, as our memorialists made clear, was no more than a recreational activity; a few years later, it had become a serious school (although not yet inter-school) sport. 1870 appears to have been the key year for this metamorphosis. How far this had

187. *Berrow's Worcester Journal*, 2 Dec. 1871; *HT*, 15 March 1873, p.2.

188. *Ibid.*, 12 March 1870, p.7; 24 Feb. 1872, p.8; 1 March 1873, p.2; 14 Nov. 1874, p.3. The HCS team in the 1874 encounter included J.A. Bevan, for whom see below, p.263 and note 98.

189. *Ibid.*, 26 Sept. 1868, p.7; and 4 May 1872, p.8; 3 May 1873, p.3, for reports of the first two Hereford meetings, which included HCS runners for the junior events.

190. *Ibid.*, 25 Oct. 1873, p.3; 22 Oct. 1874, p.7. See also the report for 14 Oct. 1871, p.14.

been inspired by other school races – such as the four-oared race between Shrewsbury School and Cheltenham College, in its seventh year by the time it was raced at Hereford on 12 June 1870[191] – is not known. However, we do know that the famous varsity boat race provided the immediate inspiration for Hereford's own 'Oxford' versus 'Cambridge' challenge, which started in 1870 more than 40 years after the first university boat race of 1829.[192] On 8 April 1871, the second year of the Hereford race, the *Hereford Times* gave a full report of the event:

> The crews belonging to this [Cathedral] School have, for some time past, been practising for a race which took place Saturday last, the same day as the great race between the Oxford and Cambridge crews on the Thames ... At 3.30, the time appointed for the race, the bank of the river about 'Jordan's Boating House' became pretty well lined with spectators, amongst whom we could see here and there the 'square board' of the young collegiates, who were eagerly looking on, and who wore a light or dark blue favour as the badge of the party to which they belonged. The race was from Hunderton to Jordan's ... The Oxford led nearly all the way, till within about half-a-dozen yards of the winning post, where the Cambridge made a spurt and came in ahead by about a foot ... Last year, as in the real race, the 'Hereford' Cambridge were [also] victorious, but the Oxford are not disheartened. They are quite content to 'wait for the turn of the tide'.[193]

Fig. 5.6 Jordan's boatyard around 1870, when rowing began to be taken seriously at HCS as a competitive sport.

191. *Ibid.,* 18 June 1870, p.2, where it was described as 'one of the finest contests we have ever had the pleasure of witnessing on the Wye', despite the disputed result and the collapse of Hughes, the number two Shrewsbury oar.

192. *TH,* no. 8 (Sept. 1881), p.103.

193. *Ibid.,* 8 April 1871, p.2.

It would have pleased the Headmaster that that particular tide only turned once under Rudd in 1872, after which 'the light blues' were victorious in the three successive years 1873-75. By the latter year, the race, like the athletics, had become something of a school institution and the focal point of a regatta.[194] So began an annual tradition which lasted until 1913.

There are only fragments of evidence to suggest how else a boy might occupy his time outside class. Fives was still popular, judging by the Dean and Chapter's 3 guinea donation in June 1874 towards the repair of the school court.[195] No doubt the other playground games of the 1860s continued to be played.[196] Drill was still provided by a militia sergeant, as was singing by Burville. Every year, the boys had an opportunity to perform their glees and part songs at the summer prize-giving, which took place annually in late July. At these gatherings, classical, French, Shakespearian recitations, and occasionally modern enactments – as in 1871 when a scene from *Nicholas Nickleby* was performed, no doubt in belated recognition of the author's death the previous year – were also given.[197] The cultural highlight of the school year, however, was the College Hall concert at the end of the Christmas term. The hall, seasonally decorated with wreaths and festoons of holly and ivy, was always filled to capacity and beyond. The best choristers and one or two masters and vicars choral – not least, the Reverend W.D.V. Duncombe, whose fine baritone voice continued to adorn these concerts for another 40 years – sang their sentimental pieces. But above all, the singing class lustily roared out such choruses as Pittman's 'Roast Beef of Old England', 'College v. Hereford Football Match' (to a tune by Monk), Hatton's 'Robin Hood', the 'Fishermen's Chorus' from Auber's 'Massaniello', and perhaps more sensitively in December 1871, following the Prince of Wales' recovery, Brinley Richards' 'God bless the Prince of Wales'. Encores were not unusual. In 1873, it was even alleged that they were given 'to prevent the audience bringing the old hall down with their applause'. That year, too, a band of 20 old boys and friends – it is significant that no boys were listed among the principal instrumentalists – played the cantata from Cummings' 'Fairy Ring' and the overture from Bishop's 'Guy Mannering'. This was trumped the following year with a band of over 30 and a school chorus of nearly 80 singing (sometimes expressively) selections from Sir W. Sterndale Bennett's 1858 composition the 'May Queen', which occupied the first part of the programme.[198]

So the period ends with good evidence of the school's corporate spirit. The year before Rudd departs, the external examiner had noted that competition ran high 'throughout most of the forms', a competitiveness which the boys clearly transferred to activities outside

194. *Ibid.*, 5 April 1873, p.3; 4 April 1874, p.3; 27 March 1875, p.3. By the latter date the two to one odds on a 'Cambridge' victory were justified by their three length win.

195. HCA, 7031/22, p.94, 25 June 1874; 7105/8, fo 149v, payment no. 68.

196. See above, p.224.

197. See, for example, the programmes performed in the early 1870s from these reports: *HT*, 23 July 1870, p.3; 22 July 1871, p.8; 27 July 1872, p.7; and 25 July 1874, p.8. The prize-giving was a month later than it had been, following Rudd's introduction of a three-term year in 1870.

198. The above account has been composed from notices in the *HT*, 18 Dec. 1869, p.6; 23 Dec. 1871, p.8; 21 Dec. 1872, p.8; 27 Dec. 1873, p.8; 26 Dec. 1874, p.6. At prize-giving in 1872, the Prince of Wales' illness became the subject of a little homily by Dean Herbert on the sacredness of family life. *Ibid.*, 27 July 1872, p.7.

the classroom. Nowhere is this spirit more in evidence than on the games field. The growth of the mid-Victorian manly ideal is well-illustrated by Canon Musgrave's speech before he presented the trophies to the winning athletes at the school's 1867 sports-day. After emphasising that his Chapter colleagues were as much interested in those games which contributed 'to the exercise and maintenance of a sound and healthy body' as the school's 'mental improvement', he is reported as having made the following remarks: 'He thought we English in a great measure might attribute our vigour and healthiness to the union of the intellect and manliness in our character in general and from the success and encouragement at our public schools on all occasions of games and sports requiring much bodily exertion'.[199] The age of 'godliness and manliness' had dawned.

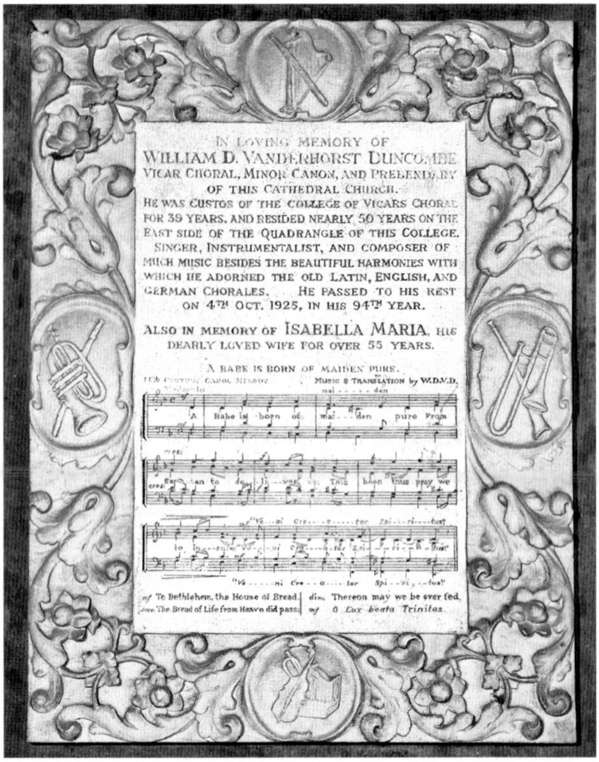

Fig. 5.7 Memorial tablet to William D. Vanderhurst Duncombe, depicting his carol 'A Babe is Born of Maiden Pure'. His singing was a feature of the school's Christmas concerts for 40 years.

199. *HJ*, 14 Sept. 1867, p.5. The trophies were described as 'a dozen electro-plated mugs', which Musgrave joked might have been intended 'as tokens of the national product of the county – cider'. C.C. Prichard, F.E. Weatherly and W. Crouch – OHs who had all won Somerset awards – presented three of them.

Chapter 6

The Transformation of the Old Endowed School, 1875-1913

Vernon Yonge was right to observe in 1909 that his school of the 1860s had changed out of all recognition, and 'that in many respects the old school stands on a distinctly higher platform than it did in years gone by'. Indeed, an old boy of Rudd's day returning to Hereford on the eve of the First World War, after an interval of 40 years, would have well appreciated the alterations which had been made to both cathedral and school in the intervening years. Had he been standing outside the west door, he would hardly have recognised the cathedral, with its restored cloister range and library (opened in 1897) and the massive 'vociferous' composition of Oldrid Scott's new west front (completed in 1908), which had replaced (depending on his taste) 'the elegant simplicity' or 'the wretched caricature' of Wyatt's late-eighteenth century design.[1] And viewing his old school from Castle Street at the east end of the Close, that same Old Herefordian (for by 1913 old boys had long been designated as such rather than as 'Old Collegians')[2] would certainly not have recognised his *alma mater.*

Physically, there had been huge changes. A new school house had been built, together with a library and specialist classrooms in the place of the old College rooms; a separate preparatory school, run as the Headmaster's private business, had been set up at the back of Harley Court; the elegant residence which was then Harley House and is now Number 1 Castle Street had been acquired for the school through the generosity of Canon Capes; and in its garden a laboratory, carpentry shed and two fives courts had been built and the corner cottage had been established as the new sanatorium in place of Foley Lodge. A mile or so up river, a games field had been created at 'Wyeside', which replaced the Barrack Field and Widemarsh Common as the school's home ground.

The 1913 school would have had a different 'feel' from the one of the early 1870s. It is true that the number of pupils did not expand as Dean Herbert had clearly anticipated at

1. The quotations are from Aylmer and Tiller, pp.166-67, 281-84 and the authorities there cited; and (for the last phrase on Wyatt), *HT,* 28 Dec. 1872, p.8.

2. The first use of the name 'Old Herefordian' I have come across occurs as early as 1875: *HT*, 25 Dec. 1875, p.5, with regard to the return of old boys to the Christmas concert of that year.

the beginning of the period. Indeed, the number of boys of July 1875 (112) was only regularly exceeded for the first few years of the new Headmaster's tenure, and despite the new buildings and growing reputation of the school, pupil numbers fell in the depression years of the last two decades of the century. Nevertheless, over the period as a whole, the number of boarders increased as a proportion of the school community. Correspondingly, among the assistant masters, the proportion of ordained clergy dramatically declined, although the Headmaster was still in Holy Orders.[3] The curriculum, too, changed with the belated introduction of Science and the establishment of French as core subjects taught by full time assistant masters, which enabled HCS to be added to the Board of Education's list of 'efficient' secondary schools by 1908. The emergence of these 'modern' subjects also meant that Classics, Divinity and Mathematics no longer dominated a cathedral schoolboy's timetable as they had done. Similarly, the methods of examining altered. Before the turn of the century, boys were tested in a range of subjects by national examining boards rather than having to run the gauntlet every July of the tests and *viva voce* examinations set by carefully chosen examiners in the three traditional disciplines. And by the Edwardian period, a pupil's 'free' time had been fiercely regulated, as Yonge indicated, in a way that his father and grandfather would have found intolerable – through the organisation of compulsory games, an officer training corps and various school societies. The devising of a school crest, based on the Chapter seal, and the making of a school shield; the intricate displays of the '*floreat*' on school occasions and the boys' proud wearing of dark blue and gold as the Hereford colours in inter-school matches and races; and the adoption of a school song, written by F.E. Weatherly for the 1881 'anniversary' celebrations – all indicate that the school itself became a more distinct entity and more readily identifiable as the Cathedral rather than the College School.[4]

The gradual change in the nature of the school's governance would have been less perceptible. Most importantly, the slow diminution of Chapter control over the school's development, which continued throughout the twentieth century, started in this period through the investigations of the Charity Commissioners and (from 1899) the Board of Education. This resulted in the inspections of 1888, 1899 and 1908, and the new schemes of governance of 1893 and 1910, which reordered the Langford and Philpotts charities through the addition of external trustees, and (in 1910, for the first time) added two laymen to the governing body and further reformed the way the school's business was conducted. It is significant that by the end of this period, the historian has to look to the educational files within the national archives and the school's own collections, rather than to the Dean and Chapter Act books, to find the main sources for the history of the school's governance.

The transformation of the cathedral's old endowed school into something at least approaching the modern school should be seen within the context of the notable advances that were taking place nationally in the fortunes of other first-grade schools.

---

3. This affected other schools as well, the percentage of ordained masters among ten 'great' public schools declining from 54 to 13.3 *per cent*, 1870-1906 (*HMC 1907 Report*, p.40). By December 1914, for the first time, ordained Headmasters were in a minority in the schools belonging to the Headmasters' Conference.

4. According to Yonge, the school colours had been first adopted (for cricket) in the 1860s: above, p.221. For the school shield: *TH*, no. 3 (Jan. 1879), p.145; and for the crest, song and '*floreat*' below, pp.249, 250, 268-69.

The major government agency for reform of grammar schools in the last quarter of the nineteenth century was the Charity Commission, which was empowered by the 1874 Act to draw up new schemes of governance for endowed schools. However, the strong opposition to W.E. Forster's proposal to set up provincial councils, which was struck out of the 1869 Endowed Schools Act, meant that there were no bodies to act as intermediaries between the Charity Commissioners and the local trustees. The absence of a forum for the gathering of local opinion and the resolution of conflict, together with the cumbersome procedures of the Act itself (simplified to an extent in 1873), often reduced the Commissioners' work to a snail's pace and necessitated the constant redrafting of schemes. This is best exemplified in the case of Leeds Grammar School, whose trustees successfully resisted the imposition of a new scheme of governance for 28 years, around 12 years longer than Dean Herbert's formal defence of the Langford and Philpotts charities.[5] Nevertheless in the period 1868 to 1883, the number of children nationally who were educated in the 189 schools where the educational endowment had been reformed more than doubled to 27,000; and by 1895, over 70 *per cent* of the total income of all endowed schools had been dealt with and nearly 1,000 new and amending schemes had been made.[6]

For the first-grade grammar schools which regularly sent boys to the universities (of which Hereford Cathedral School was one of fewer than a hundred in the country) the reforms eventually proved beneficial, despite the obstruction of trustees intent on preserving local custom and privilege.[7] Indeed, some old grammar schools with enterprising Headmasters, enlightened governors, sizeable entrance scholarships and, above all, land and other endowments (occasionally under-pinned by city companies) were able to reinvent themselves as successful boarding 'public' schools – Oundle, Repton, Sherborne, Tonbridge and (nearer home) Monmouth are good examples – as Uppingham had done under Thring in the 1860s. Hereford never had the resources wholly to transform itself in this way, but like other cathedral schools it was fortunate in being able to call upon the resources of the Ecclesiastical Commissioners under the terms of the 1869 Endowed Schools Act. Thanks in large part to the work of Arthur Leach, the assistant Charity Commissioner, its foundation was thereby eventually enriched in the early 1890s to the tune of £7,000. This was in marked contrast to the fate of some endowed schools. As Dr Jex-Blake of Rugby reminded his fellow Headmasters in 1875, numerous 'grammar schools have been depressed and made second-grade schools so that in many districts a boy cannot get any advanced teaching at all within a circle of twenty or thirty miles radius'.[8]

---

5. A new scheme for Leeds Grammar was first mooted in 1870 and successfully accomplished in 1898, three years earlier than that for Leeds (Girls') High School. Roach, (1991), pp.28-30. See below, pp.296-97, for the eventual reform of the HCS charities.

6. Roach (1991), pp.58-59, 69, Fearon's evidence before the 1886-87 select committee; and evidence given to the Bryce Commission, and the references to parliamentary papers there cited. Also see Bamford, p.187.

7. Bamford states that there were 110 schools preparing boys for the universities in 1865, with 70 sending at least one boy to Oxford and Cambridge each year (of which cohort HCS would have been one). *Ibid.*, pp.174-75. An early list compiled by the Headmasters' Conference committee (for 2 Dec. 1880) puts the number of HMC schools (including HCS) at 83, of which a considerable minority were not grammar school foundations.

8. *HMC Report 1875*, p.86, 22-23 Dec., at Clifton. Jex-Blake was moving a resolution for 'bursarships' to be found for poor boys who had passed in the first division of the Oxford or Cambridge Local junior examinations.

Eric Rudd was right to have warned his governors five years earlier that they should try to ensure that the Cathedral School was 'selected as the first-grade or high school of the county, a position which the nature of its endowment clearly assigns it'.[9] Without these endowments, the school would have been vulnerable during the years of agricultural depression in the late Victorian period; with it, even though several Somerset awards were placed in abeyance due to declining rentals on college estates in the 1880s and 1890s,[10] the school was enabled to maintain its reputation as a place of honest scholarship and become – after the reforms of the early 1890s – a school of just sufficient prosperity. This, in turn, enabled HCS successfully to resist the threats posed by the building of the new County College in 1880 and the Boys' High School in 1911.

Rudd's first attendance at the Headmasters' Conference at Winchester in 1873 – following the unanimous adoption of Thring's resolution two years earlier 'that the Head Masters of all schools of the first grade, whether they be called public schools, endowed schools, proprietary schools, or colleges, be *ex officio* members of the school conference' – placed HCS on a national footing.[11] Twenty years later, the Cathedral School's inclusion among the 'great public schools' in *Whittaker's* 1893 list is illustrative of its enhanced status, as is its own recognition of its position as a public school. A school debate like that of 4 December 1909, when the motion 'that in the opinion of this House life at a small public school is preferable to that at one of the larger public schools' was moved, would have been inconceivable 40 years earlier when the term was confined to a select number of Clarendon schools.[12]

The Cathedral School in the late Victorian and Edwardian period, then, managed both to enhance its status and to retain its identity as a place of godliness, good learning and (above all) manliness. That this was accomplished in the face of a governing body initially suspicious of change, and at a time of depression in agricultural counties, is attributable to the beliefs, strong personalities and wide-ranging talents of its three ordained Headmasters – Francis Tatham, Thomas Thistle and William Murray Ragg, the first and third of whom were significant figures in the school's evolution. It is to the most influential of these gentlemen that we must now turn.

Francis Henry Tatham, 1875-1890

Dean Herbert and his Chapter moved swiftly to secure a worthy successor to Rudd. Within days of Rudd's resignation on 24 March 1875, particulars had been drawn up for prospective applicants, outlining the Headmaster's emoluments and the school's position. These details were similar to those drawn up in 1869, except that the Headmaster's stipend had

9. HCA, 7031/21, pp.434-35, 8 Nov. 1870.

10. As it said on a school prospectus of the time: 'Several of these [awards] are at present in consequence of agricultural depression, in abeyance'. HCA, 7032/6 frontispiece. Also see below, p.272.

11. *HMC Report 1871*, p.5, 28-29 Dec., at Highgate. Thereafter, Rudd's successors periodically attended the meetings, although their attendance records were not exemplary: Tatham attended half and Thistle and Murray Ragg one third of the scheduled HMC general meetings during their tenures.

12. *TH*, NS XX (June 1893), p.6; LXIII (April 1910), p.23. In 1866 the committee of the Public Schools Club only recognised Charterhouse, Eton, Harrow, Rugby, Westminster and Winchester as public schools. Money, p.63. For a modern classification of the public schools in *c.*1900, see Honey, chapter 4.

been raised by £50 to £120 *per annum*, the pupil roll had increased to three figures, the boarding fees had gone up by over 20 *per cent* and reference was made to the 'newly built schoolrooms'. In the circumstances, this last claim was an understandable exaggeration as the rooms were not to be ready for several months, as we shall see. Candidates were then invited to send their testimonials, 'accompanied with reference to a clergyman to whom they are personally known', to the Chapter Clerk before the end of April 1875.[13] The vacancy was advertised in the same journals as in 1869, albeit at a two shilling increase in cost (13s in all) for the four line notices in the *Hereford Times*.[14]

Despite the increase to the Headmaster's salary, the riches of the university endowment – worth nearly £1,000 by this time – and the school's growing reputation, the appointment attracted a much smaller field than in 1869. There were 25 candidates all told, six of whom were laymen. This effectively meant that the Chapter's choice was limited to 19, for at a time when ordained Headmasters were still in an overwhelming majority in schools belonging to the Headmasters' Conference,[15] it was inconceivable that a layman would be appointed to the headmastership of a cathedral school. As Dean Herbert and his colleagues candidly informed the candidates: it was not 'absolutely necessary' that they should be in Holy Orders but preference would be given to ordained men 'as the Headmasters have always been so'.[16] Of the 19, the Chapter Clerk marked down nine for further consideration. Again, there is no indication as to how the final selection was made but it was done expeditiously, for on 21 May the Dean and Chapter resolved to offer the post to the Revd F.H. Tatham, subject to the approval of Lord Saye and Sele and Canon Jebb, both of whom were absent from the meeting. Three weeks later, Tatham's appointment was announced in the local press, the magisterial patent being formally registered (in time-honoured style) on 25 June 1875.[17]

Educated at Highgate School under Dr Dyne, Tatham had been a scholar at Trinity College, Cambridge, and in 1867 had taken a first-class degree in Classics, the third consecutive Headmaster to have gained this distinction. Tatham's experience of schoolmastering, however, was wider than both Woollam's and Rudd's before their appointments, having, after a brief spell at Marlborough College, served for nearly eight years at Westminster School as an assistant to its reforming Headmaster and the Dean's old Eton chum, C.B. Scott. That Tatham was soon to be married – and to a daughter of the Bishop

13. HCA, 7032/6, pp.432-33, contains the amended 1869 particulars, together with the proof copy of those for 1875.

14. The Headmastership was advertised in the *Hereford Times* for three successive weeks, 3-17 April 1875. See HCA, 7105/8, fo 192r, payment no. 8, for the overall costs of the appointment (£4 10s 11d), 5s 1d less than in 1869 – mainly because of the reduction in the postage bill.

15. In the 1875 conference at Clifton, there were only seven lay Headmasters, out of the 49 attending that year. Five years later, an early committee list indicates that there were 14 lay Headmasters in a total HMC membership of 83.

16. HCA, 7031/22, p.141, 26 April 1875. The 1869 Endowed Schools Act had in fact reserved the right of schools to appoint only ordained masters (and governors) provided, by the original operation of its statutes and 'continued observance' of the same, they could show that the school had 'been intended for and still to belong to any particular denomination'. Cathedral schools were clearly within this category.

17. *HT*, 18 June 1875, p.8; HCA, 7005/10, pp.604-05, 25 June 1875.

Fig. 6.1 Francis Tatham, whose headship transformed the school.

of London – was no doubt an additional recommendation. Whatever his reasons, Dean Herbert had again chosen well, for under Tatham's leadership the school was destined to reach new heights.

The Rebuilt School, 1875

By the time of Tatham's appointment, building plans for what was in effect a new school were already well advanced. As we have seen, in January 1875, and following the serving of a writ of ejectment from the College rooms, the cathedral had no alternative but to provide new accommodation for its school. At the same meeting that the Dean and Chapter formally gave up its possession of the College premises, they passed the following resolution:

> That new school and classrooms be forthwith built for the Cathedral School upon the site of the Canon's Bakehouse, and that the Headmaster be informed that he must make the best arrangements he can for the education of the scholars in his own house and in the house adjoining the Canon's Bakehouse during the building of the new school and classrooms.[18]

In little more than a week, William Chick, Gilbert Scott's former clerk of works who had set up an architectural practice at 20 East Street, had prepared plans and specifications for the new building; and by mid-February, James Bowers' tender for the proposal had been accepted, provided that it was reduced to £1,200 and 'some extra works recommended by the architect [Mr Chick]' were added. Before the end of March, the city council had approved the plans and had agreed to pay £30 towards the cost of rebuilding the boundary wall along Quay Street, and the contract was sealed, Bowers having reduced his tender to within 10s of the requirement.[19]

The nature of the new building at the corner of Castle and Quay Streets is clear enough from Chick's extant plans.[20] As might be expected from the accepted tender, it was a modest two-storey building, with three classrooms on the ground floor and a further two on the upper floor. Nevertheless, the rooms were a considerable improvement on what had gone before – the smallest classroom (20 x 17 feet) being far larger than the pokey College rooms;

18. HCA, 7031/22, p.126, 4 Jan. 1875. The former house of the Master of the Canon's Bakehouse was pulled down to make room for the new classrooms.

19. *Ibid.*, pp.130-31, 13 Feb.; p.132, 24 March 1875. James Bowers was presumably chosen ahead of Mr H. Walsh, who submitted the lowest tender at £1,194, because his work was known to the Chapter.

20. HARC, K 21, A/64. For Chick's other work in the county: Anderson, *passim*.

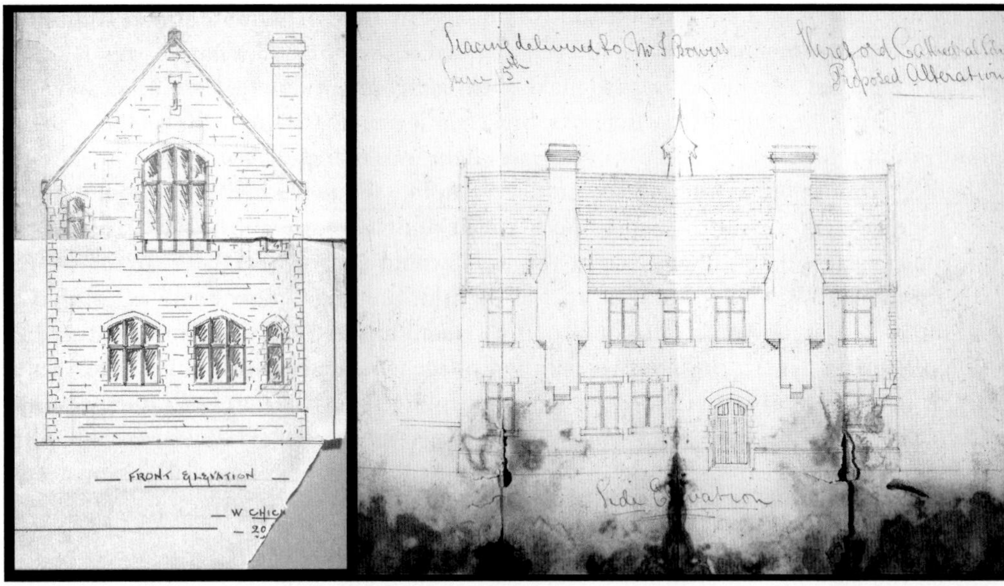

Fig. 6.2 Elevation and section of the 1875 classrooms on the corner of Castle and Quay Streets, designed by William Chick, the Dean and Chapter architect, 1863-78.

and the largest (25.6 x 44.3 feet) once again providing a decent sized room for assembly.[21] Not that these improvements weighed heavily with at least one former pupil, who wrote a furious letter to the editor of the *Hereford Times* complaining that the money that the Chapter proposed to spend on the new building was an insult to the city and totally inadequate 'for a school so long established, with such valuable scholarships and having arrived at such a high standard'.[22] A few months later, at Rudd's last speech day in July, Dean Herbert riposted in public by stating that the new rooms would be 'amply spacious', 'well adapted for the purpose of modern education' and would provide sufficient accommodation for 200 boys – a situation that was not to occur until well into the following century.[23]

Nor was this all. On the day of Tatham's formal appointment, William Chick was asked to provide plans for some additional works to School House that had been asked for by the new Headmaster. Although the details are not revealed in the Chapter Acts, it is apparent that the further proposals were quite substantial for Bowers' final bill was over £2,000, some £800 above the original estimate. Chick's surviving plans also indicate that the new works included an additional wing for dormitories – towards which Tatham himself was required to pay £100 – and servants' rooms, as well as improvements to the Headmaster's

21. For the old schoolroom (pulled down in 1851) and the College assembly room (the upper schoolroom), used between 1851 and 1875, see above, pp.180, 182; and for T.H. Parker's later memory of the old cloister rooms, the new building, school house and the playground, *TH*, NS CLXXXXVIII (May 1959), pp.9-10.

22. *HT*, 10 April 1875, p.8 letter of 'Collegian'; also see *ibid.*, 24 April, p.8, letter of 'an Old Boy', who considered that HCS would rival Marlborough, Cheltenham, Wellington, Malvern and Clifton 'had it only buildings to equal theirs'.

23. *Ibid.*, 31 July 1875, p.3. Herbert also claimed that the new building had 'a power of enlargement, if it should be regarded hereafter', as it was in a few years with the addition of the Gilbert memorial library.

own living quarters and adornments to his house.[24] The newlyweds were to be given more comfortable accommodation than had been afforded bachelor Rudd, even if they may have had to be enlarged a few years later to make them 'thoroughly commodious'.[25]

As is so often the way with contractors, Bowers was unable to complete even his original commission on time, partly because of the late alterations that had been made to the design of the Big Schoolroom.[26] After all the public trumping about the new schoolrooms being ready for the beginning of the September term, it must have caused the new Headmaster some embarrassment to announce that the term would start a week later than planned, and that the school would continue to use the old buildings rather than 'as previously announced … the new schools [schoolrooms], which are not ready for immediate use'.[27] Neither the parents' reactions nor those of the College, who had again to suffer the discomfiture of schoolboys as their immediate neighbours, are known. What is clear, however, is that the public statement hid the reality, for nearly two months later Tatham was observing that the bad weather had further delayed proceedings and that there were 'still many details to be supplied in the new buildings'. When after that Christmas the school finally entered its promised land, there were the inevitable teething troubles, magnified by the meagre sum spent on the building. After nearly a year's use, Tatham could report that the new rooms were no more than 'satisfactory', the principal drawbacks being their lack of ventilation and the thin flooring so that 'every movement in the upper room is heard below'. The cathedral responded by sealing the floorboards and providing new ventilators and window blinds. Another concern – the tapping or even breaking of windows by 'idle people' as they passed down Quay Street – was remedied by the fitting of wire grills but the Headmaster's more serious complaint about the state of the roof was dismissed for the time being. A little later it was found that the fireplaces in the main classroom were totally inadequate for heating the room and a stove had to be put in to keep the place warm. This caused another problem: the stove smoked and an additional chimney had to be built early in 1882. The following year, Tatham could still complain that the only way to open and shut the windows was by means of 'a man with a ladder', and that the flooring of the large schoolroom had come away from the wall.[28]

---

24. HCA, 7031/22, p.155, 25 June 1875; 7105/8. fo 236v, payments 114-22, totalling £2,297 9s 6d, less Tatham's £100 and the Council's £30; HCA, 5067, various plans, including the 1875 ground plan of School House and the old schoolroom prior to the alterations, and Tatham's own plans of School House, *c.*1890; HCA, 7007/1, pp.485-86, room measurements, 9 June 1888. Also see, HARC, K 21 A/64, Chick's 1875 plans; and TNA, ED 27/1606, Leach's report, 25 July 1889, p.9.

25. HCA, 7005/11, pp.471-77, agreement with Tatham, 21 July 1884, to pay interest (at 4 *per cent*) on £350 borrowed for the addition of a sitting room and two bedrooms to his residence; contract with Henry Walsh, 23 July 1884, for the improvements; HCA, 7031/22, pp.433, 435, 440, 445, 456, Acts, 8 Nov., 20 Dec. 1883, 12 May, 25 June 1884, and Tatham's report, 13 Nov. 1884.

26. HCA, 7031/22, p.155, 25 June 1875; HCA, 7105/8. fo 236v, payments 114-22, totalling £2,297 9s 6d, less Tatham's £100 and the Council's £30; 5067, various plans, including the 1875 ground plan of School House and the old schoolroom prior to the alterations, and Tatham's own plans of School House, *c.*1890. Also see, HARC, K 21 A/64, Chick's 1875 plans.

27. *HT*, 17 July 1875, p.5; 18 Sept. 1875, p.4.

28. HCA, 7031/22 pp.165, 198, 227, Tatham's reports, Nov. 1875-77; *ibid.*, pp.212, 247, 249, 300, 303, 369-70, 401, re windows, roof, floor and heating, 16 April 1877 to 6 Nov. 1882; HCA, 7105/8, 1877 audit accounts, fo

The truth was that the classrooms had been designed on a shoe-string budget and shoddily built. Tatham always considered that a great chance for building a new school on a green field site had been lost in 1875, and never came to terms with what he saw as the Chapter's failure to grasp that opportunity. Nevertheless, although it was not as Tatham would have wished, the dreams of his predecessors for new schoolrooms had been fulfilled within a few months of his appointment. The new Headmaster, however, was determined to ensure that he would bequeath a more sufficient legacy, and over the next 15 years did everything in his power to bring this about.

Academic Matters and the Failure of Reform

Tatham paid early recognition in his first report to the 'admirable system' that Rudd had established and changed it only at the margins.[29] In May 1883, the choristers' hours were again regulated. Although the Headmaster's intention to provide the choristers with over 21 hours teaching per week (including some specialist tuition from George Wargent, the new choristers' master) – necessitating the putting back of Evensong by an hour from 4 to 5pm – had subsequently to be modified, this was a successful initiative.[30] As significantly, and following the enforced retirement in July 1885 of James Brown, the 'under-school' was abolished, the pupil roll was unified and the whole school was reunited for morning prayers. The following term, Tatham expressed his satisfaction of ridding himself of a colleague 'whose main idea seemed to be the preservation of his rights and dignity'. It was, without doubt, a relief for Tatham to have the complete charge of the whole school.

By contrast, little change was made to the curriculum. The chance survival of a timetable, in Tatham's hand, for Midsummer 1889 makes strange reading for modern eyes, which are immediately struck by three things: its overwhelming concentration on Classics; its almost total inflexibility, apart from those boys in the 'modern' form (the Under IVth); and its extended periods of learning – with hour-long lessons for three or four hours in the mornings, Monday to Saturday, each day without a morning break, and then a further two and a quarter hours of classes for three afternoons each week. For the VI and Upper V, out of this near 28-hour week of formal teaching, over 18 hours were spent on Greek and Latin texts and unseens, as well as (like the rest of the school) the five hours on Mathematics and two on French. The fare was similar for the Upper and Under IVs, except that the Classics were leavened with two hours for German and a further two for English History, and either Shakespeare or Milton for the last two hours on Saturday mornings. Even in the three lowest forms the Classics predominated – although Greek (four hours per week) was not introduced until the Third Form – with eight or nine hours of Latin weekly, almost

284r, payments 110-12; 1878, fo 329v, payment 111; HCA, 7106/1, 1880, fo 43v, payments 107-08.

29. Unless otherwise indicated, the sources for the following paragraphs on the academic side of the school are contained in Tatham's audit reports to the chapter, HCA, 7031/22 and 23, *passim*, Nov. 1875 to Nov. 1889.

30. HCA, 7031/22, pp.411, 414, 416, 420, 424, 428, 426, 22 Feb.-8 Nov. 1883. The choristers' early release for the Monday practice, and the moving of Evensong to 4.30pm in the winter months (both occurring later that year) would have eroded the choristers' teaching time by at least an hour per week. Tatham, however, was not convinced that HCS benefited from the presence of choristers. See, for example, the observation of Arthur Leach, the assistant Charity Commissioner, that the Headmaster 'does not think they [the choristers] do themselves or the school good and they would be better elsewhere'. TNA, ED/1606, report, 25 July 1889, p.10.

equalling (and in the Third Form, with the addition of Greek, exceeding) the time spent on Scripture, English History, Geography and Modern Languages put together.[31] There was no Science at all recorded on the official time-table, although in his 1889 report Arthur Leach noted that the Fourth Forms were taught electricity,[32] and Tatham himself indicated that the boys attended lectures on Chemistry and then Geology for the Lent terms 1877-78, an experiment that does not appear to have been repeated. Apart from the hour of 'drill' for all boys on a Saturday morning (excepting the modern class which had two hours 'martial' at other times), and the non-timetabled singing class and games afternoons – which had been made compulsory in the mid-1880s, and extended in the Golden Jubilee year to Tuesday, Thursday and Saturday afternoons during the summer months – there was no relief from the academic treadmill. And Tatham expected that all boys (choristers and day boys included) should undertake at least two hours preparation per night on top of everything else.[33] Overall, this unremitting diet of Languages and Mathematics must have tested the stamina of the most bookish boy; and for the dullard, it would have been nothing more than an unremitting slog, tempered only by the three half-days.

That many boys found this a hard regime is indicated by the age differential in each of the classes. From Tatham's form list of June 1888, it is clear that HCS was a strict meritocracy, and that boys were not promoted until it was felt that they could cope with the increasing demands that each successive form offered.[34] Consequently, the eldest boy in the Sixth, A.G.M. Gurney, who was over 19, was more than three years older than the youngest in that form. Nor was this unusual. Indeed, the age differential averaged almost four years in each of the seven forms and over four in the middle classes. Quite apart from anything else, this must have taxed the abilities of even the most skilled master. For many boys, it also meant that they left the school in their mid-teens, having reached their academic ceiling after four or five years.

Nevertheless, the examiners' reports for Classics, Divinity and Mathematics, which nearly all survive for this period,[35] suggest that the system worked, at least in academic if not in social terms. Given that many of the school's examiners were inexperienced young graduates – albeit scholars or fellows of their colleges – it is not surprising to find that their reports vary in quality. Occasionally, as in 1879 and 1886, they are only a page or two in length and do little more than rank the pupils. More usually, detailed comments

---

31. TNA, ED 27/1605, no. 27. This was sent to the Charity Commissioners as background for Leach's report. Leach himself described Hereford's curriculum as of the 'classical grammar school type' so it was clearly not unusual for a first-grade school at this time.

32. TNA, ED/1606, 25 July 1889, p.10.

33. Having found some choristers wandering the streets in the evening, Tatham (in his own words) 'told them I considered they were subject to the same rules as day boys, who are required to observe the same hours of evening work as the boarders, viz 7 to 9'. This led to a wrangle with the Succentor who considered that the organist was 'magister puerorum'. HCA, 7031/23, pp.11-12, 6 Nov. 1886.

34. HCA, 7007/1, pp.480-82; TNA, ED/1605, no. 18. Also see no. 28, subjects for the 1888 summer examination, for some idea of the syllabus for each class.

35. Copies of the reports for 1876-80, 1882-84 and 1886-88 are to be found in the Chapter register books, HCA, 7005/11, pp.43-47, 89-92, 144-46, 198-200, 264-67, 399-404, 426-30, 465-68; HCA, 7005/12, pp.16-17, 66-69, 95-99. Abridged reports for 1881, 1889-90 (although not for 1885) were published in *The Herefordian*.

are provided on the performance of each form, especially for the senior boys in the upper Fifth and Sixth Forms who may have been tested in a dozen or more papers. By contrast, the examiner would have no time to do more than give the younger boys a cursory *viva voce* examination, which was a crude instrument of testing and could be terrifying experience for the boys involved, as those in the lower school no doubt found when W.E. Heitland grilled them on their Latin reading book in midsummer 1884.[36] 'Excellent and painstaking' as Tatham admitted the young examiners had been in his first three years as Headmaster, he suggested to the Chapter in November 1879 that a 'more mature and experienced examiner' should be appointed, partly because it eased his own burdens but mainly because their criticisms would be better considered and more acceptable to his masters. This happened the following year.[37] Tatham also improved the school's examination system by appointing his own examiner in French. This occurred in 1878, and again in 1885, as well as subsequently, to test the new arrangement of having the language taught by an Englishman, it being 'well-nigh impossible to find a Frenchman who can enter into the ways of a public school and maintain discipline'.[38] More importantly, in 1887 cathedral boys were tested for the first time by an examination board – the Oxford and Cambridge Schools Board, which had been founded less than 15 years earlier for the examination of first-grade schools – rather than by the Chapter's examiners, thereby combining the school's annual summer examination with (for select senior pupils) an examination for a 'higher' certificate. Although only W.J. Boycott and C.H. Hodgson, out of the four boys entered, managed to obtain these certificates by passing in all five subjects, Tatham found the new system to have considerable advantages: the papers were 'admirably set'; the 'formality and strictness' of the examination had 'a wholesome effect on the boys'; all the forms were examined *viva voce*, in addition to the papers set for the upper forms; and the reports were consequently 'of more value than previously'.[39] For whatever reason, Tatham did not repeat the experiment, but it was the shape of things to come.[40]

Overall, it is fair to conclude from these examiners' reports, however thin some of them seem to modern eyes, that the school's academic performance under Tatham was at worst satisfactory. Despite the demands of a narrow curriculum – and not least in the number of classical authors a senior boy was required to master for the university scholarship examinations – the examiners invariably concluded that the school was 'efficient'. The examiners

36. The majority of boys did not respond well, and Heitland was unimpressed: 'So far as I could discover, very few of these [boys in forms III and II] can be said to have any knowledge whatever of the first rudiments of Latin'. This may have been as much the examiner's fault as the boys, for when he examined again in 1890 he admitted that his first impression of the poor linguistic abilities of the lower Fourth – as a result of his *viva voce* examination – was erroneous.

37. HCA, 7031/22, pp.297, 332, Tatham's reports, Nov. 1879 and 1880.

38. The teacher was A.R. Stokes, the son of the Lucasian Professor of Mathematics at Cambridge. On his appointment to Shrewsbury in 1889, he was replaced by Herr S. Mendel, an exception apparently to the rule that foreigners could not keep good discipline. *Ibid.*, p.475; 7031/23, p.99, Tatham's reports, Nov. 1885 and 1889. Also see above, pp.218-19, for the boys' lack of respect for foreign teachers.

39. HCA, 7031/23, p.35, Tatham's report, Nov. 1887. For this more detailed and incisive report, which was published in *The Herefordian*, see HCA, 7005/12, pp.66-69.

40. The Chapter certainly gave permission for the new system to continue (HCA, 7031, p.50, 9 April 1888) but perhaps Tatham feared that the school's reputation might suffer if he continued to use the Board.

also frequently referred to the masters' careful teaching and the boys' 'honest industry', neat work and good order and discipline. And if they also alluded to the wide disparity between the top and bottom of each form, the vain attempts to learn Euclid by rote, 'the unintelligent and the unintelligible juggling' with algebraic symbols and the general lack of flair or brilliancy, that was only to be expected in a school in which the Headmaster could not afford to refuse entry to any boy, 'however stupid or backward', whose parents could meet the fees.[41] For the least intelligent, the basics of literacy, Latin and Arithmetic were drummed home; the moderately clever were given more than enough to pass the requirements for the Somerset awards; and the few high fliers, like E.J. Rapson, A.D. Brownjohn, W.J. Boycott, J.C. DuBuisson and E.W. Bowell, were able to flourish under Tatham's inspired tuition.[42]

It is unsurprising that someone like Tatham, who was used to teaching Westminster scholars, should regret the paucity of clever boys, particularly in the upper part of the school. He quickly identified the reasons: the want of competition among the boys themselves, the many Somerset scholarships actually acting as a disincentive by drawing off boys prematurely to the universities; the poor preparation many boys received before entry, HCS not being in a position to reject them on academic grounds 'unlike the larger public schools'; and, crucially, the lack of foundation scholarships. Tatham could do little to remedy the first two deficiencies but he pressed the Dean and Chapter to reform the Langfordian entry scholarships, the competition for which was minimal. Indeed, the situation seemed to have been little better than in earlier days when the awards were solely nominated by favour. Tatham claimed in 1879 that they were still usually held either by sons of gentlemen, who were 'in no need of pecuniary assistance', or by boys 'who would be better off in a national school', and were thereby 'practically wasted'. He suggested that their number should be increased by reducing the annual value of each scholarship to 12 guineas, the amount charged for tuition, and by abolishing the anomalous clothing allowance. If they were also thrown open to boys born in the county rather than simply the city, Tatham argued that they would then be attractive to the sons of the county clergy, the class 'who one [would] like to see benefit by the charity'.[43] The Chapter reminded the new Headmaster in November 1875, after Tatham had initially proposed that the Langfordian scholarships

41. G.B. Mathews, a native of Leominster, was especially severe in his criticism of the boys in his 1883 Mathematics report, but given that he was senior wrangler that year, perhaps this is not surprising. He was more tempered in 1884 but the boys' sums had also improved. For the academic quality of some of Tatham's admissions, see HCA, 7031/23, p.67, report 5 Nov. 1888.

42. The latter four boys all gained open scholarships (at Clare, Trinity Cambridge, Magdalen and Wadham), and Rapson – although a Somerset exhibitioner – in 1883 gained 'a first' in Classics, despite having known little Latin and no Greek on his entry to HCS in 1877. He later also gained a 'first' in the Indian language tripos, and eventually became professor of Sanskrit at Cambridge. At Brasenose, whose principal had suggested to Tatham in 1877 that the OH Somerset scholars at the college had 'quite held their own with the open scholars', J. Walmsley was placed above all the open scholarship candidates when he won the Somerset scholarship in 1884. Both Boycott and Walmsley were just 17 when they won their awards. HCA, 7031/ 22 and 23 *passim*, for Tatham's reports on the above. In national terms, the *Pall Mall Gazette* recorded that HCS won six Oxbridge scholarships, 1887-89, placing the school 39th from 104 public schools; or (if close awards are discounted) 65th. As cited by 'Imprimatur', *HT*, 23 Nov. 1889, p.8.

43. Tatham put forward such arguments to the Chapter in successive reports, 1875-77 and 1879. HCA, 7031/22, pp.166, 200, 226, 298.

should be open only to senior boys, that any such reform would both 'deprive boys born in Hereford of the privilege they have hitherto exclusively enjoyed, and ... postpone the claims of such boys from 9 to 15 years of age'.[44] Nevertheless, his governors were not against the reform in principle providing it was done on their own terms. But before this could be achieved, they had to face the formidable obstacle of the Charity Commissioners. Although in the long run, the Commission would be of considerable value to the school, in the short term it proved to be a major stumbling block to Tatham's immediate goal of improving the intellectual quality of the entry.

Under Dean Langford's will, as noted in chapter 2, the revenue from his lands in Disserth was to be divided between four Ludlow and four Hereford scholars, each of whom were to receive £2 13s 4d annually. Over the following two centuries, a considerable disparity had grown up between the payments made to the Hereford boys and those given to their Ludlow fellows, so that by the mid-1870s, the Hereford Langfordians were each receiving £13 5s 8d *per annum* – exclusive of the clothing allowance and the 8 guineas tuition fee paid to their Headmaster – more than double that of the Ludlow scholars. When, following the Chapter's first submission of a revised scheme for the Langford charity in July 1876, an assistant Charity Commissioner pointed out that Dean Langford had 'put Ludlow on equal terms with Hereford in respect to participation in his bounty', Dean Herbert and his colleagues 'expressed astonishment ... and unhesitatingly desired that the Ludlow School should enjoy its full share'.[45] The initial proposal was then withdrawn and a new scheme was submitted in early December 1876. This increased the annual pay of the Ludlow scholars to £8 each and reduced the number of Hereford awards from eight to seven, while maintaining a 12-14 age qualification and abolishing the place birth requirement.[46] Despite Dean Herbert's argument that the cathedral boys were entitled to a greater share of Dean Langford's legacy because he had laid down that they should attend both morning and evening services in gowns and surplices, the Chapter's concessions proved insufficient for the Charity Commissioners. While willing to prepare a new scheme broadly in line with its wishes, they further questioned whether there was a need for putative scholars to have a religious qualification, and also proposed that two nominees from the board of Ludlow Grammar School should become trustees of the charity. These proposals, both of which were anathema to the Dean and Chapter, effectively put an end to any attempt to reform the Langford charity for almost ten years. Regularisation of the Langford charity (as well as Philpotts) was eventually successfully accomplished but not in Tatham's time. Although Tatham succeeded in attracting a few bright boys by personally subsidising their education, his hopes of creating meaningful academic scholarships were stymied by his governors' innate conservatism.[47]

---

44. *Ibid.*, pp.163-64, 11 Nov. 1875.

45. The assistant Commissioner was C.H. Stanton, who, on his visit of 7 August 1876, noted both the Chapter's interest in HCS and its good local reputation. However, the school was on holiday at the time so he did not have a chance to inspect it. TNA, ED 27/1606, no. 8, Stanton's report, nd.

46. *Ibid.*, no. 11; HCA, 7005/11, p.62, 7 Dec. 1876.

47. See below, pp.296-297, for the eventual reform of these charities; and HCA, 7031/22, pp.166, 297, for Tatham's offer of subsidised places, Nov. 1875 and Nov. 1879. Rapson, the son of a Ledbury schoolmaster, who attended HCS from 1877 to 1879, may have been one boy to have benefited from Tatham's generosity.

Widening Horizons, 1878-1882

Nevertheless, Tatham was concerned to widen both the boys' intellectual horizons and their awareness of their educational heritage. Three major events, all of which were of considerable future importance, should be singled out: the creation of a school journal; the celebration of the school's foundation; and, as a permanent commemoration of the so-called quincentenary, the building of a school library and additional classrooms.

The first edition of *The Herefordian*, initially printed by the High Town firm of Jakeman and Carver, was published price 1s in January 1878. Thereafter, it came out twice each year until 1888, when it became a termly production at the reduced price of 6d per copy. Although H.P. Bull had been 'chief compiler' of a school chronicle for some years,[48] it is likely that Tatham, who probably wrote the first article on 'Cathedral Schools', encouraged the idea of publishing a magazine. However, Philip Baylis, a former student of Woollam's and Somerset exhibitioner at St John's, barrister on the Oxford circuit and secretary to the Old Herefordians' committee, seems to have written the introduction.[49] This set out the new publication's *raison d'être*, which he saw as a 'pleasurable relaxation' for former pupils at a time when the 'struggle for existence' had never been greater; and especially as 'a pleasure and a good' for those 'who still remain beneath the fostering care of … [their] *alma mater*'. *The Herefordian* would form, it was suggested, 'a written and enduring record of successes obtained in the "forms", at the universities, in the world and in … sports', the school's history thereby being 'transferred from the region of vague oral tradition to one of undoubted certainty'. Most important was the writer's moral exhortation, reminding the boys that they had:

> the honour of belonging to a foundation … ancient even in a country abounding in ancient foundations [and] that in their hands …[was] entrusted the weighty privilege of maintaining intact, and handing down untarnished and unspotted to succeeding generations, the traditions established by those who have gone before them … It cannot [he continued], in the nature of things, be that everyone will obtain in his several course either splendid success or illustrious fame … but it does lie within the powers of everyone to discharge ably, with honour and integrity, the various duties of his life, and so fulfil in the highest degree the obligations of a man and of a citizen …[50]

Tatham may have assisted its publication but two senior boys were primarily responsible for the formidable task of editing *The Herefordian*, 'a task of no light weight' as the first editor put it.[51] Indeed, in the early days, it almost folded. Three factors contributed to this:

48. *TH*, NS XXXII (Dec. 1899), p.4.

49. *Ibid.*, p.4; HCSA, for a MS copy of Bull's 'Hereford Cathedral School Record' for 1877; and T.H. Parker's obituary of G.R. Bullock-Webster (in private possession), for the suggestions about Tatham's and Baylis' authorship. For Bull's later claim that he and Bullock-Webster were the co-founders of the magazine: Eales-White, p.56; and for Baylis' excoriating remarks about 'the blighting, deadening influence of ecclesiastical corporations': *HT*, 20 July 1881, on HCS's '500th' anniversary.

50. *TH*, no. 1 (Jan. 1878), pp.4-5. The publication was welcomed by the *Hereford Times* (23 Feb. 1878, p.5) as an 'interesting and useful record of the old school's annals' and 'a healthy symptom' of HCS's 'unimpaired vigour'.

51. Although at first there were four editors, only one of whom was at school. See HCSA, for G.R. Bullock-Webster's editorial minute book, 1878-79, listing the four original editors including Bull, who was by this time

the setting up costs; the size of the second issue – at 69 pages the longest *Herefordian* ever published in this period, which meant that the editors lost at least 3d on each copy sold; and the failure of over half the school to purchase the magazine, even at the reduced price of 6d. The journal was saved, partly through strict economy – the January 1880 issue numbered 22 pages and covered only school news – and largely through the efforts of the 1880-81 editors, E.J. Boddington and J.H. Ware, whose pleas at a school meeting on 27 October 1880 resulted in a near doubling of the circulation among the boys themselves, despite them having to pay the full 1s price. The tradition of boy editors lasted throughout the period, apart from the two issues of October 1883 and February 1884 undertaken by Fred Weatherly from his Oxford home, and published in Oxford by W.R. Bowden. Weatherly resigned from his task disillusioned by the paucity of contributors and subscribers, openly declaring in his last editorial that the magazine was bankrupt. Again the journal survived, through a reduction in the number of copies printed – from 350 in September 1878 to 200 by October 1884, which roughly equated to the number of subscribers (half of whom were Old Herefordians) – so that by the end of Tatham's time the magazine was trading at a small profit. The editors still bemoaned the lack of contributions from the boys themselves, as in May 1887 when one editor predicted (erroneously as it turned out) that *The Herefordian* would not 'behold any other monarch complete the fiftieth year of his or her reign'. And while the journal may not have reached the literary heights that Weatherly had hoped for, and may indeed have been a pale imitation of the more established periodicals at the bigger public schools, its survival brought senior pupils opportunities for both editing and running a commercial enterprise and ensured that boys of a literary bent had an outlet for their talents. It also gives the historian sufficient evidence to chart an aspect of the school's modern history, if not provide him with 'undoubted certainty' as to its progress.

Indeed, in the vital respect of the school's foundation date, *The Herefordian* clouded the truth. For its first issue, a finely engraved school crest had been devised for the front cover at a cost of £2. This was based on the cathedral's own seal, and depicted an enthroned King Ethelbert, holding in his right hand a sword and in his left a flaming lamp – presumably to represent truth and wisdom – seated above the Dean's blazon, and surrounded by the motto: 'Schola Cathedralis Herefordensis 1381'. The publication of this 'stamp' gave rise in the September issue to a letter from 'Cantab' suggesting that the school's 500th anniversary should be suitably celebrated in 1881. It mattered not that in the same number an article by T.T. Davies senior, who had himself been a pupil at the school in the early years of the nineteenth century and at the time of writing was in his 85th year, had suggested that the school had been 'founded by Bishop Gilbert, December 26 1384'. This statement, although erroneous, at least had the merit of being established on the basis of the first known document mentioning the Cathedral School. Nevertheless, it was cavalierly dismissed by *The Herefordian's* boy editor, who claimed that while it was 'difficult to determine the exact period of the school's foundation', there was 'good authority for the earlier date which has been adopted as the school's crest'. What that authority was, however, he declined to state. It is clear that from the time of the magazine's first issue in January 1878, there

the Oxford representative. Unless otherwise stated, the following paragraphs are based on relevant editions of *The Herefordian.*

was no going back on the 1381 date, and that – prompted, no doubt, by the enterprising Headmaster – the school's quincentenary would be commemorated in 1881.

Over the following three years, various suggestions were put forward in the letters pages of *The Herefordian* as to how this jubilee might be best celebrated. Such ideas, together with those arising from the circulation of a questionnaire, were belatedly considered by the OH committee in April 1881. Few of these were sufficiently realistic to be adopted, much to the anger of some old boys, who vigorously expressed their indignation in the public journals. Nevertheless, the celebrations that took place in glorious weather on Thursday 30 June and Friday 1 July 1881 – dates which were convenient for most former pupils, with the exception of schoolmasters and bank managers (the former for obvious reasons, the latter because one of the dates coincided with 'settling day') – were appropriate enough. The Thursday's cricket match, narrowly won by the School XIII, was according to *The Herefordian's* correspondent 'everything that could be desired'. 'Never, perhaps,' he gushed, 'has Widemarsh witnessed so large and brilliant a concourse at a cricket match'. This was followed by a dinner of some 70 Old Herefordians at the Green Dragon – the chair being taken by Judge John Maurice Herbert, who was flanked by Bishop Atlay and the Headmaster – at which eight toasts were drunk. The near 20 speeches must have seemed interminable, at least to the younger members. Meanwhile, the boarders of School House, 'under the genial guidance of Mrs Tatham and several young ladies', rowed up river to picnic and play games at Belmont, the party not returning 'till evening had long faded into night'. The Friday morning cathedral service was attended by 'the whole body of Herefordians', the 'goodly number of old boys' wearing academicals giving a splash of colour to the occasion, and Bishop Atlay reminding them both of their educational heritage and of the importance of a liberal education. Thereafter, 200 or so friends, masters present and past (including Woollam – who used the occasion to urge the introduction of Hebrew into the curriculum – and Rudd), current and old boys packed into the 'plain and unattractive schoolroom' to witness the formal presentation by the Old Herefordians of an honours board – 'executed in oak with gothic mouldings' by Messrs Vale and Stephens, at a cost of about £35 – which was 'destined for the names of distinguished Herefordians'. (Plate 10). The two day celebrations were crowned by a grand evening concert in the Shirehall, with a 25 piece orchestra of old boys, supplemented by a further 15 for Romberg's 'Toy Symphony'. Two specially composed pieces ended each part of the programme: the festal march by the 17-year-old Francis Livesey; and Fred Weatherly's school song, '*Floreat Herefordia*', the final verse of which gives an indication of its flavour:

Then hand in hand, as here we stand
Whater'er our work may be,
We'll make a vow together now
To do it manfully.
And when the old school calls us back,
We'll answer to her call,
For all her sons are loyal ones,
And that is best of all.

It is not to modern taste, and is undoubtedly sentimental, but it spoke a truth. The Old Herefordians had not only contributed a major part to the success of the school's commemoration, but were further to answer the school's call for a new library.[52]

This was less easily accomplished. In the decades before Tatham's tenure, as Yonge revealed, a boy's access to books other than school texts was confined to the tales of Jack Sheppard and Dick Turpin and the 'penny dreadfuls' of the circulating libraries.[53] During the 1860s, however, moves were afoot within the city for the creation of a more permanent public book collection. One important source for this was the books collected by the penny readings committee, pioneered by an assistant master of the school, J.C. Hanbury, which provided 'wholesome entertainment for their fellow citizens in the shape of readings and musical performances'. The committee's donation of 234 well-bound volumes 'of the best authors', together with the collections of the Woolhope Club, formed the nucleus first for the free library and museum in King Street which was established in December 1871; and then, nearly three years later, for the grand new free library in Broad Street, opened amidst much festivity (which included the singing of the Hallelujah chorus at the cathedral service, a procession of 3,000 schoolchildren and a corporation 'déjeuner') by Mrs Rankin, the library benefactor's wife, on 8 October 1874. Two prominent Hereford citizens had played key roles in its building: the architect, Frederick Robertson Kempson, who was also to design the school library, and James Bowers, the main contractor, who, as we have seen, successfully contracted for the new classrooms.[54]

How far the cathedral schoolboys used the magnificent new facility on their doorstep is open to conjecture but certainly Tatham thought that the school was greatly disadvantaged by not having a library of its own, the subject being aired in public at the speech days of 1876 and 1877. A few months later in his report of November 1877, Tatham explained to his governors that 'the want of books and the consequent absence of all literary taste and interest among the boys, I find a very serious drawback which makes itself felt at every turn'. His strategies for remedying this deficiency – the establishment of a library fund by the charge of an extra 10s entrance fee for all new boys, the encouragement of book donations from former pupils and local worthies and the creation of a book room 'till the day comes when it may be possible to build a separate library' – were pursued with admirable determination over the next few years.[55] The first two remedies were more easily accomplished than the third. After some miscommunication, the additional entrance fees – supplemented by individual contributions from existing pupils and any profits from the *Herefordian* – were started in 1878,[56] and had brought in about £10 *per annum* by

52. The quincentenary celebrations are fully described in *TH*, vol. II no. 8 (Sept. 1881), pp.76-92, and are (less fully) remembered by T.H. Parker, *HCN*, no. 45 (Summer, 1959), pp.5-6. Livesey was organist and choirmaster of St Bee's Priory Church, 1887-1923. Weatherly's better known school song '*Floreat*' ('Let others sing of famous schools by Thames or on the hill' etc.) was published as a frontispiece to Eales-White.

53. *HT*, 14 Oct. 1909, Yonge's article XXI, 'The Concluding Paper'. Also, see above, pp.226-27.

54. *HT*, 16 Feb. 1867 (2nd sheet), for the 1d readings; and 15 March 1873, p.10, and 10 Oct. 1874, pp.2-3, for the laying of the foundation stone and the opening of the Broad Street library.

55. See HCA, 7031/22, pp.201-02, 227-28, 267-68, 299, Tatham's Nov. audit reports, 1876-79, and the references below with regard to the building of the new library.

56. Tatham had complained to the Dean and Chapter in Nov. 1877 that no notice had been taken of his proposed

November 1879. The Headmaster assured his governors that the fees were entirely spent 'on books useful for scholarships or theological reading'. By then the book collection, including Sir Herbert Croft's 1871 present of the Delphin Classics as well as many other individual donations,[57] had expanded to some 600 volumes – all according to the Headmaster 'thoroughly useful and readable' books. Most of his boys would have disagreed, judging by an entry in *The Herefordian* some months earlier which suggested that 'the number and character of the books in the library' in part accounted for the paucity of borrowing. The main problem, however, was this:

> The library will never become popular until we can have a separate room for it. At present, there is no reference library and most boys naturally prefer the quiet of the free library to the noisy schoolroom, where as everyone knows it is generally impossible to read.[58]

Still the article made clear that a school library, staffed by three boy librarians, had been operating from June 1877. It may have been inadequate but a start had been made, funds were trickling in, book donations were being made and – most crucially – the project had the full support of Old Herefordians. But where was a suitable room to be found?

An anonymous *Herefordian* correspondent appealed to the Dean and Chapter 'to supply a want which without their assistance will be impossible to overcome'. At first, they were less than helpful, particularly with regard to an approach to the Custos and vicars for the use of the old College chapel, 'formerly used as the under school', which Dean Herbert flatly refused to countenance. During the course of 1879, however, they had assisted in the replacing of the old furniture in the Sixth-form room with Osborne desks, which gave sufficient room for a new large bookcase along the wall that was freed.[59] This provided useful space but it could be nothing more than an interim solution.

By late 1880 the school's book collection had outgrown the Sixth-form room, and the Headmaster felt his position to be sufficiently strong to make an independent approach to F.R. Kempson, the city library architect, about an extension to the new building. Tatham's simple proposal was to pull down the front part of the adjoining dilapidated vicarage (leaving the back intact for a sick room 'and the accommodation of my manservant') and on its site to build a two-storey attached block, at an estimated cost of £800: a first-floor library on the same level as the large schoolroom, above an additional classroom and locker room, thus completing the original 1875 scheme. Provided the Chapter paid for the ground-floor additions, Tatham proposed to undertake an appeal for the remaining sum, and to build the library in commemoration of the quincentenary. He further suggested that such a building would attract more pupils – not a prophetic utterance – and that as the

entrance fee scheme. It had (*ibid.*, p.208, 24 March 1877), but evidently the governors' approval had not been communicated to the Headmaster.

57. Donations from members of the OH committee and others can be traced in *TH,* no. 1 (Jan. 1878), p.24; no. 2 (Sept. 1878), p.105; no. 4 (Sept. 1879), p.218; vol. II, no. 6 (September 1880), p.30.

58. *Ibid,* no. 1 (January 1878), p.24.

59. HCA, 7031/ 22, pp.267-68, 299, Tatham's Nov. 1878-79 reports; HCA, 7106/1 1879, fo 2v, payment 116, fo 3r, payment 118.

vicarage was an 'eyesore', its replacement by 'a nice building at the corner of Castle Street would be a great ornament … to the Close', a judgement that has stood the test of time.[60]

The Dean and Chapter eventually agreed to this scheme, and promised to 'give substantial aid towards the proposed work' provided the appeal raised £500, reserving to itself 'the arrangements necessary for carrying out the erection of the building'. The great and the good of Herefordshire responded quickly and generously, the benefaction list being headed by the Tathams' £50, followed by £25 from Major Rankin (the city library's great benefactor), and £20 each from Dean Herbert, Major Cazalet and H.H. Higgins. Eventually, over £550 was raised from nearly 200 individual donations, almost one third of them being reverend gentlemen.[61] Although the whole £500 had not been at that point been raised, the Chapter was sufficiently encouraged to instruct Kempson on 25 June 'to prepare plans for the proposed classrooms, with library over, adjoining the Cathedral School' at a total cost of £750, exclusive of the architect's 5 *per cent* fee. This included the pulling down of the front of the old vicarage – containing 'a very poor classroom' and locker-room on the ground floor and the sanatorium, lumber room and porter's accommodation of the upper floors – and replacing the rooms with new cellars and two new classrooms, one of which was designated for the under school and the other, the masters' room, 'for Music, Drawing, Chemistry and other small classes.'[62] Kempson's plans for the new porter's lodge and sick bay at the back of the old vicarage were approved on 12 August and completed at Tatham's personal expense (£260) by November 1881. At that year's audit, the Headmaster's report was much more cheerful than it had been three years earlier, when the problems of finding a book room had seemed insuperable:

> I rejoice that you eventually decided to my proposal to add to the schoolroom. The two new classrooms are much needed and the Gilbert memorial library (for which I am happy to inform you I have collected the required £500) will be a great boon to the school. Classrooms are almost necessarily cheerless in appearance and ours perhaps peculiarly so. I have always felt that a pleasant room for the more studious to retire to in play time was a great *desideratum*. Our increasing collection of books, too, deserve to be more worthily housed. Externally also our new buildings in place of the unsightly old vicarage house are or will be a decided improvement to the Close. I wish to move my school bell, which has remained on the roof of my own house, to the new buildings. I do not know whether you would be disposed to a small additional outlay to build us something of a belfry. It would be useful and also ornamental, and since the recent high wind has carried off the metal ventilator, the mass of roof would certainly look better if relieved by something of this kind.[63]

---

60. The above plans are outlined in HCA, 7031/22, pp.335-36, Tatham's report, 5 Nov. 1880.

61. A donors' list was later published in *TH*, no. 8 (Jan. 1882), pp.3-5. As well as the Dean, it included two bishops (the diocesan and the Bishop of London, Tatham's father-in-law), two archdeacons, the Precentor, eight prebendaries, the Custos and 45 other clergymen (of whom Woollam, Rudd and Tatham were three), the Chapter and Town Clerks, three MPs, members of the nobility and many families – headed by seven Weatherlys (F.E., E.C., F., A.W., A.J., H.H. and L.G.)

62. HCA, 7031/22, pp.340, 343, 353, Acts, 5 Feb., 24 March and 25 June 1881. *TH*, no. 9 (Sept. 1882), p.33.

63. HCA, 7031/22, pp.364-65, 5 Nov. 1881.

Given that the Chapter later opposed the construction of a new staircase and interconnecting doorway, it is doubtful whether the cathedral saw its way to providing an ornamental belfry. Nevertheless, the Gilbert memorial library, built over the period October 1881 to April 1882 for around £800,[64] and the other new rooms were greatly admired. Tatham considered them 'thoroughly convenient and well-built and a most pleasing contrast in every respect, external and internal, to the other part of the building'.[65] This verdict was echoed by *The Herefordian* editors, who in the September 1882 issue described the great room with considerable pride, drawing attention to 'the old bookcase, heightened, enlarged with a new wing and beautified with new mouldings'; the handsome furnishings, including the honours board adorning the west wall; and the glazed north window, with its four stained glass panels bearing the coats of arms of their respective donors: Thomas Llanwarne, Old Herefordian and city mayor, Bishop Atlay, Dean Herbert and Headmaster Tatham.[66] (Plate 12).

The new library's book collection was rather more important than its aesthetic effect, pleasing though that undoubtedly was after the drab schoolroom. Shortly after its opening, some 800-900 books – including many donations, as well as the purchases of the library committee – lined the shelves of the new bookcase. Although the number was comparatively small, the books had been collected over only five years – the initial impetus coming from the old boys – and (as *The Herefordian* pointed out) there was 'little lumber and less rubbish' and 'something to suit all tastes'. And over the following years, the collection was gradually expanded, not only (as might be expected) by the acquisition of works of reference, ancient, modern and local histories and classical and theological commentaries, but also by the adding of works of political economy, natural history and novels, as well as books written by Old Herefordians.[67] No catalogue or library register exists for this period, so how far these books were borrowed, let alone read and understood, is unknown. Nevertheless, and despite the library's use as a classroom for the Upper Fourth in 1885, and the inevitable wear and tear of the leather topped tables and the birch wood chairs,[68] it can

64. Kempson's plans for the library and other rooms have not been located. However, the main contract was with William Cullis and was sealed on 10 November 1881 for £1,040 for all the works, £300 being provided by the Chapter, £240 by the Headmaster (for the reconstruction of the old vicarage) and £500 by the appeal. *Ibid.*, p.360. Also see, *ibid.*, pp.373, 379 (11 March, 3 April 1882), re Cullis' orders to provide three iron tie rods in the upper schoolroom and fit gas pipes in the new classrooms, but refusing his estimate for a new staircase and interconnecting first-floor door; and HCA, 71061/1 1881, fo 93r no. 121, 1882, fo 140v, nos 115, 116, 119, fo 141r nos 121, 130, for further payments. In 1881-82, the Chapter spent over £475 (excluding chorister payments) on the school, including, and at Tatham's insistence, £2 5s on insurance – the first time that the school had been insured.

65. HCA, 7031/22, p.401, his report, 6 Nov. 1882.

66. *TH*, no. 9 (Sept. 1882), pp.34-35. Thomas Llanwarne (1837-1905) was a local solicitor, who – like J.R. Symonds OH (1850-1924) – served three terms as city mayor.

67. Acquisitions were periodically listed in *The Herefordian*. Tatham's selection of novels in summer 1888 included works by Jane Austen, Walter Scott, Whyte Melville, Besant and Rice and the inevitable Trollope's Barsetshire chronicles. Old Herefordian acquisitions included John Gwillim's *Display of Heraldry*; W.H. Cooke's *History of Herefordshire;* Charles Anthony's *Social and Political Dependence of Women* and *Popular Sovereignty*; and the young E.J. Rapson's *Struggle for Supremacy in India*.

68. *TH*, no.1 NS (Oct. 1885), p.44, letter from 'A Conservative'.

be fairly said – to use a boy editor's image – that from 1882 the school had a worthy literary shrine to add to its *genius loci*.

Wyeside and the Games Revolution

Tatham was a fine classical scholar and teacher but whether he was much of a sportsman may be doubted. As far as we know, he never played cricket with or against the 1st XI, for example, nor is there any record of his capabilities at other sports. Nevertheless, like many mid-Victorian Headmasters, he was a firm believer in *mens sana in corpore sano,* and made sure that his assistant masters were well qualified to make up for his own lack of athletic prowess. As he told his governors in 1879, his philosophy in a school where it was impossible to offer 'either large salaries at first or any prospect of increasing them' was to recruit 'the best possible man even though they are not likely to remain long'.[69] This meant a considerable turnover of staff, especially in his early years, but also resulted in the appointment of young and able men, many of whom were keen to coach the games that they had enjoyed – and often excelled in – at school and university. Tatham gave full recognition to their work in his valedictory letter of 26 May 1890:

> I have been fortunate in having masters under me who have not only devoted themselves to the work of the school but have brought much practical skill to assisting the boys in their games and sports. It is owing to them that there is no school where things are done in better style or where more brilliant results on the river, the running path or the football ground have been produced of late years than here. Witness our role of 'Blues' and a list of men representing their colleges or their hospitals on field and flood such as few schools twice our size could boast of. The school will not soon forget the names of Spencer and Poole, of Disney and Fenner, of Evors and Barton, of Daniel and Guest.[70]

We have seen how games had developed at the school under Rudd, but by 1875 they were still optional activities, which lacked coherent organisation and, above all, a central focus. As Arthur Machen later recorded, long country walks, rather than strenuous activity on the games field, were still perfectly acceptable ways for a boy to spend his half-holiday in the late 1870s.[71] Under Tatham, however, games – like sport at the bigger public schools – were gradually to become 'compulsory, organised and eulogised'.[72] The key to this transformation at Hereford was the making of a school playing-field.

It was not that the school had lacked access to games areas. The playground, a space of some 1150 square yards, was an important place for honing ball skills, even though the fives

69. HCA, 7031/22, p.296, report, 8 Nov. 1879. Also see *ibid.*, p.475, for Tatham's comment, 9 Nov. 1885: 'I am rather annoyed that I so often lose men who suit me but the fact is ... I get such good men that when other Headmasters see them, they try to lure them away'.

70. *TH*, no. 12 NS (June, 1890), pp.5-6. The masters were: Revd G.L. Spencer (1878-90), Revd S. Poole (1876-79), H.W. Disney (1881-83), G.H. Fenner (1879-82), C.A. Evors (1883-85), W.J. Barton (1883-84), J.H. Daniel (1885-90), E.P. Guest (1885-90).

71. Machen, p.88. Machen, who became a London journalist and prolific author, attended HCS (as Arthur Llewellyn Jones-Machen), 1874-80.

72. The phrase belongs to Newsome (1961), p.222.

court was dilapidated and inconveniently sited between the boots room and the covered drill shed. Much the most useful area for impromptu games was the square garden lawn, at the rear of the College buildings, which was of just sufficient length for a full-length cricket pitch (with a minuscule boundary), and also provided enough space – at a pinch – for a tennis court.[73] The lawn was retained after the College had reclaimed its buildings in 1875, and was rented personally by Tatham (at a cost of £5 *per annum*) on an insecure annual lease.[74]

In 1875, there were three principal areas for the main competitive sports. The Barrack Ground had become its home venue for rugby football and for the annual athletics sports in the 1860s, and the river Wye, aided by Jordan's boatyard, the centre for its rowing regatta from 1870.[75] Above all, Widemarsh Common, the city's cricket ground, had been used by several generations of boys for their own matches. It was good enough to host the All

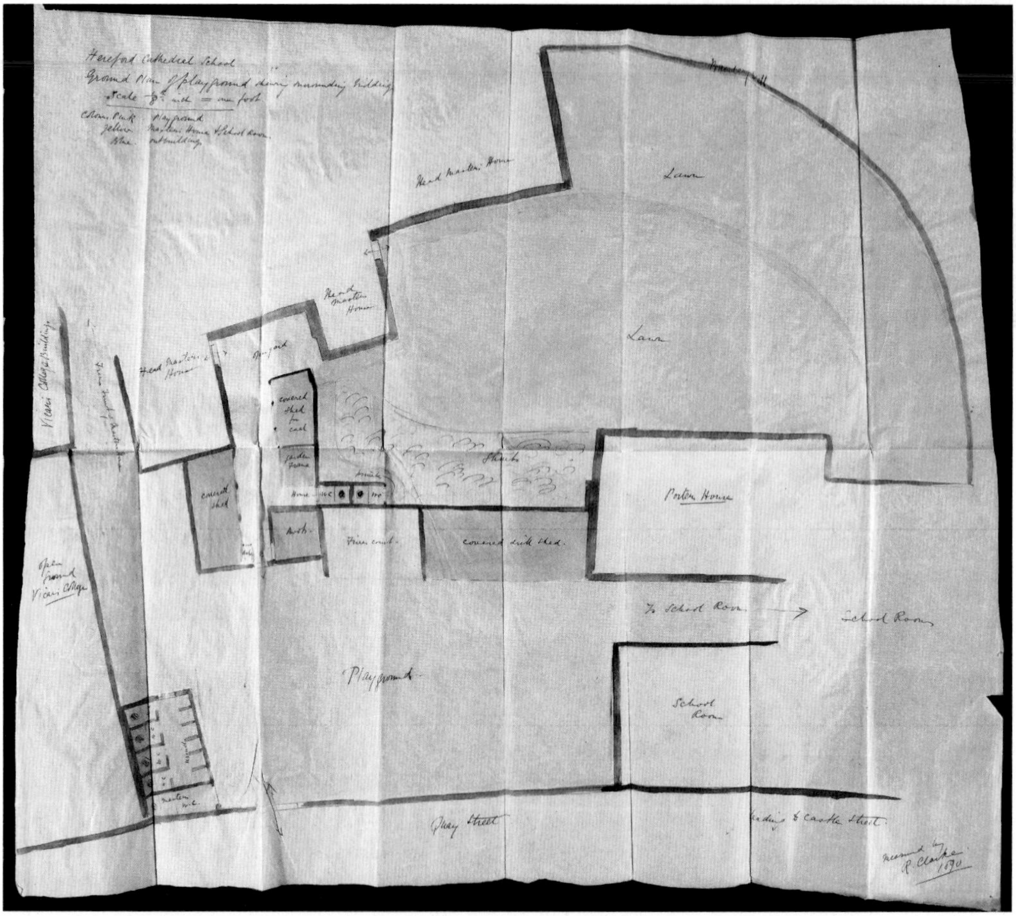

Fig. 6.3 Plan of the school playground (school yard), by R. Clarke, 1890.

73. The sizes of the two play areas were 36 by 18 and 23 by 22 yards. TNA, ED 27/1606, Leach's report, 25 July 1889, p.9. See HCA, 1541, for an 1890 plan of the school yard (Fig. 6.3), and below, p.266 and note 109, for fives and tennis.

74. It was revoked in the summer of 1889. See below, p.274, and HCA, 7003/1/6, pp.433ff, for the let to Tatham and subsequent squabbles over its terms.

75. See above, pp.262-64.

Fig. 6.4 Graffiti of a pup and the initials of John James Whitley on a garden wall of the College, carved when its north-east corner was used as part of the school playground. Whitley's initials are one of over 60 initials and names, carved on the wall in the 1870s and 1880s, that can still be deciphered. They include the name of Thomas Whitley (J.J.W.'s younger brother), who died of rheumatic fever at HCS on 4 June 1889.

England XI against 22 of Herefordshire in two three-day matches in 1850 and 1851, and was occasionally used by the school around this time.[76] A decade later, however, following the levelling of the railway side of the Common and its partial fencing in 1862, it became the school's regular home field.[77] Although property was by no means safe while a boy was playing cricket at Widemarsh – the stealing of a waistcoat and silver watch one August afternoon in 1868, allegedly by a drunken woman, was unlikely to have been the sole theft suffered by a pupil at play there in these years[78] – from a boy's viewpoint, there were certain advantages in using this venue. The turf was, at least to Yonge, 'incomparable', and the boys could engage and test their batting skills against the club professional. And having tasted the illicit delights of the city on their journey to the Common, they could enjoy themselves while they were there, well away from the confines of the Close and the watch of the school authorities, save for the occasional patrol of the drill sergeant and the friendly eye of a master or two on match days.

Not that all boys saw it in this way. The 1883 cricket captain had regarded the 'beastly fag of trudging down to Widemarsh' as the one great drawback against playing school cricket, a sentiment echoed by his immediate predecessor, who complained about 'the faithful few' who had supported the game that season at Widemarsh and 'the unreasonable demand of forming an eleven out of practically those who are tired of the river'.[79] Unsurprisingly, and for different reasons, the new Headmaster viewed Widemarsh with

76. Anthony, pp.56-65; *HT*, 28 Sept. 1850 p.8, report on the match against G.G. Hayter's school. In 1852, as we have seen (above, p.217), the England match was moved to the new racecourse ground.

77. *HT*, 22 March 1862, p.2. The previous year, at a school match during the Whitsuntide holiday, it was reported that spectators were pleased that 'Widemarsh was again likely to become what it has been – the arena for the display of our national amusement'. *Ibid.*, 25 May 1861, p.2.

78. *Ibid.*, 29 August 1868, p.7.

79. *TH*, vol III no. 9 (Sept. 1882), pp.48-9; no. 12 (Oct. 1883), p.7. The 1882 and 1883 captains were brothers: J.H. and H.S. Ware.

distaste. Indeed, before he had even witnessed a match on the Common, Tatham was pronouncing to his governors that the school's use of Widemarsh was 'most unsatisfactory in every respect', given that it could be approached only through the town, that it was 'entirely public and unenclosed', and that the boys were 'obliged to keep their things at a public house near the ground'. 'Nothing could be worse than this', he went on in his first governors' report, 'and you will agree with me that it is absolutely essential that steps should be taken to procure a fresh ground'. Tatham repeated this message – further emphasising that the people who played on the common were of 'miscellaneous character', and that for parents 'a good field within easy distance' was 'one of the first requirements of a school' – at every subsequent opportunity.[80] Fortunately for the new Headmaster, land was declining in value at this time and was cheaply available, but the key question for the school was its location.

Tatham searched for a suitable site for more than six years. Within weeks of his taking office, 12 acres near Barton station came on to the market, and he suggested that the school should form a joint stock company to buy eight of them. The Chapter refused to countenance this venture as a corporate body, as it did not consider its responsibility extended to providing 'such [a] playground', although its members were willing individually to take up shares to the value of £20 in the proposed company, 'they as citizens of Hereford considering the matter of great importance for the welfare of the school'. However, they were not obliged to honour this promise for the scheme foundered, and we hear no more about it. Two years later, in November 1877, Tatham looked at two other meadows for a cricket field – one bordering the river in Bartonsham and the other opposite the palace. Bishop Atlay, however, refused to cede this meadow to the school, 'in spite of the effectual barrier from intrusion which the river would give him'; and although Tatham still hoped as late as 1881 to acquire the land 'near the infirmary' at Bartonsham, and the Dean and Chapter made an official approach to the Ecclesiastical Commissioners for the meadow, these hopes, too, were dashed. By this time, the school's temporary exclusion from the Barrack Ground and its failure to purchase the meadow at Portfield, which it rented in 1880, made the situation more serious. In November 1882, however, Tatham was able to inform his governors that the school had at last obtained what he hoped would become 'a cricket ground of its own'. 'We are now laying down a piece 50 yards square', Tatham continued, 'and if the friends of the school help, as I hope they will, I propose to extend this further and after to build some kind of pavilion'. This had come about through the good offices of H.C. Beddoe, bishop's secretary and father of a boy at the school. Following the abortive negotiations for the Bartonsham meadow, it was Beddoe who offered Tatham the lease of 12 acres of diocesan land a mile or so further upstream. Tatham jumped at the opportunity and rented it personally on the school's behalf at a cost of £40 *per annum*, plus an additional £17 annually for rates, from 25 March 1882, although as the land was conveniently divided into two by a hedge, half of it was let to Sharp the butchers for grazing and the Chapter pledged a further £20 *per annum* towards its maintenance.[81]

80. HCA, 7031/22, pp.167, 268, 334, 402, reports, Nov. 1875, 1878, 1880 and 1882.

81. *Ibid.*, pp.164, 167, 227, 268, 334, 365, 368, 373, 402, Tatham's reports and the various responses, 1875, 1877-78, 1880-82.

A cricket ground soon arose from these pastures. G. Leigh Spencer, Tatham's Second Master, was primarily responsible for its development. By December 1883, following Spencer's two appeals in the pages of *The Herefordian*, the considerable sum of £212 8s 7d had been spent on draining, levelling, rolling and mowing the field, and erecting fences, gates and a rudimentary wooden pavilion, albeit one with running water. Nearly all the money was raised through private subscriptions and the proceeds from two evenings of amateur 'theatricals' in the Big Schoolroom.[82] Although further levelling, as well as improvements to the pavilion (a verandah and pavilion honours board of the XIs since 1883 were added in 1887-88) were still to occur, the ground was in a sufficient state of readiness to stage a cricket match on 16 May 1883, when the School XI comprehensively beat Spencer's scratch team. This was followed by the first athletics sports day there on 17 March 1884. Later that year, the first rugby football match (against the Malvern club) occurred on 18 October 1884, although the meadow at Portfield and the field opposite the Palace were also later hired for winter games, and it was not until after Tatham had left that the six acres next to the cricket field were levelled for rugby matches.[83] But before Tatham's departure, the name 'Wyeside' had been adopted for the new sports field.[84]

By the end of Tatham's headmastership, the organisation of games had also been transformed. First, the school committee of senior boys responsible for HCS's sporting administration was made more representative. Although its origins are unknown, this body certainly existed in the mid-1860s when the boys organised the first proper sports day at the Barrack Ground.[85] A decade later, by the time of the first issue of *The Herefordian*, the school committee was the nerve centre of the extra-curricular programme: issuing and accepting 'challenges' against other schools; electing cricket and football captains and 'keepers', as well as *Herefordian* editors and school librarians; organising fixture cards and regatta races; and awarding 'caps'. But it had also become a small self-perpetuating elite. In September 1877, however, its constitution was reformed by the enlarging of its membership to a maximum of nine boys – including the six senior monitors and the captains of cricket and football *ex officio*. As that year's *Herefordian* editors explained, this new committee replaced the 'inadequate' former system 'of filling up vacancies simply by the votes of the remaining committee men', which had resulted in 'the elective power… [falling] into the hands of a very small body'.[86]

---

82. For the published accounts: *TH*, no. 13 (Feb. 1884), p.32, payments to Charles Morgan, W. Pritchard, W.J. Yeomans, Ralph and Preece, P. Prosser and S. Herbert; and see *TH*, no. 10 (Jan. 1883), p.73, for the performances of 'The Cantab' and 'The Ladies Battle', featuring Misses M. Norris and E. Symonds, on 15, 16 January 1883 at which £57 7s was raised.

83. *Ibid.*, no. 12 (Oct. 1883), pp.8-9; I NS (Oct. 1884), pp.6-10; II NS (March 1885), p.18, for the reports on the first cricket, athletics and rugby on the new ground. See below, p.283, for the levelling of the second field.

84. The first usage of 'Wyeside' that I have come across occurred in the report of the rugby match against Christ's College (won by HCS) of 2 November 1889. *Ibid.*, no. VIII NS (Feb. 1889), p.4. The name was not original. See *ibid.*, IV NS (Oct. 1887), p.36, for a reference to the Wyeside lawn tennis club.

85. *Supra*, p.223. It may have gone back even earlier as at other schools. At Rugby, for instance, the first rules 'for the better observance of football', having been set out by eight boys in 1844, were written down in August 1845 by a committee of three boys, who were elected following a meeting of the Sixth Form 'Levée'. Orr, p.16.

86. *TH*, no. 1 (Jan. 1878), p.22.

The school committee also had the considerable responsibility of fixing the level of pupil sporting subscriptions. Its financial powers were further enhanced by its careful organisation of annual monetary collections, on an area basis, from the good citizens of Hereford before the autumn sports day. In Easter Term 1883, Tatham put a stop to both practices by the simple expedient of levying (as he later explained to the Dean and Chapter) 'a [compulsory] graduated charge upon the parents of the boys for the expenses of all the sports'. 'One gentleman', he continued, 'removed his son in consequence, but all the others cheerfully acceded to and approved of the arrangement'.[87] Unsurprisingly, *The Herefordian* announced the introduction of the new financial arrangement in rather different terms, explaining that 'the old system of asking for donations to meet the expenses of the sports, concert etc.' had become 'rather unwieldy'. One further consequence of the reform was the establishment of a new financial committee of four – chaired by Tatham, with his Second Master as treasurer and two pupil representatives from the school committee – in the place of the previous two-man body of a boy treasurer and a schoolmaster auditor.[88] The Headmaster had at last gained control of the school's extra-curricular funds.

As well as putting a stop to the abuses that could arise from the annual collections,[89] the new system had the additional advantage of providing a regular fee income of over £100 *per annum* for sporting and other activities. This sum, together with the £40 annual rental income from the let of the six-acre field adjoining the cricket ground, the Chapter gift of £20 *per annum*, the 'locker' money from the boys, who also continued to pay entry fees for competing at sports day and the rowing regatta, and occasional windfalls like the £11 15s raised from lemonade sales during the summer of 1884, meant that games were properly funded for the first time. One further consequence of the requirement that parents pay an extra fee for games was that cricket and football became compulsory. When club subscriptions were paid on a permissive basis by the boys themselves, it was possible for sport to remain a voluntary activity – an impossibility once the subscription was added to the parental bill. Tatham had made these games compulsory for boarders by the end of 1884, and reported that he would also like to do so for day boys if he could be sure of parental support.[90] And for the school authorities, compulsion had another beneficial side effect. As Tatham observed in that same report, through the acquisition of the cricket ground and the increase in numbers playing games, he had 'been able to check the tendency to "loaf"' which he considered was 'so very objectionable in boys during their play hours'. It was less than two decades from Woollam's resignation but Tatham was occupying a very different world.

---

87. HCA, 7031/22, p.432, 7 Nov. 1883. The termly games fee was 10s for the upper forms, 7s 6d for the fourth and 5s for the junior forms. *Ibid.*, p.414, Act of 5 Apr. 1883. T.H. Parker has left a description of how the old practice had operated in *c.*1880 in *HCN*, (Christmas, 1959), no. 47, pp.8-9.

88. *TH*, no. 12 (Oct. 1883), p.1. The new committee later absorbed *The Herefordian* accounts, following their negative balance in March 1886. Although the cricket and boat club accounts were still kept separate, they were audited by the all-powerful financial committee.

89. See above, p.223, note 161, for example, for Yonge's description of lobbying one of Hereford's parliamentary candidates in the Green Dragon in 1866.

90. HCA, 7031/22, p.456, 11 Nov. 1884. Three years later, by the time of the Golden Jubilee, when summer games were extended to three afternoons per week, this had almost certainly been achieved.

The net result of such reforms – together with Tatham's appointment of energetic and skilful games-playing masters, and the school's acquisition of a playing field – was that sport flourished as never before, in terms of both the standard to which games were played and the recognition that they were given by the school authorities.[91]

The school's sporting year in Tatham's time generally started with a quaint pastime: the paper-chase, a cross-country run of 'hounds' chasing 'hares', who laid a paper 'scent' for their pursuers. Although the race had originated in the previous century, it is not known when it started at HCS. Nevertheless, it is evident that numerous cathedral schoolboys participated in this chase in the 1870s and 1880s, even though they seldom overtook their quarry.[92] Senior boys and occasionally masters acted as the 'hares' and took great delight in laying false trails and leading their knicker-bockered and motley-costumed 'hounds', a few equipped with bugles as hunting horns, a long and less than merry dance around the Herefordshire countryside. This account of the paper-chase of Saturday 19 October 1878 will serve for many:

> The hares, Mr G.L. Spencer and C.E. Hopton, started punctually at 2pm, and were allowed 20 minutes before the hounds, about 30 in number, started. There were the usual variety of appearance from 'the complete football player' to the motley costume gathered from the cricket, rowing or Thursday's athletic wardrobe, as the troop passed down Commercial Street, over Aylestone Hill, on the top of which scent was first laid. The find announced by not a few 'halloos' downhill to the Lugg meadow was merry work. Then came awkward jumps … At the second ditch came the first check, and several of the hounds found themselves engaged on a goose-chase … The scent was at last struck off from the meadows by the River Frome, luckily at a ford. There was, however, a bridge close at hand, and most of the hounds preferred this higher level. Withington was soon reached, and the Stoke Edith grounds entered. Straight past the church some quarter of a mile from Lady Foley's mansion, the hares, half an hour in front, had run up the hill through the park on to Adam's Rocks and Backberry Hill. The hounds had already lost some ground, and these rocks in front were destined to place still wider apart pursuers and pursued … Suddenly one found again the track of the hares, and one party still stuck to the stern chase till it was too dark to see the scent. These came home by Lugwardine and Eign Hill, arriving about 7pm, some three quarters of an hour or more after Hopton and Mr Spencer … But they were not last; stragglers collected into a body again panted in not a whit less satisfied than their longer legged and winded fellows. The distance run cannot have been much less than twenty miles … It was rather too long but completely successful, if success is measured by the pleasure of the hounds and not the capture of the hares.

With the notable exception of the occasional farmer who had his crops trampled by the pursuing pack, the locals seemed to have enjoyed the spectacle. For the boarding masters,

91. Unless otherwise indicated, the evidence for the following paragraphs on games and other activities is to be found in the relevant editions of *The Herefordian*.

92. As late as 1899, paper-chases were one of the activities that some Headmasters suggested as suitable for the Lent term. *HMC 1899 Committee,* pp.15-18, athletics survey. The last recorded paper-chase to have been run at HCS was on 13 October 1914.

it occupied their charges with healthy exercise for their first afternoon of the academic year; for the non-sporty, there were the autumnal fruits and the views (one non-athletic classicist even thinking that a descent to 'the little white line' in the valley would aid understanding of '*facilis defensus Averni*'); and for the boys who took their sports more seriously, it provided useful training for the football season.

At national level, major alterations to the playing of this winter game coincided with the period of Tatham's headship, following the formation of the Rugby Football Union and the codification of its laws in 1871. Sides of 15 were introduced at the varsity match of 1875, and in the later years of that decade the universities again led the way in developing the handling game. Changes were then made to the offside rule; the practice of 'punting out' was abolished; and by the mid-1880s a points scoring system was introduced. Tatham considered that the new rules made the game 'less rough' than it had been, but he still thought it 'a dangerous game', and in 1885 organised a series of lectures for masters and senior boys 'on rendering first aid to the injured' because of 'the many accidents we have had in the football field'.[93]

The new ways of playing the game took some time to reach provincial clubs, and as late as March 1877 the school played the Hereford club side under 'Association' rules, even though HCS had long adopted the Union code.[94] There were other uncertainties. Although the number of players on each side became settled at 12 for school matches and 15 for club matches, there could be confusion as to the composition of the sides, Monmouth being guilty of playing masters against the boys of Hereford in the late 1870s, and Worcester Grammar including seven old boys and two masters in a match of February 1887.[95] Perhaps this is unsurprising in 'challenges' organised by the boys themselves. Nor is it surprising at a time when matches were either unofficiated or, at best, had boy 'umpires', to find that disputes arose over the interpretation of the laws, particularly in matches against local clubs which formed the preponderance of the fixtures.[96] And then there was the boys' failure to adapt to rugby's new subtleties, as on 17 December 1879, when they were heavily defeated by a strong 'Past' side, who (so *The Herefordian* reported) played 'the new fast game, and we have been accustomed only after the old style to take things more quietly, waiting to form a scrimmage'. These problems were compounded in the days before compulsory games when the team did not turn up for training, one captain complaining (in 1883) of the need for his successor 'to awaken some of the sleepy, fire-side novel readers, and to stir up some of those who find such enjoyment in lounging about the town'.[97] Nevertheless, despite such practices, the school established a good reputation in the game. HCS might not have been able to match Christ College, Brecon, Llandovery and the stronger 'Past' teams, and only

93. HCA, 7031/22, pp.476-77, report 9 Nov. 1885. The instruction was given by Dr Moore, 'the local lecturer acting under the Order of St John', and all 30 members of the class gained their certificate. *TH*, no. II NS (May 1886), p.2.

94. Unsurprisingly, as HCS was unaccustomed to these rules, 'there was more frequent handling than there otherwise would have been'. *HT*, 3 March 1877, p.3.

95. *Ibid.*, 16 Dec. 1876, p.3; *TH*, no. 3 (Jan. 1879), p.153; no. III NS (May 1887), pp.9-10.

96. For example, see *ibid.*, no. 3 (Jan. 1879), p.151, for a report of an ill-tempered game between HCS and the Hereford FC.

97. *Ibid.*, no. 12 (Oct. 1883), p.5.

occasionally did it do so against Bromsgrove, but it more than held its own against other schools and local club sides. And in J.A. Bevan, R.G.T. Coventry – captains of rugby, 1875-77 and 1887-88 – and C.H. Ware, HCS produced at least three outstanding players in this period.[98]

Two 'show' events of the school's sporting calendar followed the end of the football season: sports day (from 1884) and the regatta. The former, in particular, was to undergo considerable changes in the 1880s in terms of its venue, timing and organisation. Until 1884, the Barrack Ground remained the location, apart from the 1880 sports day, when Lane's Field, Broomy Hill, was used, despite 'the unevenness of the ground ... [being] somewhat against the athletes'. The school's return to its militia base, however, proved short-lived, and after a particularly wet day on 19 October 1882, good sense prevailed and the sports were moved to a spring date. As a boy meteorologist pointed out, April rainfall was then less than half that for October (2.4 inches, he recorded, compared with 5.42), and the chances for a dry day were that much better later in the academic year. This proved an accurate forecast, although it did not prevent the postponement of the event in 1889 because of flooding. As has already been told, the first sports day was held on the new cricket ground on 17 March 1884, with a track of four laps to the mile 'and an excellent course for the sprints across the centre of the field'. While the new field meant that some events such as hammer throwing – introduced at a master's suggestion in 1879, but nearly resulting in the death of a small child in the 1882 games – had to be abandoned, others such as the steeple-chase could be introduced. 'With all the Wye before us' (as a boy reported after the first Wyeside meeting), a steeple-chase course was marked out, 'under the railway embankment, going round to the left of the waterworks and back through Mr Symonds' meadow, with a water jump to wind up with'. Later other events were introduced – a tug of war, donkey races, putting the weight – heralded by *The Herefordian* as a new competition (wrongly, although perhaps this time without the run-up) – and an obstacle race, with the boys having to face the extra challenge of an addition sum on the way round. With the abolition of the athletics collections, the organisational changes were no less far-reaching, and by the time of the first Wyeside sports, it was quite clear that the 'indefatigable' Second Master, who had done so much towards creating the new field, had largely taken over the running of the day, although a committee of three (including two boys) still organised the handicapping, and to much greater effect.

The main feature of the regatta, the 'Oxford' against 'Cambridge' race – the crews now sporting the dark and light blues of their respective universities[99] – continued through this period, although some organisational changes were made: from 1881 the date (as well as the time – in the early days the race was not started until news of the result of the official boat race had been received) was no longer tied to that of the university race; the course was lengthened for some races;[100] programmes were prepared for spectators from

98. All three men followed J.E. Deakin in gaining 'Blues', and Bevan captained Wales in the first international against England on 19 Feb. 1881, when Wales lost by eight goals to nil.

99. Although some of the 1877 'Cambridge' crew wore caps of pink and white – the old Cambridge colour. *HT*, 31 March 1877, p.3.

100. For example, in 1883 it was extended from Hunderton Villa to the boathouse for the School v School House

Fig. 6.5 The winning crew of the public schools' challenge cup at Henley, July 1883: D.Ll. Rhys (bow); F.C. Palmer (2); H.S. Ware (3); N.P. Symonds (stroke); and B. Norton (cox). Their coach was H.W. Disney, who had won an Oxford rowing 'Blue' in 1879.

1884; and in 1886 and 1887 handsome trophies were awarded for the scratch fours and junior pairs events, respectively. Correspondingly, after 1884, the canoe and sailing races were abandoned – possibly a consequence of the post-race tradition of unseating the canoeists into the Wye and the fluctuating wind conditions experienced over the years by the sailors. But the oarsmen could not be immune from both the vagaries of the spring weather and the fast running of the Wye at that time of year, the river being accurately described, after the 1884 races had been rowed on a full stream, as being 'as capricious as it is lovely and sometimes knows no bounds'.[101] The greatest change, however, occurred in the quality of the school's rowing, particularly in the early 1880s, when H.W. Disney – himself a member of the 1879 Oxford crew – was a master. The highlight was his coaching of the winning crew in the public schools challenge cup at Henley in July 1883, which marked the apogee of school rowing in this period.[102]

Despite the 'alluring delights of the river', which took boys away from the summer game especially in the days when HCS still played on Widemarsh, cricket came to dominate the school's sporting year in the 1880s. Tatham acquired Wyeside primarily with a view to making a cricket ground; double the number of cricket matches were played in any one

race. The previous year, *The Herefordian* had suggested that the waterworks should be the start point, lengthening the course to three-quarters of a mile, although it is not clear whether this suggestion was adopted.

101. *TH,* no. 1 NS (Oct. 1884), p.10.

102. The crew was D.Ll. Rhys, F.C. Palmer, H.S. Ware, N.P. Symonds (stroke) and B. Norton (cox). For a full description of the race, see *TH,* no. 12 (Oct. 1883), pp.21-23. The victory was achieved against the odds. Competing at Henley was an expensive business – with costs (for 1884, when the title was unsuccessfully defended) running at over £40, which had to be raised by private subscription. Although C.O. Fowler had been elected (by his peers) as the first captain of boats in 1876-77, the school had no boats of its own. For the 1883 race, a boat had to be borrowed from Eton College; in 1884, one from Oxford was used. An HCS boat club was not formally established until the late-1880s, when a landing stage was erected by the cricket field and separate boat club accounts were published in *The Herefordian.*

season over football; and three times the amount of space was devoted to cricket in the school's annals than to any other sport. The acquisition of its own ground was to prove a major reason for the transformation of the school's cricket in this period. Although 2nd and 3rd XIs had been formed from 1880, in the last few seasons at Widemarsh the game was not always well supported by either boys or masters – with the notable exception of Revd Sealy Poole and Mr W.S. Rawson, who in 1878 had a batting average of 86 and took 30 wickets in five matches for the side. In the last season on the Common (1882), however, no master was available either to play in club games or to coach the boys. As *The Herefordian* remarked, with the move to the new ground, cricket was put on a 'much firmer footing ... than ... ever before'. From the first year at Wyeside, one Upton – described as 'a very efficient groundman', although he was not the practice bowler that HCS needed – was employed as cricket professional. Things improved over the following two seasons with the hiring of Stokes and then (in 1885) Clark, but it was not until 1886 that the services of the same cricketer-groundsman were retained. Thereby began Dick Shepherd's long association with the Cathedral School. But there were other reasons for the improved state of the school's cricket. Masters were more willing to coach and play, and with the introduction of compulsory games, the competition among the boys for places in the XIs became keener, so much so that in 1888 the school could afford to dispense with the services of masters even in club matches. This was a considerable change for the better as the vast majority of fixtures were against club sides, never more than five matches being played against schools out of the dozen or so in any one season.[103] In 1885, three further reasons were advanced by the school's correspondent for the 1st XI's record breaking season: the good wickets which had by then been laid; the finance committee's incentive of bat awards for innings of 50 and over; and the introduction of cricket 'fags' ('which no doubt is an excellent thing if properly looked after'). These golden years for HCS cricket in the mid-1880s could not last,[104] and in 1890 only one match was won. Nevertheless, in that year the standing of the school's cricket was recognised when, following improvements to the wicket over the winter, W.G. Grace brought down 11 men on 26 May 1890 to play 18 of the county at Wyeside. Two months later, it was fitting that in the last match that Tatham watched at Wyeside, one of his old boys had scored the first ever century on the ground that the Headmaster had done so much to establish.[105]

In the week before Tatham's appointment was approved in Chapter in May 1875, an article on school reports appeared in *Punch*. It imagined how a report might look in 1895

103. The three regular school fixtures in this period were Christ College, Brecon, Llandovery (played at Brecon), and (from 1882) Oswestry Grammar School (played at Church Stretton, Ludlow or Shrewsbury). The Gloucester Cathedral School match was dropped after 1880, and the only fixtures against Monmouth (home and away) were played in 1885. The annual coach outing remained a highlight of the season, as in 1882 against Garnons when according to *The Herefordian* correspondent: 'We met with a somewhat warm reception from the natives on our return to make up the lavish supply of peas with which we had favoured them as we went'.

104. In the three seasons 1884-86, the 1st XI won 33 of the 42 games played, including six successive wins against the county side.

105. The honour belonged to C.H. Ware, who scored 136 (including 'probably the biggest hit ever made on the school ground to the foot of the railway embankment') against a weak 1st XI. *TH*, no. XIII NS (Oct. 1890), pp.17-18.

when written by one Arnold Busby Brown, the fictional Headmaster of the equally mythical St Paul's College, Eastminster, in which Mr Brown ('formerly stroke of the Lady Margaret eight and captain of the Cambridge XI') made this comment on a boy's form-work: 'No observations, the weather having been so fine this term that every day has been devoted to games'.[106] HCS was too classical a school to be compared fairly to a sporting academy like St Paul's, Eastminster, and Frances Tatham was far too learned and civilised a Headmaster to be mentioned in the same breath as Arnold Brown. Moreover, the one extant report from his headmastership does not even refer to sporting pursuits.[107] Nevertheless, by 1890 boys' games at HCS had become a serious activity, if not an all-consuming passion. The outdoor sporting facilities, as well as the organisation and financing of established games, had been transformed as we have seen. New sports, too, had been promoted. At the Headmaster's direct suggestion, swimming races were held from Jordan's raft in the early hours of 22 July 1878, even though there remained 'owing to the slackness of the stream, some traces of the 2,000 gallons of creosote with which the railway company had enriched our river three days before'.[108] Two years later he bought a net for the lawn tennis court which was marked out in the lower half of the playground, the forerunner of the establishment of a tennis club and court at Wyeside in the summer of 1885, in response to the 'enormous popularity' that the game had achieved 'in an almost unparalleled short space of time'. In 1887, the school's first tennis matches were played.[109] And by Tatham's last year, a gymnastic club had been started, Instructor Bromage from the Hereford gym coming over twice a week to coach the boys during the winter months.

More importantly, it is possible to detect a decisive shift in the school's attitude towards games over this 15-year period. By 1890, sport was no longer a voluntary activity. Distinctive caps and clothing were introduced for those in the XI and rugby football XII, which (in the words on an Old Herefordian) raised 'the esteem in which members of the cricket and football team are held by outsiders and makes the present boys more anxious to obtain places in them'.[110] The publication of no-nonsense sketches of team 'characters' in *The Herefordian*, the taking of team photographs and the creation of the pavilion honours board achieved the same result in different ways. Permanent challenge cups, named and handed down from year to year, began to be presented on sports day in recognition of athletics success, instead of individual prizes. Of particular importance was the award of the *victor ludorum* cup for the overall champion – given by Joseph Carless OH, Hereford's Town Clerk and a keen sportsman, in 1887 – which replaced the Weatherlys' annual medal. The award of 'colours' was a similar recognition of excellence in team sports. Headmaster

106. The article is reproduced in *HT,* 15 March 1875, p.3. Also see Mangan, pp.94-95.

107. KCA, EFB 01/04, midsummer 1878 report on one of the founders of the cider company, E.F. Bulmer, who Tatham referred to as 'a bright and intelligent boy'.

108. Tatham reported on these races (*TH*, no. 2, Sept. 1878, pp.80-81), and this perhaps indicates where his sporting sympathies really lay.

109. Tennis's popularity was in marked contrast to fives, a game which declined at HCS in the 1880s because of the poor state of the playground court, described in the October 1884 *Herefordian* as 'a disgrace to the school'.

110. *TH*, Vol II no. 8 (Sept. 1881), p.120, letter from 'A Quondam Captain'. In autumn 1881, the new football cap 'of velvet blue with a yellow silk tassel' was considered 'a great improvement on our former blue serge polo cap'. A distinctive football jersey was also being contemplated. *Ibid.*, Vol III no. 8 (Jan. 1882), pp.17-18.

Tatham may have left the coaching of games to the masters but he took a great pride in his boys' sporting achievements, and never more so than in July 1883 when he took the whole school down to the railway station to greet the winning four on their triumphant return from Henley and escorted them back to school 'amid enthusiastic cheers'.[111] Tatham even wrote up the victory a few months later in his annual report to the governors, the first time that the Dean and Chapter had been formally told of a non-academic honour.[112] When these successful athletes subsequently left school, their sporting exploits at university were eagerly followed in the pages of *The Herefordian*. And Old Herefordians who won 'Blues' became the stuff of legends.[113]

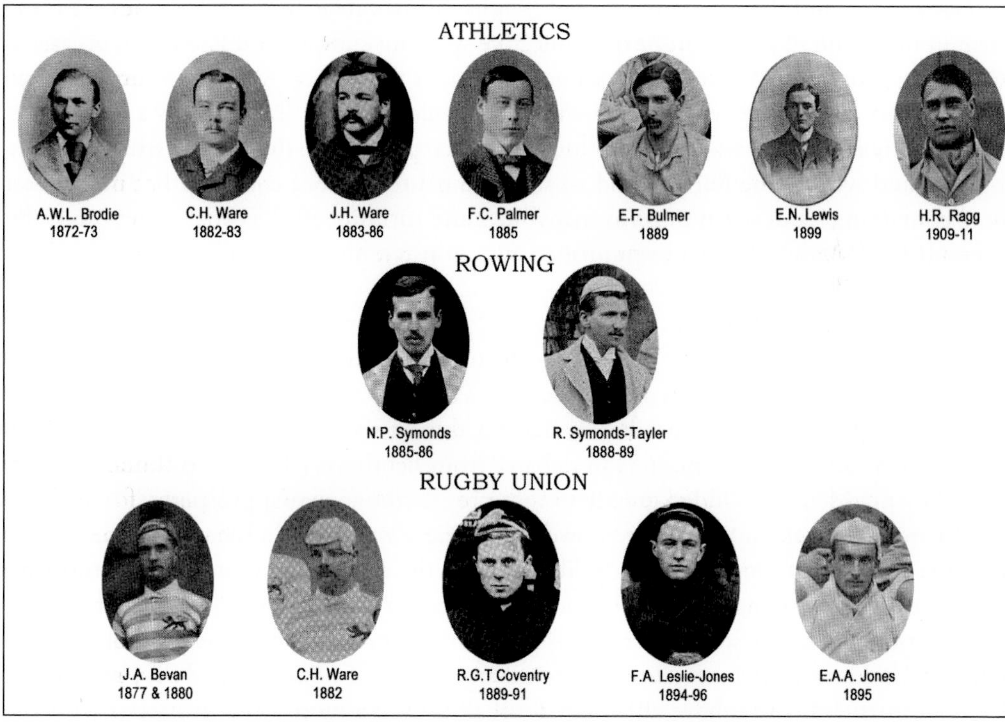

Fig. 6.6 In addition to the above Oxford and Cambridge 'Blues', the following OHs also won 'Blues' (or 'half-Blues'), 1860-1913: H.F. Baxter (Oxford, rowing, 1859-60); J.E. Deakin (rugby union, Cambridge, 1872); T.C.T. Reeve (cross-country, Cambridge, 1880); G.W. Grasett (hockey, Oxford, 1913); and W.M. Askwith (rowing, Cambridge, 1913). All told, 18 OHs won 'Blues' or 'half-Blues' at Oxford and Cambridge, 1860-1913, in five different sports, C.H. Ware winning 'Blues' in both athletics and rugby.

111. *Ibid.*, no. 12 (Oct. 1883), p.23.

112. Although he was careful to add that two of the crew had subsequently won university exhibitions. HCA, 7031/22, p.433, report 7 Nov. 1883.

113. For their names, see Fig. 6.6. Of these, C.H. Ware won 'Blues' in both rugby and athletics. His brother, J.H. Ware, who was President of OUAC in his final year, and who held the university record for 'putting the weight', also played cricket for Oxford against the MCC – 'hitting W.G. Grace out of the ground in two successive balls, though the third ball was sudden death'. See *TH*, no. II NS (Oct. 1886), p.29 and *passim*, for the records of other 'Blues'; and Honey, p.113 note, for the 'full-Blue' qualification.

Amateurism was, of course, the prevailing sporting ideal during Tatham's headship, despite his hiring of a cricket professional, an action that would have been anathema to Headmasters of an earlier generation. But many schoolmasters brought up in the mid-Victorian period held firmly to the doctrine of muscular Christianity that Charles Kingsley and Thomas Hughes had done so much to promote in the 1850s and '60s, and had an innate belief that healthiness was next to godliness and that games helped promote Christian virtues.[114] An article like 'Hints On Training', which appeared in *The Herefordian* for October 1889, could never have been written by a schoolmaster of an earlier generation.[115] If success at games brought a boy fulfilment in a way that he could not achieve in the classroom – and there were many such pupils in this category at HCS – where was the harm in that? And if, as a result of this collective sporting endeavour, HCS could occasionally triumph over the larger public schools so much the better. As Tatham explained to his governors in November 1883 following the Henley victory: 'I think it is a good thing for the school in every way that it should take its place with the public schools of the country, and we may be fairly proud of seeing our little school entering the lists against those containing six or seven times as many boys and carrying off the prize' – and especially when (as in this case) HCS had vanquished Westminster, his old school.

Debating, Music and Chapel

Aside from sport, the Debating Society was the only other formal club to exist at this time. It was revived in the mid-1870s and in Tatham's early years was in a flourishing condition, even if skating curtailed the number of debates during the hard winters of 1878-79 and 1879-80. The admission of masters to debates from February 1878 led to the resignation of the boy president but 'added greatly to increase … [the society's] prosperity'.[116] Motions became more topical, and a separate Lower Vth society was started. The change in location from the Sixth-form room to the new library, with the acquisition of a desk as a rostrum, also added to proceedings. However, from the mid-1880s debating's popularity began to wane. For the senior boys, earlier scholarship examinations precluded meetings in the Lent term; the holding of debates between 5 and 6pm on half-holidays made it difficult for day boys to attend; and (above all) rugby football proved a more attractive activity for the majority of boys. It is ironic that the motion, 'compulsory football is beneficial in schools', which was carried on 6 December 1879 when debating was at its height, sowed the seeds for the society's albeit temporary eclipse.

The reverse was true for such music as was taught. The Christmas 'dress' concerts continued much as before in a College Hall tastefully decorated by the ladies – rather than, as in bygone days, by the boys themselves – with evergreens, 'gay flags' and (in 1883) Chinese lanterns. The '*Floreat*' was always prominently displayed, although on 17 December 1878 Mrs Brown's enthusiasm got the better of her and the decoration was too

---

114. See Newsome (1997), pp.85, 87, 138, 159-60; Mack and Armytage, pp.97-99.

115. It appeared anonymously ('*verbum sap*') but given the reference to the 1878 Cambridge high jump event, it is highly likely that the piece was written by G.L. Spencer, the prime mover behind many of the school's sporting initiatives in this period.

116. *TH*, no. 2 (Sept. 1878), pp.81, 83.

heavy to be suspended, as customary, from the ceiling. The enormous popularity of these concerts also continued, the hall invariably being filled to its rafters, with old boys adding lustily to the singing and occasionally (as in 1881) disgracing themselves. Their format, too, remained largely the same, the glees, part-songs and orchestral pieces being supported by a band formed mainly of Old Herefordians, and Custos Duncombe often stealing the show with his golden voice. Perhaps the most notable innovation was the introduction of Fred Weatherly's new lyrical compositions – *Nancy Lee* in 1877, *Old Timbertoes* two years later and the school song (sung to the Custos' new tune rather than to the original German air) in 1881. By the mid-1880s, however, the quality of the school contributions to these concerts could no longer be guaranteed, and even *The Herefordian* reviewer made reference to the boys' poor rendition of the part songs in 1885 and 1886 and the lack of boy soloists. Burville was clearly losing his grip, and Tatham had little choice but to enforce his resignation from July 1887, when he retired as singing master (although not as instrumental teacher) after 25 years' service. Sixteen months later, and following the appointment of Mr Banks, the Headmaster could write that the singing class was 'now quite a different thing and our school concert at Christmas and performances at the speeches ... were a pleasing proof of the improved teaching in this department'. Encouraged by the Precentor, Sir Frederick Ouseley, who had been made a residentiary canon in 1886 and for whom Tatham had a high regard, a theory of music class had even been introduced.[117] Tatham left music, as much else, in a stronger state than he had found it, even if the school piano was on its last legs in 1890.[118]

One of Tatham's earliest initiatives was to persuade the Dean and Chapter not only to reserve seating for senior boarders at the front of the nave – the juniors occupied oak benches in the south transept – for the Sunday morning service, but also to secure the use of the Lady Chapel for two school services each term.[119] Although conditions were attached to the granting of this privilege and Tatham was by no means given a free hand in relation to the choice of dates, it at least gave the Headmaster the opportunity to preach to his school – minus, to his chagrin, the choristers – on a regular basis within the cathedral's setting.[120] He used this to good effect, as in 1878-79 when he successfully established charity collections for the Central African Mission, and the school adopted a boy from Zanzibar, christened Edwin Hereford Ramathani, through an annual payment of £6.[121] Even so, Tatham regretted the lack of a school chapel. As he mentioned to his governors in November 1885, the shortened form of daily prayer held in the school at 9am each week-day morning would be greatly improved if it could be held in the Lady Chapel:

117. See HCA, 7031/2, pp.38, 70, Tatham's reports, Nov. 1887 and 1888, for the references to Burville and Banks. Ouseley founded school prizes for reading as well as music theory.

118. A few years earlier one boy had described the piano as 'an instrument of torture'. *TH,* no. II NS (May 1886), p.18, letter from 'Orpheus'; *ibid.*, (Feb. 1890), p.28, letter from 'Antiquarian' for its state in 1890.

119. HCA, 7031/22, p.175, Chapter Clerk to Tatham, 8 Jan 1876; *HCN,* no. 43 (April-June 1959), p.5.

120. See HCA, 7031/23, pp.38-39, 66-67, 71, for Tatham's views on both the choristers' absence and restrictions on the school's use of the Lady Chapel in 1887 and 1888.

121. The story is related in successive editions of *The Herefordian*, following the sermon of the Revd T.W. Heins, the secretary of the Mission, in the school service on 24 May 1878.

> It would so far as the boys are concerned be a great benefit [for] prayers in a room are never quite the same as prayers in a church. To begin the day's work with a service in a church would have a hallowing and an elevating influence. The memories of lessons learned in a school chapel are often found to be the most enduring in a man's life, and in our case such a service would form one more link between the school and that noble church under whose shadow it stands and with which it has been for five centuries so closely associated.[122]

Even Tatham's purple prose could not influence his masters to require the Vicar of St John's to allow the school to use the Lady Chapel on a daily basis. Nor, and perhaps more importantly, could he persuade the organist either to start his choir practices at 9.15 or to hold them elsewhere than in the vestry. And he was no more successful in his later bid to acquire the old College chapel, which he described in November 1888 as 'at present used principally as a receptacle for beer bottles', for school prayers. Despite such frustrations, it was Tatham who should be given the credit for starting the practice of holding regular school services in the cathedral, and it was he who planted the seed which would eventually bear fruit in the form of a school chapel.[123]

Depression and Resignation

Tatham's last few years in office were tinged with other disappointments. One major issue was the steep decline in pupil numbers in the late 1880s: from the high water mark of 122 boys over the academic year 1881-82 to little more than 100 in each year from 1886 to 1890, more than ten boys fewer than the average for the late 1870s.[124] The boarding numbers (on which the school's and the Headmaster's prosperity depended) were particularly hard hit – down from a full senior house of 35 in 1885-86 to 15 or so fewer in 1889-90, despite a £10 reduction in the boarding fees which brought them to pre-1875 levels[125] – although day numbers were not unaffected. In a school which operated on slender margins, and where the accommodation after the building of the two additional classrooms in 1881-82 allowed for around 90 day boys and 50 boarders, such a decline was critical.

Like Power in 1857, Tatham was personally attacked towards the end of his headmastership, in a series of anonymous letters in the columns of the local press, for this state of affairs.[126] Unlike Power, however, the attacks were more widespread. For not only were Tatham's personality, judgement and relationship with his pupils and old boys vilified but the school's governance, and even its academic record, were also publicly censured.

---

122. HCA, 7031/22, p.481, 9 Nov. 1885.

123. See HCA, 7031/23, p.71 for the beer bottles and below, p.365, note 88, for the school's daily use of the Lady Chapel from September 1917.

124. The figures are taken from Tatham's annual audit reports to the Chapter, as recorded in the Act books: HCA, 7031/22 and 23 *passim*. Although the figures are incomplete, there were probably considerably fewer than 100 boys in Tatham's last year, 1889-90, only 72 of whom were inherited by his successor.

125. I.e. from £75 to £65 for senior boarders (with a £5 reduction for the sons of the clergy), and from £63 to £55 for the junior boarders in 9 St Owen's Street. In Nov. 1887, before the reduction, only seven out of 25 boarders had paid the full fee. Tatham regretted lowering the charge, which neither halted the slide in numbers nor prevented parental requests for further concessions. TNA, ED 27/1605, no. 39, Tatham to Leach, 3 July 1889.

126. See *HT* letters pages, 5 Oct. to 21 Dec. 1889.

The correspondence started innocently enough with a parental complaint about the Headmaster's apparent censorship of the published version of the 1889 examiners' report. What followed was a wave of letters. Over 60 were printed in the columns of the *Hereford Times* from more than 40 correspondents within three months in late 1889, attacking or defending the school. Many reasons were posited as to why HCS was declining since Rudd's glory days and why the County College was rising under Mr Muller's inspired leadership. Was it the Headmaster's personal fault? Was HCS too old-fashioned? Were Hereford's suburbs or its sanitary arrangements insufficient or its rents too high to attract gentlemen to the city? In the absence of any statement from the governors or the Headmaster – although a number of young OHs were not so reluctant to enter the fray on his behalf – no explanation for the school's apparent 'sluggish and sleepy mediocrity' seemed too fanciful. One correspondent even blamed the lack of spirit among Hereford's citizens and related the school's state to the 'low ebb' of the city in general. On one thing, however, most detractors were agreed: the school's governance was obsolete, and in particular (and depending on your view-point), the Dean's 'monstrous' or 'anomalous and discreditable' position as chairman of governors of both the new County College and the ancient Cathedral School should be stopped. The days of the school as a closed corporation were drawing to an end.

HCS should not have taken all the blame for its want of pupil numbers. More prosaic factors were also at work. As Tatham himself had pointed out to his governors in November 1882, the initial drop from the high point of 129 boys in the Michaelmas Term 1881 to 108 a year later coincided with the outbreak of scarlet fever in the neighbourhood which 'has given the place a bad name and deterred people from sending their sons as boarders'. A few years later, he explained the small entry of only two (day) boys in terms of local demographic trends.[127] More important than these temporary factors as explanations for the school's want of pupils were two underlying causes: the great agricultural depression, which broadly coincided with the years of Tatham's headship, and increased competition from other schools.

It is true that the depression was not as marked in Herefordshire as, for example, in the clay lands of Essex, and that the county was – at least for a while – cushioned from its full impact. Nevertheless, by the early 1880s, both estate landlords and tenant farmers in the county were feeling the pinch for by then the prices of beef and store cattle were following the rapid fall in the price of wheat of the previous decade.[128] The effect of this crisis in agriculture on Hereford Cathedral School was two-fold. First, clergymen, smaller gentry families and richer tenant farmers, upon whom HCS had depended to fill the school, were less able to meet the fees, which although modest by the standards of the bigger public schools, had increased by some 20 *per cent* for boarders during the prosperous Rudd years.[129] As early as November 1879, Tatham was warning his governors that 'the prevailing depression in trade and agriculture' was either preventing 'the classes from which our boys are for the most part drawn' from sending their sons to HCS or forcing them 'to withdraw them from school at an earlier age than usual'. By 1886, the Headmaster was bemoaning the fact that

127. HCA, 7031/22, p.398, 6 Nov. 1882; HCA, 7031/23, pp.6-7, 6 Nov. 1886.

128. For the agricultural depression in Herefordshire: Beale, pp.9, 142-44; Robinson, pp.259-78.

129. See above, p.210, and note 122.

the fees were not prepaid, as he had 'suffered from a large number of bankruptcies and bad debts'.[130] It is significant that the Headmasters' Conference debated the matter in 1881, and that Mr Ogle of Magdalen College School considered that 'owing to the recent agricultural depression' there were considerably fewer people who were able to provide for their children's education than there had been, and that £40 (some £30 less than the charge at HCS) was the maximum annual fee that small country gentlemen and clergymen dependent on glebe lands could then afford.[131]

Second, and as importantly, the fall in agricultural rental incomes had a direct impact on the number of university scholarships that the school could offer its pupils. Its own meagre foundation grants were unaffected, and despite the decline in capitular income in the 1880s,[132] the cathedral was able to meet its obligations to the school. The accumulated funds of the Philpotts charity continued to support the three Brasenose scholars (at £50 *per annum* each). Even the proceeds from the poorer Langford charity – despite the reduction of the annual rent of the Castle Crab estate (at Disserth) from £150 to its pre-1872 level of £105, which the tenant claimed was still 'more than he can make of it in these low prices of corn and cattle', and the negative balances of the early 1880s – were sufficient to fund its four scholars throughout the period.[133] St John's College, Cambridge, on the other hand, was not so committed, and having halved the number of the school's exhibitioners from four to two in 1881 and then reduced them to one the following year, gave notice in 1884 of its intention not to elect any more Hereford Somerset exhibitioners for at least two years because of the 'hopelessly insolvent position' of the March estate. Tatham considered that the sudden withdrawal of these exhibitions not only placed him in personal difficulties with parents of boys who had been entered at HCS 'on false pretences', but also reduced the attractiveness of the school, especially among those boys of moderate abilities who had hitherto been sent to board at HCS in expectation 'of getting something to help … at the university'.[134] Appended to a prospectus of the time was the footnote that several Somerset awards were in abeyance 'in consequence of agricultural depression'.[135] It hardly made for good promotion.

As Tatham ruefully admitted on hearing that St John's had created a special Hereford exhibition on the Wootton Rivers (rather than the March) estate, 'we must be thankful for

130. HCA, 7031/22, pp.295-96, 8 Nov. 1879; HCA, 7031/23, p.7, 6 Nov. 1886.

131. *HMC Report 1881*, pp.55-56, 23 Dec. 1881.

132. See HCA, 7032/6 frontispiece, for the Chapter Clerk's calculation of canonical income shortly following Canon Ouseley's death in 1889. It was anticipated that it would fall by at least £120 from the £593 *per annum* average for each canon over the 7 years, 1882-88, because of 'the great reduction already made in the tithe averages'.

133. HCA, 7104/6, *passim*; TNA, ED 27/1606, no. 23, Chapter Clerk to Charity Commissioners, 30 Nov. 1886. Two additional entrance scholarships were also offered on the Philpotts foundation from Michaelmas 1885, although these were not taken up. The Langford fund was saved by the February 1883 timber sale to W. Williams which raised nearly £300.

134. HCA, 7031/22, pp.364, 399, 451,455, 478; HCA, 7031/23, pp.6-7, Tatham's reports Nov. 1881, 1882, 1884-86; and Act, 13 Nov. 1884. Even so, 41 boys went from HCS to Oxford or Cambridge, 1882-87, about 1 in 2 of the senior pupils (TNA, ED 27/1605, no. 18); and almost one in five of Tatham's 410 admissions, 1875-90, proceeded to the ancient universities.

135. HCA, 7032/6, front cover. For the differing conditions of the St John's and BNC Somerset estates, see TNA, ED 27/1605, nos 36-38, letters to Leach, 2, 5, 14 Aug. 1889.

small mercies and hope for better days'.[136] It was a good Christian response, and although the closed Somerset awards would never be as plentiful as in the 'palmy days' of the mid-Victorian period,[137] better times would eventually dawn. Similarly, the school could do little but endure the growing strength of rival educational establishments. Towards the end of his tenure, Tatham reflected that there was 'more and more a determination' to send boys 'to the great public schools'. 'I find in my old registers', he continued, 'the names of the gentry and clergy of the county and diocese, and when I enquire where they are now, I find in nearly every case that they are at Marlborough, Cheltenham, Shrewsbury etc'.[138] But there was a more immediate threat on the doorstep in the shape of the new County College, formerly Barr's Court Proprietary School, which had been lavishly rebuilt on a six-and-a-half acre site off Aylestone Hill in 1880, at a cost of £17,000 to F.R. Kempson's design of 'red brick with stone dressings in the decorated style'.[139] It was with understandable anxiety, and not a little envy, that Tatham made reference to the new college in his speech day address of 1880, expressing the fear that HCS's 'own simple charms might be somewhat outshone by the gaudy graces of their middle-class sister on the hill'.[140] Over the course of the 1880s this is exactly what happened. Although designed as a school for the trading and farming classes, the County College was also an attraction for those clergy and poorer landed families, who in times of economic hardship could no longer afford to pay twice as much to meet the Cathedral School fees. Tatham's warnings to his governors that the new school was drawing off many local boys, some of whom might otherwise have attended HCS, were to no avail. Dean Herbert, who was also chairman of the management board of the new college, considered that the County College, intended as it was 'to supply the wants of a different class', complemented rather than competed with the Cathedral School, and he did not see his dual chairmanship of the city's main secondary schools as a potential conflict of interest. Indeed, if we are to believe A.F. Leach, he may even have 'promoted the county school on purpose to divert the "town", meaning the trading and farming class, from the Cathedral School to one of their own'.[141] In the end, as with other proprietary schools in times of commercial depression, the new college – lacking substantial endowments, burdened by mortgage payments (despite Major Rankin's munificence as a benefactor) and never having paid a dividend – found itself in difficulties. In July 1889

136. HCA, 7031/22, p.478, 9 Nov. 1885.

137. See TNA, ED 27/1605, no. 41, for Tatham's reference to 'the palmy days before the last decade' (in relation to Somerset exhibitions), letter to Leach, 30 July 1889.

138. HCA, 7031/23, p.97, report, 11 Nov. 1889. This process had begun long before Tatham's appointment. As early as November 1878, he could report that he wished 'to see the gentlemen of the county send their sons in larger numbers to the school. Though it had a large connection of this kind at one time, it seems to a great extent to have lost it'. HCA, 7031/22, p.265, 11 Nov. 1878.

139. See *BNEJ*, vol. 40 (Jan. to June 1881), pp.586-87, for a print of the original building, which contained a large schoolroom, six classrooms, seven dormitories (with accommodation for 90 boarders), numerous masters' and utility rooms and a substantial Headmasters' house 'with a lift which communicates with each floor'. The boarding fees were £36 *per annum* (and £28 for juniors), and £8 for day boys (or £6 if there were more than one from the same family.)

140. *TH*, vol. II no. 6 (Sept. 1880), p.47, speech 28 July 1880.

141. See TNA, ED 27/1606, p.11 for Leach's comment in his report of 25 July 1889, following his HCS inspection of the previous year.

the dormitories were half empty, and before Tatham left office its directors were pressing for a merger with HCS.[142] Nevertheless, we should not minimise the threat that the proprietary college posed to HCS throughout the last decade of Tatham's headship.

The exact date of Tatham's resignation is unknown. There is no mention of it in the Chapter Acts, although he admitted on 11 November 1889 that his tenure at HCS was 'not likely to last much longer', and it was known to the school in early 1890 that Lord Wantage would present him to the living of Wing in Buckinghamshire as from that mid-summer.[143] It is not difficult to understand why Tatham felt that it was the right time for him to leave. The public controversy over the running of the school would have caused immense strain; quite apart from the financial loss that Tatham suffered, probably for the first time, from the decline in pupil numbers in his last two terms. There were other issues: Dean Herbert had given George With's scientific instruments to the County College, thereby reinforcing Tatham's misguided impression that the school was less favoured than its neighbour; Thomas Whitley, son of the rector of Letton and a strong sporty boy who was 'much beloved by us all for his simple manly character and ... earnest and unaffected piety', had died from rheumatic fever in June 1889, Tatham's first experience of a boy's death in his own boarding house; during Tatham's absence on holiday in the summer of 1889, the vicars choral had carried out their long-standing threat and walled off their part of the playground, an action which not only disturbed the weekly drill but also prevented the boys from using the best area for their impromptu games and caused something of a diplomatic incident; and towards the end of 1889, the city council held a public enquiry into the school's endowments.[144] Collectively, such blows, together with the public censure, were more than the small change of a Headmaster's lot. Set against these difficulties, the lure of parochial ministry, which Tatham had tasted again as the duty priest of All Saints and Holy Trinity, Hereford, from February to May 1886, would have been a strong attraction.

Despite the mounting problems of Tatham's last months in office, his overall achievement in leading the school – and advancing several hundred pounds of his own wealth for its prosperity – during 'the best fifteen years' of his life[145] was a considerable one: at a time

---

142. See TNA, ED 27/1605, no. 41 Tatham to Leach, 30 July 1889, re its numbers; no. 171, Leach to Young, 9 July 1892, for the Chapter's attitude towards the College; and HCA, 7031/23, p.102, for the Chapter's cautious reply (undated but *c.*mid-Nov. 1889) to the directors' merger proposal. The negotiations foundered but the directors were bailed out eventually, more than a decade later, by the county and city councils, the new women's teacher training college opening in September 1904.

143. HCA, 7031/23, p.100; *TH,* NS no. XI (Feb. 1890), p.3.

144. *Ibid.,* pp.4, 30; HCA, 7031/23, pp.98, 100-01, 104; HARC, HLC A 25, p.227. Whitley's carved name can still be seen on the garden wall of the present organist's house. The 'diplomatic incident' concerned certain 'injurious and offensive' references to the College in an issue of the school magazine, for which – following the publication of a letter from the Custos in the *Hereford Times* – the Headmaster had to make a public apology. On 3 December 1889, Alderman J.H. Knight, the Chapter Clerk, ably defended cathedral and school interests before the city council. *TH,* NS XII (June 1890), pp.7-12.

145. The phrase is Tatham's own. See his valedictory letter of 26 May 1890 in *TH,* NS XII (June 1890), p.5. Tatham's financial commitment to HCS during his headship included the £400 he paid out towards building a dormitory, a porter's lodge and sick-bay; the 4 *per cent* interest repayment on the Headmaster's house improvements in 1884; and his personal liability for taking on the leases of Wyeside and the junior boarding house (9 St Owen's Street) – quite apart from his £50 donation to the library and generous subscriptions to other appeals.

of agricultural depression and economic uncertainty, he had succeeded in transforming the school. Like Rudd he was a fine scholar and teacher, but in academic terms he did little more than streamline Rudd's curriculum. However, in many other ways he moved the school substantially forward: the under school was incorporated as part of the one school; the school buildings were transformed; a library was built; *The Herefordian* was established; Wyeside was created; games were reorganised and flourished as never before; music was improved; through the regular use of the Lady Chapel for school services, the school was more closely identified with the cathedral; and perhaps above all, and with the considerable help of the Old Herefordian Club, Tatham engendered 'a corporate feeling and love for the old school' which in his own estimation was unsurpassed elsewhere – an affection in part engendered by the '500th' anniversary in 1881 and Tatham's strong sense of history. Not the least illustration of his appreciation of the past is his compilation of the first comprehensive school register. It is also indicated by the creation of honours boards, not only for sportsmen in the pavilion but also for distinguished Old Herefordians and those boys who had won university scholarships.[146] (Plates 10 and 11). All told, it is a formidable list of achievements.

At the same time, as should be expected in a school where half of the masters were in Holy Orders, and one third of the boys were still from clergy families,[147] the school's high 'tone' – to use the favourite word of educationalists of the time – was maintained. There is no need to disbelieve this claim that Tatham made to his governors in November 1887:

> Though I have not many clever boys at the present time, there is an excellent spirit of work, a conscientious sense of duty, a general steadiness and earnestness of purpose apparent throughout the school. And besides the high principle which I trust and believes prevails here, there is an *esprit de corps* and pride in their school among the boys, much fostered by my excellent colleagues, which makes my work here at once a pleasure and a ground for the deepest thankfulness.[148]

Tatham may have reflected on the missed opportunity to re-site the school in 1875, fretted about the competition from the educational palace on the hill, and worried about the intellectual quality of the entry, the failure to reform the endowments to attract

146. These boards were finally established, after considerable controversy with the old boys, before Tatham left in 1890, when the oak boards (donated at the '500th' anniversary) were completed with the names of four benefactors and ten distinguished OHs, and separate boards were provided on the east and south sides of the library for university and other distinctions (starting with F.C. Symonds in 1864) and Somerset scholars at BNC (from E.B. Smith in 1847) – although not Somerset exhibitioners at St John's. All but two of these latter boards have (sadly) disappeared. For the naming of these boards: *TH*, NS no. XII (June 1890), pp.6-7; *ibid.*, NS no. XIII (Oct. 1890), p.32, account for £32 8s 6d.

147. In June 1888, for example, three of the seven permanent masters were ordained (Tatham himself, Spencer and Higgins) – one fewer than ten years earlier – and 39 out of the 106 pupils were sons of clergymen. TNA, ED 27/1605, no. 18; HCA, 7007/1, pp.480-82.

148. HCA, 7031/23, p.39, 7 Nov. 1887. Tatham's view, which was repeated in some of his other reports, was also corroborated by outsiders: for example by Examiner Simpkinson in 1877 ('the tone of the school is all that it should be') and Canon Powell's comment on speech day 1883 about the 'good moral tone' of the boys and their excellent behaviour in the cathedral.

clever boys in sufficient numbers and his inability to fill the school, but he left HCS a much stronger school in 1890 than he had found it 15 years earlier, without sacrificing its values.

It was not all Tatham's doing, of course. His young masters, as has been indicated, were of a high calibre. Most may have stayed at the school for only two or three years but they generally made their mark, and many left for headships or senior positions at bigger schools. Moreover, it was Tatham, partly through his Westminster associations, who lured them to HCS in the first place and who had set them on their teaching careers.[149] It is also true that few of Tatham's achievements could have been accomplished without the financial, practical and moral support of Old Herefordians, who were organised into a formal association in 1876, the club being reconstituted after internal squabbles and a decline in membership 11 years later with Tatham taking the leading role in chairing the AGM on 26 July 1887, when a new constitution was adopted.[150]

Tatham could also claim support from his governors, although he had an ambivalent attitude towards them. He felt not only that the Chapter had missed an opportunity to move the school in 1875 but that they had cheese-pared in its rebuilding; he found Dean Herbert's 'markedly liberal' attitude towards the new County College and his failure to push for the reform of the Langfordian charity inexplicable; he did not feel well supported against the college; and he considered that the choristers did not 'do themselves or the school good', and that as with many other choir schools of the time, they would be better off in a separate establishment. Moreover, the Headmaster was not reticent in using the opportunity given him in his annual audit reports to express – in the politest possible terms – such views.

Tatham's perception that Dean Herbert was 'inimical to the school or to him', although strongly held, was without foundation. The Dean's view that its governors had shown 'care and generosity' towards its school – a school for which in statute they had accountability for only 16 pupils (the choristers and the Langford scholars) – has a greater authenticity.[151] This can be illustrated by the money spent 'from their divisible corporate estate ... in enlarging and rebuilding the cathedral schoolrooms and the master's residence' in the period 1874-84: some £3,121. This was £1,140 more than the sum for the building and restoration of its chancels and vicarage houses and considerably more than the actual spend on the cathedral

149. Of over 20 masters who served with Tatham, W.H. Mills, Sealy Poole and Arthur Temperley gained headships; R.W. Fowler became an HMI and E.M. Mee a tutor of Queen's, Oxford; and A.W. Hales, S.B. Guest-Williams, W.J. Barton, C.A. Evors, E.H. Kelly, J.D. Binnie, G.H. Fenner, A.R. Stokes and J.H. Daniel went on to other schools – Barton, Evors (who wrote the school history) and Kelly to Highgate, Tatham's old school. Tatham appointed at least two of his former Westminster pupils as assistant masters: W.S. Rawson and E.P. Guest. T.H. Parker's reminiscences of his teachers are recorded in *TH*, NS CLXXXXVIII (May 1959), pp.10-11 and *HCN*, no. 43 (April-June 1959), pp.7-8. For Temperley's obituary: *ibid.*, CXIV (April 1927), p.6.

150. By 1880, 129 OHs (over one in five of whom had been ordained) were listed as club members. For an account of the later internal squabbles, see *TH*, NS no. III (May 1887), pp.13-14; and *ibid.*, NS no. IV (Oct. 1887), pp.42-43, for the new constitution and 1887 AGM. By late 1890, 112 names were registered. *Ibid.*, NS XIII (Oct. 1890), pp.27-29.

151. For Tatham's and Herbert's conflicting views on the school, see TNA, ED 27/1606, A.F. Leach's report, 25 July 1889; and Tatham's reports, HCA, 7031/22 and 23 *passim*.

fabric in the same period.[152] This sum pales into insignificance against the £17,000 that it cost to build the new County College, but it was more than the Chapter had ever advanced to its school in an equivalent period before, and it was accomplished at a time when (in the words of the 1885 cathedral commission) capitular bodies were themselves experiencing considerable financial difficulties 'in consequence of the depression or actual failure of the rents of landed property'.[153]

What is true, however, is that Dean Herbert and his colleagues did not share Tatham's vision for the school. Their outlook was conservative, insular and somewhat self-satisfied: in their terms, HCS was doing well as a small first-grade classical school, and there was no need for much change beyond rebuilding the school when there was no other option – as long as it was on the same site and within convenient distance for its foundation boys – and giving the Headmaster sufficient support for his initiatives. But this had to be within defined limits. Fearing a loss of control and the threat to its independence, it is significant that the cathedral did not press for the reform of the Langford charity that Tatham considered essential to attract more bright boys to the school. This eventually occurred (after Tatham's time) but only through external pressure from the Ludlow authorities and the Charity Commissioners themselves.[154] Dean Herbert was no Dean Dawes: the Dean was united with his Chapter in this period in resisting radical change to the foundation. As Herbert responded to the question asked in 1872 by a committee of his fellows about what legislative enactment was necessary to improve 'the efficiency and increased usefulness' of his cathedral: 'None. Hereford Cathedral has already been rendered fairly efficient and useful without any help from Parliament, and if left alone will no doubt increase in usefulness and popularity still more'.[155] That was also his attitude towards the school. As Dean Herbert saw it, outside 'interference', whether from the government, the Charity Commissioners or the city, was likely to prove detrimental to HCS's best interests.

Tatham may have had a difficult last year or two but he departed in July 1890 with good-will on all sides, and with a writing table, chairs and a chiming clock as leaving gifts, which were presented jointly on his final speech day by his heads of school of 1875 and 1890.[156] In his letter of thanks, written a few weeks later from Wing vicarage, he said that the presents reminded him 'hourly of the flight of time' and his 'fifteen years of happy work and the many life-long friends' he had made in Hereford. In an earlier remarkably frank

152. HCA, 7005/11, pp.493ff, 14 Feb. 1885 return for the cathedral commissioners. Of the £3,121 18s 2d, £2,202 19s 6d was spent on the rebuilding in 1876 and no sums were recorded as having been spent in 1874 or in 1879-80. Only £662 was spent on the cathedral fabric in this decade, as opposed to £7,884 on the repayment of interest and loans for the cathedral's earlier restoration.

153. *PP 1884-85 XXI*, p.457, final report, 23 March 1885.

154. See below, pp.296-97.

155. HCA, 7005/10, p.405, 5 March 1872. He admitted that the school needed new buildings and a better endowment but pointed out that the capitular body was 'only accountable' for the education of the choristers and Langford scholars.

156. *TH*, NS no. XII (Oct. 1890), p.22. The Reverend G.L. Spencer, who left (for the Clifford benefice) with Tatham, was given an oak writing desk by the old boys, inscribed: '*XII Annorum Inter Libros Ludosque Egregie Actorum Memores DD*'.

valedictory letter, also published in *The Herefordian*,[157] he again expressed his belief that the Dean should relinquish his position as chairman of governors at the County College; and his hope that through the Charity Commissioners, open scholarships would be founded to attract clever 14 and 15 year old boys to HCS. He further apologised for leaving the school in numbers 'not quite so well off as I found', but also referred to the many advantages 'in school appliances' that he left to his successor, its recent academic successes – showing 'that we make the most of our material' – its many sporting accolades and the strong bonds of loyalty between Old Herefordians and their school. Tatham was right to reflect on his work in Hereford with pride and a sense of satisfaction, for more than a century later his reputation as one of the school's foremost Headmasters is assured.

Thomas Thistle, 1890-1897

Things did not go as smoothly for Dean Herbert's final magisterial appointment as they had done in 1869 and 1875. In part, it was the governors' fault for not moving fast enough. Tatham, as we have seen, resigned in late 1889 or early 1890 in the expectation of being able to leave before that Easter, but it was not until April 1890 that the candidates' testimonials were first examined by their prospective employers, and only on 20 May that the successful candidate was interviewed for the headmastership. As Tatham reported in his valedictory letter: 'even now in the last decade of May our governing body is still sitting and the egg is still unhatched'. By the time that letter was printed in early June, however, his successor's name had been announced in the pages of *The Herefordian*. The appointment had taken five months – more than double the time it took to select Rudd and Tatham, despite an increase in the overall cost of some £2.[158]

The Dean and Chapter had clearly been preoccupied during early 1890 with other pressing concerns, not the least of which were the tortuous negotiations with the Charity Commissioners over the remodelling of the school's charities and constitution, and, crucially, the death from influenza of the Chapter Clerk, Alderman J.H. Knight, on 3 February.[159] But there was another reason for the delay: the Revd Thomas Thistle, who was eventually offered the post, was not the governors' first choice, for on 2 May the Chapter Acts record 'that the Reverend J.H. Cohn be elected to the office of Head Master of the Cathedral School'. Quite why Cohn turned down the post is unknown, but it is clear that Thistle was subsequently elected in open competition against two other more than respectable candidates – the Reverends F.W. Hawes, a master at Dulwich, and G. Douton, a former fellow of King's, Cambridge, and an assistant at Highgate School – both of whom were also interviewed for the position.[160] His election was formally sealed

157. *Ibid.*, NS no. XII (June 1890), pp.5-6, 26 May 1890.

158. HCA, 7031/23, pp.109, 110, 113, Acts, 18, 21 April, 20 May 1890; *TH*, XVIII (June 1890), p.5, letter 26 May 1890. Total costs – including travelling expenses to the unsuccessful candidates and notices in *The Times*, *Guardian*, *Spectator* and *Saturday Review* – came to £7 2s 8d. HCA, 7106/2, 1890 audit accounts, payments 102-07. See above, pp. 202-03, 238-39, for the 1869 and 1875 appointments.

159. *TH*, NS no. XI (Feb. 1890), p.4, for Knight's obituary; and below, p.290ff, for these negotiations, about which (so Thistle later claimed) the Chapter had not thought fit to inform the candidates.

160. See HCA, 7106/2, audit accounts 1890, for the payments of their travelling expenses. Hawes was interviewed, around the same time as Cohn, in early May, and Douton on 19 May, the day before Thistle.

on 25 June 1890, under the old 'good behaviour' tenure – a form of appointment which (like Tatham's if not Rudd's), as the Charity Commissioners subsequently pointed out, had been superseded by section 22 of the 1869 Endowed Schools Act and had no force in law. This, as we will see, was later to provide Thistle with a particular bone of contention against the Commission.[161]

Thistle's academic qualifications might not have been as strong as Cohn's or Douton's – although he had gained an Oxford 'first' in Moderations – but it is not difficult to understand why he was appointed for he was a man of wide experience. Having been employed as classical master at Auckland College, New Zealand, and Warden of Christ Church College, Hobart, 1883-86, he was the first Headmaster of HCS to have taught in the colonies, returning in 1887 as assistant at Ripon Grammar School. For the boys, Thistle's sporting prowess – he had been a member of his college VIII and XI – would have been a more important recommendation, *The Herefordian*'s editors foreseeing: 'He will be able to do much for the athletics of the school, and with a river and a cricket ground ... we fully believe that under him the school will attain in this respect even greater distinction',[162] a prediction that did not altogether come about. But perhaps above all, it was Thistle's presence that stood out. The jaunty photograph of him dressed in top hat and tails, unlike the serious poses of his three immediate predecessors, shows him to have been a debonair gentleman and a Headmaster who looked right for the times.

The School Roll

It was imperative that the new Headmaster should prove sufficiently attractive to prospective parents and boys alike to reverse the decline in pupil numbers that had occurred during Tatham's last year in office. And in this Thistle was initially successful. From the low base of 86 pupils at Michaelmas 1890, there were 11 more boys in the school by the following November. Thereafter, the annual average increased steadily in each successive calendar year, as follows: 99 (1892), 101 (1893) and 106 (1894).[163] When the school roll reached the magical three figures in Easter Term 1892, the boys welcomed the achievement, which was desired (according to *The Herefordian* editor) 'for many reasons, not least the promised whole holiday'.[164] Thistle was particularly successful in increasing the boarding community, which more than doubled in three years to 38 boys, an increase which is only partly explained by the closure of the junior house at 9 St Owen's Street following Higgins' departure in July 1891.[165] The pressure on boarding space, which according to Leach's 1889

161. HCA, 7005/12, pp.157-58, Thistle's patent of 25 June. See below, pp.297-98, for Thistle's argument with the Commissioners.

162. *TH*, NS no. XII (June 1890), p.2.

163. The numbers have been collated from Thistle's reports, Nov. 1890-93, in the Chapter Acts (HCA, 7031/23, pp.119-20, 140-42, 164-65, 184), and from the new style audit accounts, 1894-97 (HCA, 7106/3, fos 45v, 98v, 118v, 169v).

164. *TH*, NS XVII (March 1892), p.1. The editorial continued: 'Does this promise, we wonder, a day and a half's holiday when the school has 150 names on its books?' Sadly, that situation was not to arise until after the Great War.

165. Thistle inherited only four junior boarders. In the 1891 census, the St Owen's Street house was listed as 'uninhabited', whereas ten years previously 18 boarders had resided there, together with James Brown (the Housemaster)

Fig. 6.7 Thomas Thistle: a Headmaster right for the times.

report was supposed to provide accommodation for a maximum of 36 boys, together with the stipulation in the 1893 scheme that HCS was to provide for 40 boarders and 80 day boys, were the driving forces behind the rebuilding of the Headmaster's house over the summer and autumn of 1894. It is ironic that at the very time when these works were in progress numbers began to decline – from the high water mark of 108 in January 1894, to 98, 88 and 84 respectively in the three following Easter terms, 1895-97, to only 68 boys in November 1897, four fewer than Thistle had inherited from Tatham.

The loss of nearly one third of the school – some 30 boys – during Thistle's last three years in office cannot solely be laid at the Headmaster's door, although his somewhat high-handed approach to parents may have cost him a few friends and potential clients. A case in point occurred in April 1896, when on the 11th of that month Thistle wrote this peremptory letter to the rector of Staunton on Wye:

> Dear Mr Ellwood. I very much regret to say that I am altogether dissatisfied with the conduct of your second son (Dick). I am of opinion that what influence he has with other boys is not for good but rather the reverse, and therefore it is my duty to ask you to remove him from the school. I am very sorry that I can find no alternative to this course. The reports on the work of the two other boys are very far from satisfactory. Unless the boys work very much harder than they have been working, it will be idle to expect them to do any good, and it will become necessary for them also to leave the school.

No specific charge was laid against Dick, although in a subsequent interview with Mrs Ellwood, the Headmaster had alleged that he smoked, used bad language, received a police warning at an Easter Monday football match and that he habitually carried 'a flash' – allegations (the smoking apart) the father vigorously denied. At the school's subsequent reassembly at the beginning of the following term, Thistle had publicly threatened to expel any boy who spoke with Dick. In these circumstances, it is not surprising to find that the Rector withdrew his two remaining sons from HCS as well, and appealed – in vain – against the Headmaster's decision. It is clear that Thistle had acted decisively against Dick Ellwood *pour encourager les autres*, as he had done at the end of his first term when he required three boys to be removed for drinking at a local public house. All three had evidently failed to uphold their oaths of office as monitors to maintain the school's discipline and act like English gentlemen.[166] The Ellwood case, however, case seems to have been badly handled: no adequate cause was shown and no warning had been given, hitherto (the father claimed) the boys' reports having been 'eminently satisfactory'. Although only one side of this story has survived, Mr Ellwood's emotional outburst to the Charity Commissioners, after the Chapter had declined to intervene, that the Headmaster should not have 'the power of

---

and his family, one 18 year old student (William Collins) and three servants.

166. For Thistle's report of the drinking incident, see HCA, 7031/23, p.141, 7 Nov. 1890. The three boys were F.A. Leslie-Jones, the captain of 'football' and future rugby international, W.C. Johns and C.H.D. Marshall, whose names were all expunged from the monitors' list in the school register. The name of R. Dew, who may also have been involved in the incident, was also deleted but – although his father subsequently removed him from the school – he only received Thistle's caution.

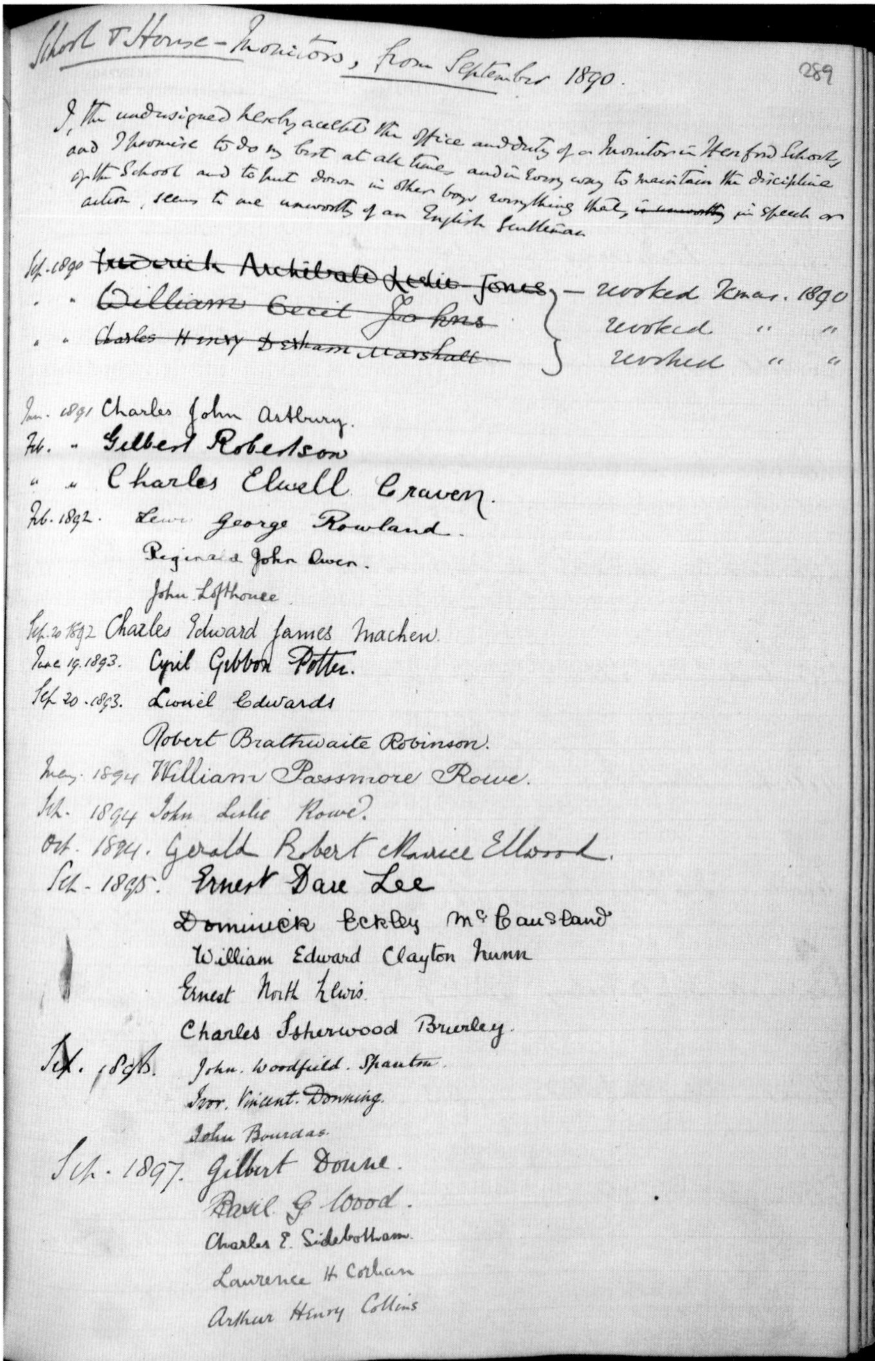

School & House-Monitors, from September 1890. 289

I, the undersigned hereby accept the office and duty of a Monitor in Hereford School, and I promise to do my best at all times and in every way to maintain the discipline of the School and to put down in other boys everything that, ~~is unworthy~~ in speech or action, seems to me unworthy of an English Gentleman.

Sep. 1890 ~~Frederick Archibald Leslie-Jones~~ — revoked Xmas. 1890
" " ~~William Cecil Johns~~ revoked " "
" " ~~Charles Henry Dextham Marshall~~ revoked " "

Jan. 1891 Charles John Astbury.
Feb. " Gilbert Robertson
" " Charles Elwell Craven.
Feb. 1892. Lewis George Rowland.
Reginald John Owen.
John Lofthouse.
Sep. 20 1892 Charles Edward James Machen.
June 19. 1893. Cyril Gibbon Potter.
Sep 20. 1893. Lionel Edwards
Robert Brathwaite Robinson.
May. 1894 William Passmore Rowe.
Sep. 1894 John Leslie Rowe.
Oct. 1894. Gerald Robert Maurice Ellwood.
Sep. 1895. Ernest Dare Lee
Dominick Eckley McCausland
William Edward Clayton Nunn
Ernest North Lewis.
Charles Isherwood Brierley.
Sep. 1896. John. Woodfield. Spaunton.
Ivor. Vincent. Downing.
John Bourdas.
Sep. 1897. Gilbert Downe.
Basil G Wood.
Charles E. Sidebotham.
Laurence H Corban
Arthur Henry Collins

Fig. 6.8 The signatures of Tatham's monitors who swore to maintain the school's discipline and put down in other boys everything 'unworthy of an English gentleman'. F.A. Leslie-Jones, one of the boys Tatham sacked from the position at Christmas 1890, later became an England rugby international and a Headmaster.

ruining for life the prospects of any boy against whom he might entertain a dislike', may command our sympathy.[167]

Parental loss of confidence in the Headmaster, therefore, might be one explanation for the mid-1890s collapse in pupil numbers. The intensification of the agricultural depression, however, is a more sufficient cause. Although there is no direct evidence of its effect on pupil recruitment – not least because after 1893 the Headmaster's reports, although initially still read at the Michaelmas Chapter, were no longer copied out into the Act books – it is apparent from the school register that entries fell markedly in Thistle's last three years.[168] It is reasonable to suppose that this decline was linked to the dire state of the local economy. The slump in wheat prices in 1893-94, the disastrous harvest of that latter year, and the continued contraction of stock prices and land values would all have severely curtailed the disposable incomes of the school's natural clientèle.[169]

Body, Mind and Character

In an address in the Lady Chapel, at the end of his fourth term, Thistle outlined his educational philosophy to his charges. The object of all education, he declared, was 'the training of the body, the mind and the moral character'. He urged every boy to try, 'as far as their natural powers would permit', to excel in these things, which he further considered were 'the essential conditions of all real happiness in life, namely to know what is true, to see what is beautiful and to do what is right'.[170] How near did he come to achieving these aims?

Thistle immediately set about improving the boys' playgrounds and sporting facilities. At Wyeside, the far field was levelled for rugby over the winter of 1890-91, although it was not until 1895-96 that a large enough area had been levelled and turfed to prevent the winter game encroaching on the cricket pitch. Nevertheless, the cricket field, which was also screened in early 1891 with a line of trees on the pavilion side, was in a good enough condition that summer for W.G. Grace's 'XII' again to play an exhibition match on the Wyeside ground, this time against 22 of Herefordshire.[171] Nearer home in the school playground, Thistle's successful appeal at last resulted in the repair (with 'granolithic pavement') and extension of the dilapidated fives court over Easter 1891, at a cost of £26 17s, which led to renewed enthusiasm for the game.[172] Such alterations no doubt added to Thistle's

167. The Ellwood case may be followed in the father's (unsuccessful) appeal letter of 1 August 1896 to the Charity Commissioners, preserved in TNA, ED 27/1608. Dick's behaviour was in marked contrast to that of his elder brother, H.W. Ellwood, to whom Thistle had awarded a special prize four years earlier 'as an expression of his regard for the boy's character and conduct', and who was elected to a Somerset scholarship at Brasenose later that year. *TH*, NS XX (June 1893), p.10; *Brasenose Reg.*, i., p.703.

168. From the high watermark of 34 in 1893-94, to an average of 19 over the three years, 1894-97.

169. See Beale, pp.163-69 and the authorities there cited, for the renewed crisis in agriculture in the county in the mid-1890s, intensified for landowners by Harcourt's 1894 'death duties budget', even though the tax was initially set at only 8 *per cent.*

170. As reported in *TH*, NS XVII (March 1892), p.7.

171. *TH*, NS XIII (Oct. 1890), p.4; XIV (Feb. 1891), p.5; XV (June 1891), pp.20-22, for an account of the W.G. Grace match on 12, 13 June 1891; XXIII (March 1896), p.19, for the list of the 59 subscribers, who raised over £27 for the further Wyeside improvements; and XXIV (July 1896), p.26, for the £30 payment to Shepherd for work on the ground.

172. *Ibid.*, XIV (Feb. 1891), pp.1, 6, 21; XV (June 1891), p.23. See HCA, 1541, R. Clarke's 1890 plan, for the

undoubted popularity among the boys, as indicated by their prolonged and hearty cheers for him at the speeches that July, when he could report on the increase in pupil numbers and the school's sporting successes.[173]

Indeed, as a college sportsman of note, Thistle's active involvement in the school's sporting life – in contrast to his predecessor – would have increased his appeal. At his first sports day on 8 April 1891, he made this declaration: 'that it always gave him the greatest pleasure to further in every way possible the athletic side of school life, and that every scheme for this purpose would always meet with his entire approval'. Thistle led from the front by coaching the 'Oxford' crew at that term's regatta and playing in the School XI – without distinction – in the crushing defeat by the Hereford club later that summer.[174] Assistants that he appointed like A.G. Jones, G. Fowler, A.G. Ford, C.H. Douton, W.W. Crosthwaite and E.A. Roberts were (as *The Herefordian* noted for the latter two) also 'thoroughly energetic masters and supporters of school games'.[175]

The pattern of the school's sporting year – the paper-chase (one of the last recorded runs, over 18 miles, being on 13 October 1896), followed by the rugby football, 'boating' and cricket seasons, with the athletic sports sandwiched midway between – had long been set and was hardly modified by Thistle. The move of sports day to early summer, 1892-95, was the most significant change but this did not prove successful. The 'tufty' state of the grass and the lack of proper training because of the heat, it was alleged, prevented any records being broken in 1892. Rowing (the season having been extended into May) also interfered with the boys' athletics preparation. Nor was there a guarantee of good weather on the day itself, as on 10 May 1893, when heavy rain made the ground 'utterly unfit' for running and jumping. In organisational terms, despite Tatham's financial reforms, much still remained within the province of the senior boys, the most important change being their decision in late 1892 that the award of colours and the selection of teams should be decided by a special committee rather than solely by the captain. Perhaps as a consequence, the award of colours was not as tightly controlled, which resulted in Pritchard's giving out 1st XI bands – 'with the utmost nonchalance', as a correspondent informed *The Herefordian* in the summer of 1897 – rather than Norton's, 'the recognised emporium' in Broad Street.[176]

The majority of Thistle's assistants were able oarsmen who had rowed for their respective colleges, so it is not surprising to find that rowing became a prominent sport in the 1890s. Indeed, with four coaches (including the Headmaster) in the school in November 1891, the complaint was that the eight weeks set aside for rowing in the late spring and early summer were insufficient for a boy's need. Nevertheless, considerable advances were made. The school regatta went on much as before, with further individual prizes of a small

---

site of the fives court (*Fig. 6.3*).

173. *Ibid.*, NS XIX (Nov. 1892), p.9. See also the encomium paid to Thistle after his departure by the boy editor of the school magazine: *ibid.*, NS XXVII (March 1898), p.1.

174. *Ibid.*, NS XV (June 1891), pp.5, 12; NS XVI (Nov. 1891), p.9. The school was bowled out for 14 (T. Thistle 0) in the 114 runs defeat at Widemarsh on 26 May 1891.

175. *Ibid.*, NS XXVII (March 1898), pp.1-2.

176. Norton's also supplied 'skull caps for choristers for use at funerals'. HCA, 7106/3, 1894 audit account, fo 48v payment 37.

silver oar – to be worn by the boys on their watch chains – for the winners of the boarders/day boy event, a sufficient incentive for the boarders to record six successive victories each year from 1892. In addition, annual boat races were arranged with Worcester Cathedral School (as it then was), first rowed at Worcester on a half-mile course form the 'Dog and Duck' on 21 May 1892 – half the length of the HCS course on the Wye ('from the Elms') the following year. Two years later, on 7 April 1894, the first boat race was rowed against Monmouth School. The 1897 double victory over both schools was celebrated at that year's speeches by Dean Leigh's presentation to the winning crew of the cups given by Lady Croft in honour of the feat. Crews were also entered for the 'Maiden Plate' in the Hereford club regatta (in 1892) and the *Hereford Times* cup (in 1896) – the fours reaching the finals on both occasions. And in 1894, for the first time, the school purchased new boats – clinker fours, built by Salters of Oxford for £64, the money being raised by public subscription over two years – although an old boy's 'bold suggestion' that a school boat house should also be built was never accomplished. Overall, the importance of rowing in this period is illustrated by the publication of the picture of the 1893 crew, successful against Worcester despite their 'crooked swing', in that year's *Herefordian* – the first photograph ever to be reproduced in the school magazine.

Rowing flourished in the 1890s but the main team games suffered contrasting fortunes. A dozen or so cricket matches were organised each season on Wednesday and Saturday afternoons from late May. Although there were no 'stars' in this period, the 1st XI generally held its own in the three annual school matches – against Oswestry Grammar, Monmouth and (from 1892) Worcester Cathedral School – and with the considerable help of the masters (especially C.H. Douton) and Shepherd, the professional, the team was generally competitive against the club sides. In 1897, perhaps to compensate for the loss of

Fig. 6.9 The Headmaster, an enthusiastic sportsman, with the 1891 1st XI

Shepherd, temporarily replaced by one Grubb – described as a useful bowler, who spared 'no pains to make a good wicket' but 'hardly the coach that Shepherd was' – the masters organised evening net sessions for the first time.[177]

By contrast, the school's performance at rugby football was little short of lamentable, despite the brilliance of two or three boys – notably F.A. Leslie-Jones (captain, 1890), who gained three Oxford 'Blues' and an international cap in 1895, E.A.A. Jones (captain, 1892-93), who gained his Cambridge 'Blue' in 1895,[178] and E.N. Lewis (captain, 1895-96), chosen for the Oxford Freshman's XV in 1896. Hereford could no longer compete against the Welsh schools and the fixtures were dropped – Brecon after 1890 and Monmouth after 1896 – and the scratch matches 'got up at a few days' notice' did 'not provoke sufficient emulation'. The school was further disadvantaged by its inability to adapt to the modern game, as in 1891-92 when the scrum lacked order, shoved 'promiscuously' and often failed to heel the ball 'in the enemy's twenty-five', a tactic the RFU had sanctioned in a school game (Magdalen College School v St Edward's) more than a decade earlier. Above all, the regular playing of 15-a-side matches – despite the belief that it was 'a great improvement on the twelve man system' – eventually proved an insuperable obstacle for a small school, even when two or three masters were added to the team.[179] The sad state of rugby football during Thistle's final terms may be gauged by these two reflections in successive issues of *The Herefordian* during and after the 1896-97 season:

> At most public schools boys are *compelled* to play football unless they can produce a doctor's certificate, but at HCS any excuse apparently, however inadequate, suffices to free them from all obligations to their school. A volume could be filled with all the different excuses put forward. Some boys are suddenly smitten with a desire to work, and find that football interferes with their good intentions; others that football is a 'nasty, rough game', while one young hopeful came to the extraordinary conclusion that it 'made him greasy'. Under such conditions football can scarcely be expected to flourish in any school.

> The most noticeable and ... most ruinous failing of the team was the almost complete inability to tackle displayed by the majority of its members ... Fellows should practise collaring low, and should not let go until the ball has been put down ... [The record of only three matches played] is nothing less than a disgrace to the school ... Boys should be made to understand that schoolwork does not constitute their only duty to the school ... it should be remembered that athletics are essential to proper mental, as well as physical, development. If this were thoroughly realised, we should see less loafing about at town matches on the part of boys who suffer from the delusion that a good game of rugby football is 'rough' or 'ungentlemanly'... School football has now reached a lower ebb than ... ever ... before, and unless some vigorous measures are adopted next season, there seems to be every probability that in no long time it will be impossible to keep the game going at all.

177. *TH*, NS XXVI (July 1897), p.26.

178. Both men were three-quarter backs, and played against each other in the 1895 varsity match.

179. For the above, see *TH*, NS XVII (March 1892), p.13; NS XX (June 1893), p.2; and (for the 'heeling' tactic), Money, p.101.

It proved an all too accurate prophecy.[180]

Like his predecessor, Thistle was unimpressed on his arrival by the school's overall academic standard. As he wrote in his first report in November 1890:

> … the attainments of the boys … are in general below the standard which I think ought to be reached in a school of this kind and position. The deficiency is especially apparent in Latin, Greek and French grammar, and in the prose composition in those languages which is generally weak and poor. The scholarship that rests on these slender foundations must … necessarily be of a loose and unsatisfactory character. I have therefore not sent in, as I at one time hoped to be able to do, any boys for the Cambridge Local Examinations at Christmas next.[181]

Over the coming years, he strove to remedy such deficiencies, and in particular – and in response to parental wishes – to strengthen Modern Languages teaching at the expense of Greek. Thistle's appointment of Robert Hermann Goetz, as Mendel's successor, in September 1890 was the key to the establishment of an effective modern language side. Unlike many of his foreign predecessors, Herr Goetz was a fine teacher – 'accurate, painstaking, zealous and successful', as his obituarist would write nearly 20 years later[182] – and under him German was established as a major feature of the curriculum. By November 1891, 28 boys were taught German and shorthand (Mr Nobbs, an expert in 'phonography', having been appointed at the same time as Goetz) in place of Greek, in three divisions; and before Thistle's departure, the subject was sufficiently well established for special German translation and grammar papers to be set and marked by an external examiner. The decline of Greek was mirrored by a change in the nature of the summer examination. The number of classical papers senior boys were expected to sit was reduced from ten in July 1891 to seven four years later, the papers in Greek and Latin verse – sat by few boys by this time – having been abandoned. At the 1897 speeches, following Thistle's rather gloomy observation about the future of HCS as a classical school, Dean Leigh took a more positive view. As *The Herefordian* reported:

> … the Dean could not help thinking that the Headmaster took somewhat a depressing view of things – he [Dean Leigh] did not take an optimistic view, but he could not quite agree with him as to the future of the school. In all schools they [the examiners] found that Classics were not now the preponderating feature of the curriculum …, and he thought it was a very good thing, as it was one of the greatest importance in

180. *TH*, NS XXV (Nov. 1896), p.28; NS XXVI (July, 1897), pp. 9-10; and below, pp.316-17, for the switch to soccer.

181. HCA, 7031/23, p.120, 10 Nov. 1890. Thistle may have had dealings with the Cambridge Board, when he was examiner for students in English Literature for the government of Tasmania, 1887-90.

182. Goetz died 'far away from the fatherland' on 19 December 1909, aged 60, the only one of Thistle's appointments still to be in post at HCS. He was undoubtedly a great teacher and a civilising influence on the school. For his photograph in 1898, see *Fig. 6.15* (wearing a hat on the front row); and for the tributes to him: *TH*, LXIII (April 1910), pp.20-21. In July 1910, the OH Club commissioned Brian Hatton (the Hereford artist whose brothers had attended HCS) to paint Goetz's portrait posthumously, at a fee of £26 5s. Hatton had completed the portrait by the following summer and for a time it hung in the school library. Its whereabouts today is unknown. For Hatton's commission: *TH*, NS LXV (Dec. 1910), p.30; LXVII (July 1911), p.38; LXVIII (Dec. 1911), p.44.

> these days that there should be a thorough knowledge of Modern Languages, because they knew how many fields were open in all parts of the world for those young men who had a good knowledge of German, French and other languages. They knew how many clerks in the city at the present time were 'made in Germany' (laughter), and they felt that there were many positions which might be filled by our own young men … instead of being obliged to send over to Germany for them.[183]

With the strengthening of the modern side came other academic developments. From the end of his first term, Thistle awarded subject prizes. These were initially for Classics and Mathematics, but later included awards for German and, when the number of forms increased to ten with the subdivision of forms I-IV, English as well. This initiative was heralded as being 'a very good arrangement', especially for those boys at the top of their form or division who following their January promotion would not have received summer prizes.[184] Similarly, following the creation of a Natural History museum in the Gilbert Library, with A.E. Boycott – who was to become a distinguished pathologist and naturalist – as its first curator, a Natural History prize was awarded (to Boycott for his matchless collection of shells) in July 1891.[185] On that same speech day, another new prize was presented – this time for General Knowledge – to Alban Coore, the top boy in the preceding Easter examination. The general test then became a feature of the school year, with the boys' 'howlers' forming an occasional amusing article in the magazine and a diversion from the endless sporting reports.[186]

One measure of the success of such initiatives is again provided by the examiners' annual reports.[187] The boys' progress in German was recognised in 1891, and by the following year W.E. Heitland commented on 'the excellence of the instruction' in the language, as well as 'the great value of the German language in all classical and scientific studies'. After the more formal examination five years later, W.L. Walter, a Cambridge graduate and exhibitioner of St John's who had studied at Kiel University, also commended the care taken in the boys' preparation, even if 'finer shades of meaning' had been missed in translation and their syntax in the grammar paper was a little suspect. Nor, despite the reduction in numbers studying Greek, was there a decline in the standard of classical learning. The Headmaster may have been worried on his arrival about the boys' deficiencies in grammar and composition, but there was little indication of this – at the top of the school at any rate – the following July, when the five boys of the VIth generally acquitted themselves well in the classical papers.[188] Indeed, throughout this period examiners were complimentary about the

183. *Ibid.*, NS XXVII (March 1898), p.21.

184. *Ibid.*, NS XIV (Feb. 1891), p.13.

185. No-one could follow Boycott, who by the age of 15 had published a catalogue of Herefordshire snails (and in later life was recorder of the Conchology Society, as well as the first Graham Professor of Pathology at UCH Medical School) and the Natural History prize was not awarded again in this period.

186. See, for example, *TH*, NS XXX (April 1899), pp.12-13; and HCSA, for R.S. Thompson's 1912 'General Information Paper'.

187. All their reports for this period, with the exception of the one for 1894, are printed with the speech day accounts in *The Herefordian*. Also see, TNA, ED 27/1611, for copies of the examiners' reports, 1896-98.

188. With the exception of the verse papers and Greek grammar. Unusually, their actual marks were published

standards reached, even in the unseen translations and especially in the set books. Similarly in Mathematics, despite Thistle's publicly expressed doubts in July 1891 'that the standard of Mathematics was not as high as it should be', over the period the examiners found good evidence of 'honest work everywhere', although the boys occasionally let down their side (as with the second division's performance in 1893: 'it would hardly be an exaggeration to say that the boys ... do not know any Euclid') and the teachers were sometimes too restricted in the range of their instruction. Even Thistle's predecessor but one, on his return as examiner in midsummer 1893 after an 18-year absence – by then he was the Revd Prebendary Rudd – could comment favourably on the boys' academic progress and express the hope 'that the Sixth Form and upper mathematical division would fully sustain the credit of the school', adding that their relative youth 'pointed in the same happy direction'. And generally they did so, Hereford boys of the 1890s winning 14 Somerset awards, although only A.E. Boycott gained an open scholarship.[189] Thistle and his young colleagues, the majority of whom were themselves scholars of their respective colleges, succeeded in maintaining the school's strengths in Classics and Mathematics, and in establishing a good linguistic modern side. The problem for the future was that despite the purchase of new Chemistry appliances, HCS was falling way behind in its provision for Science. By March 1894, even its new museum was described – presumably sarcastically – by a correspondent to *The Herefordian* as containing little more than 'a starling and a half and some select Roman pottery from the Withington tile works', and suggested that a 'bug and slug club' should be started. The journal's editor, agreed, observing: 'Other schools have scientific societies, and we don't really see why HCS should lag so much behind the times'.[190] It was an issue that was not seriously addressed in Thistle's time.

On the other hand, there are few indicators to suggest that the school of the 1890s failed to fulfil the Headmaster's third *desideratum* for a good education: the strengthening of moral character. As we have seen, Thistle dealt firmly – and perhaps in the Ellwood case peremptorily – with those boys whose conduct he found unacceptable, but such examples of poor behaviour seem to have been untypical. Indeed, the only other instance of collective ill-discipline (the 1890 drinking episode apart) that has come to light is an alleged case of vandalism against College property in July 1894 – the boys being accused by the vicars of 'battering' the playground party wall and breaking the Revd W.R. Innes' windows, charges which Thistle vigorously denied.[191] Even if some vandalism had occurred, what is more important is the extent to which such acts were characteristic of the general behaviour

(*TH* NS XVI, Nov. 1891, p.28). With the notable exception of A.E. Boycott, the seven boys in the Vth clearly struggled with the papers.

189. Seven were won at BNC and the same number at St John's, although the total number of OHs in residence at the two universities declined from 30 in June 1890 to 17 in October 1897. Boycott won an open classical scholarship to Oriel in 1894, but then transferred to natural Science, gaining a first in Physiology in 1898.

190. *TH*, NS XXI (March 1894), p.25. The editor was A.E. Boycott.

191. This spat is detailed in the College minute book, HCA, 7003/1/7, pp.86-89, 102-05. Damage (as opposed to 'wear and tear') may have been done, but it was no doubt exaggerated by Innes, who was notoriously difficult and litigious. Eventually the Chapter agreed to repair the wall, but the relationship between the College and HCS was so bad in this period that from 1895-97 the Big Schoolroom was used for speeches and the Christmas concert, rather than College Hall.

prevailing at HCS at the time, and how far the school succeeded in its aim to provide an education 'to fit the boys to take their places in life and to do their duty as simple, straightforward and honourable Englishmen'. And on these points, whatever HCS's limitations in this period and despite Thistle's public admission that it could 'never be a school of all the talents', there is no reason to gainsay the Headmaster's own judgement on his school in his final address of 17 December 1897:

> I am exceedingly glad and proud to think that the boys in this school – as I have already told my successor – are as good a set of fellows as is likely to be found in England. Now there is another thing, and a very pleasant one to deal with, viz: the high spirit of good conduct and good principle among the boys ... and for that I do not hesitate to attribute the credit to my colleagues who have been so many years with me. They, I know, without making any show, all the years they have lived in this school, have slowly, insensibly but surely, inspired into it a spirit of obedience and straightforwardness.[192]

As Thistle declared, a significant reason for the maintenance of a good spirit within the school was the lead taken, under the Headmaster's guidance, by young and sympathetic bachelor assistant masters, a majority resident within the boarding community in School House, and the quality of their relationships with the boys themselves.[193] Although by then Thistle was the only ordained master on the staff and there were fewer clergy sons in the school, the same ethos prevailed within its walls in 1897 as under his predecessor.[194]

New Schemes of Governance

Ironically, the most important change to occur under Thistle – the creation of new schemes of governance for the Langford and Philpotts charities, as well as for the school itself – was one of which he was kept ignorant on his appointment, and over which he had only marginal influence. The initial attempt to reform the Langford foundation on the lines laid down by the Charity Commissioners was, as we have seen, stymied in 1876 by the Chapter's intransigence.[195] They succeeded in delaying things by almost ten years, but ultimately a closed corporation had no alternative but to bend to the will of a statutory authority, and not least when, as in this case, the commission perceived that Ludlow boys were gaining an insufficient share of Dean Langford's estate compared with the Langfordian scholars at HCS.[196] After this state of affairs was brought to the notice

192. *TH*, NS XIX (Nov. 1892), p.9 (quoting Thistle's speech of 27 July); NS XXVII (March 1898), p.27.

193. As a photograph of July 1895 shows, there were four assistant masters, together with the Headmaster, in charge of the 33 boys then in School House. For the position of boarders in larger schools in the late Victorian period, see Honey, pp.122-23.

194. The last ordained assistant master in Thistle's time was F.M. Higgins, the Second Master, who left in July 1891. Correspondingly, over the 25-year period, 1878-1903, the number of ordained OHs listed in the old boy registers (HCSA) declined by 20. The number of boys entered in the school register from clerical families almost halved under Thistle, from an annual average of seven, 1875-90, to four, 1890-97.

195. See above, p.247.

196. This was strictly true. Contrary to earlier practice, by 1886 the Hereford Langfordians received more than double the allowance of £21 6s 8d given to the Ludlow boys, although the Chapter argued that this differential

of Ludlow town council in May 1885 and the alleged inequality was communicated to the Commissioners a year or so later, it was only a matter of time before a new scheme of governance for the charity would be drawn up, irrespective of the cathedral's wishes. And given the closely interlinked nature of the Langford and Philpotts charities and the school itself, it was inevitable that the Chapter's stewardship of these three bodies would be reviewed and new instruments of governance established for all three.

The story of the reform of the school's governance over these years is one of intricate negotiations between a Charity Commission determined to secure change, and a cathedral body anxious both to preserve control over its foundation and to maintain the nature and status of its school.[197] The eventual compromise in the resulting schemes was nothing short of a constitutional revolution: for the first time in over 500 years proper educational procedures were enshrined in an approved scheme of governance, and a permanent separate endowment was created for the school as a whole, rather than simply for the choristers and Langfordians. For the successful outcome of these reforms, which were entirely beneficial for its future welfare, HCS was indebted to one man more than any other: Arthur Francis Leach, whom even Dean Herbert later admitted knew 'most about our school'.[198]

Of the nine assistant Charity Commissioners working in Whitehall in the late 1880s, Leach, as a former fellow of All Souls, and a scholar who was to become the leading historian of his time on English medieval schools, was the most important in terms of historical enquiry. Indeed, he wrote nearly half of the 55 commission reports on the benefactions of endowed grammar schools published in this period, and it was Hereford's good fortune that HCS was among the 24 schools assigned to him.[199]

Leach's report on HCS of 25 July 1889 is testimony to the thoroughness of his research. For he did not simply rely on what he saw and was told on his visit to Hereford on 1 June 1888, but conducted a detailed historical enquiry into the school, its endowments and current circumstances, based on a wide range of sources. These included material supplied by the Headmaster and Chapter Clerk, statutes and cathedral documents copied by Canon Phillott, letters about the Somerset endowments from the authorities at Brasenose and St John's, and printed books and reports. The result was an impressive printed document of around 30,000 words, the first scholarly survey of the cathedral's educational foundation in the school's long history. But Leach's report is important not only because of the wealth of its historical detail, but also for its author's creative ability to relate his historical studies

was justified by the higher fees charged by HCS and the additional duties required at Hereford, where the boys were expected to attend morning and evening services (in their own gowns and surplices) on Sundays and festivals. TNA, ED 27/1606, no. 23, letter 30 Nov. 1886.

197. Unless otherwise specified, the following account is taken from the relevant Charity Commission files, TNA, ED 27/1605, 1606.

198. In a letter to Leach of 25 May 1892. Herbert was attempting to arrange a meeting with him to discuss the new schemes of governance, but wanted to avoid a date after 24 June, when 'we shall be in all the fuss of the general election'. They could not meet, however, until 5 July, when the election results were still coming in. TNA, ED 27/1605, nos 167a-170, letters 25 May to 24 June 1892.

199. As an historian of education, Leach received a bad press from the professional medievalists of his day, but the value of his researches (although not necessarily his interpretations) have been recognised by modern scholars such as John Miner.

to contemporary issues, and 'to find ways of using already existing benefactions in the best interests of new and more extensive educational demands'.[200]

Leach proposed several ways as to how the seventeenth-century charities might best be used to establish one independent endowment for the school. The Langfordian legacy was the first to be dealt with. Although the Chapter had objected to the first draft of a new scheme, produced (although not published) by December 1887 – and indeed had sought counsel's opinion as to whether the Commissioners had legal authority to devise such a scheme in the first place[201] – Leach's visit on 1 June resulted in two important concessions: the Commissioners' agreement in principle that the Ludlow portion could be paid off with stock that would produce the equivalent of half the income of the Langford charity (then about £45 *per annum*), and that the Langford and Philpotts charities could be merged to found internal scholarships. Provided that the three Philpottine exhibitions at Brasenose were withdrawn, the Chapter estimated that this would provide revenue of about £340 for the school, thereby achieving Tatham's long-held ambitions for the establishment of size-able entrance scholarships. Leach also hoped that the Somerset bequest might be used to support the school's foundation. In the light of HCS's extensive provision of close awards – more generous (in terms of number), Leach estimated, than those at Eton or Winchester, his own *alma mater* – and the school's inability in the 1880s to fill them,[202] he put forward a strong case for dividing the Somerset foundation between the Brasenose and St John's colleges and the school. Overall, provided that the cathedral was prepared to secure £250 *per annum*, Leach estimated that his proposals for re-ordering the seventeenth-century endowments would have given HCS a total annual income of £930, 'which [he wrote] cannot be said to be inadequate' and would have more than tripled its existing revenue.

Leach's other plan for an application to be made to the Ecclesiastical Commission for funds also promised to be of immense benefit to the school. The school's case rested on the revenue losses the cathedral had suffered from the Act of 1840, when the number of residentiary canons were reduced from six to four and individual prebendal estates were handed over to the Ecclesiastical Commissioners. Although Hereford had not given up its capitular estates, Leach estimated that the loss of both 'petty commons' and individual emoluments amounted to a net gain to the Commissioners of at least £5,000 *per annum* (after payment of the Dean's £1,000 annual salary) from the cathedral's former estates, while 'absolutely nothing' had been done 'for the cathedral fabric, its ministers or officers'. HCS, therefore, had been the poor relation compared with the nine other cathedral schools that had been given grants by the Ecclesiastical Commissioners under the 1869 Endowed Schools Act. The princely sum of £87,800 had been received by these foundations – as

200. Miner, pp.61ff, 84.

201. Unsurprisingly, John Rigby QC, who was later to be knighted and appointed Solicitor and then Attorney General, 1892-94, advised that the Charity Commissioners did indeed have the legal power. HCA, 7031/23, p.49, Act 24 March 1888. The cathedral objected to the first scheme on the grounds of the founder's intention, the real advantages of the estate to HCS despite its small surpluses, the limited value of a classical education to boys from elementary schools and the importance the Chapter attached to ensuring that its charities continued to be managed by itself.

202. According to Leach's calculations, in the years 1881-89, 20 OHs had gone up to the Somerset colleges – 10 to BNC and 10 to St John's – whereas at least 33 close awards were available, 18 at BNC and 15 at St John's.

well as, in some instances, land, and (in the case of the Archbishop of Canterbury's palace) building – from the Commissioners in the 11 years, 1873-84. These included the cathedral schools of Bristol, Rochester, Lincoln and Worcester, in which cities there were also other endowed schools, whereas in Hereford there was no other similar educational foundation to HCS. In demographic terms, too, Hereford had a sound case, its 20,000 population being more than double that of Ely and only a thousand or two fewer than cities which had received grants for their endowed cathedral schools.[203]

Leach had put forward convincing arguments for reform of the Langford and Philpotts charities and for an approach to be made to either Brasenose and St John's or the Ecclesiastical Commissioners so that a separate foundation could be established for the Cathedral School. Both the latter courses, Leach stressed, were not without their difficulties. The disentangling of the Duchess' bequest would be complicated and might well need the consent of Manchester and Marlborough Grammar Schools as well as the two colleges; while an application to the Ecclesiastical Commissioners would founder without the support of Bishop Atlay, the diocesan being an *ex officio* Commissioner. Local opinion would also need to be canvassed. And there was no guarantee that even the Chapter would be accommodating. In this regard, Leach was under no illusion as to the magnitude of the task ahead. As he observed in the conclusion to his report:

> Their [the Dean and Chapter's] position, *prima facie*, appears to be: We have done very generously by the school; the school is a good school and the kind of school we want and flourishing as we want it; except that we should like to take part of the vicars choral College for the school building, and the Philpotts exhibitions might be partly or wholly applied to the purposes of the school; [for] the school we require no change and only ask to be let alone.[204]

Leach was right in his assessment. Although Dean Herbert and his colleagues were prepared to support the proposal to merge the Langford and Philpotts funds, they considered that the management of these charities might 'with safety', and subject to a yearly account and regulation by the Commission, be left in their hands. However, Leach's other suggestions for the creation of a separate school foundation were dismissed: in their view the Duchess' bequest should not be tampered with, and the proposed appeal to the Ecclesiastical Commissioners was rejected out of hand. Above all, they were adamant that

203. The other three (of the nine) cathedral schools to have gained grants from the Ecclesiastical Commissioners in this period were at Carlisle, Chester and Peterborough. Only Southwell had been refused – partly because of the Bishop's objections. At the time of Leach's Hereford report, no applications had been received from York and Durham (each described as being 'richly endowed and flourishing'), Gloucester, Salisbury or Wells. £15,000 was the largest individual sum given: to Carlisle (£5,000 of which was conditional on £500 being raised locally), Lincoln and Worcester – together, in the latter case, with three acres of land and money for repair of the refectory. King's Canterbury's £3,000 (again dependent on £1,000 being privately subscribed), together with gift of the palace, was even more munificent. Dean and Chapter annual contributions ranged from the £1,000 at Canterbury and Rochester to £13 6s 8d at Carlisle. See TNA, ED 27/1606, Leach's report, p.29, for this table, invaluable evidence for the history of late-Victorian cathedral schools; and Barrett, pp.275-76, for the reform of cathedral schools in general.

204. TNA, ED/1606, pp.30-31.

both 'the character of the education … as is at present given in the Cathedral School' should be maintained and that the Dean and Chapter should remain as its exclusive governors.[205] Ultimately the cathedral had to back down on most of these points, but it took until 21 February 1893 – following a belated final appeal direct to the Privy Council committee on education – before its opposition 'to the proposed schemes for the further regulation of Langford's and Philpotts' charities' was finally withdrawn.[206]

The story of the evolution of the new schemes of governance for these charities and for the school itself may be briefly told. Leach's proposal to halve the Somerset bequest between HCS and its two colleges, which the Headmaster as well as the cathedral had questioned, was quietly dropped. That left the Ecclesiastical Commissioners as the only possible other source of funding to establish a sufficient school foundation. Bishop Atlay, who had sent three sons to the school and whom *The Herefordian* rightly lauded a few years later in its obituary notices,[207] was central to this process, which took much of 1890 and January 1891 to complete. As we have seen, other cathedral schools had benefited enormously from the Ecclesiastical Commissioners' largesse, but Hereford's Chapter had been reluctant to follow suit in the mistaken belief that in the event of a successful application the governing body would need to be extended.

It was Atlay who performed the crucial role of soothing fears which had been aroused by Inspector Hare in 1876 when reform of the Langford charity was first mooted.[208] By early June 1890, the Dean and Chapter had agreed to provide £273 *per annum* as a permanent foundation for HCS, provided that the Ecclesiastical Commissioners provided a similar sum, and had assented to the severing of the Ludlow portion of the Langford charity, although not to the addition of the Bishop as a governor. This was followed by the Charity Commission's formal proposal of 28 June, although it was not until 23 January 1891 that the Ecclesiastical Commissioners agreed to give £7,000 as a capital base for the school. Although this was less than the cathedral had asked for, and a later request for an additional £1,500 building grant was refused, it was a significant sum nonetheless.[209] A major hurdle had been overcome, but the considerable tasks of drafting, publishing, finalising and then

205. HCA, 7031/23, pp.59-61, 25 June 1888, in response to Leach's letter of 13 June (TNA, ED 27/ 1605, no. 22, draft of 12 June).

206. HCA, 7031/23, p.171, Act, 21 Feb. 1893.

207. *TH*, NS XXII (July 1895), pp.5-6, 9-10. Edward Wilfred, George William and Charles Cecil Atlay were all admitted by Tatham as young boys under 10 (in 1875, 1876 and 1880 respectively). All left within two years. G.W. Atlay became a missionary and was murdered in Nyasaland (aged 27) on 26 August 1895, less than a year after his father's death.

208. For Atlay's role, see TNA, ED 27/1605, nos 46, 50, 52, draft letter to Atlay, 22 April, and notes re meetings with him, 29 April, 20 May 1890; and HCA, 7031/23, for his attendance at a Chapter meeting on 17 May 1890. An application to the Ecclesiastical Commissioners had in fact been made earlier in the 1880s (but not under the Endowed Schools Act) on behalf of the Hereford Dean and Chapter; and Leach believed that HCS had not been included in the Canterbury application of 5 May 1877 because the details of the 1840 transfer of Hereford Cathedral's estates were incomplete.

209. TNA, ED27/1605, no. 55, Leach's long 12 point draft ('from Southwell application [an unfortunate reference, given that Southwell had been refused] which was drafted in accordance with previous applications') of 26 June 1890, for an application to the Ecclesiastical Commissioners; no. 60, A De Bock Porter to Sir George Young, authorising the grant; no. 139, Same to Same, 9 April 1892.

submitting (to the Committee of Council on Education) the three schemes took more than two years, before they received the royal assent on 26 June 1893 – nearly 17 years after the first approach had been made to the Commission for the reform of the Langford charity.[210] The scheme for Hereford Cathedral Grammar School (as HCS was now named) formally provided for an endowment for its foundation, which constituted the Headmaster's house and its adjacent buildings and ground, the Chapter's £273 annual payment and the £7,000 capital sum from the Ecclesiastical Commissioners.[211] The Dean and Chapter continued as the sole governors, but they were required to keep a separate minute book, as well as accounts for public inspection. 'As soon as conveniently may be', but subject to the Charity Commissioners' approval, they were to provide from the capital endowment, 'proper buildings, suitable for not less than 80 day boys and 40 boarders and planned with a view to convenient expansion'. Their other residual powers were extensive and, for the first time, clearly delineated. These included the Headmaster's dismissal at pleasure after six months' notice or within days in the case of 'urgent cause'; and (subject to consultation with the Headmaster) jurisdiction over the numbers of assistant masters and boarders, the payment of fees, the subjects of instruction, school terms, sanitation arrangements and the proper maintenance of 'school plant or apparatus'.

Correspondingly, the Headmaster's powers were diminished and his position was made less secure. He was not to hold 'any benefice having the cure of souls' or other employment; he was not to receive payments beyond his £170 annual salary and a capitation fee of between £4 and £8 per boy; and apart from any delegated responsibilities, his duties were confined to the choice of books, methods of teaching, the arrangement of classes and school hours, the appointment and dismissal ('at pleasure') of assistants, discipline, and – subject to governor approval – chorister attendance at the cathedral. As for the boys themselves (and their parents), tuition fees (in advance) were to be fixed at a yearly rate between £12 and £18, and boarding fees at a maximum of £60 'in a hostel of the foundation' or £75 'in a master's house'; and their ages were specified, non-choristers entering at 10 – every boy having passed an entrance examination in the 'Procrustean three Rs'[212] – and leaving by the time they were 19. Religious instruction was to be 'in accordance with the doctrines of the Church of England', but any boy (the choristers apart) could be withdrawn by his parents from such lessons or from acts of worship. Other subjects – including natural science – were prescribed under nine headings, and a yearly examination was to be conducted by independent examiners approved by the governors or appointed by the Charity Commissioners, who were also to receive their annual report. General clauses included provision for a Headmaster's pensions fund if the school's resources were sufficient

210. The Dean and Chapter was primarily responsible for this inordinate delay, which occurred despite Dean Herbert's commitment on his visit to the Charity Commissioners in Whitehall on 20 June 1890, that they would 'do all in their power to help the application'. On that occasion, however, the Dean was equivocal when questioned about the Bishop's addition to the governing body and this was the nub of the matter. *Ibid.*, no. 54, Stanton's memo.

211. Copies of the final Charity Commission schemes (nos 733-735) for the school and the Langford and Philpotts foundations are kept in TNA, ED/1605 and HCSA.

212. The phrase is Armytage's, p.144. The Hereford test was graduated according to age, and included writing from dictation and 'the first four simple rules of Arithmetic with the multiplication table'.

for this to be realised; the setting aside of £20 in a separate account annually for 'repairs and improvements' to school buildings; and the formal recognition of the diocesan Bishop as Visitor. All told, this formidable 50 clause document provided the basis for the first professional regulation of the school in its entire history.

The schemes for the re-ordering of the Langford and Philpotts charities were of similar consequence. The Langford foundation was formally severed by the payment of £2,100 worth of stock from the Philpotts fund to the trustees of Ludlow Grammar School. For the first time, too, the governing body of the cathedral's educational charities included non-Dean and Chapter representatives – one from the county council, established as a result of the 1888 Local Government Act, and the other from the city council. Each of these members was to be appointed irrespective of their religious beliefs. Three cathedral representatives made up the governorship to five members, who were to elect their chairman – again this was without precedent as far as the cathedral was concerned – and to serve for a five-year term. At least two ordinary meetings were to be held each year, provision being made for special meetings; and, as with the school, separate minute books were to be kept for each foundation and regular accounts rendered and made public. The land, property, funds, stocks and securities (except mortgages) of each foundation, which produced an income of around £330 *per annum*,[213] were also to be taken away from the Dean and Chapter and vested in the Official Trustee of Charity Lands, although the estates were allowed to be managed by the governors or their agents.

For the school and its pupils, the implications were as far-reaching. £150 *per annum* continued to be reserved from the Philpotts foundation for university exhibitions and open to boys of at least two years standing in the school, but their individual value was altered to an amount between £25 and £50 and they were to be tenable 'at any university or other institution of higher or professional education approved by the governors', a timely recognition that there were other university colleges outside Oxford and Cambridge.[214] The remaining income was to be applied for entrance scholarships. Similarly, the Langford foundation was opened up to any boy who had attended a Hereford public elementary school for at least three years.[215] One award, covering the tuition fee and an annual additional sum of £5, was reserved every year for an elementary schoolboy, with preference in cases of equal merit being given to a boy born within the city. No boy was to be deprived on religious grounds. Overall, the governors were charged with the duty of making arrangements for election to these scholarships by means 'as seem to them best adapted to secure the double object of

213. The total annual returns in 1891 for the Langford and Philpotts foundations respectively were: £118 12s (plus £31 16s 6d Bank stock) from the rent of the Castle Crab estate at Disserth; and £359 11s 10d from the rent of 28 High Town let to John Grout, ironmonger, (and later to Boots), various Chapter mortgage loans to St Katherine's Hospital, Ledbury, and bank deposits – the mortgages and stock having accumulated over many years from the charity's surpluses.

214. Parliament had also recognised the fact for the first time a year or two earlier in 1889, by voting an annual sum for distribution between the university colleges. The school scheme also only stipulated that the Headmaster should be 'a graduate of some university in the United Kingdom'.

215. Although in 1899, following the election of the first five Langfordians under the 1893 scheme, the school's scholarship examination was criticised by Assistant Commissioner Bruce as not being suitable for public elementary schoolboys. TNA, ED 27/1606, Bruce's report, 27 Jan. 1900. The school was also criticised for failing to publish the charities' accounts.

attracting good scholars to Hereford Cathedral Grammar School and advancing education at the said public elementary schools'. As with the school, the cumulative effect of these changes was fundamental: the Dean and Chapter's independent and exclusive governance of the Langford and Philpotts charities no longer held, and the nature of these trusts – by these schemes known as foundations rather than charities – was for ever altered.

The balance sheet of losers and winners from these major constitutional changes is not hard to draw. Dean Herbert and his colleagues would have counted themselves among the victims of educational progress. They had succeeded, at least for the time being, in maintaining complete authority over the governorship of their school, but half – and according to the cathedral, a generous half – of the value of the Langfordian estate had been given over to the Ludlow foundation for their trustees to administer. The Dean and Chapter's control of their remaining educational endowments, most of the assets of which had been transferred elsewhere, now had to be shared. Their right to determine the religious character of the Langfordian scholars (although not the choristers) had been lost. Their requests, too, for additional safeguards that would have ensured the ordained status of the Headmaster and secured some financial control over the chorister master were ignored. Special provision was made with regard to the entry ages of choristers but they were not excluded from the payment of the Headmaster's capitation fee and their number (in terms of their entitlement to a free education) was pegged at 12 rather than 16 as the Chapter had originally wanted. And even though much of the running of HCS could be delegated to the Headmaster, the enshrining of their powers and responsibilities in a statutory instrument meant that they would have to play a more prominent and business-like part in the school's governance.

Thistle also felt threatened by the new scheme which (in his own words) was 'greatly to my detriment'. His independent authority as Headmaster could now be undermined by the governors' extensive residual powers. And even if the Chapter chose not to exercise them, in personal terms he was disadvantaged as the scheme imposed on him a new contractual arrangement by changing the nature of his tenure. He had a strong moral case, if not one in law – the Endowed Schools Act of 1868 having provided for the dismissal of all teachers at the pleasure of their governing body – and his anger is understandable. His situation was this: having been engaged in June 1890 on the old 'good behaviour' terms ('as long as you shall behave yourself diligently and religiously therein'), he was now being placed (as he confided to Leach) 'at the mercy of a shifting body of clerics', with the requirement under the scheme for him to make a formal declaration that he would 'acquiesce … and relinquish all claim to the mastership' should they decide to dismiss him. Moreover, Thistle had not known at the time of his appointment that negotiations were proceeding with the Charity Commissioners, and first learned of the proposals months later when he was sent a copy of the draft scheme. He later claimed that his original terms were the major reason for his declining the opportunity 'for … appointment as Headmaster of a school in the north'.[216] It

216. This was almost certainly Ripon Grammar School where he had been Second Master. For this and Thistle's position in general, see: TNA, ED 27/1605, no. 171, Leach's memoranda, 9 July 1892; no. 155, Thistle's objections, 20 May 1892; and Leach's (unnumbered) draft replies of 24 Nov. 1892 and 24 Jan. 1893; TNA, ED 27/1608, Thistle's application to the Council Committee on Education, 14 Dec. 1892; and HCA, 1538, containing the draft schemes sent to Thistle, with the Headmaster's vigorous scoring and occasional comments – as, for example, against sections 17 and 18 (dismissal clauses), 26 and 27 (governors' jurisdiction over fees, boarding numbers and spending), and 28 (capitation fees).

was a mess, and there was no possibility of compensation from the Charity Commissioners, although his governors succeeded in persuading the Commissioners to raise his capitation fee by one third from the original proposal to between £4 and £8 (as at Norwich). Assuming a school of 90 and a capitation fee at the highest rate, this would at least allow him to reap a profit from the tuition fees similar to that he was gaining from their direct collection.[217] Thistle may not have suffered much financially but his constitutional position was considerably weakened by the new scheme and within months he was obliged to sign a declaration which gave his governors the right to remove him from office arbitrarily.[218]

If the new scheme threatened Thistle's magisterial independence and was detrimental to him personally, it was of considerable benefit to the school as a whole. The governorship of HCS may have still been limited to the Dean and Chapter, but provision was made for the school to be managed on modern lines, the governors taking primary responsibility (at least in theory) for the payment of assistant masters and the maintenance of the plant and the Headmaster for academic and pastoral matters. The administration of the new Langford and Philpotts foundations was widened and the scope of their endowments increased. Entrance scholarships were created from the Philpotts bequest, thereby fulfilling what Tatham had wanted from the fund nearly 20 years earlier, leaving the Langford bequest to provide free places for clever boys from local elementary schools. The establishment of this principle was of fundamental importance to the school's welfare in the twentieth century, as we will see. And although a majority of city councillors – many of whom had direct connections with the school – wanted the Langfordian scholarships to be available to all boys irrespective of their background, Dean Langford's intention to give boys who were 'poor and towardly for learning' the opportunity to be educated at HCS was honoured by the new scheme. As Councillor Willis proclaimed in a vigorous debate in the Town Hall on 3 May 1892:

> The proposals to alter the scheme were most specious. It was suggested that the advantages should be thrown open to all boys. What would be the effect of that? Simply to keep things as they were. The Cathedral School boys would get all the benefits. What chance, for instance, would the boys in the St Peter's, in the Scudamore, or in the Blue Coat schools stand against those in the Cathedral, Mr Baker's or Mr Pembridge's Schools? He was not pleading today for the upper middle class of society – they had many champions in the Council – but for the interests of the poor ...[219]

217. TNA, ED 27/1605, no. 175, Chapter Clerk's calculation, 28 July 1892. The £8 capitation from 90 boys would have given Thistle £20 less than the £740 profit (£1,440 less £700 masters' salaries) he would have gained from the direct collection of 90 tuition fees at £16, his assistants' salaries being paid directly by the governors after 1893; although with the average fee at around £14, Thistle would have gained more from an £8 capitation. Thistle continued to collect the boarding fees, repaying the tuition fees to the governors but retaining the boarding profits.

218. HCSA, account book 1884-1922.

219. As reported in *HT*, 7 May 1892. At least five of the 21 Councillors present at the debate had links with the school. The Conservative majority voted in favour of a resolution to allow boys who had been 'resident in or educated in any public elementary or other school' eligible for Langfordian scholarships. This proposal, together with one for the election of an additional city councillor in place of a county councillor as a trustee of the scheme, was turned down by the Charity Commissioners. HARC, HLC A/26, pp.264-65, 397, reports of William Boycott, chairman of the Education Committee (and HCS parent), 27 April, 30 Nov. 1892.

As for leaving scholarships, the Somerset scholarships remained untouched and the same amount (£150) was maintained for Philpotts exhibitions. However, at the Headmaster's suggestion, the Philpotts awards were made more equitable – six rather than three boys could now benefit from them at any one time – and they could for the first time be held outside the confines of a single Oxford college. Finally, an independent foundation had been established for the school itself. This provided a gross annual income of £469 in 1893-94 – less than what the Chapter had wanted from the Ecclesiastical Commissioners, and half of what Leach's proposal for the dissolution of the Somerset bequest would have yielded – which more than doubled the previous Chapter allowance, and gave the wherewithal for the modernisation of the Headmaster's house.

Refurbishment

Some £265 was spent by the Chapter on refurbishments to both the Headmaster's house and the classroom accommodation in the months following Thistle's appointment. The boys' dormitories, as well as the Headmaster's lodging, were completely re-decorated; roofs, water pipes and drains were extensively repaired; a platform was made in the schoolroom for the new Headmaster; classrooms were re-painted and kitted out with new desks from the Educational Supply Association; and maps and 'Chemistry appliances' were bought to aid the boys' instruction. Although these alterations amounted to around 7 *per cent* of the cathedral's ordinary expenditure in 1890-91, compared to bigger schools the money spent was not a great deal. Such changes, however, would have had an immediate impact on the boys' daily lives, as would the walling in and heating of the 'covered drill shed' in the playground in early 1892, so that it could 'be used for joinering and other such occupations' on wet days.[220]

Even so, apart from the dormitory built in 1876, the boarding accommodation was old and was, as the Charity Commissioners admitted, 'not such as should be provided and is now expected in a school of this kind'.[221] Thistle gives an insight into the conditions endured by his boarders, when he made these objections to the Commissioners' initial proposal to increase the boarding fee to a maximum of £80:

> The school is almost entirely without the advantages of position, buildings, playground and scholarships … that are now found in almost every other school of the sort, and unless the fees were very low it would be impossible to get boarders here in any numbers. The present fees … for board and tuition combined are from £55 to £65 a year. If from this I were required to pay from £12 to £16 a year as tuition fee to the governors, it would become impossible for me to take [in] boarders at all; or at any rate to give them such attention and domestic comfort as, with the present low fees, are the only attractions I can offer to parents as an inducement to send their sons to the [house], which itself also is without any … modern conveniences, e.g. a bathroom [or] a boarders' sitting room etc.[222]

---

220. For the above, see the audit account payments: HCA, 7106/2, 1890, nos 123-45; 1891, nos 118a-125; and *HT*, NS XVII (March 1892), p.4.

221. TNA, ED 27/1605, no. 55, letter (drafted by Leach) to the Ecclesiastical Commissioners, 28 June 1890.

222. *Ibid.*, no. 155, Thistle to the Charity Commissioners, 20 May 1892. The annual boarding fees were maintained at £55 (for boys under 12) and £65 (for over 12s), including tuition fees of 12 and 14 guineas respectively.

It is a moot point as to how far matters could be improved by a continuation of the governors' patch and mend policies. Indeed, Bishop Atlay himself did not believe that the Headmaster's house could ever become 'a proper boarding house', and as late as July 1892 Leach was still advocating an amalgamation between HCS and the County College.[223] Dean and Chapter intransigence made such a solution impossible, but at least the Ecclesiastical Commission grant made it possible for the boarders to be treated to some home comforts.

£1,292 15s 9d was spent from the foundation's capital on improvements to the school buildings in 1894-95.[224] This sum was near double the original estimate. Over £450 of it, moreover, was unauthorised – an overspend that caused a row with the Charity Commissioners before an accommodation was made with them for the money to be repaid within 15 years from the school's annual surpluses.[225] Despite the financial wrangles, the rebuilding made a significant difference to the school. The north side of the Headmaster's house was reconfigured with the addition of a new drawing room and bedroom wing, complete with 'Vienna marble' chimney pieces, bay windows and oak-timbered gables. And at the southern end of the building, a boiler room was added on to the scullery, over which was built a servants' bedroom and, in the roof, a new dormitory for four boys. This was to be entered from the existing dormitory, and to have enlarged dormer windows and an elevated fireplace. At the corner of the playground the toilets were improved. These works may not seem much to modern eyes, but they considerably enhanced Thomas and Ethel Thistle's home; enabled the Headmaster to increase the boarding numbers to 40; and gave the boys better facilities, including hot running water and a bathroom for the boarders, even if it was used for only eight hours each week and the water supply proved defective. School House and its yard, as we know them today, were taking shape.[226]

The End of an Era

By the time of these developments, significant changes had occurred to the composition of the governing body. Dean Herbert had lived long enough to see through the reform of the school's constitution and to be elected chairman of trustees for the new charitable foundations. On 26 January 1894, he attended his penultimate Chapter meeting, at which the school's annual expenditure under the new scheme was set at £700 'for the purpose of maintaining assistant masters and proper school plant or apparatus', and the Headmaster's capitation fee was limited to the remaining balance from the tuition fees.[227] George Herbert's

HCA, 7031/23, p.208, Act, 26 Jan. 1894.

223. *Ibid.*, no. 50, Leach's note to Young re Atlay's visit, endorsed 8 May 1890; no. 171, Leach to Young, 9 July 1892.

224. This paragraph is based on TNA, ED 27/1610, which contains correspondence between the Charity Commissioners and the Chapter Clerk over the rebuilding. The major additions were designed by Knight and Chatters of Cheltenham; the Hereford contractors were Bowers and Company for the main works, W.P. Lewis and Company for the new coke house and toilets, and Vaughan and Son for an additional water supply.

225. TNA, ED 27/1605, retrospective order, 3 Sept. 1895, for the overspend. Surpluses averaged out at around £78 10s *per annum* during Thistle's last four years in office, 1894-97.

226. A pen and ink drawing of School House (without the dormitories, but from this period) exists in HCA, 1541; and tracings of its three floors, executed by Beavan and Hodges in 1911, are to be found in the school archives.

227. HCSA, Philpotts foundation minute book, meeting 13 Jan. 1894; HCA, 7031/23, p.208, Act 26 Jan. 1894.

death on 15 March 1894, after 27 years as Dean and chairman of governors, together with several other changes in the Chapter in the early and mid-1890s,[228] marked the end of an era in the governance of the cathedral and its school. The Honourable James Wentworth Leigh, his successor, although as well born, bred and educated as Herbert, was a Dean of a different stamp. Like Bishop Percival, who succeeded Atlay as bishop of Hereford – and Visitor to the school – in 1895, Leigh was a progressive educationalist: his open support for the modern side at the expense of Classics in his 1897 speech day address would never have been publicly acknowledged by his predecessor.[229]

Thistle's sudden resignation in November that year completed the break with the past. With the change to the nature of his tenure, the alterations in the school's constitution and the rapid decline in pupil numbers in his last months, his had been a difficult few years in office. Nevertheless, despite a certain northern directness, he was a man of considerable charm, and a Headmaster who inspired affection among both masters and boys. He will not be remembered for his gifts as a scholar or administrator, but as his successor observed, he successfully inculcated a 'tone of manliness combined with discipline' among his boys, and kept the ship steady through an important period of constitutional change. His great work, however, occurred after he had left Hereford: his memorial lies at Eling Church, Southampton, where the Thistle Chapel stands as testimony to his 38-year ministry in that parish.[230]

William Henry Murray Ragg, 1898-1913

Thistle's mid-term resignation occurred the day before the formal appointment of the second outstanding Headmaster of the period, William Henry Murray Ragg, whom the Dean and Chapter appointed on 12 November 1897 from six short-listed candidates.[231] Given the desperate need for a Headmaster who could quickly build up the school roll, it was essential that the governors appointed someone of experience; and in Ragg they found a man with nine successful years behind him as Headmaster of Great Yarmouth Grammar School, who brought with him (as we will see) eight boarders from his old school in his first term. As a scholar – like Tatham, he had taken a first in Classics at Cambridge – and a person of wide intellectual interests, he would also be well able both to maintain a high standard of teaching in the Classical Sixth and improve the school's general reputation. That he further proved himself at a time of national educational reform to be a moderniser and an influential voice in educational circles within the city, was a considerable bonus. And, unlike Tatham and Thistle, he kept the complete confidence of his governors throughout his tenure – a confidence shown by his installation as a cathedral prebendary (of Bullinghope) in October 1911, towards the end of his 46 term reign.

228. Notably (as far as HCS is concerned) Canon Musgrave, who died in April 1892 after nearly 50 years as a residentiary; Canon George Whitaker, who resigned in the summer of 1892; and Canon Henry Phillott – a considerable scholar who acted as an examiner for the school, and who died on 4 December 1895, aged 79.

229. See above, pp.287-88. For Bishop Henson's favourable judgement on Dean Leigh, see Aylmer and Tiller, p.166.

230. *TH*, NS XXIX (Dec. 1898), p.11, report of Murray Ragg's speech 28 July 1898; *ibid.*, NS CXLI (April 1936), for Thistle's obituary.

231. HCA, 7031/23, p.292, Act 12 Nov. 1897. The other five candidates were S.W. Finn, C.G. Lowe, C.H. Moreland (an assistant master at Norwich School), H.A.P. Sawyer (an assistant at Highgate) and A.H. Worrall. HCA, 7106/3 fo 262r, account of the names and the £16 2s 10d spent on the appointment.

Fig. 6.10 William Henry Murray Ragg, the one Headmaster of the period who became a prebendary.

Academic Advances

The new Headmaster set about his initial task to increase pupil numbers and restore the school's standing with considerable vigour. Among his first initiatives, and following the replacement of three masters who had left with Thistle,[232] was his establishment of a preparatory department by leasing part of Harley Court from the Dean and Chapter. Although it was a private venture, the Headmaster being 'solely responsible' for its 'expenses and profits', the risk was lessened by his taking over of an existing school – a Miss Earle having gained the cathedral's consent to erect 'a corrugated iron schoolroom' in the Harley Court garden some nine years earlier.[233] The house was also rented on favourable terms: a non-repairing annual lease of £42, the Chapter further contributing towards the purchase of major fittings.[234] The yearly tuition fees of just four boys at 12 guineas each would more than cover these costs; and the fees of a few more day pupils and boarders (at £55 *per annum*) – within the year the house was able to accommodate 10 junior boarders[235] – would leave the Headmaster with a handsome profit, even allowing for the schoolmistress' salary and the £30 Housemaster's allowance.

The success of this move was soon apparent. The school had increased from 12 boys by the end of 1898 to 18 (including three boarders) in January 1901. This necessitated the appointment of a second mistress. Thereafter numbers were sufficient to sustain at least two forms, taught simultaneously at each end of the green tin tabernacle. More importantly, as most of the boys transferred at 11 to the Cathedral School proper, it guaranteed an entry of boys who had been well grounded in Latin, Scripture, History and Geography, in addition to the three Rs. Stanley Thompson was just one of many old boys who remained indebted to the end of his long life to the formidable Miss Ellen Dance, the Headmistress, who instilled into him the importance of academic rigour.[236] The Headmaster's favourable speech day reports of his annual inspection of the preparatory department provide further evidence of the high pedagogical standards that the mistresses achieved.

Murray Ragg also moved swiftly to enhance the school's academic standing by changing the examination system. Thistle, as we have seen, took fright from doing this in 1890 and it was left to his successor to seek external validation of the boys' work by requiring them

232. Messrs Roberts, Crosthwaite and Wargent (the former chorister master) were replaced by the Revd T.F.H. Berwick and Messrs W.G. Sheriff and H.R. Yates. Berwick and Yates lasted only 18 months. With the notable exceptions of Herr Goetz, who died in post on 19 December 1909, and Hugo Sharpley, who served under Murray Ragg continuously from September 1899, the Headmaster's problems of retaining his six full-time assistants for any length of time remained. The only period of stability was the three years, 1903-06.

233. HCA, 7031/23, p.86, Act 35 June 1889; p.304, Act 24 March 1898.

234. HCA, 7106/3, 1898 account, fos 248r, 303v for the leases; HCA, 7106/4, 1902 account, fo 93r, payment of £39 15s 1d for a kitchen range. From September 1903, Murray Ragg took over the whole of Harley Court (now Numbers 4 & 5) at an additional rent of £18 15s. *Ibid.*, 1903 account, fo 196v.

235. Initially under the care of Mr and Mrs Douton, and after Douton's untimely death on 3 August 1899, under Hugo Sharpley and his wife.

236. R.S. Thompson (OH 1908-14) was a Philpotts junior scholar from September 1911. He became a successful Sherborne schoolmaster and then Headmaster of Bloxham School, where he was affectionately known as 'the Bishop of Bloxham'. The school archives contain his reminiscences of his time at HCS, together with three immaculate exercise books and some reports and other papers. See *TH*, NS LXXX (April 1915), p.28, for Murray Ragg's obituary tribute to Miss Dance whom he had first appointed at Great Yarmouth.

to take tests set by national examination boards. 1898 was the last year of the cosy old regime of the school being examined by hand-picked dons, a scheme that by the end of the century was thoroughly outmoded;[237] and 1899 was the first year of the Sixth Form being entered for the Oxford and Cambridge Board Higher Certificate (instituted in 1887), and the Fourth Forms for the Oxford junior 'locals'. The following year, the Fifth Form was put in for the lower certificate. The advantages were considerable in that a higher certificate was accepted as a test of efficiency by many professional bodies and also gained a boy exemption from matriculation examinations at the ancient universities. The risks, however, were also manifest. As the Headmaster warned his audiences on successive speech days in 1899 and 1900, HCS was being tested by comparison with the best public schools and their hopes should not be raised too high.[238] Nevertheless, over the years the results again justified Murray Ragg's decision, particularly following the abandonment in 1905 of the Oxford and Cambridge higher and lower certificates in favour of the Oxford local senior and junior equivalents. Thereafter, the school's results, particularly in the Sixth Form, were above the national average, a not inconsiderable achievement given the school's policy to enter whole forms, rather than just the cleverest boys, and to teach beyond the confines of the examination syllabus.[239]

There was a price to be paid, however, for the onset of Board examinations: the external imposition of an examination timetable for the last two weeks of the summer term. One immediate consequence was the omission of the boys' recitations and plays from the speech day programme. 'We really doubt whether the public appreciate them sufficiently', wrote one boy in his report on the day's proceedings in July 1900, 'to make it worthwhile to continue them, considering the extra pressure that has to be put on us to get them up at a time when all our energies are particularly required to satisfy the exorbitant demands of the examiners'.[240] Speech day was also affected in other ways: the ending (in 1899) of the 'time honoured tradition' of the Headmaster reading out the examiners' reports; and from 1904, the moving of the ceremony itself to an autumn date so that prizes could be appropriately awarded following the publication of examination results.

The necessity for a new kind of speech day address – together with the boys' examination successes, detailed in the speech day programme – gave Murray Ragg the opportunity to convince his parents about the value of a liberal education and to justify the school's (in his own words) 'somewhat classical' curriculum. On 28 September 1904, the first autumnal speech day, for example, he outlined his educational philosophy:

---

237. L.B. Radford, a fellow of St John's, Cambridge, was lavish in his praise of the school's work in 1898 (TNA, ED 27/1611 report, 27 July 1898), which perhaps convinced Ragg that it was time to change the system, although from 1903 a separate Mathematics examination was set and marked in the old way by an external examiner.

238. *TH*, NS XXXII (Dec. 1899), p.8; NS XXXV (Dec. 1900), p.33.

239. Prior to the 1905 change, about half the candidature gained the Oxford and Cambridge certificates, which required passes in at least five subjects, in any one year. Thereafter, the vast majority of boys (except those put in a year early, 1905-08) passed the Oxford local papers compared with a national pass rate of around 70 *per cent.* The honours and subject distinctions gained by HCS in these years were also well above the national average for Oxford board schools.

240. *TH*, NS XXXV (Dec. 1900), p.15. They were revived again – at least for a few years – in 1906.

> Our aim is to give a boy of average intelligence by the time he is sixteen an all-round education, to develop his various faculties rather than teaching things definitely useful ... to develop his mind thereby and, if possible, give him a taste for learning ... I believe we should be untrue to the principles of education if we had a lower aim – the aim of specialising the teaching of young boys in what is 'going to be useful to him' in commercial subjects ...

And the following year, Murray Ragg argued that languages were the best basis for education, and that Latin held the key to language training. 'There is no medium to compare with it', he declared, 'for training the mind at once in memory, observation, reasoning, thought and taste', observing that the Americans perceived its value having 'entirely reinstated' the subject in their schools. He continued:

> There is great danger that all too soon after leaving school a boy's attention may be limited almost entirely to that which bears on making him a money-making machine. I deprecate the tendency to turn his attention to so narrow a groove, and so lamentable a groove, while he is still at school.

Two years later, his message was similar: book-keeping, typewriting and shorthand were not educative subjects and were not taught at the school. 'In this matter', he observed, 'we are completely in accord with the Board of Education'.[241]

HCS's curriculum could be justified on philosophical grounds but it could be fairly criticised for its narrow focus, its lack of a proper modern side and the excessive hours worked by the younger boys. It is true that some changes had been made to the timetable over the ten years from the end of Tatham to the start of Murray Ragg's headship. Although the length of the taught week (nearly 28 hours) was similar, hour long lessons were no longer the norm, a ten-minute mid-morning break had been created and Wednesday (rather than Tuesday and Thursday) was the designated mid-week games afternoon. In subject terms, more time had been allocated to Mathematics, French, Scripture and, in the lower forms, English grammar and composition, at the expense of Latin and Greek – although Greek was started a year earlier; German and shorthand (for a time) were established as modern options instead of Greek for forms II-V; drill was no longer timetabled, and drawing was available as a voluntary activity for 40 minutes on Saturday afternoons. Despite these developments, at the turn of the century languages accounted for well over half the lessons for the top four forms, and Mathematics, with six-and-a-half hours weekly for each form, occupied much of the remaining time. And there was still no place for Science as a separate academic discipline, a point emphasised by W.N. Bruce, the assistant charity commissioner, following his inspection on 11 July 1899.[242]

Bruce had also drawn attention to the omission of Drawing, drill and vocal Music from the curriculum. Murray Ragg soon remedied these deficiencies by re-introducing half an hour per week for drill as well as for singing, and adding two junior drawing lessons

---

241. *Ibid.*, NS XLVII (Dec. 1904), p.10; NS L (Dec.1905), p.9; NS LIII (Dec. 1906), p.10; NS (Dec. 1907), p.9.

242. TNA, ED 27/1609, timetable for 1899 (Summer term?), and the Bruce report, 3 Oct. 1899. See above, pp.243-44, for the situation in 1889.

to the curriculum.[243] Competent instructors were also appointed in these disciplines, none more so than that loyal Old Herefordian, Percy Clarke Hull, who not only transformed the school's singing in these years but also donated a cup for cross-country running.[244] Other modifications – the rearrangement of Mathematics teaching by form, the adoption of new methods in geometry and algebra, the changing of Latin pronunciation and the teaching of colloquial French[245] - could be made relatively easily. The introduction of Science as a major subject in a predominately classical school, however, was a much more difficult proposition and only gradually achieved.

Fig. 6.11 A young Percy Hull, from a photograph taken c.*1908, when he was singing-master at the school.*

As we have seen, Murray Ragg's predecessors had introduced some scientific instruction and bought Chemistry appliances but this had been done in a random and limited fashion.[246] In 1899 Bruce could observe that although a few boys received private tuition in science, there was 'a meagre supply of apparatus for teaching elementary Chemistry' and 'no proper room for laboratory work'. Such experiments that were carried out caused 'obnoxious effluvias' to drift around the school and were no doubt potentially dangerous.[247] Four years on, the situation had not improved. Called to give evidence at the enquiry into the city's educational needs in July 1903, Murray Ragg had made his reservations about Science education quite clear, pointing out that HCS had no facilities for the subject, no-one qualified to teach it and that very few boys would be interested in pursuing it.[248] A few days later, he expanded on these thoughts on speech day:

243. These subjects were all in place by the time of the 1908 inspection, but Bruce's report indicates that Murray Ragg was making arrangements for their re-introduction soon after his 1899 visit.

244. Hull had been a chorister at Hereford Cathedral and attended the school from 1889 to 1894. He was then apprenticed as an articled pupil to the organist (George Robertson Sinclair), and became the school's singingmaster from early 1900 to August 1914, when he was interned as a German prisoner of war. He was organist and master of choristers, 1918-49, and was knighted in 1947. See below, pp.319, 354, for the Hull Cup and his internment.

245. Murray Ragg made reference to these changes in his addresses of 28 September 1904 and 1 October 1906. In December 1906, in the only speech he is known to have made at an HMC conference, he also referred to the 'small amount of difficulty' that had been caused at HCS by its adoption of the Italianate pronunciation of Latin – even though only one master had been familiar with it – and that it promoted a new interest in the subject among the boys. *HMC 1906 Report*, pp.27-28. C.A. Alington (pp.41-44) had a contrary view.

246. See above, pp.193, 244, 289, 299.

247. As a boy noted in an anonymous letter: *TH*, NS XXX (April 1899), p.21, letter signed 'Ododa'.

248. HARC, J65/932, summary of evidence, 24 July 1903. Murray Ragg played a prominent part in the hearing, submitting a perceptive paper which outlined Hereford's educational needs as he saw them.

There was perhaps one point [he was reported as saying] in which the Cathedral School had not yet fulfilled its duty and that was with regard to scientific teaching, but they hoped to do more than they were doing which was practically nothing. (Laughter) For his own part, he held very strong views on the relative value of Science and Languages as a means of education, and in giving the latter a preference, he found he was upheld in his opinion by Sir William Anson, President of the Board of Education. (Applause)[249]

The report is revealing, as much for the audience's reaction as for Murray Ragg's views on the value of science teaching: an acknowledgment by all that compared with the classical languages, Science was a less useful means of learning. Still, despite the expense, something needed to be done to bring HCS into line with other public schools, if not with Oundle.[250]

Prompted by the city enquiry, where he had admitted that a small laboratory could be provided if the buildings were modified, a room was converted in the old lodge by early 1904 at an expense of £100, enabling 'Chemistry classes and "stinks" to flourish and abound once again'. Later that year, two hour-long lessons per week were devoted to teaching Science to non-classicists. This was an important step forward and involved about half the boys in those forms but the cleverest pupils were still excluded from the subject. It is not surprising, therefore, that the school's Science provision was again criticised following an inspection by the Oxford and Cambridge Board in June 1905. The inspector's suggestions were taken up, and a Science prize named in memory of that distinguished Hereford scientist, George With, was awarded for the first time in many years at the 1905 speech day. By 1908, elementary Science had been introduced for all boys in their first three years, science then being carried on in forms Four and Five as part of the modern curriculum.[251] The Board of Education inspectors later that year, however, reported that the chemical laboratory could accommodate no more than 14 boys. Despite the 'very conscientious and systematic teaching' of the Science master, the inspectors considered that 'a good standard of science work' could not be reached until Physics had been included within the curriculum.[252] The situation was partly remedied (as we will see) by the building of a new laboratory, following the school's acquisition of Harley House School (Number 1, Castle Street) in 1910-11.

Science apart, the 1908 inspectors had also alluded to other academic weaknesses including the school's failure to provide a Modern Sixth, the lack of 'really vigorous

249. *TH*, NS XLIV (Dec. 1903), p.14.

250. For the developments in Science at Rugby in an earlier generation, see above, p.208. The great advances in Science teaching in public schools of this period were being promoted by F.W. Sanderson, first as an assistant at Dulwich College, and then as Headmaster of Oundle, 1892-1922.

251. See HCA, 7106/4, fo 169r, payments to Beavan & Hodges and Harris & Co.; and *TH*, NS XLV (April 1904), p.3; XLVII (Dec. 1904), pp.9-10; L (Dec. 1905), pp.9, 11; LVI (Dec. 1907), p.9 for these developments. Science prizes, such as 'Mr Lane's Chemistry prize' of July 1884, had occasionally been awarded in the past. For George With, who died on 15 September 1904, see above, p.193. His memorial Science prize was presented five times, the last year being 1909, when Mathematics and Science prizes for Forms I and II were instituted.

252. TNA, ED 35/995, inspection of 26, 27 March; report dated, 25 May 1908.

individual work' for senior pupils and the balance of the lower school work.[253] Such criticisms were no doubt justified but Murray Ragg had done much in ten years to improve the taught curriculum, especially given the constraints within which he had to work. But he showed equal concern to offer opportunities for boys to broaden their intellectual interests outside the classroom. He and his colleagues did this in three main ways: by organising a winter lecture programme, establishing a senior literary society and breathing new life into moribund activities.

Activities

The 'Big School' lectures, interspersed with occasional monitors' concerts and masters' entertainments, would in part have been arranged to occupy the boarding community in gainful employment on a Saturday evening, but they also had real educative value. The Headmaster led the way by giving one or two lectures each year on topics as diverse as the human body, English architecture, Naples and Pompeii, great painters like G.F. Watts, and above all, his beloved Tennyson. Guest lecturers included local worthies like Alfred Watkins (on 'Herefordshire Scenery' and 'Across England with Little Nell') and 'the enthusiastic philo-Hungarian', W.H. Shrubsole; academic parents, such as C. Carus-Wilson FRS FRGS, who spoke on various geological themes; old boys like Fred Weatherly ('33 Years of Song Writing'); local clergymen (including Canon Bannister on the early history of Herefordshire); the journalist, G.H. Head, who commemorated Nelson 100 years after Trafalgar, although the school flag was prominent by its absence on Trafalgar day itself; and even one or two ladies, although what the boys made of Miss S.F. Bacon's 'adventures in cloud-land' on 19 November 1906 is unknown. These lectures were often illustrated by demonstrations, as well as slides projected by the school's unreliable oxygen-powered lantern, and, on one occasion, by cinematograph. Few speakers, however, would have been able to match Sir Ernest Shackleton, who spoke at the new Shirehall on 1 March 1910. The lecture was attended by most of the boys, one of them claiming that it had been 'well worth three bob', 'which', as *The Herefordian* reported, 'for some fellows is saying a good deal'.[254] Overall, Murray Ragg spent significant sums on these school lectures, to the boys' considerable benefit.[255]

Beyond offering his drawing-room and his wife's 'lavish hospitality' for occasional meetings, the Headmaster made no direct contributions to the success of the Literary Society. The Society was the brain-child of Hugo Sharpley, senior classical master and published versifier.[256] He also had a great love for English literature. Indeed, one of his junior boys over

253. The school's governorship, business arrangements and premises were also criticised. Despite all this, the school was recognised as 'efficient' under chapter VIII of the regulations for secondary schools. See below, p.323.

254. *Ibid.*, LXIII (April 1910), p.22.

255. From November 1904 to March 1911, £111 4s 8d – about £17 *per annum* – was spent on slides and lecturers' expenses, more than the annual average spent at Jakeman and Carver on prize books. HCA, 7106/4, 5 *passim*; HCSA, account book.

256. Several of Sharpley's verses, including 'To A Parting Guest' – on the 'diablo' craze, which had flourished at HCS – and 'Lapps Linguae Latinae', were published in *Punch*. He also had his translation of *The Trachinian Maidens of Sophocles* published, and presented the volume to the Gilbert Library. See *TH*, NS LI (March 1906), p.38; LVII (April 1908), pp.26-27; NS LXI (July 1909), p.4.

70 years later still remembered with affection the times when his Housemaster would read from the works of Scott, Dickens, Matthew Arnold and Lewis Carroll on Sunday evenings in front of the Harley Court fire. Sharpley, however, was as concerned to cultivate an appreciation of literature among the Sixth Form as he was for his preparatory boys. He did this by inviting ten senior boys to form a select society, where papers would be read and poems recited on alternate Tuesday evenings in the congenial surroundings of masters' rooms. The first meeting was held 'in Mr Clayton's room' on 21 November 1905, when the President (Sharpley) read a paper on Milton. H.P.W. Burton was the first boy to read a paper – on Coleridge – the following February, at the society's fourth gathering. Thereafter, the boys generally took the lead. Over the next few years, papers were read on many of the luminaries of literature from Shakespeare to Walt Whitman, including one or two lesser lights like Walter Savage Landor and Charles Stuart Calverley – the latter, it was observed, 'to the scathing criticism of some ... members'. And although the fortnightly rule was eventually broken – there were no summer term events from 1909 because of the 'stress of work' – 75 meetings were held from November 1905 to April 1913, when Murray Ragg left the school. The vision of that 'impressive, dignified figure', Hugo Sharpley, to acquaint boys with the works of 'great poets and authors' had triumphantly succeeded.[257]

It is an invariable law that school societies wax and wane, and that their fortunes are totally dependent at any one time on the expertise and enthusiasms of the community within which they operate. Nevertheless, and with due regard to this axiom, the malaise among several HCS activities appears to have been particularly acute at the end of Thistle's reign. Rugby football was on its last legs as the school's winter game. *The Herefordian*'s financial prospects, as its editors warned, were 'none too rosy', even though only one issue had been produced in 1897 (as in 1893-95). The Debating Society had long been dormant; little interest was taken in the Natural History 'museum', which stood, so it was said, as 'a silent reproach to all past and present Herefordians'; and the OH Club was experiencing one of its periodic bouts of decline.[258] How far this was the responsibility of Thistle, his assistants and the Old Herefordians, and how far that of the boys themselves, who even in 1897 would have had a greater influence on the organisation of their free time than today, is open to question. But what is indisputable is that when Murray Ragg came into post, all was not well with his magisterial inheritance. It did not take long for things to change.

The Herefordian was soon put on a new footing. A sub-committee was established for the magazine, and its accounts, previously managed by the games club treasurer, separately audited and published.[259] Its finances were then restored, partly through generous

257. The quotation (and other recollections) about Sharpley belong to R.S. Thompson (1910-14), whose reminiscences are held in the school archives. The Literary Society's constitution was published in *TH*, NS LI (March 1906), p.32. Its proceedings were then written up by the boy secretary in this and subsequent editions. A junior society was established in 1908 but was less successful.

258. *TH*, NS XXVII (March 1898), p.2; above, p.286, for the state of rugby; and below, p.341, note 352, for the OH Club in this period.

259. The account was audited by Murray Ragg himself, together with a member of the school committee – which was by this time clearly dominated by the Headmaster – and published annually in *The Herefordian* each December. The same system was adopted for the library and later for other societies. *Ibid.*, NS XXIX (Dec. 1898), p.26, school committee resolutions, 16 Oct. 1898.

donations from Dean Leigh, Canon Palmer and Canon Williams, and in part through an appreciable increase in its circulation as a result of the halving of its sale price to 6d per copy from July 1899. However, this was not the end of its troubles, caused by a temporary loss of sales through pupil racketeering, and, more importantly, the increase in its length – itself a reflection of the expansion in the number of school societies – and consequently its printing costs.[260] Old Herefordians had to bail out the magazine in 1906-07, and from 1908, 1s was charged for each December issue. This gave temporary relief, although deficits again mounted from 1911. Despite such difficulties, throughout Murray Ragg's headmastership, the boy editors succeeded in publishing three issues of *The Herefordian* every year, even though many of their contemporaries showed an extreme reluctance to contribute to its pages.

The boys were more enthusiastic about debating. The society was revived under a new constitution in November 1903, with the Headmaster as president. It then flourished until the last years of Murray Ragg's headship, with a regular attendance of between 30 and 40 boys. H.P.W. Burton, secretary 1906-07, who was to become President of the Cambridge Union, was the most prominent of a number of notable debaters in this period, and it is likely that it was through his initiative that Old Herefordian debates were held every December from 1909 to 1911, occasions which attracted record houses of over 50 in each of these years. The society's motions varied widely from historical subjects such as Charles I's execution, a 1906 debate which 'excited an extraordinary amount of fervour' (it was narrowly held that the King had been unjustly beheaded); to social issues like the 'sordid and unedifying' amusements of 1912 (the motion to this effect was carried, Mr Sharpley having excoriated 'cinematograph palaces' and other forms of popular entertainment); to the hardy perennial 'this house believes in the existence of ghosts' (it did in 1908 but in 1905 and 1910 the boys were more sceptical). However, the temper of the society – and undoubtedly, the school – is best shown by the outcome of political motions, which almost without exception went in favour of the Conservative and Unionist cause, the house endorsing Chamberlain's fiscal policy in 1903, expressing confidence in Balfour's government in 1904, deploring the prospect of a Liberal government in 1905, declaring that the Liberal victory in 1906 was 'largely due to gross misrepresentations', and deprecating many of the Liberal government's subsequent policies thereafter. The vote in favour of women's suffrage on 17 February 1912 was the first radical motion that the society had espoused in living memory and was something of a milestone. It was not that there were no boys of a Liberal or radical persuasion in the school – at an impromptu debate in March 1906, it was reported that 'the rabid radicals were drawn to speak for Tory motions and *vice versa*' – but just that there were fewer of them. And although they were among the best debaters, most members, as the 1911 secretary complained, had 'extremely one-sided and … narrow views on a subject', and 'no amount of oratory, reasoning or logic' could persuade them to change their minds'.[261]

260. The pupil scam involved some boarders, who had received their copies early, trading their magazines to day boys at reduced prices. The annual printing costs (to Wilson & Phillips) increased by over £5 (on the previous year) to £20 4s 6d in 1903-04, and by more than £4 to £24 12s 6d in 1905-06. *TH*, XLVII (Dec. 1904), p.3; and *TH*, *passim*, for the December annual accounts.

261. *Ibid.*, NS LXVIII (Dec. 1911), p.35.

The Nature Club – the 'bug and slug', as the boys termed it – which had been started under Thistle, was resurrected twice under his successor. In the summer of 1899, a new club was established to study every branch of Natural History 'to train the eye to see and the brain to distinguish and classify, not primarily to encourage collecting merely for collecting's sake'. Twenty-five boys signed up as members, together with the Headmaster, Mrs Ragg and Herr Goetz, and three excursions – by brake or bicycle – arranged to the Woolhope hills and Symonds Yat, T.A. Boycott following in his brother's footsteps by capturing 60 varieties of beetle in the first expedition to Stoke Edith park. Thereafter, enthusiasm again waned until March 1906, when Murray Ragg decided to try once more. This time the society was managed by a committee of five boys, with the Headmaster as president, and a subscription of 6d per term was levied on each member. Resources for the study of nature, too, were improved by additions being made to both the Natural History volumes and the museum collections (now under two boy curators) in the Gilbert Library. Fifty boys immediately joined the club, and while interest was not maintained at that level, nature study – with lectures and demonstrations (the Revd E.V. Martin's preparation of killing bottles of potassium cyanide perhaps being the most dangerous) over the winter months, prizes for collections, and summer expeditions – became a feature of HCS life for many boys over the next five years. And this time, the Headmaster's presidential role was anything but nominal: Murray Ragg read papers on topics as diverse as insects and fertilisation, the microscope, protective mimicry and slate quarries; told the boys on outings about the entomology of the Woolhope valley and the geological formations of Merbach Hill; and generally lent moral support to enable his pupils to examine the world around them in a school which was (as an early convert explained) 'in the centre of one of the most beautiful counties for natural scenery and one of the richest for the study of nature'.[262]

Outdoor education was a central aspect of Murray Ragg's educational philosophy. As early as his first speech day in July 1898, he emphasised its importance as one of the higher strands of learning and more difficult for a schoolmaster to teach because there was no 'beaten path' to this aspect of education. And ultimately, it was of greater consequence than the intellectual side because it promoted the development of character. He expounded:

> The training of character was, after all, when they looked into the distance, more important than the training of the mind – the power of self-reliance, the power of endurance, the power of self-denial, the power to win well or lose well, the power to govern others as well as to be governed – these were the great qualities which made the English nation famous, and for these great qualities in a large measure … the English public schools were responsible.

Such a task, he believed, was not accomplished in the classroom, but 'in the cricket field [and] on the river' (said to the accompaniment of boys' 'cheers'), as well, of course, 'in the intercourse between master and boy … between boys and boys … [and] in the

262. *Ibid.*, NS XXXI (July 1899), p.17. The club declined during Murray Ragg's last years. No accounts appeared in *The Herefordian* after December 1910, and by 1912 the museum had been removed from the library and deposited in a locked room in School House. *Ibid.*, NS LXX (July 1912), p.39, letter from 'Anti-Wasteful'.

school chapel, which was their noble cathedral'.[263] Later, this emphasis was reflected in his communications with prospective parents, 'outdoor life' being featured prominently in the school prospectus. These included such pursuits as natural history, the major school sports but also 'military drill'. 'Practically all boys over 13 years of age belong to the cadet corps', Murray Ragg wrote in the 1907 edition, 'and special attention is given to musketry training'.[264]

Weekly drill for an hour or so, under the watchful eye of a sergeant instructor, had long been a feature of the HCS curriculum. Unlike some of the bigger public schools, however, this did not lead to the establishment of a rifle corps, despite suggestions in 1878 from OHs in the county volunteers that one should be formed.[265] Twenty years later the national climate had changed with the onset of the Boer War, in which at least 27 Old Herefordians were to serve. (Plate 13). Murray Ragg used the opportunity at speeches in 1900, when the news from the South African veldt was at long last encouraging to British arms, both to eulogise the bravery of one OH soldier – Gilbert Donne, his first captain of boats, who had been wounded in the conflict – and to announce that he was enquiring of the War Office whether a cadet corps could be started at the school, 'now that ... [it was] lessening the expense'.[266] The wave of patriotism that swept the country at the beginning of the South African war had clearly influenced the Headmaster to make such an enquiry. It had also enabled the War Office, following strong lobbying from the Headmasters' Conference that a school corps should be treated 'as a separate corps for military instruction' rather than as a part of the volunteer force,[267] to provide the means for it to be fulfilled.

It is clear that a form of military training took place in the school prior to and concurrent with the Headmaster's formal application to the War Office authorities, which he eventually submitted in late September 1902. Senior boys had had the use of the Morris tube range in the town drill hall from April 1902,[268] and during the autumn term later that year the boys paraded weekly on Castle Green. But it was not until early 1903 – the school

263. *Ibid.*, NS XXIX (Dec. 1898), pp.10-11.

264. TNA, ED 35/995.

265. Tatham had vetoed the proposal. *TH*, no. 2 (Sept. 1878), p.80. Rossall was the first public school to enrol volunteers on 1 February 1860, at the time of the war scare with France, followed a few weeks later by Eton and other schools.

266. *TH*, NS XXXV (Dec. 1900), pp.11-12. Donne was mistakenly reported as having been killed at Heilbron on 4 June 1900. After recovering from his wound, he returned to South Africa (this time with a commission) in early 1902. Murray Ragg presented him as an 'honourable, self-reliant, modest and God-fearing' man and an example to which the whole school could aspire, even though he 'never got above the Fourth Form'.

267. An HMC special committee, which reported in 1901 following a debate on national defence at the Bradfield meeting the previous December, further recommended that a permanent standing committee should be formed to safeguard the interests of school corps, and that governing bodies should be urged to secure 'adequate consideration' for masters who trained the school corps. *HMC 1901 Committee Report*, p.5.

268. The Morris tube was a device, first introduced by the War Office in November 1883, to reduce the power of the military rifle for training purposes, by the insertion of a small calibre barrel (the Morris tube) inside the rifle. The Morris target, available for a number of short ranges from 5 to 25 yards, consisted of a tall vertical target box within which were various targets to represent ranges from 100 yards at the bottom to 800 yards at the top of each printed sheet. Given the system's numerous limitations, its indoor use – and not least in a schoolroom (below, p.314, note 272) – would have been hazardous.

Fig. 6.12 The school's first CCF camp: the Isle of Man, July 1903.

having received official approval on Christmas Eve – that real progress was made. The boys returned in January to see an announcement on the new notice board of the corps' formation and the appointment of Sergeant-Major Brisland of the 1st Herefordshire Regiment Volunteer Corps, to which the school was attached, as staff instructor. A company of 61 was formed under an assistant master, the Revd E.V. Martin, who with Brisland's help advanced its skills in marching, company drill and firing exercises, each cadet now being allowed to fire seven rounds every fortnight in the drill hall. Space was found in the lodge for an orderly room and racks made for 88 carbines, although these were less than half filled by the first consignment of arms in mid-March. The War Office was also slow to respond to the request for the new style volunteer uniforms, and 'decidedly smart' though they were when they eventually arrived, they came without headgear, which meant the postponement of the planned 'marching and skirmishing' exercise. This finally took place at Hampton Court on Saturday 16 May 1903 – the first field day in the school's history – when the cadets succeeded in capturing Hen House Farm from the HRVC by the early afternoon. Despite the frustrations of dealing with Whitehall bureaucracy, Martin could observe in July 1903 that the school corps was 'a going concern', the fact being enshrined by the appearance in *The Herefordian* of a photograph of the school party of 23 officers and cadets, in the midst of a forest of bell tents, at the Isle of Man army camp that summer.[269]

Before long the corps was fully established. Aided by the government grants, which reached £70 in 1905, and the annual guinea subscriptions for each cadet, the organisation

269. *The Herefordian* gives a full account of the corps' formation and early activities in NS XLII (April 1903), pp.22-24; NS XLIII (July1903), pp.27-30 and photograph.

had wiped off its deficit within eight terms and begun to invest in new equipment. And although the corps was still a voluntary body, Murray Ragg impressed on his boys that it was their patriotic duty – which, he said, meant 'death to the jingo spirit, and the encouraging of all that is good morally and physically'[270] – to join it. Most boys responded by obeying their Headmaster's call and the corps' strength rarely fell below 50 cadets throughout the period. Whatever their motives, led by a succession of able contingent commanders and the 'manly form' of Sergeant Brisland,[271] the boys were soon involved in a programme of strenuous training: close order drill on Castle Green during the winter months, relieved by skirmishes on the banks of the Wye in the summer as preparation for the annual inspection; promotion examinations in drill tactics and signalling; and firing exercises and shooting competitions at the Ross range and, following the erection of a Morris tube range in April 1906, in the Big Schoolroom.[272] Then there were the bi-annual field days, played out in the rolling Marches countryside, occasionally with Christ College, Brecon, or Monmouth. And finally as the academic year ended, there were summer camps for the committed – and perhaps, for some of those going to Scarborough in August 1907, at the height of the holiday season, the less committed cadets. For eight years these were organised in conjunction with the local volunteer force, the last of this type being the 50 mile camp march from Ledbury to Garnons in 1908.

Thereafter, the corps was organised on different lines. Its connection with the Hereford Volunteers was severed, and it became a branch of the junior division of the Officer Training Corps. This was a result of a national reorganisation, one of the many army reforms initiated by R.B. Haldane as Secretary for War but eventually of crucial importance in providing officers for 'the new armies' in the First World War. Its effect at Hereford can be seen as a microcosm of the changes that were happening at public and secondary schools throughout the country. From 1909 the OTC, as is should now be called, was controlled by the chief of the general staff and not by the county association. Annual inspections were now conducted by regular staff officers – including Major Arthur Percival DSO, the Bishop's son, in 1912[273] – rather than the local adjutant. Training became more focused: senior NCOs were given responsibility for drilling their sections; additional weekly sessions were arranged for infantry training to enable the cadets to meet the more demanding standards set for 'Certificate A', which every 15-year-old was required to pass; a new OTC musketry drill was practised on half-holidays, long rifles eventually replacing the antiquated carbines

270. *Ibid.*, NS LVI (Dec. 1907), p.10, speech, 1 Oct.1907.

271. The commanding officers, who were all assistant masters, in this period were: Captains E.V. Martin (1903-06), N.W. Clayton (1906-07), T.H. Porter (1907-08) and H. Hughes (1908-12). Brisland left for Berkshire in April 1912 after over nine years' service at the school (at £8 per term).

272. The Big School range was unserviceable in bad light and had only a 20-yard carry, which limited its effectiveness for competition purposes – as in 1913, when the Hereford cadets were penalised in the *Country Life* inter-school OTC trophy for not having a 25-yard range. It was replaced in Henson's first term by a 30-yard outdoor range ('rendered bullet-proof by sheets of corrugated iron packed with clinker') between the Headmaster's garden and the fives court at the back of Number 1, Castle Street.

273. Arthur Jex-Blake Percival had a distinguished military career. He fought at Omdurman and served in the South African War, where he won his DSO at Modder River. Later, he won the Legion of Honour in the retreat from Mons. He was killed in action at Ypres, one of six of Bishop Percival's eight children to predecease him.

in the summer of 1911. There was a new intensity about field days, as shown by the one held with six other western schools on 22 October 1909, when Hereford was given the responsibility, with Malvern and Cheltenham Colleges, of repelling an imaginary invasion force around the town of Upton-on-Severn. Summer camps, too, were better directed towards school needs with the cadets being commanded by hand-picked regular officers and gaining a wider experience of military life than the volunteers had allowed them. They were also better attended, the government denying the school a full grant unless at least half the senior cadets were present.[274]

The improved 'professionalism' that such reforms achieved among school OTCs in these years is best illustrated by the Windsor royal review which took place on Monday 3 July 1911, when 30 HCS boys under Captain Hughes joined cadets from every university and school OTC in the country to receive the royal salute. The troops were drawn up to receive their King on three sides of a hollow square, each line being 1,000 and more yards long and surrounding the massed bands of the guards; the salute being followed by a march past of cavalry, artillery and five infantry brigades, 'marching company after company to the strains of the massed bands with an accuracy of dressing and a precision of step that would have brought no shame on regular troops'. For the young men who witnessed it, it must have been an experience like no other. As *The Herefordian* also recorded:

> The sight, as 18,000 bayonets flashed in the sunlight from the 'slope' to the 'present', and the long line of officers' swords came down to the salute, the whole thrown into relief by the background of the noble trees of the park, was not one likely to be forgotten by those whose privilege it was to see it.[275]

The Times report of the following day was no less graphic, the correspondent pointing out that those 18,000 boys represented the many in the public schools 'who were giving themselves in a very real sense to the service of their country'. How many of them, one wonders, survived the Great War?

'It is no mere game', observed Murray Ragg one speech day, for boys 'to fit themselves to be defenders of their country if need arises'. Nevertheless, he considered games important in that these activities, like the corps, played 'a great part in the formation of character and making of "the man"'. Character was built up through a healthy life-style – keeping windows open, he believed, was the best immunity against coughs and colds – physical fitness, and good competition; and success in games was judged by the spirit and enthusiasm shown, rather than by the number of matches won and lost. Indeed, as he reminded the boys in 1908, 'that finest thing of all' was 'to play through an unsuccessful season when it comes, as come it must, with energy and enthusiasm'.[276] Not that Murray Ragg failed

274. Pleas were regularly made in *The Herefordian* urging the cadets to attend and asking parents to arrange their summer holidays after the camps had broken up. Twenty-nine HCS cadets went to Tidworth in 1912, the largest camp contingent in the Murray Ragg years. In 1913, the War Office divided (for camp purposes) school OTCs into three groups, each 2,700 strong, and directed that over the summers 1913-15 each group was to attend a camp in a different locality.

275. *TH*, NS LXVII (July 1911), p.29.

276. All these views were expressed on various speech days. *Ibid.*, NS XLVII (Dec.1904), p.8; LVI (Dec.1907),

to gain satisfaction from the boys' sporting achievements, and he was justly proud of the school's athletic records and the successes of former pupils, particularly those who had achieved 'Blues'.[277] However, the point was that success was not an end in itself, and that sporting endeavour was only one aspect of a meaningful education: the physical capacities of the young life were to be drawn out to the full but only in conjunction with their intellectual, moral and spiritual qualities. To Murray Ragg, this was the true meaning of education 'in its fullest sense'.

Consequently, Murray Ragg was fully committed to maintaining the school's reputation in games, even if it meant breaking with a long-held tradition. Like his immediate predecessors, he appointed young schoolmasters as his assistants – they were also cheap to employ – who were keen games players. Although collectively they were not as distinguished sportsmen as their predecessors a generation earlier, and in 1913 one OH could complain that games (rowing apart) were deteriorating throughout the school because of the lack of a 'thorough games master',[278] men like A.G. Jones, C.H. Douton, F.F. Fison, N.W. Clayton, T.H. Porter, T.M.F. Roberts, H. Hughes and C.E.H. Thomas contributed significantly to HCS sport in this period. Murray Ragg, too, was not as proficient a sportsman as Thistle, but was more actively involved in coaching the younger boys, rightly believing that 'half the success in games' was by laying a solid foundation in the junior years.[279] He also extended opportunities for juniors to play inter-school matches, and increased competition within the school itself by providing trophies for internal matches in cricket and football, 'as at all the large public schools'. His stated aim was to enable those boys 'who are now not over keen, to represent their House at Wyeside'.[280] Initially, these matches were keenly contested, although after 1902 the choristers were too weak to raise a side and 'the House' gradually asserted their authority over the day boys. The football competition eventually lapsed after 1906, only for the day boys of 1912 to dispute the boarders' right 'to keep the inter-house cup in unchallenged supremacy' (they lost 2-1).

One of the most controversial decisions Murray Ragg ever took – and this in his first term – was the introduction of soccer as the main winter game. It was one thing to insist (as he did in early 1898) that every boarder went on a Sunday afternoon walk, but given HCS's proud tradition in the handling game, quite another to abandon rugby and introduce soccer in its stead. This bold move produced an outcry which remained deeply seared on Ragg's memory over 30 years later. It involved 'great friction' with the boys, not least the Sixth Form who made it clear that the school committee had not been consulted over the

---

pp.9-10; LIX (Dec. 1908), p.10. Also see his comment in 1905: 'the grit of Hereford boys will be seen when the battle goes against them'. *Ibid.*, NS L (Dec.1908), p.10.

277. At the 1909 sports day, he pointed out that apart from G.R. Connop's mediocre 1899 high jump record (5 foot 1 inch), the school records were 'good and hard to beat' (especially the long jump and cricket ball records, which had stood since the 1860s; see note 291), and that apart from cricket and association football, HCS had had a 'Blue' 'in almost every department of sport'. *Ibid.*, NS LXI (July 1909), p.8.

278. *Ibid.*, NS LXXIII (July 1913), p.32, letter from '*Floreat Schola*' (who I am assuming was an OH).

279. *Ibid.*, NS LIX (Dec. 1908), p.10, speech, 2 Oct. 1908.

280. *Ibid.*, NS XXX (April 1899), p.21, Murray Ragg's letter appealing for House trophies. House cricket matches were played on half-holidays from summer 1899 and football matches from early 1903. A House competition was started on sports day for the first time in 1903.

change. Old Herefordians, brought up under the old lore to believe that the matter should have rested with the boys themselves, were also vociferous in their complaints. The sentiments expressed by an outraged anonymous correspondent to *The Herefordian* must have represented the feelings of many old boys who had learnt to play the old game during their Hereford schooldays:

> I have just heard with mingled feelings of surprise and indignation that one more of the institutions of the ancient school is threatened with abolition ... [It] is a most serious and ... lamentable step to change a game held in the highest honour at our public schools and universities for a game the chief exponents of which are the hirelings of Birmingham, Sheffield and Sunderland. It will be a sorry day indeed when the school shall descend into the arena of the Barrack Ground or Edgar Street to reap its rewards in the delicate sarcasms of the *Hereford Journal* and the *Hereford Times*.[281]

Ragg had acted decisively but the change of codes was not without precedent at other schools – Radley being among the more prominent schools to have gone over to soccer (in 1881) – and the change was fully justified by the results. In the autumn term of 1897, the last in which the school played rugby football for more than a generation, although the spirit of the side was said to be better than in 1896-97, the XV failed to register a single point against any of its three opponents. In the first soccer season of 1898-99, encouraged by the new masters, nine out of 15 1st XI matches were won – including, decisively but unsurprisingly, the game against the old boys who it was reported 'would probably have played a better game of rugby' – 57 goals were scored (against 28) and three XIs were put out. Thereafter, in only four of the 15 seasons during the time of Ragg's headmastership did the first team lose more matches than it won. There were other advantages: more school sides – local grammar schools, as well as Dean Close, King's, Worcester, Malvern A and for a couple of years, Shrewsbury A – could be challenged; House football competitions, as we have seen, could flourish; and scratch six a-side football matches could be arranged during fallow weeks in the winter term for 'dry bobs' and non-fives players. If the hope expressed by the editor of *The Herefordian* in July 1898 that the football XI would 'win for themselves the name that the "15" once held' did not quite come about, the doom-mongers were proved wrong and the Headmaster right in his judgement that a small school could better sustain the association game.

Murray Ragg was prepared to break with the main winter game of a generation by abandoning rugby but was anxious both to improve the school's sporting facilities and to maintain its prowess in traditional games. Cricket in its 'golden age' kept pride of place in the school's sporting calendar. Improvements continued to be made at Wyeside, the Headmaster paying for a flagstaff in 1900 and finding funds the following year for a railed enclosure in front of the pavilion which became 'sacred ground' on match days. Two years later, the pavilion itself was refurbished and a new cricket pitch was laid down on the adjoining meadow. Better

281. *Ibid.*, NS XXVII (March 1898), p.30. The prophecy (in part) was fulfilled in December 1910 and again the following season, when flooding at Wyeside caused both OH matches to be played on the Edgar Street ground. For Murray Ragg's later memory of the change: *TH*, NS CXXV (Dec. 1930), speech day report.

practice wickets followed in 1907.[282] And with the introduction of House matches and the expansion of school fixtures for younger players, more boys could enjoy the game. Under the guidance of the professional coach,[283] and with the encouragement of a succession of enthusiastic schoolmasters, able captains and the brilliance of one or two outstanding cricketers – notably M.C. Parry, who played first class cricket for Warwickshire less than three years after breaking the school batting record in 1905[284] – standards also improved. After some indifferent seasons around the turn of the century, 1st XI wins exceeded losses every year from 1905 to 1912, although the team never recorded an unbeaten season or even achieved the feat of winning every school match in one year in this period.[285]

Rowing was still called 'boating', which Murray Ragg described in his prospectus as 'the regular exercise of senior boys during the Lent Term'. By his time, however, as has been mentioned, it had advanced well beyond its origins as a recreational activity, even though as late as 1907, boys were apparently given 'many opportunities' in the summer term to explore 'the beautiful reaches of the Wye'.[286] But it was the serious business of the school regatta and the boat races against Worcester and Monmouth that preoccupied most boys each spring. Not every boy could take an active part, numbers being circumscribed by the Headmaster's insistence that an oarsman should first obtain a swimming certificate. And while the majority of boarders seemed to have met this requirement, and swimming rates probably improved through the re-institution of river races and a diving competition in July 1899 and by the boys' use of the public 'baths' in Venn Road for six months of the year (they were closed from November to mid-March),[287] competitive rowing was necessarily limited by the nature of the regatta itself.[288] Nevertheless, the regatta was eagerly followed on the day

282. *Ibid.*, NS XXXIV (July 1900), p.2; NS XLIII (July 1903), p.10; NS XLIV (Dec. 1903), pp.13, 54 (item re pavilion alteration costing £42 1s 7d); NS LVI (Dec. 1907), p.25, re £18 13s 6d raised by the appeal for practice wickets.

283. Shore was hired as professional for each summer, 1900-04; Carlin from Nottinghamshire ('a cousin of the famous wicket-keeper' who had stood as umpire in the first test that summer) for the 1905 season (at £28 16s); and the incomparable Shepherd (again) from 1906.

284. M.C. Parry scored 597 runs (including three centuries) at an average of 54.27 in 1905. He then went on to Birmingham University (and played for Warwickshire and Ireland). No OH succeeded (or has succeeded) in winning a cricket 'Blue'. G.W. Grasett, who played for the Oxford Authentics and had one first class match for the university (against H.K. Foster's XI, 30 May-1 June 1912) in 1912, came nearest in this period. He gained his hockey 'Blue' the following year.

285. In terms of results, 1907 was the best 1st XI season (played 15, won 9, drawn 4, lost 2), although only one school match was lost in 1905 – against Dean Close, HCS's nemesis in this period. The following schools were played annually: Christ College, Brecon, Dean Close (started 1898), King's, Worcester, Monmouth, Oswestry Grammar (played at either Ludlow or Shrewsbury) and (from 1909) KES Birmingham; but local club and friendly sides (including 'the Past', which was defeated every year, 1907-12) still made up the majority of fixtures.

286. According to the prospectus, preserved among the paper in TNA, ED 35/995. See above, pp.222-23, 231-33, 263-64, 264-85, for the development of rowing at HCS in the Victorian period.

287. Thirty-eight out of 40 boys in School House were certified swimmers in July 1902. Revd J.M. Donne gave a challenge cup in 1899 for the winner of the senior swimming race – originally in memory of his son (see above, note 266); and in 1900 the diving was judged by Revd A.B. Wynne Wilson who did much 'to foster swimming in the town'. For the city baths in this period: O'Donnell (2007), pp.83-88.

288. The regatta comprised junior pairs (although attracting 14 entries in 1902), junior fours and scratch fours races, culminating in the 'Oxford' v 'Cambridge' race from which the senior four was chosen for the Monmouth

itself even by non-participants, as well as Old Herefordians and other well-wishers, and once the school four had been chosen, the two boat races became something of a school obsession for a few weeks each year. As *The Herefordian* reported in April 1911, after the school colours had been lowered for only the third time in 16 races, defeat on the river was a more demoralising influence than losing at cricket or football. But it did not happen too often, and was more than made up for by the nine glory years, when HCS recorded victories over both Monmouth and Worcester in the same season, despite the school having a heavy boat until 1912. A lighter craft was then built which gave 'every satisfaction'.[289]

Outside the three major sports, other games competed for the boys' attention. Fives continued to attract its admirers. The playground court was again patched up in 1902, the walls being so rough that a new ball lost its bounce after one game. Good entries were then generally recorded for the annual senior and junior competitions (singles and pairs). But it was the building of two new Winchester fives courts in the grounds of Harley House in 1912 that really increased the game's popularity. It also enabled the school team to give King's, Worcester, a good match on their own courts, the away teams having hitherto been disadvantaged 'as the games were so unlike in the two schools'.[290] The athletic sports, too, continued to be held each April and promoted some good competition, even if few records were broken in this period.[291] There was little time for serious training, which in any case was frowned upon by some of those in authority.[292]

One important athletics initiative was the establishment of a winter 'steeple-chase' over the Breinton course, which took the place of the sports day event. It was first run – for a 'challenge bowl' presented by Percy Hull – on 11 December 1907, and soon became a feature of the school's sporting calendar.[293] Although a rudimentary form of hockey had been played in the playground from the late 1880s, it was not until this period that proper fixtures were arranged.[294] Three or four matches were played each spring against local clubs from 1904 to 1912, when after a disastrous season (goals for 3, against 26), the school

---

and Worcester races.

289. In 1898, 1900, 1903-05, 1908, 1910 and 1912-13 under Murray Ragg (as well as in 1895 and 1897 under Thistle). Both the 1907 races were cancelled because of a mumps outbreak. Although HCS acquired a new (and probably fixed-seat) four – costing £30 from Salter of Oxford – in June 1903, it was of clinker construction and cumbersome. The 1912 boat was built by Rough of Oxford for £32 3s, plus £3 14s for the oars from Ayling of Putney.

290. The old playground court did not have a buttress as HCS had played Rugby fives. Unsurprisingly, the change to Winchester fives and buttressed courts meant that 'it took fellows some time to get out of their old style of play'. *TH*, LXIX (April 1912), p.16. For the purchase of Harley House (Number 1), see below, p.325ff.

291. A.F. Wilding's 1862 long jump of 20 feet 6 inches and A.W. Brodie's 1869 cricket ball throw of 110 yards 2 and a half feet remained inviolable; and even H.R. Ragg, who was to gain three 'blues' for the 100 yards at Cambridge, 1909-11, failed to beat (by .2 seconds) in 1908 H.L. Coath's 1895 time of 10.4 seconds for the school 100 yards.

292. Competitors (according to one boy in 1911) were expected to turn up for their events 'just as one would run for one's train and leap over the luggage trolley which some casual porter had left in the way'; and the sports committee was likened (by the same correspondent) to the porter who 'put every obstacle' they could 'in the way of the keenly inclined'. *TH*, NS LXVI (April 1911), pp.26-27, letter from 'Knock-kneed'.

293. See *ibid.*, NS LVII (April 1908), p.18, for Hull's donation and the comment about his 'unflagging devotion' to his old school. For Hull's career: above, note 244.

294. For the earlier form of hockey at HCS: *TH*, NS CXXXIII (July 1933).

committee decided to drop the sport. Against the rival claims of fives, rowing and the athletic sports, it was felt to be impossible 'to get up a team in any way representative of the school', despite the services of two masters who tried to shore up the defence.

Despite HCS's lamentable performances at hockey, it is difficult to imagine how a school of around 100 boys could have crammed much more 'outdoor life' into a school year. Not all boys participated fully – *The Herefordian* editors often claiming that the day boys failed to pull their weight – but there is substance to Murray Ragg's observation that among all these activities every boy should have been able to find 'something to interest him and help him to self-improvement'. There is something, too, in the claim he made three years earlier:

> As regards outdoor life, I question whether there is any other school which has such opportunities of sending boys out into the world equally likely to be able to handle a rifle or a cricket bat, equally proficient on the football field or on the river, equally at home on the land or in the water. For in a small public school like this it is an advantage as well as a disadvantage that the same boys have to support every branch of school outdoor life.[295]

The boys did indeed have (as the 1908 inspectors observed) 'a vigorous and hearty life' at HCS during this period. And it was the energetic Headmaster who set the lead and the tone: as on that foul afternoon of 25 March 1899 when he escorted 'a plucky cohort of cyclists' from Hereford to Monmouth to cheer on the school four in the annual boat race;[296] or when leading natural history expeditions; or in his coaching of junior games and 'his splendid example of keenness and sportsmanship' on the cricket field.[297]

New Buildings and Further Schemes

Despite the improvements of preceding years, the limitations of the school's buildings were made apparent in W.N. Bruce's report, following his inspection visit of 11 July 1899, 18 months on from Murray Ragg's arrival. He considered the classrooms (Big School and the library apart) to be poorly arranged and inadequately lit for teaching; one of them, indeed, he described as being 'so unsatisfactory' that he believed it would not be recognised 'if the school were subject to an inspection which now takes place in Wales'. There were other issues: the sanatorium in the porter's lodge was ill-suited for its purposes, adjacent as it was to the boys' changing rooms and classrooms; the boarding provision – the dining-room was too small and some of the dormitories were 'rather low [ceilinged] and old fashioned' – was inadequate; and the small playground was hardly compensated for by its recent paving (at a cost of £80) and the 'well-kept and automatically flushed' toilets in one corner of the yard.[298] Over the next few years, the Headmaster and his governors successfully addressed many of these problems.

---

295. *Ibid.*, NS XLIV (Dec. 1903), p.13, speech 28 July 1903; NS LIII (Dec. 1906), p.11, speech 1 Oct. 1906.

296. Thirteen years later, on 21 March 1912, the Hereford party went in two 'motor brakes' to the same event, an indication of both the development of the internal combustion engine in this period and (perhaps) the Headmaster's increasing age (at 50).

297. *Ibid.*, NS LXXXI (Dec. 1912), p.14.

298. TNA, ED 27/1609, Bruce's report, 3 Oct. 1899.

Of these issues, the provision of a proper sanatorium was the most pressing. It is true that by this time some necessary health precautions had been taken by the school's authorities to limit the spread of infectious diseases. The boarders were required to pay 7s 6d per term for the services of a medical officer (Dr Thomas Turner in 1899). All boys had to present health certificates at the beginning of each term or following a boy's return to school after illness at home, as with the two sons of the poor rector of Stoke Prior, the Revd Alfred T. Peppercorn, who complained when the Headmaster refused to reduce their tuition fees after they had incurred a severe bout of measles and an absence from several weeks schooling.[299] It is also evident that some epidemics, notably scarlet fever, which had ravaged boarding schools earlier in the century, were less prevalent by its end. Nevertheless, as we will see, infections were common enough at HCS in this period.

The finding of a sanatorium became a major priority for Murray Ragg following the conversion of the porter's lodge into classrooms and better changing accommodation in March 1901.[300] It took him a year before he discovered a suitable property – Foley Lodge, a solid detached villa, built in 1867 and situated a mile from the school. He reported that the house had an 'entirely open prospect' and was sited in a quiet and healthy neighbourhood, and that it would provide rooms for six patients and a caretaker. The house was purchased out of the school's capital assets for £365 in June 1902. It then served as the school sanatorium for nine years until, following the acquisition of Harley House, it was sold in November 1911 for £30 less than the purchase price, its medical use having rendered it less attractive to prospective buyers.[301] How many boys recovered there over this time is unknown. But despite the Headmaster's public rejoicing that the new sanatorium had remained empty for the first two years of its existence, given the later outbreaks of measles, mumps, whooping cough and chicken-pox – all of which disrupted the school's routine in subsequent years – it is unlikely to have been a complete white elephant.[302]

299. See TNA, ED 27/1609, letter 19 Sept. 1901, for the concern of Peppercorn, a Mr Quiverfull with 12 children to educate, one of whom became the celebrated railway engineer. HCS's health requirements were clearly outlined in the school's first extant prospectus of 1899, although as medical certificates had been introduced at many public schools as early as the 1870s, it is likely that they well preceded Murray Ragg's tenure. Honey (pp.164-67) gives an analysis of health issues in the late-Victorian public school.

300. The classrooms were later converted into a laboratory, day rooms, and an orderly room and armoury. (See pp.307, 329, 490.) The changing rooms were damp – until a proper heating system was installed in 1905 – which, in the boys' view, contributed to the school's ill-health. A cottage, at an annual rental of £12, was provided for the porter at the entrance to Wyeside.

301. HCA, 7031/23, pp.348, 460, Acts, 24 March 1902, 9 Nov. 1911, sanctioning purchase and sale; HCA, 7005/13, pp.6-8, conveyance, 9 Nov. 1911; TNA, ED 27/1610, correspondence relating to the purchase; TNA, ED 35/995, Robert Wood's (auctioneer's) catalogue description of Foley Lodge (5 Foley Street) for 5 Sept. 1911 auction; TNA, ED 43/325, Board of Education material relating to its sale; HCSA, GMB 1908-21, pp.36, 37, 29 May, 6 Sept. 1911. The bulk of the sale money was used towards defraying the cost of alterations to the Headmaster's new house and the adaptation of 7 Ferrers Street as the new sanatorium, although the Board insisted that the sum should be fully repaid to the school's capital account within 30 years.

302. As in March 1910 when many boys caught that 'horribly modern epidemic' (chicken-pox), which resulted in the school breaking up for the Easter holidays a week earlier than had been planned. Other infectious outbreaks occurred in March/April 1907 (mumps), late 1907 (measles), early 1908 (chicken-pox) and summer 1911 (mumps). As inferred, the health issue was serious enough for the Headmaster to refer to it each year in his speech day report.

Within months of the purchase of Foley Lodge, Murray Ragg was asking his governors to find £60 for the lease of 3 and 4 Castle Street to provide additional boys' boarding accommodation, rooms for two masters and, incongruously enough, an armoury – an idea which he soon abandoned. The Chapter accepted his proposal, initially on a three year lease, provided he took personal responsibility for its implementation.[303] The need seemed evident enough at the time, for by autumn 1902 the pupil roll had reached 118, excluding the 20 or so boys at Harley Court. Of these, 44 or so were senior boarders, who were crammed into School House, together with the preparatory schoolmistress, three masters, eight servants and the Murray Ragg household of five.[304] Castle House (as it was named) was put under the charge of Mr and Mrs Fison, and was ready to receive its first inmates in January 1903. Sadly, it never reached its full capacity of 12 boys for it opened just as the boarding tide had turned. Over the next four years the number of senior boarders dropped gradually year by year until by 1906 there were 16 fewer at HCS than there had been when Murray Ragg made the decision to lease the property. So Castle House too became something of an extravagance, although its existence eased the pressure on the numbers in School House and gave some relief to its residents.[305]

In the years following the 1899 inspection, Murray Ragg had done much to answer Bruce's criticisms of the school buildings: a little more teaching and recreational accommodation had been found; an isolation unit had been established; and the setting up of Castle House had created better living space for the boarders. He had also managed to persuade his governors to replace the coal fires with radiators in the classrooms, even if the ungrateful boys preferred the old hearths to the new hot water pipes as a means of keeping warm.[306] Such advances were not inconsequential but the age-old issue remained. How could the school possibly develop any further on such a restricted site? This problem was brought into sharper focus by the proposal to build a public high school within the city, a decision which was to have enormous consequences not only for secondary education within Hereford but also for the future of the Cathedral School itself.

Murray Ragg was in a good position to know. As a leading educationalist, he was one of the four co-opted members of the city council education committee, established in March 1903 as a result of the 1902 Education Act. A key responsibility of this body, in conjunction with the county education authorities, was to make provision for the building of a secondary school for 150 boys in Hereford. In January 1907, the committee proposed that this new school should:

---

303. HCA, 7031/23, pp.353-54, Act, 13 Nov. 1902.

304. The occupants are detailed in the 1901 census. A nurse, matron, cook, parlour maid, two house maids, a nursery maid and a kitchen maid tended to the needs of the Headmaster, his wife and three children; the four teachers; and the 28 boarders. Eighteen months later, there were 16 more boarders to accommodate according to the 1908 inspection report. TNA, ED 109/1975, p.2.

305. *Ibid.*, average pupil numbers, 1902-06. The only reference I have found to the number of boarders in Castle House is in *TH*, NS (Dec. 1903), p.3, which states that there were six boarders under the Fisons' care during that autumn term.

306. HCA, 7031/23, pp.327, 372, Acts, 24 March 1900, 24 March 1905 (extending the system to the old porter's lodge). Coal fires were restored for a while in late 1907, after the system had broken down, and the motion 'fires are superior to hot water pipes' was almost unanimously carried in an impromptu debate on 14 December of that year. *TH*, NS LVII (April 1908), p.14.

be so arranged as best to fill the gap between the elementary school and the Cathedral School, and so provide a thoroughly practical education for boys who have to leave school and begin their work in life at the age of 16 or 17; whilst it would pass on to the Cathedral School, at a suitable age, any pupil whose parents might wish them to continue at school to the age of 18 or 19.[307]

In April of that year, Murray Ragg became a member of the executive committee which made the detailed plans for the building of the Boys' High School, and subsequently a member of the county education committee.

These local developments were sufficient to prompt the governors to apply to the Board of Education for HCS to be listed as an efficient secondary school, which under the terms of the 1902 Act would give HCS some measure of protection against unfair competition from a state secondary school.[308] This was granted (on 25 May 1908) following a formal inspection by E.M. Battiscombe, F.G.L. Bertram, and J.W. Headlam on 26 and 27 March 1908. The three inspectors, while criticising the irregularities of Chapter governance, the quality of some buildings – especially School House which 'compare[s] unfavourably with most boarding schools of similar standing' – and the lack of Science provision, also found much to commend. Indeed, they considered HCS to be 'a good example of those smaller boarding schools which have for so long filled a part in the educational system of the country'. Despite such plaudits, however, serious doubts were cast about the school's future. A new High School with lower fees could, they predicted, reduce numbers at HCS to 'below the level necessary for financial security and educational efficiency' unless radical changes were made. Either the school could try to increase its boarding numbers by providing additional accommodation; or it could try to secure a deal with the local authority which would preserve its endowments at the expense of its constitution, buildings and identity. 'Under any circumstances', the inspectors concluded, 'there should be an agreement between the governors and the local authority so as to prevent the attempt to maintain in the city two schools competing with one another'.[309]

That the Dean and Chapter at first inclined towards a merger on educational grounds shows the extent to which that body had changed from its conservative predecessor of a generation earlier. Their initial view, however, soon altered when Murray Ragg informed them that if HCS became part of the new secondary school, even with him as Headmaster, his boarders – 'the backbone' of his upper forms – would leave and 'the lamp of classical education would burn out in Hereford'. At a difficult conference between the governors and the Local Education Authority on 27 June 1908, a general understanding was reached: while no commitment was made to exclude any specific subject, 'except perhaps Greek', the new school would not offer a classical education.[310] Now that the way forward had been

307. HARC, HLC/A32, p.118, education committee report, 25 Jan. 1907. Murray Ragg (with Bishop Percival and Mrs Eastland) had been re-appointed as a co-opted members of the education committee on 30 October 1906.

308. 2 Ed VII cap. 42, s. 2 (2).

309. TNA, ED 35/995, inspectors' report, issued 25 May 1908; TNA, ED 109/1975, final copy of same; HCSA, GMB 1908-21, pp.1-4, 28 March 1908.

310. *Ibid.*, pp.8-9, governors' resolution, 26 June 1908; pp.10-14, copy letter to the Board of Education, 25 July 1908, the original of which is in TNA, ED 35/995. Although there was a clear split on the LEA between

established, over the next three years the energies of Murray Ragg and his governors were directed towards finding additional teaching and boarding space to enable HCS (in the inspectors' words) 'to be of most service to the city and district' and so 'usefully supplement the work of the new county school'. This not only involved a major appeal but also another significant change to the Cathedral School's constitution.

The drawing up of a new scheme for HCS and its charities was not as extended a process as the one in the early 1890s, but to Murray Ragg and his governors it must have seemed prolonged enough.[311] It was made necessary by the school's hope that the Castle Crab estate, the capital endowment of the Langford charity, might be sold and the proceeds – some £2,000 was anticipated from the sale – used as a basis of an appeal for new buildings. The essence of the governors' case, which had the unanimous support of the Langford trustees as well as the Dean and Chapter, was this: the new secondary school, with its free places for many primary boys, would effectively render the Langford endowment redundant; the redirecting of its funds would be as much in accord with the founder's intentions as the 1893 scheme; and ultimately the sale would be of greater benefit for education within the city of Hereford. It was a convenient argument but it did not initially convince the Board of Education. On 25 March 1909, it rejected the proposal, primarily because it would have deprived public elementary boys 'of the benefit to which they are entitled' but also on financial grounds, the Board reckoning that the sale of property for £2,000 on an anticipated annual return of £100 was bad business. The governors responded by agreeing to elect one elementary boy annually to a free place for four years, on the same terms as the Langford scholars, 'thereby exactly following the object for which the trust was intended by the 1894 scheme'. On this basis, the Board agreed to draft a new scheme which would provide for the sale of the Langford estate.

The school made a formal application for the new constitution on 25 May 1909 but it took over a year of tortuous legal argument and redrafting before the final document was sealed on 20 July 1910. The governors successfully resisted the use of the Philpotts endowment for further entrance scholarships but were unable to persuade the Board to lessen the value of the Langford awards or sanction the use of any unapplied Langford funds for the building programme. The Board's position was made perfectly clear in Bruce's memorandum of 10 March 1910:

> The school has a rather exclusive character as a first grade Church of England boarding school, and if we allow the capital of a poor boys' scholarship fund to be sunk in buildings for such a school, we must jealously guard their right to the full benefit of the income secured to them in return.

---

the supportive city members, led by Alderman Symonds, and some of the county members, led by Colonel Decie, chairman of the county council, who suggested that 'they would be ready to step in and compete with the Cathedral School at the first sign of weakness'. The High School curriculum, as eventually established in 1914, allowed for around three hours of Latin instruction per week, as an option against business subjects for the senior classes. HARC, HLC/EM 130, p.58.

311. For the following, see HCSA, GMB 1908-21, pp.15, 20-25, 28-29, meetings 12 Nov. 1908 to 16 April 1910; TNA, ED 35/996 and HCA, 7005/12, p.563, re application of 25 May 1909. Murray Ragg played a leading role in many of these negotiations, as at the Whitehall meeting on 24 April 1909 (scheduled to coincide with his return from a three week holiday abroad) when the Board agreed to the sale of the Langford estate.

This apparent intransigence provoked a furious but understandable response from the governors:

> The object of the new scheme was to use some part of the Langfordian endowment to meet the needs pointed out by the Board's inspectors, yet the Board insist on [the] continuance of scholarships equal in number and value to those given at present which absorb the whole income of the endowment. The result is that the scheme is quite valueless for its sole object. Under the circumstances, the governors do not in the least care about its being proceeded with, though they will not oppose it if the Board desire it.

The Board did desire it, as (in the words on one of its officials) 'the scheme would at all events bring the grammar school scheme more or less up to date, and perhaps the introduction into the governing body of city and county representatives may be thought an advantage'. The scheme was finally published amidst further controversy as to whether, as the Board claimed, the HCS site was 'clothed with an educational trust in favour of the school', and therefore inalienable, or whether the land was safeguarded by the cathedral's Caroline statutes.[312]

The struggle between the school's governors and the Board of Education over the Langford endowment is a perfect example of the law of unintended consequences. The Dean and Chapter had eventually gained permission to realise capital from the sale of the Castle Crab estate, but was hamstrung by the Board's insistence that it should still provide four full Langford scholarships which would use up most of the invested proceeds from any sale. In addition, it had reluctantly accepted a new scheme of governance. This added James Corner and Reginald Symonds (as, respectively, county and city council representatives) to the governing body as the first lay governors in our long history, and updated the school's management and other procedures.[313] It is ironic that although the amalgamation of the Langford and HCS foundations as one distinct Trust had furthered the school's modernisation, it had not been achieved in the way that the Chapter had anticipated. The school's physical development was now to be accomplished by different means.

It is likely that the school had had its eye on Harley House (Number 1, Castle Street) for some time. It was well suited by location and size for its purposes. Adjoining the Deanery, the building was set in an acre of ground. Moreover, under the management of Miss Earle, who had started the Harley Court schoolroom in the 1880s, it had already been adapted as a private girls' school, which in 1903 was sufficient to accommodate over 100 girls – 32 of whom had boarded – in 12 classes.[314] The school entered into negotiations for its purchase

312. For the detailed arguments on this issue, see TNA, ED 35/995, letters 3, 26 August and 5 Sept. 1910, and the Board's notes with regard to the legal position.

313. Such as clauses relating to the institution of a contract of service for assistant masters, the limitation of the Headmaster's powers of dismissal and the regularisation of examinations. For the first time, it was also stipulated that no master was to be debarred from employment on account of his not being ordained.

314. HARC, J 65/932, Hereford schools' hearing, 24 July 1903. In 1903, Miss Earle employed seven resident mistresses and a drawing teacher, and charged between 6 and 12 guineas for tuition, and between 27 and 37 guineas for board and tuition. The girls' ages ranged from 5 to 18.

Fig. 6.13 Canon Capes, whose generosity enabled the school to acquire Number 1, Castle Street.

in late May 1909, and by the following spring the Earle family had agreed to part with their desirable property for £5,000, the house coming into the school's possession in January 1911. The steep purchase price could only be afforded thanks to the generosity of Canon William Wolfe Capes, who had been admitted as a residentiary in March 1904. Despite his advanced age of 70, for HCS it was an inspired appointment because Capes was not only a distinguished classical scholar and historian but also an experienced school governor (of St Paul's, his own *alma mater*), and a wealthy and generous man with a personal fortune in excess of £40,000. From these means, he gave £2,500 towards the purchase of Harley House, and – after the stalling of negotiations for the other half to be provided from the school's capital reserves held by the Board of Education – also arranged for a further loan of £2,500. It was agreed that the property would remain in the possession of the Dean and Chapter, the governors paying an annual rent of £100 for its use as a school building. This sum corresponded to 3 *per cent* interest on the funds that Canon Capes had secured plus a further £25.[315] As the Chapter Clerk observed in a letter to the Board of 1 June 1911, Canon Capes was 'the active promoter of the scheme ... [who] contributed very largely to it [by] the fixing of the reserve and other details connected with the sale'.[316]

Capes was also instrumental in raising further sums to enable the conversions of Harley House and School House to proceed. This was accomplished by means of three successive public appeals from 1909 to 1911. It was not an auspicious time to ask the county's great and good for money, the appeal coinciding with Lloyd George's 1909 budget, which eventually led to unprecedented increases in death duties, income tax and land value duties. Mr Cotterell of Garnons, courteously declining Capes' request for a donation in June 1909 because of the new tax proposals, must have been typical of a number of big landowners who in earlier years would have supported the cause. More forthright was this letter of July 1910 from Arthur Chambers of Hatfield Court, Leominster:

> The present government have vindictively put in every possible way extra burdens on all owners of land, and kindly promised to increase those they have put already as soon as they can bribe themselves into power with a sufficient majority to do so; anything I can personally save must be sent abroad to be invested with a view to the future for my descendants.

The landowners' reticence contrasted with the generous, although necessarily more limited, response from country parsons like the Reverend H.T. Dutton of Lotherdale Rectory, Keighley, who 'as a very poor rector and a very big paterfamilias' subscribed one guinea

315. HCSA, GMB 1908-21, pp.23, 30, 33, meetings 25 May 1909, 16 April, 19 Nov. 1910. The purchase price of £5,000 comprised £4,000 to Mrs Emma Earle for the freehold and £1,000 to 'the Misses Earle' for the surrender of their leasehold interests in the property. Of the additional £2,500 loan, Capes personally advanced a further £1,500, the remaining £1,000 coming from the Fabric and St Ethelbert's Hospital funds. HCA, 7016/5, fos 197v-198r; HCA, 7005/13, retrospective rental agreement, 29 July 1913.

316. TNA, ED 35/995, Underwood and Steel to the Secretary of the Board, 1 June 1911. This file contains further details about the negotiations with the Board over the sale. Capes' wealth at probate on 3 December 1914 is given as £41,977 9s. His school obituary (almost certainly written by Murray Ragg) gives this tribute: 'to him the school is indebted for all the possibilities that lie before it'. *TH*, NS LXXVII (Dec. 1914), p.42.

in recognition of the good education that HCS had given his two sons.[317] By the time of the final appeal in February 1911, over £1,380 had been subscribed or promised by 115 donors, the list being headed by Canon Capes' own gift and donations of £100 each from the Reverend E.H. Browne and Sir James Rankin.[318] When the list was closed a few months later, subscriptions had been received from 160 people, half of whom were Old Herefordians. In hard times, it was an impressive response.

Months before the final appeal, the school's plans had been formulated. These were for the use of Harley House as a residence for Murray Ragg, his family and the school servants, with a new boys' dining-room and additional accommodation for 15 boarders; the conversion of the detached classroom into a laboratory, and the building of a carpenter's shop and fives courts within the grounds; and the use of one of the detached East Street cottages for the caretaker and the other as a sanatorium. This would leave School House with the old Headmaster's residence to be converted into a boarding house for 40 boys, with accommodation for two masters and a resident matron; and following the pulling down of outhouses, an enlarged playground. HMI Bertram, who acted as intermediary with the school, thought the proposal 'a very satisfactory way out of a difficult situation' and it was accepted by the Board of Education, despite the governors' refusal – on grounds of expense – to employ an architect.[319]

The governors' failure to take professional advice was a frustration to the Board because it meant that detailed architectural plans for the refurbishment of Harley House could not be submitted for its approval. Nevertheless, the school was well enough served by its builders, Beavan and Hodges, a substantial local firm with offices and showrooms in Victoria Street and further yards in Portland and West Streets. All told in 1911 and 1912, they executed contracts worth over £1,800, which together with the £5,000 purchase of Number 1, made it the most extensive building programme that HCS had ever undertaken.[320]

Harley House was in the builders' hands by early 1911.[321] The two new fives courts, built next to the cottage along Ferrers Street, had been completed by that May but at a cost of £145, over £100 more than the original estimate. Over the following weeks, the dining-room and kitchen area – with a new range and hot water system (which proved inadequate for its purpose) – were made ready, the coach house was converted into a workshop, the domestic arrangements were improved and the house decorated inside and out. The detached classroom, too, was converted into a new laboratory for 24 boys, with some

317. HCSA, Cotterell to Capes, 7 June 1909; Chambers to Capes, 1 July 1910; Dutton to Capes, 13 July 1910.

318. HCSA, Capes' printed subscription list Feb. 1911. Capes added (in his own hand) an additional 20 names of people who had contributed to the 1911 appeal. Of these 135 donors, 36 (*c.*27 *per cent*) were clergymen, who gave over £600 (44 *per cent* of the total) between them. This list is incomplete and does not take into account the final gifts which came in later that year.

319. TNA, ED 35/995, Bertram's memoranda, 1 Oct., 19 Dec. 1910, 15, 27 May 1911.

320. HCSA, various bills paid to Beavan and Hodges totalling £1,800 11s 4d, paid in five cheques, 30 Aug. 1911 to 23 Dec. 1912. The cost was not covered by the sum (perhaps about £1,550) raised by the three appeals, the shortfall being met by the proceeds from the sale of Foley Lodge.

321. The details in the following paragraphs are taken from the correspondence in TNA, ED 35/995, and the contracts (and plans for School House and the playground) in the school archives. The cost of Harley House's conversion, and the setting up of the laboratory and sanatorium, came to just over £1,000.

fittings from the old lab but with new and wider benches and re-waxed teak table tops and, following the Board's intervention, roof ventilation. Finally, the Ferrers Street cottage was adapted as the new sanatorium.

Integrating the Headmaster's old residence with the boarding accommodation – a 'rabbit warren of a place', as the HMI had observed – also proved a costly operation.[322] Extensive alterations were made to many of the 31 rooms that constituted the new School House. The boarders' space was improved by the creation of a reading room, a playroom, studies and three new changing rooms, one of which included 'a Doulton's shower and spray bath'; and the masters' living area, through the provision of a Common Room and additional studies. The Headmaster still retained a strategic foothold in the place with an eyrie that overlooked the playground. Tucked away on the first floor of the east wing, the former maids' bedrooms were converted into an armoury. And to satisfy the Board officials, who did not seem to worry about the storage of arms in a boarding house, an Ihne's steel ladder was fixed as an external fire escape from the junior dormitory above. The utilities, too, were improved: £235 was spent on a new hot water and heating systems (with 20 radiators); £50 on the installation of 'incandescent gas' (as it was later recorded) for lighting; and £8 13s 6d on a telephone connection with 1 Castle Street and an electric bell for the playground. Day boys also benefited by the provision of separate changing facilities and sitting rooms, decorated with clematis flowers, in the old half-timbered lodge, as did the whole school through the provision of a 30-foot cycle shed. The playground, too, was enlarged by the removal of the fives court and out-houses and integrating the Headmaster's old garden, which tripled the space for the boys' recreation. Although Mrs Ragg's shrubbery was levelled, some trees remained, providing shade in hot weather and a sanctuary soon to be known as the 'Acropolis'.[323] Not as much was done to improve the teaching environment as her husband would have liked. He had hoped that there would have been sufficient money to do more than install a limited ventilation system in the teaching block, but at least the classrooms were decorated and 64 second-hand single desks (with backs) were bought and re-varnished.[324]

The official opening of the new buildings on 4 October 1911, when Dean Leigh announced the Bishop's grant to the Headmaster of a prebendal stall, represented the apogee of Murray Ragg's headship. It also marked a new beginning for the old foundation on a site that was situated outside the cathedral precincts; although Alderman Symonds expressed sentiment that his *alma mater* would both continue to serve the universities, the public services and the professions and remain 'a great asset to this ancient city', doubtless echoed the views of many Old Herefordians who had attended HCS in less propitious times. Following the speeches ceremony in the Town Hall, hundreds of people processed

322. The total cost was almost £760. The quotation is HMI Bertram's in his memorandum of 15 May 1911. (See above, note 319).

323. The area had been named the 'Acropolis' within a few weeks of the opening of the new buildings in October 1911. See *TH*, LXVIII (Dec. 1911), p.12.

324. Two classrooms out of the five were fitted up with rudimentary ventilation rather than the full system which would have cost *c.*£110, Murray Ragg making a virtue out of necessity by claiming that the full expense might not be necessary given that the senior boarders would now do their prep in the School House studies. The desks for the three classrooms (and one master's desk) were bought for 11 guineas at a girls' high school sale in 1911.

Fig. 6.14 The 1911 alterations, as seen by the Hereford Times. *The top view shows the back of the improved School House, the enlarged playground, the 'Acropolis' and the half-timbered lodge; the bottom photograph of Number 1 garden, the sanatorium (on the corner of East and Ferrers Streets) at the rear of the new fives courts and the converted laboratory.*

to the new playground, where under the shade of the lime and beech trees, Dean Leigh led a short dedication service. This was then repeated on the Headmaster's lawn, the service there being followed by tours of the new buildings which lasted long after the late autumnal sunshine had given way to nightfall.

Remembered Schooldays: Flindell Bird and Kingsley Martin

Flindell Bird and Kingsley Martin were both HCS pupils under Murray Ragg, Flindell for seven terms, 1898-1900, Kingsley for nearly six years from September 1907 to April 1913, following his one year in the preparatory school. Both were clever boys: Philpotts scholars who went on to take good Cambridge degrees. And importantly for our purposes, both left reminiscences of their time at the Cathedral School, written over 50 years after they had left. Flindell's memoir was unpublished; Kingsley's was published as a chapter in *Father Figures,* the first volume of his autobiography.[325] There the similarities end. The boys were of different generations, being almost 16 years apart in age. Flindell came from a comfortable middle-class Ipswich home, which could find the £90 annual boarding fee; Kingsley was the son of the Eignbrook Congregationalist minister, whose circumstances were more modest. Flindell was of the established Church; Kingsley, of nonconformist background. Flindell was a boarder; Kingsley a day boy. Flindell started HCS at 17 in a senior form; Kingsley had to work his way up the school, leaving just as he had reached the Sixth Form following his father's appointment as minister of Finchley Unitarian Church. Above all, for this study, the remembered experiences of their Hereford schooldays contrast markedly. Nevertheless, when considered together, these testimonies give fascinating insights into two differing schoolboy lives during the Murray Ragg era.

Flindell began his account by explaining why he, as a Suffolk boy, attended a school in the west of England. The answer he gave was that his village parson, Richard Hutton Cantley, then rector of Westerfield, had strongly recommended Hereford to Flindell's father, Cantley having discovered from the public schools handbook that HCS was one of two English schools (with Pocklington) richest in closed university scholarships. Flindell's father was no doubt further influenced by Murray Ragg's strong local reputation as Headmaster of Great Yarmouth Grammar School. Indeed, it is this circumstance which persuaded others to switch their allegiances. Flindell assures us that Murray Ragg did not 'tout' for business. It was the parents of boys like Connop ma and mi, Porter, Parry, Wilson and 'Punch' and 'Judy' Nutman – all senior boys who had begun to specialise in Classics under Murray Ragg – who 'wished their sons to continue with him', fearing that a change of teacher at Great Yarmouth might affect their chances of gaining a university scholarship. All told, eight of the 12 new boarders admitted in January 1898 came with the new Headmaster from his previous school. They settled in quickly, Flindell explaining that they were not 'hazed' [bullied] as new boys because they formed 'the cream of the school in work and athletics' and were 'too big and strong' to have been intimidated. So when he arrived in Hereford a few months later, he was immediately accepted as another East Anglian.[326]

325. HCSA, F. Woolner-Bird's typescript (he having assumed the new surname after he left school); Martin, chapter 3, *passim.*

326. The eight boys were: G. Bristow, G.R. Connop, J.R. Nutman ('Judy'), B.K. Nutman ('Punch'), L.J. Parry,

Fig. 6.15 Murray Ragg and the boarding community, including the boys from Great Yarmouth School, summer or autumn of 1898. Flindell Bird (in spectacles and slightly hidden) is sixth from left on the back row.

Flindell drew pen-portraits of his fellow countrymen. There was Geoffrey Connop (Connop ma), 'tall, handsome, good-natured, generous, lazy, debonair'. He soon became 'cock of the walk' as captain of boats and cricket, full back in the soccer team and winner of the sprints and high jump, being just pipped as victor ludorum by Basil Nutman ('Punch') by a few points. 'Punch', the red-haired and freckled younger brother, was also captain of football and a good cricketer and oarsman, who rowed bow in the school boat one year and stroked it to victory the next. 'Judy' Nutman, although the better footballer, was less gifted as an athlete and less clever than his younger brother. He left after three terms to join his father's fishing business in Yarmouth, while 'Punch' went to Cambridge and then pursued a medical career, but the brothers were on the best of terms and there was no jealousy of the younger's brilliance. Thomas Porter, nicknamed 'T.H.' (he being Thomas Henry, like Huxley) or 'Slosh' ('because he slobbered a little when talking excitedly') or 'Fry' and 'C.B.' (after his cricketing hero), was another of Flindell's eastern compatriots. 'T.H.' was a member of both XIs but also studious and like his elder brother, who became rector of East Ham, devout ('but no prig'). After Cambridge, he returned to HCS in 1903 to become (in the Headmaster's words) 'an invaluable master' until he was forced

T.H. Porter, C. Stanford and G. Wilson. All had left by July 1900, with the exception of Wilson (1901) and Stanford (1904). Their parents' faith in HCS and its Headmaster was rewarded: five of the nine (including Bird) won awards, four to Cambridge and one (Connop) to Oxford. Porter became Murray Ragg's 'invaluable' colleague at HCS, 1903-11, leaving because of his consumption. S.M. Connop (Connop mi in Bird's account) did not enter HCS until May 1900, the beginning of Bird's last term. Three other boys from Great Yarmouth joined the school, 1900-06, making 13 in all from East Anglia during Murray Ragg's Headmastership.

to leave because of consumption. And then there was Gardiner Wilson, Flindell's especial friend, a boy who was good at both games and Classics 'but rather indolent … [and] a bit of a poseur about the laziness as he sometimes worked on the sly'. These close friends – 'Punch', 'T.H.', Wilson and Flindell himself (his own and his best chum's nicknames, if they had them, are not vouchsafed) – formed a brotherhood, 'not like Kipling's' *Stalky and Co.* to rag masters and get into mischief, but just for friendship and to do things together'. All four went up to Cambridge, two on Somerset exhibitions, and kept up their friendships there.

Flindell acknowledged other contemporaries outside both the East Anglian circle and the 'sign of four'. Sidebotham, Corban and Janvrin ma were Sixth-form day boys, parsons' sons, who all took Orders themselves. Two young men he mentioned were of an older vintage but were also from a clerical background. Oakeley had left HCS nearly three years before and was reported to have been 'the best fixed seat oar in Cambridge' (although he never gained a 'Blue'), who looked up the gang of four on his return as a bronzed soldier from the Boer War. Gilbert Donne crossed with Flindell for one term and was captain of boats before Connop. As a boarder, he used to go poaching at night, allegedly in 'Tabby' Boycott's father's trout stream. After leaving school, he fought, as we have seen, in the Boer War. Reported missing, he turned up later to read his own obituary in *The Herefordian*, part of which read: 'a type of the best breed of Englishmen … which has made our Empire what it is'. Another character among the non-Yarmouth boarders was Embiricos, a Greek boy. He was nicknamed 'Slampy', because of his great strength, after Umslopogaas, Rider Haggard's Zulu hero. When the school performed *Twelfth Night*, 'Slampy' was an excellent Sir Toby, and 'T.H.', with his fair hair and fresh complexion, made up well as Maria.[327]

Flindell recorded more nefarious activities. In a snowy winter, boarders fought day boys in the Cathedral Close. The seniors were to the forefront, with a bevy of younger boys behind, making and handing up the ammunition. Fire ceased if a cathedral dignitary passed by. Other townsfolk, however, took their chance, including, one day, a local solicitor and old boy, 'in full rig, top hat, frock coat and brief case', caught a 'fourpenny one', perhaps thrown by Bourdas, a cricketer 'who had never missed a catch and could throw down the stumps from anywhere on the field'.[328]

But rowing became Flindell's favourite form of recreation. He could not row when he came to Hereford, and first learned to scull by taking out whiffs from Jordan's boatyard for free, the school paying a termly fee. Sometimes he had the 'great honour' of being coached by Connop, who occasionally treated him to tea at Bevan's. It was Connop as captain of boats, together with two masters, Jones and 'Piggy' Douton, who 'tubbed' the boys by taking them out two at a time in tub pair oars, the coach sitting in the stern and coxing. Flindell trained for the school regattas. In his first term, he stroked the 'Red' junior four,

327. C.E. Sidebotham (1893-98), L.H.L.B. Corban (1891-98), R.B.Le.B. Janvrin (1894-99), H.H.E. Oakeley (1887-95), J.G.V. Donne (1891-98), T.A. Boycott (1891-99) and P.N. Embericos (1896-99). Oakeley was one of five brothers to have attended HCS; Boycott, one of four. For Donne's obituary: *TH*, NS XXXIV (July 1900), pp.4-5.

328. Bird mentioned that a Carless was the snowball victim. This may have been either Joseph Carless, the Town Clerk, or Wilfred Carless, his son. Edgar Bourdas attended HCS, 1895-99.

choosing red when tossing for colours because he was then fond of a girl called Ruby. They won their race against the 'Yellow' crew, the prize being two small crossed silver oars which he gave to his mother (not to Ruby) to wear as a brooch. In 1899, he had advanced to the 'Cambridge' boat and was again in the winning crew; and in his last year was reserve for the school four, which meant running beside Jones or 'Piggy' as they coached, on bikes, from the tow path, and sometimes in practice rows taking Raymond Woods' place when he was bilious, as he often was.[329] All rowing and sculling was on fixed seats, which stood Flindell in good stead at his Cambridge college.

And days boating on the Wye on Dean Leigh's annual midsummer 'wholes', a holiday which Murray Ragg unsuccessfully tried to persuade him to abolish, were for ever etched in Flindell's memory. In 1898, not being invited to form a river party, he took out a canoe and went eight miles up the river by himself, getting through the fast 'rapids' – impossible in a canoe in mid-stream – by rushing through the backwater. On the same holidays over the next two years, he joined his other three friends in a rowing boat. One 'whole' he remembered as an idyllic carefree day:

> Most of us boarders were up and on the river soon after 5am. A few lazy devils stayed for school breakfast at 8. We four took a tub pair, with oars and sculls. Two would row in turn, the other two [would] sit in the stern and share the steering. 'Punch' had a spinning bait trailing behind; I forget whether he caught anything. Breakfast was at Bevan's or Betty's some miles upstream. For lunch we had a veal pie, cherries, strawberries and cream, tins of apricot, peach, pear and pineapple, cheese and cream cracker biscuits and a two gallon jar of cider. During the day we must have bathed seven or eight times, as the fancy took us. Tea at Betty's or Bevan's on the return. We went up 16 miles as far as Monowden Falls and came back downstream (thank goodness!) tired and happy. Halcyon days indeed!

What of academic work? We learn something of Flindell's classical tuition. He did Latin with the Fifth and began Greek with Form II – 'a great lout' (in his own words), 'standing around and "taking places" for oral work with kids half my height'. The kids 'got their heads punched or back-sides kicked if they did too much "taking down"'. However, he moved up every term and reached the Fifth for Greek, studying Lucian's *Timon and Menippus* and a gospel in Greek for 'Little Go' with Wilson.[330] Looking back, Flindell expressed gratitude to Hereford for having taught him rowing and Greek, but it was at Mathematics that he excelled. His village priest had encouraged his love for the subject and helped him with Euclid, Book Three, when he was younger. At the Cathedral School, Jones, a former Oriel scholar, coached him privately out of school hours. Flindell said nothing about what he learned in these sessions or how they were conducted, but they were sufficiently successful

329. A.G. Jones, an assistant master from 1891, and Second Master from 1911 (above, p.350); C.H. Douton, an assistant master from 1893, who died in office in early August 1899; and R.W. Woods (1895-1901), who (being 'always sculling and [who] practically lived in a whiff') won the Symonds sculls against Bird in his last year. He was made CBE in 1918 and later knighted.

330. 'Little Go' was the examination held at Cambridge in the second year of residence. It was also called 'the previous examination' because it preceded the examination for a degree. The Oxford equivalent was 'The Smalls'.

for him to be awarded an open scholarship at St Catherine's College, Cambridge. His name was the first to appear on the school's library honour board with a Mathematics scholarship.[331] Flindell's solitary success makes it apparent that at this time HCS was still a predominately classical school which produced few university mathematicians. Murray Ragg emphasised the point in October 1912, when he pressed his governors to alter the terms of Power's bequest, which had never at that time been awarded 'owing to the absence of mathematical candidates'.[332]

Flindell concluded his account by quoting the long cathedral bidding prayer, which he had heard spoken Sunday by Sunday before the sermon all those years before and had remembered. It included the lines:

> And for a due supply of just persons to serve God both in Church and State, ye shall likewise implore his blessing on all seminaries of sound learning and religious education, especially on our famous universities and on the school attached to this cathedral church.

And in a postscript, he apologised to posterity for his ingratitude to his old school and school-friends both for taking everything and everyone for granted and for his failings as an old boy. He had returned only once or twice, 'the return fare ... [being] ... heavy for a poor schoolmaster' but had come to realise that he should have done more.[333] Had he 'come into money', he confessed, he would have built the school a boathouse, but it was not to be. Overall, Flindell looked back on his time in Hereford with great fondness. Although admitting to being a 'homebird', he claimed that he was never 'homesick'. It was not for nothing – or simply good form – that he entitled his reminiscences 'Happy Days'. Memory is kind but there is no reason why we should not believe him.

How different all this is from Kingsley Martin's recollections of HCS under the same Headmaster. His is an unflattering portrait, to say the least, and an antidote to the school's 'high tone' as discerned by Murray Ragg.[334] Miss Dance, the preparatory school Headmistress, was depicted as a 'kindly white-haired lady' and an effective teacher of grammar – learnt by heart in the 'long tin hut'; but she was also seen also as 'an extremely stupid woman' in disciplinary matters and when it came to her intimidation of poor, dull Warburton. Kingsley himself escaped the cane but she used it on others by hitting them on the hand 'when they fooled', sometimes threatening boys with a caning from

---

331. Although earlier, a few old boys – such as Richard Gwatkin, W.F. Burville, J.T. Lingen (above, pp.120, 209, 229 and note 181) and J.G. Easton, who became 18th wrangler in 1876 – had gained distinctions in the subject. Bird himself was first Junior Optime in the 1903 Cambridge tripos.

332. Murray Ragg stated that only once in every four or five years did a boy leave to study the subject at Oxford or Cambridge, and argued that the £10 prize ('of far greater value than any other') should not be limited to boys holding a Cambridge mathematical award as Power had bequeathed. HCSA, GMB 1908-21, pp.52-54, letter 14 Oct. 1912. For Power's bequest, see above, p.187, note 48.

333. He was an assistant master at Lincoln Cathedral Choir School, 1903-06, and then at Ashby-de-la-Zouch Grammar School, 1907-11; ending his career as assistant Headmaster at Loughton Grammar School in North London. In retirement, he coached Cambridge graduates, regularly cycling the 48 miles from his Essex home to the university in his eighties. HCSA, letter from his friend, Henry Frost, to Barry Sutton, 11 Dec. 1979.

334. Martin, chapter 3, *passim*.

the 'awe-inspiring' figure of the Headmaster. Once Kingsley had arrived at HCS proper, he gives this description of the annual 'ceremony', known by the boys as 'the day of stars and stripes':

> The Headmaster solemnly read a list of boys who had done particularly well, and of others whose inattention, stupidity, bad work or other form of wickedness could only be expatiated by an exemplary whipping. They were sent to his study and came back rubbing themselves.

And then, having referred to the disastrous effect that such punishment had had on a chorister, he repudiates the occasion as an 'absurd method of reforming small boys' – which, indeed, it may well have been.

Even more notorious was the bullying that Kingsley experienced at the hands of a boy he named Hull:

> This boy … was himself always in trouble and he was continuously caned. I remember, for instance, that one day he annoyed his History master and could show large weals on his behind, adding to them next day by indiscreetly setting fire to some paper, which, in the old fashioned lavatories of those days, would float along and burn his next-door neighbour's bottom. As it happened, this was a monitor, who flogged Hull quite unmercifully. He spent most of the next day with his trousers down in the lavatory, showing off his two sets of weals to admiring boys who drifted across the playground, all apparently afflicted that day with diarrhoea. Unfortunately, he took this kind of treatment out on me … Hull would wait for me as I came out of school, trip me and kick me, and delight a crowd of boys by showing his superior strength. I would go back to the class with my collar rumpled, my clothes filthy and myself in a pitiable condition of breathless misery. I remember today his grey worsted stockings, his green suit and his malicious enjoyment of my humiliation.

The end came after three years of torment, when Kingsley blurted out the truth to his parents, following his arrival at home covered in mud after 'Hull' had pushed him into a ditch. 'Hull' was caned and his victim branded as a sneak and 'deprived of all self-respect'.

Nor is Kingsley more complimentary about the teaching he received in the junior forms, which, he claimed, were 'far too crowded and noisy for any real work': ink was splashed on white collars, paper darts thrown when the master's back was turned and boys' desks moved when they stood up to translate. Once, an organ-grinder was bribed to play 'Yip I addi' outside the classroom window and, despite the masters' entreaties, refused to go away, which wasted most of that morning's lessons. And, according to Kingsley's memory, there was no serious effort to learn anything but Greek and Latin. The Science lessons only provided 'comic relief'; no encouragement was given to speak (as opposed to translate) French; in Mathematics 'no-one bothered to explain what the figures were about'; and History meant 'the dates and doings of the Tudors, Stuarts and Georges'. 'As for the rest', he continued:

> No boy was expected to be concerned with Music or the Arts, or Politics or the world round us. We were bored beyond belief. An agony of boredom. We ragged when we dared and dozed when we could. While the lesson droned on, we planned to reach one of the fives courts after school before any competitor …

But things were eventually to change, and the agent of that change was Hugo Sharpley.

As this extract illustrates, it was he who first awoke in Kingsley a joy of History – in a spare hour after an examination, when his talk about the civilisations of India and China opened 'a new world' to him – as well as a love of learning:

> A change came in the Fifth Form, where I sat at the feet of Mr Sharpley. He was responsible for a lot. I used to sit in his class, admiring, and shivering, and waiting for a chance to show off. I was very conceited and even more thin-skinned. His comments on my character were often accurate but too wounding to be valuable … But my respect for him was unlimited. He taught me to look for ideas in Euripides, and he made me so at home in the last century of the Roman republic that I have never been able to hate the Romans as they deserved. On one occasion he unconsciously transformed life for me. We were reaching a passage where Euripides describes how Iphigenia was stripped for sacrifice. Mr Sharpley led us through it … [And] for the first time I knew that these poets did something special and splendid about words. I suspect that this was one of the important moments of my life. I suppose if I had gone on doing Classics with Mr Sharpley, I might have become a scholar. He would, I think, have soon become a father figure if I had remained his pupil. The right mixture of awe, affection, and revolt was already brewing in my mind. But we moved to London soon afterwards and Mr Sharpley went to Canterbury.[335]

Of the two schoolmasters described in chapter three of *Father Figures*, Kingsley acknowledges Hugo Sharpley rather than his later teacher, John Haydon, the pedantic pedagogue of Mill Hill, as by far the greater influence.

It is impossible to establish the accuracy of Kingsley's portrait of HCS at this time: there is no similar contemporary source against which we might compare these 1960s recollections of an Edwardian childhood at the Cathedral School. There is no reason to disbelieve his story of 'Hull's' bullying, although his name is not recorded in Murray Ragg's register and is clearly a pseudonym. However, the boy Warburton, humiliated by Miss Dance, was certainly a pupil.[336] And Kingsley Martin, who, by his own admission half a century later, was an insufferable prig at this time, 'mentally advanced and emotionally a baby, offering a shrill defence to the world', and just the sort of small boy who might well have been tormented by a stronger, stupid fellow.

---

335. *Father Figures* spells Sharpley's name as 'Sharply' throughout; the correct spelling has been has been given here. After having failed in his bid to become Murray Ragg's successor (below, p.348), Sharpley left HCS in December 1913 to become Headmaster of Richmond School, before his appointment to the preparatory headship at King's Canterbury.

336. After his time at the preparatory school, H.W. Warburton entered HCS in Form I in January 1907 and had only reached Form II when he left in May 1910 to attend Lucton School.

But what of the school regime? Here we need to be a little more careful. At a time when corporal punishment was widespread in schools, the 'stars and stripes day' no doubt happened. Although no punishment book for his period survives, even if one was ever kept, Murray Ragg, like Sir John Maclure, the Headmaster of Mill Hill who publicly flogged a boy in Kingsley's time, would have used the cane as a means of correction. The open sewer and row of 'bogs', too, doubtless existed. Godfrey Winn, a boy at HCS a decade later, attested to this.[337] But did the monitor beat 'Hull' black and blue after having had his back-side scorched? Maybe this happened. Indeed, in January 1906, Murray Ragg had given the monitors powers to cane 'for the better upholding of discipline', with the provisos that several other monitors should witness the act and that every boy should first be asked whether he would prefer to appeal to the Headmaster.[338] Regarding 'Hull's' caning, however, we also need to remember that Kingsley Martin was a leading advocate in the 1960s for the abolition of corporal punishment in schools and that in chapter three of *Father Figures*, where he spends several pages describing its allegedly evil effects, he was making a case for its prohibition. As for the HCS curriculum at the turn of the twentieth century, it is to modern eyes tedious in the extreme and Kingsley's observations on then minority subjects like Science – 'there was no prestige or scholarships in Science' – ring true. But even with mechanistic teaching methods, by the standards of the time, as the 1908 inspectors recognised, good work was done in many subjects and exams were passed, not least by Kingsley himself who gained a high honours certificate in the junior Oxford locals in the summer of 1912 and won the senior English essay prize the following year.

And perhaps Kingsley was happier at HCS than he made out half a century later. He was certainly involved in the school's life. Towards the end of his time at Hereford, he was listed as one of the new day boy recruits admitted to the ranks of the Debating Society, where on 19 October 1912 he supported the motion 'arbitration should take the place of war in all international disputes'. A few weeks later, he backed his beloved form-master when he proposed the motion: 'Amusements of the present day tend to be sordid and unedifying'. Kingsley was also a useful athlete, coxing the winning junior pair in the school regatta in February 1913 and scoring a goal in a house match the previous term.[339] Moreover, he was not without friends at the school. His friendship with Tom Applebee may not have fully blossomed until his Mill Hill days but as a fellow Philpotts scholar he would have been known to him;[340] and T.J.P. York was a close schoolboy companion, who also enjoyed their imaginative two-man cricket game on his walks home from school. Half a century later, when *Father Figures* was published, it was York who thought that Kingsley's memories of his Hereford schooldays were 'highly selective'.[341]

---

337. Winn, p.135.

338. HCSA, Old Register (to 1919), p.331.

339. As he himself admitted in *Father Figures*, he was 'very quick and tricky at soccer' and was worse off at Mill Hill which was a rugger school. For Martin's later career at HCS, see *TH*, NS LXXI (Dec. 1912), pp.12, 33, 41, 42; NS LXXII (April 1913), pp.7, 11.

340. Applebee joined the First Form at HCS in September 1906 and left in April 1911. He was a Philpotts senior scholar for his last two terms (gaining the scholarship with high marks – 322 out of 400), Martin taking over the residue of his scholarship in September 1911.

341. Rolph, p.29, where York's initials are incorrect. York, who was also Martin's Cambridge contemporary, was

Whatever the truth, during his time at HCS Kingsley Martin met two people who were to have a profound influence on his subsequent development: Tom Applebee, whose death at the front in 1916 'was a grief that Kingsley carried with him always';[342] and his form-master, Hugo Sharpley, who was almost a father-figure to him. What is equally certain is that the son of a Congregationalist minister was far from typical of the Cathedral schoolboys of the Edwardian period. And Kingsley was to remain a nonconformist, although an avowedly non-religious one, and a difficult and 'often dangerously opinionated and dogmatic man' throughout his controversial life.[343]

A 'Kindly Yet Stern' Headmaster

A little more than a year after the opening of the new buildings, Murray Ragg announced that he was leaving his new house for the parsonage at Tenbury. After 15 years, the burdens of office had taken their toll. As *The Herefordian*'s Oxford correspondent observed, 'the strain and fatigue of superintending so much in addition to his ordinary duties' was enough to have taxed the strength of any man.[344] Not that the Headmaster would have agreed that his powers were waning. Indeed, he informed his governors that he had hoped to enjoy 'the excellent premises' of the new Headmaster's house and continue his work at the school 'with unimpaired energy' a little longer, had it not been for the 'quite unsolicited' offer of the Tenbury vicarage.[345] Moreover, at an Old Herefordian dinner given in his honour in April 1913, he would only admit that men sometimes needed a change to give them new vigour. On that occasion, he made his own assessment of his time in office. The period, he said, was inauspicious in terms of scholarship, but the standards that had been reached in sport were such that 'Hereford could proudly hold up its head against any school of its size in the kingdom'. And, like Thistle, he pointed to something more fundamental than scholarship or athletics: the 'high tone' of the school during his tenure.[346] Over a hundred years later, how are we to judge Murray Ragg's 'kindly yet stern rule'?[347]

History should pay a fuller tribute to Murray Ragg than the one he gave himself. For his era coincided with a restoration of the school's fortunes after a period of decline in the mid-1890s. This may be most clearly seen in the increase in pupil numbers from 72 in December 1897, just before his arrival, to 118 five years later, their high-water mark in this period. Thereafter, apart from 1905 to 1907, numbers averaged above 100 boys annually,

---

appointed Headmaster of Derby School (at 32) in 1931 and Headmaster of Merchant Taylors' School, Crosby, in 1942. Eales-White, p.129; Luft, p.255.

342. Rolph, p.44.

343. The phrase is Morgan's (2007), p.61. After war-time service in the Friends' Ambulance Unit and his undergraduate years at Magdalene, Cambridge, Kingsley Martin had a short career as a History don at the LSE and journalist on the *Manchester Guardian*. In 1931, he became the first editor of *The New Statesman and Nation*, that flagship journal of the left, and later a founder member of the Campaign for Nuclear Disarmament.

344. *TH*, NS LXXI (Dec. 1912), p.47. The letter was probably written by H.W. Yeomans, who had won the Somerset Brasenose scholarship the previous year.

345. HCSA, GMB 1908-21, pp.55-56, copy of his resignation letter, 4 Nov. 1912.

346. *TH.*, NS LXXXIII (July 1913), p.28; *HT*, 5 April 1913, pp.5-6.

347. Or so it seemed to the then *Herefordian* editor: *TH*, NS LXXI (Dec. 1912), p.2.

Fig. 6.15 Nineteen of the twenty-two who played in the last football match against the Old Herefordians of Murray Ragg's tenure, on 20 December 1912, pose in front of the first *wooden pavilion at Wyeside. HCS lost the game 9-0,* The Herefordian *reporting that the school team 'allowed itself to be knocked off the ball in a most dispiriting manner'. Four of that day's school XI were to die on active service during the Great War.*

although during his last two years the increase in boarders did not occur, as had been anticipated prior to the improvement of the boarding accommodation.

Murray Ragg, as we have seen, not only successfully maintained the school's sporting reputation but also, through the introduction of a cadet corps and the revival of a natural history club, extended the range of its outdoor activities. Simultaneously, the revived Debating Society, the new Literary Society and the extensive lecture programme gave the boys further opportunities to widen their intellectual interests. Inside the classroom, underpinned by the fitting out of the school's first laboratories and the appointment of the first master to hold a Science degree, Science was accorded a place, albeit a minor one, within the curriculum.[348] The general standard of the school's scholarship may have disappointed Murray Ragg himself, but several open awards were achieved and the Somerset exhibitions were regularly filled.[349] And for the first time in this period, all boys were

348. The first Science master was E.W. Holman B.Sc. (Lond.), who taught at HCS from April 1907 to July 1910, and who was recognised by the 1908 inspectors as being 'a very conscientious and systematic teacher'.

349. There were six open award-winners in this period: F. Bird, 1900 (in Mathematics, St Catherine's Cambridge); P.J. Lewis, 1903 (in Classics, St John's, Cambridge); H.P.W. Burton, 1907 (in History, St John's, Cambridge);

subject to the more exacting demands of examination by public boards. Reporting to parents, too, improved, with the introduction of merit holidays as a further incentive to scholastic endeavour, in addition to the traditional 'halves' granted on special occasions or for significant achievements.[350] Murray Ragg was also intent that HCS should be subject to external validation by qualified inspectors. Many of these came by invitation of the Headmaster himself, as with the three in 1908 when the school was declared 'efficient' by the Board of Education, an important landmark in its history. As importantly, these officials gave the spur (albeit an unintended one) to the further modification of its governance and the eventual acquisition of its new buildings. And such inspections invariably recognised the school's *esprit de corps*, a spirit that Murray Ragg did his utmost to foster by the promotion of inter-house as well as inter-school competitions and the further development of its own sense of identity. It is significant that a recognisably modern prospectus, new notepaper 'adorned with a dainty school coat of arms and a scroll', and picture postcards with four different views of HCS and its surroundings were all produced in this period.[351]

Not that Murray Ragg did it all, even as a hard-working Headmaster and in an age when his power – at least, at HCS, until the 1910 scheme – was almost unbridled. He was well served by some able assistant masters, notably by Hugo Sharpley, an early appointment who stayed with him for nearly 14 years. He was fortunate, too, that his headmastership coincided with that of a progressive Dean and Chapter, and that in Aldermen Corner and Symonds, he had two influential Old Herefordians as his first lay governors. He also enjoyed the support of many other Old Herefordians, who rallied around their old school at a time of great need.[352] But it was Murray Ragg who was the lynch-pin of the edifice.

'The much-beloved Headmaster', whose 'wise control' and experience had seen HCS through a period of considerable educational change, left Hereford with the respect and affection of his governors, colleagues and boys.[353] He was a person of high ideals but also a reformer and a man of business who was not afraid to break new ground and move

---

A.J. Winnington-Ingram, 1907 (in Mathematics, St John's, Oxford); W.J. Oatfield, 1910 (in History, King's, Cambridge); and A.F.J. Hopewell, 1911 (in Classics, Queen's, Cambridge). With regard to the Somerset awards, the Brasenose scholarships were held in higher regard than the St John's exhibitions, which after 1908 were not deemed sufficiently worthy to warrant the award of a half-day's holiday.

350. Merit holidays were awarded two or three times each term (when brief reports were also sent to parents) for good conduct, regular attendance and satisfactory work in at least nine out of 12 subjects. Further half-holidays continued to be given at the request of important visitors, in celebration of royal or national events, or in recognition of local honours or significant achievements by Old Herefordians – the record being held by E.J. Rapson and then A.E. Boycott with some 13 'halves' between them (including five in this period).

351. For the prospectuses of 1899 and 1907, see TNA, ED 27/1609 and ED 35/995; and the new notepaper and postcard views, *TH*, NS XLV (April 1904), p.3.

352. Although Murray Ragg himself had been instrumental in resurrecting the Old Herefordian Club, which in *c.*1898 had been pronounced as 'dead as herrings'. (HARC, M 90/1, p.57, undated *HT* extract.) Thereafter, the membership rapidly increased, reaching over 150 by December 1903. By July 1904, Murray Ragg had been elected the club's President, and held this office throughout his remaining headmastership.

353. The quotations are from *TH*, NS LXXII (April 1913), p.27, undated Cambridge letter; and TNA, ED 109/1975, 1908 inspection report.

with the times if the school's interests would be best served by his so doing. He left his successor with a much sounder legacy than the one he had inherited but some traditions remained. Each Sunday the boarders heard the bidding prayer, already cited, which pleaded for 'a due supply of just persons' to serve God in Church and State. This sense of service inculcated in Cathedral schoolboys of this period was perhaps best exemplified by the courage of D.N. Buchanan and F.J. Williams, both of whom received the Royal Humane Society's vellum for a life-saving rescue from the Wye.[354] In subsequent years such bravery would be needed by Murray Ragg's old boys in even greater measure.

---

354. *TH*, NS LX (March 1909), p. 18; LXIII (April 1910), p.4.

Chapter 7

In Peace and War, 1913-1945

> The wheel of time seems to have turned full circle, which through the vicissitudes of war and peace, the life of our little community on the Wye has flowed like the river with floods and low-water, rough and smooth, alternating.[1]

During this time of unprecedented change, stimulated by two world wars lasting 10 of the 32 years, Hereford Cathedral School was fortunate to be led by three experienced Headmasters of considerable but contrasting gifts: John Henson, James Crees and Christopher Scott. Henson and Scott saw the school through the two wars and Crees (for 61 terms) through the difficult inter-war period. Only one assistant master, F.W. Brookes, survived from the age of Henson to that of Scott; and the only staff continuity from the Victorian to the inter-war periods was provided by two loyal retainers: 'Dick' Shepherd, the cricket professional, who retired in his mid-70s in 1926; and 'Scribble' Lewis, the porter, who died in post in 1932 following a period of illness – when (so *The Herefordian* reported) 'fires burned out, shoes went uncleaned and ink-pots grew empty' – after 34 years at HCS under three Headmasters.[2] Importantly, although not a member of staff, A.D. Steel's name should be added to this list for as Chapter Clerk (singly or in partnership) he helped administer the school from 1898 to the 1930s. His length of service, together with the long tenures of Deans Leigh (1894-1919) and Waterfield (1919-46), whom he served, ensured that the school's governance and administration gradually evolved rather than dynamically changed during this period.

Yet changes there were, principally as a result of demands from the Board of Education and (in 1940) the new Headmaster. Although the Dean of Hereford continued to chair the governing body – thankfully with regard to Dean Waterfield, who as a former Headmaster (of Cheltenham College) knew about education and was impressively supportive of the school – lay voices were increasingly heard at governor level. The new scheme of 1919 required, for the first time in history, that lay would exceed clerical representation, although how far this reduced the cathedral's influence in decision making is open to question. But

1. Harry Wardle, 'Rowing Retrospect', *TH,* NS CLXX (April 1947), p.11.

2. For Dr Crees' admirable obituary of 'the school's faithful henchman' (with the inevitable quotation from Horace), see *TH,* CXXXI (Dec. 1932); and for Shepherd, see below, p.409.

over the period as a whole, the governors undoubtedly became a more professional body. Their officer's schoolwork was actually recognised in September 1918, when Steel received £50 *per annum* in addition to his salary as Chapter Clerk and was given the title of Clerk to the Governors. And despite opposition from his successor (and son), by the end of the period the Clerk was directly receiving (via the bank) parental fees, as well as paying the masters' salaries. As a consequence, by January 1941, when the parental payments were first directly collected by the Clerk rather than the Headmaster, the Clerk, again for the first time, had a complete list of the boys in the school. Around this time, too, the school joined the Governing Bodies Association (the GBA) at or shortly after its inaugural meeting in the Grocers' Hall (London) on 10 July 1941, thereby ensuring, at least in the longer term, the adoption of higher professional standards. By June 1945, however incomplete the paperwork in the earlier years, a recognisably modern agenda could be produced for governors' meetings: the reading of the previous minutes; the Headmaster's report (school and personal); the confirmation of teachers' appointments; the approval of free places, scholarships and reduced fees; and the confirmation of pupil numbers and the amounts raised by tuition fees compared with the expense of staff salaries.[3]

Not that the school was altogether modern in its practices by this date. To take the most obvious example: although by January 1944 the Headmaster had ceased to have direct responsibility for the boarders' welfare, no boarding accounts were ever presented to the governors throughout this period. So when the GBA asked for a return about the boarding side in 1942, all the Clerk could do was to reply that he had 'no record' of matrons, nurses and charges for domestic staff and 'no information' on either feeding (the sole concern of the Headmaster) or boarding as 'the Housemaster retains all profits and bears all losses'.[4] And although the Headmaster's conditions of service were changed at the time of Scott's appointment in 1940, when he was given a realistic annual salary (£800) in place of the over-generous capitation fee (£4 10s per boy) that Crees had enjoyed, the demarcation line between his personal and professional incomes was still somewhat blurred. One significant illustration of this is the Headmaster's continued ownership throughout this period of the preparatory school, which Crees had established at Number 28 Castle Street in 1925. Scott purchased the freehold of this building (although not Langford House, which Crees had also owned) from his predecessor, the governors thereby missing the chance to buy the school at the reasonable price of £2,500. They were to miss out again at the next change of headship in 1945.

Financially, the most important reform of the period – and, indeed, the most significant for the school's future for the rest of the twentieth century – was its recognition by the Board of Education in 1918-19 as a grant-earning secondary school for advanced courses in Classics and Mathematics/Science. At the time, HCS was the smallest school in the country to be so recognised. And while these grants, the value of which doubled over the period to around £2,000 *per annum*, by no means covered the annual deficit on the fees account (the difference between fees income and salary payments), they did provide well over half the school's income each year. Without them, the school would soon have found itself in

3. HCSA, draft agenda for 5 June 1945.

4. HCSA, draft return of GBA financial questionnaire, stamped 4 Feb. 1942.

difficulty. However, these grants, together with the increase in pupil numbers – boarding, initially, and then day – from the low point of 67 in January 1915 to well over 200 in Scott's later years, enabled the school to survive and eventually prosper. The increase in the number of free (and largely day) places to around one third of the school in 1944-45 also did much to change its nature, if only to make it less remote from the local population.

John Henson, the school's last ordained Headmaster, laid the foundation by acquiring the first grant in Classics, in part because his own teaching of the subject had been judged exceptional by the 1915 inspectors. After his early years in office, he also expanded the pupil roll, especially by increasing its boarding element through attracting more Welsh boys to the school – he had been Headmaster of Haverfordwest Grammar School and had a home in the Principality – and by doubling the size of the preparatory school. But his successor, the extraordinary Dr Crees, was the real architect of its success in this period. The furthering of its reputation in the 1920s enabled HCS to survive the depression years of the 1930s without serious embarrassment. In part this was achieved, after a decade of stagnation, through the improvement of its plant. Although the Headmasters were reluctant to dissipate their profits by spending too much on boarding costs, electric lighting was installed in School House, as well as the classrooms, in 1922. And partly through Crees' own generosity – of particular importance at a time when the governors were reluctant to risk the school's reserves on capital projects – his appeals for a pavilion and gymnasium, the freehold to Wyeside and new Science laboratories were successfully concluded. But the root cause of the Cathedral School's success at this time was the growth of its formidable academic reputation in Classics, Mathematics and, to a lesser extent, Science. The school's progress in these and other subjects can be measured through the increasingly complimentary inspection reports of 1915, 1924 and 1933, as well as by the unprecedented number of scholarships it won and its successes in the new (in 1918) Higher and School Certificate examinations.

The school's corporate life, too, was enhanced, not least through Dean Leigh's generosity in acquiring the Lady Chapel for its daily use from September 1917 and enabling a school chaplain to be appointed the following term. In sport, the switch in football codes was accomplished again in 1922 but this time without the acrimony of 1898. In main part thanks to the Welsh boys, the rugby game was played with considerable success throughout the inter-war years. Dr Crees' obsession with 'the game and plaie of cricket' and his passionate coaching of the 1st XI also ensured that cricketing standards improved. But from its low base at the end of the First World War and through the genius of Harry Wardle's coaching, it was rowing that became the school sport *non pareil* in these years. Despite changes in command, the corps, too, continued to thrive, particularly during wartime (when games suffered), over half the school being involved in its operations during these war years. Of other activities, debating attracted good audiences (among the boarders), chess and draughts were introduced, Dean Waterfield started a Shakespeare reading society and nature and science clubs ebbed and flowed. Culturally, apart from the regular monitors' concerts and the memorable production of *Twelfth Night* in 1941, boys had little opportunity to perform, although their musical appreciation was aided by Dr Crees' occasional gramophone concerts. So although outdoor life continued to dominate a boy's non-lesson time, HCS was a little more civilised by the end of the period than it had been a generation or two earlier.

Even in an age of teaching Heads – and Henson, Crees and Scott (the first Headmaster in modern times not to hold a Classics degree) were all outstanding teachers – and in a period dominated by Dr Crees whose control (he liked to think) was near total, the three Headmasters should not take all the credit for the school's enhanced status. The vast majority of the 80 or so assistant masters appointed during their tenures stayed for less than five years. A number, no doubt (and perhaps especially among those with the shortest HCS lives) were duds. But there were also many long-standing stalwarts such as Ralph Williamson, Duncan Felton and John Hudson who did much to see the school through the First World War; and post 1918, F.W. Brookes, C.M. Scott, Harry Wardle, J.C. Wordsworth, George Hunt and Elwy ApIvor, who served through most of the inter-war period. And then there were the younger masters, not least the six successive senior Mathematics teachers, 1920-38, with first-class degrees, and the civilised older men (or at least some of them) appointed by Scott during the Second World War, who made a distinctive contribution to the boys' welfare and the school's success. Crees and Scott, in particular, knew good assistants when they saw them, even if like their predecessors they could not always retain them for long.

Can we come to a meaningful view of the boys' collective well-being from 1913 to 1945? Certainly, they were not free from serious illness. Killer diseases may have been gradually brought under control and life expectancy increased from some 50 years to about 65 during this period,[5] but fatalities at HCS were not unknown. In the 1920s, for example, Eric Addison and Douglas Watt, both former choristers, died in their late teens (the latter from diabetes) and Sydney Hall, the senior mathematics master, passed away aged 25 following an epileptic fit at Wyeside. Epidemics, too, continued to disrupt school routine. Infectious diseases – for instance, mumps in 1913-14, influenza in 1918, chicken-pox in 1919 and nameless infections in 1920 – were especially prevalent in the earlier period, and the 'monster influenza' bug struck again in 1929. In the following decade, the school medical officer closed down the school (much to Crees' annoyance) before the end of term in March 1936, and as late as 1938 'old man scarlet fever' made a brief re-appearance at Langford House, necessitating its isolation for a few days during that summer term.[6]

With regard to food and general living conditions, the evidence is patchy and contradictory. House-mastering (until 1944) and food provision was the personal domain of the Headmaster and more importantly their wives, rather than the school, and no household accounts of the period survive. But there is no suggestion that the three wives were negligent in the discharge of their house-keeping duties and some good evidence to the contrary.[7] This may not always have been the boys' perception and certainly 'Queen' (the matron who became Mrs Crees) sometimes received a bad press. The food served up to the boarders may have been execrable to some, notably Godfrey Winn as he remembered his

5. Kynaston, (2008), p.20.

6. See *HMC 1936 Committee Report*, p.12 re Crees' complaint about the closing of HCS, and *The Herefordian, passim,* for references to the deaths and other epidemics.

7. See below, pp.374, 393, 419.

schooldays from the safe vantage point of 40 years and J.E.W. Scougall (OH 1924-29), who returned to the school as a teacher in June 1935.[8] In 1933, however, the inspectors had found school dinners to be ample (and reasonably priced), although whether Mrs Crees put on special meals for them is unknown. During the rationing days of the Second World War, the food – inevitably – was unappetising and insufficient for growing boys. The official food needed to be supplemented. One Old Herefordian remembers 'wolfing down' bread bought from the town; another adding white chocolate, purchased (with coupons) from Wathen's sweet shop, to the rice pudding.[9]

As for the boys' happiness, who is to say? Godfrey Winn hated the school he experienced in the early 1920s, but Sydney Addison, his near contemporary, in the only contemporaneous schoolboy diary we have, seemed to have enjoyed his schooldays (or most of them) in 1919. Bullying, initiation rites (a water tank in the Close during the Second World War was occasionally used to 'baptise' new choristers), fagging, beatings and other physical punishments – Harry Wardle was especially adept at painfully tweaking a boy's hair – occurred, but as at other public schools of the period they were accepted as an inescapable part of a pupil's daily existence. To our mind, too, boarding conditions were primitive, especially in School House, but for many boys from modest backgrounds they were probably no worse than they experienced at home. And there is little suggestion that the conditions at HCS were anything like as dire as those experienced by Paul Selver during his time as a teacher at a small town grammar school in the early 1920s.[10]

HCS may still have been a hard school but for the increasing number of parents who sought admission for their sons, its annual fee (of around £100 for boarders by 1945, one third more than in 1913, although day tuition fees had more than doubled) represented good value for money. And the Cathedral School was particularly successful in weathering economic storms during the inter-war period. Like other grant-aided schools, which constituted about one third of the HMC membership by 1934, this was in part due to its government subsidies, competitive fees and essentially regional nature. But it was also a result of the expert management of Dr Crees, who as the first chairman of the HMC grant-aided schools group was in a good position to monitor national trends.

Over the whole period, HCS, whilst maintaining its vigorous corporate life and reputation for godliness and good learning, also succeeded in adapting to the times: from an endowed school with no external financial support to one of sufficient importance to be recognised in 1918 as worthy of grant-aided status; from a school governed by a cathedral majority to one with a majority of lay governors; from a school where there was a preponderance of ordained masters (in the First World War) to a largely lay and more

8. '… School House boarders will learn with interest that polony still appears on the breakfast menu, sausage swill still resurrects itself on Mondays, pilchards still flourish on Mondays at 8am, cat is still the aperitif of the military on Thursdays, that bugs-in-the-bolster and bloody baby are still considered magnificent for the footballers on Wednesdays and Saturdays at lunch time, and that well-boiled split peas from the night before still masquerade as cream in the tea at next morning's breakfast'. HCSA, *OH Club Handbook 1937-38*, p.5.

9. I am indebted to the late Geoffrey Hughes and the late Colin Manning for these observations.

10. 'The masters in the school in which he taught were cheap, seedy, mean and sensual, the Headmaster was a pompous titan and the whole atmosphere was one of boredom, dirt and neglect'. Mack (1941), p.345 note, quoting from Selver's 'very amusingly bitter book called *Schooling*' of 1925.

professional staff; from a school where the Headmaster did almost everything to one which was recognisably modern in its administration; from a school with little Science to one with two Science masters and adequate Science laboratories; from a school with fewer than 100 boys to one more than double that size; from a school that was essentially insular and self-satisfied to one that was less isolated and more progressive in outlook. So that by 1945, more fortunate than many in not having to evacuate during the war from 'the green and pleasant places of this lovely town',[11] the Cathedral School was strong enough to meet the challenges of the austere post-war world.

John Henson, 1913-1919

The school's enhanced reputation under Murray Ragg's sternly benevolent rule is indicated by the impressive short-list of candidates for the vacant headmastership. Out of the 41 applicants, two of the five selected for final consideration were already Headmasters of endowed schools and three were experienced schoolmasters. Included in this list were Hugo Sharpley and the Revd John Henson.[12] We know nothing of the selection process, but on Thursday 2 January 1913 Henson was chosen as Murray Ragg's successor. In a masterfully worded public announcement, designed both to appease the supporters of the internal candidate and to stress the preference for continuity, it was made known that the governors favoured 'one in Holy Orders' and that this was the deciding factor in the appointment. The notice also stressed Henson's 'experience of boarders', his 'pre-eminently successful headmastership' of Haverfordwest Grammar School, and his 'keen intellectual features' which displayed 'a force of character that at once arrests attention'.[13]

In the same article, the Headmaster elect outlined his educational ideals and his intended policy for 'the future management of Hereford's first school', stressing the importance of inculcating 'independence of character and originality of thought' as well as 'actual book learning'. He further emphasised that HCS would continue as a classical school, 'with facilities for entering the army and preparing for the medical and other professions as necessary'. Three months later, replying to the toast at the Old Herefordian dinner held in Murray Ragg's honour, the new Headmaster pointed out the similarity in 'methods, ideals and aims' between himself and his predecessor, confirming his belief 'by training, association, inclination and conviction' in the 'humane arts' and decrying 'the new fashioned methods of education'. Following Henson's peroration that the school's independence should be preserved from the Board of Education's 'despoiling hands', because in schools such as HCS 'the English character was developed at its best', the speech was greeted with loud applause.[14] As Murray Ragg had written to his parents a few weeks before, apart from the change of Headmasters bringing 'an accession of fresh vigour to the school', it seemed likely

11. The phrase is G.H. Dhenin's from his (last) editorial in *TH*, NS CXLII (July 1936).

12. *HT*, 4 January 1913, p.5. The other short-listed candidates were the Revd O.E. Hayden, Headmaster of King's, Gloucester, and the Revd J.L. Phillips and Mr A.B. Roberts, respectively assistant masters at St Paul's and Uppingham.

13. *Ibid.* Henson had gained a first in Classical Moderations (in 1893) at Oxford – although only a second in Greats two years later – and had then taught at Cheam and Reading Schools before his appointment to Haverfordwest in 1906. For his Headmastership at Haverfordwest: PRO, SSR 2/7/2, pp.228ff.

14. *HT*, 5 April 1913, p.6.

Fig. 7.1 John Henson, the Headmaster who successfully steered HCS through the First World War.

that things would continue 'on much the same lines as before'.[15] It was a reasonable statement but Murray Ragg could not have been more wrong in his prediction.

1913-1914

And yet, the rhythm of school life changed little in Henson's first 15 months in office. The terms opened in familiar fashion with the school service in the Lady Chapel, the sermon being preached by the Headmaster and the collection taken for the Universities' Mission to Central Africa. 'Merits' and 'halves' continued to be awarded – Henson's first one being on 2 June 1913 in honour of the award of F.E. Oakeley's international rugby cap – and the usual Monday holiday for Whitsuntide observed. Apart from the cutting down of the tree outside the Close entrance and the building of the new rifle range in the Headmaster's garden,[16] the school's appearance was not much altered. Boarders' 'lock-up' was brought forward to five o'clock in the winter months but few changes were made to other aspects of the school's routine. The timings of lessons remained the same and although some minor modifications were made to the curriculum and Oxford and Cambridge Board examination papers were temporarily reintroduced, Henson kept his promise to run the school on classical lines, while maintaining a strong modern side.[17] Above all for the boys, the yearly round of activities remained untouched, Henson, like his predecessor, being elected President of the Debating and Old Herefordian Clubs. He also showed his support for games by presenting a cup for the quarter mile and playing (in 1913) in the masters' cricket team against the 1st XI.[18] His support for school traditions was further exemplified in October 1913 by the resurrection of the speech day Latin recitation, and a year later by the resumption of the paper-chase for which a half-holiday was awarded. Even the usual illnesses, such as German measles in late 1913 and early 1914 and mumps in the following

15. *Ibid.*, 11 January 1913, p.4. Henson was 39 on his appointment.

16. For the rifle range, see above, p.314, note 272.

17. See below, pp.355-56, 358-59, for the 1915 inspection report, and HCS gaining Board of Education grants for advanced courses in Classics and Science in 1918-19.

18. Batting at no. 7, he was bowled by Barnett for 8. *TH*, NS LXXIV (Dec. 1913), p.13.

summer term, resumed, much to the exasperation of *The Herefordian*'s editor. Like the Big School clock which remained stuck at thirteen minutes to nine for much of 1913, HCS time, it seemed, had stood still in the first five terms of Henson's headmastership.[19]

Contrary to outward appearances, however, the new Headmaster had to face some adverse trends, the most serious of which was a steep decline in pupil numbers. Henson inherited a school of 92 pupils in May 1913 but less than two years later the roll had been reduced by nearly one third to 67 boys, the lowest number for over 50 years.[20] The reason for the dayboy decline – and day numbers decreased at double the rate to boarding – is not hard to fathom, for HCS was facing increasingly fierce competition from the new Hereford Secondary School for boys, which had opened its doors in September 1912. Built at a cost of £10,000, with accommodation for 150, free places for a quarter of its pupils and low fees (£2 5s per term, including stationery and books) for the remainder, a progressive curriculum, and a scientist, A. Redway Allen, as its first Headmaster, it would have looked a distinctly attractive alternative to HCS for some local parents.[21] And although boarding numbers held up better, the beginning of the war led, as we shall see, to a number of withdrawals.

Simultaneous to the pupil decline, the new Headmaster had to deal with a rapid turnover among his staff. Two of the three 'old and well-tried friends', as the Oxford correspondent put it in April 1913, the revered Hugo Sharpley and loyal Arthur Jones, whom Murray Ragg had brought back as Housemaster of School House and Henson had made Second Master, had both left by the end of 1914.[22] Six other assistant masters also departed within two years of Henson's appointment. Even though most of these men had good reasons for leaving,[23] their departure did not make the task of a new Headmaster, who had yet to find his voice, any easier.

Indeed, such losses severely undermined the school's efficiency. Foremost, a declining roll depleted the school's income, two thirds of which was derived from the fees. For the

---

19. For the recitation and paper-chase (neither of which survived the Great War): *Ibid.*, p.8; *TH*, NS LXXVII (Dec. 1914), pp.23-24; for the infectious diseases: *TH*, NS LXXVI (July 1914), p.2; and for the clock: *TH*, LXXIV (Dec. 1913), p.42, letter from 'Punctual'.

20. Numbers dropped term by term from May 1913 to January 1915 as follows: 92, 88, 81, 81, 74 and 67. Excluding the choristers, boarding numbers declined from 39 to 29 and day from 39 to 21 during this time. HCSA, Register (to 1919), p.419; HCSA, account book 1894-1922, *passim*. However, following an intensive advertising campaign, numbers in the preparatory school, which was still run as the Headmaster's private business, reached 33 boys (aged 7 to 12) in March 1915. For the pupils entered at this school, see HCJSA, admissions register, 1912-31.

21. HARC, HLC/EM 130, pp.1-75, minutes 1911-14.

22. *TH*, NS LXXII (April 1913), p.25. The other, the Revd T.M.F. Roberts, stayed until December 1916, and later returned as a part-time 'visiting' woodwork master, finally leaving in December 1921 after nearly 20 years as a teacher at HCS. For Murray Ragg's obituary notice of Arthur G. Jones, see *TH*, NS CIV (April 1924), p.19.

23. Of the eight assistant masters who departed HCS from July 1913 to December 1914, four left for promotion elsewhere: P.S. Wilkinson, in July 1913, for Berkhamsted (as senior modern language master); H. Sharpley, in December 1913, for Richmond Grammar School (as Headmaster); S.S. Horsley, in April 1914, for St Edmund's, Canterbury; and H.D. Broadhead, in December 1914, for a professorship in New Zealand. P.C. Hull was interned in Germany from August 1914 for most of the war; and A.G. Jones left in December 1914 on account of his health. E.W. Clarke and H.S. Davies were both dismissed, respectively in December 1913 and July 1914.

financial year 1913-14, the masters' salary bill (including Henson's capitation) exceeded the incoming fees by nearly £240, the Headmaster agreeing to pay around £70 of the deficit from his own pocket. The following year the deficit had been reduced by around £100, but this was still a sizeable sum for a foundation with an ordinary annual income of less than £600.[24] And in each year the deficiency would have been far worse had not Henson consistently reduced the number of his assistants, from eight in April 1913 to five within two years.

The reduction in the number of boys and masters in 1913-14 inevitably affected the quality of education that HCS provided. Although some classes were amalgamated, academic standards may not have fallen, thanks in part to Henson's heavy timetable and the brilliance of his teaching,[25] but given the decrease in the numbers of senior boys, it is not surprising that these were not memorable years for sporting achievement. To take just one example, the traditional 'Oxford' versus 'Cambridge' boat race was dropped from the 1914 regatta programme 'owing to the paucity of oarsmen, the majority of the seniors being either unable to swim or too delicate to row'.[26] And the school's reputation suffered. In the summer of 1913, an Old Herefordian had put down the deterioration in the standard of games to the lack of a 'thorough games coach'. A year later another furious correspondent was scandalised by the lack of a rowing coach and that HCS was seemingly blind 'to the glorious past of rowing'. The lack of a competent games coach was bad enough, but even worse was the want of a commanding officer for the corps which meant that HCS was unable to arrange field days in that fateful summer of 1914.[27]

The Great War was, in one sense, not entirely unexpected. War clouds had been gathering for some time before August 1914, and the prospect of war had even pierced the consciousness of some Hereford boys. In a remarkably prescient editorial of December 1909, W.J. Oatfield, later Fielder exhibitioner of King's College, Cambridge, made this observation:

> We are living in an age of revolution – an age that seems unable to rest for mobility ... Those who in these troublous times enter a public school must remember that they have during their life there to prepare themselves for a struggle which is bound to come sooner or later, in which they will have to vindicate their position as rulers of this race, as members of this Empire which stands at the head of all empires.[28]

---

24. HCSA, account book, 1894-1922 *passim*. The termly deficits on the fees account over this period are recorded in HCSA, GMB 1908-21, meetings, 29 July 1913, 25 May, 24 July, 21 Oct. 1914.

25. See below, p.355, for the 1915 inspectors' comments. It is worth noting, however, that there were far fewer boys taking public examinations in the summer of 1914 than there had been a year earlier. *TH,* NS LXXIV (Dec. 1913), p.9; NS LXXVII (Dec.1914), p.9.

26. *TH,* NS LXXV (April 1914), p.10. Daly Briscoe (the 'Cambridge' cox at a little over 5 stone), in an unpublished memoir written nearly 30 years later, remembered the 1913 regatta, the 'Oxford' crew wearing 'violets especially ordered for the occasion as a sort of emblem', and both 'Oxford' and 'Cambridge' walking to Jordan's boathouse 'linked arm in arm in order of rowing'. The regatta was followed by a celebration of the ending of training at the Imperial Café. HCSA, Daly Briscoe collection.

27. *TH,* NS LXXIII (July 1913), p.32, letter from '*Floreat Schola*'; NS LXXVI (July 1914), p.27, letter from '*Remex*'.

28. *TH,* NS LXII (Dec. 1909), p.2.

The first of Daly Briscoe's picture postcards to his parents, posted on 31 July 1914, depicting the previous year's scene at the Mytchett Farm camp. Daly remarked that the food was 'jolly good'; that 'cash does go'; and that F.J.A. Downing (who was to serve in France with the Gloucestershire Regiment, 1917-19) had fainted on one of the long marches.

Three years later, one of Oatfield's successors as senior *Herefordian* editor commented that the 'outside world' viewed the Balkan unrest 'with considerable alarm … for fear that the flame of war should be kindled widespread throughout Europe by the contagion of this outbreak'. He added, however, that there seemed (in December 1912) 'no serious danger of the great powers becoming embroiled in this struggle'.[29] Even a member of the school Debating Society in the year before the war's outbreak, pointed out the dangers of a channel tunnel being built given the prospect of war with Germany.[30]

And yet when war was declared later the following summer, it came as a surprise to many. HCS broke up on 28 July 1914 after the final cricket fixture – and another loss – against the Old Herefordians. A contingent of 28 then departed for the OTC public schools' camp in the idyllic surroundings, with its lake for swimming and canal for boating, of Mytchett Farm, Aldershot. From there a 14-year-old cadet sent two picture postcards to his parents at Bewell House, Hereford. On the second card, which caught the evening post on Sunday 2 August, after again complaining about his lack of 'cash', he casually remarked: 'I think the war a jolly fine thing, don't you?'[31] It was a common enough sentiment at the

29. *TH*, NS LXXXI (Dec. 1912), p.2. The author was probably H.B. Hodgson, later senior mathematical master at Chesterfield Grammar School.

30. R.G. Prichard on 8 November 1913, when opposing the motion: 'A channel tunnel will be most beneficial to both England and France'. *TH*, NS LXXIV (Dec. 1913), p.36. Prichard was killed in action on 28 April 1915.

31. HCSA, Daly Briscoe collection. The school archives also contain his unpublished memoir, which gives a more

time – and not only among boys – but with the aid of hindsight causes surprise to the modern reader. The next day after reveille, the cadets were ordered to return home and the camp was disbanded after less than five days, the boys arriving back in Hereford late that afternoon 'tired, dusty and full of the war'.[32]

1914-1918 : Strain and Salvation

In mid-September 1914, an extraordinary meeting of the Headmasters' Conference standing committee was convened, in response to requests from some Headmasters for 'lines of common policy in regard to various emergencies created by the war' to be drawn up. Three principal issues were considered: the withdrawal of boys without notice, the volunteering of masters for military service and new arrangements for school OTCs, it being suggested that in the case of boys leaving to undertake military service with the Headmaster's approval, fees should be remitted; that the first duty of assistant masters were to their respective OTCs; and that the most urgent task for the school corps was the special training of all boys over 17 in readiness for their impending commissions, the extra hours for the prescribed programme being found 'mainly from time usually given to games'.[33] Such were some of John Henson's concerns following the outbreak of war, as he contemplated the prospects for the new academic year from his house in Montgomeryshire over the summer holidays of 1914.[34]

Henson had good cause to worry, for over those weeks from late July to mid-September, 18 newly registered boarders were withdrawn from his lists, thereby reducing the school's potential income by nearly £1,000. At a time when the Headmaster, despite the 1893 scheme, was still responsible for collecting the school fees and paying his staff, such a loss was also likely to have caused Henson financial embarrassment.[35] In addition, many of the older boys had left,[36] so Henson was faced with the prospect of a tiny Sixth Form, which was down to eight pupils by early 1915, and a young and inexperienced group of monitors. The exception was his Head of School, T.M. Ragg, but in early October he also (in the Headmaster's phrase) 'discarded the pen for the sword' and joined the many Old Herefordians who had flocked to the Colours in the first weeks of the war.[37]

---

extended description of the camp.

32. *TH, NS* LXXVII (Dec. 1914), pp.26-27. The two battalion camp officers ('the best we have had for a long time') attached to HCS were both Irish guardsmen: Captain Berners, who was killed in action the following month, and Lieutenant the Honourable Harold Alexander, later Field Marshal Earl Alexander of Tunis. Also see, Brittain, pp.95-96, for her brother's return from the Aldershot camp on the same day.

33. *HMC Committee 1914*, pp.130-31, minutes, 15 Sept. 1914.

34. I am making an assumption here but Henson's address in March 1918 is recorded in the school archives as being: 'Eithnog', Llanfair Caereinion, Montgomery, which may have been his holiday home.

35. TNA, ED 35/995, figures from (unpublished) appendix to 1915 inspection. At the time the basic annual boarding fee was £42 8s for boys under 12 and £50 for the remainder.

36. Of the 31 boys who left during the 1913-14 academic year, 15 were seniors (16 to 19) and 9 others were aged 15 to 16.

37. Over 60 OHs had enlisted by the end of September and 137 by early December 1914. *HT*, 3 Oct. 1914, p.5; *TH*, NS LXXVII (Dec. 1914), pp.29-32. More than half of the men in these printed lists are known to have been commissioned as officers. Also note Henson's comment on 27 October 1915 that the school term had begun 'with no single boy [at HCS] of military age who could pass an army medical test'. *TH*, NS LXXX (Dec. 1915), p.8.

Correspondingly, Henson's staff had been reduced to six assistant masters by September 1914. Henson was more fortunate than some of his HMC colleagues in that no teacher had left voluntarily that summer to serve their King and Country but Percy Hull, the music master and Dr Sinclair's assistant as cathedral organist, having left England in early August to undertake a walking tour in the Black Forest, had been caught by the outbreak of war and interned in Germany.[38] The autumn term activities of the OTC, too, were disrupted by the successive loss of two sergeant instructors, whom the War Office recalled for senior training duties, and the resignation of H.D. Broadhead, the newly appointed commanding officer. Major W.J. Phillips OH had been called in to drill the boys, but given that he was 60 and had to brush up on his instructions from the 1914 infantry training manual, he may not have been able to instruct the cadets as well as his predecessors, however favourable his end of term report on the state of the corps.[39] To cap it all, Henson had to announce at speeches on 9 October 1914, held in Big School for the first time in many years as the Town Hall was unavailable owing to the war, that A.G. Jones had tendered his resignation because of ill health. After Sharpley's departure the year before, this further blow came at a time when Henson might have reasonably expected his experienced Second Master to have stayed at HCS long enough to have seen him through the war years.

In these circumstances, it is not surprising that HCS's declining reputation suffered further damage. Indeed by early 1915, parental complaints about the school's poor 'discipline and administration' had become so vociferous that the governors passed a resolution of no-confidence in their Headmaster and asked him to consider his position, not least given the fall in numbers and the school's desperate financial plight.[40] But all was not as it appeared for it seems as though influential members of the local community had deliberately blackened HCS's good name in an attempt to benefit the new High School. As one of the HMIs had reported, following a post-inspection conference in Hereford in March 1915:

> The governors explained their difficulties with the utmost frankness. They thought the school was in a desperate position. The school and the Headmaster were constantly attacked by parents, by the towns-people and by the neighbourhood generally. Trivial incidents had been seized upon and magnified into scandals. The Headmaster gave me a typical case. A big boy with conspicuously red hair [having] got a bad kick on the head during a football match … walked unsteadily back to school through the streets of Hereford. This became the origin of a legend that drunkenness was one of the prevailing vices of the Cathedral School.[41]

---

38. For his internment, see the reports in the *HT*, 15 August 1914, p.7; 29 August 1914, p.6. Henson appointed J.H. Oscar Jones to take on Hull's music duties.

39. He had, however, been a commissioned officer with the Hereford volunteers for 33 years (1878-1911), being awarded the territorial decoration in 1909. See Eales-White, pp.96-97 (photograph), and his long entry on pp.98-99; and Phillips' OTC report in *TH*, NS LXXVII (Dec. 1914), pp.28-19. For the difficulties experienced by Canon Chappel, Headmaster of King's, Worcester,, in recruiting sergeant instructors, as well as other problems that the war posed for school OTCs: *HMC 1914*, minutes of 22, 23 Dec. conference, pp.49ff.

40. HCSA, GMB 1908-21, meeting, 20 Feb. 1915. The governors accepted Henson's explanations about the complaints but asked him 'to consider whether the prospects of a recovery under his headmastership' were 'such as to make it expedient in his own interest for him to retain his office'.

41. TNA, ED 35/995, E.R. Edwards' supplementary report, 25 March 1915.

HCS was indeed in a 'desperate position' in these early war months yet Henson survived thanks, in part, to the favourable inspection report which helped still the 'injurious tittle-tattle' and the unfair attacks that the Headmaster had endured.[42]

Although Henson may have feared the worst when four inspectors descended on HCS on 16 and 17 March 1915, he was personally vindicated, being described as 'a teacher of exceptional ability … with unusual powers of hard and continuous work'.[43] He may have taught an excessive weekly timetable of 31 periods, but the best teaching in the school (in History and Classics) was conducted by the Headmaster himself. Henson's introduction of a systematic History scheme would make it impossible for a Sixth-former ever again 'to be entirely ignorant of the history of his own country'; and in Classics, although only 15 boys now studied Greek (in four sets), the success of the Headmaster's decision to reduce the amount of reading was shown by 'the extremely promising work' of the best boys in Form IV no less than by 'the accuracy and taste' of the VIth in their translations.

Attainment in other subjects was more variable. The work of the senior boys in Mathematics, despite being taught by the brilliant Ralph Williamson – known to the boys as 'Sandy Bill' – who had been listed 19th wrangler in 1909, was disappointing;[44] Modern Languages teaching had clearly fallen off since Goetz's day;[45] and there were difficulties in English caused by the teaching being shared out among the whole staff.[46] Even so, the attainment achieved in these three disciplines was considered 'fair'. The same could not be said for other areas. Science still occupied a subordinate position in the curriculum. There was no Sixth Form Science teaching at all; the subject could be dropped entirely by boys opting for German or Greek at the end of Form III; less than five hours per week was allocated to Science in the whole school; there was no master with a Science degree; and the laboratory, although well equipped, was insufficiently used, it being 'cold and damp' in winter. Criticisms were also made of the school's provision in Geography, which was not taught beyond Form IV and where the master had no special qualification or aptitude for the subject;[47] in Art, taught in two junior forms, where Drawing instruction was 'not on good lines … [being] very largely from copies, and the teaching in Form III was disrupted by the master having simultaneously to teach Mathematics to a different group of boys; and in Music, where the 30 minutes weekly allocation for the two divisions, plus a Saturday 'sing-song' for the older boys, was considered insufficient, and the boys were 'thoroughly bored' with having to sing hymn tunes which they well knew. Part of the problem was that

42. The quoted phrase is from E.R. Edwards' contemporaneous draft memorandum of the above conference. *Ibid.*, 25 March 1915.

43. The inspectors were S.F. Dufton, E.R. Edwards, A. Somervell and R.W. White-Jones. The following is taken from the printed copy of the inspection report, issued 5 May 1915, and related correspondence in TNA, ED 35/995. A further copy exists in TNA, ED 109/1976.

44. Williamson was Headmaster of Oswestry Grammar School, 1920-58. For S.R.J. Addison's affectionate obituary notice of him, see *TH,* CCIX (Oct. 1965), pp.46-47.

45. However, the master, D.D.W. Felton, who had passed the Cambridge Modern Languages 'special' degree in 1913, was held to be competent.

46. This was thought especially undesirable in Form II, where 'some of the boys can barely read aloud intelligibly, and few of them have any knowledge of grammar, either Latin or English …'

47. J.K. Hudson, who had an Oxford 'first' in Classics, taught the bulk of the Geography syllabus.

the choristers were withdrawn from these and other lessons. Indeed, to the inspectors, the choristers with their special timetable were 'a nuisance to the rest of the school'. It was hardly a new observation.

Other weaknesses – namely the indifferent pupil grading; the low masters' salaries;[48] the problems posed by the Oxford Junior examination; the lack of a systematic medical examination; and the need for more 'modern single desks' and pictures – were alluded to, but it was by no means a negative report. The improvements that had been made to the accommodation, the classrooms apart, since the 1908 inspection and the school's 'vigorous corporate life', for example, were commended. But most important of all, in terms of the school's survival, was the general conclusion:

> Since the date of the last full inspection report, there has been established in Hereford a well-equipped county secondary school for boys. In an important provincial centre like Hereford there should be ample space for at least two efficient boys' schools, differing not necessarily in grade but in type. The Cathedral School, with its traditions and endowment, can offer a predominantly classical education up to a high point. Under the present Headmaster, the classical tradition is in excellent hands, and the school should continue to fill a most useful place in the educational scheme of the district.

Given this affirmation and the governors' belief that 'some powerful outside help was necessary to save the school and the Headmaster', it is not surprising to find that the report was published.[49]

The spring term of the inspection marked the nadir in the school's fortunes during Henson's tenure. Thereafter, the school roll increased steadily, term by term: from 71 boys in May 1915 to 121 by September 1919, the increase almost entirely being accounted for by the expansion of boarding, one in four of Henson's admissions having Welsh home addresses. By September 1917, when the number of boarders had reached 70 in total, the additional accommodation provided by the acquisition of Number 1 had been filled up and extra dormitories had to be found.[50] A term later, a new boarding house opened in Broomy Hill under Mr and Mrs Felton's management.[51] This enabled the boarding community to expand to 84 (including the 12 preparatory boys) by the end of the war. A year later, at the end of Henson's tenure, boarders comprised two out of every three boys at the school,

48. The annual salaries ranged from Henson's £170 (excluding his £4 capitation allowance) to the £130 paid to Roberts. Williamson and Hudson both received a £50 boarding allowance in addition to their respective salaries of £150 and £140.

49. Not quite in full, the governors having asked the Board of Education for permission to leave out the statistical survey. Five hundred copies of the report were ordered to be printed. Unauthorised summaries were published in the local press. HCSA, GMB 1908-21, meetings 22 May 1915, 1 Aug. 1916; *HT*, 19 June 1915, p.11.

50. By using the armoury, day boys' reading room and monitors' study. *TH*, NS LXXXVI (Dec. 1917), p.2.

51. Premises were found at the old Broomy Hill Academy, Felton being given an additional £30 *per annum* towards the rent. Like other masters, his salary was steadily increased through the war, and in June 1919 there was a proposal to increase it further from £250 to £325 *per annum*, for two years only conditional on his acquiring Castle Pool House as a boarding house, an offer which was never taken up. HCSA, GMB 1908-21, meeting, 24 June 1919.

compared with one out of three in May 1913. The boarders had saved the Cathedral School, and the policy of turning HCS into a predominantly boarding establishment, to counter the threat posed by the new High School, had been vindicated; as had the Headmaster's strong promotion of his preparatory school, which by January 1918 had grown to over 50 boys (and one girl, Joanna Henson, who accompanied the boys in dancing the minuet in the front room of Number 1), occupying four rooms in School House.[52] The school in these years may have been bottom heavy, which caused all sorts of nuisances to the seniors,[53] but in numerical terms at least it was growing out of its difficulties.

The growth of the school roll enabled Henson to augment his staff, a necessary requirement given his overloaded timetable and the inspectors' criticism that he had insufficient time for supervision and administration. But it was far from easy for Henson to find suitable assistants in war time, and he had periodically to rely on the services of local clergymen, six of whom were appointed to the staff (out of 16 appointments) during his tenure. Not all were suited to the school-mastering profession. The Revd G.L. Harvey, vicar of Allensmore, whose part-time salary was privately paid by the Headmaster, was described by the inspectors as 'an obvious amateur' and was dispensed with in December 1915 when he took up an army chaplaincy. Even worse, although we do not know in what way, was the Revd E.S. Andrew, who was sacked for unspecified reasons in November 1917 after having taught at the school for less than a term. In such circumstances, it was imperative for Henson to hang on to good teachers, one of whom, the mathematician, Ralph Williamson, was repeatedly protected from taking up military duties.[54] Despite such difficulties and the dreadful physical condition of the masters' Common Room, the staff was gradually enlarged so that by the end of the war six full-time masters were in post, together with the part-time assistants in woodwork/drawing and music.[55] By the time Henson left in December 1919, although the school still lacked a rowing master, the staff had increased to seven full-time masters, including a school chaplain.[56] It was also one which was much better remunerated.

52. 32 pupils were enrolled at the preparatory school in October 1914. The following January a third classroom was added, and by April 1915 numbers had increased to 42. Henson ended his tenancy of 5, Harley Court (following Sharpley's departure) in February 1914, but the preparatory school first gained a classroom in School House the previous year (*HT*, 10 July 1943, p.4, C.F. Scott's tribute to Miss Gamlen). Henson, as effective proprietor, advertised the school locally as a department of the Cathedral School conducted in 'well lighted and well ventilated premises in the old School House'. For the dancing: HCSA, letter of L.C. Dugdale to the Headmaster, 3 Dec. 2004.

53. See, for example, the complaints about junior boarders vandalising the fives courts; First-formers 'walking about with both hands in their pockets', a 'privilege' customarily allowed only to boys in the Fifth and Sixth; and comments about the 'derogatory and degrading' conduct of the preparatory boys. *TH*, NS LXXX (Dec. 1915), pp.42-43; LXXXI (April 1916), pp.14, 31; LXXXVII (April 1918), pp.35, 37.

54. HCSA, GMB `1908-21, meetings, 10 Nov. 1915, 24 March 1917, 25 June 1918. Following Andrew's dismissal, his solicitor withdrew a threat of action against the governors at their meeting on 7 Nov. 1917.

55. *Ibid.*, meetings, 24 March, 7 Nov. 1917.

56. S.H. Burgess was the school's first chaplain. His appointment was made possible through Dean Leigh's generous provision, the Dean, as the new vicar of St John, allocating the curate's stipend to Burgess, which paid for half of his (£200) annual salary. Burgess was appointed in January 1918 but left after 18 months and was replaced as chaplain by A.J. Reed.

Indeed, increased salaries as a result of war-time inflation was one of the main reasons for the school's increasing financial strain as the war years progressed.[57] Of the three masters (including Henson) who remained at HCS from January 1915 to December 1919, the Headmaster's combined annual salary and capitation allowance increased by over 40 *per cent* to £660; and Williamson's and Felton's salaries more or less doubled to £350 and £280 respectively. This was reflected in the staff salary bill as a whole which increased over the four years from £963 at its lowest point in 1915/16 to £2,235 in 1919/20, the major increases (over £900) coming in the two years from April 1918. This is partly explained by the increase in the number of staff as the school expanded but also by the payment of substantially enhanced salaries from autumn 1918. And apart from the two years from 1915 to 1917, the salary bill was never covered by the fees income during the whole of this period, the gap widening alarmingly each year from April 1917.[58] Until the school was rescued (and we shall see shortly how this was accomplished), such deficits could only be found from the relatively meagre and largely static revenue of a foundation which could only boast an average annual income of around £750, from which had to be found all the necessary expenses for running a school at a time when costs were spiralling.[59]

Despite the growth in boarding numbers and the meagre sums spent on maintenance during the war,[60] towards its end the school, like the nation at large, was in acute financial difficulty. As with other old endowed schools, salvation came in the form of the Board of Education, whose provision for secondary schools had been extended in 1917 by the allocation of grants for advanced courses. The Hereford governors were quick off the mark, and in early March 1918 Dean Leigh approached Dr Edwards, the local HMI who had already advised the Dean of Worcester, about how his cathedral school might qualify for a grant.[61] Edwards was encouraging, and in his 15 March meeting in Hereford expressed the view that given the excellent Classics report of 1915, the school would qualify for an advanced course in Classics 'if all other conditions were satisfied' – conditions which were determined by the regulations for secondary schools of June 1904 and their subsequent revisions. Three in particular were of crucial importance to HCS: the obligation (under the 1907 Liberal amendment) on grant-earning schools to admit one quarter of its pupils free of charge; the requirement that parents 'opt in' if they agreed that their child should receive denominational

57. The following figures are taken from HCSA, account book 1894-1922, *passim*.

58. There was a £55 deficit for 1917/18; £334 for 1918/19; and £719 for 1919/20 (figures from April to April). For part of the last two years, as we will see, the deficit was more than covered by the Board of Education grants.

59. No boarding accounts from this period survive, but some indication of escalating costs of goods and services in 1917-18 may be gleaned from Henson's allowances for cleaning, lighting and heating, which were increased (by £5) to £50 in 1917/18 and to £91 12s 10 (nearer their real cost, following the governors' resolution of 13 Dec. 1918 to pay 'all expenses incurred in connection with the teaching, as opposed to the boarding, portion of the school') in 1918/19. Also see the choristers' housekeeper's claim for an additional weekly allowance of 1s 6d for each boy 'in view of the further increased prices'. HCA, 7031/24, p.19, 21 July 1917.

60. Only £25 7s 7d was spent on repairs over the two financial years, 1915-17. HCSA undated pencil calculations, *c.*May 1918.

61. On Dean Leigh's strong support for the initiative, this comment of W.N. Bruce, who had known HCS since his 1899 inspection, is revealing: '... under the influence of the present Dean, the school has long been moving in this direction'. See TNA, ED 35/995, Bruce to Mackail, 20 March 1918. The following is based on these documents: TNA, ED 35/995, 997; HCSA, GMB 1908-21, meetings, 9 Feb., 25 March, 25 June and 21 Sept. 1918.

religious instruction, rather than 'opt out' if they objected; and the necessity that representative governors should be reduced. Given the financial imperatives, the good will towards the school shown by Dean Leigh and his Chapter and the firm support of the Headmaster, the governors were willing to meet such conditions, particularly when the HMI had explained to them that it was unlikely that the Board would insist on the full 25 *per cent* free place requirement.[62] It is an indication of the extent to which the governing board had moved its position from that taken by the old Dean and his colleagues a generation or two earlier.

The negotiations between the Board of Education officials and the governors need not concern us here. What is notable, however, is the speed with which the changes were made. The detailed forms on the school finances and the organisation of the curriculum (a time analysis sheet included), together with a staff register, plans of the school premises and certificate of its sanitary condition – this caused a little difficulty, as will be related – and copies of its instruments of government, regulations for religious instruction and prospectus, were all returned to the Board a month or so before the deadline of 1 July 1918.[63] And the amendment to the scheme of government was sealed on 20 May 1919, just over a year from the initial application – in marked contrast to the delays over passage of the 1894 scheme and, to a lesser extent, the 1910 amendment. A number of ameliorating factors enabled the necessary alterations to be made with relative ease: the school's financial necessity; the governors' compliant attitude; the Board's willingness to be flexible with regard to the number of free elementary places (10 *per cent* of new admissions, estimated at 33 each year, was the agreed figure for 1918-19); and its recognition that the choristers could be excepted from the denominational rubric.[64] The governors' and Henson's relief when they received the news in mid-September 1918 that HCS had been placed on the list of recognised grant-earning secondary schools can well be imagined.[65] The precedent of government financial support for the school had been set, support which was to continue in different guises throughout much of the century.

The importance of this change to the school's prosperity can hardly be over-stated. In financial terms it meant the eventual infusion of much needed cash, the first instalment finally coming through on 29 May 1919. The grants were sizeable, amounting to £1,185 in 1918-19 and £1,585 the following year, when an advanced course in Science and Mathematics was offered as well as in Classics.[66] Consequently by April 1920, the school

62. Given that there were two boys' secondary schools in Hereford, one (the High School) allowing free places to the full 25 *per cent* of its pupils, 'and the other to a large extent a boarding school'.

63. Drafts of some of these forms are still contained in the school archives.

64. As with Southwell Minster, it was agreed by the Board's legal department that 'any religious duties required of choristers could be regarded as a condition of choristership and not as a condition of admission to or retention in the school as a pupil'. TNA, ED 35/997, Freehill to Mackail, 14 Aug. 1918.

65. Although further conditions were imposed: the passage of the new scheme; the improvement of the sanitation and premises; the provision of a single and inclusive fee covering all extras, and the separation of the boarding and tuition fees; the inclusion within the curriculum of 'manual instruction [woodwork] ... when circumstances are less abnormal'; and the printing and circulation to parents of the new regulations concerning religious instruction. The governors accepted these conditions by letter of 24 September, the maximum boarding fee being set at £54 *per annum* and the annual tuition fees at £15 3s and £17 5s (for under 12s and over 12s respectively).

66. In addition to the advanced courses grants, *per capita* payments were made of £7 per pupil (£2 for under 11s) as well as examinations fees. HCSA, Board of Education returns, 28 May 1919; account book, 1894-1922.

accounts showed a favourable balance of over £425, the largest in its history. The school's plant, too, was improved as a consequence of the grant. The Board had insisted, following the surveyor's report in May 1918 that the school's latrines, which were 'unprovided with a disconnecting chamber and a ventilatory shaft at the upper end', and its drains should be brought up to standard. Unsurprisingly, this was speedily accomplished.[67] Dr Edwards' stipulation that the classroom ceilings should be whitened, the laboratory and workshop improved and the Science equipment enhanced, 'as soon as circumstances permit', was also acted upon in the following months.[68]

Correspondingly, the award of advanced subject grants enabled the appointment of two additional staff: one to relieve the masters teaching the new Classics course, and, crucially, F.W. Brookes in May 1919 to teach advanced Science.[69] It also meant a long-needed overhaul of a curriculum that had hardly moved with the times. The major change came with the appointment of Brookes, who devised the first scheme of work for Physics and Chemistry for the six weekly lessons allocated for Sixth-form Science teaching in September 1919.[70] Nor should the impact of the Board's requirement for schemes of work in other subjects – however inadequate they seem to modern eyes – or its issue of circulars of best practice in their teaching, be underestimated.[71]

The Board's requirements further necessitated the improvement of the school's administration and governance. For example, Henson was required to devise a new admissions form, based on the Board's template, for parents to signify their approval of their son receiving 'religious instruction distinctive of the Church of England'. He also used the opportunity to state, probably for the first time, that if a boy was peremptorily withdrawn, a full term's fees was to be paid in default of one term's notice. Attendance registers likewise needed to be improved: the Board examined them yearly before sanctioning a grant to ensure that they were 'in every respect complete'. In terms of governance, the governing body under the 1919 scheme was remodelled so that it now consisted of five representative governors, three (rather than five) of whom were appointed by the Dean and Chapter, and two *ex officio* governors. Lay expertise was thereby strengthened and the Chapter's in-built majority eliminated.[72] In addition, as the Board observed in its accompanying letter of early

---

67. By W. Rowberry, at a cost of £25 10s, plus £6 16s 6d to James Taylor, the Hereford surveyor, for his report, specification and supervision of the works. The rebuilding of the urinal walls, however, was not done until the following year, when W. Preece was paid the substantial sum of £45 18s 9d for the works.

68. In 1919-20, £38 0s 3d was spent on improvements to the laboratory and workshop and £84 13s 11d (to W. Preece and Dredge, the cabinet maker) on other repairs.

69. Brookes spent almost 25 years at HCS, dying (in post) in tragic circumstances in November 1943. See below, p.426.

70. An indication of the advances made under Brookes in 1919 is provided by an examination of the five page Science scheme, submitted to the Board 28 May 1919, in the school archives, one page of which was devoted to Chemistry (inorganic, organic and practical) and four to Physics (heat, light, sound, magnetism, electricity and general Physics). This should be compared with the sketchy Science submission of the previous year.

71. Although at least one educationalist, who was to become Headmaster of HCS, poured scorn on both these circulars and their author, W.N. Bruce: Crees (1915), pp.102-03.

72. The other two representative governors were to be appointed by the city council and county council respectively, the mayor and the chairman of the county council completing (as the *ex officio* governors) the seven members of the new governing body.

February 1919, some amendments to the earlier schemes were introduced and 'rendered desirable by modern conditions in secondary education, changes in the regulations and recent legislation'. These included the repeal of the 1893 clause relating to the Headmaster's pension fund 'in view of the passing of the School Teachers (Superannuation) Act, 1918', legislation which the newly designated and salaried Clerk to the Governors had difficulty in locating.[73]

The 1918 Act was also of consequence for the further development of the school's constitution. For less than four months after the sealing of the 1919 amendment, enquiries were made to the Board to see whether the scheme could again be altered to enable the preparatory mistresses to benefit from the Act's superannuation provisions in the same way as the senior masters, the mistresses being debarred from the provisions of the 1893 scheme which prevented the admission to the school of boys under 10 (the choristers apart). A formal application was then made in early 1920 (shortly after Henson's departure) to bring the preparatory department under the governors' financial control, the amending scheme finally being sealed on 11 June 1920.[74] Given that the new Headmaster made a tidy income from the preparatory enterprise, it was not, as we shall see, the most carefully considered initiative.

1914-1918 : Play and Service

How was the school's 'vigorous corporate life' (as witnessed by the 1915 inspectors) carried on during the war? The boys returned for the beginning of term on 18 September 1914 to find, as one of them later reported, 'that Hereford was in a military whirlwind'. 'Wherever one went', he continued, 'one met soldiers either drilling or strolling about', adding 'but in spite of these things the time-honoured routine of school life went on as before'.[75] This may have been the perspective in the autumn of 1914, but as the conflict continued not only beyond that Christmas but well beyond the next three festive seasons, the school's activities, like those of English society at large, became increasingly determined by the demands of a war the like of which had never before been experienced in human history.

Games, which the Board had recognised played such 'a necessary part' in HCS life,[76] inevitably suffered. The assistant masters, not least Duncan Felton, did a valiant job to keep them going, but in the circumstances of the times Henson was unable to appoint an all-round sportsman to replace Arthur Jones or find an oarsman to coach rowing. That sport declined, relying as it did in these war years on the captain of the Hereford club or a senior pupil to coach the crews, and a small pool of older boys few of whom could swim let alone row. Similarly, the call to arms of senior boys, especially in the early war years when the school roll was decreasing, resulted in some weak cricket and football XIs. The difficulty

73. A.D. Steel's responsibilities to the school were recognised, for the first time, in September 1918, when he was paid £50 *per annum* in addition to his salary as Chapter Clerk. By 1920, he had also become mayor and an *ex officio* governor.

74. TNA, ED 35/998.

75. *TH*, NS LXXVII (Dec. 1918), p.1.

76. TNA, ED 35/995, letter to clerks, 13 Sept. 1918, when suggesting that games expenses were included within the tuition fee.

of war-time travel after August 1916, when petrol was rationed and (later that year) rail services were slashed and train fares doubled,[77] also meant that fixtures were curtailed. Local games against the two Worcester schools and Bradley Court, and Lucton and St Michael's Tenbury for the junior teams, survived; other pre-war matches were lost, an early casualty being the games against 'the Past' because (as it was described in *The Herefordian* following the demise of the rowing challenge against the OHs in July 1915) 'all available men' were 'serving in the army'. So HCS found itself playing more home matches, when they could be arranged, against men from local military or works stations, like the Monmouthshire Royal Engineers, the Rotherwas Barracks, the Rotherwas Munitions Works, the Army Ordnance Depot at Credenhill and the Wireless Training Centre at Worcester. And the school was usually beaten.[78] The number of competitive matches may have declined but the war years were witness to the enduring popularity of fives, especially among the boarders, and the damaged courts were rebuilt by the end of 1917.[79]

Other activities were also affected by the war, if only indirectly. The Debating Society chose such motions as 'young men under 20 … should not go into the firing line', 'this House greatly appreciates the efforts of those who, although under military age, try to enlist' and 'this House does not deplore the cutting down of the height limit of the army'. That the first motion was lost and the second and third were won gives some idea of the temper of the school in December 1915. Lectures, like those on trench warfare, the war in Palestine and the air service, invariably had a military theme. Even Canon Bannister, when he gave his paper in his high-pitched voice to the Literary Society to mark its 100th meeting on 31 March 1916, could refer to 'the cruel and immoral tyranny of Prussian savagery', his talk being followed by readings of patriotic poetry. And then there were the war charities, money, for example, being raised for the National Egg Fund (£4 6s 8 ½d in November 1915) and the Public Schools Hospital, nearly £16 being collected from a special entertainment and in lieu of sports day prizes in the spring of 1916.[80]

But one organisation flourished in the war years as no other: the Officer Training Corps. Even so, it was not an easy time to be commanding officer of a school contingent. Following the rapid departures of Horsley and Broadland, the lot eventually fell to Duncan Felton, who was gazetted second lieutenant from January 1915. The sergeant instructors proved impossible to replace, the school relying for professional support on Major Phillips, as we have seen, and then on flying visits from old boys on leave. But for the most part it was

77. Marwick, pp.210, 218; *HMC Report 1916*, minutes of the Rugby meeting, 21-22 Dec. 1916, p.75. The Board of Trade subsequently refused an HMC request in October 1917 for more school journeys to be allowed. For petrol rationing, also see Henson, p.265. The new Bishop of Hereford had visited the petrol controller's office in Berkeley Street, London, on 28 February 1918 (noting the 'excited and incompetent flappers'), and was promised by 'a dejected female' a monthly supply of 30 gallons.

78. Although the XI won by an innings against 12 men of the 4th Loyal North Lancashire regiment on 26 June 1915, one of three victories that summer. Daly Briscoe, in an unpublished memoir in the school archives, describes playing cricket in these years against the polar explorer R.E. Priestley (later Sir Raymond), who served at the Wireless Training Centre 1914-17, as well as a first-class cricketer named Lawson.

79. *TH*, NS LXXXI (April 1916), p.14, for the 'deplorable' state of the junior court; and NS LXXXVI (Dec. 1917), p. 44, letter from 'Fives Enthusiast' about the new courts. Also see note 53 above.

80. By October 1919, subscriptions to the Public Schools Hospital fund from all schools amounted to over £35,000. *HMC 1919 Committee Report*, p.53.

down to Felton and boy NCOs to command a corps which doubled in size to over 70 cadets by 1918. Their charges, moreover, did not always take kindly to the discipline imposed, and had to be reminded 'that position in school and rank in the corps' were 'totally independent of each other' and that in the case of breaches of corps discipline, corps rank was the only one that counted. And at least on one occasion towards the end of the war, when the commanding officer was perhaps not as sensitive as he might have been, matters came to a head in the form of open defiance, as a senior cadet later remembered:

> We had one serious rag which was in the nature of a revolt in the corps. We had drills at all times which were, of course, accepted by all as part of our duty, but the chosen afternoon for the school regatta in this particular year, either 1917 or 1918, the master commanding the OTC decided should be given up also to extra drill. This was felt to be a real injustice and the NCOs connived at almost open rebellion. Most of the ranks paraded slovenly with buttons and collars undone; one or two with shoes instead of boots, and one boy with a red sock on one foot and a yellow one on the other (part of the colour scheme for the junior forms) which were ... visible below the puttees. The outcome was that the Head Boy was deprived of his monitorship by the Headmaster. The remaining monitors, of whom I was one, had been also involved, as were all NCOs, and we sought an interview with the HM and elected to be treated similarly; which was done, and for the rest of that term there were no monitors.[81]

OTCs, too, were not high on the list of War Office priorities. Some of the War Office instructions issued to school contingents in September 1914 were found to be difficult to implement, particularly when rifles and ammunition were taken away and the public school field days and camps, together with the 'Certificate A' examinations, were suspended.[82] Still, the HCS corps seems to have muddled through better than most. The instruction that 'any kind of physical training tending to harden the boys and to train them to endurance of fatigue', especially, was taken seriously. Route marches were regularly practised, despite the difficulties in making them successful 'owing to the differences in sizes'. None was more testing than that of 27 February 1918, when the cadets endured an eight-hour-day's march in snowy weather to Credenhill (via Breinton) and back. Moreover, they had rations for just one meal, the days of January 1915 when the entire contents of a baker's cart were bought to stave off hunger on a field day being long gone. Only two casualties were reported.[83] Other activities, such as uniform parades (twice weekly on Mondays and Thursday afternoons from January 1916), local field exercises, semaphore signalling, musketry practices (including sticking bayonets into mounted sacks on Wyeside for the over 16s) and endless drill, made up most of the rest of the time. And then there were the summer camps, which although voluntary attracted good numbers and were organised on a school basis – at Garway in 1916, Credenhill in 1917 and, under the auspices of the Ministry of National

81. HCSA, Daly Briscoe collection, unpublished memoir.

82. See, for example, the Headmaster of Sedbergh's criticisms in his speech of 22 December 1915, *HMC Report 1915*, p.13; and above, note 33, for the September 1914 War Office instructions.

83. The juniors were due to return by train but it never turned up (a war-time hazard), and they were diverted by having to fight a rear-guard action all the way back to Hereford. *TH*, NS LXXXVII (April 1918), p.24.

Service, Crickhowell for three weeks from mid-August 1918, when the boys helped to bring home the local harvest.[84]

Overall, the value of some of these activities might be questioned, or even today derided, but it is undeniable that the backbone of the young British officers on the western front before conscription was provided by men who had first served in their school corps. The War Office well recognised the value of this service, and referred (in a letter of 20 March 1919, sent to all school contingents) to their 'great work' during the war. The same letter continued:

> In the early months of the war, the number of vacancies filled in the commissioned ranks of the army by ex-cadets ... fully justified the formations of the corps in 1908, and afforded an able testimony of the standard of training and powers of leadership which had been inculcated ... The lists of those who have fallen and of those who have been mentioned in despatches and decorated show how grandly the ex-Officers' Training Corps cadets have fought for King and Country, and form a record of which the schools may be justly proud.[85]

And for a relatively small corps, the Cathedral School's war record was commendable. At the signing of the Armistice, of the boys on the school roll at the beginning of the war and who had joined the forces during the conflict – that is those young men between the ages of 18 and 22 – 48 were officers (or waiting to be commissioned) and eight were in the ranks; eight had been killed, eight wounded and two taken prisoner; and two had won the Military Cross.[86] All told, nearly 500 Old Herefordians (including 50 or so former choristers) had joined up, 79 are known to have lost their lives, around one in five had been wounded, 47 had been awarded the Military Cross and 62 mentioned in official despatches.[87] The school, like many others, had played its part in the eventual victory but it had been a costly sacrifice. (Plates 14 and 15).

A hundred years on, it is hard to appreciate the spirit of patriotism that swept through a small public school on the English borders during these war years; or how torn Henson must have been as he signed character references for his young men as they applied for commissions. It is equally difficult to recreate the atmosphere at HCS during that time as the roll of honour lengthened and the Headmaster read out the names of the fallen in Big School and later in the Lady Chapel, the new school chapel which was used for morning

---

84. *TH*, NS LXXXIX (Dec. 1918), pp.26-29. The competition for the longest hours worked by any boy in any one day was won by O.W. Richards (13 hours). 4,500 boys were involved from over 100 schools in 1917 and around double the number in 1918. Recommended payment (in 1917) was between £4 10s and £5 for 25 boys, each working a seven hour day. On the operation of the public school land camps in 1917-18, see the *HMC Committee Reports*, 16 May 1917, 14 Feb. 1918; *HMC Report 1917*, pp.41ff.

85. *TH*, NS XC (April 1919), p.13, letter from B.B. Cubitt. The British Expeditionary Force of 1914 comprised some 100,000 men and about 7,000 officers, the vast majority of whom would have been former public schoolboys who had served in their school corps. Seldon and Walsh, p.39.

86. *Ibid.*, NS LXXXIX (Dec. 1918), p.27.

87. Martin Everett OH has generously given me access to his extensive research on Old Herefordians who saw active service in the Great War. He has calculated that 163 decorations in all were made to OHs. For incomplete lists: Eales-White, pp.130-41.

assemblies from September 1917.[88] Nor can we at this distance fully understand, as Old Herefordian decorations mounted, the sense of pride as half-holidays were awarded in recognition of acts of bravery as well as academic achievement. Nor, apart from the occasional reference, do we know much about the deprivations suffered by the school community as food prices continued to rise and rationing was imposed during the last two war years. The letter to *The Herefordian* in early 1918 from the boy who signed himself 'iron rations', suggesting that every boarder should be able to claim his half pound weekly sugar ration (rather than the rations being pooled) and that puddings should be sugar free, is one tiny indication of the hardships endured.[89] Another is provided by the evidence of the aptly named HMC War Economies sub-committee, which suggested that school communities could save money by simplifying dress, reducing the number and cost of books, ensuring that both sides of the paper were written on, spending less on games, limiting pocket money and substituting margarine for butter, as well as anthracite instead of coke for heating.[90] There is reason to believe, as we have seen with the abolition of athletic prizes, that HCS adopted some of these measures. What we know with certainty, however, after such a time of 'patience and fortitude', is the unrestrained joy of 11 November 1918, following the signing of the Armistice, when 'the schools were all let out and the boys were rushing about cheering'.[91] The event inspired this editorial:

> After Christmas, we were at last able to return to our studies freed from the doubt and anxiety of war, and several of us who expected in a short time to have the privilege of serving our King and Country find ourselves destined for the quiet peacefulness of yet another year at school. We fully agree with the sentiment of *dulce et decorum est pro patria mori* ... yet still few of us are sorry that instead of having to die for our country we are now called upon to live for it.[92]

How one boy responded in the first year of peace will be examined in some detail.

S.R.J. Addison's Diary, 1919

The son of a London hotelier, Sydney Robert James Addison attended HCS as a boarder between the ages of 9 and 16 from 1913 to 1920. He spent the first five of these years as a cathedral chorister, first under Dr Sinclair and then under the two temporary organists who were employed between Sinclair's death in February 1917 and Percy Hull's appointment

---

88. Dean Leigh, when he became vicar of St John's, put the Lady Chapel at the school's disposal not only for Sunday Matins (as Bishop Percival had suggested) but also for morning prayer at 9am on week-days. For his provision for a school chaplain, see above p.357, note 56.

89. On food prices, shortages and rationing in general during the war, see Marwick, pp.205-18; and in public schools, *HMC Committee Report*, 14 March 1918, pp.34-36.

90. *HMC Committee Report*, 14 March 1916, pp.34-36.

91. 'Patience and fortitude' were the words used by Major Walker, the school's inspecting officer, when referring to the 'great push' in the summer of 1916. *TH*, NS LXXXII (July 1916), p.19. For the description of Armistice Day in Hereford, see HCSA, Daly Briscoe memoir.

92. *TH*, NS XC (April 1919), p.2. Daly Briscoe, who had left HCS in July 1918, had more mixed feelings about the Armistice, believing (incorrectly as it turned out) that he had missed 'the one big thing' that was likely to happen in his life-time.

in late 1918.[93] We know that Sydney was a bright boy who showed academic strengths on the Arts side, passing the Oxford Junior Locals with a distinction in Scripture in 1918, and winning school prizes the following year in German, English and History. He was also a gifted sportsman, who by the time he was 15 had played for the 1st cricket and football XIs. Had he not left the school at 16 – quite why we do not know – he might well have gone on to emulate his elder brother's achievements.[94] So Sydney's HCS career is not dissimilar to hundreds of other former choristers, who over the centuries have gone on to excel in other spheres once their treble days were over – except in one important respect: he kept a continuous record of his doings at the school for the whole of a calendar year, an account that provides a unique insight into the life of a 14/15 year old boarder during that momentous first year of peace and in the last year of Henson's headship.

Produced by Charles Letts & Co and bound in 'art linen with back loop pencil' at a cost of 1s 6d (there was also an edition bound in French Moroccan leather at twice the price), Sydney's journal was as much a schoolboy's note-book as a pocket diary, containing as it did 'much useful information and many tables helpful for his work and play, and £1,000 accident insurance'.[95] Most prominent of these tables were the double spread pages on the inside covers, with 32 colour illustrations (at the front) depicting 'decorations awarded for honourable service in the great European and other wars of recent years' and (at the back) a black and white map of the western front during the Great War, a reminder that the war may not have ended as the diary was being printed. Although the young Addison did not part with the shilling to the General Accident Fire and Life Assurance Corporation Ltd in Perth to claim the insurance benefit – the insurance 'coupon' still remains intact, uncompleted and neatly folded in the diary nearly a century later – the 1919 diary clearly became a prize possession for its owner.

Although, as might be expected, the diary is essentially a personal school record, it inevitably reflects the nature of the times in that new post-war world. 'Tuck' provision, after wartime privations, played a major part in Addison's life in 1919. So we learn that on 28 January, he paid 1s 6d for éclairs, doughnuts and iced cakes 'just like old times'. A few days later, he reported that 'much better sweets and tuck' could be obtained 'all over town', Addison again spending 1s 6d on toffee and cakes. Pre-war flour may have returned but some foodstuffs were still rationed, as indicated by his receipt on 1 March of a small parcel of butter from his mother in Newbury. At this time, 'reconstruction' had for many months been the watchword of every politician, the Ministry of Reconstruction as war ended being in the hands of Sydney's namesake, Dr Christopher Addison. At a local level, this was reflected in the provision of a series of Oxford extension lectures in Hereford Town Hall by G.S. Horsborough, Sydney with the rest of the Fifth and Sixth attending a talk on 17 February on 'Industrial

93. He sang in the cathedral choir from 1913 to 1918, coinciding with his brother Eric for the first four of those years. HCA, 7104/6, Tomson's charity accounts 1913-18, *passim*.

94. Eric Arthur Addison was also a chorister (1912-16). By 1920, he had been appointed Head of School, as well as captain of rowing and cricket. His died that year, 'leaving behind him a very fine influence and example on the boys at the school of his period'. Eales-White, p.44.

95. It was compiled by Marc Cope of Whitgift, the version in the school archives (without the pencil) being embossed with 'Hereford Cathedral School' in white lettering. For the paucity of extant schoolboy diaries in the period before 1914, see Fletcher (2008), chapter 20.

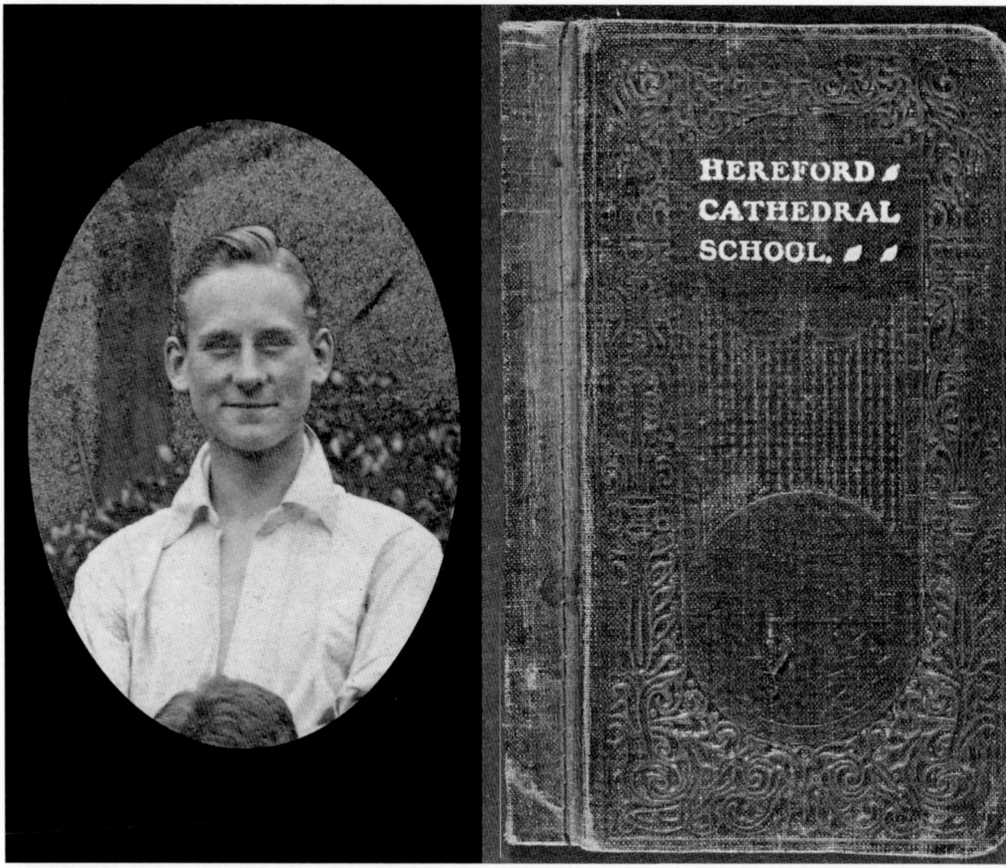

Fig. 7.3 Sydney Addison, aged 15, and the front cover of his 1919 diary.

Reconstruction'.[96] But post-war reconstruction was to be bedevilled by industrial unrest, making 1919 a year of strikes. Even young Addison was sufficiently concerned to note on 21 February that the 'labour outlook was very bad', the miners having voted for a general strike. By early autumn, on 27 September, he recorded that a 'great universal strike' (the national railway strike) had begun. Such was its impact on the school that the interviews for Henson's successor, initially scheduled for 30 September, had to be postponed. Not that Sydney would have known this, but on the weekend of 5 October he listened – more attentively, perhaps, than some of his friends – to Bishop Hensley Henson's 45 minute sermon on the strike, pronouncing it 'very fine'.[97] That afternoon, on returning to the Palace after Evensong, the Bishop discovered that the strike had ended – at 4.15 according to our young scribe – the railwaymen having won their main point, the abandonment of a proposed wage cut.

96. In these extension lectures, which first started as early as 1878, Oxford dons provided a programme of thematic talks 'beyond the limits of the university'. By 1919, there would have been scores of extension centres (including the one in Hereford) throughout the country.

97. HCSA, GMB 1908-21, meeting, 30 Sept. 1919. Bishop Henson referred to his sermon in his autobiography (vol i., pp.316-17). He observed that he had needed 'to suppress the coughing of the choir boys and school at the beginning of the sermon' but that the congregation then 'listened closely throughout'.

By this time, the cathedral's musical establishment had returned to its pre-war strength. Percy Hull, having been interned in Germany for most of the war, had been appointed organist (initially for one year) in October 1918, the place having been temporarily filled for some 20 months following Dr Sinclair's death in February 1917.[98] The lay clerks' ranks, too, were soon complete after their release from war-time service, Addison noting as early as 2 February 1919 that a Handel anthem had been sung by 'a whole pre-war-men choir' for Evensong, a Candlemas service that (Canon Bannister's sermon apart) he had much enjoyed.[99] Indeed, as a former Hereford chorister, Sydney was in a good position to comment on the two Sunday services that each boarder was required to attend. Now that the school was using the Lady Chapel for its own service,[100] the Sunday morning regime was presumably more palatable for boarders in 1919 than it had been a few years earlier, but this did not prevent the astute younger Addison from making critical comments about the services. On 9 March, for example, he confided to his diary that chapel was 'hopeless', Brown's playing and Burgess (the chaplain's) sermon coming in for particular censure. Still, things were better when the Headmaster or Mr Scott[101] preached or when he was able to join his brother Eric at the harmonium. And following the arrival of a new chaplain, Mr Reed, in September, the services (to Sydney's mind) showed a distinct improvement.[102]

In between morning chapel at 10 and evening prayer (with sermon) at 6.30, Sydney Addison could experience the quiet delights of Sunday afternoons in the Herefordshire countryside. His Sunday walks took him on 9 February over Aylestone Hill where he watched people skating on Lugg Meadows; on 23 March, he visited Belmont Abbey for the first time ('didn't like it much'); and on 26 October, he 'got heaps of lovely apples' from an unnamed local orchard. 'These "slacks" are so enjoyable', he confided to his diary on 4 May after a leisurely walk on the banks of the Wye to Belmont woods. And sometimes the enjoyment was enhanced by an invitation to Sunday tea, perhaps at Mrs George's, the Gores, the Dunnetts, or, on one occasion, Mr Felton's at Broomy Hill.[103]

Sydney, as one of the more senior boarders, experienced a good deal of freedom at other times. Before the beginning of each term, he was allowed to go the Kemble Theatre, paying 2 shillings for the privilege on the evening of 1 May, when he saw a good show including 'some motoring in mid-air'. During the course of the year, there were also a

98. HCA, 7031/24, pp.40, 46, Acts of 10 Oct. 1918 and 2 Jan. 1919, appointing Hull (from 11 Nov.) and remunerating George Banks and Gordon Brown for their services.

99. At least three permanent or temporary lay clerks – Messrs Jinks, Proctor and Jones – had joined the forces and another had been allowed to work on the land. HCA, 7031/23, p. 498, Act, 11 Nov. 1915; HCA, 7031/24, p.4, Act, 6 June 1916; HCA, 7003/1/7, College Act, 24 Oct. 1918 re war bonuses.

100. See above, pp. 365, note 88. The boarders, however, continued to attend special Sunday morning services in the body of the cathedral, as (in 1919) on 'Thanksgiving Sunday' on 6 July and to hear Bishop Henson on 5 October.

101. Revd C.H. Scott, assistant master at HCS September 1918 to March 1920, when he left for a curacy at St Jude's, Acton Green.

102. For Burgess, who left in July 1919 after 18 months for Ardingly College, see above, pp. 357, note 56. Reed also had a short tenure as chaplain, leaving HCS in December 1920 to become rector of Withington. Addison received a number of impositions from Burgess (who was his Housemaster) and this may in part explain the boy's attitude towards him in chapel.

103. For D.G.W. Felton, assistant master in French and German (1913-20), see above, pp.356, 361, 362. The other names have not been traced.

number of 'halves' – half-days outside the normal Wednesday and Saturday games afternoons, awarded at the Headmaster's discretion. As a clever boy, he gained all four 'merit' holidays, although on 4 March he had dropped two places to sixth 'because of my wretched averages in Maths, French and Science'. In addition, Henson allowed eight more that year: one for H.H. Grimwade's Brasenose exhibition; one at the special request of Bishop Walmsley OH, the Bishop of Sierra Leone; two seemingly as a result of the weather: on 14 February during the arctic freeze, and 11 July in the midst of a heat wave; several for no specified reason (at least none that our diarist could fathom); and, importantly, one on Monday 30 June 'in honour of signing of peace'.[104] The 'half' that was Addison's due after his Confirmation on 4 April was cancelled because 'some rotter bagged Thomas' razor [and] wouldn't own up'. The boys were detained for three-and-a-half hours and the razor was later found in Mr Glennie's garden.[105] Otherwise, he used these occasions for outdoor pursuits or simply (as he admitted on 11 November) to play the fool. 'Halves' in 1919 came about once every three weeks on average, but even on a weekly basis the grind of a near 25-hour academic timetable – with the exception of the periods set aside for the OTC and PT – was relieved each day by an extended lunch break. Time could sometimes be found in these 100 minutes for occasional visits to the town to replenish tuck boxes. And then there were the periodic excursions and treats, such as visits to the Town Hall on 31 March, when 'Mr Gethen OH showed and explained to us all the city plate and charters'; to the Racecourse to watch H.K. Foster's XI be humbled by the Australians on 16 and 17 July;[106] and to the Green Dragon on 25 November, when a Mr Bailey of Malvern treated Sydney to lunch and gave him £1, a present which stabilised his pocket money account.[107]

The diary reveals something of Sydney's pastimes and amusements: skating, ice hockey and playground sliding during the frosty days of February; unofficial boxing matches in early March after Lewis had been given 'some topping boxing gloves'; boating and bathing in the Wye on hot summer afternoons; and games of bridge at other idle moments. We also learn about the occasional dormitory frolics, as on the nights of 23 January, when the seniors 'ragged' the lower seniors, and 6 April when a 'great rag' was described as being well worth both Burgess' wrath and copying out 20 pages as a punishment. It seems to have mattered little that both revels took place on Sunday nights.

We can also gauge a little of the small – and in the case of illness, large – change of a boarders' world. Sydney's weekly baths (he only once mentions taking a shower) on Sunday evenings were of sufficient novelty to warrant a few entries. School haircuts were periodically recorded, as on 18 February. ('Abominably done! I must look a wreck!') A strict order

104. The Peace of Versailles was 'signed between belligerent nations' on 28 June 1919, as Sydney recorded (in capital letters) in his diary. On Sunday 6 July, the boarders attended a 'very impressive' thanksgiving service in the cathedral, and they were given an additional exeat weekend on 19 and 20 July for the national peace celebrations.

105. Revd W.B. Glennie lived in the College and was later (in 1933) elected Custos, the last before the 1936 dissolution. The culprit presumably threw the razor from a back window in School House into Glennie's garden.

106. Henry Knolls Foster ('Harry') (1873-1950), was the eldest of the seven Foster brothers who all played cricket for Worcestershire. He was a land agent in the town, who from 1918 (after the retirement of C.B. Beddoe) acted for the vicars choral. HCA, 7003/1/7, pp.259, 261, 263, College Acts, 5 Feb. to 24 Oct. 1918.

107. Sydney described this day, which ended with him going to a choral concert, as 'one of the best days in my existence'. Mr Bailey ('about the nicest chap I ever met') has not been identified.

governed boarders' places for prep. Pocket-money was 6d a week. Boarders' possessions could be traded, as with the loan of Addison's skates to Peacock for 5d on 12 February, and items were occasionally raffled. Betting (in eggs) on the results of the regatta was rife. Two types of punishments were recorded: pages, Sydney receiving nearly 200, many from his Housemaster, Mr Burgess, in 27 separate incidents during 1919; and (from NCOs in the corps) punishment drills, which could last hours and be spread over several days. But Sydney was never beaten nor is there any indication of fagging or bullying. In an age when a boarder might stay at school continuously for 13 weeks, correspondence with home was an important task, Sydney replying to some 35 letters received in the first two terms of 1919. A boarders' vulnerability to illness, perhaps especially in the aftermath of the First World War,[108] was exposed by the prevalence of infectious diseases, the outbreak of chicken-pox in late November being especially severe and resulting in 'a general exodus' and the cancellation of nine football fixtures.

Apart from recording the occasional test, the timings of examinations – 31 March to 4 April for internal exams and the ten days from 17 July for the Oxford Local Senior certificate[109] – and one or two other references, young Addison reveals little about the academic side of the school. The historian would have liked to know more as to why he found Tuesday lessons so 'rotten', and what was so 'topping' about PT on 3 June. As a former chorister, he also sometimes mentions his weekly music lessons but what he thought about them is again unknown. And there are only tangential comments about the masters. He liked both Henson and Brookes, the new science master, despised Burgess, his Housemaster, and once described 'old Scott', his form-master, as a 'silly idiot', following 'a great rag' in his lesson.

Addison's diary, then, is essentially an extra-curricular record. When, as on 24 November, he writes 'nothing happened at all' – and 'nothing happened' very rarely – what he really means is that there were no games or other diversions that he considered worthy of record. On the other hand, entries referring to his non-academic activities abound. Sometimes these are of a cultural bent, such as concerts or debates, as on 22 February when Sydney, 'in a degree conducive to laughter', supported his elder brother's motion that 'a League of Nations is desirable'.[110] But, overwhelmingly, and the daily weather reports apart, the diary is a record of outdoor activities, a reflection of Sydney's own inclinations as much as the nature of HCS at the time.

For the young man had a passionate interest in sport. References are even made to national events like the billiards championship,[111] a game Sydney enjoyed at his club in the holidays and occasionally at the YMCA in Hereford, and the Carpentier versus Beckett

108. A virulent influenza epidemic broke out throughout Britain (and many other countries) in 1918-19, with a particularly high incidence among young adults. Marwick, pp.277-78.

109. These Oxford locals were interrupted by a weekend away at the Lloyds (K.A. Lloyd, was a contemporary of his brother) in Radnorshire for the national peace thanksgiving on 19 July. For the ceremonies on this day in Hereford: Henson, pp.312-13.

110. See *TH*, NS XC (April 1919), pp.14-15, for an account of this debate. The motion was lost by 15 votes.

111. After noting the scores over several rounds, Addison lovingly records the final result on Monday 24 March, Inman winning the championship from Stevenson by 6,532 points, the cup being presented (presumably on the previous Saturday) by Horatio Bottomley, the journalist and financier and Independent MP for South Hackney at the time.

boxing match for the European title, and the dates of the horse racing 'classics' and the Eton-Harrow cricket match are noted. But, above all, at a more humble level, it is his own trials and tribulations in school sport that he lovingly records. Through Sydney's eyes, we see his efforts to support his elder brother, who was captain of rowing. Having 'tubbed' for the first time, he attempts to get fit in the frosty days of early February by an early morning regimen of PT and cold baths, together with attempting to refrain from eating between meals. His training regime, however, was soon interrupted, partly by his chilblains and hunger but in the main because of ice and then floods, and it was not until 17 March that he resumed his physical exertions. Despite these interruptions, he rowed with Owain Richards[112] in the heats of the coxed junior pairs, the crew starting as favourites only to lose by a foot, 'owing to misunderstanding the course and a crab by me'. So Sydney spent regatta day itself in the appreciative company of Miss Lloyd – she gave him a rosette – rather than exerting himself on the river.

That winter term, however, his real passion was that 'most enjoyable game', fives. Sydney lost no opportunity to have a game, sometimes playing twice a day after morning and afternoon school and lamenting one Sunday (23 March) that the courts were out of bounds in such gorgeous weather. And although he was not selected for the representative fixtures against Brecon and King's, Worcester, and was beaten in the early rounds of the junior singles and doubles competitions, his game showed rapid improvement so that by the end of the season in early April, he was beating his great rival, Yendoll, more often than not. Around the same time, he won the junior high jump and throwing the cricket ball contests on sports day, gaining 'a WHS pen and a decent pair of pads' for his efforts.

In the glorious summer of 1919, Sydney's favourite sport was leavened by bathing, usually up river although occasionally in the cold public baths, boating, and more seriously towards the end of term, sculling, in which he reached the junior finals before 'collapsing after leading by half a length'. But it was cricket that predominated, with nets after school on Mondays and Fridays and practices or matches on Wednesday and Saturday afternoons. The diary gives us some idea of his prowess at the game. He played five times for the 1st XI and despite, to his brother's annoyance, his 'funk' of leg balls in the nets, he proved himself a useful bat with a top score of 27 not out against Monmouth. At just 15, it was a reasonable hope that he would eventually have emulated Eric's feat (at the end on the 1919 season and with the aid of his new 'imperial driver') in winning the Woods batting cup.

It was the same that autumn, as a young player on the fringes of the 1st football XI. He had kept goal (at 14) once or twice for the XI the previous season, when his captain, his brother's friend Kenneth Lloyd, who had represented the public schools against the Woolwich RMA, reported that his keeping suffered 'from lack of size' and that he needed to 'improve his ground saves'.[113] Sydney kept his position for the first few games of 1919, but after the 7-2 drubbing against King's, Worcester, he was dropped to the 2nd XI. That match, however, was only one of three losses from 17 representative games all told, and it was unfortunate that the chicken-pox outbreak meant that for the last month of the season, practice matches – like the Sixth against the rest (including Mr Felton and Dr Tasker, a

112. Owain Westmacott Richards (1901-84), who became a distinguished entomologist.

113. *TH*, XC (April 1919), p.11.

former Bristol City forward) – replaced the official fixture list. And sometimes there were other diversions. On Saturday 6 December, for example, our diarist writes that 'many chaps went to see football matches in the town' in the place of watching the return match against the High School Old Boys that was due to be played that afternoon. Sydney was not one of them. But how far his 'ground saves' had improved and how much he had grown (he was 5 feet 6 inches and under 9 stone in early 1919) is unrecorded.[114]

One other activity, which continued throughout the year, occupied a prominent place both in Sydney's record and his life at school, and that was the corps. Now with a time-tabled lesson on Thursday afternoon, he invariably commented on the weekly parade: whether the elements would mean that it was cancelled; whether it was to be 'undress' or uniform; where it happened (usually in the playground, with platoon drill on Castle Green, and occasionally at Wyeside); and who took it – sometimes 'the parade maniac', F.J.P. Parker of the Fosse;[115] but more usually a master, the popular Mr Felton (who nevertheless ordered a full uniform parade on 27 February, lasting two hours, because it was alleged that he had overheard someone say 'he was a slacker about parades') or the 'jolly decent' Mr Brookes. And at the beginning of term, after Thursday morning school, time was spent cleaning rifles and side arms in preparation for the afternoon martial exercises. Then there were the 'highlights' of each term: the section competition, popularly won by Eric's section that April, with his younger brother's platoon, as Sydney had forecast, trailing by 50 points under the 'slack and indifferent' Corporal G.W.H. Davies;[116] the escorting of the colours of the returning 1st Herefords from the station through the great crowds in High Town on 23 May, when the school was given another half-day; the inspection on 17 July by Major E.A. Capel MC OH of that same regiment, who was 'very bucked with us'; and the two field days on 17 June, consisting of a route march 'in skirmishing order' from Ashperton to Hereford on which the boys averaged 4 miles per hour, and the inter-school competition on 31 October at Wellington, Shropshire, when 'we beat Shrewsbury all ends up', only for Sydney and his chums to be later rewarded with six hours punishment drill 'for Friday's escapade', the details of which are unknown. It is not hard to conclude that in 1919 the OTC was among Sydney's least favourite pursuits.

Yet it was in his character to make the best of it. He had a sunny disposition, which (as in the debate on 22 February) made people laugh, and his energy and enthusiasm for whatever HCS had to offer is apparent throughout the diary. On most days, for Sydney (as he recorded on 16 May) it was 'absolutely a joy to be alive', despite the deprivations of the post-war world and, as it seems to us, the hardships of being a boarder in School House in the grim winter and stifling summer of 1919. And he was a talented and popular boy. Like many former choristers before and since, he set himself high standards in work and play, even though he was competing in lessons and in games against boys two or three years older

---

114. Not much, perhaps we should conclude, given Lloyd's comment a year later that he was still 'very weak', although he added: 'but fortunately [he] still retains his proverbial luck'. *TH*, NS XCIII (April 1920), p.7.

115. The 'Jacobean' villa, probably built to the design of Robert Smirke in *c.*1825 (who at this time was engaged to build a pedimented constable's cottage on Castle Green), north of Castle Cliffe.

116. *TH*, NS XCIII (April 1920), p.12. Davies later made good, becoming Head Monitor and platoon Sergeant in 1920. Following his Oxford degree, he was ordained in December 1925, and was subsequently appointed a minor canon of Brecon Cathedral. Eales-White, p.66.

than himself. It is not too much of an exaggeration to suggest that Sydney Addison, by devoting himself 'strictly' in all that he attempted (as *The Herefordian* editor had exhorted), had done his small part in 1919 to build up the post-war world.[117]

All's Well?

There can scarcely have been a more challenging time to lead a school than the period of Henson's headmastership, particularly during the Great War when the nation experienced the most cataclysmic conflict of modern history. The emotional effects of this war on the Cathedral School community, and not least its Headmaster, are barely comprehensible. But it was not only a time of great anguish, but also one of considerable uncertainty for the school – uncertainty as to its pupil population in Henson's first two years; uncertainty as to the retention of its staff; uncertainty as to the school's health; above all, uncertainty as to whether it could possibly continue against the competing claims of the Boys' High School and the background of running a boarding school in a period of scarcity, rising prices and escalating salaries. That the school would survive these adverse conditions was by no means a foregone conclusion.

Although for the Headmaster it cannot always have seemed like it – when, for example, he was dealing with the latest epidemic, the news of yet another old boy fatality or the official complaint that an entrance scholarship had been awarded to the son of a German alien[118] – HCS did more than survive. Henson may not have been as highly regarded by some of his pupils as his predecessor. Nevertheless, his years may be seen, if we could adapt his own words of 1917, as ones of 'steady progress and [eventual] prosperity'.[119] With the notable exceptions of the use of the Lady Chapel, which became the school's spiritual home for half a century, and the lease of the old Broomy Hill Academy as a boarding house, this was not an era of great physical development. In other ways, however, HCS made a number of advances between 1913 and 1919: from the relatively modest, like the publication of a new school history, the generous endowment of a prize fund for Modern Languages and the successful introduction of the Higher School Certificate;[120] to the fundamental change in the nature of the school's constitution and its recognition by the Board of Education as a grant-earning school for two advanced courses in 1918-19, the smallest school in the country to have received this stamp of approval. The Science grant, in particular, was of importance and helped to balance the modern side of the curriculum. Cumulatively, these

117. For the exhortation, see above, note 92. Following his brother Eric's death in 1920, Sydney left HCS. He later became a member of the Honourable Artillery Company, winning the regimental King's Prize in 1925, and was a member of the London Stock Exchange, 1936-65. Eales-White, p.44; *TH*, CCXIX (Oct. 1973), p.68.

118. Hubert Reade made the allegation that Max Purcell, tailor of 9 Bridge Street, Hereford, was an enemy alien, and questioned whether the son was entitled to hold a scholarship. The row presumably reached Henson's ears. For the correspondence between Reade and the Board of Education, see TNA, ED 35/995, letters, 13-22 Nov. 1915. The outcome of the case is unknown.

119. *TH*, NS LXXXVI (Dec. 1917), p.13, speech, 24 Nov. 1917. Henson is compared unfavourably with Murray Ragg in *TH*, CCXX (Oct. 1974), p.42, letter of L.S. Munn (HCS 1913-15), 4 Jan. 1974.

120. For Carless' history, see above, p.ix; for the prize fund, see TNA, ED 35/995, correspondence between W.C. Bull and the Board of Education, 26 Nov. to 12 Dec. 1917, re purchase (for around £112) of 200 consuls. In 1918, J.G.M. Richards was the first HCS boy to gain the new Higher School Certificate (with a distinction in Greek).

grants seemed to ensure a prosperous future, not least because his legacy, unlike his inheritance, also included a full school of 122 boys, as well as 67 in the preparatory department (and including100 boarders all told), a doubling of the roll since its low point in early 1915 when Henson nearly lost his job. As was reported on Henson's final speech day, the Headmaster 'ventured to think that all was well with the school, and his successor would find in it all the best elements of the public school spirit'.[121] There is no reason to doubt this claim.

It was not, of course, all Henson's doing. He was hugely supported by the three stalwart assistant masters, Ralph Williamson, Duncan Felton and John Hudson, who were the mainstays of his Common Room. The unconventional Dean Leigh, who retired at 80 after over a quarter of a century as chairman of governors in the same year as his Headmaster, had also done much to move the school forward, particularly in securing its financial recognition by the Board of Education by accepting that it could no longer remain under the direct control of the Dean and Chapter. Nevertheless, it is Henson who deserves most of the plaudits, whatever his regime's shortcomings in terms of administration and discipline, as unearthed by his successor. *The Herefordian*'s view of Henson as a Headmaster, who through his 'strong personality and never ceasing work', his abilities as a teacher, his support for games and 'keen interest in every society' overcame the school's war-time difficulties, is a fair characterisation.[122] But it is also incomplete for it says nothing about his considerable pastoral gifts – or, indeed, the support his wife, who bore the burden of war-time catering, gave him. To gain a more rounded picture, the school's tribute should be read in conjunction with the following account of his leadership towards the end of 1918, at a time of grave danger for the boarding community:

> Difficulties to him were faced with a quiet thoroughness that always won through … A vivid memory recalls the influenza scourge of 1918, when boarding schools suffered so grievously and many brilliant promising scholars were lost. Shortage of food, milk, medicine and of nurses did not help the situation. At Hereford, where the writer was honoured to be on the staff, there were at one time only 11 boys … who were not victims. Here was Mr Henson (and his wife) at his best – supplies were conjured up as if by miracle, nurses were secured from 'nowhere'. It was quite usual to find Mr Henson going round the dormitories as late as 11.30pm with requisites for the invalids. Not a single fatality occurred, and it was just his example of courage and inner strength that helped us all in that grievous time of trial.[123]

121. For the above claim (for HCS) and pupil numbers, see the report of Henson's speech of 16 October 1919 in the *HT*, 16 Oct. 1919, p.11. In Henson's final governors' report, he presented the same figures and made a similar claim. HCSA, GMB 1908-21, meeting, 7 Oct. 1919. That meeting also saw an increase in his annual salary from £220 to £270 (backdated to Sept. 1918), exclusive of his £4 capitation fee and boarding profits. When Henson left in December 1919, his final entry in the school register records 121 boys at HCS: 77 boarders, 30 day boys and 14 choristers; and 67 preparatory boys, 23 of whom were boarders.

122. *TH*, NS XCIII (April 1920), p.5.

123. *HDM*, (Nov. 1946), p.10. The obituary was written by the Revd George Hoyle, who taught briefly at HCS from September 1918 to April 1919 and (as rector of Hopton Wafers) was Henson's 'close and intimate' friend for 30 years. For one indication of his wife's support, see Eales-White, p.4.

A year later, it was fitting that his farewell sermon should be based on the text: 'we are members one of another' (*Ephesians* 4.25). And there we must take our leave of a dedicated Headmaster, whose final years were to be spent in cure of different souls – still within the Hereford diocese but in a Worcester College living as rector of Neen Sollars with Milson.[124]

James Harold Edward Crees, 1920-1940

Around the time of Henson's resignation at the end of the summer term 1919, another Headmaster living in a nearby cathedral city was pondering his future. That man had also successfully seen his school through the war years. Indeed, his achievements at the Crypt School, Gloucester, from 1911 (when appointed he was 28, the youngest secondary Headmaster in the country) had eclipsed those of Henson in Hereford. One hundred or so pupils had been added to the school's roll; the size of the Sixth Form had near doubled (to 22); 20 boys had won scholarships to the ancient universities; and nearly 200, over half with honours, had passed the Cambridge Local examinations. Despite the Crypt's considerable advance, recognised in 1916 by the Headmasters' Conference, its Headmaster was feeling unappreciated – and not least financially – by his governors. And so in August 1919 he tendered his resignation. Within a week of its announcement, he had received an invitation to meet the governors of a neighbouring school, 'where the financial prospects were immensely better', his appointment to Hereford being made in early October a few days before the old Dean's retirement and three weeks before his own successor had been appointed at Gloucester.[125] And so began the long association between James Harold Edward Crees and Hereford Cathedral School.

Fig. 7.4 Dr J.H.E. Crees, aged 37, the most remarkable HCS Headmaster of the twentieth century.

124. For Henson's ministry there (1920-46), compare the retrospective views of his organist, Mrs Butcher – 'he was rather remote' and 'too good for us' – with those of Hoyle, who referred in his obituary to 'the love his parishioners bore him'. I am indebted to the late Colin Oldroyd for giving me Mrs Butcher's observation.

125. For the above: Crees (1920), pp.10-11, 14, 15; Lepper, pp.67-68; *HT*, 2 Aug. p.4, 11 Oct. p.5, 18 Oct. p.4 (for the announcements of Henson's resignation, Dean Leigh's retirement and Crees' appointment.) The governors used the national rail strike (above, p.367) as an opportunity to prune the final short-list from five to three, Crees being appointed on 7 October 1919, following the interviewing of the Revd T.A. Moxon, F.T. Nott (OH) and Crees himself. Nott was appointed Headmaster of King Edward VI School, Stafford, in 1924.

In some ways it was a surprising appointment. Dr Crees (at 37) was unmarried; he had not been educated at a public school; and he was not in Holy Orders. Of these, the latter two short-comings were the least serious. After all, Crees' humble origins at Westminster City School – a far cry from its famous neighbour – had been consistently trumped by his brilliant scholastic achievements thereafter. Even his lay status mattered less for a prospective Headmaster of a school which boasted an ordained chaplain, and in a world where well over half the public schools were headed by laymen.[126] By 1919, too, for an appointments board where (for the first time under the 1919 scheme) the three Dean and Chapter representatives were outnumbered by laymen, it was a less important issue. Dr Crees' bachelorhood, however, may have been more of an impediment. Later, it became common gossip amongst the boys that the governors had hesitated in offering him the post because it was strongly felt that the boarders needed the motherly influence of a Headmaster's wife. Indeed, it was even rumoured that there was an understanding on Crees' appointment that he should find a wife within a reasonable time. Although he was eventually to make amends in 1925 by his marriage to the school's matron, in 1919 as far as we know he had no potential bride in mind. Be this as it may, the deficiency was an insufficient reason to prevent the governors from choosing, by a majority of one, the remarkable Dr Crees – the first layman and the most erudite Headmaster of modern times – as Henson's successor.[127]

Despite his detractors, Dr Crees was indeed a remarkable man. As a classical scholar, from a lowly beginning he rose to some eminence. As he wrote in his educational manifesto, *Didascalus Patiens*:

> The writer was not brought up in the 'grand old fortifying curriculum' of the Classics ... After dallying as a schoolboy with Mathematics, the Sciences and Modern Languages, he found suddenly that he was in danger of starving on this thin diet ... renounced his allegiance to the moderns, enlisted in the ranks of the ancients, and contrived by grievous labour, despite the handicap of years, to get level with most of his rivals in the race of learning.[128]

He did this with marked success, his London first being crowned by firsts in both parts of the Cambridge classical tripos in 1904-05, the Thirlwall essay prize (published as *Claudian as an Historical Authority*) in 1907 and the award of a London doctorate in the same year. Other publications on classical subjects followed: in 1911, *The Reign of the Emperor Probus*, heralded by *The Times* as 'a very erudite examination of the best of the late Emperors', in 1911; and in 1927 (with J.C. Wordsworth, the HCS Classics master) a useful commentary on Books III and IV of Apollonius' *Argonautica*.

Nor should it be imagined that Crees' intellectual interests were confined to the Classics. He wrote a study of the novelist and poet George Meredith, one reviewer of Crees' 1918 literary criticism considering him 'a true Meredithian, for he writes with dexterity in language and a wide range of metaphor and allusion that reminds us of Meredith himself'.

126. By 1914, for the first time among HMC schools, lay Headmasters outnumbered ordained by 61 to 53. By 1919, the comparative figures were 79 to 51.

127. Hidden, pp.39-40, for the rumour; Crees himself (1920, p.14 note) for the majority.

128. Crees (1915), pp.151-52.

But it was not simply Meredith. His immense literary range and general intellectual interests and other concerns are further evident in *Meredith Revisited and Other Essays* of 1921, a compilation of 12 pieces on writers as diverse as Homer, Newman and J.D. Beresford, together with a prophetic article on 'smoke nuisance' and an essay entitled 'Literature versus Science', written in response to the Cambridge University Senate's vote on 17 January 1919 that Greek should no longer be a compulsory subject in the 'Previous' examination.[129] Similarly in *Didascalus Patiens*, quite apart from the wealth of educational sources, quotations are found from Dante and numerous English poets; references are made to Thackeray, *Middlemarch* and H.G. Wells; and his admiration for Bach, Mozart and Rachmaninoff is evident.

But it is Crees the Headmaster that is more important for our purposes, and again *Didascalus Patiens* is an important source for his views. And it is here, and in his memoir of his time at the Crypt, that we see that he was a self-confessed 'Headmaster of the old style, with his privileges and his autocracy'. Imitating Carlyle, he viewed the history of the great public schools as largely the biographies of their great Headmasters. Correspondingly, he saw the advance of bureaucracy in education, and particularly after the 1902 Act the growth of the local authority in administering and developing secondary education, as pernicious in its effect, especially in its diminution of the powers and prestige of Headmasters, 'the gravest danger which now [*c.*1914] threatens higher education'. For the way to build up a great school, he believed, was for its governors to appoint a good Headmaster and then give him a free hand. A Headmaster had to be an autocrat 'because expert knowledge and the earnestness which will generally be combined with expert knowledge are needed at the helm in times of trial'. If these conditions pertained, provided that the Headmaster insisted on high standards of work, punctuality and attention to detail from masters and boys alike, there was no knowing what a school might achieve. As he wrote: 'If a man puts from him with scorn the notion of an eight hours day, resolves to hate shams and never if he can to shirk an issue, to cultivate convictions as well as tastes, he may be surprised in the end to find what will-power and unhasting, unresting energy can do'.

Given Crees' belief that a Headmaster should be 'an intelligent despot' and his view that work above all was the foundation for success in education, it is not surprising to find that he drove his schools hard. Anxious as he was to 'get the last ounce of work out of his assistants', his staff were subject to a strict regime. His rules for assistant masters at the Crypt survive – although not those for Hereford – and it is illustrative to quote from some of them. The Headmaster was to be acquainted if a master wished to leave the school premises; the Headmaster 'in no wise pledges himself to diminish the amount of duty required' if the number of assistants increased; no master had any right to a fixed number of free periods, which were to be used solely for school purposes; term holidays were also 'purely matters of grace'; the Headmaster was to be informed of all parental complaints and, on attendance returns, of all cases of lateness 'for whatever cause'; and so on.[130] Crees expected similar high standards from the boys, whose behaviour at HCS was governed by 57 written rules and a host of unwritten ones. For example, almost everywhere outside the

129. For a definition, see above, p.334, note 330.

130. CSA, Crees' rules for assistant masters, 30 June 1913 and 26 Jan. 1918.

Cathedral Close was out of bounds, not least the café where cathedral boys furtively met High School girls; and if boarders made purchases, they needed a written permit signed by the Headmaster specifying the shop, the article to be bought and the time of return. Many of these regulations, such as the notorious 'hands in pocket rule' (never allowed for juniors, one hand for the Fourth Form, both hands – with jacket buttoned – or one hand with jacket unbuttoned for the Fifth, and total freedom for the Sixth) had been built up over time, but under Crees they were no doubt both added to and more rigorously enforced by a strict Headmaster who, like many of his assistants, did not spare the use of the cane or *in extremis* expulsions.[131]

Crees' authoritarian tendencies, matched as they were by his severe countenance and a character that did not exude warmth, did not make him popular, a fact admitted even by Canon Bannister, his long-serving governor.[132] Parents could find him impatient and dismissive, and to many boys he appeared formidable, remote and a little odd. Many years later, the writer Godfrey Winn, who spent two unhappy years at HCS in the early 1920s, described Crees as 'that bird-like figure, with the long talons, the ivory skin, the ageless and ignoring face, holding no conversation with his neighbours [at meals in the dining-hall], gazing fastidiously into space ... utterly aloof and impregnable ... desiccated [in] appearance and manner'. It was hardly a fair portrait. One old boy of a different vintage remembers observing Crees at the top of the senior table in the dining-hall, talking animatedly to the bright boys of the school. Even more valuable is the testimony of Norman Hidden, whose school career was more fulfilled and successful than Winn's and who knew his old Headmaster a good deal better. 'He had high standards and a considerable sense of duty ...' he wrote, 'he did many kindly intended things to inspire his VIth Form and I experienced many of these in my own relationship with him. These personal touches unfortunately were experienced only in the VIth Form and only by those taking Classics'. He might also have added that they were also evident on the cricket field, where even Winn admitted he revealed 'a glimmer of personal pleasure' and where there was a sixpence reward awaiting any boy who took a catch in the deep from his lofted straight drives.[133] The good fieldsman must have found this unusual pecuniary source a useful supplement to his pocket money.

For Crees, like the best public school Headmasters of the period, was more than a teacher. As he remarked, he devoted almost as much time at the Crypt – and certainly at Hereford, where he was also cricket master from 1921 to 1939 – to teaching the theory of the off-drive and the cut, with personal illustrations, as to Greek and Latin moods and tenses. 'I was never a mere schoolmaster', he wrote, 'and my devotion to cricket, music, chess and literature will attest the variety of my interests'. It was this concern to communicate his unbridled enthusiasm for these passions to receptive young minds which

131. See Hidden, pp.1-2, and his letter to the author, 17 Nov. 2004, in the school archives.

132. To the HMIs after the 1924 inspection. TNA, ED 109/1977, post-inspection conference, 22 Feb. 1924.

133. For the above reminiscences, see Winn, pp.136-37; Hidden, pp.37, 39; and HCSA, letters to the author, 17 Nov. 2004 (N.F. Hidden) and 11 Jan. 2012 (Geoffrey Hughes). The late Michael Morris, having once caught out his Headmaster, remembered (interview, 9 Jan. 2015) collecting his 6d from Crees' study the next day and being invited to return in the afternoon to listen to the Test Match broadcast.

humanised him and which left its indelible mark on HCS between the wars. For the Cathedral School as much as the Crypt, Crees' work stands as the embodiment of his own ideals and convictions and, in a real sense, an expression of himself.[134]

All Change

On 20 December 1919, within weeks of Crees' appointment, Reginald Waterfield had been installed as Dean of Hereford. The new Headmaster was fortunate that the new Dean, who as was customary was soon elected chairman of governors, was not only a fine classicist – with a first in both Mods and Greats – but also someone with wide experience of the workings of public schools: as an assistant master at Rugby (1893-99); a reforming Principal of Cheltenham College (1899-1919), where his 'good sense, good manners and enchantingly warm-hearted Australian wife' won him many admirers; and an energetic member of the Headmasters' Conference.[135] The Dean further complemented his Headmaster in matters of temperament. As the *Hereford Times* said of him: 'He is far from the old stern type of Headmaster and is gifted with a keen sense of humour … On the platform he can be felicitous and entertaining, and his kindly and sometimes subtle humour will no doubt be appreciated by Hereford audiences'. That this sentiment was not mere propaganda is shown by Dean Waterfield's first Hereford speech day at the Town Hall on 17 December 1920, when after waiving his right to chair the proceedings, and following the Headmaster's and Bishop Linton Smith's worthy addresses, his vote of thanks was given 'in a lighter vein'.[136] And then there was the practical support that the Dean was able to give – as chaplain (for a time in 1921-22) and a leading light in the Shakespeare Society, as well as chairman of governors.

Crees soon had an opportunity to stamp his authority on the school. For at the beginning of his second term, in May 1920, he sacked ten boys, whom he had 'discovered to be engaged in various objectionable and indecent practices', and who had admitted their guilt. One other boy, 'who was undoubtedly guilty', was withdrawn by his parents. The exact nature of their misdeeds is unknown but it led to a governors' enquiry, the parents demanding a return of their fees and threatening legal action. The governors, after consulting the Board of Education, resolved that the Headmaster had acted within the terms of the 1893 scheme but decided to return the fees 'as a matter of grace', as the incident had occurred at the end of the previous term.[137] It was, no doubt, a painful incident for all concerned but it enabled Crees to show that he was not the soft option that his predecessor may have been.

---

134. Crees (1920), p.23, for the quotation; and p.67, for his own comments in this vein in his valedictory address at the Crypt, 19 Dec. 1919.

135. For his time at Cheltenham, see Morgan (1968), pp.88-89, 120-21 (on his wife's winning ways) and 158-59. During the Great War, Waterfield was also a member of the HMC professional, war economies and military committees.

136. *HT*, 22 Nov. 1919, p.5; *TH*, NS XCVI (July 1921), p.7. For one other instance (from many) of Waterfield's humour on public occasions, see below, p.392, for his remarks at the opening of the new laboratory, 28 September 1935.

137. HCSA, GMB 1908-21, meetings, 8, 22 May 1920. Clause 26 of the 1893 scheme had given the Headmaster power to expel or suspend boys 'for any adequate cause to be judged of by him'.

The swift departure of two of Henson's masters gave Crees the further opportunity to appoint his own lieutenants: A.B. Mayne as chief mathematical master and senior Housemaster, and C.M. Scott as a Housemaster and form teacher. Both were to become key supporters of the new regime.[138] Before long other staff changes were made so that by the end of 1920 all Henson's clerics had left – how far they were encouraged to do so, we do not know – as had Duncan Felton six months later.[139] These masters were replaced by such stalwarts as Harry Wardle, Harry Kedge and Emile Maurer, who were then followed by two Crypt men: Crees' former pupil, George Hunt, and J.C. Wordsworth, one of Crees' first appointments at his old school. By January 1921, F.W. Brookes was the only one of Henson's assistants to remain on the staff. Four months later, for the first time in the school's long history and with the exception of the part-time woodwork teacher, HCS was without a master in Holy Orders, the gap being filled by Dean Waterfield who acted as chaplain for five terms from summer 1921.[140]

With the Common Room changes came an overhaul of systems, societies, dress and routine. The new Headmaster took direct control of the library fund, with the inevitable consequence that newly purchased library books invariably reflected Crees' own interests;[141] the number of speech day prizes was cut down, the money being funnelled into entrance exhibitions;[142] a Shakespeare Society replaced the moribund Literary Society, a Chess Club was formed and rugby was re-introduced to the school; the school cap was adopted for universal wear, except for monitors and first team colours, mortar-boards being worn by the boarders on Sundays; and a ten minute pre-interval PT session (taken initially by Brookes and later by the monitors) was made compulsory for all boys, instead of the pre-breakfast classes for boarders, and morning school was prolonged to 12.40. Even the choristers' timetable was altered so that they would have more time in school, their morning practice being brought forward to 8.30 before Matins at 9.30.[143] Such was the pace of change that a senior boy could remark:

> As it were by Aladdin's lamp … in the twinkling of an eye, our leisure, our work and our punishments have all been equally affected. Those who bewail the departure of a cherished privilege or protest against the inauguration of a new rule are met with the

138. And both being paid £100 more than their predecessors, Mayne with an annual salary of £450 and Scott with £250. Mayne stayed only three years, leaving for the headmastership of the Cambridge and County School for boys in December 1922, although C.M. Scott stayed at HCS for the rest of his career (until 1945), becoming Crees' Second Master in September 1925.

139. The Revds C.H. Scott, A.J. Potter and A.J. Reed, left respectively in March, July and December 1920. The Revd H.R. Collins (appointed by Crees) survived one year, until March 1921, when he moved to Falmouth Grammar School. For a tribute to Felton: *TH*, NS XCVI (July 1921), pp.13-14.

140. Until W.M.R. Vonberg's appointment, who was followed as chaplain by Elwy ApIvor in September 1925.

141. Books on Science, Mathematics and other subjects were, of course, occasionally purchased but reference volumes aside (the new 29 volume set of the Encyclopaedia Britannica, for example, was purchased during the autumn term 1929), the preponderance of the hundreds of volumes bought through the library fund, 1920-40, related to the classics, ancient and modern history, cricket, music and travel.

142. On speech day 1918, 44 prizes were awarded, compared with nine two years later. For Crees' explanation of his policy in this regard, see *TH*, NS XCVI (July 1921), p.6, speech, 17 Dec. 1920.

143. HCA, 5983/4, Choristers' Magazine no. 2 (April 1921), pp.3-4.

unanswerable – *nous avons changé tout cela* ... With the new order we must learn 'to shun delights and live laborious days'.[144]

Such changes did not always bring Crees popularity – the published poem 'Sartor Resartus', including the line 'a new King reigns in the city, with rod he governs not flowers', expressed the feelings of many – but by July 1922 a perceptive boy could acknowledge the school's new sense of purposefulness, driven by the Headmaster's tireless example.[145] This was symbolised later that summer by the installation of electricity in both the classrooms and School House.[146] The fitful flame of incandescent gas was being replaced by the searching beam of electric light in all the corners of the school. Much had been done in Crees' first three years in office but it was a strenuous period and his achievements had come at a high personal price. 'Had I known,' he reflected, 'to what an inheritance of chaos and disorder and debt I was succeeding, I am doubtful whether I should have faced the difficulties of such a post'.[147]

The Weathering of Economic Storms

The economic conditions of the inter-war period caused public school Headmasters considerable anxiety. In general, despite the sudden end of the post-war boom in 1920-21, the 1920s were (in the words of Cyril Norwood, who had presided over a period of expansion at Harrow) 'years of the greatest popularity that the public schools have ever known'.[148] Thereafter, the consequences of the depression on the disposable incomes of the middle and upper classes, higher taxation, a falling birth rate – a trend which so alarmed leading Headmasters that they invited a woman (Miss Leybourne of the population investigation committee) to address their 1937 conference[149] – and the growing danger of war made the future for such schools far less clear.

The magisterial worries caused by cyclical boom and slump can be further illustrated by reference to the Headmasters' Conference debates over the period as a whole. In early 1921, for example, at a time of rising fuel prices and escalating rates and wages, the Headmaster of Shrewsbury led a discussion on how economies in boarding schools could best be undertaken. Apart from a denunciation of Eton boys for wearing homburgs rather than top hats

144. *TH*, NS XCIII (April 1920), pp.1-2. For the reintroduction of rugby and the new societies, see below, pp.402-03, 404-05.

145. *TH*, NS XCIII (April 1920), p.5; *TH*, NS XCIV (July 1922), p.2, including the observation: 'There seems to be a greater inclination on the part of all both to play and work harder'. One element of this (and a consequence of an expanding school) was the increase in ink usage, the payments for which increased from £1 10s (to 'Mr Brumwell') in 1920-21 to £4 15s 6d in 1922-23. HCSA, account book 1922-45.

146. HCSA, GMB 1921-45, meetings, 20 Jun, 16 Oct. 1922. The installation was made by A.J. Rowberry at a cost of £25. HCSA, account book 1922-45. For the cathedral's electrification in this period: HCA, 7031/24, pp.140, 157, 185, 245, 262, 268, 270, 308, Acts, 8 Nov. 1923 to 7 Nov. 1933.

147. HCSA, GMB 1921-45, Crees' February 1923 report to the governors' meeting, 23 March 1923.

148. Quoted in Mack (1941), p.381, from Norwood's *The English Tradition of Education* (1929) p.129. Mack also gives figures for the increase in numbers at the leading boarding schools during the 1920s.

149. She was the first woman ever to do so. *HMC 1937 Conference Report*, p.68

at Henley, there was little consensus.[150] More than ten years later in December 1931, the exigencies of the financial crisis – the Charterhouse conference of that year took place little more than three months after the government's emergency budget and the suspension of the gold standard – made agreement easier. So the Headmasters, after a long debate, unanimously accepted a resolution advocating general economies 'by saving in administrative expenses, a postponement where practicable of structural improvements, and a withdrawal of all demands for expenditure on purposes which are not of essential value to the school'. At the same conference the recently formed grant-aided schools sub-committee of HMC, including Dr Crees who for the previous two years had chaired the group, passed the resolution that 'all such schools should make a 10 *per cent* cut in salaries', although they were under no legal obligation to do so.[151] In subsequent years, motions condemning the use of agents and demanding that advertising was confined to the *Public Schools Yearbook* reveal the extent of competition between public schools and the difficulties Headmasters faced filling their over-expanded schools. By December 1938, the decline in numbers, especially in non-grant-aided schools, was so acute that an HMC resolution was passed recommending that the matter should be investigated by a Royal Commission, a resolution that was dropped at an extraordinary meeting the following July when there were more pressing matters to worry about.[152] Being a public school Headmaster in such a period of economic turbulence and uncertainty was an unenviable occupation.

Hereford Cathedral School fared better than most during these two troublesome decades. One indication of its growing reputation, if not its prosperity, is given by the pupil roll which rose inexorably from a base of 110 in January 1920 to a peak of 200 in the autumn of 1928, the first and only time Crees reached a double century at HCS. Numbers then remained steady during 1929-30 before they dropped away in the depression years, averaging 167 for the four years 1930-31 to 1933-34. After substantial influxes in the autumns of 1934 and 1935, Crees averaged 176 during his last five complete years in office. These numbers were far higher than any HCS Headmaster had ever achieved and look good for a school on a cramped site with a limited capacity. Indeed, they were considered so at the time. The 1924 inspectors reported that 184 boys, which represented almost a trebling of the 1915 figure, was especially satisfactory considering the 'substantial rise in fees' since the previous inspection.[153] Similarly, their colleagues in November 1933 thought that despite the decline in numbers from the high watermark of 1928-29 (194 average), the 170 boys then *in statu pupillari* was a 'highly satisfactory [figure] when

150. *HMC 1921 Conference Report*, p.34ff, debate, 4 Jan. 1921.

151. *HMC 1931 Conference Report*, pp.61, 64, resolutions, 23 Dec. 1931. The emergency budget of 8 September 1931 had initially proposed a 15 *per cent* cut for teachers but this figure was eventually revised to 10 *per cent* which brought the reduction into line with other public workers. (Taylor [1965], p.295.) The salaries of HCS staff were cut from October.

152. *HMC 1938 Conference Report*, pp.78-79; *HMC 1939 Conference Report*, pp.18-19; *The Times*, 10 July 1939, p.9. For the *Times* reference, figures for the decline in numbers at Harrow, Cheltenham and Clifton from 1929 to 1938, and an indication of the even worse plight of smaller schools by the end of the 1930s, see Mack (1941), pp.394-95, and p.395, notes 59, 60.

153. See below, pp.384-85, for an analysis of the school's fee structure in this period.

the recent economic crisis is borne in mind'.[154] As significantly, boarding numbers, which Henson had built up to over 70 when he left, after an initial drop under his successor, increased throughout the 1920s. These culminated in the 104, 'drawn from all quarters of the globe', that gathered in their Houses – including Langford House, which Crees had purchased for £1,400 in 1921 – in autumn 1929. At speeches shortly after the beginning of that term, Crees proudly announced (to boarder cheers) that day pupils were at last outnumbered. Thereafter, boarding numbers remained steady at over 80 – less than 20 below maximum capacity – even during the depression years, so that in September 1935 Crees could report that 'the school was divided almost equally into day boys and boarders, and two different systems of education were being tried out side by side'.[155] It was an impressive achievement.

As Crees himself had written of his years at the Crypt, 'increase of numbers proves nothing'.[156] While not wholly subscribing to Crees' dictum, it is true that numbers give only a general impression of a school's well-being, particularly at HCS as it was between the wars when there were some 14 choristers and many other boys on free places, and a considerable number paying less than the full fee.[157] For a better indication of the school's prosperity during these years, we need a fuller examination of the school's accounts.[158]

Although the Headmaster's capitation allowance of £4 and then £4 10s per pupil,[159] together with his assistants' salaries, always exceeded the incoming tuition fees – any profit on the boarding fee being the Housemasters' perquisite – the deficit was always well covered by the Board of Education grant. Consequently, the school's current account was in deficit only in exceptional years (the early 1920s, 1934-35 and 1936-38). As the 1933

154. Pupil numbers during this period have been averaged out from the termly figures listed in the account books in the school archives. For this and subsequent references to the 1924 and 1933 inspection reports: TNA, ED 109/1977 and 1978; and for Crees' references to the effects of the depression: HCSA, GMB 1921-45, meetings, 20 Dec. 1930 (re St John's reduction of close awards), 18 Nov. 1931, 22 June and 15 Dec. 1932.

155. HCSA, GMB 1921-45, Crees' 14 Nov. governors' report for their meeting, 18 Nov. 1929 (for Langford House). *TH*, NS CXXII (Dec. 1929), speech, 4 Oct. 1929; NS CXL (Dec. 1935), speech, 28 Sept. 1935. It should be remembered that a number of boys – especially those from farming families – were full or weekly boarders, even though they lived within the county boundaries. See HCSA admission registers for the 1920s, *passim*.

156. Crees (1920), p.11. Crees' observation was made in reference to how a school's progress might best be measured.

157. Over the 60 terms from summer 1920 to spring 1940, the number of non-choristers on free places averaged out at 47 per term, well above the Board of Education's 25 *per cent* requirement for grant-aided schools. The averages for full fee-payers, part fee-payers and non fee-payers, including choristers, for the three financial years 1938-40 – respectively 34, 30 and 36 *per cent* – are instructive. See HCSA, account prepared for C.F. Scott, 23 Nov. 1940.

158. The following figures are taken from the account books for the period in the school archives.

159. Crees' £4 capitation fee (on each boy, including non or part fee-payers, *per annum*) was four times the Crypt allowance. The fee was raised to £4 10s in September 1925 as compensation for the removal of the preparatory school from School House. Crees gained around £14,589 from these fees, 1920-40. This considerable sum averages out at £729 *per annum* over the whole period, some 17 *per cent* of the average total annual salary bill. From the capitation fee alone (excluding the Headmaster's salary and other income derived from the masters' accommodation fees, his ownership of the preparatory school and Langford House), Crees was gaining an amount far in excess of any of his assistants' salaries. His total annual income was estimated by the 1933 inspectors to have amounted to between £1,500 and £2,000.

inspectors pointed out, a significant surplus had been built up since the 1924 inspection, following the increase in numbers and a further rise in tuition fees. By 31 March 1933, the school's cash balance had risen to £854, over £650 more than it had been in 1924, with an additional £1,000 on loan to the city corporation at an advantageous 5 *per cent* (another £1,000 was soon to be lent at a lower return), together with a further £200 loaned to the Headmaster for the purchase of Wyeside. Moreover, the annual cost of pupil maintenance – despite the rise in costs from £29 17s to £31 9s for each boy – had been improved from an imbalance of £8 17s in 1924 to a surplus of £1 6s in 1932-33. In such circumstances, it is not surprising to find that the inspectors recommended that the school should spend some of its profits on improving its premises. The governors were soon to do so with a £1,000 contribution from the school's surplus towards the new Science laboratory appeal, the only such investment that they saw fit to make between the wars. Although it might well be argued that the governors were over-cautious in their stewardship of the school's resources through this period, there was good biblical precedent for wealth being set aside during years of abundance to compensate for subsequent lean years. And this they successfully accomplished.

So HCS survived the crisis of the inter-war years and entered the first months of the Second World War with 174 boys, a recovering balance sheet, an annual income stream (from all sources) of around £2,450 and around £10,000 worth of investments.[160] It was not riches but it was sufficient to keep the school running on existing lines and was in marked contrast to the situation faced by many other public schools in early 1940. How was this achieved?

Foremost, as has been intimated, the school would have soon ceased to operate without the Board of Education's annual grants, which had first been awarded in 1918-19. The grants increased as the roll expanded and averaged over £2,000 *per annum* from the late 1920s, well over half the school's unreserved income.[161] The size of the Board's grants, however, was largely dependent on the size of the school. And the size of HCS was in part determined by the competitive nature of its fees.

Crees had inherited a fee structure which was unsustainable in the post-war inflationary world. As the Clerk to the Governors explained to the Board of Education in December 1920, when seeking to remove the prescribed £18 tuition fee cap: 'In view of the largely increased cost of salaries of teachers, repairs and other expenses, the governors find that the upper limit is no longer sufficient to enable the school to pay its way'.[162] The Board reluc-

160. The deficit on the fees account (£1,327) has been accounted for in this composite income figure (for the financial year ending 31 March 1940), which also includes an income of some £935 which was specifically reserved for the Philpotts scholarships. For the £10,000 figure, see TNA, ED 35/4441, V.C.M. memo to Birch Jones, *c.*late Feb. 1940.

161. Although the nature of the grants changed over the period. The capitation allowance increased by £2 to £9 for the majority of pupils, 1930-31, and was then reduced to £7+ during the financial crisis from 1932-33, increasing to £8+ from 1935-36. The £800 block grant for the two advanced courses (in Classics and Science/Mathematics) remained at that figure until 1935-36. It was changed to a Sixth Form grant the following year, which meant a reduction for HCS from £720 to £480 *per annum* over Crees' last four years in office. The Board continued to cover the school's examination costs, the payments increasing from £24 in 1920-21 to £106 in 1939-40.

162. TNA, ED 35/995, Steele to Board, 22 Dec. 1920. E.W. Marples, Herefordshire's Director of Education, also

tantly approved the request to increase the tuition fee to £30, despite fears – unfounded as it turned out – that a hike of the tuition charge and an £11 increase of the boarding fee (to £65, an increase made from January 1921 without the Board's permission and only authorised retrospectively) would 'have the effect of rendering the school less accessible to the children of parents of limited means'. In the Board's letter sanctioning the increase the same point was made, the governors being reminded that they should 'so far as their funds permit … give sympathetic consideration' to relieve parents of 'both existing and future pupils' who were unable to meet the fees hike.[163]

The Headmaster and his governors took good heed of the Board's advice by endeavouring in various ways to ensure that admission to HCS was not confined to the privileged few. Firstly the fees, even considering the post-war increase, became affordable for middle class families. Apart from a £3 increase in the annual tuition fee and, for boarders, a small increase in the laundry charge (from 3 guineas to £4 10s) and the establishment of a 'domus' fund (at 1 guinea, then 12s *per annum*), the fees were pegged at the 1921 level. There were reductions in favour of sons of diocesan clergy and for younger brothers. At Crees' insistence 'extras', such as the costs of games, stationery (although not books and instruments), the library and *The Herefordian* were included in the tuition fee.[164] For fee-paying boarders especially, a public school education costing less than £100 annually compared favourably with the larger schools.[165] And for those many parents who could not afford the full fee – by the end of the period two-thirds of the boys were either given free places or receiving part remission of fees[166] – there were other avenues to explore. If the son was clever and living nearby, he could hope to gain one of the free day places which were, in part, subsidised by the Langford foundation, strengthened in 1922 by the sale of the Castle Crab estate at Disserth for £2,500.[167] Crees was at pains to ensure, and the Board of Education to insist as a condition of its grant, that the number of boys from local elementary schools increased. So the six free place elementary boys in 1920-21 expanded to over 40 by 1923-24 and to 50 or more thereafter. In addition, there were Philpottine scholarships, which were held over four years and worth (from 1921) £20 annually for seniors and

---

sought and gained permission to raise annual fees (from 9 to 12 guineas) for new pupils (over 10) at four county secondary schools from 1 August 1921. This followed their adoption of the Burnham scale and the consequent increase of expenditure to 'at least' £30 per child. *Ibid.*, letter from Marples and R.E. Campbell's reply, 7 June 1921.

163. *Ibid.*, Cookson's draft minute, 5 Jan. 1921; C. Eaton to Steele, 21 Jan. 1921; Campbell to Steele, 16 August 1921.

164. See HCSA, Crees to Steele, 19 June 1921. Although such items as OTC membership, piano tuition and school 'dinners' for day boys – at respectively £1 2s 6d, 6 guineas and £7 4s – continued to be counted as 'extras'.

165. In 1933-34, for example, although the HCS tuition fee was some £10 more than the national average of £21 14s for state secondary schools, its boarding and tuition fee combined was £50 less than the £147 18s average for public schools. *HMC Report 1937*, p.72, Miss Leybourne's figures (excluding 'extras').

166. See above, p.383, note 157.

167. See TNA, ED 27/7415, for a detailed survey of the farm (over 297 acres then let at £120 *per annum* to Thomas Prosser Bowen), conducted by Stooke & Son, 30 April 1921, when it was valued (including timber) at £3,554 14s 9d. By February 1922, the same firm suggested £3,000 as the reserve price, in view of the fall in prices of agricultural property'. The sale to H.V. Vaughan that July, however, excluded timber valued at £1,110, so the original estimate was eventually reached.

£10 for juniors, with 'increases or prolongations in special cases where the circumstances of the parent required it'. These were awarded to boys already at HCS, a few of whom could look forward to gaining university awards from the same fund.[168] And to attract bright boarders, Crees established generous House awards. One Old Herefordian remembered, following a private examination in the Headmaster's dining-room in May 1921, winning a £70 House exhibition which was followed in his first year by the award of a Philpottine scholarship so that (in his own words) 'during my time at HCS I only cost my father £5 *per annum*, plus railway fares'.[169]

Indeed, the railway line, especially the one from South Wales, played a significant part in keeping boarding buoyant during the inter-war years. As we have seen, boarding numbers had increased under Henson; a third of all his new admissions were boarders, over 40 *per cent* of whom lived in Wales.[170] Crees built on this trend so that in the years from January 1920 to September 1928 over half of the 227 boarders admitted to HCS held Welsh addresses, despite the trade depression in South Wales during the middle of this decade. Some of these boys had attended preparatory schools such as Llandaff Cathedral, St John's Porthcawl, and Westbourne House at Penarth, but a considerable number came from elementary schools in the valleys. Whatever their background – and sons of artisans, clerks and GWR railwaymen mixed in School and Langford Houses, as they did in the school in general, with those whose fathers were farmers, clergy, business or professional men[171] – the Welsh boys made a distinctive contribution to HCS life as they had done in previous and were to do in later generations. As the 1933 inspectors recognised:

> There were 170 boys in the school at the time of inspection. Of these exactly half were boarders, a large contingent of whom come from South Wales. In view of the impoverished economic conditions in this district, the maintenance of this Welsh connection speaks well for the school, and it is worthy of mention that the Welsh boys have played a conspicuous part in the school's life, both so far as the intellectual and the athletic sides are concerned.[172]

---

168. HCSA, Philpotts foundation minute book, 21 June 1922. Over the 20 years from 1920-40, 31 OHs benefited from Philpottine university grants. A further 75 senior and junior awards were made from the fund. All told, over £3,397 (average £170 *per annum)* was spent on Philpottine university awards and £3,526 (average £176 *per annum)* on Philpottine school scholarships. HCSA, Philpotts charity account book, *passim*.

169. HCSA, J.A.W. Smith letter (written in his 98th year) to the author, 13 Dec. 2004. Unsurprisingly, Mr Smith's memory in terms of the exact value of the Philpottine grant, was faulty, but this does not detract from his evidence about the school fees costing his father very little. He went on (in 1926) to win a Somerset exhibition at St John's, Cambridge.

170. These and the following figures have been taken from the extant two registers for the period in the school archives.

171. As Godfrey Winn remembered of his time as a boarder in School House (1920-22): 'we were all at close quarters, though an ill-assorted lot …' *The Infirm Glory*, p.137. Also see Crees' comment in his 1929 governors' report about the difference of parentage, 'ranging from the grandson of a peer to the son of an engine driver', among the pupils. HCSA, GMB 1921-45, Crees' report, 14 Nov. 1929.

172. TNA, ED 109/1978, report of 22-24 Nov. 1933 inspection, p.2; and HCSA, GMB 1921-45, meetings, 30 June 1926, 23 June 1927, for Crees' comments on the earlier recession in South Wales.

Such an observation fully justified Crees' policy of widely spreading the word about the school's virtues, whatever the views at the time of the Headmasters' Conference on advertising.[173]

But Crees did not only make overtures to the Welsh. From the autumn of 1938, the first of several Jewish refugees, almost all from Vienna, 'whose parents ... [had] been driven from the countries in which they were living owing to racial prejudice', were admitted as boarders on half-fee places. They were bright boys from professional families who were highly placed in their forms. And despite initial language difficulties, religious differences – the chaplain's wife used to invite them to tea during Sunday Evensong – and most of them not being attracted to games, they were soon assimilated into school life.[174]

Crees also built on Henson's work by establishing the preparatory school – the Headmaster's private enterprise, it will be remembered – in new premises. This was achieved with difficulty. Although the Headmaster's control was threatened by the passing of the new scheme of June 1920, which gave the governing body authority 'if they think fit' to assume responsibility for the prep, fear of financial loss through the obligation to enhance the (lady) teachers' salaries, which would have been the Board's requirement on the scheme's adoption, made it convenient for the governors to ignore its provisions. Instead they decided to abide by the agreement on Crees' appointment that the school should be maintained as the Headmaster's private perquisite. For Crees the pecuniary advantages were clear, and not least following his doubling of the preparatory school's tuition fees (for older boys) to £21 in September 1921, which did not result, as the governors might have feared, in a diminution in numbers. And the preparatory teachers continued to be paid less than the Burnham scale and had no pension provision.[175] So it was not constitutional matters but the very success of both the private venture and the public school that caused the problem. For as the 1924 inspectors found, as a consequence of the expansion of the senior school, HCS was desperately in need of the four School House classrooms occupied by the prep. Indeed, such was the concern about the legality of the occupation, the Board required that 'steps should at once be taken to exclude from the buildings the whole of the preparatory school'. Steps were taken. A governors' sub-committee (excluding the Headmaster) was appointed to investigate the matter and Number 2 Castle Street was mooted as a possible site. In the summer of 1925, however, Crees found his own solution by purchasing 'a well-found and dignified Georgian house' (now 28 Castle Street) for his school.[176]

---

173. See, for example, Crees' courageous defence of the right of smaller schools to advertise in the speech he made to the 1933 conference, a month after the inspection. *HMC 1933 Conference Report*, pp.69-70.

174. The following eight Jewish boys: A. Eisinger, G. Berkenau, R. Kris, G. Eisinger – the exception (as a good fives player) in terms of games – H.P. Rothbaum, R. Kimelman, L. Stöger and R. Meyer, were all admitted between September 1938 and June 1939. In September 1940, J. Taglicht (a destitute Polish refugee, who gained a classical scholarship to King's, Cambridge, in 1943 after three years at HCS) was the first of a further five war refugees admitted to HCS, 1940-42. HMC was active in helping such children: *HMC Committee Report*, 16 Feb. 1939, pp.8ff.

175. See above, p.361, for the 1920 scheme; and TNA, ED 35/4440, Cookson's memo, 12 April 1924, discussing preparatory school issues in the light of the 1924 inspection.

176. *Ibid.*, report on 20-22 Feb. 1924 inspection, p.5; J.B.L. memo, 4 April (re the legal issue); A.P. Oppé to Underwood and Steel, 15 May 1924; C.W.P. minute, 27 Jan. 1925; letter, 14 Feb. 1925; Steel letters: 16 Feb., 2 April, 7 May 1925; HCSA, GMB 1921-45, meetings, 21 March, 11 Nov. 1925, 18 Nov. 1929 (Crees' 14 Nov.

The history of the preparatory school from 1925 to 1940 is only tangentially germane to a history of HCS. Suffice it to say this. Crees did well from his investment of £2,500. Indeed, it was estimated that he was making £400 a year out of the venture (excluding the rents from the two top floor flats) by the time of his retirement in 1940.[177] But whatever profits Crees was making, the Cathedral School historian needs to be thankful to him for risking his capital, however odd the conflict of interest may seem to modern eyes. For quite apart from the preparatory school's success in educational terms, its establishment by Crees in a new home meant that it continued to sustain the senior foundation during the depression years of the 1930s.[178]

Following Crees' proud announcement at speech day on 17 November 1922 of the substitution of electric light for gas, he suggested that 'it was desirable to make other improvements as opportunity offered'. Like other public school Headmasters in the inter-war years, Crees was able periodically to refurbish the school's infrastructure; unlike many of them, he had precious few resources at his disposal to make substantial changes other than by appeal.[179] Although this limited their extent, it meant that HCS could be made more attractive without incurring heavy financial liabilities.

In 1920, it was clear that something needed to be done to smarten up a school that had been untended for far too long. Godfrey Winn's description of School House as 'Bleak House', and his criticisms of the open 'bogs' and other aspects of the school as it was in the early 1920s, might be dismissed as an unfair account, penned by a writer from a comfortable background who was unhappy at the school; except that they are repeated by other old boys who were not so disaffected.[180] Nevertheless, Crees strove hard to improve the plant, the insurance for which almost doubled to £5,250 in March 1922.[181] Early on, the work primarily involved routine maintenance, including (for the 1924 inspection) 'a great deal of painting and redecoration', but apart from the provision of electricity, the ventilation of the classrooms and dormitories was also improved as was, at a cost of £350, 'the external sanitary accommodation'. Much of the latter item related to works at the Headmaster's house and the School House dormitories, where in the summer of 1923 'practically a new system of drainage' was required following the corporation's inspection. But perhaps – even though they still froze in hard winters – the external lavatories in school yard were also up-graded.[182]

---

report stating that the purchase price was £2,000).

177. For these figures, see TNA, ED 35/4441, Steel to Board, 26 Jan. 1940; R.E. Williams' memo, 22 Feb. 1940. Miss Gamlen, the Headmistress, also lived (perhaps rent free) in the house.

178. The preparatory school admission registers (HCJSA), indicate that 220 out of the 410 boys admitted in the 1920-40 period came on to HCS. See TNA, ED/4441, for a copy of the preparatory school prospectus, *c.*Feb. 1940. There were 71 boys (around 7 of whom were boarders) in the school at this time.

179. Compare, for example, Crees' position with that of F.B. Malim, Master of Wellington College (1921-37), who was able to spend a large portion of the average yearly profits of around £5,000 on capital projects. Newsome (1959), p.318ff.

180. For the descriptions of Winn, who admittedly conceded that the Welsh boarders were 'less surprised by the conditions': *The Infirm Glory*, pp.135-37. For further criticisms of the outside lavatories and the buildings in general, see Hidden, pp.9, 35, 43; and HCSA, reminiscences of B. Butcher, A.A. Jones and Geoffrey Morgan-Jones.

181. HCSA, GMB 1921-45, meeting, 16 March 1922.

182. For these improvements: HCSA, GMB 1921-45, meetings, 30 March, 21 June, 3 Oct. 1921, 23 March, 7

The most notable addition to the school premises in the early 1920s, however, was the new pavilion and gymnasium at Wyeside.

By this time the old pavilion, which had served generations of boys adequately, was 'quite unworthy of the school': its accommodation 'incommodious' and its roof resembling a 'sieve-like structure'.[183] An attempt in 1919 by the Old Herefordians to raise money for its reconstruction had failed – because of inadequate planning, so Crees believed – but the new Headmaster and cricket obsessive was not to be denied. In November 1922 he made his appeal to raise £1,000, suggesting that 5 guineas might be the average subscription from the parents of the 200 boys then attending the preparatory and upper schools. Crees himself pledged £300, and promised, if there was a short-fall, to provide the balance so that the building could be completed within 12 months. The parents and friends responded generously and quickly, the £700 being raised by the end of the following term, and Crees was as good as his word. Messrs Spencer, Heath and George, a firm with 'a long and highly satisfactory record for the building of gymnasia and pavilions', was then engaged to construct the new building. This was opened to great fanfare, and the accompaniment of a Latin ode recited by a monitor garbed as a river god, on 16 October 1923 by Sir Sydney Robinson OH, the Chief Justice of Burma.[184] With its verandah, balcony, cupola and flagstaff, it was

Fig. 7.5 The second Wyeside pavilion of 1923, which despite the dilapidations caused by the Wye in flood, lasted for over 40 years.

May, 2 Nov. 1923; HCSA, accounts 1920-24, payments to Beavan and Hodges, W. Preece and L.E. Reece; HCA, 7031/24, pp.93, 96, re a loan for repairs at Number 1, 6 April, 25 June 1921; TNA, ED 35/4440, letters, 27 June, 3 August, 11 Sept. 1923, 18 Jan. 1924; ED 27/7415, Board order, 4 July 1924; ED 109/1977, 1924 inspection report, p.4. The school's annual average repair bill, 1920-24, came to around £218, some 7 *per cent* of its income.

183. So described by Crees and an Oxford OH in *TH*, NS C (Dec. 1922), pp.6, 27.

184. For an account of the appeal, building and opening, see *TH*, NS C (Dec. 1922), pp.6-7; CII (July 1923), pp.10-11; CIV (April 1924), pp.15-16. The December 1923 volume, which would have described the opening, is missing, but a full report, with photographs, appears in *HT*, 20 Oct. 1923, p.5.

rightly described as a 'handsome and commodious building', and one which the school was initially able to show off with pride. Sadly, however, the wooden structure was unable to withstand the ravages of the Wye in flood, and only ten years later, the gymnasium (when inspected on a muddy November day in 1933) was considered too small and not altogether fit for use, the floor being 'so dirty as to be unsuitable for the lying and sitting exercises performed on it'.[185]

The success of the pavilion appeal depended on its extension to purchase the land on which the new building stood, together with the rest of Wyeside, the Ecclesiastical Commissioners who owned the 13 or so acres being hesitant about sanctioning the expenditure of 'so large a sum' on property held on a yearly tenancy (of £38). Prompted by Dr Linton Smith, the new Bishop of Hereford, the Commissioners agreed to sell the two fields for 'the exceedingly moderate price' of £800. The sale went ahead in October 1923, even though less than half the money had then been raised, the governors lending the balance to the Headmaster from accumulated surpluses. When Crees finally closed the appeal in July 1927, he was able to congratulate the school and its wider community on having raised over £1,600 for the new pavilion and gymnasium and, as importantly, the acquisition of Wyeside's freehold 'in perpetuity'. No-one deserved the plaudits more than Crees himself.[186]

For a school with limited resources, a great deal had been achieved in a short time, but as the 1924 inspectors observed: 'while it is true that much has been done ... to improve the material conditions of the school, much remains still to be done before they can be considered quite satisfactory'. Some of their recommendations – the provision of desks 'of the modern type' and the extension of the bicycle shed, the improvement of washing facilities in the boarding houses and, crucially, the adoption of better fire safety measures – could be implemented relatively quickly;[187] others, like the removal of the preparatory school from School House and the increase of classroom space, as we have seen, took a little longer; yet the major building recommendation, the provision of a Physics laboratory, took more than a decade to achieve.

As with the pavilion, Crees attempted to raise the money for the new building by turning to the school's friends, and like Tatham 50 years earlier, he used an anniversary to promote an appeal. The '550th' celebrations over the week-end of 20-21 June 1931 comprised the annual speech day, this time in the Shirehall, a Town Hall luncheon and two cathedral services, followed by a grand concert on the Monday. At their centre on the Saturday and

185. TNA, ED/1978, report on the inspection of 22-24 November 1933, pp.4, 11. Such defects were not to be remedied until the opening of the new gym (behind Number 1) in 1958 and the third Wyeside pavilion a decade later. See below, pp.487, 516.

186. The final appeal total was £1,629 7s 5d. *TH*, CXV (July 1927), p.24. For the acquisition of the playing field, see TNA, ED 35/4440, letters, 9 April 1923, 8 April 1924 (including the conveyance of 18 October 1923) and 15 May 1924. Crees repaid the governors' loan in instalments from the games fund, the final payment being made on 8 October 1935.

187. *Ibid.*, Crees to Cookson, 27 Sept. 1924, re the adoption of fire-safety measures following advice from Mr Rawson, the Chief Constable, who was also in charge of Hereford's fire brigade; HCSA, accounts for 1923-25, payments of £60 for new desks; £51 14s for new lavatories and bathroom; £32 2s for the new cycle shed. Langford House, which Crees owned, was enlarged and improved in 1930 following Harry Kedge's replacement by Harry Wardle as Housemaster. At the time of the 1933 inspection, the fire escapes were still considered inadequate.

Fig. 7.6 Masters, governors and guests outside the Shirehall, Speeches, 20 June 1931. Seated on the front row (from left to right) are: the headmaster of King's, Worcester (C. Creighton); Sir Sydney Robinson OH; the principal of Brasenose (C.H. Sampson); Dr Crees; the Bishop of Durham (Hensley Henson); the Dean of Hereford (Reginald Waterfield) and Sir Frederick Kenyon, a former director of the British Museum. Father H.P. Bull OH, co-founder of The Herefordian, *stands in the second row, second from the right.*

Sunday was the returning Bishop of Durham, Hensley Henson, who at speeches gave a wide-ranging disquisition on the development of grammar schools from the time of Wat Tyler, proposed the toast to HCS at the luncheon and on the Sunday preached on 'the whole duty of man', relating the verse in Ecclesiastes (XII, 13) to the Christian doctrine of education. But Dr Crees more than held his own with the Fellow of All Souls, using his opportunities to emphasise the importance of the appeal for £3,500 (launched earlier that year) for improved Science facilities. Turning to 'the unknown and uncharted region which extends as far before us as the past behind us', he concluded his luncheon address on 'the unchanging boy' by surmising that in future it would be necessary:

> to confront new problems and adapt the school to the needs of the present age, in particular to attempt to bring the Science accommodation up to date. Amid such changes as none could forecast and such difficulties as none could surmise, the loyal Herefordian could picture his beloved school still passing on, fulfilling its appointed mission and accomplishing its age-long task.[188]

188. For a full account of the '550th' anniversary celebrations, which included 'distinguished representatives of the church and prominent men of education, Science and [the] civil service' connected with HCS: *HT*, 20 June, p.6.

Such noble sentiments deserved an immediate a response from the school's well-wishers as in 1922-23. The trouble was in the timing: there was no worse year between the wars to have launched an appeal than 1931, and no worse time to be asking for money than the depression years of the early 1930s. An initial £650 had been raised by July 1931 but by the following term, 'the alarums and excursions of the financial crisis' meant the appeal made slow progress; by July 1932, when over £900 had been raised, such was the climate that Crees believed that 'the present trying times ... made the time of a year ago seem like a golden age'. It was not until early 1934, when the total stood at over £1,300, that the governors – prompted by the findings of the 1933 inspection report – were prepared to pledge £1,000 towards the project; and not until the following year that they were sufficiently confident to order the demolition of the old laboratory and the building of the new Science block. By the time the appeal was finally closed in July 1936, almost one half of the total of £3,042 18s 6d had come from three sources: £400 from Crees, 100 guineas from A.U. Zimmerman, then President of the OH Club, and £1,000 from the school's surplus. But as *The Herefordian* reported 'the spirit of self-help' was evident too, the boys contributing almost £115, the assistant masters nearly £100 and over £150 being raised from school concerts.[189]

Even so, the original design needed to be altered and old fittings required to be used, the revised estimates of £2,174 for the two new laboratories (for Chemistry and Physics) and £410 for the fittings, tendered respectively by W.A. Sherrat and Halstead Bros, being accepted by the Board in March 1935.[190] Over the course of that summer term, the boys had 'to take their meals to the music of the pick and the trowel' and 'to labour to the bricklayers' song', but the building was ready for the beginning of the new academic year and was opened by the Mayor of Hereford, Dr J.V. Shaw – the city's 554th mayor in the '554th year' of the school's existence – on 28 September 1935. In the speeches ceremony which followed in the crowded Physics laboratory, the Headmaster described the new two-storey block as a 'minor palace' compared with the old 'converted stable'; the mayor hoped that Biology would now be taught and – optimistically – that the school might soon be able to prepare boys for the first medical examination; and the Dean mischievously suggested that Dr Shaw should give a lecture on hydrostatics in aid of the £200 that was still needed for equipment.[191] This jolly affair marked the end of the fund-raising projects (the shooting range excepted) of Dr Crees' reign. Given his prodigious efforts over the years, Crees' failure to realise his dream to establish an endowment fund to make HCS 'independent of the whims and fiats of administrators and politicians' comes as no surprise.[192]

---

189. For the Crees quotations: *TH*, NS CXXVIII (Dec. 1931) and NS CXXXI (Dec. 1932), speech, 23 July 1932; and for the final appeal account: *TH*, NS CXLII (July 1936).

190. See TNA, ED 35/4440, A.E. Munby (the architect) to Kendall (at the Board), 16, 31 July 1934, 21 Feb. 1935; correspondence between A.D. Steel and the Board, 14, 27 Aug. 1934; and TNA, ED 35/4441, statement of final cost, 18 May 1936. Munby, a former Science teacher, rightly countermanded the inspectors, who wanted a Science building on the playground site.

191. *TH*, NS CXXXIX (July 1935), editorial by G.H. Dhenin; *HT*, 5 Oct. 1935, p.7.

192. *Ibid.* speech 28 Sept. 1935. Crees mentioned the need for an endowment fund in the context of the anticipated annual loss of £350 from the Board's recalculation of its grant for advanced work. For the building of the shooting range in the preparatory school moat, see below, p.412.

One further factor which enabled HCS to withstand the buffetings of unpredictable financial winds in the inter-war years was its economic efficiency. This was one advantage from the roles of Headmaster and bursar being vested in one man, who still collected the fees, chased up late payers and had supervision of routine expenditure, even if masters were now paid directly by the Clerk to the Governors from his office in Castle Street. Although individual salaries were not pegged to the Burnham scale, which put masters at a disadvantage compared with teachers at some other schools, they gradually increased over the period. With the Headmaster's capitation, indeed, they constituted around three-quarters of the school's annual expenditure, although Crees was adept at both employing young (cheaper) men on a part-time basis and reducing staff numbers and costs if necessary.[193] Crees had little control over other fixed costs, such as the price of fuel which, despite the switch from gas to electric lighting, increased by over 40 *per cent* in this period.[194] But, burst boilers and other emergencies apart, he could do something to control the expense of building repairs, which averaged little more than £100 annually over the whole period.[195]

Miss Amy Mary Martin, the School House nurse known to the boys as 'Queen' – who in a quiet (almost furtive) service in the Lady Chapel on 8 August 1925 became Mrs Crees[196] – was an important accomplice in the school's efficient management. Indeed, years later an old boy reckoned that the marriage arose principally from Crees' high sense of duty, for they seemed to have little in common. Queen's 'capabilities as a manager and organiser, ruthless and direct', he wrote, 'were important to the running of the boarding side of the school. This freed him [Dr Crees] to concentrate on teaching and the establishing of academic standards'. Whatever the reasons for the marriage, it was a successful union as far as HCS was concerned for 'Queen' proved a staunch ally of her husband and an effective housekeeper and manager of the domestic staff. Whether the boarders always saw it this way is another question for she was a matron of the old school, who did not suffer 'lead-swingers' gladly and who kept a watchful eye on boys who had a fondness or necessity to change their clothes more than the regulated once a week. As well as supervising the sick bay and linen cupboard, her further responsibility for the provision of food may not have aided her popularity.[197]

---

193. Staff costs (including the Headmaster's capitation) averaged £4,408 *per annum* over the whole period. From their peak of £5,090+ in 1928-29, they declined in successive years to £4,376+ in 1933-34 during the worst years of the depression, partly as a result of the 10 *per cent* salary cut in October 1931, which was reduced to 5 *per cent* in July 1934 and abolished the following year. Thereafter, they remained well below the peak years of 1927-30, declining to £4,280+ in 1939-40.

194. From £68 7s 8d in 1920-21 to £96 13s 1d in 1939-40. There was only a three-year cost saving (from 1922 to 1925) following the switch from gas to electricity, although lighting costs again fell in 1939-40 (by almost £4 to £11 9s 1d) as a result of the blackout. Apart from 1925-26, expenditure on coal remained stable until the late 1930s.

195. And this includes the expensive 'sanitation' and other repairs, which amounted to over £1,070 (more than half the total cost for the whole period), during his first five years in office, 1920-25. The renewal of all the boilers (by December 1937) and the addition of new library radiators may partly explain the rise in fuel costs, 1938-40.

196. 'So secret had the event become that there was barely half a dozen persons present when the ceremony took place', as reported: *HT*, 15 Aug. 1925, p.4. The service was conducted by the bride's brother, the Revd E.V. Martin.

197. HCSA, N.F. Hidden, letter to the author, 17 Nov. 2004. See Hidden, pp.37-38, for an unaffectionate portrait of 'Queen', and *TH*, NS CLII (March 1940), pp.2 and 4, for an encomium. The evidence re the quality

So helped by his capable wife, Crees the businessman Headmaster, who owned a boarding house and a preparatory school and made a small fortune from his position, ran a tight ship. The school with a maximum staff of 12 full-time masters (including Crees himself) for no more than 200 boys became an efficient unit and its finances were stabilised. Its plant was old and costly to maintain but it was improved so that by 1933 the inspectors considered it 'solid, well-heated and on the whole, well-ventilated'. Significant additions, moreover, were made to the buildings through two major appeals. These were successful in part because of Crees' financial contributions and in the main through his own drive. And these buildings were kept tolerably full in the depression years because the fees were competitive, numerous scholarships, discretionary grants and free places were awarded, and Welsh boys were courted to help fill the boarding houses. One further advantage Hereford had over some of its rivals, which had a definite but incalculable affect, was that it belonged to an England which suffered less than other parts of the country during the 1930s; in J.B. Priestley's words it was a part of 'old England, the country of the cathedrals and minsters and manor houses and inns, of parsons and squire, guide-book and quaint highway and byways England'.[198] But as Priestley also observed, it had 'long ceased to earn its own living' and Hereford Cathedral School could no longer simply rely on its heritage to attract custom. Of much greater regard in the Twenties and Thirties was the Headmaster's significant enhancement of its academic reputation. It is to this that we must now turn.

Academic Flood-Tide

'The Headmaster, in presenting his report, said that in spite of government economic alarms, the school was proceeding on its way placidly, and in so far as work was concerned seemed indeed to be on the flood-tide of prosperity'. In this manner, Dr Crees, following on from A.E. Scott's Latin oration, opened his speech day address in the Shirehall on 29 July 1933. Ironically, perhaps partly because of the state of the economy – to which his Head Monitor, as befitted a young man who had just won a Balliol Classics scholarship, had elegantly referred in his ode – Old Herefordians and boys alike had excelled academically during that year: gaining two first class honours and a number of second-class degrees; three Oxford scholarships, including two state scholarships; 13 Higher Certificates, with 10 distinctions; and 24 School Certificates, a third with honours.[199] For a small school of 170 boys, with fewer than 40 in the Sixth Form, it was a fine record.

---

of the boys' meals in this period is, almost inevitably, contradictory. Compare, for example, Winn's retrospective comment about 'a diet of squashed swedes for every meal and pieces of gristle floating in a sea of congealed fat' (*Infirm Glory*, p.135) with the 1933 inspectors' observation that 'the dietary seems excellent'. TNA, ED 109/1978, report on 22-24 Nov. 1933 inspection, p.4. Also note the inspectors' (unpublished) comment that Crees 'has improved and mellowed since he married his housekeeper, a most capable woman'. TNA, ED 1090/1978, typescript, p.2.

198. Priestley, p.297. Although the nearest Priestley came to Hereford on his famous tour of the country in the early 1930s was the Cotswolds.

199. *TH*, NS CXXXIV (Dec. 1933), report on 29 July speech day. Following Scott's Balliol scholarship, T.A. Jones won an open scholarship in Mathematics to Trinity, Cambridge, in early 1934. Two blue ribands of the educational world were thus won by Hereford boys in successive academic years.

And although 1932-33 may be regarded as one high point of academic achievement, the successes of that year were not without parallel. For example: five Oxford and Cambridge scholarships were won in 1925-26 and 1931-32; there were 11 first-class honours in the School Certificate examination of 1929; in 1931, three out of the five distinctions in Mathematics nationally for the Oxford Higher Certificate fell to HCS boys, as well as several others in Classics; and, on average, ten boys passed the Higher Certificate each year between 1938 and 1940. Overall during Crees' time around 50 scholarships, half of which were open and almost all of which were in Classics or Mathematics, were won to the ancient universities;[200] at least ten of these scholars gained first-class degrees, a number going on to distinguished academic and teaching careers;[201] state and county university scholarships were regularly won on the basis of distinctions in Higher Certificate examinations; and an increasingly high proportion of boys, some 40 *per cent* by the 1930s, stayed on to work for certificated examinations, the average leaving age (of boys aged 14 and above) increasing year by year in the early 1930s, as the depression gathered, to over 17 – a leaving age far higher than at most schools – and the average length of stay to over five years.[202]

The school's academic progress in this period can be measured by reference to the three inspection reports of 1915, 1924 and 1933.[203] In 1915, as we have seen, the quality of teaching was variable in the extreme. Nine years later, and after Crees' four strenuous years at the helm, the inspectors could report that 'remarkable progress in every way' had been made and not least through the Headmaster's efforts to stimulate work in Classics and Mathematics. With its masters possessing 'unusually high qualifications', 55 clever boys studying Greek, all boys taking Latin for five years and a timetable which gave the subject (in Form V) over 40 *per cent* of curriculum time (some 11 hours per week), it is perhaps not surprising that standards in Classics were considered 'much better than in any school within about 50 miles'. Similarly, the five masters responsible for teaching Mathematics, led by a well-qualified young graduate with a 'broad outlook',[204] were clear and thorough in their approach and effective in their teaching of specialists and non-specialists alike. Science teaching, too, under the 'well qualified and forceful' F.W. Brookes, despite the limitations of the rudimentary laboratory and its equipment, was considered more than competent. Standards reached in other subjects, however, were less satisfactory. English work suffered from 'from lack of organisation and responsible control' and was consequently done 'in a rather haphazard fashion'. The History syllabus, an outline of English history from 55 BC,

---

200. It should be noted that in this period colleges seem to have expected a higher standard of attainment (at least in Classics) from students competing for 'closed' scholarships (like the Somerset awards). See *HMC Report 1928*, pp.70-72, Crees' speech, 21 Dec. 1928.

201. Prominent among these were O.W. Richards, later professor of Zoology at Imperial College; Raphael Powell who became professor of Roman Law at UCL; V.M.C. Pennington, who was the only first in his year in each part of the Law tripos and headed the Bar final examination; R.W. Morris and J.M. Burch.

202. TNA, ED 35/4440, inspection statistics, 31 March 1933. Crees himself estimated that of the 850 or so HCS boys who had passed through his hands, 400 obtained the School Certificate and 135 the Higher Certificate. *HT*, 23 March 1940, p.8.

203. For copies of the three inspection reports, see TNA, ED/1976-1978.

204. The young man was Sydney Hall, who died in post on 9 July 1924 following an epileptic seizure at Wyeside. The department had been built up by A.B. Mayne, 1920-22.

Fig. 7.7 C.M. Scott, Second Master, teaches a group of Sixth-formers outside the Armoury building in school yard. This photograph of an obviously posed lesson appeared in successive editions of the school prospectus in the 1930s and early 1940s.

was repeated three times in five years to the total exclusion of European history. There was only one specialist Modern Languages teacher, the elementary course being repeated in the third year – where the class in the Big Schoolroom was separated from another form by means of a curtain – because the junior French teaching was so poor. Above all, with the honourable exceptions of PE and Manual Instruction (although the admirable local cabinet maker, who came in on two mornings each week, worked in cramped conditions where the risk of accident was 'very great'), the practical subjects came in for criticism, the work in both Art and Music being judged as falling well below the standards by then achieved in other secondary schools. As the governors observed, in four years Dr Crees had 'done magnificently for the school', but in 1924 HCS was still very much an unfinished work.

By November 1933, the school's academic record had been 'maintained and developed'. Over the previous four academic years, 42 boys had gained Higher Certificates and six state scholarships, six open scholarships and a number of exhibitions had been won. From the 93 boys who had left during the same period, 30 had gone on to Oxford and Cambridge, a number to other universities – the part played by the school in 'creating good material for a university career' being considered 'remarkable' – and 34 'to some clerical or commercial occupation'. Improvements were noted in certain subjects: in English, although there was still no specialist teacher, the work of the six masters was now well co-ordinated; standards in French had risen since 1924, with sympathetic masters teaching the juniors and the less gifted, and were now 'eminently satisfactory'; instruction in Religious Knowledge, which included the literary study of certain Bible passages, was now based on the Revised Version rather than a 'scripture history', and was held to be a 'very suitable course'. But there were also deficiencies. The History syllabus had been somewhat re-modelled but European history was still only taught in one year (Form III), and Classical history held 'an abnormal part' of the syllabus so that the average boy was not being properly trained in 'intelligent citizenship'. Geography fared even worse, and not simply because a boy had informed an inspector that Manitoba was a horse that ran in the Derby rather than a Canadian province (or lake). For the subject was in the hands of a master with no relevant qualifications; Europe, America and matters of 'human interest' were excluded from the syllabus; the same text book was used for every form; the teaching failed 'to arouse the interest and capture the imagination of the boys' and, unsurprisingly, the results were moderate. The practical subjects, too, had stood still. The Art teacher, an Old Herefordian, had to teach with borrowed equipment in a room totally unsuitable for the subject; the standard of work in Physical Education, taught by an ex-Army instructor unacquainted with developments in modern gym theory and practice, was low; and Manual Instruction, despite the overhauling of its equipment, required 'a progressive course of instruction' to be adopted. Like the Humanities, there was a lack of trained specialist teachers in these disciplines, with the inevitable consequence that the subjects suffered.

And so the advanced subjects, as recognised by the Board of Education, continued to constitute the school's real academic strengths. Although the teaching was 'very seriously handicapped' by the old laboratory and the syllabus was little changed from 1924, 15 boys were undertaking advanced Science, with Chemistry as the main and Physics as the subsidiary subjects, one boy having gained a distinction in 1933 in the Higher Certificate examination. In Mathematics, the senior teaching was 'vigorous and thorough' and the syllabus suitable, with the boys 'responding readily and intelligently' to any demands made upon them. The school was congratulated for its mathematical results, especially considering the size and strength of its classical side. But Classics continued to be the department *nonpareil*. Almost every boy offered Latin, 'the backbone of the ... curriculum', for the School Certificate and one third of the school (55 boys) still learned Greek. Twenty-four boys, moreover, were taking the advanced classical course, the scholarships and higher certificate passes over the past three years being 'results of which any school of this size might justly be proud'. With half the staff teaching the subject at some level, Dr Crees led a strong team, as did (one man apart) the young senior maths master. So the achievements in Classics and Mathematics were impressive, but even the inspectors had to admit that as a consequence other subjects may have been 'cramped'. Still, within narrowly defined limits, the Headmaster had raised the school to a high standard.

Most of the plaudits for raising academic standards should go to Crees himself. And in an age of teaching Headmasters – and Crees taught a good portion of the advanced Classics course, in addition to School Certificate Latin and English to the whole Sixth Form – foremost among his many qualities was his prowess as a teacher. This signal accomplishment was well recognised by the inspectorate, who while accepting his limitations with parents, fully acknowledged his outstanding abilities in the classroom.[205] His senior pupils paid him similar compliments, if only retrospectively. For instance, Charles Cook, who left HCS with a state scholarship in 1940, remembered his teaching with these affectionate words:

> Imbued with an undying love for classical literature, he expected and often achieved the impossible from the semi-literates in his charge. His lessons of Virgil's Georgics and Aeneid or Homer's Iliad and Odyssey, and especially the great Greek tragedies, were conducted with the greatest possible verve. He had the magic gift of communicating his enthusiasm, to the degree that after two years in his charge even the most reluctant learned to share his life-long devotion to the values inherent in these disciplines.[206]

It was here in the Gilbert Library with the Classical Sixth that he revealed something of his personal emotions, which he normally concealed, and (in the words of another pupil from an earlier generation) 'did many kindly intended things to inspire' his charges. If you were not among this elite, you found less favour.[207]

But Crees inculcated a habit of disciplined learning among all boys. As he observed in his valedictory address at Gloucester: 'Enduring success in intellectual work is rarely achieved except by self-denial, diligence and strength of purpose'; or, more prosaically, in *Didascalus Patiens*: Boys need 'the heartiest encouragement to row themselves out' more

205. Note, for example, the private remarks of the 1933 inspectors: 'HM is a first class teacher and fond of [the] boys, but careless with parents whom he is too apt to look on as a nuisance'. TNA, ED 109/1978, inspectors' unpublished report following their meeting with governors, 24 Nov. 1933.

206. HCSA, F.C. Cook's article, 'Oil Lamps and Earth Closets'.

207. HCSA, N.F. Hidden's letter to the author, 17 Nov. 2004. Compare Hidden's approving attitude with that of Professor P.W.M. John, a mathematician, who still held Crees in contempt over 50 years after he had left HCS. HCSA, John to Bob Adams, 22 Sept. 1996.

than the 'comfortable words' and 'egregious utterances' of speech day addresses.[208] And, as we have seen, it did not take long for him to change the comfortable culture that his predecessor had established.

In appointing his assistants, Crees generally found men with the intellectual capacity and drive to carry out his wishes. This was especially true of his Sixth Form teaching appointments, not less than 11 of whom – five classicists and six successive senior mathematical masters – had gained firsts in at least one part of their degrees. A number of these masters later moved on to senior positions at other schools.[209] As we have seen, among the classicists who saw out more than a generation of pupils were two men from the Crypt: the erudite and austere J.C. Wordsworth ('Wo' or 'Woe'), the form master of the Classical Sixth; and G.W. Hunt, a Crypt pupil from 1910 to 1918. Both, in their way, were influential teachers. Some of Crees' other assistants, such as the Second Master C.M. Scott and Housemasters like Harry Wardle, may have been less academically inclined but they were considerably gifted in the teaching of less able pupils in lower forms, to say nothing of their varied contributions elsewhere.[210] Even Emile Maurer, who in the tradition of native foreign language masters was badly treated by some boys, was given a clean bill of health by the inspectors. Indeed, in the 1933 inspection only one of Crees appointments, I.L. Beynon, was considered to be a poor teacher despite his Oxford diploma in education.[211]

These were some of the men who guided HCS boys through their formative years during the inter-war period. And despite Crees making what a modern generation would feel to be excessive demands on their time and their freedom – 'he could be seen standing outside the old Common Room after chapel, watch in hand, checking the masters' arrival', as one old boy remembered – the turn-over of his staff was not rapid. Indeed, nine of his assistants stayed for ten or more years and a number outlived him at the school. Not the least of the many reasons which could be advanced for this relative stability was the paucity of jobs elsewhere in this period and the fact that Crees believed that a labourer was worthy of his hire and remunerated his teachers accordingly.[212] The consequence for HCS, and schools like it, was the provision of a stable educational environment. So during these two decades,

---

208. Crees, *Gloucester, 1911*-19, p.65; *Didascalus Patiens*, p.245.

209. The following gained firsts. Classicists: V.J. Dunstan (1921-28), G.W. Hunt (1921-53), J.C. Wordsworth (1923-45), G.F. Pollard (1928-34), E. Rushworth (1936-40); Mathematicians: A.B. Mayne (1920-22), S. Hall (1922-24), F.L. Dawney (1924-26), R.J. Marsh (1926-33), J.B. Morgan (1933-38), L.S. Brown (1938-40). At least two of these men later ran their own schools: Mayne, who became Headmaster of Cambridge County School for Boys; and Dunstan, who after Liverpool Collegiate was appointed Headmaster of Carlisle Grammar School.

210. This may also have been true, to a lesser extent, of the chaplain, Elwy ApIvor. He had a gift for bringing out the best among the less talented members of his Lower Vth Form but had his limitations as a teacher with bright boys, one OH remembering his lessons as being 'repetitious, dull and uninspiring … made worse by his furious use of the cane'. HCSA, Geoffrey Hughes to the author, 11 Jan. 2012.

211. Despite the criticism about his Geography and Mathematics teaching, Beynon was kept on until April 1935 when he left for Newbury Grammar School after over ten years at HCS.

212. By 1934, the Burnham basic annual scale for graduate masters started at £234 and then increased by annual £15 increments to a maximum of £480 *per annum*. Crees the previous year had appointed J.B. Morgan as senior mathematical master (at the age of 23) at a salary of £300 (less the 10 *per cent* cut and £50 for board and lodging), which then rose to £350 in September 1934. It should be noted, however, that he was less generous with other young junior assistants, whose salaries tended to start at £200 in the mid-1930s.

Crees drove a small, highly efficient and dedicated body of teachers, whom the boys got to know well. It was one recipe for academic distinction.

In many ways, however, it was still a limited curriculum. Given Crees' belief that man and his history, 'the greatest and most difficult of all subjects', should take central place in the curriculum and that the Classics were the best vehicle for this exploration, it could hardly be other.[213] But despite this essentially Victorian educational perspective, Crees did not entirely look back to the past. He kept up with current educational developments: visiting Toronto as the representative of the Headmasters' Association in the autumn of 1927; representing HCS on the councils of the Classical Association, the Society for the Promotion of Roman Studies and the Oxford Delegacy (for examinations); and chairing the HMC grant-aided schools' group, 1929-30. Among his most important educational initiatives at his own school, after the provision of its first purpose-built Science block, was the appointment in 1938 of a second scientist, F.L. Ward, to teach Sixth Form Biology. Such developments gave the Modern Sixth more opportunities for individual scientific investigation and promoted a greater interest in the subject, but Science still came a poor third behind Classics and Mathematics and F.W. Brookes, the Science master, ploughed a lonely furrow for much of his HCS career. Yet however narrow the curriculum, and however poor the facilities for practical subjects – even with the building of a new gymnasium, which among its other faults lacked electricity, limiting its use on dark winter afternoons – in terms of academic results, the numbers of boys taking certificated examinations and the staying-on rate, HCS had never experienced a more prosperous time.

But academic success was only one part of the Creesian ideal. It was imperative that body and character should be developed as well as the mind. As he pronounced:

> ... the highly intellectualised conception of education may be chilling, poverty-stricken and sterile. It needs the glow of moral enthusiasm, it must be fertilised by active endeavour. Neither men nor boys are intellectual machines, and a conception of education which leaves no scope for the virtues of good citizenship, which divides a school into those who work and do not play and those who play and do not work, is incomplete. The moral and the intellectual interpenetrate.[214]

Civility and Heartiness

Crees' intent to make his boys good citizens involved an inculcation of values designed to enable boys to live together well in the school community, and eventually the wider world, and also the encouragement of virtues which would help civilise them. Such values and virtues were not only to be extolled in the classroom and the chapel but also in and around the school through a boy's exposure to cultural activities and games, where the maturing adolescent would have opportunities both to cultivate his mind and strengthen his body. There was nothing new about all of this, except perhaps that music and 'King Willow', together with the Classics, were his own chosen instruments for civilising his school.

---

213. Crees (1915), p.158.

214. Crees (1920), p.65, Crypt valedictory address, 19 Dec. 1919. Also note, for example, this observation of Crees in June 1922: HCS 'has never fulfilled more effectively than at present its task of sending out into the world boys well equipped both in mind, body and character'. HCSA, GMB 1921-45, meeting, 22 June 1932.

Christian virtues were not, of course, neglected. How could they possibly be in a Cathedral School with a Lady Chapel as the school chapel and a Dean as chairman of governors, who also acted as chaplain during an inter-regnum? It was just that Crees as the first lay Headmaster was inevitably less central to the boys' spiritual development than his predecessors had been. He left spiritual matters to his chaplains, notably from 1925, after the hiatus of four chaplains in five years, the Revd Elwy ApIvor, a stern moralist, who was to serve the remainder of his ministry in Hereford until his sudden death in 1944.[215] Although until his last few years in office, Crees was not neglectful of his duties as a preacher – how effectively we do not know – in Sunday morning chapel.[216] He preached on a wide range of biblical texts but also on such magisterial themes as friendship, humility, authority, justice and mercy, high ideals and bad language. And he was not afraid to use the pulpit to educate the boarders about political events – sermons on 'the present crisis' and 'Anti-Christ', preached respectively on 27 September 1931 and 11 February 1940 are cases in point – or, as on 7 June 1931, their 'founder' and benefactors.[217] Historical figures, Virgil, St Francis, Samuel Johnson and John Wesley among them, were also subjects of his sermons, as were Beethoven and Schubert on 27 March 1927 and 18 November 1928 respectively, during the weekends of the school's centenary celebrations of their deaths.

For music was also the Headmaster's passion. Crees himself was an accomplished musician and despite his right-hand deformity, he was good enough to play duets with Reggie West, the music master who was later to become organist of Armagh Cathedral.[218] These included arrangements of Beethoven's 'Eroica' symphony and the first two movements of Schubert's C Major symphony during the centenary celebratory concerts. Senior pupils (and sometimes younger boys) were also given opportunities to appreciate classical music through attending occasional gramophone concerts – Crees had an extensive record collection – and other gala concerts, such as those organised in the early 1930s in aid of the Science appeal.[219] The actual practice of Music, however, was a different matter. The prospectus claimed that piano tuition was available at 6 guineas a year and violin and organ lessons 'as arranged', but choristers apart, few boys seemed to have taken advantage of these

215. The son of a village postmaster from North Wales, whose early ministry included a time in rural parishes during the rebellion and civil war in Ireland, ApIvor was an enthusiastic convert to Anglo-Catholic ritual. He was also a robust disciplinarian, with a sharp tongue, who did not spare the rod.

216. For the following, see HCSA, register of school services, from 28 March 1924.

217. Two years after this '550th' anniversary service, a Commemoration Service was held for the first time on 25 June 1933, when the 1931 commemoration hymn (with words written by J.C. Wordsworth) was used. From then onwards, the service was held annually throughout the 1930s on the Sunday of the patronal festival (the octave of St John the Baptist).

218. R.H. West, as assistant organist of Hereford Cathedral, was the school's music master from January 1923 to July 1935, when he left for Armagh. For a time he also acted as joint secretary (with his brother N.E. West) of the Old Herefordian Club.

219. Like the Town Hall concert of 15 June 1931, which raised over £50 for the Science appeal. It was reported (*HT*, 20 June 1931, p.7) that although the cathedral choristers' singing 'seemed subdued', the concert gave Herefordians an all too rare opportunity of hearing singers with whom they were acquainted 'only through the medium of wireless or gramophone record'.

terms, and orchestral players were virtually non-existent.[220] There was, of course, a school choir which sang at school services and monitors' concerts, but in general boys' participation in musical activities advanced little in this period. Crees may have had some success in raising awareness of classical music but by 1940 music making was still for an elite.

The same may be said for Dr Crees' occasional treats for budding classicists. The Cicero and Catullus 'XIs' were select gatherings of boys who had performed exceptionally well in their School Certificate examinations. Crees dined each team once, respectively on 15 October 1927 and 26 September 1931, in recognition of their results of the previous summer.[221] We have just one description, that of the Cicero XI's six-course meal in 1927, the proceedings beginning with a Latin grace and the Headmaster's own Latin verses, and ending with his toast to the orator's 'immortal memory', a reading from Cicero's second *Philippic* (the best done paper) and replies from the boys. Before they departed they were each presented with a copy of J. Wright Duff's *The Writers of Rome*. It was a civilised and memorable evening. Similarly, Dr Crees organised, and in part paid for, at least two Mediterranean cruises for the Classical Sixth, the details of the one in April 1935 having survived.[222] Preparations were carefully laid: the prospect of travel scholarships (dependent on internal examinations) were offered; Baedeker's among other guides, as well as two volumes of the Proceedings of the Hellenic Travellers' Club, were bought for the library; and a party of seven staff and nine boys was gathered together for the trip. Despite the news of another attempted Greek coup – the boys who knew their Greek history and predicted that in one week all would be 'lost and won' being proved right – the party sailed that April on the *SS Letitia* from Marseilles and onwards to the Greek islands, Naples and Gibraltar. The promotional aspect of the tour was almost as valuable as its cultural value: it was the subject of paragraphs in the London press; mentioned in a wireless broadcast when the ship ran aground; and the Hereford boys won the on-board tug-of-war competition against Eton, Harrow, Marlborough and Mill Hill.

The Shakespearean Society, too, was for a select number of Sixth-formers. The Dean's Bard's club first met in the autumn of 1921, replacing the defunct Literary Society. Its passing was mourned by at least one old boy, who regretted that there was 'too little of our old-time catholicity' about school life. 'If in the past', he continued, 'we always tended to be superficial, we were not without a certain versatility ... There ... [were] just a few papers read in the Literary Society whose recollections will ever be keen and delightful'.[223] He had a point. Crees' boys no longer had the opportunity afforded to a previous generation to research and write pieces on a wide range of literary figures, although the Headmaster

220. Denis ApIvor (1927-33), who became a distinguished composer, recalled that he was the only boy at HCS to play the clarinet during his time at the school (1927-33). HCSA, ApIvor to Alan Morris, 2 Nov. 1996.

221. In the July 1927 School Certificate, 24 boys (out of an entry of 32) passed, with 6 gaining honours; of these, 8 out of the treated 11 gained 'very good' or 'good' Latin passes. In the equivalent 1931 examination, 25 (out of 32) passed, 8 with honours. Of the 7 distinctions, 3 were in Latin from the 5 boys who gained first-class honours that year. HCSA, GMB 1921-45, meetings, 8 Oct. 1927 and 18 Nov. 1931.

222. *TH*, NS CXVI (Dec. 1927), p.23 for the dinner; and *TH*, NS CXLII (July 1936), for Dhenin's personal reminiscences of the cruise. Two or so years later, 24 boys went on a trip to Belgium, the first (it was optimistically hoped) of regular annual tours abroad. HCSA, *OH Club Handbook, 1937-38*, p.5.

223. *TH*, NS XCVII (Dec. 1921), p.22, Oxford letter.

may well have felt that his Sixth Form English teaching was sufficient for the average boy. Occasionally, too, *The Herefordian* still provided an outlet for literary 'masterpieces'.[224] On the other hand, 14 or so senior boys would now be able to read through perhaps six of Shakespeare's works during their time in the Sixth Form, the society meeting at least twice each term through the academic year. And they would also have the chance to listen to the memorable renditions of Dean Waterfield and Canon Lilley, at that time reputed to be the best reader in the Church of England. For these two gentlemen invariably took the principal parts, leaving the boys to fill – sometimes no doubt in a desultory way – the more minor roles. The range, too, was remarkable. At least 19 of Shakespeare's plays, half the surviving canon – tragedies, histories and (usually in the summer) comedies, many several times over – were read in the Deanery through this period.[225] And if a boy disliked a play, he could always look forward to the refreshments, provided by the Dean's wife, or (at least in the summer of 1936) marvel at Miss Phoebe Waterfield's enchanting performance of Rosalind in *As You Like It.*

It was all very wonderful but, ultimately, a little limiting, as the 1933 inspectors indicated in the one negative comment about the school's 'corporate life':

> A school magazine appears terminally [termly] and there are in existence both a Debating Society and a Shakespeare Society which meets in the Deanery. Certain Sixth Form essays suggest that in these societies a rather wider selection of plays and topics for discussion, especially current events, would help to develop the high standard of scholarship in the school.

It is a fair criticism of the Shakespearean Society but not a wholly accurate reflection on the school's debating record. While it is true that the outcome of school debates tended, as in the past, to favour the Conservative cause – although a national Liberal (N.F. Hidden) won the 'mock' election on 31 October 1931, and the results of debates were by no means foregone conclusions – there was no shortage of motions about current affairs in these feverish political years. For example, the 1920s witnessed debates on Ireland, the Lloyd George coalition, Stanley Baldwin, strikes, the two party system, the League of Nations, state welfare and votes for 'flappers'; and during the following decade debates were held about 'aeronautical enterprises' (in relation to the R101 disaster), the nationalisation of mines, democracy, the public school system of education, communism and fascism, sanctions against Italy (in the light of the Abyssinian crisis), the government's policy of re-armament and (on 8 October 1938) the Munich crisis, a motion on the purchase of peace 'at too high a price'

---

224. Most notably Norman Hidden's excellent article on Thomas Traherne in the April 1932 edition. Over 70 years later, Hidden, who in 1974 received a civil list pension for his services to literature, wrote this in his own literary profile: 'A few snatched paragraphs from his [Traherne's] *Centuries* which I came across in the town library drove me to roam the streets and their buildings at the end of the old town [in Hereford] – haunts which inspired me with something like an echo of what the boy Traherne had felt …'

225. Including the plays read more than once, this amounted to over 50 works (or part works) being read from autumn 1921 to February 1940, the most popular being the five recitals each of *Julius Caesar* and *The Tempest.* Canon Alfred Lilley retired in 1936 but returned to make a final appearance as Falstaff in *The Merry Wives of Windsor* in early 1938. His brilliant renditions were well recognised in successive reports of the meetings in *The Herefordian.*

being defeated in a 'keenly contested' debate by four votes. Moreover, apart from the 'mock' general elections, a 'mock' trial was held on 2 April 1938 – the boy jury declaring guilty verdicts in each case – and, on 25 March 1939, a 'mock' parliament was conducted, the no confidence motion being defeated by 39 votes to 27. It was to be the last debate for some time, the blackout preventing the resumption of meetings during the first year of the war.

Debating held a time-honoured place in the school's annals but new games were also introduced in these decades. A Chess and Draughts Club was started in early 1920, no doubt through the Headmaster's influence. Dr Crees himself was a sufficiently good chess-player to be the first board for the masters against the boys, sometimes (as on 5 March 1928) winning two games in the same match, and he had some able chess lieutenants, notably J.C. Wordsworth who was the county chess champion in 1929. With fees set at one shilling for new members and sixpence for old, the club flourished with a membership of over 60 at its height in March 1929. Several internal competitions were held in the Michaelmas and Lent terms, and the first inter-school chess match took place against the High School on 26 November 1935 (which ended in a draw). For young and old alike, chess and draughts were enjoyable and instructive activities on winter evenings between the wars. But before the end of the period, the ancient game of chess had been challenged by a modern rival, the School House boarders being 'royally' entertained every Sunday evening to a 'cinematograph show' (featuring 'Pop-Eye' among others) in the winter of 1939-40. And then there were the unofficial playground games, a cross between rounders and baseball ousting cricket from school yard in May and June 1932, only to be ended by a 90 degree heat-wave and by the yo-yo craze the following term.[226]

But the staple diet for outdoor games continued to be football, rowing and cricket, interspersed with fives and athletics. The nature of one of the three major sports, however, was to change, the 'association' game being discarded in early 1922 in favour of rugby football. As in 1898, the change was not made without disquiet, the following letter (from 'non-egg punter') to *The Herefordian* of midsummer 1920 echoing in many respects one written more than 22 years earlier against the change to soccer:

> Why should a game, which is the cause of such healthy rivalry, be abolished for a game that is the chief source of amusement for Welsh colliers and the hirelings of Swansea, Pontypool etc.? Last year the school soccer team had a most successful season, why should it be changed at this stage? Is it not a matter for the sports master and the boys, not for the masters? Because the staff has changed why should the games of this ancient school? ... If the change comes about the *Hereford Times* will have scope for their delicate sarcasm and journalistic genius.

Leaving aside the 'genius' of the *Hereford Times* reporting, the letter was firmly answered by 'punter in alternam' in the next issue of the magazine:

> Whatever be the wishes of the 'powers that be' as regards the code played at the school, I consider that your correspondent's reference to 'Welsh colliers' and 'the hirelings of Swansea, Pontypool etc.' is quite out of order. It is only necessary to compare the

226. 1932 has been named, by Blythe (p.134), as 'the year of the yo-yo'.

records of association and rugby footballers in the late war to see which game has produced most 'MEN' ... In conclusion, it is interesting to recall that at least one of Swansea's many fine footballers was an Old Herefordian.

Nevertheless, 'non-egg punter' clearly represented a strand of opinion that was against a precipitate change of code. And Crees was sufficiently acute a politician not to make the same mistake as Murray Ragg and enforce a change of game until he could carry the school and, especially, the old boy community with him. In the end, on 13 December 1921, 18 months after a unanimous decision that rugby should not be re-introduced, the school committee decided that rugby football 'be adopted as the school game for the future', the news being 'received with much applause' the following month at the London OH dinner.[227] The change made good sense: Felton, the main 'association' master had left the previous December; HCS possessed worthy rugby coaches in A.B. Mayne and C.M. Scott; rugby would have been a second religion for many of the Welsh boys, the school was growing and there was a good chance of a successful transition to the new game; and, perhaps most important of all, other schools were also adopting the rugby code.[228]

So the final soccer season ended on 17 December 1921, the school appropriately losing five goals to two against a strong OH team in the last fixture of the Michaelmas term. Unlike the 1st XV in its ignominious final rugby season in the autumn of 1897, the 1st XI soccer team, with a record of six wins and two defeats, had bowed out with some dignity. In January 1922 all boys, with the exception of the two junior forms, took up the oval ball, one game for seniors and one for juniors being organised on the two weekly half-holidays. Despite poor weather limiting the effectiveness of practices and the boys indulging in some 'serious faults' – everyone was advised, among other things, to 'learn to tackle low and hard and to have infinite patience with the referee' – Mayne predicted that it would be possible 'to field a fair XV' later that year.[229]

That proved an accurate enough prediction, although it took some time and considerable efforts on behalf of the rugby masters, and particularly the first team captains who coached the juniors in the arts of the game and often refereed their practice matches, before HCS could be considered a good rugby school. But the number of representative teams was soon increased to include regular matches for the 1st, 2nd and junior (under 15) sides. The quality and the suitability of the fixture list was also improved, with (for the seniors) a reduction in the number of club matches – and correspondingly less reliance on masters playing in the same team[230] – and their replacement by new school fixtures. These included estab-

227. For the above: *TH*, NS XCIV (July 1920), p.33; NS XCV (Dec. 1920), p.38; NS XCIV (July 1920), p.3; NS (April 1922), pp.3, 13.

228. King's, Worcester, switched codes at the same time as HCS but there were other public schools following suit up and down the country. By December 1925, the situation nationally had become so worrying for soccer-playing schools that a motion was carried (by 36 to 10), when HMC met at Shrewsbury that month, regretting the prospect of 'a wholesale defection of public schools from association to rugby football'. *HMC 1925 Report*, pp.33-34.

229. *TH*, NS (April 1922), pp.7-8.

230. Although as late as October 1936, when a record score of 81-nil was run-up against Worcester 'B', the school team included 'Messrs Scougall and Cooper'; similarly, 'Mr Lewis' played in the 1938 away match against BNC, reputedly the strongest college team in Oxford at that time.

Fig. 7.8 The 1933-34 1st XV, captained by J.H. Morgan and coached by C.M. Scott, was the most successful of the school's inter-war rugby teams.

lished rugby academies like Bromsgrove, Newport High School, Christ College, Brecon, and Wycliffe, but also Lucton, Abergavenny and Ludlow grammar schools and RGS Worcester who all adopted the game in the late 1920s. Gradually some fine players emerged.[231] Some strong sides were also produced, especially in the early 1930s, when the 1st XV went undefeated for two years (from 16 November 1932 to 10 October 1934) against a school side and Wyeside became something of a rugby fortress. The 1st XV of 1933-34, whose only defeat came in the last match of the season against the Old Herefordians when the team was 'hopelessly out-weighted', was the most notable of these sides. This outstanding XV just happened to come together in an inspection term. After describing the preparations for the inspector's visit – 'new paint, new desks, new rules ... [and] new vigilance' – the editor of *The Herefordian*, who also played in the winning XV, was in no doubt that the inspection took second place that term 'to those heroes who have shoved so manfully, run so swiftly and play[ed] so whole-heartedly on the football field'.[232] The team's record was never again

231. Notably A.E. Brookes, who played a number of games for Oxford between 1929 and 1931 without winning a blue; and J.E.W. Scougall, E.C.N Adams and R.H. Jerrome who played representative public school fixtures, 1928-30. But there were others: Gower Davies, 'the one player of genius' in the 1929-30 side; W.L. Davies, who scored 36 tries in 1933-34; and G.H. Dhenin, captain for two seasons, 1934-36, and the inspiration of those sides.

232. *TH*, NS CXXXIV (Dec. 1933). The editor was W.W.M. Cooper, who played as a forward in the team. C.M. Scott, who coached the 1st XV (after Mayne's departure in December 1922) throughout the inter-war years, ascribed much of the team's success to the fact that there were 12 Sixth-formers in the side who well displayed their 'brains' by playing 'clever football'.

emulated in this period.[233] Nevertheless, well before this time, the Headmaster must have concluded that the change in codes was fully justified by the results – even though there is no evidence to show that Crees took the slightest interest in the game.

Cricket, on the other hand, was one of Crees' passions. How much of a passion may be gauged from these three reports in *The Herefordian*.[234] The first was penned in July 1926, 'after a glorious baking afternoon spent on the cricket field'; the second on Dick Shepherd's retirement as cricket professional later that year; and the third on the eve of Crees' own retirement and following the declaration of war in 1939:

> On such a day it is not hard to recognise that cricket is the grandest of all games, the most dignified, the most beautiful as a spectacle, the finest in its development of the moral qualities (what more hopeless condemnation of a thing than to say that it is not cricket?), the least selfish, the most truly English and the most symbolical of life itself with its sudden changes, its drama, its swift retribution for errors made, its punishment for chances not taken.

> Was cricket languishing? Was it too tame a game for this hectic, fretful, bustling age? Was the long-drawn drama of a three days' match unsatisfying to a generation which demanded a result in ninety minutes? If that were so, and cricket were destined to dwindle into the past-time of a few select votaries, the survivors from an earlier age, there would pass out of English life something beautiful, noble, for which the feverish sentiments of more popular games would offer inadequate compensation.

> Whether our playing fields will in 1940 afford the usual spectacle of flannelled figures – we will not call them fools – only 1940 can tell. 'Business as usual' may prove an impossible aspiration, and even school cricket – one of our greatest institutions just as cricket itself is one of our country's greatest institutions – may not go on unaltered ... Not inappropriately the present chronicler will seize the opportunity and lay down his pen. He will depart from the cricket scene with enthusiasm undiminished and affection unabated for this noble pastime, which has given him ... so many hours of great delight, delight not untempered with failures and reverses, yet even our cricket failures bring their consolations and teach their lessons. In this strange, crazy world in which we find ourselves, how small a portion of our lives can we discover in retrospect in which we have won so great a measure of satisfaction as in those golden hours spent in 'the game and plaie of cricket'!

As the school's first, but by no means last, cricketing Headmaster, Crees was a fair performer at the game: a steady bat, with a wristy cut as his trademark shot, and a wily left arm spin bowler. His record in 1919, before his arrival in Hereford – in school games for the Crypt at any rate – was impressive: 462 runs in 15 innings and an average of under 6 for his 70 wickets.[235] This record was never exceeded at HCS but in the 1920s he put in

233. Although the records of the 1935-36 1st XV (played 17, won 12, lost 4, drawn 1) and the 1938-39 2nd XV (played 11, won 11) should also be noted.

234. *TH*, NS CXII (July 1926), p.8; CXIII (Dec. 1926), p.15; CLI (Dec. 1939), p.6.

235. Crees (1920), p.23 note.

some memorable performances with ball and bat, notably his 105 not out for the masters XI against the school in 1922. As his batting powers waned and he dropped down the order in the 1930s, he was still able to take the occasional wicket. And in his last match against the 2nd XI in July 1939, his reflexes (at 57) were sharp enough to win the match with a running catch at wide long-on.

His time as cricket master for 19 successive seasons, a record unlikely to have been surpassed by any other twentieth-century Headmaster, deserves further scrutiny. New equipment was bought: a slip machine in 1924, an extra net in 1927 and new sight screens in 1931. The pitches, too, were re-laid (at a cost of £50) for the 1920 season, and both fields were in use for cricket by 1930. In 1928, Crees described Wyeside as the best ground in the county, although seven years later his fulminations against the city – 'too anxious for the welfare of its hideous Hunderton suburb' – for reducing the water pressure 'on this side of the river', suggest that during the hot summers of the 1930s, the wickets were not always as well prepared as they might have been.[236] The Headmaster was also a tireless, demanding and enthusiastic coach, who laid down strict rules for practices. He had high standards – Spofforth and Bosanquet, Fry and Rhodes, Bradman, Woodfull and Grimmett were held up to the boys as exemplars – and his expectations were considerable. His strictures could be devastating and his published character sketches of the XI severe, as in 1924 when he declined to write up any member of the team 'because so many of them have no character'. Such methods eventually achieved results and the general standard of cricket improved, not least in fielding. The number of school fixtures increased – the Crypt, Newport and Hereford High schools and Abergavenny and Cheltenham grammar schools were all added to the list; the Christ College, Brecon, game was revived in 1935

Fig. 7.9 Dick Shepherd, the school's cricket professional and groundsman, 1885-1926, who (in Dr Crees' opinion) 'so mightily and so magnificently played the game'.

236. Judging by Crees' cricket reports, hardly a game or practice was cancelled in Hereford during the summer terms, 1929-30, 1933-35. See *TH*, NS CXXXIX (July 1935), for his invective against 'our municipality'.

and Llandovery in 1939 – and there were more opportunities for boys to play in 2nd XI and junior matches. But at the top level, there were too few good players to ensure regular victories against other schools.[237] In club matches, which still dominated the fixture list, all too often the team relied on the performances of Dr Crees himself and one or two other masters (notably J.E.W. Scougall in the mid-1930s), as well as the cricket professionals, Dick Shepherd – until his generous testimonial and final school match in July 1926[238] – and (from 1928) Joe Woodward. And, as the Headmaster admitted in 1937, a small school needed the services of both 'wet' and 'dry bobs' (oarsmen and cricketers) if a high cricketing standard was to be maintained, and by that date the best oarsmen had for many years been unavailable until late in the season. So despite Crees' devotion, it was in rowing, rather than cricket, that the Cathedral School was to excel between the wars.

The captain of boats recognised that with Mr Wardle's appointment in September 1920, there was once again 'a zealous advocate on the staff' to promote rowing.[239] Yet it was an uphill task. Like the previous year, there were too few entries to justify a school regatta in 1921, only two boys having rowed competitively before. Moreover, the disastrous race on 9 March, when both crews were swamped and the Monmouth stroke was drowned, resulted the following year in the abandonment of the traditional rowing fixtures, both Monmouth and Worcester deciding to move their rowing to the summer term. It seemed in 1922 that the sequence of races might come to an end but in March 1923 the regatta was revived, and despite the inevitable interference with cricket, the Headmaster was persuaded – how we will never know – to allow the school crew to continue rowing for the first three weeks of the summer term. So the pattern was now set for the revival of both school races, participation in the town regatta over Whitsun, and eventually (from 1929) in the Marlow public schools fours championship. By this time there was a solid base on which Wardle could build strong school crews: over 50 boys in ten or more crews (in clinkers or tub fours) would compete in the school regatta, the highlight of which would now be the races against Old Herefordian crews – who invariably lost, partly because they were used to using 'slides' in their college rowing – rather than the pre-war 'Oxford' versus 'Cambridge' races. Nevertheless, the successes of the first coxed four from the late 1920s onwards speak eloquently for Wardle's abilities as a rowing coach and the boys' determination (in the words on the 1920 captain of boats) 'to live up to the reputation earned by the crew of 1883' and (we might now add) that of 1929.

The 1929 win at Marlow was less of a surprise but as great a triumph as the one at Henley 46 years earlier. For the first four were unbeaten since 1926 in both the Worcester

---

237. For example, it was not until 1927 that the 1st XI recorded its first victory against King's, Worcester, since the end of the war. The team's best seasons in the inter-war period were 1926 (won 16, drawn 5, lost 6), which Crees heralded with the line from an Aeschylus chorus: 'Sing woe, sing woe but let the good prevail', and 1934 (won 9, lost 3, drawn 7).

238. Following the match against Bradley Court on 26 July 1926 which was won by the record margin of 279 runs (Shepherd 6 for 12), he was presented with an illuminated address and a cheque for £212 0s 7d, towards which Crees contributed £20. For Crees' tributes to Shepherd (including a Latin ode) and an account of his 50 years as a professional cricketer: *TH*, NS CXI (March 1926), pp.9-11; CXII (July 1926), pp.21-27; CXIII (Dec. 1926), pp.14-17.

239. *TH*, NS XCV (Dec 1920), p.19.

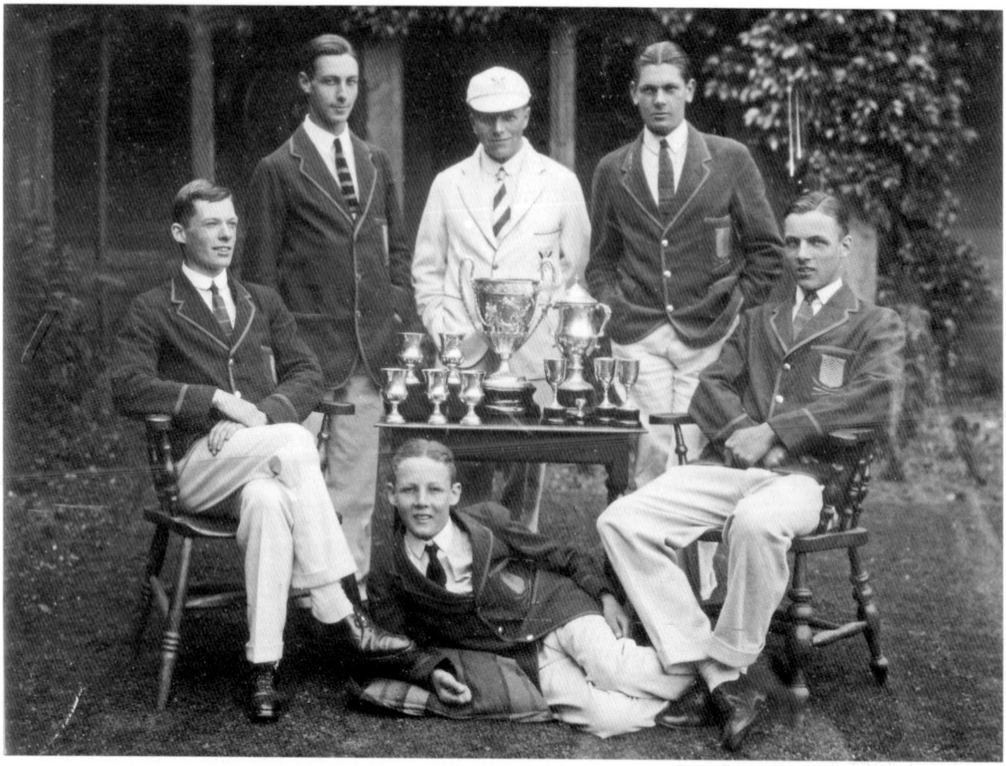

Fig. 7.10 Harry Wardle with his victorious 1929 coxed four, the second HCS crew to win the public schools' challenge cup: C.E. Crocker (stroke); E.C.N. Adams (3); W.A. McLay (2); E. Bettington (bow); F.F.J.C. Adams (cox).

and Monmouth races – and apart from 1932 and 1936 were to remain so throughout the 1930s; and the challenge cup, presented by the city chamber of commerce for the public schools race in the Hereford regatta, had occupied a permanent place underneath the schoolroom clock from the first race in 1927. But 1929 was the first time in this era that the school crew had been tested at a national level and there was a record entry of 16 schools for the coxed fours that year. However, on 21 and 22 June, Tonbridge, Stroud, Bedford Modern, Winchester, Cheltenham and Tiffin succumbed over the three races to the 'solidly hard-working' Hereford crew, which if it did not quite attain the elegance of the 1928 four, showed courage, determination and stamina in sweeping all before them.[240] Although the school came close to repeating its Marlow victory in 1930, 1935 and 1939, it never succeeded in doing so but HCS in its seven further attempts to win the Marlow public schools fours had (as Wardle earlier claimed) 'a record of consistency excelled by none'.[241] The school may never have produced a 'Blue' in this period and its crews may

240. Unsurprisingly, Wardle thought that the Marlow victory was superior to the one at Henley because 'many more races were rowed during the season and there was far more competition'. See *TH*, NS CXXI (July 1929), pp.29-30 for a full account of the races.

241. HCS competed nine times in the coxed fours at Marlow, 1929-39 (no crew was entered in 1936 or 1937), and was never beaten by more than two lengths. For Wardle's observation, see *TH*, NS CXXXIII (July 1933).

generally have been outweighed by their opponents; their boats may not have been of the best, despite the successful appeal in the wake of the Marlow win; and the boys may have had to battle against high winds and fast currents in their winter and spring training on the Wye, conditions which may have produced a stream of oarsmen who had (in Wardle's words) 'learned in a hard school how to manage an oar' but did not produce the prettiest crews.[242] Nevertheless, there was a discernible spirit about HCS rowing in this period for the revival of which the rowing master was chiefly responsible.[243]

Of the minor sports, athletics and fives, which were crammed into the school sporting programme in the last weeks of the spring term, and often suffered from the competing claims of rowing and junior rugby and (more seriously) the weather, a little needs to be said. In athletics, high winds and rain sometimes (as in late March 1928) made the Wyeside sports day races farcical, but occasionally conditions were sufficiently benign to enable the competitors – including E.C.N. Adams who broke the high jump record (admittedly with a jump of only 5 feet one) in 1929 – to achieve their best. Attempts, too, were made to improve the standard of performance by the introduction of inter-school fixtures – regularly (from 1930) against Monmouth and (from 1932) against the Crypt, and occasionally against the Worcester schools; the appointment of an athletics captain and the adoption of new rules for sports day.[244] Fives, on the other hand, flourished following the repair of the courts in 1921. Although the master in charge had once to remind the school of the 'nonsense' that it was merely 'an old woman's game',[245] the number of boys participating in the sport increased to over 50, the masters were generally able to raise four men to play against the first and second pairs and, despite the difficulty of playing against schools where courts were without a back wall and a buttress (as at Monmouth) or even (as at RGS, Worcester) where they were of a different size, new fixtures were organised.[246] These included (in 1938) a triangular contest with Brecon, as well as King's. Christ College scratched before it could take place in 1939 but it was optimistically reported at the end of that season that a similar match would be arranged the following year.

It is not surprising that the OTC during the inter-war period initially played a less prominent part in the school's activities, despite the proud display of some captured War

---

242. *TH*, NS CXLIX (April 1939). It should be noted that G.M. Lewis, who left HCS at 14 but started his rowing on the Wye, gained a Cambridge rowing 'Blue' in 1936; that the school four generally averaged around 11 stone, around a stone a man lighter than most of their Marlow opponents; and that as a result of the 1930 appeal, which raised over £223, the school bought two new tub fours, two second hand tub pairs and a light clinker four.

243. Wardle also revived sculling from 1926, entries averaging around 30 for the Symonds sculls (won by D.W.D. Heathcote for the fourth time in succession in 1934) and the junior cup. The competitions were rowed off towards the end of the summer term, although it should be admitted that the boys were not always able to steer a straight course and that sometimes (as in 1927) the Hunderton 'refreshments' sign 'seemed to exercise a potent attraction'.

244. The new rules, passed at a meeting of the school committee on 9 July, 1933, involved the establishment of three different age groups and the replacement of sports day entry fees with a 2s compulsory levy on every boy in the school. School athletics colours were also to be awarded on the basis of performances in inter-school matches.

245. *TH*, NS CXXIX (April 1932), report on the season by R.J. Marsh, senior mathematical master and the school's most successful fives coach in this period.

246. The traditional fives fixture against King's, Worcester, remained, although even at Worcester where the courts were similar in style to those at HCS, the Hereford boys complained when they played away that they were put off by their lurid pink colour. HCS's 1931 victory against their old rival was its first for 20 years.

Office trophies, which included a German field gun (a Krupp five inch howitzer) placed as a souvenir, rather ironically, on the 'Acropolis' for the younger boys to clamber over. Parades were cut to once a week – and the lengthening of morning school made less time for the cleaning of equipment in the lunch break beforehand – and there was an initial dip in the number of recruits. The corps' fortunes, however, soon revived following F.W. Brookes' elevation as commanding officer in January 1922, only to slump again after his enforced retirement in July 1929. One possible explanation for this 'rather dismal period' in the corps' history may have been the influence of the peace movement on the school, as exemplified at Oxford by the famous Union debate of 9 February 1933, when the motion 'that this House will in no circumstances fight for its King and Country' was carried by 122 votes.[247] A far more likely reason, however, was the appointment of the uninspiring Beynon as commanding officer in Brookes' place and the refusal of parents to cough up the extra guinea annual fee in a time of financial stringency.[248] And once Beynon was himself replaced by J.B. Morgan in April 1935, morale recovered and rapid progress was made with the introduction of House competitions, a regular field day at Lugwardine and, following the building of the miniature range at the back of the prep school, the establishment of a shooting team which once again competed against other schools.[249] On 15 June 1939, in the final OTC inspection before the outbreak of war and with Brookes back in charge, the inspecting officer praised the corps' high standards, and during the field day on Dinedor three weeks later, the NCOs were able to lead sections 'in conditions comparable to those of war-time'.[250] It was a timely exercise.

Such were the outdoor activities offered by the school in the inter-war period. They were conducted with a great deal of enthusiasm and no little skill by many masters and perhaps with the exception of the ten minutes of 'brisk exercises' during mid-morning break, were taken up enthusiastically by most of the boys. Not all, of course, enjoyed them and fewer enjoyed all of them, but only a handful thought like H.J. Sutters that sport played too great a part in HCS life.[251] And for the non-sporting intelligentsia, masters like J.C. Wordsworth, G.F. Pollard and, at least for his favoured Sixth Form classicists, Dr Crees himself, provided sufficient sweetness and light. But even these masters would have agreed with their colleague, Harry Wardle, that 'much self-denial and strenuous labour' was a prerequisite for success, and that outdoor activity was an essential part of a school curriculum. So let the final words on 'civility and heartiness' at this time go to HCS's most

247. Although there is no evidence about the effects of the peace movement in the early 1930s on HCS boys. For one of the few OTC reports for this period (which may itself be indicative): *TH*, NS CXXVII (July 1931).

248. For an indication of the state of the corps in these years, compare Brookes' meticulous account keeping in the 1920s with that of Beynon in the early 1930s, as well as the decline in the boys' subscriptions and the government grants for the period 1930-35. See HCSA, OTC cash book, 1919-35.

249. *TH*, NS CXLVII (July 1938), OTC report; HCSA, *OH Club Handbook 1937-38*, p.4. £134 9s was subscribed for the shooting range as a result of Crees' appeal letter of 10 March 1937, urging that at such a time 'it would be undesirable for the corps to fall behind in any department of its work'. The building of the range was started in late 1937 and completed early the following year.

250. *TH*, NS CL (July 1939), p.32.

251. *TH*, NS CXV (Dec. 1930), for a report of the 18 October debate: 'sport has too great a place in the public school life of today', the motion (proposed by Sutters, who garnered only eight votes) being lost by 40.

successful games coach of the Twenties and Thirties, words which well characterise the general nature of the school's corporate endeavour during these decades:

> In these days of newspaper lamentations about the predilection of the younger generation for 'soft' games, even the oldest of old fogies, the most rabid boaster of the manly things they used to do in his day, must have been gratified to see the crowded state of Jordan's [the boat-house] this term. For no sport demands more of the spirit of endurance, discipline and self-sacrifice than does rowing ...[252]

War and Retirement, 1939-1940

Dr Crees' last two terms in office from September 1939 to April 1940 coincided almost exactly with (in Evelyn Waugh's words) 'that odd period before the Churchillian renaissance which people called at the time the great bore war', subsequently known to history by the American usage 'phoney war'. But even at Hereford Cathedral School during these strange war-time months of inactivity, the effects of Chamberlain's declaration of war on 3 September 1939 were felt. Whereas in the autumn of 1938, the gas masks promised in the aftermath of the Munich crisis had got no further than Gloucester, a year later even a school on the furthest fringes of England could not escape the requirements of war.[253]

Within Hereford itself, there was frenetic activity during the month of September 1939 for which Dr Crees, as a prominent member of its education committee, took considerable responsibility.[254] Towards the end of that month, he could report to the city council that history had been made through the accommodation of 98 teachers and 850 children who had been evacuated from the Birmingham area. The blackout requirements, too, had proceeded apace, not least in the schools, the secondary schools being ordered not to re-open until the ARP (Air Raid Precautions) committee was satisfied that the necessary measures had been taken.[255] Other air-raid precautions were less well advanced. By early October, for example, there were still over 1,000 children unprovided for in shelter trenches; the shelter provisions for the High Schools were not finally approved (at a cost of £935) until late November; the first testing of the air raid siren on the Shirehall roof did not occur until 16 December; and the first 300 Anderson shelters (out of over 4,000 ordered) for ordinary householders did not arrive until late February 1940.

From the beginning of the previous autumn term, the impact of war was immediately felt at HCS.[256] On its outbreak, George Hunt had left the staff to be gazetted lieutenant in the Herefordshire regiment, the first of many masters to be called up; and within days news of the first OH casualty, J.A. Blackledge (1931-37), who was among those missing when *HMS Rawalpindi* was sunk in the North Sea, had filtered back to the school. That autumn term, the exigencies of the time meant that only ten Old Herefordians returned to visit

252. *TH*, NS CXIV (April 1927), p.11.

253. Waugh, dedication to Randolph Churchill; *TH*, NS CXLVIII (Dec. 1938), editorial.

254. For the following see *HT*, 30 Sept. 1939, p.4; 28 Oct. p.8; 2 Dec. p.9; 23 Dec. p.9; 24 Feb. 1940, p.7.

255. Thus delaying the start of term for the High Schools by two weeks (to 25 September). HCS started on the following day, around the usual time, apart from the Classical Sixth which returned three days earlier.

256. The following paragraph is largely based on D.P. Lloyd's editorial and the subsequent notes in *TH*, NS CLI (Dec. 1939), pp.2-4.

their *alma mater*, compared with 30 or more each term before the war, the school hearing intelligence day by day 'about this or that old boy who is in the air force, the navy or the army'. But it was the blackout, which gradually grew earlier as the leaves fell and autumn turned to winter, that caused the biggest disruption.[257] Although little lesson time seems to have been lost 'by the darkness', the decision not to blackout the schoolroom – even though £200 had been set aside in the annual budget towards ARP expenditure and the Board of Education would find half of these costs – inevitably restricted its use and disrupted routine. The boarders could no longer do prep there and were now dispersed between the music, day and reading rooms, new boys missing (it was reported) 'the thrill of hearing for the first time the authoritative voice of the monitor who stalks majestically up and down the room'. It was impossible, too, to hold debates on Saturday nights, although (as we have seen) boarders had the enjoyment of films in School House on Sunday evenings; and on account of the blackout, the annual confirmation service on 14 December had to be held in All Saints rather than the cathedral. Other changes were enforced. The rugby fixture list, for example, was reconstructed, the matches against King's, Worcester, and the Gloucester schools being replaced by more local games 'owing to the difficulties of transport'. The shooting match arranged against the 217th Searchlight Training Regiment was also a sign of the times.

Still, D.P. Lloyd, the Head Monitor who was to lose his life in the war, put a brave face on things. In December 1939 he wrote: 'We are very fortunate in not having been moved from our ancient seat … We have experienced rations and restrictions, inconveniences and innovations but on the whole the old order doesn't change'. 'This term,' he concluded, 'has been … a happy medium between the extremes of lunacy and sanity'. And to what extent were these lines from his published soliloquy: 'the cerulean tranquillity of a star-lit sky, which ever holds new wonders for those who scan its unfathomable galaxy', prompted by those jet black winter nights in the early weeks of war?[258]

But despite the soliloquies and reassuring editorials, an old order was giving way to a new. Crees' decision to retire had been building up for some time. As he mentioned to the governors in June 1936, the burdens of the headmastership at HCS, which included the management of a boarding House and heavy secretarial duties (undertaken without the assistance of an official secretary), required 'the attention and energy of two, if not three, men'. The previous term, he had taken an extended sea cruise on medical advice, another 'mid-term breathing-space' being repeated that summer. Crees had also been thinking about his pension provision, and enquired of his governors the following March whether the additional £200 given to him for masters' board could be paid as part of his salary for pension purposes. And retirement was certainly on his mind when he wrote to his former tutor at Cambridge in June 1939. So when on 2 October 1939, he gave his governors six months' notice of his intention to retire, it could not have caused any surprise.[259]

257. By November 1939, it had been agreed that the blackout should begin half an hour after sunset and end half an hour before sunrise. Calder, p.73.

258. *TH*, NS (Dec. 1939), pp.27-28.

259. HCSA, GMB 1921-45, meetings, 13 June 1936, 24 March 1937, 19 Oct. 1939; SJCA, 11/3/37, Crees to T.R. Glover, 13 June 1939: '… if I could myself attain to *otium cum dignitate* shortly I should feel that I deserved to be congratulated'.

Crees had certainly earned a long rest from his magisterial labours. The job had aged him, to which the photographs taken at the beginning and end of his tenure bear witness: the spectacles were similar, the intensity of the stare the same but like the disappearance of the winged collar, the fresh faced young tyro of late 1919 had given way to the drawn and greyed veteran of February 1940. As Crees himself had put it years earlier, any Head who had survived 20 years 'richly deserved an honourable leisure', and after nine years at the Crypt and more than double that at HCS, Crees had long ago fulfilled his own dictum.[260] And it was not as though he was without things to occupy his leisure time. Indeed, few men were better equipped to put retirement to good use for quite apart from his many interests, he had been elected a city councillor in the Liberal interest in November 1937, and 18 months later he was chairman of one committee and vice-chairman of two more.[261] There was every prospect in the summer of 1939 that the exhausted warrior could look forward to a long and profitable retirement.

Crees' decision to leave must have been confirmed by the outbreak of war. Although as Lloyd had observed, the Cathedral School was much better off than the evacuated schools,[262] the Headmaster during that autumn term at the beginning of the war was beset with nagging difficulties which however much foreseen affected the smooth running of his school and which were largely outside his power to control. He reported to his governors in mid-October 1939:

> Since the governors last met, the country has been involved in a war involving difficulties and dangers without precedent. Though Hereford has been classified as a reception area, it has not escaped the problems of less sheltered areas. It has been considered necessary to make certain adaptabilities for air raid precaution purposes and the expense of these adaptations may prove a heavy burden. The school was a few days late in resuming but has not been appreciably affected in its numbers, the few who have dropped out having been made up for by some newcomers from more dangerous areas. At present work is proceeding normally. One master has been called up for military service, the woodwork instructor is … absent, as is also the school porter.[263]

Such problems were compounded by the onset in early 1940 of the worst winter of the century. Pipes burst; the five courts were snowed up; the Wye froze and then drift ice smashed up Jordan's raft, the floes crashing into the city bridges (according to the *Hereford Times*) 'with almost frightening noises as if being rent and torn by demonic forces'; the regatta was cancelled, football on Wyeside became impossible, attendance was affected, and influenza and measles decimated the school ranks. Harry Wardle's comment that it was his

---

260. Crees (1920), p.29.

261. Crees was elected (with 738 votes) as the second councillor for the Monmouth ward on 1 November 1937, and before the end of that month had become a member of the rating, library and education committees. HARC, BO 35/19, fos 5, 25, 38, 67. See Crees' letter to Glover (note 259 above) for his chairmanship of these committees. Given his tirades against local councillors earlier in his career, his joining their ranks was a strange reversal of the past as Crees himself acknowledged.

262. Some ten HMC schools had been affected by enforced evacuation by December 1939, quite apart from those evacuated voluntarily (like St Paul's). *HMC 1939 Report* pp.22ff, debate at Shrewsbury School, 21 Dec. 1939.

263. HCSA, GMB 1921-45, 17 Oct. report for meeting on 19 Oct. 1939.

worst term in 20 years was put more diplomatically to the governors by his Headmaster – he described the term as 'the most remarkable and unusual in living memory' – but the message was essentially the same.[264]

The term was mercifully short as Easter fell almost as early as it could fall in that year of 1940. Dr Crees preached his last school sermon on 17 March – his text is unrecorded – and the term ended three days later. By April, the preparatory school had been sold at a generous price to his successor,[265] and Dr and Mrs Crees had taken to the country, to 'Wonder View', the house which had been built to their specification at Much Birch, with its balcony inscribed with the legend (in Greek) from Psalm 121: 'I will lift up mine eyes unto the hills ...' There he could read his committee papers, listen to his gramophone records and contemplate the serene beauty of the Welsh mountains. And from here, he could roam on his bicycle through (in his own words) 'the sequestered peace of ... a region where the English landscape is still scarcely touched or disfigured'.[266] Alas, it was not to be for long. For on 29 December 1941, after his morning cycle ride, Dr Crees collapsed and died from a cerebral haemorrhage. So passed a great figure in the school's history. It is appropriate that his last head monitor, who like many of his predecessors was to win a Somerset Thornhill classical scholarship at Brasenose, should have the final say on a career which had taken the Cathedral School to new heights, even if the light was dimming by the time Crees handed over the torch to his successor:

> We would venture to say that Dr Crees' testimonial remains impressed upon the minds of generations of boys whose education he made his life's work. Dr Crees may well say with Horace: *Exige monumentum aere perennius*. It is now Dr Crees' turn to hand on the torch. It burns brightly.[267]

---

264. The mean January temperature (at Ross) in 1940 was 30°F, the coldest since 1881: *HT*, 17 Feb. 1940, p.10; and 10 Feb. 1940, p.7, for an account of the coldest Hereford winters, 1814-1940. See *HT*, 3 Feb. 1940, p.7, for the devastation locally; and *TH*, NS CLII (March 1940), pp.17-18, 20-21, 23, for that winter's effect on HCS life; and HCSA, GMB 1921-45, for Crees' final report, 26 March 1940.

265. Crees sold the preparatory school to his successor in a private deal for around £2,500, the price he had paid for it, without apparently insisting on an additional 'goodwill' payment. The HCS governors, who had initially wanted to buy the school – a move favoured by the Board of Education – backed down when there was a possibility of their acquiring Number 2 Castle Street for the Langford boarders. Crees eventually sold Langford House at the end of the summer term 1940, the boys moving to Number 2 (rented by HCS on six months' notice at £70 *per annum*) the following September. For all this, see TNA, ED 35/4441, *passim*.

266. SJCA, 11/3/37, Crees to T.R. Glover, 13 June 1939. In this letter Crees estimates that he cycled 4,000 miles per year. His love of bicycling is also recorded in reminiscences by two Old Herefordians: Basil Butcher (1919-29), who later sold his former Headmaster (and taught him to drive) a Morris Six, specially fitted with a bicycle rack; and F.C. Cook (1933-40), who had the misfortune to be caught absconding from games one afternoon 'by a familiar figure [Crees] sitting astride his machine' at the top of Bewdley Hill.

267. *TH*, NS CLII (March 1940), p.2, D.P. Lloyd's editorial, the translation of the Latin phrase reading in English: 'I have erected a monument more lasting than bronze'. Crees allowed any member of the Classical Sixth, 1920-40, to take one book from his personal library as a souvenir, but his residuary estate, valued at £16,773 gross and £13,355 net, was bequeathed to St John's College, Cambridge, subject to his wife's life interest. Following Mrs Crees' death in 1973, the college received £21,599.59 from the estate, the income from which is still used for the benefit of St John's students.

Christopher Fairfax Scott, 1940-1945

In late January 1940, Dean Waterfield and his governors appointed Christopher Fairfax Scott – 'Kit' to his friends, 'Boko' subsequently to the Hereford boys – as Headmaster, from a strong list of candidates, after a search lasting little more than six weeks.[268] They were again fortunate in being able to entice at a modest annual salary of £800, plus rent-free occupation of Number 1, another relatively young but experienced Headmaster: even more so given that the Head's rights to capitation fees had been abolished, although he was still able to retain the boarding profits and (following Scott's purchase of the property from Crees) the income from the preparatory school.[269] Only 43 at the time of his appointment, Scott had already 12 years' experience leading three HMC schools: Monmouth (1928-36), Brighton College (1937-39) and Taunton School (1939-40). He could have achieved little of permanence during his two terms as acting Head in Somerset but in his first two headmasterships he made, in different ways, a distinct impression. At Monmouth, he was remembered as having built up boarding numbers, improved its buildings and enhanced the school's academic and athletic reputation; and at Brighton, he had made a number of discerning staff appointments and had introduced some timely reforms. There, however, he had fallen foul of his Council over certain financial matters and his proposal to evacuate the College, his chairman unhesitatingly accepting his second letter of resignation in January 1939, 22 months after his first attempt to resign, so terminating 'the shortest and stormiest' tenure in the college's history.[270]

The relationship between Headmaster and Dean at Hereford was to be much less stormy than that between Scott and his no-nonsense chairman on the Sussex coast. Indeed Dean Waterfield, whose influence on the governing body was decisive, must have felt that despite the turbulence of his Brighton career, in Scott they had uncovered a leader who had not only the experience but also the strength of character to steer the school through the war years. From his time at Monmouth, moreover, he was someone who knew both the school and the area well, and who could be relied on to sustain boarding numbers, a view endorsed by the Board's inspector.[271] And although Scott was the first HCS Headmaster in modern times not to have possessed a Classics degree – having been invalided out of the Army in 1915, he returned to Oxford to read for the final honours school of English – his wide literary interests and record as an outstanding teacher, and not least at Cheltenham College, made him a more than suitable Headmaster for the Cathedral School. On Scott's part, he realised that the £400 drop from his Brighton salary could be more than made up from

268. The post was advertised in *The Times* and *The Spectator* (for £4 10s and £4 respectively) in late 1939. Scott was appointed (he was the only candidate to be interviewed from an initial short-list of four) on 29 January 1940; and the announcement was made in early February. HCSA, HCS Cashbook 1925-46, fo 74, payment 21 Dec. 1939; HCSA, GMB 1921-45, meetings, 23 and 29 Jan. 1940; *HT*, 10 Feb. 1940, p. 8.

269. Capitation fees had been prohibited by the Board of Education's 1935 regulations for secondary schools. For the sale of the preparatory school, see above, note 265. The preparatory school was an excellent business, its profits for the four years 1941-44 averaging out at over £675 *per annum*. This more than made up for the poor return that Scott made (at least at first) from the boarders. HCSA, Scott to Waterfield, 1 Dec. 1945.

270. *The Monmothian* (March 1937), pp.4-5; Jones (1995), pp.208-15, 224.

271. TNA, ED 35/4441, R.E. Williams to V.C. Martin, 11 May 1940. Although Williams also commented (without elaborating) that Scott was 'a queer customer in some ways'.

Fig. 7.11 Christopher Fairfax Scott, an imposing Headmaster, who took over the school 'at a most difficult time in the world's history', but who initiated important reforms during his five year tenure.

the preparatory school's profits; and that in the Dean of Hereford he had a like-minded and sympathetic chairman with whom he could do business. Indeed, the few letters that survive from Scott to Waterfield show that by late 1945 the relationship was one of some intimacy.[272]

The school welcomed the appointment. Scott was known to senior masters from his Monmouth days – he had even attended an OH dinner in the Green Dragon – and *The Herefordian* felt that 'a trusted friend was coming to rule over the school'.[273] And even if young boys were over-awed, if not actually frightened, by the tall, imposing be-tweeded figure with a forceful personality and powerful bass voice, some of their seniors recognised, at least in retrospect, that the new Headmaster was (in the words of one of them) 'an enormous breath of much needed fresh air'. Although not less, and possibly more, mean-handed with the cane, the contrast with the oppressive and apparently humourless Crees was marked. Here was a more sympathetic and 'a lighter freer task-master', whose style was to encourage and who was more prepared to give and take.[274]

With the announcement of Scott's appointment, there was also recognition that he had taken over the school 'at a most difficult time in the world's history', and that he and Mrs Scott, whose burden as war-time housekeeper of Number 1 was considerable and ultimately wore her down, needed all possible support. But it was not simply a time of acute uncertainty internationally, for as the Board of Education confessed in early 1940, the impact of a prolonged war upon direct grant boarding schools could not possibly be foreseen.[275] And at Hereford, despite Crees' success in moving HCS forward academically and in other ways, in April 1940 the school's structural weaknesses were apparent. The new Headmaster's conditions of service may have changed but through the preparatory school and such boarding profits as there were, he could still make money at the school's expense. And initially at any rate, he still directly collected parental fees and 'extras', often sent 'by the grubby hands of their children'.[276] This hardly made for efficiency. Moreover, the financial state of the school, with a current account balance of £73 10s 6d for 1939-40, hardly bred confidence. Pupil numbers had largely been sustained, but only on the boarding side – where the average fee was around half the proper amount – by Crees's generous offers of free and cut-price places. And despite the improvements since 1920, the classrooms and boarding houses were antiquated and fitfully heated by coal fires and stoves, apart from the

---

272. HCSA, letters 19, 26 Sept, 1, 15 Dec. 1945; 8 March 1946.

273. *TH*, NS CLIII (July 1940), p.4.

274. Compare, for example, Peter Williams' memory of C.F. Scott on his first day at HCS in September 1940 (*Old Herefordians' Newsletter* 2009, pp.30-31), with the appreciations of P.W.M. John and Geoffrey Hughes in their respective letters to Bob Adams (22 Sept. 1996) and the author (27 Nov. 2010) in the school archives. Interestingly, one of the senior boys at Brighton College also (like John) used the phrase 'breath of fresh air' about Scott's arrival there as Headmaster. See Jones (1995), p.215, for this and other reminiscences of Scott.

275. TNA, ED 35/4441, Birch-Jones' report, 12 March 1940.

276. HCSA, GMB 1921-45, meeting, 11 Nov. 1940; HCSA, Scott to Waterfield, 1 Dec. 1945. Despite opposition from Tom Steel, the Chapter Clerk, of whom Scott had a low opinion, the matter was resolved largely through Scott's and Dean Waterfield's efforts, and from January 1941 all fees were paid directly to Lloyds' Bank and accounted for by the Clerk (and the invaluable Mr Parker) who for the first time had a complete school roll and a list of parental addresses. For Scott's tribute to Parker: HCSA, GMB 1921-45, report, 3 Aug. 1944.

new Science building which had its own central heating system. The installation of central heating throughout the school, however, was to remain a distant and unfulfilled dream of the new Headmaster. Scott could console himself that the school's academic side was sound, if still biased towards the Classics and Mathematics, and that its sporting traditions and corporate life were strong. This was illustrated at the end of his first term when three state scholarships in Classics and two exhibitions in Mathematics were won and the 1st cricket XI went almost unbeaten.[277] These were essentially Creesian triumphs.

If HCS was not in the rudest of health in April 1940, during the war it was more fortunate than most. Unlike around 30 HMC schools and thousands of others, it had not suffered evacuation from a danger area; it had not been commandeered like its near neighbour, Malvern College; it had not been bombed like Wellington College.[278] As the *Hereford Times* noted at the end of the war, the Cathedral School and other schools in the district had been spared 'the most disruptive war-time influences'. But as the 1945 report goes on to state, these war years:

> presented many worries and difficulties to those whose task is the guidance of educational foundations ... [and] no-one will gainsay that its [the Cathedral School's] administration during these grim years has called for outstanding qualities of leadership allied to education ability.[279]

That HCS came through the war with its numbers enhanced and its reputation secure was in no small measure due to the work of its resolute new Headmaster and his ageing friend, Dean Waterfield.

A Community At War

During the course of the war Hereford underwent a remarkable transformation: from a population of some 26,000 to one of near 50,000 at its peak; from a city in which 'nearly all the residents were on nodding acquaintance with each other' to a place of many strangers; from a quiet county capital to a busy centre of military activity.[280] The influx of population 'brought about conditions of over-crowding in all houses, ruthlessly swept aside the habitual reserve of the average Herefordian, made the already difficult task of shopping a nightmare ... and crowded the streets, the cinemas, the dance halls ... the public houses, hotels and cafes'.

---

277. The three state scholars were J.M. Burch, F.C. Cook and D.P. Lloyd. The Somerset exhibitions in Mathematics were awarded to R.E. Curtis and I.P. Williams. The 1st XI in 1940 won 8 of their 11 matches, losing only to Monmouth.

278. By October 1940, 29 HMC schools, some 15 *per cent* of the Conference membership, had been evacuated. Two of these schools came to Herefordshire – Felsted to Goodrich Court and Westminster to Saltmarshe Castle, Bromyard. *HMC Committee Report 1940*, p. 46.

279. *HT*, 16 June 1945, p.4.

280. Hereford's history during the Second World War remains to be written. The following is drawn from various issues of the *Hereford Times* for the war years, especially that of 12 May 1945, p.6. The pre-war population figure (25,890, for 1938) is given in TNA, ED 151/43, Ministry memo, 13 Dec. 1944; and the near 50,000 estimate is extrapolated from the amounts raised per head of population (for Hereford and district) in the three war savings campaigns, 1941-43: *HT*, 8 May 1943, p.5; 15 May 1943, p.5.

A number of schoolchildren were evacuated, as we have seen, but there was also an influx of hundreds of workers for the war production factories at Holmer, Withington and Rotherwas, as well as a migratory population of refugees from bombed cities. The majority of 'invaders', however, were forces personnel, the city's streets being filled during the war years with people in Army khaki and RAF blue, 'with a sprinkling of Royal Navy blue uniforms'. First came the searchlight batteries of the Royal Artillery, who camped on the Racecourse during the spring and summer months of 1940 and then moved in August to the new Bradbury barracks. In the first year of war, their training lights did much to relieve the blackout gloom, when up to 20 powerful beams at a time could be seen penetrating the night sky, the blackout suddenly returning as the lights were simultaneously shut down and the city was again 'plunged into Cimmerian darkness'. Then after Dunkirk, there were the men from numerous other regiments, who, 'footsore and weary beyond words', began to arrive at Hereford railway station to recuperate at the barracks and even on the grass within the Close where trespass was forbidden. One young officer, on seeing two choristers dressed in their Eton suits and mortar boards on the Barrs Court Road, emptied the ammunition from his revolver and declared: 'Now I know I'm home!'[281] In the following months and years thousands more soldiers and airmen came to the area to be trained, including after Pearl Harbour 'white and coloured' (so the *Hereford Times* revealingly informs us) American troops – the old Wye Bridge being strengthened to carry their tanks and equipment – only to be replaced after D-day by the wounded.

The impact of war on Hereford's civilian population was further heightened by the nature of the conflict, for this was the people's war, and unlike the first time around 'blighty' was the front line. Not that Hereford suffered much by the way of bombardment. The solitary bomb that was dropped on the city fell on open ground on Red Hill and caused little damage, but close by, the lone aircraft raid on the Royal Ordnance factory at Rotherwas just after dawn on 27 July 1942 killed 17 and injured 24 people. Less than two years later, an explosion there – one of several during the war – was the equivalent of 31 x 2,000 lb bombs going off, which could have wrecked a large part of the city had it not been for the bravery of many people.[282] All told, 700 high explosive bombs and thousands of incendiaries were dropped in various parts of the county, nearly all in open countryside. And the mighty drones of enemy aircraft not infrequently passed over Hereford on their way to bomb the industrial cities, their handiwork in the Midlands and South Wales, where an Old Herefordian was busy organising the Swansea defences, sometimes being visible from vantage points on the Herefordshire hills. During such nights the HCS boarders were woken up and marched down in their dressing-gowns to the spartan ARP shelter, constructed in the Number 1 cellars, often staying there for several hours from the first siren to the all-clear signal.[283] All told, there were 69 air raid alerts (apart from the monthly

281. HCSA, letter of H.J. Downes to the author, 31 Aug. 2010.

282. This serious incident happened on 30 May 1944 but it was not fully made known until the following January. The damage was extensive but only two people were killed and 30 injured even though some 700 people were at work at the factory at the time. Subsequently, 50 honours and commendations for gallantry, including five George Medals, were made to the factory managers and workers. See *HT*, 13 Jan. 1945, p.4 for the full report.

283. HCSA, Geoffrey Hughes to the author, 11 Jan. 2012. Hughes added: 'Hereford was ignored. We thought the Luftwaffe very inconsiderate'. The Swansea OH was H.L. Lang-Coath (previously H.L. Coath), who was awarded

tests) in Hereford city from the first one on the night of 25 August 1940 until the last in anger on the 14 August 1944, the biggest number of consecutive alerts being sounded for eight nights in early May 1941.

So in Hereford, the fear of air raid attack was prevalent for more than four years. As J.P.L. Thomas, the city's MP, put it to his Unionist Association on 22 June 1940: 'We are, every one of us, now defenders of this country. The weariness of inaction has gone and there is now no-one who has not some part to play in the battle ahead'. By that date, a government order had prohibited the use of church bells except when giving warning of enemy invasion, the responsibility for their ringing being handed over to the military or defence volunteers. The fear of invasion was made more real in Hereford by the civil defence exercises such as the one on Sunday 25 May 1941 during the period of the heaviest concentration of air-raid warnings. The public were asked to co-operate in the exercise, following the 'bombing' of the Town Hall and a three-pronged ground attack on the city, by carrying their respirators, producing their identity cards when asked (under threat of a £5 penalty and/or imprisonment) and acting as casualties; and in the search for 'quislings', all people entering Hereford were stopped by the home guard. Fire-watching, too, became a vital requirement of war, the Dean appealing in January 1941 for the assistance of roof watchers to ensure the cathedral's safety. Cathedral schoolboys, as we will see, answered this call, as did – by October 1941 – 5,671 volunteers for the city as a whole.

For the cathedral authorities, the Second World War caused more problems than that of 1914-18.[284] In September 1940, Dean Waterfield gave over his Deanery to the military – it was later used to house American troops – and moved with his wife into the College Cloisters. The archives, Mappa Mundi and other treasures were removed for safe-keeping from the cathedral to more remote locations. More permanently, in January 1943 the cathedral lost its railings, although not its massive screen which with its 11,200 lbs of iron and 5,000 lbs of copper and brass some felt should also have been salvaged for the war effort.[285] The cathedral's establishment, too, was reduced. Philip Wilson, a lay clerk, joined the army on 25 March 1941 – a locally stationed airman and Freeman Newton, the Chief Constable, were later brought in as supernumeraries – and Walter Gittens, the College gardener, was recruited the following July. The Chapter's (and school's) effectiveness was also impeded by the absence of both Canon Moreton – leaving Canons Warner and Jordan to alternate their residences – and Tom Steel, the Chapter Clerk, on military service. On top of all the trials of running a cathedral with a depleted staff at a time of national crisis and local need, the Dean had other responsibilities. Not the least among these was his role as chairman of the Cathedral Commission for England. And as an active chairman of governors of HCS – and according to Scott himself, the only governor during the war years to take a real interest in

the CBE in 1941 for his services as Town Clerk and ARP Controller in organising the civil defences during the heavy raids on that city. He attended HCS, 1890-95, and held the school 100 yards record for many years. (See below, p.500, note 198.) For his obituary: *TH*, NS CLXXX (Oct. 1950), p.48.

284. For the cathedral and its treasures during these war years, see Aylmer and Tiller, pp.175-76, 531, 553-54; and HCA, 7031/24, *passim*.

285. For this controversy about the screen, see the following letters between 'Realist' and Herbert Powell (later the school's architect): *HT*, 16 Jan. 1943, p.6; 23 Jan. 1943, p.7; 30 Jan. 1943, p.6; and 6 Feb. 1943, p.5.

the school or who 'knew the least thing about it' – he had the school to watch over.[286] The strain on a man in his seventies, even a sprightly one who was to live to a hundred, must have been immense.

The Headmaster's burdens were almost as great. Unlike Scott's previous headmasterships, any grandiose ambitions he might have had for the Cathedral School needed to be put on one side. There were limited occasions, too, for his formidable presence to make an impression on a popular platform: speech days were abandoned; OH Club dinners were made impossible; public performances were few and far between. As Scott himself admitted at the end of his tenure: 'I realise how little of what I wished for has in these years been possible. My stay with you has coincided with the period of the war so that personal contacts, offers of hospitality and reunions have, to my deep regret, been out of the question'. So for C.F. Scott, make do and mend was the order of the day, together with the dreary circumstances of total war: the blackout, rationing, supply problems, escalating costs, travel restrictions, the call-up of young masters and the near impossibility of adequately replacing them, the premature leaving of boys and all the other difficulties associated with 'austerity and … that gloomy dame's brisker brother, utility'.[287]

Scott was dealt a weak hand, yet he played it with some aplomb. One outcome of the war for public schools was that while some schools – those suffering dislocation or high fees (or both) – were struggling, others were profiting. As Spencer Leeson, the long-serving HMC chairman during the war explained to the Haileybury Conference in December 1940, despite the country being over supplied with boarding places, schools 'in remote districts with a fee of £150 or less' were 'doing very well'.[288] This certainly applied at HCS where the £98 annual boarding fee, minus extras but including the £33 tuition fee, remained unchanged apart from a 'temporary war-time surcharge' of £6. And the Headmaster was not slow to promote his new school. Better contacts were made with preparatory schools. A new prospectus was commissioned from John Bellows of Gloucester for his second term, the firm reprinting more than a thousand extra copies over the next five years. School advertisements were also regularly placed in regional newspapers – as well as more locally – with a coverage which extended to Devon and Cornwall, Bristol, Gloucestershire, all parts of Wales and the West Midlands.[289] Boarding numbers grew to around 70, which as Scott

286. Dean Waterfield was a member of the commission throughout the 11 years of its existence, and chaired the body for its last seven years until its cessation on 31 July 1942. All told, it devised 77 new schemes for all the old foundations, some modern cathedrals and all parish church cathedrals; and dissolved all but one of the ancient minor corporations (including the Hereford College of Vicars). *HT*, 30 May 1942, p.4. For the Headmaster's observation on the Dean: HCSA, Scott to Waterfield, 1 Dec. 1945. Waterfield's dominance as chairman of the governing body, whom he represented on the newly-formed Governing Bodies Association from 1941, is apparent from the governors' minute book for the period.

287. For the Scott and 'austerity' quotations: *TH*, NS CLXVI (Sept. 1945), p.8, Scott to Wardle, 31 July 1945, in acknowledgement of his £45 leaving gift from the OHs; and Calder, p.322.

288. *HMC 1940 Report*, p.15, 20 Dec. 1940. Scott is not listed as having attended any of the five conferences held during his tenure at Hereford.

289. HCSA, Cash Book 1925-46, fo 78, payment to John Bellows Ltd, 24 Oct. 1940; and *passim* for the other payments to the Bellows company and various newspapers. Three of the Scott prospectuses survive in the school archives, one of which includes an old clothes list with the heading: 'some concessions are made in this list in war time'. These included soft collar shirts and sports coats and trousers replacing the pre-war Eton collars and grey

observed when the 60 mark had been reached was 'more than we can contain', and would have been impossible had not Number 2 housed over 20 boarders. Day numbers expanded even more rapidly, one indication of which was the purchase of 120 'stelcon' bicycle blocks for the 1941 summer term.[290] Another was Scott's geographical reorganisation of the day boys into two distinct Houses, East and West – as he had done at Monmouth – at the beginning of the 1940 autumn term, under Harry Wardle and William Harley as their respective Housemasters.[291] This enabled more meaningful House competitions to occur, although it needs to be said that in the war period the boarders invariably beat the combined strength of the new day Houses in most games. Overall, the steady increase of the pupil roll averaged over five academic years from 1940/41 to 1944/45 makes impressive reading as this progression shows: 181, 187, 210, 220 and 235.

Recruitment at the preparatory school was also stimulated by the war. One extra form, making five in all, was added in September 1940 and in the summer of 1943, Miss Gamlen's last term, when the school was at last recognised as efficient by the Board of Education, the hundred mark was reached, 30 or so above the average pre-war figure.[292] During the one-year tenure of her successor, Miss Emmerson, a record 52 boys were enrolled. Entries fell the following year but in September 1944 under Miss Phillips, who had started at the prep with Miss Gamlen in 1912, the boys were regrouped into four houses named after benefactors, thus anticipating a similar re-organisation at the senior school by 30 years. A thriving preparatory school was one explanation for the expansion of HCS during the war years, even if only one in two boys passed on to the senior school.

The school's expansion did not result in a marked improvement in its financial position, as might have been expected had the preparatory school surpluses been available to help balance the Cathedral School's books rather than line Scott's pocket. And Crees gave the governors every opportunity of purchasing his school in 1940 and the Board of Education every encouragement to do so. This opportunity was squandered through the governors' holding out the prospect that a new Headmaster might be able to retain the preparatory's profits, and their attempt to purchase Number 2 Castle Street in preference to the prep. In the end they missed out on both, Number 2 eventually being rented (rather than bought) to accommodate the Langford boarders.[293] Consequently, the school's finances were not as

---

flannel suits. HCSA, Geoffrey Hughes to the author, 11 Jan. 2012.

290. HCSA, GMB 1921-45, meetings, 30 June 1942 (for the Scott observation); and 30 Nov. 1944 (re 27 boarders in Number 2 at that time). HCSA, Cash Book1925-46, fo 89, payment for £34 10s to Stelcon Industrial Floors Ltd, 16 June 1941. The bike blocks were then hired out to the boys for a nominal sum. The boarding numbers are based on the March 1941 and March 1943 figures (59 and 66 respectively), which exclude the preparatory boarders. HCSA, GBA surveys, 4 Feb. 1942, 3 June 1943.

291. In 1928 at Monmouth, Scott had divided the 'Country House' boys into separate Monmouthshire and Herefordshire (including Gloucestershire) units. Ward, p.32.

292. Recognition followed the inspection of 16 and 17 June 1942, the first in the school's history and one which Scott had specifically requested, and a further HMI visit on 19 May 1943. See TNA, ED 35/4442, Scott to the Board, 23 Jan. 1942; and TNA, ED109/1979, for the request, the inspection report and subsequent correspondence.

293. See TNA, ED 35/4441 for these negotiations, which at one point led an exasperated Board of Education official to express the view that 'the governors seem a little over fond of broaching hypothetical schemes and putting them tentatively to us'. V.C. Martin to R.E. Williams (HMI), 20 March 1940.

favourable as they otherwise would have been, exhibiting annual deficits (apart from 1942-43) on the general account which amounted to almost £550 by 31 March 1945. The exception was the Philpotts scholarship fund which had a balance of over £679 by the same date, despite the increase in the amount spent on internal scholarships – an average of nearly £350 *per annum* (1940-45), benefiting 29 boys by 1945.[294]

The indifferent state of the school's general account is not hard to explain. For although the Board's annual grant remained fairly steady at around £2,000 and the increase in fees income more than kept pace with the rise in the salary bill, there was still an annual average deficit on the fees account of over £1,300. Other costs continued to rise. Some of these were directly to do with the war: for example, the £115 14s paid to the Herefordshire County Council for the school's contribution towards the cost of the air raid shelter constructed in 1939;[295] the £38 13s 9d spent by Scott on the blackout of Big School in early 1943; the £21 12s 8d paid annually, 1941-45, under the War Damage Act; and a doubling of the fire insurance premium to the Royal Exchange Assurance Company, the new policy from the end of 1944 covering the school to the extent of £15,300. The cost of electric lighting was the only expense to come in below the pre-war level – for obvious reasons – averaging around £10 *per annum* until 1944-45 when costs tripled. Fuel costs, too, rose markedly during that year, doubling to over £68. There were other new liabilities: the making of the sick-bay on the top floor of Number 1 in 1941, the old sanatorium in Number 7 Ferrers Street being (in Scott's view) 'grossly unsatisfactory'; the expense of taking on Number 2, its annual rental being increased from £70 to £90 in January 1945; the first ever rental increase in January 1943 (by £50 to £150) for Number 1 and 7 Ferrers Street;[296] and the hundreds of pounds worth of repairs to the school plant, after years of minimal maintenance, in 1944 and 1945. These included the rebuilding of Number 1, the construction of the cellar air-raid shelter earlier in the war having considerably weakened its foundations.[297] And then there were the many incidental costs, not least the frequent and unprecedented payments associated with promoting the school and advertising and interviewing staff.[298]

For in these years, the task of finding suitable staff was a constant worry for any Headmaster. At HCS, a school with a war-time Common Room of never more than a

294. HCSA, Philpotts account book *passim*. The increase in the number of internal scholarships more than compensated (in financial terms) for the decline in university grants, caused by the early call-up of young men to the forces.

295. See HCSA, Cash Book 1925-46, fo 82, payment 13 Feb. 1941. The sum represented 37 *per cent* of the £312 14s total cost of the air raid shelter in 1939.

296. The Dean and Chapter claimed that the new £150 rent was based on 'the value taken by the income tax and rating authorities for very many years'. The increase was further consequent on the raising of £2,000 to repay the loans made by the Fabric and St Ethelbert's Hospital accounts to complete the original purchase. HCA, 7031/24, pp.426, 429, Acts, 4, 9 Dec. 1942.

297. The total cost of repairs during these two years amounted to £1,061 18s 5d. Significant sums were also spent on refurbishing 7 Ferrers Street (for the Scotts), School House and the school lavatories. HCSA, E.A. Roiser to Waterfield, 3 Nov. 1943 (on the playground); and Rosier to Waterfield, 9 March 1944, enclosing the report (running to 21 items) for the governors on the poor, and in certain respects dangerous, state of the school buildings.

298. For example, the high sum (for HCS) of £34 11s 9d was spent on staff advertising and interviewing in 1944-45.

dozen full-timers and three occasional teachers, Scott made over 20 appointments in five years, double the annual average during Crees' tenure. The problem confronted Scott within weeks of his arrival, when following the government's decision in May 1940 to raise the age of reservation for schoolmasters from 25 to 30, his senior mathematician was called up, to be followed in the autumn by his second scientist, and by his most effective junior Classics teacher and the 2nd XV coach.[299] Two of these conscriptions were in mid-term when replacements were almost impossible to find. Even more traumatic were the deaths of four colleagues within a year in 1943-44. F.W. Brookes died at the hands of a hit and run driver while bicycling with his wife on Ledbury Road in the gloom of a November evening (but just before blackout) in 1943. As the long-serving senior Science master and commanding officer of the corps, who had given valuable instruction to the Home Guard in the early days of its formation and who was Tupsley's senior air raid warden at the time of his death, his was a great loss for both the school and the local community. And then just before the start of the next autumn term, Brookes' successor, the deaf David Price, died of heart failure while at work in an agricultural camp. Three weeks later, Andre van der Meersch, died after a short illness; and in the first week of October, Elwy ApIvor, school chaplain for almost 20 years, died following a gall-bladder operation. Well might John Henson, himself greatly affected by the death of his immediate predecessor a few weeks earlier, write in sympathy to his last but one successor about these losses. And well might Scott inform his governors of 'the numerous adjustments' that he made to staff timetables.[300]

The difficulties Scott experienced in gaining adequate replacements for such men, especially in Science and Mathematics, were experienced by Headmasters through the country. Indeed, a few resorted to poaching teachers at short notice from other schools, thus breaking professional etiquette and HMC rules.[301] One person who indulged in this practice was William Harley, who 'after an intrigue with the Headmaster of Wrekin' gave Scott three weeks' notice of his intended departure from Hereford. 'The conduct of both these gentlemen', wrote Scott, 'has been deplorable and I have told them so'. For Scott in this sellers' market, it was sometimes a case, especially with temporary stop-gaps, of hiring women teachers, like the charming Mrs Jepps or Mrs Elsie Wardle, or of engaging masters whom he knew to be unsuitable. Dr Plaut, a German Jewish refugee with no teaching experience, whose tiny chalk characters are explained by his having been near blinded in a Nazi concentration camp, was one of these. He was a brilliant mathematician, very charming, but also expensive and (in Scott's words) 'quite incompetent as a schoolmaster', and was eventually sacked without notice. Scott also persuaded others to come out of retirement: Mr Harre after L.S. Brown's abrupt departure; Jackie Storr-Best, a former Brighton colleague, until the onset of pneumonia caused by fire-watching and station duty resulted in long absences and forced him to retire a second time; and Andre

299. Respectively, L.S. Brown, F.L. Ward and E. Rushworth. Country-wide, the raising of the reservation age meant that those men aged 25 to 30 were not now protected from call-up, and resulted in a loss to schools of around 11,000 teachers, including over 2,000 from secondary schools. Dent, p.63.

300. HCSA, GMB 1921-45, Scott's reports for the meetings, 10 Jan., 30 Nov. 1944; *HT*, 20 Nov. 1943, p.5; 27 Nov. 1943, p.5; *TH*, NS CLXV (Dec. 1944), pp.17-18, for the obituaries of ApIvor, Van der Meersch and Price; HCSA, Henson to Scott, 3 Nov. 1944.

301. For evidence of this practice, see *HMC 1943 Committee Report*, p.21.

Van der Meersch ('Vandy'), the chief Physics master, a retired engineer who had spent much of his career constructing railways in French West Africa, who reformed the Physics syllabus and did valiant service over four years, his lessons being spiced with tales of his colonial past or blackboard sketches of African wildlife. Among the other older masters, Charles Scott continued to teach for a couple of years past his 65th birthday in 1943, although in September 1944, having handed over the second mastership to Harry Wardle, he went part-time; the excellent Emile Maurer was brought out of retirement (aged 67) in 1945 to teach Modern Languages in his most arresting fashion; and, most revealing of all, F.R.H Hora, a 75-year-old fresh from service at Worksop College, who celebrated his appointment as a Science master in late 1944 by getting married. It is no surprise to find that an Old Herefordian remembers that Hora's classes had to be conducted 'in a loud voice in order to be heard above the hubbub'. Other appointments were more successful. These included the ungentlemanly William Harley and Francis Clayton, two young men in their twenties, who with A.P. Grundy – a bombed-out Headmaster from Acton – made a real contribution to the intellectual and cultural life of the school; and Bernard Edwards, invalided out of the Army to teach French, who was to have a long and successful post-war career at the school.[302]

But Scott's most important appointment was that of A.F.J. ('Jack') Hopewell. Having hastily been evacuated with Victoria College, Jersey, to Bedford School, he had taught at the Elms in Colwall for a few months in 1943 before being appointed boarding Housemaster at HCS. As the first assistant master to undertake the charge of Number 1 and School House, it was a significant move for the school, for Hopewell and for Scott himself. Like the divesting of his responsibilities for fee collection to the Chapter Clerk in 1940, Scott's off-loading of the housemastership – not least because of the strain it had put upon his wife – enabled him to concentrate his declining energies on running the school. Scott's mood as he and his wife prepared to leave Number 1 for 7 Ferrers Street, the old sanatorium which was being vacated by its American occupiers, may be gauged from his letter to a parent in November 1943:

> We shall certainly miss the boys, and the sound of a treeful of magpies that floats along the passage to our bedroom in the mornings. The irrepressible vitality of boys – even at breakfast – and the innumerable things that make them laugh at all sorts of times are a splendid tonic, and also a reproach to those of us who are no longer young! But it's unwise to try to do too many things if one is not going to do them efficiently.[303]

How far the boys' war-time education was affected by the frequent change of their teachers, the poor quality of some of their teaching and the larger classes (at least until the Sixth) is difficult to assess. Certainly their academic results seem to suggest that it was:

302. HCSA, GMB 1921-45, Scott's reports for meetings, 11 Nov. 1940 to 22 March 1945, *passim*. For Harley's ungentlemanly conduct, see above, p.426. I am indebted to a number of OHs for sending me character sketches of their war-time teachers, especially David Apperley, B.K. Coalbran, Geoffrey Hughes and Ronald Perry.

303. HCSA, Scott to Dr James, 13 Nov. 1943; HCSA, GMB 1921-45, special meeting, 18 Sept. 1943, authorising Scott's withdrawal from housemastering and Hopewell's appointment.

there was a marked decline in the number of state and open scholarships and a drop in the number of 'Highers' to a mere handful, although the number of School Certificates held up at around 20 each year. War conditions, however, make such results a misleading indicator: there were fewer boys staying on to the Sixth; and with the lowering in September 1939 of the age of obligation for military service to 18, together with the gradual lowering of the actual call-up age over the following two years, fewer going on straight to university. What we can say with more certainty is that Science subjects were beginning to grow in importance at the school. This is suggested by the award of the first (for HCS) Somerset exhibitions in the Natural Sciences, and by the increase in the number of Old Herefordians going on to study Science and Medicine at redbrick universities – partly explained, no doubt, by the government's decision to defer military service for undergraduates studying scientific subjects.[304] The corollary to this was that Classics became less dominant, although this should not be taken too far. Crees' retirement and the absence of Hunt and Rushworth (who was never to return to HCS) were massive blows to the teaching of the subject, but although past his best years 'Wo' (J.C. Wordsworth) did not retire until 1945, and double the number of awards were won in Classics than in any other subject in this period.[305]

Classics may have been reduced but the war gave boys opportunities outside the classroom that had been denied their predecessors in the inter-war period. Like the nation at large, there was an enhancement of the school's intellectual and cultural life.[306] New societies were formed or revived in a different guise. The Scientific or Natural History Society (both titles were used) was active until the foundation in November 1943 of an Engineering Society. 'Vandy' was prominent in both – giving talks on his West African experiences to the one, and then as vice-president of the new club, explaining about bridge building and technical drawing, and in the summer before his death, starting an engineering competition. Visits were later made to local engineering works, including the REME workshop in Friars Street. A few years earlier, on 5 July 1940 and within days of the fall of France, Canon Moreton had been instrumental in organising the first meeting of the French Society. Thereafter, through William Harley's enthusiasm and the co-operation of the city branch of the 'Friends of Fighting France', several meetings were held each year. The senior boys of this period, therefore, became more aware of the resistance movement, the 'empty promises of Vichy' and French politics and culture generally, as well as a little more fluent in the French language. In addition, through the courtesy of F.C. Morgan, the city librarian, they regularly watched showings of Ministry of Information propaganda films and heard

---

304. The Natural Science exhibitions were won by D.B.J. Wardle in 1942 and P.V. Skinner in 1944, respectively at St John's, Cambridge, and Brasenose. For university education in general in this period, see Dent, pp.137-44.

305. Awards in Classics (over the four years from *c.*December 1940) were won by J.M. Burch (Oriel), D.A. Roberts (Jesus, Oxford), J. Taglicht (King's, Cambridge) and G.T. Hughes (Brasenose). No timetable survives so it is impossible to ascertain whether Scott actually reduced the amount of Classics teaching.

306. An indication of renewed intellectual activity within Hereford itself may be gleaned from the increased number of visits to the art gallery and museum and loans from the city library (there were a record 44,822 visits and 240,889 loans in the year ending 31 March 1943, for example), and the establishment of a Hereford 'Brains Trust' in September 1942 and a 'Recreation Society' over the winter of 1942-43. Such trends and activities cannot simply be explained by the increase in the city's population.

lectures at the library, which was increasingly used by senior boys. And informed people came in to give talks at the school: Mr Alexander Cheshnakov, for example, on Russian folk songs in February 1943, during Hereford's 'Aid to Russia week', as well as servicemen like Squadron-Leader Frank Aikens OH AFC on 'night operations' during 'Wings for Victory' week in May 1943.[307]

There was also something of a renaissance in the performing arts at the school. This was directly linked to the formation of a Dramatic Society on the arrival in October 1940 of A.P. Grundy, who spread much sweetness and light during his 21-month stay in Hereford. By the end of his first term, at the last of the old monitors' concerts, two scenes from Shakespeare were performed despite numerous difficulties 'including our old friend, the blackout'. And at the end of the academic year, *Twelfth Night* was produced in College Hall. It was well received, despite the temporary extinction of the lights on loan from the Kemble Theatre, the *Hereford Times* reporting:

> The school has not moved publicly in the world of drama for some time. Watching the play one was conscious of regret that the dramatic ability generally displayed has not been uncovered in the past.

It was a good observation and not one entirely answered by the Shakespeare Society, which continued to meet in the cloisters with the Dean invariably in the title role. After Grundy's departure in July 1942 things never again reached these heights, but Francis Clayton's appointment ensured that public performances continued in the form of concerts and House entertainments. The most notable of these was the production of J.B. Priestley's *Laburnum Grove* over three nights in December 1944. Given the author's war-time links with the county and his 1940 exhortation to 'have the bands playing and the people singing in the streets', it was an appropriate choice. It also raised £12 for the Red Cross.[308] The war, indeed, gave an impetus to school saving and community service. A national savings group was formed and raised several thousand pounds during the war savings campaigns. A party of 14 boys joined the Dean's nightly squad of fire-watchers, following his plea in January 1941 for volunteers to ensure the cathedral's safety.[309] One Old Herefordian remembers trying to reach the Lady Chapel roof, carrying a bucket of water and a stirrup pump, within a minute and, not surprisingly, failing; another recollects riding his bicycle around the nave during air raid warnings; and a third, the 'gothic experience' of climbing around the roofs of the deserted building in the dark with faint

307. Squadron-Leader Aikens was the second son of a remarkable family of five boys – sons of a lay clerk – all of whom were educated at the school and four of whom (in 1927) sang in the cathedral choir simultaneously, an achievement unlikely to be surpassed. All five boys served in the forces during the Second World War. During 'wings week', 1-8 May 1943, the city and district raised £477,161 4s 5d through the purchase of national savings certificates and war bonds, a record for a Hereford savings week. *HT*, 11 Oct. 1941, p.4; 15 May 1943, p.5.

308. For the above: *TH*, NS CLIV (Dec. 1940), p.19; *HT*, 2 Aug. 1941, p.5 (re *Laburnum Grove* for which Hopewell is also credited). Priestley's wife opened her first hostel for mothers and babies at Broxwood Court, near Leominster, which Priestley occasionally visited during the war.

309. *HT*, 25 Jan. 1941, p.2.

torches. Such larks must have more than made up for the privations of sleeping on camp beds in a cold and draughty cathedral.[310] Later in the war in the early summer of 1943, following the lifting of the prohibition on the normal ringing of church bells, a school band of change ringers was formed, which provided useful service in the All Saints and cathedral belfries and continued for a generation.[311]

The junior training corps (as it became known) continued to provide the main opportunity for active service at HCS during the war. The annual War Office grant near doubled to over £90 and cadet numbers increased to near one hundred. There were limitations: the use of First World War uniforms, at least until the arrival of battledress in early 1942 for the lucky few; parading with old and rickety rifles, allegedly captured from Italian colonial troops in East Africa, which replaced the short Lee-Enfields after Dunkirk and were too long for arms drill and incapable of being fired; and field days and camps being confined to the immediate vicinity because of travel restrictions. But the activities were more interesting than in peace time. Full use was made of the expertise of local infantry training units; bren guns and anti-tank projectiles were fired, and even (in March 1945) a training flight taken in a de Havilland Rapide; and the contingent became less isolated as it marched with other service organisations in church parades, like the one in February 1944 at the end of Hereford military exhibition week or the parade a few months later at the beginning of 'salute the soldier' week.

The corps flourished but competitive inter-school games floundered. Even though Wyeside was not given over to the cultivation of cabbages and parsnips, as Crees surmised might happen, fixtures were reduced. For much of the war travel difficulties curtailed the number of matches – by mid-1943 the Ministry of War Transport had requested that away fixtures should not be played on Saturdays for the war's duration – and school games were hard to find.[312] Matches against two evacuated schools – King Edward's Fiveways, evacuated from Birmingham to Monmouth, and Felsted School which found a home at Goodrich Court – were occasionally played but the deficit was largely made up against forces' sides. So the names of unusual opponents entered the fixture lists: in rugby, the 1st Battalion Queen Victoria Rifles, the Border Regiment, Sussex Yeomanry, Bradbury Lines, the 348th Battery Searchlights Company and RAF Credenhill and Shobdon; and in cricket (as well as RAF Credenhill), the No. 9 Bomb Disposal Company, the Royal Army Service Corps and the Physical Development Centre, Harold Street. It was men – and men on good rations – against boys, and often younger boys as in late 1943 when the average age of the XV was under 16.[313] The end result, in rugger at any rate, was predictable, especially as there were

310. I am indebted to John Ockey, Ronald Perry, John Downes and Geoffrey Hughes for these reminiscences in their respective letters of 8, 12 July, 31 Aug. and 27 Nov. 2010. The College gardener was paid 1s 6d per week for 15 weeks fire-watching (HCA, 7031/24, p.403, 30 June 1941); the boys nothing.

311. The ban on church bells was not completely lifted until Easter 1943, although the first peals were rung, after an interval of over two years, on Sunday 15 November 1942 to celebrate the El Alamein victory, and again the following Christmas. *HT*, 21 Nov. 1942, p.5; 26 Dec. 1942, p.3; 24 April 1943, p.5; and (for the condition of St Martin's belfry) 22 May 1943, p.4. For the school band of change ringers in the later period, see below, pp.463, 498.

312. *TH*, NS CLI (Dec. 1939), p.6 (for Crees' observation); *HMC 1943 Committee Report*, p.22 (away fixtures).

313. See, for example, *HMC 1944 Committee* Report, p.29, for the observation about Army technical schools being given double bacon rations, among other food, after a school game.

few younger teachers able – and none willing – to bolster the school sides and following C.M. Scott's retirement (at 65), few good coaches.[314]

On the Wye it was different. Rowing remained popular, so much so that Hopewell having taken over cricket's ailing cause, could lament at the end of the 1944 season that:

> The apparently well-nigh irresistible attraction of the river Wye has quite naturally, since the choice is open, lured many a potential member of the 1st XI to the comparative strenuousness of an oarsman's life, leaving us with a sadly immature first game and no second game at all.[315]

But there were few opponents to row against: Monmouth in 1940-41, King's, Worcester, in 1944, an army four and two scratch OH crews representing the sum total of the school's opposition on the river during the war years. That the 1st IV remained unbeaten did not mean that much. So with the cancellation of races – as well as the national schools regatta – Harry Wardle had to content himself with organising the annual HCS regatta (moved to July) and sharing in the glory of his son winning a war-time Cambridge 'Blue', rowing bow in the 1945 boat race at Henley. It was some consolation for his one competitive race during his two years as captain of boats at school.

At the end of an idyllic summer term in 1941 – during which the boys had experienced fine weather, good cricket, rowing and bathing, an enjoyable field day and the acclaimed production of *Twelfth Night*, although 'no striking adventures' – P.M.W. John, *The Herefordian*'s (boy) editor, could reflect that 'probably few schools had been so blessed'.[316] This term, it should be remembered, also coincided with the greatest concentration of air-raid alerts in Hereford during the entire war. But John was right. For during the war years, Hereford was better off than most cities and HCS was more fortunate than many other schools. Despite the blackout, the rationing, the meals in British Restaurants and the other privations,[317] the school's routine of chapel, lessons, games, corps, society meetings and occasional exams continued uninterrupted, even if some masters were older and crankier. So did beatings, fagging, and other daily realities of school life like Charlie Revell's jabbering as he went about his business each morning stoking the open fires in the classrooms.[318] And notwithstanding the presence of servicemen in the city, some of whom spoiled Sunday morning worship in 1941 by their lack of appreciation of the school's 'amateurish efforts at chants, psalms [and] misereres';[319] and despite the air-raid warnings,

314. The exception in rugby was the Revd S.Z. Edwards who coached a relatively successful 1st XV during the 1941-42 season. This is not to gainsay the contributions of William Henley who was games master, 1943-44, and T.C. Hay, who succeeded Henley in the post. E.J. Wright, who represented the English public schools against Wales in April 1945, was the best HCS rugby player of the war generation.

315. *TH*, NS CLXIV (Sept. 1944), p.4.

316. *TH*, NS CLVI (July 1941), p.3. John later became Professor of Mathematics at the University of Texas.

317. Although it is a moot point how far these meals were a real privation, at least for the day boys who enjoyed their mid-day meal off rations. For the frequenting of the two Hereford British Restaurants at Eignbrook and St Martin's by HCS boys: *HT*, 1 Aug. 1942, p.5.

318. See HCSA, Scott to Waterfield, 1 Dec. 1945; and David Apperley's typescript 'Song Schools and Stall' pp.84-85, for two evocative descriptions of the school caretaker.

319. HCSA, GMB 1921-45, Scott's report, 18 March 1941.

the field day exercises and the stories of heroism of scores of Old Herefordians recounted in the pages of *The Herefordian*, compared with the industrial cities, the actuality of war was a long way off. This episode, remembered by one old boy 70 years later, is illustrative:

> Soon after the war-time blitz on Birmingham ... a few of my friends and I decided to cycle to the city to have an idea as to what had occurred. We told our parents that we were staying with our friends' parents for the night. We cycled to the outskirts ... and were so upset at what we had seen – houses smashed to pieces and a terrible smell of gas and sewage with detritus everywhere – that we turned tail and returned to the peace of Hereford.[320]

Nearer the time, a young Old Herefordian soldier fighting in Italy in 1944, made the same point in a different way:

> Castle Street is one of the things I long to see after the war. I want to stand in the Close when the moon is full and see it as I used to see it while watching for the fires that never broke out. Whatever else may have changed, the massive realities must stay. The cathedral must still have its Evensong, the school have its chapel and the Dean his Shakespearean Society.[321]

Not all these 'massive realities' were to survive after the war, but for its duration survive they did to the inestimable benefit of a generation of cathedral schoolboys.

Peace and Retirement

In spite of the inclement morning weather, Tuesday 8 May 1945, VE-day, saw much revelry in Hereford as in the nation at large. Bunting and the allied flags bedecked the city centre; a line of washing (representing the Siegfried Line) with the Fuehrer's effigy upside-down, hung across Church Street, its residents collecting over £40 of the £125 gathered for the 'Welcome Home Fund' over the two day holiday; the cathedral was flood-lit by 26 projectors, beaming upward lights totalling 6,000 candle power, which intersected to make a V for victory sign on the central tower; its bells pealed long and hard before and after the evening service; and lines of people irrespective of rank or station – men and women of the British forces, American and French allied troops and land girls – danced the Palais Glide, the Lambeth Walk and the night away.[322]

Although we know that the preparatory school lined up in the playground to make a V and an E in celebration of the victory, the change ringers helped in the peal and the choristers did their normal duty, during this day of celebration when all the local schools were given a holiday, the Cathedral School worked a normal day. Whether much actual study went on is to be doubted. On the following Sunday, however, among the special services

320. HCSA, John Ockey to the author, 8 July 2010.

321. *TH*, NS CLXIV (Sept. 1944), pp.31-32, letter from D.A. Roberts (son of a vicar of Neath), who later had a distinguished career in the Foreign Office and following his retirement as ambassador in Lebanon became a governor of HCS. See below, p.551, note 336.

322. *HT*, 5 May 1945, p.5; 12 May 1945, p.5.

Fig. 7.12 The hut, the original 1898 preparatory classroom, at the back of Number 1, Castle Street, c.*1940. It was moved to this location in 1914 to serve as a playroom for junior boarders. Post 1945, it became a dining-room for day boys.*

of thanksgiving, Prebendary Green gave belated recognition to the moment by preaching a sermon on 'victory' at the boarders' morning service.[323]

By this time Scott would have known that he would not stay in Hereford beyond the end of the summer, although he delayed the announcement of his retirement until after half-term. His lot had been to see the school through the war. Despite all the difficulties, during his 16 terms HCS had done more than merely survive. Numbers had increased to overflowing; the overdraft had been kept to manageable proportions; and the Headmaster's role had been enhanced by the divesting of his responsibilities for housemastering, fee collection and other payments.[324] By 1945, the Creesian era of total control had long since passed. And even though many of Scott's appointments were of necessity no more than stop-gaps, a few lifted the boys' horizons in new and interesting ways. The division of the day boys into two Houses, moreover, enhanced friendly internal competition even if the opportunities for sporting rivalry against other schools were more limited. The reforming Headmaster could, no doubt, have done greater things in peace-time, but as it was, his war-time reign should be judged a success. He left to his chosen successor a full school and a competent staff, despite its 50-year age range, who at the end of the war were rewarded for the first time with salary increases in accordance with the Burnham scale. Scott also laid

323. There is no mention of VE-day in *The Herefordian* but John Bullock OH has made clear (letter to the author, 10 July 2010) that HCS was not given the day off. Prebendary R.D.R. Green's sermon is listed in the school register of services. I am indebted to Anthony Weston OH for the information about the preparatory school.

324. During the war, Harry Wardle accounted for games, books, exams and the OH Club fees, although the Headmaster's responsibilities for various payments were still considerable.

a solid foundation for post-war improvement, an application to the Ministry of Education for the recognition of HCS as a direct grant school under the 1944 Education Act being sanctioned by the governors in June 1945. And following his final governors' meeting that July, he could leave with the knowledge that the school had acquired the use of the Deanery for its burgeoning boarding population.[325]

As at Monmouth and Brighton, Scott's health collapsed at the end of his tenure. He then spent several weeks in the Lakes Nursing Home at Swainshill, under the tender care of Mrs Gertrude Wood, thereby delaying his departure for Cornwall by nearly three months until the faithful Revell saw him off on the 4.15 train one morning in November 1945. From the nursing home and from Point House, Devoran, he corresponded with Dean Waterfield about two pieces of unfinished business: the possible sale of Number 28 (the preparatory school), and the disposal of the 'hut' in the Headmaster's garden. Both properties were owned by Scott and neither was wanted by his successor. The governors again missed the chance to acquire the prep school but they eventually bought the 'hut' for the generous price of £60 for which Scott was thankful.[326] And so from the Scotts' delightful new home overlooking Restronguet Creek, after a few more weeks recuperation, Kit Scott started on the final – and perhaps happiest – leg of his well-travelled professional career, as an assistant master at Truro Cathedral School.[327]

---

325. HCSA, GMB 1945-82, meetings, 5 June, 26 July 1945; and below, pp.451-52.

326. For the story of the sale of the 'hut' and the abortive preparatory school negotiations: HCSA, Scott's letters to Waterfield 19, 26 Sept., 1, 15 Dec. 1945 and 8 March 1946.

327. Scott taught at Truro Cathedral School (his eighth school, excluding his time at the Imperial Naval College, Japan, 1917-19) from January 1946 to July 1953 and appears to have been in charge of English teaching there until shortly before the school's inspection in February 1952. CRO, AD 1531/1, HMI report, 19-22 Feb. 1952.

Plate 1a Master Richard Burgehyll, a late fifteenth-century Headmaster. The drawing (c.1680) is from his lost memorial brass, formerly in the nave of Hereford Cathedral.

Plate 1b The original (extant) Latin inscription from the Burgehyll memorial brass. In part, it reads: 'quondam instructor gramatice istius civitatis' *('formerly teacher of grammar in this city').*

Plate 2 Bishop Miles Smith, who was born at Hereford and became a cathedral residentiary, wrote the Preface to the King James Bible. The artist is unknown.

Plate 3 Richard Gardiner (1590/91-1670), who attended 'Hereford's Free School … to good effect' in the early seventeenth century, was a benefactor to the College of vicars choral as well as his native city. This Latin inscription on his rebus (a riddle in picture form) reads: 'Hortulanus rigat dat fructum Deus' *('the gardener waters but God gives the fruit').*

Plate 4 Sir William Gregory in his judicial robes by John Riley (1646-91). As the Duchess' agent in Herefordshire, he was instrumental in acquiring Somerset scholarships for Old Herefordians.

Plate 5 Daniel Rowland, the co-founder and leader of Welsh Methodism, as depicted in a miniature by Robert Bowyer, 1790.

Plate 6 The fallen west front of Hereford Cathedral in the late 1780s by Edward Abbot (1737-1791). The painting shows two bays (with the lower windows blocked up) of the Great Room, which was used as the schoolroom, 1778-1835.

Plate 7 James Wathen's watercolour of the south-east view of Hereford Cathedral, taken from Robert Squire's (the Headmaster's) garden, 'Friday even 7 o'clock', 21 May 1799. The corner of his newly bricked house (now School House) may be seen in the left foreground.

Plate 8 Dean Richard Dawes, a radical educationist and the prime mover in the school's improvement in the mid-nineteenth century.

Plate 9 The effigy of Dean Dawes, with books depicted under his head-cushion, by Sir George Gilbert Scott.

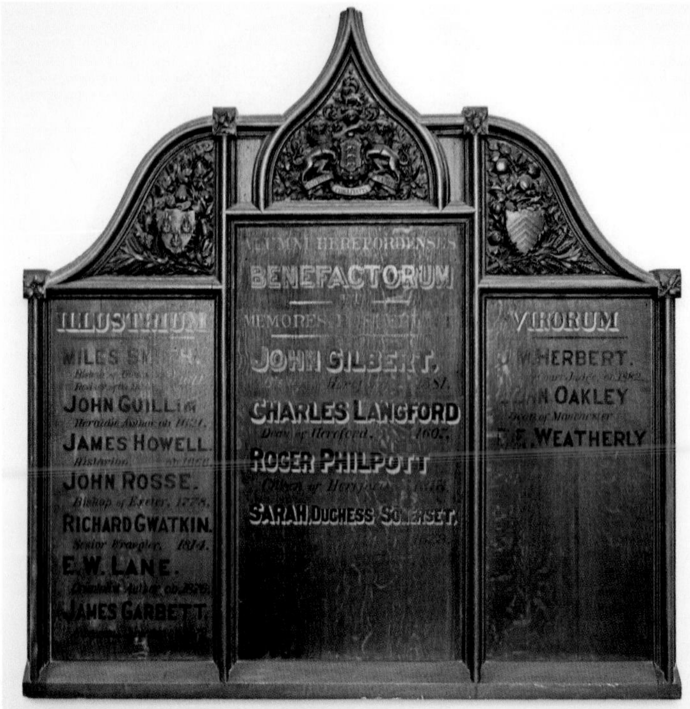

Plate 10 The honours board, 'executed in oak with gothic mouldings', presented to the school by Old Herefordians, 1 July 1881, but not completed until 1890. Over the three panels are carved (with suitable foliage) the Hereford city arms, surrounded by those of the see and cathedral and surmounted by a bishop's mitre. Although 'expressly designed as to admit of indefinite expansion', it was never so used.

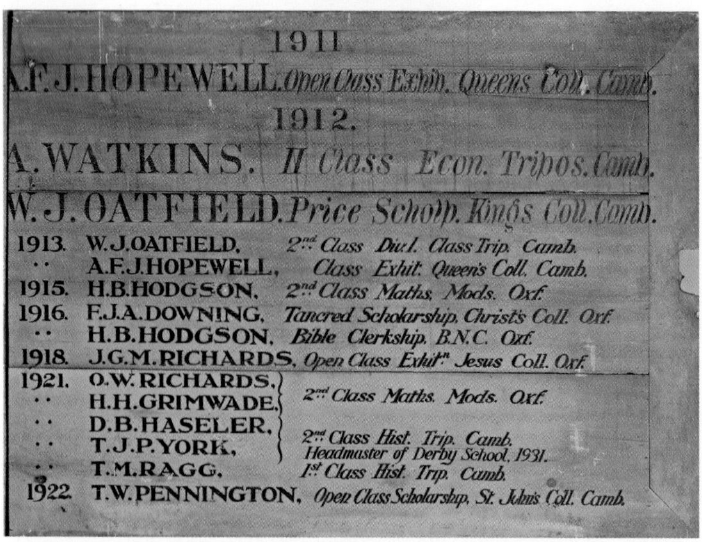

Plate 11 A school honours board, one of a number mounted in the old Gilbert Library from 1882, before James Peebles had them removed in 1959. In Hopewell, York, the Richards brothers and Ragg, this board names five who appear in the list of notable OHs (Appendix 2).

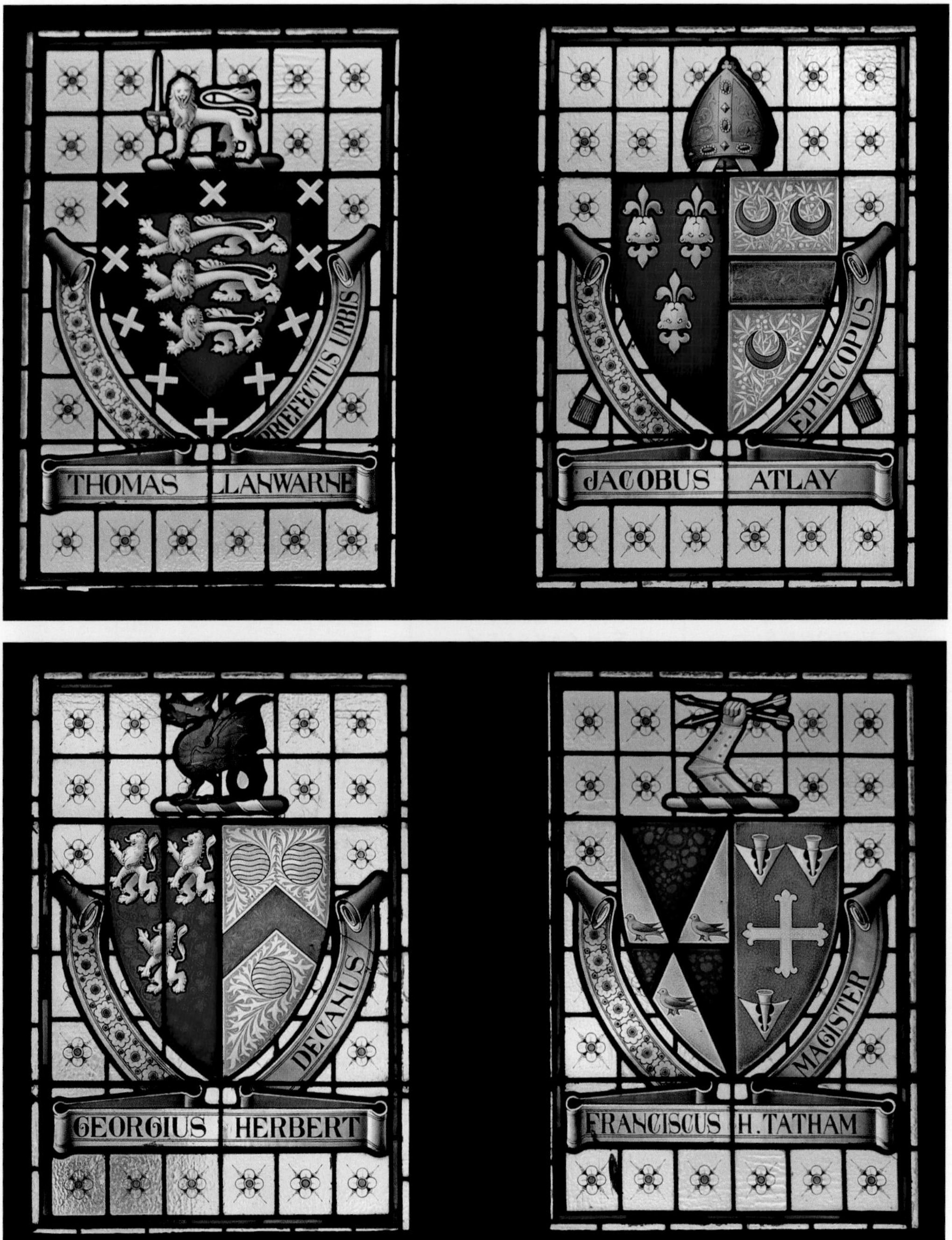

Plate 12 The stained glass panels of the glazed north window of the Gilbert Library, built in 1882, with the coats of arms of the mayor (Thomas Llanwarne OH), the Dean (George Herbert), the Bishop (James Atlay) and the Headmaster (Francis Tatham).

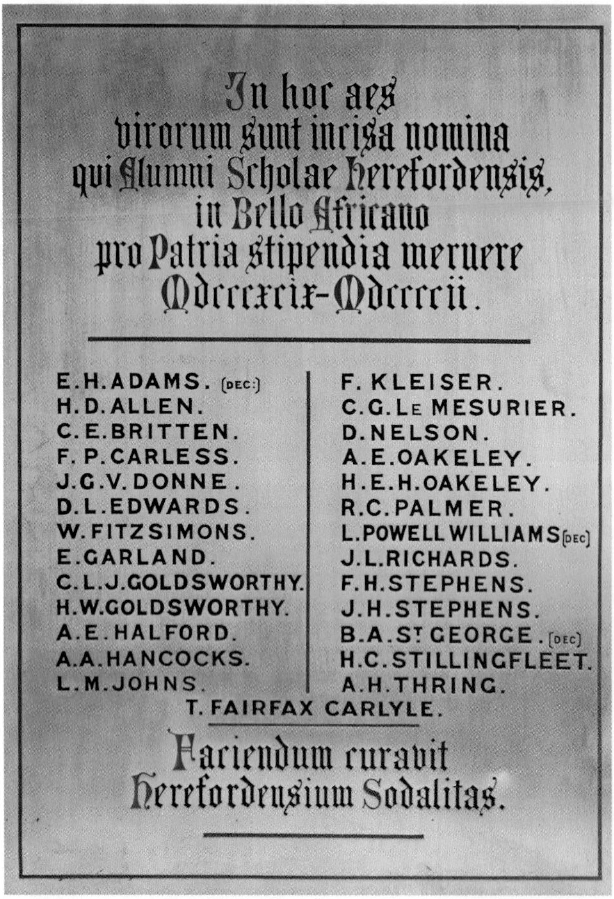

In hoc aere
virorum sunt incisa nomina
qui Alumni Scholae Herefordensis,
in Bello Africano
pro Patria stipendia meruere
Mdcccxcix-Mdccccii.
E.H.ADAMS. (DEC:)
H.D.ALLEN.
C.E.BRITTEN.
F.P.CARLESS.
J.G.V.DONNE.
D.L.EDWARDS.
W.FITZSIMONS.
E.GARLAND.
C.L.J.GOLDSWORTHY.
H.W.GOLDSWORTHY.
A.E.HALFORD.
A.A.HANCOCKS.
L.M.JOHNS.
F.KLEISER.
C.G.LE MESURIER.
D.NELSON.
A.E.OAKELEY.
H.E.H.OAKELEY.
R.C.PALMER.
L.POWELL WILLIAMS (DEC)
J.L.RICHARDS.
F.H.STEPHENS.
J.H.STEPHENS.
B.A.ST GEORGE. (DEC)
H.C.STILLINGFLEET.
A.H.THRING.
T. FAIRFAX CARLYLE.
Faciendum curavit
Herefordensium Sodalitas.

Plate 13 A plaque honouring Old Herefordians, who fought in the Boer War, given to HCS by the OH Club in early 1903. Twenty-six OHs are named. The name of C.I. Brierley, a civil surgeon with the imperial light horse, should be added to this list.

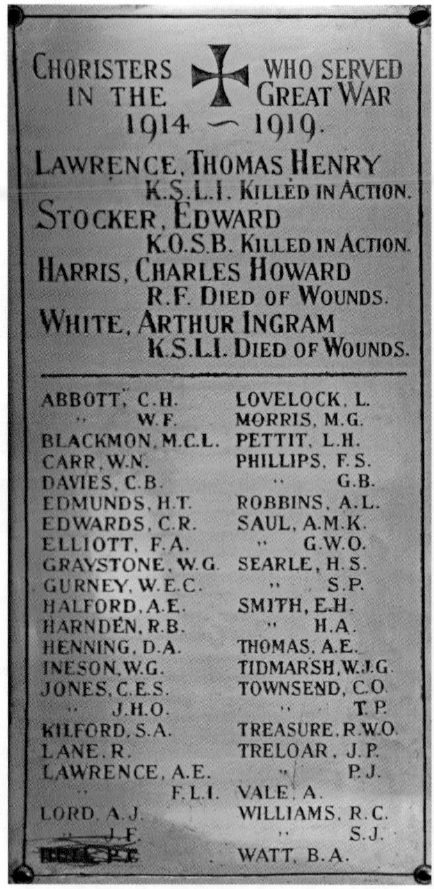

CHORISTERS IN THE GREAT WAR
WHO SERVED
1914 – 1919.
LAWRENCE, THOMAS HENRY
K.S.L.I. KILLED IN ACTION.
STOCKER, EDWARD
K.O.S.B. KILLED IN ACTION.
HARRIS, CHARLES HOWARD
R.F. DIED OF WOUNDS.
WHITE, ARTHUR INGRAM
K.S.L.I. DIED OF WOUNDS.
ABBOTT, C.H.
" W.F.
BLACKMON, M.C.L.
CARR, W.N.
DAVIES, C.B.
EDMUNDS, H.T.
EDWARDS, C.R.
ELLIOTT, F.A.
GRAYSTONE, W.G.
GURNEY, W.E.C.
HALFORD, A.E.
HARNDEN, R.B.
HENNING, D.A.
INESON, W.G.
JONES, C.E.S.
" J.H.O.
KILFORD, S.A.
LANE, R.
LAWRENCE, A.E.
" F.L.I.
LORD, A.J.
LOVELOCK, L.
MORRIS, M.G.
PETTIT, L.H.
PHILLIPS, F.S.
" G.B.
ROBBINS, A.L.
SAUL, A.M.K.
" G.W.O.
SEARLE, H.S.
" S.P.
SMITH, E.H.
" H.A.
THOMAS, A.E.
TIDMARSH, W.J.G.
TOWNSEND, C.O.
" T.P.
TREASURE, R.W.O.
TRELOAR, J.P.
" P.J.
VALE, A.
WILLIAMS, R.C.
" S.J.
WATT, B.A.

Plate 14 The commemorative plaque to Old Herefordian choristers who served in the Great War.

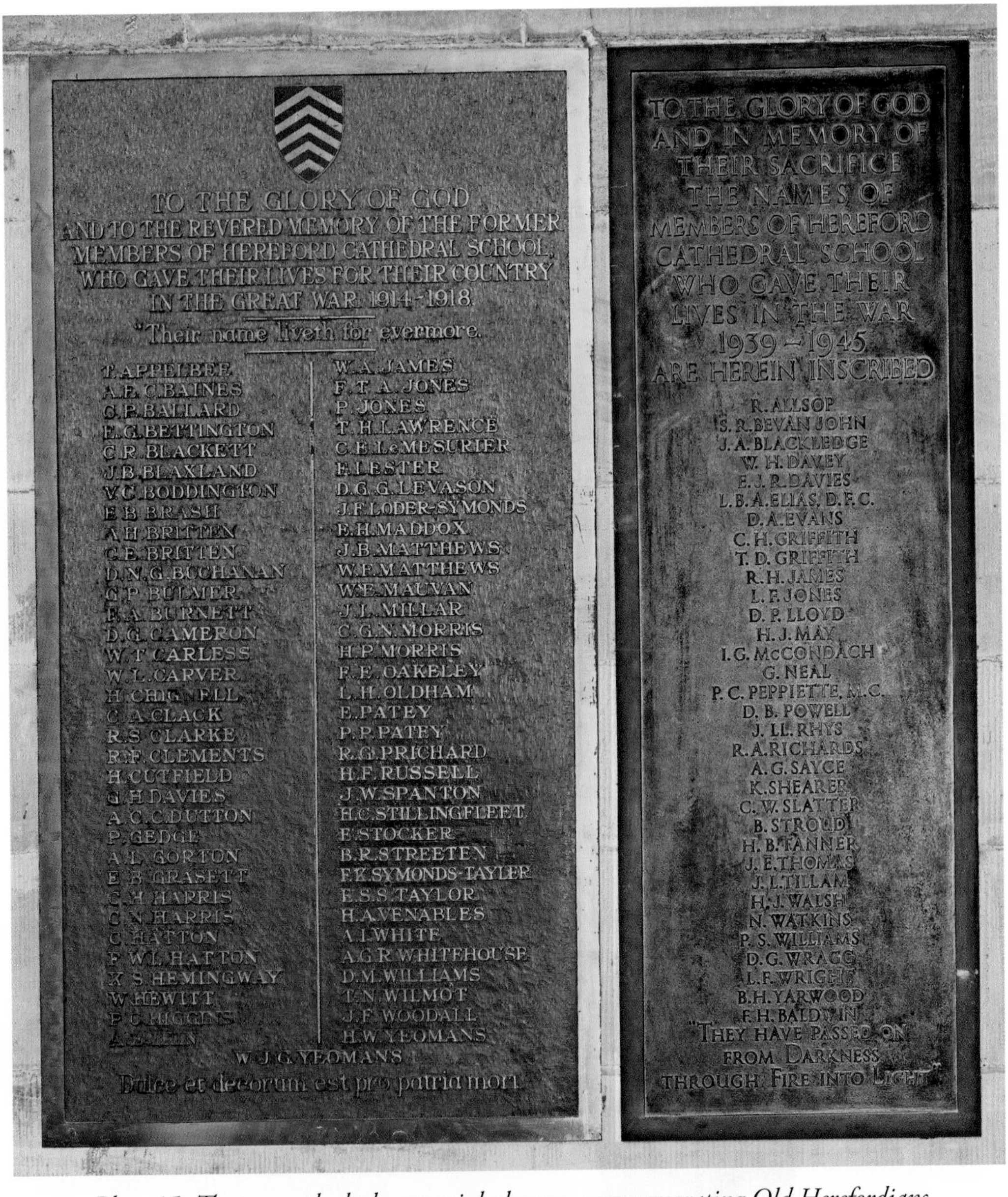

Plate 15 The two cathedral memorial plaques, commemorating Old Herefordians who fell in the First and Second World Wars.

Plate 16 The school mace, made by Alan Johansson, and dedicated by Bishop Eastaugh in March 1983 to the memory of Major Michael Forge of the Royal Corps of Signals, who died on 6 June 1982, the one OH fatality of the Falklands War. Above the school crest, the letters of the school motto form a balustrade, which is surmounted by a three-dimensional image of St Ethelbert holding his head in his hands.

Plate 17 HCS forwards win the ball in the Yorkshire mud, barely two minutes into the national quarter-final (under-18s) against Bradford Grammar School, February 1995. The team loses the match, however, 23-10.

Plate 18 Cantabile, the girls' senior choir, in concert in Hereford Cathedral, June 2016.

Plate 19 Arthur Ulrich Zimmerman OH, the school's greatest benefactor of the twentieth century.

Plate 20 Roy Blackler OH, former governor and then chairman of the OH Trustees, flanked by Dean Willis and the Headmaster, opens the Zimmerman Building, 12 July 1997.

Plate 21 Daly Briscoe OH cuts the tape with a flourish to open the new Gilbert Library in December 1998. He was in his 99th year, and it was over 80 years since he had left HCS (as Head of School) in July 1918.

Plate 22 Paul Smith, the current Headmaster, plants a tree in the forecourt of Number 1 Castle Street, watched by his three immediate predecessors and some younger pupils, 11 November 2014.

Plate 23 The glass-walled Portman Building (for Technology, Art and Computer Science), opened by Lord Portman on 12 December 1992.

Plate 24 The extension to the Gilbert Library (formerly Big School), incorporating the old studio theatre.

Plate 25 The pre-preparatory classrooms ('The Moat'), situated by Castle Hill to the rear of Numbers 28 and 29 Castle Street, and opened by the Duke of Kent on 5 June 2003.

Plate 26 The sports hall, the refurbished Science Block and the new (autumn 2017) courts at the back of Number 1, Castle Street.

Plate 27 A school Eucharist, 27 September 2017, with Dean Michael Tavinor as celebrant.

Chapter 8

The Embracing of Change, 1945-1987

Of those two young boys who sat an entrance examination to HCS – one did so in 1950 and another in 1978 – both passed and after a fulfilled seven years at the school were accepted as undergraduates at an ancient university. Both in time were to become successful writers. Alick Rowe and Matthew Hall were schooled in the shadow of Hereford Cathedral 28 years apart from each other, but as these reminiscences reveal, such was the gulf between their eras that they seem to have been educated in different worlds.[1]

> In 1950, when one cold February morning I took the entrance examination, the Cathedral School still enjoyed its misty mystique of superiority. Herded into a large chocolate and cream hall, we were settled into carved and ancient desks, musty with the grime of many years, and here old, unsmiling men shuffled us through tests of reading, writing and arithmetic, with an interview at the end with A.F.J. Hopewell, the Headmaster ... The school seemed vast and dirty but incredibly impressive. Nevertheless, when I took up my county scholarship later in the year, I was glad to be placed in brand-new premises in Castle Street. My seven years at the school were almost entirely happy: they began averagely and ended very well indeed for me. It was all so different from anything that had gone before. In those early post-war days, a rich crew of eccentrics still manned the posts. Instead of Scripture, the Revd Jack, on hands and knees, chalked complex rail layouts beneath our desks. Geography, with the weird Mr Faulkner, became an endless running quiz ... There were others, too: 'Tiger', a shambling hulk of a man, whom I later came to like, vacillating between sentimentality and barely controlled fury; and if George was due to teach us the period after lunch, we knew we had 20 minutes as he weaved an unsteady path back to the school from the Booth Hall. I think it was the sheer noise that most surprised me: not the steady sound of industry but the shrieking of wild animals in which one soon joined. We spent our time half in fear and half in hysteria. I understand it better now: there was little pleasure in Britain at that time – even in 1957 when I left,

1. Alick Rowe, who died in 2009, was a prolific writer for radio and television from the early 1970s. M.R. Hall has written numerous screenplays and (at the time of writing) is the author of six crime novels, published in successive years from 2009. I am indebted to Matthew Hall for composing a companion piece to the one written by Alick Rowe, which was originally published in *HT*, 2 March 1973, p.10 ('My Boyhood in Hereford').

there was only one record-player possessed by one senior boy and only one member of the school's rugby team was blessed with a track suit, and life in school was very uncertain. Senior boys slapped faces, whacked heads, beat bottoms much as they pleased and usually for no good reason ... Of lessons in those first years, I remember only English with a much-respected Pablo Baylis … and the academic excitement of learning French, albeit with the terrifying slapper-down … Woodwork … never materialised for those of us in the A stream and Art, like Music, was completely uninstructive … The prevailing ideology was strictly Victorian: culture was seen as a waste of time, luring us from our twin gods of work and games … From the age of fifteen, all things began to work in my favour, and when I left I had become Lord High Everything … All this seems very small beer in these days and even faintly ridiculous, but in the inward-looking small world of school, there was tremendous satisfaction in the middle-class value of 'moving up' and the total success was a disability that took years to overcome … I went to Cambridge … believing myself invincible. I had come to believe that anything less than getting to the very top was paramount to failure. It was a shock to realise that I was a pygmy chief in a land of giants, and that the most magnificent school in Britain had been a small, rather smug back-water.

It was 1978 ... I nearly didn't get in ... Then came a summons to interview with the Headmaster, Barry Sutton. His oak-panelled study smelt of beeswax and pipe smoke that drifted over from the staff Common Room ... He questioned me gently but firmly and sent me away with an exhilarating, 'see you in September'. The first term began with Mrs Howard-Jones, vowels as immaculate as her hair, teaching us the history of the cathedral ... I took it all to heart. Within a few short weeks that magnificent building ... had become a permanent refuge in my imagination and the yardstick by which I still measure centuries. My seven years in Castle Street would give me two things: an enduring sense of permanence and, by mixture of accident and design, intellectual freedom. These were Thatcher's years. A social revolution was underway. The older tweed-jacketed masters, some of whom had served in the war, still cast an avuncular and occasionally austere shadow ... but the younger generation was setting the tone. Colin Gray took chapel shortly after the sinking of the Belgrano. From behind the cathedral lectern he waved a copy of *The Sun* with its now infamous headline 'Gotcha', and inveighed against the Falklands War. The air crackled. We all sensed the schism in the staff room. From 30 years distance I can see that the school, like the rest of the country, was unshackling itself from the rigidity of the past. There was no single ethos, rather an atmosphere of creative tension layered on top of tradition. Artistic talent bubbled up like springs ... After four mostly studious years I fell prey to teenage distractions, particularly girls, and fell dramatically in love with several ... Some masters privately grumbled that the arrival of females had spoiled things ... but I couldn't have disagreed more. As far as most pupils were concerned ... we were truly equals in every respect. In the Sixth Form the school let me have my head and indulged me and several others to an over-generous extent. Ege Parker taught us History as if we were undergraduates ... Colin Gray led us through Chaucer and Hamlet with a modern critical eye … and Barry Sutton, proving himself a true liberal, allowed me to print a polemical magazine, 'Coup De Grace', which from the safety of our ivory tower espoused anarchism and pacifism ... Throughout the Lower Sixth, I kicked against authority while secretly longing to be anointed as a prefect. Sadly, by then my copybook bore too many blots, but I was admitted to Oxbridge classes with

> Barry Sutton and the wonderfully eccentric polymath, Dick Rhodes. During many heated and searching lunchtime debates, I acquired sufficient critical skills to win a place to read Law at Oxford ... Existential threats aside, the 1980s marked a uniquely carefree moment. We were set free from formalism, rewarded for individual flair and remained unoppressed by league tables and continual assessments that would dog our successors ... The Mappa Mundi places Jerusalem at the centre of the world; we have the cathedral, the school and the green hills beyond as the centre of ours. It's a beautiful and increasingly privileged perspective. We weren't served up doctrine, but [came] ... away knowing what matters.

As these recollections indicate, Rowe's school-world of the 1950s was an insular place where Victorian values predominated, presided over by some eccentric schoolmasters, and situated in buildings which apart from its one new addition hardly seemed to have changed since Hopewell had attended HCS in Edwardian times. Hall's world of the 1980s was totally different. The school was still dominated by its cathedral – which apart from a few adornments, notably the beautification of the Lady Chapel in the early Fifties and the controversial removal of the Skidmore screen in 1967, remained much the same – but it had shed its Victorian ethos and narrow curriculum. The noisy, shabby school that languished (at least in the early Fifties) under the shadow of post-war austerity had given way, in a more prosperous age, to a less capricious and more ordered co-educational establishment, run by an enlightened Headmaster and staffed by a number of teachers keen to promote intellectual enquiry and encourage artistic endeavour. What these recollections point to is a fundamental shift in the nature of the Cathedral School, and, indeed, a revolutionary change in educational values over the 40 years following the end of the Second World War.

Almost every aspect of the school was transformed during this period. In terms of accommodation, it spread its wings around the Close and eastwards up Castle Street. Aside from its periodic renting of Chapter properties and one or two minor buildings, it acquired, re-built or new built the following: the Old Deanery (1945); New Block, now the Portman Centre (1950); the old gymnasium (1958); the laboratories (added to in 1952, 1958 and 1973); the extension to Old Block (built in two stages in 1960 and 1965); the dining-hall (1964); the old day change room (now the CCF office) (1968); 29 and 30 Castle Street and St David's Hall (1976 and 1978), followed by Numbers 2 (1984) and 28 and 34 in 1987; the Quay Street 'Buttery' in 1979; and 5 and 6 St John Street (1984 and 1987) for girls' boarding. Off-site sports facilities were improved with the building of the new stilted pavilion in 1967-68, the extension of Wyeside in 1978 and 1986 and the creation of the tennis and netball courts on the site of the Bishop's old vegetable patch in 1980. Landmarks familiar to generations of boys, notably the 'Acropolis' and the decrepit wooden pavilion, disappeared. New uses were found for old buildings and rooms, particularly School House which was changed from boarding to day use in 1979-80, and Big School which became the new studio theatre in 1983. 5, Harley Court replaced Number 1 as the Headmaster's house in 1970; his study moved twice within Number 1 and finally (for two decades) to Number 29; the Common Room after its dingy quarters in School House had been extended in 1957, moved to more gracious living in Number 1 and then 29. The Gilbert Library was transformed twice in 1959 and 1977; the Zimmerman Library was created in

1959 and disappeared in 1977; and by the Eighties school yard, rather than the playground that it had been for more than a century, had become – after a brief period as a netball court – a staff car-park.

This seemingly continuous extension and adaptation of the school's plant reflected both an expansion in the number of its pupils and staff and a marked change in their character. The school's roll more than doubled in size from 252 in September 1945 to 591 in April 1987, each total being a record for its day. The bare figures hardly tell the whole story. Day numbers more than tripled; boarding declined by 14; and the size of the Sixth Form increased exponentially, from perhaps one in 12 pupils in 1945 to more than one in four 40 years later. Above all, with the coming of co-education in the 1970s, more than 20 years after a motion extolling its virtues had been 'triumphantly carried' in a school debate,[2] 260 or so girls had been added to the boy population by 1987. Although rugby, cricket and rowing (mostly) were denied them, by this time, as Hall reveals, girls were treated as equal school citizens. Even within the corps, at the biennial CCF inspection in May 1981, the parade was taken by a female cadet, the first in the country – so the Headmaster claimed – to have had such a responsibility. By then, the school's governing body and the OH Club committee had also succumbed to female membership.[3]

As with the pupils so with their teachers. Staff numbers increased from 13 assistant masters and an assortment of five part-timers in the mid-1940s to a Common Room of almost 50 by the mid-1980s, one third of whom were women and almost all of whom – unlike their predecessors in 1945 – held a professional teaching qualification. There may have been fewer eccentrics among the staff in 1987 than there had been 40 years earlier but there were more good teachers and the general quality of a pupil's learning experience had improved immeasurably.[4] And the days when it was expected that a lady teacher such as Miss Milligan, the Art mistress in 1948, should retire on her marriage, were long gone.

The consequences of HCS's remarkable transformation from an all-male to a mixed establishment can hardly be over-emphasised. The impact on the school's academic and cultural life is obvious enough. What is less apparent is the more subtle change that co-education made to its character through the 1970s. An example is provided with the decline in the use of nicknames, which were so prevalent among 'Tiger' Bell's pupils in the Forties and Fifties – 'Tiny', 'Bambino', 'Picaninny', 'Glider', 'Hob-Goblin', 'Old Father William' and 'Verge' are some of them – and the increasing use of forenames. Although there is evidence from *The Herefordian* that surnames were being abandoned by the late Sixties, a decade later it had clearly become official school policy for all pupils to be addressed by their first name as is illustrated by the 1979 speech day programme, the first to use given names rather than

2. The motion that 'co-education should be introduced in public schools' was proposed by R.D. Lancaster on 20 November 1948 and carried by 42 votes to 20. Lancaster lived to see its fulfilment at HCS while still in post as a teacher at the school.

3. Nicola Smith took the 1981 parade; Anthea McIntyre (appointed in 1978) was the first female governor; and Maureen Morris, the first woman to serve on the OH Club committee.

4. For some eccentric HCS schoolmasters of the 1940s, see Peter Williams' anonymous Franklin Barnes Flowers advertisement on the back cover of *The Herefordian* for 1976. However, his comment that: 'perhaps each generation produces its own quota of personalities who strike their contemporaries just as oddly and vividly' should also be borne in mind.

initials. In this way, the arrival of girls in the Seventies accelerated a process of liberalisation which was already underway. Similarly with discipline. The 1960s had seen an end to boys beating boys, and while the Headmaster retained the right to administer corporal punishment, its use had become infrequent long before its formal abolition in 1987. When almost half the school was protected from the cane by reason of their gender, this could hardly have been otherwise. The last Headmaster of the period could even make a joke at an Old Herefordian dinner in 1980 of a letter he had received from a Chatham supplier offering to provide any quantity of regulation 34 inch punishment canes at £1.25 each.[5] It no doubt went down well with old boys brought up in the Forties and Fifties when corporal punishment, as Rowe records, was a matter of course but by 1980 there could be no return to the good old days.

Indeed, the closing of School House that very year left the Old Deanery as the only boarding house for senior boys (with Number 1 for juniors); the two Houses being soon joined in the mid-Eighties by St John House, which set new standards of luxury for the girl boarders. But even before its closure, the hallowed traditions of the school's oldest House had long since been moderated: personal fagging had been reorganised on a study basis before its complete abolition in the 1970s; new boy initiation rites had ceased; bounds had been loosened and weekly boarding introduced; and the OH Club dinner night was no longer one of excessive licence.[6] As with the Old Deanery, following the introduction of central feeding in the new dining-hall in 1963, there was an inevitable curtailing of House independence. Only the tuck shops – the School House one, following that of Old Deanery (which started in 1953) – remained, until the Buttery's opening in 1979. As significant was the change in the Housemasters' terms. After the Wardles' retirement in 1950, the Old Deanery Housemaster and his wife were salaried and no longer ran the House as a private business enterprise. In 1955 School House followed suit, although the Headmaster continued nominally to run the House until the late Sixties. So by the end of this period the character of boarding had markedly changed: boarders were now a distinct minority – albeit an important one – within the community, and they had a less pervasive influence over the school as a whole. Day pupils, on the other hand, were in the ascendant. To accommodate their growing numbers the old East and West divisions were abolished in 1971 and four day Houses, named appropriately after benefactors, created. Much had been lost, but pupil pastoral care – the phrase was not current in 1945 – had vastly improved.

Less obvious, but as important in its way to the school's well-being and perhaps even its survival, was the change in the nature of the school's foundation and governance. From 1947 the Philpotts foundation, now less needed for entry scholarships, was applied to financing school improvements before eventually being wound up as a separate fund following the sale of its High Town property in 1966. New schemes to widen participation in governance were sealed in 1953, when *ex officio* governors were abolished, and in 1971 when co-opted governors were officially sanctioned, a move which captured the two most

5. There is no evidence in the surviving copy of the speech that the joke was made, but the fact that the Chatham letter from P.D. and N.J. Durant is stapled to the original script is suggestive.

6. Michael Walling reviewed some of the rituals and excesses associated with boarding at School House in *TH*, CCXXVI (1980), pp.7-8.

influential governors of the period. Later, by internal agreement, the governing body was extended to 12 and the first lay chairman of governors was appointed. By the end of the period, HCS had even been incorporated as a company limited by guarantee.

Underpinning these constitutional changes were alterations to the school's management practices and structures. Double-entry book-keeping was abandoned at the end of March 1956, as was the manuscript audit account book, signed off by Little and Co. on 4 August 1972, 16 years later. A governors' finance sub-committee was appointed in 1971, the first of many such standing committees. In 1972, the school's first ever bursar was appointed, his additional responsibility as Clerk to the Governors being added to his brief three years later following the Chapter Clerk's retirement. This increased the school's independence from the cathedral even if it meant that the governors lost their permanent meeting place in Number 30a Castle Street and had for a time to endure a peripatetic existence by gathering in odd rooms around the school. But there were other aids to efficiency. For example, the minutes of governors' meetings were typed (from 16 March 1976 and seven years before those of the Chapter), copied and circulated rather than being read out at each meeting; an accounting machine was acquired in 1981 to ease administration; and the school's human infrastructure was strengthened. By the end of the period, the Headmaster's secretary was no longer his personal employee and was working full-time; an architect was retained on a consultancy basis to keep watch over the school's fabric, reporting to the governing body on his findings from 1957; an on-site caretaker, who was originally also employed as a laboratory technician, had replaced the old stoker, no longer needed following the change from coke to oil-fired boilers (the Old Deanery excepted) in 1962-63; a full-time manager had replaced the Headmaster's wife as domestic supervisor; and a versatile works team had been established to maintain the school's expanding plant. Compared with today it was a small skeleton support staff, and the school continued to rely on teachers to take charge of the library and man such services as careers but it was a vast improvement on earlier days. Although the school of 1987 could hardly be described as prosperous, its governance and administration was being conducted on a more professional basis than at any time in its history.

This chapter will examine how such changes were made under successive Headmasters, sometimes reluctantly, invariably pragmatically, not least in response to political threats of the Seventies when its very existence came into question. It will find that despite the alteration in the school's status from a direct grant grammar to an independent school by the time the period ends, its adoption of the assisted places scheme in 1981 ensured that the school continued to attract pupils from as wide a range of backgrounds in 1987 as in 1945. Little else, however, remained the same as is indicated by even a cursory glance at the glossy colour prospectus of the mid-Eighties compared to its buff counterpart 40 years earlier. By 1987, all pupils could aspire to further education; and all were receiving a more rounded education, with a greater subject choice and in a less confined environment, where in addition to traditional games, the corps and more transient societies, the performing arts were beginning to flourish in a way never achieved before. And, in general, pupils were healthier – the last epidemic to close the school occurred in 1957 – and happier, the easy relationship with their teachers being one of the features of HCS in the Eighties. Even the pattern of school speech had changed. The slang associated with fagging and corporal punishment

Fig. 8.1 School yard in the mid-1950s: a boy (far left) crossing to the bike sheds; another (far right) waiting to return serve.

passed into obsolescence when these practices ceased. Like the fading of nicknames, by the end of the period talk of 'the dap', 'tonking', 'four down' and 'four up' (four strikes of the cane with trousers down or up) – and also, among others no doubt, 'dibs' (for prayers) and 'demonning' (for the deprivation of office) – was heard no more.[7]

And the whole community lived and worked within a sanctuary which had lost its solitude. Much of the damage was done by the motor car. Although the Headmaster of the time had warned his governors as early as November 1957 about the dangers of incompetent learner drivers practising backing and turning at Quay Street, there were few cars at that time in Castle Street – many day pupils then came to school on foot or by bicycle – and no parking in school yard which was reserved for impromptu games of football and the like. As late as March 1969, an advertisement in *The Herefordian* made the claim that the Castle Pool Hotel was situated in the city centre 'yet devoid of traffic'. Life was also quieter within the Close itself, where car-parking was limited until the Sixties. There, too, in the earliest year of that decade, Dean Hedley Burrows, dressed in frock-coat and clerical gaiters, might still be spied hastening from his house in the cloisters to catch the post at the old Broad Street Post Office.[8]

7. On this, see A.J. Weston's observations in *TH*, CCXXIII (Nov. 1977), p.28. I am grateful for his further comments in a letter to me of 1 June 2014.

8. I am indebted to John Eisel, a boarder in School House at the time, for this recollection.

Hedley Burrows, as Dean of Hereford 1947-61, was the longest serving chairman of governors during these years. Of the central characters, however, no-one survived the whole period, although one master (R.D. Lancaster) spanned 40 years, several 30 years and a governor (T.W. Barnes) nearly 29. On the other hand, the four Headmasters (two of whom died in office), important though they were, averaged a mere ten years in office each. Of the four, Jack Hopewell, to his generation at least, was the most revered.

Alan Francis John Hopewell, 1945-1957

Jack Hopewell's elevation from Housemaster to Headmaster was completed in haste, the public announcement of Scott's retirement and his successor's appointment being made on 16 June 1945 just days after the school had been informed. The post was not advertised, it later being explained to the Ministry of Education which had queried the decision that 'owing to the breakdown in health of both the Headmaster … and Mrs Scott, the matter was one of great urgency and as Mr Hopewell was already in charge of the boarding house it was considered that compliance with the regulations … was inexpedient, particularly in view of the prevailing war conditions'.[9] And despite his age – at 53 he was the oldest HCS Headmaster to have been appointed in modern times – in Hopewell the governors had found a safe pair of hands. His wide experience of school-mastering in nine schools had included a five-year spell in charge of Victoria College Preparatory, Jersey; as Housemaster of School House for near five terms, he knew much about the working of the Cathedral School; he and his family were already in residence at the Headmaster's house, Number 1 Castle Street; and he was well liked and widely respected, not least by his predecessor. Hopewell had one further advantage. As an Old Herefordian, there was a good prospect of his being able to use the old boy network for the considerable benefit of his *alma mater*. And so in August 1945 A.F.J. Hopewell, a favoured son who as head boy in 1910-11 had won many academic and sporting accolades,[10] took over the reins of his old school, the first Old Herefordian to do so since Charles Taylor in 1826. At school he had been described as the best all-round cricketer in the 1st XI of 1911. Over 100 years later, posterity's verdict would be that he was the school's best loved Headmaster of the twentieth century. The governors, as *The Herefordian* acknowledged, were indeed fortunate 'to have such a man ready to step into the breach'.[11]

Within weeks, their decision to make an internal appointment had been vindicated. For following Scott's collapse shortly after his final assembly in late July, many of the school's immediate problems could only have been effectively dealt with by a resident senior man who knew its workings. Indeed, there was much unfinished business to engage the mind and energies of the new Headmaster over the summer holidays. Would the new boarding house, due to replace Number 2 Castle Street, be ready in time for the influx of additional

9. HCSA, GMB 1945-82, p.26, minute, 19 June 1946.

10. In 1910-11 (his last year), Hopewell was school captain, captain of football (association), three times cricket colour, OTC corporal, and winner of six school prizes, the Philpottine university exhibition and an open classical exhibition to Queens', Cambridge, for which he won a half-holiday for the school (taken on 30 May 1911). At Cambridge, he did not fulfil his academic potential, leaving with a third class degree in the classical tripos of 1914.

11. *TH*, NS CLXVI (Sept. 1945), p.5.

boarders at the start of the autumn term? How could the school's run-down buildings be made good? How were senior men like Chas Scott and 'Wordy' to be replaced? Would the four masters in His Majesty's forces return and when would they be demobilised? Above all, would the application for the new form of direct grant, submitted on 25 June 1945, be accepted by a Labour Minister of Education?[12] Such issues, together with the myriad daily concerns of a Headmaster who was also both Housemaster and bursar, were to be faced during a period of post-war deprivation almost as severe as the war years. And in the summer of 1945, it was by no means a foregone conclusion that 'Hoppy' or 'Bop' as he was affectionately known to his pupils, would be able to lead his 'troops' (as he called the boys[13]) successfully through the hardships of post-war Britain; just as it was by no means clear how long it would take the country at large, and Hereford in particular, to emerge from the drab years of post-war austerity.

Fig. 8.2 Jack Hopewell: the first Old Herefordian HCS Headmaster for over a century.

Emergence from Austerity

Within days of taking over his new duties, and following the Japanese surrender, world peace was restored in the earliest hour of Wednesday 15 August 1945. VJ Day in Hereford was greeted with a sense of anti-climax. The crowds in High Town were nowhere near as great as those on VE Day, partly no doubt because there were now fewer American soldiers and service women in the city, and the decorations were more subdued. That evening the cathedral, this time more dimly lit by the corporation gas department, was little more than three-quarters full for the service of thanksgiving. Bishop Parsons struck the right note when he proclaimed that peace should not be made 'on the cheap' and that the British people would

12. This was the fiery left-winger, 'Red' Ellen Wilkinson, who was in office from 3 August 1945, and who, in contravention of her predecessor's (R.A. Butler's) policy, was known to want to impose a strict limit on the number of direct grant schools. Gosden, p.363. At Hereford, two HMIs and the County Education Director (A.P. Whitehead) had informed the governors on 5 June 1945 that 'the great age of the school would carry weight with the Minister if … the deficiencies could be made good but pointed out that in the present conditions the deficiencies were such as to afford no hope of recognition'. The Old Deanery's subsequent acquisition helped persuade the Minister to recognise HCS as a direct grant school under the terms of the 1944 Education Act, on 12 October 1945. HCSA, GMB 1945-82, pp.4, 13, minutes, 5 June, 29 Nov. 1945.

13. For Hopewell's description of the boys as 'troops', see the editorial obituary tribute (probably written by Alick Rowe) in *TH*, NS CLXXXXVI [*sic*] (May 1957), p.3. The origin of 'Hoppy' (and its diminutive 'Bop') was presumably derived from Hopewell's lop-sided walk, a serious war-time injury at Suvla Bay in August 1915 resulting in the loss of his right lung and the permanent lowering of his left shoulder.

need to continue to show 'steadfastness and self-sacrifice'.[14] For the onset of world peace was to usher in a period of deprivation as severe as the war years. As one historian of this period has observed of the middle classes: 'the staples of the middle-class lifestyle – domestic service, ample food and clothes, consumer durables, motor cars and luxuries such as travel, entertainment and subscriptions – were squeezed by labour shortage and rationing as well as high taxation and rising prices'.[15] And for those below them it was much worse.

Post-war Hereford reflected the austerity of the nation at large. It was, as one Herefordian remembered, a time of 'drabness, poverty and depression'. The coming of peace saw similar endeavours to those practised during the years of conflict. Victory was itself celebrated by a thanksgiving savings week in early November 1945 which apart from its object differed little from the war savings campaigns. The hunt for paper, rags and bones also continued, with Herefordshire raising more of this kind of salvage than any of its neighbouring west midland counties in the three months to the end of September 1945. A year later there was a renewed drive to collect wastepaper, with 40 tons set as a two-week target, the *Hereford Times* being reduced to its war-time length of eight pages for most weeks during 1947.[16]

More serious than the lack of newsprint was the chronic housing shortage and the interruption of fuel supplies. The appeal to householders to give up their spare rooms was the council's initial response to the housing crisis but new permanent houses were also built – the first post-war council house on the Hunderton estate being officially opened in April 1946 – as well as 'temporary' prefabricated homes. These, however, were erected at a rate which could not possibly satisfy the thousands clamouring for new accommodation. It was little comfort to the homeless that in the first year of peace the city corporation had built more new houses than many local authorities. Squatting, including the illegal occupation of Langford House, the former Cathedral School boarding house, for several months in late 1945, was the inevitable consequence.[17]

And even if you possessed your own home, there was little likelihood that it would have been warm and well-lit, especially during the dreadful winter of 1947. Even before then, the shortage of coal meant that there was a need to economise on street and shop lighting and domestic consumption, but the coldest winter in living memory brought things to a head. By early 1947, with worse weather to come, demand for gas had exceeded figures for any previous winter and the consumers in Hereford's 9,000 houses that used gas were urged to save supplies. A month later, the same Arctic conditions resulted in the diminution of coal stocks at the corporation gas works to an estimated five days. Street lighting was suspended in its entirety, gas supplies were reduced and electricity cut off. There was a renewed appeal to householders to show neighbourliness – 'always a characteristic of Hereford citizens', the mayor alleged – by sharing their meagre stocks of often poor quality coal. Given these conditions, it is hardly surprising that there should have been a public complaint about

14. *HT*, 18 August 1945, p.5.

15. Ina Zweiniger-Bargielowska, 'Rationing, Austerity and the Conservative Party Recovery After 1945', *Historical Journal*, 37/1 (1994), p. 180, as quoted by Kynaston (2008), p.260.

16. Rowe, p.118. *HT*, 10 Nov. 1945, p.5; 26 Jan. 1946, p.4; 21 Sept. 1946, p.4; 5 Oct. 1946, p.5.

17. *Ibid.*, 24 Nov. 1945, p.5; 13 April 1946, pp.4, 5; 4 May 1946, p.8; 2 Nov. 1946, pp.4, 5; 7 Dec. 1946, p.7; 21 Dec. 1946, p.7; 4 Jan. 1947, p.7 (for Langford House).

the cathedral's 'woefully inadequate heating arrangements', the complainant reporting that sitting through Evensong in February 1947 was like spending 'a night on an ice pack'.[18] At HCS, cisterns froze, Wyeside was unusable and there were outbreaks of influenza, chicken pox and measles – over 100 boys were laid low at one time and hardly a day passed with a full complement of staff – but the school stoically carried on despite the 'extreme precariousness' of the fuel supplies. Unsurprisingly, Charlie Revell, school caretaker and stoker for seven years of austerity, decided to call it a day at the end of term.[19] That winter was the worst it got but power cuts and gloomy streets were a regular feature of the post-war scene for a number of years.

The greatest daily irritant in this post-war age of austerity, however, was the continuation of rationing. Fruit from abroad was more easily available, as indicated by the arrival in Hereford of bunches of bananas in early February 1946, heralded in the *Hereford Times* by a photograph of the first two Hereford children to taste that 'unaccustomed fruit'. But the rationing of bread for the first time later that summer, with 11 to 18 year olds having the highest weekly ration (12 ounces) apart from manual workers, meant that a staple food actually became less plentiful than during the war. New restrictions were imposed in August 1947, following the drain in dollars from the country and a run on the pound, which reduced meat and other rations, as well as limiting the basic petrol allowance and suspending foreign travel. Although things were getting better by the end of the decade, a wide range of consumables remained on the ration in 1950, including meat, cheese, fats, sugar, sweets (after the 'false dawn' of 1949) and tea.[20]

Austere as times were, following the havoc wreaked by global conflict, many desired to return to pre-war certainties, to 'familiar ways, familiar rituals and familiar relations'.[21] In Hereford, once demobilisation was under way – and by late January 1946, the 100,000th serviceman had been demobbed from Bradbury Lines[22] – this manifested itself in various ways in the first years of peace. For instance, the first Oxford University extension lecture since 1939, the Second World War having marked the only break in the series since 1888, was given in February 1946; later that spring the May Fair was again held in the city's streets 'as a further token of a return to more normal times'; the race-course, having finally been de-requisitioned in late June, again became a venue for sporting activities (and later for commercial flights); and early in the New Year, a repertory company was revived at the Palladium, which was renamed the County Theatre.[23] But for music lovers, the most important revival was that of the Three Choirs Festival.

---

18. *Ibid.*, 27 July 1946, p.6; 4 Jan. 1947, p.7; 25 Jan. 1947, p.6; 8 Feb. 1947, p.5; 15 Feb. 1947, p.5; 22 Feb. 1947, pp.5, 6.

19. *TH*, NS CLXX (April 1947), *passim*; HCSA, GMB 1945-82, pp.32-35, Hopewell's report for 6 March 1947 meeting.

20. *HT*, 9 Feb. 1947, p.8; 27 April 1947, p.4; 29 June 1947, pp.4, 5; 30 August 1947, p.5. For the convertibility crisis of July/August 1947 and rationing in general: Kynaston (2008), pp.106, 192, 226-28, 246, 249, 297-98, 358, 509.

21. The phrase is Kynaston's (2010), p.134.

22. Gunner F.G. Dabbs from Liverpool. *HT*, 2 Feb. 1946, p.8. All told some four million British service personnel were demobilised between June 1945 and January 1947.

23. *HT*, 23 Feb. 1946, p.4; 11 May 1946, p.5; 29 June 1946, p.6; 12 Oct. 1946, p.6.

An analysis of the 1946 Hereford Three Choirs is instructive because it illustrates the acute difficulties faced by a small local community in organising a national festival in the grim months after the war. Although it was by no means a foregone conclusion, it was given the green light by a vote of 25 to 6 at a special meeting in the cathedral library on 27 October 1945. The *Hereford Times* welcomed the decision. 'Out of the blood and sweat and tears of the war', its editor asserted, '... there is discoverable among the more hopeful signs of true progress, a greatly increased interest in music and the arts'. But the risks were considerable. Anticipated costs of over £6,000, 40 or so *per cent* higher than in 1936; the fear that stewardship subscriptions would be down; the lack of accommodation; food and labour shortages; and transport difficulties were among the biggest headaches for Tom Steel, the new secretary. One by one they were overcome – in some cases belatedly, the Green Dragon being de-requisitioned just days before the festival's start – and the festival went ahead between 8 and 13 September. And although it was a less grand affair – cathedral flood-lighting was prohibited, for example, and a Town Hall tea replaced the traditional civic banquet and choir breakfast – it was both a musical and financial success. In the words of one Three Choirs devotee, it had proved to be 'the one real return of pre-war civilisation we have been permitted to enjoy'.[24]

Among the school community, too, there was a natural desire to return to pre-war plenitude. In the late 1940s, however, this was a forlorn wish. The Old Herefordians, for example, managed to have 'a cheery and not unpalatable dinner' at the Green Dragon, their pre-war rendezvous, in December 1946 but by the following year a Ministry of Food order had restricted their number to 100. In the event only 75 attended, the shortfall being explained by a cut in the petrol ration. OH functions at the school told a similar story, Hopewell regretting, with catering problems 'more difficult than ever', that the OH cricket match in the summer of 1946 could 'not regain something of its pre-war splendour' as he had hoped.

Indeed given the extension of rationing, institutional catering – including the provision of 'dinners' at HCS for an increasing number of day boys from January 1947[25] – can by no means have been easy operation in the post-war world. Even so, the quality of meals at the Cathedral School is open to question, despite the repetition in the prospectus of Scott's war-time claim that 'fresh fruit, vegetables and milk' were available daily for the boarders. This was no doubt true for milk, not least because Labour's 1946 Act provided (during the week) one third of a pint of milk free for all schoolchildren under 18,[26] but what about the fresh fruit and veg? Certainly concern was expressed in the 1952 inspection report about the catering arrangements in the boarding houses, 'especially the uncontrolled supply of

24. *Ibid.*, 3 Nov. 1945, p.4; 1 Feb. 1946, p.7; 10 August 1946, p.4; 14 Sept. 1946, pp.4, 5; 21 Sept. 1946 p.4; 4 Jan. 1947, p.7. For a musical appreciation: Boden and Hedley, pp.227-28.

25. Day-boy lunches at 8d per day (supervised by a master at 1s per day) were provided in the hut at the back of Number 1, which had a capacity for 25 boys, from January 1947. A number also ate at the cathedral café in Church Street (where a meal cost 2s 3d) for the autumn term 1951 and then the following term at the British Restaurant in St Martin's (at 1s 5d). The school subsidised these 'dinners' although it received 4d for each meal taken by a direct grant boy. HCSA, GMB 1945-82, *passim*; Cash Books 1946-51, 1951-56 *passim*.

26. In the autumn term 1954 alone, Hereford Co-operative Society supplied over 430 gallons (at 4s 8d per gallon) for the boys at mid-break, the subsidy amounting to £102 12s 6d. HCSA, Cash Book 1946-51, fos 125v, 126v, 133v.

tuck and its effect on the variety of the menu and the use of all rationed and other foods available'.[27] The recollections of former boarders also suggest that the food was distinctly mediocre in these years. Invariably it was supplemented by the contents of the ubiquitous tuck box, home food parcels, and by visits to the West Street fish and chip shop. Wathens, the back room of which was also used a smoking den, was an even closer source of supply. Provisions were especially poor in the Old Deanery, but there is good reason to believe that the 1953 change in house staff there – from the Wardles to the Grays – resulted in a marked improvement in the standard of the meals.[28] What is also clear is that soon after their arrival, and following the final ending of sweet rationing on 4 February 1953, the Grays also opened a House tuck shop which was soon stocked with the complete range of Lovells sweets, Mrs Gray being a member of that sweet manufacturing dynasty.[29] Provisioning was getting better even if it did not always appear so to some boys at the time.

Other pre-war school necessities were in short supply in the immediate post-war period. The chairman of the Headmasters' Conference was reminded by the government as late as 1951, when rearmament demands were again restricting supply (clothes rationing having formally ended on 15 March 1949), about the importance of boarding schools limiting the number of non-utility items on clothing lists.[30] In Hereford, Hopewell had already responded to this emergency by instituting a new colours blazer, with gold braid, pocket lettering and crest, in place of the old cricket and rugger blazers, because of the 'impossibility of obtaining cloth at an economic price'. By the following summer, it was reported that there seemed 'less prospect than ever' of getting these blazers, although by October 1951 Pritchard's was able to supply OH blazers (in all sizes) at £9 5s each. There were other shortages: of fives balls for example, over the winter of 1946; and of film for the Photographic Society during the summer term 1948. Earlier that year, *The Herefordian* was slimmer than usual and published late, its editor attributing such deficiencies 'to the universal need for economy … the blessings of staggered holidays and the five day week (or is it the five *hour* week?)'. More significantly, new library books were difficult to procure. Stephen Bell, the master in charge, consequently issued an appeal in April 1947 for library donations, particularly English novels and poetry, newer editions of Greek and Latin texts and modern theology, excepting 'volumes of sermons by Victorian divines'.[31]

Repairs, too, were held up. As a result of the five day working week, the boys' 'handy squad' – by 1947 led by 'Poo' Baylis (with his 'formidable' tool set) – was able to undertake even more maintenance jobs. However, although self-help was continued for much of the period, it could not provide the professional expertise needed for the long awaited new building which took nearly two years to complete from autumn 1948. This was quite apart

27. TNA, ED 109/8825, p.3, report on inspection, 18-21 March 1952. Although the boys' rations were not fully utilised, it was specifically mentioned in the post-inspection meeting with the governors that there was no evidence of 'sharp practice'.

28. The employment of Mrs Sullivan, 'a very competent and pleasant Irish lady', as cook was of particular importance in making the difference. I am grateful to Victor Jordan for this reference.

29. I am indebted to Peter Fairman-Bourne for this observation.

30. *HMC Committee Minutes 1951*, pp.26-27, R.N. Heaton to R. Birley, 2 April 1951.

31. *TH*, NS CLXXII (Jan. 1948), p.4; NS CLXX (April 1947), pp.26-27. Hopewell himself was the (anonymous) editor, as he was throughout much of his career as Headmaster.

from the preparatory works in the preceding years. When the building work eventually started on the Old Deanery lawn and stable yard, an exasperated Headmaster could report:

> For some considerable time vague rumours have been afloat that we are to have a welcome addition to our buildings. For so long, in fact, that even the most sanguine may perhaps have been beginning to wonder whether all the necessary permits and sanctions, labour and materials, not to mention the very necessary cash, would be forthcoming in time for the work to be completed before our present buildings collapse – a disaster which we hope is now less likely to occur owing to the presence in our midst for many months of vast quantities of scaffolding and the occasional appearance of a workman for an hour or two.[32]

Such were some of the peculiar frustrations of running a school in the immediate post-war period.

By the mid-1950s, when the austerity of the immediate post-war years had become a distant memory, there were more opportunities for Herefordians to enjoy the growth in prosperity of the early part of that decade. The emergence from austerity is to be seen in the fitful abolition of rationing. Ration books were widespread until 1952 but that October tea came off the ration, followed (as we have seen) by sweets – this time for good – in February 1953. But the real breakthrough came that autumn with the appearance of 'that strong prize symbol of pre-war good living', the pure white loaf, and the disappearance of sugar rationing. The ending of meat rationing at midnight on 3 July 1954 was the final step, after 14 years, in the dismantling of war-time rationing. That its demise was largely uncelebrated is an indication that unofficially rationing had been abandoned months earlier, about the time (according to the *Hereford Times*) when the Food Ministry had 'failed ignominiously to persuade the shrewd British housewife that tough old Australian ewe meat was delightfully edible'.[33]

The building boom of the early 1950s was a further sign that the country was emerging from austerity. In Hereford, by the end of 1954, over 1,700 new council homes had been provided in the city since the end of the war. The following April, the opening of 12 shops on the Newton Farm estate was heralded as 'another milestone' in the city's post-war development.[34] The same was true of schools. In early 1956, Maurice Edge, the county's Director of Education, presented a favourable report on school development over the ten post-war years. The recent opening of the new Whitecross secondary school, described in the local press as 'an educational palace of light, space and colour', helped substantiate his claim that enormous progress had been achieved since 1945. Equally, the building of the new Girls' High School on the Broadlands site, as well as the start of what became the Bishop's School at Tupsley, gave credence to his claim that the county would be able to provide secondary education for all within five or six years.[35]

---

32. *Ibid.*, NS CLXXV (Jan. 1949), p.5.

33. *HT*, 2 July 1954, editorial, p.8. For the end of rationing also see, Kynaston (2010), pp.254, 317, 324, 371, 392, 394.

34. *HT*, 11 Feb. 1955, p.6; 15 April 1955, p.6.

35. *Ibid.*, 21 Jan 1955, p.5, 27 May 1955, p.6, for Whitecross; 1 April 1955, p.10, 2 Dec. 1955, p.10, for the new Girls' High School; and 28 Oct 1955, p.8, 4 Nov. 1955, p.9, 5 Oct. 1956, p.8, for the Tupsley school.

But there was to be no permanent return to 'pre-war civilisation' as that Three Choirs friend may have hoped following the first post-war festival. Even the Three Choirs did not remain set in aspic. And in his second Hereford festival in 1955, Meredith Davies, Dr Hull's young successor, broke from tradition by omitting morning cathedral performances, increasing the proportion of orchestral to choral music and introducing 'unusual items' such as Stravinsky's *Symphony of Psalms,* Poulenc's *Stabat Mater* and Huber's *The Prodigal Son*, at the expense of such works as *Messiah* (dropped for the first time since 1875) and *Elijah*. Had Mr Davies gone too fast too quickly? Conservative opinion in Hereford suggested that he might have done.[36]

Other forms of entertainment, outside the rarefied atmosphere of a cathedral festival, had changed by the mid-1950s. The repertory company had been disbanded, and the County Theatre had become the city's fourth cinema, even though it was facing competition from a newer medium, television. In October 1954, more TV licenses were issued than in any other previous month, taking the national total to 3.8 million. Some public school Headmasters were worried about such developments in mass communication, but in Hereford the new medium was given official blessing when the city's first televised service was broadcast on Rogation Sunday 1955.[37]

One fixture of Hereford life, the May Fair, did not change, but in 1955 the wisdom of holding a fun fair in the crowded thoroughfares of a city with an essentially medieval street-plan was questioned. The great increase in motorised traffic – vehicle registrations had more than doubled in ten years – and the loss of trade were advanced as powerful reasons for banning the fair from the city centre. Although the fair stayed put, by 1956 such was the concern over the volume of vehicles going through the city – at an average speed of 4 mph, the same speed as carts in the first Elizabethan era according to one chamber of commerce member – that a new one way system was introduced, not for the last time, in August 1956.[38]

These were some of the local developments which form the back-drop to the 11 post-war years of Hopewell's headmastership. Few tenures coincided with a greater period of change. Many, of course, were for the good. Despite the growth of price inflation in the mid-1950s, the standard and quality of living had improved immeasurably for most people in these years. By then the convertibility crisis of the summer of 1947 had long passed and a holiday abroad was also becoming a realistic ambition for some families. Schools, too, ventured overseas, as in January 1951, when a Cathedral School party went on a skiing holiday to Arosa in Switzerland, the school's first expedition abroad since the Belgium trip of 1938. The boys, many kitted out in a motley collection of ex-government clothing from Jessons of Hereford, came back loaded with sweets and chocolate bars to a country still under rationing.[39]

---

36. *Ibid.*, 9 Sept. 1955, p.9, 16 Sept. 1955, p.8; Boden and Hedley, pp.236-38.

37. Kynaston (2010), p.434; *HMC Report 1953*, pp.32ff, (debate on commercial TV); *HMC Report 1954*, pp.37ff (debate on mass communication); *HT*, 6 May 1955, p.8, 20 May 1955 (photographs pp.8, 10).

38. *Ibid.*, 6 May 1955, p.9; 1 June 1955, pp.8, 10; 20 July 1955, p.8; 27 July 1956, p.9 (plan).

39. I am indebted to Richard Hammonds and Robert Hall for their recollections of this trip. The 1938 visit to Belgium is recorded in the *OH Club Handbook, 1937-38,* p.5.

Life chances also increased. One measure of this was the introduction of poliomyelitis vaccination for children between the ages of 2 and 9 in the summer of 1956. Tragically, this was several years too late for Michael Allsebrook and thousands of other victims of this crippling disease.[40]

Historians continue to debate how far British society had actually altered during this decade of rapid change but in terms of youth culture there are suggestions that the age of deference was beginning to crumble. At HCS in 1956, there are indications of an independent spirit being fostered by a new generation of masters. In Hopewell's last year *The Herefordian* had again come under the editorial control of the boys rather than the Headmaster, an intellectual society (named after the Duchess of Somerset) had been established by enterprising Sixth-formers and the Old Deanery cellars had become home to a Jazz Appreciation Society. And among the youth of Hereford in general there were even incipient signs of rebellion. To take just one example. In late September 1956, within the first week of what proved to be Jack Hopewell's final term, a disturbance took place outside the Ritz cinema, when hundreds of gyrating 'teenagers' – a new phenomenon this – caused mayhem in the streets after the late night showing of 'Rock Around the Clock'.[41] Whether any Cathedral schoolboys were among them is unknown.

A Time of Addition

After a short but most impressive service of dedication, the Bishop expressed his pleasure at being allowed to perform the ceremony, and referred to the school's long and honourable history which he said could be described as chequered, especially in respect of its buildings. It had been largely a matter of addition and subtraction, but latterly he was pleased to observe that it had been all addition. And this latest addition was conveniently situated, well designed, solidly constructed and built to last.

Thus Bishop Longworth dedicated what came to be known as New Block (and later the Portman Centre) in the late afternoon of Saturday 22 July 1950.[42] And while Hopewell's headmastership was not one of inexorable increase, as might be mistakenly implied from the Bishop's words, it may be characterised generally as a time of addition: in numbers, in buildings and, more ominously, in costs.

After the down-turn of their fortunes in the late Thirties and early Forties, public schools revived in the following decade.[43] At HCS under Hopewell, the trend of increasing boy numbers continued: from an average of 252 in 1945-46 to 301, the first time the 300 mark had been passed, in 1951-52, when the increase in the age limit to 16 for the new General Certificate examination meant an inevitable over-crowding of the Fifth Forms. After this,

40. Michael Allsebrook contracted polio, aged 19, while still at school. He died in the early hours of 20 July 1952 after a 10 day illness, his funeral taking place in the Lady Chapel on 24 July, towards the end of that summer term. The memorial plaque to this outstanding schoolboy sportsman, originally placed in the Wyeside pavilion, is now in the Zimmerman archives room.

41. *HT*, 21 Sept. 1956, p.10; 28 Sept. 1956, p.9.

42. The opening ceremony, on a day of 'steady downpour', is described in *TH*, NS CLXXX (Oct. 1950), pp.34-36.

43. Spencer Leeson, the war-time chairman of HMC, charts their revival from 1942 in *The Public Schools Question* (1948), p.15. Cited by Gosden, p.356, note 93.

the roll stabilised.[44] The first 'whole school' photograph, taken on 21 July 1953, shows a satisfied Headmaster, with 19 assistants, presiding over his cohort of troops. This is not a complete representation: it shows neither his wife, who was soon to receive the governors' commendation for her many services 'in connection with the comfort of the boys and the well-running of the school',[45] nor all the part-time staff, and 21 boys were absent that July day. Nevertheless, it is a permanent reminder of the school's apparent well-being in this Coronation term.

What is also significant is that the number of boarders increased markedly so that in September 1950, for the last time, the boarders outnumbered the day boys (by one, 144 to 143). Overall, almost half the boys admitted under Hopewell boarded at the school and over one third of these still had Welsh addresses.[46] Without Dean Waterfield's generosity this could never have been achieved. For following the war department's release of his Deanery, which had been accomplished by July 1945 'mainly to satisfy the urgent need of the school for extra accommodation for boarding and teaching' and the consequent securing of its direct grant status, it was the Dean who, with Bishop Parsons' approval, was instrumental in gaining the necessary consents to enable the school to occupy the building by the beginning of the September term.[47] Its availability came just in time: the school's hold on Number 2 Castle Street, which had provided extra war-time accommodation, was becoming increasingly precarious and additional boarders were being signed up for the start of the new academic year.[48] Number 2 was then released – Mr Hubbard, its owner, complaining that the boys had damaged some rooms by 'using air-guns on targets placed on the walls' – and its incumbent Housemaster, Harry Wardle, was given the charge of

---

44. At 297, 292, 300, 296 and 291 in the following five years. The 300 mark was passed for the first time in the autumn term 1951, the number being exceeded five years later with a record roll of 306. Even Hopewell admitted that at 300 the school had reached 'about saturation point'. With 303 boys in the school at the end of 1951, many classrooms in the main building were operating beyond their normal capacities, the direct grant regulations of a maximum class of 30 being exceeded in four rooms out of ten (including Big School). *TH*, NS CLXXXVII (Feb. 1953), p.5; HCSA, GMB 1945-51, back cover.

45. Brittain MSS, Tom Steel to Barbara Hopewell, 27 Nov. 1953, recording the governors' minute of 26 Nov. 1953. I am grateful to Mrs Brittain for permission to cite from this and other family documents in her possession.

46. Of the 718 boy admitted from the autumn term 1945 to the autumn term 1956 (inclusive), 357 (49.7 *per cent*) were boarders. 128 boys (36 *per cent* of all boarders) came from Wales.

47. HCA, 7031/24, pp.452, 457-58, Acts, 17 July, 19 Sept. 1945. HCSA, J.R. Brown, Secretary to the Ecclesiastical Commissioners, to Dean Waterfield, 6 July, 7 August 1945, together with Stooke and Son's valuation of 15 August 1945, correspondence about the lease and a draft lease, which was not finally agreed until after the school had occupied the premises. A school use for the Deanery was contemplated as early as 1940. A printed prospectus (undated but *c.*July 1940) for the opening of a Victoria College (Jersey) House at the Deanery, under Mr and Mrs Grummitt, the Jersey Headmaster and his wife, but in conjunction with HCS, is to be found among the Hopewell papers in the Brittain MSS.

48. The school initially leased Number 2 from August 1940 at £70 *per annum*. The house was then sold in June 1944 to Arthur H.F. Hubbard, C.F. Scott's £1,700 bid being insufficient to acquire the property. Hubbard wanted Number 2 as an annexe to the Residence Hotel (which he leased from the Chapter), business at that time being 'so good that he is panting for more premises'. Having given the school notice to quit, he eventually leased Number 2 (on a termly basis) to the governors at a rent of £90 per annum. For the background to this: TNA, ED 35/4441, R.E. Williams to Stephenson, 22 June 1944.

the Deanery, soon to become known as the Old Deanery.[49] The terms were favourable to all parties. Dean Waterfield was freed from the expense of living in a property which (as Bishop Parsons observed) was outside the means of his office. The governing body gained a large building on favourable terms: a 21-year lease, with power to terminate at 7 or 14 years, at a rent of £250 *per annum*, the money being well covered by the Housemaster's fee and the incoming rent from the two sitting tenants.[50] Their sub-tenant, Harry Wardle, apart from having to pay a capitation fee of £2 per boarder per term, which averaged out at well over £300 *per annum* during his tenure, continued to enjoy the profits of running a boarding house as a private business. And the school itself acquired the largest, if not the finest, of the Close residences with space for eight dormitories, other House rooms and an additional classroom, all set with out-buildings in almost an acre of ground.

Whether the boys – 50 of them, some of whom had been previously boarded out in private houses because Number 2 was full, that autumn term – appreciated their new accommodation is doubtful. Certainly, there is no recorded recollection from among the surviving Deanery old boys of 1945 of their appreciation of the new space; just memories of a spartan house with no carpets or curtains and little heating. Things gradually improved. Early the following year general repairs were made, a new bath and basins were added to the end bedroom and radiators were transferred to the ground-floor rooms. The school bore little more than £100 of the total cost (£673 7s 3d), the remainder being found by the military on account of war-time 'dilapidations'.[51] As importantly, it was not long before Harry Wardle forged a new House spirit through events like the annual Old Deanery summer entertainments; the House soon competing for sporting honours, too, winning its first junior rugby trophy in 1948 and finally 'putting an end to a long series of victories by School House' by winning the senior competition in 1951. The House food, as we have seen, became more palatable with the arrival of Colonel and Mrs Gray in September 1953. With their appointment, the House was also established on a new financial basis as the previous year's inspectors had wanted: the Grays were salaried and given new titles, being paid £100 and £250 respectively as bursar and housekeeper; and the House accounts were incorporated into the school general account, the school reaping the profits and bearing any losses.[52] The practice was extended to School House in

---

49. HCSA, A.D. Steel and Son to Dean Waterfield, 19 Sept. 1945; HCSA, Harry Wardle to A.D. Steel and Son, 1 Dec. 1945.

50. From the Dean's view-point, the income also subsidised his residence in the cloisters (Number 17, as it then was), the rent of which was now borne by the Chapter. Over the summer of 1945, the Dean and Chapter had apparently decided against purchasing 34 Castle Street as the new Deanery, probably on grounds of expense. HCA, 7031/24, pp.452, 457-58, Acts, 17 July, 19 Sept. 1945.

51. HCSA, Roiser (the architect) to Dean Waterfield, 16 Jan. 1946; HCSA, Account Book 1945-72, fo 3r (1945-46); HCSA, GMB 1945-82, pp.19-20, 20 Feb. 1946. The installation of showers, baths and basins in the old pantry, which would have meant a new tank and boiler (all at an estimated cost of £461 8s), was not carried out.

52. The Old Deanery account (under the management of the Grays and from April 1955, the Prestons) was in deficit for the two financial years 1954 to 1956 (for £702 14s 4d and £142 1s 11d respectively) but made a small profit (£46 19s 5d) in 1956-57. School House (and Number 1) made a profit of £237 10s 10d in 1955-56, the last complete year of the Hopewells' tenure. *Ibid.*, fos 80, 89r, 90r, 98r, 99r. At the time of the 1952 inspection, the governors had feared that 'incentives and efficiency would be lost' if the Housemasters received a fixed emolument. TNA, ED 109/8825, report on post-inspection meeting between the HMIs and governors, 21 March 1952.

1955, the governors paying £2,100 for the Hopewells' furniture and fittings in Number 1 and School House and giving each of them a £250 salary for their House responsibilities.[53] The era of modern house-mastering had at last arrived at the Cathedral School. With the boarding houses no longer being run as private enterprises, it was the most important administrative reform of this period.

The pupil roll was also sustained by the continuance of the direct grant, the number of free places (excluding the choristers) rising to near 100, one third of the total, in the early 1950s. As has been mentioned, few schools could be certain of the outcome of their applications for direct grant status following the Labour landslide of 1945.[54] In an attempt to satisfy the Ministry's requirements, HCS made its pitch on the grounds of its long history, its endowments (even 'by kings'), the support it received from the Chapter and its former pupils, its non-local character and its purpose as an ancient foundation of godliness and good learning. 'Perhaps in the frenzied modern world', the governors argued, 'this influence will be even more marked than in the leisurely days of our ancestors'.[55] In retrospect, given the admitted deficiencies – the school's cramped site, its inadequate premises (although with de-requisitioning the application held out the prospect 'of immediate and admirable expansion adjoining the school') and its ageing equipment 'as a result of six years of war' – it does not seem the strongest of submissions. Nevertheless, it received the government's approval on 12 October 1945. HCS had done better than many other schools: the majority that applied for direct grant status were turned down and only 44 direct grant schools remained members of HMC by October 1947. In view of the extent to which it relied on its direct grant over the coming years – by the end of Hopewell's tenure over half of the school's income came from this source alone – the grant's retention was of crucial importance for the school's future character and financial stability.

With the grant came an expectation that the school would not only need to tighten up its procedures – by operating, for example, an approved sliding scale for subsidised places, based on declared parental income rather than the Headmaster's judgement following a parental interview[56] – but also improve its premises. As the governors had hinted in the direct grant submission, the Deanery, together with its grounds and outbuildings, was to provide the way to salvation. In order to convince the government that the school meant business, plans for new accommodation were drawn up in late 1945,[57] but apart from the

53. HCSA, GMB 1945-82, p.96, 25 Feb.; p.99, 23 June 1955. H.P. Barnsley & Son's certificate of valuation of £2,036 11s 5d (plus £67 10s for improvements) was made on 28 April 1955. A copy exists in the school archives. Over £500 of this amount was paid off on 5 October 1956, Mrs Hopewell generously donating the remaining £1,600 still due after her husband's death to the school's gymnasium appeal.

54. See above, p.443 and note 12. Even as early as January 1945, Spencer Leeson, the HMC chairman, had been unclear about the Ministry's exact criteria for direct grant status. *HMC Report 1945*, p.27, Leeson's speech, 5 Jan.

55. HCSA, typed copy of the application, 25 June 1945. Dean Waterfield was informed by the Clerk on 23 June that the application was 'precisely on the same lines as the application made by Mr A.P. Whitehead in respect of Lucton School, who loaned to us his copy to follow'.

56. The suggested scale for 1945-46 was a free place for parents (with one child) earning under £390 annually, with a £2 fee increase for every £26 of additional income. HCSA, T.O.D. Steel to Dean Waterfield, 30 Jan. 1946, enclosing the Ministry of Education's letter of the previous day.

57. HCSA, architectural plans and elevations (Ellery Anderson, Roiser and Falconer) 17, 24 Oct., 20, 21 Nov. 1945. The school archives also contain an undated but completed Ministry of Education form (353a G), 'estimates

creation of a larger classroom beneath the library nothing was accomplished for several years. Shortages of materials and labour and the difficulty of obtaining building licences all contributed to the delay but the main obstacle was lack of money. As a direct grant school, HCS was not entitled to financial help from public funds for capital developments. How, therefore, could a project with a preliminary estimate of £10,736, which was not much less than the entire income of the school in 1945-46, possibly be financed without resort to unaffordable borrowing?

A former mayor of Hereford was to provide part of the answer, for the Philpotts charity had grown into a sizeable foundation by the post-war period. Through the rent of Number 28 High Town to Boots, increased from £300 to £500 *per annum* in June 1945, it had accumulated capital assets worth over £10,500 by early 1947. Given the increase in state university funding and direct grant places, the diversion of these funds from scholarships to buildings could now be justified. Accordingly, the alteration of the Philpotts scheme on 13 March 1947 enabled the governors to use its assets to improve the school's premises, and most of its capital stock – excluding the house, valued at £7,500 in December 1947 – was transferred to the general account.[58] A further £9,000 from the school's unreserved endowment fund, together with a £1,500 loan from Mrs R.E.A. Steel, was also used to meet the £22,000 eventually needed for the new accommodation.[59]

The new building was in essence two separate constructions. The first part of the design, while continuing the character of the existing façade to the street elevation, subtly converted the old stable block into shower baths and changing rooms. A new two-storey building, faced in stone on the Castle Street side, was then erected behind the old Deanery coach house which was knocked down. This provided four classrooms, an Art room 'worthy of the name', a sound-proof workshop, a day boys' room and various other amenities. It also freed up space in the boarding houses and meant that inappropriate rooms (including Big School) no longer needed to be used as form bases. On his return from the summer holiday, Hopewell proudly announced that the changes resulting from the new accommodation were as significant as any in the school's long history.[60] This was justifiable hyperbole – his troops needed to be made aware of their privileged new existence – but even with hindsight it can be truthfully said that the new building was the most important addition to the school's teaching facilities since 1875. However, the improvements were costly. As the

and particulars of proposed building works'; and letters from Roiser to Ministry of Education, 27 Dec. 1945; Roiser to Dean Waterfield, 24 Sept. 1945, 21 Feb. 1946; Roiser to A.D. Steel & Son, 6 Feb. 1946.

58. £9,914 11s 7d worth of Philpotts stock was sold and transferred between April 1948 and October 1950. The award of university exhibitions and senior and junior scholarships from this fund was thus brought to an end, after more than 300 years, the last scholarship payments being made in 1952-53. Thereafter, most of the Boots rental money was made over each year to the general account. Philpotts' name lived on through the award of a Philpottine scholarship to the boy with the highest mark in the school's 11 plus examination (won by a pupil from St Owen's Primary in successive years, 1951-54).

59. Tom Steel, as Clerk to the Governors, had visited the Ministry of Education on 14 December 1949 to ascertain how the building might be best financed given the decline in the value of the school's securities (to £18, 630). See HCSA, GMB 1945-82, between pp.67 and 68, for the minutes of that meeting. The exact cost of the building (including £448+ for furniture) was £22,198 0s 3d. The building was designed by E.A. Roiser, the cathedral architect, and built by W.H. Peake and Son, with George Laing as the Quantity Surveyor.

60. *TH*, NS CLXXXI (Feb. 1951), p.5.

Archdeacon had mentioned at the opening in July 1950, HCS was now 'practically without endowments [and] more or less living from hand to mouth'.[61] For the time being, further building could only possibly be funded through the generosity of Old Herefordians.

And there was a pressing need for other facilities. Some of these had been identified by old boys who wished to establish a further memorial to the 34 Old Herefordians who had lost their lives on service in the Second World War. This was to be distinct from the Lady Chapel tablet, unveiled by Vice-Admiral Loder-Symonds OH and dedicated by Dean Burrows on 11 December 1948.[62] A special meeting of the OH Club was called on 19 July 1947 to draw up a short list of six projects. Following a postal vote, the building of an on-site gymnasium and a Biology laboratory, at an estimated combined cost of £7,000, were the choices of the majority of old boys.[63] The preferences accorded with both the Ministry's views and the Headmaster's wishes,[64] Hopewell having followed Arthur Zimmerman as president of the club in December 1946. However, it took the old president to make part of the vision a reality through his covenanting of £1,120, worth £2,000 to the club with tax relief and almost half of the money raised from OHs during Hopewell's tenure. And even all the contributions – the Headmaster himself gifting £20 and covenanting £106 15s – were insufficient to complete the whole project, a decision being made to proceed only with the building of the laboratory, appropriately opened by Zimmerman on 13 December 1952.[65] Despite Hopewell's best efforts to ensure that the full scheme became 'something more than an idle dream', the gymnasium was not built until after his death, when it became his own school memorial rather than a tribute to the fallen of the Second World War.

Two other physical developments which took place during Hopewell's time should be mentioned. Although these alterations occurred in the cloisters and the cathedral, they undoubtedly improved the quality of the boys' experience. In early 1949, College Hall was re-floored 'with semastic tiles' and redecorated. A new electric heating system was also installed and the stage was raised and enlarged, the purchase of tubular scaffolding enabling the school to erect a proscenium and scenery for its plays. The work was completed in time for the examinations and the end of term summer entertainment, although the cost

---

61. With annual re-payments of the endowment capital fixed at £418 16s, it would take many years to refill the coffers. The Archdeacon was A.J. Winnington-Ingram OH, a governor and vice-president of the OH Club. When he retired nearly 11 years later, his fellow governors recorded their appreciation of his 'immense service' and 'the assistance they had received from his long experience and great knowledge of the school and its affairs'. HCSA, GMB 1945-82, p.144, 26 May 1961.

62. The name of J.H. Wilmore OH was missed from the list of 33 inscribed on the tablet. The inscription: 'They passed from darkness through fire into light' was chosen by the Dean from words spoken by Lord Allenby when unveiling a Belfast memorial after the Great War. *HT*, 18 Dec. 1948, p.5.

63. These two items (the first and second on the list) received 457 and 338 votes respectively. The other suggested projects were an OH rugby club-house (181 votes), the provision of scholarships for the sons of OHs (138), an organ for the Lady Chapel (91) and a school boat house (56). Each OH was asked to rank three projects in order of preference, although it is unclear how the actual counting of votes actually operated.

64. The Ministry of Education's dissatisfaction with the existing arrangements for PT were conveyed by the HMI to the architect. HCSA, Roiser to A.D. Steel & Son, 6 Feb. 1946.

65. The laboratory was designed by Herbert Powell OH so that it could be built independently. He was also responsible for the design of the memorial tablet. His plans were published in *TH*, NS CLXXIV (Sept. 1948).

of using the hall more than doubled to a guinea for each hire.[66] There was no charge, of course, for the school's daily use of the Lady Chapel. Through the generosity of Lennox B. Lee of How Caple Court, the chapel was cleaned, redecorated and restored in 1949 and then refurnished and adorned over the next two years. The gifts included a new altar, the burnished gold reredos, return and choir stalls and a new chamber organ, the school's contribution being a revolving lectern designed by the architect 'to be in perfect keeping with the other furnishings' and dedicated on 26 July 1951, two months after the official consecration. These alterations disrupted services for several months but on the school's return from temporary exile in the north transept to its spiritual home, the quality of worship was immeasurably enhanced, not least the singing, the harmonium having been abandoned and the choir now sitting collegiately.[67]

The cathedral environment became more attractive and the school grew. These were the positive aspects but there were also downsides to the school's apparent prosperity. One major consequence of the expansion was that HCS became more costly to run. Over the 11 financial years from 1945, teaching salaries more than doubled from £6,856 (1945-46) to £16,603 (1955-56), even though the number of full-time masters increased by only five: from 13 to 18.[68] As a result, there was a growing annual deficit on the fees account (the difference between fees income, excluding the direct grant, and staff payments) from £1,890 to £7,022, despite basic fee rises from £104 (for boarders) and £33 (day) to £153 and £48 *per annum* respectively in the same period. This deficit was well covered by the direct grant, which more than trebled from £4,277 in 1946 to £12,897 in 1956, but the school was becoming increasingly dependent on the government subsidy. And if salaries are excluded, general costs almost doubled (to over £22,000) in these years. Let us take just one illustration of this price rise: the school's bill for cleaning, lighting and heating (including payments for the porter and stokers) rose from £300 in 1945-46 to £836 ten years later, fuel costs alone increasing from £80 to £328. There were two main reasons for this: the increase in the price of coal/coke from around £2 16s per ton in September 1948 to £6 14s in February 1956, the increase being particularly steep from 1955 to 1956;[69] and the coming on stream of New Block, which doubled the school's fuel costs over one year. The servicing of a new building, amidst the upkeep of old ones – there were nine boilers, for example, in the six school buildings by November 1951[70] – was an expensive business.

66. HCA, 7031/24, p.458, 19 Sept. 1945 (hire charge); 7031/25, p.17, 30 Nov. 1948 (W.J. Morris & Son's flooring estimate); p.41, 26 Oct. 1949 (new hire charge). *TH*, NS CLXXVII (Oct. 1949), pp. 5, 31-33.

67. *Ibid.*, p.7; NS CLXXXIII (Oct. 1951), pp.5, 29-30; HCA, 7031/25, pp.34, 36-37, re Lee's offer and the new scheme, 24 June, 2 Aug.1949; pp.86, 87, 90, re service of dedication and HCS gift, 29 May, 26 June and 31 July 1951; HCSA, GMB 1945-82, between pp.77-78, Hopewell's report for 5 June 1951 meeting. The architect was W.H. Randoll Blacking. For Lennox Lee's benefactions: Aylmer and Tiller, pp.174, 176, 177, 285, 492.

68. Including Hopewell, whose basic annual salary (excluding house-mastering) increased from £800 in 1945-46 to £1,283 in 1955-56. His most junior assistants in 1945-46 (John Basil) and 1955-56 (M.R. Stafford) received basic annual salaries of £315 and £460 16s 8d respectively. In 1945-46, two members of the full-time staff, F.R.H. Hora and E.R.B. Gray, were not being paid on the Burnham scale.

69. The cost in April 1955 was around £5 13s per ton, the price having been more or less stable for over two years, the following year's price rise stemming from the 18 *per cent* increase – the largest ever – announced by the National Coal Board in July 1955.

70. HCSA, Cash Book 1946-51, fo 178v, payment (1 Feb. 1951) of £58 1s 3d to the Royal Exchange Assurance

Given such trends, it is no great surprise to find that there were only two years over this period when the general account showed a surplus. More alarmingly, the deficit increased annually from 1951-52 until it reached £5,698 at the end of the financial year, 1955-56.[71] So despite the expansion of the Hopewell years, the financial outlook was less than rosy by the end of his tenure. Costs were rising and the overdraft increasing at a time when the school had cashed in most of its endowment income to pay for improvements to the academic infrastructure. The additions came at a price, a price which was just about affordable as long as the political weather remained fine.

The Felling of the 'Acropolis' and Academic Concerns

Fig. 8.3 A solitary senior boy reads in school yard in the mid-1950s, but no longer in the shade of the 'Acropolis'.

A momentous event took place in January 1954, while the boys were away on their Christmas holidays: the two massive beech trees which towered over one corner of the playground were felled because they were considered 'very far from safe'. The 'Acropolis', which for generations had provided a play space and shelter for the boys; a trophy cabinet for a captured German gun; a platform for both magisterial announcements and pupil orators during 'mock' general elections; or, more prosaically, simply a vantage point for ogling passing girls, was thus shorn of its greatest adornment. Only two untidy stumps and the mound remained. The felling of these trees was of such significance to the school that it merited a paragraph in the pages of *The Herefordian*.[72] Nearly 60 years later, their destruction can be used as a metaphor for the weakening of the Classics stronghold during the Hopewell era.

for boiler policy insurance, 1950-51. At that time, the school employed Hubert J. Jones (also the porter and corps sergeant-major) as stoker at £3 10s per week and Joe Woodward, the cricket professional, as the relief weekend stoker at 15s per week. The boiler-rooms also served a function as places of refuge for miscreant boys. I am indebted to Geoffrey Burgess for this observation.

71. There was a surplus of £132 at the end of the financial year 1947-48 and one of £378 for the year ending 1950-51. For these and other figures in this paragraph, see HCSA, Account Book 1945-72, fos 1-99.

72. *TH*, NS CLXXXX (May 1954), pp.6-7; HCSA, Cash Book 1951-56, fo 93v, £10 payment to H. Wragg & Sons. I am indebted to David Hedwoth and Derek Wintle for their recollections of the 'Acropolis'. For the German field gun, see above, p.412.

As in the war years, the argument should not be pushed too far. For although there was a relative decline in the number of boys studying Classics, from around one half of the Sixth Form taking a predominantly classical Higher Certificate (1946-50) to about one quarter taking classical subjects at Advanced-level (1951-56), the classicists tended to gain the better results. Certainly at the highest level, of the 14 Oxford and Cambridge awards won between 1946 and 1956, 11 were won by classicists and only three by the Modern Sixth.[73] So the Classics department still attracted clever boys. It also was the best resourced department, had the best Sixth Form room (in the Gilbert Library) and further kept its privileged place in the curriculum. Until after the 1952 inspection, five or six periods of Latin per week continued to be the staple diet for all boys up to and including the Fourth Forms, and the Grecians, who dropped Science in place of Greek after Form II, had six periods each week for two years and then eight in the Fifth.

So Classics was still well favoured but standards in classical subjects had dropped since Crees' time. In the 1952 inspection report, the first objective measure we have of the school's academic performance for over 18 years, attainment in Latin below the Classical Sixth was held to be 'very disappointing', the work of the 'B' forms, and even some of the 'A' sets, being regarded as poor at best. In Greek, the picture was brighter, although the fact that only two boys had taken the Ordinary-level paper in 1951 was criticised, perhaps unfairly given the age restrictions then in force.[74] Two teachers were exempt from the general criticism: a younger master (John Brookes) appointed in 1951; and the senior classical master, who had been successful 'in instilling a love of the Classics and a good standard of proficiency in translation and prose' among the Classical Sixth, and who 'from his own ripe scholarship and experience' had worked a remarkable improvement in standards. Stephen ('Tiger') Bell's idiosyncratic teaching methods, 'with his extraordinary system of post-cards, each covered with eight or nine weird sentences or phrases', are remembered with affection by his former pupils and clearly produced impressive results.[75] Yet the inspectors considered that changes were imperative and that Bell would need 'to descend into the arena and take part in the work of the Fifth' if the Classics were to be saved at the school. This indictment of the Classics department is in marked contrast to the encomiums lavished upon it by the HMIs a generation earlier, when there were 24 boys in the Classical Sixth, as opposed to 6 in 1952.[76]

Correspondingly, the size of the Modern Sixth had grown from 15 in 1933 to 25 in 1952. Despite Hopewell's difficulties in finding suitable Science teachers, almost all

---

73. The classical awards were won (in chronological order) by P. Davies, J.E. Hammond, P.H. Williams, H.K. Hill, D.L. Watkins, G.D. Dunn, P.N. Challenger, J.B. Evans, P.J.C. Murray, V.F.J. Jordan and A.J. Weston; and those for Mathematics or Science by I.E. Hughes, F.E. Roberts and P.G. Fuller Lewis. Almost all of these were close awards and no open scholarships were won during this period.

74. For John Wolfenden's criticism (as chairman of HMC) of the Labour government's decision to impose this age limit, see *HMC 1948 Report*, p.14ff, 27 Sept. 1948.

75. One of Bell's most distinguished former pupils, the late Professor A.D. Nuttall, wrote the following about his mentor (in *Why Does Tragedy Give Pleasure*? [Oxford, 1996], p.4): 'I spent the first ten years of my adult life arguing in my head with the man who taught me Latin and Greek at school'. I am indebted to John Ward for this reference and to him and Victor Jordan for insights into Bell's teaching methods, for which also see John Meredith's affectionate portrait in *TH*, CCX (July 1966), pp.28-30.

76. TNA, ED 109/8825, report issued on 15 July 1952 of inspection, 18-21 March 1952. For the 1933 inspection, see above, pp.397-98.

of these boys were taking advanced courses in Mathematics or Science and the inspectorate suggested that the form might be more aptly named the Science Sixth. Standards in Mathematics had fallen back but better work was being done in Science, despite its being too closely circumscribed by examination requirements. According to the inspectors, 'the understandable desire to "make sure" for the weaker brethren [in the Sixth]' was 'the enemy of more adventurous teaching and the cultivation of an experimental scientific outlook'.

So the Sciences had grown in prominence but no subject on the Arts side had begun to compete with Classics. To modern eyes, what is striking about the Sixth Form curriculum in 1952 is that there were no advanced courses in History and Geography and apart from the solitary boy studying French (and taking a correspondence course in German) none in Modern Languages. English was taught to good purpose to all the Sixth as was Divinity throughout the school but neither subject was taken at Advanced-level. And, in curriculum terms, practical subjects, all taught by part-timers, were almost non-existent. Despite the new dedicated room – not equipped, incidentally, with water supply at this time – Art made only a slight contribution to the boys' education with one lesson a week in the first two years and two for some in the Fifth; there was no craft; Music, again taught for one period a week (although for the first three years) but this time in the 'dingy and uninspiring' Big School, played 'a very small part in the life of the school'; and the visiting PE instructor, a local publican, had no experience in modern civilian physical training and so did not 'get beyond the dull, static and uninspiring type of lesson for which the boys do not change apart from discarding their jackets'.

The inspectors had other criticisms: the lack of specialist rooms was hindering progress, particularly in French and Geography; the Common Room, which the staff had outgrown, was 'dismal and unattractive'; the Old Block classrooms were 'drab and dingy' and filled with worn and broken furniture; there were deficiencies in equipment, text books and resources and the library contained 'merely the beginnings of a collection' in most subjects. More serious were the complaints about unimaginative teaching, 'lacking in vigour, tied to the text book and often ill-adjusted to the mental calibre of the boys'.[77] Here was a school still in recovery from the war and one which had not yet adjusted to its rapid post-war expansion. It had also still to provide a suitable curriculum for the less academically gifted, who were pushed to cope (many in only four years) with the demands of the new Ordinary-level syllabus. The lamp of Classics may have dimmed but most other subjects were still in its shadow and awaiting a fuller place in the curriculum. So the Headmaster, who was recognised as devoting himself to the school's best interests, was charged with the task of remedying these deficiencies. As it turned out, Hopewell had little more than four academic years to accomplish an assignment which took more than a generation to fulfil.

Had an HCS inspection taken place in 1956 – eight years before the next one actually happened – what might the inspectors have written about the school's academic progress? In one sense, had none of the earlier recommendations been implemented there would still have been visible signs of improvement, for despite the advent of the new building, 1952

77. For these criticisms: TNA, ED 109/8825, 1952 report, especially pp.3-5.10-11. The Boys' High School was inspected (the team being led by the same RI, R. Sibson) almost a year later than HCS and received a much more favourable report, which emphasised its strengths on the Science side, the well maintained plant, good resources and competent staff (language teaching apart). *Ibid.*, report, issued 24 June 1953, for 10-13 March inspection.

was an unfortunate date for a formal academic review. At that time, almost half the staff had started their careers around the end of the First World War; none of them had been professionally trained; all had taught the old School and Higher Certificate courses for most of their time as teachers and were having to adapt, within a few years of retirement, to the more rigorous demands of the new General Certificate of Education. By 1956, Harry Wardle, George Hunt, Ernest Gray, Emile Maurer (re-appointed in September 1951 at the age of 74!) and Evan Morgan had all departed.[78] And in terms of results, in the first two years of the new GCE (1951 and 1952), only candidates above the age of 16 could sit the examination. This precluded HCS from entering clever younger boys (many of whom were classicists) early for the Ordinary-level. After the age requirement was made discretionary in 1953, the school's O-level performance markedly improved.[79]

Nevertheless, changes were also made which improved the school's academic performance. Early in 1953, it was made possible for those finding 'the pace exhausting and the going heavy' to take an extra year before O-level.[80] Hopewell's new appointments were generally well chosen and reduced the average age of the academic staff (including the Headmaster) by five years to around 40 in the summer of 1956. The Common Room base, however, remained in School House, a fire that occurred on 17 January 1955 proving the inspectors' point about the cramped nature of the masters' quarters.[81] With the opening of the new laboratory, the biologists moved from their temporary home in New Block, which then became the woodwork room as had been originally intended. Separate labs for each Science and the coming together of a new set of Science teachers provided the platform for excellence in that area.[82] A form room for the modern linguists was created, together with a languages bookcase in memory of Colonel Gray; annual expenditure on text books increased from £218 (1951/52) to £423 (1955/56), a substantial amount even allowing for mid-Fifties inflation; and other important resources were bought, including a Roneo duplicator (for £34 12s 7d). There was an expansion, too, in the number of subjects offered at Advanced-level, English Literature, French, German, History and Geography all being added to the list by 1955. The number taking A-level, and consequently the size of the

78. Harry Wardle resigned (aged 61), and left after 33 years service in July 1953. He was succeeded as Second Master for one term by George ('Squitty') Hunt, who took early retirement (aged 54) at Christmas 1953, thus severing the last link (among the academic staff) with Crees' staff. Morgan retired, aged 63, in July 1954; and Gray, who had missed the inspection because of illness (Maurer having taken his place), died in post, aged 60, on 21 January 1955. Of Hopewell's contemporaries (i.e. those born in the 1890s), only Arden-Davis and Bell remained in 1956.

79. At least in terms of the number of boys gaining five or more passes – from 9 and 14 respectively in 1951-52 to 24 in 1953-54 and 1956, and 26 in 1955.

80. *TH*, NS CLXXXVII (Feb. 1953), p.5.

81. The fire, 'apparently caused by a spark from a cigarette', badly charred the door, damaged the floor and destroyed three gowns and a mat. HCSA, GMB 1945-82, between pp.95-96, Hopewell's report 24 Feb. 1955. See HCSA, Cash Book 1951-56, fos 157v, 161r, 163v, for payments to Hornby and Moorse for gowns, Reece & Co for Common Room repairs and insurance claim (£27 8s 6d), 27 May to 24 June 1955.

82. Hopewell's Science appointments included two fine teachers who spent most of their careers at the school, W.J. Rumsey (1948) and J.W. Rowlands, the first full-time Biology teacher (1950); the chaplain, E.D. Preston, who also had a 'first' and a higher degree in Chemistry (1951); H.A. Hornby (1954) and B.C.L. Kemp, formerly Head of Science at Wellington College, who died following an accident on 26 December 1956 after one term at HCS.

Sixth Form, was also growing, to 23 advanced and scholarship candidates by 1956. This cohort gained 51 passes, the most yet achieved, with two boys winning state scholarships that year.[83] Hopewell had succeeded in maintaining the average leaving rate at around 17 years, a cause for satisfaction as the inspectors had observed, given the numbers of farmers' boys and choristers who tended to leave early. The harmonious relationship between the school and the county educational authority, which from 1951 nominated 10 boys each year for free places on the results of its own selective examination, was beginning to bear fruit.[84]

There was no attempt to do much in curriculum terms about the practical subjects, still taught by a motley collection of part-timers who however talented did not have the period allocation to make much of a difference. Indeed with Physical Education, once Sergeant Birch, the publican, had retired in July 1955, the subject went backwards in that it was farmed out to the PT instructors of the boys' artillery battery at Bradbury Lines. It was not until a gymnasium had been built in the next reign that a proper course of physical instruction could begin. As for the other initiatives, it would have been too much to have expected root and branch reform from a Headmaster in his sixties, but at the very least these piece-meal changes laid the foundations for the considerable academic advances under Hopewell's successor.

New and Old Occupations

The inspectors made passing reference to the 'keen interest' shown by staff and boys in games and athletics, and they cursorily mentioned the school's 'flourishing' CCF, its dramatic productions and the 'vigorous organisation' of the OH Club with its 600 members. Overall, however, they did less than justice to the strengths of the school's corporate life, which flourished under the Headmaster's benevolent rule. In this sphere, as a former Housemaster and man of wide interests, Hopewell was in his element.

One of his most innovative ideas was the institution, on Friday afternoons but within the school day, of a compulsory programme of pursuits or 'occupations' for all boys and staff. Apart from the Fifth Forms and those others required for extra work under Wardle's and Hunt's supervision, the school was split 'without regard for seniority or degree' into groups 'as far as possible in accordance with each boy's taste and inclination'. Fifteen or more clubs were offered each term. Some existing societies were incorporated into the new programme; some, like boxing or swimming in the summer, were sporting; others were cultural, such as the Recorded Music Society where classical music was played – initially from the radio, then via a wind-up gramophone, and later on the Headmaster's three valve portable electric record player 'of considerable power and beauty'. By this time, a library of 650 classical records had been built up. A number of handicraft hobbies were also offered. The Model-Aero Club's activities included the flying of a control-line model at 70 mph in school yard, with 9 inch

83. The two state scholars were D.E.N.B. Jones and A.J. Weston. They followed J.C. Gittins and A.D. Nuttall, who won state scholarships in 1955 and were to become distinguished academics.

84. In 1951, Hopewell had been permitted to select any 10 boys from the first 16 on the list who had given HCS as their first choice school. HCSA, GMB 1945-82, between pp.77-78, report 3 June 1951. How far this 'quite satisfactory arrangement' carried on in subsequent years is unknown.

clearance between the walls; the Printing Club, led by the Headmaster himself, did useful work on the new high speed 'Adana' press, printing invitation and fixtures cards, school programmes and stationery and occasionally the junior entrance examination; and members of the Photographic Society snapped local scenes and monuments thanks to the gifts of a plate camera, lens and tripod, and eventually processed their images in the darkroom, incorporated into New Block at the Headmaster's insistence. Such hobbies were in tune with the spirit of the times, the school's efforts being exhibited in the Shirehall at the Hereford Rotary Club exhibition in May 1950. By then, however, the Friday afternoon programme had almost run its course. After five years, compulsory occupations were abandoned 'with some reluctance' in July 1951, a victim of timetable pressures, choice limitations and (according to *The Herefordian*) the 'couldn't care less attitude ... all too prevalent today'.[85]

However true this was – and each generation's young has been castigated in this way – the school provided other opportunities for enrichment outside the classroom. There were perhaps three or four of these 'diversions', as Hopewell called them, each term. There were occasional whole school visits to special showings of films at the Odeon: for example, *The XIVth Olympiad* (15 October 1948), *Scott of the Antarctic* (24 June 1949), *Hamlet* (1 December 1949), *A Queen is Crowned* (17 June 1953) and (at the Ritz) *The Conquest of Everest* (17 February 1954), the subject of the most popular book in the Gilbert Library. Smaller groups visited the theatre, sometimes (from the summer of 1950) at Stratford; more often to Shakespearean productions at the local County Theatre; and occasionally to recitals and lectures at the Shirehall or, less conventionally, at the Girls' High School. But more regularly, entertainments came to the school. By the aid of several staff wireless sets, the boys were able to listen to Princess Elizabeth's wedding day broadcast on 20 November 1947, as well as John Snagge's commentary on the varsity boat race in 1949 and 1953. Richard Dimbleby's Hereford *Down Your Way* – featuring (among ten interviewees) James Poulter, the venerable cathedral verger, and Hubert Jones, the school porter – was broadcast on a Sunday (23 January 1949), but it was no doubt listened to by many boarders after their afternoon walks.[86] The boarders also continued to have the pleasure of film presentations on Saturday evenings, but with sound from late 1952, as well as occasional talks, including the Revd S.J. Davey OH on sex and Dean Alington on humorous poetry.[87] And then there were the entertainments and plays.

One distinguishing mark of the Hopewell era is the great expansion of theatricals. The Shakespeare Society continued until the last meeting in the Number 1 garden in late July

85. *TH*, NS CLXXXIII (Oct. 1951), p.54. See *ibid.*, NS CLXIX (Jan. 1947), pp.25-31 for the beginnings of this scheme; subsequent editions for its progress; and Kynaston (2010), p.185, for the general pursuit of hobbies in this period.

86. No full transcript of this broadcast exists, although an outline survives at the BBC Written Archives, Caversham, which shows that Poulter selected Elgar's *Dream of Gerontius* and Jones Bing Crosby's *If I Had My Way* as their chosen pieces. Herefordshire had been featured 'on the air' a dozen or so times since 1936. See *HT*, 22 Jan. 1949, pp.4, 5, for this and details of the 1949 broadcast.

87. Davey, who was rector of Great Witley, gave a series of talks during the autumn term 1947. He dealt mainly 'with the spiritual aspect of sexual relations and personal respect'. I am grateful to Alan Gooch for this recollection. Dean Alington's lecture of 21 July 1953 captured the imagination of at least one pupil, who even today is able to cite quantities of the Dean's verse.

1951 but despite the support of the Headmaster, the Archdeacon and Stephen Bell, it was never quite the same after Dean Waterfield's swan-song (as Shylock) on 16 November 1946. By this time performances were superseding play readings. Summer term boarding House entertainments of the late 1940s had given way by 1955-56 to a House acting competition. At this time, too, there were experiments in broadcast drama with the King's supper sequence in *The Man Born to be King* and *Judas Iscariot* being recorded and played before an audience in the Lady Chapel in 1954-55. But it was the December production of a full-length school play that was the annual dramatic highlight.[88] There were difficulties however. The small College Hall stage comprised three-sided 'flats' with only three entrances and little indoor room back-stage; there was the obvious problem of boys playing female parts, one reviewer of *Busman's Holiday* (1948) suggesting that an experienced actress should be engaged to show these boys how to walk, sit and hold their hands; there was always the danger of power failure; and the production budget was limited to £10. The biggest issue concerned the choice of plays. Pinero's *Dandy Dick* (1951) and Du Maurier's *Rebecca* (1952) were among those 'of a repertory type' which some considered unsuitable for a school production in that they did not stand as good plays irrespective of performance. This could not be said of Gogol's *The Government Inspector* and Marlowe's *Dr Faustus* presented (with A.E. Rowe and N.J. Pocknell in the lead roles) to considerable acclaim in 1955 and 1956. The society had come a long way in little more than a decade.

Musical performance was less prevalent. There was little serious singing of secular music, the one known entry of the school choir in the Herefordshire music festival being in 1947, when it was given a harsh report, the adjudicator being under the mistaken impression that it was the cathedral choir. The chapel choir, consisting of masters and boys, made progress, however, in hymn singing and psalmody. And the pupils sang heartily in services, sometimes too much so as on one St David's day when there was a too vigorous rendering of Cwm Rhondda. The hymn was banned the following year.[89] The playing of instruments was more limited. A corps marching band (drummers and buglers) was started in 1949 and by the following year was sufficiently established to impress at the annual inspection, but this said more about the CCF than school music. Similarly, the ringing of hand bells at the annual carol service from 1950 was more an eloquent testament to the proficiency of members of the Society of Change Ringers – that unique school campanological society, which in this period became affiliated to the Hereford diocesan guild and was the subject of an article in *Ringing World*[90] – than an indication of the strength of instrumental music. The inspectors' suggestion that the 40 pupils then taking piano and violin lessons should all be taught on the premises, thereby integrating their work in to the general life of the school, was not implemented. And it was to be another generation or two before a school orchestra was formed.

88. The producers of these and other plays from 1945 were John Basil, who as chairman of the Herefordshire playgoers' circle had a significant role in promoting the local repertory company (which in 1947 included Arthur Rowe) at the County Theatre; R.D. Lancaster, P.G.S. Baylis and J.A.M. Baldwin. I am indebted to John Ward for his observations about the College Hall staging.

89. I am grateful to Lionel Meredith for this information.

90. On 10 August 1951. The society continued to ring at the cathedral and All Saints through most of this period, with regular summer expeditions (1945-51) to ring at outlying towers within the Hereford and Gloucester dioceses.

Musical appreciation was a different matter. There were occasional recitals at the school but better opportunities to hear a Gilbert and Sullivan opera or concert in the town, although few boys were present at the choral society's performance of Edward German's *Merrie England* at the Shirehall on 10 November 1949 which marked the end of Sir Percy Hull's 60-year connection with the cathedral and school. However, the Recorded Music Society, founded in May 1945 by the then chaplain (J.L. Lawson), flourished in the late 1940s. As well as meeting on Friday afternoons in the hut, it also met for a time on Sunday evenings in the Gilbert Library, a more suitable venue apart from the time that the doorhandle broke and the imprisoned listeners had to make their escape by ladder to school yard. Still, the society gave Sixth-formers a broader appreciation of classical music and opera – 'nearly all the members are suffering from chronic romanticism aggravated by severe Italian-operitis' reported 'Tiger' one term[91] – until it came to an end with the abolition of compulsory 'occupations'. It was revived nearly six years later in a less elitist form, the membership of the new Gramophone Society being spread across the school, the records of 'a certain guitar player' being a frequent choice at meetings.

By this time, as we have seen, a new intellectualism was abroad, at least in the Sixth Form. In 1954-55, the Debating Society, having gone through one of its periodic fits of quiescence, was on the rise. The society's mock election of May 1955 again returned a Tory candidate, although the Welsh nationalist garnered 27 votes and the Communist the lowest poll with the finest speech.[92] The society's own elections later that year saw almost a clean-sweep among the office-holders. A 'brains trust' panel was instituted as a new feature of the society's activities that year. Change was also afoot at *The Herefordian*. The May 1956 edition saw the first post-war boy editorial, a plea for literary contribution of general interest 'provided that the laws of libel, blasphemy and obscenity are observed'.[93] As in the past there was a disappointing response. But the boldest initiative of the mid-Fifties was the formation by the boys themselves of a Sixth Form society named after the school's greatest benefactor. The Somerset Society did not last long but gave that generation of Sixth-formers a taste of university life and a greater awareness of the workings of the professions. That it also met outside school at the Residence, a hotel – albeit one of temperance – in Broad Street, was no doubt an added bonus.[94]

Cultural activities, however lively, could not yet compete with sport, which Hopewell as a games enthusiast encouraged. New competitive sports were added to the list. Boxing, which had started in the autumn term of 1944, flourished briefly in the late 1940s. Successful tournaments were arranged against King's and then RGS Worcester in 1946-47; the Headmaster helped pay for a portable boxing ring for use in Big School; and the annual sequence of matches against Monmouth began in 1948, Hereford generally being

91. *TH*, NS CLXXIV (Sept. 1948), p.33.

92. These three candidates were (respectively): J.P. Ward, D.B. Roberts and J.C. Gittins.

93. The senior editor was A.E. Rowe, who (after Hopewell's collapse in health) led the editorial team for the following two editions.

94. In that first year (1955-56), T.S. Eliot and Kingsley Martin ('I am not very good at being an old boy') declined the opportunity to give talks but Frank Owen, one time editor of the *Daily Mail*, accepted as did local luminaries. The Residence Hotel, situated on the corner of Broad Street and long since demolished, was sold by the Dean and Chapter for £6,200 in December 1951 (HCA, 7031/25, p.96) and managed by an HCS parent at this time.

Fig. 8.4 Boys celebrate with tea (and the occasional pipe) at a Somerset Society meeting at the Residence Hotel, c.*1956.*

out-classed by their opponents, apart from three years (1952-53, 1955) when Monmouthian measles or mumps were the victors. Lawn tennis, which Crees had dismissed as 'pat ball', was again played on the back lawn of Number 1, which became the venue for school matches in 1949 and 1950. An unofficial day-boy soccer team, the Cathedral Rangers, also made its appearance, but without the Headmaster's knowledge or blessing. Their reward for winning the St Dunstan's cup final in 1948, before a large Edgar Street crowd, was one hour a week's compulsory rolling of the cricket square at Wyeside for the whole team.[95] The punishment seemed to fit the crime of playing the wrong kind of football and thereby contravening the winter games code.

Not that this was a vintage era for the winter sports. Fives were popular enough but only two inter-school matches were won throughout the period, lack of equipment, the poor maintenance of the courts and bad weather often militating against proper practice and good play. Neither did the continued holding of sports day in late March make for good competition, the athletics being cancelled three times in this period: in 1946, when the pavilion was flooded to a depth of three feet and the hut was swept away; in 1947, when Wyeside was unusable for the whole term; and in 1955. In other years, conditions

95. Typically, Hopewell congratulated the boys before imposing the punishment. I am grateful to John Chadd and George Warley for these details.

were rarely ideal for either training or record breaking. Although junior records were occasionally set, eight of the nine pre-1918 records which were unbroken in 1948 still stood in 1957.[96] Rugby was stronger, although over the period as a whole the 1st XV won little more than one third of its matches, the late 1940s sides being particularly weak. Results improved in the early 1950s, Christ College being beaten for the first time on the Brecon ground in 1951 and the XV winning more matches than they lost in each of the three seasons 1951-53 and again in 1956.[97] And sometimes good reasons could be put forward for disappointing performances, notably in the matches following the team's three weeks in quarantine (E.M. Geddes, a member of the team had contracted polio) in November 1947, and the week in early December 1954 when an influenza epidemic closed the school and put paid to any hope of victory in the last match against the Old Herefordians. More often, it was injuries to key players that were the cause of poor results. Nevertheless by 1956-57, four school teams had been well established, and with the Junior Colts winning all seven of their games that season and R.C. Gristy being selected for the English schoolboys' junior XV, the future for the school's rugby looked brighter than it had done in 1945.

If the late 1940s were winters of discontent for fives, athletics and rugby football, they were glorious summers of promise and fulfilment for rowing and cricket. In 1946, the school crews, much perhaps to their coach's surprise, swept all before them, the first crew tying with Haileybury in the final of the coxed fours at Marlow. At the season's end, Harry Wardle stepped down 'to rest on his oars and his laurels' after 26 years of unparalleled success as rowing coach.[98] 1947 was again a successful season; 1948, the school's first year of using slides, less so. The outstanding triumph of these years, however, was the victory of the first four at Marlow in 1949 in Harold Lush's first year as coach and with the early help of Harry Wardle's son 'which laid the foundation of their long swinging style'. It was the fourth and last time that the school was to hold this challenge cup.[99] In cricket, too, the appointment of a new master in charge (R.D. Lancaster) was to bear immediate fruit in the shape the victorious 1948 season: played 14, won 14, the first time that the XI had won all their matches and a feat never yet equalled. The expertise of the groundsman, Joe Woodward, then in his early sixties and nearly ten years before his eventual retirement; the enthusiasm – and perhaps over-indulgence as an umpire – of the young cricket master; and the encouragement of the Headmaster are among the ingredients for their success. But the

---

96. However, B.T. Thom's achievement of wining the senior *victor ludorum* trophy in three successive years (1949-51) should be recorded. Although eight boys had won the trophy twice since J. Carless presented the cup in 1887, this was the first time that this particular feat had been achieved. Thom kept the cup and presented a new one to the school the following year.

97. Notable rugby players of the period included J.T. Harries (captain 1951), who later played outside-half for Wasps; L.P. Evans (captain 1952 and 1953), who although he missed out on a 'Blue' played games for Oxford University; and R.M. Milne (vice-captain 1953), who captained Edinburgh University. I am grateful to John Powell Ward for these details.

98. Since 1920, the school had rowed over 100 races, of which fewer than 20 had been lost. For Wardle's record and his explanation of the school's success during these years, see his 'Rowing Retrospect': *TH*, NS CLXX (April 1947), pp.11-15. M.R. Jones, D.F. James, J.B. Jacob, R.S.J.N. Barton, with W.B. Turner as cox, comprised the 1946 first crew. T.D. Briden took over from Wardle and was the coach in 1947-48.

99. The event and the season are described in *TH*, NS CLXXVII (Oct. 1949), pp.10-15. For D.B.J. Wardle and the previous victories (1883, 1929 and 1946), see above, pp.264, 409-10, 466.

Fig. 8.5 The third HCS crew to win outright the coxed four public schools' challenge cup, 1949: B.T. Thom (bow); C.T. Brooke (2); M.P. Moreton (3); J.S.Vaughan (stroke); H.J.R. Hammonds (cox). The photograph appeared at the front of the school prospectus for more than a decade.

Fig. 8.6 The 1948 1st XI, captained by Peter Richardson, coached by R.D. Lancaster: played 14, won 14.

main reason was the talent of the boys themselves, especially that displayed by the opening bowlers and by the captain P.E. Richardson, who again averaged over 50 for the season.[100] His Headmaster and school coach both lived long enough to congratulate (by letter-gram) their former pupil and protégé after he had scored a century for England against Australia in 'the Laker Test' at Old Trafford in July 1956.[101]

Neither rowing nor cricket again reached the heights achieved in the late Forties but there were developments and successes in both sports in the following decade. The record of the first crews was distinctly meagre in the Fifties but the net of competitive rowing was spread wider. More boys opted for the sport; third and fourth crews were formed as well as an occasional eight; other regattas, apart from Hereford and Marlow, were entered; new fixtures were arranged and new races, such as the monitors' pairs and the coxswain's sculls, devised. In 1956, there was even a race against a masters' four, a powerful school crew striking 25 to the minute against their opponents 30, plus five air shots, or so it was reported. In cricket, the 1st XI had five good seasons in succession, 1950-54, each team winning more matches than they lost, with the 1953 XI losing only twice (in 13 games) and the 1954 side (that 'could give and take two hundred') remaining undefeated against school sides.[102]

The Ministry's 1952 inspection of the Combined Cadet Corps (rather than the Junior Training Corps, the name having been changed in 1948) was cursory at best, but it was right to have described it as 'flourishing'. Indeed, under the successive commands of Gray (1945-49), Daniels (1949-52) and Lush (from April 1952), it flourished throughout the period. The training could be arduous and the organisation was not every boy's idea of happiness. This observation in the summer of 1947 from the Recorded Music Society's secretary – that would-be members had been 'reluctantly lured from the soothing strains of Mozart or Delius to face the raucous orders of a drill-sergeant' (following the use of Friday afternoons for extra parades after the hard winter) – was one of the few voices of dissent in contemporary records.[103] Nevertheless, despite the 10s termly fee and other costs, many boys volunteered. Indeed, with an average strength of around 100 in the late Forties and early Fifties, the corps had grown to a record 132 cadets (including four officers) by early 1954. It is clear then that in this period, and in marked contrast to the early 1930s, the CCF was an attractive option, even though, proportionately, boarders by far outnumbered day cadets - at least until 1955, when the Old Deanery was taken over by the chaplain, who may have been less enthusiastic about encouraging his boys to join the corps.

100. The averages of the opening bowlers, C.L. Davies and G.T. Warley (respectively, 40 wickets at 5.25 and 51 at 5.41), although bettered by L.R. Browne in 1888, have never been surpassed in the modern period. Peter Richardson's batting figures in the 1947 and 1948 seasons (565 runs at 56.5 and 602 at 50.17), together with his total aggregate of over 1600 runs for the 1st XI (1945-48), were superior to any other HCS boy up to this time. They have since been bettered by Edward Symonds, Stephen Price and Ben Stebbings.

101. Peter Richardson scored 104, while Laker took a record 19 wickets (for 90 runs) in this famous test match. Peter played 34 times for England, appearing in one Test (against the West Indies in 1957 at Trent Bridge) with his Old Herefordian brother, D.W. Richardson.

102. Over these years, the cricketing achievements of two boys, J.E. Chadd and G.V. Miller, should be recorded. Chadd took more than 100 wickets for the 1st XI over three years (1949-51), and G.V. Miller scored 446 runs at 49.54 in the 1954 season.

103. *TH*, NS CLXXI (Sept. 1947), p.44. Over 40 years later, during the present author's headship, Peter Williams, the writer of this piece, became a governor of his old school.

There are, no doubt, as many reasons to explain why a boy opted into the CCF – or in the case of a reluctant boarder was volunteered into its ranks – as there were cadets but a few general observations about its popularity in this period may be given. In the immediate post-war period, especially, there was still a strong sense that joining the corps was a duty to those who had gone before. The HCS corps was an efficiently led unit which offered a variety of courses and activities, including (by 1956) the band, marksmanship and signalling (an automatic telephone exchange, George Mark II, had been established in the CCF office). During a period of overwhelming public support for the monarchy, the corps gave further opportunities for boys to represent the school (and in a battle-dress uniform), as they did at King George VI's memorial service in February 1952, the Coronation of the following year and the Queen's visit to Hereford in April 1957. And, most significant of all, at a time when almost every 18-year-old boy was required to join one of the armed services – a peace-time conscription unique in modern British history – experience in a school cadet corps stood him in good stead when it came to National Service.[104]

As a distinguished old soldier, who had been seriously wounded at Suvla Bay in 1915, the corps in any case received the Headmaster's full support. But, as has been shown, he also widened opportunities and encouraged participation in many other pursuits, and not least through his active involvement in the Printing Club which he founded; *The Herefordian*, which he edited almost throughout his tenure; and despite his collapsed lung, his playing cricket against the boys in his own XI (with the captain of school as his runner when he was batting) until his late fifties. Although the number of societies reduced from the 15 or more available in the days of compulsory 'occupations', at least 10 were still active in early 1957. Many of these were of a craft or cultural kind, which did something to counteract the dominance of the outdoor regime. Jack Hopewell did much to promote a more rounded educational experience for most of his troops, even if this education was only half observed – and less than fully reported on – by the six men (and two ladies) from the Ministry.

'Our Much Beloved Headmaster'

Jack Hopewell's funeral on Wednesday 23 January 1957 was a family affair. Two days later the cathedral was packed for his memorial service. And among the mourning cards attached to one of the many beautiful wreaths was this heart-felt message: 'To our much beloved Headmaster from all his monitors: A trusty friend and constant guide to every one of his troops'.

Hopewell was not only the first Old Herefordian since Charles Taylor in 1826 to have become Headmaster of his *alma mater* but also the first HCS Headmaster in modern times to have died in office. He had not been in good health for some time – indeed given the loss of his lung, he must have been in discomfort for much of his life – but like the officer and gentleman he was, he carried on his duties until mid-October 1956 when he was taken to Hereford General Hospital 'for respiratory aid'.[105] His condition was sufficiently serious

104. Senior cadets with sufficient training experience, for example, could choose which service they wished to join. National Service was instituted in 1947 and extended from 18 months to two years in 1950. Some 2.3 million men all told were called up between 1945 and 1960.

105. Around 15 October, Hopewell developed a heavy bronchial cold which caused him breathing difficulties. He

that it prompted Mrs Hopewell, on her husband's behalf, to tender a letter of resignation to the governors to take effect from the end of the following term. This was accepted at their meeting on 8 November 'only because … it was inevitable and in his own interest', the governors simultaneously recording in their minutes 'their sincere appreciation of the long and invaluable service rendered to the school by Mr Hopewell'.[106] From this evidence, it is apparent that although there was no hope of him resuming his career, there was still an expectation that he would make a partial recovery. Indeed, when a number of senior boys visited him in hospital later that term, he was found reading the latest issue of *The Herefordian* and was strong enough to chat about the school. After Christmas, the move to a nursing home also suggests that his strength was returning. There was a relapse, however, and on 17 January he returned to hospital. He died there, in his 65th year, in the early hours of Monday 21 January 1957. The school reconvened the following day to hear the sad news, the Dean speaking 'in very touching terms' about their great loss at the opening chapel service.[107]

Tributes came flooding in to his widow. The Old Herefordians at their reunion of 15 December – a dinner disrupted by petrol rationing following the Suez crisis – had already given their president a toast 'with musical honours'. In proposing a toast to the school, Maurice Edge, the Director of Education for Herefordshire, had also publicly saluted the Headmaster's fortitude and acknowledged 'the modesty of a man who had no need to be modest'.[108] Now private condolences were paid by Church dignitaries, his Cambridge college, his colleagues and the domestic staff, and by his school contemporaries and other Old Herefordians throughout the world. Jack's untiring work for the school, his example as a man and schoolmaster and his great gift for friendship were recurrent themes in these private letters as well as in official obituaries. This published eulogy by Stephen Bell, his devoted Second Master, stands for many:

> I have never known a kinder and more understanding Headmaster than Jack Hopewell. Always courteous, always scrupulously fair and upright, always sympathetic with the problems and worries of boys or masters, he was the wisest of counsellors and the staunchest of friends … As a schoolmaster he had great gifts as an administrator, with a meticulous attention to detail and a real love for boys and particularly of his old school. But above all, he set the example of a 'verray parfit gentil knight', a man of the utmost humility and courtesy, in fact the living example of the fifteenth psalm that he loved to quote.[109]

---

was admitted to hospital on the 19th. The following day, Stephen Bell as Second Master, informed the school that their Headmaster was seriously (although not dangerously) ill. HCSA, GMB 1945-82, between pp.105-06, Bell's report for 8 Nov. 1956 meeting.

106. *Ibid*; Brittain MSS, T.O.D. Steel to Mrs Hopewell, 12 Nov.; and HCSA, GMB 1945-82, between pp.105-06, for her reply, 17 Nov. 1956.

107. For his last months, see *Ibid.*, between pp.109-10, Bell's report 1 March 1957; *TH*, NS CLXXXXVI (*sic*) (May 1957), pp.2-3, 9.

108. *Ibid.*, p.52. One of the diners was R.S.F. Edwards OH, the then director of sea transport and civil aviation, who 'welcomed the guests with an urbanity quite unruffled by his experience as a modern Duke of York – having marched all his men out to Suez, he was now about to march them all back again'.

109. *HDM* (April 1957), p.12.

The school owes an immense debt to this 'kind and devoted commander'.[110] For in the 11 active years of his headship, he guided HCS through significant changes which helped secure its future. By 1956, despite deficiencies which his successor well identified, the school was more efficiently managed; its buildings had expanded; its pupils, both boarding and day, had increased; its staffing had been strengthened; its curriculum had been developed and its extra-curricular programme widened. These were, of course, important changes. Equally telling, but less easily identifiable, was the improved spirit that Hopewell engendered. Unlike Dr Crees, this was not achieved by dynamic performance, by rallying his troops on speech day or by stirring their hearts in chapel. In fact during this era, there were no public speech days as we now know them and only one known instance of the Headmaster having preached in a Sunday service. No, 'Hoppy' – as his former pupils remember – fostered a new spirit through his respectful dealings with masters and boys alike and his constant encouragement of them. Consequently, HCS became less oppressive and a more open and kindly place.[111] And inspired by the Headmaster's optimism and example, it also grew in confidence and success.

In the absence of a diagnosis, the conclusion must be that years of strain and over-work at the Cathedral School contributed significantly to Jack Hopewell's premature death. At the end of the memorial service on 25 January, it was fitting that Dean Burrows, chairman of governors and the Headmaster's close associate for much of his tenure, recited this bidding prayer:

> Let us today remember and always keep in remembrance Alan Francis John Hopewell. Let us thank God for his loyalty to King and Country and for his war service at Gallipoli given at cost to himself; for his years of teaching and administration and especially for 12 years as Headmaster of this Cathedral School; for his sense of duty and concentrated industry. Let us praise God for his devotion to the members of this school, past and present, the school in which he was once a boy; for his love and service to the church and to this cathedral ... Finally, let us give thanks for what he was in himself – modest, humble and loving – our brother, and the disciple of his master and ours, the Lord Jesus Christ.[112]

It was fitting, too, that the Dean and his Chapter allowed the ashes to be interred in the Lady Arbour, under a simple headstone and not far from the school that Jack had loved and so loyally served.[113]

James Ross Peebles, 1957-1967

Any death within a small community inevitably has an unsettling effect on its life. When the death was that of a well-loved Headmaster, still technically in office, the shock felt

110. The quoted words are probably those of Alick Rowe, as printed in *The Herefordian* editorial of May 1957.

111. This is not to say that Hopewell was a push-over; nor did he refrain from corporal punishment. However, he always shook hands with a boy after 'tonking' him. Unlike some of his predecessors, he did not rule by fear.

112. *HT*, 1 Feb. 1957, p.5.

113. HCA, 7031/25, p.186, 30 Jan. 1957. His ashes were buried in the Lady Arbour on 18 March 1957; those of Barbara, his wife, being interred there in 1980.

by its members must have been even more chastening. It fell to Stephen Bell, Second Master since January 1954, Hopewell family friend and next door neighbour (in Number 2 Castle Street), to guide the school through nearly six months of uncertainty from mid-October 1956 to the end of the following term. There was a never a more reluctant acting Headmaster. Having been given a unanimous endorsement by his colleagues at an extraordinary staff meeting on 22 October, he expressed these concerns to the governors a few days later:

Fig. 8.7 Stephen Bell: a reluctant acting Headmaster but an extraordinary teacher of Classics.

> I am endeavouring [to carry on] ... but I do find the job difficult, and I have had to give up a good deal of my teaching which I love and in which I think I have done the school some service ... My talents do not lie in administration and I hope that the emergency will not last longer than is absolutely necessary'.[114]

Nevertheless, Bell was an experienced and respected schoolmaster who had the background if not the appearance or temperament for the task. Although not quite the senior member of the Common Room in terms of length of service, he was among Hopewell's first appointments and was both well acquainted with the school's routine and hugely supportive of all its activities. He was also respected by both his colleagues and the boys. For as was observed in his retirement notice a few years later, 'beneath the stern classical teacher, there was a very human being – the real schoolmaster who cared deeply for his pupils'.[115] Moreover, at this time of crisis the school rallied round, as Bell made abundantly clear in this letter of condolence to Hopewell's widow:

> I have been very greatly helped in my task of carrying on Jack's work by the loyalty of the staff ... Alick Rowe and the monitors also have been of the greatest help. This loyalty has been and still is beyond all praise.[116]

And so during the interregnum the school went determinedly about its business. Indeed, judging by the events described in *The Herefordian*, there hardly appears to have been an

114. HCSA, GMB 1945-82, between pp.105-06, report for 8 Nov. 1956 meeting.

115. *TH*, CCII (Oct. 1961), p.3.

116. Brittain MSS, Bell to Barbara Hopewell, 2 Feb. 1957. Alick Rowe was 'captain of the school' for four terms from the autumn of 1956. He was to return to HCS as an English teacher in 1963.

interruption to its daily round. Thirty-one boys were confirmed (on 29 November 1956); a gaggle of boys took Ordinary-level examinations that December and many passed; the school play (*The Tragical History of Dr Faustus*) was considered 'the most ambitious and the most splendidly successful production we have had from the dramatic society for many years'; and the 1st XV beat the Old Herefordians by 11 points to 6 in a 'mud bath' on 15 December. The following Spring Term brought other news: the cadets had undergone 'freezing parades' that January; 'an army of un-cooperative fags' had helped repair the fives courts; some geographers had set up a weather station on the Old Deanery front lawn; 84 hopefuls had sat the junior scholarship and entrance examination on 2 March; and the annual sports day had taken place on a miserable afternoon later that month. And there was an unusual crop of mid-year retirements, the last link with the Crees era being broken with the departure at the age of 72 of Joe Woodward, school groundsman and 'presiding genius of the pavilion', after 29 seasons; and one of the two ties with the Scott years being severed with Arden-Davis' resignation on grounds of ill-health after nearly 14 years.[117]

Public recognition was given in *The Herefordian* for May 1957 'to all those who have done so much to further the smooth running of the school in a time of stress'. How stressful these traumatic weeks were for a man nearing the end of his career and who never wanted the burden can only be a matter of conjecture, but this passage from Bell's letter to Barbara Hopewell already cited, whilst revealing something of his anguish tells us more about his sacrificial service to the Cathedral School:

> One thing that this emergency has brought me to realise is the great love I have for the school. As long as I am spared to work in the school's service, I shall do so with the utmost devotion. True, a younger man must cope with the major problems; when one is approaching sixty they get harder to bear. But I trust God will grant me several more years to support the new Head with all my loyalty.

He was to enjoy four more years of active service before ill health forced the early retirement of an extraordinary schoolmaster.[118]

The governors moved swiftly to secure the permanent succession, but this time – unlike 1945 – the post was advertised. Following their meeting on 8 November, when Dean Burrows read out Mrs Hopewell's letter tendering her husband's resignation, notices were placed in the *Times Educational Supplement* and other journals advertising the vacancy. There was an immediate response: 74 applications were posted to Tom Steel, the governors' clerk, between 21 November and 6 December 1956. The list was an impressive one and included 12 existing Headmasters, nine reverend gentlemen, two Old Herefordians (T.A.

117. For other staffing difficulties during the interregnum, see Bell's report to the governors of 1 March 1957: HCSA, GMB 1945-82, between pp.109-10.

118. Bell, having been replaced as Second Master by P.G.S. Baylis in September 1960, retired at the end of that academic year, although ill health forced him to give up teaching early in the Summer Term of 1961. He died 'peacefully and suddenly' two years later, his funeral taking place at All Saints on Saturday 18 May 1963. The school was closed at 10.30 that morning so that many boys, as well as former colleagues and governors, could attend the service, 'a moving tribute to the affection in which Mr Bell was held'. *TH*, CCV (May 1963), p.3. For Bell's idiosyncratic teaching methods, see above, p.458.

Jones and M. Ricketts) and one internal candidate (J.L.T. Brookes). Five men were selected for interview on 10 January 1957, when James Ross Peebles, Housemaster and Head of English and History at Westminster School, was appointed Headmaster, at the age of 47, on 10 January 1957 at an annual salary of some £2,000.[119]

As the application of the 49th candidate on the Clerk's alphabetical list, that of Peebles himself, is missing from the school archives – all the others survive – there is no way of knowing the details of his submission for the post. We have a fair idea, however, of what his Headmaster might have written about him from this posthumous notice in the Westminster School magazine:

> He was educated at Glasgow Academy and at University College, Oxford, and he brought with him a reputation as a cricketer … and a Scottish pertinacity which stood the school in good stead in later more difficult days. From 1932 to 1939 he was a member of the light-hearted band of bachelor masters … coaching cricket and football and rowing, and teaching devotedly at the leisurely pace which was all that was required in those days when most Oxbridge colleges were glad to take any boy who had not actually failed his O-levels. In the war Peebles went with the school to Hurstpierpoint, to Exeter and finally to Bromyard. Here he began to prove himself. Entrusted with the care of 60 day boys who had overnight become boarders, and confronted with the usual difficulties of evacuation, including at first a lunatic landlord who thought his stables too good for boys' sleeping quarters, he yet managed to make a success of his assignment. He served in the Intelligence Corps from 1941 to 1946 when he returned to Westminster, and in 1948 he took over the housemastership of Rigaud's. It was there that his principal work for the school was done. He always had time for any boy wanting to discuss his present problems and future prospects. He would defend any member of his house doggedly against the slightest indictment from any outside quarter. He would do anything for his House, except get his House accounts in on time … Two generations of boys … [have] good reason to be grateful to him.

From such an account of Peebles' career, perhaps three things would have most impressed his prospective employers: his war-time Herefordshire connection; his war record (he had held a major's commission, attached for service to the War Office); and, as the Dean later observed, his thorough understanding of 'both the day and boarding aspects of an old public school'.[120] In addition, his wife's experience of presiding over the domestic side of one of Westminster's 'catering houses' would have been valued, particularly as the governors evidently preferred that the new Headmaster, supported by his wife (all five short-listed candidates were married), should also continue as Housemaster of School House. This enabled the governors to offer an acceptable salary, as well as maintain the existing domestic arrangements.

---

119. The other short-listed candidates were J.D. Eastwood, Headmaster of Ludlow School; B.M.S. Hoban, assistant master at Shrewsbury School (and later Head of St Edmund's, Canterbury, Bradfield and Harrow); J.D. Neil, Headmaster of Queen Elizabeth Grammar School, Wimborne Minster; and J.H. Woodroffe, senior Biology master at Shrewsbury. Peebles was paid £2,043 8s 9d in 1957-58, including his Housemaster's allowance.

120. WSA, *The Elizabethan*, XXX no. 1 (March 1968), p.143; *HCN*, no. 37 (Spring 1957), p.6.

Fig. 8.8 James Peebles, the Headmaster whose reforms moved HCS forward into the second half of the twentieth century.

What kind of man had the governors engaged? Clues as to Peebles' character and interests have already been given: his native 'pertinacity'; his love of games; his resourcefulness; his dedicated teaching; his dogged defence of his boys; and his waywardness as an accountant. These traits can all be illustrated from surviving letters at Westminster, perhaps none more so than the one written to him by his Headmaster, after Peebles had quarrelled with the bursar:

> Fundamentally no doubt there's an incompatibility. He has a bit of the Army high-handedness as it seems to you. And you appear to him, as you did to his two forerunners, as a man of pitiless tenacity and rather late in getting your bills and so on into his office.

But there were other qualities. Although a games enthusiast, he was a cultivated man, who in his undergraduate days had been the first secretary of his college musical society at a time when University College had a reputation for heartiness.[121] These cultural interests stayed with him throughout his life. And while he was conservative both in taste and politics, he could be progressive in educational matters as we will see. Above all, as a son of the manse – his father was Minister of Birnie, near Elgin – Peebles was a man of strong faith and a gifted lay preacher, who was to preach regularly in school services, as well as occasionally in churches within the wider Hereford diocese. As he declared on Education Sunday in Holy Trinity, Hereford, in October 1964: 'Our aim must surely be to help young people to grow up, to develop their own resources to the full and to prepare them to live a full and useful life founded on the rock of Christian principles.'[122]

Educational and Social Change, 1957-1967

James Peebles' tenure coincided with a time of uncertainty for all selective secondary school Heads, not least – given Labour's hostile attitude towards both private schooling and the 11 plus – for those like him who presided over direct grant schools. Direct grants, funded by the government directly to the school, were vulnerable, and although the Conservatives were in power for over seven years of Peebles' headship, the election of a Labour government in 1964 heralded a particularly anxious time for him and his colleagues. As for the free places bought for good reason by LEAs at direct grant schools, attitudes depended on the political complexion of the local authorities and their continuance was not guaranteed. The political outlook was uncertain but the stirrings of the teenage young were a more immediate problem for secondary Heads. This applied quite as much to independent school Headmasters as those in charge of grammars and secondary moderns. In an age of relativism in morals and scepticism in religion, when (as one Headmaster despairingly wrote) all that was left was what de Tocqueville had called 'a kind of virtuous materialism',

121. WSA, Peebles' file, Christie to Peebles, 25 March 1949 (for the quotation); and Darwall-Smith, p.460 for the foundation of the musical society at University College, and 456ff ('The Pub on the High') for the atmosphere of the college between the wars.

122. Steele MSS, sermon 25 Oct. 1964, one of over 20 of his sermons extant in the family's archive. I am grateful to Jillie Steele for the use of family documents in her possession.

the old public school values seemed to be disappearing.[123] How far direct grant schools were affected by these winds of political and social change provides the context for the Cathedral School's remarkable period of growth during the Peebles decade.

The expansion of the school's pupil roll over these years is indeed significant. From a base of 299 boys in the summer term of 1957, numbers had increased to 375 by November 1964 and remained not far short of that figure for the remainder of Peebles' tenure. This advance is wholly accounted for by the increase in day numbers, the boy boarding community remaining stable at around 125. What is most remarkable about this increase is the doubling in size of the Sixth Form, from 54 in October 1957 to over 100 from early 1964 onwards, getting on for one-third of the whole school. This expansion in day numbers can partly be explained by local demographic factors: Hereford's population increased by more than 10,000 to an estimated 45,870 in June 1966.[124] Correspondingly, there was an unprecedented expansion in the provision of secondary education within the city. Secondary modern schools at Tupsley, Redhill and Grafton, together with the new Girls' High School at Broadlands, were all opened within this period (at a combined cost of over £500,000) to try to accommodate the children of the post-war baby boom in a growing city.

HCS's growth was not untypical of the independent sector as a whole and direct grant schools in particular. In October 1961, the chairman of HMC could report that independent education was 'flourishing as it has probably never flourished before'; a year later, it was reckoned that the bigger public schools all had five-year waiting-lists at the very least.[125] Direct grant schools did not operate in this way but most were bulging at the seams by the early 1960s, and four out of five of their pupils were now staying on into the Sixth Form.[126] As James Peebles was to experience, managing an expanding school was not without difficulty for any Headmaster, but it was far preferable to leading a school through a period of falling rolls.

That direct grant schools were in demand is shown by Hereford's experience in this period when scores of local boys attempted each year to qualify for one of the ten free county places or other day places. By the 1960s there were some 60 county place holders at HCS, which together with the 30 or so boys who also gained free places because their parents annual income was £450 or less, constituted one in four of the school's population. In addition, there were an increasing number of day boys (around 90 by 1966) whose fees were scaled down according to their parents' means. By the mid-1960s, if the choristers are included, the education of more than half the boys in the school was subsidised to a greater or lesser extent. For those parents able to pay, the fees were competitive, and although the

123. Dancy, p.70.

124. *HT*, 13 Jan. 1967, p.1, citing the Registrar-General's estimate. It compared with an estimate of 33,200 in 1958 (*ibid.*, 23 Nov. 1960, p.1) and the 1961 census figure of 40,431.

125. *HMC 1961 Report*, p.10, C.P.C. Smith's speech at Durham, 2 Oct.; Dancy, p.146.

126. *HMC 1966 Committee Report*, p.39, minute of Direct Grant Committee, 6 May. The growth of other direct grant schools in this period may be gauged from individual school histories. For example: Luft, pp.255ff (the Headmaster of Merchant Taylors' School, Crosby, in this period was T.J.P. York, an Old Herefordian); Bentley, pp.113ff; Hinde and Parker, p.149.

annual tuition fee doubled over the period from £48 to £97 10s, it was still towards the lower end of charges made by similar HMC schools.[127]

Unsurprisingly, the direct grant schools – there were 180 of them in England and Wales in January 1968 – were stoutly defended by those with a vested interest in their continuance, not least by their Heads, around 60 of whom were members of the Headmasters' Conference. James Peebles himself on speech day in July 1964, with the general election only weeks away, described the direct grant system – notwithstanding the government's refusal to extend grants to boarders – as 'the ideal and most democratic' type of education. 'There can be few schools in the western world', he declared, 'where the sons of a Bishop, an MP and a vice-Chancellor can mix on terms of complete equality with the sons of a fitter, a cotton operative and an invalid widow on public assistance'. Cotton operatives, if not fitters or invalid widows, were in short supply in Herefordshire but the school registrations of the period shows that among the cohort of county free places each year were sons of parents of very modest means.[128]

The trouble was that the selective system of education, which gave rise to genuine social mobility, was vulnerable in the febrile atmosphere of educational politics in this period. And after maintained selective schools, the direct grant grammar schools (as they were officially termed) were in the front line of fire after the election of a Labour government, particularly following the issue of Circular 10/65 by the Department of Education and Science on 14 July 1965. This requested that each of the 163 local authorities then in existence should submit plans within one year for a comprehensive system of secondary education. At the same time direct grant schools were encouraged to negotiate locally with a view to participating in the move towards comprehensive status. The alarm bells sounded even more shrilly in the ears of direct grant heads following a speech in Harrogate by Anthony Crosland, the then Secretary of State, in early January 1966, during which he said that if the direct grant schools were unable to co-operate with their local authorities the future of the direct grant system would 'inevitably come into question'. The *Hereford Times* covered the speech and compared Crosland's remarks with Peebles' comments the previous July when he had presciently argued against both over-large comprehensives and 'hasty experiments in education'.[129]

The immediate future of direct grant schools, therefore, was dependent on the outcome of negotiations between the school and its local authority. The Cathedral School was more fortunate than many in that it had maintained a good relationship with Herefordshire County Council and particularly with its Director of Education, Maurice Edge, a pragmatist

127. The annual tuition fees of HMC direct grant schools ranged from around £60 to £85 in September 1959 and from around £80 to £130 in October 1966. *HMC 1959 Report*, p.80; *HMC 1966 Report*, p.56. HCS's tuition fees were £66 and £97 10s at these two dates. Between 1957 and 1967, its annual boarding fee (including tuition) increased from £165 to £262 10s.

128. Steele MSS, speech 10 July 1964. A sheet metal worker, a train guard, a school caretaker, a cellulose sprayer, a saddler, a maintenance fitter, crane and fork-lift drivers and a Baptist minister are among the parental occupations listed for the county free place boys, 1957-67. HCSA, Registration Book 1928-67, *passim*.

129. *HT*, 14 January 1966, p.20; Steele MSS, speech 9 July 1965. At speech day in 1966, Peebles hoped that the local authority would have second thoughts about a Sixth Form college, and the following year he spoke against the proposed raising of the school leaving age (to 16).

rather than an ideologue whose main concern was the improvement of education for all the county's children in whatever ways that might best be accomplished.[130] Under his guidance the education committee, which following the opening of Weobley and Wigmore schools had completed its plans to provide separate secondary schools for all children of the appropriate age, had anticipated Circular 10/65 by six months through its decision to launch an enquiry into the nature of secondary education within Herefordshire. From the outset it was established that there would be no attempt to curtail the allocation of places at HCS, Lucton and the Monmouth schools.[131] On the other hand, it was clear from the working party interim report of April 1966 and the final report to the Secretary of State a few weeks later that there was to be no place for the Cathedral School in the county plan. Indeed, it is doubtful whether the inclusion of HCS would have been welcomed by either side. Quite apart from the difficulty of housing an 11-16 non-selective school (as was eventually envisaged for all the Hereford city schools) on a limited site, for the governing body there was the impossibility of reconciling two incompatible viewpoints: belief in a comprehensive framework for secondary education, and a commitment to a selective system in conformity with the regulations for direct grant schools. The latter view could also be held to be in accord with the spirit of Circular 10/65 which emphasised the importance of 'preserving what is best in existing schools' and warned against the 'adoption of plans whose educational disadvantages more than off-set the benefits which will flow from the adoption of comprehensive schooling'.[132]

It was a satisfactory outcome for HCS, at least for the time being. The school had been the beneficiary of a shortage of grammar school places, caused by both Hereford's population explosion and its failure to build another grammar school on the Fayre Oaks site.[133] Indeed, even with the additional independent provision, around 65 city children selected for grammar school education had to be allocated places each year at rural grammar schools. And even after the government's approval (by March 1967) of the county's educational plan, one of the few schemes to be accepted in its entirety, Herefordshire's 'comprehensive crawl' (as the *Hereford Times* aptly named it[134]) ensured that the local authority would continue both to select at 11 plus and to allocate free places to HCS for a few more years. The direct grant, too, was to be retained, at least until after the public schools commission had reported, following the Secretary of State's belated decision in November 1967 to include the direct grant schools within its terms of reference. However, the government's refusal that autumn – for the first time – to match (or come near to matching) the

130. The situation was very different in other areas. In Bristol, for example, the local authority proposed to withdraw its places from the Bristol direct grant schools as early as 1964. *HMC 1964 Report*, p.109, minute of the direct grant schools' meeting, 30 Sept.

131. In addition to the ten each year at HCS, there were three at Monmouth School, two at Monmouth girls and up to eight at Lucton.

132. *HMC 1965 Committee Report*, p.71, Direct Grant Committee report, *c.*Sept. 1965.

133. A 500-place mixed grammar school in the Whitecross area was projected as early as 1959, and the school was included in the county's educational building programme from 1961/62. By the time the Fayre Oaks site was acquired, the planners had been overtaken by events, although Fayre Oaks was still a part (as a 600-place comprehensive) of the 1966 scheme for Hereford city secondary schools.

134. *HT*, 22 Sept. 1967, editorial, p.12.

Burnham pay award of the previous April through an increased grant, was a clear indication that the long-term future of direct grant schools was by no means assured.

During the course of one of the periodic bouts of soul-searching undertaken by the Headmasters' Conference in the early 1960s, the 1963 discussions on 'public schools and public service' and 'freedom, authority and the older boy' stand out as landmark debates.[135] Donald Lindsay, Headmaster of Malvern College, made this pronouncement as he introduced the latter topic: 'It is our fate to be Headmasters at a time of great perplexity and uncertainty'. He was referring not to the political threat, real though that was in October 1963, but to the peculiar problems that many secondary Heads were then experiencing from their senior pupils. Lindsay continued: '... at this difficult time, we are faced with problems to which there is no easy solution ... [the guidance] of a generation who (in the words of the Crowther report) have substituted "the public opinion of their peers for the wisdom of the ages."'[136] It was hyperbole, of course. Youth had always been inclined to rebel against authority and indulge in illicit pleasures. But there was substance to the contention that traditional morality was breaking down by the early 1960s and that teenagers were taking a lead from the youth of their own generation rather than their elders and supposed betters. Many Headmasters – and other authority figures – educated in the more ordered and hierarchical world between the wars, were genuinely bemused. As another of them observed at that autumn's conference: 'We have some excuse for bewilderment when we survey a landscape in which many of the traditional signposts have been up-rooted and the general vista reveals what to many looks like a blasted heath [littered] with dustbins and the odd kitchen sink'.

Tom Howarth, High Master of St Paul's School and Lindsay's seconder, wryly pointed out that these traditional pillars which had customarily underpinned the public schools' moral edifice all began with C: chapel, corps, cricket and cold baths.[137] All four were beginning to flake by the early 1960s. The influence of religion had declined in the face of the secular assumptions that increasingly characterised society; the conflict between a generally accepted – in the public school chapel at least – understanding of God's providence and a belief that man could master his own destiny was being won by scientists rather than theologians.[138] The importance of the corps, too, had been lessened with the abolition of National Service, the last call-ups having been made as 1960 came to a close. Even cricket, with the 1963 abolition of the distinction between gentlemen and players in the first-class

---

135. *HMC 1963 Report*, pp.19-39, 90-112. The following is principally based on the speeches of P.G. Mason, High Master of Manchester Grammar School (introducing the public service debate), and D.D.A. Lindsay and T.E.B. Howarth (opening the freedom debate), Southampton University, 1 and 2 Oct. 1963.

136. HMC had debated the progressive Crowther Report on 15-18 education (published in 1959) at their 1960 conference. Lord James of Rusholme, then High Master of Manchester Grammar School, argued that it was important for HMC to back the report, 'not only for the raising of the school leaving age but the whole opportunity for advance which the report offers'. *HMC 1960 Report*, p.23, speech, St John's College, Cambridge, 27 Sept. 1960.

137. Michael McCrum when chairman of HMC a few years later added three more: Classics, conceit and corporal punishment. *HMC 1974 Conference Report*, p.11, speech 30 Sept. 1974.

138. E.R. Wickham, Bishop of Middleton, had given an acute exposition of the religious issue at the previous year's conference at New College, Oxford, *HMC 1962 Report*, pp.73ff.

game, was not immune to change. In future there would be no need for the Cathedral School to make a printed public apology to four members of the Headmaster's 1957 XI for omitting their initials 'thus giving them professional status'.[139] As for cold baths, modern plumbing was ensuring running hot water in most public school boarding houses, even those in Hereford.

The weakening of these and other props of the old public school order ran parallel to the growth in number, affluence and independence of a teenage population during these years.[140] As has already been noted, public schoolboys now began to identify as much with their wider peer group as their school. Donald Lindsay in that same debate referred to the earlier maturity of boys and girls and 'the curiously greater danger' of Sixties' youths drinking in mixed company in coffee bars – no doubt each containing a juke box, as in the one licensed in Hereford in February 1958[141] – rather than the secret underage cherry-brandy swigging of previous generations in more innocent days. Boys, he alleged, were becoming increasingly bored with school by 17, which led to greater ill-discipline and a growing unwillingness to become prefects.

The old verities were then questioned. Was the prefect-fag relationship, useful as a model for colonial officers caring for native populations, relevant in a new world order? Should chapel be voluntary? Would Sixth-formers be better off in separate houses? Their colleagues were urged to establish closer links with parents; to prepare boys for confirmation only when they were ready; to stop the pretence that the members of the 1st XI were the nicest boys in the school; to agree that there was as much merit in visiting old people's homes as in polishing corps boots; and, above all, to educate more and nag less. A new vision was necessary which could challenge the prevailing mood of disillusion and cynicism. Part of the answer might lie in a new conception of public service through the establishment of voluntary service programmes, not in a missionary sense 'but with sympathy and a willing hand and eye'. Other experiments had been tried, including the zanier one of setting up of smoking rooms for senior pupils – in an era when the connection between smoking and lung cancer had been established. But it was not all doom and gloom. Although it was acknowledged that it was easier to run a disciplinary system based on corporal punishment than one dependent on trust and persuasion, boys of this generation were regarded as being more thoughtful and persuadable; they may also have been less deferential but they were held to be more open and confident in their relationships with masters than in the past; and the appeal of the voluntary service overseas, their generous response in world refugee year and their deep interest in distant continents like Africa suggested that their idealism was genuine.

Peebles agreed with these latter observations. Indeed, a few months earlier, at speech day in July 1963, he had stood up for the younger generation with these words:

---

139. *TH*, NS CLXXXXVI (March 1958), p.2.

140. Mark Abrams in an influential survey estimated that there were more than five million British teenagers (which he defined as unmarried young people between 15 and 25) in early 1960, commanding around 10 *per cent* of the population's total personal income. As cited by Sandbrook, (2006), p.435.

141. *HT*, 12 Feb. 1958, p.8, licence granted to L.J. Slade.

> ... what I value so much in this generation...is that they are friendly, frank and straightforward ... I am time and again impressed by the honesty, frankness and willingness to discuss things that matter. I am sure, too, they have more independence, initiative and sense of adventure both in thought and action than some of us had at their age ... I see no grounds for being pessimistic about the future.[142]

His sense of optimism was not misplaced for he steered the Cathedral School through much of the Sixties with astonishingly little trouble from its pupil body. In part this was a direct result of Peebles' own attitudes as well as his timely reforms. Remembered by some Old Herefordians today as an authoritarian figure, he was in fact an enlightened disciplinarian as this magisterial pronouncement, given in a school assembly after a series of petty thefts, shows:

> It is an easy thing to run a school on a strict set of rules, each having its appropriate punishment if broken or disregarded. But that is not what I want; it is irksome to the more intelligent and does not make for happy relations or understanding and certainly doesn't help people to grow up. My own aim, perhaps just an ideal which can't be quite realised, is to have as much freedom and absence of petty rules as possible.[143]

And despite mockingly describing himself as a reactionary,[144] like the good Conservative he actually was, he gradually changed some harsher aspects of the school regime. Caning by monitors came to an end in the early Sixties; with the introduction of the Duke of Edinburgh's award scheme and other reforms, the CCF became more noted for adventure activities than square bashing; Sunday chapel was re-organised, the special school service and the boarders' requirement to attend two Sunday services both being discontinued in October 1965; much to the boys' alarm, and perhaps even to the misgivings of some staff, parents' receptions were introduced for the first time in 1957-58 – and reported on as being a tremendous success with around 80 parents attending each occasion; and day pastoral care was improved following the introduction in 1959 of two additional tutors for both East and West Houses. Although it was to be another generation before corporal punishment, boarder initiation rights and fagging in School House and Deanery were to be abolished, some of the lesser boarding house rituals like the unofficial House food eating records, disappeared with the introduction of central dining in 1964.[145] So in this period the Cathedral School was beginning to open up: to parents, to the wide world and to itself.

---

142. Steele MSS, speech, 12 July 1963; reported on in *HT,* 17 July 1963, p.3 ('Head Impressed by Younger Generation ...'), and *TH*, CCVI (Oct. 1963), p.4.

143. Steele MSS, undated hand-written note. The meeting may have taken place in the summer term of 1959 as he refers to a special assembly he called in College Hall in his governors' report (HCSA) of 10 July 1959. However, his report indicates that he threatened a public caning for any boy found pilfering and this does not square with Peebles' own note of the proceedings.

144. In relation to his opposition to raising the school leaving age to 16 (as had in fact been originally provided for in the 1944 Act). *Ibid.*, speech 7 July 1967.

145. I am grateful to Andrew Singer, who as Head of School House in 1964 strongly opposed the change, for this observation.

Aided by the appointment of a younger generation of masters, it became a freer and more civilised place. And while co-education was a few years away, even girls began to make their appearance – on stage in the school's annual drama productions, as well as at the Christmas dances in the Booth Hall.[146]

Managing a secondary school during this decade of increasing teenage independence was a challenging assignment. Although Peebles was more fortunate than his metropolitan colleagues or those in charge of large boarding establishments, the tensions even in a small school in a provincial city which was hardly at the centre of the so-called 'swinging Sixties', were real enough. Among these frictions were the potential conflicts of interest between a day Sixth-former and his wage-earning contemporaries. As James Peebles himself observed in his contribution to that 1963 HMC debate on 'freedom, authority and the older boy':

> Where one has day boys, more particularly in a town the size of Hereford, and where as a direct grant school one has a wide range of income groups, there is a very real tension … Many of the boys come from districts where their contemporaries … live in the same road. We are trying to keep the intelligent boys at school until 17, 18 or 19 for university places and so on. They are under certain disciplines. They have prep to do in the evening. They can get only as much pocket money as perhaps not very well off parents will allow or we advise … But further down the road there live boys whom they have known since their childhood, working in our case in Bulmers, Wiggins or Painters and firms like that, and bringing fairly large wage packets home each week. They have no prep to do, they are absolutely free … I have asked many of the boys about this and they tell me they are pointed at as schoolboys with a very small amount of pocket money, having to go home to do some work and in trouble if they go to the cinemas during the week. This makes a tension which is very difficult for them.[147]

Nevertheless, such tensions were managed. As we have seen, the Cathedral School's Sixth Form (and its numbers overall) grew to record proportions; and as we will see, HCS emerged from the Peebles decade with its reputation substantially enhanced.

The School Makes Strides

On a hot afternoon on Saturday 19 July 1958, a speech day was held in the Shirehall before a large gathering of around 750 people. The occasion was significant, not so much for the Lord Lieutenant's charming speech – his recommendation that adventurous boys should look for a career in the British colonies was singularly unfortunate in its timing[148] – but for its novelty (it was the school's first speech day since the war) and promotional value. The new Headmaster took his opportunity well, reporting on the progress that had been made

146. Lynda Lewis, who played the part of Alice in André Obey's *Frost at Midnight* in 1961, was the first girl to appear in an HCS production. Thereafter, apart from the 1965 production of *Billy Budd* (an all-male line-up), girls were cast in every major school play during this period.

147. *HMC 1963 Report*, p.109, speech, 2 Oct. 1963.

148. The Lord Lieutenant was Lord Cilcennin, who (as J.P.L. Thomas) was MP for Hereford 1931-55 and served as First Lord of the Admiralty in Churchill's final administration. He was a good friend of HCS, lending his name to the 1959 appeal and taking the CCF inspection on 3 June 1960, one of his last public engagements.

with the new buildings, the close co-operation that had been established between parents and the school and the vibrancy of the Sixth Form. Likewise his chairman of governors, Dean Burrows, spoke of the occasion as a landmark event. The 'great strides' that had been recently made, he said, despite the strain that had been placed on the school's slender resources, were a tribute to Mr Peebles' 'hard work and enthusiasm'.[149]

Quick strides had indeed been made in only four terms, a pace that was to continue throughout Peebles' tenure. Conscious perhaps at the age of 47 of a need to make up lost time, and even more aware that he had inherited a school that despite his predecessor's devotion required considerable modernisation, the new Headmaster set about his task with purpose. The summer of 1957 was not a bad time to be starting. Five days before term began, on the morrow of St George's Day, he was presented to the Queen on her first visit to the city; a few weeks later F.R.W. Blackler, an Old Herefordian, was installed as the 576th mayor of Hereford at the early age of 37; and before the term had ended, two other Old Herefordians, P.E. and D.W. Richardson, played together in the Trent Bridge Test, the first brothers to represent England in the same cricket match since 1892. These events could all be used to promote the school: members of the CCF were given prominent places lining the Queen's route; the Dean did not fail to mention Mr Blackler's old school at the mayor's Sunday service in late May; and the boys were given half-holidays in honour of the Richardsons' achievement. But the most notable celebration that term was the revival of the commemoration service after nearly 20 years on 23 July, but this time it was before a large congregation, with the full choir, in the cathedral nave. The like had not been seen since the '550th' anniversary in 1931.[150]

HCS's external profile was rising but much needed to happen internally to improve its standing.[151] Peebles' first impressions of his new school were mixed. He felt fortunate in his colleagues, who although lacking academic distinction, were held to be competent, hard-working and cooperative. However, they were shy of taking responsibility and he involved them in reorganising that 'thing of shreds and patches', the timetable. Something was immediately achieved by starting chapel ten minutes later at nine, enabling the whole school (at least in theory and with the exception of the choristers) to be present for corporate worship. Among the pupils, he found boys of 'character and independence' but they had not been given the best chance to develop intellectually. They had been allowed to take too many subjects at Ordinary and Advanced-levels; the senior work had been handicapped by the absence of a reading room for private study; and the timetable demands for junior pupils, with 36 taught periods plus two games lessons each week, were considered excessive. Choristers, in particular, suffered from missing ten lessons every week,[152] and the day

149. *HT*, 25 July 1958; *TH*, NS CLXXXVII (*sic*) (Nov. 1958), pp.5-6. Also see, *HCN*, no. 38 (Summer 1957), p.11, where the Dean wrote: 'The new Head Master is full of energy and keenness and the school is taking strides'.

150. *TH*, NS CLXXXXV (Nov. 1957), pp.11-13. In 1958 speech day was re-introduced and held (except for 1959) in the Shirehall. For three years, it took place on Saturday afternoon after the morning Commemoration. From 1961, it was held on the Friday immediately preceding Commemoration.

151. For the following: HCSA, Peebles' first report to the chairman of governors, 4 June 1957.

152. The proposed remedy was ending the school day at 3.20 for the first two years, the cathedral organist (Dr Cook) having agreed to restrict the morning practice to half an hour from 8.45 in return for an extended afternoon practice.

boys in general were too '9 to 4pm minded'. Remedies were proposed: a circular letter to all parents setting out what the school expected; the institution (introduced for the autumn term 1957) of parents' 'gatherings'; and the strengthening of the position of the two day-boy Housemasters by giving them studies – two ante-rooms in the new classroom block were soon provided – where they could see boys and parents privately in proper surroundings. In general, the boys' dress was held to be 'slovenly and varied' and the school's appearance poor. In late 1957 a new striped tie was devised and the boys were given three months to conform to the school's dress code.[153] More immediate measures were taken to improve the boarders' food, particularly in School House, where the breakfasts were inadequate, the evening meals lacking – for three evenings each week, the boys brought in their own food for re-heating in the kitchens – and there was an unhealthy reliance on 'tuck' and cooking in studies.

The improvement of the school buildings was 'a major question'. The new Headmaster again did not pull his punches in his first governors' report: the masters' Common Room he considered could not have had a 'rival in England' such was its state; much of the fabric of School House was dangerous; the Old Deanery required external decoration; the desks and beds were 'less than sub-standard'; the new groundsman's equipment at Wyeside consisted of not much more than an old motor mower, a rotor scythe and a roller. Six months later, Peebles vented his feelings in public, observing at his first old boys' dinner that he had inherited 'one of the shabbiest schools in England'. 'The original coat of wood', he continued, 'dating back to the days of Bishop Putta, I believe, is showing distinct signs of wear. Frankly, gentlemen, this is not a good thing either for our good name or as an environment for education'.[154] His concern to refurbish and new build became a central pre-occupation of his headship.

It was the age of re-development. Hereford city itself underwent its own 'renaissance' over this decade.[155] The new town plan, praised at the time (in 1963) as a model for other cathedral cities, in retrospect seems like (to borrow Geoffrey Moorhouse's phrase from his survey of Gloucester in the early Sixties) a desperate attempt 'to suppress history'.[156] For re-development came at a price. Among the historic buildings to be demolished in Broad Street alone during the Sixties – to say nothing of the timber-framed buildings and ancient city defences lost with the building of the inner relief road and new bridge (1964-66) – were the Residence Hotel, the old hop market and the Kemble Theatre. Their replacements were undistinguished but at least the city was spared the building of a 22-storey council block adjacent to the Shirehall, proposed in 1967 as the answer to the county's administrative problems.[157]

---

153. *TH*, NS CLXXXXV (Nov. 1957), p.8.

154. Steele MSS, speech at the Green Dragon, 14 Dec. 1957.

155. Dean Burrows and Mayor Blundstone both referred in 1961 to the 'renaissance' taking place in Hereford at this time. *HT*, 7 June 1961, p.3; 25 Oct. 1961, p.6.

156. Moorhouse, p.57. Also note the comment made in early 1965 by F. Noble, President of the Woolhope Club, that the new road network would mean that history was 'likely to be bulldozed': *HT*, 12 Feb. 1965, p.1. The plan had been praised earlier by Ian Nairn and Ken Browne in an article in *The Architectural Review*. *HT*, 25 Sept. 1963, p.4.

157. For this inappropriate design: *HT*, 5 May 1967, p.1.

The change in the school's physical appearance during these years was also held to be a 'renaissance'.[158] A detailed report in September 1957 by Herbert Powell, the school's first retained architect, 'who combined skill with devotion to his old school', showed that Peebles had not much exaggerated when he termed HCS the shabbiest school in the country. School House, in particular, had suffered from neglect but the lack of proper maintenance was everywhere apparent. Powell estimated that around £4,000 was required for essential repairs and redecoration, without rewiring, the improvement of the heating supply and the provision of a proper system of locks.[159] The spending of around two-thirds of this amount was initially sanctioned but at least a start had been made and over the following months the plant was gradually improved: first in School House; then the Old Block classrooms, where the ancient 'perch and high' desks and chocolate brown classroom paint and 'margarine colour' wash on the upper walls hardly relieved the gloomy atmosphere, and elsewhere.

The impact on the school's appearance and comfort was considerable. Within two years, School House had been refurbished and its front restored, the rampaging ivy having been tastefully replaced in time for the 1958 speeches ceremony by three coats of arms – the central cathedral shield being flanked by the ancient and modern arms of the diocese – painted by the Art master. By September 1958, the face of the Headmaster's house (Number 1) had also been restored, its white stucco gleaming brightly in the late summer sunshine, and some classrooms had been redecorated in light pastel colours and framed pictures hung (unlabelled) on the walls. New desks, too, had been provided, the old ones having been broken up in the holidays by a gang of boys, who reflected ruefully (it was reported) as they hit the desks with pickaxes that a few weeks previously they 'would have been beaten for scratching their names on them'. All told, an average of £2,790 was expended annually on repairs, redecoration and maintenance in the four years from 1957 to 1961. It was not a fortune but the money was now being spent more effectively and it trebled the repair bill of the previous four years. Eventually, even the heating system was improved through the rationalisation of the many boilers and their conversion from coke to oil in 1962-63 and 1965 (for the Old Deanery). In School House at least, this came about just before the extended winter freeze of early 1963, and after the greatcoat, that time-honoured bed blanket, had been replaced (in Summer Term 1962) by the cape as standard cadet issue.[160]

New schemes were also sanctioned. These included (in 1957-58): a new workshop, on the site of a derelict greenhouse in the Old Deanery garden; the conversion of the old woodwork room into the Zimmerman Reading Room (subsequently the Zimmerman Library, following the division of the Gilbert Library in 1959); and the extension of the masters' Common Room by the addition of glass panels in school yard, making the room

158. By the anonymous 'Cathedral School Correspondent': *TH*, NS CLXXXXVI (March 1958), p.24. The following year the correspondent referred to the 'wonderful metamorphosis' that had occurred over the summer holidays (1958). *TH*, NS CLXXXXVIII (May 1959), p.8.

159. HCSA, Herbert J. Powell's report on the condition of school buildings, Sept. 1957.

160. HCSA, GMB 1945-82, pp.151-73, various minutes from 21 June 1962 to 10 June 1965; Account Book 1945-72, *passim*; Peebles reports to governors, Nov. 1958 to Oct. 67, *passim*; *TH*, NS CLXXXVII (*sic*) (Nov. 1958), pp.33-34; CLXXXXVIII (May 1959), p.8; CCIII (May 1962), p.20. The following paragraphs are mainly based on the relevant editions of *The Herefordian*, the above minutes, account book and reports, and Herbert Powell's typescript on the evolution of the school buildings.

lighter, larger, but also considerably colder and more vulnerable to damage from a stray football. But there were more significant additions during these early years.

The building of an on-site gymnasium and new laboratories were both inherited projects. As has been indicated, a gym and Biology laboratory had been designed by Herbert Powell ten years earlier as a proposed memorial to fallen Old Herefordians of the Second World War. The monies collected were only sufficient to build the laboratory (in 1952). The gymnasium, however, became a reality after Hopewell's death. His widow generously released the school from its obligation to pay the remaining £1,600 owed for the purchase of the family's furniture and fittings, enabling the OH Club to undertake the building without a loan. The scheme, which cost £4,500, was thereby completed as originally envisaged, except that the gymnasium became the Hopewell memorial.[161] In March 1958, the site was cleared and the new foundations dug. Despite the difficulty of attaching the gymnasium to the pre-war laboratories, it was ready for use by the beginning of the autumn term, D.W. Theakston having been appointed that summer as the school's first properly qualified instructor in Physical Education.

The addition of two further laboratories was the responsibility of the school rather than the old boys. The project was underwritten in part by the Industrial Fund – that important organisation set up in 1955 to raise funds to reform Science education in independent and direct grant schools[162] – to the tune of £6,000 provided that HCS itself could find

Fig. 8.9 Don Theakston supervises boys climbing ropes in the new gymnasium, 1957.

161. See above, p.455; and Brittain MSS, Peter Williams (OH Club Secretary) to Barbara Hopewell, 1 March 1958.

162. The fund's trustees secured £3.2 million from 141 companies. Building and apparatus grants were distributed to 187 schools; a further 143 being awarded apparatus grants only. In the end HCS benefited from a total grant of £7,700 of which £1,700 was to go towards equipment.

a further £4,000. The school was only able to raise its portion through the generosity of Arthur Zimmerman OH who made a £4,000 loan at a nominal interest rate, a sum he later increased to £5,000. Henry Wiggin and company made a further contribution of £100 for Science books, a generous gesture given that the school had indirectly benefited from the firm's support of the Industrial Fund. The new Physics and Chemistry laboratories, to be built as a second storey on top of the existing ones, were started in October 1957 and completed on budget by the following July.[163] As Peebles had observed at his first OH dinner the previous December, with five laboratories all told – a sixth room (used as a Science lecture theatre) was inexpensively added, at the rear of 7 Ferrers Street on the site of the Headmaster's garden rubbish dump, in 1961-62 – the school would be able to hold its own 'in this scientific age', an observation confirmed by the pupils' growing interest in Science during this decade.

By the end of the summer term 1958, following the introduction of parents' visits and speech day, the erection of new buildings and the refurbishment of old, the school (in the caustic words of a senior pupil) had begun 'to look like a school'. But this was just a beginning; the Headmaster had other dreams. As he informed Old Herefordians at their annual dinner on 13 December 1958, after the official opening of the gymnasium and laboratories:

> I sit in my study and hatch vain empires – or perhaps they may not be so vain ... I have a plan to suit every income; like – is it Montague Burton? – I can fit any figure ... when you win your next football pool do come and see me.

In the same speech he had listed his priorities: more form-rooms and playing fields; the enlargement of Big School and its furnishing as an assembly hall for the whole school 'to say things pleasant or unpleasant as the case may be'; and a proper dining-hall.[164] It is a mark of Peebles' tenacity and his governors' support that these projects were all realised during his tenure.

As Peebles had intimated, the major problem was – as ever – one of money. The early building work had stretched the school's own resources to the limit and there was a need to find other funding streams. A direct appeal to the Old Herefordians could hardly be repeated so soon after the last one but a wider appeal to the county might be more successful. This was launched in the summer of 1959 with the support of Lord Cilcennin, the Lord Lieutenant, and the Headmaster as effective manager. The £25,000 target – ten times less than the money raised during the 1950s when Cilcennin was chairman of the board at Rugby School[165] – was modest enough but even that sum proved elusive and less than £10,000 was eventually collected. Nevertheless, it proved sufficient to enable HCS to embark 'in faith, hope and charity' upon the next stage of its development.

---

163. H.A. Hornby, Science master at HCS 1954-56 and then Head of Physics at Portsmouth Grammar School, was helpful with his advice, the new Portsmouth Science wing having been completed a year earlier in 1957. Hereford's scheme cost just over £11,626 (including furniture and professional fees), Bayley Brothers being paid £10,268 18s 6d for its building.

164. Steele MSS, Peebles' speech, 13 Dec. 1958. His priorities were also outlined in various reports to the governors over the following months and they were incorporated in the appeal document of 24 June 1959.

165. As reported: *HT*, 25 June 1958, p.4.

For a school that was growing 'like a good healthy plant, not as a result of deliberate policy and planning',[166] the provision of more classrooms was an absolute priority. The hiring of extra rooms in Castle Street to accommodate increased numbers in the Modern Sixth, which had grown to 24 boys by early 1959, could be no more than a temporary measure. A solution was found in the partition of the Gilbert Library in the summer of 1959. This involved the transference of non-classical and Modern Language books to the Zimmerman Reading Room which Peebles rightly saw as advantageous in that it provided the opportunity to establish a new library that was likely to be better used. But it also meant the removal of old honours boards. These, he argued, did 'scant credit' to the school and, aesthetically, would have done 'little credit ... to British Railways'. The partition eased the pressure on Sixth-form teaching accommodation even if the division of a lovely (although neglected) room had meant the sacrifice of a part of the school's heritage.

The plan to provide additional classrooms and improved facilities for the rest of the school also involved the destruction of a part of the school's past. In January 1959, Herbert Powell designed another building which could be added to at a later date. This 'new wing' comprised a cloakroom for 200 day boys, seven lavatories and a day monitors' room, and on the first floor, two classrooms and a room for the printing press.[167] It was to be integrated

Fig. 8.10 The old Gilbert Library before its partition (and the removal of the honours boards) in the summer of 1959.

166. Steele MSS, Peebles' speech, 14 July 1961.

167. The school archives contain Herbert Powell's plans for the two stages of the extension, dated 14 January 1959 and 30 June 1964.

with Old Block and built in school yard on the site of the old armoury building, an early brick building with half-timbered gables which was originally the porter's lodge. Since 1901, when the porter moved to a cottage by Wyeside, it had undergone various conversions and by this time housed day changing rooms and studies, as well as the armoury and CCF office on the first floor. The loss of this old cottage and the final levelling of the 'Acropolis' do not seem to have caused much heartache: the armoury building was in a poor state of repair, with a pronounced westward lean, and the removal of an attenuated 'Acropolis' provided more space for yard games and corps parades. But if there were some who were sentimentally attached to the old armoury and mound, there could have been none who regretted the destruction of those (in the Headmaster's words) 'ancient inconveniences' in the south-east corner of the yard, not least the cathedral organist whose garden stood adjacent to them. A home was found for the armoury in a disused passageway in Old Block and the new extension was started in October 1959 and in use by the following summer, its £7,000 cost being covered by the promised appeal donations. By 1965, when the two second floor classrooms and music practice rooms were added, building costs had risen sharply, the total cost of the new wing being in excess of £12,000. Meanwhile, over the 1960 summer holidays, Big School had been extended by 20 feet with the building of a gallery extension (on stilts), enabling the holding of Saturday morning assemblies in school rather than the Lady Chapel. At long last, the Headmaster had a suitable time and place for berating and praising the boys.[168]

A new dining-hall had been planned as early as February 1958 and the appeal included a scheme for a new hall capable of seating 220 boys. Appeal receipts were insufficient for this to be realised and it was not until Zimmerman again came to the rescue just before his death in March 1963 that the facility could be built by which time costs had doubled.[169] Work began immediately after term had ended in July 1963. Site clearing involved some heavy constructional work, including the demolition of the old workshop, where names of unknown past generations had been carved into its structure, and despite the Headmaster's impatience at the contractors' delay, the dining-hall was ready by January 1964. The following month, Peebles could report that considerable savings were being made. Of the 229 lunches provided each day, 95 were for day boys who at 1s 3d (he had asked the Ministry for 1s 4d) were charged 3d more than they had been. This meant an extra 23s 8d per day. In addition, the school was saved the £5 daily subsidy which helped pay for day-boy meals in the decrepit civic restaurant where they had previously lunched.[170]

---

168. He had occasionally used College Hall as a place to admonish the pupils but felt the lack of an assembly hall large enough 'to see the school under proper dignified conditions'. HCSA, report to governors, 10 July 1959.

169. In the appeal, it was estimated that the building would cost £6,000; Zimmerman gave £14,000, the agreement being sealed on 9 March 1963, the day before his death; actual building costs came to £12,522 7s 6d. The hall was built by C. Honey Ltd of Hereford. Also see: HCSA, for dining-hall plans, 11 Feb. 1958 and 28 Sept. 1962.

170. Over the course of a year the savings were considerable: the school's annual average subsidy for day lunches – their costs being carefully controlled by the Ministry of Education – was £263 over the six financial years, 1958-64. Costs incurred by increased wages (of £3 and 30s weekly for the chef and assistant cook respectively in 1964) and the employment of a further assistant cook were offset by the Old Deanery requiring fewer staff and the unquantifiable savings made by central purchasing.

Some boarders resented the loss of traditions that central dining brought about, although the boarding houses retained something of their own identity in the new building and more dayroom space was created in their Houses. For the staff it was all gain, their odd glass-panelled room in School House being replaced by the Georgian elegance of their new Common Room, the old School House dining-room in Number 1. Alan Morris, the young Chemistry master from King Edward's School, Birmingham, would not have been the only teacher to have been impressed by the civilised atmosphere of these surroundings.

The physical appearance of HCS changed markedly over the ten years from 1957: in Castle Street, old buildings were refurbished and new ones added on both sides of the school; and at Wyeside, as we shall see, the field was drained, beautified and screened, the pavilion shored up and the foundations of a new one laid. Overall, over £50,000 was spent on new premises during this decade. It was not a huge amount and insufficient for the needs of every boy – as Peebles told his governors in June 1964, in an 'affluent society with its many outside attractions', the school had very little to offer by way of amenities – but for the Cathedral School it was unprecedented. In the process of new building some of the school's heritage was lost, but overall the school gained: within two generations, the teaching and living conditions of masters and boys had been transformed.

Like Tatham more than 80 years earlier, Peebles soon appreciated the difference between Hereford boys and those he had taught at Westminster. While impressed by the enthusiasm and talent displayed outside the classroom, he was surprised by the complacency many of them showed in their attitude to academic work. In his early governors' reports he tried to analyse why. Was this lack of urgency to do with the mock exams giving a false sense of security? Or was it more to do with Hereford's climate or the innate qualities of Herefordians? Whatever the cause, the end result, he concluded, made teaching too often 'like punching dough'. Peebles determined to do something about it, and while he was not wholly successful in his endeavours, there was a marked improvement in the school's academic standing over the course of his tenure. As ever, the keys to success related to the quality of the intake, the ability and enthusiasm of the teachers, class sizes and the learning resources.

No entrance test scores are extant so little can be said about the quality of the entry in these years. It is clear, however, that while the competition for day places was considerable, with well over two applications for every place (aside from the county 11 plus applicants), boarding demand, with the exception of the years around the turn of the decade, was less intense. By May 1962, the Headmaster could report to his governors that it would not be wise for them to contemplate expansion on the boarding side, a stance justified by the fall-off in boarder applications by the mid-Sixties. And throughout his tenure, Peebles was disappointed that Headmasters from the better preparatory schools – whom, he claimed, did not understand the direct grant system and were suspicious of Hereford's low fees – did not send him candidates at common entrance (13 plus). Here again this was totally contrary to his experience as a Westminster Housemaster.

The quality of teaching, however, improved. As HCS expanded, Peebles had opportunities to make additional appointments, the Common Room increasing from 16 to 23 full-time masters in these years. The turn-over rate was still slow, Peebles making 20 full-time appointments, around two a year. Of these, three out of four were educated at Oxford or Cambridge, and a number even held a professional teaching qualification. Most were in their twenties and were (in the Headmaster's words about two of them) 'young, vigorous and capable'. Not all of Peebles' appointments worked, and he occasionally had difficulty in filling posts in subjects like Mathematics and Modern Languages, but the vast majority were successful. So as Hopewell's men retired or moved on, they were replaced by outstanding young teachers who re-energised the school.[171] As the 1964 inspectors noted:

> the newer appointments have added considerable strength to the teaching ... Though they represent a blend of youth and experience, they are a staff young in age, only two being over 50 ... Many of them have the qualities of the good schoolmaster; they have a sense of vocation and give freely of their time to the interests of the school and of the boys.[172]

And, among the Common Room as a whole, there was a real camaraderie which is still fondly remembered.[173]

Despite the increase in the number of teachers, the staff pupil ratio hardly altered. By February 1965, Peebles reckoned that at 1:23 (on a weighted ratio counting Sixth-formers as double), HCS exceeded the average for direct grant and maintained grammar schools. Consequently, class sizes remained stubbornly high, particularly in the Fourth and Fifth Forms where some classes approached 30. In the Sixth, however, the problem was even more acute. Whereas admissions in the lower forms did not markedly change, the Sixth Form grew exponentially as we have seen, the decisive change occurring in the late Fifties when the number of leavers aged 16 to 17 reduced from 107 in the three years 1954-57 to 50 from 1957 to 1960. The Sixth Form almost doubled in size (to 90) during these years, and then increased again to 100 or more, despite Peebles' doubt as to whether all those who stayed on were capable of undertaking Advanced courses. This put considerable pressure on the Sixth Form masters, particularly those teaching subjects like Classics, Modern Languages and Biology, where two or three year groups were likely to be taught together and the ability and age range was wide. As a two-form entry, the school was just not big enough to provide specialist teachers in every subject for each of the Sixth Form year groups.

Still, Peebles successfully harried his governors into improving conditions for study and resources for learning. The removal of the woodwork room from New Block – and the subject from the timetable – in 1957 gave the opportunity for the creation of the Zimmerman Reading Room for private study. Additional study facilities were also eventually found for both boarders and day boys. And although a fine room was temporarily

171. Of the younger men (in their twenties) appointed in this period, Bill Glover, Bruce Andrews and Martin Woodgett went on to senior posts at larger schools; Alick Rowe became a freelance writer; while Don Theakston, Peter Skinner, Alex Shave, Alan Morris and Dick Rhodes remained at HCS until their retirements, as did Martin Nicholson for most of his career.

172. For this and subsequent references to the 1964 inspection: TNA, ED 109/9473.

173. The late Bill Glover, in particular, had happy memories of his eight years (1957-65) as a young teacher at HCS. I am grateful for his recollections of his time at the school.

lost with the partitioning of the old Gilbert Library, it resulted in the establishment of a more modern and accessible library in the Zimmerman Library. Five years after its opening in April 1959, the inspectors described this as a 'well lighted room of ample size', albeit one with a rough floor and nondescript furniture which did nothing 'to suggest scholarship'. Nevertheless, 924 new books had been added over these years, during which time the annual grant had increased from £36 to £114.[174] Between £4 and £5 was also spent on binding from the sale of old paper-backs (the first Penguins appear to have been bought for the Gilbert Library in early 1959), thus simultaneously helping the library and encouraging private collections.

Peebles had been proclaiming the virtue of private libraries for some time, advising his governors that this was one of the ways to convert 'a good natural brain into a good intellect', particularly among those boys who came from non-academic home backgrounds. Even senior boys, he found, were reluctant to buy suitable books. So in late 1958, during the second round of the 'parents' parties' (as he called them), he suggested that a parent of an older boy might put aside £1 each term for the purchase of relevant books. He reiterated the point on speech day 1960, while modifying the amount to between 10s and £1 despite the inflationary pressures of the previous 18 months. As he pronounced, 'even in an age of TV and the lottery' – 'Ernie' had been extravagantly launched in Hereford a few days before, bringing traffic in High Town to a standstill for several hours[175] – books were 'still the essential part of the wider education'. They were more likely to be valued if they were owned rather than borrowed, and they lasted for life, long after joints had become 'too stiff and the wind too short for the more energetic pursuits'. How much notice was taken of Peebles' exhortations is impossible to establish, but we do know that the amount spent on text books trebled during his tenure and that the winning of book prizes again became a reality for a good few and an aspiration for many more.[176] The cumulative effect of such developments was a significant improvement in the school's academic standing.

Peebles was not satisfied with the academic results, like much else, on his arrival. In public speeches, as well as privately to his governors, few punches were pulled. 'I sometimes feel if they [the boys] took on the GCE examiners in the same spirit [as their rugby opponents]', he told the Old Herefordians in December 1959, 'we should have some remarkable successes'. The Ordinary-level results in particular disappointed him. There was too much 'dead wood', he confided to his governors, and a lack of proper grounding in the junior forms. Over the following years, however, despite his continuing the policy of entering the better boys for O-level at 15 plus, after only four years, so that they had the opportunity

174. The inspectors thought this amount inadequate and in the following three years the sums spent on library books increased annually, reaching almost £175 by 1966-67.

175. *HT*, 6 July 1960, p.8.

176. The amount spent on text books rose from £358 17s 7d (1957-58) to £1,058 1s (1967-68), a considerable increase even allowing for inflation. Around 50 prizes were awarded annually from the 1958 speech day. The Arden-Davies memorial, the Norris Chemistry and the Raphael Powell prizes were all properly endowed in this period. These, together with the Murray-Ragg classical essay prize, the Bull French prizes and the Power memorial prize for Mathematics, made up the six prize endowments in existence in 1967. Money for the remaining prizes (the annual prize bill averaged nearly £90 in the three years from 1965) came from individual donations and school funds.

to spend a longer time in the Sixth Form, things were gradually turned around. In the four years 1957-61, out of an annual entry of around 70, only once did 20 candidates gain five passes or more; in the six following years, 25 boys on average achieved this bench-mark each year. The Sixth Form story was similar. As the numbers taking Advanced examinations increased from an average of 32 in the late Fifties to 50 or so in the Sixties, so did the proportion passing at least two A-levels. In terms of public examinations, general standards were rising.

The university patterns of entry over the period as a whole are complicated by the large expansion in the number of university students in the Sixties.[177] So as the decade unfolded and the new post-Robbins universities were built,[178] the opportunities for university education increased and, as importantly, the guarantee of some government funding for all, rather than only the select state or county scholars. The Cathedral School followed the trend of the times. Over the four years 1957-61, one in three leavers went on to higher or further education, compared with one in two from 1960 to 1963. As significantly, over the same three years in the early Sixties, farming, the armed forces and the merchant navy claimed only 12 leavers, compared with 48 in the three years before the 1952 inspection.[179] By 1967, three out of four Sixth-formers went on to some kind of further education.

One of Peebles' missions was to try to improve the school's representation at Oxford and Cambridge. This was harder to do than in the past, given the increased competition as Sixth Forms expanded nationally and entry standards rose. This applied as much to close award holders as open scholars and commoners. So at the two ancient English universities, the number of the school's award-winners during this decade could almost be counted on the fingers of one hand.[180] The numbers winning places, however, increased considerably, averaging five each year from 1962 to 1967, one in ten of the A-level candidates, with a record nine in Peebles' last year. The school's representation at other universities also improved, the Headmaster proclaiming as early as December 1960 that there was an Old Herefordian at almost every university in the country, including (he said patriotically) St Andrews. And in May 1963 even *The Herefordian*, that most conservative of journals which had from its beginning published missives (but only spasmodically in this period) from its Oxford and Cambridge correspondents, printed a letter from an OH extolling the virtues of Nottingham University.

---

177. Some 216,000 people were enrolled at British universities in 1962; by 1965, this number had increased to 310,000, around one in ten of the age group. It continued to rise through the rest of the decade.

178. The case for a University of Hereford was twice examined (in early 1959 and 1964-65) and twice rejected, presumably on account of costs and the difficulty of finding a suitable 100-200 acre site. The second time, following an initiative by David Gibson-Watt MP, the Lord Lieutenant (Col J.F. MacLean), chaired an exploratory committee which may have included James Peebles who favoured the scheme. *HT*, 1 April 1959; 4, 11 Dec. 1964.

179. Figures from Steele MSS, Peebles' speech, 13 July 1962; TNA, ED 109/9473, inspection report, p.2. The annual average for these three occupational categories over the four years, 1957- 61, was seven.

180. During this period, A. Butcher (Brasenose, Oxford), K.J. Henley (St John's, Cambridge), P.F. Barnett (Corpus Christi, Cambridge), P.H. Baxendale (St John's, Cambridge) and C.J. Harding (Brasenose, Oxford) gained open or Somerset awards. G.A. Williams, E.S. Judge and G.F. Howard won state scholarships in 1958, 1960 and 1962 respectively. By this period, close-award winners had to be of open award standard. See Dancy, p.58 note 1, for an analysis of the close awards made at Oxford and Cambridge in 1961-62.

The 1964 inspection report is a good indicator of HCS's academic progress. Led by W. Peach, soon to become an HCS parent, the nine HMIs recognised the improvement that had been made in working conditions and the school's rising academic standards. 'Steady, competent work' was being accomplished in most subjects, with Classics, English, Science and the higher Mathematics leading the way. A less academic approach was advocated in Modern Languages and Geography, but only the History teaching was regarded as calamitous.[181] As in 1952, however, the lack of a laboratory assistant was held to be a serious deficiency. The organisation of the curriculum was also criticised: the failure to provide a broadly based Science course in the junior years was a weakness; the late introduction of German and limited Spanish precluded the development of a full Modern Languages course; insufficient time was allowed for private study in the Sixth Form; and the provision for the creative subjects was inadequate – a situation in part remedied some two years later by the appointment of D.W. Rix as the school's first full-time Art master.[182] This left Music as the Cinderella subject: taught (and as a core subject only to the first two years) part-time by a lay clerk, with Big School as the inadequate music room. Nevertheless, in marked contrast to 12 years earlier, the 1964 report was, as Peebles observed, 'lucid, helpful and on the whole encouraging'. The four governors (out of six) who troubled to turn up to the 90 minute de-brief on the afternoon of 29 May 1964 must, like the Headmaster, have been reasonably content with the outcome.

Overall, as the inspectors recognised, the Peebles era was 'an important development phase in the school's history'. Despite the academic limitations – in particular subjects, class sizes, specialist rooms, and in the poverty of the creative curriculum and non-existence of support staff – a far greater number of boys benefited from learning at the Cathedral School in 1967 than had done so a decade earlier. One attractive aspect of that learning (as the HMIs also observed) was that it was accomplished in a relaxed atmosphere 'with a marked lack of regimentation'. Another was the hospitality enjoyed by senior boys: like the cider, cake and croquet on the Bishop's lawn on a summer evening after Sunday Evensong, and the more forbidding Headmaster's dinner parties.[183] By such means they were encouraged to achieve their best both in and out of the classroom.

More clubs were made available for widening a Sixth-former's intellectual horizons. For the period as a whole, as well as for the year 1965-66 when the statement was made, the Scientific Society was 'the most successful, alive and active society in the school', even taking into consideration its dramatic slump in membership by 1967.[184] Founded in June 1957 with 'Danny' Rumsey as its president, it met fortnightly (at least at first) in the Physics laboratory with the avowed aim to encourage an active interest in all branches of Science. The society caught the mood of the times and over the next ten years had a regular membership of around 40 budding scientists. With the support of the local branch of the

181. Although by 1970 the teaching of the subject had 'much improved'. See below, p.526, note 276.

182. As Peebles reported to his governors, Rix had spent several weeks of his summer holiday, before starting in September 1966, making 'the Art room what it ought to be'.

183. And remembered today by Richard Blott, Angus Craig and John Dauncey, to all of whom I am indebted for this observation. The Bishop, who is still held in affection by Old Herefordians, was Mark Hodson.

184. The following paragraphs are largely based on the relevant editions of *The Herefordian*.

British Association for the Advancement of Science, which until 1967 did not charge for its lecture services, and the use of the extensive film libraries of industrial corporations, over 100 talks were given and numerous films shown. Lectures and demonstrations were often prepared by the boys themselves as well as by guest lecturers. The range of the talks was impressively wide. For two hours on a Thursday evening, the boys learned about such topics as evolution, thermo-nuclear energy, earth satellites and moon probes, radio astronomy and (by the mid-Sixties) colour television, the use of computers, Concorde and the North Sea gas industry.[185] Nor were such local topics as the Ross-Tewkesbury motorway, the new road bridge and cider-making neglected.[186] But it was not simply a home-based organisation. Visits were made to local works and to industries wider afield: to British Nylon Spinners at Pontypool, Ebbw Vale steelworks and the Royal Radar Research establishment at Malvern, for example. There were also regular invitations to the annual meetings of the Mullard Film Society at the Green Dragon and the BAAS at Birmingham University. And while the society may have lost support by 1966-67, and (as with all activities) exams meant there were fewer meetings in the summer term at the end of the period than the beginning, this enterprising association did much to promote both the cause of Science within the school and the career of Science within the wider world.

Although the 'Science harms the mind' motion at a joint meeting with the Arts Society in the 1966 autumn term was defeated, that the debate was held at all was indicative of a move away from Science towards the Arts. The size of the Maths/Science Sixth had declined from 70 or more in 1964-65 to 55 by September 1967, the number of boys studying Arts subjects having correspondingly increased from 34 to almost parity in the same three-year period. The swing away from Science subjects followed national trends, the issue being first raised at HMC in 1964 when two-thirds of the Conference had noticed the shift.[187] But there was an additional factor to account for at HCS: the return of Alick Rowe to his old school as an English teacher in 1963. His influence may be discerned in the re-awakening of the Arts Society.

By this time the Somerset Society had almost run its course. Although mentioned in the 1964 inspection report as 'a small elected discussion group' under the Headmaster's presidency, there was no further account of its activities in *The Herefordian* after May 1959. It had, in effect, been superseded by the Arts Society. Founded in early 1960 under the lively patronage of J.A.M. Baldwin, it became a vehicle for theatre visits and talks on modern art, poetry, music and other topics. It was by no means an establishment club. In 1962-63, for example, the playwright and CND activist Margaret Wood had given a talk at an angry meeting on 'the artist and the bomb', and at the end of that year's programme – with four meetings at different locations in successive nights, a kind of Arts festival as the secretary

185. In Hereford, by July 1967, the county council was considering the purchase of its first computer and the city's first colour television sets were received for demonstration purposes. *HT*, 21 July 1967, p.22; 28 July 1967, p.1.

186. Brian Nelson, then chief chemist for H.P. Bulmer, gave the 'cider' lecture in the autumn of 1961, thus beginning an association with HCS that lasted more than 30 years. The 7-mile Hereford section of the M50 was started in early 1958 and finished (for £860,000) before the end of 1960; the new road bridge, which took over two years to complete (at a cost of £608,000), was first opened to traffic on 20 December 1966.

187. *HMC 1964 Report*, pp.33ff, Headmasters' comments during a discussion on 'the Sixth Form in the Robbins era'.

observed – the society heard the recitations of a performance poet, the boys being stirred by his 'shaggy shoulder length hair, crimson velvet bow-tie and other decorations'. Thereafter, activity waned until the mid-Sixties when Rowe assumed the presidency. After this things never looked back, talks on anarchy, religious and literary forums and a showing of Orson Welles' film 'The Trial', for instance, being some of the highlights of the 1966 spring term. By November 1967, membership (at 61) was somewhat reduced, but the 5s fee (for card and admission) represented good value for that term's nine events; and by then Rowe could trumpet: 'culture is in the ascendancy ... we're winning'.

This was certainly true for creative writing and drama; less so for art and music. With Alick Rowe's arrival literary items again appeared in *The Herefordian* (from May 1964), poems, an 'important questionnaire' (on school monitorship) and a rather good James Bond spoof ('Goldnavel') being the pieces reprinted from 'Conspirator', an in-house rag that lasted three issues before being re-born in an improved guise in March 1967.[188] Meanwhile, prize-winning entries from poetry competitions filled the literary pages of further editions of the school magazine (October 1966 and March 1968) and the juniors continued composing endless sheaves of uncontrolled verse. Not much of all this was fit to be printed and the 1967 entries for the Headmaster's short story competition failed to produce much of worth, but, encouraged by their mentor, at least many more boys were now involved in the arts of composition and (for the Bishop's prize) recital.

The annual school play was already well established as the cultural highlight of the autumn term. John Baldwin's casting of girls in 1961 enabled him to widen the choice of play performed and having taken over the Old Deanery in September 1959 (a school play was not produced that year), he signed off in 1962 with an acclaimed production of Golding's *The Brass Butterfly*. What followed thereafter were a succession of extravaganzas directed by Alick Rowe: *The Merchant of Venice* (1963); *Nightmare Abbey* (1964), an adaptation of Thomas Love Peacock's novel and played not entirely convincingly as burlesque rather than satire; *Billy Budd* (1965), which involved the turning (in College Hall) of a four-square proscenium 'into a heavy creaking ship of the line'; *Macbeth* (1966), 'a well disciplined and original production' according to J.K. Richards of the *Hereford Times*; and T.S. Eliot's *Murder in the Cathedral* (1967), performed in the cathedral itself. These productions (in Richards' words) were all 'dominated by the director's personality', but what made them really memorable was not simply their increasing professionalism but the involvement of large numbers of boys and girls (including in 1967 a chorus of ten 'women of Canterbury' from the training college) as actors, with masters and many others as managers, technicians, stage hands and backroom-staff. The total complement was rarely less than 50 and in 1966 exceeded 100 people. There can have been few schools of a similar size in the Sixties that could have produced as notable a theatrical education on such slender resources.

By contrast, creativity in Art and Music was in its infancy. A succession of part-time Art masters had done little to encourage the development of the subject. Art exhibitions became a feature of the speech day programme but it was not until the 1967 display,

188. It was not the first time that the school produced an in-house publication in this period. For details of 'The Bugle', a news-sheet produced by two enterprising 13-year-olds, Dudley Ankerson and John Williamson, together with a photograph of the boys: *HT*, 14 Feb. 1962.

when 250 works in a variety of media were displayed, that we have evidence of something worthwhile being produced despite the technical limitations. In the light of that exhibition, what might be called the school's first Art manifesto was published. However, Rix's hope that Art at HCS would achieve the status it enjoyed at other schools, 'and that it will come to play its full part in the education of the complete man', was not realised during Peebles' tenure.[189] In Music, there were hardly the resources to produce a quality concert. Music appreciations groups fell in popularity – the old Gramophone Society, for example, did not survive Rowe's first departure in December 1957 – and piano and recorder were the only instruments taught. The 1964 inspectors spied five school pianos but found that instrumental resources did 'not amount to orchestral strength', although a four part choir of 30 was by then in existence and later a senior madrigal group, with Sixth-formers from the Girls' High School, was formed. By the end of the period, as the May 1967 carol concert indicates, ensemble playing was also being developed but the Hereford youth orchestras benefited more from such talent available than the school itself.[190]

With other pastimes there was little continuity. The golden age of hobbies was drawing to a close. The Photographic Society continued until Dennis Mack left in December 1962. The Railway Club survived a little longer until the summer of 1964, by which time, in the age of Dr Beeching, making model railways and visiting locomotive depots held less of an appeal. Similarly, the Cycling Club, which had started in September 1958 as a Sixth-form alternative to rugby, foundered four years later, put paid to by other sports, influenza and exams. The Antiquarian Society (formed in October 1961) died within a couple of years, although its descendant, the Local History Society, was still going strong at the end of this period. Other new societies sprang up: for bridge and squash players and even, for a short time, anglers. Yet others were resurrected, notably the change ringers for a few years from 1962, inspired no doubt by its past master's record length peal of over 40,000 changes.[191] Following its restoration in 1965, the Debating Society also resumed its activities with considerable enthusiasm, again drawing wide audiences which often included pupils not normally engaged in extra-curricular activities. Throughout most of this period of pastime turbulence, the Chess Club continued to provide a valuable service, as did the Cathedral Junior Friends, fortified by their annual summer outings which were uninterrupted between 1952 and 1966.

Even the corps, which remained an important part of the school's corporate life, changed its practices. At the national level, there was a time of uncertainty following the abolition of National Service and a fear that school CCFs might become little more than vocational classes for potential officers. In 1962-63, however, the aims were redefined to emphasise the development of 'qualities of endurance, resourcefulness, self-reliance, leadership and responsibility and a sense of public service' among all cadets.[192] HCS adapted well to this

---

189. See *TH*, CCXIII (March 1968), pp.35-36, for a description of the exhibition and Rix's plea.

190. It should be pointed out, however, that in this period the school helped nurture the talents of Michael Hankinson and Noel Davies, both of whom were to become distinguished professional musicians.

191. John Eisel rang the fourth in the peal of Plain Bob Major at the Loughborough Bell Foundry on 17 July 1963, a feat which took 18 hours ringing to complete.

192. *HMC 1962 Report*, pp.57ff (especially p.68), debate on the future of the school CCF.

change of direction. As well as developing specialist units – to the signals section was added a civil defence group in the late 1950s and an engineers' troop (from January 1960) – there was a renewed emphasis on arduous training. The school's adoption in autumn 1959 of the Duke of Edinburgh's award scheme within the CCF programme, gave an added impetus to expeditioning, and by the time of Sir John Hunt's visit on 11 May 1960, many boys were competing for these awards, the first 'golds' being won by five boys in the summer of 1961.[193] And when the number of recruits began to decline in the mid-Sixties, Peebles replaced the regular 'barrack square parade' with three short field days per term. A weekly instruction hour after school on Fridays enabled the syllabus requirements for the military tests to be met. These reforms, together with the establishment of an RAF section, authorised from 12 January 1967, enabled the corps to survive.[194]

There was, therefore, a considerable change in the nature of these voluntary activities over the decade. As masters moved on some societies waned; as new men arrived, so the enthusiasms of another generation were kindled and new clubs were formed. Fashions, too, changed: by 1967, practical hobby clubs were less in evidence than ten years earlier; by then, the Science Society was giving way to the Arts and the CCF had adapted its practices. More opportunities were provided for outward bound activities, and not simply within the corps. From as early as May 1957, Peebles allowed each Ascension Day to be used for outings, sometimes organised by the boys themselves, after a morning cathedral service. And as the day element became stronger so meeting times altered to a spot after school rather than in the evening. Exams also intervened so that it became more difficult to convene a society in the summer term. This was especially so from 1965 when, much to Peebles' consternation, the schedules of most Boards were brought forward so that all GCEs could be completed by the end of June.[195] Not that this mattered to every boy, as the periodic references to 'trade unionist' attitudes, pupil laziness and indifference in *The Herefordian's* editorials testify. And even Peebles worried about the boredom that could set in, particularly among 'the undistinguished rank and file' in the Fourth Forms and Lower Sixth when examinations seemed a long way off.[196] Yet for those who wished to get involved, and not least the sportsmen, life was more than full enough.

The athletes, especially, were better organised and took longer strides during this period. John Brookes' reorganisation of athletic competition in the latter part of the spring term was a key element in this development. His introduction of an inter-House standards competition in 1958 revitalised the athletics season, as did the replacement of the throwing the cricket ball and the tug-of-war competitions by the javelin, discus and shot. These

193. The boys were: R.J.S. Blackhall, C. Chambers, I. Fairley, S.F.M. Kings and J.K. Webb. By 1965, 55 boys were taking part in the scheme within and outside the corps.

194. In 1966 its future was in doubt. The governors were not in favour of a compulsory corps 'even for a limited time' (GMB1945-82, p.178, 10 Feb. 1966), but by November of that year Peebles could report to them that: 'The experiment which I have made to try and keep the CCF in being seems to be working quite well'. The corps' strength was around 100 by September 1967, about 23 fewer than at the end of 1961-62.

195. Peebles held that there was no justification for this on educational grounds, and that it had been first instigated by the Board of Trade to help stagger summer holidays. HCSA, governors' report, 8 Feb. 1965.

196. For example (for the editorials): *TH*, NS CLXXXXV (Nov. 1957), p.2; CCI (Oct. 1960), p.3; CCV (May 1964), pp.3-4. And for the Headmaster's worries: HCSA, Peebles' report to the governors, 8 June 1964.

reforms meant improved fitness levels and greater numbers being involved in the athletics programme. Despite the continuance of sports day in late March, when conditions were far from ideal,[197] the end result was an improvement in performance. Records were regularly set – as with A.T. Foxton's 1960 mile and 880 yards times, which broke records which had stood for over 50 years – so that by 1967 only a handful of pre-war records remained.[198] Cross-country, too, was reinvigorated. Entrants for 'the Hull' increased annually until reaching an unprecedented 276 runners (junior and senior) in 1963, with record times being set in 1962-63.[199] Inter-school fixtures were again organised and teams entered for the schools and county championships.

If it was something of a golden age for record-breaking in track and field, it is not obvious that the same could be said for other sports. The school's performance in rowing, in particular, lacked consistency, and the judgement on the 1967 first crew that it 'was never able to achieve a standard of skill and control sufficient to provide a good performance on demand' could well be applied to the rowing in general over this decade. Few pots were won and there were only occasional triumphs, such as the beating of the Monmouth and King's, Worcester, first boats in 1962 and 1964 respectively, and the creditable row in the schools' head of the river race at Putney in 1967. Nevertheless, there were significant developments in the sport. The most important of these, with the aid of the magnificent new facilities opened at the Hereford rowing club on Whit Sunday 1958,[200] was the move to rowing in eights. This was not without its problems. In an eight rather than a four, it was more difficult to find a sufficiency of quality rowers of the right stature; there were fewer suitable local regattas; and costs were greater. Nevertheless, by the end of the period better equipment ('spade' blades and a new £500 'shell') had been acquired and the 1967 first eight was hailed as the best for some years, even if at less than 11 stone per man it was lighter than all its opponents. And throughout the period, 60 or more boys could be seen on the water on Wednesday and Saturday afternoons. Fully half of them could expect to represent HCS in the eight summer regattas which, despite the pressure of public examinations, still formed the core of the school's rowing programme.

The traditional team games, as the Headmaster was fond of saying, could often be David against Goliath contests. This applied particularly to rugby, where the first team was exposed, in an era of no substitutes for injuries, to four or five fixtures annually against tough

---

197. Although no sports was cancelled in this period, the 1964 event was postponed to late April, the standards competition was abandoned in the fierce winter of 1963 and frequently the weather was poor either for standards, sports day or both.

198. Foxton's times in 1960 were 4 min. 46.4 secs. for the mile and 2 min. 9.8 secs. for the 880 yards, surpassing records which had stood since 1896 and 1906 respectively. Five early records still stood in 1967: open (senior) 100 yards (10.4 secs., H.L. Coath 1895), 440 yards (53.8 secs., W.R. Hereford 1906), Long jump (20 ft. 6 ins., A.F. Wilding 1862); under 15s 100 yards (11.4 secs., T.M. Ragg 1911), High jump (4 ft. 11½ ins., E. Bourdas 1898). When throwing the cricket ball was abandoned after the 1957 sports, despite A. Howgate's best efforts that year, A.W. Brodie's record 1869 throw of 110 yds. 2 ft. 6 ins. remained unbeaten, although (as *The Herefordian*) put it: 'perhaps in 1869 the wonders of Science had not unfolded to sports officials the accuracy of the measuring tape'.

199. In 1962, for the Senior and Junior Hull respectively, by R.J. Rowlands (24 mins. 53 secs.) and M.H. Blott (17 mins.12.7 secs.); and in 1963, for the junior Hull by E.E. Cronin (17 mins. 6.8 secs.).

200. The development, which cost £40,000, was opened by Mrs H.J. Hammonds, who referred to the club-house as the most modern in Europe. *HT*, 28 May 1958, p.1.

Welsh sides: Christ College, Brecon; Cardiff High School; West Monmouth, Pontypool; and Monmouth (to 1960), Newport High School (to 1963) or Llandovery College (from 1964). If the 1st XV won any of these matches, they were doing well; if they won half of their 12 fixtures in a season and scored more points overall than their opponents – as in 1958 and 1963, when Don Theakston took over the team – they had enjoyed a very good season. It was the same with the junior sides, although they generally fared better than the seniors. Cricket, although it did not dominate the summer term as it once had done – the abbreviated cricket scores published in the magazine from 1958 being an indication of both its relative decline and increased printing costs – was the stronger game in this period. The 1st XI won more matches than it lost in five seasons (1957, 1963-65 and 1967), the biggest number of wins being the seven recorded in 1957, when the Headmaster had the satisfaction in the penultimate fixture of gaining a leg-before decision against the captain, R.B. Brown, the best bat of the period.[201] Matches for the seconds and two colts XIs, increased, numbering around 35 each season between the four teams. In two seasons all four won more matches than they lost, the colts being undefeated in 1963 and the junior colts in 1965.

Not that winning was everything but victories were 'nice now and then', as Peebles observed at the 1964 Old Herefordians dinner. This was at the end of a rugby season which – even though the school had not adapted to the new offside laws (introduced to encourage open play) as well as some of its opponents – saw all four teams defeat King's, Worcester, on the same afternoon. But what was even more important was the vigour and enthusiasm shown by the boys. 'That is what counts', he told parents in 1962. 'It reflects the quality both of the boys and the masters who devote so much time and energy to help'. And on the games field such qualities were invariably displayed.

Overall, the facilities for sport improved, as did the variety of games played. At Wyeside, following the project undertaken by the River Wye Board in 1959, the 'duck pond' was drained and four rugby pitches became available for regular use. In that year, too, a new chain fence was erected along the length of the two fields and 12 flowering trees were planted. Some six years later, 36 Italian poplars were interspersed between these trees to screen 'the extensive housing development' across the river. A second cricket pitch was laid in time for the 1961 season. And while the old wooden pavilion, vulnerable as it was to damage by floods and hooligans, was little more than shored up, by 1967 the foundations of a new one had been laid. By then, the fives courts had been roofed in, lighted and re-plastered, which made them usable in the evenings and the wet, just at the time (in late 1965) when the game's popularity was waning. Improvements at Wyeside and in school did not necessarily lead to enhanced performances. Nevertheless, by the end of the period there was greater variety in the school's games programme, especially for senior boys. Athletics was available for increasing numbers in the summer term; squash was regularly played from October 1964 on the new Whitecross courts; and in February 1968, a House sevens

201. Brown scored 538 runs that season at an average of 48.91, by far the highest annual aggregate and average over the 11 seasons, 1957-67. Peebles put himself down as no. 11 (he did not bat) but opened the bowling for the Headmaster's XI – the last time the fixture was played in this era – his figures being 1 for 25. The name of the umpire who gave the decision in his favour is not recorded.

competition (involving 176 boys) was held at Wyeside for the first time. There may not have been something for everyone but more games were being played, and perhaps enjoyed, than ever before.

A Landmark Tenure

It was a poignant end to Autumn Term 1967, and for the nine masters who remembered Hopewell's death, it must have seemed like history repeating itself. Like his predecessor, Peebles was unexpectedly taken ill shortly before half-term; and as in 1956, the Second Master became acting Headmaster.[202] Apart from the boys' enforced silence in the vicinity of Number 1, where the Headmaster lay dying, the term was completed as though nothing much had happened. On the actual day of his death, Friday 15 December 1967, *Murder in the Cathedral* continued its run; and the Debating Society entertained the Girls' High School to a joint debate, the motion condemning modern youth 'for succumbing to pop culture' narrowly being carried. The day after, the Old Herefordian rugby match took place, despite the outbreak of foot and mouth – the school lost by 21 points – and the OH dinner was held; and on the following Monday there was the annual service of lessons and carols. There must have been a sombre tone to all these proceedings. Term ended with the Headmaster's funeral on Tuesday 19 December.

The cathedral was filled from end to end that day, a mark of the esteem in which the Headmaster was held and his friends' sense of loss at his untimely passing. Among the packed congregation were the Lord Lieutenant, the governors, all 23 masters, diocesan and educational representatives, the Headmaster of Westminster and other HMC and local Heads, and many parents, pupils and Old Herefordians. At the front were the nine family mourners: Anna, his wife; their three children; his brother, who had played cricket for England, and sister-in-law; his sister, who taught the Eton choristers, and two nieces. In the service, the choristers sang the 23rd Psalm, which the Headmaster had learned by heart in early childhood, and Dean Price gave a moving eulogy. Few people, he said, had served the school more loyally: James Ross Peebles had lived, worked, thought, planned and almost breathed the school and it had prospered; a tribute later amplified in *The Herefordian*, which held that his headmastership would stand 'as another clear landmark in the long history of the school'.[203]

James Peebles' death at the early age of 58 was a tragedy for his family and a set-back for the school. Like his immediate predecessors, he had worn himself out in its service: more than 30 terms in charge had taken its toll. As photographs show, he had changed from a young looking 47-year-old on his arrival to a man who less than ten years later had prematurely aged. But despite the ravages of time, he had kept the promise he made to Old Herefordians in 1957 that he would do what he could for their old school; and what he could was a considerable work.

---

202. J.W. Rowlands, the Deanery Housemaster, had only taken over as Second Master in September, following P.G.S. Baylis' retirement. The first indication of Peebles' illness had been the paralysis he had experienced at his silver wedding anniversary party. Half-term that year was from 3 to 9 November.

203. *HT*, 22 Dec. 1967, p.17; *TH*, CCXIII (March 1968), p.5. I am indebted to Jillie Steele and Charles Peebles for some of the details which appear in this paragraph and the preceding note.

It was not achieved by popularity. Peebles was not as well-loved as Hopewell. Younger pupils feared visiting his study; his uninvited presence in Common Room caused resentment; and some old boys found him off-hand. Despite his gregarious nature, generous hospitality and great 'style', there was something about his well-bred gentility and patrician manner which did not always endear him to Herefordians.[204] But he was also misunderstood. More enlightened than he appeared, he was a firm believer in the precepts of a liberal and well-rounded education. Some perceived him as trying to turn the Cathedral School into a Westminster of the Marches. Yet Peebles used his Westminster connections to the school's advantage. Inviting friends and former colleagues as guests of honour at commemoration and speech day – both of which occasions he resurrected – helped raise the school's profile. These connections could also be useful behind the scenes, as in 1962 when one of them was instrumental in giving advice about the new Nuffield Physics course.[205]

Peebles worked hard to foster good relations between the school and the local community. As an accomplished wordsmith with a keen sense of humour, he was in demand as a preacher and after-dinner speaker, whether at a harvest festival at Kilpeck, a Burns night supper or the High School PTA, where shortly after his arrival in Hereford he had stressed the importance of establishing a close co-operation between home and school. It was not long before he had introduced parents' receptions at his new school, a timely and well-appreciated innovation. The maintenance of friendly relationships with the cathedral also bore fruit at a time when the Dean and Chapter's influence on school policy was still preponderant.[206] One obvious result was the school's increasing use of the nave rather than the Lady Chapel: first for the new special services (often with guest preachers) on All Saints, Ash Wednesday and Ascension Day, and then, from the summer term 1962, for morning assemblies.

As has been shown, during the Peebles decade, the school's work ethic and general academic standards improved; it became a school of greater freedom with a more varied corporate life; and its pastoral care systems were more effectively organised through the appointment of additional day tutors, the system of regular meetings between tutor and tutee being recognised by the 1964 inspectors as a 'notable feature' of school life. As we have seen, too, its buildings on both sides of Castle Street were transformed and its playing fields were drained and screened.

This is not to suggest that HCS was more secure in 1967 than it had been or that it did not suffer from structural weaknesses. Financially, the school's position was not much stronger than it had been a decade earlier. Despite the expansion in the pupil roll and the rise in fees, tuition income could not keep pace with the increase in teachers' salaries.[207]

204. For an unfavourable account of one of Peebles' dinner parties: Rowe, p.49.

205. HCSA, Peebles' report to the governors, 20 Nov. 1962. The former colleague was at that time Head of Science at Rugby School.

206. The size of the governing body was determined by the scheme of 3 February 1953, which provided for a board of six representative governors: three from the Dean and Chapter, two from the county council and one from the city council. The Dean continued to act as chairman.

207. Teachers' salaries (including the Headmaster and part-time staff) more than doubled: from £18,646 11s in 1957-58 to £38,083 4s in 1966-67. The deficit on the school fees account (the difference between tuition income and teachers' salaries) rose from £5,364 in 1957-58 to £12,454 in 1966-67.

Boarding made a surplus in only three years during this period and became increasingly less profitable through the Sixties, there being an alarming loss on the boarding account of over £3,500 in 1966-67.[208] Overall, the school traded at a profit in only four years (1958-59, 1961-64), its bank overdraft increasing each year from 1964 to 1967 when it totalled over £7,000. Two bright spots in the shape of the Philpotts charity and a potential legacy did something to relieve the general financial gloom. Throughout the period, most of the £600 annual rent for the lease of Number 28 High Town to Boots had been transferred from Philpotts to the school's main account. In 1966, the governors took the decision to sell the property, the school's last remaining substantial asset, £39,000 being raised from the sale that October. In the short term, at least, it was a sensible move, the money being reinvested for future developments. Secondly, Arthur Zimmerman's death on 10 March 1963 held out the prospect of a substantial windfall. Although this was not to be realised in Peebles' life-time, the legacy eventually became of inestimable value to the school and established Zimmerman as our greatest benefactor in modern times.[209] (Plate 19). Of more immediate concern for the school's financial stability, as has been indicated, was the political threat to its direct grant, worth nearly £35,000 in 1966-67, over half the school's total income. The threat had been seen off for the time being but it was an ever-present concern for Peebles' successor.

If the school's finances were precarious, its organisational structure also left much to be desired. Despite plans to enlarge the board, the school was governed throughout this period by only six men, of whom three were Dean and Chapter representatives. This was too small a body for a growing school and did not ensure a sufficiently wide spectrum of expertise. With such a small number, moreover, there was always the possibility of a rapid turn-over of a good proportion of its members as happened in the early Sixties with the changes in Chapter.[210] Even though (as the inspectors recognised) the governors met regularly, were 'keenly interested' in the school and enjoyed the Headmaster's confidence, Peebles was at times both disappointed with the poor turn-out and frustrated that his requests for strategy meetings went unheeded. And so a disproportionate burden fell on the shoulders of the 'works manager', as Peebles once described himself.

In truth, the school's staff infrastructure was painfully thin. In February 1962, besides the Headmaster, the administrative and maintenance strength amounted to four: a part-time secretary, an accounts clerk (also part-time), a non-resident caretaker and boiler-man – who lived three miles out and was coming up to his 65th birthday – and an unskilled groundsman. As Peebles informed his governors:

---

208. The surplus years were: 1957-58, 1959-60 and 1961-62. For the years in which separate accounts are available (1957-64), the Old Deanery ran at a profit (£1,076) whereas School House, which was more expensive to run in that it included Number 1, lost £2,703.

209. Despite this, a badly drawn will meant that three-fifths of his estate was taken up in death duties; and his legacy to the OH Club was realised much later than it might have been. For all this: HCSA, P.H. Williams file, especially the copy letter from T. Pennington to Miss C. Whiting, 7 Dec. 1965; and below, note 333.

210. Dean Burrows wrote to the Ministry of Education on 27 March 1961 to enquire about how the governing body might best be enlarged while ensuring that the Dean and Chapter representatives were in the majority. The proposal for additional governors was revived in 1966 but not implemented until 1 November 1971. HCSA, typed copy letter from the Ministry to the Dean, 7 Apr. 1961; HCA, 7031/25, 26 July 1966; below, p.513.

> Our difficulties were underlined this term when both caretaker and groundsman were ill and of course we have no reserves of labour. It does mean, as I have stressed on previous occasions, that a great deal centres on the Headmaster beyond his duties as such. One finds oneself performing the duties of bursar, caretaker and general dogsbody. When things are running smoothly we just manage ... but when the teaching staff are absent or the caretaker etc., the situation becomes difficult and one has the fear that one's more important duties ... may suffer through lack of time or sheer weariness of the flesh and spirit ... I think the governors should realise how very near the margin we operate.

The appointment of a fuller-time secretary and (from September 1964) a 30-year-old former merchant seaman as resident caretaker and laboratory assistant eased the situation, but the governors did nothing to remedy the 'rather unusual arrangement' (as the inspectors saw it) of a Headmaster-bursar with his wife as domestic supervisor.[211]

The final word about HCS during this decade should be left to the man who through his 'sturdy persistence' did more than anyone else to move the school forward – despite the weaknesses still evident in 1967 – into the second half of the twentieth century. 'What gives me great hopes for the future', he declared to the Old Herefordians in December 1957, 'is that there is plenty of vitality in the school and vitality is the main essential. If there is life, you can do something'. Or as he told parents in July 1962: 'My criterion for judging a school [is] what can it do for the average boy to develop the best in him. The quality I would like to see above all is vitality. Is the school alive? Is it doing things, not necessarily winning?' By this measure alone, the new opportunities James Peebles helped provide for learning – in its widest sense – made his headmastership of lasting significance.

David Michael Richards, 1968-1975

For the second time in a generation, the school faced the prospect of an interregnum following the serious illness and premature death of its Headmaster. As in 1956, the Second Master succeeded as acting Headmaster from halfway through the autumn term. John Rowlands, however, had himself been in office as Peebles' right hand man for only a few weeks before his elevation from 1 November 1967.[212] It was the beginning of a challenging year for the first scientist ever to assume the headship.

New as he was to high office, as a forthright Welshman with a powerful voice, Rowlands was tougher and temperamentally better suited to the role than Bell had been a decade earlier. And by 1967, he was also an experienced schoolmaster. Appointed in 1950, after four years in the RAF and a further four at Rutlish School, at the princely annual salary of £465 – a higher point on the scale than warranted because Hopewell considered him 'valuable', as indeed he was given the Headmaster's desperate search for Science teachers in

211. HCSA, Peebles' report to the governors, 16 Feb. 1962. The groundsman, who helped out with the CCF, was (Sgt) W. Matthews; and the old caretaker, described by Peebles as 'a treasure in every way', Jim Brown. Mrs Cooper, who replaced Mrs Newey in April 1963, was still technically part-time, although the pay of the Headmaster's secretary increased from £6 5s to £8 per week on her appointment. The new caretaker, 'Jock' Adamson, resided at 77 East Street, living there until his retirement some 35 years later. His emolument on appointment was £12 per week, the groundsman's wage being increased to that amount in November 1965.

212. HCSA, GMB 1945-82, p.190, 2 Jan. 1968.

the late 1940s – Rowlands had established Biology as an Advanced Science subject within the curriculum. Later he was given responsibility for advising on careers and organising public examinations. And in 1965 the Headmaster had awarded him one of the few plums in his orchard, the housemastership of the Old Deanery. Peebles considered Rowlands to be 'very able' and a natural successor two years later to P.G.S. Baylis as Second Master.[213]

Fig. 8.11 John Rowlands, who introduced Advanced Biology to HCS and was an effective acting Headmaster, 1967-68.

Taking charge of the school, however, was a different matter and Rowlands' ride, which was to last for two-and-a-half terms, was not an easy one. There was the immediate problem of maintaining the school's morale and efficiency during Peebles' last weeks and the uncertainties as to how the domestic side would be managed after his death, although like her predecessor his widow did the school inestimable service in agreeing to continue to reside in Number 1 and administer the house boarding and the general catering for another two terms. And then there were the inevitable magisterial problems and the peculiar worries associated with running a direct grant school to be faced. Let us take just a few examples. Within days of his taking over, some boys were accused of hooliganism on Widemarsh Common, prompting unwanted headlines in the local press;[214] for other reasons, two members of staff had to be moved on and three more resigned, leaving an unusual number of new men to be appointed for September 1968;[215] there were indications that the direct grant would be cut by £20 per boy from September 1968; losses continued to be made on school 'dinners', which remained fixed (by the government) at the January 1964 price of 1s 3d, even though food cost had risen by some 20 *per cent* since then; and the fall in boarding numbers appeared to be an increasing trend.[216]

But the school's latest projects progressed. The new day boy changing rooms were completed early in the New Year, and the latest pavilion, following the authorisation of the spending of £12,000 on its construction, was well advanced by the summer of 1968.

---

213. Rowlands also had the benefit of being 'on the spot': HCSA, Peebles' report to the governors, 9 Feb. 1967. Baylis died suddenly in December 1970, having spent part of his short retirement transcribing the cathedral's sixteenth century Act books, to the benefit of numerous scholars (including the present author). His three volumes of transcripts are held in the cathedral library.

214. *HT*, 17 Nov. p.18; 8 Dec. 1967, p.21.

215. A.E. Rowe and G.G. Williams were both advised to leave; W.R. Marsh and J.A. Streule left for posts at Shrewsbury and Epsom respectively; and D.W. Rix returned to Rhodesia.

216. On these issues: HCSA, Rowlands' report to the governors, 9 Feb. 1968.

Fig. 8.11 David Richards: a Headmaster whose introduction of co-education in the early 1970s was crucial to the school's future development.

School life, moreover, continued unscathed. The fact that this happened with the minimum of disruption was in large part due to the acting Headmaster, the governors appropriately recording their appreciation of his services in their minute book. This was later publicly acknowledged, Dean Price, presiding at his last speech day on 12 July 1968, recognising John Rowlands' 'efficiency and cheerfulness' in shouldering the burden of the headship. 'It was largely due to him', he continued, 'that what might have been a difficult time had in fact passed so smoothly'.[217] And Rowlands left a tolerably full school of 359 pupils (including 124 boarders) – 58 boys having been admitted for the autumn term 1968, a number on a par with previous autumnal entries – and a younger and reinvigorated Common Room for his new Headmaster.

Meanwhile, the governors lost little time in expediting the search for Peebles' permanent successor. Five of them met on the second day of 1968 'to consider the circumstances arising from the death of the Headmaster'. Advertisements for the vacancy were placed in *The Times* and *The Times Educational Supplement* and a special governors' meeting was called for 19 February. At that gathering, which included the presence of Donald Lindsay, Headmaster of Malvern College and Chairman of The Headmasters' Conference, 'in an advisory capacity', the decision was made to interview eight candidates on 6 March. The interviews were to be held in the Dean's study, followed by a buffet lunch in College Hall 'to which wives should be invited'. On the appointed day, three candidates underwent a second interview in the afternoon, and the post was offered to David Richards, subject to his wife (unavoidably absent 'having recently given birth to a son') undertaking the school catering for at least a year. Richards immediately accepted the position, no doubt reassured by the governors' promise that after a year the catering arrangements could be reviewed.[218] At 36, he was the school's youngest Headmaster of the century.

The governors had chosen wisely. Tall and good looking; relatively youthful and energetic; and a former Bishop's Chorister at Salisbury, Cheltenham College boy, Cambridge

217. HCSA, GMB1945-82, p.191, 9 Feb. 1968; p.197, 13 June 1968; *TH*, CCXV (March 1969), p.6.

218. HCSA, GMB 1945-82, pp.190, 193, 194, minutes of meetings on 2 Jan., 19 Feb. and 6 March 1968. John Rowlands applied for the post but was not interviewed. The eight short-listed candidates were: E.H.S. Dillon, B. Fielding, R.C. Giles, C.J. Grimwade, P.K. Ledger, J.W. Phillips, D.M. Richards and R.A. Stobbs. Dillon, Richards and Stobbs were given second interviews.

graduate, and Haileybury Housemaster, who had seen service in Germany as a second lieutenant in the Royal Horse Artillery and had captained Wiltshire at cricket, David Richards was well suited to the post. Above all as a reformer, he was just the man needed to run a direct grant school in difficult times. He was, as Dean Price publicly confirmed: 'a dedicated master who would value the traditions of the school and be open to new ideas of the time'.[219]

Challenge and Opportunity

David Richards' magisterial tenure was the second shortest of the twentieth century but it encompassed a period of considerable turbulence in the independent school and wider world. The years from 1968 to 1975 were indeed a momentous time to be a head teacher, especially of a selective school. Over 30 years after he had left, Richards himself acknowledged the challenges posed by his period in Hereford. Describing a short but influential visit he and the new Dean made to Church House to see Sir Hubert Ashton – a Church Commissioner, Chairman of the Direct Grant Joint Committee and one of the famous Ashton cricketing brothers – he accurately remembered the time as one of 'uncertainty, challenge and change'.[220] For events tested his and his colleagues' skills, the governors' resolve and the school's resources to the full.

Dean Price, presiding at his last speech day in July 1968, had expressed his confidence in the school's future. It was important that the assembled company heard this optimistic message but there were no guarantees that the school would survive in a hostile political climate. As we have seen, despite declarations of intent, the Labour government had allowed schools to retain their grants pending the deliberations of the public schools' commission. The Newsome report, published in the summer before the new Headmaster came into office, was encouraging in so far as it accepted the partnership of independent and maintained schools. But the task of reviewing the principle of central funding for direct grant schools and advising the government as to how they might participate in the move towards comprehensive status, was the subject of a separate enquiry. And Professor Donnison's response in the second report, published on 24 March 1970, sounded the early death knell of the direct grant system.[221] The Conservatives' unexpected General Election victory three months later gave the schools only a temporary respite. As an educational correspondent put it in late March 1971: 'Without some bold new thinking, the direct grant schools are doomed, even though now reprieved for a season'.[222] Although the day remission scale was made more generous and capitation grants were increased, this was no more than tinkering with

219. *HT*, 19 July 1968, p.13, report of Dean Price's 12 July speech.

220. HCSA, Richards to the author, 10 Aug. 2007. The meeting ended 'with a clarity of conclusion I have seldom experienced', the pair being advised to extend the governing body, appoint a bursar and launch an appeal. I have not been able to find a contemporary record but the meeting may have taken place in the summer of 1970 following the strong letter from the DES about the state of the school's finances. See below, p.512.

221. Donnison recommended that day direct grant schools 'must participate in the movement towards comprehensive reorganisation in some way that accords with local needs and plans'; that the arrangements must be worked out between the schools and the LEAs on terms approved by the Secretary of State; and that no fees should be charged in such schools. *Report on Independent Day Schools and Direct Grant Grammar Schools*, (HMSO 1970), p.108.

222. *Times Educational Supplement*, 26 March 1971, as quoted in *HMC 1971 Committee Report*, p.45.

the system: bold initiatives for the independent sector were not a priority, even for a Tory administration with Margaret Thatcher as the responsible Secretary of State. And hostility to direct grant schools in some areas was unabated as indicated by the reluctance of some primary Heads to recommend them to their pupils, the continued widespread opposition to selection and the refusal of certain local authorities to take up their allocation of places.[223]

With the return of a Labour government in early March 1974, it was only a question of when, not if, direct grant schools would go. It was not long coming, the government announcing its intention the following March to withdraw direct grants from September 1976, while safeguarding the position of those pupils already in receipt of a grant. The mass lobbying of MPs and a big rally of direct grant supporters in Westminster Central Hall in late June 1975 made little practical difference; nor, locally, did David Richards' impassioned defence of the system.[224] Since 1945, the direct grant system had enabled HCS to establish a strong partnership with the maintained sector to the mutual benefit of both parties at a time of shortage of appropriate secondary places in maintained local schools. But by 1975 there was no chance of the policy to abolish direct grants being reversed.

To meet just such circumstances, the governors had decided as early as 28 May 1970 to opt for independence.[225] Following this momentous decision, Richards' headship was dominated by measures to strengthen the school in preparation for this eventuality. As has been shown, HCS had been given a breathing space for several years by the rotation of the national political compass but it was also aided by the local political situation. Relations with the local authority remained cordial and the ten free county places continued throughout the period, although in June 1972 the LEA decided against increasing their number and making the places available beyond the High School catchments.[226] When the 11 plus was abolished, the school administered its own entrance examination for the county places, resulting in the record entries of 165, 185 and 195 candidates respectively for around 50 places annually for the three years from 1973 to 1975. But following the merger of Herefordshire and Worcestershire on 1 April 1974 and the retirement of Maurice Edge as Director of Education that July, and given the anticipated capacities of the county's comprehensive schools, the governors' hope that the local arrangement might continue 'in places where primary school heads or the authority consider it advantageous' was an unlikely one in the longer term.[227]

223. The Inner London Education Authority, Surrey and Exeter are examples. In 1972-73, Birkenhead School Governors were even driven to sue (successfully as it turned out) their local authority for breach of contract. *Ibid.*, p.4; *HMC 1973 Committee Report*, p.60.

224. *HT*, 4 July, p.9; 18 July 1975, p.15. See also the hostile letters of Stephen Williams and others, and the supportive ones of Barbara Cooper, Alan Morris and R.B. Boddington. *Ibid*, 11 July, p.9; 18 July, p.15; 25 July, p.9; 8 Aug. 1975, p.9.

225. HCSA, GMB 1945-82, p.215: 'The implications of the report of the Donnison Commission were considered and it was decided, if necessary, to continue Hereford Cathedral School as an independent school'.

226. The scheme was scotched partly through the opposition of the socialist mayor, Joan Prendergast, a former HCS parent. *HT*, 21 Jan. 1972, p.1; 30 June 1972, p.11.

227. HCSA, D.M. Richards to M.J. Gifford, 25 March and Gifford's reply of 16 May 1975. E.H.G. Moreton, a county representative governor, felt that a strong protest was necessary because 'an approved and authorised system of education in Herefordshire was being superseded without proper discussion at Council level'. GMB 1945-82, p.289, 18 June 1975. For the authority's abandonment of county places at HCS, see below, p.536.

Richards' challenge, however, was not just the political one. The actual business of headship in the late Sixties and early Seventies was far harder than it had been a decade earlier: the county towns in this period were 'catching up' with the bigger cities in terms of youth culture, much to the horror of many middle-aged parents and schoolteachers. Although the Cathedral School did not have the problems of 'walk-outs' and 'sit-ins' experienced by some Hereford educational establishments, Richards had to manage other problems unknown to his predecessors.[228] Two instances may be cited. In October 1969, the Head of School together with seven other senior boys, all on the Modern side and egged on by a disaffected former member of staff, signed and presented to the Headmaster a poorly typed and occasionally mis-spelt petition. This demanded an end to the monitorial system and the formation of a representative committee to be both 'a permanent channel for the conveyance of Sixth-form grievances' and a forum for the presentation of ideas, 'which will be expected to be considered very seriously indeed' ('implemented' had been crossed out), about the running of the school. 'Since the state regards 18 year olds to be sufficiently mature and responsible members of society to enfranchise them', the letter continued, 'it is reasonable that the school should treat members of the Sixth Form in a similarly adult fashion'.[229] Less than two years later, there was the food strike of 26 April 1971, which was similar to the one at the Royal Grammar School, Worcester, the previous term, when 120 boarders refused to eat their lunch as a protest against monotonous menus and 'carelessly presented food'.[230] And then in this age of growing spontaneity, informality and excess, when unauthorised applause broke out even at the Three Choirs Festival, there were the problems associated with pupils' appearance – boys' hair grew to almost shoulder length in some cases over the period – and the increasing availability of soft drugs.[231]

Equally, the school could not be isolated from the social unrest and economic uncertainties of the period. By 1968, the heady mood of optimism and glamour of the mid-Sixties had given way to a more sober outlook, crystallised by the humiliations of the pound's devaluation and de Gaulle's veto of Britain's bid to join the Common Market in November 1967. Nor, with five states of emergency in three years, did the national temper lighten in the early 1970s.[232] It was a wretched time to be an executive officer

228. For youth culture in general in the early 1970s, and the 1974 'walkout' at Haywood Comprehensive and the 'sit-in' at the College of Education in particular: Sandbrook (2011), p.327; *HT*, 8 Feb., p.2; 28 June 1974, p.22.

229. I am grateful to the late David Richards for having shown me this document which is now in the school archives. In November 1969, he informed his governors that the group 'had not counted for much'. Nevertheless, he had responded to the demand by calling an emergency staff meeting, banning the boys from seeing their former teacher and by setting up a Sixth Form council. The Girls' High School had abandoned their prefectorial system a year earlier. *HT*, 6 Dec. 1968.

230. HCSA, Richards' report to the governors, 17 June 1971. A local press report (*HT*, 30 April 1971, p.11) carried the unfortunate headline: 'Pupils go on stew strike'. Richards was quoted as having 'enjoyed' the stew. Nevertheless, he promised to investigate the complaint.

231. For the applause: HCA, 7031/25, pp.492-93, 498, Chapter minutes, 10 Sept., 25 Nov. 1969; and *HT*, 28 Aug., p.1, 25 Sept. 1970, p.12 (letter of R.S. Thompson). For pupil untidiness: HCSA, notebook of monitors' meetings, 1 March (1971). For Hereford's drugs problem and Richards' suspicion of pupil drug-taking: *HT*, 9 July 1971, p.12, 22 Oct. 1971, p.1; and HCSA, Richards' reports to the governors, 7 Nov. 1969, 9 Nov. 1971.

232. See Sandbrook, (2007) pp.427-33, 606-08; Sandbrook (2011), p.8 and *passim*.

and Richards must at times have been driven to distraction by such inconveniences as the national postal, building workers and transport strikes, random power cuts, the 90 day wage and prices 'freeze' and the oil crisis. Moreover, double digit inflation – average annual pay settlements reached 30 *per cent* and living costs rose by 25 *per cent* in Richards' last year – made annual budgeting difficult and longer term planning hazardous. In the midst of such dislocation, well might the editor of the school magazine try to lift his readers' spirits by writing this up-beat editorial to the first edition of the new-style *Herefordian* in October 1974:

> While Greeks and Turks, Arabs and Israelis do battle in the Middle East, world-wide inflation is rife, general elections come and go and pressures – both economical and political – increasingly hedge about the direct grant schools, life goes on at HCS. In contrast to the prevailing gloom, this issue of *The Herefordian* seeks to strike an optimistic note.[233]

There were other concerns which were more immediate but more readily within the school's control. Of the many issues facing the new Headmaster, the domestic situation caused him the most anxiety. Despite the efforts that had been made over the summer of 1968 to make his accommodation a little more private and comfortable, the rooms in Number 1 were hardly ideal for a young family. It took a further two years before this was resolved with the Richards' move to the Chapter property where the preparatory school had started in 1898: 5, Harley Court, which was let at the 'economic' annual rent of £450.[234] Meanwhile, there was a need to address the question of domestic staffing, which was (as the young Headmaster admitted to his governors at his first November meeting) 'the most frustrating and energy-absorbing … [problem] that we have so far had to cope with'. The governors could hardly have been surprised when they heard that Margaret Richards, her baby son only a few months old, could not manage the full responsibilities of her predecessor. These gradually lessened with the appointment in early 1969 of Mrs Woods as the resident housekeeper, and at the end of that year of Mrs Wyatt as domestic supervisor in charge of all catering and domestic cleaning. With these appointments, the unreasonable expectation that the Headmaster's wife should devote herself to the school's domestic arrangements had come to an end. And the three Ws of Woods, Wyatt and Witts (School House matron, 1968-71), Richards remembered, were 'a trio formidable enough to hold their own with Muriel Smith [the Old Deanery matron] across the great divide'.[235]

Richards himself was also freed from some of the burdens his predecessors had carried. Through his own initiative, the anomalous position of the Headmaster being nominal Housemaster of School House was immediately remedied, the resident senior tutor properly receiving the recognition together with an increased allowance. Similarly, the following year, Richards was relieved of the onerous responsibility, for which he had little inclination

233. *TH*, CCXX (Oct. 1974), p.3, R.G.N. Rhodes' editorial.

234. Together with the rent and rate free house, the Headmaster's heating, lighting and telephone bills were to be borne by the school and his salary was increased by £500 *per annum* as compensation for 'loss of amenities'. GMB 1945-82, pp.214, 216, minutes of 13 March, 28 May 1970.

235. HCSA, Richards to the author, 26 Jan. 2012.

or aptitude, for the routine supervision of the buildings, a duty which was handed over to the school architect.[236]

The further anomaly of the Headmaster managing the school's day to day finances, although less easy and more expensive to put right, desperately needed resolving. The antiquated financial system had changed little since the Chapter Clerk's agreement to account for the fees at the height of the Second World War. And even in 1968, there was not one accounts official in the school's direct employ as David Richards recollected:

> All entries in the single huge accounts ledger were made by Tom Steel's [the Chapter Clerk's] clerk, a very patient Mr Lovesy. You will not be surprised to hear that the words 'miscellaneous expenditure' were commonly heard in ... [his] office, and that the column of that name provoked the occasional enquiry at governors' meetings.[237]

In practice this meant that the Headmaster's financial role was significant, there being no bursar. Richards' early governors' reports reveal the extent of that responsibility, the Headmaster bringing to the governors' attention such routine concerns as book and stationery expenditure, requests for equipment purchase, games costs, laboratory allowances, Housemasters' accounting (parents' bills for extra charges still being laboriously prepared by them) and the school clothing stock (handed over from Pritchards to Chadds on 3 February 1969). Consequently, governors' meetings were weighed down by consideration of these and other matters such as outstanding fees. There was no finance subcommittee, although occasionally an *ad hoc* one was called into existence to discuss these negligent parents and the Headmaster's salary. It was all, no doubt, very gentlemanly but quite unbusiness-like.

By the late Sixties, there was a gradual realisation among the governors, pressed hard by the Headmaster, that three gentlemen of the cloth, together with a further three representative governors and one solicitor were insufficient to guide the fortunes of a business with a turnover of over £90,000.[238] There was no single catalyst for change but the visit to Sir Hubert Ashton already described must have been influential. Sharp criticism from the Department of Education and Science in July 1970 over the governors' failure to control expenditure also played its part.[239] A year later things had not improved as David Richards' hard-hitting memorandum to his governors makes evident:

> I believe that the Clerk's task of presenting a meaningful estimate of future expenditure to the DES a reasonable time in advance is virtually impossible (hence the last

236. HCSA, Richards' report to the governors, 14 Nov. 1968; HCSA, GMB 1945-82, pp.200, 207, 210, minutes of 14 Nov. 1968, 9 Oct., 7 Nov. 1969. Peter Skinner's allowance was increased to £150 *per annum* (backdated to September 1968) and Herbert Powell's annual retainer was raised from £50 to £175 and then to £300 in 1970-71.

237. HCSA, Richards to the author, 10 Aug. 2007.

238. The school's expenditure in the three financial years 1968-71 (to the nearest £) was: £93,552; £94,573; and £99,577. It topped £100,000 the following year.

239. The department further questioned the balance between tuition and boarding fees. For Richards' anxiety about how these criticisms might affect the school's future: HCSA, letters to Dean Rathbone and Tom Steel, 3 and 7 July; and for the criticisms: HCSA, GMB 1945-82, p.219, meeting, 2 Sept. 1970.

> two years delay in writing for permission to increase fees) for two main reasons: (1) No allocation of money to various departments/functions ever takes place, except with regard to the Music department and to the bulk of the masters' salaries which are in any case governed by Burnham … (2) During a financial year, it is virtually impossible to see how money is going out – not until weeks after March 31st does one discover that (as this year and last) we are £5,000 overspent … This inability to assess or control our financial situation at any given time may be attributed to many things, among them: … the absence of meaningful budgetary figures against which to make periodic checks … the absence of adequate staff to make such checks … the fact that the Headmaster somewhat indiscriminately authorises (because someone has to) expenditure on virtually everything from bus excursions to overhead projectors, from Shirehall bookings to washing-machines … the fact that so many people are involved in the business of making our accounts. Six Housemasters are now responsible for this … and yet a seventh person, Mr Lovesy, sends the account out and receives payment from the parent.[240]

As Richards concluded, it all added up to a serious weakness in the management system: the Headmaster did not have access to the proper machinery to control the expenditure for which he was ultimately responsible.

By the time the paper was written, the means to a solution was close at hand. An enquiry as to how governor numbers might be increased had been made in 1961, and Dean Price's final advice to his fellow governors in September 1968 was that they consider expanding the board. It was not until 1 November 1971, however, that a new scheme was sealed. Prompted by the need to provide for a new constitution for the admission of Sixth-form girls, the opportunity was taken to add two co-opted governors to the representative members.[241] Dean Rathbone's new appointees could hardly have been better chosen. Sir Humphrey Mynors (whose ancestral connections with the county dated from the twelfth century) was a former director and deputy governor of the Bank of England and chairman of the Finance Corporation for Industry; and Peter Prior, then group managing director of H.P. Bulmer Ltd, was hailed locally as one of the new breed of top management to be found in British industry in the 1970s. Despite their contrasting temperaments, their wide experience and complementary professional expertise in banking and commerce made them a powerful combination.[242] Three years later they were joined by Maurice Edge, who was both the first educationalist and the first Common Room representative to sit on the

240. HCSA, 'A Memorandum on Finance', 7 June 1971. Mrs Cooper, the Headmaster's secretary, made such checks for correct entries on parental accounts as were done but her temporary absence at the beginning of that term had brought home to the Headmaster 'the absurd extent of the school's administrative reliance on one person'.

241. The scheme allowing for girl pupils also contained a clause limiting a governor's tenure to three years initially (he/she then being eligible for re-appointment), in addition to the provision of the two additional governors. HCSA, GMB 1945-82, p.227, 19 March 1971.

242. For Prior, note: *HT*, 9 Jan. 1970, p.12, 'City and County Personalities, no. 10'; and for Mynors, Richards' view that he was 'a highly respected person of good sense, practicality [and] wisdom', who 'was able to temper Peter Prior's dynamism and so ensure that we did not overreach'. HCSA, Richards to the author, 10 Aug. 2007.

board, as the third co-opted governor.[243] New life was breathed into what had been a parochial governing body.

Even before the 1971 scheme had been sealed, Humphrey Mynors was invited to join the Dean and Tom Barnes on the new finance sub-committee which spear-headed the drive for reform. It met eight times within little over a year from the inaugural meeting on 30 November 1971 and reviewed many aspects of the school's financial operation: fee levels and wages increases were scrutinised; heads of departments' estimates were examined; resources for repairs and maintenance were allocated; tenders for new projects were chosen; and (with the help of an auditor recommended by Peter Prior) budgets were revised. Most importantly, the committee was the mechanism used for a bursar's appointment. The governors made the decision on 15 February 1972 that 'under modern conditions' such an appointment was 'almost essential'. Having ascertained that the Department for Education was likely to favour the appointment and that there would be no objections on grounds of cost,[244] it was left to the finance committee to provide a job description, which eventually ran to 11 distinct areas of responsibility, and (with Peter Prior) to select the short-listed candidates. The interviews took place at a special governors' meeting on 28 June 1972, and despite the presence of a Group Captain, a Squadron Leader and two Lieutenant-Colonels on the final list, the post was offered at a salary of £2,500 to A.P. Hollingworth. As David Richards again recollected:

> Here was a trained accountant, relatively young and inexperienced alongside the other ... temptingly 'safe' choices ... But the governing body, constituted as it now was, saw that Tony [Hollingworth], while trained in accountancy and therefore at ease with books and ledgers, was also a hands-on man, and this indeed he proved to be ... The whole management set-up changed and the Headmaster could become Head-teacher.[245]

It was not quite done in the way Richards would have wanted. As early as November 1969, he had suggested that management consultants should be called in to advise over the appointment of a domestic supervisor; and again in June 1971, he had presented his governors with an article putting the case for their use in schools.[246] These requests, which

243. The change was brought about by the Charity Commissioners, who had taken over jurisdiction of educational charities from the education department. They pointed out that HCS did not accord with the 1959 direct grant school regulations which stated that there should be nine trustees on the governing body, including a third representative governor from the new Hereford and Worcester authority (rather than one of the three being appointed by the Hereford City Council) and a third co-opted governor. HCSA, Richards' agenda, 10 Sept. 1974, for a special governors' meeting; HCSA, GMB 1945-82, pp.277, 280, minutes, 23 Sept., 19 Nov. 1974.

244. At an important meeting – one of several at the DES during this period – attended by Humphrey Mynors and the Headmaster on 1 March 1972. Confirmation was also given on that occasion that the department would raise no objection to the introduction of girls at 11 plus. Mynors' memorandum of the discussion on these and other issues exists in the school archives.

245. HCSA, Richards to the author, 10 Aug. 2007.

246. J.B.C. Miller-Bakewell's article, 'Belling the Cat: The Case for School Consultants', was from the HMC *Conference* magazine. Richards attached the piece with his financial memorandum but had little hope that the governors would call in the management consultants.

might have been taken up had Peter Prior then been a governor, were not heeded and the problems were resolved piece-meal. In a haphazard way and over a three-year period, a solution was found and a new management structure implemented, banishing forever a domestic arrangement which, as the 1964 inspectors had subtly intimated, was outmoded even in Peebles' time.

It was hard work for the new bursar, despite his being given a part-time clerical assistant. For he took over all the school duties of the solicitor's office with one important exception: while in attendance at governors' meetings, he was not appointed their officer until the end of December 1974, Tom Steel's retirement that month after 36 years as both Chapter and governors' Clerk, ending the joint office which had been held by a member of his family for 135 years.[247] And in addition, he assumed all the routine daily financial work and buildings oversight previously undertaken respectively by the Headmaster and architect, as well as having the charge of all the non-teaching staff. It was a frenetic first year and (as he recollects) 'work descended from all quarters'.

> The domestic bursar's department worked well and no changes were made but daily maintenance and small repairs were considerable and a manual accounting system had to be devised and executed quickly to deal with payments for supplies and staff salaries and domestic wages. Obviously, I had to take over the preparation of bills for parents, and at the end of the first term I was up until the early hours of Christmas morning completing them.[248]

Hollingworth's memories are corroborated by the contemporary evidence. The governors' minute book and surviving accounts show the extent of the bursar's more official tasks in his first months in post: taking action on the outstanding fees list; appointing a new groundsman in Kurt Winsel at £20 per month, £3 more than old Matthews, despite his inability to prepare a decent cricket wicket; and producing for the governors, for the first time and eventually typed, schedules of non-teachers' wages and the state of the school's decoration, projected cash-flows, estimates of actual expenditure compared with budget, and proper accounts of future income and expenditure under recognisable headings in which 'miscellaneous' did not predominate. The minute book of the 1970s also shows the gradual use of a business vocabulary long common at that time in the commercial world – including, as we will see, the term 'public relations' – alongside the introduction of a more effective system of financial management.

Such innovations made an immediate difference to the bottom-line. The annual trading losses of the late Sixties and early Seventies were reversed, the school making a few hundred pounds surplus in 1972-73, despite the £30,000 overdraft agreement with Lloyd's Bank

247. Although there is a discrepancy of five years between the Chapter and governors' minutes as to the family's length of service. Compare: HCA, 7031/26, p.132, 6 Jan. 1975 (135 years); with HCSA, GMB 1945-82, p.284, 16 Jan. 1975 (140 years). The correct figure seems to have been recorded in the Chapter Acts, as suggested by Richard Underwood's appointment on 14 November 1839 as the new Chapter Clerk (HCA, 7031/19, p.458). Following Tom Steel's departure, governors' meetings were transferred from 30 Castle Street to the Zimmerman Library.

248. HCSA, Hollingworth to the author, 13 Jan. 2013.

being exceeded. Well might the governors record their congratulations to the bursar 'on getting the school finances onto a comparatively firm basis so quickly' little more than a year after his appointment. The good times, however, did not last long, the balance sheet turning from black to dark red following a £6,000 loss in 1973-74, wholly accounted for by the increase of salaries and wages under the governments' threshold payment agreement. And although a surplus of just under £500 was recorded in 1974-75, it was only achieved through a £30 parental levy as a result of the implementation and backdating of the Houghton teachers' pay award. These were exceptional years for (as the bursar explained to the governors in November 1974) in addition to the unprecedented pay rises, 'the increased cost of food, fuel and other consumable items' was also outside the school's control. At the Headmaster's final governors' meeting the following June, Hollingworth presented estimates for 1975-76 which allowed for an inflation rate of 25 *per cent*. In this tough economic climate, had the school not had the services of such an efficient and hard-working bursar, the consequences are barely imaginable.[249]

For a year after Richards' appointment, as we have seen, the routine superintendence of the fabric, like the day to day accounting, was in the Headmaster's hands. And although the plant was in much better fettle than it had been on Peebles' arrival a decade earlier, there were still grounds for concern. Number 1 roof was in a 'risky state'; the furniture in the boarding houses was shabby compared with the classroom desks; the School House bathroom was 'in such deplorable condition' that the young Headmaster was embarrassed to show it to prospective parents; and the laboratories were out of date – a visiting inspector being fascinated by an ancient fume cupboard, the like of which he had never seen before – and insufficient. Overall, the school was under resourced on all fronts.[250]

The picture was not a totally negative one, however. Like his predecessor, Richards had inherited new buildings. A day changing room had been built in the corner of the yard, and the new Wyeside pavilion, erected on a reinforced concrete frame and positioned so that it could overlook both playing fields, was nearing completion. The flood-proof pavilion was opened on 3 May 1969 with due ceremony by the Lord Lieutenant, Colonel J.F. MacLean, who used the occasion to speak about sport's eternal verities, sentiments which would have been truer of his own playing days as a gentleman first class cricketer.[251] It was also possible to do something to improve the two worst boarding houses. In 1969, the School House washrooms were renovated and its south wing replanned. And in the early Seventies, Number 1 was subject to a make-over. Following the timely move of the Headmaster and his family to Harley Court, the rooms were reordered for occupation by Egerton Parker, the new Housemaster, three boarders and two Sixth-form girls. Downstairs, the masters were given improved accommodation in the old drawing room, the former Common Room

249. For the above two paragraphs: HCSA, GMB 1945-82, pp.256ff; HCSA, Account Book 1945-72, fos 195ff; and miscellaneous income, expenditure and other accounts, 1972-75.

250. HCSA, Richards' report to governors, 14 Nov. 1968; HCSA, Richards to the author, 10 Aug. 2007.

251. This is not to downplay all of what he said; only to suggest that (sadly) some of his observations ('one may rest assured that if a man has a reputation for being a good sportsman, he is always a good Christian and a good citizen') no longer held good for the late 1960s. MacLean kept wicket for both Worcestershire (1920-22) and Gloucestershire (1930-32), and was a member of the MCC tour to Australia and New Zealand in 1922-23. For the pavilion's opening: *HT*, 9 May 1969, p.11; *TH*, CCXV (ii), p.11.

being converted into a Sixth-form English classroom. Over the next two years there were other improvements: the roof was renewed, the internal gutter removed and extra service rooms were created in the freed space.

Such improvements were necessary but expensive. The new pavilion cost near £14,500 and the School House renovation £5,280, both improvements being financed from capital which the DES insisted was replenished. Given that the school, following the sale of 28 High Town, had no substantial assets – the school's overdraft at Lloyds was only secured in 1973 through a charge on Chapter buildings[252] – there were limits as to as to what could be financed through borrowing by other means. And direct grant schools were prevented from financing new building through their tuition fees. If HCS was to compete successfully as a fully independent school against the city comprehensives and the new Sixth Form College, to say nothing of other public schools, another way had to be found to fund its further development.[253]

The chosen way was by means of an appeal, but an appeal which was more effective than the one in 1959 or, indeed, any before. It was run by Hooker Craigmyle, a fund-raising consultancy which had directed successful campaigns in several schools in the 1960s.[254] After a series of exploratory visits, the governors engaged the company on 3 May 1971, their suggested target of £70,000 being increased to £100,000 at the insistence of Peter Prior, who became campaign chairman and mobilised local industry behind the school's cause. Directed by the 'amiable, methodical, pipe-smoking' Colonel Hazelton (a Craigmyle employee) with Yvonne James as his secretary, the campaign was meticulously planned and effectively executed. And despite the economic climate of the early Seventies being less propitious for fund-raising than a decade earlier, by 1 September 1973 – little more than 18 months after the launch – almost £97,000 had been given or pledged. Despite the Headmaster's disappointment with the response from Old Herefordians – only 165 out of 1,300 OHs whose names were traced subscribed – it was a decent effort with contributions from over 50 companies (the list being headed by Henry Wiggin & Co. Ltd with £10,000, followed by H.P. Bulmer and Sun Valley with £5,000 each) and more than 500 individuals.[255]

Even so, the money raised was insufficient to realise many of the objectives as originally stated in the *Development for the Seventies* appeal brochure. This fanciful wish-list, estimated to cost £46,500, included a heated swimming pool, a new pottery and art centre, wood and metal workshops, a renewed Big School and refurbished departmental rooms,

252. HCA, 7031/26, pp.89-90, minute, 1 May 1973.

253. The College, in its new premises, was not formally opened until 9 September 1974, a year later than planned, having spent its first year in Broadlands House. For its inception and planning: Barnes, *passim*.

254. According to a company document of January 1971, £1,639,400 was raised through Hooker Craigmyle campaigns in 12 boys' schools from 1960 to 1970, St Paul's £429,500 being by far the largest individual school total.

255. The appeal's progress may be traced in the various company and other documents in the school archives. For Richards' disappointment: HCSA, Old Herefordian Dinner speech, 9 Dec. 1972. The figures are taken from *Hereford Cathedral School: Development for the Seventies*, (Second Progress Report, 1973), p.2. The final amount actually raised when the appeal was closed in early 1974 was around £95,000, the published figure being reduced because of a change in taxation rates. HCSA, Richards' report to the governors, 13 Feb. 1974.

as well as (had the appeal target been 'significantly exceeded') other buildings like a sports hall that the school did not acquire until 2009. The reasons for this failure to execute half the intended plans are clear: in a period of escalating building costs, the 1971 estimates proved wildly inaccurate;[256] and insufficient allowance was made for the steep rise in interest rates charged by the banks for bridging loans. Nevertheless, the appeal had tangible results. From its proceeds, Number 1 was renovated (at a cost of around £13,000); a careers centre was created in Old Block, better it was said than that enjoyed by the area careers officer; a squash court was built; and, most importantly, a modern Science complex was created on the East Street site.[257] When, after a year of disrupted teaching, the new laboratories were opened, fittingly by the chairman of Wiggins, on 26 October 1973, the appeal's major objective had been achieved. As Richards observed at the time, it had been a close run thing, and 'in these days of inflation and higher interest rates', had the appeal been delayed, it was doubtful whether even the new Science building would have been completed. But as he also remarked more than 30 years later, in the long term perhaps 'the greatest benefit of the exercise lay less in the immediate objectives reached than in the people whose interest and commitment the appeal seemed to attract'.[258] Among these were Peter Prior; Viscount Portman, whose acceptance of the presidency was not his last service for HCS; leaders of local industry and commerce; and many smaller donors who had no direct connection with the school.[259]

So during the four years' respite which the Conservatives' unexpected 1970 General Election victory afforded, HCS met the threat that Donnison had posed to its status by accepting change: in its governance; in its administration and financial method; and by means of a professional appeal. By these methods, and a growing awareness of the importance of increasing its profile, if not the enthusiastic adoption of a formal public relations policy,[260] the school became better equipped to meet the challenges of full independence. But significant as these factors were, another development over these years proved an even greater safeguard of its future: the advent of girls.

Co-Educational Pioneers

The start of what became an irreversible trend towards full co-education in boys' public schools coincided with the period of David Richards' tenure. Marlborough College's

256. For example, despite constant paring, the published estimate of £43,000 for the new laboratories and squash court was exceeded by over £10,000.

257. The Science block comprised new Biology and Chemistry laboratories, the latter underpinning the improved Geography room and the advanced Physics laboratory on the first floor. The extension considerably improved the Number 1 garden elevation.

258. HCSA, speeches, 24 May, 14 Dec. 1974; Richards to the author, 10 Aug. 2007.

259. Captain Leonard G. Garbett RN, who was in his early nineties by the time of the appeal, was the donor with perhaps the most remarkable story of all. Although not an Old Herefordian, he had strong family links with Hereford and the school. His father, the Revd Charles Garbett (1813-95), was a Brasenose Somerset scholar and one of seven brothers to have attended HCS; and his grandfather, the Revd James Garbett (1775-1857) was (as we have seen) a classical master at the school and a cathedral prebendary. For Lord Portman: below, pp.579, 581.

260. Peter Prior was again the prime mover in this initiative. After discussion with masters and senior boys, he drew up a draft public relations policy which was the subject of 'considerable discussion' at the governors' meeting on 19 November 1974 but was not whole-heartedly endorsed by the Headmaster and his colleagues.

admittance of 15 Sixth-form girl boarders to join the school's 800 boys in September 1968 was perhaps the most influential change. A year later, there were 29 girls out of the 400 pupils in the Marlborough Sixth, their Headmaster outlining to the assembled company at HMC that September the school's selection criteria, the girls' programme – with cookery, dressmaking, pottery and flower arranging one afternoon each week – and the uniform rules, including a requirement that a skirt hemline should be no more than seven inches above the knee. More locally to Hereford, Christ College, Brecon, had made an arrangement enabling the St David's Convent girls to attend certain Sixth-form classes at the college from September 1968; and by the end of the decade, the single girl among 250 boys at Belmont, were joined by 11 other Sixth-form girls, the new Headmaster admitting that he did not know how the monks would cope with co-education but that it was right for the abbey to try it 'in all humility and with an open mind'. So when two 16-year-olds, Diane Lidster and Catherine Whittaker, became the first two girls at Hereford Cathedral School in September 1970, although a huge break with tradition – 'after more than 600 years ... one of Hereford's male strongholds has fallen to the fair sex' were the first words of one local press report – it was by no means a novel occurrence in the public school world.[261]

Fig. 8.13 Catherine Whittaker (left) and Diane Lidster cross the Close as HCS sixth-formers in September 1970, thereby setting in train a social revolution at the school.

261. *HMC 1969 Conference Report*, pp.67-69, report of speech by J.C. Dancy, 26 Sept. 1969; *HT*, 7 June 1968, p.13; 16 May 1969, p.24; 26 June 1970, p.22; 18 Sept. 1970, p.11. It should be pointed out, however, that even by January 1973, girls accounted for only 2 *per cent* of all pupils in HMC schools and 3 *per cent* of all Sixth-formers. *HMC 1973 Committee Report*, p.84, January 1973 census.

Girl numbers at HCS did not increase overnight. Indeed, Diane and Catherine were not joined by any other girls during their Sixth-form careers. Surrounded as they were by 370 and more boys, and with (for their first year) no female teachers on the staff – they had a day-room to themselves in Number 1 where they were under the charge Mrs Woods, the housekeeper – it must at times have been a strange existence, despite the Headmaster's claim that they had 'settled in most satisfactorily and without fuss'. And despite the press headlines, no fuss was made of their arrival in *The Herefordian*, although a discerning reader of the school magazine for that year would have noticed that the girls had taken parts in the December 1970 production of *Zigger Zagger*, that 'the mini-skirted duo' had represented the school at badminton and that Catherine Whittaker was a double prize-winner in May 1971, a feat she repeated the following year. Towards the end of their two-year stay, the Headmaster rightly paid tribute to the two pioneers, 'for the start they have given us in this new departure, for the full part they have played in school life and for being who they are'.[262]

Thereafter, there was a slow increase in the number of Sixth-form girls: four in September 1972, increasing to six by the end of that academic year; nine by April 1974; and 12 by the following September. Although still a tiny proportion of a Sixth Form of around 100 boys, as *The Herefordian* of October 1973 indicated (an edition which had on its back cover a wordy advertisement entitled 'a lesson in love'), the greater numbers made their presence a little more obvious: on the Whitecross squash court (the school court not being in use until spring 1974), the balconies always being crowded, it was reported, whenever the girls played; on the athletics field, their participation in the 100 metres and high jump (the new girls' events) on sports day in late May 1973 drawing 'warm appreciation and applause for the onlookers'; on the river, history also being made that same month with the formation of a girls four ('resplendent in bright yellow rowing shirts, they added a splash (or two!) of colour and beauty to mundane training afternoons on the Wye – their rowing wasn't bad either!', wrote the captain of boats); and in the Debating Society, Ann Wignall being 'the first lady member to be more than just an ornament' by giving a speech from the platform. When read over 40 years later, such comments seem patronising at best but as this recollection reveals, the second wave of Sixth-form girls – all refugees from girls' only schools – well survived the experience:

> The four of us who started in September 1972 … were again novelties, spoilt to bits, included automatically as a point of honour in just about everything as 'the girls' rather than on merit. All the boys … knew who we were, while we hadn't the slightest idea who they were, especially if they were below us. We were treated very cautiously as potentially explosive material. Little preparation had been made or, possibly, it was impossible to plan for a gang of four. We were assigned seats in the cathedral choir stalls which necessitated clambering over a tomb each morning. We were given a grand Common Room over the entrance hall to Number 1 … The uniform for girls was vague, and the instructions relayed through Mrs Woods … stated grey suits 'like secretaries going to an office' – a demand for subfusc that we young feminists thought hilarious as none of us ever intended going anywhere near an office. These were the

262. For the quotations: HCSA, Richards' report to the governors, 22 Oct. 1970, and his speech, 26 May 1972.

days of the beat generation ...We used Biba ochre eye shadow and maroon lipstick to get that intense, hollowed-out intellectual effect, and I remember Annie [Wignall] striding through the door of Number 1 in her boyfriend's Sun Valley wellies, with distinctive red rubber sun patches. Pretty soon we won the case for trousers in winter.

... we constructed part of our own timetable to make good certain deficiencies. This is how we ended up taking pottery classes on games afternoons at the Art College ... Certain masters also turned the gaps in the provision for girls into great opportunities. Mr Shave took us into the squash club ... Mr Skinner set up a girls' rowing four and we thrashed up and down the river in vivid yellow t-shirts ... Rowing did not prevent two of us being temporarily stranded on a canoe trip down the Wye ... No-one in charge noticed. One really did sink or swim at HCS. Or catch up, in this case.

It seemed that all the teachers had other more serious interests beyond their allotted subjects and this was something entirely new to me. Mr Lancaster, apart from his expertise in history, was legendary for his composition of poems, classes on literary criticism and cycle-rides for inspiration ... Subsidiary Art, it turned out, was simply the place where the first XV discussed rugby tactics ... Dick Heald, it was said, taught maths so that he had ample time for music. He ran the madrigal group on Tuesday evenings and because my family lived so far out, provided there were no sick children in the san, I was allowed to stay overnight ... We had great affection and respect for the staff who had, it seemed, endless time and courtesy, provided one was witty and deserving ... At my girls' school there was no banter at all between staff and pupils but at the Cathedral School wit and repartee were expected, indeed were the very lifeblood of the Debating Society ...

The school must have served 'us' very well: we worked hard and did end up with good results and places at the destinations of our choices ... The experience made us very resilient and enterprising. I stayed on for a further term of a third year to sit the Oxbridge entrance ... So it was that I, almost seventeen and a half, became the first girl at HCS to gain a place at Oxford, at Brasenose, to read Classics. I was informed by telegram on Christmas Eve, 1974.[263]

In retrospect, the decision to admit Sixth-form girls seems to have been taken in a fit of absence of mind. There was no formal governors' resolution; as late as 23 June 1970, the Headmaster had not received DES permission for their admission; and a new scheme of governance, formally recognising the change, was not sealed until 1 November 1971.[264] By contrast, the decision for the school to open its gates to 11-year-old girls was carefully planned. With the arrival of girls in the Sixth Form, Richards soon came under pressure, 'from all sorts

263. I am grateful to Elizabeth Locke (née Whittaker) for these reminiscences. The other three members of the 'gang of four' of September 1972 were Liz Hellyer, Fiona Strange (now Mason) and Annie Wignall. They came from (respectively) Adcote, Malvern and Monmouth Girls' Schools, Elizabeth Whittaker having spent 'four years enclosed at Shrewsbury High School ... a strict, serious place intent on academic achievement for girls' before her arrival at HCS.

264. It was not until April 1970 that it was realised that the scheme would have to be altered. On his return from holiday that month, the Headmaster not only found a letter awaiting him from the Clerk's office to say that an intake of girls would be illegal but also discovered that nothing had been done to mend the broken gateway pillar which was lying in the Number 1 forecourt. HCSA, Richards' note, 18 April 1970. It was not a good start to the new term.

of people' he later reported, to admit girls at 11. He himself favoured 'breaking the barrier of the sexes' (as he had put it in September 1970) but sold it to his governors by reporting that it was the best practical response to the threat to remove the direct grant because it doubled the potential intake, even if it meant reordering a boarding house. Following an informal approach to Maurice Edge, who strongly supported the change and even suggested that the local authority might allow an additional ten girls as free place-holders, the governors agreed in principle (on 15 February 1972) to admit girl pupils at 11 plus and, if necessary, to change to a three-form entry, the Headmaster being authorised to reduce the number of boarder acceptances following that month's junior entrance examination. It was the most momentous decision ever taken by that or any set of governors.[265] Although at that stage the DES was not prepared to sanction a three-form entry, in late May 1972 it authorised the admission in September 1973 of ten day girls at 11 plus within the existing two-form system, and a further ten (later increased to 15) the following year. Various conditions, however, were attached to the agreement: a new approach should be made before the 1975 intake (girls were subsequently admitted on parity); more female staff were to be appointed at the first opportunity; in addition to the new facilities, special curricular requirements were to be provided for the girls; and curiously, since no extra provision was made for the boys in this regard, care was to be taken to ensure that young girls were 'not at risk when crossing from one side [of Castle Street] to the other or even in the school grounds'.[266]

Not all of this could be accomplished within 15 months, and the Headmaster took to warning prospective parents and their daughters before the first junior intake that the curriculum did not include Domestic Science and that the girls' athletics facilities were limited. This did not deter them from applying. 57 day girl hopefuls turned up with the 98 day boy applicants for the preliminary junior entrance examination on 10 February 1973, Richards later declaring that 'no Headmaster on a Saturday morning had seen Big School look so attractive or so pretty'.[267] And slowly preparations were made: the appointment of female teachers, the organisation of a makeshift games timetable and the designation of lavatories in Number 1 for that September; and by September 1974 (at a cost, financed from capital, of £6,000), the conversion of the old School House music rooms into cloakroom facilities and the making of a changing room at the new Wyeside pavilion, as well as the provision of a grass hockey pitch and lessons in dress design and needlecraft.[268] One

265. HCSA, Richards' report to governors, 9 Nov. 1971; letter to the finance committee, 20 Jan. 1972; HCSA, GMB 1945-82, p.240, minute, 15 Feb. 1972. Despite Edge's optimism, the LEA were not prepared to increase the school's allocation of free place-holders, the ten places being shared among boys and girls in the three entries from 1973 to 1975.

266. HCSA, K.L.R. English to Richards, 28 May 1972, and his acknowledgment of 24 May. It is not clear which date is the correct one. Also: HCSA, for Mynors' memorandum on the DES visit, 1 March 1972.

267. HCSA, speech, 25 May 1973. The number of 11 plus day girl/boy applications, 1974-75, was respectively: 76/93, 64/112. By way of contrast, the first year (boy) boarding applications averaged around 13 annually, 1973-75.

268. Taught by Mrs Acheson. All told eight female teachers were appointed by David Richards in four successive years: in 1972, Mrs M.M. Barfield (Mathematics, 1972), the first woman teacher for over 20 years; in 1973, Mrs P.E.G. Sadler, the first ever female Head of department (English), Miss V.J. Speake, later Mrs Green (Mathematics and Physics), Mrs L.J. Howard-Jones (English) and Mrs P.M. Theakston (PE); in 1974, Mrs S.P. Acheson (French, Art and Design); and in 1975, Mrs M. Lowther (PE) and Mrs M.M. Nitek (Biology).

Fig. 8.14 More pioneers: girls as well as boys sit the Junior Entrance examination for HCS, 10 February 1973.

fruit of these efforts was the creation of a patchwork quilt which was presented to the Headmaster as a leaving present.[269]

Despite the initial difficulties, the junior girls soon began to make a real contribution to school life. Given the severity of the competition at entry, it comes as no surprise to find that among the September 1974 entry list there was the first girl winner of the Langfordian scholarship and that girls swept the board with the junior form prizes in 1974-75.[270] In sport, they could not compete on equal terms with the boys, although they were allowed to run in the Junior Hull in 1975, and on sports day three special events were introduced in both the senior and under-12 girls' competitions. There were other activities – debating, music (a recorder group was formed in the first year) and acting, two brave girls even taking part in *The Man in a Trilby*, Stuart House's entry in the junior House drama competition. And their life at school was made easier than it would have been a few years earlier, a new House system having been introduced in April 1971 when 'East' and 'West' were replaced by four new Houses named after former benefactors. The day pastoral unit was

269. I am grateful to Jennifer Jones OH for this detail and for other recollections of her early years at HCS.

270. The first girl Langfordian was Suzanne Watson, and the girl prize-winners were Rachel Williams, Judith Goodsell (in successive years), Christine Morris, Clare Parry, Miranda Holt and Clare Wood.

thereby halved to around 60 pupils. And when the young girls arrived, one senior girl was appointed as a monitor to each of the two forms.[271]

It was only natural if girls occasionally experienced problems settling into a predominantly male establishment but it cannot always have been easy for the masters themselves. The advent of co-education gave a new lease of life to some but for other older men who had neither experience of teaching mixed classes nor of women being members of their Common Room, it must have been an unnerving experience. And how should 11-year-old girls be addressed? Surnames were hardly appropriate for girls and the experiment of prefixing each girl's name with 'miss' was soon abandoned. It is significant that in October 1974 for the first time in an '*avete*' notice in the school magazine, the first name of each girl was printed, even though initials were still used for the boys. It was only a matter of time before the use of surnames fell into disuse for all pupils.[272] Similarly with the growth of girl numbers, it could only be a matter of time before old customs like fagging (formally abolished in 1976) were abandoned.

So this was an important time of transition in the history of HCS. And the majority of the girl pioneers, even if with hindsight they realised that the school was hardly well prepared for co-education, seem to have enjoyed the experience. Moreover, through the gradual increase in the total girl population – by September 1975, following the lifting of the 11 plus entry cap, the 66 girls comprised 17 *per cent* of the pupil roll, and there were only two all boy year groups – their impact on all areas of school life was increasingly being felt. This applied not least in the academic sphere. The reduction in the number of boarding places and the admittance of girls on the basis of parity of performance in the junior entrance examination would soon result in improved performance in public examinations. And although it had not quite happened by 1975, soon it would become the norm for all boys to treat girls in the school as they would their sisters at home, rather than as 'the fairer sex'. Just as HCS owes a debt of gratitude to that generation of parents who were prepared to send their daughters to a boys' secondary school embarking on the experiment of co-education, so the school is indebted to these girl pioneers brave and talented enough to take their places and succeed in a boys' world.

Diversification, Choice and Responsibility

The lowering of the age of adult franchise (to 18) and of medical consent (to 16) by the Family Reform Act of 1969 ensured that all Sixth Forms would include a minority of pupils who were allowed to vote, marry and enter into contracts without consultation, and a majority for whom parental consent was unnecessary before any medical treatment. Simultaneously, there were numerous calls through the Sixties for there to be greater choice

271. Respectively, Deborah Barker (who came to HCS from the Girls' High School in January 1974), the first girl school monitor, and Fiona Strange, the first girl to be a Head of House (Somerset). The first Housemasters of the new day Houses were R.D. Lancaster (Langford), J.L.T. Brookes (Somerset), F.G. Hallowell (Cornwall) and A.N.L. Shave (Stuart). Boarding pastoral care for younger boys, too, was immeasurably improved with the creation of a junior boarding house in Number 1, under Egerton Parker, in September 1972.

272. This was clearly happening to some extent already, especially with senior boys. The earliest use of first names I have found for any report in *The Herefordian* occurs in the October 1969 edition, and by December 1971 they were being used for all pupils in the school play (*A Man for all Seasons* that year) cast list.

and freedom for teenagers in schools and colleges: an increasing degree of 'consumerism' within contemporary society was being extended to the world of education.[273]

Richards' response at the Cathedral School was to meet such demands by broadening the curriculum and increasing the range of activities, especially for Sixth-formers, thereby giving his charges a degree of freedom of choice unknown to their predecessors, while stressing the need for pupils to take individual responsibility for their decisions. His general approach is best encapsulated in this extract from his speech of May 1974:

> Thinking back over the last five years or so, it seems to me that two issues have really dominated any remarks about the general health of the school that I have made on occasions such as this: the diversification of activities, in the form-rooms and out, which has progressively taken place and which is still taking place; and, secondly, the increasing measure of personal choice – freedom, opportunity to opt in or out of things, which is available these days to members of the school at all levels and especially in the Sixth Form.

As he had explained earlier, choice applied to which game to play or to which club to belong, or whether to accept responsibility or whether indeed: 'to co-operate, co-exist or obstruct; in the last resort whether or not to surrender to the glamorous appeal of the mythical world outside where routine or regulations will not inhibit and discipline does not intrude – or that, I think, is how the arch opter-out sees it'. In the age 'of fashionable apathy and the illusions of synthetic escape', it was the school's function to provide that stable background 'against which may be played out this business of choosing between endeavour and apathy, fulfilment and frustration, the real and the synthetic in an atmosphere where there is a properly judged balance between encouragement, tolerance and respect for principle'. And it required 'a good deal more courage and initiative for a young person to follow the paths of faith and leadership' than in times past when 'rules and regulations concerning bounds, haircuts, manners, number of jacket buttons done up' were all laid down, and 'responsibility was delegated from above and accepted from below as part almost of a natural law'. It was a brave educational philosophy but the only sensible response in an age which saw the rise of what one historian has called 'a new kind of populist individualism'.[274]

Academically, a pupil might choose not to do much work but there was little opportunity for him to opt out of formal lessons. Nevertheless, the curriculum was made more attractive by a gradual relaxation of its former rigours, even if as late as 1972-73 it was still in part straitjacketed by the disproportionate number of classicists on the teaching staff.[275] The four year accelerated stream from entry to Ordinary-level was discontinued from 1970, all boys then entering the First rather than the Second Forms and taking five years in most subjects to public examination to the benefit of the vast majority. Correspondingly, the

273. See Barnes, pp.45-46, for an analysis of what he terms 'clientele education' and its general impact on the Hereford Sixth Form College.

274. Sandbrook (2011), p.468. For the above: HCSA, Richards' speeches, 28 May 1971, 26 May 1972 and 24 May 1974.

275. In that year there were five classicists among the 26 assistant teachers. For the difficulties this caused in terms of staff deployment: HCSA, Richards' reports to the governors for 20 June, 21 Nov. 1972 meetings.

rather arbitrary streaming of new boys after one term was delayed until the end of their second year. New subjects were introduced, including Biology at the Fourth Form level from 1971 and Computer Science throughout the lower school in 1973. The timetable was also made more flexible to enable obvious combinations (like two Modern Languages, and Economics and Mathematics) at Advanced-level from 1969; and the increase in the number of weekly lessons from 34 to 38 two years later then enabled greater flexibility in subject choices in the middle school. The Sixth Form general studies programme, too, became more considered, comprising (in 1972-73) of the Esso business game, courses in architecture, Art and current affairs, as well as lectures and visits to historic sites and national galleries. And better university and careers advice was proffered, through the appointment of a universities master (in 1969), the use of computerised 'Birkbeck' careers tests (administered by the new Independent Schools Careers Organisation) on a voluntary basis and the creation of a modern careers centre. It was evolutionary rather than revolutionary change but the curriculum underwent a timely overhaul during these seven years, choice increased and guidance improved.[276]

The diversification of extra-curricular activity produced as big a change. From the very beginning, Richards had indicated that traditional games would no longer hold total sway, warning some no doubt sceptical Old Herefordians at their dinner in December 1968 that 'a wide variety of games and sports' was 'of very considerable importance these days, when mass support of a single game is so much on the wane'. The following year games afternoons were staggered, making better use of the facilities and enabling more boys – including the choristers, the Headmaster wisely informed his governors – to play but giving them less time to watch the first teams. Moreover, boys in their final Sixth-form year were given the opportunity to take up an activity from six options – four sports, estates work and community service.[277] Soccer was introduced for senior boys from Spring Term 1970, and badminton was started 'for those unsound in wind and limb who tremble at the onset of winter's rigours' to join other court games as an alternative Wednesday afternoon activity. By 1972-73, squash rackets, tennis, association football, sailing, shooting and badminton, in addition to the traditional games, had all been recognised as school sports, as signified by the longer list of games captains printed in *The Herefordian*. But there were casualties, the captains of cross-country and fives disappearing from the records after 1970. Although the Hull continued, the brief flourishing of cross-country in the Sixties came to an end with the advent of soccer; and, more significantly given its history, fives

276. An unofficial inspection report early in Richards' tenure indicates the extent to which the curriculum needed to be improved. The three HMIs pointed out the problems caused by a 34-period week and the 'express stream'; the lack of provision for 'handicraft' and 'practical/aesthetic activities'; the limited O-level subject choices; and the imbalance among the staff caused by the excessive number of classicists. HCSA, HMI memorandum (on the curriculum and the Geography department), 2/3 June 1970. Also see: HCSA, Richards' notes on individual departments (including History, the teaching of which had 'much improved since 64') of June 1970.

277. The games choices (in autumn term 1971) were rugby, squash, badminton, and shooting, soccer and rowing being added to the list for the following term. There were maximum limits (in terms of numbers) for all activities except rugby. Choices for the Lower Sixth were more restricted and Fifth-form boys 'normally' played rugby. The success of James McManus in winning the city's 1969 Franklin award for community service should be noted. He was one of the first Old Herefordians to spend his Gap year with VSO (Voluntary Service Overseas), teaching on a remote mission station in New Guinea.

gave way to squash, two walls of the old courts, after suitable treatment, forming part of the new court's perimeters.

The Fives IV disappeared with the old courts for ever, but the other major team games, together with athletics, continued in reasonable health, even if results were not always favourable. Despite the dropping of most of the rugby fixtures against the Welsh schools (Brecon apart) by the early Seventies, in only two seasons (1971-72 and 1973-74) did the 1st XV win more games than it lost. The 1st VII, on the other hand, reached the quarter-finals of the Rosslyn Park competition at the first attempt in 1975. Similarly with the 1st XI, only in the 1972 and 1973 seasons did wins predominate, there being few batsmen who could be relied on to score consistently on sub-standard Wyeside pitches. In rowing, Peter Skinner, by himself for the most part, heroically turned out three or four crews each year – and seven in 1973 – which regularly competed in the Tideway Head of the River, as well as summer regattas. Only occasionally were pots won, although the acquisition of a new racing four in 1973 made the first crew more competitive. At least in athletics, with the moving of sports day from March to May and the need for new track times (from 1971) with metrification, records continued to be broken, with the notable exception of Wilding's 1862 leap of 6.24 metres in the long jump, the only pre-1914 record still standing in 1975.[278] Overall, this was not a vintage period for traditional games. But as the Headmaster observed in December 1971, although the XV, XI, VIII and IV were having a lean time, these sports continued to be enjoyed by those opting to participate in them.[279] And except at the second team level, the inconsistent performance of such teams has to be explained by factors other than the introduction of alternative attractions.

New recreational clubs were founded. The Canoe Club, launched in September 1968, flourished throughout the period, winning three trophies in the Herefordshire canoe sports of 1975; a Croquet Club was formed in autumn 1970 and was well patronised, although the treasurer was worried in 1975 about its viability given the near 50 *per cent* rise in equipment costs; sailing started at Llangorse in the summer of 1972; and the Mathematics department's 1973 purchase (at a cost of £640) of a 'Busicom' computer, described at the time as 'a sophisticated calculating machine', gave rise to a Sixth Form Computer Club. There was also an increase in activities for younger boys (and later girls) with the re-formation of the Junior Debating Society in autumn 1969, which was itself soon transformed into a Junior Debating and Literary Society. Following Egerton Parker's arrival in 1970, junior musicals became a highlight of the school calendar, the 1972 production of *Oliver* – involving a cast of nearly 50 and the support of many staff as well as Evans, an undertaker – being followed by two Julian Slade pieces, the author himself making a personal appearance in March 1975 on the first night of *Salad Days.* And the younger boys and girls themselves made an indirect contribution towards the welfare of clubs and societies through their collecting some 450 books of green-shield stamps, which were a major source

278. Field event records, which remained unaffected by metrification, were simply converted. T. Ragg's 1911 run of 11.4 seconds for the under 15s 100 yards was finally broken (by .1secs.) when D. Keyte and D.R. Wood tied for first place in the event in 1969; and in 1973, N.R. Towell broke the 1898 under 15 high jump record of E. Bourdas (converted to 1.505 metres) with a jump of 1.51.

279. HCSA, Richards' speech at the OH dinner, 11 Dec. 1971.

of funding for the school's first minibus. This was eventually purchased in early 1974, after an 18-month funding drive by the newly formed Parent Teacher Association, despite the threat of petrol rationing at that time.[280] Minority activities were not now so reliant on staff transport, capacious though the 'admiral's barge' (Mr Nicholson's Rolls) was.

By then, Sixth-form cultural life had proliferated in unexpected ways. The performance of John Arden's *Sergeant Musgrave's Dance* in December 1972 brought to an end the long succession of set-piece end of year school plays. Thereafter, much of the impetus for performance was generated by a talented group of senior pupils who formed the 'Spyder Arts Movement'. Through its initiative, Pinter's *Birthday Party* was produced; trips were organised to avant-garde events at Cardiff's Chapter Arts Centre and elsewhere; performances were improvised in experimental workshops, revues and musical extravaganzas; and, directed by Sixth-formers, an experimental production of Aristophanes' *The Frogs* was performed – until it rained on the third night – in the Number 1 garden. Elizabeth Locke (née Whittaker) – one of the 1972 'gang of four' – who was on the fringes of all this, now fondly recollects this movement's influence:

> This movement … was entirely a student initiative and unstoppable, though considered quite subversive by some. This was exactly what the school was so good at, whether by design or default – allowing individuals to flourish and tolerating eccentrics. So many good things came from below.

In a different genre, much of the material for the new look *Herefordian* (from the October 1974 edition) 'was the product of the imagination and strenuous efforts of a team of [pupil] writers, sub-editors and artists', many of whom had been involved in the production of a fortnightly news-sheet called 'Blue and Gold'. It was all very different from what had gone before.

The rise of improvised performance does not imply that more formal music-making was in decline; quite the opposite. Despite their dual role with both school and cathedral, the appointments of Robert Green as the school's first Director of Music in April 1969 and then Roy Massey as his successor in September 1974 (Green then becoming Assistant Director), were significant advances. And for the first time Music was given a proper base, at first in the east wing of School House and from mid-1974 in 7 Ferrers Street. However modest the accommodation and the budget – in 1969, the governors agreed to an initial £100 grant, with an additional £150 for musical instruments and a promise of £50 termly thereafter – a music department had been created. As a result, more pupils took a serious interest in music than ever before, exemplified by the establishment of a madrigal group in the summer of 1970 and a new Music Society the following spring; an increased demand for instrumental tuition; the foundation of a school orchestra, nearly 40 strong by 1975, and other ensembles; and the school's greater involvement in the city's musical life. On his arrival, Roy Massey was 'surprised and delighted' with the school's musical talent and thought that HCS music stood comparison with that of his previous school (King Edward's,

280. The PTA was founded in 1970-71 and its purchase of the 12 seater Bedford minibus for *c.*£1,500 was its first major school project.

Birmingham). 'We have a very bright musical future,' he wrote after his first year in charge. It was a prescient remark.[281]

By the mid-Seventies, the school's extra-curricular life had been reinvigorated and the apathy senior boys had shown towards some activities around the decade's turn seems to have lessened. It is not clear when the tide turned, although Richards himself noticed in December 1971 that the numbers opting out of the major games was declining. Two years later the Sixth Form was fizzing. A report in *The Herefordian* written during Richards' first year suggesting that there were a 'tremendous' number of boys who could not 'be bothered to do anything' could not justly have been made on his departure.[282] And it was not just in Music and the performing arts that progress had been made. The Debating Society, for example, grew in stature under the benign and inspiring guidance of R.G.N. Rhodes. An annual debating competition was introduced, regular friendly debates were organised with neighbouring schools and HCS became involved for the first time in national contests. As suggested by M.E. Pope's and S.E.D. Williams' victory in the 1972 *Observer* Mace, one of the school's most notable achievements, high standards were set during this period by members of the school's oldest society.

Fig. 8.15 M.E. Pope and S.E.D. Williams (both seated, respectively third from the right and third from the left) bring home the Observer Mace: pictured here with the vice-president (R.G.N. Rhodes) and senior members of the school Debating Society, summer 1972.

281. For this 'personal view': *TH*, CCXXI (Oct. 1975), p.32. The new Director's optimism was shared by the Headmaster in his governors' report for the 19 Nov. 1974 meeting.

282. HCSA, Richards' speech at the OH dinner, 11 Dec. 1971; *TH*, CCXV (ii) (Oct. 1969), p.24.

Even the corps and chapel – two of the four C traditional pillars[283] – well survived the storm. It is difficult to judge the health of the CCF in the late Sixties and early Seventies such is the paucity of the reports of their routine activities – that in itself, of course, may tell a story – but it is apparent that adventure training expeditions continued to be well supported. And after the retirement of Major Lush, who had pioneered the introduction of such arduous pursuits within the corps, as commanding officer in 1973 after a record service of 21 years, there is plenty of evidence to suggest a revival. A total strength of 76 cadets in 1974-75 did not compare favourably with the old days but for a school of under 400 it was quite sufficient.[284]

As regards chapel, there were signs of a growing discontent among a number of senior boys in the late Sixties and early Seventies. One of the 'most inconclusive and serious exchanges' (Richards reported) in an early meeting of the Sixth Form council concerned the daily morning service. Should it be compulsory for all every day or once a week or voluntary for seniors or held for different levels of the school each day? None of these ideas were adopted but subtle changes were made to the weekday service with the introduction of non-biblical texts and modern hymn tunes, and periodically – as on Wednesdays in Lent 1971, when the chaplain addressed the Sixth Form on the church in contemporary society – whole school chapels were abandoned. And for the boarders on Sundays, the number of school services was reduced to two or three each term, the boys being given the freedom to choose which cathedral services to attend on the other days. On state occasions there were also adjustments. At the 1972 carol service (for one year only) the voice of the Lord God walking in the garden in the cool of the day was not heard; and at Commemoration the following May, perhaps partly in response to a major disturbance by some senior boys two years earlier, the congregation took a more active part in the service, school singers replacing the cathedral choir in the process. So over these years, the nature of school worship did not remain static but its traditional pattern was maintained. And any unrest among senior pupils was largely contained by the sensitive response of an excellent chaplain, who in 1974-75 prepared a record 51 candidates (including the first four girls) for confirmation.[285]

At a meeting on 1 March 1971, following unspecified public complaints, the Headmaster spoke to the monitors about the importance of the school's appearance being tidied up. There was no intention, he said, to withdraw the more flexible uniform regulations or (he implied) to go back to the days when a boy would be castigated for the narrowness of his tie or the check of his suit. The rumour that a tape would be taken to measure boys' hair was also mistaken. But tidiness, cleanliness and, above all, good manners mattered and it was up to the monitors to keep these principles uppermost in their minds. This meeting provides a tiny illustration of what Richards was striving to achieve by 'diversification': pupils should respond to being given greater choice by not abusing their freedom and by being mindful

---

283. With cricket and cold baths: see above, p.480.

284. For J.L.T. B(rookes)'s reports on the corps' wide-range of activities in 1974-75: *TH*, CCXX (Oct. 1974), p.12; CCXXI (Oct. 1975), p.16.

285. The paragraph is based on Richards' governors' reports for the meetings on 16 Feb. and 17 June 1971 (for the Sixth Form council discussion and the 'serious misconduct by senior boys') and Charles Neill's chaplain reports: *TH*, March 1969 to October 1975, *passim*. The first HCS girls to be confirmed were Carolyn Baker, Judith Heald and Jennifer Jones (on 25 October 1974), followed by Alison Evans on 11 July 1975.

of their wider responsibilities. It was a message those in authority were trying to get across to their charges throughout the country. As the Headmaster of Charterhouse observed at the 1969 HMC conference: 'We are evolving a blend of understanding and tolerance and discipline which is in the only true sense liberal and democratic'.[286] And, in general, like the successful change to a self-service catering system in 1970, the school responded positively to the more relaxed atmosphere, varied curriculum and increased choice of activity. But it was at a cost: for a small school, it meant the stretching of slender resources; it required older staff to adapt to changing times and learn the art of disciplining with a less definite rule-book; and it needed a more sophisticated response from the pupils themselves. And inevitably some pupils abused their position by making wrong choices, taking advantage of a relaxation of the rules or simply opting out of school life altogether. The making of such mistakes was an inescapable part of growing up in a world with greater freedom than ever before.

A Man of Vision

This time *The Herefordian's* leaving notice was not in the form of an obituary. For in the summer of 1975, having reached the semi-final of the croquet competition and scored a half century for the Old Herefordians, the Headmaster departed for a second headship at Portsmouth Grammar School rather than the Elysian Fields. His work at Hereford, however, prompted suitable appreciations from his chairman as well as the Second Master. Dean Rathbone stressed 'the happiest relationship' that he had established with his governing body; while John Rowlands mentioned that his boss had 'proved to be a man of vision' who had laid strong foundations for the school's independence.[287]

David Richards was certainly the right man for the school and for the times. As a former cathedral chorister, he appreciated the importance of (in Rathbone's words) 'cementing the bonds between cathedral and school'. Before he had taken up the post, he had commented to the press that the link with the cathedral held great appeal for him and throughout his tenure he was fully conscious of the importance of that relationship. One example of this was his effort to secure Roy Massey as the school's Director of Music; another was the lengths he went to in preparing the ground for an amicable settlement with the Dean and Chapter over the cathedral choristers.[288] But as with Dean Rathbone, he realised that the old ways of governance and domestic administration would no longer do in the modern world. The governors did not bring in a management consultant as the Headmaster wanted, but he did secure their agreement to a new domestic arrangement and to the hiring of a firm specialising in school appeals. And Dean Price's recommendation for an enlargement

286. HCSA, Richards' notebook of monitors' meetings, 1 March (1971); *HMC 1969 Conference Report*, p.24, speech of Oliver Van Oss at the University of York, 25 Sept. 1969.

287. *TH*, CCXI (Oct. 1975), p.3. For Richards' work at Portsmouth Grammar School, where his reforming instincts continued: Watson (2008), pp.114-20.

288. See HCSA, Richards' detailed 'Memorandum on Choristerships' of March 1975, which outlined the terms of the 1973 agreement whereby the governors agreed to pay the tuition fees of 12 choristers plus those of half the remaining choristers in the school; and urged (with the impending demise of direct grants) that a new system was implemented which was both more rational and allowed for the introduction of choristers to the cathedral choir at an earlier age.

of the governing body was well heeded by his successor. A bursar, too, was appointed who eventually assumed all the responsibilities of the old Chapter Clerk. Not all of this was the Headmaster's doing but it would not have happened so amicably without the co-operation and mutual trust that had been established between the Headmaster and his governors.

And Richards can take the main credit for the broadening of the curriculum in the widest sense, as well as ensuring that girls were admitted at both Sixth Form and junior levels. He also understood the importance that parents attached to a school having an efficient system of pastoral care and one allowing more regular access to their children – hence his establishment of four day Houses and a junior boarding house and his encouragement (without fee reduction) of weekly boarding. And in October 1970, he set about establishing a Parents' Teacher Association 'to further communication and co-operation' between parents and school and to provide 'an organisation dedicated to the encouragement and support of the school's activities and welfare'.[289]

As the Headmaster put together his report for speech day in May 1972, he pondered this issue:

> I have quite often wondered how a historian of the future might look and view this year. Against the enormous and rather frightening background of international and national affairs, he would see a Herefordshire fighting for its life and name; and within the county dare one hope that he might see our small school making significant adjustments to its course, to assure its future so it can be worthy of its long and historic past?

It was a perceptive muse, for although temporarily the county lost its struggle to maintain its independence, the school during these years of shelter afforded by the Conservative government made sound preparations for the time it would no longer have state support. Mistakes were made, notably the failure again to secure the preparatory school on Mr Thomas' retirement in 1973,[290] but its general development during these years was crucial to its later survival. Not the least of these was the decision to admit girls at 11 plus, which Richards rightly saw as 'one of the biggest and most significant policy decisions taken in the long history of our school'.[291]

But on Richards' departure the task was only half complete and the future still uncertain. Peter Prior's public relations policy proposal – following his wide consultation with staff and pupils in autumn 1974 – which suggested among other things that a public relations committee should be formed 'under the chairmanship of a senior, lively and enterprising master' (the names of John Brookes and Egerton Parker were mentioned for this role), was not altogether welcomed but it was on the right lines. As Prior himself observed:

289. HCSA, Richards' letter to parents, 24 Oct. 1970, setting up the first meeting on 27 November. Richards then chaired the main PTA committee from the first meeting of the working party on 21 January 1971.

290. According to the valuation undertaken on the governors' behalf in early 1972, the preparatory school was worth £19,900 which was over £5,000 below the asking price. Moreover, the governors were not prepared to commit themselves to continuing the school as it then existed; and by the end of that year they had decided that they were 'not in a position to purchase' the building. HCSA, GMB 1945-82, pp.241, 255, minutes, 15 Feb., 21 Nov. 1972.

291. HCSA, speech, 24 May 1974.

> The school's prospects were less certain now than at any time in its history. With the advent of a Labour government, it is possible that the school may have to fight hard for its very existence. The better it is thought of, the more likely it is to win through.[292]

And there were a number of key unanswered questions. Could HCS continue to exist as a two-form entry and a school of under 400? How could additional accommodation on a restricted site be provided if the school needed to expand? Could two large boarding Houses be sustained? Was there a sufficient fee-paying day market at 11 plus to replace the free county scholars and the direct grant entry? Would parents continue to be able to afford fees which (in the case of the day fee) had trebled in seven years?[293] How serious would the competition be from the new Sixth Form College? It was left to Richards' successor, the bursar and the re-vamped governing board to try to resolve such questions.

As for David Richards, he had seen a generation of pupils come and go and had successfully steered the school through the tribulations of the late Sixties and Seventies. That it was by 1975 a more open and less stuffy establishment at greater ease with society and itself was largely due to this progressive, conscientious and scrupulously fair-minded Headmaster. As importantly, his personal example had helped elevate the culture and tone of the school. Typically, in his last speech day address he paid due acknowledgment to the Second Master and the bursar for their 'staunch loyalty and firm friendship', as well as those on whom 'a Headmaster depends most of all' – the teachers. He was a fine teacher himself, inspiring his students with a love of Shakespeare and Milton, and despite occasional difficulties with the Common Room, he recognised that it was the staff who determined 'the true worth of a school'. It was they, he pronounced, who would see HCS 'through whatever political shoals there may be, beyond the 70s and 80s, into a future as distinguished as its past'.[294]

Barry Bridge Sutton, 1975-1987

As in 1968, the governors moved quickly to replace their Headmaster. The post had already been advertised by the time of the specially convened meeting on 11 December 1974, when Richards' resignation was received 'with regret' and the 'unreasonable request' of the Portsmouth chairman for the date of his release to be advanced was turned down. At that meeting, too, particulars of the appointment were finalised, applications being invited to reach the new clerk to the governors by 25 January 1975. Although the exact number of applicants is unknown, it is evident that many aspiring Cathedral School Headmasters applied for the position, their number being so large that the external adviser indicated that it was impractical for him to give due consideration to them all. A governors' sub-committee was therefore formed to undertake the initial sift, the panel recommending 21 aspirants for further discussion. On the last day of January, when unusually all nine governors were

292. HCSA, Prior to Richards, 5 Nov. 1974; and Prior's 'Public Relations Policy' paper, 12 Nov. 1974.

293. The annual day fees increased from £133 10s in September 1968 to £414 in March 1975; and the (inclusive) boarding fee increased from £289 10s to £666 (in 1974).

294. *TH*, CCXXI (Oct. 1975), p.8, speech 23 May 1975. I am grateful to David James (Head of School, Autumn Term 1973) for his recollections of David Richards' headship and teaching. Richards, in fact, took over the running of English during Mrs Sadler's illness in 1973-74, and left a note for his successor about his concerns for the department.

present, the list was whittled down to seven, the date of the preliminary interviews being brought forward to 21 February. A week later from a short-list of three, Barry Sutton, senior History master and Housemaster at Wycliffe College, was chosen as Richards' successor.[295]

Fig. 8.16 Barry Sutton: during his 14 years as Headmaster, HCS became established as a successful co-educational school.

Although there is no record of the interviews, it is clear that Peter Prior was a prime mover in the appointment. It was he who re-fashioned the job specification; it was Prior (with Dean Rathbone and Maurice Edge) who helped with the initial sift and suggested that in framing a letter to referees a definite question should be asked 'as to each candidate's suitability for the post in view of independence in the near future'; and it was he who subjected Mrs Sutton to a lengthy telephone call before her husband's interview. Barry Sutton's outward bound activities – his wide experience of scouting (he was assistant county commissioner for venture scouting in Gloucestershire) and interest in expeditioning and rock climbing – were also likely to have appealed to the Bulmer's chief, who had not only been president of the local scout council but had himself a distinct taste for adventure.[296]

But the other governors also needed to be convinced, and they would have been impressed by Sutton's churchmanship, his strong sense of history, his erudition and quick wit. For a set of governors whose 'unequivocal aim' (as the candidates were informed) was to make HCS fully independent in the likely event of the abolition of the direct grant, Barry Sutton's experience over 14 years as an 'integral part' of the life of an independent boarding school was also an important recommendation.[297] And although, given the

295. HCSA, GMB 1945-82, pp.283-85, minutes, 11 Dec. 1974, 16, 31 Jan. 1975. The external adviser was D.M. Annett, Headmaster of King's, Worcester. Barry Sutton remembered (interview, 11 Nov. 2013) that J.V. Tyson and P.H. Hutton, future Headmasters of St Edmund's, Canterbury and Wolverhampton Grammar School, were the other two short-listed candidates. I am also indebted to him for the loan of his speeches and for his general help in the writing of this section.

296. As pilot, diver, free-fall parachutist and rider of powerful motor-bikes. For an indication of Prior's own interests and his preference for leaders who could develop 'idiosyncratic activities': Prior, p.39; and *HT*, 7 Oct. 1977, p.14 (review of Prior's book).

297. And, not least, a school such as Wycliffe College, which, as a nonconformist foundation, embodied a self-help culture that directly involved the whole community. This attitude was to inform Sutton's Hereford years. I am indebted to Mark Sutton for this observation.

domestic rearrangements, it was less vital for a wife to be involved in housekeeping duties in 1975 than it had been in 1968, Margaret Sutton's reputation for warm hospitality at Springfield (her husband's Wycliffe House), quite apart from her own teaching career as an Oxford physicist, would have gone before her. In short, the Suttons had all the qualities necessary to take up residency within the environs of a cathedral. And as Peter Prior informed the chairman of Wiggins a few months later, in the new Headmaster the school had captured 'an energetic and imaginative young man' (he had just turned 38 at the time of appointment) who had the drive to lead the school forward to the independent future that appeared to be its inescapable lot.[298]

Independence and Growth

On 11 March 1975, within days of Sutton's appointment, Reg Prentice, the new Secretary of State for Education and Science announced in the Commons that the government intended to withdraw financial support (with the important exception of current pupils whose interests were safeguarded) from the 174 direct grant schools from September 1976. Given Labour's manifesto pledge, the statement hardly came as a surprise but now each school was required to make an unequivocal response to the government's mandate. Faced with an imposed 31 December deadline, the Hereford governors on 18 November 1975 re-stated their unanimous resolve for the school to become fully independent. In reality, the education authority having already indicated that there was no place for the Cathedral School in local plans for comprehensivisation, they were left with no choice.

As with many direct grant schools, the projected move to full independence was not warmly embraced. Dean Rathbone announced in the local press that he regretted the ending of the direct grant system, 'especially the passing of the fee remission scheme that allowed pupils to come to the school irrespective of parental income', and the young Headmaster called the government's decision 'a tragedy' and one motivated purely by political considerations.[299] And as other sensible observers also pointed out, the abolition of the direct grant was quite self-defeating. As *The Times* put it, the government's plan would 'reinforce both the principles of selective secondary education and the power of independent schools', thereby sacrificing genuine social mobility to 'the demands of egalitarianism without any corresponding gain'. This proved an accurate enough forecast for in the end HCS was one of 119 direct grant schools to become fully independent. Prentice's hope that the direct grant schools would become 'an integral part of the local system of comprehensive education' was confounded, and as a consequence the Labour government created in one year more private schools than any other administration since the Reformation.[300]

The Cathedral School was more fortunate than some: a handful closed and a number, particularly the Roman Catholic schools, were too poorly endowed to contemplate independence. Indeed, had there been a necessity for HCS to declare independence unilaterally,

298. The Suttons careers at Wycliffe may be traced through various editions of the *Wycliffe Star*, from no. 222 (Sept.-Dec. 1961) to no. 260 (Jan.-July 1975). I am grateful to Catherine Roberts, Foundation Manager, Wycliffe College, for providing these references. For Prior's observation: HCSA, P.J. Prior to A.T. Shadforth, 28 Oct. 1975.

299. *HT*, 21 Nov. 1975 p.1, 'Public School decides to go it alone'.

300. Sandbrook (2012), pp.198-200; *The Times* (as quoted by Sandbrook), 13 March 1975; Rae, pp.49, 54-55.

it might have been difficult – and perhaps impossible, as David Richards believed[301] – for HCS to have survived. However, the phasing out rather than the immediate abolition of the direct grant meant that the last direct grant pupil would not leave until 1982, thereby giving the school some breathing space. Despite the hike in tuition fees of over 50 *per cent* in 1975 from £95 to £155 per term (boarding fees were raised by around 20 *per cent* from £265 to £320 per term in the same year), the market remained buoyant. 178 candidates, 100 more than there were places for, sat the Junior Entrance examination in February 1976. It is true that 45 of these entries were for 'free places only', but for the time being the county scholarships continued, the full council having voted (against the advice of its own education committee) for the continuation of the 50 county awards in Hereford and Worcester on 13 November 1975.

At a time of educational cuts in the maintained sector and the completion of the reorganisation of education in Hereford city on comprehensive lines (insufficient grammar school provision being one reason for the continuance of county places), the school was unlikely to hang on to these free places for long. And so it proved in 1976-77, when the county finally abandoned its support for independent education (with the important exception of cathedral choristers),[302] despite Sutton's persistent lobbying for the adoption of a means tested scheme. There was now no possibility of any further public subsidy until the election of a Conservative government. But this was in the future, and despite the Tory Party's adoption of an assisted places scheme in 1977, given the unpopularity of their leader among the nation at large for much of the late 1970s, there was no guarantee that they would win the next election.[303]

And so from the beginning of his tenure, Sutton was charged with the task of leading (in the clumsy official phrase of the time) a 'direct grant school moving towards independence'. Although some element of DES control remained, principally in the setting of fees for subsidised pupils, the move towards independence had its advantages. The governors were given the freedom to determine the fees and other charges for the non-direct grant pupils; the Secretary of State's approval was no longer required for new buildings or alterations; and the strict requirement of local representation on the governing body was lifted. But as Richards had pointed out in November 1974, it was to be independence at a price.[304] And the price to be paid was the inevitable exclusion of many local families – nearly half of the 382 pupils in September 1975 were in receipt of a subsidised place – who were being priced out of the market. In Richards' own words, the 'cramped and old' school was in desperate need of modernisation, both physically and in terms of its infrastructure and governance.

---

301. HCSA, GMB 1945-82, p.281, 19 Nov. 1974.

302. 'Apparently the comprehensive cathedral choir, like the comprehensive ballet company, is not yet to be forced upon us' was Sutton's pointed comment in his report for the governors' meeting of 29 June 1976.

303. The complicated story of HCS's loss of its county places in the mid-1970s may be traced in the correspondence (now in the school archives) between Barry Sutton, M.J. Gifford (the LEA's chief education officer), and T.W. Barnes and E.G.H. Moreton (the county council governors), 10 Sept. 1975 to 26 May 1977. Also see: *HT*, 28 Nov. 1975, p.13 (letter from Cyril Jones, 'Grants to Independent Schools Indefensible'); 19 Nov. 1976, p.3 ('AP plan scrapes through Council'); 14 Jan. 1977, p.1 (educational cuts); and below, pp.538-39, for the assisted places scheme.

304. HCSA, 'What Price Independence?', Richards' prescient paper, 15 Nov. 1974.

In sum, HCS had to become a more modern and business-like operation, as well as a larger and fully co-educational school, if it was to prosper. And if it was to continue to fulfil its stated aim of service to the community, it also required new funding streams.

From September 1976, ways were found to fund three £300 scholarships annually, as well as means-tested benefits (up to a maximum of one third of the tuition fees) to children of diocesan clergy. It was a start but more substantial measures were clearly needed. Might not local industries – and the school had particularly close links with Wiggins and Bulmers (26 HCS parents were identified as being employed by these two companies alone in late 1975) – be able to help out? The energetic new Headmaster certainly thought that they might do so for within weeks of taking office he had proposed an industrial scholarships scheme, an idea enthusiastically endorsed by Peter Prior who attempted to sell the scheme as one of mutual advantage. For the sponsor it would provide a tax free benefit to selective employees of local firms, and for the school it would preserve (in Prior's words) 'the broad range of social classes from which the pupils of the school are at present drawn'. In April 1976 an approach was made to 27 local firms, seven of which were represented at a meeting at 5, Harley Court in late May. An outline Trust document was drawn up, counsel consulted and other schools drawn in but in the end only Sun Valley was prepared to commit to the scheme. As the bursar reported on 31 May 1977, 'nothing further would be gained by talking to additional industrial firms'. At a time when even the Prime Minister was lamenting the poor relations between schools and industry, it was an imaginative attempt to improve the links at a local level but in the end difficult trading conditions put paid to the scheme.[305]

So the school would have to go it alone by the time-honoured means of an appeal. Sutton's suggestion in November 1976 that an appeal be launched for improving the school's facilities was taken up by his governors the following year when it was clear the industrial scholarships scheme had foundered. The principal objective, however, changed to an appeal for a bursaries fund 'to mitigate the effects of losing the direct grant and fee remissions scheme'. Craigmyle was again used but this time on a consultancy basis, the Headmaster trusting that he and his bursar would make up 'for any amateurishness in their approach by the conviction of their commitment'. His instincts were right for the 1978 appeal, launched at the end of the Easter term that year, was hardly less successful than the one earlier in the decade. Twenty of the county's great and good under the Lord Lieutenant's presidency were again called upon to lend their name to the venture and an 11-man (no woman was appointed) appeal committee was established under the chairmanship of Brian Nelson, Bulmer's Managing Director and a recently co-opted governor. The brochure was less glossy than *Development for the Seventies* but its content was more impressive. The tone was up-beat, the Headmaster claiming that the school had 'never been in better heart or more strongly placed to assume the responsibilities of independence'; the appeal was put in the context of its impending celebration of 'the sixth century

305. There are eight letters (from 24 Feb. to 12 May 1976) in the school archives from local firms expressing doubts about the scheme. The negative response of Anvil Enterprises Ltd of Withington on 12 May 1976 ('in these difficult times in the big industry, the Ensor Group of which we are a part have decided to conserve as much cash as possible') is typical of many. In the end, even Bulmers pulled out. For the Prior observation: HCSA, draft letter, 12 May 1976; and for Callaghan's criticism in his Ruskin speech, 18 October 1976: Sandbrook (2012), p.686.

of the reform of its foundation'; and with a basic tax rate of 34 *per cent* and corporation tax at 52 *per* cent, the advantages of individuals contributing under deeds of covenant and limited companies making covenanted gifts were clearly spelled out. Although the response from Old Herefordians was again disappointing – despite Sir Horace Cutler, the leader of the Greater London Council, having invited London OHs to a County Hall reception – by mid-July 1979 almost £100,000 had been donated or promised. The Headmaster expressed disappointment on that speech day that the final £20,500 had proved so slow to come in but, as he explained to the assembled company, the new government's assisted places proposal had made it more difficult for the appeal to reach its designated target. Nevertheless, through gradual additions and careful investments the assets of this useful reserve fund had reached almost £150,000 by 1988 when a trust deed was finally registered with the Charity Commission.[306]

The 1978 appeal brochure had rightly emphasised the school's obligation to work towards 'responsible independence' in its provision for continuity of education from 11 to 18 for as many children from the region as possible. In reality, this could only be substantially achieved by a government financial measure similar in scope to the old direct grant. The school's aspiration to enhance opportunities for all local children who could benefit from the education it offered was made possible by the assisted places scheme, introduced by the new Conservative government in its second education bill, which received the royal assent on 3 April 1980 and came into operation for the first time in September 1981. The Act was passed at a time when expenditure on the maintained sector was being cut and was fiercely resisted. Opposition came from many quarters and not least from the Labour opposition which pledged the immediate ending of the scheme, including the withdrawal of benefits from existing assisted place holders, when it returned to power. But for its supporters – and by 19 February 1980, 446 schools (representing *c.*13,000 pupils) had expressed an interest in the scheme, of which 218 (offering around 5,500 places) were eventually invited to participate – the scheme had distinct advantages over its direct grant predecessor. It was based on a means test and was clearly aimed at lower income families (the limits of the sliding scale in 1981 for a family with one child ranging from £4,166 to £7,800); there was no element of local funding or control; schools did not need to wait for permission before any proposed fee increase, although the Secretary of State had reserve powers with regard to the setting of unreasonable fees; and participating schools preserved their independent legal status.[307]

The Cathedral School's participation in the assisted places scheme did not go through without debate. At a near two hour special governors' meeting held on the afternoon of 15 January 1980, reservations were expressed about details of the scheme but only Canon

306. For the above: HCSA, *Hereford Cathedral School Appeal: Six Hundred Years* (the appeal brochure); HCSA, Sutton's reports for governors' meetings, 16 Nov. 1976 to15 May 1979; *TH*, CCXXIV (Nov. 1978), pp.7-8; HCSA, G.B. Nelson to the author, 14 March 1988, enclosing draft Trust deed.

307. The history of the origins and implementation of the assisted places scheme may be traced through the regular bulletins sent to Direct Grant Heads by the indefatigable James Cobban, Chairman of the Direct Grant Joint Committee. See HCSA, for those of Oct. 1976, 4 and 14 Dec. 1979, 16 Feb. and 18 June 1980. For the general opposition to the scheme: Simon (1991), pp.476-77; and for the doubts of the Headmaster of Westminster School: Rae, pp.179-80.

Acheson, perhaps surprisingly for an HCS parent, objected on principle. This prevented a unanimous vote in favour of a bid being made to the DES for 60 assisted places annually.[308] Despite the one abstention, and although a bid was later made for only 40 places, which were all eventually awarded, there is little doubt that Brian Nelson's contention that the school's participation in the scheme would both broaden its base and improve its academic standards proved to be an accurate forecast.[309] But the risk of Labour abolition of the scheme remained. And as the numbers of assisted place holders grew so the financial dependence on the scheme increased: by 1986-87, over one quarter of the school's gross income (of £1,392,000) came from assisted place holders who represented more than one third of the total number of pupils (592). On 10 January 1987, five months before the general election, David Langstaff, the new bursar, brought to the governors' attention the financial implications for the Cathedral School should a Labour government be voted in. He estimated that over a four year period there was likely to be a 45 *per cent* drop in tuition revenue of £559,000. In such circumstances, a complete rationalisation of the school would inevitably follow. The Conservative victory at the polls on 11 June that year meant that that particular problem would not yet have to be faced, to the relief of the incoming headmaster.[310]

Richards had suggested in November 1974 that following independence HCS would need to become a three-form entry school and that 'a further programme of modernisation' would 'have to be initiated if we are to hold our own with new schools built with state money'. He was right on both counts, although even he could not have predicted the pace of change that would take place within a few years of his departure. For in the five years from 1975, the school roll grew year on year as never before: from 382 to 556 pupils by September 1980, the Sixth Form expanding from 93 to 141 in the same period. This astonishing increase was followed by more modest growth with the introduction of assisted places in 1981, the school expanding to 591 by Sutton's last term. Over the whole period, the Sixth Form increased by 50 (to 142), day numbers by 200 (to 496), and after a dip in the late Seventies, the boarders by 12 (to 95). The expansion should mainly be seen in terms of co-education, apart from one windfall: Lucton School's overnight closure on 25 October 1984, which resulted in an unexpected addition to the HCS roll of 27 pupils (12 of whom were in their final O-level year) after that half-term, making an uncomfortably large Fifth Form that year.

Within two years of Sutton's arrival, all forms had become mixed; in the academic year 1979-80 for the first time more girls were admitted than boys; and in the junior

308. HCSA, GMB 1945-82, pp.322-25; and p.336, 28 October 1980, when 'unanimously' was replaced by 'nem. con.' in the minute book regarding the motion agreeing to the formal application for 40 assisted places.

309. An analysis of parental occupations as listed in the school's admissions register in the two years 1984-86, compared with those admitted from 1977-79, show an increase in the numbers of children from non-professional backgrounds, although as a national survey also discovered (Simon [1991], pp.517-18, note 7) there were still 'relatively few assisted place holders [in the 1980s] from unambiguously working class backgrounds'. The improvement in the school's academic standards, however, is clearly shown in the 1986 O-level results (for the first assisted place 11 plus cohort), where the pass rate increased by around 7 percentage points (to 74.6 *per cent*) on the previous year, close to the level of the last direct grant cohorts in the late 1970s.

310. HCSA, 'Financial Implications of Political Change', written for the Development and Finance Committee meeting, 9-10 Jan. 1987. There is no evidence to suggest that the paper was ever discussed.

intake for September 1986, boys were outnumbered by girls (again for the first time), the Headmaster explaining the decline in boy applicants as 'a phenomenon experienced by many other co-educational schools'. Overall from 1975 to 1987, although the number of boy boarders declined by 20, boy numbers in total hardly changed from around 320. By contrast, the girl population mushroomed. The increase in number of day girls (from 66 to 264) mirrored the increase in the day population overall; and by 1986-87, one third (32 girls) of the boarding community were female, the first girl boarders – living, by courtesy of Bridget Eastaugh, *en famille* in the Bishop's Palace – being admitted in January 1979. And gradually women (or more decorously 'ladies' in the language of the day) were being appointed to the staff Common Room, which by 1986 contained 16 female teachers (out of 53) compared with the five women (out of 29) in 1975. Within a year one of their number, Linda Miles, had been designated 'senior mistress'. By this time, too, many of the old stagers, masters who had served the school loyally for 30 and more years, had retired or were on the verge or retirement.[311] The Common Room's move from Number 1 to 29 Castle Street in 1977 was slowly being matched by a subtle alteration to its character.

The change to the nature of the school created by the female tide during these years can hardly be over-emphasised. From a boys' school with some girls attached, it became a fully co-educational establishment in less than a decade. This was reflected both in the girls' recognition by the school authorities and the scope of their contributions to school life. In terms of the pupil hierarchy, the first deputy Head of School (Julia Budd) was appointed to office for 1978-79. For this year, too, the girl captains of two sports (badminton and hockey) were listed for the first time in the roll-call of school officials printed in *The Herefordian*. Three years later, Olivia Morris became the first girl Head of School. From the turn of the decade, girls were successful in increasing numbers in the Oxbridge stakes: seven out of the 26 OHs in residence at the ancient universities in June 1984 were female, including Celia Lind Jackson, the first girl but last OH to win a close Somerset award (in 1979) before their abolition after 300 years. But girls also began to make major contributions to artistic and other aspects of school life, not least in those areas which had hitherto been male preserves. In 1976-77, for example, the first girls, 18 of them, joined the CCF, it being reported 'in these days of equality and economy' that they wore the same uniform 'from berets to boots' as the boys and 'rapidly reached the high standard expected of them'. And even the rowing club succumbed to the exhortations of a female cox, Hilary Burnham being the first girl to win a regatta event, coxing four boys to victory in the under 14s Ironbridge sprint in 1979. And as successes mounted, particularly on the games field – in 1979-80, the first senior girls' hockey and netball teams were established, and within a few years girls' teams at all levels were beginning to win county tournaments – the boys' patronising attitudes began to disappear. The affectionate cartoon in the 1978 magazine of a hockey girl encouraging her team with the

311. The following assistant masters retired, with 30 or more years service each and 165 years combined service between them, during Sutton's time: B.E. Edwards (Jan. 1945 to Dec. 1980), the last of C.F. Scott's appointments; J.W. Rowlands (1950-80); J.L.T. Brookes (1951-86); H.J. Lush (1948-81); and M.R. Stafford (1955-87). They were soon followed (in 1988) by R.D. Lancaster (1947-88) and W.J. Rumsey (1948-88).

shout 'Come on girls! We haven't lost yet!' (with a scoreboard HCS 0, Visitors 10 in the background) would have been an irrelevant contribution by the mid-1980s.[312]

So, above all, the school's atmosphere gradually changed and HCS became a more civilised place. One indication of this is to be found in the wider use of Christian names. First names rather than initials became the norm in public lists, as with the 1977-78 list of school officials and the 1979 prize list (both for the first time). As R.D. Lancaster acutely observed in his poem 'Love to Jump', published in *The Herefordian* centenary edition of 1978:

> You never know with names these days, so many,
> Lost the plain upstanding surname in this flutter
> Of Rebeccas, Rachels, Carolines and Nicolas.

But the new climate is perhaps best exemplified in this piece written by Richard Errington, an Old Herefordian who had returned to teach music at his old school:

> When I was a boy ... where were all the girls? Then they were things glimpsed fleetingly across the Close or seen fleetingly through the window of a passing bus. Now they can be spotted in every nook and cranny of the school, bringing with them something special that cannot be pin-pointed but was sadly lacking fifteen years ago. The introduction of the girls ... also heralded the arrival of ladies in the Common Room. I often wonder if this most sacred of rooms sparkled all those years ago as it occasionally does now ... I can say that my three years here as a 'new boy' have provided me with more pleasure, happiness and fun ... than my seven years as an 'old boy' ever did, which for me speaks volumes for the type of place this ancient establishment must have become.[313]

In these Sutton years then, the school changed in character and grew out of all recognition from previous generations. How was this expansion managed and the unprecedented increase in numbers accommodated?

As HCS prepared for the loss of the direct grant in 1975, both outgoing and incoming headmasters had no hesitation in informing their governors that the school was poorly equipped for independence. Richards, as we have seen, thought modernisation essential if the school was to survive. As he observed in 'What Price Independence?', 'somehow we must be made to look a better buy at £500+ p.a.' At that time, however, the state of the school hardly suggested value for money, and unless conducted tours ended at the new laboratories, there was no avoiding a visitor going away 'with an impression of age and drabness'. His successor on the other hand was as concerned with the poor impression

312. Also note Mrs Martin's comment, when reviewing girl's games in 1976-77: '[Next Year] we hope ... to change the general feeling of amusement held by most of the boys to one of respect and even, who knows, pride'. *TH*, CCXXIII (Nov. 1977), p.26. The under-18s hockey XI was the first team to win a county trophy (in 1983-84). All told, the girls won seven county hockey or netball tournaments in the four years from 1983. Marilyn ('Lynn') Martin and (from January 1981) Marise Williams (née Vater) were instrumental in the improvement of standards in girls' games during these years.

313. Reprinted from 'Term Times': *TH*, CCXXIV (1983), p.5.

given by the state of Number 1 front garden as parents first approached the school. This was only one of a catalogue of suggestions in Sutton's development plan of November 1975. The document was divided into three sections: cosmetic improvements; additional facilities; and the better use of existing plant. The cosmetic included making the most of Number 1 lawn which could be 'a great aesthetic asset' if the garden was developed 'as a college court'; the improvement of notice boards which 'proclaim a school's activities to the world at large and will be keenly studied by visitors and prospective parents'; the refurbishment of the library, 'the heart of an academic institution'; and the provision of a girls' changing rooms and garden access to the Science block. Among the additional facilities, there was a need for a craft workshop, more music rooms, tennis courts, classrooms on East Street (to complete 'Castle Street Court') and a swimming pool or sports hall. Finally, he suggested that the use of Big School, Numbers 4 Castle Street and 4 Harley Court, School House and even College Hall should all be examined to see if these premises could be employed to better purpose. It is a mark of the school's progress during this period that many of these ambitions were realised during his tenure. To adapt BBS's own observation of October 1976, moving and improving were characteristics of the school's physical development during the Sutton years.

A taste of what was to follow over the coming decade was experienced by the bewildered pupils returning to school at the beginning of Autumn Term 1976. As the Headmaster reported, form rooms had moved; the old book room was no longer a book room so that even John Brookes, the master in charge, seemed at a loss; the Biology laboratory could only be approached through an incomplete changing room; the squash players had no longer to run the gauntlet of Ferrers Street; the Art department was ('like Henry IV') in two parts; and 'someone had taken down the old, ugly comforting black notice boards in Old Block and replaced them with shining, white, empty new ones'. Underneath the account of these changes, as if to emphasise the point, was a photograph of a dismantled Gilbert Library and a warning that with the school poised to move into Numbers 29 and 30 Castle Street, its newly acquired properties, the real upheaval was yet to come.[314]

Thanks to the Old Herefordian Fund, the renovation of the Gilbert Library was almost completed by the following September by which time the 1959 partition and remaining honours boards – behind which extensive damp had been found – had been taken down, and the old heavy bookcases and desks had been replaced by modern library furniture. Through the generosity of the PTA's £1,000 grant and the discernment of Paul Latcham of the Hereford Bookshop, the library had also been re-stocked with new reference books. Books were also transferred from the old Zimmerman Library, which from 1977 only existed in name (or, more accurately, in initial as room Z). But the Gilbert Library had again been made whole, and two gloomy classrooms replaced by a light and spacious facility which was to serve the school well for another generation. As Sutton later informed Old Herefordians at their 1984 dinner, the library no longer exuded 'that atmosphere of academic decay that was so close to a former generation of classical scholars'.

By that autumn term, too, a gem of a building, which became the jewel in the crown of all the school's properties, had been acquired. 'Old College' was the name that had long

314. *TH*, CCXXII (Oct. 1976), p.3.

been given to Number 29 Castle Street because at its heart was the late medieval hall of the College of Vicars Choral.[315] Next door in Numbers 30 and 30A were the former offices of the Steels' legal practice, which included the room where much of the cathedral's business had been conducted during the Steels' long tenures as Chapter Clerks. And outside there was a beautiful walled garden and sunken rose garden, which had one time formed part of the castle moat, flanked by two seventeenth-century gazebos, one of which incorporated a small cottage and a coach house. So not only did this building, or more accurately collection of buildings, possess a scholastic name which would make an impressive school address but (as Sutton remarked) it served 'as a permanent visual aid for the history of domestic architecture'.[316] For apart from the original medieval college hall with its magnificent (but hidden) timber roof, it included a seventeenth-century oak-panelled dining-room with an italianate plaster ceiling, an elegant eighteenth-century drawing room and nineteenth-century offices. With its 27 rooms and extensive grounds, it was a unique opportunity for the school to acquire the most extensive accommodation and the largest parcel of land in Castle Street; and all at a price of £59,000. By the end of 1976, thanks to Zimmerman's generous legacy and the good offices of Tom Steel (whose own plan for a modern town house on the site had been rejected), the property had been bought and leased to the school (at a rent of £6,000 *per annum*) by the Old Herefordian Fund trustees. Over the following months it was renovated for school use so that by the beginning of the 1977-78 academic year, Numbers 29 and 30 had become the home of the Headmaster and Common Room; rooms had been found there for the Classics, Economics and Music departments; and additional residential and study accommodation had been provided. Its timely acquisition also resulted in the establishment of two extra form-rooms in Number 1, and the consequent establishment of three forms throughout the school from 11 to 16, as well as the creation of a staff dining-room and a monitors' Common Room. It also enabled the PTA to embark on its conversion of the half-timbered coach house, restored to a high standard by using timbers recovered from the 'Black Swan' in Widemarsh Street, into a school 'Buttery'. The restored building was opened in September 1979 with this quotation from *The Taming of the Shrew*: 'Go, Sirrah, take them to the Buttery / And give them friendly welcome everyone' – which is just what Peter Skinner, as master in charge, did, as in so many walks of school life.[317]

The acquisition of Old College, vital though it was, was only one step in the school's development during these years. There was further need for an additional junior classroom in September 1978. Fortune again smiled on the school following the county council's plans to dispose of its surplus building stock, including St David's Hall, the old mission hall in Castle Street which was built in 1923 and acquired by the council in 1937. It was leased by the school in time to house one of the First Forms in September 1978 and purchased

315. Built after the incorporation of the vicars choral as a college in 1395, before its move around 80 years later to the new cloistered college adjoining the cathedral. Aylmer and Tiller, pp.444-45.

316. *TH*, CCXXIII (Nov. 1977), p.8.

317. In 1980, its architect, Derek Preece (who was also an HCS parent) was awarded the city council's first conservation award, for his conversion of the old coach-house. The design had been commended by the Civic Trust as 'an imaginative use of an otherwise neglected piece of seventeenth-century Hereford'. *TH*, CCXXVI (1980), p.3; *HT*, 17 Feb. 1978, p.5. The Buttery's opening signalled the end of the boarding tuck shops.

by the governors for £25,900 in February 1980, thus becoming the first piece of real estate ever owned (albeit with a £15,000 mortgage) by the school.[318] At the end of the following summer term, School House was abandoned as a boarding house. Although given the decline in demand the rationalisation of senior boys' boarding was inevitable, it was a sad end to a long and venerable House tradition. As Michael Walling observed, 'there was more than a hint of melancholy when the last three boys left … for School House, though to the end of its days it kept a reputation for tough conditions, had a character and atmosphere all of its own'.[319] But at least the building was put to good use, the boarding accommodation being converted into study space for the Lower Sixth, four classrooms, a TV room (with video recorder courtesy of the PTA), an English book room and a scout store.

As one boarding house closed another opened. Number 4 Castle Street was leased from the Chapter, renovated and used as a boarding house for a few girls from September 1979. But no more than six could be accommodated there, and the *en famille* arrangements at the Bishop's Palace and in other homes around the Close could be no more than temporary. The Canon's House, St John Street, was considered as a possible alternative but it was too small – only 17 girls could be accommodated there – required extensive rebuilding, and the Chapter's likely asking price of £120,000 was considered by the governors to be 'far too high'. Of all the buildings available for girls' boarding, 5 St John Street was the most suitable, the property being purchased from Dr Langford by the OH Trustees for £91,000 in late 1983 in sufficient time for it to be renovated before receiving its first 20 boarders in September 1984. With the addition of Number 6 next door (again purchased

Fig. 8.17 Bill and Geraldine Rumsey preside as house-parents over the first girl boarders at Number 5, St John Street, September 1984.

318. The hall was then converted to two classrooms for the Geography department, its old base in the Science block becoming in turn the upper Biology laboratory.

319. See *TH*, CCXXVI (1980), pp.7-8, for Walling's beautifully written and nostalgic piece about the halcyon days of boarding in School House.

by the Trust) nearly three years later, the school had sufficient accommodation for 40 girl boarders. By this time, 2 Castle Street – described by Herbert Powell as 'a good example of Regency jerry building', and one which stood 'in a midden' – had also been acquired by the OH Fund. It was restored by the school at considerable expense over the best part of two years (1984-86) – the central wall had to be completely rebuilt, its foundations being sunk 16 feet lower than originally intended – and brought into use as additional accommodation for junior boys, a form-room and staff flats.[320] By 1987, therefore, the school's boarding needs had been met, and boarding had been turned from a loss-making into a profitable enterprise.[321]

Better recreational amenities were also essential. Although Sutton soon realised that the building of a swimming pool or sports hall was unaffordable – and in the case of a pool, given the new municipal facility, unnecessary – the school's games facilities were insufficient. This was certainly the case for the girls, their occasional netball practice being confined to School House yard and their tennis games to the courts on Bishop's Meadow. So there was some urgency to develop new games areas but these took time to achieve. Following Bishop Eastaugh's suggestion in 1976 that the school could have the use of part of the Palace vegetable garden, it took months of intricate negotiations with the Church Commissioners (who owned the land and at first were not prepared to give security of tenure), the department of the environment and the city planning authorities – given its

Fig. 8.18 Then first purpose-built girls' courts off Gwynne Street: the Headmaster with Lynn Martin, John and Bridget Eastaugh and the netball squad, autumn 1980.

320. Kevin Mason, an influential new governor, negotiated the £70,000 asking price down to £58,500, but an additional £90,000 was spent to make it fit for school use. The OH Trustees bought Number 2 by means of a loan (of the whole purchase price) from the 1978 Appeal Fund, the monies being repaid in three equal instalments plus interest at 1 *per cent* above bank minimum lending rate.

321. For the four financial years 1976-80, boarding losses (which were particularly severe, 1978-80) averaged over £5,000 *per annum*; and for the three years 1984-87, following the rationalisation of boys' boarding and the opening of St John's House for the girls, boarding made an annual surplus of over £10,000.

location, it was a sensitive archaeological site – before a suitable lease was signed and the scheme for two tennis/netball courts given the go-ahead. And it was not until late in the autumn term of 1980 that they were ready for use. It was an important additional facility for girls' games, even if an article in that year's *Herefordian* had suggested that as the courts were built on the possible site of Nell Gwynne's birthplace, 'real, royal tennis' would have been the more appropriate game for these courts.[322]

Sports facilities at Wyeside were also coming under increasing pressure as the number of hockey matches increased and new games like rounders were introduced. This again took time to remedy. However, in September 1978 the school acquired from the city council – through the good offices of its senior governor, Tom Barnes – and signed a 21 year lease for eight acres of land: the 'Red Ash Field' (or 'black ash' as the Headmaster termed it), adjoining Wyeside. It was one thing to sign a favourable lease at £350 *per annum* rent; quite another to level, drain, repair and sow ground to make it fit for playing games. But helped by the pupils themselves, who were used *en masse* to clear the field of stones with hardly a parental complaint, the 'Red Ash' was ready for sowing by the autumn of 1979. By then the state of the main ground was giving great cause for concern, the 1st XI cricket fixtures that season having been curtailed or rearranged as away matches. A year later, following Brian Goode's appointment, the Headmaster could observe that the new groundsman had 'made an immense difference to the quality of the facilities at Wyeside and also to the appearance of the ground as a whole ... we now have a wicket that is safe to play on and it has become a pleasure to watch the games'.[323] By late 1982, a governor reported that Wyeside's 25 acres now provided two cricket squares, three rugby and hockey fields, four rounders pitches, and a 400 metre athletics track; that the area was effectively managed; and that the head groundsman was satisfied with the plant and machinery at his disposal.[324] It was a far cry from the days of Kurt Winsel, Goode's predecessor.

Nor were the performing arts neglected. The drama facilities that Sutton inherited were totally inadequate. College Hall, although still occasionally used by the school for dramatic purposes, had ceased to be the venue for school plays. The school was therefore dependent on the use of other spaces: the Great Hall of the Palace for *Hamlet* (1979); All Saints for the original rock opera, *Murderers* (1980); the cathedral for *The Vigil* (1980); and 'Old College' garden for *Charley's Aunt* (1980). Big School, it is true, was also available for plays but that space – while not quite deserving its description as the 'elephant's graveyard of lost causes' as it was called in a review of *A Little Lampoon* (1979) – was also in demand as a venue for lectures, films, concerts, examinations, CCF functions and shooting practice. And as the number of productions increased following Colin Gray's arrival as Head of English and

---

322. *TH*, CCXXV (1980), back cover, 'Anyone for Tennis?', one of Peter Williams' inimitable articles advertising Franklin Barnes.

323. HCSA, Sutton's report for the governors' meeting, 22 May 1980. For one further indicator of the wicket's improvement that year – the first 1st XI century scored at Wyeside for ten years – see below, p.569, note 376.

324. HCSA, Ernest Moreton's report for the governors' meting, 3 Nov. 1982. Although 18 months later, when Peter Prior inspected Wyeside, he was made aware of the damage caused to machinery when the Wye flooded and the pavilion's limitations in terms of girls' accommodation and storage space. HCSA, Prior to Sutton, 18 May 1984. Further land above the flood-plain – the site of the old Broomy Hill tennis courts – was acquired for around £9,000 in 1986.

Drama in September 1979 – indicated not only by the plays produced in 1979-80 but also by the prominence that Drama was then given in *The Herefordian*[325] – so the demands on Big School escalated. And Big School could not even be used for the experimental Drama and Theatre studies O-level course, undertaken by 12 Sixth-formers in 1981-82, which had to be taught in the School House 'yellow room'.

It was Gray's vision to see the potential that Big School afforded for public productions, as well as school performance and teaching; and it fell to John Seely, his colleague, to turn the vision into reality. In June 1982, the governors unanimously approved Seely's design against three other proposals for a studio theatre for an audience of 80 to 120 and at a likely cost of £28,000.[326] The main building work was completed by the late autumn of 1982, the fire officers' demands having been met, the long staircase lengthened, the careers room shortened, John Brookes' room temporarily demolished, and the balcony halved and turned into a control room with a new staircase. The amateurs – parents, and pupils for more menial roles – then took over the demanding tasks of cleaning and painting a wall area of over 2,000 square feet, installing the light and sound systems and undertaking the myriad of jobs required to turn a basic shell into a proper theatre. The 1 March 1983 deadline was met and five varied entertainments were put on during the opening week, followed by *As You Like It* as the first major production. The creation of this new and flexible facility had an immediate effect on HCS life. In the academic year 1983-84, Drama was taught for the first time to all First and Second-formers; and in that year too the studio was the scene for seven professional company visits, three school productions, a Gilbert consort concert and a wildlife lecture featuring several large birds of prey. And in subsequent years, following the appointment of the school's first professional Head

Fig. 8.19 Colin Gray overlooks a performance from the sound box of the new Big School studio, c.1984.

325. From virtually no Drama reports for the mid/late-Seventies, the 1980 edition (for the academic year 1979-80) contained no less than four pages of text and nearly two of visual images, including a cartoon of the four 1980 producers. From then onwards, a separate Drama section was always featured in *The Herefordian*.

326. The actual cost was £28,211, plus £1,490 additional expenditure to meet the fire safety requirements and an extra £500 fee to a designer. Of this sum, £11,560 was found from the 'Mediaeval Fayre' monies and £4,000 from the OH Trust. HCSA, Sutton's report for the governors' meeting, 7 June 1983. John Seely described the process of building the theatre: *TH*, CCXXIX (1983), pp.25, 27.

of Drama,[327] the studio saw the performance of musicals, plays by Bennett, Pinter and Stoppard, a production of *King Lear* as well as professional productions and courses. The Head of Drama's claim that the New Hereford Theatre apart, the studio was 'the only regular promoter of theatre and dance in the city' was no idle boast. Drama at HCS had come of age.

Music had suffered in a similar way to Drama: facilities were poor for both class teaching and individual tuition. While acknowledging that 'Music is our strong non-athletic extra-mural suit', Sutton made the following comments about the inadequate nature of the school's musical provision in his buildings review of June 1976: 'Ferrers Street unsatisfactory. Teaching rooms for peripatetics uncongenial. Poor practice facilities. Inadequate storage of instruments'. The acquisition of Old College enabled the creation of a music room 'worthy of the name' in the elegant first-floor bedroom at the back of the house, but even this addition was insufficient for the school's needs. By November 1982, as Sutton admitted, the physical constraints of space restricted the amount of music taught. More than three years later the Headmaster's drawing room was in use most weekdays for individual piano tuition, the new Director of Music taught Sixth-form groups in his own house and other music staff often scrabbled around for spare teaching rooms. So the finding of suitable premises for music teaching was given a high priority. Number 31 Castle Street, a late seventeenth-century town house with Victorian additions, a fine staircase, ornate plasterwork and wisteria trailed garden, had been identified as a possible music school as early as April 1982. Next door to Old College, it was located in the right place; and its 14 rooms covering 3,500 square feet of space, with over 1,100 square feet in the extensive medieval cellars, would provide the space for recitals, class teaching and individual tuition and create the right atmosphere for music making. It was also the wish of the owners that the school should be given the opportunity to buy it but it was not until April 1987 that the school finally purchased the building at a cost of £85,000.[328] Even though conversion costs were estimated at around £30,000, it was not an unreasonable price to pay for a building that was to be of fundamental importance to the school's future development.

Music facilities were patchy at best until the Headmaster opened the music school, only the ground floor of which was refurbished, on his final Hereford speech day. And for much of this period, the same might be said about the quality of the school's music making. It is true that the development of HCS as a fully co-educational school had increased interest in musical activities. The November 1983 inspectors found a full orchestra with a strength of 50, a chamber orchestra of 25 and a CCF band of the same number; a junior choir for the first and second years (mostly girls) and a chamber choir of 15; together with the more specialist Gilbert consort and recorder and guitar groups. Such activity was a considerable advance on the situation a decade earlier. And the standard that some of these groups attained was commendable. The chamber choir reached the finals of a national competition in 1983, and in the Herefordshire Music Festivals of the late-Seventies and early-Eighties,

327. Christine Borrett-Sykes, who was formerly Arts Officer for Stoke and Newcastle Arts Project Ltd and had wide experience of the theatrical world.

328. On Mrs Victor's death in December 1985, the ownership of the house passed to her sister, Miss Cicely Cholmeley, who sold it to the school. A few boarders had been housed there for a short time in 1983.

HCS pupils won more trophies and classes than those from any other school.[329] But not everything was sweetness and light. As the 1983 inspectors found, Music at HCS was 'essentially a recreational pursuit rather than an educational activity'. And when in September 1985 John Williams took office as Director of Music – and the school's first Head of Music unencumbered by cathedral responsibilities – he compared HCS unfavourably with the musically established Cranbrook School from which he had hailed. But there were compensations and a real base on which to build. Within two years, a jazz band and a hundred member choral society, which performed *African Sanctus* and *Carmina Burana* in its first year, had been founded; 13 students had gained grade 8 distinctions or merits; new academic courses had been provided; chamber music had been incorporated as part of the Tuesday activity programme; and resources, including the acquisition of the 20-volume *New Grove Dictionary of Music and Musicians*, had improved. There was still much to be done but the possession of Number 31 meant that the department could now be properly directed. And in the new Director of Music the school had the man with the expertise, vision and energy to enable HCS to become in time a nationally respected musical school. When that happened, as Williams himself accurately forecast, the school's future would be strengthened and the quality of life enhanced for all.[330]

One further major initiative occurred in Sutton's final year when the governing body grasped the opportunity that its predecessors had been unable to take in 1940, 1945 and 1972, and acquired the privately owned Cathedral Preparatory School. Keith Hill, its joint owner, had been made aware of the governors' interest in 28 Castle Street as early as June 1983, but it was not until three years later that serious negotiations took place over its acquisition. Heads of agreement were signed by mid-October 1986, with HCS initially leasing the property for £30,000 *per annum* (plus an agreed sum for its assets), with an option to buy at a later date. This enabled the headmastership to be advertised the following month, Stephen Sides, then Director of Music at Prestfelde, being appointed as the first non-proprietorial Headmaster of the Cathedral Preparatory School on 23 January 1987. The acquiring of CPS (as it then was) was not without its difficulties, and HCS made a significant loss in the first year of the lease.[331] In the longer term, however, its acquisition was to prove of vital significance to the senior school's prosperity.

Mention should finally be made of important infrastructure projects undertaken during these years: the provision of girls' lavatories and a girls' changing room for PE; the

329. HCS entries for the festival often reached 100 in the late-Seventies and early-Eighties. Of these, perhaps one quarter would be placed first, second or third; several trophies were won in most years; and the school orchestra was placed first in its class on at least three occasions (1978, 1981 and 1982). However, it should be acknowledged that entries in some classes were in the low single figures, and – given that there were few other musical secondary schools in the vicinity – that standards were variable.

330. HCSA, unpublished report of the HMI inspection, 21-25 Nov. 1983 (pp.8-9 on music); and *TH*, CCXXXII (1986), p.25; CCXXXIII (1987), p.56 for Williams' perceptive comments on the state of HCS music on his arrival and his own estimation of the progress made in his first two years.

331. The break-even figure for the acquisition was a roll of 135 boys. However, following an outflow of pupils, the budget for 1987/88 was revised to forecast a loss of £34,500 on a school population of 111 pupils, roughly the number inherited by Stephen Sides. As Brian Nelson, who negotiated the transaction, had accurately predicted: 'it may well be that the first year could present us with a loss as it may be impossible to attain the requisite pupil numbers in the time available'. HCSA, G.B. Nelson to P.J. Prior, 2 June 1987.

acquisition of new boilers and central heating systems; the extension of fire precaution work throughout the school; and the improvement and re-equipping of the dining-hall and kitchens. As significantly in terms of pupil learning was the development of computing. The county system of running school computer programmes having proved too inefficient, a North Star Horizon machine with 48 Kbytes of main store was bought in June 1979; and the school's first computer centre, complete with eight BBC microcomputers, each with a colour monitor connected together by an econet system, was opened on 15 February 1984.[332] The conversion was undertaken entirely by members of the estates department, led by Geoff Pinches, who together with Herbert Powell, the school architect, played such an important part in the school's maintenance and development during these and subsequent years.

All told, around £670,000 was spent on capital projects, 1976-87, far more than in any other decade hitherto. One half of this sum was provided by the Old Herefordian Trust Fund.[333] Without Zimmerman's legacy, such development would have been impossible; with it, HCS could afford to implement a programme of expansion and modernisation unparalleled in its history. It is true that not everything in Sutton's 1976 wish-list had been accomplished by the time he came to leave. For example, little had been done to improve the facilities either for Art and Technology, the projected appeal planned for 1986-87 having been shelved, or for indoor sports. It is also evident that opportunities, such as the possible purchase of the Castle Pool Hotel – set, it was claimed (in 1982), 'in quiet and secluded country-like surroundings' – and a field study centre near Aberystwyth, were missed.[334] Nevertheless, that so much was accomplished in a comparatively short time reflects great credit not only on the Headmaster and his bursars but also on governors who were prepared to move with the times.

Governance and Finance

As guest of honour on his final speech day in July 1987, Peter Prior – governor for almost 16 years and the board's first ever lay chairman – made reference to the school's financial state:

---

332. HCS was the first Herefordshire school to provide a computer exclusively for pupil use: *HT,* 1 Feb. 1980, p.13, for Roger Toll's letter and the acknowledgment of John Chapman, Headmaster of Bishop's; and *TH,* CCXXX (1984), pp.6-7, for the opening of the computer centre (formerly Room G) in Old Block.

333. Zimmerman's estate at the time of his death in 1963 amounted to some £250,000 but the sum was severely reduced by death duties. So only £104,429.86p was actually received by the OH Trustees – the Trust being formally established in January 1975 – the monies being handed over in two tranches on 5 August 1974 and 27 January 1979 after the deaths of the life tenants, Mrs Folkes and Miss Whiting. Excluding the sum for the Gilbert Library's restoration, the OH Trustees paid the following: £60,955 in 1976 (for Numbers 29-30, Castle Street); £4,000 in 1982-83 (towards the Studio); £18,743 in 1983-84 (for the renovation of the gazebos in Number 29 garden); £93,550 in 1983 (for Number 5 St John Street); £59,750 in 1984-85 (for Number 2 Castle Street); and £97,250 in 1986 (for Number 6 St John Street). The Fund's net current assets (derived mainly from the school's rents, which had reached £25,000 by 1986-87) had increased to £266,792 by April 1987.

334. Although both were considered: HCSA, for the bursar's report, 9 Aug. 1982, on Grogwynion House, Llanafan, (offers 'in region of' £30,000); and GMB 1982-86, minutes, 3 Nov. 1982, p.3, re the Castle Pool (then on sale for around £185,000 for the business and its assets). The school's failure to purchase the High School's playing fields may be added to this list, although at the time (as Sutton observed) the £65,000 asking price seemed a lot of money to pay for 12 acres. HCSA, B.B. Sutton to K.G. Mason, 20 Jan. 1983.

> Sound education is, of course, what this school is all about. But it can develop only if the school is financially successful. We are at present on a sound financial footing and can remain so provided that everybody concerned with the school's management understands that we must break even. The school has no hidden crock of gold; there is I fear no substitute for hard graft.

In the next breath, he paid tribute to his governing colleagues:

> But I'm leaving the place in very safe hands with Wallace [Garland, Prior's successor as chairman] and his colleagues. They are energetic, dedicated, informed and perceptive. They have varied backgrounds, business executives, clerics and a housewife. What is important is that they are all equally capable of counting the pennies.[335]

A sound financial base; and a committed and varied board composed of governors who were financially aware. It had not always been the case.

Despite its male dominance, the 1987 governing board was indeed a capable body. Aside from the chairman and Dean, who had recently been appointed its President, its membership comprised a city alderman; the managing director of Bulmers; the second ever lady governor, a professional speech therapist as well as a 'housewife'; another businessman with wide experience of youth work; a young executive of Knight Frank and Rutley; two able cathedral canons; an Oxford don who had taught a number of promising OH physicists at Brasenose; and a recently appointed manager of the Royal Bank of Scotland.[336] With the exception of the cathedral representatives and the city father, they had been appointed to the board because of the contributions they could make to its deliberations rather than as a result of their position. This marked a significant shift in the nature of the board's constitution and was a far cry from the position 12 years earlier when two-thirds of the nine governors held representative governorships. How was this transformation, which was of crucial importance to the school's development, brought about?

As with any constitutional change, the development of a modern system of governance evolved gradually. Within the first year of Sutton's tenure both Humphrey Mynors and Peter Prior supported an immediate expansion of the board's membership and pressed particularly for the appointment of a woman governor. By May 1977, Brian Nelson, at Prior's suggestion, had been added as a co-opted governor. Less than a year later, Anthea McIntyre, a recently elected county councillor and member of the county Education Committee, had the honour of becoming both the first woman and the youngest governor in the school's history.[337] Elizabeth Evans' admission in May 1978 brought the member-

335. *TH*, CCXXXIII (1987), p.8. The speech was in fact read by the Headmaster, Prior's voice having broken down.

336. The governors were respectively: Peter Prior, Peter Haynes, Roy Blackler, Brian Nelson, Elizabeth Evans, Wallace Garland, Kevin Mason, Paul Iles, John Tiller, John Peach and Alastair McConnachie. The newest member of the board (and a potential chairman), Sir David Roberts, a distinguished diplomat and an Old Herefordian, had died on 7 June 1987, a few weeks before speech day.

337. Anthea McIntyre (at the time of writing, Conservative MEP for the West Midlands) was elected a county councillor at the age of 22 in May 1977 and replaced Tom Barnes as an LEA governor. Her governorship was not an unqualified success: she missed half of the ten meetings from September 1978 to June 1981 – her last

ship to 12 in accord with the maximum number prescribed by the Charity Commission. The total membership had been increased by three and two women had been appointed. However, there still remained the need for new blood, and in 1981-82, following Dean Rathbone's retirement and the demise of the LEA representative governors with the departure of the last direct grant pupils, a new constitution was essential. But there could be no instant remedies.

Before new blood could be transfused, the old had to be disposed of and without any retirement provision this was not an easy operation. Peter Prior, who tended to view school governors as the equivalent of company directors, was again the prime mover. His opinion of many of his early governing colleagues was not high. In May 1980, he wrote confidentially to the Headmaster:

> You will know that I feel that the average age and the capabilities which are offered by some of the present governors are unsuitable. One problem is how to lose a number of them. In my view, there are at least six who make a very minimal contribution and four who make none at all. It behoves us to recruit other more useful members.[338]

This was easier said than done but the resignation of Anthea McIntyre, and the retirement to Australia of Tom Barnes, a member of the board for nearly 30 years, gave an opportunity for new faces.[339] Henrietta Dunne, wife of the Lord Lieutenant and an HCS parent; and Wallace Garland, a senior executive at DRG plastics, and a scout leader and sportsman who had already helped the school with Young Enterprise, answered the call and were nominated as governors in late 1981. Over the following five years, a further seven able governors were added to the board as a result of resignations or retirements so that on that July 1987 speech day only Peter Prior, the retiring chairman, and Roy Blackler remained of the nine governors who had appointed the leaving Headmaster.

The board's constitution, too, was to be fundamentally changed in the early-Eighties. That Peter Prior should have consulted Humphrey Mynors – perhaps the only governor who could keep Prior 'at bay' (as Mynors termed it) and who somewhat reluctantly continued as a governor until into his 80th year – as to the best way of doing this is one indication of the esteem in which he was held. Mynors had in fact tried to interest the old Dean in reform some time earlier but Rathbone had shied away from the task. 'As Murray Irvine [Canon Chancellor and governor, 1965-78] once said to me in most affectionate terms', Mynors commented to the Headmaster in early October 1981, 'he [Rathbone] is a great non-grasper of nettles'. Now, with the impending retirements of both the Dean and Tom Barnes (his deputy on the board), there was little time to formulate a new arrangement. And there was an urgent need to do this so as to avoid the alarming prospect (from Sutton's

attendance before her resignation in late 1981 being the meeting on 29 January 1980 – and had the worst attendance record of any governor of the period.

338. HCSA, P.J. Prior to B.B. Sutton, 8 May 1980. That there were 10 dead-weights among a governing body of 12 seems unlikely, but Prior's view received qualified support from the Headmaster who in his reply of 16 May said that he would welcome 'a more rigorous scrutiny of our activities … and a larger injection of ideas from the board'.

339. Tom Barnes' governorship from 22 June 1953 to 3 November 1981 (first and last meetings) represented the longest period of continuous service for any governor in the twentieth century.

viewpoint) of the Precentor becoming acting chairman as well as acting Dean. For Peter Prior, it was more of a case of devising a different instrument of government in order to enforce a mass clear-out of unsatisfactory governors.[340]

As we have seen this did not happen as Prior wanted; nor was the new constitution in place by September 1981 as he had originally anticipated. But after consultation with the Dean, Headmaster and select governors, a set of rules for future governors were drafted in time for consideration that November. Most of these were formally adopted in February 1982. They regularised the number of governors (12, nine co-opted), the frequency of their meetings, governors' service and retirement (to 65 and then 70 with agreement), attendance, voting and the quorum (five governors).

The new rules, however, did not resolve the chairmanship issue, Peter Prior having only been elected acting-chairman. Peter Haynes' arrival as Dean concentrated governors' minds. Little more than a month after his installation, Prior raised the question as to whether the chairman should be elected by his colleagues. He wrote to the new Dean in a typically forceful manner:

> I could not have raised this with the former Dean ... To do so might have implied unkind assessments which would have been reprehensible ... I am looking into the unknowns of the future however. A future Dean might be of an unusual type (there was once a red Dean of Canterbury!). The welfare of the school might then be better served if the chairman came from amongst the other governors but if there is no break with tradition now, this might be impossible.

And when the Chapter decided that it would be wrong to alter the historic link 'at the present moment', Prior's attitude was even more direct:

> It is ... vital to maintain the standards of business management [already established] and it is questionable whether this is likely to be achieved if the chairmanship of the governing body depends on chance rather than merit ... [During my time] such measures of reform as have resulted in its financial viability have been effected in spite of rather than because of the contribution in management terms which has arisen from the Chapter and its nominees.

In essence, the problem was this: the new Dean wanted Prior to continue as chairman – understandably given the cathedral's own weighty problems – but his Chapter wished to reserve the Dean's right to be chairman *ex officio*. On the other hand, most of the governors, Humphrey Mynors being the most notable exception, felt strongly that it was in the school's best interests (as Prior explained) 'to elect as chairman whichever of their number seems most suitable'.[341] Prior's viewpoint eventually prevailed, the issue being resolved on

340. For these issues: HCSA, P.J. Prior to Dean Rathbone, 12 Dec. 1980, 8 Jan. 1981; H.B. Mynors to B.B. Sutton, 12 Jan., 4 Oct. 1981; H.B. Mynors to A.P. Hollingworth, 22 Sept. and Sutton's reply, 26 Sept. 1981. Philip Barrett in his eulogy at Dean Rathbone's memorial service (24 September 1995) referred to the Dean's reluctance to grasp nettles 'as perhaps his only failing'. *Friends of Hereford Cathedral*, 62nd Report (1996), p.16. For Canon Precentor Allan Shaw, see below, p.558.

341. For the above, see HCSA, P.J. Prior to Dean Haynes, 28 Jan., 6 May 1983; B.B. Sutton to H.B. Mynors,

7 June 1983 when it was agreed that 'the governors shall elect a chairman by a simple majority, provided that the Dean is a part of it, to serve for a period of five years'. At the following November meeting, Peter Prior was unanimously elected chairman and Wallace Garland vice-chairman.

With the completion of these new rules a great forward step had been taken. And although the requirement that a canon should be in post for six months before becoming a governor was to prove so contentious that it was never enforced, and there was to be a further hiatus in 1986-87 when Peter Prior announced his intention to stand down as chairman, these rules set down important new principles of governance. For the first time it was established that a chairman and deputy should be elected by their colleagues; that all governors would retire at 70; and that they could be removed if they failed to attend three consecutive meetings or engaged in inappropriate behaviour. Moreover, with the exception of the Dean and two Chapter representatives, the desirable principle of co-option over representation was enshrined in an agreed document, even if agreement was limited to the governors themselves and the changes were not incorporated as formal amendments to the scheme of governance.

The second major constitutional change of the period arose from an event which could not have been foreseen when the 1983 rules were drafted. The overnight closing of Lucton School, after 276 years of its existence, on 25 October 1984 not only left 166 pupils stranded but also sent shock waves through the county. Lucton's closure resulted in the resignation of its third lady governor from the Cathedral School's board.[342] It also persuaded the HCS governors that it was now imperative to implement the proposal that its solicitors had advised four years earlier: the incorporation of the Cathedral School as a company limited by guarantee. This time the proposal met with the Chapter's approval as well as the board's endorsement. A memorandum and articles for the proposed company, which reflected both the school's existing constitution and its close links with the cathedral, were drafted. After consultation with the Chapter and its officers and due consideration by the governors themselves, they were submitted to the Charity Commissioners by 1 August 1986 and formally endorsed by the time the new Headmaster had taken up his post. Incorporation in this way had much to recommend it. Although it did not cover maladministration or negligence, it protected the individual liability of any governor should the school go into receivership through misfortune; it protected Dean and Chapter interests, the two other Chapter members being included as company directors in addition to the 12 governors, the Chapter also reserving its rights over the school's religious education, the status and number of its choristers and the appointment of the Headmaster; and it guaranteed the school's £100,000 Lloyd's Bank overdraft, which since 1973 had been secured on Dean and Chapter property. The question 'By what authority do ye do these things?' which Humphrey Mynors had posed several years before could now be given this answer: by the

27 April, 5 May and Mynors reply, 1 May 1983; P.J. Prior to all governors, 3 June 1983. For the relationship between Hewlett Johnson (the 'red Dean' referred to by Prior) and John Shirley, Headmaster of the King's School, Canterbury: Butler, pp.62-67, 101-03, 150, 205-06, 231.

342. Henrietta Dunne, the wife of the Lucton chairman, resigned on 11 December 1984. Peter Prior acknowledged her 'enthusiastic support and spirited advice' over her three-year governorship, the following day. HCSA, P.J. Prior to Henrietta Dunne, 12 Dec. 1984.

authority of an externally validated, modern system of corporate governance. It was the most significant constitutional change since the establishment of the original 1893 scheme. The *ancient régime* had at last been brought to an end.[343]

In pressing his case for an elected chairman, Prior had emphasised to the new Dean the operating changes that had recently been made, contrasting the school's 'Dickensian' accounting procedures of the previous decade to its business-like methods in 1983. The acting chairman was clearly making the point that standards of business management were not necessarily likely to be advanced by an *ex officio* head of the board, but there was substance to his claim that the school's management procedures had improved out of all recognition since he had become a governor.

Efficient business practices, however, were not easily established. A considerable start had been made with the bursar's appointment in 1972 but as Hollingworth explained to the governors in September 1979, the nature of his job had changed markedly during a period of unprecedented expansion. In 1972, he had been appointed principally to concentrate on the school's accounting functions; seven years later he was also acting as the Headmaster's general manager 'to assist him in planning and to be responsible for undertaking the many improvements which the school needs and ought to have'.

Matters had come to a head at a governors' meeting in September 1978 when the failure to produce the previous two years audited accounts gave rise to a general discussion on the bursar's role. Should he still be answerable to the board or, as with 'modern business methods where the head of finance reports to the chief executive', to the Headmaster? It was decided to follow modern practice but this did nothing to improve the completion of the audited accounts which were three years overdue by September 1979. This was the signal for a heated discussion as to whether a school should be run as a normal commercial undertaking or whether (as Mynors maintained) 'jobs that seemed the most important to the Headmaster should be dealt with first'. Nevertheless, it was clear that the situation could not be allowed to get completely out of hand. An experienced accountant was brought in to deal with the backlog and the accounts brought up to date by the time of the January 1980 meeting. That year interim financial accounts were produced for the first time, giving the governors regular four-monthly updates on the school's financial state; and in mid-1981 an accounting machine, the Kienzle 2200, was purchased (at a cost of over £12,000) to deal with salaries, purchases and fees. These measures did not always produce accurate forecasts; nor were draft accounts always produced in sufficient time or in the way that governors wanted; nor were the bursar's priorities always as his chairman would have wished; but by the time of Hollingworth's retirement in 1986, the school's financial management was immeasurably better than it had been a decade earlier. And David Langstaff, his successor, lost no time in further improving the efficiency of his accounts team.

The work of a new governors' committee in reforming the school's finances and longer-term planning should also be emphasised. Elizabeth Evans had first suggested in May 1980 that standing-committees should be appointed to support the executive but it was not until the autumn of 1982 that a formal committee was established to deal with the school's

343. Mynors makes his observation in a letter to the Clerk to the Governors: HCSA, H.B. Mynors to A.P. Hollingworth, 22 Sept. 1981. For the 1893 scheme, see above, pp.295-6.

development. It was chaired by Wallace Garland, who had already taken over the audit brief from Peter Prior, and included three other able younger governors. Its business expanded (as its chairman admitted) 'outside any terms of reference' but it proved to be the power-house of the school's administration over the next five years: revising budgets, examining bad debts and rental demands, improving financial information, planning expansion and monitoring developments. It also became an important sounding board for the Headmaster and his bursar and occasionally a point of reference for governor criticisms. Without its work, the school's governance and development in the Eighties would have been very much the poorer.[344]

The success of the school's improved governance and financial management is partly reflected in its trading position. In the five years from 1975 to 1980, only in one year (1977-78) did it make a surplus; in the seven years from 1980 to 1987, only in one year (1982-83) did it make a loss.[345] It is true that the margins were small – in the best year (1984-85: the Lucton year), the surplus represented little over 3 *per cent* of turnover – but the cumulative effect was palpable, as is indicated by the bursar's report of May 1985, when for the first time the balance sheet showed an excess of current assets over current liabilities. It did not last but it was a milestone in the school's growth towards financial stability. Much of this improvement should be put down to its first lay chairman. As his successor remarked, Peter Prior's contribution had been 'immense'.[346] By the time he departed in July 1987, the governors were better informed and the school better managed than ever before. His chairmanship was not without friction; nor were his fellow governors always in sympathy with his commercial approach; nor (to use his own phrase) was his 'brash goodwill' always appreciated, but he more than anyone dragged the school's governance into the late twentieth century.

Fig. 8.20 Peter Prior: the school's first lay chairman of governors.

344. The Development and Finance Sub-Committee (the 'Finance' title was first added in October 1983, although it had been dealing with financial matters since its inception) met 18 times between autumn 1982 and May 1985. Its first extant minutes date from 5 March 1983. The committee comprised four governors, Wallace Garland, Elizabeth Evans, Kevin Mason and (from June 1984) Paul Iles, the Headmaster and bursar always being in attendance. For Garland's worries about the expansion of its business: HCSA, W.L. Garland to B.B. Sutton, 17 Oct. 1983.

345. The losses for the years 1975-77, 1978-80 and 1982-83 respectively were: £1,843; £6,592; 16,606; £3,637 plus £6,670 (for the four months 1 April to 31 July 1980, the school's financial year then changing to coincide with the academic year); and £3,003. And its surpluses for the years 1980-82 and 1983-87 respectively were: £17,291; £2,004; £19,762; £37,683; £6,722; and £31,500 (as forecast). It is true that trading conditions were easier in the Eighties than the Seventies, when inflation rates and teachers' salary settlements were both higher. Government grants in the form of assisted places should also be taken into account for the period from 1981, as should the lifting of the government's 'repressive controls' (as the bursar put it) which inhibited development in the days of the direct grant.

346. HCSA, W.L. Garland to P.J. Prior, 13 Oct. 1986.

School and Cathedral

> The concept of a single foundation underlying the school and the cathedral, with each constituent part supporting the work of the other, seemed to me to be right … The real sadness for me is that the Dean and Chapter do not share this vision of a single foundation with a common purpose. Reservations about 'private' education; misconceptions about the school's finances and tenancies of cathedral property; impatience with children in the Cathedral Close and Castle Street all preoccupy the Chapter. Fundamental issues have not been faced nor the exciting challenge and opportunity of a community of over 500 young people on the doorstep ever been grasped … If my vision is wrong or unacceptable I should have been told long ago, and my successor deserves a clear statement from the Dean and Chapter if only to save him from the frustration and heartbreak that I have suffered.[347]

Barry Sutton's *cri de coeur*, written in confidence to the four members of the governors' finance and development committee on the penultimate day of 1986, was born of years of frustration with the cathedral authorities, but how had the relationship between school and cathedral become so strained?

There were immediate catalysts for the Headmaster's outburst. At the end of the previous term, the Chapter Clerk had issued a mild rebuke over the alleged over-running of a school congregational practice and the school's failure to inform the cathedral of the designation of its carol service collection. More serious was the Chapter's failure to inform the school directly of its proposal to raise the nave sanctuary crossing, an operation that would inevitably have affected its use of the cathedral. Most serious of all was the publication of an unfortunate phrase in 'The Hereford Commission', which commented upon recent 'tensions' between school and cathedral.[348] The matter was discussed at a full governors' meeting in February 1987, when the Dean firmly denied that this impression had ever been given to the commission, adding that the Chapter regarded the school as an integral part of the cathedral foundation.

The trouble was that it did not always feel that way.[349] Incidents relating to the school's use of the cathedral were not commonplace but were troubling when they occurred. The school did its best to obviate difficulties. The broderers objected to pupil use of kneelers so

347. HCSA, B.B. Sutton's paper, 'Cathedral/School Relationship', for the Finance and Development Committee, 30 Dec. 1986.

348. The Hereford Commission had been established by Bishop Eastaugh in June 1985 'to consider the whole life of Hereford City Deanery, the background of growth and change over past years and the developing needs of the Deanery over the next fifteen years …' As the Headmaster also pointed out, the commission did not call upon the school to give evidence and the report failed to mention the opportunities for evangelism provided by the daily use of the cathedral as a school chapel.

349. For the following: HCSA, notes on the author's interview (11 Nov. 2013) with Sutton; Sutton's subsequent letter, 11 Sept. 2014; and his paper, 30 Dec. 1986. Also see: HCSA, A.P. Hollingworth to B.B. Sutton, 21 Sept. 1981 re disturbances caused by fabric repairs. The date of the snow storm is unknown, but see HCA, 7031/27, p.241 re Archdeacon Woodhouse's suggestion (2 Dec. 1985) that 'large canvas druggets' should be placed inside the north and St John doors for school assemblies during snowy weather; and HCSA, B.B. Sutton to R. Kingsley-Taylor, 10 March 1987, re the potential hazard of the stoking of the St John door stove as pupils entered for chapel. Mats may not have been provided by the school until the author's headmastership.

with good medieval precedent the school stood for prayers; the school's use of the cathedral's *Hymns Ancient and Modern* caused problems, so each boy and girl was issued with their own pocketable copy of the *English Hymnal*; the canon in residence once tried to stop school chapel during a snow storm – he was ignored, but the school later provided mats for the wiping of feet. Sutton was the first to recognise that young people could be (in his own words) 'exasperating, careless, noisy and selfish, and ... over familiar with a sacred place' but such irritations, he argued, should be dealt with in a spirit of goodwill. What rankled with him was that the school seemed to be blamed for anything that went wrong in the cathedral and that its morning chapel – accompanied as it occasionally was by the noise of workmen or more often 'enlivened by processions of coal trucks and brooms' (for the Gurney stoves) – did not seem to be regarded by the cathedral authorities as a proper service. And yet that service, and not least the minute's silence which in Sutton's view was 'as impressive and precious as any moment in the cathedral year', was a golden opportunity for bringing people closer to God:

> I think I may be forgiven [he wrote in that desperate December memorandum] for believing that the daily school service must be amongst one of the most important things that happens regularly in the cathedral – 500 young people coming together every day of the term for praise and prayer, an opportunity to preach to the unconverted and to welcome them into God's house second to none in the diocese.

Although the Headmaster was generally successful in getting the vergers on-side, not least the unpredictable Ted Pannell with whom Sutton established a good personal relationship following his agreement to supervise the seating in the choir during the Three Choirs Festival, the attitude of some cathedral dignitaries reinforced the impression of indifference towards the school. Canon Shaw, for example, was a particular thorn in Sutton's side. Although he had a certain boyish charm and could be helpful – as in 1976 with his talk to senior pupils on central Africa (he had been Dean of Bulawayo) – there was, as one governor observed, 'too much lack of a feeling of responsibility and too much cultural and social pretension' for him to be a reliable colleague. And this Precentor, as opposed to Paul Iles, his well-disposed successor, did not make it easy for the Headmaster for (in Sutton's view) he was an obstructive presence in Chapter who lost no opportunity to rattle the chaplain and pass on grumbles for other governors to deal with. One incident will suffice. In May 1982, Shaw threatened to resign as a governor because of his embarrassment about the school's public behaviour, the final straw being a boy's surly response following a cheerful morning greeting. Complaints were investigated and the resignation did not happen but it must have been a considerable relief all round when the Precentor announced the following month that he had been translated to Ely, despite Shaw's protestation to the General Chapter that he was leaving with regret and that his time in Hereford had been 'the happiest seven years of his life'.[350]

---

350. For the above: HCSA, W.D. Ledwich to Dean Haynes, 27 May 1983; *TH*, CCXXII (Oct. 1976), p.4 and CCXXV (Nov. 1979), p.4; B.B. Sutton to H.B. Mynors, 26 Sept. 1981 and Mynors' reply of 4 Oct.; C.A Shaw's two letters of 21 May 1982 and Sutton's reply of same date. Shaw's appointment as Dean of Ely was announced to the Hereford General Chapter on 24 June 1982. He was installed at Ely on 4 December 1982 and was Dean

One other controversial figure, but in this instance a member of the school team, was Father William Ledwich, chaplain from 1979-84. He followed Charles Neill, a traditional clergyman and a safe pair of hands who was well respected by both the school and cathedral communities. Ledwich, although a man of real spiritual gifts, was less emollient, less well-balanced and less well-suited to a dual-position with cathedral and school. Admitted, like his predecessor, as a vicar choral (without audition) on his school appointment, he lasted barely a year in that role before being moved for 'organisational and musical' reasons. Once his new contract had been sorted out – he was relieved of all cathedral duties, remuneration and housing but continued as an honorary member of the foundation – Canon Shaw hoped that his personal relationship with the chaplain would improve, and that the new arrangement would 'prevent the kind of misunderstanding which … had spoilt things recently'.[351]

The freeing of the chaplain from his cathedral duties benefited both parties but it did not end the tension. The difficulties caused by Ledwich borrowing vestments, without permission, for a service at Llanthony Abbey and returning them soiled; or those resulting from the Head Verger's official complaint about the manner in which the pupils set out chairs for the school assembly were, perhaps, par for the course.[352] What caused more general disquiet were the changes in the nature of school worship, especially those practices which some felt smacked of Roman Catholicism. The alterations made to the 1980 Commemoration service were of particular concern. After parental complaints to Chapter governors expressing disquiet 'at the undue emphasis shown over the patronal festival of the Virgin Mary', it was even discussed at a governors' meeting despite Dean Rathbone's efforts to keep the matter off the agenda.[353] Later that year, parents and candidates of a 'low church' persuasion, and perhaps others, were distressed at the imposition of formal confession before the school Confirmation on 11 May when 72 pupils, more at one service than ever before or since, were confirmed. The setting up of a Walsingham 'cell' and the organisation of regular school pilgrimages also seemed to point away from mainstream Anglicanism. However, there is no denying Ledwich's profound spiritual influence on the pupil community. Here is how one former pupil remembers him:

> Father Ledwich, whose Irish identity had earned him the legendary nick-name 'Daddy Paddy', was an impulsive, charismatic priest who served as HCS chaplain and live-in assistant housemaster in Number 1. An Anglo-Catholic with a deep respect for the exactness of ritual, he provided a firm and unapologetic leadership of the Christian

---

there for less than a year.

351. HCA, 7031/26, pp.358, 368, Chapter Acts, 8 Oct., 3 Dec. 1979; HCSA, A. Shaw to B.B. Sutton, 3 Dec. 1979. Shaw added: '… in my view the whole episode ought never to have occurred and would not have done had this kind of consultation with the whole Chapter taken place and we had known where he stood before the appointment was made'.

352. HCA, 7031/26, pp.462-63, Chapter Acts, 13 July 1981; HCSA, W.D. Ledwich to Dean Haynes, 27 May 1983, expressing his disagreement 'in the strongest possible terms' to the complaint of Ted Pannell, the Head Verger.

353. HCSA, Dean Rathbone to B.B. Sutton, 11 April 1980 ('I cannot think that the Mariolatious or Mariological or plain Marian Commemoration should be on the agenda of the governors' meeting.'); GMB 1945-82, pp.331-32, 22 May 1980.

> life of the school. The termly Eucharist was a lavish affair, a procession of well-drilled altar boys, with Fr Ledwich robed in highly decorated chasuble at the rear, hands crossed in intense prayer, incense filling the air as the altar party made its way forward … The purpose was no shallow indulgence of personal taste, however. For Fr Ledwich, bringing the school community to the altar was the source and summit of his ministry … His sense of prayerfulness, along with an occasional fiery temper and an impish sense of humour, combined to present to teenagers a figure at once deeply authentic and yet, unorthodox … [Yet] it was not his doctrinal orthodoxy which was ever in doubt, but rather his quirkiness. Many of us found him to be fun first and foremost, and for some of us this admiration for the man drew us to a personal appreciation of what he stood for.[354]

Some teachers, at the time, saw it rather differently: the cathedral organist was not the only member of staff to feel that the establishment of a 'rather effete holy huddle around the chaplain' was not entirely healthy.[355]

Although far from being a crypto-Catholic, it is true that the chaplain was ill at ease with liberal opinion within the Church of England. During what proved to be the final months of Ledwich's tenure, he became involved in a national rather than local controversy. Indeed, Ledwich himself called 'the Durham affair' 'a crisis which attracted public and media attention like no Anglican dispute this century'. Written in the immediate aftermath of the dispute this is a pardonable exaggeration but it could be fairly said that the Durham 'crisis' was the Church's biggest disputation since the publication of the Bishop of Woolwich's *Honest to God* in 1963. The details need not concern us here except to say that following the television broadcast on 29 April 1984 of an interview with Dr Jenkins, Bishop designate of Durham, in which he had denied the historicity of the Virgin birth and the physical resurrection of Christ, Ledwich, having been alerted to the broadcast by two of his Fourth Form pupils, organised a national petition. This urged the Archbishop of York to 'seriously question' whether Jenkins' should be consecrated bishop if he refused to affirm publicly his belief in the creeds 'as the Church has consistently interpreted them'. The petition, which eventually gathered nearly 14,000 signatures, was presented to the Archbishop of York by a delegation headed by Ledwich (and including one of his pupils) on 1 July. The Archbishop stood his ground, Jenkins refused to renounce his views and the consecration went ahead in York Minster on 6 July. At this point, after listening to the broadcast of the service, Ledwich crossed the Close to the Bishop's Palace, via All Saints Church where he 'lit a candle under the statue of our Lady', and resigned his Orders. By so doing, he was no longer able to exercise his ministry as chaplain – a fact that the *Daily Mail* reporter, one of the many journalists to besiege the school during that summer term, found hard to comprehend – but there remained the question of his teaching. Sutton had originally hoped that he would be able to continue as a teacher for one more term, but Ledwich resigned his teaching post, following a direct intervention from the Bishop of Hereford, fully supported by the Dean and Chapter, at an extraordinary governors' meeting. It was

354. HCSA, Stephen Morris to the author, 27 Jan. 2015. I am indebted to Stephen Morris for this recollection.

355. HCSA, R. Massey to B.B. Sutton, 12 July 1983. An insight into Ledwich's remarkable ministry at HCS is provided by Michael Walling in his article 'Classrooms and Cassocks', *TH*, CCXXVI (1980), pp.11-12.

done without rancour. As the Headmaster observed in a generous tribute that speech day, the chaplain had shown that 'he was a man of principle'. So ended the HCS career of a gifted priest and schoolmaster whose time at Hereford had contributed towards his disenchantment with the Church of England.[356]

On a more prosaic level but of more lasting consequence to the school's material well-being, there were issues relating to the school's leases and the rental it paid for the occupation of Chapter property. This brought into question the exact nature of the relationship between the cathedral and its school. It was a complicated and uncertain picture. Until the property purchases of the Seventies, the school rented all its buildings from the Dean and Chapter. Although economic rents (at least when settled at the beginning of the tenancy) were mostly paid for recently rented houses at Harley Court, 4 Castle Street and 6 St Ethelbert's Street, the school's annual rentals for its three major properties were time-honoured: 6s 8d for School House and its yard, the same rent as originally prescribed in the Caroline statutes; £150 for Number 1 and its garden and adjacent buildings, as set on 9 December 1942; and £250, the original 1945 rent, for the Old Deanery. There were other questions. Was the Dean and Chapter entitled to charge a higher rent for School House? Was Number 1 bought for school use by the Dean and Chapter as governors rather than beneficially for the cathedral? Did the considerable capital expenditure spent by the governors on Dean and Chapter property give the school any additional rights? Should any rental review be related to the school's contributions towards the choir and the maintenance of boarding for the cathedral choristers? How secure was the school's tenure of these buildings? And, most important of all, should the Cathedral School be treated as a foundation distinct from the cathedral, necessitating arm's length agreements, or as part of the same family? These were far-reaching issues for both parties. Some of them were resolved by legal opinion during this period even if it took another decade before there was a final settlement on the vexed question of rents.

The question of security of tenure was first raised by Peter Prior. If the present tenancies at will continued, he stated at a governors' meeting in May 1980, he could not see how the school could show improvements made to those buildings on its balance sheet. He modified his stance when reassured by Anthony Weston, the school's solicitor, that although the governors did not have a formal leasehold interest, the school's equitable interest through its improvements to these properties was likely to be recognised by the courts. But as to its security of tenure, Weston could go no further than express the view – acting this time as Chapter Clerk, he held both posts at the time – that he could not 'foresee any probable circumstances that would prompt the Chapter to bring the school's tenancy to an end'. There matters stood: although the school did not have security of tenure, its balance sheet could record as assets sums spent on improving its rented buildings. It comes as no surprise to find that some time later the school auditors suggested that this messy situation needed regularising.[357]

356. For this *cause célèbre*: Ledwich, *passim*; HCSA, GMB 1982-86, for Bishop Eastaugh's letter to Peter Prior of 13 July and minutes of 18 July meeting; *HT*, 2 Nov. 1984, p.21 ('Pressurised out of a job – allegation'), and Ledwich's letter to its editor of 5 Nov. Ledwich was later received into the Greek Orthodox Church as Archimandrite Athanasius. He died on 20 July 2011, the feast day (in the Carmelite Order) of St Elias (Elijah).

357. HCSA, A.J. Weston to B.B. Sutton, 22 Feb. 1980; GMB 1945-82, p.331, 22 May 1980; R. Mainwaring (Little & Co) to the Governors, 3 Feb. 1986.

Before the end of the period, however, light had been shed on the legal position regarding the school's occupation of the School House site. The Chapter's own counsel in June 1983 had found unequivocally in favour of the school. 'The cathedral is not entitled to procure an increase in the rent of 6s 8d', he advised, '... and is not entitled to resume possession of these buildings'.[358] With Number 1, the position was far less clear-cut. Sutton strongly held the view that the house 'was always intended for school use right from the beginning of the negotiations [to acquire it]' and went to some lengths to prove it. At the very least, he argued, Number 1 was a special case corresponding more nearly to school yard than to 4 Castle Street. It was a doughty defence but the weight of evidence was against him. As the Chapter Clerk informed the Headmaster in January 1984 – his letter being based on the vicar choral's extensive research – the Dean and Chapter regarded its acquisition as property for the cathedral and not for the school. This was suggested by the source of the funding and the fact that the premises were leased to the governors (not quite the same body of men by the time of the 1911 yearly tenancy) from the outset and not placed under a deed of trust for the school beneficially.[359] This legal opinion was never tested and there the matter rested, at least for the time being.

What of the actual payment of rents? Here there was a distinct change over the period, for understandable reasons, in the Dean and Chapter's position. Under Dean Rathbone, the view prevailed that the cathedral and school were one foundation and that the school's maintenance was one of the basic matters laid down in the cathedral statutes. The nominal rents on its long established leases could be justified provided that the cathedral's aims were carried out 'in seeking to provide a distinctively Christian education'.[360] This view changed following Dean Rathbone's retirement in early 1982. This was hardly surprising given the cathedral's dire financial straits at that time.[361] Within weeks of the new Dean's arrival, the Chapter had obtained the services of a new land agent to advise about the level of rents for cathedral properties within the city, and by the end of 1983, he had been instructed to negotiate realistic rents for all properties on the north side of Castle Street. It took a change of agent and another three years before a crude valuation 'by contractors' method'

358. HCSA, Opinion of G.R.A. Argles, 24 June 1983. A further opinion of 13 July 1983 found that if formal leasing arrangements were established, the school would have a right of compensation for any improvements (as opposed to maintenance) it had made to its Chapter properties, and that the amount of compensation would not be 'in any way limited by the "under payment" of rent by the school over the years'. Also see HCSA, paper by P.L.S. Barrett, 25 March 1983 and HCA, 7031/27, pp.91, 113, 114, for the wide terms of reference of the first opinion and the Chapter's acceptance of the advice for the adoption of a 'new look' agreement between school and cathedral.

359. See HCSA, B.B. Sutton to A.J. Weston, 20 Dec. 1983, and Weston's reply of 17 Jan. 1984. The minutes of the governors' meeting of 16 April, 19 Nov., 16 Dec. 1911 (GMB 1908-21, pp.30, 33, 43) would suggest that Weston was right in his view. Sutton's submission was in part based on J.C. Wordsworth's erroneous statement (Wordsworth, pp.13-14) as to the sources of funding for the purchase.

360. As articulated, for example, by the Dean and Chapter Clerk at the governors' meeting on 22 May 1980. HCSA, GMB 1945-82, p.331.

361. The £24,000 deficit reported to the General Chapter in June 1982 had increased by over £30,000 a year later, necessitating an increase in the cathedral's bank overdraft to £70,000. HCA, 7031/27, pp. 40, 91, 108, reports, 24 June 1982, 7 March and 24 June 1983.

of all the school Chapter properties had been completed.[362] A letter was then sent by the Canon Treasurer on 10 February 1987 proposing annual rents with a collective value of £114,670 – an increase of some £100,000 – on all the school's Chapter properties, emphasising (contrary to the Headmaster's view) that contributions which the school made to the choral foundation 'should be regularised as an entirely separate matter'.[363] The negotiations which followed, skilfully handled by Kevin Mason on the governors' behalf, need not detain us here, except to say that it was several more years before a settlement was finally reached.

In reviewing the relationship between school and cathedral over this period, there is a danger with hindsight of over-stressing the clashes between the two. Given the school's rapid growth and its increasing use of the cathedral, some friction was inevitable, as in May 1982 at the time of the denouement with Canon Shaw, when Sutton had to remind the Precentor that he had 545 'hostages to fortune' only a few of whom let him down. On a day to day basis, however, the two bodies no doubt rubbed along happily enough. And quite apart from the formal contributions made to cathedral worship by the cathedral choir and growing band of pupil servers, over 30 strong (including the first girls) by 1986, there are also plenty of instances of the school's support in other ways: whether over its employment of lay clerks, which did not always work to the school's advantage; its increasing involvement in the home Three Choirs Festival; or its co-operation in more mundane matters like the redecoration of College Hall (1978) or the restoration of the St Ethelbert gardens in 1983-84 or its contributions in the mid-Eighties to the cathedral appeal. In a family it should be so.

And yet by 1987, it was a matter of debate as to whether HCS was still a brother or a more distant cousin. Certainly, there is good evidence of a weakening of the tight bonds of that relationship over this period. With the acquisition of Old College, the centre of the school had moved away physically from the cathedral, symbolised after the academic year 1981-82 by the change in the venue of the photograph of the Headmaster with his monitors from the cloisters to the garden of Number 29. This is significant because during that year Dean Rathbone retired, a retirement that led to the appointment of a lay chairman and the relinquishing of the 'common control' exercised by the Dean as chairman of governors. The old unwritten familiar relationship, described by Mynors on the verge of his own retirement as a governor 'as intimate and real as a marriage',[364] with its potential conflicts of interests but undoubted mutual benefits was slowly breaking down. Although more

362. *Ibid.*, pp.121, 177, 240, 248, 279, 295, Acts, 5 Dec. 1983 to 4 Aug. 1986; HCA, 7031/28, p.3, 12 Jan. 1987.

363. HCSA, R.A. Masters to P.J. Prior, 10 Feb. 1987. The proposed rents included £39,800 for School House and Old Block (despite the earlier Counsel opinion); £34,230 for Number 1, 7 Ferrers Street and 77 East Street; and £40,087 for the Old Deanery. Had such rents been paid it would clearly have placed the school in severe financial difficulty. Sutton regarded the proposals as 'inept', the figures having taken no account of the circumstances of occupation or the law. HCSA, B.B. Sutton to P.R. Iles, 12 Feb. 1987.

364. HCSA, H.B. Mynors to B.B. Sutton, 1 May 1983. As with other matters, Mynors' view was diametrically opposed to that of Peter Prior, who in a letter to Canon Masters later that year agreed that the correct relationship should be 'that of two separate bodies conducting transactions at arm's length and in a way which was equitable to both sides'. The letter produced a vigorous response from the Headmaster (HCSA, P.J. Prior to R.A. Masters, 15 Dec.; B.B. Sutton to P.J. Prior, 16 Dec. 1983) but it is Prior's view that has ultimately prevailed.

formalised by the school's incorporation in 1987, the process of change was not to be completed until the establishment of arm's length agreements and independent managements (with the Chapter's eventual withdrawal from active governance) after this period had ended. In retrospect, Sutton's headship marked a difficult time of transition in the nature of the relationship between the school and its cathedral.

Not that this was fully recognised at the time but Sutton feared the worst. In that most personal of responses on the eve of the 1987 New Year, in which he recognised that his emotions might have clouded his judgement, he pointed out the possible consequences of the establishment of arm's length agreements. The charging of 'economic rents' would make the boarding element too expensive to run and the employment of the master of choristers impossible to afford. In that sense, even though the new Headmaster and his chairman of governors worked hard to improve the relationship with the Dean and Chapter, it was a prophetic utterance.

Jubilees and Other Celebrations

A visiting Australian teacher, writing in late 1977 about his impressions of the home country after two months at the Cathedral School, was attracted by its patriotism. 'England and in particular London', he observed, 'is unashamedly ablaze with the Silver Jubilee'.[365] This acute comment was made some time after the height of the junketing on 5 and 6 June, which in spite of the gainsayers, had proved to be a time of great national celebration. As the *Hereford Times* reported: 'It was the British family demonstrating solidarity and togetherness in a way hardly seen since the last war'.

In Hereford, as with towns across the land, the jubilee was commemorated in glorious style. The fair in High Town was opened by the mayor, June Carter, dressed in red, white and blue, and an estimated 5,000 people packed into the square 'for the old time atmosphere'. Donkey rides and a children's fancy dress competition were held there; old steam engines were on show; stalls included 'boweling for the pigge' and guessing the weight of other livestock; the Hereford Morris men danced and the city silver band belted out medleys of traditional English songs; and the jubilee cake, made by students from Hereford Technical College, was appropriately cut. Within the wider city, over 100 street parties were held – the mayor visiting 63 of them – and 44 businesses entered the jubilee window display competition, the prize being won by Franklin Barnes Flowers, a firm managed by an Old Herefordian. And within the Close itself, members of the cathedral guild of bell-ringers rang a full peal of 5040 changes of Plain Bob Royal, the number six bell being the responsibility of another former pupil.[366]

The Silver Jubilee was not the only reason for local celebration during this period. For example, there were the centenaries in 1978 and 1979, celebrating respectively the birth of John Masefield and the death of Francis Kilvert, Herefordshire worthies to whom the Cathedral School could lay no claim; the 1980-81 rugby season saw the centenary of the

365. *TH*, CCXXIII (Nov. 1977), p.4, 'First Impressions' by A.K. Beavis, then Senior Master at St Andrew's Cathedral School in Sydney, who had undertaken a year's exchange with Martin Nicholson.

366. *HT*, 10 June 1977, p.1. The two Old Herefordians were (respectively) Peter Williams and John Eisel. For the Silver Jubilee celebrations in general: Sandbrook (2012), pp.628-40.

Welsh Rugby Union, its first ever captain (James Bevan), as with its 100th captain (Paul Thorburn), being an Old Herefordian; and there were important civic and corporate landmarks, represented by the 600th city mayoralty in 1981 and the H.P. Bulmer centenary in 1987. Whether the city's mayor attended the Cathedral School is unknown but Percy and Fred Bulmer, who set up their cider business in Ryelands Street in 1887, were both old boys.

There were important ecclesiastical anniversaries. In 1976, the church in Hereford commemorated the 1300th year of the foundation of its diocese with a remarkable festival. Reflecting on the thirteenth centenary celebrations, Dean Rathbone called 1976 an *annus mirabilis* for the cathedral as well as the diocese. The cathedral became the scene of a number of great occasions: the Queen's distribution of the Royal Maundy on 15 April, the Children of the Chapel Royal, brought to sing in the service with the Hereford choristers, being boarded in Number 1;[367] the service on 20 May, the feast of St Ethelbert, when the cathedral's ancient cross was returned after its progress through the diocese's 13 Deaneries; a diocesan service of thanksgiving for the Mothers' Union centenary which was addressed by the grand-daughter of its founder; and the solemn Eucharist on 2 October, the feast of St Thomas of Hereford, which marked the festival's end. During these months, too, a stream of pilgrims visited the cathedral to pray the pilgrim's prayer and sign the pilgrim's book. Many groups also expressed their gratitude and affection for their mother church with offerings of music, drama and art. Despite the disruption of the cathedral's normal routine, it was an exhilarating year for the choristers and all those involved in the celebrations. And Bishop Hodson's proclamation at the closing service that the festival had placed Hereford 'well and truly back on the ecclesiastical map' proved more accurate than the reported rumour that at the festival's end Hereford would relapse once more into its customary slumber for another century.[368]

Indeed, within six years there was another significant anniversary, this time of the cathedral's own. For 1982 marked the 700th anniversary of St Thomas Cantilupe's death, remembered by the publication of a book of essays on the Bishop's life and work, the creation of the ill-fated 'nimbus' above his shrine, the Friends' pilgrimage (on the 50th anniversary of their foundation) to Hambleden where Cantilupe was born, and by the 'goose fair' held on 9 October when it was reported that 'animals, jesters, musicians and players ... produce[d] medieval mayhem' in High Town. On this occasion, the school played a more prominent part in the festivities. Jamie Eastaugh, Head of School, and Alison Ford, his deputy, enjoyed lengthy spells in the stocks; choristers processed; the 'green man and his maidens' controlled the crowds; parents, staff and pupils manned information booths, sold programmes and served in stalls; and in the growing gloom, the boarders tidied up the Close. The success of the day owed much to the school's efforts.[369]

---

367. The Hereford boys were put out to stay with staff and parents, thereby disappointing the Chapel Royal matron who thought that all the boys would get on well together boarding in Number 1, as 'we feared that the intense indignation of our choristers, who saw the importation of foreigners as an implied insult, might lead to murder and mayhem'. HCSA, Sutton to the author, 11 Sept. 2014.

368. *Friends of Hereford Cathedral 43rd Annual Report* (1977), pp.7-9; *HT*, 8 Oct. 1976 p.3; *TH*, CCXXII (Oct. 1976), p.6.

369. See *TH*, CCXXIX (1983), p.4, for A.E. P[arker]'s account of the goose fair.

And then there were the school's own commemorations. The least noticed by the outside world but the most important for the school community were the regular commemorative occasions within the cathedral itself. These included its annual use from July 1978, the school having outgrown the Shirehall, as a setting for speech day. Indeed, as the school grew and fragmented through the acquisition of new properties, the cathedral assumed an increased significance for preserving the school's communal identity on a daily basis. New-style chapels were started. The number of external speakers was increased to enliven assemblies and a period of silence introduced (by William Ledwich) to aid contemplation. The pattern of worship also developed. The first whole-school Eucharist occurred on 13 May 1976. By 1977-78, it had become a termly celebration, replacing the formal sermons that had occurred on All Saints, Ash Wednesday and Ascension, with (from 1980-81) the service being enhanced by the affectionately christened 'Missa Wiburiensis', harmonised by Roy Massey and composed by Dick Heald, who trained the school to sing the liturgy and brought a new enthusiasm to its hymn-singing. More controversially as has been shown, changes were made to the 1980 commemoration service. A less problematic and more poignant commemoration was held three years later on 26 March 1983, when a specially commissioned and finely crafted school mace was dedicated by Bishop Eastaugh to the memory of Major Michael Forge, the one Old Herefordian fatality of the Falklands War.[370] (Plate 16).

There were also centenary commemorations, the most important of which was the school's '600th'. Despite the certain knowledge that the so-called 1381 foundation date was a myth,[371] Sutton decided that the pattern established for the 'quincentenary' should be maintained. But the celebration on 27 June 1981, which took the form of a 'mediaeval fayre', was vastly different from the events organised in 1881 and 1931. Formality was eschewed in favour of a fun day for all. The day opened with a grand procession, led by a Hereford bull and a court jester, from Castle Green through High Town to Castle Street, which for five hours became a medieval market with stalls and entertainments of every kind. As *The Herefordian* correspondent described it:

> Castle Street was a blaze of colour on this, one of the most glorious days of the year. It was closed to traffic for a day and transformed into a mediaeval fayre-ground, festooned with flags, streamers and bunting in blue and gold. Mingling with the huge crowds were serving wenches, archers, lords and ladies in their fine silks and velvets, cattle, jesters, maypoles, green men, stocks, crumhorns, 'quainte maides' … mummers, morris men, falconers, greasy poles, Gilbert consorts, wrestling, gurning contests [a rustic pastime of face contortions], ponies, tugs o' war … and all infected by the euphoria of the occasion.[372]

370. Michael Lancaster Forge attended HCS as a School House boarder from 1954 to 1957, when he left to go to Welbeck College. For his friendship with Alick Rowe: *Boy at the Commercial*, pp.123ff.

371. As Alan Morris had pointed out four years earlier in his piece on the history of the school. *TH*, CCXXIII (Nov. 1977, p.9). Also see the editorial, '1384 and All That', in the 1984 edition of the magazine: *TH*, CCXXX, p.1.

372. *TH*, CCXXVII (1981), p.14, 'The Medieval Fayre' remembered by Andrew Price. Also see: *HT*, 3 July 1981, p.24, 'All the fun of a bygone age'.

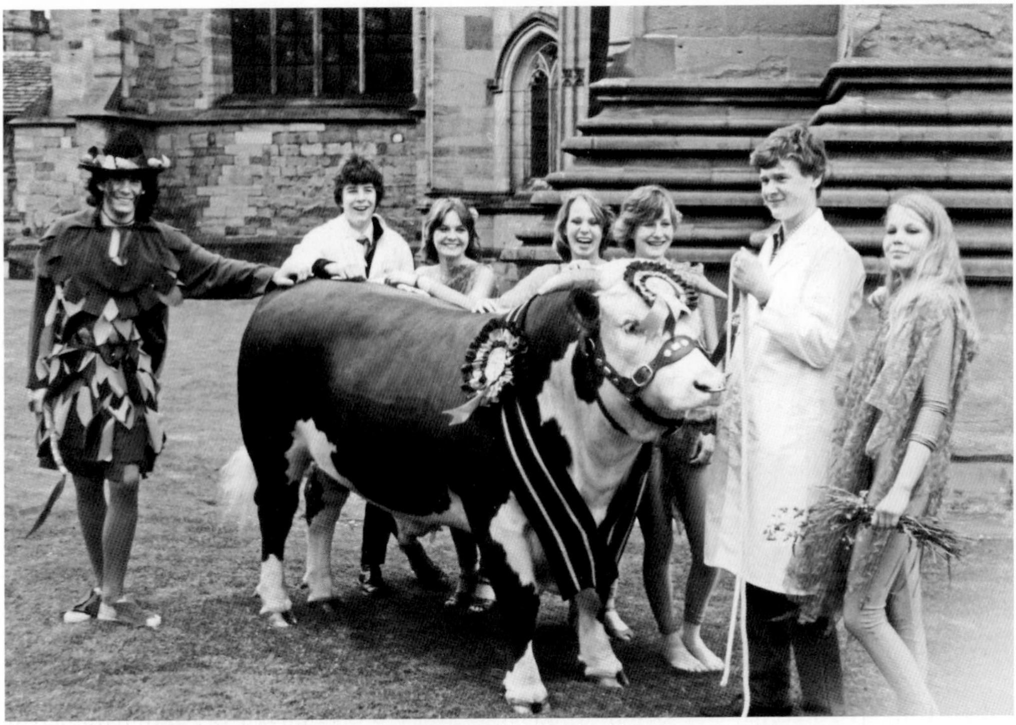

Fig. 8.21 The Hereford bull that led the 'Mediaeval Fayre' procession, with a group of pupil admirers, outside the Lady Chapel, 27 June 1981.

It was a spectacular celebration, which brought together the school and its wider community in a way hardly ever before achieved. That around £10,000 was raised for the Big School conversion, a sum which beat the King's, Worcester total for their summer fair, was of lesser import.

Two other school centenaries were thought worthy of celebration in Sutton's time, the first being rugby football. A rudimentary form of football, as we have seen, was played by the boys up to the mid-Victorian period but it was not until the 1870s that the school adopted the Union code. On the basis of the acceptance of the 15-a-side rule by the English Rugby Union in 1876, it was decided to celebrate the centenary of the start of HCS rugby in the 1976 autumn term, even though we now know that the numbers and composition of school teams in the late 1870s were far from settled.[373] So like the 1881 school 'quincentenary', the 1976 rugby 'centenary' was of doubtful provenance. But in the absence of official HCS records for the 1876 season, the adoption of the XV club rule was as good a reason as any for a hundred year celebration. It was also a shrewd year to choose in another sense for with 13 boys having had experience of regular first team rugby, the school could expect to field a strong 1st XV for the 1976-77 season. And although the team was to lose three of its 16 matches, it captured some good scalps, notably RGS Worcester (for the first

373. See above, pp.262; and *TH*, CCXXII (Oct. 1976), p.13, for Don Theakston's rationale on the reason for the centenary celebration.

Fig. 8.22 The 'centenary' 1st XV, 1976-77, coached by Bob Talbot and captained by Gareth Williams: played 16, won 12, drawn 1, lost 3.

time), King's, Worcester, and Belmont Abbey.[374] There was one further rugby celebration at the end of that season. On 2 and 3 April 1977, an inaugural 'centenary sevens' for 16 schools was held at Wyeside, the HCS VII narrowly losing to Rydal in the semi-finals, its best result to date.

If the origins of 15-a-side rugby football at HCS were shrouded by the mists of time, there was nothing mysterious about the date of the original issue of *The Herefordian* which was first published in January 1878. Although the centenary edition (number 224) came out towards the end rather than at the beginning of the year, it was an imaginatively compiled commemorative issue. There were reprints of the first pages of the January and September 1878 editions, an original librarian's report and early published football, rowing and OH notices; evocative caricatures; articles on the school and the wider world as it was in 1878; a commissioned poem from 'an established poet of our own' (R.D. Lancaster) to mirror Fred Weatherly's verses of a century earlier; a suitably wistful letter from the school's Oxford correspondent; and a deeply researched back-cover advertisement. It was the editor's stated intent that these historical pieces, together with the usual school articles, should (like those 100 years earlier) serve 'to remind the readers of their part in an ancient and continuing tradition'. So it comes as little surprise to find that on 21 November 1978, a representative from Maylord Jakemans attended the luncheon party to mark the publication of the magazine's centenary, a direct link with 'Jakeman and Carver', the firm which had printed the earliest editions.

374. In terms of results (played 16, won 12, drawn 1, lost 3) this was the best 1st XV of the period, closely followed by the teams of 1975-76, 1977-78 and 1983-84. With regard to individual players, P.G. Cobb (1977 and 1978) and A.J. Thorburn (1979) were both awarded England schools' trials and G. Hiscoke was selected for the England under-18s side against New Zealand in 1985.

The school's rugby history and its long-standing magazine were both appropriately celebrated, but Tatham's reforms a century earlier had given other opportunities for commemoration which were not taken up. For example, the centenaries of C.O. Fowler's election (by his peers) as the first captain of 'the boat' in 1877 and the first Wyeside cricket match on 16 May 1883, as well as the 75th anniversary of the corps' foundation in 1903, might all have been recognised by jubilee events but their anniversaries went unheeded.[375] Irrespective of these missed opportunities, there were sufficient grounds for celebration in all three areas. In rowing, it was fitting that a century after the winning of the public schools cup at Henley in 1883, Mark Waddington and Hugh Slee should have gained the gold medal in the coxless pairs at that year's national championships. Sustained by funding from the Buttery's profits, the rigorous training schedules of a new coach, Dr Michael Budd, and the ever faithful Peter Skinner, the boat club achieved other creditable results: seven pots in 1979, 11 in 1981, a bronze in the national schools of 1984 and success at Henley with 'an ecumenical eight' (with Belmont Abbey) in the first heat of the Ladies' Plate at Henley in 1982. Overall, it was not a bad record for a small club of around 20 boys and the occasional ladies' four and girl cox.

The same could not always be said for cricket and the corps but both activities had gained in strength by the end of the period. Cricket reached its nadir in the late Seventies because of a shortage of coaches and the woeful state of the Wyeside wicket, the school's maintenance man being seconded to help with the pitches in 1978. With the appointment of a new groundsman in Brian Goode, the wickets and results gradually improved. The first 1st XI century for ten years was scored at Wyeside in 1980. The next one in 1984 ensured an HCS victory against a more formidable opponent, RGS Worcester, in the first cricket fixture against the school, a feat repeated in 1985. By the time of the 1986-87 seasons, following the appointment of Andy Connop as the new cricket master, winter nets at Hereford's recently built Leisure Centre and the school's acquisition of a bowling machine, the 1st XI was beaten only once in 25 matches. The coach was able to record in 1987 that despite the one loss (by 15 runs), he had trained a squad of strength, depth and undoubted talent.[376]

A similar story can be written about the corps, which at times during this period was close to extinction. Despite the admittance of 18 girls in 1976-77, the number of cadets had declined to barely 50, with 33 on show at Captain Morris' first parade as commanding officer in January 1978. A policy change, with the CCF being brought into the timetable, led to an increase in recruits. However, it was not until Captain (soon to be Major) Howard Briggs' appointment as commanding officer in January 1981, and the

375. Fowler's election was in anticipation of a boat race against Malvern College which was arranged for 23 June 1877. Ten days before the appointed date a letter was received from the Malvern captain of boats 'by which … after 4 mistakes in spelling, he withdrew from the race on a most frivolous pretext'. HCSA, 'Hereford Cathedral School Record' (*c.*1877), attached to the school's admission register, 1967-93. For the inaugural Wyeside cricket match and the corps' foundation: see above, pp.259, 312-13.

376. The 1980 and 1984 centuries were scored respectively by Gary Withers (104* against Lady Hawkins' School) and Peter Butler (102* against RGS). J.G. Caiger's 310 runs (at 62 per innings) and 24 wickets (at 4.83 for each wicket) in 1976; P. Butler's 450 runs (at 50) in 1984; N.R. Denny's 421 runs (at 46.8) in 1986; and A. Herbert's 30 wickets (at 7.63) in 1987 were among the best seasonal averages during this period.

introduction of compulsory corps for the Third Form from September 1981, that things radically improved. This latter move was not without controversy at a time of national resurgence of unilateralism and anti-militarism among a vocal minority at HCS. A Royal Naval section was formed (May 1982) and the RAF section resumed (in 1986); contacts with the regular forces were strengthened; and more adventurous exercises were promoted. By the end of the period, the corps had been built up to over 200 cadets. It was a remarkable turnaround.[377]

One 75th birthday that was properly celebrated was the anniversary of Baden-Powell's first scout camp on Brownsea Island in August 1907. The school troop (16th Hereford) had been formed with Roger Toll as scout leader during the 1976 summer term. Encouraged by the Headmaster's active support, it was built up into a thriving troop with a full programme of adventurous activities. A venture unit under the chaplain's leadership was added in 1980-81. For the 75th anniversary in 1982, the year of the scout, seven scouts walked 75 miles across Wales, from its eastern border to the sea, in 98 hours. Further scouting celebrations and challenges occurred in 1985 to mark the Hereford city district's 75th anniversary. By the time of the 16th Hereford's tenth birthday the following year, 120 boys had been enrolled as scouts over the ten year period, and the small troop of 1976 had expanded into a much larger unit with the Headmaster as group scout leader.

HCS also celebrated one of its own with the launch in November 1975 of the Traherne Society 'to celebrate our distinguished, if underrated, *alumnus* in the year following the tercentenary of his death'. This was a Sixth-form Literary Society in the tradition of its Somerset forebear of the Fifties and Sixties. Over the next three years distinguished speakers gathered to give papers in the Suttons' magnificent timbered hall at Harley Court. The cast included such luminaries as Dr Bernard Richards, who had taught OHs at Brasenose, on Traherne's life and verse; Dr Roy Strong on Nicholas Hilliard; and Lord Blake on Disraeli. The society did not survive the Seventies but was briefly revived in 1984 as the Traherne lecture series.

There were other reasons for celebration. Although the school's participation in national team competitions – often promoted by media outlets as with *Country Life* for shooting, the *Daily Mail* for bridge and the *Sunday Times* for chess – did not often go beyond regional rounds, finals were occasionally reached. Slee and Waddington's gold medal aside, the chamber choir were finalists in the Granada school choir of the year competition in 1983; a team of Sixth-form economists came fifth out of 950 entries in the 1985 'Running the British Economy' competition sponsored by Herriot-Watt, Hewlett Packard and British Petroleum; and Michael Walling and Gary Withers won the 1981 Observer Mace competition, HCS thereby becoming one of only five schools in the country to have twice won the coveted silver owl. And then there were the more esoteric individual national triumphs. To name but four: in 1984 Miss Radio Wyvern and the *Daily Star*'s young cartoonist of the year were both HCS pupils; and the 1986 Boy Bishop came to national notice when he helped launch that year's 34p Christmas stamp, as did the choristers in general in early 1987

377. This paragraph has been written with the aid of Alan Morris' recollections. For an indication of radicalism within the Debating Society and the extent of the controversy over a compulsory corps: *TH*, CCXXVIII (1982), p.17; CCXXIX (1983), pp.6-8 ('the case for compulsion', an interview between Anne Goodsell and Major Briggs).

Fig. 8.23 Gary Withers (left) and Michael Walling with the Observer Mace, May 1981.

with the national screening of 'A Sort of Innocence' on BBC television.[378]

Here then was a school conscious of and determined to celebrate its heritage but not hidebound by its history. Centenaries were appropriately used as vantage points in time to celebrate the present and consider the future as well as the past. Indeed, it was essential that this was so for although schools are the most conservative of institutions, traditions can only carry them so far. And of the many new opportunities offered to boys and increasingly to girls at HCS during the late Seventies and Eighties, none was more important than the opportunity to widen their experiences beyond the classroom: through placements in the world of work; through increasing their understanding of industry by educative (often Bulmer sponsored) courses and their involvement in business-gaming and Young Enterprise; through voluntary service and community projects; through an expansion of adventurous activities and leadership training; through an emphasis on the importance of charitable giving to good causes of which they might have been only dimly aware. As Sutton observed in his penultimate speech day address: 'I have always felt it was one of the advantages of being a school on the pavement that we were in contact with the outside world'. During these years he and his colleagues exploited this to the full.

A Man For All Seasons

In 1983, two very different inspections were made of the Cathedral School: one a brief tour by the chairman of governors at the beginning of the year; the other an inspection over several days later that November by a panel of six HMIs.[379] Both complimented the school's

378. The individual pupils were (respectively) Rachel Welsh, David Jones and Rupert Broad. 'A Sort of Innocence', Alick Rowe's screenplay, was filmed during the 1986 autumn term. The first of six episodes was broadcast on BBC1 on the evening of 13 January 1987.

379. HCSA, P.J. Prior to B.B. Sutton, 28 Jan. 1983; HMI (Unpublished draft) Report on Hereford Cathedral School, inspected 21-25 November 1983. For Abram Khan, a new Science inspector, a later visit to HCS – and perhaps particularly the dinner Peter Prior hosted for the verbal report (delivered at 11pm on 21 Feb. 1984) at the Red Lion, Weobley – was his 'inspectorial high-spot'. HCSA, B.P. Fitzgerald to P.J. Prior, 24 Feb. 1984.

leadership. Peter Prior left his tour with the feeling that solid progress had been made in many directions over the previous few years. Not least was he impressed by the pupils' mature response to his questions, the relaxed and happy atmosphere and the Headmaster's ability to address almost every pupil on sight by their given name.

The report on the HMI visit several months later was more critical. The inspectors commented about weaknesses in certain departments, the poor O-level results 'for a small but significant minority', the absence of curriculum guidelines and working documents, the bleak appearance of parts of the school, the limited facilities for Physical Education, poor heating and shortcomings and safety hazards in the boarding accommodation. But on the strength of HCS as a community the report was unequivocal:

> The success of the school as a community lies in the achievement of the leadership in uniting positively so many different aspects of the school's life and organisation which suggests management skills of a very high order. To be so successful with a minimum of written directions or personal promotion or [it was later added] clarion calls to arms, demonstrates leadership of a high order. The school demonstrates convincingly the aims it espouses …[380]

That this should be so owed much to the Headmaster's personal qualities and example.

For Barry Sutton was a Headmaster who cared deeply about the Cathedral School and its wider community, and despite his 1982 protestation that he found it 'difficult to be everywhere', he more than most Heads was personally involved in its activities. Not one to be tied to his desk, he knew every nook and cranny of the school, which included an extensive knowledge of its many cellars. His was an approachable presence in Castle Street and its environs: conducting tours; talking over issues with parents in the street or after events before they became major problems; greeting pupils; dealing with a recalcitrant estates bursar when he locked out the children from their classrooms; and teaching a magisterially heavy timetable of 12 or so periods each week. 'He will turn his hand to anything', Sutton once said of his bursar, but the same could be said of the Headmaster himself for he had a practical as well as an academic disposition: screwing gallery prints of famous artists to corridor walls; rodding drains, as the new chaplain found on his first HCS visit; or energetically clearing snow with his bursar from the Old Deanery roof in early 1982 during that year's severe winter weather, which had delayed the start of term by five days. Although not a cricketer like his predecessor and successor, he was the first Headmaster to canoe across Wyeside in flood and the only one ever likely to undertake the 54-foot abseil down the Strongbow cider vat.[381] And of the many adventurous training days he supervised during

380. These were outlined for the first time in the 1977 prospectus as follows: 'Hereford Cathedral School sets out to be a community on a scale that encourages the establishment of good personal relationships, in which the pupils may develop their academic, cultural and athletic talents with the maximum personal attention of members of staff. The school strives to maintain a balance between individual and corporate interest so that boys and girls may learn to fulfil their potential within a framework of self-discipline and hard work in a way which will stand them in good stead as adults'.

381. The feats were undertaken in early January 1980, with the Wye around 18 feet in flood, and for a sponsored event on 1 June 1982, when 12 people made 538 abseils giving a total descent of 29,052 feet – the Headmaster making the day's final abseil.

his 12 years at the school, it is good to picture him at a suitably elevated check-point on top of Waun Fach on a summer field day in 1986. Characteristically, however, it is Father Ledwich's celebration of the Eucharist under canvas during the Ventures' expedition to Norway four years earlier that he most vividly remembered, for this occasion reflected both his love of the outdoors and his sincere faith.

As important but more difficult to capture was Sutton's style as Headmaster. As Prior recognised, the inspectors picked up on and his former Head of School observed, he helped promote 'a friendly, relaxed and positive atmosphere' which enabled pupils to fulfil their potential even if that meant a regime which was too liberal for some traditionalists.[382] Although his successor was the first Headmaster never to apply the cane, Sutton was sparing in its use and abandoned the practice following the formal abolition of corporal punishment in state schools.[383] As with the pupils, so with the Common Room. Staff morale was not high on his arrival in 1975 but this was soon turned around. A former colleague recollects:

> The arrival of BBS and his charming wife Margaret was greeted by the staff with great enthusiasm. They quickly ingratiated themselves by entertaining the staff to dinner at Harley Court. Gone were the formalities of the Peebles and Richards eras – a formal dinner, the lady of the house rising after the meal to lead the other ladies to the drawing room, leaving the men to enjoy the port and the cigars ... He was, therefore, very approachable.[384]

He was also skilled at appointing dynamic teachers, who brought new energy and expertise to certain areas. English is a case in point. From a department that was so dysfunctional in 1975 that Richards left a note on file expressing his concerns to his successor, following Colin Gray's appointment it became one of the strongest departments. Gray, with John Seely, was also instrumental in transforming Drama, laying the foundations for a distinct Drama department. The same may be said about the appointments of Lynn Martin and later Marise Williams (née Vater) for girls' games and John Williams as Director of Music in 1985. Such gifted members of staff combined with others to create, as Michael Walling remembers, an enriching and creative learning environment which could be transformational. It is instructive to learn that at least five members of the cast of *The Crucible*, Gray's first HCS production, went on to careers in the professional theatre. Several novelists (of whom Matthew Hall was but one), many musicians and at least one cartoonist were also nurtured at HCS during the Sutton years. HCS was a stimulating place to be in the late-Seventies and Eighties. The easy relationships, particularly in the Sixth Form, between staff

382. The former Head of School's tribute was paid by Gary Withers. *TH*, CCXXXIII (1987), p.10. Also see *ibid.*, pp.9-10 for tributes by Dean Haynes, W.J. R[umsey], A.N. S[have], G.J. M[arsh] and Angus Macdonald, Head of School, 1986-87.

383. By the Education (no. 2) Act of 1986. The Act abolished corporal punishment for all pupils supported by public funds, including assisted place holders, as from August 1987. In the light of this enactment, the governors on 3 June 1987 endorsed the Headmaster's decision to cease the practice.

384. I am indebted to Alan Morris for this reminiscence. For an indication of the restrained atmosphere at one of Peebles' dinner parties: Rowe, p.49.

and pupils were evident. And in the days before regular inspections, continuous assessment and league tables, all this was managed with a light touch and (as the HMIs found out) a minimum of paper procedures.[385]

The changes during Sutton's tenure were greater than during any previous decade in the school's history. As we have seen, full co-education was established and 200 pupils added to its roll; its governance and finances were dramatically improved; its plant altered out of all recognition as the school extended eastwards up Castle Street and northwards into St John Street; its community links were strengthened; and the opportunities for its pupils increased. Overall, its reputation was immeasurably enhanced.

Many, of course, contributed to these developments. Sutton owed a considerable debt of gratitude to Bishop John Eastaugh. Although not involved in governance, the Bishop knew HCS as a parent – and with his wife, Bridget, as a quasi-houseparent – appreciated the larger picture, and provided invaluable counsel behind the scenes. More visibly, the first lay chairman of governors gave his headmaster great support and encouragement. Indeed, Peter Prior was a remarkable man, whose drive was an essential element in the school's success. Its governing body of the mid-Eighties was the best it had ever been, and the stimulating presence on that board of the Bulmer chairman and managing director gave the school access to the expertise and sponsorship of the then flourishing company. Tony Hollingworth, that conscientious servant of both the board and Headmaster, also deserves praise. He was (in Sutton's words) an 'indefatigable worker whom I drove relentlessly but with whom I had a wonderful working relationship'. 'The achievements', he modestly added, 'were as much his as mine'. But Sutton also had good fortune on his side: Zimmerman's legacy came on stream at just the right time for the school's expansion; and from 1981, the assisted places scheme widened the school's catchment and social mix in a way that would not otherwise have been possible. Above all, the school was blessed with some dedicated teachers, without whose support much less would have been achieved. Sutton himself reflected in his late retirement on some 'remarkable members of staff ... who were willing to go the extra mile'. Among those not already mentioned, he remembered Dick Heald and Ege Parker as being 'pure gold'; Bill Rumsey as a fine Physics teacher and great support as Second Master; John Brookes and Dick Rhodes as important members of a department which maintained the school's classical reputation and continued to produce excellent results; the dual act of Dunn and Morris which 'made Chemistry really worth doing'; the contributions of Bill Suttle and Roger Lancaster which 'brought real distinction' in their very different ways; Linda Miles' revitalisation of the Geography department; and Geoffrey Marsh's gifts as 'a remarkable pastor' and teacher who revolutionised the teaching of Divinity at O and A-levels.[386] These tributes are just, but it was the Headmaster who admitted the pupils and made the appointments; it was he who provided the dynamic for much of the school's

385. This paragraph could not have been written without the invaluable insights of Michael Walling and Matthew Hall. The five members of *The Crucible* cast (of December 1980) who later made careers in the professional theatre world were: Catherine George, Rachel Preece, Andrew Price, Michael Walling and Suzanne Watson. The previous March, Walling had produced 'Murderers', an original and elaborate rock opera that was composed and almost entirely managed by members of the Sixth Form.

386. For the above observations: HCSA, Sutton to the author, 11 Sept. 2014; Michael Walling to the author, 27 April 2014.

advance; and it was he who helped create a unique environment for learning. As Michael Walling again observes:

> I think [Sutton's] ... greatest talent was to balance ['modernisation' and expansion] ... with the preservation of a distinct and idiosyncratic eccentricity that was every bit as important to the education of young people as the institutional framework within which it operated.

So on Sutton's departure, the school was a larger, more secure, self-confident, open, civilised and comfortable place than the one he had inherited. This is not, of course, to imply that there were no areas of concern. A survey of parents – 40 *per cent* of whom returned their questionnaire – conducted in the summer of 1986 suggested among other things that pupils' dress, manners and behaviour needed to be improved; that they should be more carefully guided in their homework; that the curriculum should be developed by the inclusion of more practical subjects; that various clubs and societies existed more in theory than practice; and that some members of staff were not pulling their weight. A number of these complaints were hardy perennials which were liable to be raised by any parent body at any school. Some had substance, however, and called for a response when they were incorporated into an impressively wide-ranging report which proved to be a useful blueprint for Sutton's successor.[387] Financially, too, HCS was by no means in a strong position. Although the school was less encumbered by debt than it had been a decade earlier, its surpluses were small and it was stretched by its spate of property acquisitions. It was also over-dependent on the income from assisted places, although in the short term the political threat to their existence was eased with the Tory victory in the General Election on 11 June 1987. More immediate were the looming increases of its rental bill for Chapter properties and the wider issue of the school's relationship with the cathedral.[388] Such pressing matters would soon be the concern of a different chairman of governors and a new Headmaster rather than Peter Prior and Barry Sutton, who both departed the scene in July 1987. While lamenting the departures, the new regime was welcomed in *The Herefordian*'s pages. Both chairman and Headmaster, it was said, would 'bring a new drive and youthful vigour to the task of directing and running this community'.

After 16 years as a governor Peter Prior deserved his retirement. It was the right time, too, for Barry Sutton to move on to a second headship at Taunton School after 12 years of unstinting service to the Cathedral School and its wider community. In his formal letter of resignation he had observed that he was leaving Hereford with mixed feelings, and that his one regret was that HCS seemed as 'encompassed with enemies' in 1987 as it had been in

387. Sutton established a 'curriculum development working party', under the chairmanship of the chaplain (Father Geoffrey Marsh), on 21 January 1986, to review the curriculum and timetable, to explore developments in educational philosophy and policy, including the examination system, and to explore the school's role in the wider community. Its report was not finally completed until January 1987, too late for the recommendations to be implemented by the Sutton regime.

388. The Chapter soon set an agenda for its first meeting, proposed for 19 September 1987, with the new Headmaster and chairman of governors. Discipline, the school's use of the cathedral for its daily assembly and its future development plans were among the items it wished to see discussed. HCA, 7031/28, p.39, 6 Aug. 1987.

1975.[389] This was the response of a man who was upset at his increasingly strained relationship with the cathedral authorities and who was growing weary of defending the school's interests. But in calmer moments, he could look back with justifiable pride on both his pupils' accomplishments and the way that the Cathedral School had developed under his steadfast leadership in a less incessantly demanding and litigious age.

389. It should be pointed out, however, that the letter was written to Peter Prior on 10 February 1987, a time of considerable anxiety and before the settling of the question of the chairmanship and the Dean's election as president *ex officio* at the following day's governors' meeting.

Chapter 9

The Past Thirty Years

At the beginning of his first speech day address on 14 July 1988, the Headmaster made the following observation:

> As an historian who has grappled with the problems of oral testimony, I know that memory is kind. As an historian-Headmaster, I am also conscious that objective truth is a chimera. At the best of times it is difficult, if not impossible, for a Head to stand back and take an unbiased and comprehensive view of how his school is getting on, particularly on a speech day when his objectivity may not be at a premium. If this is so for an experienced Head, how can a new Headmaster possibly do justice to reviewing his school in his first breathless year in office?

Almost 30 years on, as I near the end of this history, I am even more conscious of an historian's need for perspective, especially when writing about the recent past of a school which for 18 years I helped shape. Historians, in any case, are generally happier writing about the dead than the living. Above all, they need to be aware of the dangers of recalling so-called 'golden ages' and treat the phrase 'things were better in my day' with extreme caution. So for this writer at least, events at HCS over the past 30 years are both too close in time and too near to the author's heart to be given anything more than cursory treatment. A due appreciation of the period and its actors will have to wait until this history is continued by another hand. For now, this penultimate chapter, which brings the story of our school up to the early twenty-first century, can be little more than an interim report, based on publicly available material and fallible memory. Other more sensitive records have been subjected to a self-imposed 30-year confidentiality rule: it is not only cabinet papers and other government records which require temporary censorship.

Nevertheless, an outline can still be given of the school's developments since 1987. So what changes occurred during the headmastership of Howard Tomlinson (1987-2005), including the temporary rule during my sabbatical of Guy Rawlinson (1997-98), the school's first Deputy Headmaster? And what are the landmarks of the past 12 years under Paul Smith, the first scientist – John Rowlands' interim administration apart – to be appointed to the headship in the school's long history?

The story cannot be effectively told, however, without a brief consideration of the nature of educational change over the past generation. In the mid-Eighties, the position of schools could hardly have been more different from today. In 1987, when I succeeded Barry Sutton, GCSEs had just been introduced and pupils were still being taught – mostly by 'chalk and talk' – for the old-style Ordinary and Advanced-level examinations; corporal punishment in schools had only recently been abolished; the school leaving age had been raised to 16 within recent memory; neither the national curriculum, nor modular examinations, nor coursework and controlled assessments, nor academic league tables and performance measures, nor the Ofsted inspection regime, nor the 'EBacc' existed; school policies, such as the one relating to health and safety legislation, were limited;[1] there was no Children Act; teacher in-service training and staff appraisal were in their infancy; fewer than one in five school-leavers proceeded to Higher Education; government support for independent education was strong through the assisted place scheme; and traditional boarding schools flourished. Thirty years later, in a digital age of instant global communication and a diverse educational market-place – where schools are over-burdened with the requirement to produce ever more extensive policies for health and safety, risk assessment and numerous educational and welfare matters[2] – how distant that world seems.

Transitional Times, 1987-2005

Although it is still too early to know what themes will ultimately prove most significant, no future historian of HCS is likely to deny the importance of the Education (Schools) Act of 31 July 1997, when the new Labour government scrapped the assisted places scheme. My time in office, therefore, may be seen in retrospect as an interim period during which the Cathedral School built up its infrastructure in preparation for full independence in 2004, when the last cohort of assisted place pupils left the school.

The senior school roll could not but be influenced by the phasing out of assisted places. In 1987, I inherited a school of around 590 pupils, with a further 109 junior boys under Stephen Sides in Number 28 Castle Street. Forty *per cent* of the senior pupils were subsidised by the government and there were about 100 boarders between the two schools in three boarding houses. HCS numbers remained around 600 for the following few years, enabling the school to expand from a three to a four-form entry in September 1993. By the mid-Nineties, following the closure of Belmont Abbey School in 1994, the school reached its all-time record peak of 634 pupils (in 1994-95). These healthy numbers, together with the school's offering of 20 means-tested bursaries for its junior entry in September 1998, and subsequently grants from the Old Herefordian Trust to the tune of £100,000 (by 2005-06), did something to soften the blow of the phasing out of £1,000,000 of government funding. Numbers, however, inevitably declined. The delicate state of the local economy post the 2001 outbreak of foot and mouth made matters worse. The result was that in 2002-03, for the first time for many years, the school's income and expenditure account

1. The school's first brief (two clause) 'health and safety' policy document (concerning the 1974 Health and Safety at Work Act) was not formally adopted by the governors until 10 June 1982.

2. For the Cathedral School alone, 34 policy documents (for both seniors and juniors) that it is 'obliged to publish to parents' are detailed on its website, even though it is 'not an exhaustive list' of its policies.

was in deficit. This had painful consequences but led to the creation of a more streamlined and cost-effective curriculum.

The decline in senior numbers, however, does not tell the whole story for the senior school's continued success was in part due to the growth of Hereford Cathedral Junior School, as it soon became. Although it remained a separate school with an autonomous Headmaster – albeit under the same governing body – it is in 1987 that the history of HCS intersects with that of its junior partner. Alongside the name change, it soon became a 3 to 11 establishment rather than a traditional preparatory school to 13. The junior school had access from the start to senior facilities so lunches were taken in the HCS dining-room, games were scheduled at Wyeside and juniors were able to use the music school and drama studio in Castle Street. As importantly, the governors having taken on Number 28 on a full repairing lease, the senior school's works department were on call to maintain an old building in a poor state of repair.[3] The change to co-education also aided the junior school's expansion. Its first eight girls were admitted in September 1990 and before the end of that decade girls constituted one third of the school. Above all, its two Headmasters, Stephen Sides (1987-95) and Tim Lowe (1995-2008), ably supported by their deputy, Bob Hall (1977-2008), provided the dynamic leadership required to move the junior school forward. Each Headmaster added more than a hundred pupils during their tenure, making a junior school of 350, sending 50 or so boys and girls yearly to HCS, by the early years of the century.[4] The increased junior numbers helped offset the demise of boarding and eventual withdrawal of assisted places. It resulted in a 3 to 18 all-day foundation of nearly 890 by the time of my retirement, a near doubling of day numbers since 1987.

In terms of buildings, the school also developed substantially. As under Barry Sutton, the reconfiguration of the school campus resembled an elaborate game of musical chairs as HCS gave up many of its Castle Street properties to the junior school. But the first major development was a new senior base for practical subjects. The existing Art and Computer rooms were inadequate for a school of 600. The facilities for Technology, introduced by Bob Clarke in the early 1980s as an after school club, with a few hand tools in a corner of a Physics laboratory, before moving to the music school basement in 1989, were no better. The eventual solution, after the abandonment of the original scheme for an extensive building on East Street, necessitated New Block's re-modelling. An appeal, 'Design for the future', raised £400,000 at a time of economic recession in little more than two years, and the new centre for Art and Technology was opened by Lord Portman on 12 December 1992. Meanwhile, the Old Herefordian Trustees' acquisition of 34 Castle Street provided an adequate temporary teaching base for the New Block departments and form-rooms. The Portman Centre, including the Clive Richards computing rooms on the new upper floor with its striking glass wall, won an RIBA regional award and has stood the test of time. (Plate 23).

3. And with the purchase of the freehold in 1994, a full programme of refurbishment was possible. Gas central heating was installed, leaking roofs fixed, new toilets provided and serious faults – including major repairs to the hall floor and staircase – corrected.

4. Stephen Sides started with 109 boys in the main school and five boys and girls in the nursery. By the time he left in 1995, there were over 250 in the school, with a two-form entry from Reception to Year 6. Tim Lowe established a three-form entry throughout the pre-prep and main school. For a history of HCJS during these years (to 1998): Howard-Jones, pp.61-76.

Almost simultaneously, space had to be found for the burgeoning numbers in the junior school. An interim but unsatisfactory solution was the releasing of two classrooms on the first floor of Number 29 and the creation of a play area at the back of the music school for September 1993. But the establishment of a proper campus for HCJS had to wait until the senior school released the whole of Old College in the summer of 1995, followed by St David's Hall two years later and the Quay Street buttery in 1999. In the previous year, the junior school had celebrated its centenary from the time of its origins within Harley Court as Murray Ragg's private business. One aim of the celebrations was to fund a new library which would involve creating an internal link between Numbers 28 and 29. This was successfully achieved, the centenary library being opened by the Duchess of York in 2002. The stage was now set for the most complicated – and expensive – project of them all: a classroom development for the pre-preparatory department on the dry moat of the medieval Hereford Castle. The moat was the boundary of a scheduled ancient monument at the back of 28 and 29 Castle Street that also abutted onto listed buildings, and this led to local opposition which was eventually overcome.[5] The imaginatively designed high-tech building, originally with a grass roof, was opened by the Duke of Kent on 5 June 2003 and again won an award for its architect, Angus Jamieson, and the contractors, Wheatstone and Plant. (Plate 25).

The establishment of suitable accommodation for an expanding junior school on the south side of Castle Street could not have happened without HCS adapting its three remaining boarding houses for other uses, a process which occurred gradually through the 1990s. During this decade, boarding became both unfashionable and unaffordable, even for professional families, despite the competitive annual fee of £8,355 by the middle of the decade. The inexorable decline in boarding numbers was also accelerated by the abandonment of Saturday morning academic lessons from September 1996. In these circumstances, and with the continued demand for day places, some rationalisation of our boarding provision was inevitable. In the summer of 1993, Number 1 was converted to day use, thus bringing Egerton Parker's exemplary service over 21 years as its Housemaster to a close. A new mixed house for junior pupils was maintained in Number 2 for a few years before it, too, was re-established. Senior boarding did not last much longer, boarding in Old Deanery coming to an end after 50 years in 1995, and the new mixed (Philpotts) house in 5 and 6 St John Street in 1999, when numbers had fallen to fewer than 20. It should be recorded that Robin Baggott, a chorister, continued as the solitary boarder in the school for a year until he, too, left (in 2001), thereby bringing to an end – perhaps temporarily – hundreds of years of boarding provision at the school.

It was a sad decline but the boarding houses were put to good use: Number 1 for First-form (Year 7) classrooms, a base for the History and Economic departments and eventually for new Upper Sixth (Year 13) studies; Number 2 as a nursery; and 5 and 6 St John Street as a temporary Music department until 2003, when it was released back to the Old Herefordian trustees, who were then able to increase their award of scholarships and bursaries. As significantly, the move of boarding from the Old Deanery gave sufficient room for a

5. The cost was almost £600,000. Half the sum was provided by the OH Fund, the remainder by bank loan on the security of the Fund's assets.

proper reception area for the senior school, as well as space for the Headmaster's study, the Common Room, two classrooms and administrative offices, including a conference room, named after Dr Daly Briscoe OH, which houses much of his old library. The school's focal point had shifted once again towards its historic heart opposite the cathedral.

HCS's acquisition of the old British Telecom Exchange in Church Street completed its return to the Close. This huge building, acquired in 1996 by the Old Herefordian Trust Fund, provided over 25,000 square feet of extra space for the school.[6] Over the following two years, it was skilfully adapted into classrooms for two departments, an extensive room for multi-purpose use, a games hall and a theatre. It was appropriately named after Arthur Ulrich Zimmerman, the school's greatest benefactor in modern times, and formally opened by Roy Blackler, then chairman of the OH Trust, on 12 July 1997. (Plates 19 and 20). Two years later, a new buttery was created in the old engine house. By the late 1990s, the extensive halls were also being used for public examinations, which with the advent of modularity now included January as well as the early summer months. From 1997, College Hall, which had served as the school's examinations room for generations of pupils, was no longer required for that purpose. So ended, after many decades (as Roger Lancaster, with pardonable poetic licence put it) the practice of 'one of those gilt-edged Deans on the wall … trying to examine what goes on / beneath him in the body of this hall …'[7] One consequence of the adaptation of the old Exchange was the opening of the Powell Theatre (named in recognition of the generous legacy of Herbert Powell, school architect for 30 years, and his wife) in December 1997, the first production being Alick Rowe's commissioned burlesque on the history of HCS. Another was the incorporation of the studio theatre in Old Block into the former Gilbert Library. As well as doubling in size, the new library was completely remodelled, its south window, composed of more than 1,000 pieces of fractured and stressed glass, paying tribute to Lord Portman's generosity to the school. It was opened with a magnificent flourish by Daly Briscoe, in his 99th year, on 9 December 1998. (Plate 21). The restored library of September 1977 thereby became a modern resources-centre for a different generation.

Nor were outdoor games facilities neglected. A pavilion was built adjacent to the Gwynne Street netball and tennis courts in 1988 and the playing-fields were properly fenced in 1991 – both by courtesy of the PTA – by which time the Wyeside pavilion itself had been extended for girls' changing. Other Wyeside developments occurred early in the new century: the pavilion itself was refurbished, an extra field for junior games was acquired and the drive was improved.

So by the end of my period in office the school site had been extended, many of its buildings had been renewed, and new infrastructure had been put in place, notably the establishment of a co-ordinated telephone system and an extended computer network across Castle Street. It was a complicated jigsaw for a school with 17 listed buildings in a conservation area, and looking back mistakes were made. Plans for new buildings on

---

6. The Fund borrowed £300,000 to buy the building, the loan being repaid by 2003. Its purchase was – as Peter Williams, the OH Trust correspondent, has observed – 'game-changing in the school's operation'.

7. At least as far as HCS examinations were concerned. For this wonderful poem, entitled 'Understanding of Literary Material under Controlled Conditions', see *TH* (1999), p.14.

East Street were aborted and premature announcements were given about other developments which were not realised. Nevertheless, thanks to the generosity, time and commitment of many individuals and the resources of the Old Herefordian Trust Fund, which through its property and other investments could boast net assets in excess of £2,000,000 by the end of the period, substantial improvements to the school's built environment were made. In my last speech day address on 9 July 2005, I put forward this wish-list in terms of desired future physical developments: a refurbished science block; a new sports hall; more space for children in the early learning years; an all-weather games surface; and a commemorative stained-glass window in the cathedral. As we will see, the first three of those wishes (and much else) have been achieved under my successor and the fourth is under consideration.

Changes in the nature of the governing body mirrored the four different sites for their board during my years of attendance at their meetings: the old Gilbert Library, Number 29, Number 1 and the Briscoe room in the Old Deanery, its present location. Three chairmen of governors served the school through my 18 years, Wallace Garland (1987-93), Robert Willis (1993-2001) and Meriel Oliver (2001-05), all of whom brought special leadership qualities to the board. The cathedral links were continued through the Dean's presence as an active governor – Robert Willis, indeed, may prove to be the last Dean ever to chair the board – and the dedicated service of two residentiary canons, notably Paul Iles and John Tiller in my time. Two former Headmasters, Richard Bull from 1992 followed by John Chapman five years later, acted as staff representative governors, since when the board has always included a former head-teacher. Links with Brasenose were strengthened through the hosting by John Peach and then John Rowett of an academic policy sub-committee at the college, which eventually morphed into a home-based education committee led by Adrian Silcock. Ties with Bulmer's, too, were maintained, through Brian Nelson, Ian Richardson, Trevor Gregory and David Hitchiner; as were those with the Old Herefordian Trust, Peter Williams and Bill Morris following on from Roy Blackler, the last of the old city council representative governors. No governor served throughout my tenure, although David Langstaff almost did as

Fig. 9.1 Howard Charles Tomlinson, Headmaster 1987-2005.

bursar and Clerk to the Governors from 1986 to 2003; but many proved to be invaluable stewards – a stewardship which has continued after my time under two other chairmen: Adam Darnley (2006-12) and Rob Haydn Jones (2012-17).

Just as the governing body became more business-like in its methods in the last decades of the twentieth century, so too did the full-time staff. Thanks in part to Wallace Garland's expertise, teacher appraisals were introduced and job descriptions drafted. A senior management team was formed and committee structures introduced. The titles of colleagues slowly changed. So the term 'senior master' was replaced by 'deputy head administration'; the 'senior mistress' by 'deputy head pastoral'; and the bursar by 'director of finance and administration'. Following the 1988 Education Reform Act, regular staff training days were started; internal posts were advertised for the first time; an increased number of heads of department were appointed from outside; and more younger staff moved on to higher positions in other places. But as in the past, many dedicated teachers saw out their careers at the Cathedral School. Among those who retired or left in my time and whose service to HCS amounted to at least 30 years were the final survivors of the Hopewell regime: Roger Lancaster (1947-88) and Bill Rumsey (1948-88); the last of Peebles' masters, Peter Skinner (1957-93), Don Theakston (1958-91), Alex Shave (1964-95), Alan Morris (1965-98) and Dick Rhodes (1966-2000); the last of Rowlands' appointments, Bob Talbot (1968-2002) and Jim Dunn (1968-2005); and the last of Richards' men in the person of Roger Toll (1973-2003). So these ten schoolmasters, with a combined service of almost 350 years, retired within 15 years of each other. Given the tendency for today's staff to move jobs more frequently, it is unlikely that so many teachers will ever again register such long stays at the Cathedral School.[8]

The careers of women teachers have inevitably been shorter, given that few were appointed before co-education. However, several who retired in or shortly after my time completed long tenures at HCS: notably, Jill Howard-Jones (1973-97), Anita Pritchard (1979-2006), Hilary Gould (1980-2005), Marise Williams (1980-2008), Linda Miles (1981-2001) and Ann Bigley (1983-2007). During their careers, the Common Room, like the school as a whole, became more gender balanced. In 1987, women comprised one-third of the academic staff; by 2005, the ratio was almost fifty-fifty. During these years, HCS became a more civilised as well as a more professional place.

Between these dates, the number of academic teachers grew by six and the support staff by as many, with the addition of a 'learning support' department, further science technicians, a new computing technician (later, in 1999, an 'ICT systems manager'), as well as assistants in Languages, Technology and Art. And before my departure, in a world increasingly demanding ever greater specialisation, the tradition of teachers trying their hand at various offices became unsustainable. So Bill Walling was appointed the school's first specialist careers advisor in 1989; and Rachel Ayers-Nelson our first professional librarian in 1997. The secretariat, too, increased. No longer was it possible, as Yvonne James had so admirably done over nearly three decades, for the Headmaster's secretary to cope with

8. Although for those retiring with at least 30 years service under my successor, Jim Shutt (1981-2011), Molly Ball (1983-2015) and Sue Connop (1984-2014) have done so, together with Jonathan Priday OH and Marnie Wooderson (appointed respectively in 1982 and 1985), who are both still in post.

the increasing expectations of parents so a school secretary was appointed following our move to the Old Deanery, and – belatedly – an admissions secretary from September 2002. There was a need, too, for the school to be more vigorously marketed which led to Bob Adams' appointment as our first development officer, with responsibilities for promotion and public relations, in 1993. Some three years later, following the abolition of Saturday morning school, the first open morning was tentatively held in the Portman Centre. By then, a mission statement had already been published (in 1992). A first development plan, '2000 Plus', was to follow in 1997. We were slowly feeling our way towards a time when HCS would become fully independent.

Yet its old mix of assisted and fee-paying pupils had served us well. The gradual improvement in our external examination performance, which could not altogether be explained by grade inflation, culminated in 2004, when the last cohort of assisted place pupils took their 'A' levels and gained the best academic results at that time in the school's history. With a near 70 *per cent* gaining the top two grades, almost all students won entry to their preferred university. These not only included Oxford and Cambridge – although fewer than the one in ten now proceeded to the ancient universities as happened in our best years in the 1990s – but also a spread of higher education institutions throughout the country. Moreover, at GCSE that year, every pupil gained at least five A to C passes and one in five at least ten of the two top grades, with an A*/A rate overall of 56.6 *per cent.* What was particularly pleasing, given the base-line testing that we had started for this group at 11 in 1999, was that nationally recognised criteria proved that HCS had added academic value over most other schools. All this boded well for the future.

But HCS has always been about much more than what goes on in the classroom and examination hall. In my final speech day address, I also reflected with pride on pupil achievement over my time in Music, with more than 20 music groups then giving 40 or so concerts each year; Drama and Design-Technology, now both firmly embedded in the curriculum; Art, including a national prize-winner that year;[9] and in debating, not least James Probert's debating triumphs in the world championships among many other successes in local and Oxford and Cambridge Union competitions. I also recalled HCS pupils who had won national titles or gained national sporting recognition during their time at the school;[10] as well as teams that had competed to a high level in national sporting competitions, reminding my audience that such successes were invariably achieved against much larger schools.[11] And I further acknowledged our consistent level of performance

9. Following on from Maxim Devereaux in 1994 (for 'A' level Chemistry), Tim Sarson in 1995 ('A' level Geography) and Iain Mackay in 2000 (for both GCSE Economics and English Literature), there were three national prize-winners for examination performance in 2004 – Felicity Watkins ('A' level Art), Christine Batchelor and Pia Dowse (both for GCSE English Literature) – and one (Liam Dunachie) for GCSE Music in 2005. Anthony Goddard (in 1996) and Simon Middleton (in 2001) also won national Arkwright awards in Design-Technology.

10. The list included Helen Aitcheson, Rob Allen, Adam Billig, David and John Bray, Toby Eckley, Helen Ellison, Joel Evans, Alex Gallagher, James and Robert Lewis, Harriet Lowe, Stephen Price (in two sports), Rachel Smith, Robbie Symonds and George Thomas. Adam Billig holds the record as the most capped Herefordshire boy for England schools' rugby; and Robert Lewis the equivalent record for Wales.

11. I highlighted three boys' teams – the under-18s in 1995 (see Plate 17), and the under-15s in 1996 and 2003 – all of which had reached the quarter-final stages of the *Daily Mail* rugby competition, and the Old Herefordian

through our extensive outward bound programmes: the Duke of Edinburgh's award scheme and the CCF, one mark of which was the 150 or so Old Herefordians who had successfully completed officer training in Her Majesty's forces since 1990. And there were a host of other activities. Thirty-three societies, any of which I could have focussed upon, were then listed in the 2005 Summer Term calendar. Over 18 years, as staff had moved on or retired and student enthusiasms had waxed and waned, some clubs – the Traherne and Austro-Hungarian Societies are good examples – had disappeared but many more had taken their place. We had become a much busier school.

Sport, the CCF and debating had long been staple diets but in this generation HCS had done much to stimulate artistic endeavour and creation, in its widest sense, among its pupils. During my time, the school managed both to retain and improve its traditional academic and extra-curricular strengths, as well as widen its cultural horizons. One reason for this was the maintenance of old and the building of new facilities, already described. Many different agencies were responsible for this advance: a progressive governing body; the Old Herefordian Club and Trust which were instrumental to the school's expansion; the Parent Teacher Association, who raised in excess of £100,000 to the benefit of many departments, activities and projects; and, not least, the bursar and estates staff, whose hard work maintained and renewed our plant and beautified our gardens. But nothing could have been achieved in my time without the aptitude and receptiveness of three generations of pupils, the support of their parents and the expertise and inspiration of some 130 teachers with whom I worked. As the original mission statement proclaimed: 'To realise our ideals demands a talented and committed staff and the full moral and practical support of parents. The boys and girls of Hereford Cathedral School will be best served within such a spirit of trust and co-operation'.

As for me, I had at least seen the entire school through to full independence, free from any form of government pupil subsidy for the first time in nearly a century. I had appointed three out of every four members of Common Room, only 14 of my predecessor's appointments having survived my tenure; about 2,350 pupils (according to my last Head of School) had studied at HCS during my period in office; and I had served with some 40 governors, none of whom at my retirement had been responsible for my appointment. And although I did not break Dr Crees' inter-war record for the longest modern stint as Headmaster, 18 years over 52 terms was long enough for present times. A future historian will need both to evaluate the accuracy of the sentiments expressed in my retirement messages of appreciation, and to analyse whether the generous tributes in the *Hereford Times* and *The Herefordian* are anything more than mere hyperbole.[12] For the moment, this judgement of the 2002 inspectors must suffice: 'The Headmaster offers sensitive and thoughtful leadership, is readily accessible, and is deeply concerned to maintain the ethos of the school as a Christian foundation that "fosters good manners, the highest personal standards, respect and compassion, commitment, participation and an open mind"'.

XI (under Richard Skyrme's captaincy) that won the Brewers' old boys cricket cup in 2003.

12. *HT*, 21 July 2005, p.27; *TH 2005*, p.7. Of the cricketing allusions which headline each article, the newspaper's 'good innings' seems to me to be nearest to the mark.

Full Independence, 2005-Present

Although historians should not be called upon to be prophets, in my final speech day address I had given public expression to my faith in the school's future and listed some of its assets: a progressive governing board; an able and committed staff; an admirable pupil body; a thriving junior school; good links with local primary and preparatory schools; a reputation for all-round excellence; and, above all, a special ethos and atmosphere which attained (as a prospective parent had described it to me) 'a tangible balance of tradition with progression ... where the individual is obviously cared for'. I also referred approvingly to my successor, Paul Smith, whose leadership and strategic vision over the past decade has more than demonstrated my approbation and, far more importantly, the governors' trust.

However, by July 2005, although HCS had come through a painful few years to full independence, we needed to continue to improve all aspects of our operation. Peter Prior had recognised this 25 years earlier, in the interim period between the loss of direct grants and the advent of assisted places. Writing to Barry Sutton, he observed: 'I am still of the view that we might as well declare ourselves unashamedly as an independent public school, develop a strong marketing policy, sell our places at the highest going price and create a reputation for being a first-class school with a high-grade staff'.[13] Although a totally independent Cathedral School was far better able to face the future in 2005 than it would have been (without assisted places) in 1980, not all of Prior's conditions had been fully met by the end of my tenure. The most urgent tasks related to the continued need to strengthen the school's financial position; further rationalise its plant and improve its facilities for science and sport; more fully integrate its junior school; and develop its marketing strategy and transport links. All these *desiderata* have been accomplished over the past decade, during which time the school's reputation for excellence has been consolidated.

The turnaround in the school's financial fortunes, following the serious impact of the withdrawal of assisted places, had begun in the earlier years of the century. However, costs have continued to be rigorously controlled following my departure, by Simon Jones, the bursar from 2004 to 2009, and his three successors.[14] By 2007, a surplus of £170,000 had been secured, since when its balance sheet has always been favourable, and the school has built up an investment pot in excess of £1,000,000.[15] This is a considerable achievement, as is the maintenance of overall pupil numbers at 786 (for September 2016), despite the credit crunch following the banking crisis of 2008 and the demographic decline in the number of school-age children in Herefordshire, 2006-15.[16]

---

13. HCSA, Peter Prior to Barry Sutton, 8 May 1980.

14. Jacqui Millar (2009-11), Norman Moon (2011-13) and Rob Pizii (2014-present).

15. The favourable balance sheet has in part been achieved through the generosity of the Old Herefordian trustees, whose scholarship and bursary grants amounted (in 2016-17) to £163,000 annually. HCS now receives back in grants almost all the money that it paid to the Trust in rents for the school buildings owned by the OH Fund. The Trust continues to improve its reserves, through the setting up of an investment fund managed by professional brokers, in which some £240,000 has so far been set aside for long-term growth.

16. Senior school pupils in the county declined from 11,000 to 9,595; and juniors from 13,800 to 12,984 between these dates.

Fig. 9.2 Paul Anthony Smith, Headmaster, 2005-Present.

Even more so has been the money spent – some £2,400,000 over the decade from 2005 – on improving the school's facilities. The long-discussed Sixth Form centre, including computer-hub and café, was developed on the ground floor of the Zimmerman building for the start of the 2006-07 academic year. The development deprived the school of its indoor cricket nets and games hall but within three years a sports hall had been built on the East Street site at the back of Number 1. (Plate 26). It was opened by Dame Kelly Holmes on 22 April 2009. By then, the dining-hall had been enlarged and refurbished, all forms below the Sixth being required to eat lunch there from 2008. By this time, too, the old 1950s gymnasium had been converted into two laboratories and the squash court into an additional new Science space. An artificial surface behind Number 1 also enabled the CCF to parade undisturbed by the growing number of cars parked in School House yard. It had been a frenetic few years for the new regime. Within four years of Paul Smith's appointment, the Science building on the Ferrers Street site had been renewed and a multi-purpose hall for various sports had been created on East Street. A site which had been earmarked for development for the previous two decades, but apart from a portacabin for junior Science had remained untouched, had been transformed. A few years later, the old buttery was converted into a new Art and Technology facility for the junior school. The acquisition of Quay House, with its walled garden and open-plan design, also provided an excellent centre for its pre-school provision, the nursery moving into the renovated building from Number 2 in 2014.

At the beginning of this decade, it was finally resolved that HCS and HCJS were one school. With both Stephen Sides and Tim Lowe, the understanding had been that we were two schools within the one foundation. Although in my last year Tim Lowe had periodically attended senior management meetings, by the time of Paul Smith's arrival, the governors wished to promote a stronger sense of the Cathedral School providing a seamless education from 3 to 18, with the senior Head overseeing development strategy for the whole school. The new approach worked well from the appointment of Tim Wheeler (HCJS Headmaster, 2008-14) and under his successor, Chris Wright. As part of the whole school ethos, the obligatory entrance examination for junior pupils soon ceased; senior forms were renumbered consecutively from Year 7 upwards; further facilities were made available for junior use; and, in a symbolic display of unity, both Headmasters were invited to take part in cathedral processions on formal occasions. *The Herefordian*, moreover, has now developed into one magazine for both senior and junior sections of the school.

This unified approach has been emphasised in the school's expanded marketing operation. The 1990s had witnessed the appointment of our first development officer. Early in the following decade, a marketing group and parent public relations committee was established, as well as a professional secretary for the Old Herefordian Club. However, in the last few years marketing has been elevated to a new level of expertise. One key to this transformation was the appointment in 2010 of two new and separate 'directors': one for development, the other for marketing. Another has been the digital revolution. So HCS, like other schools, has implemented a social media strategy. The school's website, 'Twitter' and 'Instagram' sites have largely usurped the place of the traditional prospectus, and while glossies – notably 'Blue and Gold' – still have a part to play in spreading word about the school's activities, electronic communication rather than paper has become the chief means of promotion. And the school has been rebranded at least twice. The strap-line 'an education for life' was replaced by 'remember and dream' and now by: 'Arrive a member of your family; become one of ours', the theme of a promotional film released in October 2017. That autumn, too, following the design of a new logo in 2009, a more traditional school crest once again became the school's distinctive marketing symbol.

So HCS has reached out to its several constituencies as never before. With the development office now more firmly established, HCS has become much more active in organising *alumni* gatherings and other corporate events. It has also established new outreach programmes. An innovative scheme to admit Whitecross students into its CCF has been created; active programmes to advance the teaching locally of such subjects as Classics and Physics have been established; and at a time of cutbacks to local music provision, extensive support has been given to county musical activities. And the school's name is carried about the far-flung reaches of the Marches by a fleet of minibuses, as children are transported around the county and beyond.

Although with the demise of assisted places, there is now a longer academic tail at HCS than formerly, pupil achievements over the past decade have continued to impress.

Academic results, with 69.6 *per cent* (A*-B) at A-level and 81 *per cent* (A*-B) at GCSE in 2017, remain the best in the county. National Board prizes continue to be won.[17] Students almost invariably gain places at one of their chosen universities. Extra-curricular activities are just as highly regarded, as suggested by the recent appointment of the school's first Assistant Head (in 2015) with responsibility to oversee their provision. With a PE/Games department of 18, sport retains its place as an important part of the school calendar. And the school still excels in this regard, despite often being pitted against larger schools: the girls regularly win county hockey and netball tournaments at all age groups and periodically produce international players;[18] and boys' teams continue to achieve good results – and sometimes, as with the 1st XV in 2005-06, impressive ones – and include outstanding individual players who have broken records and achieved national recognition.[19] Rowing has enjoyed a period of revival; soccer has again made its appearance as a school representative sport; and the CCF and Duke of Edinburgh's award scheme thrive.[20]

Among a myriad of other activities – some 33 clubs and societies, from Abel Set to Young Enterprise, are listed in the Autumn Term 2017 calendar – pride of place must go to music. The two cathedral organists apart, the Director of Music oversees a department of two academic musicians, three music administrators and a staff of 32 peripatetic instrumentalists. At the last count, around 500 individual music lessons are taught to over 300 pupils on a weekly basis, and there are 23 different music groups within the school. HCS is now well provided for, musically, in everything except a new music school.[21] There can be few other schools, moreover, which can match its consistently high level of performance. One significant illustration of this is the outstanding achievements in 2015 – the *annus mirabilis* for our choral singing – of both Cantabile, the senior girls' choir (Plate 18), and the junior school chamber choir in winning national competitions.[22]

One final activity, charitable giving, is worthy of permanent record. Regular charitable donations have long been practised but their scope has recently increased, over £10,000 being given to ten local and national charities in 2015. As significantly, a charity which now has a national profile was initially founded at the junior school: The Little

17. In GCSE Economics (Richard Watkins, 2007); GCSE Religious Studies (India Benjamin and Megan Corder, 2008); and in 'A' level Art (Christine Batchelor, Pia Dowse, Elizabeth Marlow, Rhianna Williams, Sarah Boulton and Miranda Harris, 2006-08).

18. Notably in rounders, 12 girls having represented England at various age groups, 2006-14.

19. The 1st XV in October 2005 was chosen by *Rugby World* for the first time as its team of the month, and by winning 13 of its 16 matches over the season became the most successful senior rugby team in the school's history. The Lewis twins have both played rugby sevens for Wales, and Will Butler has represented England for rugby at under-18 and under-20 levels. In cricket, Ben Stebbings' seasonal record of 904 runs for the 1st XI in 2006 should also be noted.

20. During the 21 years that Mike Moffatt was school staff instructor of the CCF (1989-2010), 252 of his former cadets joined Her Majesty's armed forces; and in December 2012, Sarah Hunter-Choat OH became only the fourth woman in the history of the RMA Sandhurst to have been awarded the sword of honour.

21. David Evans' initial judgement of his area as 'a happy but tatty department of outstanding people' (*TH* 2007, p.16) should still stand, despite an extension of music facilities and the department's enhanced national reputation after his 11-year tenure as Director of Music.

22. Respectively winners of the BBC 'Songs of Praise' school choir of the year and Barnardo's choir of the year competitions. Both choirs performed before HRH the Duke of Kent on the occasion of his royal visit that year.

Princess Trust has raised an astonishing £11,000,000 since its inception little more than a decade ago.[23]

So the school has developed commendably under new management in the 12 years since my retirement. Its reputation as a place of all-round excellence has been confirmed by the 2014 inspection report; its status among like establishments endorsed by the *Good Schools Guide*, in which HCS is described as 'a school with a great deal to offer and an ethos of careful, thoughtful nurture ... with truly outstanding arts and music, a wide curriculum, a great sense of community and a genuine commitment to develop courage, confidence and a sense of adventure in even the quietest child'.

Not least of the changes since 2005 has been among the personnel. Only one governor, together with the Dean (now president), remain from my era. For the first time in its history, a Bishop rather than a member of Chapter is a working member of the board. Only a fifth of an HCS Common Room of nearly 60 teachers are still left from my staff room; only Jonathan Priday, who has recently completed a century of terms, and Marnie Wooderson, who has almost done so, survive from Barry Sutton's time. Mrs Wooderson's observations about the nature of the teaching staff on her arrival in 1985 are instructive:

> Once I started teaching here, I wondered whether I had walked into a time-warp. The Common Room seemed dominated by elderly gentlemen who regarded the place as something akin to a gentlemen's club and were really rather disconcerted to see women allowed within its hallowed portals. I can still remember receiving looks askance when I first wore trousers and ... [being told] that I must wear a skirt or dress for Commemoration. There was even a rule in the constitution about women not being allowed to knit in the Common Room.

Now, although teachers have remained as committed to HCS as they ever were, with a majority of women on the staff – and occasionally (as in 2007) a majority of female students – things could hardly be more different. We have long become a proper co-educational school.

Until her recent retirement, there was only one person within the wider establishment with a continuous record of service, who could remember HCS as it was in David Richards' time.[24] Mary Lawrence – 'Aunty Mary' to generations of children – stood as a representative of a long line of support staff who have loyally served the school over many years. Robert Goode, although his record does not go back as far, was first employed in Barry Sutton's early days in what was then known as the 'works department' under the superintendence of a 'foreman'. His long service and present title as 'estates manager' are reminders of how much things have stayed the same and how far they have changed.[25]

---

23. This Trust, founded in memory of Hannah Tarplee, a junior school pupil who died of a Wilms tumour in June 2005, helps children who have lost their hair as a result of cancer treatment. It supplied 1,076 wigs in 2016 and receives up to 3,000 hair donations a month. Recently, the charity donated £500,000 for research into childhood cancers and their treatment. In 2012, it received the Queen's Award for Voluntary Service.

24. Following Katherine Soulsby's retirement in 2015 after 42 years as a bassoon teacher.

25. Note should also be made here of an HCS parent, Bob Binnersley, who sent his four children (Richard, Rachel, James and Thomas) to the school, their attendances (from eldest to youngest) covering a 41-year period from 1976

The balance over the past decade, however, has necessarily tilted towards the latter pole. Among the administrative staff, a host of new offices have emerged which did not exist in my time. These include a receptionist, an examinations officer, a human resources officer, a transport organiser and a website and communications co-ordinator. The days of the Headmaster teaching an Advanced-level set and coaching a cricket team are long gone, and there are fewer all-round schoolmasters and mistresses than there were. Nomenclature, too, has continued to change. The Headmaster's secretary has become his PA; the study, his office; the senior management team, the senior leadership team; and the school secretary, the school office administrator.

As the school's administration has been professionalised, so its pupils have become more engrossed in the modern digital world than any previous generation. British Telecom's removal of the school's two telephone booths in 2003 because they were insufficiently profitable illustrates the extent to which mobiles were by then being used by the pupil body. More recently, the rapid spread of smart-phones among children of all ages marks a further stage in the advance of the knowledge economy but brings with it unprecedented problems for any institution.[26]

The world is evolving at a faster pace than ever before and the Cathedral School must adapt accordingly, living in the present and looking to the future. It is no easier now for someone writing in 2017 to know what that future will bring than it would have been in say the mid-Victorian period in the aftermath of the Endowed Schools' Commission. But despite Brexit, it is certain, as the present Headmaster is well aware, that 'with ever increasing globalisation ... working within an international industry or marketplace will become more commonplace for our students, as ... [will] working with colleagues from overseas'.[27] One way that HCS is preparing its pupils for our increasingly multicultural and interconnected world, is by extending its exchange programme with St Catherine's and King's Parramatta in Sydney, and through its growing links with The Phillips Academy in New Hampshire as well as a German school in Flensburg. Another is by making places available in the Sixth Form for international students. The first six Chinese Sixth-formers were admitted in 2012, followed by a similar number each year since then. They have been successfully integrated into the school, gaining much from it and giving much to it. One illustration must suffice. In 2014, Kevin Chang was awarded the Withers Elective,[28] and at prize-giving that year he gave a short speech of welcome to his Chinese family, surely the first time that Mandarin has ever been spoken aloud in the cathedral. Plans are now afoot to broaden the countries from which international students are drawn by expanding the homestay arrangements, and perhaps eventually by acquiring a property to house senior boarders.

---

to 2017 – a record unlikely ever to be surpassed.

26. The Headmaster has written an excellent letter (of 4 September 2016) to parents banning their use in school for pupils below the Sixth Form, unless specific permission has been granted, in order to protect 'our strong ethos of tolerance, understanding and self-improvement'.

27. *TH 2012*, p.6, from Paul Smith's speech day address, 7 July 2012.

28. A prize endowed by Gary Withers OH and awarded annually to the person who in the pupils' view (following a secret ballot) has contributed most to the school community that year. In 2017, another Chinese boy, Frank Zeng, also gained this distinction.

Whatever the threat to the charitable status of independent schools or the proposal to impose VAT on independent school fees,[29] the school can look to the future with confidence. After more than a decade of full independence, during which the school has weathered its fair share of storms with (in the Headmaster's words) 'resilience, determination and an amazing camaraderie to move on and get things done',[30] much has been achieved. No school, however, can afford to stand still, and even though there is still much to be done, the structures are now in place to take it to new heights. Its assets are considerable: a senior Headmaster who, together with his junior colleague, is ever striving for success for his school; a renewed governing body of 12 with a suitably wide breadth of professional expertise; and committed support from its parental body, the Old Herefordians, its recently established 'Friends' and other well-wishers in and beyond the county. And at a time when less than half of England's teachers have ten years' experience, among its own staff there remains a judicious balance of age and youth, which – like the solera system of sherry production – by retaining a portion of earlier good vintages, helps maintain the quality of current blends.[31] Above all, its pupil body continues to be refreshed each year by delightful groups of young people who on the whole bring credit to their parents and the school. In the words of a former colleague: 'there is something about HCS which transcends time and ensures a continuity of community and loyalty'. That mystique has everything to do with its Christian heritage.

---

29. A current Labour Party policy recently endorsed by the retiring Principal of the Hereford Sixth Form College: *HT*, 20 April 2017, p.39.

30. *TH 2008*, p.5, from Paul Smith's speech day address, 12 July 2008.

31. Even though many of the names have changed, John Morrill's observations in his speech day address of 6 July 1991 still hold true more than 25 years later.

Epilogue

Eternal Verities

There is a tendency for all institutions as they develop to ignore their *raison d'être*. And as this school responds to the modern world, it should not divorce itself from its permanent roots. For if this history has proved anything, it is that educational fashions are transient. Clerical governors and masters have almost entirely been replaced by lay men and women; the all-pervading dominance of the Classics has given way to a broader curriculum; terms have changed from two to three each year, and Saturdays excluded from the working week; attitudes to discipline have altered from the sanction of the birch to pro-active pastoral care; buildings have been acquired and released, adapted and built; school 'traditions' have tended to last little more than two or three generations before new ones have been invented; unsupervised freedom outside the classroom has been replaced by supervised activities throughout the school day; the domination of sport and the CCF for most of the last century has lessened; other pastimes, clubs and societies have waxed and waned; a male, part-boarding, government-assisted school has given way to a mixed, day and wholly independent establishment; and parents who were once kept at arm's length are now welcomed to the school as a vital part of the educational process. Such are some of the mutations of the past 800 years.

The school's relationship with its cathedral church has also evolved over time. For centuries, the Dean and Chapter were the school's sole governors; its Chapter Clerk administered its affairs; its masters were often selected from old boys within the College of Vicars Choral. This pattern has gradually and haphazardly changed over the past 200 years: the last vicar choral masters working in tandem were Picart and Garbett in the early 1800s; from the end of that century – after 1893, when in the light of the Endowed Schools Act of 1869 the school was first constituted as a separate entity – there has been a gradual dilution and eventual withdrawal of the Dean and Chapter from its active governance; and during the 1970s a school bursar took the place of the Chapter Clerk as the school's chief administrative officer.

Nevertheless, today's Chapter still retains influence over school affairs through two legal instruments and one formal agreement. So by the terms of the cathedral constitution of 2000, the Chapter is enjoined to 'maintain a school or schools for the primary purpose of educating choristers and others'; and from the school's side, its establishment in 1987 as a limited company both included the Chapter among its members and recognised the Dean's right to chair its annual general meeting. And in 2006, following the resignation of the Dean and Precentor as governors, the office of president was resurrected. By the terms of this office, the Dean presides over major school occasions in the cathedral; he is involved in the appointment of the Head and the chaplain; he holds the right of nomination for two members of the board; he oversees policy with regard to the choristers; and he supports the Headmaster in maintaining the school's Christian ethos. Although school and cathedral are now distinct institutions, by such mechanisms channels of communication are kept open and the Chapter – while reserving its powers over the choristers – keeps a general watching brief over the school and its activities.

Other links have disappeared within the past 50 years. Roy Massey was the last cathedral organist simultaneously to hold the post of Director of Music at the school; Peter Dyke, the last assistant organist to teach at HCS. The Chapter Clerk is no longer in charge of the school CCF.[1] School groups, like the Society of Change Ringers, the junior 'Friends' and the band of Sunday servers, which actively supported the church's witness, have long disappeared. The favour of allowing senior pupils the privilege of parking within the Cathedral Close was withdrawn in 1989. Rental negotiations are now conducted at arm's length, and as required by charity law, conflicts of interest cannot now occur. The school is no longer part of the cathedral family as Barry Sutton hoped that it might have been in the 1980s.

Yet there is still far more to unite than divide the two corporations. The Dean, as we have seen, has important responsibilities as president of governors; both Headmasters are Chapter officers with their own named stalls in the quire; the school rents one third of its buildings from the Chapter, to the mutual benefit of each body; scholars are admitted annually as 'Dean's scholars' at a special service of Evensong; and the boy choristers, whose choir house is in the College where the school was once situated, continue to receive their education at the school.[2] Other individuals help bind the two institutions together. There is a long tradition of HCS teachers singing as lay clerks in the cathedral choir;[3] and a shorter one of tutors being employed by both school and Chapter to care for the choristers. Not least, the cathedral remains the school's *genius loci* and is still the place which preserves its identity and is central to its life.

Indeed, as the school has moved westwards in recent years, the Cathedral Close – the cutting of the Old Deanery hedge during the precinct's redevelopment in 2011 indicating the school's re-integration with its surroundings – has again become its thoroughfare if not its playground as in times past. And even though HCS no longer assembles daily within its portals as a whole school community, the cathedral remains at the heart of the school. It is here that the grand school occasions – the carol service, commemoration and speeches – which end each term are held; it is at its altar that pupils receive communion or a blessing

1. As Lt Col Andrew Eames was during his distinguished tenure as commanding officer, 1996-2011.

2. And play a vital part in its musical life after their voices change, as suggested by their recent record in gaining music awards – John Challenger, Liam Dunachie, Luke Fisher, Ruairi Bowen (a St Paul's chorister before HCS) and Patrick Dunachie all having gained organ or choral scholarships at Oxford or Cambridge colleges, 2006-12.

3. Following Jeremy Crowhurst's recent retirement (in October 2016) after over 30 years as a lay clerk, the present representative is Andrew Semple, Head of Academic Music at the school.

at the bi-termly Eucharist, presided over by the Dean (Plate 27); it is within its midst that the fallen are remembered each year on Armistice Day, an act of remembrance still taking place at the war memorial below the Lady Chapel where the school worshipped for much of the twentieth century.[4] As was said of another school chapel, 'Every stone is eloquent with the memories of a personal past. The chapel is not a monument, it is a biography'.[5] Or, in the words of my last Head of School on his final speech day: 'This magnificent cathedral will always leave a subtle sense of history on all of us who have spent our school years in and around it'.[6] And as is attested by many other Old Herefordians – and now children of Old Herefordians[7] – among them those who have been married or had their babies baptised within the building, the moments they spent as young people within the cathedral are among their most precious school memories.

So Christian ideals stand as the inspiration for the present generation. Such ideals have inspired many hundreds of teachers and tens of thousands of their pupils over more than 800 years from the time the school was a small society of scholars in a remote north-western corner of Christendom. Its site has changed several times over the centuries but it has always nestled under the shadow of that great building which has dominated Hereford throughout the ages, its massive Norman pillars and Gothic arches still pointing us today to the creating and loving God worshipped by our ancestors.

It was in this cathedral, at the school's first chapel of the new millennium, that the chaplain opened the service with the following prayer of celebration:

> God of all ages, you dwell among us in our world of time and space. Yet our days cannot confine you and our world cannot contain you. Your mercy and love sustain us, and you hold the universe in being by your powerful word. We rejoice in your goodness to us, in bringing us to this day and revealing to us your glory in the everyday wonder of human birth. Throughout your world this new era is celebrated. As we rejoice and sing, put a new joy in our hearts, a new song on our lips, set the praise of Christ in all our living and the good news of Christ throughout the world.[8]

It is a prayer which echoes down the centuries; a reminder of the continuity of the Cathedral School community with one belonging to another realm.

---

4. For the tree-planting ceremony following the 2014 Armistice Day service, attended by the present Headmaster and his three immediate predecessors, see Plate 22.

5. Tyerman, p.565, quoting Joseph Wood's 1907 speech commemorating the 50th anniversary of the consecration of Harrow School's chapel.

6. *TH 2005*, p.8, from Ralph Dickinson's speech, 9 July 2005.

7. The first child to enter the school, where both parents were Old Herefordians, was Edward Watkins in September 1992.

8. As read on 11 January 2000 by Andrew Law, chaplain of Hereford Cathedral School, 1997-2001.

Appendix I

Headmasters of Hereford Cathedral School to 2017

The list of Headmasters is incomplete until the late seventeenth century. Before then, the dates listed do not necessarily indicate the length of tenure, simply the date given in an extant document. No confirmation has been found for the headmasterships of John (?) Taylor and Lane other than the names of Hereford schoolmasters recorded by Joseph Harvey in April 1674, as given to him 'in the remembrance of those who have longest lived here' (CCCA, 390/1, fo 209). The other sources are as those cited in the main body of the text.

John Lelamour possibly Headmaster 1373
Richard Cornwaille 1384
Thomas More possibly Headmaster late 1380s/early 1390s
Richard Burgehyll possibly Headmaster late fifteenth century
John Dornell 1535
William May 1583-*c*.84
Thomas Rastall possibly Headmaster 1587
Thomas Cooke 1591-*c*.93
James or Thomas Povey 1595
Richard Harley 1600
Richard Dugard 1613 (resigned 1616)
Thomas Dugard 1616
John White Osgood 1619
Clement Barksdale 1637-*c*.46
William Seaborne 1646-47 (still in office)
John? Taylor 1650s (?)
John or Richard Morris 1660-61
? Barrow 1661
? Lane 1661-62 (?)
Thomas Smyth 1662-63
William Wakeman 1663-71
Joseph Harvey 1671-85

Robert Phillips 1685-97
Richard Traherne 1699-*c*.1731
Thomas Willim 1731-49
John Stephens 1749-62
Gibbons Bagnall 1762-78
Abraham Rudd 1778-82
Gibbons Bagnall 1782-84
Robert D'Lambert Squire 1784-1803
Samuel Picart 1803-07
Charles Taylor 1807-26
Charles Taylor (junior) 1826-39
William Henry Ley 1839-42
John Woolley 1842-44
Thomas Layng 1844-51
Thomas Barratt Power 1851-57
John Woollam 1857-69
Eric John Sutherland Rudd 1869-75
Francis Henry Tatham 1875-90
Thomas Thistle 1890-97
William Henry Murray Ragg 1898-1913
John Henson 1913-19
James Harold Crees 1920-40
Christopher Fairfax Scott 1940-45
Alan Francis John Hopewell 1945-57
James Ross Peebles 1957-67
David Michael Richards 1968-75
Barry Bridge Sutton 1975-87
Howard Charles Tomlinson 1987-2005
Paul Anthony Smith 2005-Present

Appendix II

Some Notable Past Old Herefordians

Hereford Cathedral School may not have produced many great men (or, as yet, great women), defined somewhat arbitrarily by Bishop Lisle Carr at the '550th' celebrations as those who have 'won a title or an elaborate tombstone'. Nevertheless, as this appendix indicates, a number of Old Herefordians have gained national recognition, as well as local prominence, over the centuries.

All those listed below are deceased. In compiling this appendix, I have included all OHs who can be found in either the *Oxford Dictionary of National Biography* or in Philip Weaver's *A Dictionary of Herefordshire Biography*; or (for the past few years) OHs who have received major obituary notices in national newspapers. I have also added to this list the names of some figures who have either been important in the school's history or had significant careers in other respects.

The task of identifying the non-foundationers who attended HCS before the first extant school register, Dr Taylor's incomplete one from 1807, is not straightforward. However, before this date, attendance at HCS can sometimes be verified from admission registers at Brasenose College, Oxford, and St John's, Cambridge; or, for those who organised the earliest OH dinners from 1784, from the relevant entries in the *Hereford Journal*. Where, as with Thomas Traherne and some other names in this appendix, there is sufficient circumstantial evidence to suggest that they were educated at HCS, they have been claimed for the school.

ApIvor, Denis (1916-2004), composer
Askwith, Wilfred Marcus (1890-1962), Bishop of Gloucester

Beavan, Richard John (1950-2012), geophysicist
Berry, Francis (1915-2006), poet and university professor
Bevan, Edward (1770-1860), physician and apiarist
Bevan, James Alfred (1858-1938), Church of England clergyman and first captain of Wales for rugby union
Bird, Charles John (1777-1854), Church of England clergyman and antiquary
Bird, Thomas (1772-1836), lawyer and antiquary

Blaxland, Alan Bruce (1892-1963), major-general
Boycott, Arthur Edwin (1877-1938), pathologist and university professor
Bradford, John (1750-1805), Church of England clergyman and Independent minister
Brewster, William (1665-1715), physician and antiquary
Briscoe, (Arnold) Daly (1900-2002), doctor, author and HCS benefactor
Bull, John (*c.*1563-1628), organist and composer
Bullock-Webster, George Russell (1858-1934), Church of England clergyman, author and co-founder (with H.P. Bull) of *The Herefordian*
Bulmer, Edward Frederick (1865-1941), cider-maker
Bulmer, Henry Percival (1867-1919), cider-maker
Bury, John (1925-2000), theatre designer

Carless, Joseph (*c.*1843-1909), Town Clerk of Hereford
Christmas, William Jeffery (1950-2017), electrical engineer and university teacher
Coningsby, Fitzwilliam (*c.*1596-1666), MP and Royalist leader
Cooke, William Henry (1811-94), judge and antiquary
Cotterell, Sir John Geers, first Baronet (1757-1845), MP and builder of Garnons
Cox, David (junior) (1809-85), watercolour artist
Cutler, Sir Horace Walter (1912-97), local politician

Davies, John (1565?-1618), poet and writing-master
Davies, Noel (1945-2008), operatic conductor
Davies, Stephen Harris (1883-1961), Bishop of Carpentaria
Davis, Hugh (d.1644), organist, Hereford Cathedral
Dhenin, Sir Geoffrey (1918-2011), RAF doctor and air marshal
Du Buisson, John Clement (1871-1938), Dean of St Asaph

Eagles, Henry Cecil (1855-1929), Commandant Royal Marines and general

Garbett, Edward (1817-87), Church of England clergyman, journalist and evangelical apologist
Garbett, James (1802-79), Church of England clergyman and Oxford professor of poetry
Gardiner, Richard (1590/91-1670), Church of England clergyman and benefactor
Gething, Richard (1585?-1652?), writing-master
Goaman, (Geoffrey) Michael (1921-2009), postage stamp designer
Gregory, Sir William (1625-96), judge and Speaker of the House of Commons
Griffiths, Silvanus (*c.*1576-1624), Dean of Hereford
Guillim, John (1550-1621), herald
Gwatkin, Richard (1791-1870), senior wrangler and Church of England clergyman

Herbert, John Maurice (1808-82), judge
Hidden, Norman Frederick (1913-2006), teacher and poet
Higgins, Edward (1808-84), Church of England clergyman, antiquary and rebuilder of Bosbury House
Hopewell, Alan Francis John (1892-1957), Headmaster, Hereford Cathedral School
Howell, James (1594?-1666), historian, political writer and first historiographer-royal

Hoskyns, Sir Hungerford, fourth Baronet (*c.*1677-1767), MP and owner of Harewood
Hull, Sir Percy Clarke (1878-1968), organist and master of choristers, Hereford Cathedral
Jancey, Robert Christopher (1934-96), plant scientist and university professor
Jesse, William (1870-1945), Principal, Meerut College; Headmaster, Kenton College, Kenya
John, Peter William Meredith (1923-2015), statistician and university professor

Lafford, Lindsay Arthur James (1912-2014), organist, composer and university professor
Lambe, William (1765-1847), physician
Lane, Edward William (1801-76), orientalist
Lechmere (alias Stratford), Edmund (*c.*1586-1640), Roman Catholic priest
Leslie-Jones, Frederick Archibald (1874-1946), England rugby union international, and Principal, Aitchison College, Lahore, and Mayo College, Ajmer
Leslie-Jones, Leycester Hudson (1872-1935), judge, Chief Court of the Punjab
Lewis, Thomas (1689-*c.*1737), polemicist
Loder-Symonds, Frederick Parland (1876-1952), vice-admiral

Mace, Arthur Cruttenden (1874-1928), Egyptologist
Machen, Arthur (1863-1947), writer
Maddy, Watkin (1798-1857), astronomer
Mansell, Francis (1579-1665), Principal, Jesus College, Oxford
Martin, (Basil) Kingsley (1897-1969), political journalist and journal editor
Mayo, John (1761-1818), physician
Morris, Christopher John (1922-2014), organist and music publisher

Nicholls, Howard Charles Warrender (1931-2011), Wales rugby union international
Nott, Frederick Trevor (1885-1950), Headmaster, King Edward VI School, Stafford
Nuttall, Anthony David (Tony) (1937-2007), literary scholar

Oakeley, Francis Eckley (1891-1914), England rugby union international
Oakley, John (1834-90), Dean of Manchester and social reformer
Owens, Frank Arthur Robert (1912-95), newspaper editor

Pain, John Freeman (1899-1976), bridge engineer
Parry, Matthew Croose (1885-1931), cricketer, Warwickshire and Ireland
Peppercorn, Arthur Henry (1889-1951), railway locomotive engineer
Phillips, John Spencer (1848-1909), chairman, Lloyds Bank
Powell, Raphael (1904-65), professor of Roman Law
Powell, William (1735/6-69), actor and theatre manager

Ragg, Harry Richard (1889-1967), athlete and Bishop of Calgary
Ragg, Thomas Murray (1897-1953), historian and editor
Rapson, Edward James (1861-1937), Sanskritist and university professor
Rawcliffe, Gordon Hindle (1910-79), electrical engineer and university teacher
Rhodes, Sir Robert Heaton (1875-1980), New Zealand politician and cabinet minister
Rhys, John Llewellyn (1911-40), RAF pilot and author

Richards, John Gower Meredith (1900-68), HMI and civil servant
Richards, Owain Westmacott (1901-84), entomologist and university professor
Richardson, Peter (1931-2017), cricketer, Worcestershire, Kent and England
Roberts, Sir David Arthur (1924-87), ambassador to Syria, UAE and Lebanon
Robinson, Sir Sydney Maddock (1865-1945), Chief Justice, High Court of Burma
Ross (Rosse), John (1719-92), Bishop of Exeter
Rowe, Alick Edward (1939-2009), teacher and writer
Rowland, Daniel (1711?-90), Church of England clergyman and Methodist preacher

Scobie, Mackay John Graham (1852-1930), hon. colonel, the Herefordshire Regiment
Sheppard, Sir William Didsbury (1865-1933), member of the Council of India
Smith, Frederick William Boyton (1837-1911), composer
Smith, Miles (d.1614), Bible translator and Bishop of Gloucester
Steer, Philip Wilson (1860-1942), painter
Symonds, John Reginald (1850-1924), three times Mayor of Hereford and (with J. Corner) first lay governor of HCS
Symonds-Tayler, Sir Richard Victor (1897-1971), admiral

Thompson, (Reginald) Stanley (1899-1994), Headmaster, Bloxham School
Traherne, Thomas (*c.*1637-74), Church of England clergyman, poet and writer

Vevers, Geoffrey Marr (1890-1970), zoologist and zoo superintendent

Walley, Sir John (1906-2002), civil servant
Walmsley, John (1867-1922), Bishop of Sierra Leone
Watkins, Ivor Stanley (1896-1960), Bishop of Guildford
Watts, Arthur Herbert (1886-1960), Headmaster, St George's School, Harpenden
Weatherly, Frederick Edward (1848-1929), songwriter and barrister
Williams, Arthur Nicholl (1894-1982), major-general
Williams, David (1926-2003), advertising executive and crime writer
Winn, Godfrey Herbert (1906-71), popular author and journalist
Woods, Sir Raymond Wybrow (1882-1943), government solicitor to the Post Office

Yeld, George (junior) (1845-1938), Newdigate prize-winner, schoolmaster, Alpinist and horticulturalist
York, Thomas John Pinches (1898-1970), Headmaster, Derby School and Merchant Taylors', Crosby

Zimmerman, Arthur Ulrich (1889-1963), HCS benefactor

Bibliography

Adamson, J.W. (1930). *English Education, 1789-1902.* Cambridge.
Alington, C.A. (1914). *A Schoolmaster's Apology.* London.
Allfield, C.E. (1985-87). 'Hereford in the 1850s', *TWNFC,* XLV, pp.347-70.
Allsobrook, D.I. (1986). *School for the Shires: the Reform of Middle Class Education in mid-Victorian England.* Manchester.
Anderson, P.J. (2010). 'William Chick, Herefordshire architect', *TWNFC,* 58, pp.156-79.
Anthony, E. (1903). *Herefordshire Cricket.* Hereford.
Archer, I.W. (2002). 'The Charity of Early Modern Londoners', *TRHS,* 6th Series 12, pp.234-45.
Armytage, W.H. (1970). *Four Hundred Years of English Education.* Cambridge.
Arnold, R. (1961). *The Whiston Matter.* London.
Askwith, G.R. (1930). *Lord James of Hereford.* London.
Aston, N. (2004), 'Ross [Rosse], John (1719-92)', *ODNB,* 47, pp.825-26.
Aylmer, G.E. (1972). 'Who was ruling in Herefodshire from 1645 to 1661?', *TWNFC,* XL, pp.373-87.
Aylmer, G.E., and Tiller, J. (Eds.). (2000). *Hereford Cathedral: A History.* London and Rio Grande.
Bagnall, G. (1765). *Education an Essay.* London.
Bamford, T.W. (1960). *Thomas Arnold.* London.
Bamford, T.W. (1967). *Rise of the Public Schools: A Study of Boys' Public Boarding Schools in England and Wales from 1837 to the Present Day.* London.
Bannister, A.T. (1924). *The Cathedral Church of Hereford: Its History and Constitution.* London.
Barker, G.F. (1895). *Memoir of Richard Busby, DD (1601-95).* London.
Barksdale, C. (1651). *Nymphal Libethris or The Cotswold Muse.* London.
Barnes, G. (2008). *The Founding of Hereford Sixth Form College: An Episode in Change Management, 1964-73.* Hereford.
Barrett, P. (1993). *Barchester: English Cathedral Life in the Nineteenth Century.* London.
Bateson, M. (Ed.). (1895). *Letters from the Bishops to the Privy Council, 1564.* Camden Miscellany, IX.
Beale, C. (2006). *Champagne and Shambles: The Arkwrights and the Downfall of the Landed Artistocracy.* Stroud.
Bell, A. (1817). *Instructions for Conducting Schools.* London: 6th Edition.
Bennett, P. (1977). *A Very Desolate Position: The Story of the Birth and Establishment of a mid-Victorian Public School.* Blackpool.
Bentley, J. (1990). *Dare To Be Wise: A History of The Manchester Grammar School.* London.
Besse, J. (1753). *A Collection of the Sufferings of the People called Quakers,* 2 vols. London.
Best, G.C. (1971). *Mid-Victorian Britain 1851-75.* London.
Blumenau, R. (1965). *A History of Malvern College, 1865 to 1965.* London.
Blythe, R. (2010). *The Age of Illusion: England in the Twenties and Thirties, 1919-40.* London, reprint.
Boden, A., and Hedley, P. (2017). *The Three Choirs Festival: A History.* Woodbridge.
Bradshaw, H., and Wordsworth, C. (Eds.). (1892-97). *Statutes of Lincoln Cathedral.* 3 vols. Cambridge.
Brittain, V. (1979). *Testament of Youth.* Glasgow, reprint.
Britton, J. (1831). *The History and Antiquities of the Cathedral Church of Hereford.* London.
Brock, M.G., and Curthoys, M.C. (Eds.). (1997). *The History of the University of Oxford, vol. VI, Nineteenth Century Oxford, part I.* Oxford.

Bullock, J. (1821). *A Fair, Candid and Impartial State of the Case Between the Masters of the College School and the Rev. James Bullock.* Hereford.
Burnett, C. (1995). 'Mathematics and Astronomy in Hereford and its Region in the Twelfth Century', *Medieval Art, Architecture and Archaelogy at Hereford.* (D. Whitehead, Ed.) British Archaeological Association Conference and Transactions, XV, pp.50-59.
Butler, J. (2011). *The Red Dean of Canterbury: The Public and Private Faces of Hewlett Johnson.* London.
Caird, R. (2000). 'The Georgian Music room at Hereford Cathedral, 1760-1835', *Hereford Three Choirs Festival Programme 2000*, pp.28-31.
Calder, A. (1982). *The People's War: Britain 1939-45.* London, reprint.
Capes, W.W. (1908). *Charters and Records of Hereford Cathedral.* Hereford.
Carless, W.T. (1914). *A Short History of Hereford Cathedral School.* Hereford.
Carlisle, N. (1818). *A Concise Description of the Endowed Grammar Schools in England and Wales.* 2 vols. London.
Chandos, J. (1985). *Boys Together: English Public Schools, 1800-1864.* Oxford.
Charles, B.G., and Emanuel, H.D. (1955). A Calendar of the Earlier Hereford Cathedral Monuments. 3 vols. HCL Typescript.
Cheney, C.R. (1932). 'Letters of William Wickwane, Chancellor of York, 1266-68', *English Historical Review,* 47, pp.626-42.
Clarke, M.L. (1945). *Greek Studies in England 1700-1830.* Cambridge.
Clarke, M.L. (1959). *Classical Education in Britain, 1500-1900.* Cambridge.
Coffey, J. (2004). 'Barksdale, Clement (1609-1687)', *ODNB,* 3, pp.907-08.
Coxe, H.O. (1852). *Catalogus codicum MSS in collegiis aulisque Oxoniensibus.* 2 vols. Oxford.
Crees, J.H. (1915). *Didascalus Patiens: A Satire, A Medley, A Romance.* London.
Crees, J.H. (1920). *Gloucester 1911-1919: A Record of the Crypt Grammar School During Those Years.* Gloucester.
Cressy, D. (1975). *Education in Tudor and Stuart England.* London.
Crook, J.M. (2008). *Brasenose: the Biography of an Oxford College.* Oxford.
Currie, D.C. (1967-69). 'Improvement in Hereford', *TWNFC*, XXIX, pp.389-401.
Dancy, J.C. (1963). *The Public Schools and the Future.* London.
Darwall-Smith, R. (2008). *A History of University College, Oxford.* Oxford.
Dawes, R. (1849). *Observations on the Workings of the Government Scheme of Education and on School Inspection.* London.
Dawes, R. (1854). *Remarks on the Re-organisation of the Civil Service and its Bearing on Educational Progress.* London.
Defoe, D. (1962). *A Tour Through the Whole Island of Great Britain.* (G. D. Cole, and D. C. Browning, Eds.) 2 vols. London.
Dent, H.C. (1948). *Education In Transition: A Sociological Study Of The Impact Of War On English Education, 1939-44.* London.
Drinkwater, N. (1949-51). 'The Old Market Hall, Hereford', *TWNFC,* XXXIII, pp.1-13.
Duncumb, J. (1804-12). *Collections towards the History and Antiquities of the County of Hereford.* 2 Vols. Hereford.
Dyer, J.P. (2001). '"As We May Live in Peace and Quieteness": Regulations in the age of Reformation: Hereford, 1470-1610'. University of Colorado: Ph.D Thesis.
Eales, J. (1990). *Puritans and Roundheads: The Harleys of Brampton Bryan and the outbreak of the English Civil War.* Cambridge.
Eales-White, J.C. (1931). *Records of Hereford Cathedral School.* Hereford.
Edwards, K. (1967). *The English Secular Cathedrals in the Middle Ages.* 2nd Edition. Manchester.
Eisel, J.C. (2005). 'Notes on the former Hereford Market Hall and the Tolsey', *TWNFC,* 53, pp.25-40.
Eisel, J.C. (2014). 'Jordan's Boatyard in Hereford', *TWNFC,* 62, pp.134-45.
Emden, A.B. (1957-59). *A Biographical Register of the University of Oxford to A.D. 1500.* 3 vols. Oxford.
Fincham, K., and Tyacke, N. (2007). *Altars Restored: The Changing Face of English Religious Worship, 1547-c.1700.* Oxford.
Firth, C.H., and Rait, R.S. (Eds.). (1911). *Acts and Ordinances of the Interregnum, 1642-60.* 3 vols. London.

Fisher, G.W. (1911). *Annals of Shrewsbury School.* London.
Fletcher, A.J. (1981). *The Outbreak of the English Civil War.* London.
Fletcher, A.J. (2008). *Growing Up in England: The Experience of Childhood, 1600-1914.* Yale.
Foster, J. (1887-8). *Alumni Oxonienses: the members of the University of Oxford, 1715-1886; their parentage, birthplace, and year of birth, with a record of their degrees; being the Matriculation Register of the University.* 4 vols., Oxford and London.
Foster, J. (1891-2). *Alumni Oxonienses: the members of the University of Oxford, 1500-1714; their parentage, birthplace, and year of birth, with a record of their degrees; being the Matriculation Register of the University.* 4 vols., Oxford and London.
Frere, W.H., and Kennedy, M.N. (Eds.). (1910). *Visitation Articles and Injunction of the Period of the Reformation, 1536-75.* 3 vols, Alcuin Club Collections, 14-16.
Gosden, J.H. (2007). *Education in the Second World War: A Study in Policy and Administration.* London.
Green, I.M. (2006). 'Libraries for school education and personal devotion', in *The Cambridge History of Libraries in Britain and Ireland,* (G. Mantelbrote and K.A. Manley, Eds.), vol. 2, pp.47-64. Cambridge.
Gretton, F.E. (1889). *Memory's Harkback ... 1808 to 1858.* London.
Grundy, J.E. (1985-87). 'Population Movements in Nineteenth Century Herefordshire', *TWNFC,* XLV, pp. 488-97.
Hackett, M. (1827). *A Brief Account of Cathedral and Collegiate Schools ...* London.
Hans, N. (1951). *New Trends in Education in the Eighteenth Century.* London.
Harries, R., Caltermole, P., and Mackintosh, P. (1991). *History of Norwich School; King Edward VI Grammar School at Norwich.* Norwich.
Henson, H.H. (1942). *Retrospect of an Unimportant Life: vol I, 1863-1920.* Oxford.
Heseltine, P., and Stuchfield, H.M. (2005). *The Monumental Brasses of Hereford Cathedral.* Colchester.
Hidden, N. (1973). *Dr Kink and his old-style boarding school: Fragments of autobiography.* London.
Holmes, G. (1982). *Augustan England: Professions, State and Society, 1680-1730.* London.
Honey, J.R. (1977). *Tom Brown's Universe: The Development of the Victorian Public School.* London.
Hope Simpson, J.B. (1967). *Rugby Since Arnold: A History of Rugby School From 1842.* London.
Howard-Jones, J. (1998). *From Teddy Tail Collars to Itchy Tights.* Logaston.
Hunt, R.W. (1936). 'English Learning in the late Twelfth Century', *TRHS,* 4th Series ,19, pp.19-42.
Jacobs, J. (Ed.). (1890). *Epistolae Ho-elianae: The Familiar Letters of James Howell.* London.
James, D. (2008-2009). 'Chapel Farm, Deerfold, Herefordshire: a re-appraisal', *TWNFC,* 56, pp.73-98; and 57, pp.65-88.
Jebb, J., and Phillott, H.W. (1882). *The Statutes of the Cathedral Church of Hereford, promulgated AD 1637.* Oxford.
Jewell, H.M. (1998). *Education in Early Modern England.* Basingstoke.
Johnson, A., and Shoesmith, R. (Eds.). (2016). *The Story of Hereford.* Logaston.
Johnson, R. (1882). *The Ancient Customs of the City of Hereford.* 2nd Edition. London.
Jones, M.D. (1995). *Brighton College, 1845-1995.* Chichester.
Jones, T. (1858). *Hereford, Cathedral and City.* 2nd Edition. Hereford.
Jordan, W.K. (1960). *The Charities of London , 1480 - 1660: The Aspirations and Achievements of the Urban Society.* London.
Keeler, M.F. (1954). *The Long Parliament, 1640-41: A Biographical Study of its Members.* Philadelphia.
Kynaston, D. (2008). *Austerity Britain, 1945-51.* London.
Kynaston, D. (2010). *Family Britain, 1951-57.* London.
Lascelles and Co. (1851). *Directory and Gazetteer of Herefordshire.* Birmingham.
Latham, R., and Matthews, W. (Eds.). (1970-83). *The Diary of Samuel Pepys.* 11 vols. London.
Le Neve, J. (2002). *Fasti Ecclesiae Anglicanae 1066-1300, VIII: Hereford.* (J.S. Barrow, Ed.) London.
Le Neve, J. (2009). *Fasti Ecclesiae Anglicanae, 1300-1541, Hereford Diocese.* (J.M. Horne, and D. Lepine, Eds.) London.
Le Neve, J. (2014). *Fasti Ecclesiae Anglicanae 1541-1857, XIII Hereford Diocese.* (W.H. Campbell, Ed.) London.
Leach, A.F. (1896). *English School of the Reformation, 1546-48.* Westminster.
Leach, A.F. (1907). 'Schools', *Victoria County History: Sussex, vol. 2.* London.

Leach, A.F. (1911). *Educational Charters and Documents, 598-1909.* Cambridge.
Leach, A.F. (1916). *The Schools of Medieval England* (2nd ed.). London.
Ledwich, W. (1985). *The Durham Affair.* Welshpool.
Lehmberg, S.E. (1988). *The Reformation of Cathedrals: Cathedrals in English Society, 1485-1603.* Princeton.
Lepine, D. (2002). '"A Long Way from University". Cathedral Canons and Learning at Hereford in the Fifteenth Century' in *The Church and Learning in Later Medieval Society: Essays in Honour of R. B. Dobson.* (C. Barron, & J. Stratford, Eds.) pp.178-95.
Lepper, C. (1989). *The Crypt School, Gloucester, 1539-1989.* Gloucester.
Lewis, T.T. (1853). *Letters of Lady Brilliana Harley*, Camden Soc., vol. 53.
Lineham, P. (Ed.). (2011). *St John's College Cambridge: a History.* Woodbridge.
Lloyd, D.J. (1977). *Country Grammar School: A History of Ludlow Grammar School through Eight Centuries.* Birmingham.
Lobel, M.D. (1969). *Historic Towns: vol.1.* London and Oxford.
Luft, H.M. (1970). *A History of Merchant Taylors' School, Crosby.* Liverpool.
Lysons, D. (1895). *Origins and Progress of the Meetings of the Three Choirs.* Gloucester.
Mack E.C., and Armytage W.H.G. (1952). *Thomas Hughes: The Life Of The Author of Tom Brown's Schooldays.* London.
Mack, E.C. (1938). *Public Schools And British Opinion, 1780 to 1860.* London.
Mack, E.C. (1941). *Public Schools and British Opinion Since 1860.* New York.
Macken, A. (1922). *Far Off Things.* London.
Macky, J. (1714, 1722). *A Journey Through England.* 2 vols. London.
Mangan, J.A. (1981). *Athleticism in the Victorian and Edwardian Public School.* Cambridge.
Margoliouth, H.M. (1958). *T. Traherne Centuries, Poems and Thanksgivings.* 2 vols. Oxford.
Marshall, W. (2004). 'Croft, Herbert (1603-91)', *ODNB*, 14, p.240.
Marshall, W. (2009). *Church Life in Hereford and Oxford, 1660-1760: A Study of Two Sees.* Lancaster.
Martin, K. (1969). *Father Figures: The First Volume of Autobiography, 1897-1931.* Harmondsworth, reprint.
Marwick, A. (1965). *The Deluge.* London.
Matthews, A.G. (1934). *Calamy Revised.* Oxford.
Mayor, J.E. (1882-1931). *Admissions to the College of St John the Evangelist in the University of Cambridge.* (R. F. Scott, Ed.). 4 parts in 3 vols. Cambridge.
Miner, J.N. (1990). *The Grammar Schools of Medieval England: A. F. Leach in Historiographical Perspective.* Montreal.
Money, A. (1997). *Manly and Muscular Diversions: Public Schools and the Nineteenth Century Sporting Revival.* London.
Moorhouse, G. (1964). *Britain in the Sixties: The Other England.* London.
Moran, J.A. (1979). *Education and Learning in the City of York, 1300-1560.* Borthwick Papers 55. York.
Morgan, F.C. (1942-45). 'A Hereford Booksellers Catalogue of 1695', *TWNFC*, XXXI, pp.22-36.
Morgan, K.O. (2007). *Michael Foot: A Life.* London.
Morgan, M.C. (1968). *Cheltenham College: The First Hundred Years.* Chalfont.
Morgan, P. (1981). 'Early Printing and Binding in York', *The Book Collector*, 30, pp.216-24.
Morgan, P.E. (1985). 'The Library of Lady Hawkins' School, Kington, Herefordshire', *The National Library of Wales Journal*, XXIV no.1, pp.46-62.
Morris, C. (1982). *The Illustrated Journeys of Celia Fiennes, 1685-c.1712.* London and Exeter.
Mould, A. (2007). *The English Chorister: A History.* London.
Mynors, R. and Thomson, R. (1993). *Catalogue of the Manuscripts of Hereford Cathedral Library.* Cambridge.
Newsome, D. (1959). *A History of Wellington College, 1859-1959.* London.
Newsome, D. (1961). *Godliness and Good Learning: Four Studies on a Victorian Ideal.* London.
Newsome, D. (1997). *The Victorian World Picture.* London.
Nuttall, A.D. (1996). *Why Does Tragedy Give Pleasure?* Oxford.
O'Day, R. (1982). *Education and Society 1500-1800: The social foundations of education in early modern Britain.* London and New York.
O'Donnell, J. (2007). *John Venn and the Friends of the Hereford Poor.* Logaston.
Orme, N. (1976). *Education in the West of England, 1066-1548.* Exeter.

Orme, N. (1989). *Education and Society in Medieval and Renaissance England*. London.
Orme, N. (1996). 'The Medieval Schools of Herefordshire', *Nottingham Medieval Studies*, 40, pp.47-62.
Orme, N. (2006). *Medieval Schools: From Roman Britain to Renaissance England.* New Haven and London.
Orme, N. (2013). *English School Exercises, 1420-1530.* Toronto.
Orr, L. (2003). 'On the Playing Fields of Rugby: Williams Webb Ellis and the Invention of a Tradition'. Oxford BA Modern History Thesis.
Outhwaite, R.B. (1969). *Inflation in Tudor and Early Stuart England.* London.
Parkinson, R. (1845). *The Life of Adam Martindale written by himself.* Chetham Soc.
Parry, J.H. (Ed.). (1913, 1915). *The Register of John Gilbert, Bishop of Hereford, 1375-89.* Vol. 18. Cantilupe Soc. Canterbury and York Soc.
Pickles, J.D. (2004), 'Weatherly, Frederick Edward (1848-1929)', *ODNB*, 57, pp.790-91.
Phillott, H.W. (1888). *Diocesan Histories.* Hereford.
Pitman, L. (2016). *The Parish that Disappeared: A History of St. John's, Hereford.* Logaston.
Price, J. (1796). *An Historical Account of the City of Hereford*. Hereford.
Priestley, J.B. (1984, Jubilee Edition). *English Journey.* London.
Prior, P.J. (1977). *Leadership is not a Bowler Hat.* Newton Abbot.
Rae, J. (1981). *The Public School Revolution: Britain's Independent Schools, 1946-79.* London.
Rawlinson, R. (1717). *The History and Antiquities of the City and Cathedral Church of Hereford.* London.
Redgrave, G.R. (1891). *David Cox and Peter De Wint.* New York.
Rees, W.J. (1808). *The Hereford Guide: Containing a Concise History of the City of Hereford* (2nd ed.). Hereford.
Roach, J. (1971). *Public Examinations in England, 1850-1900.* Cambridge.
Roach, J. (1991). *Secondary Education in England, 1870-1902: Public Activity and Private Enterprise.* London.
Roberts, G. (2001). *The Shaping of Modern Hereford.* Logaston.
Robinson, G.M. (1976-78). 'Agricultural depression, 1870-1900', *TWNFC*, 42, pp.259-78.
Rolph, C.H. (1973). *Kingsley: The life, Letters and Diaries of Kingsley Martin.* London.
Ross, D. (2012). *Royalist But ... Herefordshire in the English Civil War. 1640-51.* Logaston.
Rowbotham, J.F. (1901). *The History of Rossall School.* Manchester and London.
Rowe, A. (1978). *Boy at the Commercial.* London.
Rudd, A.B. (1786). *Sermons on Religious and Practical Subjects.* Ludlow.
Sandbrook, D. (2006). *Never Had It So Good: A History of Britain from Suez to the Beatles.* London.
Sandbrook, D. (2007). *White Heat: A History of Britain in the Swinging Sixties.* London.
Sandbrook, D. (2011). *State of Emergency: the Way We Were, Britain, 1970-74.* London.
Sandbrook, D. (2012). *Seasons in the Sun: The Battle for Britain, 1974-79.* London.
Seaborne, M. (1971). *The English School: Its Architecture and Organisation, 1370-1870.* London.
Searby, P. (1997). *A History of the University of Cambridge, volume III: 1750-1870.* Cambridge.
Seldon, A., and Walsh, D. (2013). *Public Schools and the Great War: The Generation Lost.* Barnsley.
Sheils, W.J. (2004). 'Whitgift, John (1530/31-1604)', *ODNB*, 58, pp.717-28.
Simon, B. (1960). *Studies in the History of Education, 1780-1870.* London.
Simon, B. (1991). *Education and the Social Order, 1940-90.* London.
Simon, J. (1966). *Education and Society in Tudor England.* Cambridge.
Stanley, A.P. (1844). *The Life and Correspondence of Thomas Arnold D.D.* 2 vols., 3rd Edition. London.
Storer, J., and H.S. (1815). *The History and Antiquities of the Cathedral Church of Hereford.* London.
Strype, J. (1822). *The Life and Acts of John Whitgift DD.* 3 vols. Oxford.
Sutherland, L.S., & Mitchell, L.G. (Eds.). (1986). *The History of the University of Oxford, vol. V: The Eighteenth Century.* Oxford.
Symonds, R. (1859). *Diary of the Marches of the Royal Army during the Great Civil War.* (C. J. Long, Ed.) Camden Soc., vol. 74.
Taylor, A.J.P. (1965). *English History, 1914-45.* Oxford.
Taylor, C. (1823). *A Latin Grammar Arranged According to the Principles of the Madras System.* Hereford.
Taylor, I. (1820). *Self-Cultivation Recommended or Hints to a Youth Leaving School.* 4th edition. London.
Thomas, K. (1976). *Rule and Misrule in the Schools of early Modern England.* Reading.
Tiller, J. (2004). 'Smith, Miles (d.1624)', *ODNB*, 51, pp.259-60.

Tomlinson, H.C. (2014). 'Seymour, Sarah, Fourth Duchess of Somerset (1632-1692)', *ODNB* Online.
Tompson, R.S. (1971). *Classics Or Charity? The Dilemma of the 18th Century Grammar School.* Manchester.
Tonkin, J., and M. (1975). *The Book of Hereford.* Chesham.
Tyerman, C. (2000). *A History of Harrow School.* Oxford.
Venn, J., & J.A. (1922-54). *Alumni Cantabrigienses: A Biographical List of all Known Students, Graduates and Holders of Office at the University of Cambridge ... to 1900.* Cambridge, part I in 4 vols., part II in 6 vols.
Vincent, W.A. (1950). *The State and School Education 1640-60 in England and Wales.* London.
Vincent, W.A. (1969). *The Grammar Schools: Their Continuing Tradition, 1660-1714.* London.
Ward, H.A. (1964). *Monmouth School, 1614-1964.* London.
Wase, C. (1678). *Considerations concerning Free Schools, as settled in England* . Oxford.
Watkins, A. (1918-20). 'Three Early Timber Halls in the city of Hereford', *TWNFC* (1918-20), pp.164-71.
Watson, F. (1908). *The English Grammar Schools to 1660: Their Curriculum and Practice.* London.
Watson, N. (2008). *Independent Vision: A History of the Portsmouth Grammar School.* London.
Waugh, E. (1942). *Put Out More Flags.* London.
Weatherly, F.E. (1926). *Piano and Gown.* London.
Weaver, P. (2015). *A Dictionary of Herefordshire Biography.* Logaston.
Webb, J., and T.W. (1873). *Military Memoir of Colonel John Birch.* Camden Soc., new series, vol. 7.
Webb, J., and T.W. (1879). *Memorials of the Civil War … as it Affected Herefordshire and the Adjacent Counties.* 2 Vols. London.
White, R.J. (1972). *From Peterloo to the Crystal Palace.* London.
Whitehead, D. (2007). *The Castle Green at Hereford: A Landscape of Ritual, Royalty and Recreation.* Logaston.
Whitehead, D., and Shoesmith, R. (Eds.). (1994). *James Wathen's Herefordshire, 1770-1820: A Collection of his sketches and paintings.* Logaston.
Winn, G. (1967). *The Infirm Glory.* London.
Winnington-Ingram, A.J. (1972). *Monumental Brasses in Hereford Cathedral.* Revised Edition. Hereford.
Wood, A.A. (1820). *Athenae Oxoniensis.* 4 vols. London.
Wood, G. (2003). *Railways of Hereford.* Cleckheaton.
Woolley. (1847). *Sermons Preached in the Chapel of Rossall College, Fleetwood.* London.
Wordsworth, H.B. (1892-97). *Statutes of Lincoln Cathedral.* 3 vols. Cambridge.
Wordsworth, J C. (1941). *A Shorter History of The Cathedral School, Hereford.* Cardiff.

Index of Names

General Index